# THE

# TRAFALGAR
## COMPANION

# THE
# TRAFALGAR
## COMPANION

*A Guide to History's Most Famous Sea Battle and the Life of Admiral Lord Nelson*

## MARK ADKIN

*with illustrations by Clive Farmer*

AURUM PRESS

**Also by Mark Adkin**

*The Waterloo Companion*
*The Sharpe Companion*
*Urgent Fury*
*The Last Eleven?*
*Goose Green*
*The Bear Trap (with Mohammad Yousaf)*
*The Quiet Operator (with John Simpson)*
*Prisoner of the Turnip Heads (with George Wright-Nooth)*
*The Charge*

*In acknowledgement of the debt owed by Britannia*
*to all ranks of the Royal Navy, past and present.*

First published in Great Britain
2005 by Aurum Press Ltd
25 Bedford Avenue, London WC1B 3AT

Text copyright © 2005 Mark Adkin

The moral right of Mark Adkin to be identified as author of this work has been asserted by him in accordance with the Copyright, Designs and Patents Act 1988.

All rights reserved. No part of this book may be reproduced or utilized in any form or by any means, electronic or mechanical, including photocopying, recording or by any information storage and retrieval system, without permission in writing from Aurum Press Ltd.

A catalogue record for this book is available from the British Library.

ISBN 1 84513 018 9

1 3 5 7 9 8 6 4 2
2005 2007 2009 2008 2006

Book design by Robert Updegraff

Diagrams by Robert Updegraff

Plates and illustrations by Clive Farmer

Maps by Sandra Oakins

Editorial project management by Phoebe Clapham

The author and publishers are grateful for permission
to reproduce the following material:
Nelson's letters to Jervis; Nelson's battle plan sketch
and reverse, all © National Maritime Museum
Bowles' Map of London and Westminster, 1799 © Museum of London
Portrait of Horatio, Viscount Nelson (oil on canvas) by Sir William Beechey
(1753–1839), Norfolk Museums Service (Norwich Castle Museum)
Portrait of Emma Hamilton (oil on canvas) by George Romney
(1734–1802), private collection

Printed and bound by Kyodo, Singapore

# Contents

# ACKNOWLEDGEMENTS

As with *The Waterloo Companion* I am indebted to many individuals and organizations who have assisted me with my research either by sharing their expertise or by pointing me in the right direction to locate a particular book or document. Assembling all the information I needed not just on Trafalgar but on Nelson's life would have proved an endless and frustrating task had I not received guidance and help from many people. I offer them all a very sincere 'thank you', and I hope they all read and enjoy *The Trafalgar Companion* that they helped put together.

In addition to this general acknowledgement a number of individuals and organizations require a more personal mention. Once again Philip Haythornthwaite heads the list. His knowledge of both military and naval affairs is vast, as is his library of books and journals. Any query I raised was always answered promptly either over the telephone or through copies of documents that he generously provided by post. Nothing was too much trouble.

If anyone is an expert on Nelson then it must surely be Colin White. He has written several books on the subject and has carried out a huge amount of original research into Nelson's letters, in the process discovering fresh evidence on various aspects of Nelson's life and battles. As Director of Trafalgar 200 and Chairman of the Official Commemoration Committee he is an immensely busy man so I offer him my grateful thanks for taking the time to help and advise me on a number of occasions.

Similarly, there can be nobody with a greater detailed knowledge of *HMS Victory* than Peter Goodwin. He has the wonderful job of Keeper and Curator of the *Victory* and has written extensively about her. My thanks go to him for the valuable discussions we had and the advice he gave me with regard to that magnificent ship's construction and manning.

Mark Barker of the 'Inshore Squadron' at Portsmouth gave unstintingly of his time in responding to queries and in meeting with me at Portsmouth and helping to resolve issues that I found puzzling. In connection with Nelson's death, wounds and illnesses I am most grateful for the advice and opinions of Professor Leslie Le Quesne and Dr Ann-Marie Hills. Both have greatly helped my better understanding of a highly technical aspect of the Nelson story.

Other individuals who I would like to thank personally for their help are le contre-amiral Alain Bellot of the French Naval Historical Service, Captain Barry Kent RN, Victor Turon in Spain for his information on the Spanish Fleet and Derek Haynes, Chairman of The Nelson Society.

It only remains for me to add my appreciation to the staff of the following organizations who have gone out of their way to provide information or to find books or documents, and whose assistance was both friendly and invaluable: the Association des Amis du Musée de la Marine (French ships at Trafalgar), the National Maritime Museum, Greenwich, the Royal Naval Museum, Portsmouth, the Royal Marines Museum at Southsea and the Royal United Services Institute Library in Whitehall, which is a treasure trove of many long out-of-print books. Finally, I should like to thank the Bedford Central Library, whose librarians successfully located some most obscure, out-of-print books and allowed me to borrow them for long periods.

# INTRODUCTION

IT IS NOW two hundred years since the Battle of Trafalgar, the most famous naval action in human history. For the British it is the best-remembered battle of them all, taking a place above even Waterloo in the national consciousness. Victory at Trafalgar gave Britain unchallenged mastery of the seas for a hundred years. An island nation dependent on trade, with a huge merchant fleet to protect and overseas possessions scattered around the globe, Britain's economic as well as military survival was heavily dependent on the Royal Navy. Not until the indecisive Battle of Jutland in 1916 did an enemy again challenge Britannia's rule over the waves.

The nation has two great physical memorials of the battle. The first, and most obvious, is Trafalgar Square in central London. Countless millions of people from virtually every country in the world have visited this famous plaza, a focal point for tourists and Londoners alike. Crowds, demonstrators and marchers inevitably gather there. It is the nation's centre for protests and celebrations. Towering 170 feet above the Square, guarded by four British lions, is a column crowned by a statue of the admiral who won the victory but died at the moment of triumph. For over 150 years, since the square was completed in 1842, Nelson's sightless eyes have gazed out over the London he died defending. He is a permanent reminder to the country of her naval heritage.

Britain's second memorial is *HMS Victory*. Nelson's flagship has been preserved in the Historic Dockyard at Portsmouth and is visited by an average of 300,000 people every year. They see the spot on the quarterdeck where Nelson fell and the cockpit below where he lay dying. They visit his cabin and the gundecks, all beautifully preserved as close as possible to their state when the *Victory* sailed out of Portsmouth in September 1805. When she returned in early December she was bringing Nelson's body home in a barrel of brandy. On 21 October each year, Trafalgar Day, the Royal Navy celebrates by hoisting Nelson's famous signal 'England expects that every man will do his duty' on the *Victory*'s halyards. A special service of remembrance is held on board, a tribute to Nelson and all those who fought and died with him, and the day ends with a formal dinner in his cabin at which the toast to 'The Immortal Memory' is drunk.

The scale and importance of Trafalgar is demonstrated by the figures involved. It was a struggle between giants in terms of firepower. 33 French and Spanish ships-of-the-line (the Combined Fleet) faced 27 British. These 60 ships, all massive floating gun platforms, could produce a huge theoretical weight of shot. The Combined Fleet's 2,636 long guns could fire a combined broadside of 27.5 tons of iron, while the British ships carried 2,026 guns that could deliver 19.5 tons. There were some 4,662 guns (mostly heavy) at Trafalgar, in comparison to 537 (mostly light) at Waterloo. Although not all ships participated to the same extent at Trafalgar, it was a close-quarter fight with ships often slugging it out at less than 50 yards, sometimes with their sides grinding together so that guns could not be run out before firing. At these ranges it was difficult to miss. The battle raged for four hours. At the end many ships on both sides were dismasted and crippled, numerous holds flooded and hundreds of dead bodies were thrown over the side. Hundreds more men lay in agony on bloodstained decks. Dozens of casks full of amputated limbs were emptied overboard. A French ship exploded, and at the end the British had captured 17 enemy vessels – a huge haul and an extraordinary achievement.

Trafalgar cannot be divorced from Nelson or vice versa. Because he died at the battle and because it was such a stunning, overwhelming triumph, this *Companion* examines and discusses not only the battle but also the highlights of Nelson's life, from his early successes through to international fame and the tragic culmination of his career.

Nelson was, and is, one of Britain's most celebrated heroes. His fame has outshone that of Wellington (probably partly because of Trafalgar Square), his only rival in more modern times being Sir Winston Churchill. But Nelson's character was one of contrasts, almost of opposites. On the one hand he was a man of great personal courage, physical courage. Of frail appearance, slight in build and only five feet six inches tall, he did not possess great strength but he never shrank from exposing himself to danger, nor let excruciating pain defeat him. He had his right arm amputated without anaesthetic, lost the use of his right eye, was hit in the stomach at St Vincent and on the head at the Nile. Finally, at Trafalgar, he lay dying for over three hours in terrible pain with little or no complaint. He was a superb leader who inspired those under him of every rank. It is no exaggeration to say that his men adored him. Those who served on his ship clamoured to go with him when he transferred his captaincy or his flag. He led by personal example at the head of a boarding party at St Vincent, on the leading boat at the landings at Santa Cruz and exposed on his quarterdeck at Trafalgar. He looked after his sailors, ensured they were given fresh rations at every opportunity, he kept them healthy, and although he used the lash he did so justly and never to excess. With his captains, his 'band of brothers', he had a special relationship. He took them into his confidence, he sought their opinions, he gave them clear instructions, ensured they knew what was expected of them and allowed them to get on with the task with the minimum of supervision. This was (and is) a highly effective form of command – but rare for the time. Nelson was also a supreme professional. His seamanship and navigational skills were exceptional, and he was a first-rate tactician who understood the need to concentrate ships and firepower at close range at an enemy's weak points. He understood his opponent's vulnerabilities and he exploited them – as at Trafalgar. This combination of courage, leadership, seamanship and tactical skill made him one of the most successful admirals of all time. Little wonder hardened seamen wept openly at his death – many would have preferred defeat to the loss of their admiral.

Some of Nelson's other characteristics, however, were less appealing. His vanity was excessive, and he revelled in his public fame although he pretended not to. Admiral Lord Keith wrote shortly after Nelson's promotion to vice-admiral in January 1801, as he travelled across Europe with his mistress Emma Hamilton, 'Poor man! He is devoured with vanity, weakness and folly; was strung with ribbons, medals etc. and yet pretended that he wished to avoid the honour and ceremonies he everywhere met on the road.' Even earlier, after Nelson's victory at the Nile, General Sir John Moore remarked, 'He looks more like a Prince of the Opera than the Conqueror of the Nile.' The Sultan of Turkey created a special award for him (the Turkish Order of the Crescent) as no existing order could be given to a Christian. Nelson wore it on every occasion along with his insignia of a Knight Grand Commander, awarded by the Chapter of the Order of St Joachim. His four stars of knighthood and his two gold medals for St Vincent and the Nile made a dazzling display, which, at a time when medals on uniform were very rare, made him look boastful, if not ridiculous. Decorations were usually worn only when in full dress uniform but Nelson had copies made with sequins and wire for his everyday undress uniform – the uniform in which he was shot.

His other unattractive characteristic was his cruelty to his wife Fanny, whom he abandoned in a strikingly brutal manner. This callous act sprang from his blatantly adulterous relationship with Emma, Lady Hamilton, which developed after the Nile. He became publicly besotted with Emma, who returned his love and pandered to his whims and vanity. The liaison cost him the friendship of several of his captains – even the King ignored his presence on one social occasion – and eventually

## The Pigeons of Trafalgar Square

Trafalgar Square has long been famous for two things – Nelson and the pigeons. Until recently, several thousand of the birds descended on the square every day to be fed. Their tameness was a delight to children. They landed on your head, they ate out of your hand and they swirled up in a cloud of rushing wings at any sudden noise. They were photographed as much as Nelson on his column, and they provided a living for at least one seller of birdseed. Over the years they became almost as much of a tourist attraction as the admiral. But they made a dreadful mess and, in 2000, the Mayor of London declared war on what he described as 'rats with wings'. Birdseed sellers were banned from the square in 2001, with a new by-law authorizing a fine of £50 for those who disobey. The following year a firm was hired at a cost of £55,000 a year to bring a hunting hawk to the square every day. The hawk, named Squirt, has now become a tourist attraction in its own right, while the mayor claims it has been such an effective deterrent to the pigeons – whose numbers have shrunk to perhaps 200 – that it has saved £140,000 on cleaning up feathers and bird droppings. Nelson suffered as much as the rest of the square from pigeon detritus, so perhaps he too welcomed the hawk's arrival.

affected his personal judgement and duty to the extent that he used every excuse not to leave his lover's side, ultimately even disobeying orders. This behaviour led to his recall from the Mediterranean in July 1800.

Nevertheless, he won his battles, and that was what mattered. He gave his country victories in time of war, and against this personal defects and human weaknesses counted, rightly, as nothing.

*The Trafalgar Companion*, like its predecessor *The Waterloo Companion*, does not have to be read from cover to cover. Of course you can do that, but you can also dip in for facts, figures, analyses or recollections from the seamen who fought in the battle. About two-thirds of the book deals with Trafalgar or some aspect of it relevant to the three navies that took part. In addition to the campaign there are sections devoted to ships and seamanship, the officers and warrant officers, petty officers and seamen, guns, gunnery and tactics, a fleet comparison and command and control. Each of these is related to the battle and enhanced by numerous boxes that contain relevant anecdotes or further information to enliven the main text. There is analysis and discussion of most aspects of the fleets and their commanders. These preliminary sections are designed to give the reader a clear understanding of the ships, the commanders, their plans and how they intended to fight. The final two sections analyse the battle and the equally destructive storm afterwards. In every section coloured maps, plans, diagrams and drawings are used to illustrate the text.

At the end of each of the first seven sections there is a sub-section covering a period of Nelson's life. These sections do not purport to form a complete biography of the man, but, with the aid of numerous maps, aim to give the reader an understanding of Nelson's career and of the events and circumstances that made him what he was. These sub-sections can be read in sequence and thus form a book within a book. The Prologue takes the reader to the mizzentop of the *Redoutable*, locked alongside the *Victory*, as a French sharpshooter fires the fatal shot, and to the cockpit as Nelson lies dying there. The Epilogue describes the bringing of his body home, the funeral barge procession on the Thames and the endlessly long, melancholy march to St Paul's Cathedral the following day for the burial service.

# SYMBOLS FOR DIAGRAMS AND MAPS

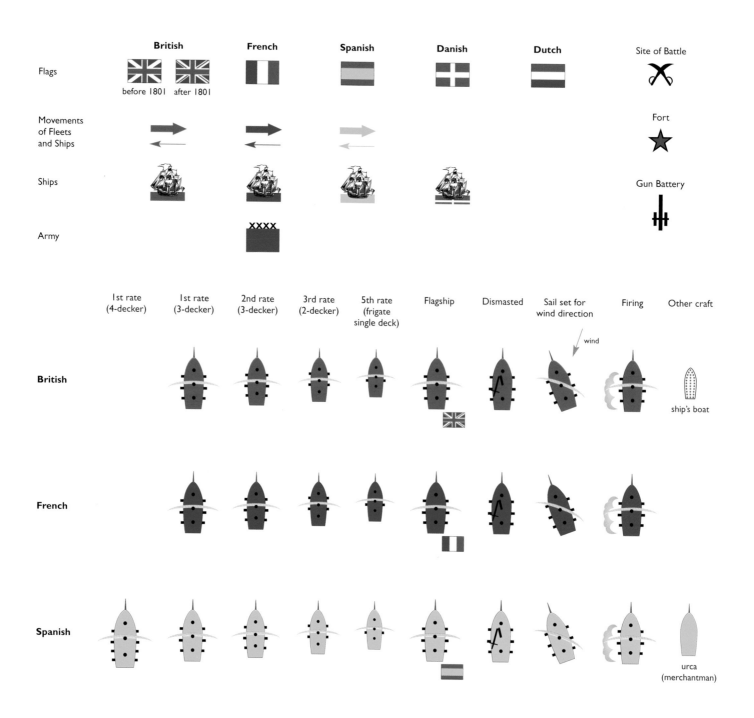

# *Prologue*
# THE DEATH OF NELSON

### NELSON: THE WOUNDING

The musket ball that slammed into Nelson's left shoulder had only travelled 70 feet. It was a massive sledgehammer blow that sent the admiral staggering forward onto his knees and then down onto the deck. The ball, weighing just under an ounce and with a diameter of almost three-quarters of an inch, tore through his epaulette carrying part of the braid right through his body – pieces of it were still attached to the ball when it came to rest. As it smashed through Nelson's torso it fractured two ribs, penetrated the left lobe of his lung and severed a branch of the pulmonary artery before lodging in his backbone and wounding the spinal cord. It was a monstrous, mortal wound. Nelson felt it break his back and knew he was finished. 'They have done for me at last, Hardy.' 'I hope not,' answered Captain Hardy. 'Yes, my backbone is shot through.'

*A view of Nelson on the* Victory's *quarterdeck, just before he received his fatal wound.*

It was 1.15 p.m. on 21 October 1805 and the *Victory* had broken through the enemy line astern of Villeneuve's flagship the *Bucentaure* some forty-five minutes earlier. Now her starboard side was grinding together with the larboard side of the French 74-gun *Redoutable*. By then the British *Téméraire* had swung in on the *Redoutable*'s starboard beam so that the French ship was sandwiched between the two. The *Victory*'s surgeon, William Beatty, was later to describe the situation thus:

> The *Redoutable* commenced a heavy fire of musketry from the tops, which was continued for a considerable time with destructive effect to the *Victory*'s crew: her great guns however being silent [Captain Lucas of the *Redoutable* disputes this], it was supposed that at different times she had surrendered; and in consequence of this opinion, the *Victory* twice ceased fire upon her by orders transmitted from the quarterdeck.
>
> At this period, scarcely a person in the *Victory* escaped unhurt who was exposed to the enemy's musketry....

To subject the enemy's exposed upper decks to a hail of musket fire and showers of grenades from the tops was a deliberate tactic of Lucas. He had trained his men remorselessly in this method of sweeping his opponent's decks clear preparatory to boarding, and it was highly effective. Nelson had refused to let his Royal Marines into the tops so their response against superior numbers of musketeers and grenade-throwers was limited, and for much of the time they had to fire upwards through the swirling smoke at figures 35 feet or more above them. It was a one-sided contest. However, below on the gundecks the situation was far more favourable. Beatty wrote:

> ... the starboard guns of the middle and lower decks were depressed, and fired with a diminished charge of powder, and three shot each, into the *Redoutable*.... When the guns on this [lower] deck were run out, their muzzles came into contact with the *Redoutable*'s side; and consequently at every discharge there was reason to fear that the enemy would take fire, and both the *Victory* and the *Téméraire* be involved in her flames. Here then was the astonishing spectacle of the fireman of each gun standing ready with a bucket full of water, which as soon as his gun was discharged he dashed into the enemy through the holes made in her side by the shot.

Such was the situation when the unknown Frenchman fired his fatal shot.

The 'fighting tops' were the D-shaped platforms about a third of the way up the ship's masts, where they were stepped. From the outer edges of these platforms the shrouds to support the foretopmast, maintopmast and mizzen-topmast were fixed. For the battle a canvas screen (banded in the blue, white, red of the Tricolour, according to Fraser in *The Sailors Whom Nelson Led*) had been placed around the tops so that the musketeers and grenade-throwers could duck out of sight to reload or ready the next missile. The man who shot Nelson did so from the mizzentop of the *Redoutable*. He was one of several soldiers in this top at the time. It is possible he was a seaman, but unlikely, as seamen were scarce on French ships whereas soldiers were in plentiful supply – and it was their job to fire muskets. A mizzentop could take some eight sharpshooters but at this stage, after three-quarters of an hour of furious fighting, probably only four or five remained.

According to Captain Lucas the two ships were locked together so that 'our poop was abeam of her [*Victory*'s] quarterdeck'. This is borne out by Beatty who states, 'the enemy's mizzen top ... was brought just abaft [nearer the stern, or to the rear of], and rather below, the *Victory*'s main yard, and of course not more than fifteen yards distant from that part of the deck where his Lordship stood'. The diagram opposite makes the relative positions of the ships clear. The French musketeers were some 50 feet above their own deck but nearer 40 above the *Victory*'s quarterdeck. As noted above, the distance from marksman to target was a mere 70 feet.

The range may have been short but shooting accurately was not easy. It has often been asserted that Nelson was shot by a 'sharpshooter' in the proper meaning of the word – what we would today term a sniper. It has been suggested that because he was so obvious in his admiral's uniform ablaze with decorations the Frenchman singled him out, took deliberate aim and brought him down. This is highly unlikely. The weapon used was a standard 1777-pattern infantry musket with a 44.5-inch barrel. This must have been extraordinarily cumbersome to use in the restricted space in the tops. Shrouds would get in the way and it would be impossible to avoid jostling with comrades who were struggling to fire or reload – one wonders what happened to wounded men and dead bodies. Then there was the heavy swell. As the ships rose and fell, the masts moved, creating a highly unstable platform. Add to this fear, excitement, the feeling of exposure, and the sight of comrades bleeding or

## Nelson is Hit – the Line of Shot

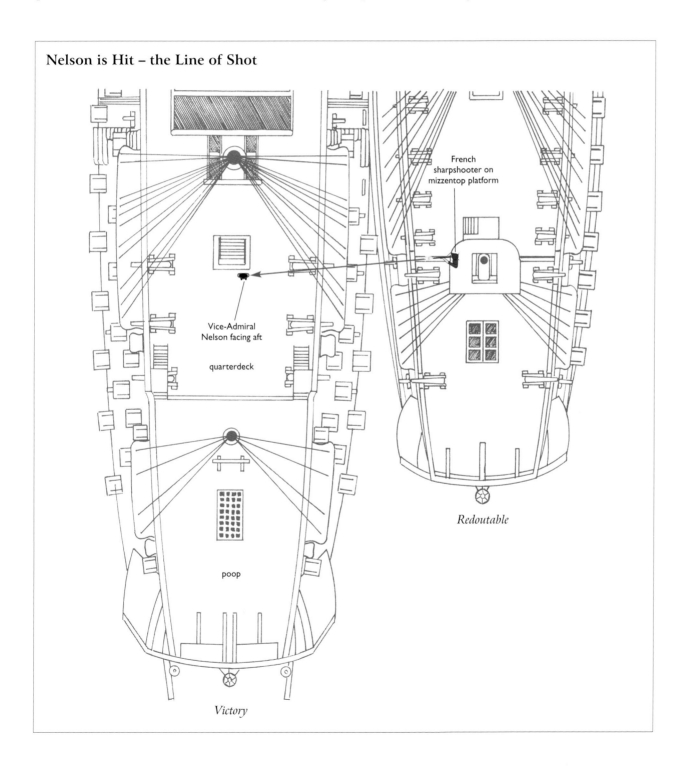

French
sharpshooter on
mizzentop platform

Vice-Admiral
Nelson facing aft

quarterdeck

*Redoutable*

poop

*Victory*

dying alongside, and taking a calm, steady aim must have been very difficult. But undoubtedly the biggest factor in preventing good shooting was the problem of not being able to see any target clearly. Everything was shrouded in smoke. Dozens of guns were continuously firing at point-blank range creating huge banks of smoke, and the lack of wind meant that they never cleared. Figures below appeared dimly through the haze, often disappearing completely as the guns fired.

Our soldier had been in action for some forty-five minutes. During that time he probably fired perhaps twenty to thirty times. Reloading would have become increasingly difficult as the fouling in the barrel accumulated; he had almost certainly had one or two misfires already. Ducking out of sight below the canvas might have made him feel safer but created great difficulties for using his long ramrod. At around 1.15 p.m. he bobbed up above the screen and thrust the long barrel through the shrouds, pointing it down in the direction of the enemy's quarterdeck. Perhaps he saw two figures walking below amongst the swirling fog of smoke and dust, perhaps he noticed their cocked hats denoting officers, perhaps he had seen and fired at them before – we can never know. He hastily aligned the barrel in their general direction and pulled the trigger. Almost certainly he never knew the damage he had done.

Nelson and Hardy had been pacing up and down the twenty or so feet between the wrecked binnacle and wheel and the main hatch for some time. Nelson was probably on Hardy's right (the more exposed position, as Hardy was a much bigger man and most of the firing was coming from the starboard side) as they walked forward. The only other naval officer on the quarterdeck when Nelson was hit apart from Captain Hardy was the first lieutenant, John Quilliam. Mr Atkinson, the master, had gone below to rig temporary steering after the wheel had been smashed. The deck around them was, however, far from deserted. The two officers had to keep amidships during their short walk as on either side 12-pounder guns were firing and leaping back with every recoil. Apart from the gun crews there were two or three midshipmen and a similar number of powdermen all crowded into a comparatively small piece of deck space. At about 1.15 p.m. Nelson turned just before reaching the hatchway. It is uncertain whether he turned to his left or right but either way he had taken perhaps one pace towards the stern when his left shoulder was hit by an enormous blow. As Hardy turned, about a second later than Nelson, the first thing he saw was his friend on his knees.

As Hardy bent over the wounded Nelson he shouted orders to Sergeant James Seckar of the Royal Marines and two seamen to carry their admiral below to the cockpit. Carefully they lifted him from the deck and to the hatchway just a pace or two from where he fell. Then came the awful business of getting him down the companionway through the upper, middle and lower gundecks before finally descending to the cockpit on the orlop deck. Although Nelson was no heavyweight the stairs are extremely steep and the head beams very low, as any visitor to *Victory* will know. It was a slow and painful descent, with Seckar and his two helpers desperate not to drop or further injure their burden. Nelson remained conscious and sufficiently aware to notice that the tiller ropes had not been replaced and to instruct a midshipman to go to the quarterdeck and remind Hardy that new ones should be rove (put through the blocks). He then had enough strength to take out his large handkerchief and spread it over his face and decorations in the hope that he would not be recognized. Just how he managed this with no right arm and his left shoulder smashed is hard to explain.

## NELSON: THE DYING

The scene below in the cockpit was grim. At least forty or more men were lying around waiting for the surgeon's attention. The midshipman's mess table was black with encrusted blood, and the lanterns swinging over it gave but poor illumination as Beatty probed and cut while his unfortunate patients were held down by loblolly men. The noise of the cries and groans was largely drowned out by the thunder and crash of the large lower-deck guns firing only a few feet overhead. The Reverend Scott had returned below after finding the quarterdeck almost as hellish as the cockpit. He had been particularly shocked by the death of young Lieutenant William Ram. Ram had his legs smashed by a roundshot and had had the bleeding checked by the application of tourniquets, but when left alone, knowing he was certain to die, he tore off the tourniquets in order to bleed to death more quickly. The sheer horror of seeing this had sent the chaplain dashing up to the quarterdeck – only to return within a few minutes.

As Sergeant Seckar and his companions, stooping low to avoid the overhead beams, carried Nelson slowly through the lines of wounded looking for a place to set him down, the handkerchief slipped from his face and chest. He was instantly recognized. Beatty was alerted by cries of, 'Mr. Beatty, Lord Nelson is here! Mr. Beatty the admiral is wounded!' Beatty turned and through the gloom saw the three figures stumbling towards him bearing their admiral. He and Mr Walter Burke, the purser, at once ran over. They took Nelson from the arms of the seamen and carried him over to a rough mattress in a space on the larboard side of the ship just forward of the after hanging magazine. He was propped up by leaning against one of the large frames of the ship's side. As he was being carried Nelson had called out, 'Who is carrying me?'

'Beatty, my Lord, and Burke.'

'Ah, Mr. Beatty! You can do nothing for me. I have but a short time to live: my back is shot through.'

'I hope the wound is not as dangerous as your Lordship imagines and that you will live to see your glorious victory.'

As he was laid down the chaplain, who had been giving lemonade to the injured, came at once to his side and 'in the anguish of grief wrung his hands, saying "Alas, how prophetic you were!"', an allusion to remarks made by the surgeon before the battle about Nelson's vulnerability. Beatty, who in his account always refers to himself as 'the surgeon', described what happened next.

> His lordship was laid upon a bed, stripped of his clothes and covered with a sheet. While this was affecting, he said to Dr Scott, 'Doctor, I told you so. Doctor, I am gone;' and after a short pause added in a low voice, 'I have to leave Lady Hamilton, and my adopted daughter, Horatia, as a legacy to my country.'
>
> The surgeon then examined the wound, assuring his Lordship that he would not put him to much pain in endeavouring to discover the course of the ball; which he soon found had penetrated deep into the chest, and had probably lodged in the spine. This being explained to his Lordship; he replied, 'he was confident his back was shot through.' The back was then examined externally, but without any injury being perceived; on which his Lordship was requested by the surgeon to make him acquainted with all his sensations.

In a low voice and with some difficulty Nelson replied, 'I feel a gush of blood every minute in my breast. I have no feeling in the lower part of my body and my breathing is difficult, and gives me great pain about the part of my spine where the ball struck. I felt it break my back.' The symptoms were fully consistent with the ball severing a branch of the pulmonary artery so that the heart pumped blood into the chest and damaging the spinal cord, producing paralysis and loss of feeling below the ball. Nelson's pulse was low and the sensations he described told Beatty that his admiral was dying and that there was little he could usefully do. For the sake of the others around him and for the morale of the ship's company Beatty did not disclose his true thoughts. The only persons to whom he subsequently indicated the mortal nature of the wounds were Captain Hardy, Dr Scott, Mr Burke and the two assistant surgeons Mr Smith and Mr Westenburg.

## Nelson's Wound

All the paintings of Nelson's last hours have been sanitized. They do not try to depict the very real suffering he went through, or the blood loss from his shoulder. During the three hours or more that he lay in the cockpit he was slowly drowning in his own blood from internal bleeding into his chest. He was not able to feel anything below his lower chest, as the ball in his back had paralysed him. His internal wounds were excruciatingly painful but he was given no opium or other palliative to alleviate his suffering – possibly because none was available, or for fear it would make him vomit. He could have gained possible slight relief only from being in a semi-upright position and perhaps having his chest gently rubbed. However, turning him onto his right side would probably have hastened the end. Even had the ball not severed a branch of the pulmonary artery the injury would have been fatal. The cutting of the spinal cord meant he would be paraplegic, and thus his bladder could not function and the small arteries in his legs would have dilated and blood collected there leading to infection. Medical science in 1805 could not cope with these sorts of injuries.

Even had Nelson received his wounds on a modern battlefield with immediate helicopter evacuation to a fully equipped field hospital, his recovery would have been doubtful. To survive he would have needed a drip in his arm to give a blood transfusion – which was not practical, as his only arm was shattered at the shoulder. He would have had to go onto a life-support machine and undergo major thoracic surgery. The best he could have expected in these circumstances was to survive paralysed from the lower chest downwards. Nelson would surely have preferred death on his ship.

When the sound of cheering was heard from the deck above Nelson enquired what was happening. Lieutenant Pasco, lying wounded nearby, raised himself up to reply that another enemy ship must have struck, which appeared to please him. As time passed Nelson kept a tenuous hold on life, lying in great pain, pale and with his breathing fast and shallow. He soon developed a raging thirst and frequently called for a drink or to be fanned. According to Beatty he maintained his pleas for 'Fan, fan!' and 'Drink, drink!' until shortly before his death. Dr Scott knelt beside him giving him sips of lemonade or wine and water, fanning with a piece of paper, rubbing his chest and reassuring him. Mr Burke was on the opposite side with his arm behind the admiral's shoulders – a position that caused him considerable discomfort as the hours passed. Nelson continually asked after Captain Hardy, insisting that he needed to see him. Dr Scott and Mr Burke did their best to reassure him that the battle was going well and that Hardy would come as soon as possible. The purser went so far as to tell him that the enemy were decisively defeated, and that he hoped his Lordship would live to be the bearer of the joyful tidings to his country. To which Nelson replied, 'It is nonsense, Mr Burke, to suppose I can live; my sufferings are great, but they will all be soon over.' Dr Scott's plea for him not to despair and that with God's help he would be restored to his country and friends drew the immediate response, 'Ah Doctor! It's all over, it's all over!'

As Nelson's life slipped away, the battle raged above. More wounded were brought below and Beatty and his assistants had to move away to attend to other duties, leaving the admiral under the care of Scott and Burke with his steward, Henry Chevalier, and valet, Gaetano Spedilo, hovering nearby anxious to help. Lying on one side was his signals officer John Pasco with grapeshot in his side, and on the other Midshipman George Westphal with a head wound. Westphal had been given Nelson's rolled-up jacket (now soaked in the blood of three men) as a pillow.

Nelson became increasingly weak, but agitated by the non-appearance of Hardy, often exclaiming, 'Will no one bring Hardy to me? He must be killed: he is surely destroyed.' Midshipman Richard Bulkeley, just sixteen years old and acting as the captain's orderly, came below to reassure his lordship that Captain Hardy was still unharmed and would come to visit him as soon as the battle above allowed. Nelson, his eyes closed, was only semi-conscious and did not see the young man, but he understood the message and asked who brought it. Mr Burke responded, 'It is Mr Bulkeley, my Lord.' 'It is his voice,' replied Nelson before whispering to Westphal, 'Remember me to your father.'

It was well over an hour after Nelson was hit before Captain Hardy could clamber down to see his friend. Beatty's account is as follows:

> They shook hands affectionately, and Lord Nelson said, 'Well Hardy, how goes the battle? How goes the day with us?'
>
> 'Very well, my Lord,' replied Captain Hardy: 'we have got twelve or fourteen of the enemy's ships in our possession; but five of their van have tacked and shew an intention of bearing down upon the *Victory*. I have therefore called two or three of our fresh ships round us, and have no doubt of giving them a drubbing.'
>
> 'I hope,' said his Lordship, 'none of *our* ships have struck, Hardy.'
>
> 'No, my Lord,' replied Captain Hardy, 'there is no fear of that.'
>
> Lord Nelson then said, 'I am a dead man, Hardy. I am going fast: it will all be over with me soon. Come nearer to me. Pray let my dear Lady Hamilton have my hair, and all other things belonging to me.' Mr Burke was about to withdraw at the commencement of this conversation; but his Lordship, perceiving his intention, desired he would remain.
>
> Captain Hardy observed that 'he hoped that Mr Beatty could yet hold out some prospect of life'.
>
> 'Oh! No', answered his Lordship; 'it is impossible. My back is shot through. Beatty will tell you so.'

Captain Hardy then returned on deck.

## Reverend Alexander J. Scott

Scott was a man of many talents, who served not just as chaplain on the *Victory* but as Nelson's private secretary, interpreter and close friend. He was devoted to Nelson, remaining at his side constantly in the cockpit throughout his dying hours, giving what comfort and encouragement he could. After Nelson died Scott refused to be parted from the body. He accompanied it home, remained with it throughout the nights of Nelson's lying in state at Greenwich, and was in attendance during the funeral processions and burial service at St Paul's Cathedral. Nelson's death had devastated him. In a letter to a friend after the battle he wrote:

> Men are not always themselves and put on their behaviour with their clothes, but if you live with a man on board ship for years; if you are continually with him in his cabin, your mind will soon find out how to appreciate him. I could forever tell of the qualities of this beloved man, Horatio Nelson. I have not shed a tear before the 21st October, and since whenever I am alone, I am quite like a child.

Scott was thirty-seven at Trafalgar, the son of a naval lieutenant. He had been educated at Charterhouse. From there he obtained a scholarship at St John's College, Cambridge, graduating in 1792. He was ordained the following year, joining the Royal Navy as a chaplain in 1793 on the *Berwick* under Lord Hood in the Mediterranean. His main talent was in his extraordinary linguistic abilities – he was fluent in French, Spanish and Italian. He was introduced to Captain Nelson of the *Agamemnon* while in the Mediterranean, but declined the position of chaplain that was offered on that occasion. He was chaplain on the 98-gun *St George* and 100-gun *Britannia* under Sir Hyde Parker and on the 98-gun *London* at Copenhagen in 1801, assisting Nelson in drawing up the treaties after the battle.

His talents were put to use in translating documents and spying, or at least eavesdropping in foreign ports. In the West Indies Admiral Duckworth, while Scott was chaplain on the frigate *Topaz*, made use of his abilities by inviting him to dinner with the French General LeClerc to try to ascertain French intentions in the Caribbean.

Scott had a severe shaking in a freak incident while on the *Topaz*. He was struck by lightning while asleep in his cabin, and the bolt also ignited some powder and cartridges stored above him. The resultant explosion and electric shock knocked out several teeth, badly injured his jaw and affected his hearing and eyesight. Although he recovered he was never again in good health and suffered from 'nerves'. In 1804 Nelson had to petition the Treasury to get him appointed as his 'foreign secretary' on the *Victory*. The blood, the smells, the screams and the hideous sights in the cockpit at the height of the battle were almost more than he could bear.

His life after Trafalgar was, however, a tranquil one, as Vicar of Southminster, Chaplain to the Prince Regent and then incumbent of a government living in Catterick, South Yorkshire. He died at Ecclesfield vicarage, Yorkshire in 1840, aged seventy-two.

Nelson had to insist several times that Beatty attend the other wounded before the surgeon could be persuaded to return to his assistants, who were at that time attending the needs of the two Royal Marine officers, James Peake and Lewis Reeves. However, he had been gone only a few minutes before Dr Scott called him back. As the surgeon stooped over his admiral so that he could be recognized Nelson said, 'Ah, Mr Beatty. I have sent for you to say what I forgot to tell you before, that all power of motion and feeling below my breast are gone; and you very well know I can live but a short time.'

Beatty replied, 'My Lord, you told me so before.' He then tested for feeling in Nelson's legs upon which Nelson whispered, 'Ah, Beatty, I am too certain of it: Scott and Burke have tried it already. *You know* I am gone.'

Finally Beatty admitted it to his face. 'My Lord, unhappily for our country nothing can be done for you.' Having confirmed the death sentence poor Beatty had to turn away to hide his tears. Nelson's response was to repeat 'I know it,' and then add, 'I feel something rising in my breast which tells me I am gone. God be praised, I have done my duty.'

When the surgeon enquired as to the severity of the pain Nelson declared, 'it continues so very severe that I wish I were dead. Yet one would like to live a little longer too.' There was then a long pause followed by, 'What would become of poor Lady Hamilton, if she knew my situation?' Beatty then quietly withdrew, unable to do anything to relieve his suffering.

Almost another hour had passed before Hardy could find the time to visit Nelson for the second time. Beatty is again the best witness of the last meeting between the dying admiral and his lifelong friend.

Lord Nelson and Captain Hardy shook hands again: and while the captain retained his Lordship's hand, he congratulated him even in the arms of Death on his brilliant victory; 'which,' he said, 'was complete; though he did not know how many of the enemy were captured, as it was impossible to perceive every ship distinctly. He was certain however of fourteen or fifteen having surrendered.'

His Lordship answered, 'That is well, but I bargained for twenty:' and then emphatically exclaimed, '*Anchor*, Hardy, *anchor!*'

To this the captain replied: 'I suppose, my Lord, Admiral Collingwood will now take it upon himself the direction of affairs.'

'Not while I live, I hope, Hardy!' cried the dying chief; and at that moment endeavoured ineffectually to raise himself from the bed.

'No,' he added, 'do *you* anchor, Hardy.'

Captain Hardy then said: 'Shall we make the signal, Sir?'

'Yes,' answered his Lordship; 'for if I live I'll anchor.' The energetic manner in which he uttered these his last orders to Captain Hardy, accompanied with his efforts to raise himself, evinced his determination never to resign command while he retained the exercise of his transcendent faculties …

He then told Captain Hardy, 'he felt that in a few minutes he should be no more;' adding in a low tone, 'Don't throw me overboard, Hardy.'

The Captain answered: 'Oh! no, certainly not.'

'Then,' replied his Lordship, 'you know what to do:' and continued, 'take care of my dear Lady Hamilton, Hardy; take care of poor Lady Hamilton. Kiss me Hardy.'

The captain now knelt down and kissed his cheek; when his Lordship said, 'Now I am satisfied, Thank God, I have done my duty.'

Captain Hardy stood for a minute or two in silent contemplation: he then knelt down again and kissed his Lordship's forehead.

His Lordship said: 'Who is that?'

The captain answered: 'It is Hardy;' to which his Lordship replied, 'God bless you, Hardy!'

After this affecting scene Captain Hardy withdrew, and returned to the quarter deck; having spent about eight minutes in this his last interview with his dying friend.

After Hardy's departure at about 4.10 p.m. Nelson's life drained away fast. The pain was becoming unbearably prolonged. He weakly asked his steward to turn him onto his side, thinking it might give him some relief. As this was being done he muttered, 'I wish I had not left the deck, for I shall soon be gone.' Shortly afterwards, turning his head slightly towards the chaplain, he said, 'I have not been a great sinner.' There was a pause before he continued, 'Remember, that I leave Lady Hamilton and my daughter Horatia as a legacy to my country: and, never forget Horatia.' Then, as if suddenly thinking the attempts at soothing administrations had stopped, he called, 'Drink, drink', 'Fan, fan!' and 'Rub, rub'.

He was now, mercifully, slipping in and out of consciousness. With his eyes closed he murmured, softly and repeatedly, 'Thank God, I have done my duty.' Dr Scott now gave up trying to give him drinks and the fanning ceased but he continued to rub his chest, while Mr Burke still supported Nelson's shoulders. Neither made any further attempt to speak. After five minutes of silence his steward, Chevalier, went to fetch Beatty as he feared the admiral had at last gone. Beatty knelt down and took his hand but could feel no pulse in the wrist. He placed his hand on Nelson's forehead – it was cold. At that moment the dying admiral opened his eyes, looked up, and closed them again. Beatty returned to his duties.

Five minutes later, at 4.30 p.m., Chevalier again went over to the surgeon to say he thought Nelson was dead. Beatty went back to find Scott still rubbing his chest and Burke still supporting him. He confirmed to them both that the admiral was no more. At the moment of triumph in what was to become the most famous naval victory of all time the victor, the architect of success, had lost his life. It was a tragedy that many thought was too high a price to pay.

## NELSON: THE AVENGING

The scene reverts to the poop and quarterdeck of the *Victory*. Long after his retirement Major Lewis Rotely, Royal Marines, gave a talk on his experiences as a young second-lieutenant at Trafalgar. What he said in relation to the weight of fire sweeping the upper works of the flagship that afternoon bears repeating.

It was like a hailstorm of bullets passing over our heads on the poop, where we had forty marines stationed with small arms. It has been stated that Lord Nelson ordered them to lie down at their quarters until wanted, but no such order was given, and no man went down until knocked down …

Captain Adair's party was reduced to less than ten men, himself wounded in the forehead by splinters. One of his last orders to me was, 'Roteley, fire away as fast as you can,' when a ball struck him on the back of the neck and he was a corpse in a moment – and at the same time [slightly earlier] our revered Chief fell, having received his mortal wound from a soldier in the mizzen top of the *Redoutable* …

Some Frenchman has vaunted that he shot Nelson and survived the battle, and I have heard that a book had been published so stating, but it must be a romance, as I know the man was shot in five minutes after Nelson fell [it probably took a little longer].

If nothing else Roteley's account of the heavy weight of musket fire that poured down onto *Victory*'s upper decks suggests it is very unlikely that the ball that hit Nelson was deliberately aimed.

## Midshipman Pollard's Later Career

For a young midshipman of eighteen who had already been in the service for eight years and survived a shipwreck off Jersey aged thirteen, John Pollard's career after Trafalgar was something less than inspiring. He was on the *Victory* during the chase after Villeneuve to the Caribbean and back in early 1805, and at Trafalgar he held a key appointment as signals midshipman, armed with telescope and slate to spot signals and write down messages. Although slightly wounded early in the engagement he carried on with his duties on the exposed poop deck, and afterwards he was acknowledged to be the man who avenged Nelson's death by shooting down the French soldiers in the *Redoutable's* mizzentop. All this would surely indicate a sparkling future ahead.

It was not to be. Although he was promoted lieutenant in 1806 that was effectively the end of his career. He served in the boats of the 74-gun *Brunswick* at the attack and capture of the Danish brig *Fama* and the cutter *Salorman*. However, he was invalided home in 1814 when still a lieutenant. After remaining on half pay for fourteen years he obtained a three-year appointment in Chatham Dockyard. Another five years on half pay followed before he accepted an appointment as a lieutenant in the Coast Guard. In 1853, with the Crimean War only a year away and almost fifty years after Trafalgar, Pollard, aged sixty-five, was appointed to the staff at Greenwich Hospital – still a lieutenant! Ten years later he had received no promotion. Finally, in 1864, he retired after fifty-eight years as a lieutenant and a grateful government rewarded him with the rank of commander. He died four years after his retirement in 1868, aged eighty-one, having served throughout the Napoleonic Wars and lived through the Crimean and American Civil Wars.

Despite some arguments along the way, history now seems to accept that the man who avenged Nelson's death was the signals midshipman, John Pollard. Like everybody else on the poop or quarterdeck that afternoon Pollard, who was only eighteen and came from Cornwall, was shocked at the hail of fire directed at him and his comrades. He was one of the first to be wounded, being struck by a splinter on his right arm, and he then had his telescope struck from his hand by a musket ball just before another smashed into his leg. But the ball shattered the watch in his pocket rather than his thigh bone, and he was only bruised. The events as far as Pollard was concerned after Nelson had been taken below are best described by himself. Writing in 1836, when he was a forty-nine-year-old lieutenant in the Coast Guard, Pollard gave his account of what happened to the soldier who killed Nelson.

> After being engaged with the *Redoutable* for some time, I observed the officers and men falling very fast, both on the poop and quarter deck, when my attention was arrested by seeing in the tops of the *Redoutable* a number of soldiers in a crouching position loading and directing their destructive fire on the poop and quarter deck of the *Victory*. The Signal Quarter-Master call'd King was standing by me at the time. I pointed them out to him, and there being a number of spare muskets on the Signal Chest for the use of the marines, I took up one – King supplying me with the Ball cartridges from 2 barrels kept on the after part of the poop for the use of the marines. Captain Adair of the Marines and the small party he had left (the others being either killed or wounded), was firing from the starboard of the *Victory* into the *Redoutable's* deck when Captain Adair was killed. The two Lieutenants of Marines were previously wounded by musket balls. As often as I saw the French soldiers rise breast high in the Tops to fire on the *Victory's* deck, I continued firing, until there was not one to be seen. King, the Quarter-Master, in the act of giving me the last parcel of Ball cartridges, was shot through the forehead and fell dead before me; this event gave my feelings a great shock. I was the only officer left alive on the poop after the action ceased (that was stationed there). Thus originated the belief that I was the Person who shot the Man that killed Lord Nelson.

This was not the end of the story. In the early 1860s a series of letters appeared in *The Times* under the heading of 'Who Shot the Man that Killed Nelson?' These letters implied that the honour should be shared with another (acting) midshipman, Edward Collingwood (no relation of the admiral). This correspondence prompted an elderly Pollard to pick up his pen once more. His letter was published in *The Times* on 13 May 1863.

Having seen several letters in *The Times* lately with reference to my name, I feel at length called on to come forward to state a few particulars, which differ materially from your correspondent's statements of yesterday.

It is true my old shipmate Collingwood, who has now been dead some years, did come on the poop for a short time. I had discovered the men crouching in the tops of the *Redoutable*, and pointed them out to him, when he took up a musket and fired once: he then left the poop, I conclude, to return to his station on the quarter-deck.

I remained there firing till there was not a man to be seen in the top; the last one was coming down the mizzen rigging and he fell from my fire also.

King, the quarter-master, was killed while in the act of handing me a parcel of ball cartridge, long after Collingwood had left the poop. I remained there for some time after the action was concluded, assisting in rigging the jurymast; then I was ushered into the wardroom, where Sir Thomas Hardy and other officers were assembled, and complimented by them as the person who avenged Lord Nelson's death which fact was afterwards gazetted [actually a statement in the *Gibraltar Chronicle*].

Far from wishing to disparage my old friend Collingwood, I only wish he had received the honours due to him for having shared in that great naval action.

## France and the Western Mediterranean in 1804 — Map 1

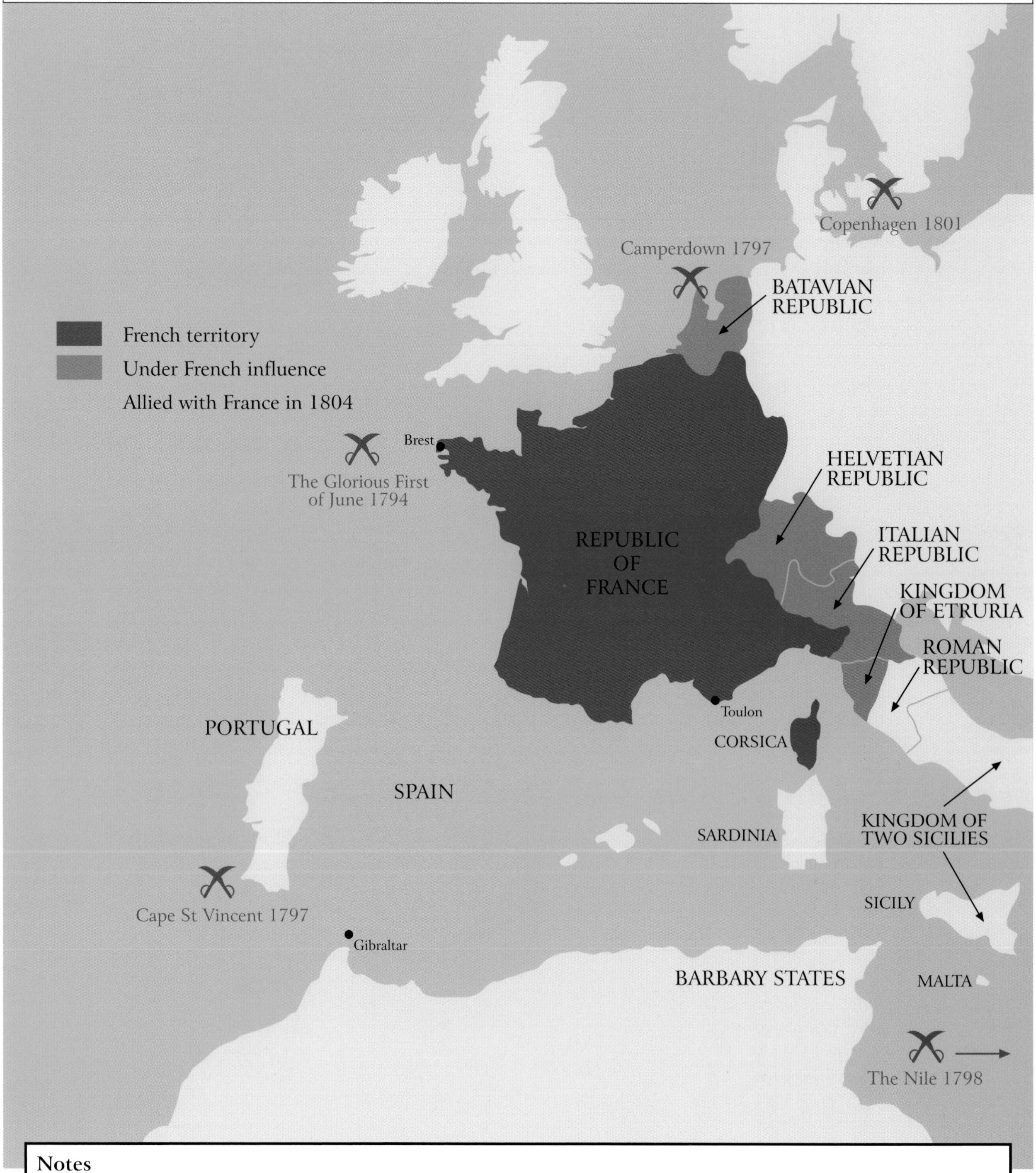

Copenhagen 1801

Camperdown 1797

BATAVIAN REPUBLIC

French territory

Under French influence

Allied with France in 1804

Brest

The Glorious First of June 1794

HELVETIAN REPUBLIC

ITALIAN REPUBLIC

REPUBLIC OF FRANCE

KINGDOM OF ETRURIA

ROMAN REPUBLIC

PORTUGAL

Toulon

CORSICA

SPAIN

SARDINIA

KINGDOM OF TWO SICILIES

SICILY

Cape St Vincent 1797

Gibraltar

BARBARY STATES

MALTA

The Nile 1798

### Notes

- In the seven years prior to the 1802 Peace of Amiens there were five major defeats at sea for France and her allies. Nelson played an important role at Cape St Vincent and Copenhagen and led the fleet to victory at the Nile.

- On land the French had been much more successful. The Peace confirmed France's extended boundaries to the Rhine and her influence in the western Mediterranean. Spain's re-entry into the war on the French side in 1804 was a strategic blow of considerable consequence to Britain.

- The alliance of France and Spain meant that Nelson, when in command in the Mediterranean, was faced with a mainly hostile coastline, which severely restricted his ability to resupply and refit his fleet. He also feared that French influence would expand further down Italy and to Sicily and Sardinia.

# The Campaign

## EUROPE IN EARLY 1805

An exhausted, punch-drunk Europe heaved a collective sigh of relief when the Treaty of Amiens was finally concluded on 25 March 1802. It brought a temporary halt to a ten-year struggle against Revolutionary France, led from 1799 by Napoleon Bonaparte, who during the war rose from unknown artillery captain to First Consul (for life) of France and most of her recently acquired dominions. These long years of war had begun with the triumph of the 'red cap' of *Liberté, Fraternité* and *Egalité* throughout France. The revolutionaries had been most noticeably zealous in ensuring *Egalité*. In a twelve-month period during 1793–4 more than 2,500 aristocratic heads (including those of King Louis XVI and his wife Marie Antoinette) bounced into bloody baskets after receiving a quick kiss from 'Madame Guillotine' at the touch of her consort – the bare-chested man in a black hood. The other countries of Europe – still ruled by monarchs – were appalled and terrified by these events, and in 1792 Austria and Prussia went to war with France, soon followed by most of the rest of Europe.

Throughout the last decade of the eighteenth century, French revolutionary armies became accustomed to victory on land, particularly in Europe. France beat the Prussians at Valmy and the Austrians at Jemappes, and then, with monotonous regularity, at Montenotte, Castiglione, Arcole, Rivoli and Marengo (after which Napoleon was to name one of his horses). Two more defeats at Hochstadt and Hohenlinden finally brought the dispirited Austrians to the peace table in early 1802. In the West Indies the sugar islands were the scene of a bewildering scramble for possession, with most of today's tourist destinations changing hands again and again. With news taking weeks to arrive, neither London nor Paris could be certain who owned what at any one time. Only in Egypt did Bonaparte fare less well; his initial victories at the Pyramids and Jaffa were overturned by the British at Alexandria in March 1801, and in August of that year 20,000 French troops surrendered. At sea it was different: France and her allies received a series of hammer blows at the hands of the British, who first defeated the French navy at 'The Glorious First of June' (1794), then the Spanish at Cape St Vincent (1797), the Dutch at Camperdown (1797), the French again at the Nile (1798) and finally the Danes at Copenhagen (1801). Trafalgar was to be the *coup de grâce*.

The Treaty of Amiens was signed by Britain, France, Spain and Holland. Paris was jubilant at its contents. Despite defeat at Copenhagen the previous year, despite the loss of Egypt, despite surrendering several Caribbean islands, France appeared to recoup (or at least deny to Britain) almost as much by the pen as she had lost by the sword. Although compelled to give up the Papal States and the Kingdom of the Two Sicilies, she retained Nice, Savoy, Piedmont and the territories she had seized on the west bank of the Rhine, as well as Holland. With overseas possessions she did particularly well. Britain obligingly agreed to hand back the Cape (to the Dutch), Egypt (to the Egyptians), Malta (to the Knights of St John), and in the Caribbean Tobago, Martinique, Demerara (Guyana), Berbice (Guyana) and Curaçao (to the Dutch). She hung on to Trinidad and Ceylon (Sri Lanka) and steadfastly refused to vacate Malta.

As has been the case on numerous notable occasions in the two centuries since, Britain became too concerned with greedily grabbing a 'peace dividend'. Doing so seriously weakened her security. The fourteen months of peace following Amiens were bad for Britain. Her manufacturers found to their cost that the ports of Europe remained closed to their goods. But although commerce might be dead, Britain's wealthier citizens delighted in visiting the continent on sightseeing trips. Their coaches clattered happily through the streets of Paris, stopping to view the paintings in the Louvre, to admire the splendour of Notre Dame cathedral or to sample the novelty of French cuisine and wines. In the Place de Carrousel they were sometimes able to watch and listen in awe to the military pomp and precision, accompanied by the blare and thump of martial music, as the First Consul carried out one of his frequent reviews of his veterans.

Napoleon used the peace to prepare for war – economically, militarily and diplomatically. He forged cannons, he filled arsenals, he replenished scores of warehouses that had been emptied by the British blockade, he built more ships and he recruited more sailors and soldiers. He became president of a republic that included Milan, Modena, Bologna and Romagna, in total a very substantial swathe of northern Italy. He controlled Genoa and Switzerland (then known as the Helvetic Republic). His rapidly expanding navy began once more to pose a serious threat to the eastern Mediterranean, including Naples, Sicily, Greece and Egypt (again). Even India seemed endangered.

While the First Consul openly built up his military and economic muscle, the Prime Minister in Britain did the opposite. Henry Addington (later Viscount Sidmouth) was, by and large, a

dithering and incompetent premier. During this period he succeeded in halving the Army, paying off 60 per cent of the Navy's
ships-of-the-line and discharging over 40,000 trained seamen –
the hardened veterans of long years of blockade duty and of the
battles that had trounced the Spanish, French and Danish fleets.
Addington's reckless disarmament programme was ably supervised by a man who should have known much better, Admiral
Earl St Vincent, who had earned his title as the victor at the great
battle of that name five years earlier. Huge quantities of war
stores were auctioned off cheaply, much of them to French agents
who, scarcely able to contain their glee, shipped them home over
the Channel to an astonished but grateful government.

But what of Spain? How did she come to be fighting alongside France in the events that led, ultimately, to the crushing
defeat of the Combined French and Spanish Fleet on the grey
waters off Cape Trafalgar? At the start of the French Revolution
the fate of the Bourbon King Louis along with hundreds of
France's nobility horrified, indeed terrified, the Spanish
Bourbon monarchy. It was this fear of the anti-royalist revolution spreading, of Spanish peasants donning the dreaded 'red
cap' and baying for aristocratic blood in Madrid, that ensured
Spain joined the First Coalition against France (1793–5). Her
allies were Britain, Austria, Prussia, several smaller German
monarchies and Russia, together with the Kingdom of Sardinia
and Naples. Nevertheless, within two years Spain dropped out.

She had become ever more fearful of Britain's imperialist ambi-
tions in both the Mediterranean and the Caribbean. Islands
such as Cuba, Puerto Rico and Trinidad, in particular, were seen
as vital sources of revenue for the Spanish government coffers.
Sugar was a hugely expanding industry, for Spain second only to
gold and silver as a source of income from her overseas territories. Worries that Britain was intending to seize these colonies
outweighed anxiety over French revolutionary expansion in
Europe. From withdrawal from the anti-French alliance, it was
but a short step to siding with her in armed conflict. Thus Spain
declared war on Britain on 11 October 1796. An extract from
her declaration makes her principal motive abundantly clear.

> That ambitious and greedy nation [Britain] has once more
> proclaimed to the world that she recognizes no law but
> that of aggrandizement of her own trade, achieved by her
> global despotism on the high seas; our patience is spent,
> our forbearance is exhausted; we must now turn our gaze
> to the dignity of our throne ... we must declare war on the
> King of England and on the English nation.

Spain's act had the effect of almost doubling the opposition to
the Royal Navy. In the Mediterranean the pressure was enough to
force Admiral John Jervis to abandon naval bases on Corsica and
Elba, and transfer his command to Gibraltar and his fleet activities to the Atlantic coasts of Spain and Portugal. However, within

---

## Spanish Reluctance to Join the War in 1804

The renewal of the war between France and England in May
1803, following fourteen months of peace after the Treaty of
Amiens, posed something of a dilemma for Spain. How could she
remain neutral without giving offence to either of the
belligerents? In the end Spain yielded to the pressure of
Napoleon, who was massing troops on her borders, and tried to
buy her neutrality by paying a substantial subsidy to France. This
was the pretext for England to attack, without any declaration of
war, four Spanish ships bringing treasure from South America.
Four British frigates, the *Indefatigable* (44), *Medusa* (38), *Lively*
(38) and *Amphion* (32), intercepted the supposedly neutral
Spanish off Cape St Mary, west of Cadiz, on 5 October 1804.
Commodore Graham Moore (*Indefatigable*), the younger brother
of General Sir Thomas Moore who was killed at the Battle of
Corunna five years later, commanded the British squadron tasked
with hunting for the neutral frigates in the waters between Cadiz
and Gibraltar. Early on 5 October the Spanish ships were sighted.
They were the *Medea* (42), flying the flag of Rear-Admiral Don
José Bustamente and the 36-gun *La Mercedes*, *La Fama* and *La
Clara*. Moore's report to Cornwallis describes events:

> My orders were to detain his [Bustamente's] squadron ...
> it was my earnest wish to execute them [his orders]
> without bloodshed ... after hailing them to make them
> shorten sail without effect, I fired a shot across the rear-
> admiral's fore-foot [foremast sail], on which he shortened
> sail, and I sent Lieutenant Ascott [in a boat] to inform
> him that my orders were to detain his squadron ... . As
> soon as the officer returned, with an unsatisfactory
> answer, I fired another shot ahead of the admiral, and
> bore down close on his weather bow. At this moment the

> admiral's second stern fired into the *Amphion*, and the
> admiral fired into the *Indefatigable*, and I made the signal
> for close battle. ... In less than ten minutes the *La
> Mercedes* ... blew up alongside the *Amphion* with a
> tremendous explosion.

Within half an hour the *La Fama* and *La Clara* struck their colours
while the *Medea* fled but was chased and later captured by the
*Lively*. Moore continued, 'As soon as our boats had taken possession
of the rear-admiral, we made sail for the floating fragments of the
unfortunate Spanish frigate that blew up; but, except forty taken
up by the *Amphion*'s boats, all on board perished.'

Although over a million silver dollars had disappeared with
the *La Mercedes*, the treasure seized was well worth the effort. The
main haul consisted of 3,166,850 silver dollars, 1,119,658 gold
dollars, 150,011 ingots of gold, 1,735 pigs of copper, 4,723 bars
of tin and 25,925 seal skins. Despite this flagrant breach of
neutrality and robbery, Spain still dithered about joining
Napoleon again until the end of December.

There is a tragic but interesting footnote to this incident. A
Captain Alvear was returning home on the *Mercedes* after thirty
years in Montevideo, during which time he had accumulated a
wife, five sons, four daughters and a modest £30,000 with which
to enjoy his retirement. On the approach of the English ships,
for some unexplained reason he and his eldest son transferred to
the *Medea*. From her deck he watched with utter horror as the
*Mercedes* exploded, annihilating nine of his family and his
fortune in a sheet of flame. Nothing could replace the human
loss but, in an age when it was possible for politicians to be
gentlemen, the British government later restored the grief-
stricken captain his money.

a few months the situation swung dramatically in Britain's favour, with Jervis' resounding victory with fifteen ships-of-the-line over a Spanish fleet of twenty-three off Cape St Vincent on 14 February 1797. In this battle Nelson, flying his commodore's broad pennant on the 74-gun *Captain*, greatly distinguished himself in a boarding action (see Section Three). Jervis became Earl St Vincent. In the same year Britain seemed to justify Spanish commercial concerns in the West Indies by annexing Trinidad.

The Spanish Navy was, however, allowed several years of grace to recover. The great naval victories of Nelson over the French at the Nile (August 1798) and the Danes (then allied to France along with Sweden and Prussia) at Copenhagen (April 1801) did not involve Spanish ships. It was Bonaparte's victories on land, especially against the Austrians, that brought down the Second Coalition (Britain, Austria, Portugal, Russia and Naples). All involved were looking forward to the peace following the Treaty of Amiens – although for differing reasons.

Amiens turned out to be a truce rather than a peace. During the fourteen months when open hostilities ceased Napoleon continued to amass his huge invasion flotilla across the Channel and annexed Switzerland and Piedmont, which he described as 'mere bagatelles'. After failing to withdraw his troops from occupied Holland, Switzerland, Piedmont and the Italian Republic he imposed high trade tariffs on British imports, and soon afterwards used Britain's refusal to evacuate Malta to declare war again.

Spain's re-entry into the conflict was triggered by Britain's persistence in the time-honoured activity of plundering Spanish treasure ships – despite Spain's supposed neutrality. In November 1804 four such ships were seized on their way back from Montevideo (South America). Spain declared war the following month.

## THE WAR AT SEA

'A ship in port is safe, but that is not what ships are made for.' This anonymous quote aptly describes, in general terms, the strategy of both the British and French fleets in the two years leading up to Trafalgar. Until January 1805 the object of the British admirals in the Channel (Cornwallis) and the Mediterranean (Nelson) was to keep their fleets at sea. During the same period the French admirals were mostly content to keep their ships secure in port. The British were blockading, the French being blockaded. From May 1803, when Britain again declared war on France, until 11 January 1805, when Rear-Admiral Missiessy slipped out of Rochefort en route to the West Indies, there was little serious warlike activity either on land or sea in Europe. It was a 'phoney war' similar in some respects (although of much longer duration) to that which existed between Britain's declaration of war on Germany in 1939 and Hitler's lightning drive through France in May 1940 after months of waiting, watching, planning and preparing.

Throughout 1803, 1804 and the first nine months of 1805 there was not a single major battle on land in Europe. Only in the Caribbean did the squabble over islands resume. The British captured St Lucia, Tobago, Demerara and Essequibo (Guyana) in 1803 and Surinam the following year. Not until Napoleon's triumph on the Ulm, where 30,000 Austrians raised the white flag of surrender on 20 October 1805, the day before Trafalgar, were the Napoleonic Wars dramatically re-ignited on land. Trafalgar was the climax of a seeming eternity of blockade, of searching an empty ocean, of chasing over many thousands of miles for an eternally elusive enemy.

# BRITISH NAVAL STRATEGY 1803–5

As Earl St Vincent liked to boast, 'I don't say the French can't come, I only say they can't come by sea.' He was referring to the possibility of an attempted French invasion of England from across the Channel. His words give a clue to Britain's basic strategy during the two years before Trafalgar – it was primarily (but not entirely) defensive. The overriding requirement during this period was defence against invasion. Next came the defence of Britain's trade, for Britain's prosperity, as today, depended on overseas commerce. Without the ability of merchant ships to fetch and carry goods across the oceans, her economy would face ruin. For protection, merchant ships were grouped into large convoys, which then sailed with warships (often frigates) as escorts scurrying to and fro, much as a sheepdog darts about protecting his unruly flock. Protecting trade, and the overseas possessions from which the raw materials traded mostly came, was a task second only to preventing invasion. During much of the Napoleonic Wars a large proportion of these duties were carried out in the clear blue waters around the Caribbean, or the 4,500 miles of much duller Atlantic waters that separated them from Britain. These islands were, as we have seen, continually changing hands. The only one to be spared a bloody history of conquest was Barbados. Peacefully annexed by Britain in 1605, it remained a

colony for over 350 years – the only enemy faced ashore being, as throughout the West Indies, 'yellow jack' (yellow fever).

At the same time as ensuring unimpeded passage for British merchantmen, the Royal Navy was tasked with attacking those of the enemy. British captains were forever on the lookout for opportunities to seize the slow, overloaded merchant ships of France or Spain – sometimes by scattering and plundering a convoy or, more often, by snatching a straggler. Any captured vessel became a prize to be sailed (occasionally towed) home to be sold off by a prize agent. Eventually, months or even years later, the proceeds would be distributed among the officers and crew of the ship that took her (see pp. 141–2). Prize money was one of the eagerly anticipated perks of naval service, and one to which Nelson attached considerable personal importance. Many senior officers made handsome fortunes through this system (see Section Three), which was the Navy's equivalent to the Army's plundering cities taken by storm. Both soldiers and sailors regarded these opportunities as essential compensation for their low pay and tough, dangerous conditions.

The final major task of the Royal Navy was to bring the enemy fleet to battle. A successful major action was the surest way of safeguarding Britain from invasion and, at the same time,

## British Fleet/Squadron Deployment, 1805

### Irish Squadron

**Tasks**: Protecting trade and Ireland. In 1805, providing a frigate screen from Southern Ireland to Cape Finisterre
**Base**: Cork
**Strength**: 12 frigates
8 sloops

### North Sea Fleet

**Task**: Blocking invasion from the North Sea
**Bases**: Downs, Ramsgate, Dungeness, Yarmouth, Leith
**Strength** (in 5 squadrons): 11 ships-of-the-line
16 frigates

### North America (Newfoundland) Squadron

**Tasks**: Convoy protection, 'cruising'
**Bases**: St John's, Newfoundland
**Strength**: 4 frigates
9 smaller ships

### North America (Nova Scotia) Squadron

**Tasks**: Convoy protection, 'cruising'
**Base**: Halifax
**Strength**: 4 frigates
4 smaller ships

### Jamaica Squadron

**Tasks**: Attacking enemy convoys and territories
**Base**: Port Royal
**Strength**: 3 ships-of-the-line
15 frigates
8 sloops

### Leeward Islands Squadron

**Tasks**: Protecting British colonies and merchant ships, escorting, 'cruising' and attacking enemy islands and shipping
**Bases**: Antigua and Barbados
**Strength**: 6 ships-of-the-line
13 frigates
13 sloops

### Channel Fleet (Cornwallis)

**Tasks**: Defending Britain against invasion
**Bases**: Portsmouth and Plymouth
**Strength**: 35 ships-of-the-line
16 frigates

### Notes

• These are the approximate numbers of ships-of-the-line, frigates and, where known, sloops and smaller ships. The actual numbers available varied from day to day as ships went off for victualling, repair or on detached duties.

• Main tasks and bases only are shown.

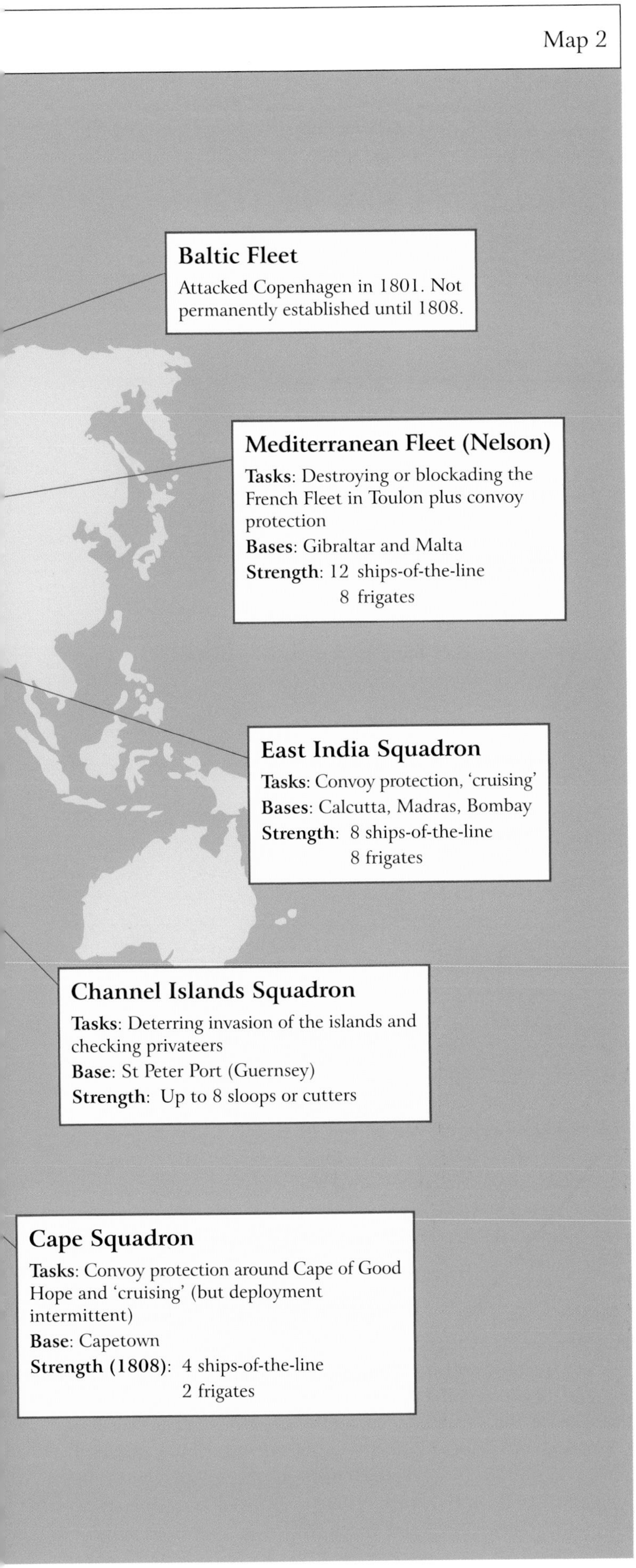

Map 2

### Baltic Fleet

Attacked Copenhagen in 1801. Not permanently established until 1808.

### Mediterranean Fleet (Nelson)

**Tasks**: Destroying or blockading the French Fleet in Toulon plus convoy protection
**Bases**: Gibraltar and Malta
**Strength**: 12 ships-of-the-line
8 frigates

### East India Squadron

**Tasks**: Convoy protection, 'cruising'
**Bases**: Calcutta, Madras, Bombay
**Strength**:  8 ships-of-the-line
8 frigates

### Channel Islands Squadron

**Tasks**: Deterring invasion of the islands and checking privateers
**Base**: St Peter Port (Guernsey)
**Strength**:  Up to 8 sloops or cutters

### Cape Squadron

**Tasks**: Convoy protection around Cape of Good Hope and 'cruising' (but deployment intermittent)
**Base**: Capetown
**Strength (1808)**:  4 ships-of-the-line
2 frigates

protecting her trade and colonies. This was aggressive defence. To rule the seas, which is what Britain did for over a hundred years after Trafalgar, was the ultimate triumph for an island nation. The problem lay in finding, catching and forcing a battle on an enemy that was increasingly reluctant to accept such a trial of strength. After Nelson's brilliant victory over the French at the Nile, it was to be seven years before they were forced to fight a decisive fleet action again, at Cape Trafalgar.

Britain implemented her naval strategy by the maintenance and deployment of the Royal Navy around the world. The Navy was divided into a number of fleets and squadrons, each with an area of operations, responsibilities and duties. The cornerstone of this strategy during the two years prior to Trafalgar was the blockade. To understand Trafalgar it is necessary to understand the system of fleets, their deployment and the blockade policy.

## THE FLEETS AND SQUADRONS

In 1804 Britain had a Royal Navy of some 726 ships. Of these 189 were modern, two- or three-decker line-of-battle ships with between 64 and 120 guns – details of the ships and how they were 'rated', armed and operated are in Section Two. Another 27 were obsolete, smaller, line-of-battle ships with 50 to 60 guns. About 204 were frigates with 22 to 46 guns – smaller, faster, jack-of-all-trade ships primarily used as an admiral's eyes and ears. The balance of 324 was made up of sloops, brig/sloops, brigs, schooners and cutters with anything from 2 to 20 guns, together with bomb vessels and transports. Of these up to half might be unavailable for sea duties for various reasons – serving as guard or hospital ships, 'in ordinary' (in reserve in port with masts taken out), or in port for resupply, refitting or repairs. In March 1805, at the start of the Trafalgar campaign, although more ships had been built and commissioned, the actual number of ships-of-the-line at sea in the Channel and Mediterranean Fleets was only 45. Around the world there were some 79 ships-of-the-line and 98 frigates in commission at sea.

The majority of ships in commission were divided into fleets under a senior admiral (which in turn could consist of several squadrons) or independent squadrons usually under a subordinate admiral (see Section Seven: Command and Control). The crucial ships in any large fleet were the line-of-battle ships and the frigates – the former to fight the enemy fleet in a major action, the latter to find them, tail them and relay information. A fleet might have fewer ships than a squadron in total but it always had more ships-of-the-line. During the period under review, their deployment and strategic roles were as follows.

### Fleets (Map 2)

*The Channel Fleet* (also known as the Western Squadron or Atlantic Fleet)
This was the most crucial fleet in the Royal Navy, since its primary task was the close defence of Britain against invasion. As its various titles imply, its ships were deployed to the west or southwest of the British Isles; its area of operations covered the coasts of France, Spain and Portugal. Its duties included the blockade of all French ports from Brest southwards to Rochefort and Lorient, together with the Spanish ones of Ferrol and Corunna, and it patrolled the 600 miles of Portugal's coast. In March 1805 the newly formed 'Spanish Squadron' under Rear-Admiral Orde, watching Cadiz and the western approaches to Gibraltar (until

---

## Convoys

---

Convoys were often unpopular with both the merchantmen and their naval escorts. While many better-class shipowners demanded proper protection from the Admiralty, there were other owners who did all they could to avoid the convoy system, since a fast ship contriving to slip through with her cargo at a time of shortage was sure of a large profit, whereas when a convoy arrived a glut was inevitably created so prices fell. Such a single ship ran the risk of capture, but it was the business of Lloyds underwriters to reimburse her owners for that. Some owners were in league with the enemy, and welcomed capture and the subsequent insurance scam. To check these practices a number of convoy laws were passed, the most important of which, in 1798, ruled that no ship was to leave a British port without a convoy, under penalty of a £1,000 fine.

The general unpopularity of convoys, even among reputable shipowners, was due to delays (often of weeks) in collecting ships at the terminal ports, followed by snail-like progress, as all were compelled to keep station with the slowest sailers. The arrangement caused an enormous loss of time and money. In addition, the average merchantman did not want to have any more to do with the navy than was necessary because of the activities of the press gang. One way of evading these problems was to take out a privateer's commission or obtain Letters of Marque, for privateers were permitted to sail without a convoy. A privateer's commission permitted a large East Indiaman, for example, to fire first without her officers being hanged for piracy.

Convoy escort duties could involve any Royal Navy ship but were most often given to 74s or frigates. The merchant ships of that day included every possible rig. Their speed and handiness varied considerably, with those without copper plates below the waterline becoming so fouled with weed and barnacles that they could scarcely move through the water. The difficulty of organizing and controlling a large convoy of such diverse vessels was a nightmare for the escort commander. If they were given reasonable sea room the convoy would be so spread out that effective protection would be impossible. One convoy in 1794 consisted of 600 sail escorted by three dozen warships. Another in the same year, carrying war stores from Sweden, contained 1,000 ships. With such an ungainly charge it is little wonder even the best naval captains were liable to lose many ships.

---

then part of the Mediterranean Fleet's area), was also effectively part of the Channel Fleet (see Map 3). The Channel Fleet's priority, in terms of observing and blockading, was the main French naval base at Brest. There was always a considerable number of enemy warships in this harbour, which was located at the western entrance to the Channel – the area most threatened by a potential French invasion. For this reason the squadron blockading Brest always consisted of a substantial number of ships-of-the-line as they had to be prepared to fight a major action if the French fleet sailed. It was the fundamental principle of British naval strategy at the time that the Channel Fleet must be strong and, except in really appalling weather, in position – the bulk of it normally off Ushant (the tiny rocky island just west of Brest). Other fleets or squadrons were under instructions to make for Ushant if uncertain of their orders, in circumstances of confusion or when their immediate enemy had disappeared. It was rather like the Army's dictum that a general in doubt should march to the sound of the guns: in the Royal Navy an admiral should make for the Channel. If the Channel was safe, Britain was safe.

During the years 1803–6 this most crucial of naval commands was under Admiral Sir William Cornwallis (younger brother of General Charles Cornwallis, who, in 1781 had been forced to surrender at Yorktown, a defeat that finally gave the American colonies their independence). Admiral Cornwallis flew his flag as commander-in-chief of the fleet on the 110-gun three-decker *Ville de Paris*. His second-in-command was Vice-Admiral Sir Charles Cotton. As Map 3 indicates, in March 1805, at the opening of moves that marked the seven-month run-up to the Battle of Trafalgar, he had under him two subordinate admirals each with their own squadron: Rear-Admiral Sir Thomas Graves off Rochefort and Vice-Admiral Sir Robert Calder off Ferrol. Rear-Admiral Sir John Orde's squadron off Cadiz was a semi-independent force supposedly directly under the Admiralty. In early 1805 the Channel Fleet had a combined strength of thirty-five ships-of-the-line and sixteen frigates.

The main bases of this fleet were Portsmouth and Plymouth. These two ports contained naval dockyards, from which the ships were fitted out, victualled and repaired. However, the fleet's main place of assembly, and of shelter from severe westerly gales, was Torbay in south Devon. Plymouth was far too open and exposed, while Torbay provided protection from northerly, southerly and westerly winds, deep water and good holding ground for anchors. It was also not much over a hundred miles from Ushant (a twenty-four-hour sail given a reasonable wind, less with a good one). Nevertheless, although Torbay was often used, there was a major risk involved – that of being caught by a strong easterly or south-easterly wind. A wind from these directions was exactly what French ships at Brest needed in order to gain the open sea quickly, whereas ships at anchor in Torbay were stuck. This had happened to Admiral Howe in 1795 with thirty-four ships-of-the-line and sixteen frigates, many of which broke their cables and were driven into shallow water. Ship's masters and officers-of-the-watch in Torbay were forever watching the wind. A hint of it swinging eastwards and the ships had to sail at once. Cornwallis himself wrote in 1805, 'In the middle of last month we put into Torbay, where we were a week, but the being in Torbay is no great relief, for no person or boat goes onshore. We visit our friends and neighbours in the fleet, but have no communication with the rest of the world.'

### The North Sea Fleet

In 1803, at the renewed outbreak of war, the hitherto separate squadrons responsible for the eastern half of the Channel and the coast of Belgium and Holland were combined under one command called the 'Eastern Command' (as opposed to the 'Western Command' or Channel Fleet). Its area of responsibility stretched from Selsey Bill (near Portsmouth) in the south up to the Shetland Islands in the north. This gave control over the narrowest part of the Channel and was intended as a blocking force to any invasion threat from the North Sea – just as the Channel

Fleet blocked off an approach from the Atlantic. In 1805 Admiral Lord Keith, flying his flag in the 64-gun *St Albans*, commanded this fleet, which at that time had eleven ships-of-the-line and twenty frigates divided into five squadrons, with bases at Downs, Ramsgate, Dungeness, Yarmouth and Leith.

During the two years preceding Trafalgar, it was the Downs Squadron (part of the North Sea Fleet) that had the task of harrying and disrupting the build-up of the French invasion flotilla based at Boulogne. In other respects this fleet did not play a specific role in the Trafalgar campaign.

### The Baltic Fleet

This fleet was a powerful force in 1801 when, under Admiral Sir Hyde Parker and with Nelson as his second-in-command, it carried out the successful attack on Copenhagen (see Section Seven). For this operation it had twenty-one ships-of-the-line and eleven frigates and 50s, plus seven bomb vessels, nine brigs and a number of cutters and schooners. However, it was a fleet that was only formed when it was needed. Although the Baltic was always important to British naval strategy, in 1805 activity in that area was negligible and consequently there was no fleet. Only in 1808 was a permanent Baltic fleet established.

### The Mediterranean Fleet

The importance of this Fleet was second only to that of the Channel, so it had always been the command of a senior and competent admiral. Vice-Admiral Viscount Nelson hoisted his flag on the *Victory* on 18 May 1803 and joined his fleet off Toulon on 6 July. He was to be at sea from then on, with only a short break of six weeks in August/September 1805, until his death at Trafalgar that autumn. Nelson's primary task was to destroy or blockade the French Mediterranean Fleet based at Toulon. However, the Mediterranean Fleet also had responsibilities outside the Mediterranean, being required to observe the port of Cadiz and the Portuguese coast as far north as Cape Finisterre. With the renewed declaration of war by the Spanish in late 1804, this task was given to the 'Spanish Squadron' under Orde – a newly formed squadron with five ships-of-the-line under the control of the Admiralty in London. The additional twenty-five operational ships-of-the-line that this declaration gave to overall French naval strength, plus the added hostile coastline, were deemed, rightly, too much for Nelson to control with his existing resources. Nelson was far from happy with the appointment of Orde and his lack of authority over him. For one thing Orde would get the best chance of grabbing Spanish galleons, and for another Nelson's personal relationship with Orde had been soured by the Battle of the Nile (see Section Five).

Apart from watching the French Fleet in Toulon, much of Nelson's time and resources were spent in the protection of British trade. The hundreds of islands, narrow waters and the feebleness of many of the tiny littoral states encouraged privateers. As Captain Mahan in his *Life of Nelson* puts it:

> Under these conditions, small privateers, often mere rowboats, but under the colours of France or the Italian Republic, swarmed in every port and inlet; in the Adriatic, – a deep, secluded pocket, particularly favourable to marauding, – in the Ionian Islands, along the Barbary coast, upon the shores of Spain, and especially in Sicily.

Nelson had bases only in Gibraltar and Malta, which Britain had refused to surrender even though obliged to do so under the Treaty of Amiens. The numerous, small neutral states gave sanctuary to the privateers, whose depredations were unending. British merchants ceaselessly demanded naval protection. 'I am pulled to pieces by the demands of merchants for convoys,' Nelson complained. The problem was lack of sufficient ships for the multitude of tasks. His twelve or so ships-of-the-line were to confront and defeat the enemy warships sheltering in Toulon. In order to seek out, deter, chase and destroy privateers and to escort convoys, as well as keeping a close watch on the French Fleet, Nelson needed fast frigates and sloops. Not long after taking up his command he complained, 'I wrote to the Admiralty for more cruisers [meaning frigates or sloops] until I was tired.' 'I am distressed for frigates … From Cape St. Vincent to the head of the Adriatic I have only eight … absolutely not one half enough.' 'I want ten more [frigates] than I have in order to watch that the French do not escape me, and ten sloops besides.'

His pleas were in vain. Throughout his two years he struggled to dominate his three million square kilometres of sea, always woefully short of cruisers. His strength in 1805 was twelve ships-of-the-line and eight frigates. As we shall see, Nelson twice failed to prevent the French Fleet in Toulon from sailing and then disappearing. On the first occasion, in January 1805, he sailed all the way to Alexandria in a frantic but fruitless search for his enemy. On the second, some three months later, he had to chase all the way to the Caribbean and back – again without ever catching up.

## Squadrons

### The Irish Squadron

This squadron was normally based at Cork with responsibility for protecting trade to the west and guarding Ireland, which was regarded by Bonaparte as ripe for rebellion and a possible stepping stone to the conquest of England. The squadron was, in reality, an extension of the Channel Fleet. In 1805 it was given the special task of establishing a screen of frigates from the southern tip of Ireland to Cape Finisterre. For this it had twelve frigates and eight sloops.

### The Channel Islands Squadron

This was a small squadron established at Guernsey to deter invasion of the islands and to give check to the privateers sallying forth from St Malo. Consisting of several sloops and cutters, it was really an add-on to the Channel Fleet.

### The North American Squadrons

There were two squadrons located off the North American coast since the loss of the American colonies. One was based at Halifax (Nova Scotia) and the other at Newfoundland. Neither was large or considered of great significance during this period, and in fact the admirals in command were also the governors of their respective colonies. In 1805 the Halifax Squadron had eight ships, none larger than a frigate, while the Newfoundland Squadron had thirteen.

### The Jamaica Squadron

The West Indies was always an exciting place as the British, French, Spanish and Dutch staked out their claims to colonies on the islands or the South or Central American mainland. Trade was the driving force for possession. The more colonies owned, the greater the trade and wealth that flowed into the government's and individuals' pockets. But the colonies required protection and ships and soldiers were frequently needed to defend and attack the island territories as they changed hands. The vast flow of merchant ships needed escorts, and privateers abounded.

The Caribbean was divided into two commands (squadrons). One, the Jamaica Squadron, was based at the splendid harbour of Port Royal. It was well sited to attack the Spanish mainland colonies from Venezuela to Mexico or, more lucratively, waylay their convoys as they crawled sluggishly home with heavy holds. In 1805 this fleet had three ships-of-the-line, fifteen frigates and seven sloops.

### The Leeward Islands Squadron

During the late 1790s, when the struggle for ownership of the islands was at its height, this squadron had been more important than that at Jamaica. With the capture of many enemy possessions its size had decreased substantially by 1801, but by 1805 it was once again an important command with six ships-of-the-line, thirteen frigates and as many sloops – a larger force than Nelson's entire fleet in the Mediterranean. Its main bases were in Antigua (where English Harbour, as it is still called, is well worth a visit) and Barbados. For two hundred years Barbados boasted a smaller version of Nelson's column in its own Trafalgar Square – now replaced by a statue of a local politician in a renamed 'National Heroes Square'.

### The East India Squadron

There was a constant struggle for territory in the East Indies (India, Malaya, Sumatra, Java and Borneo) just as there was in the West Indies. As always, the driving force was commerce and wealth. In India Arthur Wellesley (later the Duke of Wellington) and others extended British rule, while the Royal Navy was required to protect the resultant flood of merchant ships in convoys, sometimes of over a hundred ships, demanding escorts. In 1805 this squadron had eight ships-of-the-line and as many as twenty-one frigates, sloops and cutters.

### The Cape Squadron

The Cape was a Dutch possession until 1795, when Britain began to govern it in the name of the Prince of Orange, who had taken refuge in England after the seizure of Holland by the French (who renamed it the Batavian Republic). Under the Treaty of Amiens it was restored to Holland. However, three months after Trafalgar the British arrived again to take it over from Holland (which was still a dependency of France). The Cape Squadron, based at Capetown, was never large. Its existence was intermittent and, when on station, its duties mainly involved escorting convoys and providing cruisers to prey on the trade route around the Cape of Good Hope.

### Other ships

All ships deployed in fleets or squadrons around the world were under the command of admirals, but there were also a substantial number of individual ships that did not belong to a fleet or squadron but sailed under the direct orders of the Admiralty. Invariably they were escorting merchant convoys (although fleet ships also performed this duty) or on a 'cruise' hunting enemy trading vessels or privateers. This was a popular duty with captains, as they could keep the large share of any prize money that would usually go to the flag officer (admiral) in overall command.

## THE BLOCKADE

### An open blockade (Nelson off Toulon)

The object of an open blockade was to entice the enemy out of port, then attack him before he could return or elude the blockading force. Nelson, writing to the Lord Mayor of London in August 1804, stated his tactics plainly: 'I beg to inform your Lordship that the port of Toulon has never been blockaded by me: quite the reverse – every opportunity has been offered to the Enemy to put to sea, for it is there that we hope to realize the hopes and expectations of our Country.'

Nevertheless, the commander of any blockading force had to have a continuous supply of information on what the enemy was doing, how many ships were in port, whether they were getting ready to sail, what their intentions were and, if they left port, where they were going. To gain this information, they had to have an uninterrupted presence outside the blockaded port. This was invariably the duty of frigates and sloops, which had enough firepower to confront similar or smaller enemy ships and, more importantly, the speed to deliver messages or catch up with escaping vessels and hang on their flanks, reporting movements.

One of the many problems facing the commander of the open blockade was ensuring sufficient frigates and/or sloops were on duty outside the port. There needed to be enough to set up a chain of ships between the port and main fleet or inshore squadron (see below) so that signals could be quickly relayed back to the commander – by night this was done by a combination of lights, gunfire and rocket flares. There also needed to be enough ships close to the port to prevent their being chased away by a greater number of enemy frigates or corvettes. If this happened, the blockading force would be blinded as to what the main enemy fleet was doing or the direction it was sailing. On the other hand, too strong a presence visible outside a port might put the enemy admiral off attempting to venture out at all – which would defeat the main purpose of the open blockade.

As with all ships, frigates and sloops could not stay at sea without replenishment for much longer than three months (they had sufficient stocks onboard to last six, but for health reasons needed fresh fruit, vegetables and water much sooner than that). Supplies could be sent out in supply ships, or the ships of the fleet could take it in turns to leave their station to find a friendly port. For Nelson Gibraltar and Malta were out because of distance so he was forced to rely on supply ships or find supplies where he could. Maddalena could not offer much in terms of provisions, so he depended on making purchases along the Barbary States (North Africa). Tunis did a lively and regular trade with Nelson's ships, but even then it was over 400 miles from Toulon, so an absence of ten days would not have been exceptional. Vice-Admiral Collingwood, Nelson's second-in-command at Trafalgar, complained:

> It would be a happy day that would relieve me of this cruising, which is really wearing me to a lath. The great difficulty I have is to keep up the health of the men. We get good beef from the Moors; but to bring it requires a number of ships, which I can ill spare. Two hundred bullocks do not serve us a week, and a transport laden with wine about a month. How we are to keep up our water I do not know.

## The Strategic Blockade Situation, March 1805

Map 3

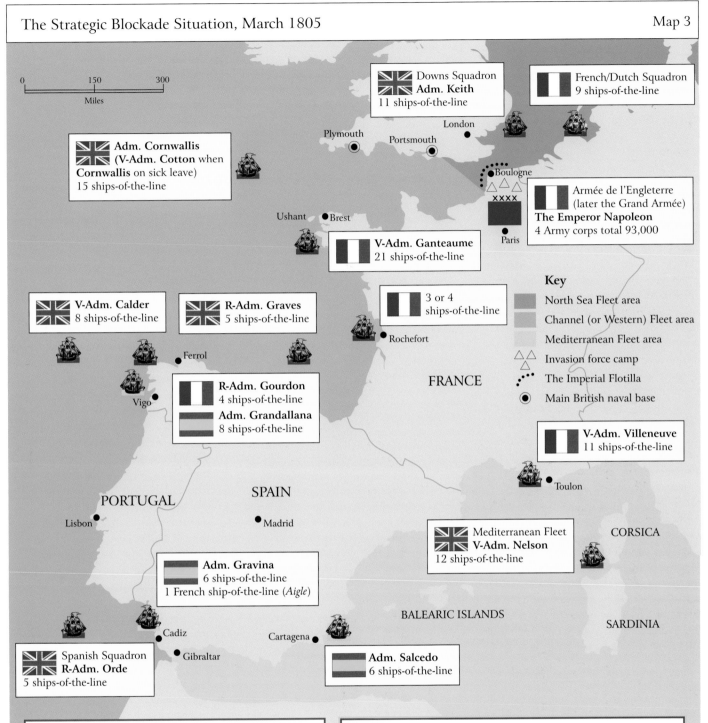

### Key

- North Sea Fleet area
- Channel (or Western) Fleet area
- Mediterranean Fleet area
- △△△ Invasion force camp
- •••• The Imperial Flotilla
- ⊙ Main British naval base

**Downs Squadron**
**Adm. Keith**
11 ships-of-the-line

**French/Dutch Squadron**
9 ships-of-the-line

**Adm. Cornwallis**
**(V-Adm. Cotton** when
**Cornwallis** on sick leave)
15 ships-of-the-line

**Armée de l'Engleterre**
(later the Grand Armée)
**The Emperor Napoleon**
4 Army corps total 93,000

**V-Adm. Ganteaume**
21 ships-of-the-line

**V-Adm. Calder**
8 ships-of-the-line

**R-Adm. Graves**
5 ships-of-the-line

3 or 4
ships-of-the-line

**R-Adm. Gourdon**
4 ships-of-the-line
**Adm. Grandallana**
8 ships-of-the-line

**V-Adm. Villeneuve**
11 ships-of-the-line

**Mediterranean Fleet**
**V-Adm. Nelson**
12 ships-of-the-line

**Adm. Gravina**
6 ships-of-the-line
1 French ship-of-the-line (*Aigle*)

**Spanish Squadron**
**R-Adm. Orde**
5 ships-of-the-line

**Adm. Salcedo**
6 ships-of-the-line

Plymouth, Portsmouth, London, Boulogne, Paris, Ushant, Brest, Rochefort, FRANCE, Ferrol, Vigo, PORTUGAL, SPAIN, Madrid, Lisbon, Toulon, CORSICA, BALEARIC ISLANDS, SARDINIA, Cadiz, Gibraltar, Cartagena

0 150 300
Miles

### British Notes

- Ships from the Channel and Mediterranean Fleets were involved in the campaign leading to Trafalgar. The Spanish squadron was an extension of the Channel Fleet.
- Only ships-of-the-line are indicated. Numbers are approximately those actually at sea on blockade duties. Frigates, which played a critical blockade role, are not shown.
- Rear-Adm. Cochrane with 6 ships-of-the-line had been sent from watching Rochefort in pursuit of Missiessy when the French broke out and sailed for the Caribbean in January.
- At any one time during March about 45 ships-of-the-line were on blockade duties – 33 in the Channel Fleet, 12 in the Mediterranean. The Downs Squadron was not involved in the Trafalgar campaign.

### French/Spanish Notes

- All ships were confined to port by blockading British squadrons.
- The numbers indicate the numbers of ships-of-the-line estimated to be ready for sea during March 1805. No attempt has been made to show the number of frigates or smaller vessels, which would have been substantial.
- Discounting ships in the Dutch Squadron area, which played no part in the Trafalgar campaign, the French had approximately 40, and the Spanish 20, ships-of-the-line available.
- The invasion force had about 90,000 troops ready on the coast to embark immediately once the Channel was secure. Other reserve formations were available near Paris.
- The ships at Rochefort were left behind by Missiessy when he broke out and sailed to the Caribbean with 5 ships-of-the-line in January.

To compensate for having too few frigates, the commander of an open blockade would sometimes deploy an inshore squadron. This would consist of several ships-of-the-line under their own squadron commander. They would normally stay just out of sight of the port so that the enemy would not know of their presence – and thus, hopefully, would not be deterred from coming out given a favourable wind. If the enemy sailed, the inshore squadron could assist the frigates in tracking it, delaying it and providing more relay ships to pass signals to the main fleet.

In January 1805 Nelson only had two frigates (*Active* and *Seahorse*) on patrol outside Toulon where Villeneuve's fleet was bottled up. Nelson had, throughout his time in the Mediterranean, been chronically short of frigates. While these two ships watched, his ships-of-the-line sheltered from the blasts of the winter storms at Maddalena two hundred miles away. There was no inshore squadron. When Villeneuve sailed on 18 January with his eleven ships-of-the-line and nine cruisers (frigates and corvettes) all the English frigates could do was shadow them. This they did for some twelve hours in atrocious weather. Then, when approximately west of Ajaccio (the capital of Corsica) at about 10 p.m., they both abandoned Villeneuve to take their news to Nelson, at the time only about sixty miles away – five hours sailing in the high wind. This was their error. Neither of the frigates stayed to tail the enemy fleet through the night. For at least one, probably two, complete days there could be no contact even if the French continued on the same course. If they altered course, who was to know?

### A close blockade (Cornwallis off Brest)
The object of the close blockade was to keep the enemy ships in port, and, if that was not possible, to attack them when they came out. Brest was always the most important blockade station for the British fleet as it was in the Brest anchorage that the main French fleet was based. Any enemy leaving Brest soon reached the entrance to the Channel. If unopposed by a substantial force, French ships-of-the-line, possibly escorting troop-laden transports, would be threatening the southern coast of England or heading for Ireland within a few hours.

The Channel Fleet had the responsibility for the blockade of Brest. The disadvantage of a close blockade was that it required a large number of ships at sea. To keep ships continuously on blockade for months, even years, on end was impossible unless a proportion could be sent back to port for refit as necessary. Allowance had to be made for ships, or groups of ships, leaving and rejoining the fleet at regular intervals. It was to be expected

## On the Brest Blockade

Although strenuous efforts were made to restock ships with fresh food at every opportunity, and the rottenness of the food has been exaggerated, there were occasions when it was anything but appetizing. Very few seamen wrote describing their life. A rare exception was a young boy of eleven called Bernard Coleridge who wrote home to his parents while on blockade duty off Brest in 1804. Despite the conditions, he seemed happy with his lot.

> Indeed we live on beef which has been ten or eleven years in corn and on biscuit which quite makes your throat cold in eating it owing to the maggots which are very cold when you eat them, like calves-foot jelly or blomonge being very fat indeed. Indeed, I do like this life very much, but I cannot help laughing heartily when I think of sculling about the old cider-tub in the pond, and Mary Anne Cosserat capsizing into the pond just by the mulberry bush. I often think what I would give for two or three quarendons [apples] off the tree on the lawn with their rosy cheeks! We drink water of the colour of the bark of a pear-tree with plenty of little maggots and weavils in it and wine which is exactly like bullock's blood and sawdust mixed together. I hope I shall not learn to swear, and by God's assistance I hope I shall not.

His parents had good reason to keep and treasure his letters, as he died from a fall from the rigging when only fourteen – by no means an uncommon way of being killed.

that up to a third of the Channel Fleet might be absent from its station at any one time. Lord Melville, when First Lord of the Admiralty, went so far as to declare, 'the portion of the Channel fleet apportioned to the blockade of Brest ought to be double of what is requisite for the actual blockade'.

Each ship put to sea with provisions for six months. They were supposed to be resupplied by a small fleet of victuallers and water-hoys visiting them at regular intervals. Only for vital repairs, or when the weather was blowing a gale from the west, was a ship given permission to put back to Cawsand or Plymouth. Even then, seamen were not allowed ashore and officers could not travel more than five miles from the beach and had to sleep onboard.

Although during the two years immediately preceding Trafalgar Brest was the prime example of a close, tightly enforced, blockade, this had not always been the case. For many years before this Brest had been 'under observation' as a part of an open blockade. The main fleet had spent its time sheltered at Spithead (Portsmouth) – ready to put to sea, but protected from the hazards of wind, weather, rock or shoal. The advantage of this policy, as well as keeping the ships safe, was that it might tempt the enemy out, thus providing the opportunity to destroy him. The problem was, as Nelson was to find in the Mediterranean, that once out, the French could only be brought to battle if they wanted to be. A dangerous disadvantage was that officers and men became bored, idle and lost their training edge – in short, soft. It is significant that the two mutinies that occurred in 1797 at Spithead and the Nore were among the crews of ships in port.

When Admiral Jervis (Earl St Vincent) took command of the Channel Fleet in 1800, he immediately enforced a close blockade on Brest. Five years earlier, when he had been appointed commander-in-chief in the Mediterranean, he had kept the French in Toulon bottled up very securely. His arrival was not anticipated with much enthusiasm by many of the officers who had grown accustomed to the less than rigorous regime at Portsmouth. There is a story that at a dinner a captain of the Channel Fleet proposed a toast: 'May the discipline of the Mediterranean Fleet never be introduced into the Channel Fleet.' The toast was supposedly drunk by all present without comment – including an admiral.

This unknown captain was to be disappointed. In the years that followed the blockade of Brest was rigidly applied. When war was declared again in 1803, the close blockade was standard practice. St Vincent wrote of the wisdom of keeping ships 'in constant movement'. There was certainly no time for boredom on blockade. On the contrary, there was a heavy and incessant strain on

## The Close Blockade of Brest by the Channel Fleet

Map 4

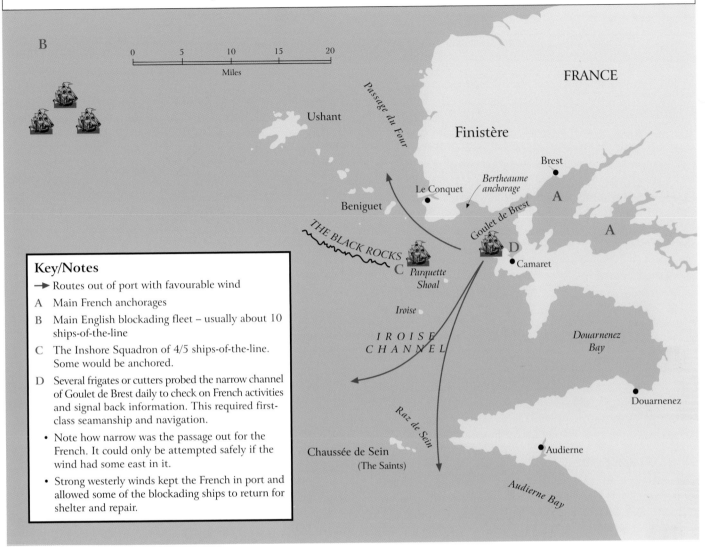

B

0    5    10    15    20
Miles

FRANCE

Ushant

*Passage du Four*

Finistère

Brest

Le Conquet

*Bertheaume anchorage*

Beniguet

A

*Goulet de Brest*

A

THE BLACK ROCKS

D

Camaret

C *Parquette Shoal*

*Iroise*

*I R O I S E*
*C H A N N E L*

*Douarnenez Bay*

Douarnenez

*Raz de Sein*

Chaussée de Sein
(The Saints)

Audierne

*Audierne Bay*

### Key/Notes

→ Routes out of port with favourable wind

A  Main French anchorages

B  Main English blockading fleet – usually about 10 ships-of-the-line

C  The Inshore Squadron of 4/5 ships-of-the-line. Some would be anchored.

D  Several frigates or cutters probed the narrow channel of Goulet de Brest daily to check on French activities and signal back information. This required first-class seamanship and navigation.

• Note how narrow was the passage out for the French. It could only be attempted safely if the wind had some east in it.

• Strong westerly winds kept the French in port and allowed some of the blockading ships to return for shelter and repair.

## The Royal Navy Mutinies at Spithead and the Nore, 1797

In April 1797 the Channel Fleet refused to put to sea on blockade duty. The sailors' demands, which had been simmering for some time, were:

• a revision of pay – they received less than soldiers
• an end to the practice of pursers fiddling the ration issue
• an issue of fresh vegetables in port
• proper care of the sick or wounded and payment until they recovered
• shore leave
• a fairer share of prize money.

Little emphasis was put on the supposedly brutal discipline, the overuse of flogging, the laws and customs of the Navy or poor food. Generally the complaints were of an administrative nature against the Admiralty or the government rather than their own officers – although a number of unpopular ones were sent ashore. Despite flying red flags instead of ensigns at the mastheads, the seamen were still loyal to their country and willing to fight her enemies. Indeed, once normality was restored, the same crews sailed to victory at Camperdown and the Nile. The demands were recognized as reasonable by an Admiralty Board of Inquiry but, although prepared to concede, the government mishandled its response by a belligerently worded letter to captains – which was leaked. The Spithead crews again refused to sail. Lord Howe, pulled out of retirement, was given full powers to redress grievances and grant pardons. He did both and the Channel Fleet sailed for Brest.

Despite this, a rabble-rouser called Richard Parker (a disgruntled former midshipman) stirred up another mutiny at the Nore, which spread to the North Sea Fleet at Yarmouth. Parker wanted to lead a revolt rather than correct wrongs so there was little sympathy for the mutineers, since agreement had already been reached on genuine complaints. Eventually Parker was himself seized by the mutineers and then, with about four hundred other ringleaders, was put on trial. There was some leniency: most were pardoned, some flogged or imprisoned, and twenty-eight, including Parker, were hanged. In all the mutinies had lasted two months.

ships and crews struggling to maintain position in gales, torrential rain, mountainous seas and biting winds. The stress experienced by the officers-of-the-watch (two hours was the maximum instead of the usual four) in keeping the ship in position is not hard to imagine. Ceaseless vigilance, combined with a strict and careful lookout and the best of discipline, was needed to avoid disaster. Vice-Admiral Lovell wrote of the Channel Fleet, 'To the very credit of the officers of the watch scarce an accident occurred during the long, tiresome and harassing blockade of Brest.'

In calmer weather other duties kept officers and men alert and active. Privateers were chased, merchantmen stopped and searched, and the inshore squadron probed and tested the defences, navigating round the rocks and shoals that made Brest so hazardous a port to approach or leave. Further out the main fleet practised gunnery, signalling and manoeuvres. Frigates, however, were constantly coming within cannon shot of the onshore batteries as they sought to discover every possible detail of which enemy ships were in harbour and what they were doing. A report submitted to Admiral Cornwallis in 1805 by Lieutenant Beauman of the frigate *Aigle* shows how comprehensive they were:

> In obedience to your signal of this morning, I ... reconnoitred the enemy's force in Brest harbour at 3pm; had a favourable opportunity of getting a very distinct view of the fleet, and found them to consist of twenty-one sail-of-the-line, four of which are three-decked ships, four frigates, two corvettes, two brigs and one cutter, with one admiral and two rear-admiral's flags flying.

He must have had an exciting time getting in close enough to provide such an accurate count.

The usual tactic was for about ten ships-of-the-line to provide the main squadron of the fleet. These ships could be expected to follow the advice of St Vincent to 'never be further than six or eight leagues [eighteen to twenty-four miles] from Ushant with the wind easterly'. If the wind was from the west the French could not leave their anchorage. Ahead of this force were the five or six ships-of-the-line of the inshore squadron. They were: 'always anchored during an easterly wind between the Black Rocks and the Parquette shoal [see Map 4]. Inside, between them and the Goulet, cruise a squadron of frigates and cutters plying day and night in the opening of the Goulet'.

# FRENCH GRAND STRATEGY 1802–5

For the three years from 1802 to 1804 Napoleon had two basic objectives. The first was entirely civil – to consolidate and strengthen his personal grip on France. The second was military – to build up his navy and army for the invasion of England.

## CIVIL STRATEGY

The words 'I fear a revolt caused by lack of bread more than a great battle' aptly summed up Napoleon's thinking. A strong economy, security under the law, personal prosperity and patriotism must be combined to produce a contented people. Like the Roman emperors, Napoleon understood that he needed the 'masses' behind him; they had to see him as the ultimate provider of economic success and national glory. As early as 1798 he set out to ensure the population had their 'bread and circuses', and he implemented a highly effective combination of the carrot and the stick. The main elements of his regime were:

*Rooting out opposition*
This included the setting up of a secret police force under the ruthless former headmaster and religious zealot Joseph Fouche. Military tribunals were set up throughout France to eliminate Napoleon's opponents with brutal severity. Those hauled before the tribunals were either Jacobins (ultra left-wing republicans) or fervent royalists (there was an on-going royalist rebellion in the Vendée during much of this time). Fouche's skill at discovering plots against Napoleon – real or concocted – and the apparatus of police terror that he controlled made him the most feared man in France.

*Financial reforms*
These included the creation of France's first national bank in 1800, with sole authority to issue paper money. This helped ensure economic stability. Trade was encouraged, particularly external trade with other European countries, including those under French influence. Full employment was actively sought, so people felt better off – and gave the credit to Napoleon. He made certain that land seized from the Church and the nobility by the Revolution and handed to the peasant farmers remained in the latters' hands. Keeping the population content – particularly traders, farmers and the bourgeoisie (middle class) – was the key element of Napoleon's internal rule.

*Law and order maintained*
A new national police force was established in 1802. This was followed by the promulgation of a comprehensive new Civil Code – the Code Napoleon – which has lasted in some respects to this day; it is still the basis of civil law in Mauritius (at that time Isle de France), amongst others.

*Glamour and spectacle*
Some of Napoleon's extravagant public reviews, with thousands of troops parading in Paris to the blare and thump of martial music, can be likened to the hypnotic Nazi rallies in Germany in the 1930s. The populace was held spellbound, gripped, if only temporarily, by intense feelings of pride and of patriotism – an enormously useful emotion from Napoleon's point of view. 'It is with baubles that men are led' was another of his phrases that revealed his shrewd understanding of human nature. In May of 1802 the first distribution of the Legion d'Honneur, the French order of merit, was made. The white enamel cross with its strips of red ribbon became France's premier civil and military decoration, and it remains a much-coveted honour.

*Pardons for royalists, rewards for generals*
Napoleon understood that there was much to be gained from reconciliation with the many talented royalists who had fled France to save their heads in the earlier years of the Revolution. He issued an amnesty for royalist émigrés to return to France.

Some 40,000 accepted, and a large number were appointed officers in the army. For his successful generals Napoleon created the 'marshalate'. To become a 'Marshal of the Empire' (there was never an equivalent for the navy) was the ultimate reward for a general. With the rank came the marshal's baton. Inside the red morocco case with its silver eagles and clasps was a baton over a foot long, covered with blue velvet, embroidered with thirty-two eagles and tipped with gold bands. At each end, in gold characters, was the name of the recipient. In May 1804 Napoleon created eighteen marshals. It was an important step in the creation of a new nobility.

## Reconciliation with the Papacy

'The people must have a religion and that religion must be in the hands of the government.' Napoleon had long regarded the church as a potential source of opposition. Despite the outcry from the more ardent revolutionaries, he had succeeded in persuading the Papacy to sign a formal treaty of reconciliation in July 1801.

Napoleon's zealous overhauling of France's civil administration, coupled with his years of victory as a military commander, succeeded in uniting the country in loyalty to him personally. For the great majority of the populace, their personal prosperity and their country's greatness were due to one man. In May 1804 even the most bloodthirsty men in 'red caps', who had greeted the King's appearance on the scaffold of 'Madame Guillotine' with frenzied yells of delight, accepted (with some misgivings) the monarch's replacement by an emperor. Napoleon was determined his succession would be hereditary. The title of emperor evoked memories of Rome and Charlemagne, and, like Charlemagne, Napoleon wished to be crowned by the Pope, not in Rome, but in Paris. After some hesitation Pope Pius VII acceded to the request, and on 2 December 1804 a dazzling ceremony took place at Notre Dame. The soldier of the revolution became the anointed of the Lord. So impatient was Napoleon to wear the crown that he took it from the Pope and placed it on his head himself. He created his marshals, he built up a new nobility, he gathered together a new court. France approved of everything.

## NAVAL STRATEGY: THE INVASION OF ENGLAND

The years 1802 to 1805 saw the French military mostly preoccupied with plans and preparation for a massive invasion of England. They had other objectives, including the attack on maritime trade and the capture of British overseas possessions, but their primary aim was the invasion.

In the summer of 1803 the First Consul, as he then was, took his wife Josephine to inspect progress at the Channel ports from which the invasion flotilla would sail. He travelled in style, riding a grey horse, preceded by several hundred soldiers and surrounded by a bodyguard of about thirty mamelukes in their exotic Eastern-style uniforms. Josephine sat demurely in a carriage, screened from the view of the common soldiery. Napoleon's day at Calais did little to give him confidence. During the course of his tour the Royal Navy had the audacity to send a frigate in close enough to fire on seven new landing craft that were desperately scurrying for shelter in port. The First Consul, a former artilleryman, watched with keen anticipation as the guns of the shore batteries opened fire on the daring intruder. As the shots continued to splash down well short of the target, Napoleon became increasingly agitated. Eventually it was explained to him that the guns had been accidentally loaded with the small amounts of powder used as saluting charges. Livid, he demanded to see the artillery officer in charge. When this unfortunate individual arrived, the fuming Napoleon personally ripped his epaulettes from his shoulders and dismissed him from the army.

This trivial hiccup may have spoilt the First Consul's day and ended the career of one officer, but it did nothing to hinder the build-up of the invasion force or the accumulation of boats intended to carry it across the few miles of water that separated France from England. The plan was to have Boulogne as the central port from which to launch the invasion. However, one port was totally inadequate for so vast an undertaking. Some 150,000 soldiers were to be mustered and trained in a huge camp around Boulogne. An armada of over 2,000 flat-bottomed boats was being built and assembled in all the small ports and estuaries along the Channel coast. The cost escalated enormously. Complex engineering works were required to increase the capacity of existing ports and to build new ones. Boulogne was supposed to be able to launch 800 transports from a woefully inadequate basin that lacked locks and barrages. Even using cheap labour (the army), work was estimated to cost nearly 400,000 francs a month for Boulogne alone. Tens of millions of francs were raised by bank loans, public contributions and the national budget.

It was not only the scale of the undertaking and the increasing inability to pay contractors and workers that caused delays. Both the enemy and the weather interfered with the flotilla's assembly. The Royal Navy persisted in raiding, bombarding and attacking shore establishments, the new makeshift harbours along the French coast, and the transports themselves as they sailed from the shipyards to their assembly ports. The weather, too, was exceptionally unkind to the French. Gales, often lasting many days at a time, lashed the coast bringing huge waves and high tides, which frustrated work regularly throughout 1803 and into 1804. Even the summer months were not immune.

---

### Strange French Invasion Craft

Rumours were rife in England as to the means the French would employ to get across the Channel. That the bogeyman Napoleon was coming was a threat with which many a misbehaving child in Kent was sent to bed during 1804 and 1805. He would arrive by tunnel, in troop-carrying balloons or on vast rafts. These huge rectangular platforms, fitted with forts and propelled by paddle wheels at each corner, were supposedly capable of carrying ten thousand troops. Although none of these outlandish ideas resembled the truth, there was a possible solution that nobody considered – steam power. Since 1801 a steam barge called the *Charlotte Dundas* had been pulling barges along the Forth and Clyde Canal in Scotland. In Paris in 1803 an American engineer, Robert Fulton, had built a steamer, but nobody showed any interest in its military potential. By the time Napoleon was sent into exile on St Helena ten years later, a passenger service by steamer was chugging across the Channel from Brighton to Le Havre. Trafalgar was the last time anybody would witness the awesome sight of a major sea battle fought completely under sail.

## Napoleon's Invasion Craft

**Prame**

**Notes**
The largest landing craft, initially with 12 gunports and capable of carrying up to 120 troops. Very unstable in even moderate wind.

**Chaloupe Cannonière**

Able to carry 130 troops. As for the prame, lack of keel and too much sail made it likely to capsize.

**Bateau Cannonière**

These craft were flat-bottomed for shallow water and carried one 24-pdr cannon, with a small crew of 6 and up to 106 men and 2 horses.

**Bateau Cannonière**

**Peniche**

The smallest landing craft, with three short masts and no deck. Carried a crew of 5, 2 howitzers and up to 66 men.

**Peniche**

On an unfortunate occasion on 20 July 1804, Napoleon visited Boulogne on one of his frequent inspections. He sent an ADC to tell Admiral Bruix, the commander of the flotilla, to have the sixty or so vessels moored in the roadstead to embark their troops and guns and sail in review before him on the open sea. He wanted to see the new port functioning and the flotilla in action. The Emperor was flabbergasted when the embarrassed ADC returned with a refusal from the admiral. Years later Napoleon's valet, Louis Constant, related what happened next. Bruix was instantly summoned before his enraged Emperor, who demanded to know why his order was not being carried out. The flustered admiral replied with truth that there was a severe storm brewing – the sky was black and distant rumbles of thunder could be heard. He added that to put to sea would be risking the lives of many men. Napoleon would have none of it. He again ordered Bruix to obey. Again the admiral refused. Napoleon almost lost control and stepped forward, raising his riding crop as if to strike. Bruix took a pace back and actually put his hand on his sword hilt, saying words to the effect of, 'Sire, mind what you do!' The Emperor's staff

froze, dumbfounded at the scene before them. Then Napoleon flung down his crop, sacked Bruix and replaced him by Rear-Admiral Magon. Lacking the moral courage of his predecessor, Magon scurried away to get the flotilla to sea.

Bruix was proved disastrously right. After the transports sailed, packed with troops, the storm broke. Howling winds drove dozens of the vessels onto the rocks and beach at the base of the cliffs. Many boats were completely smashed or overturned, their occupants hurled into the raging surf. Napoleon, with his entourage of admirals and generals, all drenched in the driving rain, watched helplessly as men screamed and drowned before their eyes. All present knew it was the Emperor's fault. Napoleon suddenly scrambled into a nearby boat and ordered the crew to row out to help. It was a futile gesture. Mountainous seas tossed the boat around like a cork. The Emperor was knocked to his knees, his hat disappearing in the swirling water as he was dragged ashore with great difficulty. Some 300–400 soldiers and seamen drowned, their bodies, along with the Emperor's hat, being washed ashore during the next twenty-four hours.

## Napoleon's Invasion Flotilla

In mid-1803 Napoleon began issuing orders for the building of the invasion flotilla. The first contracts required 350 vessels to be delivered in four months. Napoleon was a frighteningly hard taskmaster who invariably put intolerable pressure on his subordinates to produce administrative miracles. The unfortunate individual directly responsible to the Emperor for this huge construction programme was 'Citizen' Pierre-Alexandre Forfait, who was appointed Inspector-General of the National Flotilla (later renamed the Imperial Flotilla). Napoleon drove Forfait to despair, as he was forever 'moving the goalposts', demanding more vessels in less time. For instance he wrote to Forfait reminding him of the urgency of having the first batch of boats ready by the end of September 1803 but adding, 'Try to have twice that number. … Speed up all boat construction, there will be no shortage of money … every hour is precious.'

The clamour for additional vessels and materials meant an equivalent demand for skilled workers and labourers. Boats were to be built everywhere, not just at naval yards such as Cherbourg, Brest, Marseilles and Toulon. Wherever there was a navigable river from which they could be launched, boat-building became the only industry. The authorities at Ghent, Namur, Lyons, Strasbourg, Toulouse, Rouen and many other towns as far east as the Rhine drafted in, at bayonet point if necessary, anybody who looked as though he could handle a hammer or saw. For the Paris boatyards the order went out, 'let all the workers living along the banks of the river in the Departements of the Seine, the Seine-et-Oise, and the Seine-et-Marne be summoned to the works in Paris'.

What were they making? There were four types of vessel (see diagram), each designed to draw very little water, as they were intended for landing troops over an open beach. Each vessel would carry sufficient guns in order to protect itself on or near the landing place, though in practice such guns were so inaccurate as to be useless. They formed the 'armed flotilla', as opposed to the hundreds of unarmed transports that made up the bulk of the vessels.

*Prame – initial order 50*
The largest landing craft – 110 feet long with a 25-foot beam, three masts, virtually no keel and only drawing eight feet of water. It carried 38 crew and 120 troops. Initially, its single deck was intended to carry twelve 24-pounder cannons. It proved a disaster. Its build – schooner-rigged with high masts, heavy rigging and no keel – ensured it was unable to steer a straight course, while anything above a breeze put it in danger of capsizing. After some hair-raising trials the order was reduced to eighteen.

*Chaloupe Cannonière – initial order 300*
Another boat with no keel, drawing a mere six feet of water and armed with three 24-pounders and a howitzer. It was 80 feet long with a slim beam of 17 feet and two masts like a brig. It was manned by a crew of 32 and could transport 130 soldiers. However, like the prame, it was unstable due to its lack of keel and large square sails. Its comparatively weak construction could not withstand the heavy shock of artillery discharges, while the hull timbers proved too thin to withstand frequent grounding over stones or rocks.

*Bateau Cannonière – initial order 300*
A smaller type with three small masts, less sail area, a length of 60 feet and a narrow beam of 14 feet but, like the others, virtually flat-bottomed. It could get into shallows of four and a half feet before it touched bottom. It only required six sailors but could carry 106 men plus two horses. It was armed with one 24-pounder, one howitzer and one field artillery piece. Its drawbacks were the lack of stability when navigating, weak hull, and too little freeboard, with the result that it was easily swamped by anything resembling a wave.

*Peniche – initial order 700*
The smallest vessel with the narrowest beam (ten feet), 60 feet long, a draught of a mere three and a half feet, with three short masts but no deck – an elongated surf-boat with a crew of five, two howitzers and capable of carrying 66 soldiers. Like the others it had no keel.
The cost of all these new vessels alone touched thirty million francs.

A month later the official state of the Armée d'Engleterre (the French always liked to call their armies after the country in which they were to operate) and the transports ready to lift them showed 1,928 vessels with the capacity to carry 131,000 men and 6,212 horses. Theoretically this allowed a good margin for accidents, the enemy and the unexpected, as only 93,000 soldiers and 1,700 horses were ready to embark on the coast around Boulogne. Their actual deployment was as follows:

| Port | Vessels | Troop capacity | Horse capacity | Troops ready | Horses ready |
|---|---|---|---|---|---|
| Etaples | 365 | 27,000 | 1,390 | 20,000 | 1,200 |
| Boulogne | 1,153 | 73,000 | 3,380 | 45,000 | 1,500 |
| Wimereux | 237 | 16,000 | 769 | 13,000 | – |
| Ambleteuse | 173 | 15,000 | 673 | 15,000 | – |
| Totals | 1,928 | 131,000 | 6,212 | 93,000 | 2,700 |

Even though there were not as many troops as the Emperor had initially planned for, their quality was excellent, with many veterans from the Italian battlefields in their ranks. If they could be got across the Channel without too drastic a loss, they should prove enough for the seizing of a substantial bridgehead, and if necessary reserves could be ferried across for the march on London. The 1,700 horses comprised only a tiny fraction of the number an army of that size would need to mount its cavalry and pull its guns and wagons, since the plan envisaged the cavalry carrying their saddles and seizing English animals once ashore. But there were three main constraints: weather, time and the Royal Navy.

*Weather*

Initially, Napoleon had hoped to row the bulk of his transports across the few miles separating him from the Kent beaches. To do this he required a flat calm sea for a prolonged period – a nice long summer day, perhaps. Mist or fog would be ideal, giving the added possibility of achieving surprise. What attracted the Emperor to this scenario was that no wind and a calm sea meant enemy warships would be becalmed and unable to interrupt the crossing. That his own fleet could not be used either was of no consequence. His admirals eventually convinced him that these ideal conditions were unlikely to the extent of verging on the impossible. The frequency of the raging storms of 1803 and his own humiliating experience in July 1804 persuaded him that rowing across was not a practical option. There was also the issue of distance, linked to the stamina of the oarsmen and

the time available in daylight. The modern Channel Tunnel between Folkestone and Calais is twenty-five miles long and the Folkestone–Boulogne ferry route thirty-five – a long way to row even on a midsummer day.

Sailing across was also weather-dependent. Gales of any severity would wreck the whole enterprise (again, Napoleon's 1804 experience was relevant). Wind from the north-west would prevent the transports sailing at all. What was needed was a fair breeze coming from any direction except north-west, coupled with small waves.

*Time*

The saying 'time and tide wait for no man' had particular relevance for the French contemplating invasion. At first Napoleon thought he could 'jump the ditch' within ten hours, arguing that 'only ten hours would be needed for landing 150,000 disciplined and victorious soldiers upon a coast destitute of fortifications and undefended by a regular army'. It was a soldier's view, not a sailor's, and totally unrealistic. It would have been quite impossible to embark even 90,000 men, sail an average distance of around thirty miles and then disembark on a hostile beach in ten hours. This figure took no account of the tides or the fact that even with ideal conditions four to five knots was the likely best speed of the transports, meaning a six- to eight-hour journey. Napoleon's flotilla admirals felt that two days, possibly three, would be needed even supposing the elements and the enemy were cooperative. Which leads to the most crucial constraint of all – the Royal Navy, in particular the Channel Fleet.

*The Royal Navy*

It was obvious to anyone who considered the situation on either side of the 'ditch' that if the English fleet was present in the Channel, the French flotilla was likely to be pounded to pieces. The resultant slaughter of the troops they carried would be on a scale too vast to contemplate. The Emperor required the uninterrupted use of the Channel for two or three days to have a chance of getting his Armée d'Engleterre onto the soil after which it was named. As there was always a strong British naval presence in the Channel, the only answer was to get a much stronger French naval force in position to protect the flotilla as it made the crossing.

Napoleon took a long while summoning up the nerve to jump the 'ditch'. After several days touring the coastal area and inspecting the preparations, he wrote:

## L'Armée d'Engleterre Receives the Legion d'Honneur

On 16 August 1804 Napoleon, now the Emperor, bestowed the new imperial insignia on his officers and troops poised for the dash across the Channel. The occasion was a massive review that took place only a month after the disastrous day in July when so many seamen had perished due to Napoleon's stubbornness and stupidity (p. 37). The summer of 1804 must have been miserable, as even mid-August was unseasonably wet. As the Emperor arrived to inspect his regiments, the rain was lashing down and his soldiers were already soaked. However, the army was drawn up with the columns paraded in a huge fan formation and his arrival was greeted by some 1,300 drummers beating 'Aux Champs'. Napoleon loved the rattle of side drums and the thump of kettle and bass drums. He would surely have approved of Benjamin Hoyden's words:

> The crash of the Imperial drums, beating with the harsh unity that stamped them as the voices of veterans in war, woke me from my reverie and made my heart throb with their stony rattle. Never did I hear such drums and never shall again: there were years of battle and blood in every sound.

The drummers kept drumming despite the rain, as officers and soldiers to be decorated came forward to receive the coveted stars of the Legion d'Honneur. But the Navy that was supposed to ensure the invasion was possible was not represented – the July fiasco was far too fresh in the imperial mind. Napoleon had, and continued to have, a low opinion of admirals.

I have passed these three days amidst the camp and the port, from the heights of Ambleteuse I have seen the coast of England as one sees the Calvery from the Tuileries. One could distinguish the houses and the bustle [presumably through a powerful telescope]. It is a ditch that shall be leaped when one is daring enough to try.

Not until May 1804 did he pluck up the courage to give orders for the first of his four grandiose naval schemes that preceded Trafalgar.

**Plan 1 – July–September 1804 (Map 5)**

Napoleon's objective was the invasion of England from Boulogne by the end of September. His method was to order Admiral Latouche-Tréville, commanding at Toulon, to sail in July with ten ships-of-the-line, evade Nelson, pass through the Straits of Gibraltar and avoid Cochrane's squadron off Ferrol. He was then to pick up the six ships at Rochefort, slip past Cornwallis into the Channel and escort the flotilla across to Kent – after stopping briefly at Cherbourg for final instructions from Napoleon. As Latouche-Tréville was sailing across the Bay of Biscay, Ganteaume

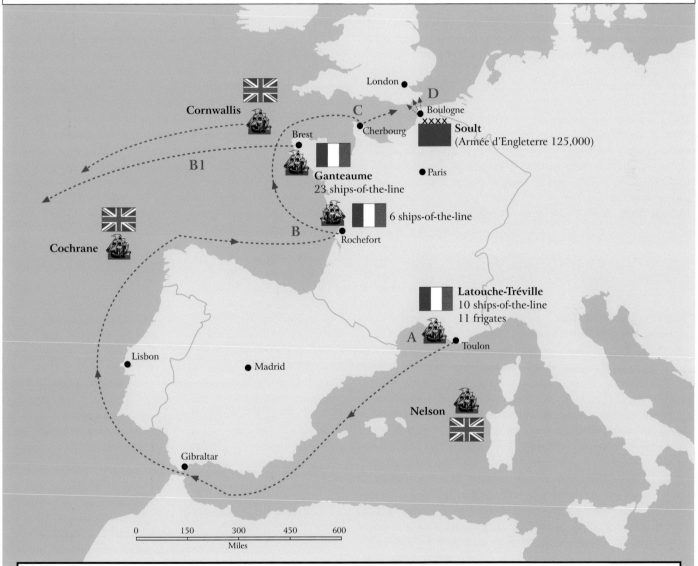

**Napoleon's First Invasion Plan (to be implemented July to September 1804)**                                        Map 5

### Key/Notes

- - - ▶ Intended French movements

- - - ▶ Intended British movements

**A**   In July 1804, Latouche-Tréville to sail through the Straits of Gibraltar to Rochefort, avoiding both Nelson and Cochrane.

**B**   Latouche-Tréville to pick up 6 ships-of-the-line at Rochefort and sail for Cherbourg.

**B1**  At about the time Latouche-Tréville arrived at Rochefort Ganteaume to sail from Brest away from the Channel, luring Cornwallis after him.

**C**   Latouche-Tréville to be briefed at Cherbourg by Napoleon for the final stage of the plan.

**D**   Latouche-Tréville with a fleet of up to 16 ships-of-the-line to protect the invasion flotilla as it carried Soult's army across to Kent. This should happen by the end of September.

The entire operation was cancelled when Latouche-Tréville died suddenly on 19 August at Toulon.

was to sail from Brest out into the Atlantic, hopefully drawing Cornwallis after him. If he succeeded, perhaps the fleet from Toulon could reach Boulogne. There were lots more 'ifs' before the final phase, the invasion, could be launched. *If* Nelson and Cochrane could be avoided (highly unlikely), *if* Cornwallis could be lured away from the Channel (a virtual impossibility) and *if* the winds and weather were always favourable (very doubtful). All these imponderables affected the timing of every move. Despite these difficulties, the scheme was comparatively simple compared to Plan 2 (see below), but even so it had all the hall-marks of a naval plan put together by a soldier. In the event it failed because it was never tried. By mid-August Latouche-Tréville was still on board the *Bucentaure* in Toulon harbour, too fearful of encountering Nelson to sail. On 19 August he died suddenly of a heart attack, brought on, it was said, by his daily habit of clambering up the telegraph tower above the port. The fact that yellow fever had weakened his constitution the previous year would not have helped. His death was also the death of Plan 1.

### Plan 2 – October 1804 through to early 1805 (Map 6)
This was a much bigger and more complex version of Plan 1. It had three objectives: to protect the crossing of the Channel by the Armée d'Engleterre; to invade Ireland; and to capture St Helena before causing mayhem in Senegal. Each mission had separate fleets assigned to it. Vice-Admiral Villeneuve (replacing the unfortunate Latouche-Tréville) was to sail from Toulon with ten ships-of-the-line and 5,600 troops on 21 October, pick up another French ship, the *Aigle*, from Cadiz (the Spanish were still neutral but

friendly to the French), then make for a rendezvous off Surinam. En route he was to detach two ships with 1,800 soldiers to capture St Helena and relieve Senegal – a side issue that only served to complicate operations and detract from the main mission.

At Surinam Villeneuve would combine with Rear-Admiral Missiessy's six ships-of-the-line and 1,200 troops. This force of some fifteen warships and 5,000 men would then capture Surinam and other Dutch colonies, and then attack British West Indian roadsteads as opportunities arose. It would then return across the Atlantic to raise the blockade of Ferrol and pick up the five ships there. The twenty ships-of-the-line would finally make for the Channel – hopefully to be joined there by Ganteaume. Before all this, Missiessy (who was to leave Rochefort on 1 November with 3,500 soldiers embarked) was to have dropped off garrisons at Martinique and Guadeloupe and captured Dominica and St Lucia.

The third strand of this hideously complex scheme was the invasion of northern Ireland. On 23 November, Ganteaume with twenty-one ships-of-the-line and 18,000 troops was to sail round Scotland and disembark the army at Louch Swilly Bay. Having done that he was to meet the returning Villeneuve, and the combined fleet of nearly forty ships-of the-line would head for the Channel. The likelihood of this happening after months of sailing over thousands of miles of ocean, not to mention almost inevitable clashes with English ships, was so remote as to be verging on the miraculous. Perhaps fortunately these amateurish, ill-considered manoeuvres were never attempted. The British intercepted the orders to Ganteaume, so the entire project was abandoned.

# THE APPROACH TO TRAFALGAR

### Plan 3 – January 1805
By the beginning of 1805, Spain was again in alliance with France against Britain, and Napoleon was becoming increasingly anxious about continental (land) affairs. Austria was becoming restive. Russia supported her and was negotiating with Britain. Of this French spies were certain. Napoleon was probably having serious second thoughts about the wisdom of committing his army across the Channel. What if another coalition was cobbled together against him? If Austria and Russia moved against him while he was embroiled with Britain, how could he deal with two fronts simultaneously? Then there were all the setbacks and frustrations of organizing an invasion over the past eighteen months. If success was doubtful, it might be better to keep his army for looming problems in central Europe. Almost certainly by the late autumn of 1804 the Emperor was looking for an escape from having to launch an invasion. So he decided to cause the British problems elsewhere, ordering both Missiessy and Villeneuve (with troops embarked) to sail from Rochefort and Toulon respectively and head for the Caribbean. There they were to cause chaos among the British colonies and traders. The eminent French historian Desbrière later wrote that their objective had:

> at that time no connexion with an invasion of England …
> nor [were they] given any instructions that could lead
> them to suppose that their operations were to be a part of
> a comprehensive plan of campaign.

Due to foul weather Missiessy, who sailed on 11 January, evaded Vice-Admiral Sir Thomas Graves' blockading squadron and headed out across the Atlantic. Rear-Admiral Cochrane did not hesitate, on his own initiative, to leave his station off Ferrol in pursuit. Both reached the West Indies and played no further part in the Trafalgar campaign. Villeneuve left Toulon a week later but within two days he was back in port, having been defeated by a combination of the weather and shaky seamanship. Villeneuve was exceptionally forthright when explaining the debacle to the Minister of Marine, Decrès:

> My fleet looked well in Toulon, but when the storm came on,
> things changed at once. The sailors were not used to storms:
> they were lost among the mass of soldiers: these from sickness
> lay in heaps about the decks: it was impossible to work the
> ships: hence yard-arms were broken and sails carried away: our
> losses amounted as much from clumsiness and inexperience as
> from defects in the materials delivered from the arsenals.

It was an embarrassing failure for Villeneuve, but had even more frustrating consequences for Nelson.

### NELSON DECEIVED
On 20 January 1805 Nelson had eleven ships-of-the-line sheltering in Maddalena Bay on the northern tip of Sardinia. It was a miserable, bone-chilling winter afternoon. A biting northwesterly gale was screaming through the Straits of Bonifacio (the channel

## Napoleon's Second Invasion Plan (to be implemented October 1804 to early 1805)   Map 6

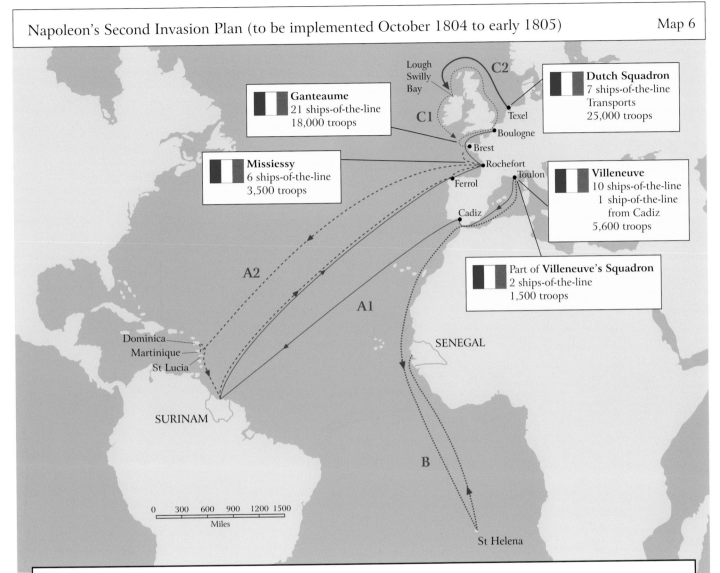

### Notes

This hugely ambitious scheme, involving almost 50 ships-of-the-line, numerous frigates and transport, and over 53,000 troops, was in fact three distinct operations.

A1  Villeneuve to sail from Toulon for Surinam and there join with Missiessy, capture Surinam before sailing back to Ferrol, pick up five more ships-of-the-line and head for Boulogne via Rochefort. When he arrived in the Channel the invasion could proceed.

A2  Missiessy to sail to the West Indies, first garrisoning Martinique and then capturing Dominica and St Lucia before joining Villeneuve for the return to Europe and the attempt on the Channel.

B  Two ships of Villeneuve's Toulon fleet to capture St Helena and then stir up trouble in Senegal and the West African coast.

C1  Ganteaume with a substantial army to sail round Scotland and land the troops in Northern Ireland, then to join Villeneuve in the Channel.

C2  The Dutch Squadron to reinforce the invasion of Ireland.

between northern Sardinia and the southern tip of Napoleon's birthplace, Corsica). Maddalena Bay, with the three tiny islands of Spargi, Caprera and San Stefano crouching opposite, now blocking the main force of the wind, had been Nelson's main refuge from the frequently appalling weather of the Gulf of Lyons for nearly two years. With the British base of Gibraltar being over 900 miles, and Malta over 1,200, from Toulon (the port he was blockading), this secluded spot a mere 200 miles away was a godsend. It gave him shelter from the worst weather, some fresh water, wood for the galley fires and perhaps a little fruit.

Although not able to keep him supplied with basic provisions, Maddalena was an anchorage that could be reached by supply ships from Gibraltar or the towns on the North African coast. It was a place to which he could bring his main fleet for a brief respite. There, with his frigates watching Toulon and elsewhere, he could still be near enough to catch the French should they venture out – or so he thought.

Both ships and seamen were tattered and tired after so many months at sea. Rigging was spliced in many places, the painted sides were peeling, while the sails were stained and patched, hulls

An Open Blockade – Nelson Chases Villeneuve (January–February 1805)          Map 7

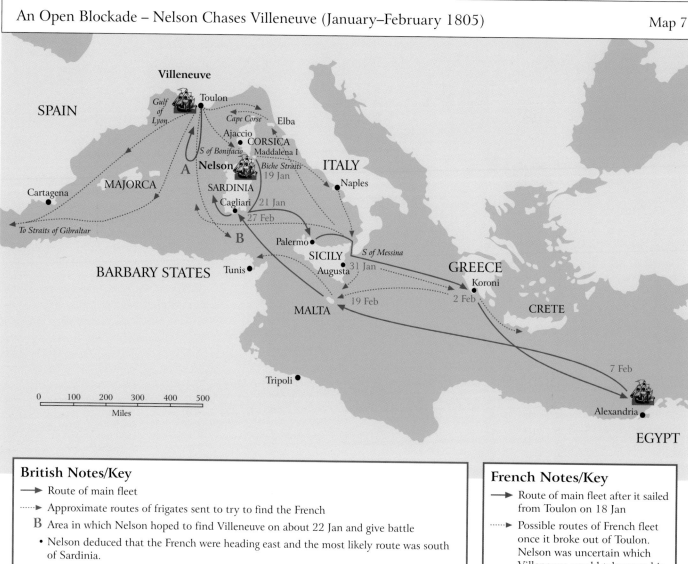

**British Notes/Key**

→ Route of main fleet

┈┈▸ Approximate routes of frigates sent to try to find the French

B  Area in which Nelson hoped to find Villeneuve on about 22 Jan and give battle

• Nelson deduced that the French were heading east and the most likely route was south of Sardinia.

• When they were not found in area B, he feared that they had slipped past him into the eastern Mediterranean. He dispatched his frigates to locate them.

• He took his fleet to Alexandria in his fruitless search. Not until he was at Malta on 19 Feb did he learn the French had been back in Toulon since 21 Jan.

**French Notes/Key**

→ Route of main fleet after it sailed from Toulon on 18 Jan

┈┈▸ Possible routes of French fleet once it broke out of Toulon. Nelson was uncertain which Villeneuve would take once his frigates lost contact.

A  French fleet badly damaged and scattered by NW gale – returns to Toulon by 21 Jan.

covered in barnacles and weed. All the ensigns were badly frayed, transparent in their wind-whipped thinness. Particularly threadbare and scruffy was the 74-gun *Superb*; she had been commissioned only four years previously, but had never been into port for a refit since. Condemned as unseaworthy twelve months before, she had hung on in the desperate hope of a battle.

On the poop deck of the 74-gun *Belleisle* (a captured French ship, previously named the *Formidable)* only the hunched and sodden figure of the signals midshipman was visible, as his duty compelled him to keep the flagship in sight. Below, on the quarterdeck, the lieutenant of the watch avoided the worst of the weather by keeping well back behind the quartermaster at the wheel. The officer leant against the bulkhead, under the awning of the poop cabins. The quartermaster glanced yet again at the hourglass just as the upper half emptied. 'Six bells by the glass, sir!' he reported. 'Make it so, quartermaster!' the lieutenant nod-

ded. The petty officer reached up to the lanyard of the bell hanging in the awning above the wheel. He double-jerked it six times. *Clang-clang, clang-clang, clang-clang, clang-clang, clang-clang, clang-clang*. It was three o'clock in the afternoon, and there was another hour before the watch changed and hands were piped to supper.

However, routine was to be abruptly ruined. Within moments of the bell sounding came the unmistakable BOOM of a single cannon shot. The sound rolled round the islets and between the cliffs. Surging in from the west, was a frigate, first plunging, then rearing up as she ploughed through the angry waves, foam cascading across her upper deck every time she brought her bows up. Even with much reduced sail in that gale, she was doing twelve knots (about 15 mph). It was the 38-gun *Active* firing her forecastle gun to attract attention to the signal she was flying. Streaming from her mizzen-masthead were flags that none of the fleet's signals midshipmen could fail to read, indeed everyone out on deck could recognize the words they had waited for so long – 'Enemy at sea!' The blockade of Toulon had been broken. Within moments a second frigate was spotted rounding the headland – another 38-gun ship, the *Seahorse*. A short pause, then another BOOM, this time from the *Victory*'s forecastle as a blank shot was fired. Even before the wind snatched away the smoke, all eyes went to the flagship's masthead to see the Blue Peter rising to the top. The fleet was to sail.

On the *Belleisle* both the First Lieutenant Thomas Fife and the Captain, William Hargood, forty-three years old and at sea since he was nine, were now on the quarterdeck. The Captain spoke crisply: 'Mr Fife, have all hands piped to prepare for sea.' 'Aye aye sir!' The first lieutenant raised his speaking trumpet to bellow, 'Bosun's mates, prepare for sea!' It was the same on the *Donegal* (74), *Superb* (74), *Canopus* (74), *Spencer* (74), *Tigre* (74), *Royal Sovereign* (100, flying the flag of Rear-Admiral Sir Richard Bickerton, Nelson's second-in-command), *Leviathan* (74), *Conqueror* (74), *Swiftsure* (74) and of course on the *Victory* (102) herself. All eleven ships-of-the-line (the twelfth was in Naples) would sail that night.

Nelson's blockade on Toulon had been an open one, deliberately so, because he wanted a battle. Now the enemy fleet was out, but there would be no battle unless the French could be found and caught. The news that Villeneuve had sailed, however, meant that Nelson at Maddalena had a problem. Like every officer and seaman in his fleet he was elated that the French were out. But he must find them, overtake them and, if possible, force them to fight. Shortly after 3 p.m. on the wild winter afternoon of 20 January, with darkness rapidly approaching, lanterns were lit and charts were spread across the table of the admiral's day cabin. Where were the enemy, where were they headed, what was their mission? When *Active* and *Seahorse* had left them, they were about 120 miles south-south-east of Toulon, sailing south-south-west. Nelson reasoned as follows (Map 7).

• Since easterly winds had been blowing for the past two weeks and Villeneuve had ignored them, he was unlikely to be heading west, through the Straits of Gibraltar. With a northwesterly gale the French must surely eventually head east.

• The French had embarked several thousand troops, so presumably a landing was contemplated somewhere. It was also likely that Villeneuve wanted to avoid a sea battle, at least until the soldiers were ashore. His destination could be Naples, Sicily, Sardinia, Malta or even further east; perhaps an attack on Greece or another one on Egypt was planned.

• Supposing the French fleet were headed for the eastern Mediterranean, then if it had intended to use the passage round the northern tip of Corsica it would already have passed Cape Corse. Its reported position the previous afternoon made this route extremely unlikely. It was also unlikely that it would take the short cut through the Straits of Bonifacio, which was just

## Lightning Strikes

For a sailing ship to be struck by lightning was not uncommon. It could result in fire and the magazine exploding – the quickest and most effective way of destroying any ship. Vice-Admiral Lovell, writing in 1800, described how, during a fierce storm in the Mediterranean, lightning hit a British squadron. The *Dragon* (74) and *Renown* (74) were both struck. The former was damaged and a man killed. The *Renown*'s mizzen-topgallant mast was smashed, as was the topmast. The mizzenmast was set on fire, while some tin and iron pots in the gunroom were perforated as if hit by a bullet. The lightning exited through a gunroom port. If the *Renown*'s mizzenmast had been stepped (had its base) in the after magazine like older 74s, she would certainly have blown up.

north of where Nelson was now weighing anchor. The passage was tricky even for competent sailors and in a fierce gale the risks were enormous, particularly for the poorly trained French. So the only remaining route was round the southern tip of Sardinia.

• To intercept Villeneuve the English fleet would have to sail immediately down the eastern coast of Sardinia. Two hundred miles would take them midway between Sardinia and the coast of North Africa. There, perhaps within two days or less, the French might be found and brought to battle.

The Fleet set sail in line, each ship desperately trying to keep sight of the light of the one ahead through the blackness and driving rain. They had to negotiate the Biche Straits, the shortest of the channels open to them from Maddalena Bay, but still a terrifying route between towering cliffs, in places less than 400 yards apart. Almost certainly it was the first time any ships of that size had attempted the passage, certainly at night in a raging storm with no pilot. On the *Belleisle* the master, William Hudson, had taken several midshipmen forward to the bowsprit heel, the better to see the hazards and follow the flickering light of the ship ahead. Through his speaking trumpet Hudson yelled instructions to make adjustments to the course steered. They were relayed aft to the quartermaster who shouted the appropriate orders to the four seamen struggling with the double wheel. A tiny error and the ship would have been smashed to pulp in moments on the huge piles of jagged rocks, whose presence was betrayed by the mountainous waves crashing over them at the foot of the cliffs. Within an hour the whole fleet was clear of the channel. It remains to this day an incredible, probably unsurpassed, piece of seamanship.

Nelson wrote in his diary late on 19 January:

Hard gales N.W. At 3.00 p.m. the *Active* and *Seahorse* arrived at Maddelena, with information that the French Fleet put to sea yesterday. … Unmoored and weighed. At 28 minutes past 4 made the general signal for each Ship to carry a light, and repeat signals during the night made by the Admiral. Ran through the Passage between Biche and Sardinia at 6 o'clock. At 35 minutes past 6 burnt a blue light. … At 7 the whole Fleet was clear of the Passage. Sent *Seahorse* round the Southern end of Sardinia to St. Peter's [a small island off the south-west of Sardinia], to look out for them … the moment Captain Boyle discovered them, to return to me. From their position when last seen, and the course they were steering, S. or S. by W., they could only be bound round the Southern end of Sardinia.

On 21 January Nelson made the general signal 'Prepare for Battle'. By then he was off the south coast of Sardinia but saw no sign of the French. For several days he remained in this location awaiting news from his handful of far-flung frigates while continuing to fight the foul weather and heavy seas. On the morning of 22 January the

*Seahorse* rejoined the fleet. At 11 a.m. Captain Boyle scrambled aboard the *Victory* with some difficulty to report. He had reached as far east as fifty miles from the southern tip of Sardinia, and he informed Nelson that the day before he had glimpsed a French frigate scurrying into the comparative shelter of Cagliari Bay – nothing more. Villeneuve had vanished – the blockade had been broken.

There is no doubt Nelson was extremely worried that the French had outmanoeuvred him. Writing to Sir John Acton, Prime Minister of the Two Sicilies in Palermo on 25 January, he complained, 'You will believe my anxiety, I have neither ate, drank or slept with any comfort since last Sunday (20th).' Once again, Nelson had been compelled to examine two unwelcome options. The first was that Villeneuve had returned to Toulon. If this was the case, then Nelson had missed the opportunity of attacking and possibly destroying his enemy – an opportunity for which he and his ships had worked ceaselessly over the past twenty gruelling months. The second possibility was that somehow the French fleet had slipped past him and was at that moment in the eastern Mediterranean heading for Greece or Egypt. If this was the case then it was absolutely imperative that he catch them. Villeneuve with his ships and soldiers could do much more damage in the east than riding at anchor at Toulon. So Nelson determined to sail east. To Acton he wrote:

> I hope that the Governor of Augusta [on the east coast of Sicily] will not give up the post to the French fleet; but if he does, I shall go in and attack them; for I consider the destruction of the enemy fleet of so much consequence, that I would gladly have half of mine burnt to effect their destruction. I am in a fever. God send I may find them!

He never did. On 26 January Nelson learnt that no French landing had been made on Sardinia and his frigate *Phoebe* returned to report that a dismasted enemy 80-gun ship had struggled into Ajaccio on the 19th. Nelson sailed for Palermo and the Straits of Messina, through which the fleet beat on the 31st. He described this feat as 'a thing unprecedented in nautical history, but although the danger from the rapidity of the current was great, yet so was the object of my pursuit; and I relied with confidence on the zeal and ability of the fleet under my command'. He now knew for certain that Sicily and Naples were not threatened. Before continuing east to Koroni (Greece), which he reached on 2 February, he sent six cruisers fanning out for news, three of which were frigates sent back to resume the watch off Toulon. There was no news of the French in Greece so he pushed on to Alexandria, arriving on 7 February. Still no news. On the 12th an angry, frustrated and exhausted Nelson turned back westwards to retrace his fruitless voyage. On 19 February, off Malta, he at last received information that Villeneuve had been back in Toulon for four weeks! As we have seen, the French fleet had been scattered, dismasted and defeated by the weather and had limped back to port by 21 January. By the time he arrived back at Cagliari on 27 February Nelson had spent nearly six weeks sailing over 2,500 miles, mostly battling mountainous seas. He was to say, 'It has been, without exception, the very worst weather I have ever seen', and his foe had been sitting safely in Toulon all along. For the entire time all ships had, as Nelson put it, 'been prepared for battle: not a bulkhead up in the fleet'.

The open blockade had succeeded in tempting Villeneuve out but a combination of too few cruisers, a frigate captain's error in leaving the French unobserved when out at sea plus the appalling weather had prevented the battle Nelson so desperately sought. The lesson to be learnt for open blockades was simple – once an enemy leaves port he should be kept under observation at all costs until the main fleet can come up. Unfortunately, it was to be a lesson that had to be relearned a few weeks later.

## THE CHASE TO THE CARIBBEAN – AND BACK

In general terms, French naval strategy was first one of evasion, then concentration for the purpose of invasion. From 1803 onwards, France sought to avoid battle at sea. In this she was largely successful. Even Vice-Admiral Calder's clash with Villeneuve in July 1805 off Cape Finisterre (see below) was indecisive. British fleets wanted to fight, and as the months and years passed they became obsessed with the idea of bringing their guns to bear on the enemy. The events in the Mediterranean, the Atlantic, the Caribbean and the Atlantic again during the spring and summer of 1805 were perfect examples of the two strategies unfolding.

### Plan 4 – March to August 1805

By early March 1805 Napoleon had received a letter from the Emperor of Austria giving assurances that his intentions were entirely peaceful, so his invasion plan was back in favour. His new scheme, like his previous one, involved the French and Spanish fleets sailing off to the West Indies with the intention of luring the British after them, then doubling back to Boulogne to guard the invasion flotilla as it crossed the Channel. The scheme therefore envisaged a gathering together in the Caribbean of almost fifty ships-of-the-line and at least twenty frigates and brigs, which would then descend on the Channel in overwhelming numbers. The commander-in-chief was to be Vice-Admiral Honoré Ganteaume, then at Brest. His orders of 2 March were as follows:

• He was to embark 3,000 troops, break out from Brest with twenty-one ships-of-the-line, six frigates and two store ships and sail for Ferrol.
• He was then to drive off or capture the British blockading squadron (under Calder) and join with Rear-Admiral Gourdon's four ships-of-the-line and the Spanish Admiral Grandallana's eight. All were then to sail west to Martinique in the Caribbean.
• At Martinique he would join with Missiessy's five and Villeneuve's eleven ships-of-the-line and his frigates.
• This huge armada was then to sail back across the Atlantic heading for Ushant and a clash with whatever ships the British had mustered there, defeat them and proceed to Boulogne.

Villeneuve's orders of 2 March were:

• At Toulon, he was to embark the 3,000 troops under the recently promoted Général de Division Jacques Lauriston (his second-in-command was Général de Brigade Honoré Reille, who ten years later was to fight as a corps commander at Waterloo). He was then to sail to Cadiz.
• At Cadiz he was to pick up the French 74-gun *Aigle* plus the six Spanish ships-of-the-line (if ready to sail) under Admiral Gravina and sail for Martinique to join Missiessy and Ganteaume. If, after forty days, there was no sign of Ganteaume, he was to disembark 1,300 troops and sail for the Canaries in order to intercept convoys from India. Thence, if Ganteaume had still not appeared, he should make for Cadiz.

────────── **Général de Division Comte Jacques Alexandre Bernard Law Lauriston (1768–1828)** ──────────

Lauriston was a general serving as a member of a band of hand-picked aides-de-camp to Napoleon. These ADCs later became the most important element of the Emperor's personal staff, known as the *Maison Militaire* (Military Household). They were specially selected and could be called upon for a wide range of key duties, such as diplomatic missions, battlefield reconnaissance, the delivery of orders to field commanders or taking charge of a particularly critical operation. In this case, Lauriston the soldier was not only the commander of the troops embarked but also had orders to be watchful of Villeneuve the sailor and to keep him to his duties (see also Section Seven: Command and Control). Lauriston was an artillery officer like his Emperor and had been an ADC to the First Consul since 1800. He was on the *Bucentaure* in the action against the British off Cape Finisterre on 22 July 1805, still describing in vitriolic terms what he saw as Villeneuve's invariable failure to carry out his duties. In August 1805, commenting on Villeneuve's sortie from Ferrol and retreat to Cadiz, he wrote to Paris:

I have the honour to be Your Majesty's aide-de-camp; I am truly humiliated at finding myself present at so many ignominious manoeuvres, powerless to do the slightest thing for the honour of Your Majesty's flag. We sail like a fleet of merchantmen who fear the attack of 4 or 5 of the line and it is a single man who is the cause of all this.

Lauriston, no doubt much to the relief of Villeneuve, missed Trafalgar. He was later appointed Governor of Austria and, in 1807, of Venice. Service in Spain as commander of the Imperial Guard artillery followed. In 1809 he was back on Napoleon's staff, and at Wagram he was given the command of the famous battery of a hundred guns. In 1811 his ADC status brought him the ambassadorship of St Petersburg. He rode into Russia with the Emperor's staff in 1812 and was selected to negotiate with Tsar Alexander but was not allowed through Russian lines. Having fought with the rearguard during the infamous winter retreat, he was a corps commander on the Elbe in 1813 at Mockern, Bautzen and Leipzig, where he was captured. He stayed loyal to Louis XVIII in 1815, and his reward was promotion to marshal in 1823.

Crucially, Villeneuve's orders, unlike Ganteaume's, made no mention of Boulogne being the final objective of the Combined Fleet. This was probably because Ganteaume, not Villeneuve, was intended to be the overall commander at that stage. Also Lauriston, as a personal ADC to the Emperor, had been given sealed orders to be opened later at sea that gave the plan in full. In a dispatch dated 16 March, Lauriston was urged, as soon as the sealed orders were opened, to galvanize the admirals into action. Napoleon had far more faith in his generals than his admirals – which is not surprising. As with Napoleon's previous grand naval plans things began to go frustratingly awry from the outset. Not only were they complex but Napoleon forever expected his admirals to manoeuvre their fleets as he did his armies, seemingly incapable of understanding the effect weather, currents and tides would have on his orders.

**Vice-Admiral Comte Honoré Ganteaume: Confined to Brest**

Ganteaume, in 1805 fifty years old, commanded the main fleet in the French Navy. The most memorable and fortunate incident of his life was undoubtedly surviving the spectacular explosion that destroyed the admiral's flagship the 120-gun *L'Orient* at the Nile in 1798. Now, despite the fact that he was junior to Villeneuve, he would take command of the combined fleet at Martinique and bring it back to cover the long postponed invasion. If the Emperor regarded any admiral with a degree of favour it was probably Ganteaume. When Napoleon had decided to leave his army in Egypt in 1799 he boarded the frigate *Muiron* to slip through the watchful ring of British cruisers. It was Ganteaume who brought him safely back to France.

Throughout mid-March the inner anchorage at Brest buzzed with activity as Ganteaume got his ships ready. The fleet had to be fully manned, which meant most ships drafting in soldiers to make up numbers. Holds had to be stocked with rations and water, armouries with powder and shot. After two weeks an impatient Emperor wrote urging haste: 'Do not forget the great destinies which you hold in your hands. If you are not wanting in enterprise, success is certain.' He wanted his fleets away by the end of the

month. On 24 March Ganteaume was ready. However, sitting outside, poised in the Iroise Channel (Map 4) was the bulk of the Channel Fleet under Vice-Admiral Cotton (Gardner did not take over until 3 April). Ganteaume's signal stations counted fifteen ships-of-the-line. If he sailed he would have to fight his way out. What should he do? The arms of the telegraph jerked and jolted as the problem was put to Paris. Ganteaume was confident: 'Success is not doubtful. I await your Majesty's orders.' He got his reply within hours. 'A naval victory,' replied Napoleon, 'in existing circumstances can lead to nothing. Keep but one end in view – to fulfil your mission. Get to sea without an action.' That was clear enough.

On 26 March Ganteaume moved cautiously out through the Goulet channel into the Bertheaume anchorage, still under the protection of shore batteries. He would wait for a fog. The next morning it came, and with it he hoisted the signal to weigh anchor. Unfortunately a gentle northerly breeze quickly blew away his convenient screen to reveal a bright spring day. The signal station indicated that Cotton was approaching with seventeen ships-of-the-line. Ganteaume signalled for the fleet to anchor where it was. Cotton closed to within five miles. With the wind now unfavourable for a return to the inner harbour Ganteaume resolved, reluctantly, to fight. The fleet was ordered to make sail and form battle order but then, to the French admiral's surprise, Cotton tacked and stood out again. With night approaching, many dangerous shoals and the proximity of heavy shore batteries, he preferred to keep the French under observation in the hope of them eventually making for the open sea. Nelson would almost certainly have attempted another Nile, but Cotton was only a temporary, acting fleet commander, so perhaps understandably he chose to be cautious.

The next morning the wind freshened from the south-west so Ganteaume was able to seek the inner harbour again. Forbidden to fight his way out, with the enemy sitting on his doorstep and no hope of escaping unobserved, the commander-in-chief of this great enterprise had no choice but to remain inactive at Brest. And so it was. Nearly half of the great combined fleet ultimately destined for Boulogne never left port.

## Vice-Admiral Pierre Charles Villeneuve: Escape from Toulon (Map 8)

Villeneuve was forty-two in 1805, and had succeeded to the vital Mediterranean command only due to the unexpected death of Latouche-Tréville. Napoleon had little confidence in either of the two possible replacements – Villeneuve and Vice-Admiral Rosily – but was persuaded by Villeneuve's friend Decrès, the Minister of Marine (who like him had escaped from the debacle of the Nile), to appoint him. As will be seen, Villeneuve had drawn an exceptionally short straw, one that fated him to meet Nelson at Trafalgar seven months later, and a gruesome, agonizing death six months after that.

As at Brest, Toulon was the scene of a frantic scramble to get ready by the end of March. Villeneuve had eleven ships-of-the-line divided into two divisions, with his second-in-command Rear-Admiral Pierre Dumanoir le Pelley commanding the second division. His fleet was organized as follows:

**1st Division**

*Bucentaure* (80)
(Villeneuve's flagship)

*Neptune* (80)
*Pluton* (74)
*Mont-Blanc* (74)
*Berwick* (74)
*Atlas* (74)

**Frigates**

*Cornélie* (40; 18-pounder)
*Rhin* (40; 18-pounder)
*Hortense* (40; 18-pounder)
*Hermione* (40; 18-pounder)
*Sirène* (36; 12-pounder)
*Thémis* (36; 12-pounder)

**2nd Division**

*Formidable* (80)
(Dumanoir's flagship)

*Indomptable* (80)
*Swiftsure* (74)
*Scipion* (74)
*Intrépide* (74)

**Brigs**

*Pleiade* (18)
*Furet* (18)

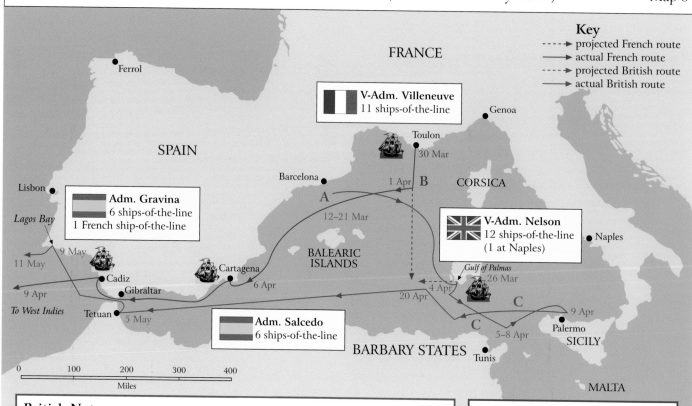

## Villeneuve Breaks Blockade and Sails for the West Indies (30 March–11 May 1805)    Map 8

**Key**
- - - -► projected French route
———► actual French route
- - - -► projected British route
———► actual British route

### British Notes

- During 12–21 March Nelson deliberately lets his fleet be identified cruising off Barcelona – area A.
- He then sails to Gulf of Palmas to meet his supply vessels and lie in ambush for the French if they sail south.
- When Villeneuve sails, Nelson's frigates lose contact and again Nelson is unsure of their location.
- As his primary duty is to protect Sardinia, Sicily and Naples, Nelson remains in area C until 9 April.
- On 18 April Villeneuve's leaving the Mediterranean is confirmed as Nelson is heading back towards Toulon.
- He remains uncertain of whether their destination is the West Indies, Brest or Ireland. He decides to follow the French fleet and leave the Mediterranean. Final confirmation that Villeneuve was heading for the West Indies is given to Nelson at Lagos Bay on 9 May.

### French Notes

- On 30 March Villeneuve sails from Toulon. He heads south to avoid area A where Nelson has recently been seen.
- On 1 April in area B he encounters a merchantman that informs him Nelson is at Gulf of Palmas, so he alters course to sail west of the Balearic Islands.
- Adm. Salcedo's ships at Cartagena do not join Villeneuve.
- On 8 April at Cadiz Villeneuve is joined by Adm. Gravina's squadron and the French *Aigle*. The combined fleet sails for the West Indies.

A shortage of sailors was made up by 1,800 men from the 2nd Régiment de Ligne, which also provided marines for the fleet, and was to fight on land at Waterloo ten years later under the Emperor's brother Prince Jérôme. Six months' supply of victuals, water and stores was lowered into the holds. Also crammed uncomfortably on board were over 3,000 troops. General Lauriston commanded, with Général de Brigade Reille as his second. This small division consisted of two battalions of the 16th Ligne and another of the 67th, with 120 artillerymen with siege and field pieces.

Villeneuve's immediate problem was to make a break without being intercepted by Nelson. The French admiral knew he could not avoid the British frigates outside Toulon, but the blockade was a loose one, so the skill (or luck) would lie not in leaving port, as at Brest, but in slipping past the main enemy fleet at sea. Hearing that Nelson had been seen off Barcelona on 17 March, Villeneuve decided that the French would sail south between the Balearics and Sardinia. At 4 p.m. on 30 March he put to sea. The following day only two enemy frigates (*Active* and *Phoebe*) could be seen shadowing his fleet. Of Nelson's ships-of-the-line there was no sign. The next day, 1 April, even the frigates had disappeared. There was, however, a solitary sail in sight. This turned out to be a neutral Sicilian merchantman, whose captain had information that changed the whole course of the campaign. Nelson's fleet had been spotted, not off the Spanish coast, but in the Gulf of Palmas on the southern tip of Sardinia. A quick glance at the chart was all Villeneuve needed to confirm what he must have already known – if he continued south Nelson would ambush him. A cannon boomed, a signal was hoisted and the French fleet swung slowly to windward, to the south-west, to hug the Spanish coast west of the Balearics.

Although he could not know it, Villeneuve had successfully opened the great attack. In fact he found it hard to credit his good fortune and still expected the dreaded Nelson's topmasts to appear on the horizon at any moment. He fumed at the weather that forced him to close haul into the wind for a week before reaching Cartagena on 7 April. Only 400 miles in seven days – it was exasperating. Although the Emperor's orders had not specifically mentioned picking up the six Spanish battleships under Admiral Salcedo at Cartagena, Villeneuve hoped they would join him. But, according to Villeneuve, the Spanish admiral felt he could not leave without specific orders from Madrid, and in any case his ships would not be ready to sail for another two or three days – too long for Villeneuve to wait with, he felt certain, Nelson on his heels. It is also possible that Villeneuve refused to take the Spanish ships when he heard that a serious epidemic had recently ravaged the port. Whatever the truth, that night (7 April) he left Cartagena with a fresh easterly wind filling his sails. The next day the Rock of Gibraltar was sighted. With the frigates standing ahead and the two divisions in column astern, the French fleet made a fine sight to watchers in both Africa and Spain as it entered the Straits. Only fourteen miles separate the so-called Pillars of Hercules – to the north the grey limestone mass of the Rock, to the south Mount Ceuta on the Moroccan coast. As the genie sailed sedately out of the bottle it was, inevitably, seen by enemy ships south of Cadiz. The 74-gun *Renown* with the frigate *Mercury* and sloop *Sophie* from Rear-Admiral Orde's squadron turned in haste to report.

Villeneuve had sent the frigate *Hortense* ahead to Cadiz to warn the French 74-gun *Aigle* and the Spanish to be ready to sail immediately. As night fell the Spanish Admiral Don Frederico

Gravina sent word that six of his ships-of-the-line, *Argonauta* (80), *San Rafaël* (80), *Firme* (74), *Terrible* (74), *America* (64) and *España* (64), plus the frigate *Maddalena*, were ready. Villeneuve, ever worrying as to Nelson's whereabouts, sent his flag lieutenant, Lieutenant Fleury, across to the Spanish flagship *Argonauta* to remind Gravina that, 'every minute was precious, that the enemy's Mediterranean squadron must be in pursuit and might effect a junction with the force that had blockaded Cadiz [Orde] up till then and that it was essential to set sail for our destination'. Fleury brought back a positive reply. Villeneuve could make the signal to get under way at once and the Spanish would follow suit. The efforts of the Spanish were later praised by the French General Reille, although he was probably justified in criticizing his own admiral's decision to leave the slower Spanish ships to make their own way across the Atlantic. He wrote:

> The activity which Admiral Gravina has displayed cannot be too highly praised. In one hour his troops [about 2,000] were on board the cables slipped, ... at 1 o'clock in the morning the signal was made for the two Squadrons to get under way and at 2 o'clock the greater part were under sail. On the 20th [9 April] at daybreak all the French ships were in company but only the Spanish flag-ship was with us. Some leagues astern some ships were sighted which were apparently the five others. ... It would have been desirable for the Fleet to heave-to and wait for them, thereby preventing separation, but they continued to carry a good deal of sail. ... Towards evening, however, the Admiral bore away for about 2 leagues [six miles], but this was not nearly sufficient in order to rejoin the stragglers. The night passed and the next day the 21st [April 10], we could only see the ... *America*, which was not able to join us until the 22nd [April 11]. No one could conceive what induced the Admiral to do so little to prevent this separation which might have had the most serious consequences. The fate of these ships was compromised, whilst their presence ensured the success of the expedition; it was only necessary to wait for two or three hours.

The fleet was to sail some 4,000 miles across the Atlantic in two groups. They were not reunited until 16 May.

## The British Plan

March of 1805 saw not only the first moves of Napoleon's grand naval combinations but also the first British moves in an offensive to support Russia in the Mediterranean. The British government had become increasingly worried about the vulnerability of Naples and Sicily. By the end of March, preparations were under way to reinforce the troops in the Mediterranean by sending a large expedition to Malta under the command of Lieutenant-General Sir James Craig. Forty-five transports were assembled to embark six infantry battalions and a dragoon regiment. This huge convoy would be escorted by the 98-gun *Queen* and the 74-gun *Dragon*, which would reinforce Orde's squadron off Cadiz and hand over escort duties to Nelson for the remainder of the voyage to Malta. The admiral commanding the escort ships was Rear-Admiral John Knight. Part of Craig's complex and wide-ranging instructions stressed the importance of the defence of Sicily. He was expected to 'use his utmost exertions, in concert with Lord Nelson, for the defence of Sicily'. Contrary winds prevented Craig's expedition from sailing until 19 April.

## Nelson Deceived – Again (Map 8)

Within ten days of returning from his fruitless chase to Egypt at the end of February, Nelson had set out his new plans in a 'Most Secret Memorandum'. His fleet had to cover Sardinia, Sicily and Naples; he knew that Villeneuve still had troops embarked and so suspected he would put to sea again shortly. That was what he wanted, so there was no question of deterring Villeneuve by imposing a close blockade. The open blockade would continue but behind it would be a trap. The best place at which to meet supply ships and to intercept the French if they made for Naples or Sicily was the Gulf of Palmas on the southern tip of Sardinia, codenamed 'Rendezvous 98'. If Villeneuve sailed south Nelson could ambush him somewhere between Sardinia and the Barbary Coast.

In order to tempt the French to come south, Nelson sailed for the north-east coast of Spain. His intention was to 'show himself off Barcelona and the coast of Spain … until the 21st of March'. Then he would return to Rendezvous 98 to meet his supply ships. The frigates Active and Phoebe would watch Toulon. On 26 March Nelson arrived back at Palmas. For a week the crews laboured under the watchful eyes of pursers and master's mates in the dark, evil-smelling holds transferring cargoes. On 3 April the fleet weighed and sailed out in quest of the enemy. The following morning the frigate Phoebe hove in sight with the magic signal 'Enemy at sea' hoisted for all to see. For the second time in three months Villeneuve was out. Unfortunately for Nelson, within five hours the Active arrived, confirming the news but having lost contact with the French during the night. For the second time in three months Nelson was left to guess their course and intentions. The frigates had clung to the French throughout daylight on 31 March but at 8 p.m. the Phoebe departed to report, leaving Active to keep track during darkness. Active steered south-west, which was the direction of the French at nightfall, but by daylight Villeneuve had vanished. The frigate had not been close enough to keep track of the fleet during the night, and there was nothing to be done except rejoin Nelson. Later that morning (1 April) Villeneuve had his fortuitous encounter with the merchantman and altered course. Nelson had been forced back to making decisions based on calculated guesswork. He was later to write, 'I am entirely adrift by my frigates losing sight of the French fleet so soon after their coming out of port.'

The next five weeks were some of the most frustrating in Nelson's life. An officer on the Victory described his admiral as, at times, 'almost raving with anger and vexation'. A chronology of those depressing days makes for interesting reading showing, as it does, how lack of reliable information combined with agonizingly slow communications multiplied the problems of command at sea.

4 April Nelson feared Villeneuve intended to disembark his troops at Naples or Sicily. If so, the most probable route was the passage between Sardinia and North Africa. He positioned himself in the centre of this passage. But what was to stop the French admiral doubling back and sailing round the north of Corsica or through the Straits of Bonifacio between Corsica and Sardinia? He had to be sure.

6 April Nelson wrote to Captain Sir John Ball, Governor of Malta, of his desperate uncertainty. 'I am in truth half dead, but what man can do to find them out shall be done. But I must not … leave Sardinia, Sicily or Naples open for them to take should I go eastward or westward without knowing more about them.' To find them he scattered his cruisers in all directions: the Ambuscade to the island of Galita north-west of Tunis, the Active between Galita and the Barbary Coast, the Moucheron to Tunis itself for information, the Seahorse and Aetna off Toro (an islet south of Sardinia), the Hydra off the east coast of Corsica and the Amazon to Naples.

6–8 April Nelson was waiting for a sighting or information in a central position between Sardinia and North Africa. Nothing. He decided to head for Palermo where he would still be in a good position to attack the French should they appear off Naples.

10 April Off Palermo he wrote again to Ball, 'I am in despair, I have not a word of news; all my Frigates are out cruising.' He had by then heard rumours that a large military expedition was being mounted in the Mediterranean in conjunction with the Russians. He continued his letter, 'I have not the most distant idea of such a thing … I am sorely vexed at the ignorance in which I have been kept.' A little later Captain Hallowell of the Tigre (80) came on board from Palermo to confirm that Craig's 'Great Expedition' had sailed from England (this was incorrect; in fact Craig sailed from Portsmouth only on 19 April, with a convoy of 67 transports). Nelson ended his letter, 'I must do my best. God bless you. I am very very miserable.' As Nelson was writing this, Villeneuve had just left Cadiz for Martinique. By now Nelson was convinced that the French had indeed sailed west and that he had been mistaken in his calculations.

11 April Nelson was now desperately trying to head west but was frustrated by head winds. For nine days his ships beat into the wind, tacking continuously in their efforts to make headway. Again he wrote to his friend Ball in Malta, 'I cannot get a fair wind, or even a side wind. Dead foul! – Dead foul!' To reach a position south of Sardinia, some 200 miles from Palermo, took the full nine days – a mere twenty-two miles a day.

16 April Nelson received a report from Leviathan (74) that Villeneuve had been seen off Cape Gata (south-west of Cartagena) on 7 April running west before an easterly wind. Two days later the sloop Childers, sent by one of Nelson's scouting frigates, the Amazon, confirmed that the French fleet had passed through the Straits on 8 April.

18 April Nelson knew for certain that the French had left the Mediterranean but was still unsure whether Villeneuve had left any ships at Toulon capable of transporting troops to Sardinia, Naples, Sicily or even Egypt. To cover this possibility Captain Bladen-Capel of the Phoebe was instructed to take command of the frigates Hydra, Juno, Niger and the bomb vessel Thunder and position them between Toro and the Barbary Coast to intercept any such expedition.

19 April Nelson considered the implications of Villeneuve leaving the Mediterranean but with his ultimate destination still unknown. Again he picked up his pen, this time setting out his conclusions and plan to William Marsden, Secretary to the Board of Admiralty.

> Seeing that the Enemy has so long ago passed the Straits and formed a junction with the Spanish Squadron at Cadiz, these are my intentions: I have sent the Amazon to Lisbon for information, I am proceeding … to Cape St Vincent where I hope to know from the Amazon what is the destination of the French Squadron. The fact that they have joined the Spanish … seems to me to prove that it is not their intention to go to the West Indies or to Brazil, but rather to raise the blockade of Ferrol, and to proceed from there to Ireland or to Brest, for I believe Villeneuve has troops on board. If I have no intelligence I shall leave Cape St Vincent and station myself fifty leagues [150 miles] west of the Scilly Isles…. My reason for taking this position is that from there I can equally well join the Fleet which is before Brest or go to Ireland.

He was leaving his station, the Mediterranean, on his own initiative. It was a bold, characteristic decision.

*1 May* The sloop *Martin* joined the fleet with the Admiralty's orders for Nelson to assume responsibility for the passage of Knight's convoy carrying Craig's troops through the Mediterranean.

*4 May* The British Fleet put into Mazri Bay, near Tetuan, and anchored a mile and a half from the beach. The following signal was hoisted: 'Ships to fill up with water, wood and fresh vegetables. *Superb* to Tetuan for beef for the Fleet.' Nelson was stocking up while waiting for a more favourable wind to take him westwards through the Straits, difficult at any time as ships had to battle against the current racing in from the Atlantic. He felt let down by Orde who, as noted above, had retired northwards on sighting Villeneuve. Nelson was particularly aggrieved as he felt Orde should at least have sent a cruiser with information on the direction the French were headed:

> I believe my ill luck is to go on for a longer time, and I now much fear that Sir John Orde has not sent his Small Ships to watch the Enemy's Fleet, and ordered them to return to the Straits' mouth, to give me information, that I might know how to direct my proceedings, for I cannot very properly run to the West Indies, without something beyond mere surmise; and if I defer Jamaica may be lost.

*7 May* Still at Tetuan waiting for wind and information. Nelson wrote: 'I am as much in the dark as ever. If I hear nothing I shall proceed to the West Indies.' Rear-Admiral Bickerton was to be left to command a Mediterranean squadron of cruisers, shifting his flag from the 100-gun, three-decker *Royal Sovereign* to the former Spanish frigate *Amfitrite.*

*8 May* A slight change in wind direction and the Fleet left Tetuan before all ships had been restocked. At last they headed through the Straits, then on to Lagos Bay, under the great cliffs of Cape St Vincent, where Orde's supply ships were still at anchor. Nelson had decided to help himself to all he needed. On the evening of 9 May Captain Sutton, commanding the frigate *Amphion*, joined, having been left on the Cadiz station by Orde. He finally confirmed that Villeneuve had not sailed north, that nothing had been seen of him for three weeks and therefore his only possible destination must be the Caribbean.

*10 May* Nelson had made up his mind. In another letter to Ball he wrote: 'My lot is cast and I am going to the West Indies.' To another friend he complained, 'Disappointment has worn me to a skeleton, and I am, in truth, very, very far from well.' He instructed that the *Royal Sovereign* (a slow sailer nicknamed the West Country Wagon) should join Knight's/Craig's convoy while the fast sloop *Martin*, under Commander Savage, should precede the fleet to Barbados.

*11 May* With ten-ships-of-the-line and three frigates Nelson began the great chase after an enemy given a thirty-one-day start. His ships were:

| Ships-of-the-line | | Frigates |
|---|---|---|
| *Victory* (102) | *Superb* (74) | *Amazon* |
| *Canopus* (80) | *Spencer* (74) | *Amphion* |
| *Tigre* (80) | *Conqueror* (74) | *Decade* |
| *Leviathan* (74) | *Belleisle* (74) | |
| *Donegal* (74) | *Swiftsure* (74) | |

At 4.00 p.m. the great convoy taking Craig's troops to Malta (and eventually to Naples) was sighted. It was the British Army's first expeditionary force of the war. The *Victory* hoisted a signal and the *Royal Sovereign* swung reluctantly away to reinforce the convoy escorts, her crew desperately disappointed to be missing the anticipated action in the West Indies. Their disappointment was unfounded – their place in history at Trafalgar was assured.

## Villeneuve in the West Indies (Map 9)

On 14 May the French fleet arrived in Fort de France Bay, Martinique. On the same day the Spanish ships *Firme, Terrible, España* and *Maddalena* were seen beating up to enter. On 16 May the *San Rafaël* arrived. As Reille wrote, 'Behold therefore, all the fleet reunited after a separation which might have been fatal to it.' Villeneuve had eighteen ships-of-the-line, five frigates and four corvettes or brigs, carrying over 5,000 troops. All were grateful to see the forest-clad peaks of the island after some five weeks at sea. Martinique was, and still is (it is now a Department of France), the jewel in the French Caribbean crown. The French acquired it in 1635 and held it until the British captured it for a year in 1762 and again in 1793 for eight years. In 1805 it had been French once more for four years.

Villeneuve's first priority after dropping anchor in the warm green waters of the bay was to take on fresh water and disembark Lauriston's seasick soldiers. His orders specified that he must wait for Ganteaume for up to six weeks – a long period of inactivity. After a week restocking and relaxing, which included several glittering formal dinners at Government House, he considered attacking the nearby British islands of Dominica or St Lucia but quickly rejected the idea as they were said to be alert and well guarded. He was also inhibited by a report that a strong squadron of British battleships might be approaching from near Puerto Rico (it consisted of the *St George* (98), *Northumberland* (74), *Spartiate* (74), *Eagle* (74), *Atlas* (74), *Centaur* (74) and *Veteran* (64) under Rear-Admiral Sir Alexander Cochrane). Until Ganteaume arrived he was on his own. Missiessy, with his five ships-of-the-line, had departed the Caribbean two days before Villeneuve left Toulon on 30 March. Napoleon had recalled Missiessy when gales had driven Villeneuve back to Toulon in January. So now Villeneuve felt it prudent to stick to his orders and not get embroiled in a serious operation. From this it would seem that Lauriston had still not shown the sealed orders to his admiral, as it was still possible that Ganteaume would arrive to assume overall command.

However, after two weeks of inactivity Villeneuve decided to send three frigates out cruising for information and to prey on trading ships. Above all he bemoaned his lack of intelligence: 'None reaches me here and I know absolutely nothing of what is happening.' It was a familiar complaint of military commanders down the ages. At the same time as looking for information, he was finally persuaded to bestir himself by the French Governor of the island, Captain-General Villaret-Joyeuse, to attack Diamond Rock, a precipitous lump of granite which the British occupied off the south-western point of Martinique (the Royal Navy had officially named it His Majesty's Sloop *Diamond Rock*). Here, for two years, as the British naval historian Julian Corbett wrote, 'the little garrison of a hundred men had lived in pure enjoyment a Robinson Crusoe life among the caves, incessantly raiding and cutting out, and proving an unendurable thorn in the side of Martinique'. A small armada containing a large sledgehammer was sent to crack

## The French and British in the West Indies (March to June 1805)    Map 9

To Europe
March 28

SANTO DOMINGO

VIRGIN
ISLANDS

PUERTO RICO

To Jamaica
17 April 6 ships-of-the-line

To Barbados
26 April with 1 ship-of-the-line

March 22

CARIBBEAN
SEA

ST KITTS
NEVIS

12 June

Missiessy 20 Feb 5 ships-of-the-line

To the Straits 13 June 11 ships-of-the-line

To Europe 11 June 20 ships-of-the-line

Villeneuve & Gravina 14 May 18 ships-of-the-line

Magon 4 June 2 ships-of-the-line

Cochrane 5 April 6 ships-of-the-line

Nelson 4 June 10 ships-of-the-line

B    St Johns
ANTIGUA
MONTSERRAT
GUADELOUPE
BARBUDA

Basse-Terre
DOMINICA
Roseau
MARTINIQUE
Fort de France
Diamond
Rock
A

LEEWARD ISLANDS

WINDWARD ISLANDS

ST LUCIA

CURACAO    (Dutch)
BONAIRE

Grenadines

Bridgetown
BARBADOS
5 June

ST VINCENT

GRENADA

TOBAGO

Dragon's Mouth

Port of Spain
8 June

NEW GRENADA

TRINIDAD

### French Notes

MARTINIQUE    French possession

- - - ▶ Missiessy

——▶ Villeneuve and Gravina

······▶ Magon

- Feb.–Mar. Missiessy carries out attacks on Dominica, Montserrat and St Kitts before sailing to Santo Domingo and then back to Europe. He does not achieve anything of significance.

- Villeneuve and Gravina are initially inactive awaiting the arrival of Ganteaume. After two weeks Villeneuve is prodded into attacking the British holding Diamond Rock A. It falls to the French on 2 June.

- Magon arrives on 4 June with 2 ships-of-the-line and more troops.

- On 30 May Villeneuve receives fresh orders from Paris to wait a month for Ganteaume and then sail for Ferrol, after capturing British islands. Villeneuve sails north.

- On 8 June he captured British convoy B and is informed that Nelson has arrived in Barbados. He sets out for Ferrol.

### British Notes

MONTSERRAT    British possession

- - - ▶ Cochrane

——▶ Nelson

- Nelson arrives in Barbados on 4 June expecting to join Cochrane's squadron, but only the *Northumberland* and *Spartiate* are at Bridgetown. Cochrane has left five ships-of-the-line in Jamaica.

- Nelson accepts false information as reliable and sails for Trinidad, hoping to catch the French/Spanish fleet there. He arrives on 8 June to find Villeneuve is in the north.

- He sails north directly to Antigua, missing the enemy by just two days.

- Nelson believes Villeneuve is making for Cadiz or Toulon, so intends to head for the Straits and catch up. He fails to make contact and arrived in Gibraltar on 19 July.

this troublesome nut. It was commanded by Captain Cosmao of the *Pluton* (74) and consisted of the *Berwick* (74), the frigate *Sirène* and two brigs. The battleships had troops on board and another 250 were embarked in four longboats and four armed cutters from Martinique. The assault began on 30 May. Although the attackers secured an early lodgement, they were unable to make progress as they had forgotten to bring scaling ladders to climb the sheer rock face. Not until 2 June did the British surrender.

By then all this was a distraction. On the day the attack was launched, the frigate *Didon* arrived with two sets of orders that, for Villeneuve, contained both good news and bad. A copy of those written on 17 April (when Nelson was sailing west from Palermo) informed him that Rear-Admiral Magon (who was carrying the original of these orders) would be arriving to reinforce him with the two 74s *Algéciras* and *Achille*, carrying a battalion of over 850 soldiers. This was part of the good news. Villeneuve was instructed to wait for a month after Magon's arrival and then return to Ferrol where:

> you will find 15 French and Spanish sail of the line in readiness there. With these 35 ships you will proceed off Brest where Ganteaume will join you with 21 and with this force of more than 50 of the line you will enter the Straits of Dover and join me off Boulogne. In the meantime, cover your expedition with glory, capture St Lucia if it is not done or any other island.

This implied that Villeneuve, not Ganteaume, would command the combined fleet – if it ever formed. Then there was a packet containing fresh orders compiled on 29 April. Decrès had written:

> with the troops you have with you, His Majesty considers it very possible to expel the English from all their Colonies in the Windward Isles. All these enterprises are to be

subordinated to the main operation which is to crown His Majesty's arms [the invasion of England] … if Ganteaume puts to sea [even as late as the end of April Decrès still hoped it might happen], he will send his fastest sailer on ahead to notify you. … The intentions of the Emperor are still the same: whether Admiral Magon joins you [or not] you will still direct your return on Ferrol.

The final piece of good news was that 'Nelson has gone off to Egypt after you.' This was dramatically misleading. On the very day – 4 June – that Magon sailed into Fort de France Bay, Martinique, Nelson was arriving in Carlisle Bay, Barbados. Only 140 miles separated them but they were not destined to clash until nearly five months later off Cape Trafalgar. It was a classic example of the communication problems that commanders of that time faced.

Villeneuve had been given an impossible task in the time available. Having sat at anchor for three weeks he was now expected to capture several islands and then set out for Europe within a month. At 4 a.m. on 5 June Villeneuve weighed anchor from Martinique with twenty French and Spanish ships-of-the-line. He sailed north, passed to the leeward (west) of Dominica, embarked more troops from Guadeloupe and continued north round Antigua when, on 7 June, he sighted a convoy of fifteen merchantmen. He swooped down on them on 8 June and captured fourteen without a fight. The prizes represented five million francs at no cost to him, and from interrogating prisoners he gained an astonishing piece of information: Nelson had arrived off Barbados! With dwindling supplies and Nelson so close, Villeneuve conferred with Gravina and both agreed their next course – north again, then west, destination Ferrol. The combined fleet set sail for Europe on 11 June. Reille expressed the exasperation of the army officers in his journal: 'We have been masters of the sea for three weeks with a landing force of 7000 to 8000 men and have not been able to attack a single island.'

## The Loss of His Majesty's Sloop *Diamond Rock*

If an officer lost the ship he was commanding he was automatically court-martialled, no matter what the circumstances. The ship could have been lost by enemy action in battle, by capture, by accidental fire, by storm or by going aground – whatever the reason, the captain faced trial. Such was the case when Captain James Maurice surrendered *Diamond Rock* to Villeneuve's attackers on 2 June 1805. The official findings of the court began:

> At a Court Martial assembled on board His Majesty's Ship Circe [28-gun frigate], at Carlisle Bay, Barbadoes the 24th June, 1805, for the Trial of James Wilkes Maurice, Esq., Commander, the Officers, and Crew of His Majesty's late sloop Diamond Rock, taken by a squadron of the enemy's ships on the 2d inst.
>
> PRESENT
> Captains,
> JONAS ROSE, President
> GEORGE TOBIN, WILLIAM CHAMPION
> R. HENDERSON, JOSEPH NOURSE
>
> The Court being duly sworn according to Act of Parliament, in pursuance of an order from the Hon. Rear-Admiral Cochrane …

Maurice's detailed account of the defence of Diamond Rock was read to the court. A brief summary of it is contained in Maurice's letter to Nelson dated 6 June 1805:

> MY LORD,
> IT is with the greatest sorrow I have to inform you of the loss of the Diamond Rock, under my command, which was obliged to surrender on the 2d inst., after three days' attack from a squadron of two sail of the line, one frigate, one brig, a schooner, eleven gun-boats and, from the nearest calculation, 1500 troops. The want of ammunition and water was the sole occasion of its unfortunate loss…. [our losses were] only two killed and one wounded. The enemy, from the nearest account I have been able to obtain, lost on shore 30 killed and 40 wounded: they also lost three gun-boats and two rowing-boats.

The court martial did not take long to reach its verdict:

> the Court is of the opinion that Captain J.W. Maurice, the Officers and Company of His Majesty's late sloop Diamond Rock did every thing in their power to the very last, in the defence of the Rock, and against a most superior force … [Maurice] did not surrender the Diamond until he was unable to make further defence for want of water and ammunition, the Court do therefore honourably acquit Captain Maurice accordingly.

## Lieutenant Carr and the *Netley*

Lieutenant Carr commanded the British 16-gun schooner *Netley*. In early June 1805 he was ordered to escort a convoy of merchantmen home from St Johns, Antigua. It was known that the French Fleet was close, but panic had gripped the merchants of St Johns and they pressurized the Governor into letting the convoy sail. Carr had also been given despatches for the Admiralty in London from his commander, Captain Nourse. On 8 June, the convoy's worst fears were realized when Villeneuve's fleet was sighted. The *Netley* was helpless in such a situation. The moment he saw the enemy frigates, Carr signalled his convoy to save themselves, while he waited and watched until the enemy was within gunshot range. Then he ran, chased by two frigates, while the enemy fleet dispersed to catch all fourteen of his wallowing, helpless merchantmen. By dusk he had lost his pursuers.

For the young lieutenant it was decision time. He had lost his convoy but he still had the despatches for London. On the other hand he knew the location of the Combined Fleet. So what should he do? He could either continue to England or return to Antigua with the information on the enemy. Carr needed to know the nature of the sealed despatches he carried. Were they critical? How urgently did they need to arrive in London? There was only one way to find out – by opening them. It was an extreme step for a very junior officer to break open secret letters addressed to the Admiralty. In the event Carr found nothing exciting or critical, only Nourse's reasons for sending the *Netley* home. All doubt removed, he sailed to find Nelson. On 13 June he joined the British Fleet about an hour after it had weighed from St Johns road. The news Carr carried as he clambered up the side of the *Victory* was to galvanize Nelson, to launch him once again in the seemingly endless chase after the ever-vanishing Villeneuve. Carr escaped censure for his opening the despatch. However his luck ran out two years later when, while he was still commanding the *Netley*, she was captured by a French frigate and brig.

### Nelson in the West Indies (Map 9)

When Nelson anchored in Carlisle Bay, Barbados, at around 5 p.m. on 4 June, he had sailed some 4,000 miles from the Straits of Gibraltar in twenty-six days. This was fast, giving an average of about 150 miles a day or a speed of over five knots. To the impatient Nelson it had seemed far from fast, but he had to keep to the speed of the slowest ship – the weed- and barnacle-encrusted *Superb*. Fearful that Captain Keats would feel he was to blame, Nelson was kind enough to write to him on 27 May saying, 'I would have you be assured that I know and feel that the *Superb* does all which is possible for a ship to accomplish.' This was a typically thoughtful 'Nelson touch'.

Villeneuve had taken thirty-five days for the same voyage, managing only 114 miles in a day – an average speed of four knots. As Nelson sailed to his anchorage at Barbados with the cannons of Fort Charles crashing out in salute, the French and Spanish fleet had only that morning left Fort de France, Martinique, steering north, a mere 150 miles away. In over four months this was the closest Nelson had come to catching his elusive foe. As always, what was needed was reliable information as to the enemy's whereabouts. The sight of the *Northumberland* (74) and *Spartiate* (74) basking in the sun, with Rear-Admiral Cochrane's flag at the mizzen of the former, was surely a sign that such information would be forthcoming.

After dropping anchor, with the ships swinging on their cables, the *Victory* signalled to fire the 21-gun Royal Salute to mark the King's birthday. Grog was served to drink His Majesty's health, while officers and men alike eagerly anticipated the possibility of a quick trip ashore. It was not to be. Hardly had the smoke from the last shot drifted away when the Blue Peter soared to the flagship's masthead, giving the message that they should prepare to sail. Nelson had been shown a letter received the previous day by the officer commanding in Barbados and the Leeward Islands, Lieutenant-General Sir William Myers, from Brigadier-General Brereton in St Lucia. Brereton had received a report from the Gros Islet signal station (on the north-western point of St Lucia) that the enemy had been seen sailing south on the night of 28 May. It was considered reliable information and the enemy's destination was thought to be either Barbados (which it was obviously not) or Trinidad. Myers was convinced the information was accurate. He suggested to Nelson that the 2,000 troops in the Barbados garrison at St Anne's Fort (now the home of the Barbados Defence Force), the 15th Foot, 96th Foot and 4th West India Regiment, should be embarked to help defend or retake Trinidad. Against his instincts Nelson agreed to sail south. He wrote:

> There is no doubt in any of the Generals' or Admirals' minds, but that Tobago and Trinidad are the Enemy's objects; and although I am anxious in the extreme to engage their 18 sail of the line, yet as Sir William Myers has offered me 2,000 men, I cannot refuse so handsome an offer.

At 9.30 a.m. on 5 June Nelson's fleet of twelve ships-of-the-line was steering for Trinidad. At 2 p.m. decks were cleared for action. At 5.30 p.m. the following day Tobago was silhouetted against a reddening sky. On 7 June, the *Curieux*, an 18-gun brig sent ahead for information, reappeared to report that an American merchant brig had told of being boarded by the French off St Vincent, and that they had then continued south. Then, as they approached Trinidad in two divisions, a private schooner was seen making the agreed signal that the French were at the island. Battle seemed a certainty. Throughout the afternoon, as the fleet slowly approached the gaping Dragon's Mouth (the narrow, islet-studded channel between Trinidad and the mainland of South America), there was unsuppressed excitement as crews craned to get a first glimpse of the Combined Fleet as they rounded the point into the bay. All hands were at quarters, guns shotted and run out, marines parading at their stations. At last the enemy was cornered.

Alas, not a French or Spanish flag was to be seen in front of the Port of Spain. The signal station on St Lucia had mistaken three French frigates for the entire fleet and the American's information had been deliberately false. Finally, by a one in a thousand coincidence, the private schooner making a pre-arranged signal with a merchant ashore that the British fleet was approaching was the one Nelson had selected to announce the French had been sighted! Unbelievably, Villeneuve had eluded them yet again.

The next morning, 8 June, as the British Fleet was negotiating the Dragon's Mouth once more, intelligence was received of the loss of Diamond Rock and that Villeneuve at Martinique had been reinforced by the whole of the Ferrol Squadron. The first piece of infor-

## Naval Deployment 22 July 1805    Map 10

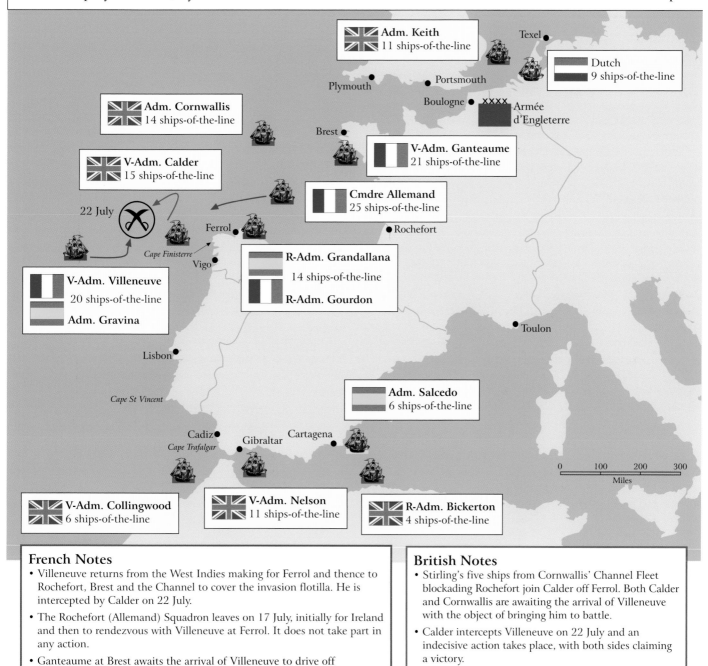

### French Notes
• Villeneuve returns from the West Indies making for Ferrol and thence to Rochefort, Brest and the Channel to cover the invasion flotilla. He is intercepted by Calder on 22 July.

• The Rochefort (Allemand) Squadron leaves on 17 July, initially for Ireland and then to rendezvous with Villeneuve at Ferrol. It does not take part in any action.

• Ganteaume at Brest awaits the arrival of Villeneuve to drive off Cornwallis and then join Villeneuve for the dash to Boulogne.

• The Armée d'Engleterre still awaits the arrival of the French navy to escort it across to Kent.

### British Notes
• Stirling's five ships from Cornwallis' Channel Fleet blockading Rochefort join Calder off Ferrol. Both Calder and Cornwallis are awaiting the arrival of Villeneuve with the object of bringing him to battle.

• Calder intercepts Villeneuve on 22 July and an indecisive action takes place, with both sides claiming a victory.

• Nelson is at Gibraltar, having failed to catch Villeneuve in the chase to and from the West Indies.

---

mation was correct but Magon's two ships had been mistaken for the Ferrol Squadron. Despite the now seemingly heavy numerical odds against him, Nelson continued north with all speed. His ships passed a succession of Caribbean jewels – Grenada, the Grenadines, St Vincent, St Lucia, Martinique, Dominica (where Nelson obtained a further report that the enemy were heading north), Guadeloupe, Montserrat and, finally, Antigua on 12 June. During these days Nelson was consumed with frustration by the way he had been deceived. 'Brereton's wrong information could not be doubted,' he told his friends, 'and by following it I lost the opportunity of fight-

ing the enemy. What a race I have run after these fellows, but God is just, and I may be repaid for all my moments of anxiety.'

At St Johns, Antigua, more information made it certain that Villeneuve was headed for Europe. Myers' troops, embarked at Barbados, were disembarked in Antigua before Nelson set out yet again in pursuit on 13 June – only two days behind his enemy. Ahead of him, with letters for the Admiralty in London explaining both Villeneuve's and his own actions, went the *Curieux*. Nelson considered that Villeneuve was making for Cadiz or Toulon so his course was set for the Straits. This misreading of the enemy's intentions led to him sailing too far south while the Combined Fleet, making for Ferrol, took a route north of the Azores. Their tracks crossed once on 17 June, but they were not destined to see each other. After meeting an American ship, the *Sally*, about 600 miles out from Antigua, which gave Nelson the enemy's position he wrote: 'I think we cannot be more than eighty leagues [240 miles] from them at this moment, and by carrying every sail, and using my utmost efforts, I shall hope to close with them before they get to either Cadiz or Toulon.' On 19 June it occurred to him that perhaps Villeneuve might make for Ferrol, so the frigate *Decade* and sloop *Martin* were sent ahead to warn the squadron watching there.

Almost a month later, with the African coast in sight, Nelson wrote of his wretchedness to the Secretary of the Admiralty (Marsden): 'Cape Spartel in sight, but no French fleet, nor any information about them – how sorrowful this makes me, but I cannot help myself!' On 19 July Nelson arrived at Rosia Bay, Gibraltar, and the following day stepped ashore for the first time since 16 June 1803. After a few days' rest, he took his fleet back through the Straits to join Cornwallis off Brest. Beating against the wind, he was not off Ushant until 15 August. Worn out and unable to shake off a feeling of failure, he took the *Victory* to Portsmouth, accompanied by the battered old *Superb*. On 18 August he went ashore to spend a few short weeks at Merton with his beloved Emma. On 14 September he boarded his flagship for the last time en route to Cape Trafalgar.

## CALDER'S CLASH WITH VILLENEUVE OFF CAPE FINISTERRE, 22 JULY 1805 (Map 10)

Captain Edmund Bettesworth commanded the 18-gun brig *Curieux*. In Antigua he had been entrusted with delivering vital letters from Nelson to the Admiralty. He set sail on 14 June and anchored at Plymouth twenty-four days later (7 July), having crossed over 4,000 miles of ocean at an average speed of some 170 miles a day. On 19 June he had spotted Villeneuve some 900 miles from Antigua – still heading north. For a while Bettesworth shadowed the enemy fleet until certain of their course, then, cramming on every possible foot of sail, he headed home with his news (Villeneuve did not turn eastward until 24 June, on a course that took him north of the Azores). Within an hour of arrival Bettesworth had set out in a post-chaise on the 200-mile journey to London. He clattered to a halt in front of the Admiralty at 11 p.m. on 8 July. The elderly Lord Barham, First Lord of the Admiralty, was asleep and his staff feared to wake him so a delay of several hours elapsed before Barham awoke in the early hours of 9 July. Still in his nightshirt, he read the despatches and, even more importantly, heard Bettesworth's report that Villeneuve had been heading north. Nelson told him that the Combined Fleet had left the West Indies on 11 June for Europe and that he, Nelson, was to follow him. Bettesworth's news, however, indicated the enemy was taking a northerly route and was therefore likely to be making for the Bay of Biscay rather than the Straits of Gibraltar as Barham had thought.

Despite his great age (over eighty) and the unseemly hour, Barham's brain was functioning clearly. The enemy was likely to attempt to raise any, or all, the blockades of Ferrol, Rochefort and Brest. If successful, a fleet of thirty, forty or even fifty ships might head for Boulogne. The key was to intercept Villeneuve. But was there time? It was a month since Villeneuve had departed from near Antigua, so by 9 July he could already be approaching the Bay or even in it. By 9 a.m. the Admiralty messenger was thun-

dering down the Portsmouth road with orders for Cornwallis, now back in command of the Channel Fleet, off Brest. The note that Barham had hastily scribbled and then amended and upon which the orders were drawn up, read:

> My idea is to send the intelligence immediately to Admiral Cornwallis who may be directed to strengthen Sir Robert Calder's squadron with the Rocheforte squadron and as many ships of his own as will make them up to 15, to cruise off Cape Finisterre from 10 to 50 leagues [30 to 150 miles] to the west. To stand to the southward and westward with his own ships, at the same distance for 10 days. Cadiz can be left to Nelson. 9th July.

The actual orders specified that Rear-Admiral Stirling's five ships-of-the-line off Rochefort were to join Calder's ten and cruise west of Cape Finisterre searching for Villeneuve for six to eight days. They reached Cornwallis on 11 July. By the 13th Stirling had raised the blockade and two days later had joined Calder. Barham's reading of the situation was uncannily accurate. The planned interception took place, in almost precisely the spot predicted, on 22 July.

On the morning of 22 July Calder had spread his two frigates, *Egyptienne* and *Sirius*, together with the two 74s, *Defiance* and *Ajax*, ahead of his fleet, which was sailing in two columns. The weather was fine, the wind light from the north-west but visibility was poor due to patches of dense fog that drifted slowly across the fleet. Towards noon, as the mist thinned and then temporarily cleared, the lookouts in the crosstrees of the *Defiance* were the first to spot strange sails far to the south-west. There was much excitement when they were eventually identified as the enemy. Officers with telescopes stared at the horizon as sails were counted. Captain Durham signalled twenty-four, then twenty-seven (an accurate reckoning – Villeneuve had twenty-seven ships-of-the-line and frigates). Calder ordered his fleet to bear to the south-west and clear for action. Some sixteen miles still separated the fleets. It would be over five hours before either side opened fire, as three knots was the best speed that the slight breeze would allow.

Villeneuve was heading west with three columns and a light squadron, the six Spanish ships-of-the-line forming the lee (southern) column. In the van was the *Argonauta* flying Admiral Gravina's flag. For some time after the first sighting by the *Defiance* visibility was often cut to under 500 yards. Not until around 1 p.m. did Villeneuve's lookouts in the forward frigates manage to convey that there was a British fleet of twenty-one sail approaching. The French admiral hoisted the signals for his three columns to form a close-hauled line of battle on the Spanish squadron. Decks were cleared for action and the fleet began to close up to a distance of half a cable (100 yards) between ships. They were riding ponderously on a heavy swell, now heading north through patches of fog, uncertain of when or where the enemy might appear.

At around 3.30 p.m. the mists parted sufficiently for both admirals to get a longer and more informative look at each other. An hour later, although the fleets were some eight miles apart, it was apparent to Calder that if he continued south and the Combined Fleet north, his enemy might escape. To prevent this he signalled for his fleet to tack in succession to come round onto a northerly course. To bring all fifteen ships onto the new course by this method would be an extremely slow process. Calder did not, seemingly, consider commanding his fleet to tack together, which would have got them sailing north much more quickly. At about the same time his 36-gun frigate *Sirius*, which was well ahead of the fleet, found herself within a short distance of the French frigate *Sirène* towing a captured treasure galleon in the Combined Fleet's rear. At a value of 15 million francs it was too rich a prize to resist. Captain William Prowse began to close to attempt to board. The *Sirène* opened fire, more to warn the fleet than to damage her attacker. Villeneuve was alerted, and feared that the British were attempting to tack round his rear to surround and attack it from two sides – as he had seen Nelson do so effectively at the Nile. He instantly signalled for the fleet to wear in succession, thus turning south with the Spanish flagship still leading the line. At this point both fleets were once again approaching each other, slipping slowly in and out of banks of fog as the distance between them gradually closed. When the visibility improved slightly they found themselves sailing almost parallel to each other on opposite tacks but just out of gunshot range.

Action was imminent. The Combined Fleet had the advantages of the weather gauge (see Section Five).

Meanwhile the British frigate *Sirius* found its attempt to seize the treasure ship frustrated when the 80-gun bulk of the *Argonauta* loomed out of the mist, towering above her like some huge mammoth. To the amazement of Captain Prowse, who was expecting to be blown from the water, not a shot was fired. The *Terrible* and *America*, which were following close behind their flagship, showed equally honourable forbearance. The *Sirius* slipped away to leeward. The action started at around 5.30 p.m. when the leading British ship, the old, slow, lumbering *Hero*, a 74 under Captain Alan Gardner, sighted the *Argonauta*. Gardner, acting on the last order from Calder's flagship (the *Prince of Wales*) at 5.09 p.m. to engage the enemy closely, yelled to the master to tack immediately to larboard. This would bring her starboard battery to bear. It was a daring manoeuvre that was followed by successive British ships as

## Calder and Villeneuve Clash off Cape Finisterre, 22 July 1805

### The fleets sight each other, about 12.00 p.m.

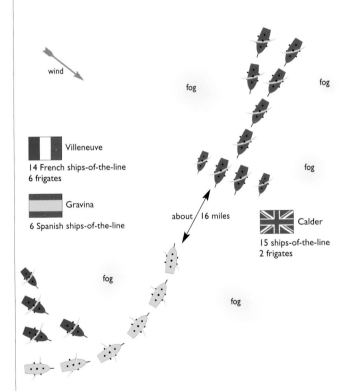

wind

fog

fog

fog

Villeneuve
14 French ships-of-the-line
6 frigates

Gravina
6 Spanish ships-of-the-line

about / 16 miles

Calder
15 ships-of-the-line
2 frigates

fog

fog

### The fleets turn towards each other, about 4.30 p.m.

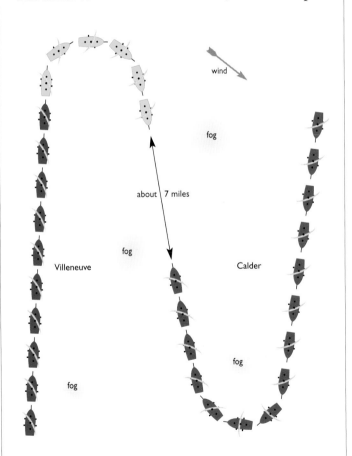

wind

fog

about | 7 miles

fog

Villeneuve

Calder

fog

fog

### Allied Notes

• Villeneuve has been sailing in 3 columns and a light column. He forms line of battle with the Spanish squadron in the van.
• Visibility is poor with patchy fog. The fleet hauls to the wind on the larboard tack and sails slowly northwards, ships half a cable (100 yards) apart.

### British Notes

• Calder sails initially in 2 columns, then forms 1 column and clears for action.
• Although numerically inferior and having the lee gauge, Calder intends to close and give battle. However, his progress is painfully slow even with topgallants set.

### Allied Notes

• Villeneuve fears that the British are intending to encircle his rear and thus attack it from two sides.
• He signals for his fleet to wear at about the same time as Calder tacks.

### British Notes

• At about 4.30 p.m. Calder realizes that his enemy could escape north without giving battle.
• He signals to the fleet to tack in succession and thus steer a northerly course.

## Calder and Villeneuve Clash off Cape Finisterre, 22 July 1805

### 5.30–9.00 p.m.

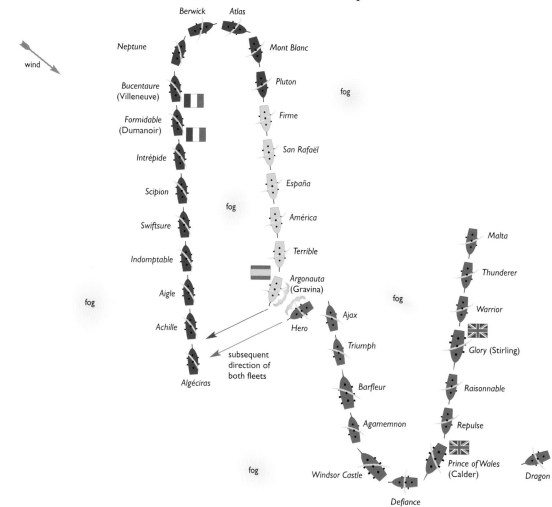

**Allied Notes**
• The Spanish ships leading the line are all heavily, if intermittently, engaged. Both fleets swing to the south-west, and firing continues until about 9.00 p.m.
• *Firme* and *San Rafaël* are crippled and drift to leeward, then taken by the British.

**British Notes**
• The vans of both fleets are about to pass each other sailing in opposite directions when the *Hero* sees the *Argonauta* through the mist. Her captain, following Calder's signal to engage more closely, turns to larboard on his own initiative and opens fire with his starboard battery.
• The remainder of the fleet follows in succession and a confused battle with poor visibility ensues.

they copied the actions of the ship in front. Unfortunately for the *Hero*, the Spanish flagship fired the first broadside of the battle just as she was completing her turn. She was raked from bow to stern. Incredibly, little serious damage was done, as the *Argonauta* was listing to larboard due to unbalanced stowage in her hold, so her lower-deck guns could not fire. As she came round, Gardner was able to return fire and the action became general as ship after ship came up and the fleets swung onto a course of west-south-west.

Once hundreds of cannons began firing, the smoke merged with the mist to produce an impenetrable blanket of cloud that enveloped each ship as it came into action. Both fleets fired almost blindly at the muzzle flashes of those opposite. The action

soon became chaotic, and by 8.30 p.m., with failing light adding to the gloom, Calder signalled to call off the action. Most ships failed to see or hear his signal so firing continued until after 9 p.m. Because the Combined Fleet's line was longer than Calder's it was the Spanish squadron that suffered the most, with Villeneuve's flagship *Bucentaure* reporting only six casualties. The eight French ships behind her took no real part in the fighting. By 9.30 p.m. both fleets were hopelessly scattered. The fifty-one-year-old *San Rafaël* and the thirty-four-year-old *Firme* were both dismasted and captured after a fearsome fight. The Combined Fleet lost 149 officers and men killed and 341 wounded plus some 1,200 Spanish prisoners from the captured ships. On the British side the *Windsor Castle*, with her foretopmast and the bulk of her foretop shot away, was the most seriously damaged vessel. Overall casualties were light, with 39 all ranks killed and 159 wounded. From these statistics Calder could claim to have got the best of the engagement. In fact both admirals claimed success. Calder's despatch the next day included the words, 'A very decisive action which lasted upwards of four hours, when I found it necessary to bring up the squadron to cover the captured ships.' Villeneuve saw it differently: 'The enemy then made off. He had several vessels crippled aloft, and the field of battle remained ours. Cries of joy and victory were heard from all our ships.'

Calder was to be court-martialled, not for what he did on 22 July but for what he failed to do during the days that followed. At daybreak on 23 July both fleets were badly scattered but still in the same area. Calder was to leeward, so still between Villeneuve and Ferrol. Although initially wanting to renew the action, Calder soon allowed his difficulties to persuade him otherwise. 'The enemy', he wrote to Cornwallis, 'are now in sight to windward and when I have secured the captured ships and put the squadron to rights … it will behove me to be on my guard against the combined squadrons at Ferrol … I may find it necessary to make a junction with you off Ushant.' In the words of the naval historian William James, Calder 'would neither attack or retreat'. On the 24th the wind was more favourable to the British but he made no use of it. The following day the fleets were many miles apart and out of sight of each other. Both admirals for their own reasons sailed away in different directions, Calder east towards Ferrol and then north to join Cornwallis off Ushant, while Villeneuve headed south-east for Vigo to replenish supplies and water, carry out repairs and offload several hundred sick. It was to be almost exactly three months later before his next encounter – off Cape Trafalgar.

If, tactically, the affair of 22 July was an inconclusive skirmish (although Calder was to call it 'a very decisive action' in his despatch), strategically it was of considerable consequence. It was

yet another serious setback to Napoleon's dream of concentrating his naval forces in the Channel to shepherd his invasion flotilla across to Kent. Instead the Emperor's frantic last-minute attempts to co-ordinate naval operations in the latter part of July unravelled. On 20 July Ganteaume remained in Brest (he had been told to fight his way out if blockaded by sixteen or fewer ships, but he counted eighteen and so sat tight). Villeneuve limped into Vigo on 28 July after claiming a victory over Calder.

Meanwhile, Napoleon was devising yet another convoluted combination for invasion involving Villeneuve and the squadrons at Cadiz, Ferrol and Brest.

On 3 August the Emperor arrived at Boulogne for the last time to inspect arrangements and await Villeneuve's arrival. On 8 August he learnt of Villeneuve's 'successful' action off Cape Finisterre on 22 July and that he intended to fulfil the plan to sail for Brest. Napoleon declared a victory, but halted the Imperial Guard's march from Paris to Boulogne. At the same time Austria signed a defence pact with Britain, thus completing the Third Coalition against France and Spain.

The Combined Fleet under Villeneuve sailed from Ferrol and Corunna on 13 August to make a rendezvous with Allemand (Missiessy's replacement commanding the Rochefort squadron) before going north to the Channel. But there was no rendezvous, as they supposedly mistook each other for the enemy and Villeneuve, fearing to meet the combined British fleets, turned south for Cadiz! This prompted one of the Emperor's frequent outbursts of rage against the navy and Villeneuve in particular: 'What a Navy! What an admiral! All those sacrifices for nought!'

Giving up hope of invading England, Napoleon turned his back forever on the Channel and the Armée d'Engleterre, now renamed the Grand Armée, began its march to the east. Napoleon's grand combinations on land from the Rhine to the Danube culminated in the defeat of the Austrians on the Ulm the day before his navy was crushed at Trafalgar. The general had returned to what he understood – soldiering.

## The Court Martial of Vice-Admiral Sir Robert Calder

Calder missed Trafalgar because he had to come home to face a court martial for his conduct during and after the action off Cape Finisterre in July 1805. His trial lasted four days, from 23 to 26 December 1805, including Christmas Day. The court martial signal was hoisted on board the three-decker 98-gun *Prince of Wales* in Portsmouth harbour. To try an admiral was a serious business that merited an impressive amount of naval gold braid as members of the court. Admiral George Montagu, commander-in-chief of the ships and vessels of war at Portsmouth and Spithead, was the president, and his court was composed of three vice-admirals, two rear-admirals and seven captains. A Judge Advocate, assisted by a solicitor, conducted the prosecution. Calder had to conduct his own defence.

The charges were:

[the] Court is hereby required and directed to inquire into the conduct and proceedings of the said Vice-Admiral Sir R. Calder, with His Majesty's squadron under command, on the said 23rd of July last, and also into his subsequent conduct and proceedings, until he finally lost the enemy's ships, and to

try him for not having done his utmost to renew the said engagement, and to take or destroy every ship of the enemy, which it was his duty to engage accordingly.

After a grim Christmas the court assembled at ten o'clock on 26 December to deliver its verdict. After a laborious and lengthy preamble Calder heard the judgement:

the Court is of the opinion, that the charge of not having done his utmost to renew the said engagement, and to take or destroy every ship of the enemy, has been proved against the said Vice-Admiral Calder; that it appears that his conduct has not been actuated either by cowardice or disaffection, but has arisen solely from error in judgement, and is highly censurable, and doth adjudge him to be severely reprimanded, and the said Vice-Admiral Sir Robert Calder is hereby severely reprimanded accordingly.

Calder never received another active command but was promoted to admiral by seniority in 1810 and, in 1815, appointed commander-in-chief of Portsmouth – the post the president of his court martial had held ten years earlier. He died in 1818 aged seventy-three.

# BOYHOOD TO HALF-PAY POST CAPTAIN

## CAPTAIN'S SERVANT AND MIDSHIPMAN

On a windy day in March 1771 a forlorn-looking young lad of twelve carrying a large valise stepped down from the stagecoach near Chatham dockyard. Other passengers from London clambered out and went their various ways while the small boy, who looked even younger than his age, glanced anxiously around to see if anyone had come to meet him. There was nobody. As the coach clattered away he picked up his bag and walked towards the quayside, his eyes searching out a name among the host of ships moored alongside or out in the Medway. The boy's name was Horatio Nelson, and he was peering up at the sterns of the totally unfamiliar ships looking for the name *Raisonnable*, a 64-gun ship-of-the-line captured from the French in the year of his birth, on whose books young Nelson was rated as a midshipman. Her captain was the boy's uncle, Captain Maurice Suckling. As he peered hard at each ship, he could not have failed to notice a huge three-decker, her masts towering high above her neighbours. It was a ship the boy would one day get to know intimately – indeed, he was destined to die on her – the 102-gun *Victory*.

At last the *Raisonnable* was identified, but she was moored in mid-stream and Nelson could find no boatman to take him out to her. At length a kindly officer spoke to him and, at the mention of Captain Suckling's name, took the chilled young lad to his house for refreshments. Later a boat was procured to take Nelson to his first ship. But on board his reception was as cold and unwelcoming as the quayside. His uncle was not on board. Nobody seemed to be expecting him, he was not shown to

---

### Nelson's Family

Horatio was the sixth of eleven children, two of whom died at birth. His surviving brothers and sisters in order of appearance were:

**Susannah** The first to leave home when she was apprenticed to a milliner at Bath, Somerset. At twenty-six she married a prosperous corn and coal merchant, Thomas Bolton. She died in 1813.

**Maurice** Five years older than Horatio; he became a clerk in the Navy Office.

**William** One year older than Horatio. Graduated from Cambridge and, like his father, entered the church. Seemingly an arrogant and pompous man, he succeeded to Nelson's title after the latter's death at Trafalgar.

**Anne** Born next after Horatio. Died young (at twenty-one), according to Nelson's letter to William Locker in 1783, 'at Bath after a nine days' illness ... occasioned by coming out of the ball-room immediately after dancing'.

**Edmund** Hoped to join the Bolton family business but was handicapped by poor health and died aged twenty-eight.

**Suckling** This was Nelson's mother's maiden name. Something of a troublesome youth, he eventually took Holy Orders but died at thirty-five after what his father described as 'a very convivial evening' in a farmer's house.

**George** Died in 1776 aged only eleven.

**Catherine** As the youngest child she was a great favourite of Nelson's. In a letter to his brother, William, Nelson wrote, 'she shall never want a protector and sincere friend while I exist'. She married George Matcham, a wealthy man with business interests in India and a passion for travelling.

---

the midshipmen's berth, indeed there was hardly anybody on the ship and no one even spoke to the bewildered boy. He later recalled spending the rest of the day and much of the night pacing endlessly back and forth along the deck. It was a lonely, depressing first day in the Navy.

However, Horatio had chosen a naval career himself. Born on 29 September 1758 some seven weeks premature, he was baptized within hours of birth, as it was feared he would not live. He had arrived in exciting times. The Seven Years War against Prussia was two years old. The year before, great battles had been fought in Europe at Prague, Rossbach and Leuthen. In India Clive had retaken Calcutta and with an army of 3,500 had trounced an Indian force of 50,000 at Plassey. The year following Horatio's birth, a British brigade in a Brunswick Army routed six regiments of French cavalry at Minden – a day still celebrated by the regiments concerned. In North America, Wolfe had climbed the Heights of Abraham to defeat the French in front of Quebec but, like Nelson forty-five years later, had been mortally wounded at the moment of victory. Nearer to home and at sea, Admiral Hawke had crushed the French Fleet in Quiberon Bay off the southern Brittany coast.

As he grew up in the small Norfolk village of Burnham Thorpe, where his father was the rector of All Saints' Church, Horatio would no doubt have got to hear of some of these great events. Although his maternal uncle was a naval officer he came from a church family. Not only was his father a clergyman, but both his grandfathers, two of his great-uncles, eight cousins and two brothers took holy orders. Little wonder Horatio grew up with a strong Christian faith. Unfortunately, when he was nine his mother, formerly a Miss Catherine Suckling and a great-niece of Sir Robert Walpole (prime minister from 1721 to 1742) died. She was only forty-two but was, perhaps, somewhat enfeebled by having borne eleven children in seventeen years. As Horatio's sister Susannah put it, she had 'bred herself to death'. His father was left with the intimidating prospect of bringing up eight children (three had died in infancy), including a nine-month-old baby. A combination of these circumstances, his father's religious faith and the authoritarian ways of the times meant Nelson grew up in a household where discipline was paramount. According to Nelson senior, shortsightedness was no reason to wear glasses and people who leant against the back of a chair should be reprimanded for slouching. The Reverend Nelson considered the essentials of a child's upbringing to be 'Air, Exercise, Warmth and Cleanliness'.

Horatio attended three schools with his elder brother William. The first was Norwich (Grammar) School, next to the cathedral, where he is commemorated by a statue standing opposite the school chapel – a hundred yards away is another of the Duke of Wellington. The second was at Downham Market. There, according to a fellow pupil, Nelson wore a green coat and liked to get the smaller boys working the village pump so he could sail paper boats on the resultant stream of water. The third was Paston (Grammar) School at North Walsham. Here the famous 'Nelson brick', taken from the old school wall and bearing the initials HN, has been preserved. His education was simple but sound, with an emphasis on the classics and Shakespeare. Bird-nesting was a favourite childhood pastime. On one such occasion there was great consternation as dinner time came and went without Horatio's return. It was feared he was at best lost, or at worst had been abducted by gypsies. A good deal of shouting and dashing about eventually revealed him sitting exhausted but composed beside a deep stream. When asked why fear or hunger had not driven him home he is alleged to have replied, 'I never saw Fear. What is it?' or alternatively, 'Fear never came near me.'

During the Christmas holidays of 1770–1 the Nelson family read with interest in the *Norwich Mercury* that uncle Maurice was to have command of the *Raisonnable*, which was being recommis-

sioned for a war with Spain. Horatio had a letter written on his behalf pleading for a place with his uncle. Captain Suckling was staggered that so young and frail-looking a boy should seek such a hard, demanding life. Nevertheless, he agreed to take him, with the comment: 'What has poor Horace [as a child he was often called by this name] done, who is so weak, that he above all the rest [of the boys] should be sent to rough it out at sea?' His uncle seemingly thought the decision was some sort of punishment of his father's, rather than Horatio's choice. He continued, 'But let him come; and the first time we go into action, a cannon ball may knock off his head, and provide for him at once.' Hardly an encouraging welcome to the Royal Navy.

In fact the *Raisonnable* did nothing. The likelihood of action against Spain died away and Midshipman Nelson, while adjusting to the routine on a warship, did little of practical use and certainly nothing exciting. After five months the ship was paid off – she later saw service at Copenhagen in 1801 and in Calder's action in July 1805. Captain Suckling took Nelson with him, this time as a 'captain's servant', to his new command, the 74-gun *Triumph*. But the *Triumph* also had a dull, dead-end job. She was the Thames guard ship tasked with protecting all shipping using the river from the Nore to the city – unlikely to provide any dramatic duties or even proper seamanship experience for a thirteen-year-old boy. Captain Suckling knew his nephew required hands-on training in navigation, mathematics and the use of charts, as well as the handling of ships at sea in differing winds and currents. If the boy ever wanted to rise above midshipman he would have exams to pass, for which sitting on a ship at anchor in the Thames estuary was no preparation. So Horatio's uncle arranged an unusual transfer. The boy was to have a period on a merchantman, the *Mary Ann*, under the command of Mr John Rathbone, who had formerly been the master of the *Dreadnought* on which Captain Suckling had served. Nelson's new ship sailed for the West Indies in August 1771. A year later he was back, having crossed the Atlantic twice and seen a new world of lush sugar-cane islands, white beaches, turquoise lagoons, coral reefs and foreign ports all the way to Venezuela. Above all he returned a

## At Paston Grammar School, North Walsham

Discipline was extremely strict at school, and the motto of the headmaster, 'Classic' Jones, could well have been 'spare the rod and spoil the child'. He was certainly renowned for his generous application of the birch – 'a keen flogger'. One story goes that there were some ripe pears growing in the garden that sorely tempted the young boys, whose school diet was meagre, basic and boring. The thought of the headmaster's wrath and strong right arm acted as an effective deterrent, but one night Nelson allowed himself to be lowered from the dormitory window by a knotted sheet. He picked a large number, which he distributed among his admiring friends but kept none for himself. He later explained that he 'only took them because every other boy was afraid'. The next day 'Classic' Jones went so far as to offer five guineas reward for any one who 'fingered' the thief. According to the writer of this anecdote Nelson was 'too much beloved for any boy to betray him'.

## A Midshipman's Berth

The living conditions in a midshipman's mess on board a ship-of-war have been well described by Frederick Chamier in his *Life of a Sailor*. Although writing in 1833, he was describing conditions that had changed little from the early part of the century:

Cups were used instead of glasses. The soup tureen, a heavy lumbering piece of block tin, pounded into shape, was, for want of a ladle, emptied with an ever-lasting tea cup; forks were wiped on the table cloth by the persons about to use them, who, to save eating more than was requisite of actual dirt, always plunged them through the table cloth to clean between the prongs. ... The rest of the furniture was not much cleaner; now and then an empty bottle served as a candlestick; and I have known both a shoe and a quadrant-case used as a soup plate. ... [The midshipmen] dressed and undressed in public; the basin was invariably of pewter; and the wet towels, dirty brush-head etc., were, after use, deposited in his chest. A hammock served as a bed and so closely were all stowed in war, that the side of one hammock always touched that of another; fourteen inches being declared quite sufficient space for one tired midshipman.

trained seaman with a lasting admiration for the officers and men of the merchant service. Many years later he was to write:

> I returned [from the West Indies] a practical seaman, with a horror of the Royal Navy, and with a saying then constant with the seamen, 'aft the most honour forward the better man'. It was many weeks before I got the least reconciled to a Man-of-War, so deep was the prejudice rooted; and what pains were taken to instill this erroneous principle in a young mind!

Nelson was referring to the harsher regime in the Royal Navy, where the gulf between officers and seamen was much greater than on a merchantman. Yet on most Royal Navy ships the best sailors, the men who worked in the tops handling the sails, had learnt their skills on merchantmen. The experience had a lasting effect on the development of Nelson's more compassionate leadership, for which he was admired when he achieved high rank. To use a modern expression, his 'man management' was unusually effective. His personal touch, his thoughtfulness, his obvious concern with the wellbeing of his officers and men, combined with his exceptional professional competence, produced in those under him an extraordinary devotion and loyalty – the seeds of which can be traced back to those twelve months in the Caribbean with the merchant service as a youngster of thirteen.

Nelson might have experienced serious difficulties settling back into doing things the Navy's way on the *Triumph,* which was still very much a 'brown-water' ship confined to the Thames, had not Captain Suckling intervened again. He ensured his nephew was kept busy with the ship's boats. Both the cutter and decked long boat were equipped for sailing as well as rowing. The cutter was the smaller of the two and used almost daily for moving stores, provisions or people. Putting Nelson in charge of them gave him considerable independence in an environment which was limited but in which he had to make decisions. Handling these boats required in microcosm many of the seamanship skills he would need later (navigation, steering, sounding for shoals, the effect of tides, raising or lowering sails and overseeing the loading of stores) when commanding a warship. During the winter of 1772 his confidence in boat handling and pilotage improved considerably. By his own account he became, 'confident of myself amongst rocks and sands, which has many times been of great comfort to me'.

Nelson's next adventure was unique for a fifteen-year-old boy. In 1773 it became known that the Admiralty were fitting out two bomb-vessels to investigate the possibility of finding a north-east passage through the Arctic to the Pacific. Nelson became determined to get a berth on one. Bomb vessels, although only from 300 to 400 tons with a complement of sixty-seven men, were especially stoutly built to allow them to withstand the recoil of heavy guns in their bows. They were, with additional reinforcement and adaptation, thought ideal for withstanding pressure from ice packs or for breaking a passage through quite thick sheet ice. It seems young Nelson's persistence and powers of persuasion, reinforced by his uncle's recommendations, were sufficient to secure him a position as the personal servant (regulations forbade boys in any other capacity) of Captain Skeffington Lutwidge of the *Carcass*. The other bomb vessel was the *Racehorse* under Captain Constantine Phipps, who commanded the expedition.

They sailed from the Nore on 2 June 1773 and got to within ten degrees of the North Pole when they found themselves, due to unfavourable winds, trapped in the ice pack. The two Greenland pilots became extremely agitated, so Captain Phipps warned all officers to make ready the ship's boats in preparation for abandoning the ships. Their intention was to set off on foot dragging the boats over the ice until clear water was found. An early start was to be made on 9 August with each man equipped with a musket, ammunition and a bag of thirty pounds of bread. Floyd, a midshipman on the *Racehorse*, was wearing 'two shirts, two waistcoats, two pairs of breeches, four pairs of socks and my best hat' – laughably inadequate by today's standards. However, during the night of 8/9 August the wind suddenly changed, and there was a desperate scramble to get the boats back on board and set sail to try to force their way out. Slowly, with much cracking and crunching of heavy ice, they made their way to open sea. They were back off Orfordness, Suffolk, by 25 September, having been away just short of four months.

Nelson's ever-helpful uncle secured him a new posting as a midshipman on the small, 20-gun frigate *Seahorse* commanded by Captain George Farmer, a former protégé of Suckling. It was bound for the East Indies. Young Nelson was full of praise for the master, Mr Surridge, who unlike many of his calling took his duties of teaching young midshipmen navigation seriously. Nelson was later to say of him, 'a very clever man and we constantly took lunar observations' – which involved much complex trigonometry. However, it would be safe to surmise that Nelson disapproved of the severity of the captain's disciplinary methods. Farmer ran an extremely 'tight ship' with frequent recourse to the cat-o-nine-tails. With a crew of about 120 men, the logbook records 300 floggings during the voyage, while the first lieutenant was relieved of his duties and court-martialled. The contrast between his experiences on the *Mary Ann* and on the *Seahorse* was another pertinent lesson on how to manage a crew, one that Nelson would never forget. Nor would he forget how, as a sixteen-year-old, he had been allowed to take control of the ship and tack her for the first time. The thrill of being in command, of giving the orders, of seeing the seamen dash to their duties, the sheets hauled, the great sails fly, thunder and then come to rest, then fill again as the ship drew away on her new tack, would have stayed with him forever. For over a year he cruised the Arabian Sea, the Indian Ocean and the Bay of Bengal. He visited Madras, Calcutta, Bombay and the naval base at Trincomalee in Ceylon. He tasted the exotic East with its vivid colours, its bustling bazaars, dirt, smells, squalor, dust and heat.

Unfortunately, Nelson also tasted its disease. In December 1775 he was struck down by a 'malignant disorder' that was almost certainly malaria – the scourge of the East Indies station as yellow fever was of the West Indies. For a time he was semi-paralysed and almost died. In March 1776 he was half carried on board the frigate *Dolphin* at the start of a six-month voyage home – much of which he spent alternately sweating or shivering, delirious in his cot. At times he 'almost wished myself overboard'. Nevertheless, as the fever and delirium eventually subsided, his depression lifted and his mood swung. His recovery was a turning point in his life. As he explained, 'a sudden glow of patriotism was kindled within me, and presented my king and country as my patron. My mind exulted in the idea ... I will be a hero, and confiding in Providence, I will brave every danger.' As he was often to tell Captain Hardy in later years, he saw before him a 'radiant orb' urging him forward.

## Confrontation with a Polar Bear

During the expedition to the Arctic in 1773 when Nelson was still only fourteen, an incident occurred that gives an insight into the character of the future admiral. The story is best told by his first biographers, Clarke and McArthur:

Among the gentlemen on the quarter-deck of the Carcass, who were not rated as midshipmen, there was, besides young Nelson, a daring shipmate of his, to whom he had become attached. One night, during the mid-watch, it was concerted between them that they should steal together from the ship, and endeavour to obtain a bear's skin. The clearness of the nights in those high latitudes rendered the accomplishment of this object extremely difficult: they, however, seem to have taken advantage of the haze of an approaching fog, and thus to have escaped unnoticed. Nelson in high spirits led the way over the frightful chasms in the ice, armed with a rusty musket. It was not, however, long before the adventurers were missed by those on board; and, as the fog had come on very thick, the anxiety of Captain Lutwidge and his officers was very great. Between three and four in the morning the mist somewhat dispersed, and the hunters were discovered at a considerable distance, attacking a bear. The signal was instantly made for their return; but it was in vain that Nelson's companion urged him to obey it. He was at this time divided by a chasm in the ice from his shaggy antagonist, which probably saved his life; for the musket had flashed in the pan [a misfire], and their ammunition was expended. 'Never mind,' exclaimed Horatio, 'do but let me get a blow at this devil with the butt-end of my musket, and we shall have him.' His companion, finding that entreaty was in vain, regained the ship. The captain, seeing the young man's danger, ordered a gun to be fired to terrify the enraged animal. This had the desired effect; but Nelson was to return without his bear, somewhat agitated with the apprehension of the consequences of this adventure. Captain Lutwidge, though he could not but admire so daring a disposition, reprimanded him rather sternly for such rashness, and for conduct so unworthy of the situation he occupied; and desired to know what motive he could have for hunting a bear? Being thought by his captain to have acted in a manner unworthy of his situation, made a deep impression on the high-minded cockswain; who, pouting his lip, as he was wont to do when agitated, replied, 'Sir, I wished to kill the bear, that I might carry its skin to my father.'

The characteristics of courage, recklessness, high-spiritedness, determination, disobedience to orders and love of family can all be seen in his behaviour on the Arctic ice.

## LIEUTENANT

Only two days after arriving home in September 1776 Nelson received a welcome surprise. His uncle, who was now the Comptroller of the Navy responsible for shipbuilding, repairs and the mustering of men, had secured him the post of acting fourth lieutenant (the most junior) on the 64-gun *Worcester*. He was only just eighteen and had yet to qualify for promotion by age, sea service or examination. That winter was spent on convoy duty in the Atlantic, where he experienced just how wild and frightening that ocean's storms could be. The War of American Independence had recently broken out and France was expected to side with the rebel colonists at any moment, but for the *Worcester* there was no battle with the enemy, only the elements.

Early in April 1777 Nelson faced his first major professional hurdle – his lieutenant's promotion exam. It was not uncommon to have midshipmen in their thirties, or even forties, who had failed the exam many times. Most had resigned themselves to their lowly status for the duration of their naval careers. In order to take the exam, which involved answering a number of technical questions put by a board of senior officers, the applicant had to have served six years at sea and be at least twenty years old, and certificates to this effect had to be produced. Nelson had six years and just over three months' sea service since that depressing first day on the *Raisonnable* – but it was another five months to his nineteenth birthday, let alone his twentieth. When Nelson entered the room to face the interviewing board of elderly captains, he was taken aback at seeing his uncle sitting in the centre of an intimidating display of gold braid. As the questions came, he noticed that Captain Suckling asked none of them. Nelson had no difficulty responding promptly and fully to the queries and easily demonstrated his competence. The interview ended with the board pronouncing him successful. Only then did Suckling stand to introduce his nephew. The captains expressed surprise at his not informing them before, as many captains would have done. The Comptroller replied, 'I did not wish the younker [sic] to be favoured, I felt convinced that he would pass a good examination; and you see, gentlemen, I have not been disappointed.' His uncle made no mention of the age discrepancy. The following day Nelson received his lieutenant's commission and a posting as the second lieutenant on the 32-gun frigate *Lowestoffe* under Captain William Locker.

The *Lowestoffe* was under orders to sail with a convoy for the Jamaica station in the West Indies, but before she could do so she needed to make up the crew numbers. For this she had to resort to the press gang and, as the first lieutenant was on leave, Nelson had to lead the party with cudgels and cutlasses, scouring the taverns and brothels of Sheerness to make up the complement. It was the only time Nelson was called on for this duty, and while engaged in these distasteful activities he suddenly became very ill and unable to speak. It was undoubtedly a recurrence of malaria. The collapse of their commander must have caused consternation (and probably a few uncomplimentary comments) in the press gang, who were then making their way with their reluctant 'recruits' to a rendezvous near the Tower of London. The situation was saved by Nelson's number two in the party, a broad-shouldered midshipman named Bromwich who, with little effort, carried his commander across his back to the rendezvous.

Once in the Caribbean, Locker's task was to hunt for American privateers, giving Nelson his first prospect of action. One of *Lowestoffe*'s first captures was a small American schooner, which Locker decided to keep as a tender for his ship rather than sending her in as a prize. He renamed her *Little Lucy* after his daughter and placed Lieutenant Nelson in charge: his first command! Nelson was delighted. 'In this vessel I made myself a complete pilot for all the passages through the Islands on the north side of Hispaniola.'

In 1778 Sir Peter Parker arrived in Jamaica as commander-in-chief. On Locker's strong recommendation he took Nelson on board his flagship, the 50-gun *Bristol*, as third lieutenant. This was a plum posting for the twenty-year-old. He was under the eye of an admiral, in daily contact with him, so if he did well his prospects of promotion were excellent. He did well. Sir Peter liked him (just as importantly, so did Lady Parker) and admired his competence. Before the year was over he was the first lieutenant, and in December 1778 he was promoted again to 'master and commander' of the brig *Badger*. Meanwhile his uncle, Captain Suckling, had died in England. Nelson had lost the patron who had launched him in his career. Nevertheless, his charm, efficiency and enthusiasm had been recognized and rewarded by his new commander-in-chief, who had promoted Nelson on his own judgement.

In the *Badger* Nelson's task was to 'protect the Mosquito shore [the bay off the north coast of Panama is still called the Gulf of Mosquitoes] and the Bay of Honduras, from the depredations of the American privateers'. He had some success: in April 1779 he captured the 80-ton *La Prudente* (and spent the next two days searching desperately for the ship's papers to prove her identity, which were finally discovered hidden in an old shoe).

## POST CAPTAIN

Within six months, on 11 June 1779, Nelson, still under twenty-one by three months, was promoted to post captain. He was given command of the 28-gun frigate *Hinchinbrooke*, formerly an enemy merchantman renamed after the First Lord of the Admiralty's ancestral home. This was the crucial promotion in any naval officer's career. It meant that from then on he merely had to survive and avoid disaster, and eventually seniority would elevate him to flag rank – he would become an admiral. Moreover, no junior could be promoted over him. That Nelson jumped this hurdle so young was exceptional, and attributable to a combination of three factors. First, his own ability as a resourceful, energetic and professional naval officer. Secondly, the patronage of the commander-in-chief. Sir Peter Parker (and his wife) knew him intimately, recognized his ability and in some ways probably regarded him as a son. Not many officers of his age could count on so powerful a patron. Thirdly, luck. It so happened that the former captain of the *Hinchinbrooke* had been killed by a random shot, so there was an immediate vacancy to fill. At the same time as he promoted Nelson, Admiral Parker also gave a Lieutenant Collingwood command of the *Badger*. These two lifelong friends climbed the promotion ladder together. At Trafalgar they led the two columns of the British Fleet into battle, and when Nelson was killed Collingwood took overall command. Sir Peter Parker, aged eighty-two, was to be the chief mourner at Nelson's funeral.

With Nelson in command, the *Hinchinbrooke* took a few small prizes that ultimately netted him £800 but there was no notable action at sea to test the new captain. Strangely, it was to be on land that Nelson first came under heavy fire. The overall plan, dreamed up in Jamaica, was to attack the Spaniards in Central America. This involved landing a force at the mouth of the San Juan River that forms the boundary between Costa Rica and Nicaragua, proceeding up it to take Fort San Juan. This would give them control of Lake Nicaragua, and from there the supposedly wealthy cities of Granada and Leon could be seized. The force would then have reached the Pacific, thus cutting America in half. The expedition took no account of the dense jungle, the atrocious climate, the rainy season or the scourge of yellow fever. To cap it all only a hotchpotch of 500 troops could be spared. Major Polson commanded the army element composed of men from the 60th and 79th Regiments, the Loyal Irish plus a hundred Jamaican volunteers. The navy element was the *Hinchinbrooke*.

Typically, Nelson went ashore to lead the naval party of marines and sailors. 'I quitted my ship, carried troops in boats one hundred miles up a river, which none but the Spaniards since the time of the buccaneers had ever ascended.' The journey became a seventeen-day nightmare, during the course of which Nelson led an attack on a small defended island from which the defenders fled without a fight. It was an exhausted, depleted and disease-ridden force that finally arrived in front of Fort San Juan. Instead of an immediate assault (which Nelson favoured), the laborious business of preparations for a siege were put in hand. Major Polson was impressed by his naval comrade. 'A light-haired boy came to me in a little frigate. In two or three days he displayed himself, and afterwards he directed all the operations.' In his official report he wrote: 'He [Nelson] was the first on every service whether by night or day. I want words to express what I owe that gentleman.' Nelson was not present when the fort surrendered, as he had been recalled to take command of the 44-gun frigate *Janus*, whose captain had died. This was just as well as, had he remained, he would have probably succumbed to the fever that was ravaging the force. Many have thought this was the deadly 'yellow jack' that was the curse of the Caribbean. But, as has been recently pointed out by Dr A.-M. E. Hills, the symptoms of yellow fever – intense fever, violent delirium, yellow skin, constant and copious black vomit, collapse and death – were not the symptoms ascribed to most of the sick on this expedition. Dr Hills considers it more likely to have been tropical sprue (diarrhoea, soreness at the corners of the mouth, muscle cramps, lassitude and weakness) made worse by the general debility of all after a seven-week journey without fresh fruit or vegetables. Indeed, many men were showing the first signs of scurvy on arrival off the San Juan River. In Nelson's case it was probably made worse by a mild dose of manchineel poisoning.

### The Poor State of Health on the *Hinchinbrooke* in 1780

Nelson's friend Captain Collingwood took over command of the *Hinchinbrooke* from Nelson. He found the crew in a dreadful state of health due to a combination of scurvy, tropical fevers and malaria. He described the seamen as showing symptoms of 'fevers, fluxes [diarrhoea] and scorbutic [scurvy] ulcers'. The remedy, put in hand by Collingwood, is recorded in the ship's log as washing down the whole ship twice with vinegar and lighting fires in iron pots that were kept burning continuously. Not surprisingly, there was little noticeable benefit. While Nelson had been in command eighty-seven men out of a complement of 200 'took to their beds in one night'. Collingwood noted that in May sixteen men died, while on one day seventy had fever. In an attempt to alleviate the suffering of the worst cases, forty men were sent ashore to sleep in tents. On many days that month the sickness rate exceeded seventy. Nelson was later to write to Dr Benjamin Mosely in a note for the latter's *Treatise on Tropical Diseases* that only ten men of the *Hinchinbrooke* survived the San Juan expedition.

## Nelson's Attack of Manchineel Poisoning

According to Clarke and McArthur, writing in their *Life of Admiral Lord Nelson KB* in 1809, Nelson was poisoned during the San Juan expedition in 1780 by drinking water contaminated by manchineel fruit. They claim that:

> On another occasion, Captain Nelson and some of his men narrowly escaped being poisoned [killed]. They had inadvertently endeavoured to quench their excessive thirst by drinking at a spring into which some branches of the manchineel apple had been thrown. Nelson suffered severely from its effects; and it is the opinion of his Royal Highness the Duke of Clarence, from whom this anecdote was received that the delicate health of his friend thus experienced a severe and lasting injury.

The manchineel is one of nature's most deadly trees. It can easily tempt the unwary with its apple-like fruit and sweet smell and (initially) taste. Every part is poisonous, particularly the juice in the bark or fruit. Contact with the sap causes severe skin blisters. Eating the fruit causes vomiting, abdominal pain, violent and bloody diarrhoea and, often, an agonizing death. Sawdust from cutting the wood and smoke from burning it can seriously affect the eyes, while drops of juice in the eye will cause blindness for several days. Native Indians dipped their arrowheads in the sap. The celebrated buccaneer Basil Ringrose recorded an incident in 1679 on an island in the Gulf of Panama, where his ship had put in for water:

> In this pond, as I was washing myself, and standing under a mancanilla tree, a small shower of rain happened to fall on the tree and from thence dropped upon my skin. These drops caused me to break out all over my body into red spots, of which I was not well for the space of a week after.

It seems probable that the water Nelson drank had substantially diluted the poison, as he was able to lay his battery of one gun the next day. He had a close call but, like most of his companions, he was still sick.

---

Nelson had to be carried ashore at Jamaica, unable to take up his new command. At the end of August 1780 he wrote to Admiral Parker:

> Having been in a very bad state of health for these last several months, so bad as to be unable to attend my duties aboard the *Janus*, and the faculty [doctors] having informed me that I cannot recover in this climate, I am therefore to request that you will be pleased to permit me to go to England for the re-establishment of my health.

Permission was granted and Nelson was able to sail home on the 64-gun *Lion*, whose captain was 'Billy Blue' Cornwallis. Sir Peter Parker never thought he would make it. Writing to the Admiralty, he said, 'Captain Nelson is so emaciated and in so bad a state of health that I doubt whether he will live to get home. I wish much for his recovery. His abilities in his profession would be a loss to the service.'

Parker was almost right. After an unusually long voyage (almost three months), Nelson was still desperately ill and weak on arrival in England. He went initially to Bath to convalesce. It was to be a lengthy and uncomfortable process. He complained of having to be 'carried to and from bed with the most excruciating tortures'. In February 1781, he told his old friend Captain Locker that he had nearly lost the use of his left arm, and in May, after moving to London, he had a relapse. Writing to his brother William, he complained, 'I have entirely lost the use of my left arm, and very nearly of my left leg and thigh.' Nelson eventually recovered sufficiently (but not completely) to take over command of the recently converted 28-gun frigate *Albemarle* (formerly the French merchantman *Menagere*) in which he spent the winter of 1781–2 on Baltic convoy duties. They revealed the *Albemarle* to be a poor sailer, a brute to handle, with, seemingly, a mind of her own. The spring saw *Albemarle* escorting a convoy of some forty ships to Newfoundland through a virtually continuous storm across the Atlantic. Nelson described St Johns as 'a disagreeable place' and was anxious to leave.

He was much happier during the summer cruising off the American coast looking for prizes. On 14 July he captured an American fishing schooner, the *Harmony*, whose owner, Mr Nathaniel Carver, was but a few miles from his home at Plymouth, Massachusetts, when the *Albemarle* caught him. The weather was squally, the shoals in Boston Bay numerous, and neither Nelson nor any person on the *Albemarle* had knowledge of them. Mr Carver was ordered on board to pilot the ships through the hazards and out of the Bay. The American did as he was told with skill and success. At that point Nelson stepped up to him, made a short speech of thanks and finished by declaring, 'I return your schooner, and with her this certificate of your good conduct.' It was signed 'Horatio Nelson'. A shaken but relieved Mr Carver took his vessel home and, in later years, when Nelson became a British national hero, had the certificate framed. It remained a highly prized family heirloom for several generations.

By September 1782 it was five months since the crew had eaten their last fresh meal in Portsmouth. For eight weeks salt beef was the sole item on the menu for officers and men alike. Not surprisingly, the first dreaded signs of scurvy began to appear – lassitude, depression, spongy gums and muscular pains. Nelson reluctantly headed north for Quebec.

There, at last free from his illness, Nelson fell in love for the first time. The object of his affection was Mary Simpson, the sixteen-year-old daughter of a gentleman called 'Sandy' Simpson of Scottish descent. So infatuated was he with the young lady that he seriously considered resigning his commission and leaving the Navy. He was, with difficulty, dissuaded from taking this drastic course, and he rejoined his ship when ordered to escort a convoy to New York.

In November, while lying in the narrows off Staten Island, New York, Nelson had occasion to visit Admiral Hood's flagship, the imposing 98-gun three-decker *Barfleur*. As he clambered on board, he was watched with some amazement by a young midshipman, Prince William Henry, son of George III, later to become the 'Sailor King', William IV. Years later the Prince was to recall his first impression of the twenty-four-year-old captain:

> [He] appeared to be the merest boy of a captain I ever beheld; and his dress was worthy of attention. He had on a full-laced uniform; his lank unpowdered hair was tied in a stiff Hessian [pig]tail, of an extraordinary length; the old-fashioned flaps of his waistcoat added to the general quaintness of his figure … I

### Problems on the *Boreas*

Nelson's journey to the West Indies in 1784 was anything but happy. The start was particularly galling. A pilot had been taken on board at Long Reach with the task of navigating the mud banks of the Medway, only to allow the fine new frigate to go aground. Nelson later wrote:

> On Monday, April 12th, we sailed at daylight, just after high water. The d——d Pilot – it makes me swear to think of it – ran the Ship aground, where she lay with so little water that people could walk round her till next high water.

Fortunately the *Boreas* had hit mud, not rocks, so the only damage was to the pilot's reputation and the ship was able to sail for Portsmouth to pick up passengers. Already on board was Nelson's elder brother William, a clergyman, who fancied a sea voyage and a sojourn in the sun away from the dull routine of his parish. Nelson was unenthusiastic, telling him, 'Come when you please, I shall be ready to receive you. Bring your canonicals [sic] and sermons. [Then, worried about overcrowding] Do not bring any Burnham servants.' Also on the ship were some thirty midshipmen, including another Maurice Suckling, a cousin of the captain. They would all eventually be dispersed to various ships in the West Indies but in the meantime Nelson was responsible for their nautical education for the next few weeks.

Further problems awaited at Portsmouth, in the form of Lady Hughes, the wife of Nelson's future commander-in-chief on the Jamaica station, and her daughter. The young lady, Rosy, was a member of the 'fishing fleet' being taken to the Caribbean to find a husband – having failed to do so in England. To Lady Hughes, the young bachelor captain of the *Boreas* was an obvious target for her scheming and incessant chatter. Nelson was not impressed by his first introduction to Rosy, claiming that 'the mother will be handsomer in a few years'. Lady Hughes was to be disappointed in her obvious matchmaking. Nelson made it plain from the outset that no amount of encouragement would induce any amorous association with the girl. She must have felt rejected when, as the voyage progressed, the other eligible officers, namely the two lieutenants and the surgeon, showed more interest in the purser's wife than in her.

Despite these minor awkwardnesses, Nelson later conceded that the admiral's wife and daughter were 'very pleasant, good people'. He made a point of attending to the instruction of the midshipmen, and he himself led races to climb to the masthead. Lady Hughes noticed how 'the young gentlemen who have the happiness of being on his quarterdeck' became devoted to their captain.

had never seen anything like it before ... [but] there was something irresistibly pleasing in his address and conversation; and an enthusiasm, when speaking on professional subjects, that showed he was no common being.

Nelson had come to ask a favour of Admiral Digby. He wanted 'a better ship and a better station'. On telling Nelson that his present station was excellent for prize money, the Admiral was startled to get the response, 'Yes, sir, but the West Indies is the station for honour.' In late November Nelson got his wish. The *Albemarle* was transferred south as part of Lord Hood's squadron to the West Indies, but not for long. Peace was in the offing, America was about to win her independence, and by June 1783 Nelson was back in England, the *Albemarle* paid off. Although he had achieved nothing dramatic and had still not managed to get involved in a proper naval action, Nelson was an experienced and popular commander who won both respect and devotion from his subordinates. His men knew a good captain when they saw one. When the *Albemarle* was paid off, the entire crew wanted to serve under Nelson again if he got another ship.

Within two weeks of his return Lord Hood (yet another admiral under Nelson's spell) took him to a levée at St James's Palace to introduce him to the King. George III was delighted to meet a friend of Prince William, warmly inviting him to Windsor to take leave of the Prince who was about to embark on an 'educational' tour of Europe. Although he was on half-pay, Nelson's name was unlikely to be forgotten in high places. He spent the next few months in France where he managed to fall in love again. But this time there seem to have been pecuniary implications as well as amorous ones in the development of the relationship. The lady in question, Miss Andrews, was the daughter of a visiting clergyman in St Omer. Nelson now had an annual income of £130, which was, as he put it, 'far too small to think of mar-

riage'. He had found out that the lady had considerably more money than he did, at least £1,000, which was embarrassingly awkward. He turned to his other uncle, William Suckling, who was a senior official in the Customs and Navy Office. His letter of 14 January 1784 makes the situation plain.

> There arrives in general a time in a man's life (that has friends) that either they place him in life in a situation that makes his application for anything further unnecessary [i.e. employment], or give him help in a pecuniary way if they can afford it, and he deserves it. The critical moment in my life has now arrived. [He knew Miss Andrews had a small fortune] ... £1,000 I understand. The whole income I possess does not exceed £130 per annum. Now I must come to the point. Will you, if I should marry, allow me a hundred a year, until my income is increased to that sum either by employment or any other way? A very few years will, I hope, turn up something, if my friends will but exert themselves. [If he could not have money then his uncle was urged to] ... exert yourself either with Lord North or Mr. Jenkinson, for me to get a guardship, or some appointment in a public office.... If nothing is done for me, I know not what I have to trust to. Life is not worth living without happiness, and I care not where I may linger out a miserable existence.

Mr Suckling was willing to help, but before his reply reached him Nelson arrived in London. Something drastic must have happened. The most likely reason was that Miss Andrews had declined the idea of marriage, although Nelson never admitted this. It was election time in England, so Nelson told everyone of influence that he was desperate for a ship, or a political career. In March 1784 his efforts were rewarded with the command of another 28-gun frigate, the *Boreas*. His destination was, yet again, the West Indies. This time he would remain there for three years.

## NELSON IN THE WEST INDIES

On arrival at Barbados Nelson found that he was the senior captain and therefore the second-in-command of the Leeward Islands station. He was not impressed with his fifty-five-year-old commander-in-chief, Admiral Sir Richard Hughes, whose wife he had just brought out to join her husband. According to Nelson, the elderly admiral, who had lost an eye in an accident trying to kill a cockroach with a table fork, was 'tolerable, but I do not like him, he bows and scrapes too much for me'. He also disapproved of an officer of his rank and importance scrimping on the pennies by residing in a common boarding house.

His three-year stint in the Caribbean came during a time of peace – part of the period between the end of the American War of Independence and the outbreak of the French Revolutionary Wars in 1793. This was not to Nelson's liking, for there was little prospect of honour or money. Much of his time was spent in Antigua, where one of the main tourist attractions today is English Harbour, then used as a naval maintenance base, with its many associations of Nelson. Nelson, however, detested the place: 'English Harbour I hate the sight of.' His prolonged stay was notable for three events. The first was his entanglement with the Commissioner of the Navy in Antigua, a retired naval captain called John Moutray, and his wife. The second, more serious matter, was his clash with Admiral Hughes over the trading rights of American vessels with British colonies. The third was his marriage.

Almost immediately after his arrival in Antigua, Nelson was writing to his commander-in-chief and the Secretary to the Admiralty. He was protesting that Admiral Hughes had allowed the Commissioner, Captain Moutray (who was retired on half pay) to fly the broad pennant of a commodore during the absence of a senior officer. It was a nitpicking complaint perhaps, but as a civilian the Commissioner was not allowed this privilege, as Admiral Hughes was well aware. While waiting for a ruling on this matter, Nelson proceeded to develop a romantic passion for Mrs Moutray. She became the one bright spot in his existence, though both realized an eventual parting was the only likely outcome. 'Was it not for Mrs Moutray, who is very, very good to me, I should almost hang myself at this infernal hole,' Nelson lamented, although almost certainly the affair was never more than a respectable passion. After eight months Commissioner Moutray was sent home in poor health, taking his wife with him. Nelson was desolate. Mooning and brooding, he exclaimed, 'Her equal I never saw in any country or in any situation.' After her departure he visited her house on the hill above English Harbour where he had spent the 'happiest days in this world'. Then, rather pathetically, 'E'en the trees drooped their heads.'

His second difficulty arose from his insistence on forbidding American traders from doing business with British colonies in the Leeward Islands. The Navigation Act was clear: only British-built and British-owned ships were permitted to trade with her colonies. This meant that Americans, who were no longer colonists, were excluded. However, Admiral Hughes had allowed the trade to continue. Both before the war, and now afterwards, it was a highly lucrative trade which neither the Americans nor the West Indian merchants saw any good reason to stop. It suited every planter, merchant and customs official in the islands – but it was contrary to the Navigation Laws. When Nelson pointed all this out to Hughes, the admiral first claimed never to have seen the laws, then agreed to enforce them, then dithered, took 'good advice' and rescinded his enforcement instructions. Nelson was furious and wrote to Admiral Hughes, the Admiralty (several times), the Secretary of State and even, with real desperation, the King. As can be imagined, Captain Nelson became probably the most unpopular man in the islands. He was ostracized by society. On a visit to the Governor, General Shirley, and in response to his comment that 'Old generals were not in the habit of taking advice from young gentlemen,' Nelson replied, 'I have the honour, sir, of being as old as the Prime Minister of England, and think myself as capable of commanding one of His Majesty's Ships as that Minister is of governing the State.'

While cruising, Nelson never hesitated to turn back American merchantmen. When four such vessels in Nevis roads failed to depart within forty-eight hours, he seized them. The tinderbox exploded. The Americans, in alliance with the merchants of Nevis, hired a lawyer to sue Nelson for assault and imprisonment. He was forced to remain on board the *Boreas* for eight weeks to avoid arrest. Three months later instructions came from England that Captain Nelson's defence costs were to be met from Treasury funds, vindicating his behaviour. But, by the same mail, Admiral Hughes was commended for his zeal in protecting British trading interests! This affair, which dragged on for months, demonstrated Nelson's moral courage. Few, if any, junior captains would have been prepared to stick to a principle with such tenacity. With his commander-in-chief, the governor, the business community and virtually all of Antigua's society against him, he refused to back down. Threatened with arrest, his career in the balance, Nelson's remarkable strength of character is revealed with startling clarity. Nobody was ever to question his physical courage. After Antigua, nobody could dispute his moral courage either.

The third highlight of Nelson's three years in the Caribbean was his meeting, and subsequent marriage to, a widow a few months older than him, Frances Herbert Nisbet. She was the daughter of William Woolward, a senior judge on Nevis, and the niece of John Richardson Herbert, the President of the Council of Nevis, whom she was staying with and looking after. At the age of eighteen she had married a doctor, Josiah Nisbet, who shortly afterwards became deranged, dying within eighteen months of their marriage and leaving her with an infant son, also called Josiah.

Nelson met her in March 1786, made up his mind to propose in June and did so in August. They were married in March the following year, exactly twelve months after meeting. Prince William, who was now commanding the 28-gun frigate *Pegasus* that had recently joined the station, gave the bride away. The Prince had earlier remarked that Nelson felt 'only esteem', rather than that thing

### English Harbour Snippets

Some interesting snippets of information on Nelson's life in the place he hated. He:

- had six buckets of water poured over his head at dawn
- walked a mile every night without fatigue, but was 'housed' all day
- took a quart of goat's milk daily
- established an officer's mess ashore
- during the hurricane season, encouraged his men to amuse themselves with music, dancing and cudgelling
- organized amateur theatricals.

## Captain Josiah Nisbet, 1780–1830

Nelson's stepson was five years old when Nelson first met his mother in Nevis. After Nelson married Josiah spent some five years at school in Norfolk. Then at the outbreak of the French Revolutionary Wars in 1793 he joined his stepfather on the 64-gun *Agamemnon* as a midshipman. Nelson was able to write favourably that Josiah's 'understanding is excellent, and his disposition really good. ... He is a seaman, every inch of him.' Early in 1797 Josiah served as a junior lieutenant on the 74-gun *Captain* at the Battle of St Vincent. On the disastrous night landing and attack at Santa Cruz later that year it was Josiah who was instrumental in saving Nelson's life. When the latter's right arm was shattered he would probably have bled to death if Josiah, helped by a seaman, had not got him into a boat and checked the profuse bleeding with a scarf as a tourniquet.

Regrettably Nelson's good opinion of his stepson was not to last. Josiah was starting to exhibit the bouts of ill-temper and drunkenness that were to blight his career in the Navy. His stepfather's patronage had him promoted lieutenant and then post-captain within a remarkably short time, and through Nelson's efforts Josiah secured command of the 36-gun frigate *Thalia* in the Mediterranean. It was not a happy ship. Captain Nisbet took to messing in the gunroom, and discipline and morale plummeted. In 1799 Nelson wrote, when sending the *Thalia* to Admiral

Duckworth at Gibraltar, that he could say 'nothing in her praise, inside or out'. He added, 'Perhaps you may be able to make something of Captain Nisbet; he has, by his conduct, almost broke my heart.' The admiral failed. He wrote in June 1800 expressing his grave concern at the low morale on the *Thalia*. The surgeon had been under arrest for three months and was demanding a court martial, while the first lieutenant had compiled a long list of grievances against his captain. Duckworth had smoothed things over and a public inquiry was avoided, but he recommended the *Thalia* be paid off. His final recommendation was that Captain Nisbet should have 'a few months with Lady Nelson'.

Part of the problem was that Josiah strongly objected to his stepfather's flaunting of his adulterous relationship with Emma Hamilton. He was intensely loyal to his mother, feeling, with reason, that she was being treated disgracefully. On one occasion, seeing the one-armed admiral struggling to climb up a rope ladder, he remarked that he wished Nelson would fall and break his neck. Despite all this, Nelson kept trying to get Captain Nisbet, an officer who would never be 'an ornament to the service', another ship. He was unsuccessful. Josiah did better ashore. He developed a talent for business, married well, made a very good living and when he died, aged fifty, left his family comfortably off.

---

'which is vulgarly called love', for Mrs Nisbet. In May the *Boreas* sailed for home, having completed her tour in the Leeward Islands. Shortly before leaving, Nelson wrote to his old friend Locker:

> No man has had more illness or trouble on a Station than I have experienced; but let me lay a balance on the other side – I am married to an amiable woman, that far makes amends for everything: indeed till I married her I never knew happiness. And I am morally certain she will continue to make me happy for the rest of my days.

Facing Nelson on his return were five years 'on the beach'. Without a war there were no jobs, even for captains as talented and experienced as him. Not until the French Revolutionary War broke out in 1793 was he called upon again. Thanks to powerful patronage and outstanding ability, his rise had been meteoric. By twenty-nine he had been at sea for seventeen years and was a post captain with eight years' seniority. He was seen to be a master of his profession by all who came in contact with him, from seaman to admiral. But despite all this Nelson, along with hundreds of his contemporaries, was destined for a long period of half pay.

## Nelson's Ships 1771–87

| Date | Name | Station | Guns | Rate | Nelson's rank |
|---|---|---|---|---|---|
| 1771 | *Raisonnable* | Medway | 64 | 3rd | Midshipman |
| 1771 | *Triumph* | Thames | 74 | 3rd | Captain's servant |
| 1771–2 | *Mary Ann* | West Indies | Merchantman | | – |
| 1772 | *Triumph* | Thames | 74 | 3rd | Midshipman |
| 1773 | *Carcass* | Arctic | Bomb | unrated | Captain's servant |
| 1774–6 | *Seahorse* | East Indies | 20 | 6th | Midshipman |
| 1776 | *Dolphin* | returning sick | 44 | 5th | Midshipman (passenger) |
| 1776–7 | *Worcester* | Baltic | 64 | 3rd | Acting Lieutenant |
| 1777 | *Lowestoffe* | West Indies | 32 | 5th | Lieutenant |
| 1778 | *Little Lucy* | West Indies | 4 | unrated | Lieutenant |
| 1778 | *Bristol* | West Indies | 50 | 4th | Lieutenant |
| 1778–9 | *Badger* | West Indies | 14 | unrated | Commander |
| 1779 | *Hinchinbrooke* | West Indies | 28 | 6th | Post captain |
| 1780 | *Janus* | West Indies | 44 | 5th | Post captain |
| 1780–1 | *Lion* | returning sick | 64 | 3rd | Passenger |
| 1781–2 | *Albemarle* | Baltic/N. America | 28 | 6th | Post captain |
| 1784–7 | *Boreas* | West Indies | 28 | 6th | Post captain |

# Ships and Seamanship

All sixty of the British, French and Spanish line-of-battle ships that slogged it out for five hours at Trafalgar were floating gun platforms or, more accurately, floating castles. They each had a crew (garrison) of several hundred (the Spanish *Santa Ana* had 1,188); they defended themselves behind walls, oak rather than stone, averaging about $2^1/_2$ feet thick at the waterline. Each ship, like a castle, was self-contained with water, food, ammunition, powder and stores, as those within it could be cut off from replenishment for long periods. Once battle was joined, some 88 per cent of the officers and crew were employed firing the guns or humping powder and shot. During action on the 102-gun *Victory* at Trafalgar, out of a total complement of 820 men no fewer than 727 were, in one way or another, involved in serving the guns. This did not leave many for other duties – such as sailing. The sole purpose of the ship-of-the-line was to bring its guns to bear on the enemy. Everything on board one of these warships was geared to moving and firing the 'long guns', as they were called (the French called them 'great guns'). Even an average ship, such as the French 74-gun *Pluton*, carried a battery almost equal in number to the entire French 'Grand Battery' that pounded the British line at Waterloo, and in terms of the size of the cannons, weight of shot and range, the *Pluton* far outgunned the 'Grand Battery'.

If the tactical purpose of a ship-of-the-line was to destroy enemy ships (or bombard coastal installations), its strategic purpose was to secure command of the seas. For European continental countries a large and powerful navy was useful but not absolutely critical. For France under Napoleon, being defeated at Trafalgar was an annoyance, not a catastrophe. France built more ships but never really used them. She became master of Europe by marching soldiers across land frontiers rather than sailing ships around continental coasts. For Britain, however, command of the sea in time of war was a basic requirement for survival. Sea trade was vital; her merchant fleet was therefore large and needed protection. As big ships beat smaller ones, so Britain, despite numerous weaknesses and setbacks, was forced out of sheer necessity to maintain sufficient battleships to ensure an edge over her opponents. At the same time these ships were the means by which Britain could deter or defeat invasion. As described in Section One, Napoleon needed to outnumber British battleships in the Channel for perhaps two days in order to ferry his army across to Kent. He was never able to do so.

Unlike her enemies at Trafalgar, Britain spent more on her navy than on her army. Britain could survive defeat on land but not at sea. In 1800 the Royal Navy cost £12.6 million, or 47 per cent of the country's war chest. By 1814 the figure had peaked at £22 million, of which £6.5 million was on victualling. However, the navy did not always get good value for money, as a substantial percentage disappeared through wastage and corruption. In France, throughout the long years of war, naval costs were always dwarfed by those of the army.

When assessing relative naval strengths, the important figure was normally the number of ships-of-the-line in commission; all navies had up to a third or more of their fleets 'in ordinary' (awaiting major refits) at any one time. A ship-of-the-line, or battleship, was a ship capable of holding its own against an enemy ship in a line of battle, and they acted as a deterrent to large-scale naval adventures by an enemy. A country's battleships were seldom in action as a fleet. In the ten years prior to Trafalgar, only five major battles took place: the Glorious First of June, 1794; Cape St Vincent, 1797; Camperdown, 1797; the Nile, 1798; and Copenhagen, 1801. The real day-to-day jack of all naval duties was the frigate. Although too under-gunned to have a place in the line of battle, she was, for Britain in particular, an absolutely indispensable element of the navy. The frigate blockaded, scouted, repeated signals, escorted convoys, transported troops, acted as a courier and cruised on the lookout for enemy privateers or merchantmen. She did everything except fight against battleships in a major action.

In the year of Trafalgar, 1805, the strength of the navies of each nation involved in the battle were as shown below. The main figures indicate the approximate number of ships actually available (at any time there would be up to a third more of both categories that were victualling, acting as guardships, or in port for minor repairs but able to put to sea at short notice). The number in brackets is the number present at the battle of Trafalgar, with the percentage this formed of the entire fleet.

|                    | British        | French        | Spanish       |
|--------------------|----------------|---------------|---------------|
| Ships-of-the-line  | 79 (27; 34%)   | 41 (18; 44%)  | 38 (15; 40%)  |
| Frigates           | 98 (4; 4%)     | 35 (5; 14%)   | 26 (0; 0%)    |
| **Total**          | 177 (31; 17%)  | 76 (23; 30%)  | 64 (15; 23%)  |

The figures illustrate the following:
• The British, with their worldwide naval commitments and blockade duties, could only muster about a third of their battleships at Trafalgar. A statement made to the House of Lords in May 1805 on ships in commission declared that 37 might last five years and 27 three years, while 17 were only fit for home or limited service.

• Together the French and Spanish had about the same number of battleships theoretically available (mostly in Europe) as the British but despite this, largely due to the British blockade, only just over 40 per cent were available for the battle.
• Only a tiny proportion of frigates were involved in a major action.

# CLASSIFICATION

## Classes of battle fleets

Ships at that time were classed according to their armament – that is, the number of long guns (cannons) they carried. The largest, mounting 100 guns or more in their broadsides, were **first rates**. Examples at Trafalgar were the British 102-gun *Victory* and the Spanish 136-gun *Santisima Trinidad*; strangely, the French had no first-rate ship at the battle. Those with 90 to 98 guns were **second rates**, such as the British 98-gun *Neptune*, *Téméraire* and *Prince*; neither the French or Spanish had ships of this rating. Those with 64 to 80 guns were **third rates**; for instance, the British 80-gun *Tonnant*, 74-gun *Bellerophon*, 64-gun *Agamemnon*, French 80-gun *Bucentaure* and Spanish 64-gun *San Leandro*. The guns in the first two rates were distributed between three gundecks – hence the term three-decker. The Spanish *Santisima Trinidad*, the largest ship in the world, was unique in having four gundecks. Ships with 64 to 80 guns had them divided between two gundecks and were two-deckers.

In 1805 these three rates comprised the ships-of-the-line that made up a nation's battle fleet – anything smaller could not withstand a battering from these larger ships in action, nor could they deliver the weight of broadside required to defeat them. The system of 'rating' was also (and still is) used to classify the grades/ranks of seamen (see Section Four).

## Classes of other ships

All other ships were 'below the line' and therefore not normally part of the battle fleet. Those with 50 to 60 guns were **fourth rates** with their armament on two gundecks. These had, in the middle of the previous century, been ships-of-the-line, but by the beginning of the nineteenth they were so seriously out-gunned by the higher rates that they were regarded as large frigates rather than battleships. As they became unserviceable, they were not replaced. The Royal Navy had no 60-gun ships and had only fifteen with 50 guns in 1805. There were none at Trafalgar.

The **fifth** and **sixth** rates were frigates. By 1805 the **fifth rate** was by far the most common. These ships had 32 to 44 guns on one gundeck. Nelson had four at Trafalgar, the largest being the 38-gun *Naiad*, the others (*Euryalus*, *Phoebe* and *Sirius*) having 36 guns. Only the French contributed frigates to the Combined Fleet – four with 40 guns each (*Cornélie*, *Hermione*, *Hortense* and *Rhin*) plus the 32-gun *Thémis*. Sixth-rate ships, small frigates usually with 28 guns, dated back to 1748, but as they only carried 9-pounder guns they were easily out-gunned. None was added to the British fleet after 1793 and there was none at Trafalgar.

All smaller ships or vessels were **unrated**. These included sloops (ship-sloops and brig sloops), brigs, bomb vessels, fireships, schooners and cutters. The French equivalent of the British sloop was the 20-gun corvette. At Trafalgar the British had two unrated ships, the schooner *Pickle* with ten carronades (a short gun with a relatively large bore) and the cutter *Entreprenante* with twelve. The French deployed two brigs, the 18-gun *Furet* and 16-gun *Argus*.

## FIRST RATES (100+ GUNS)

The largest in any navy, first rates were constructed to act as floating ambassadors of naval power. To command a first rate was a highly prestigious appointment for a post captain. It was a plum job, often under the eye of his admiral, since first rates were built to accommodate an admiral and his staff in addition to the normal complement. When an admiral was on board, they wore (flew) an admiral's flag at the masthead, and so the captain of the ship was known as the fleet's 'flag captain'. No fewer than six admirals wore their flag on the 102-gun *Victory* before Nelson. In battle the flagships usually took station in the centre of the fleet or squadron line so the admiral's signals could be more easily seen and repeated by frigates and other ships. They provided an enormous weight of fire, which could only be matched by another first rate. At Trafalgar the 136-gun *Santisima Trinidad*, carrying the flag of the Spanish Rear-Admiral Cisneros, had double the firepower of a third-rate 74. It was from these giants that the battle was planned, orders given and the action controlled.

At Trafalgar the first rates present were:

**British**   102-gun *Victory* (Vice-Admiral Nelson)
100-gun *Royal Sovereign* (Vice-Admiral Collingwood)
100-gun *Britannia* (Rear-Admiral the Earl of Northesk)

**French**   none

**Spanish**   136-gun *Santisima Trinidad* (Rear-Admiral Cisneros)
112-gun *Principe de Asturias* (Admiral Gravina)
112-gun *Santa Anna* (Vice-Admiral Alava)
100-gun *Rayo* (Commodore Macdonnell)

## Characteristics

• First rates were expensive both to build and maintain. However, they tended to last longer than lesser rates as, being so large and representing so substantial an investment, they seem to have been looked after with more care. If money was short, the tendency was to spend it on the first rates before others. The *Victory*, which was built in 1765, cost almost £30 a ton – about £63,000 (the equivalent of at least £63 million today).
• They required an exceptionally large complement of officers, seamen and marines, so recruitment of quality crew was sometimes a problem. At Trafalgar the *Victory* had 14 commissioned officers, 29 warrant officers, 70 petty officers, 565 seamen or administrative personnel, and 142 marines. This total

## Deck Arrangements of Main British Ships at Trafalgar

First Rate – *HMS Victory*, 102 guns + carronades

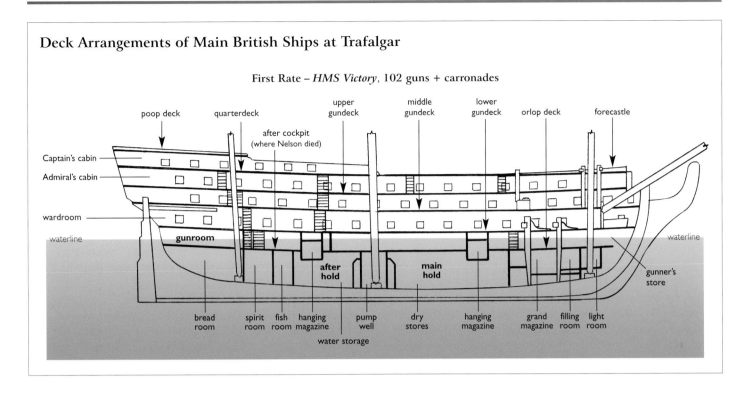

### The hold

Located at the very bottom of the ship, the hold was a giant warehouse. In the *Victory* it was some 150 feet long, 50 feet wide and 20 feet high, with curving sides. Here were stowed hundreds of barrels of food (mainly meat and cheese), drinking water, beer, wood (for the galley fire), cannonballs, spare sails, ropes and a variety of ship's stores. They might have to last up to six months. The stowage of these items had to be carefully planned so they were readily accessible when needed, but also distributed evenly so a good sailing trim (balance) was maintained as they were consumed. The stowage was therefore the overall responsibility of the master, while their issue was that of the purser. A hold was divided into compartments by partitions called bulkheads. Special rooms were reserved for bread (raised up to keep bilge water out), fish (to keep the smell in), spirits (to keep pilferers out) and shot. The grand (main) magazine was also partitioned off as a precaution against fire and explosion, while in the centre of the hold was the pump well with space around it to allow access for repairs. In addition, at the bottom of the hold was the ballast. This consisted of pig iron (about 200 tons in a first rate, 70 in a fifth) with loose shingle on top. The ballast kept the centre of gravity low and the shingle created a flat surface on which the barrels could rest. After weeks at sea, the hold usually became infested with rats and awash with foetid bilge water, the stench of which made men unused to it gag.

### The orlop deck

This got its name from a Dutch word meaning 'overlap', because it overlapped the hold. Aft was the upper part of the bread room, then came the after cockpit containing the slop (clothes) room, steward's room (from which daily provisions were issued), store rooms for officers, and cabins for the purser and surgeon. Forward of the cabins on each side was the midship-

of 820 was still 30 below the full entitlement. The *Santisima Trinidad* carried a crew of 1,100, but the most labour-intensive ship at Trafalgar was the Spanish 112-gun *Santa Ana,* which required almost 1,200 officers and men. During heavy weather 150 men were needed to man her pumps; it took 250 to raise her five large anchors of 3.5 tons each.

• They had massive firepower. Until around 1790 the lower gundeck had carried 42-pounders, but their weight proved a disadvantage and so by Trafalgar the British had replaced them with 32-pounders. At the battle the *Victory* carried thirty 32-pounders, twenty-eight 24-pounders, forty-four 12-pounders, two 68-pounder carronades plus one 28-pounder carronade for use in the launch. One broadside sent 1,148 lbs of iron travelling at 1,600 feet per second hurtling towards the enemy. By comparison the *Santa Ana*'s armament consisted of thirty 36-pounders, thirty-two 24-pounders, thirty 12-pounders and twenty 8-pounders – a broadside of 1,184 lbs, almost identical.

• Most were difficult to handle in a high wind or sea. Even with a large crew the heavy sails were hard to manoeuvre, so these ships tended to be ponderous and slow moving. The *Victory* was an exception. She was a good sailer for her size and could compete with the smaller 74s for speed and manoeuvrability. A speed of eight to ten knots (10 mph) was not unusual for her, and with a following wind she could put on another two knots.

## Construction

Like all rated ships, the first rates were three masted and square rigged, i.e. the main sails were rectangular and hung from yards at right angles to the hull. The difference in construction between them and smaller ships lay in the overall length, beam, weight and, except for second rates, number of gundecks. Apart from the *Santisima Trinidad*, all first and second rates were three-deckers (that is, they had three gundecks stretching the full length of the ship). Starting at the bottom and working upwards, all first and second rates had:

men's berth, where they ate and slept. In battle this space was taken over by the surgeon as his operating theatre. The middle of the orlop deck was devoted to cable storage, although a few petty officers and privileged seamen slung their hammocks there. Forward on the orlop deck were the storerooms and cabins of the boatswain and carpenter, together with the gunner's store. It was on the orlop deck, in the cockpit, that Nelson died at Trafalgar.

### The lower gundeck

This deck had the heaviest guns down each side – in the case of the British first rates, 32-pounders, while the French and Spanish had 36-pounders. It was on this deck that the great majority of the seamen slung their hammocks and mess tables, from the beams and between the guns.

### The middle gundeck

This deck housed the 24-pounder guns on both the British and Combined Fleet ships. On the *Victory* there were twenty-eight in all, fourteen to each broadside. The galley (kitchen) was located forward under the forecastle. The gallery burnt wood in a furnace beneath an iron stove with two large copper kettles for boiling the food. The officers fared better, since their cooks had access to an oven, grill and turnspit. Their food was also more likely to be eaten hot, as their cabins and wardroom (dining/living room) were at the stern on this deck.

### The upper gundeck

Unlike the lower or middle deck, the upper deck was open to the weather in the centre, so was sometimes called the 'weather deck'. Three of the ship's boats were stored on this deck, which carried 12-pounder guns – thirty on the *Victory*. At the stern were the admiral's spacious living quarters.

### The forecastle

This was a raised deck that covered the bow area of the ship. Many of the ship's sails were controlled from here (jibs and foremast) and it usually armed with lighter guns and carronades. The *Victory* carried two of the former (medium 12-pounders) and two of the latter (68-pounders) on her forecastle.

### The quarterdeck

This raised deck at the stern of the ship, the equivalent to the 'bridge' on modern ships, was normally reserved for the admiral, captain, master and other officers plus helmsmen, whose duties were directly concerned with the command and control of the ship (or fleet). The *Victory* had twelve short 12-pounders on this deck. It was here that Nelson received his mortal wound, close to the wheel, by which the ship was steered. Aft of the quarterdeck were the captain's quarters and the master's and secretary's cabins.

### The poop deck

The highest deck on the ship, this was located at the stern and formed the roof of the captain's quarters. It did not carry guns but housed the flag locker, as officers and the signal lieutenant and his assistants used it when hoisting signal flags or stern lanterns. It was also the working platform for controlling the sheets, braces and halyards of the mizzenmast.

## SECOND RATES (90–98 GUNS)

A second-rate was a large ship-of-the-line commanded by a post captain, which could be used to carry the flag of an admiral, possibly on colonial expeditions. Intended as a cheaper alternative to the first-rate ship, they originally carried 90 guns, but from 1771 onwards another eight were added to the quarterdeck. This type of ship was only built by Britain, and in 1804 there were only twenty-one in service, nineteen with 98 guns and two with 90. Four fought at Trafalgar, all with 98 guns. They were the *Témeraré*, *Neptune*, *Prince* and *Dreadnought*.

### Characteristics

• Marginally cheaper than first rates, they were three decked, three masted and square rigged but sailed poorly because they were comparatively short for their height and were forced to carry a disproportionate amount of ballast to compensate for the increased weight. They were unpopular with most captains and even when they were available, admirals, such as Lord Keith when in the Mediterranean, preferred to have their flag on an 80-gun ship.
• The complement of these ships was about 750.
• Originally these ships had 12-pounder guns on the upper deck, but by the 1790s these were being replaced by 18-pounders. The armament was distributed on the three gundecks as follows, using the British *Dreadnought* as an example:

lower deck: twenty-eight 32-pounders
middle deck: thirty-two 24-pounders
upper deck: thirty 18-pounders.

These gave a maximum broadside loaded with single shot of 1,102 lbs – a mere 46 lbs lighter than the *Victory*'s. Indeed, the *Dreadnought* was later reclassified as a 104-gun first rate, although she fought at Trafalgar as a second rate.

### Construction

The deck layout and usage was as for first rates.

## THIRD RATES (64–80 GUNS)

Senior post captains commanded third rates, whose primary role was, as battleships, to stand in the line to trade shot for shot, broadside for broadside with the enemy. As full-scale battles were something of a rarity, third rates usually did duty on blockade, sometimes as an inshore squadron serving as a link between the foremost frigates and the flagship and main fleet well back over the horizon. 74s were to be found escorting convoys, and they also formed the bulk of the more important detached squadrons around the colonies. They were to be seen in the West Indies, basking in the sunshine of Carlisle Bay, Barbados or English Harbour at Antigua. Or perhaps they might be disembarking boats filled with troops for an attack over an open beach on an enemy-held island. Others would take on, and probably overwhelm, shore batteries in a decidedly unequal gunnery duel. They formed the bulk of the fighting navy for all major maritime nations.

In 1804 there were thirteen 80-gun ships, ninety-four 74s and forty-two 64s in service. At Trafalgar, Nelson had one 80, the *Tonnant* (built in Toulon and captured at the Nile), sixteen 74s and two 64s, one of which was his former favourite command – the *Agamemnon*. The French deployed four 80s, one of which, the *Bucentaure*, wore the flag of the commander-in-chief of the

## Deck Arrangements of Main British Ships at Trafalgar

### Third Rate – *HMS Mars*, 74 guns

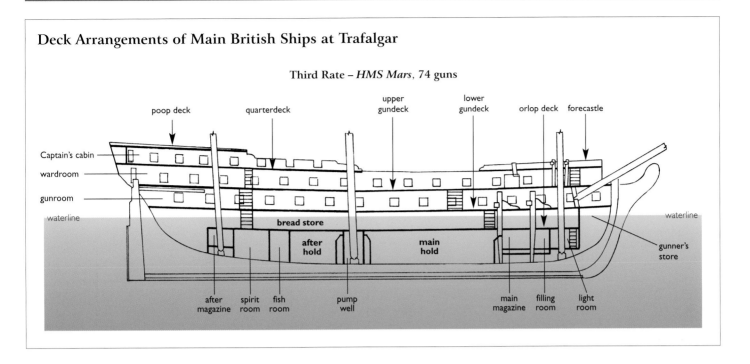

Combined Fleet, Vice-Admiral Villeneuve, and fourteen 74s. Their Spanish allies had two 80s, eight 74s and one 64. In both fleets the 74 predominated.

The 64s were, in practice, cut-down cheaper 74s. They lacked the firepower (carrying 24-pounders rather than 32) and sailing ability of the 74, but their lower cost made them useful in making up numbers in the squadrons that were scattered around the world. Although by the 1780s 64s were regarded as obsolete, they still made up a large proportion of the Royal Navy.

### Characteristics
• The two British 80-gun ships launched during the Revolutionary/Napoleonic Wars (*Caesar* and *Foudroyant*) were two-deckers, neither of which fought at Trafalgar. Until 1750 these ships had three decks, but as they proved unsuccessful they were largely replaced by 74s. However, the two-decker 80s were powerful ships with 32-pounders on the lower deck and 24-pounders on the upper, making them able to take on second rates or even first rates – for a while.
• The 74s were a great success, proving an ideal compromise between the conflicting need for good sailing qualities and maximum firepower. Their 1789 cost was almost £43,000 each, or about £28 per ton. There were two classes of British 74s, the Large Class and the Common Class, the main difference being in the weight of the guns on the upper deck – the former had 24-pounders, the latter 18-pounders. By the 1770s the Large Class consisted mainly of captured French ships or copies of them.
• The complement of these ships was between 500 and 600, their average speed in fair conditions five or six knots (6–7 mph). The large majority of the Common Class had twenty-eight 32-pounders on the lower deck and twenty-eight 18-pounders on the upper, plus eighteen 9-pounders on the forecastle and quarterdeck. This gave a single shot broadside of 781 lbs from the long guns.

### Construction
Three-masted, square-rigged two-deckers.

## FOURTH RATES (50–60 GUNS)
Formerly classed as ships-of-the-line, by the latter half of the eighteenth century these were badly out-gunned, forming a hybrid class of their own between battleships and frigates. However, the 50-gun ship, carrying 24-pounders on the lower deck, 12-pounders on the upper and 6-pounders on the quarterdeck and forecastle, had a revival in the 1770s as a patrol vessel or a squadron flagship in peacetime. They also proved useful in the North Sea or the Baltic where a shallow draft could be advantageous. Several 50-gun ships fought in the line at the turn of the century at Camperdown (*Isis* and *Adamant*), the Nile (*Leander*) and Copenhagen in 1801 (*Isis*). They were two-deckers, but with a gundeck of around 145 feet they were too stubby to make good sailers. In 1804 the Royal Navy had twenty-five fourth rates – thirteen 50s, seven 54s, three 56s and two 60s. None was present at Trafalgar on either side.

## FIFTH RATES (LARGE FRIGATES; 32–44 GUNS)
To command a frigate was the ambition of most commanders just promoted post captain. It presented them with a great deal of independence and the opportunity to make both their reputation and – they hoped – their fortune at the same time. As noted above, a frigate's duties were wide-ranging and exciting. They were the eyes and ears of the fleet or squadron and, as such, they were expected to navigate the shoals and narrows of the approaches to enemy harbours, under the guns of shore batteries, in order to count the ships hidden at anchor. They were expected to hunt out and fight enemy frigates. A frigate captain particularly relished a cruising role. His ship was faster than any ship-of-the-line in a light wind and could easily overhaul a merchantman in any weather. It was these latter vessels that were the desired prey of the cruiser, for their capture meant a generous allocation of prize money to the captain – with a pro-rata distribution to the crew.

## Deck Arrangements of Main British Ships at Trafalgar

### Fifth Rate – HMS Euryalus (frigate), 36 guns

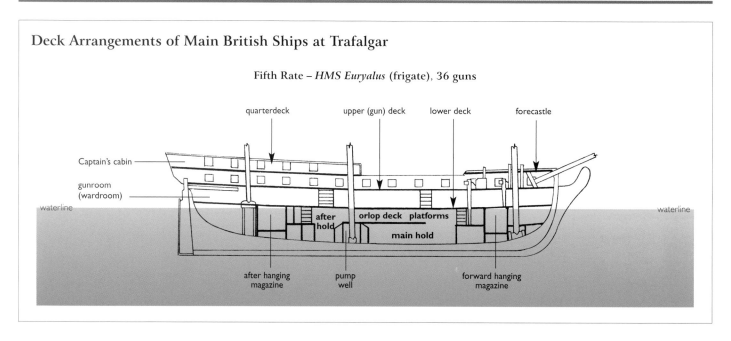

The frigate patrolled, escorted convoys and carried despatches. The only task not required of her was joining the fighting in a major battle, since her firepower and comparatively flimsy hull made her unfit to trade shots with a ship-of-the-line. A 38-gun frigate had only two-fifths the weight of broadside of a 74, and it was an unwritten rule that in a full-scale engagement a ship-of-the-line would not open fire on a frigate – unless provoked. Thus the frigate *Euryalus* at Trafalgar, although in the thick of the action, repeating signals first for Nelson then for Collingwood, sustained no casualties or damage. The frigate's task in a chase was to hang onto the enemy, find out his strength and direction of sailing and signal them back to the main fleet. At a distance, with her hull down below the horizon, it was impossible to distinguish a frigate from a 74. The masts and sail plan were identical and the length was similar, so it was only when the distance closed and all the gunports were visible that a lookout could be certain what he had seen. Once battle was joined, the frigates kept out of the line on a flank, the better able to see what was happening and to repeat the flagship's signals. At Trafalgar the 38-gun *Naiad* and the 36-gun *Euryalus*, *Phoebe* and *Sirius* performed these duties for Nelson. Villeneuve had the 40-gun *Cornélie*, *Hermione*, *Hortense* and *Rhin* plus the 32-gun *Thémis*. There were no Spanish frigates at the battle.

Nelson never seemed to have enough frigates. When chasing round the Mediterranean searching for the French expedition to Egypt, he almost exploded with exasperation, declaring, 'Frigates! Were I to die this moment, want of frigates would be engraved on my heart!' Although at the height of the wars the main strength of the Royal Navy was in third-rate 74s and fifth-rate frigates, the latter suffered few losses. Throughout twenty-two years of hostilities only three frigates foundered at sea. During the same period the British lost seventeen to the French (of which nine were recaptured), whereas the French lost 229 to the British – a ratio of one to thirteen.

### Characteristics

These ships were three masted and square rigged, with a speed of two or three knots faster than most higher rates, and a top speed in ideal conditions of twelve or thirteen knots (15 mph). With one

notable exception (the 44-gun ship), they had their main armament on the upper 'weather' deck, with the accommodation (except for the captain) on what was, on higher rates, the gundeck below. This arrangement meant the gun ports were well over five feet above the waterline, enabling the ship to keep her ports open and guns firing when heeling over in quite heavy seas. Frigates could sail better in light winds and make better progress to windward than larger ships. The more junior post captains commanded them, with a crew of 200 to 300. By the 1790s there was still no standard gun arrangement for British frigates. Many were comparatively weak in terms of firepower in comparison with the French equivalent – the French 18-pounders outclassed the British 12-pounders. However, as the wars progressed, the Royal Navy up-gunned many of their ships, thus ending up with something of a hotchpotch of six different types:

• 32-gun frigates with twenty-six 12-pounders on the upper deck and six 6-pounders on the quarterdeck (none at Trafalgar)

• 32-gun frigates with twenty-six 18-pounders and six 6-pounders or carronades on the quarterdeck (such as the French *Thémis* at Trafalgar; there were no British ships of this class at the battle)

• 36-gun ships with twenty-six 18-pounders on the upper deck and eight 6- or 9-pounders (or 32-pounder carronades) on the upper works (the British *Euryalus*, *Phoebe* and *Sirius* were the only 36-gun frigates at Trafalgar)

• 38-gun frigates (many captured from the French). The only difference from the 36-gun type was the additional two guns on the upper deck (the British *Naiad*, which was copied from the French, was the only ship of this type at Trafalgar)

• 40-gun frigates. These were few in number, and a high proportion were razees – ships that had had a deck removed in order to reduce them to a lower rate with fewer guns (such as the French *Hermione* at Trafalgar)

• 44-gun ships, an older type with two decks carrying guns. Twenty 18-pounders were on the lower deck, twenty-two 12-pounders on the upper deck and two 6-pounders on the forecastle. These frigates had occasionally worn the flag of an admiral or commodore of a small squadron in peacetime, but by the 1790s they were most frequently used as transports or troopships rather than warships (none at Trafalgar).

## SIXTH RATES (SMALL FRIGATES; 20–28 GUNS)

Three masted and square rigged with guns on the upper deck and forecastle, these were smaller versions of the fifth rate, commanded by a junior post captain. The most common was the 28-gun ship. Their problem was the lightness of their armament, as 9-pounders were just too light to take on even a 32-gun frigate. Nelson gained his experience as a junior post captain in the *Hinchinbrooke*, *Albemarle* and *Boreas*, all 28-gun ships, which he commanded in turn for a period of five years around the sunshine islands of the Caribbean. There were also a handful of 20-, 22- and 24-gun ships called 'post ships' as they were still a post captain's command, but too small and lightly armed (with 9-pounders only) to do much more than protect coastal convoys. They did, however, prove useful in anti-invasion duties or amphibious operations where their shallow draft (15 feet) enabled them to come close inshore. A good example is the 24-gun *Ariadne,* which did useful service with Sir Home Popham's attack on Ostend in 1798 and against Napoleon's invasion flotilla in 1805.

### Key Characteristics of Typical British Ships-of-the-line and Frigates in 1805

| Rate | Weight (burthen)* | Guns | Crew | Length (gundeck) | Breadth (extreme) | Draft |
|---|---|---|---|---|---|---|
| 1st (*Victory*) | 2,162 | 102 | 850 | 186ft | 51ft 10in | 24ft 5in |
| 3rd (*Conqueror*) | 1,842 | 74 | 650 | 176ft | 48ft 2in | 20ft 10in |
| 5th (*Euryalus*) | 946 | 36 | 250 | 145ft | 38ft | 19ft |

*Burthen: old builder's tonnage.

## UNRATED SHIPS (UP TO 18 GUNS)

There were a host of unrated ships and vessels, including two types of sloop, two types of brigs, bomb vessels, fireships, schooners, cutters and gunboats. At Trafalgar the British Fleet had the 10-gun schooner *Pickle* and the 12-gun cutter *Entreprenante*, while the French had two brigs, the 16-gun *Argus* and the 18-gun *Furet*. Sloops-of-war were commanded by officers of the rank of commander; brigs, cutters, schooners and others were normally commanded by senior lieutenants.

# THE CONSTRUCTION PROCESS

## WHO BUILT THE BEST SHIPS?

If there is any truth in the saying 'imitation is the highest form of flattery', then the answer to this question during most of the latter half of the eighteenth century was probably the French or Spanish. By 1800 the British shipbuilders had copied many of the French features or were using captured French or Spanish ships. At Trafalgar three of Nelson's 74s were formerly French (*Belleisle*, *Spartiate* and *Tonnant*), as was the solitary cutter present (*Entreprenante*). The *Tonnant* was said to be 'the finest two-decker ever seen in the Royal Navy', while the frigate *Egyptienne* taken in 1800 was 'the finest ship of one deck we ever had'. A few early English shipbuilding disasters included the *Deptford,* built under the supervision of the Surveyor of the Navy and thus expected to be a huge success, which was soon found to be so unstable and heavy that the number of her guns had to be cut from 60 to 50. Even this did not prevent her hurried abandonment as a hulk. The 60-gun *Pembroke*, launched a year before Nelson was born, was so deficient that she became known as the 'Carpenter's Mistake', and also ended her limited life at sea as a hulk. One ship was so lopsided when launched that 35 tons of ballast were needed to bring her upright. Even the *Victory,* when she first slid slowly into the water at Chatham in 1765, had her lower-deck gunports too low above the waterline – a mere 3 feet 11 inches instead of the required 6 feet (unloaded) – despite being designed by Sir Thomas Slade, who was to be Surveyor of the Navy for sixteen years and whose ship designs were often adaptations of the French. In contrast the Spanish *San Josef,* even with six months' stores in her hold, had 5 feet 4 inches of timber between her lowest gunport and the sea. Spain had the services of an Irishman called Mullins, who proved himself to be a shipwright of genius. In Britain heavy dependence was placed on copying.

Examples of direct copying of French ships were the 74s *Northumberland* and *Superb*: the former, built at Deptford, was a copy of the *Imperieux,* the latter of the *Pompée*. The frigates *Minerva,* *Phaeton* and *Latona*, regarded as superb sailers by their English captains, all owed their qualities to the copying of plans of captured French frigates. The real puzzle for British shipbuilders came with the discovery that the French seemed able to produce 80-gun ships that were longer and narrower than some British ships with 100 guns. The French third-rate *Juste* with 80 guns was 193 feet on the gundeck – 7 feet longer than the 102-gun *Victory*. Because the *Juste* was longer and narrower, she was also faster. At about the same time, in the 1790s, it was established that 80-gun French ships had higher masts than 100-gun British ones (with some 4 feet extra on the lower masts). So the answer appeared to be longer, narrower ships with taller masts. What was baffling was that some Spanish ships seemed to contradict this simple rule of thumb. In 1797 it was discovered that two Spanish 74s, known to be good sailers, taken at the Battle of Cape St Vincent, were only 179 and 176 feet on the gundeck. This was substantially shorter than the French *Juste*'s 193 feet and the British *Caesar*'s 181. They were shorter and broader in the beam – positively stubby – but could still sail well. Building a sailing ship, it seemed, was an art much more than a science!

## DESIGN

A warship designer was forever solving conflicting requirements by compromise, and for this he needed considerable experience and knowledge of the qualities or deficiencies of existing ships. For the Royal Navy, design was the responsibility of the Surveyors of the Navy, of whom the best known is Sir Thomas Slade, who drew the lines of the *Victory*. In practice, the Admiralty or Navy Board approved the basic requirements of a new ship in terms of length of gundeck, number of guns to be carried, maximum breadth and depth in hold. It was usual for a Surveyor of the Navy to have overall responsibility of the plan – which he signed. It was then for senior shipwrights to supervise the construction of the ship. A sailing warship had several crucial needs:

## A stable gun platform

Warships were built and sailed in order to fight and threaten. Ships of the first three rates in particular had to carry a heavy armament – the total weight of metal on *Victory*'s three gun-decks was some 206 tons. For stability it was desirable to keep the centre of gravity of the ship low, so the heaviest guns (British 32-pounders) had to be on the lower deck, which in turn had to be as low as possible. However, it was even more important to keep the lower-deck gunports well above the water level. A three-decker that had to keep her lower gunports shut in heavy seas or when rolling badly was effectively reduced to a two-decker if forced to fight in these circumstances. The aim was to have six feet between the lower edge of the lower gun-deck ports and the sea, but most ships had to be satisfied with something over five feet.

## To carry sail well

The ship had to be able to carry maximum sail without loss of control. Masts had to be of the right proportion to her upper works. Of real significance was the ship's ability to sail close to the wind (close-hauled) without making too much leeway (being pushed sideways). The designer had to decide whether a ship should be best in heavy weather and strong winds or in a light breeze – few could sail well in both conditions.

## To steer well

In other words, she should react quickly to rudder changes when the wheel was operated. This was critical when she needed to come about (turn round) or tack. The safety of the ship depended on being able to tack quickly, often when faced with a head wind and the need to navigate through a narrow channel or beat out to sea away from rocks on a lee shore.

## To be able to take punishment – from the enemy and the weather

To withstand enemy fire and absorb cannon shot, at least at the longer ranges, a ship required thick, heavy timbers in the hull. Heavy seas and violent winds could be as dangerous as enemy gunfire if a ship was poorly built. The ship had to rise to meet oncoming waves in a heavy sea rather than burying her bows. Neither pitching or rolling, or the stomach-churning corkscrewing motion that is a combination of the two when a ship's course is oblique to the waves, should put undue stress on the hull or masts. While rolling and corkscrewing are often more noticeable and decidedly more unpleasant for passengers and crew, it was pitching that was more liable to hurt the wooden walls in Nelson's day. The main strains put on a ship's structure by pitching were of two types. 'Hogging' occurs when the centre of the ship is supported by a wave while the two ends are in the air and tend to droop. 'Sagging' takes place when the ends are supported but the centre is not. Alternate hogging and sagging is called 'working'. As an example, the 74-gun *Kent* at one time was found to have drooped at the ends by 17 inches both fore and aft due largely to having a lower gundeck of 181 feet – some 5 feet longer than the average for that rate of ship. The main strain was amidships, and the groaning and protesting timbers were clearly audible in wooden vessels. If the strain was severe and prolonged and

---

## The Shipbuilding Yard at Buckler's Hard

Not all warships were built in navy yards. Probably the best known private yard was Buckler's Hard on the Beaulieu River in Hampshire, conveniently situated near the oaks of the New Forest. In 1743 the shipbuilding firm of Wyatt and Company took over a piece of land measuring 170 feet deep with a frontage of 40 feet at Buckler's Hard. 'Hards' were patches of sand or gravel that were convenient for shipbuilders, for which they paid an annual rental of six shillings and eight pence. Two years later the company's first ship, the 24-gun frigate *Surprise*, was launched. A Mr Henry Adams became the Master-Shipwright at the yard – a post he retained for the next fifty years. He lived until the year of Trafalgar, by which time he had reached the great age of ninety-two. He would have been proud to know that three of his ships fought well at that famous victory – the 64-gun *Agamemnon* (according to Nelson 'the finest 64 in the Service'), the 74-gun *Swiftsure* and the 36-gun frigate *Euryalus*. Most ships constructed at the yard were fifth or sixth rates with the occasional 64, however in 1789 the yard launched a 74 – the *Illustrious*.

This was the largest ship built by Adams. The launch was celebrated in regal style – the King and Queen went in state to nearby Beaulieu to stay with Lord Montagu. On the day of the launch the royal couple proceeded down river in the state barge to the Hard, and on their arrival the *Illustrious*, still on the slipway, fired a 21-gun royal salute. Unfortunately, the *Illustrious'* career, belying her name, was short and disappointing. In action with the French off Toulon in 1795 she was sufficiently badly damaged to need a tow. During a sudden storm the tow broke and the

*Illustrious* limped to an anchorage in Valence Bay to ride out the weather. This time her anchor cable parted and all efforts to save her failed; eventually the captain was forced to order the ship set on fire to prevent her being driven ashore and captured. The crew was saved but the ship burnt down to the waterline and her back was broken by exploding gunpowder before she sank.

Apart from the *Agamemnon*, probably the most famous ship built at the Hard was the 24-gun *Pandora*. Launched in 1779, she was sent out in search of the *Bounty* and those of her mutinous crew who cast Captain Bligh and eighteen of his crew adrift in the ship's boat. Captain Valentine Edwards of the *Pandora* ran the fourteen mutineers to ground in Tahiti and arrested them. They were placed in a special roundhouse that had been constructed on the quarterdeck – called, inevitably, Pandora's Box. On the homeward voyage the *Pandora* was wrecked in the Torres Strait between Australia and New Guinea. But for the action of a seaman in assisting the prisoners to get free of their leg irons, all would have drowned (four drowned anyway, along with thirty of the ship's company).

The *Repulse*, a small Revenue cutter, was the fifty-second and last ship to be launched from Buckler's Hard in 1818 after over seventy years of building 'wooden walls'. The last few years at the Hard had been difficult as after old Henry Adam died his sons became over-ambitious, contracted to build four ships simultaneously, failed to deliver them on time and unwisely went into litigation when the Admiralty refused to accept the delay. The brothers lost the case and with it their money, thus bringing to a sad close the activities of one of England's most famous shipbuilding yards.

## Corruption and Fraud in the British Navy Yards

Fraud, theft and negligence were rife in many yards. For a ship to leave port after a refit in more or less the same condition as when she went in was not unknown. Nelson, writing in December 1803, said of the 74-gun *Excellent* that had just arrived from England, 'It is much to be lamented that a ship ... coming direct abroad from a king's yard should have sailed in such a state. The master attendant at Portsmouth must either have been blind to the situation of the rigging, or not to have given himself trouble to discover its miserable state.' To her captain he was more forthright: 'It was shameful for the dockyard to send a ship to sea with such rigging.'

Cheating and stealing were commonplace in the public service, but seemingly the Navy gave its employees more and bigger opportunities. In July 1801 copper merchants in London were condemned for 'knowingly having in their possession certain naval stores (copper nails, etc) marked with the broad arrow [government mark]'. The actual amount seemed small, but in his speech for the prosecution the attorney-general said, 'The jury would hear with astonishment, but it was a fact capable of the strictest proof, that the depredations upon the king's naval stores did not annually amount to less than £500,000.' In 1803 the *Naval Chronicle* commented, 'The loss sustained by the public during the course of the late war, in consequence of the peculation or negligence of its servants in the naval departments, is said to have amounted to no less than twenty millions.'

Two typical instances of dishonesty are worth noting: 'the keys of the victualling storehouses at Portsmouth have been entrusted to improper persons, and particularly to John Freeborne, the foreman of labourers, who had access to the stores at all hours,' and in partnership with the storekeeper's clerk, 'kept hogs in the storehouse, and that these were fed with the king's serviceable biscuit'. Freeborne also kept a shop in town that did a good trade in mops and brooms – all filched from Navy stores. A Parliamentary Committee in 1783 stated that, 'from an examination of accounts it appears in 1780 there were deficient in Portsmouth alone, 27,8042 lbs. of bread; 9,672 bags of bread; 11,162 pieces of beef; 4,649 pieces of pork; 3,748 lbs. of flour, and 2,798 pieces of suet; besides considerable deficiencies in other species of victualling stores'.

All this was in a large measure due to the mistaken policy of the government, which considered it a prudent economy to miserably underpay its officials and then permit them to eke out their salaries by 'fees' and 'gifts'. Thus, for example, the Chief Clerk in the Navy Office in 1783, on a salary of £250 a year, received no less than £2,500 in 'gifts'.

---

if the ship was old or poorly constructed, seams would open up, causing, in extreme situations, the ship to founder. It has been calculated that a hole of just one square inch deep below the waterline would admit about 30 tons of water an hour.

*To maintain a good speed*

A fair speed for a third rate was six to eight knots with a favourable wind. Speed was more important for frigates than for ships-of-the-line, as the formers' duties required them to overhaul merchantmen, carry despatches or escape from a superior enemy. All sailors liked a fast ship but some speed usually had to be sacrificed for more critical characteristics.

## PLANNING

Before a new British ship could be built, the Admiralty had to authorize its construction and set out the basic specifications – for example, 74 guns, gundeck length 176 feet, beam 48 feet, depth in hold (depth of hull below lower deck) 24 feet. The actual design and drawing up of the plan was the responsibility of the Surveyors of the Navy (members of the Navy Board) who, at this time, were two elderly gentlemen called John Henslow and William Rule, who had joined the service in 1745 and 1758 respectively. Often, if it was not a direct copy or close adaptation of a French ship, the plan was a joint effort between them. A surveyor might draw the plans himself or delegate to one of the three skilled draughtsmen on the staff of the Navy Board. However, one surveyor would normally sign the plans and directly supervise the construction. When completed, the main plan (four views of the ship on one sheet of paper on a scale of 1:48) went to the Admiralty and Navy Board to be given the rubber stamp of approval. It was then copied by placing sheets of paper under the original and then pricking through the plan before laboriously joining up the tiny holes on the blank sheets –

rather like a giant children's puzzle whereby dots are joined to reveal a picture.

The plans then went to the dockyard where the ship was to be built. There were fifty-one government and fifty-nine private yards in southern England, concentrated at Plymouth, Solent, Medway, and the Thames. The main French dockyards were at Brest, Rochefort and Toulon, while Spain had Ferrol, Corunna, Santander and Cartagena, with a large overseas yard at Havana, Cuba, where the huge *Santisima Trinidad* was built. At the yard the plans of the ship were drawn out full size on the vast floor of what was called the mould loft. This was carried out by a master shipwright and was known as 'lofting'. From these drawings moulds, or patterns, were made of thin pieces of wood, which in turn were used as master templates for cutting out parts of the actual framework of the ship. The ship itself would be built on 'stocks' on a slipway leading down to the water.

## TIMBER

Until the introduction of ironclad ships, large stocks of timber were as essential to the economy of maritime nations as oil is today. Britain had to maintain a huge merchant fleet as well as a large navy, and so timber not only secured Britain's shores from invasion but was also essential for her economic growth. The rapid expansion of her overseas empire, the demands of war for more ships for the navy and dwindling forests meant that much timber, particularly for masts, had to be imported.

During the Seven Years War (1756–63), timber had accounted for a sixth of British imports, mostly from Prussia, Russia and, to a lesser extent, the American colonies. During the French Revolutionary War, Britain undertook a massive shipbuilding programme. The rush to build meant that many ships were constructed from unseasoned wood that quickly dried out and shrank, thus necessitating repair or rebuilding – which in

## Timber-shaped Oak Required in Ship Construction

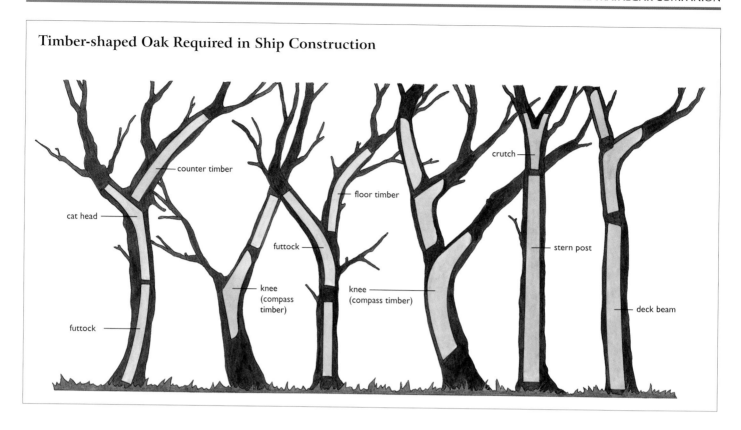

turn increased demand. Soon home-grown supplies were almost exhausted, and there was a critical shortage of 'compass' timber – wood with a natural curve in it essential for hulls. During the Peace of Amiens, timber stocks were allowed to dwindle to less than a year's supply, funding was cut, dockyard workers laid off and contracts cancelled. The resumption of the war in 1803 found the Navy in a parlous state. Not until the following year, after a change of government, did the situation begin to improve. As contracts were renewed and supplies became available, the building programme gathered momentum but, as it took about three years to build a 74, the initial emphasis was on repairing ships in reserve and getting them to sea. Fresh timber stocks allowed thirty-nine ships to be fitted out in the two years prior to Trafalgar. Of the twenty-seven ships-of-the-line in Nelson's fleet at the battle, all but four had undergone major repairs in the previous two years. The 100-gun *Royal Sovereign* sailed just six weeks prior to Trafalgar, having had £60,000 worth of repairs completed in eight weeks – a clear indication of the urgency of the situation.

Not all timber was suitable for ships. There was an insatiable demand for two types – oak for hulls and pine (fir) for masts and spars. Vice-Admiral Collingwood, who commanded the lee column at Trafalgar, made a point of making a personal contribution to the future of Britain's oak supply. Every time he went for a walk from his home in Yorkshire, he took a pocket full of acorns and, when he saw an appropriate spot, pressed one into the soil. Some of these acorns may now be 200-year-old oaks. For hundreds of years the oak tree was an all-important raw material for any maritime nation. The hull of the *Victory* required some 6,000 unshaped oak trees, which at around 60 trees to the acre represented 100 acres of forest. As a rule of thumb, every long gun represented one acre of oaks. On this basis the amount of timber in the ships-of-the-line of both fleets at Trafalgar is staggering.

| British Fleet | Ships | Acres | Trees |
|---|---|---|---|
| | 3 x 100-gun | 300 | 18,000 |
| | 4 x 98-gun | 392 | 23,520 |
| | 1 x 80-gun | 80 | 4,800 |
| | 16 x 74-gun | 1,184 | 71,040 |
| | 3 x 64-gun | 192 | 11,520 |
| **Total** | **27** | **2,148** | **128,880** |
| **Combined Fleet** | | | |
| | 1 x 136-gun | 136 | 8,160 |
| | 2 x 112-gun | 224 | 13,440 |
| | 1 x 100-gun | 100 | 6,000 |
| | 6 x 80-gun | 480 | 28,800 |
| | 22 x 74-gun | 1,628 | 97,680 |
| | 1 x 64-gun | 64 | 3,840 |
| **Total** | **33** | **2,632** | **157,920** |
| **Grand Total** | **60** | **4,780** | **286,800** |

290,000 oak trees equates to approximately seven and a half square miles of forest felled to produce these sixty ships-of-the-line. The figures take no account of the timber that had been needed over the years in repairs to keep them at sea – possibly half as much again. It has been estimated that the Spanish Navy consumed over three million trees during the eighteenth century. Of course, not all the trees came from the same forest, or even region. Each nation tried to exercise tight control over felling and planting so that forests were conserved. It is of interest to examine the system of forestry employed by France for her navy – the British and Spanish only differed in the detail.

Since mediaeval times France had been passing laws to preserve a proportion of oak trees in forests for the King and the navy. Sixteen trees in every acre of coppice over 40 years, and ten in every acre of forest over 120 years, were reserved. In addition, no person was permitted to fell any tree within 15 leagues (45 miles) of the sea or six leagues (18 miles) of any navigable river. Reserved trees were 'hammered' – that is, a piece of bark close to the ground was removed with an axe and the official government mark was 'hammered' in. The hammer used was called the 'King's' hammer; on it was the *fleur-de-lys* surmounted by an embossed anchor, and the hammers were kept locked in a casket with three locks, the keys of which were kept by three different officials. The hammering was the task of Surveyors of the Navy, assisted by warrant or petty officers. The hammered trees were listed in a legal document and merchants with a felling contract were responsible for each tree and whether it was preserved or felled.

The French classified the oak timber according to whether it came from a coppice, a forest or a hedgerow. The coppice was a piece of land planted with younger trees, some of which were cut after a period of between eight and forty years. There was a careful conservation plan for these trees so that a proportion of each age group was always maintained. They tended to grow with more curved branches than other types and with heavier timber. Coppice timber represented what today might be called a medium-term investment. The long-term investment was the forest oak. In this type of woodland there were only mature trees classified according to age. 'Young' oaks were from fifty to eighty years old and 'full grown' from 100 to 300 years old. Because of the need for light and air, forest trees tended to grow straight and to a considerable height. However, due to the lack of light and dampness in the forest, their timber was somewhat fragile and consequently was only used for well-ventilated timber. The law allowed felling in these forests at intervals of 100 to 300 years. The third type of oak was that planted along the edge of fields, bordering roads or single isolated trees. These were known as 'hedgerow' oaks. They were probably the most prized by the navy, as their unrestricted growth led to large branches which yielded good 'knees' (see diagram opposite).

In France the oaks were felled in late autumn or early winter but not during frosty weather when the sap would freeze. The stumps were never pulled up despite the large roots yielding compass timber. Once felled, the timber was 'squared', i.e. cut up into logs by axe (saws were prohibited), and

## Shortage of Oak Timber in England

By 1806 the Royal Navy had a total tonnage of ships amounting to 776,000 tons. The amount of oak required to build and maintain so vast a fleet was staggering. In 1783 the House of Commons became so concerned that timber resources in England were running out that it instituted a survey of the country's forests. The object was to discover how many 'loads' were available – a load being 50 cubic feet (a ton was 40 cubic feet). About 800 loads equalled 1,000 tons. Six forests were surveyed and the results compared with a previous one carried out in 1608. The results were extremely alarming. Whereas in 1608 English forests had been able to produce 234,000 loads, capacity had now dropped to a miserable 50,000. Sherwood Forest had fallen from 31,000 to 2,000, the New Forest from 115,000 to 33,000. What was really frightening was that from the six forests there was only enough oak for about twenty-five to thirty ships-of-the-line. Put another way, the 50,000 loads available would only supply the timber needs of the Royal Navy and merchant fleet for one year. By 1791, two years after the start of the French Revolution, the actual annual consumption of timber for new building and repairs had risen to 385,000 loads (Royal Navy 218,000 and merchant fleet 167,000). Desperate needs led to desperate measures. English woodlands were combed and imports were dramatically stepped up from such places as Italy, Danzig, Holstein (a German province), Canada and America – although all these woods were, in varying degrees, acknowledged as much inferior to English oak.

## Nelson Oaks to Restore *HMS Victory*

At the time of writing, September 2004, oaks planted some 200 years ago on Nelson's recommendation have been felled to be used in the restoration of HMS *Victory* in time for the bicentenary of Trafalgar in 2005. In a report to Parliament about timber availability for warships, Nelson asked for the trees to be planted in the Forest of Dean, Gloucestershire, when he learned that many of its oaks had been plundered for charcoal. The two trees that have been felled will be collected by *HMS Victory*'s current commanding officer.

then the bark was removed. The timber was transported during the winter to the dockyards by floating or transportation by ship. At the dockyard the timber was preserved, usually by submerging in a river (as at Brest or Toulon) or by being kept in drying sheds (as at Rochefort). Timber that has absorbed water must be given time to dry out before use. Unless it was possible to move the logs by water, the cost of transportation could become prohibitive. This was the reason, in England in particular, that large quantities of timber needed to be imported. Indeed, the need to import was the reason why Britain was always anxious to keep the Baltic open.

Oak was supposed to be seasoned for up to fifteen years before use, but due to the unprecedented demands of a long war, shortcuts were inevitably taken. These involved using unseasoned timber, some suspect types of foreign timber and pine in hulls. A notorious example in Britain was the 100-gun *Queen Charlotte*, launched at Deptford in 1810. Despite previous bad experience, she was built, except for the frame timbers, of Canadian oak and pine. Without ever having been on service, she was badly infested with dry rot within a year. Incredibly, having uselessly occupied dock space at Plymouth for eighteen months, she was virtually dismantled and rebuilt – with the same kind of timber!

There were alternatives to oak. Elm was sometimes used (for the *Victory*'s keel, for instance) but it was not satisfactory for hulls. Pine was used frequently by the British in the early 1800s to build frigates and sloops, of which, as noted by Nelson in the Mediterranean, Britain was so desperately short. They did not last – a number were condemned for firewood in as little as three years – and were found to be unpopular and a false economy. The only hardwoods that could outlast oak were teak and mahogany. Teak was common in India, and after 1801 a number of excellent ships were built of teak in Indian dockyards at Bombay and Calcutta. Spain used teak and mahogany from the unlimited supplies available from her colonies in Cuba and Central America. However, it was found that teak suffered from one serious drawback: like other timber, it shattered into splinters when hit by cannon balls, and wounds caused by these splinters tended to become septic, often killing the victim, whereas wounds from oak splinters were not so liable to become infected in this way.

## Ship Construction – Keel and Frame

### The frame (ribcage) of a small ship

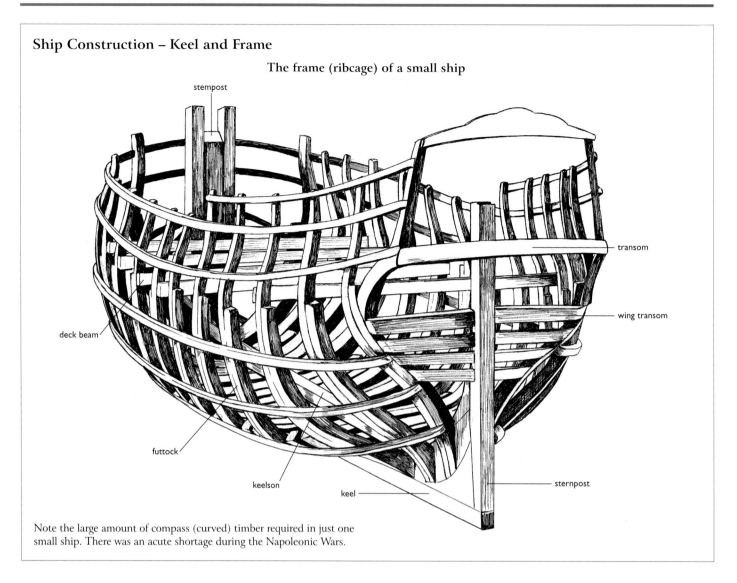

Note the large amount of compass (curved) timber required in just one small ship. There was an acute shortage during the Napoleonic Wars.

Pine trees were regarded as the best for masts and spars. Pine is a softwood which is flexible, elastic and light, all qualities needed for ship's masts and yards. France had only limited resources. The Pyrenees and Corsica supplied some, but reliance was placed on imports from the vast forests of Poland, Lithuania, Norway and Russia. The French shipbuilders especially prized the pine from the forests of Ukraine, which was floated down the Dwina River and sold at Riga. It was purchased by navy contractors, who then arranged transportation to the dockyards where master mast-makers checked the quality. Trees were stripped of their bark and 'topped', a process that involved exposing both ends of the log with an axe 'in order to *taste* the grain, which should be fine, and filled with resin, which ought to be reddish and shiny, and smell of dilute turpentine – all signs of an excellent quality'. The French reserved the best timber for the topmasts of first rates. The mast-wood was stored submerged in mast-ponds to prevent it drying out and losing its resin. Both seawater and fresh water were used. The former was regarded as the best but there was a risk of it being attacked by worm.

As many as forty pine trees were required to make the twenty-two masts and yards of a single 74. First rates had more (the *Victory* twenty-eight). On the basis of this figure, the masts and yards of the two fleets at Trafalgar represented some 3,000 pine trees.

## CONSTRUCTION

Although there were variations in technique from country to country the basic principles were the same at whatever dockyard a ship was built.

### Keel and Frame

The keel was laid first. It needed to be absolutely straight (so it was made from elm rather than oak) and was normally constructed from up to eight pieces of overlapping 'scarphed' (joined) timbers. Below it was a thinner, false keel designed to give protection to the main keel if the ship ran aground or scraped rocks. At the stern, sloping aft at about ten degrees from the vertical, was the sternpost – usually made from the trunk of a single oak tree. It was strongly reinforced by a false sternpost and internal knee. At the bow was the stempost, curved in shape and made of several pieces of timber scarphed together. Forward of the stempost was the knee of the head, which formed a cutwater and supported the ship's figurehead.

It was not possible to make the frames (ribs) of a ship from single pieces of timber, so several were joined together. Called futtocks, they were curved to form the framework on which to fix the hull timbers and cross beams that supported the decks. The frames curved up from the keel in pairs. When all in position, they gave the familiar brandy-glass shape to a cross section of the hull. Alternatively, at this stage the ship could be likened to the ribcage of some huge prehistoric monster. The frames that ran from the keel to the top of the ship's sides were known as full frames and were fitted first. The remainder, known as filling frames, were fitted above and below the gunports.

## Decks

The deck beams had to be slightly curved to allow water to run off the surface, and they had to be of thick solid oak, strong enough to carry the weight of thirty cannons. In ships-of-the-line they consisted of several pieces scarphed together and ran athwartships (across the hull at right angles from the sides). Lighter pieces, known as carlines, ran fore and aft linking the beams. More, even lighter pieces were fixed athwartships between the carlines. On this framework the timber of the decks was secured in strakes (planks) that were two inches thick and a foot wide, running fore and aft. At the sides of the deck were waterways, thicker strakes positioned to keep deck water off the sides and channel it into the scuppers. Scuppers were apertures cut through the sides of the ship at deck level to allow boarding sea to drain over the side. The expression to 'be scuppered', meaning to be defeated, originally described a ship on the point of foundering with the sea coming in through the scuppers. The edges of the hatchways and gratings were surrounded by coamings (pieces of wood raised above deck level) to keep water swilling around on the deck from falling below.

### Construction Statistics of the *Bellerophon*

The 74-gun *Bellerophon* was a typical British third-rate ship-of-the-line that fought at Trafalgar. Her particulars were:

| | |
|---|---|
| Keel length | 138 feet |
| Gundeck length | 168 feet |
| Beam | 46 feet 10.5 inches |
| Displacement | 1,600 tons |
| Cost | £30,232 14s 4d |
| Guns | 74 |
| Trees required | 2,000 (50 acres) |
| Iron bolts | 100 tons |
| Copper bolts | 30 tons |
| Treenails | 30,000 |
| Copper sheets | 4,000 |
| Tar | 12 tons |
| Linseed oil | 400 gallons |
| Paint | 5 tons |
| Sails | 10,000 square yards of canvas |
| Shot | 80 tons |
| Gunpowder | 20 tons |
| Provisions | 200 tons |
| Fresh water | 260 tons |

## Planking

On the outside of the frames (ribs), extra-thick planks known as 'wales' were placed along the length of the hull under the gunports to provide additional strength. The hull consisted of planking between two and four inches thick held in place by treenails, pronounced trennels, which were round or octagonal pieces of oak driven into undersized holes in the planking, frames or other timbers. Metal bolts were used at the ends of each plank with the treenails in between. The hull was of double thickness, as it was also planked internally. When the planking was complete, the caulkers got to work hammering twists of cotton into the gaps between the planks. This was a long and tedious process.

## Decoration

The two features on rated ships that could be termed decorative were the stern galleries, or balconies (one for each deck), and the figurehead. The stern galleries were either open or closed with a row of windows and woodwork decorated with carved figures and elaborate paintwork. They enhanced the ends of the admiral's and captain's quarters with a touch of elegance, even opulence. However, although they looked fine, they were rightly deemed the soft and vulnerable 'underbelly' of any warship. A broadside into the stern turned the windows and woodwork into thousands of shards of flying glass and splinters, causing catastrophic casualties for those unfortunate enough to be nearby.

---

### Cleaning the Paintwork

Maintenance of high standards of cleanliness on board ship has always been a strong tradition in the Royal Navy. The phrase 'spick and span' originated from the nautical word 'spick', which was a nail, and 'span', which was a chip of wood just struck from a new piece of timber. A 'spick and span' ship was one in which every nail and piece of timber was as new. In Nelson's navy there was much daily drudgery in keeping everything clean, such as scrubbing decks and cleaning paintwork. A Lieutenant A.D. Fordyce produced a lengthy manuscript in the 1820s on the subject of commissioning and maintaining a warship. On the matter of cleaning the paintwork he wrote:

> Putting on the paint was a serious business, equally momentous was the task of keeping it clean. The best mode of doing this was to let a hand [seaman] wipe it round every morning with a clean soft rag, such as a piece of old hammock, and fresh water, directly after the decks were washed. When very dirty, however, other means were requisite. The best was

scrubbing with soap and hot water, but as this might be too expensive for the outside the next best is a mixture of wood ashes, vinegar and fresh water. In the first place the cook is ordered to save the ashes, which are then carefully separated from the cinders, next a quantity of vinegar sufficient to liquidate the ashes is poured over them, while five or six times that quantity of fresh water is added last of all. When well mixed the paintwork is to be scrubbed with it and with canvas rubbers, taking care that it be washed down promptly with plenty of salt water, a mop and scrub broom. If the washing and rinsing-down be delayed the mixture will speedily dry, be difficult to get off, and turn quite white. If all these methods fail, sand and water, with canvas rubbers, had better be used, but sand as fine as possible.

Cleaning paintwork was, unsurprisingly, a duty to be avoided. It would normally have been given to a 'landsman' or 'idler' – not to a trained seaman.

Figureheads were fixed high in the bows just under the bowsprit and were intended as a decorative emblem that usually represented some part of the ship's name or function. They had no practical purpose, hence the expression today that a leader without authority is 'only a figurehead'. Many sailors were superstitious men and often regarded damage to the figurehead of their ships as foretelling bad luck. At the Battle of the Glorious First of June in 1794 the 74-gun *Brunswick* had the Duke of Brunswick wearing a cocked hat as her figurehead. When the duke's hat was shot away, the crew were so upset that the captain gave the carpenter his own hat to nail on the hatless figure. Eyes were an important feature of figureheads due to the belief that a ship needed to be able to see her way around rocks or through dangerous shoals.

## Painting

Not until the 1790s did it become normal practice to paint the hull of warships. The colours most commonly used were yellow ochre, red and black or a combination of these. Captains had a say in the colour scheme adopted. At Trafalgar, Nelson's fleet had largely adopted the colours of the *Victory*. The bottom of her hull and the hull above each gundeck was black, while the hull between each gunport was yellow. The gunports were also black, so when shut the hull had a distinctive chequerboard appearance. This striking effect became famous, and following the battle, ships in these colours became known as 'Nelson's chequer players'. The ship's name was painted on the stern while the figurehead was frequently left white with the colouring done later according to the captain's wishes.

## Launching

The time taken to build a warship depended on many factors, not least the availability of timber, the degree of urgency and therefore priority. On average a sloop could be built in six months, a 74 in two to three years and a first rate in around seven or eight (although the *Victory* was completed in six). The day of launching was one of celebration. On 10 April 1781 the 64-gun *Agamemnon* was launched. Twelve years afterwards Nelson took command of her and wrote to his brother, 'My ship is, without exception, the finest sixty-four in the Service, and has the character of sailing most remarkably well.' On that April morning the *Agamemnon* was sitting on the slip at Buckler's Hard on the Solent with her stern towards the water. She was slightly higher in the bow than the stern, resting on a launching cradle which ran on wooden rails to the water, and she was held in position by wooden props. The shipbuilder, a Mr Adams, had chosen a high spring tide and informed the Admiralty of the date. A number of local dignitaries had been invited, but much of the crowd was made up of those workers involved in her construction, their families and the curious. At this stage the *Agamemnon* was still an empty shell. She was a hull, without masts, without copper on her bottom and without any fittings or stores. At the appointed time the props were knocked away and she began her slow slide into the Solent. Heavy ropes prevented her drifting away on the tide. The crowd cheered. Mr Adams watched anxiously as his ship settled in the water – accidents were far from unknown. All went well: she floated. So it was that Adams, with a tinge of relief as well as pride, was able to report a successful launch to the Admiralty and qualify for his final payment. Later the *Agamemnon* would be towed across to Portsmouth dockyard for her masts and fitting out.

## Masts and yards

All rated ships were square rigged or 'ship rigged', meaning they all had three masts with horizontal yards attached carrying square (rectangular) sails – they also had staysails but these were of secondary importance (see below, p. 85). As noted above, the masts and yards were made from fir trees for their flexibility. Even though all fir tree trunks were long and straight, after the loss of the American colonies with their ready supply of tall trees it became necessary to make masts in three separate components that were then joined together – a method copied from the French. Their actual construction was complex, with various shaped cross sections, tapering and for the lower sections long strengthening pieces known as fishes attached. Rope lashings or iron bands further reinforced these sections.

The masts (including the bowsprit) were, from the bow, bowsprit, foremast, mainmast and mizzenmast. However, each of the three vertical masts was divided into three sections or components. It was only the lowest sections, those passing through the deck to be stepped (secured) to the keel, that were actually called the foremast, mainmast or mizzenmast. The middle sections were, somewhat confusingly, 'topmasts', thus they were termed the foretopmast, maintopmast and mizzen-topmast. The upper sections were 'gallants', hence foretopgallant mast, maintopgallant mast and mizzen-topgallant mast.

The height and diameter of the masts varied with the size of the ship. The *Victory*'s lower main- and foremasts were three feet in diameter, her mizzen two feet. In a 74 the lower masts would rise to about 70 feet above the deck (the mainmast being slightly higher). Near the top of each lower mast was the 'fighting top' or just 'top' (foretop, maintop and mizzentop). These were platforms on which sharpshooters could be stationed in battle to pick off enemy on the decks of nearby ships – it was from the mizzentop of the *Redoutable* that Nelson received his mortal wound, as described in the Prologue. The topmasts were lighter and shorter, rising up to some 60 feet above the fighting tops. The third and highest extension of the masts were the topgallant masts, which on a 74 rose to around 155 feet above the deck. In a severe storm these topgallant masts were usually lowered to the deck.

The bowsprit was the mast that projected forward at an angle from the bow of the ship. A separate spar called a jibboom extended it and, on a first rate such as the *Victory*, a third spar called a flying jibboom could be attached if needed.

The spars holding the square sails were known as yards. They were octagonal in cross section near the centre and then circular as they tapered towards each end. The ends were known as yardarms – from which mutineers or others guilty of capital offences were sometimes hung. They could be made of one piece of timber or be several joined together. The mizzen could carry up to four yards plus a boom and gaff pointing aft to carry the mizzen sail or spanker. Additional smaller yards and booms could be attached to the main yards to extend them to carry studding sails in very light winds. Their names, working up from the deck and in decreasing length, were:

**foremast**: foremast yard, foretopmast yard, foretopgallant mast yard and, at the top if needed, a fore royal yard
**mainmast**: main yard, maintopsail yard, maintopgallant yard and main royal yard

## Maintop or Fighting Top

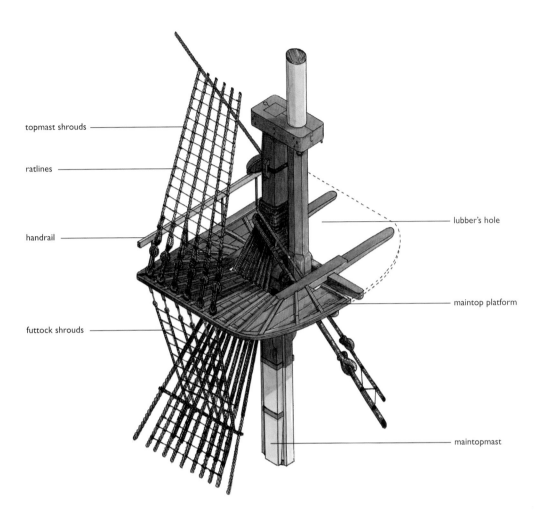

topmast shrouds

ratlines

handrail

futtock shrouds

lubber's hole

maintop platform

maintopmast

### Notes
- Topmen or able seamen would almost always use the futtock shrouds to climb onto the maintop. The lubber's hole was for those whose agility or head for heights was suspect, such as 'idlers' or marines.
- The tops were used as a platform on which to assemble the topmen before going out onto the yards or, in action, for sharpshooters to fire down onto enemy decks.
- The top had only one rail on the aft side and so was not a particularly secure place to stand while firing a musket.

**mizzenmast:** mizzen boom, mizzen gaff, crossjack yard, mizzen-topsail yard, mizzen-topgallant yard and mizzen royal yard
**bowsprit:** spritsail yard and sprit topsail yard.

### Rigging
A ship's rigging was extraordinarily complex, and 'getting to know the ropes' could take a long time and considerable practical experience. Officers and seamen had to tell the difference between jeers, lifts, halyards, braces, tacks, sheets, clewlines, bowlines, leechlines and brails – surely something of a young midshipman's nightmare. Without this knowledge a ship could not be sailed. The *Victory* had over 26 miles of rope in her rigging, all of which was divided into two groups, standing rigging and running rigging.

*Standing rigging*
This was permanent rigging used to support the masts in the same way guy ropes support a tent pole. Because they had to last a long time, all these ropes were coated in black tar. This rigging was further divided into shrouds, forestays and backstays. Each mast and each part (topmast, topgallant, etc.) had its own set of shrouds and stays. The shrouds ran from the lower masts (under the top) to the side of the ships and from the higher masts to the top or crosstrees of the mast below. Shrouds were joined by ratlines to make a rope ladder, enabling the seamen to climb to the tops and thence out along the yards (standing precariously on a footrope) to attend the sails. Forestays ran forward from each mast to meet another mast, the deck or the bowsprit. Backstays ran from the mast aft to the deck.

## Masts and Yards of Square-rigged Ships

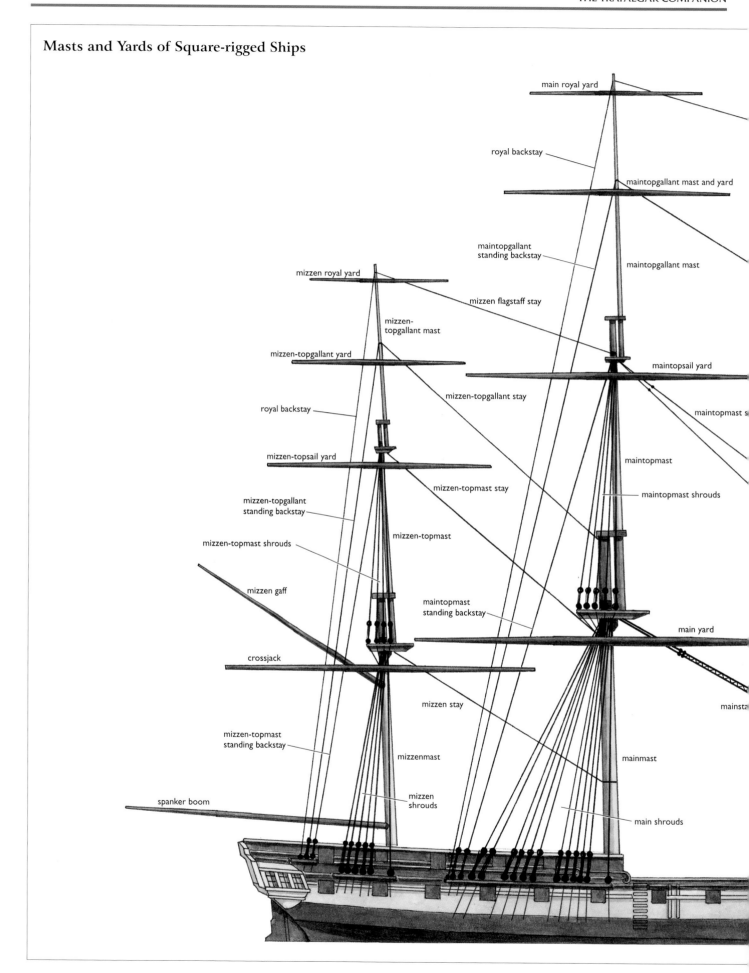

main royal yard

royal backstay

maintopgallant mast and yard

maintopgallant
standing backstay

maintopgallant mast

mizzen royal yard

mizzen flagstaff stay

mizzen-
topgallant mast

mizzen-topgallant yard

maintopsail yard

mizzen-topgallant stay

royal backstay

maintopmast s

mizzen-topsail yard

maintopmast

mizzen-topmast stay

maintopmast shrouds

mizzen-topgallant
standing backstay

mizzen-topmast

mizzen-topmast shrouds

maintopmast
standing backstay

mizzen gaff

main yard

crossjack

mizzen stay

mainsta

mizzen-topmast
standing backstay

mizzenmast

mainmast

spanker boom

mizzen
shrouds

main shrouds

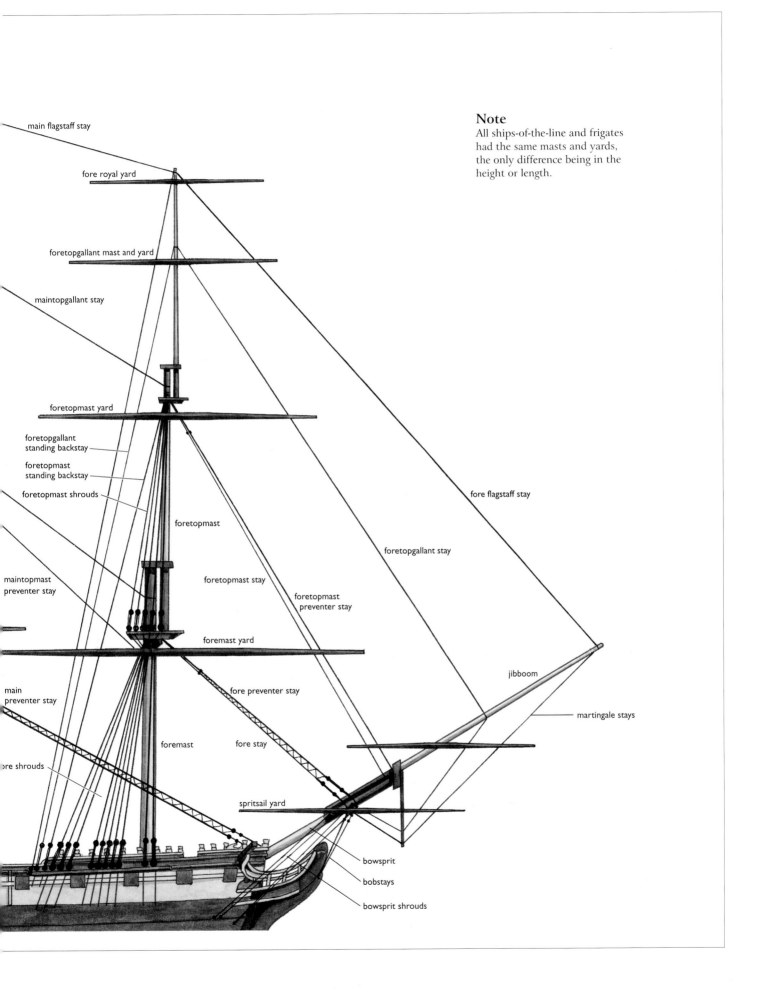

main flagstaff stay

fore royal yard

foretopgallant mast and yard

maintopgallant stay

foretopmast yard

foretopgallant
standing backstay

foretopmast
standing backstay

foretopmast shrouds

foretopmast

maintopmast
preventer stay

main
preventer stay

foremast

ore shrouds

**Note**
All ships-of-the-line and frigates
had the same masts and yards,
the only difference being in the
height or length.

fore flagstaff stay

foretopgallant stay

foretopmast stay

foretopmast
preventer stay

foremast yard

fore preventer stay

fore stay

spritsail yard

jibboom

martingale stays

bowsprit

bobstays

bowsprit shrouds

# Running Rigging

The box (right) shows a square sail
with all its ropes marked and labelled.

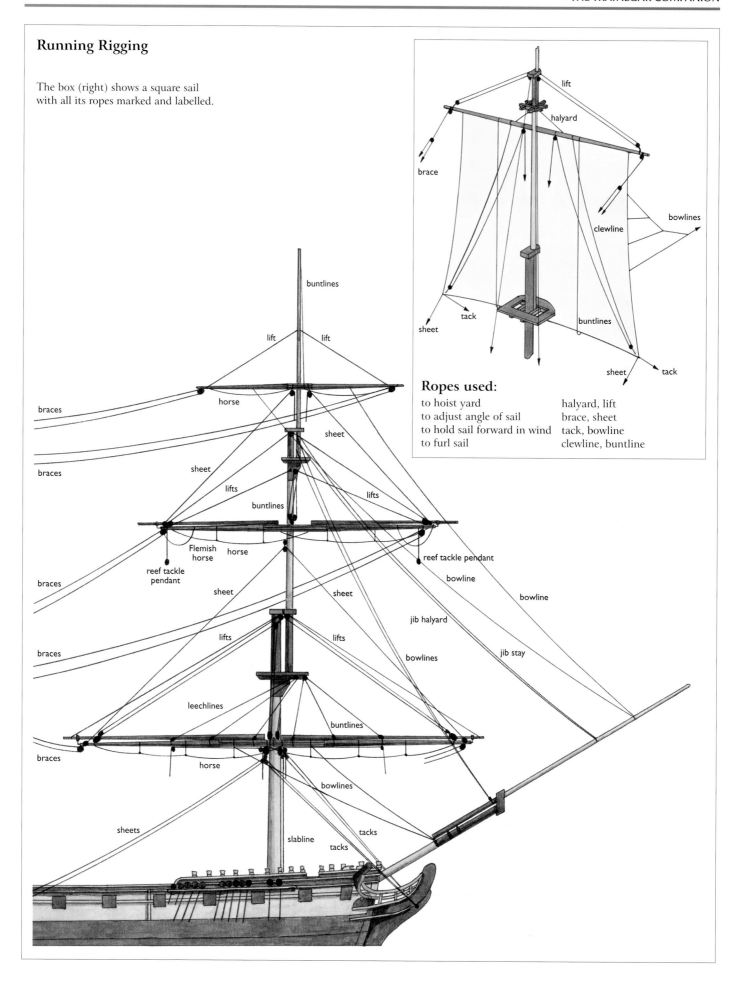

**Ropes used:**

| | |
|---|---|
| to hoist yard | halyard, lift |
| to adjust angle of sail | brace, sheet |
| to hold sail forward in wind | tack, bowline |
| to furl sail | clewline, buntline |

## Running rigging

This rigging comprised all the ropes (untarred) that were handled by the crew to turn the yards and operate the sails. Yards had to be turned (rotated) as far as possible round the mast to catch as much of the wind as possible from various directions. They had also to be raised or lowered as circumstances required. It was also running rigging that was used to set or furl the sails. To work this rigging required the use of hundreds (768 on the *Victory*) of wooden (ash, elm or beech) pulley blocks.

## Sails

Sailmaking in Nelson's day was a tiring, immensely tedious and poorly paid trade. A master sailmaker could expect £1 15s 0d a month, his mate £1 8s 0d and a sailmaker £1 5s 0d. Their weeks, months and often years were spent sewing long strips of canvas called bolts. Mills in Dundee, Dorset and Northern Ireland supplied the bolts, which were thirty-nine yards long and two feet wide. The *Victory* could set (carry) up to thirty-seven sails with a total area of nearly 5,500 square yards – equal to one and a third football pitches

– and at least another twenty replacement sails would be carried. To distinguish Royal Navy canvas a thin wavy blue line was painted down the centre of each bolt. The sails were cut and sewed for the *Victory* in a huge sail loft at Chatham. It required over 58,000 yards of seams to complete a set of her sails, and with twenty sailmakers each would have to sew over 2,900 yards of stitching – 35 yards a day for 83 days with rough, heavy canvas.

The sails were divided into two types: square, and fore and aft. The square sails were rectangular in shape and hung from the yards, while the fore and aft were triangular and set on stays between the masts or between foremast and boom or jib; hence they were known as staysails. The names of sails were related to the masts and yards to which they were set. For example, the sails on the mainmast were, from bottom to top, the main course, main-topsail, maintopgallant and main royal. Royals were only set in light winds, like those during the approach to battle at Trafalgar, as were studding sails. Studding sails were only rigged on the fore- and mainmasts. They were rectangular in shape and were set in pairs on booms that extended on either side of the yards.

## A Foretopsail

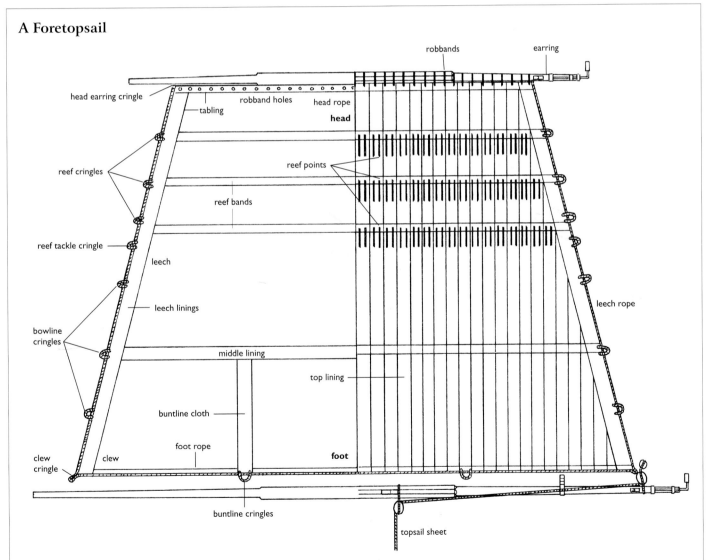

## Note

This diagram is included to show the complexity of one sail. There are 24 different parts, each of which had its own specific function and had to be understood by all able seamen and most petty officers and officers.

Selected Sails, Square Rig

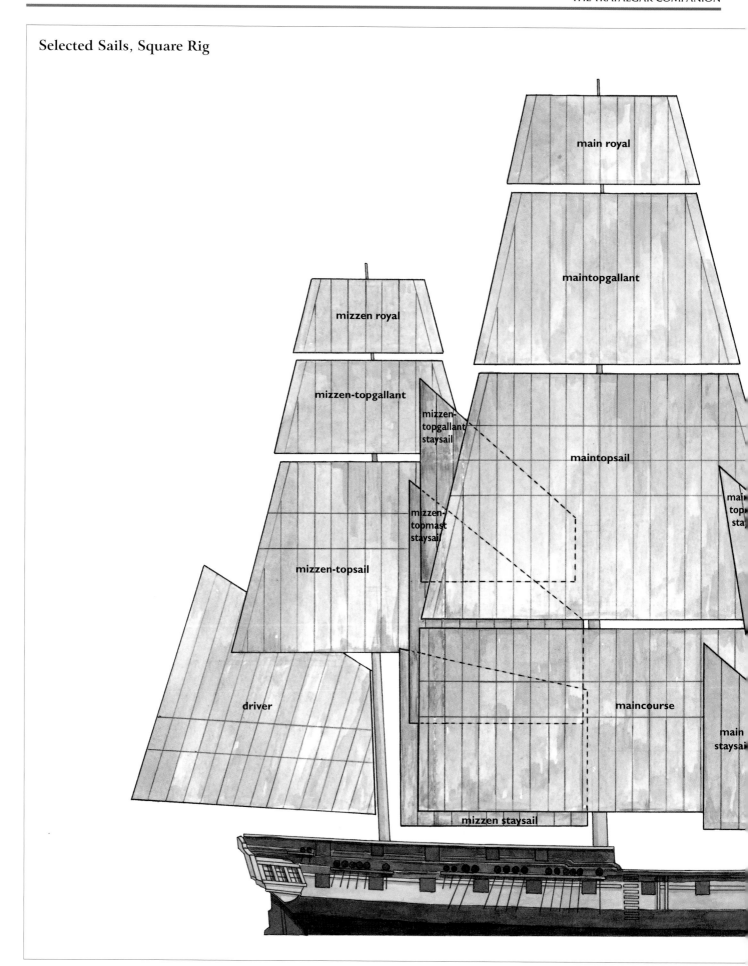

main royal

maintopgallant

mizzen royal

mizzen-topgallant

mizzen-
topgallant
staysail

maintopsail

mai
top
sta

mizzen-
topmast
staysail

mizzen-topsail

driver

maincourse

main
staysai

mizzen staysail

**Note**
Smaller versions of each staysail, known as storm staysails, were used in bad weather. They were as small as possible to keep the ship under way without completely losing control in a 'driving' (strong) wind.

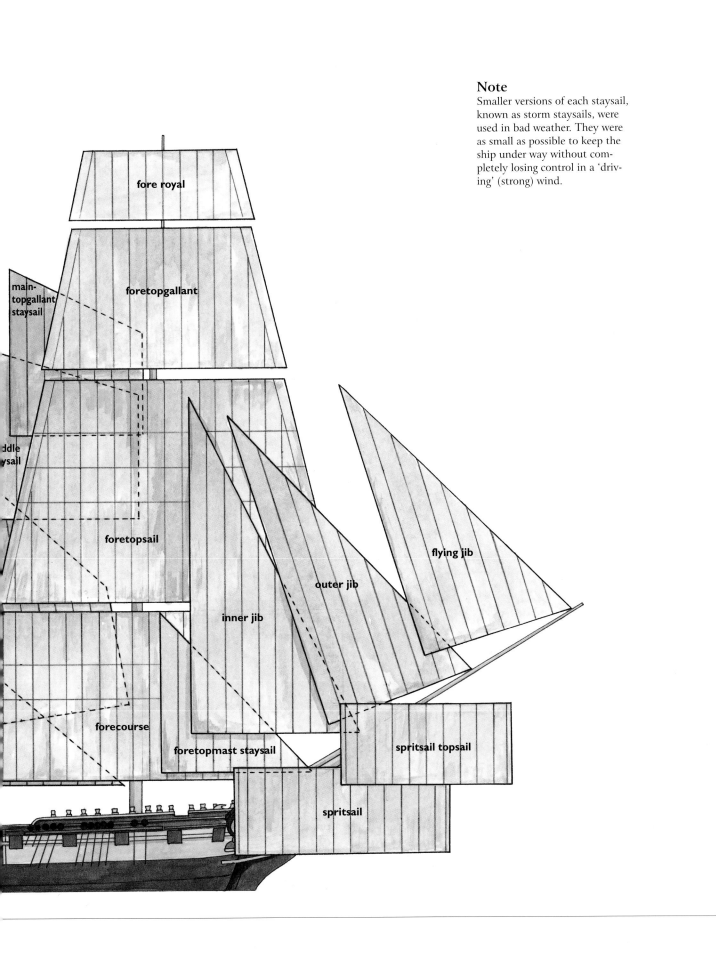

fore royal

main-
topgallant
staysail

foretopgallant

ddle
ysail

foretopsail

flying jib

outer jib

inner jib

forecourse

foretopmast staysail

spritsail topsail

spritsail

## Coppering the ship's bottom

The expression 'copper bottomed' has come to mean that something is safe, secure and reliable. It derives from the discovery that covering the bottom of a ship with copper plates gave excellent protection against the ravages of the teredo worm and the accumulation of weed and barnacles. Before copper was introduced, ships in tropical waters had been plagued by the worm, which could eat its way into the planks of the hull below the waterline, eventually making the ship unsafe. Weed and barnacles clinging to the lower hull dramatically reduced speed. The only satisfactory answer had been frequent careening – scraping the bottom and, if the hull was worm-eaten, full-scale replacement of the timber. With wooden bottoms this tedious process had to take place as frequently as every six weeks for cruisers in home waters. Line-of-battle ships usually came in three or four times a year. With the larger ships a spring tide was needed to dock them but, working day and night, it was possible to careen a ship in two tides. With a copper bottom a ship was faster and needed to be refitted in port only about every two years instead of every few months. Despite the initial high cost (£1,500 for a 74) the dividends in terms of economics and increased availability of ships at sea were substantial. One captain could barely recognize his ship after her bottom had been sheathed. It had, 'answered beyond my hopes as her superiority in sailing is hardly credible'.

The programme to put copper sheathing on all ships-of-the-line began in earnest in Britain in 1779. Within two years half of them (83 ships) had been completed. So had 115 frigates and 182 sloops and cutters. All the ships of both fleets at Trafalgar had copper bottoms. The standard size of each sheet was 4 feet by 14 inches. They were held on with copper nails, the thicker plates being at the bows. After 1783, extra wooden protection having been found unsatisfactory, regulations required that the plates extend 16 inches above the waterline.

The problem, a serious one, was that the copper reacted with the iron bolts that held the hull together, causing them to gradually rust away. The solution – replacing every iron bolt with a suitable alloy bolt – was a laborious and expensive process. By 1783 a suitable mix of copper and zinc had been found to be effective, so instructions were given that as ships came in for refit their iron nails would be replaced. It was a long process, but by Trafalgar it had been completed.

## FITTING OUT

The hull was built and launched, masts and yards were fitted, the bottom was sheathed in copper, but the ship was still a long way from being ready for sea. The process of fitting out had still to be undertaken.

### *HMS Victory*: Some Statistics

| | |
|---|---|
| Overall length | 227 feet 6 inches |
| Length of gundeck | 186 feet |
| Breadth | 51 feet 10 inches |
| Displacement | 3,500 tons |
| Rope used in rigging 22,880 fathoms (26 miles) | |
| Cooper plates used to sheath lower hull | 3,923 |
| Nails required for copper sheathing | 550,000 approx. |
| Canvas in one set of sails | 5,468 square metres |
| Cost at launch | £63,176 |
| Complement at Trafalgar | 820 |

Typical provisions carried (varying according to whether she was destined for Channel or foreign service): coal 50 tons, beef and pork 30 tons, bread and biscuit 45 tons, beer 50 tons, fresh water 300 tons, gunpowder 35 tons and shot 120 tons.

### 'Starboard' and 'Larboard'

These were two basic terms of seafaring. Starboard is the right-hand side of the ship when looking forward. It originates from the Anglo-Saxon word 'steorbord', meaning a board or oar hung over the right-hand side of a vessel and used for steering before the invention of the hanging rudder. It was hung on the right side because most men were right-handed, and the steersman was able to face forward comfortably holding the steering oar in his right hand. In Nelson's navy the starboard side of a ship was the captain's side. The starboard side of the poop deck was reserved for him if he came up for exercise, and he used the starboard ladder when leaving or boarding the ship.

The left side was called 'larboard', from the old English word 'ladeborde' meaning loading side. When a vessel came alongside to load, it was obviously better for the side unencumbered with the steering oar to come close to the wharf or jetty for loading. However, starboard and larboard sound very similar when shouted in a stiff breeze and dangerous confusion could result from misheard orders. So gradually larboard was dropped in favour of 'port' – the side a ship used to receive stores over when in port. Larboard was not dropped officially until 1844.

## Steering gear

The steering gear consisted of three basic components – rudder, tiller and wheel. The rudder was fitted to the sternpost of the ship by means of hinges (six or seven on a ship-of-the-line). The hinges, resembling a series of large hooks and eyes, consisted of two parts: the gudgeons and the pintles. A gudgeon was bolted to the hull by arms that fitted round the sternpost and held a ring (the eye) just aft of the post. A pintle was bolted to the rudder and had a pin (the hook) that fitted into the ring of the gudgeon. The tiller was the means of moving the rudder from side to side. In frigates and ships-of-the-line it was fitted just under the upper deck (or middle deck in first rates). One end of the tiller was slotted through a hole near the top of the rudder and the other, which reached inboard almost to the mizzenmast, was attached to a sweep by a piece of wood called a goose neck. The sweep was a curved piece of timber placed above the tiller and attached to the deck beams above it. The tiller ropes ran round the sweep, guided by wooden rollers, and up through holes in the decks to the wheel on the quarterdeck. The middle of the tiller rope was nailed to the barrel of the wheel. The bigger the wheel, the more the leverage, but the size was limited by the need for it to fit under the poop and for the spoke that was parallel to the deck to be about three feet above it, so that the helmsman could exert maximum downward pressure. In most ships the wheel was about five feet in diameter and was a double wheel, i.e. a wheel on either end of the central barrel.

### Anchors and cables

Depending on the size of the ship, between four to seven anchors were carried. The *Victory* had seven anchors: one best bower, one small bower, two sheet, one stream, one large and one small kedge. The bowers, the main anchors, each weighing over four and a half tons, were to hold the ship in deep water. The name bower derived from the fact that they were both carried at the bow, the best bower on the starboard side, the smaller on the larboard. Sheet anchors, each

## Steering Gear (Ship-of-the-line)

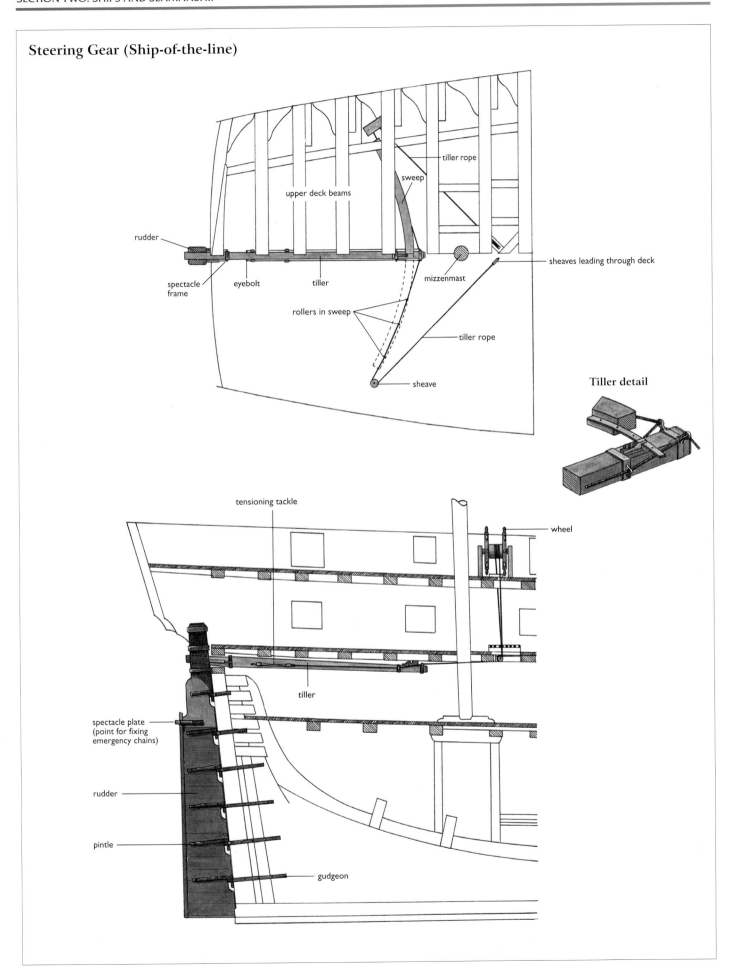

tiller rope

sweep

upper deck beams

rudder

spectacle frame

eyebolt

tiller

rollers in sweep

mizzenmast

sheaves leading through deck

tiller rope

sheave

Tiller detail

tensioning tackle

wheel

tiller

spectacle plate
(point for fixing
emergency chains)

rudder

pintle

gudgeon

## Best Bower Anchor

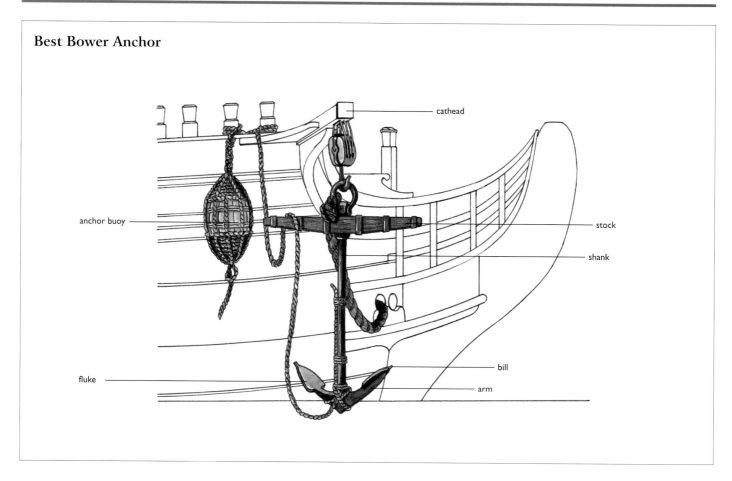

weighing a little over two tons, were also carried one on each side. They served as spares or for additional security in heavy weather, or as a lightweight anchor used in shallow waters such as rivers at low tide. The kedge anchors were the smallest and lightest. They were designed to be slung under a boat and rowed out ahead of the ship, then dropped, so the ship could haul in her cable and thus pull herself forward up to the anchor. The procedure was then repeated as necessary. It was called 'kedging' and was done when the ship had to manoeuvre in confined water or in a flat calm. The combined weight of all the anchors on the *Victory* was 15.27 tons.

All ships carried a number of cables. A 74 had eight, the *Victory* fourteen. They were made of rope varying in thickness (circumference) from 7 to 24 inches. Each was 120 fathoms long or 720 feet. A third rate would therefore carry some 5,760 feet (1,800 yards) of cable. Several could be joined together if required in very deep water.

### Capstans and messengers

All ships had capstans for lifting weights too heavy for muscle power and pulleys, such as anchors, stores, guns and yards. Two-decker ships normally had two, the main capstan and the jeer (fore) capstan, three-deckers sometimes three (although the *Victory* only had two). Frigates and smaller vessels had one. The main one, usually double in that it operated over two decks with barrels (resembling enormous cotton-reels) and bars at both levels, was used to lift anchors. The jeer capstan's head was usually situated in the open so that it could be used for lifting yards, guns or stores. Removable capstan bars were fitted into square holes

around the barrel, each bar being long enough to have up to ten men pushing. Bars could be slotted into the barrel on both deck levels. On the *Victory*, for example, the main capstan could take fourteen bars on the middle-deck barrel and another twelve on the lower deck. When fully manned this capstan could take 240 men (a third rate would have 192). With this number it could lift 10 tons. However, weighing anchor could be a long process, taking up to six or even eight hours depending on the length of cable out. In these circumstances the men on the bars became exhausted quickly and were changed over regularly. Marines were useful extra manpower for this purpose. While the capstan was in use it was customary for a sailor to play lively tunes on a fiddle to take men's minds off their back-aching drudgery.

The problem with capstans was that most cables were too large and heavy to be wound round the barrel. This was overcome by the use of a 'messenger' – a smaller, thinner endless cable of about 200 feet. It was passed a few turns round the capstan and led forward over appropriate guides and blocks, so that it would run close alongside the anchor cable from the hawse hole to the cable tier amidships; it then returned to the capstan. As the capstan turned, the anchor cable was quickly but temporarily fastened to the messenger by short lengths of rope called 'nippers'. This meant that it was the messenger cable that went round the capstan, not the anchor cable, as the nippers were quickly removed to allow the anchor cable to be stowed below. Often ship's boys or young seamen were employed on attaching the messenger rope to the anchor cable as they had to be nimble and quick – hence 'nipper' become a common term for a small boy, full of energy and mischief.

## Pumps

It was never possible to keep wooden ships entirely watertight. Caulking worked loose with the movement of the ship. Rain, sea spray and the smashing of waves over the weather deck in a storm all contributed to the gradual accumulation of water in the bilges at the bottom of the ship. In battle there was the added danger of water pouring in through holes made by enemy shot. The carpenter and his mates could not always cope adequately with makeshift repairs, and if the slowly rising water was not removed by pumps the ship could founder. There were four pumps in ships-of-the-line (frigates and sloops had two), grouped around the mainmast on the gundeck, picking up water from the lowest part of the hold.

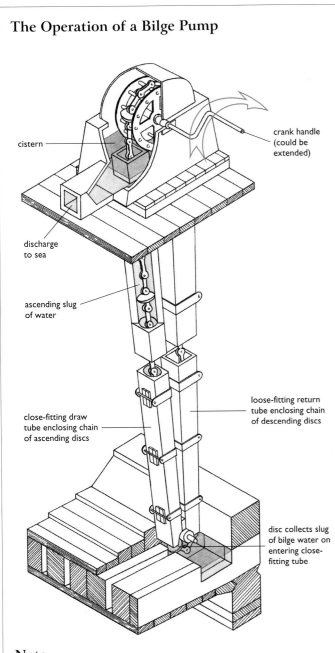

## The Operation of a Bilge Pump

cistern

crank handle (could be extended)

discharge to sea

ascending slug of water

close-fitting draw tube enclosing chain of ascending discs

loose-fitting return tube enclosing chain of descending discs

disc collects slug of bilge water on entering close-fitting tube

### Note

Up to 30 men on a first-rate could man the extended handle. However, it was a most unpopular duty as the circular movement soon caused severe muscle and joint pains.

Each consisted of a chain, not unlike a large bicycle chain, with discs, or collars, attached at regular intervals. It was these collars that scooped up the water. The chain passed over a large wheel, turned by crank handles on the gundeck, down a loose-fitting wooden tube to the bilge, thence round a roller and up through another tube in which the discs fitted closely. Just before the discs entered the upward tube, they scooped up the water, which on reaching the gundeck was discharged into a cistern and then over the side. It was of basic design, easily repaired but exhausting to operate. The pump handles could be extended to allow up to thirty men (on a three-decker) at a time to work them using a rotary action. However, pumping was a crippling and much-dreaded experience. An officer described how it was not uncommon for men to have to be driven to man 'the pumps of leaking ships, when obliged to keep them constantly going. It strains their loins, affects the muscular parts of their arms like violent rheumatic pains, and galls their hands'. It has been calculated that the capacity of four pumps was similar to that of a water main supplying a town of 30,000 people. So long as the intake of water was kept below this amount, the ship would not founder. As with hauling in anchors, marines were often employed on this demanding duty.

## Ship's boats

It is not always apparent how important ship's boats could be to a rated ship. It is hardly an exaggeration to say that without them the warship could not function. All ship's boats could be sailed (the masts were removable) or rowed with sweeps (oars). The principal tasks carried out by these boats were:

### Moving men, supplies and equipment

Rated warships seldom came alongside a wharf or jetty due to fear that pressed men would desert and the difficulty of manoeuvring a large sailing ship without oars. Everything the ship required had to be taken out to the ship at anchor by small boats.

### Carrying messages and personnel between ships

If an admiral or captain wanted to send a complex message the best, if not the only, way to do so was to send a boat across to the ship concerned, either rowed or sailed – probably with a midshipman in charge. If an admiral wanted a conference of his captains on the flagship, as Nelson did before Trafalgar, these officers would arrive in one of their ship's boats.

### Moving the ship

Being dependent on the wind for movement meant that in some circumstances, such as when becalmed or in a confined space with an unfavourable wind, it was impossible or unsafe to use the ship's sails. The boats could then tow the ship. Several boats would usually be needed, and even then progress was very slow and the boat's crews quickly tired. They were mostly used in a real emergency, to pull the ship away from a shoal or in pursuit of an enemy in a flat calm in deep water. Kedging was used in more shallow water. This involved the boat taking a kedge anchor out ahead of the ship and dropping it; the cable was then hauled in, pulling the ship forward. The process could be repeated over and over again. The disadvantage was the huge physical demands made on both the rowers in the boat and those toiling on the capstan. A better technique was warping, whereby the boat would take the cable to a fixed object such as a mooring buoy or perhaps a convenient tree ashore.

## Weighing Anchor with Main Capstan and Messenger

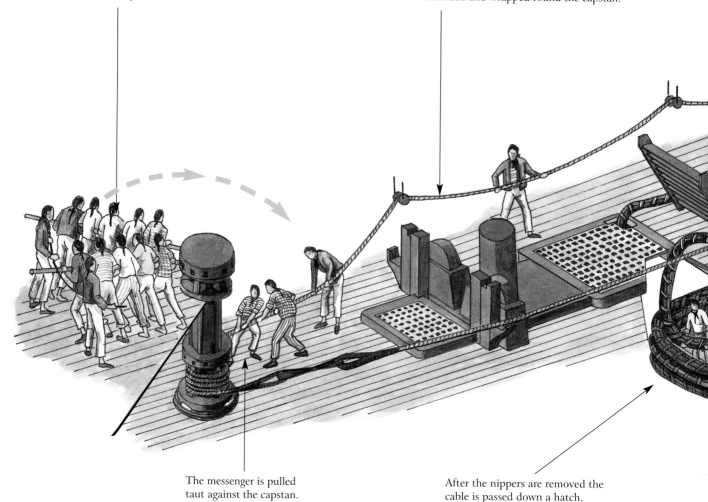

All hands helped haul in the anchor cable. The men at the capstan are mainly marines.

The anchor cable was too thick to wind directly around the capstan so the crew tied the cable to a thinner one called the messenger. The messenger, which is endless, is passed back through a series of rollers attached to the deckhead and wrapped round the capstan.

The messenger is pulled taut against the capstan.

After the nippers are removed the cable is passed down a hatch.

### The 'Silent Service'

The British Royal Navy has always been called the 'silent service', in contrast to the old Merchant Service, who invariably sang working songs and sea shanties as they heaved on the ropes. Such frivolity had no place in the Royal Navy; Napoleon was most impressed with how the crew of the 74-gun *Northumberland* taking him to exile on St Helena in 1816 performed their duties efficiently without undue noise or shouting. Nevertheless, there was music aboard Nelson's warships. When grog was served, the ship's fiddler often played 'Nancy Dawson' or 'Sally in our Alley'. When the crew was drummed to quarters, the tune was 'Heart of Oak', and when the anchor was weighed (a task that could take hours and scores of men) the fiddler would sit on the capstan and strike up a variety of tunes, a popular one being 'Drops of Brandy'. The singing of songs and ballads was done mostly by off-duty men on their mess decks – a Saturday night at sea being a suitable occasion.

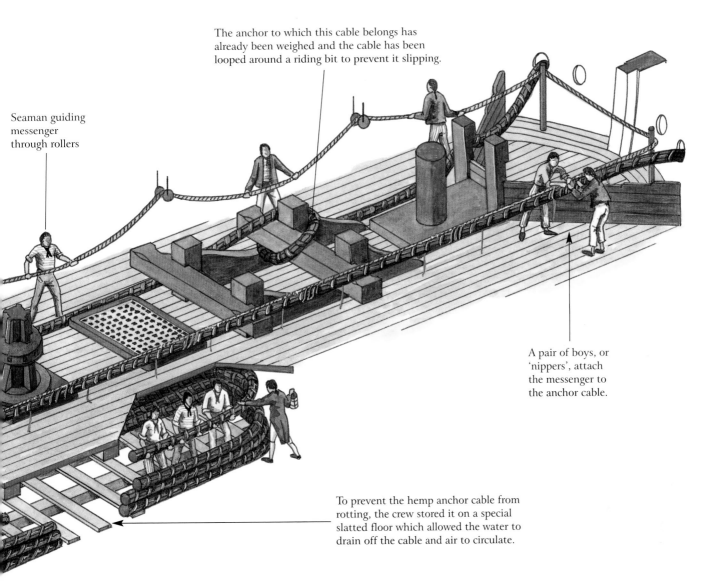

The anchor to which this cable belongs has already been weighed and the cable has been looped around a riding bit to prevent it slipping.

Seaman guiding messenger through rollers

A pair of boys, or 'nippers', attach the messenger to the anchor cable.

To prevent the hemp anchor cable from rotting, the crew stored it on a special slatted floor which allowed the water to drain off the cable and air to circulate.

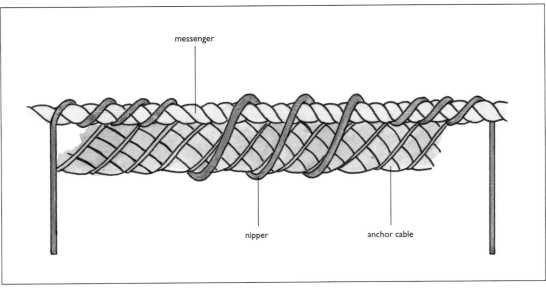

messenger

nipper

anchor cable

*Military tasks*

The most dramatic of these were 'cutting out' expeditions. A ship's boats would be crammed with armed men and rowed into an enemy harbour (normally at night) in great secrecy to carry out an attack on an enemy ship. The object was to board the ship, capture it and sail her out of the harbour as a prize. Other military activities included landing marines, seamen and guns on a beach in an amphibious attack, perhaps against a shore battery.

*Rescue work*

Ship's boats were never regarded as lifeboats at this time. If a man fell overboard, it took a long time to get a boat and crew launched, and as few seamen could swim attempting a rescue was regarded as somewhat futile and rarely tried. However, boats were sometimes used to pick up survivors from a shipwreck or after a battle. The best example of the latter was the rescue of some seventy men by boats from several British ships of the crew of the French flagship *L'Orient* after she blew up at the Battle of the Nile in 1798. As to their use as lifeboats, the only well-known incidence is the survival of Captain William Bligh and his party in 1789 after they had been set adrift in a launch in the Pacific by the mutinous crew of his ship, the *Bounty*. Bligh and his companions drifted 4,000 miles before landing in Timor. Bligh commanded the 54-gun *Glatton* at Copenhagen in 1801.

By 1793 the allocation of boats to British rated ships had been more or less standardized, certainly in terms of numbers carried. Ships-of-the-line had six, with a typical 74 carrying a launch, a barge, a pinnace, two cutters and a small jolly boat. The launch (similar to the old longboat) was primarily designed to carry out the heavy work – carrying stores or kedging for example. It could also mount a carronade in the bow for military operations. The barge and pinnace were very similar, although the barge was slightly more prestigious and often carried admirals to or from the shore or ships, while the pinnace was more likely to be carrying captains. Cutters were also popular with officers for dashing around, as they were fast and good sailers. The jolly boats were very light, small (between 16 and 18 feet long) and easily hoisted in and out of the water.

The boats were stored on beams fixed athwartships between the two gangways in the waist of the ship, where it was possible to stow three boats (launch, barge and pinnace) side by side. Cutters were stowed under the quarter davits (beams of timber acting as cranes) on either side of the stern. The jolly boat was usually hung from the stern davits. The French and Spanish tended to save space by removing the thwarts (benches in the boat on which rowers sat) and stowing the smaller boats inside the larger ones. They could also be towed astern – something often done in action, as it usually prevented their being damaged and reduced the number of splinters that might otherwise be flying around the upper deck.

## REFITTING AND REPAIRING

Most warships put to sea with plenty of provisions in their hold, often up to six months' worth. All captains sought to replenish fresh stocks of drinking water, fruit and vegetables as frequently as possible to avoid scurvy which, by the time of Trafalgar, was known to be prevented by lime juice. A warship on patrol or blockade would be victualled either by calling at a port or by having regular visits from supply ships, preferably long before the hold was empty.

While crews sometimes suffered from disease or malnutrition, their ships inevitably succumbed to the slow but deadly disease of wood rot. This problem was additional to those created by barnacles and teredo worms for which coppering was the answer. Due to ignorance of the causes of wood rot, combined with the pressure to take shortcuts with the seasoning of timber, the so-called 'wood cancer' was often already present as the bands thumped out their martial music while the ship slid down the slipway at her launching. As Dudley Pope put it, she was frequently 'a beautiful woman already riddled with a fatal disease'. How rot spread was not properly understood. Green timber was often, of necessity, used. This wood shrank as it eventually dried out, leaving cracks which held moisture that bred the spores of rot. Also, because of the shortage of compass timber, it was common practice to take such timber from old ships due to be abandoned as hulks. Often this old wood would have a soft patch that was, or had to be, ignored, and would then spread rot to new adjoining timber. Ships taking perhaps two, three or more years to build were often left in the open exposed to frequent drenching by rain, and damp became endemic. This water slowly seeped into all corners and cracks of the hull, starting rot or spreading it from old compass timbers. The problem was exacerbated by lack of wood preservatives, inadequate ventilation and the need for tiny cavities built into the ship's structure. All this meant that despite constant vigilance by the ship's carpenter, whose ability to tackle the problem was limited anyway, all ships required frequent and extensive overhauls. These were not cheap.

Every ship would cost considerably more to keep seaworthy than she had to be constructed in the first place – in many cases up to seven or eight times as much. The *Victory* cost £63,176 at her launch in 1765 (over £5 million of today's money), and during the fifteen years between 1790 and Trafalgar another £147,330 was needed to keep her in reasonable repair. A House of Commons report in 1814 stated that twenty-three 74s had cost £1.07 million to build but, after from one to eight years, another £1.15 million had been spent to keep them afloat.

### Estimated Cost of HMS *Victory* from Launching to 1800

Most ships whose seagoing life extended for over fifteen years cost more in repair and refit costs than in their original construction and fitting out. *Victory* was forty years old at Trafalgar and in the thirty-five years between her launch and 1800 she cost the government well over three times her original cost.

Expenditure was:

| | |
|---|---|
| Launch 1765 | £63,176 |
| Refit | £15,373 |
| Major repair 1787 | £37,524 |
| Repairs 1799 | £23,500 |
| Repairs 1800 | £70,933 |
| **Total repairs** | **£147,330** |
| **Total costs** | **£210,506** |

*Victory*'s annual costs over the thirty-five-year period were £4,209. Today she is priceless, still in commission and still costing large sums for renovation and maintenance.

# SEAMANSHIP

A sailor (as distinct from a landsman or idler; see pp. 143 and 172 for a definition of these terms) in Nelson's navy had not only to be physically hard, but also to acquire a host of seamanship skills if both he and his ship were to survive the enemy and – more pressingly – the elements. Life at sea could be short and brutal, and disease and accidents killed far more effectively than the efforts of the French, Spanish and Dutch combined. Although muscle power was essential, as a sailor spent most of his days at sea pulling and lifting (hernias were the most common injury), agility, stamina and a cool courage had to be combined with an exact knowledge of his duties and how to work the ship. Seamanship was complex, with the unexpected always ready to pounce, and men had to become accustomed to acting instinctively. It was sometimes said that a seaman had two hands, one for the ship and one for himself. In nautical terms a 'hand' is a sailor (although it could equally apply to every man on board, including marines). The cry 'All hands on deck' meant every man was needed from both watches to deal with some dangerous or difficult situation.

As an example of a few of the basic skills a sailor needed, we shall look at the likely duties in the months leading up to Trafalgar of Benjamin Hawkins, a twenty-six-year-old Able Seaman from London, who had been on the *Victory* since November 1803.

## BASIC SEAMANSHIP

From 19 August to 14 September 1805 the *Victory* was at anchor at St Helen's, Portsmouth. Although Vice-Admiral Nelson had gone on leave to Merton, Hawkins had probably not been so fortunate. It was well over two years since the *Victory* had been in a home port, so there was a massive amount of repair, maintenance and restocking to be done. If Hawkins was lucky, he might have got some shore leave, but for most of those four weeks he and his comrades would have been working ceaselessly. As an able seamen of twenty-six, it is likely he was a topman and as such he would have been concerned with stripping down the ship. The greatest concern was for the sails, all thirty-seven of which had to be checked and repaired. They had to be thoroughly dried and unbent (taken down) from the yards – otherwise they would rot. Sailmakers, probably including Hawkins (to be rated AB he had to be able to 'sew a seam'), would spend many hours sewing up the stiff canvas and repairing rents. For stowage in the sail locker, sails were always 'made up' (folded) in a certain way. Each was marked with a tally and stored in the position laid down so that all seamen knew exactly where to look when they were needed again. A good deal of the running rigging (ropes) also came down with the sails. It was examined for fraying, then repaired (by splicing) or replaced as necessary. When the rigging was properly serviceable, it was coiled, tallied and stored away. Other jobs included repairs to yards and spars, painting, caulking decks and tarring the standing rigging. The hold had to be restocked with six months' supplies under the keen eye of the master, Thomas Atkinson. Atkinson was assisted by the purser, Walter Burke, fussing around with his endless lists as the hundreds of casks and barrels were ferried out and swung on board. The tasks were endless, the activity unceasing.

Hawkins was detailed to join the party to man the admiral's barge to fetch Nelson from the wharf. It was an emotional send-off with the crowd pressing forward, in some instances into the water, as the barge pulled away. Nelson waved his hat to his well-wishers. As Hawkins heaved on his sweep and the blades found their rhythm in the flat calm sea, Nelson turned to Captain Hardy and said, 'I had their huzzas before. I have their hearts now.' That evening the admiral hosted an elaborate dinner party for London dignitaries and senior officers. Waiting at table was not one of Hawkins' duties – such tasks were not given to able seamen but taken by the admiral's personal servants.

The next morning at 8.00 the *Victory* weighed. All hands were required to get her under way. The capstan was manned, the long, slow haul on the cable began and the 'nippers' darted about below tying and untying the dripping cable to the messenger. Yards were hoisted, the most awkward being the yards for the topsails, topgallants and royals, which had to be lifted vertically to get them up without snagging the rigging. A seaman was positioned on the crosstrees and another on the shrouds to guide them through. Then Hawkins and the other topmen went aloft, by running up the shrouds using the ratlines. The topmen tended to be the younger, fitter men with considerable skill and experience. Most, like Hawkins, were able seamen. As they climbed to the tops they used the windward side if possible, as the shrouds were tauter and any wind would push the climber against them. This was not of much consequence in a light wind in port but could make the difference between hanging on or falling in a high wind and rough sea.

As Hawkins neared the underside of the top he was faced with a choice. Either he could continue through the 'lubber's hole' (there to make things easier and safer, especially in bad weather or for non-seamen such as marines sent up as sharpshooters who were not used to heights) and clamber onto the top (platform) that way, or he could climb out round the outer edge of the top using the futtock shrouds (see diagram p. 81). If his duty was to bend (fasten) the main course, for example, he and his fellow topmen (probably seven of them) would go out along the yard and bend the sails to their yards by lashing them through eyelets along the upper edge

## 'Hands'

The nautical word 'hands' has given the English language a number of quaint expressions. Some examples:

*a dab hand* a seamen with a lot of experience in painting the ship

*Do you want a hand?* 'Do you want another crew member?'

*an old hand* a seaman well versed in his skills, a man of great experience

*short-handed* short of crew members

*come to hand* from the seaman's ability to identify every rope or piece of rigging without having to peer at it or search for it

*handy* A ship was said to be 'handy' if it was easy to sail and manoeuvre. One of the most useful tackles on board was known as 'handy billy', a simple rope-pulley arrangement for lifting heavy weights.

of the sail. If the maintopsail or maintopgallant were to be bent then he had more climbing to do. Bending sails required considerable nerve, skill and strength. When working on the yards, the men had to stand on foot-ropes suspended under the after side of the yard by short lengths of line called stirrups. Except at the ends, the foot-rope was adjusted so that the yard came just over his waist, allowing him to lean against it and have his hands free to work. A captain of the tops (a petty officer) usually sat astride each end of the yard to supervise the task in hand. A foot-rope breaking or a sudden violent, unexpected movement of the ship in bad weather could, and often did, cause a fatal fall onto the deck or, less often, into the sea. At a hundred feet up in a strong wind with the ship corkscrewing, the mast tops dancing wildly in all directions, with all one's instincts screaming at one to cling on, it took an exceptionally courageous and experienced man to do the job.

The amount of canvas that a ship required to give her steerage way and make her manageable depended entirely on the strength of the wind. If it was blowing at any strength, the topsails and topgallants on each mast were sufficient to give her a fair speed and keep her under control. When the *Victory* left her anchorage, she steered south-south-east before turning west round the Isle of Wight. Thereafter the wind freshened considerably and at one point it was feared she would be blown into Weymouth on the lee shore. Hawkins and his fellow topmen were then out along the yards taking in sail. This could be done by either reefing (partially reducing the surface area) or furling (taking in the entire sail). To reef, men on deck hauled on the reef tackles of the sail to take the weight and pull it up towards the topmen spread out along the yard. The topmen leaned over the yard to grab the appropriate reef line (short lengths of rope fixed in rows through the sail). Having taken hold of the reef line he would pull the sail onto the yard, find the other end on the other side of the sail and tie the two together over the yard – using a reef knot. This way an adjustable proportion of the sail could be brought out of use. Furling involved the entire sail being tied to the yard. In a high wind this had to be done quickly, so it was common practice for the ship to be luffed up slightly (turned into the wind) when the order to shorten sail was given. This had the effect of spilling wind from the sails, thus making work aloft easier. On a dark gusty night in winter reefing was one of the worst jobs seamen would face. Men could be fighting for hours to get in a reef. When an armful of canvas had been gathered, and just as the man was about to pass the reef lines round it, a gust of wind could tear it from his grasp, forcing him to start all over again. Not surprisingly,

when they came down such men were totally drained, frozen, trembling with exhaustion and with every fingernail bleeding.

After an anxious hour, some skilful ship handling and strenuous activity by Hawkins and his fellow topmen on the yards, the *Victory* was able to avoid the indignity of being pushed into Weymouth Bay. On the afternoon of 16 September Nelson wrote, 'Off Portland [Bill]. My fate is fixed, and I am gone, and beating down Channel with a foul wind.' On 28 September the *Victory* joined the fleet off Cadiz – Trafalgar was only four weeks away.

The voyage out had been uneventful. It is likely that during those weeks Hawkins had to demonstrate another skill that his rating as an able seaman required of him: steering. Under the eye of a quartermaster (petty officer) Hawkins would have been the main helmsman standing on the weather side of the wheel. There he was responsible for controlling the movement of the wheel. On the lee side was a more inexperienced man, learning the job, whose task was merely to add muscle power to the wheel. The officer of the watch decided which method, or combination of methods, the helmsman should use to steer the ship. It could be by compass when out of sight of land or at night, although Hawkins would have been trained only to glance at the compass while spending most of his time watching the ship's bow, the sea, the clouds or other objects. Alternatively, he could steer by a landmark or another ship, but Hawkins' vision was partially obscured, so the quartermaster would sometimes have to climb into the rigging and shout down helm orders. The third method was by the wind. This entailed steering into the wind but at the same time trying to keep the sails filled (the nautical term being 'full and by'). This was not easy. The helm was slow to react – there was a delay of several seconds between moving the wheel and the ship starting to turn, and once a turn had begun it continued until the helm was turned back some way in the opposite direction. For a novice helmsman it took a while to get used to the fact that an order 'Hard a-starboard' would turn the bow to larboard and vice versa. Hawkins needed to have enough experience to interpret the 'feel' of the helm and ship's reactions. He would have kept a careful eye on one sail that he could see clearly – probably the topgallant or royal. If it started to shiver or flutter, it meant he was sailing too close to the wind. If uncorrected the ship could get into serious difficulties, with all sails flogging (flapping), emptied of wind, the ship wallowing and not reacting to the helm. Similarly, with a strong wind astern an inattentive helmsman could broach the ship (bring it broadside on to the waves). If heavy seas then struck it could founder. To a considerable extent the safety of the ship was in Hawkins' hands when he took the helm.

# SHIP HANDLING

Ship handling was the job of the sea officers. For every hour of every day at sea there was an officer-of-the-watch, usually a lieutenant or the master on a ship-of-the-line, on duty on the quarterdeck. It was he who initiated any changes in course and decided whether to reduce or put on sail or tack. He gave the order to the quartermaster who repeated it to the helmsman. The officer had command of the ship and in a sudden emergency had to make decisions that could affect the safety of all on board.

To handle a ship required an understanding of the wind and its effect on the sails and therefore the behaviour of the ship. It also needed the ability to navigate. Ship handling was an art, not a science. Every ship was slightly different and reacted to a different degree to given sets of sails in various wind strengths or direction. Some were faster, some sluggish, some could sail closer to the wind. But the overriding factor was the wind. Its strength could vary from nothing to a violent gale, and it could come from any point of the compass.

# Going Aloft

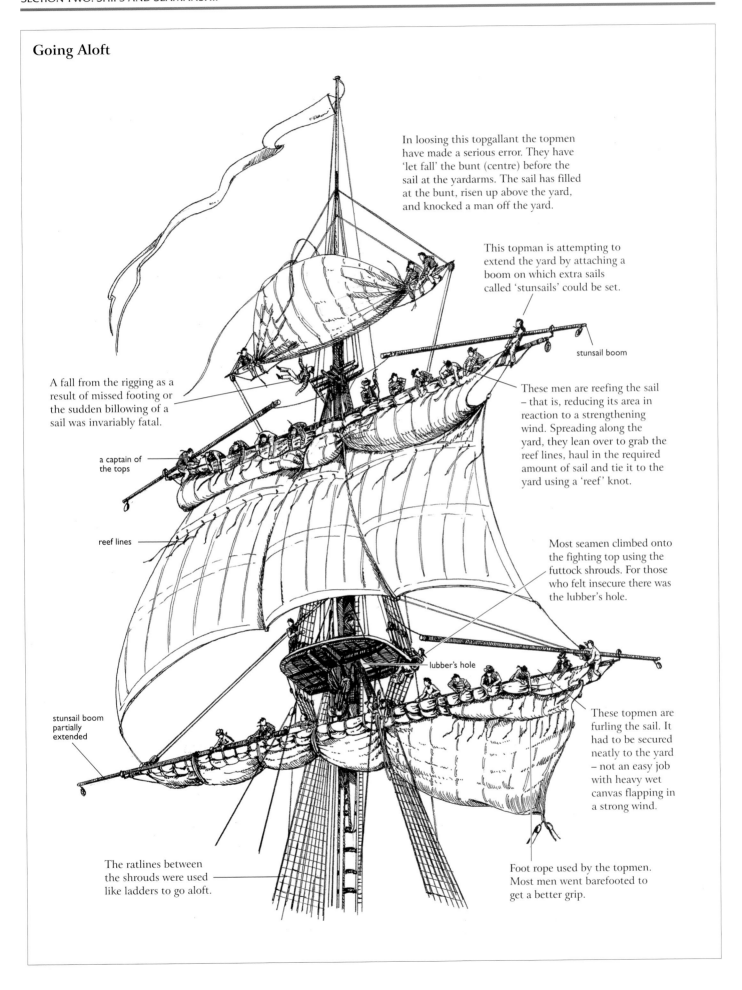

In loosing this topgallant the topmen have made a serious error. They have 'let fall' the bunt (centre) before the sail at the yardarms. The sail has filled at the bunt, risen up above the yard, and knocked a man off the yard.

This topman is attempting to extend the yard by attaching a boom on which extra sails called 'stunsails' could be set.

stunsail boom

A fall from the rigging as a result of missed footing or the sudden billowing of a sail was invariably fatal.

a captain of the tops

reef lines

These men are reefing the sail – that is, reducing its area in reaction to a strengthening wind. Spreading along the yard, they lean over to grab the reef lines, haul in the required amount of sail and tie it to the yard using a 'reef' knot.

Most seamen climbed onto the fighting top using the futtock shrouds. For those who felt insecure there was the lubber's hole.

lubber's hole

stunsail boom partially extended

These topmen are furling the sail. It had to be secured neatly to the yard – not an easy job with heavy wet canvas flapping in a strong wind.

The ratlines between the shrouds were used like ladders to go aloft.

Foot rope used by the topmen. Most men went barefooted to get a better grip.

Vitally relevant to the manoeuvring of ships and battle tactics are the terms 'weather', 'windward' and 'leeward'. The weather side is the windward side, the side from which the wind is blowing. The lee side is the sheltered side. So a rocky weather shore lying to windward of a ship posed no threat, whereas a ship blown towards a rocky lee shore was in very serious danger. There were distinct advantages (and some disadvantages – see Section Five) in having the 'weather gauge' (being up wind of the enemy) in a naval action. The fleet with the weather gauge could choose the moment of attack against ships to leeward. Leeward is the opposite direction to windward. To make a lot of leeway meant the ship was being pushed (sideways) off her course by the action of wind or tide. At Trafalgar Nelson led the weather (windward) column of ships in the attack while Collingwood had the lee (sheltered) column, but both had the weather gauge vis-à-vis the Combined Fleet.

Certain words were used to describe a relative position or bearing from the ship. 'Starboard' was right, 'larboard' was left. An object might be lying 'ahead', 'abeam' (at right angles to the hull) or 'astern', 'on the starboard bow', 'on the larboard beam', or 'fine on the starboard beam'. However, it was common practice when indicating a side to use 'to windward' or 'a-weather' and to 'leeward' or 'a-lee' rather than 'starboard' or 'larboard'. Another ship could be sighted on the 'weather bow' for example.

### Points of Sailing

The 360-degree circle of the horizon was divided into thirty-two points of the compass, each measuring 11 degrees and 15 minutes. No sailing ship can sail directly into the wind as she will soon lose headway (the forward motion of the ship). In fact there is a 'dead' angle of six points either side of the wind into which a ship cannot sail without tacking. When a ship was sailing as close as possible to the wind, she was said to be 'close hauled'. To be close hauled on the starboard tack was to have the wind hitting the starboard side; on the larboard tack the wind came from the larboard side. At Trafalgar both fleets were on the larboard tack. When a ship was close hauled, the yards were braced as far forward as possible on the starboard side and back on the larboard side to catch some wind. This made for slow sailing, minimum headway and a lot of leeway being lost as the wind forced the ship sideways. To sail too close to the wind made the leading edge of the sails begin to shiver. If the ship continued to point further into the wind, or if there was a sudden wind shift, the sails would be 'put a-back', bringing the ship to a standstill, or 'put about' (turned) on the wrong tack (direction). Particular care had to taken to avoid shaking the sails if there were men aloft, as the motion could throw them from the yards with fatal consequences. As noted above, when sailing close to the wind, in order to make a reasonable speed and reduce leeway the helmsman would be ordered to sail 'full and by' – that is, with sails filled but still keeping into the wind as much as possible.

With a more favourable wind the ship could sail 'large'. This meant the yards could be almost at right angles to the line of the ship. A ship could be up to six points large on either tack. With the wind two points large, or abeam, a ship was said to have a 'soldier's wind', fair for two ships sailing in opposite directions, making sailing so simple that even a soldier could master it. The best speed and least leeway, however, came when the ship had the wind on her quarter so the sails did not mask each other, as happened with the wind directly aft. In this situation the ship was said to be 'sailing before the wind' with the yards at right angles to the hull.

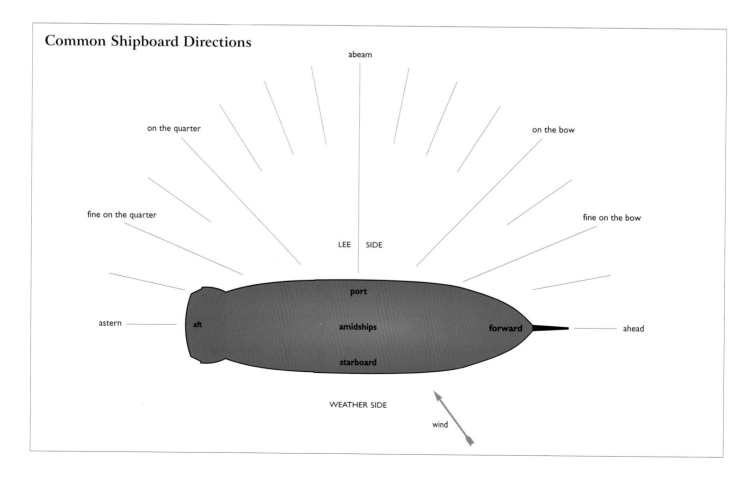

## Common Shipboard Directions

abeam

on the quarter

on the bow

fine on the quarter

fine on the bow

LEE | SIDE

port

astern — aft   amidships   forward — ahead

starboard

WEATHER SIDE

wind

## Points of Sailing

Ship in eye of wind. Fore and aft sails not drawing. Square sails 'flat aback'. Ship makes sternway.

Ship running before wind. Forestaysail not drawing and taken in. Main course brailed up to reduce strain on mainmast. Spanker brailed up to reduce risk of broaching to, i.e. slewing suddenly and uncontrollably across wind and sea.

direction of wind

Ship 'all in the wind'. Yards not braced and sails shivering. Ship slowly drifts to leeward.

Ship further off the wind. With full quartering breeze she is 'sailing large'. Studding sails may be set or weather clew of main course may be lifted, depending upon wind strength.

Ship on the wind. Yards braced, everything drawing, she is close-hauled on the starboard tack.

Ship off the wind. Sheets eased, she is sailing free with a quartering sea.

## The Nautical Compass

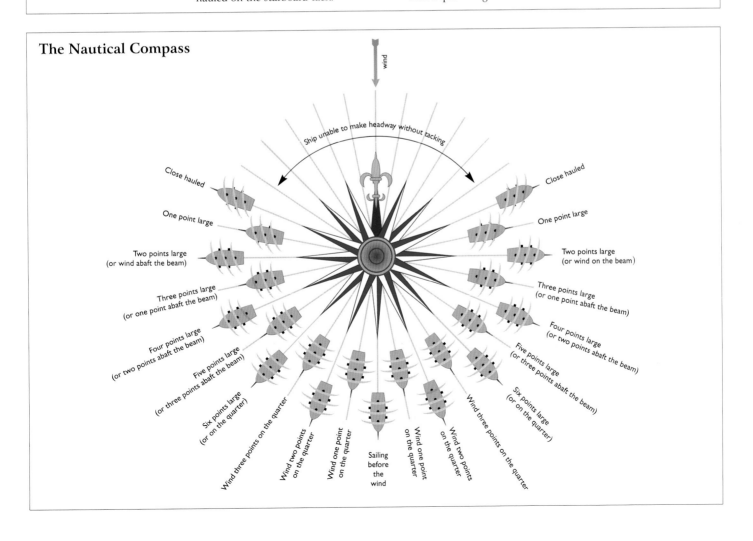

wind

Ship unable to make headway without tacking

Close hauled

One point large

Two points large (or wind abaft the beam)

Three points large (or one point abaft the beam)

Four points large (or two points abaft the beam)

Five points large (or three points abaft the beam)

Six points large (or on the quarter)

Wind three points on the quarter

Wind two points on the quarter

Wind one point on the quarter

Sailing before the wind

Wind one point on the quarter

Wind two points on the quarter

Wind three points on the quarter

Six points large (or on the quarter)

Five points large (or three points abaft the beam)

Four points large (or two points abaft the beam)

Three points large (or one point abaft the beam)

Two points large (or wind on the beam)

One point large

Close hauled

## Trimming the yards

Trimming the yards meant adjusting the sails to get the best possible advantage of the wind. The alteration of the sails was done by the use of the sheets, tacks, braces and bowlines (all ropes connected with the adjustment of the yards or sails). Keeping the sails on good trim was only part of the officer's duty when in charge of the ship. He was also required to maintain a constant eye on the course steered and to give orders to the quartermaster at the helm as appropriate.

## Tacking

As noted above, a ship could not sail into a head wind. So if such a wind prevented her from sailing direct to her destination, she was compelled to tack in order to make progress in the desired direction. Such progress was made in a series of ninety-degree zigzags, also known as beating to windward. The tacking (turning) was achieved by pointing her head into and through the wind until it blew on the other side of the ship. Tacking was also used to 'go about' (turn round). It was one of the most frequent manoeuvres undertaken by a ship at sea. Continuous tacking was necessary when a ship was trying to navigate a narrow channel against an unfavourable wind. Leaving Portsmouth was a case in point. No matter what the direction of the wind, at least one or two short tacks were needed to clear the mouth of the Solent, the shallows off Selsey Bill in the east and the Isle of Wight in the west. In open sea, such as the Atlantic crossing to the West Indies, huge distances of several hundred miles could be covered before a tack (or change of course) was required.

There were risks involved with tacking and always the chance of a mishap through poor judgement. For this reason, when it was done with a lee shore nearby or during the passage of a channel, the captain was almost certainly in charge on the quarterdeck. However, if far out to sea, the officer of the watch would probably be trusted to tack. All hands were needed on deck, so a common practice was to tack as one watch was being relieved – for the sailors, a few minutes' delay in getting off watch and to sleep was far better than having to be rousted out when off watch. The vital point was to give the ship enough way (movement) to keep her under control until the operation was completed. Three things could go wrong. First, the ship might not go round and thus fall back onto her original course. Second, the wind might be so light that she would not get any way. Third, a head of sea (large wave) might hit her bow and prevent her head from completing its circuit. A failure to tack in narrow waters could put the ship in serious danger. There were ways of recovering from these predicaments but they all took time, during which the ship would drift downwind towards any hazards that lay astern or to leeward.

---

## Trimming the Yards

Braces are used to swing, or trim, the yards to various angles for the purposes of shiphandling or to take advantage of wind from a given direction. Some terminology is as follows:

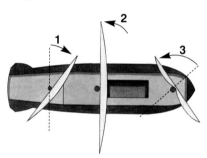

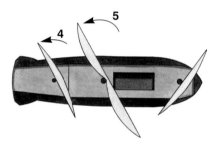

### Notes

1 Yard 'braced up' as wind direction moves farther forward.
2 Yard 'braced in' ('squared') for running directly before wind, which direction has moved farther aft.
3 Yard 'braced aback', bringing wind on forward side of sail to take way off ship.

### Notes

4 Yard 'braced about' as wind moves to opposite side on going about.
5 Yard 'braced by' the forces in the backed mainsails balancing those in the fore sails, causing the ship to 'lie to' or be 'hove to'.

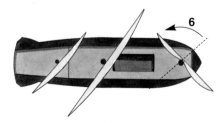

### Notes

6 Yard 'braced abox', the fore sails being backed, again to slow or stop the ship.

### Notes

7 Yard 'braced to', easing the sail as the ship comes more before the wind.

# Tacking

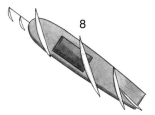

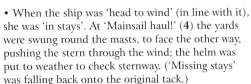

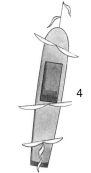

## Notes

To sail in the wind, a ship needed the wind coming over her port or starboard bow (when she was said to be on the port or starboard tack), and to gain distance to windward she tacked or sailed across the wind in a series of legs, at the end of each one bringing the bows through the wind until the wind was on the other side.

## Tacking a square-rigged ship

• The helm was put to leeward, bringing the head to windward, into the eye of the wind: 'The helm's a-lee!' (**3**)
• 'Raise the tacks and sheets!' The ropes confining the tacks (lower weather corners) of the lower sails were loosened, allowing the ship's head to come up into the wind.
• When the weather edges of the mainsails shivered, they could bring her no closer to the wind, so let go: 'Off tacks and sheets!'

• When the ship was 'head to wind' (in line with it), she was 'in stays'. At 'Mainsail haul!' (**4**) the yards were swung round the masts, to face the other way, pushing the stern through the wind; the helm was put to weather to check sternway. ('Missing stays' was falling back onto the original tack.)
• When the after sails were full, and the ship had fallen off five or six points, the fore sails were brought into the wind again: 'Haul off all!' or 'Let go and haul!' (**6**). The windward fore sheet was gathered aft, bringing the yard around and the sail to the wind, the yards were braced sharp up and the ship had tacked.

*The Illustrated Companion to Nelson's Navy*
Blake, N. and Lawrence, R. (Chatham Publishing, 2000)

# Path of Ship Tacking

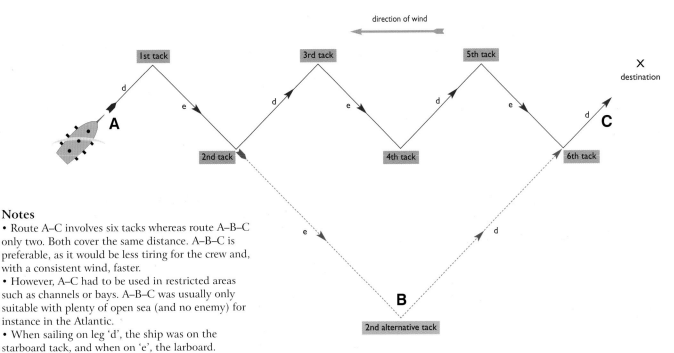

## Notes

• Route A–C involves six tacks whereas route A–B–C only two. Both cover the same distance. A–B–C is preferable, as it would be less tiring for the crew and, with a consistent wind, faster.
• However, A–C had to be used in restricted areas such as channels or bays. A–B–C was usually only suitable with plenty of open sea (and no enemy) for instance in the Atlantic.
• When sailing on leg 'd', the ship was on the starboard tack, and when on 'e', the larboard.

## Wearing

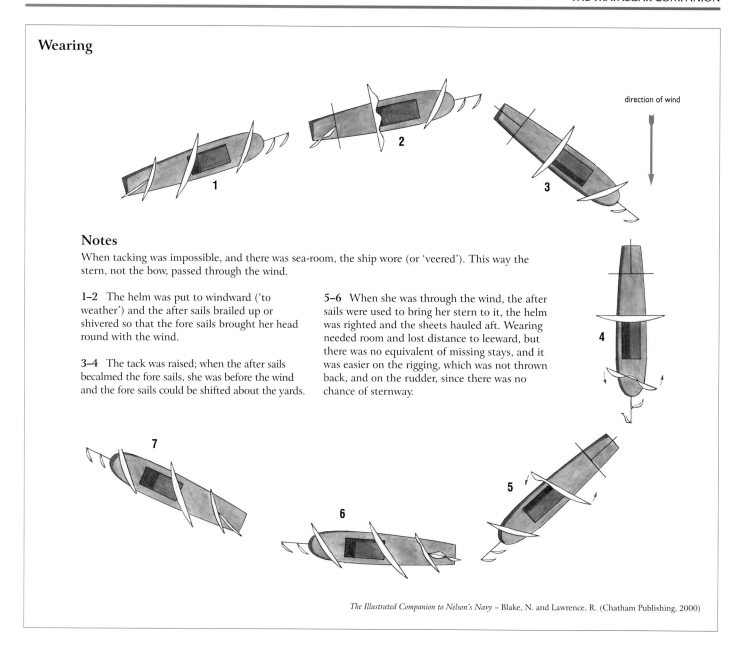

direction of wind

### Notes

When tacking was impossible, and there was sea-room, the ship wore (or 'veered'). This way the stern, not the bow, passed through the wind.

**1–2** The helm was put to windward ('to weather') and the after sails brailed up or shivered so that the fore sails brought her head round with the wind.

**3–4** The tack was raised; when the after sails becalmed the fore sails, she was before the wind and the fore sails could be shifted about the yards.

**5–6** When she was through the wind, the after sails were used to bring her stern to it, the helm was righted and the sheets hauled aft. Wearing needed room and lost distance to leeward, but there was no equivalent of missing stays, and it was easier on the rigging, which was not thrown back, and on the rudder, since there was no chance of sternway.

*The Illustrated Companion to Nelson's Navy* – Blake, N. and Lawrence, R. (Chatham Publishing, 2000)

The actual technique of tacking was somewhat complex in terms of what sails were adjusted and when. Essentially, what happened was that the ship gathered a little extra way (speed) by bearing away from the wind slightly, then, when ready, the helm was put 'hard a-lee' to bring her head sharply back into the wind. When the wind was about a point on the weather bow, or almost dead ahead, the sails on the foremast were thrown a-back. With luck, this, plus the ship's momentum, would push the bow through the wind. Once the wind was on the other side of the ship success was assured. The sails on the main and mizzen were braced round and filled and the helmsman had control again.

## Wearing

Wearing (or veering) was an alternative to tacking as a method of turning a ship round. Villeneuve used it several hours before the battle off Cape Trafalgar to reverse the direction of his entire fleet from almost south to almost north. It was only possible to tack if there was sufficient way (speed) to turn the ship's bow

through the wind, whereas wearing involved turning her stern through the wind. This manoeuvre was only possible with plenty of sea room, as it took considerably longer than tacking and a lot of leeway could be lost. Its advantage was that it could be done in virtually any condition of sea or wind – so it never failed. It was also easier on the rigging, because nothing was thrown aback, and on the rudder fastenings as the ship was at no point sailing backwards.

## Heaving to

This was a commonplace manoeuvre used to stop a ship and hold it stationary, or nearly so. It was necessary when riding out a storm, lowering a boat, allowing another ship to catch up, keeping station on blockade or (sometimes) engaging an enemy. It involved putting the helm down so that the ship tended to turn into the wind while some sails were filled and others backed to counteract any forward movement. One way was to take in the courses and have the fore sails backed but the main and mizzen sails filled.

## Heavy weather manoeuvres

### Scudding

In a severe gale, with perhaps mountainous waves, a possible option was to run before the storm, heading directly down wind. This was resorted to if there was enough sea room to leeward and if the course to be taken was roughly in the desired direction. All sails were taken in except for the fore- and maintopsails, which might be reefed (reefing must have been a terrifying experience). In a wind that was so violent that no sails could be carried, a ship could run with bare masts, but the danger then was that the helm would become ineffective and the ship would yaw, fly up into the wind or broach to.

### Heaving to or lying to

Caught in a bad storm in confined waters, this was the only real option.

## Anchoring

The ability to drop anchor quickly could prevent the ship foundering on a lee shore in a storm or after a battle. Even then, care had to be taken to control the speed of the cable going out and water thrown on the beams to prevent fire caused by the friction. With heavy seas and a violent wind driving a ship towards a rocky shore, cliffs or dangerous shoals, dropping anchor to stop or slow the ship was essential to avoid disaster. Similarly after a battle, with ships damaged, masts and sails destroyed and the ability to sail therefore drastically reduced, it was sometimes prudent to anchor to make repairs or, as in a storm, avoid being blown onto a lee shore. It was this danger that Nelson foresaw after Trafalgar. His last order as he lay dying was that the fleet must anchor after the battle, as he feared his ships being driven onto the jagged coast of Cape Trafalgar. However, despite the storm that blew up after the battle, Collingwood did not anchor.

An anchor was designed to bury one of its spade-like flukes in the bottom and resist any horizontal pull. This was fine in theory, but in practice on either a rocky or soft sandy or muddy bottom the ship would not be held and would drag her anchor(s). The closer to horizontal the cable, the more effective the pull of the anchor – anchoring in more than 40 fathoms (240 feet) was seldom attempted, because the depth meant the anchor cable would be almost vertical. To drop anchor involved the following procedures:

- The anchor, with a buoy attached, was allowed to hang vertically from the cathead by a single rope known as a stopper.
- Estimates were made from the charts as to the depth of water the ship would anchor in.
- An appropriate length of cable was brought up from the orlop deck and laid out on the lower deck.
- The inboard end of the cable was secured to the bitts while the outer end was fed through the hawse hole and bent (attached) to the anchor.
- The leadsman would call out the depth of water as the ship approached the anchorage.
- Normally, the ship's speed would be reduced by putting the helm over to steer the ship into the wind. The ship would stop

## Path of Ship Wearing

X destination

direction of wind

### Notes

- This was the manoeuvre used by Villeneuve prior to Trafalgar, although he only did so once, not eight times as in this diagram.
- The opposite of tacking, wearing involved turning the ship's stern through the wind; because it needed plenty of space, this could only be done in open sea.
- Its advantage was that it was a simpler operation than tacking, but it took longer and considerable leeway could be lost.
- The path of a ship wearing to windward looked like a series of copperplate flourishes. The distance covered from start point to destination far exceeded that for tacking.

## Anchoring

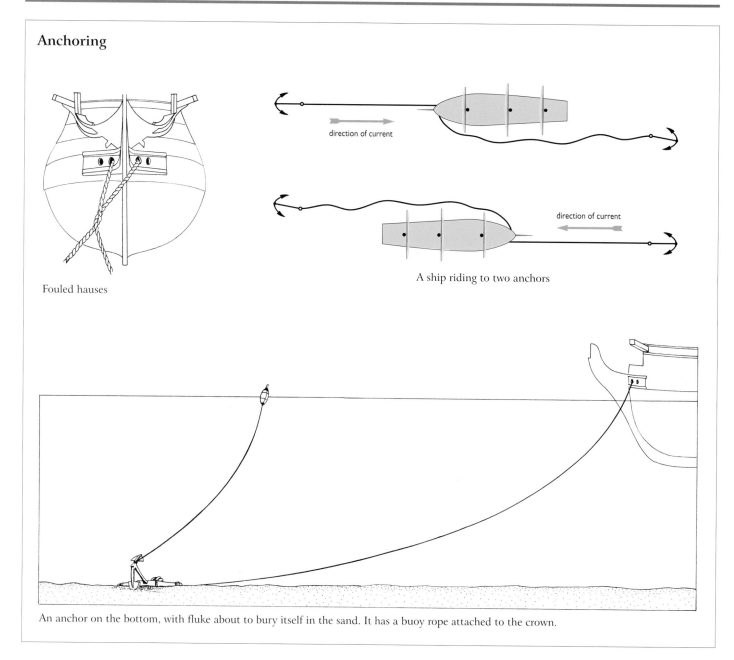

Fouled hauses

direction of current

direction of current

A ship riding to two anchors

An anchor on the bottom, with fluke about to bury itself in the sand. It has a buoy rope attached to the crown.

and begin to gather sternway (go backwards), the stopper would be released and the anchor would fall to the bottom.
• As the ship continued to make sternway, the cable was let out gradually until it ran out. The ship was then riding at anchor.

When held by a single anchor a ship would tend to swing with the tide in a wide circle about equal in radius to the length of cable let out. If the ship was to remain at anchor for any length of time, two anchors would be used – such a ship was then regarded as 'moored'. This greatly reduced the swing of the ship but risked it becoming entangled with the changing tides; using the sails to manoeuvre the ship at each turn of tide prevented this.

Unlike anchoring, methods of weighing anchor varied according to wind and sea conditions. The first method was to sail the ship slowly towards the anchor, taking in the slack of the cable with the capstan as the ship moved. The second was to haul the cable in with the capstan and thus use muscle power rather than the wind to drag the ship forward onto the anchor.

### Dangers If Anchors Failed

It was frequently impossible to make ground to windward – one captain reported beating (tacking) painfully up the Channel for four weeks to make port. More serious was when heavy seas forced a ship inexorably towards a lee shore. She could easily find herself embayed – trapped in a bay, unable to clear the headlands. In these circumstances there was no hope but the anchors. In addition, captains sometimes cut away their masts to reduce windage aloft. Even these extreme measures could not always prevent anchors dragging or cables breaking, followed by the ship foundering on the shore. A gale in Plymouth Sound in 1762 forced seven ships to cut away their masts, five of which foundered due to anchors failing and two of which collided with each other.

# NAVIGATION

All officers in Nelson's navy had to understand navigation; indeed, budding midshipmen were rigorously tested in their application of navigational skills before promotion to lieutenant. But it was the master who was the specialist, with ultimate responsibility under the captain. Navigation can be divided into two parts – pilotage (coastal navigation) and deep-sea navigation. To conduct a ship safely across the high seas to a distant port the navigator required first a chart embracing his starting point and destination, on which he could lay off the course or courses he must steer. He also needed some means of keeping his ship on her predetermined course, and some way of knowing what speed she was making through the water at any time. These two needs were met, respectively, by the compass and the log – not to be confused with the log book, in which the events of the voyage were recorded. Furthermore, while his ship was anywhere near the coast he had to determine at frequent intervals, by the hand-lead, the depth of the water in which he was navigating, and also check her position by making observations of recognizable points on land or buoys. Finally, when out of sight of land he could not trust to 'dead reckoning' – that is, assume that because he had steered due west (by compass) for 500 miles (by the log) he was necessarily 500 miles due west of his starting point. By reason of a combination of currents, tide or bad steering he might be many miles from his estimated position. He therefore had to keep an accurate check on his latitude and longitude by taking observations from the sun or stars. Brief notes on the navigator's art and equipment are given below.

## The binnacle

This was a sideboard-like cupboard positioned athwartships in front of the wheel on the quarterdeck. The top was divided into three compartments, with a compass on either side and a lantern in the centre to illuminate the compass at night. There were usually drawers in the binnacle to store the slate, a telescope (called a 'bring 'em near'), log and lead lines, hour-glasses and a night glass. The latter took some getting used to as it gave an inverted image – a ship would appear upside down and seemingly on the opposite tack to the one it was actually sailing.

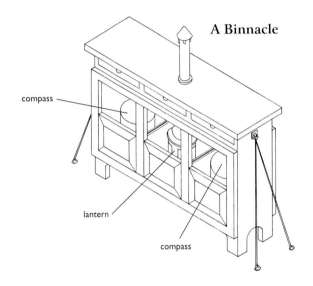

A Binnacle

compass

lantern

compass

## Nelson's Navigation

Two of Nelson's great victories required considerable navigational and seamanship skills dangerously close inshore: the Nile and Copenhagen. However, if asked which incident involving navigation he was most proud of, he would probably have chosen his passage of the Harwich Channel in 1801. On 10 August of that year Admiral Nelson came aboard his flagship the 36-gun frigate *Medusa*, which was lying at anchor off Harwich. She had been imprisoned for two days by a strong easterly wind and Nelson urgently needed her to take him to the Nore that night. Nelson himself explained the situation to a Mr Spence, the Maritime Surveyor of that part of the coast: 'We have got the *Medusa* into this hole, but cannot get her out again, through the proper channel, while this wind remains, and although I have two or three pilots on board, neither they, nor the Harwich pilots will take charge of her. I must get to the Nore tonight in her.' As she had inched her way to her anchorage through the passage between the Ridge and Andrew's Shoal, her keel had scraped the bottom twice. The pilots refused outright to attempt to get her into Harwich and Hollesley Bay over the flats extending seawards from The Naze. Nelson, however, persuaded Mr Spence to overrule the pilots and attempt the passage at high tide. His success was a record for ships of that size and the channel was thereafter named Medusa Channel.

## The Mariner's Compass

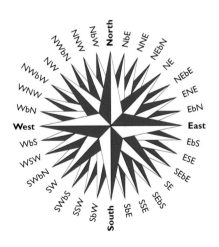

### Notes
• The compass was divided into 32 points.
• The small 'b' indicated 'by', thus SEbE meant 'South-east by east'.

## Log lines and lead lines

The log line was used to measure the speed of the ship through the water. The 'log' was a weighted piece of triangular wood and was attached to a light cord about 150 fathoms (900 feet) long, which had knots tied in it at 48-foot intervals. The log was cast off the stern and the line allowed to pull out from its reel as the log floated stationary in the water. When the first knot was reached a small sand timer that ran for 28 seconds was turned, and the number of knots that passed in this period counted. The ship had a speed of one knot or one nautical mile per hour for every knot that passed; knots are still used today to measure ship or aircraft speeds. It was normal routine for the log line to be cast every half-hour. The officer-of-the-watch recorded the results, the course steered, wind directions and strength during the previous half-hour on the log slate (blackboard) situated close to the wheel. All data was later transcribed into the master's log – which in turn the captain often copied, although he was supposed to keep his log independently.

The lead line was used for measuring the depth of the water. It consisted of a 20-fathom (120-foot) length of line attached to a conical piece of lead that was hollow and filled with tallow so that it could pick up a sample of the bottom. The hand lead, which could be used while the ship was moving, weighed about 7 lbs, while the deep-sea lead, with a 200-fathom line, weighed from 14 to 30 lbs. The ship had to heave to in order to use this heavy line. The lead was cast by a seaman standing in the channel, which

### A Seaman Swinging the Lead Line

### A Quadrant

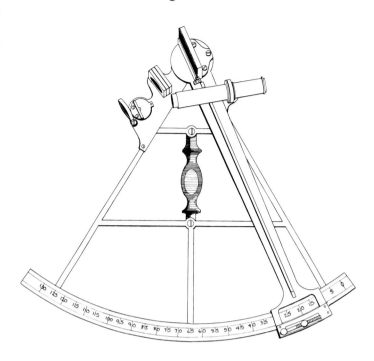

overhung the side of the ship. All lines were marked at intervals to indicate various depths in fathoms – for example, a piece of black leather indicted 3 fathoms, a white rag 5 fathoms.

## Glasses

Time-keeping was critical, not only for navigation but also for the smooth running of life on board ship, the change of watches, soundings taken and log entries made. Several types of sandglass were used. A normal watch of four hours had a four-hour watch glass; a half-watch (dog-watch) glass lasted two hours. There were half-hour glasses to indicate when lookouts or helmsmen were to be changed over, together with much smaller ones of four, one and one-half minutes for use when the log line was run out.

## Quadrants and sextants

Hadley's quadrant, invented in 1731 for measuring the angles of the sun, was made of wood and consisted of an arm that pivoted on a frame shaped as a sector of a circle, on which a scale of 45 degrees was marked. A system of mirrors doubled the 45-degree angle on the frame (hence the name quadrant, meaning a quarter of a circle) and shades were fitted to protect the eyes of the observer. At noon every day the master, the officer-of-the-watch and sometimes the captain would take navigational sightings and calculations to fix the position of the ship accurately. This would involve dead reckoning, celestial observation or taking bearings on shore objects. The results would be plotted on the chart table in the master's cabin (which served as a chart room) using dividers, scale rulers and compass.

The sextant, which could measure 60 degrees, a sixth of a circle (hence the name sextant), doubled by mirrors, was a more accurate version of the quadrant. It was made of brass rather than wood and was expensive. Probably for this reason it did not entirely replace the quadrant in Nelson's navy, although many officers (and virtually all masters) purchased their own.

## PILOTAGE

In Britain pilots were required to go on board ships entering or leaving ports whose approaches were dangerous due to complex tidal flows, shoals, shallows or channels. This included virtually all the coastal waters around England. Pilots were supplied by the Navy Board for the River Thames and its estuary, and by the Society of Pilots at Dover for the Downs. They were only to be used when authorized for a particular port. If one had to be employed due to the ignorance of the master, his fees were to be deducted from the master's wages! For some overseas destinations pilots were taken on as part of the crew. They were rated as warrant officers and given a berth in the gunroom.

However, the inaccuracy of the charts and the incompetence of many pilots was notorious. Pilots were often troublesome, indolent and always expensive. One exasperated captain of the time remarked, 'The insolence and ignorance of these fellows occasion frequent delays and inconveniences to the Service.'

## TIDES AND CURRENTS

Of all the dangers seamen faced when piloting a ship, tides presented the greatest problems. Not only do tides alter the amount of water under the keel, but their flow can push a ship off course and hasten or slow her progress. In the landlocked Mediterranean, with a maximum variation in sea level of three feet and weak tidal flows, there was seldom cause for concern. Around the coasts of north-west Europe, however, the situation was alarmingly different. Along these constricted shores, tides could rise or fall 30 feet, with tidal streams of perhaps 4 knots. In narrow channels 8 knots was not impossible. Being able to 'work the tides' was one of the most demanding tasks of a master or pilot.

Equally important to a master was his knowledge of the ocean currents, whose set and drift could add or subtract many miles to his ship's daily run. The usual method of discovering what current a ship was experiencing, still in use in Nelson's day, had been documented as early as the beginning of the seventeenth century. It was described in 1844 in the thirteenth edition of J. W. Norie's *Practical Navigation* as, 'take a boat in calm weather, a small distance from the ship, and being provided with a half minute glass, a log, a heavy iron pot ... and a small boat compass, to let down the pot ... by a rope fastened to the boat's stem, to a depth of about 100 fathoms [600 feet], by which the boat will remain as steady as at anchor; the log being hove, its bearing will be the setting of the current and the number of knots run out in half a minute will be its drift per hour'.

# *HMS Agamemnon*, 1793 TO 1796

## HALF PAY

Five years without a ship was an eternity for an officer as dedicated to the navy as Nelson. He wrote frequently, but unavailingly, to all in authority, reminding them of his existence and pleading for a command. The odds, however, were stacked against him. He was far from the only captain struggling on half pay. Britain was at peace, and for every ship that was kept in commission and needed, a captain the Admiralty could choose from at least a dozen possible candidates. Nelson's competence was never in doubt, but he had alienated people in high places. His officious insistence on applying the Navigation Act in the Caribbean was recalled with annoyance by many. He had quarrelled with, and disobeyed, his admiral, while his exposure of peculation by Leeward Island officials had stirred up further enmity by powerful individuals. But perhaps most damning of all, King George III had turned against him. Nelson, on a visit to Lord Hood, had been informed frostily that, 'the king was impressed with an unfavourable impression' of him. This was the result of Nelson's friendship with the King's son, Prince William, Duke of Clarence, then at the centre of an almost daily round of scandals and outrageous behaviour that infuriated the King and made him highly suspicious of his son's associates.

Life at the parsonage at Burnham Thorpe was not without its problems either. Although Nelson was devoted to his new wife, Fanny, she failed to conceive by him and it became apparent that Josiah, Nelson's stepson, would be her only child. Additionally, she was forever ill. The bleak winters, the icy winds sweeping across the flat fields and fens of Norfolk from the Arctic or Siberia, were torture for a woman brought up in the glorious sunshine of tropical islands. When she was not suffering from rheumatism or arthritis, she was just plain cold or afflicted with the 'vapours', something that modern medicine would probably describe as a psychosomatic illness. Nevertheless, Fanny was to outlive most of her family, including her son. Despite her persistent and painful ailments she lived to be seventy-three.

Then there were the family's financial difficulties. A hundred pounds a year half pay spelt serious poverty. Nelson could only maintain reasonable standards and pay regular visits to Bath so Fanny could visit the spa because he lived in his father's house, and because of the generosity of his uncle, William Suckling, who gave him an allowance of another hundred pounds a year. Fanny received a similar amount from her uncle.

The months and seasons passed slowly. Life for Nelson revolved around gardening, writing letters to their Lordships, reading (Dampier's *Voyages* was a favourite), visiting relatives, taking Fanny to the spas, enduring the long winters and, in the spring, some birds-nesting and coursing – a favourite pastime. There were sometimes invitations for the naval captain to go shooting, but unfortunately Nelson was a lousy shot, to the extent that many of his companions considered him more dangerous to themselves than the birds. He carried his gun loaded and cocked at all times and blasted off, often from the hip, at the first bird he saw. It is reported that he once shot a partridge.

### *HMS Agamemnon*

In January 1793 things changed dramatically. In France the Revolutionary mob put King Louis XVI's head on the block, war became imminent and Nelson, in London, was told he would get a ship, not just any ship, but a ship-of-the-line. He was to command a 64 initially but with the prospect of a 74 a little later. He was ecstatic. By 26 January he was 'fixed for the *Agamemnon* at Chatham'. Nelson had no wish to be fobbed off with scores of jail-birds and the victims of the press gangs, so he embarked on frantic efforts to get together a reliable crew, helped by his old friend Locker, who was then commodore at Sheerness. Nelson's cousin, Lieutenant Maurice Suckling, was discharged from Locker's flagship, the *Sandwich*, to the '*Eggs and Bacon*', as the *Agamemnon* was affectionately known. Joseph King, formerly Nelson's boatswain on the *Boreas*, was transferred from the *Valiant*; Nelson wrote of him that he was 'one of the best boatswains I have seen in His Majesty's service'. Fanny sent her twelve year-old son Josiah Nisbet to join the midshipmen's mess in the gunroom of the *Agamemnon*. Even Nelson's old servant from a previous ship, Frank, was mustered as his steward once more. With the crew Nelson 'sent out a lieutenant, and four mids, to get men at every sea port in Norfolk'. The muster book was thereby filled with a high proportion of volunteers from Norfolk and Suffolk. Her captain was as pleased with the crew as he was with the ship, which, in the twelve years since her launch from Buckler's Hard, had gained an excellent reputation for being both fast and hard hitting.

### Cadiz, Toulon and the *Melpomène* (Map 11)

In June 1793, Lord Hood with eleven ships-of-the-line, including the *Agamemnon*, sailed for the Mediterranean. As Spain was still neutral, Hood detached the *Agamemnon* with several other ships to pay a friendly call to Cadiz, headquarters of the Spanish treasure fleet and the wealthiest port in Western Europe. Spanish hospitality was open and generous, and the British ships' captains were able to inspect the Spanish fleet in port and discuss its merits (and

## Nelson and *Agamemnon* in the Mediterranean (June to December 1793)    Map 11

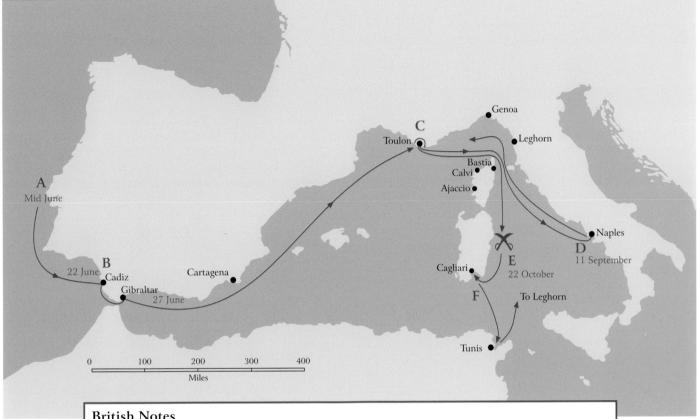

**British Notes**

A   Nelson in *Agamemnon* and Lord Hood in *Victory* sail for the Mediterranean with 11 ships-of-the-line.

B   Nelson calls at Cadiz and samples Spanish hospitality, including a gory bullfight.

C   Hood, now reinforced to 15 ships, blockades Toulon and the port, along with the French fleet, is handed to the British on 27 August. The British are then besieged until forced to withdraw in December.

D   Meanwhile Nelson is sent to Naples to secure troop reinforcements for the defence of Toulon. He meets Sir William and Lady (Emma) Hamilton for the first time.

E   After returning to Toulon, Nelson is sent to join a British squadron at Cagliari. En route he chases and engages the French frigate *Melpomène*, which is badly damaged and only rescued by four other French ships.

F   Nelson accompanies the squadron (under Linzee) to Tunis, and in December returns to Leghorn for a refit.

---

note its failings) with its officers. Nelson commented, 'They have four first-rates in commission at Cadiz, and very fine ships, but shockingly manned. ... The Dons make fine ships, they cannot however make men.' A Spanish frigate captain explained the high level of sickness among his crew by saying it was to be expected after sixty days at sea. Nelson kept his response to himself. The visitors were also permitted to cast a professional eye over the port defences. They inspected the naval arsenal of Isla de Leon, the fortifications of Cortadura and the extensive dockyards. Nelson was wined and dined by the Spanish admiral on board his 112-gun flagship, the *Concepcion*. It had been a very worthwhile visit, but was spoiled by the final day.

Saturday 22 June 1793 was hot as only a Spanish midsummer day can be. The Spanish authorities had invited the officers from the six Royal Navy ships to a farewell entertainment on a rocky island in the middle of some salt marshes on the southern side of the bay. The officers were ushered into the best seats in an amphitheatre that could hold 16,000 people. They had come to

watch what we know as a bullfight but which was translated to Nelson as a 'Bull-Feast'. The atmosphere was much as it would have been in Roman times, when the same crowd packed into the same seats to sweat and scream in the boiling sun as gladiators and wild animals died in the sand. The spectators were the same mix of patricians and plebs, gentry and peasants, high-class ladies and low-class whores. The Spanish hosts explained that society ladies came to pick their lovers from those who showed courage and skill in despatching the bulls – even this aspect had not changed in nearly two thousand years. Ten bulls died painfully that day, five horses were disembowelled and two of the bulls' tormentors seriously gored – it was considered an excellent day. But Nelson and his officers were appalled, sickened by the seemingly endless slaughter and by the all too frequent shrieks of female delight at the bloody struggle. He later wrote, 'How women can even sit out, much more applaud, such sights, is astonishing. It even turned us sick, and we could hardly go through it: the dead mangled horses with their entrails torn out, and the bulls covered with blood, were too much.'

## Toulon Defies the Tricolor

It is often forgotten that for a time in 1793 British forces occupied Toulon, France's most important naval arsenal and the key to her control of the Mediterranean. In August of that year, the city rebelled against the revolutionaries, admitting an Anglo-Spanish fleet (Spain was not at that time allied to France). Its loss through treachery was a major blow, and the French government feared that the idea of revolt could spread – the reputation, indeed the success, of the Revolution was at stake. Toulon must be retaken regardless of the cost. Meanwhile, British ships had been pouring troops in to bolster the garrison – it would eventually total 15,000.

A Corsican artillery captain, Napoleon Bonaparte, was given charge of the siege artillery when the existing commander was wounded. In a truly amazing demonstration of energy, zeal, perseverance and leadership eleven new batteries had been set up by the end of November. One particular site was unpopular with the gunners as it was extremely uncomfortable and dangerously exposed. Bonaparte quickly demonstrated his understanding of soldiers by erecting a large notice at the battery entrance with the words, '*Batterie*

*des hommes sans peur*' (Battery of the men without fear). Thereafter it was never short of volunteers. Despite his lowly rank it was Bonaparte's plan of attack that was accepted by his superiors. There was a setback, however, when the British under General O'Hara led a strong sortie, which was driven off by a counter-attack headed by Bonaparte in which O'Hara was wounded and captured. When the main assault went in on 17 December, covered by an immense bombardment, several outlying defensive forts were captured – in the course of which Bonaparte had a horse shot under him and received a bayonet wound in the thigh. Guns could then be advanced to fire on the British ships in the port with red-hot shot. As the artillery opened fire, Admiral Hood ordered the evacuation to begin. The arsenal was deliberately blown up – a sure sign that the garrison had had enough. On 18 December the last of the British and Allied troops, along with numerous citizens of Toulon who feared for their necks, sailed out of the harbour. Toulon belonged to the Republic again, while Napoleon Bonaparte had made a spectacular start to what was to become an even more spectacular career.

---

July and August saw Nelson with the *Agamemnon* as part of Hood's fleet off Toulon. Initially, the fleet kept the French bottled up in the port but it was by no means certain what was happening on land. Toulon had a powerful anti-Revolutionary movement that desperately clung to control of France's premier Mediterranean port. On 27 August this faction gained the upper hand and, to secure their future and save their heads, handed Toulon, together with the French Fleet, over to the British. Hood had to occupy the port and prepare to defend it against what would surely become a serious siege. Reinforcements were essential, and Nelson was sent to Naples in early September to expedite the dispatch of more troops: some 4,000 were eventually forthcoming. To fulfil his mission in Naples, Nelson had to present himself to Sir William Hamilton, the British Envoy and Minister Plenipotentiary to the Court of the Two Sicilies, and to Sir John Acton, officially Secretary for War and Minister of

Marine and in practice the most powerful man in the Neapolitan government. Sir William, an efficient but elderly gentleman in his sixties, had recently acquired a young and voluptuous wife, Emma, with whom Nelson was suitably impressed. He was not to see her again for five years, although he corresponded regularly with Sir William. Then she would dramatically change his personal life and enter the history books alongside him.

Acton arranged for the transportation of the troops, who arrived at Toulon on 5 October, the same day as the *Agamemnon* returned. Within three days Hood ordered Nelson south with orders for Commodore Robert Linzee's squadron at Cagliari in southern Sardinia. Due to sickness, his crew could only muster 345 men – not enough to man all her guns. On 22 October, *Agamemnon* was in action off the north-west coast of Sardinia. An excited young midshipman, twelve-year-old William Hoste, wrote to his father describing his first encounter with the enemy:

---

## Nelson's 'Roving Eye'

There is little doubt that Nelson had a sailor's eye for a pretty girl. Even before his passionate affair with Emma Hamilton, he had undoubtedly committed adultery. His contemporary biographer James Harrison hinted at this when he wrote: 'though by no means ever an unprincipled seducer of the wives and daughters of his friends, he was always well known to maintain rather more partiality for the fair sex than is quite consistent with the highest degree of Christian purity'.

Captain Freemantle, who commanded the frigate *Inconstant* in the action against the *Ça Ira* and was one of Nelson's 'band of brothers', corroborates Harrison's somewhat priggish comment. Freemantle noted of his time with Nelson at Leghorn:

> December 1794. Wed. 3. Dined at Nelson's and his Dolly. Called on old Udney [British Consul], went to the opera with him. He introduced me to a very handsome Greek woman.

> August 1795. A convoy arrived from Genoa. Dined with Nelson. Dolly aboard who has a sort of abscess in her side, he makes himself ridiculous with that woman.

> August. Sat. 28. Dined with Nelson and his Dolly.

> September. Sun. 27. Dined with Nelson and Dolly. Very bad dinner indeed.

In early 1782 Nelson suffered from a 'fleshy excrescence' between his upper lip and jawbone that was painful when he shaved. Doctors at Haslar naval hospital, Portsmouth, diagnosed a venereal infection and suggested mercurial treatment. Nelson agreed the remedy, but a French dentist offered to cut it off with a scalpel, to which Nelson consented. The growth was removed and the problem was, seemingly, solved, but this is clear evidence that Nelson knew he had been at risk from venereal infection.

On the 22nd of October, when running down the island of Sardinia, about two o'clock in the morning ... we saw five sail of ships standing to the NW. On observing us, they tacked and stood to the eastward. Captain Nelson, suspecting them to be a French convoy, immediately stood after them. About three o'clock we were very near up with the hindmost, and at four within gunshot. We hailed her in French, but receiving no answer, fired a gun for her to bring to, and shorten sail, when we observed her making signals with sky-rockets to her consorts, who were some distance to windward. After we had repeatedly hailed her to no purpose, we fired one of our eighteen-pounders at her, to oblige them to shorten sail.

It did not have the desired effect, as the French frigate, identified as the 44-gun *Melpomène*, crammed on more sail to get away. The *Agamemnon*, although a larger and therefore slower ship, was able to keep her within range for over three hours. During this time, however, skilful sailing by the frigate enabled her to fire broadsides at the *Agamemnon* while only receiving shots from Nelson's bow guns in return. Not until the end of the engagement was the *Melpomène* to feel the full weight of a broadside. Hoste continued:

> She bravely engaged us in this manner for three hours, both ships sailing at the rate of six knots an hour ... . The other frigates were coming after us with a fresh breeze, consequently we expected to have warm work, and were therefore anxious to dispatch this gentleman before they arrived, but, at about eight o'clock, by an alteration of the wind our antagonist got out of reach of our guns. Our last broadside did initiate damage, nor was what we received inconsiderable, as our rigging was shot away, and our main top-mast broken ...

The other French frigates arrived to take the crippled *Melpomène* in tow. They neglected to press home an attack on the *Agamemnon*, while Nelson, after consulting his officers, allowed the enemy to sail slowly away, taking their almost sinking frigate to Calvi on the north-east coast of Corsica.

After arrival in Cagliari, Hood's orders were opened and Linzee found he was to take his squadron to Tunis on a semi-diplomatic mission that also served as a show of force. By Christmas, Nelson at long last was able to take *Agamemnon* into Leghorn for a refit. A few days before he arrived, the French, under the guidance of a little known artillery captain called Napoleon Bonaparte had bombarded Toulon into submission. Hood carried out a hasty evacuation that included burning the French ships in port before turning his attentions to Corsica (Captain Bonaparte's birthplace) as a suitable island on which to establish a British base.

## 1794: THE CORSICAN CAMPAIGN (Maps 12 and 13)

### San Fiorenzo

The *Agamemnon* left Leghorn on 3 January 1794 en route for Corsica. Nelson had been entrusted with yet another diplomatic mission, this time to settle with the Corsican patriot General de Paoli, who had agreed the island should be ceded to Britain provided the British expelled the French, who had garrisons at San Fiorenzo, Bastia and Calvi. Unfortunately, 'the hardest gale of wind ever remembered here' drove him off station with the loss of most of *Agamemnon*'s sails. Hood's fleet, loaded with hundreds of violently seasick soldiers, was similarly scattered to seek shelter at Elba. Nevertheless, while blockading Bastia Nelson was able to carry out several pinprick raids ashore, mostly north of the town, to draw the French attention away from San Fiorenzo where Hood intended to make a landing. Nelson and his men enjoyed the variety and excitement these small-scale coastal raids provided. Shortly before the storm spoiled his fun, Nelson led an attack on a flour store near San Fiorenzo: 'I seized a happy moment, landed sixty soldiers and seamen. In spite of opposition at the landing the sailors threw all the flour into the sea, burned the mill, the only one they have, and returned on board without the loss of a man.' Other successes included burning twelve vessels loaded with wine (an unusual destruction of such a prized commodity!) and capturing a small fort north of Bastia, together with a small castle from which Nelson personally tore down the French colours.

### The Tower at Mortella Point, San Fiorenzo

The tower on Mortella Point on the western coast of the Gulf of Fiorenzo was a tough nut to crack. It was a solitary, circular tower with solid masonry 15 feet thick mounting two 18- and one 6-pounder gun with a small but determined garrison of thirty-eight soldiers. On 8 February 1794 a 32-gun frigate, *Juno*, and a 74-gun ship-of-the-line, *Fortitude*, opened fire on the tower. Between them they deployed twenty-eight 32-pounders, twenty-eight 18-pounders, twenty-six 12-pounders, eighteen 9-pounders and six 6-pounders – 106 guns against three! For two and a half hours they pounded away. Most shots missed, while those that did fall on target seemed to have little visible effect. Meanwhile, the tower's response had been nothing short of devastating. Using hot shot, the French gunners had set the *Fortitude* on fire and inflicted over sixty casualties. Both ships were forced to retire surprised and hurt. Not a single defender had been scratched.

It was only after Dundas had established a shore battery of four guns protected by earthworks within 150 yards of the tower and bombarded it continuously for two days with hot shot that the gallant garrison surrendered. The strong resistance offered by these three guns led to the conclusion that towers of this description were especially formidable. Britain, calling them Martello Towers, built large numbers, at heavy expense, along the shores of England, particularly along the south and east coasts, where a number remain to this day. They contain vaulted rooms for the garrison, and a platform at the top for two or three guns that fire over a low masonry parapet. Access was provided by a ladder, communicating with a door some 20 feet above the ground. In some cases a ditch was provided around the base. Little did the handful of French soldiers in that remote, forgotten tower know that their efforts would inspire a new type of defence along many miles of their enemy's shores.

## Capturing San Fiorenzo and Bastia, 1794   Map 12

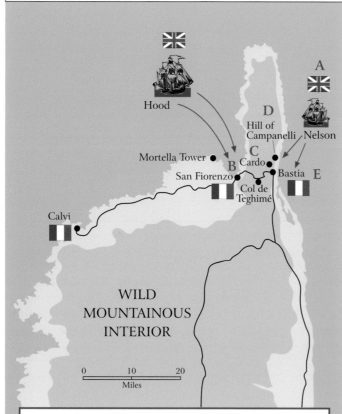

**British Notes**

A   Jan 1794 Nelson in *Agamemnon* makes coastal raids around Bastia while blockading it.

B   19 Feb British occupy San Fiorenzo and French retreat to Bastia.

C   23–27 Feb Maj-Gen. Dundas sends Corsican force to Cardo but they are driven off. He decides to wait and see what effect the blockade has.

D   4–9 April Nelson lands eight of *Agamemnon*'s guns to be part of the battery on Campanelli Hill above Bastia.

E   21 May The garrison at Bastia surrenders to the British.

In mid-February the British took San Fiorenzo with something over 2,000 troops. The only real opposition came from the gallant garrison of the Tower of Mortella at the point of that name on the western side of the Gulf of San Fiorenzo, which resisted a close-range bombardment for twenty-six hours. Eventually the French withdrew along the mountain road to Bastia, leaving the British Army to settle down at San Fiorenzo under Major-General Dundas. From there, on 23 and 24 February he advanced two battalions halfway to Bastia under Lieutenant-Colonel John Moore (later of light infantry fame and destined, as a general, to die at Corunna in 1809). From the Col de Teghimé it was possible to survey the defences of Bastia. Dundas sent forward a reconnaissance in force of Corsican allies to the Cardo ridge, but they were quickly driven off by a spirited sally from Bastia, burning Cardo village in the process. On 27 February, Dundas retreated back almost to San Fiorenzo, then refused to budge, preferring to await the effects of the blockade on the French garrison at Bastia and further British reinforcements from Gibraltar.

## Bastia

The Army gave Nelson the nickname 'The Brigadier', so keen was he that Bastia could be taken with a dash of determination. He forthrightly condemned Dundas for his supposed timidity. Hood supported Nelson, so there was a bitter clash of personalities between the admiral and the general. On 11 March, Dundas sailed home on sick leave, leaving command of his forces not to Moore but to the senior officer, Colonel D'Aubant of the engineers – described by the British Army's historian, Sir John Fortescue, as 'a feeble and incompetent officer'. A council of war between the naval flag officers and army field officers on 20 March at San Fiorenzo resulted in deadlock. The naval officers, who had not seen the ground, unanimously declared in favour of an attack; the army officers, who had, unanimously pronounced against it. On 2 April Hood sailed away to play the soldier off Bastia, at the same time vainly urging the Army to advance from the west.

Two days later Nelson landed eight 24-pounders from *Agamemnon*'s gundeck, and these, along with eight 13-inch mortars recently arrived from Naples, were dragged into position atop Campanelli Hill. A Sub-Lieutenant Duncan of the artillery had recommended this position, some 2,500 yards north of the citadel in Bastia. Getting the guns into position was a herculean effort that also demonstrated the ingenuity of Nelson's sailors. Sir Gilbert Elliot, the future British envoy on the island, watched with amazement as these enormous loads were hauled up the mountainside:

> They fastened great straps round the rocks, and then fastened to the straps the largest and most powerful purchases, or pullies, and tackle, that are used on board a man-of-war. The cannon were placed on a sledge at one end of the tackle, the men walked down hill with the other end of the tackle. The surprise of our friends the Corsicans, and our enemies the French, was equal to the occasion.

Nelson and a Lieutenant-Colonel Vilettes had also brought some 1,250 men ashore to man the battery while Hood's fleet anchored in a crescent formation round the harbour just out of effective range of the garrison's guns. Further inshore a floating battery of gunboats and launches was deployed. The *Agamemnon*'s log reads:

> Saturday 5 April: Landed the troops equipage & 2 days provisions. Left on shore several sail for tents for the officers and seamen. People employed making sandbags for the batteries. Empd [employed] getting into launch two 24-pounders, sent them on shore with sundry other stores.
> Wednesday 9 April: Landed 150 barrels of powder with a quantity of grape & canister shot.
> Friday 11 April: At ½ past 9 our Batteries opened upon the Enemy Redoubts, the Mortars upon the Town. ...

But the bombardment by Nelson's battery on the hill and the inshore flotilla in the harbour failed to produce dramatic results. The floating battery was speedily destroyed or dispersed with red-hot shot while the range to the citadel from the hill proved too great for effective shooting. Days then weeks passed in stalemate while the mutual pounding continued. Casualties were inflicted on both sides (five 'Agamemnons' were killed) but nothing decisive was achieved. During this time Nelson was slightly wounded, being struck by a piece of flying metal that inflicted a 'sharp cut in the back' as he and others went forward to reconnoitre a better gun position closer to the town. However, he was in no way incapacitated and continued to enjoy his role of artillery commander.

On 15 May some fresh drafts arrived for the Army at San Fiorenzo and an emboldened Colonel D'Aubant marched his men up the hill to the Col de Teghimé. It was little more than a parade. On 21 May, before he could make up his mind to do anything interesting, the garrison in Bastia surrendered, having exhausted their food and virtually all their ammunition. General Paoli transferred Corsica's allegiance to the British and the *Agamemnon* was sent to Gibraltar for a long-overdue emergency refit, before returning to take part in the final part of the operation, the taking of Calvi.

## Calvi

At around 7.00 on the morning of 10 July, Nelson was in the main battery overlooking Fort Mozzello, about 700 metres down the ridge leading to Calvi. Firing by both sides had already begun and Nelson was watching the strike of the shots from the battery. At that moment an enemy cannonball hit the sandbag and stone embankment protecting the guns. There was an instantaneous blast of stone fragments and sand, some of which struck Nelson in the chest and face, while the ball itself was either buried in the gun emplacement or ricocheted away to the rear. Nelson was knocked back with blood pouring from his face. A surgeon was summoned. Once the blood flow was stopped it became clear that the lacerations to his face were superficial, but there was a deep cut just on the right eyebrow, and a piece of stone had penetrated the eyelid and eye. It looked a mess and the pain was intense, but the surgeon was optimistic that he would recover at least some measure of sight. Nelson was soon making light of his injury. That evening, in his report to Lord Hood, he stated that he was 'a little hurt this morning: not much as you may judge from my writing'. Hood showed deep concern and wanted to send his surgeon, but Nelson, although he must still have been suffering discomfort, if not pain, declared himself capable of supervising the construction of another battery, claiming, 'My eye is better, and I hope not entirely to lose the sight.' His hopes were unfounded and Nelson remained blind in his right eye for the remainder of his life – although outwardly the eye looked normal.

### Nelson's Loss of his Right Eye

It can never be certain what medical condition caused Nelson's blindness after his injury at Calvi. All that is known is that he lost his sight in the right eye, and that two certificates to this effect were signed in August 1794, one by the Physician of the Fleet and the other by the Surgeon-General in the Mediterranean. However, there was nothing abnormal in the appearance of the eye itself. The only visible sign of injury was a scar on the eyelid below the eyebrow.

Blindness in the right eye was not Nelson's only problem with his eyes. It is well documented that he had a pterygium growing at the inner side of both eyes. Lord Elgin described Nelson in 1799, when he was forty-one, as 'a prematurely aged man who appeared to have a film growing over both eyes'. Two years later Dr Thomas Trotter, when examining Nelson's 'good eye' on the *San Josef* in Torbay, stated he had 'a membranous substance seemingly growing fast over the pupil'. This led to Trotter recommending Nelson wear a green shade over his eyes; one was sewn into the front of his hat. William Beatty (*Victory*'s surgeon at Trafalgar) was later to state that Nelson's vision in his left eye was impaired and that he always wore the green shield over his forehead to protect this eye from sunlight. However, it is by no means certain that had Nelson lived he would have become totally blind, as has been suggested.

It should be emphasized that at no time did Nelson wear a black patch over his right eye!

Calvi stands at the end of a peninsula formed by a ridge of rocky hills some 900 feet high. The town itself was strongly fortified and further protected by important outworks. These were Fort Mozzello, a pentagon built of stone with a heavy gun on each face situated on rising ground about 750 yards west of the town, coupled with a battery of six guns, called the Fountain Battery, on its northern side and the Francesco Battery, with three guns, standing on a rocky hill washed by the waves. The final outwork was more isolated. This was Fort Monteciesco, with one heavy gun and five or six field pieces built on a steep rock about 2,000 yards south-west of Calvi. Its task, in conjunction with the two frigates in the bay, was to cover the approaches to the town from the south. On 20 June, *Agamemnon*, the 44-gun frigate *Dolphin* and the 18-gun sloop *Lutine*, together with fifteen transports and stores ships, came as close as they dared to the tiny cove of Port Agro, which had been selected two days previously by Nelson and Lieutenant-General Charles Stuart. It was to be a classic combined operation with Nelson commanding the naval aspects and Stuart the military operations ashore. At 3 a.m. troops and sailors began to disembark, along with provisions and stores. The wind was freshening and Nelson soon became anxious of the danger of having to anchor in over 50 fathoms (300 feet) of water so close to a rocky lee shore.

By 22 June the disembarkation had not been completed and a howling gale with thunder, lightning and torrential rain had developed. All three ships had to put to sea in great haste. There was no time to spend hours at the capstan hauling in the best bower, so the hawser cable was buoyed and then cut. The ships were able to beat seaward to sit out the storm. Four days later they returned, and during the next few days guns for the shore batteries, ammunition and rations for the men were taken ashore. Landing them on the beach was just the beginning. The real work was in building a road, dragging everything up into the hills and in building the first battery position able to fire on Fort Monteciesco. That they did it by 4 July (the date the British guns opened fire on this fort) with malaria rampant and under the intolerable heat of a Corsican summer sun (known to the locals as the Lion Sun) was a staggering achievement. Nelson was extremely proud of the efforts of his men ashore during those searing weeks of July: 'By computation we may be supposed to have dragged one 26-pounder with its ammunition and every requisite for making a battery upwards of eighty miles, 17 of which were up a very steep mountain.' But the price was high. He wrote to the Duke of Clarence, 'we have upwards of one thousand sick out of two thousand, and others not much better than so

## The Siege and Capture of Calvi, 20 June to 10 August 1794

Map 13

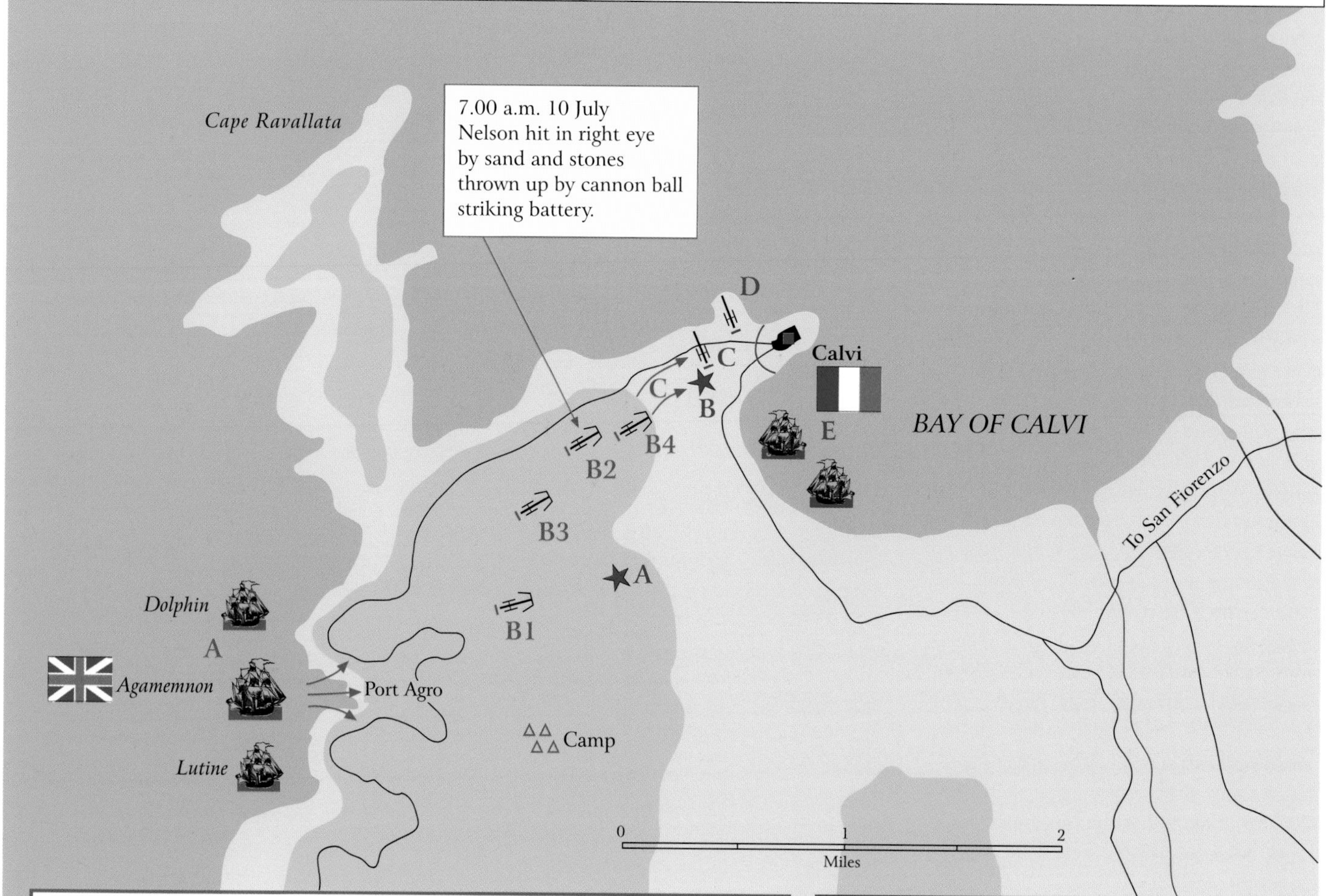

*Cape Ravallata*

7.00 a.m. 10 July
Nelson hit in right eye
by sand and stones
thrown up by cannon ball
striking battery.

D

C

C

B

**Calvi**

B4

B2

E

*BAY OF CALVI*

B3

*To San Fiorenzo*

★A

B1

*Dolphin*

A

*Agamemnon*

→ Port Agro

*Lutine*

△△
△△ Camp

0                    1                    2
Miles

### British Notes

A    20 June *Agamemnon*, *Dolphin* (44) and *Lutine* (18) with 15 transport and store ships begin disembarking over 2,000 troops under Lt-Gen. Charles Stuart. Bulk of Hood's fleet remained at San Fiorenzo.

B1   First battery is established. On 4 July it opens fire on Fort Monteciesco.

B2 & B3   6 July Stuart makes feint night attack on Monteciesco and sets up a battery (B2) within 700 metres of Fort Mozzello and a separate covering battery (B3).

C    19 July Lt-Col. Wemyss leads assault on Fountain Battery and Lt-Col. Moore on Fort Mozzello. Both are taken and another battery is set up (B4). After a short bombardment of the town a 25-day truce is arranged and the French finally surrender on 10 August.

### French Notes

A    Fort Monteciesco (seven guns) built on steep rock to command approach to Calvi from south.

B    Fort Mozzello (five guns)

C    Fountain Battery (six guns)

D    San Francesco Battery (three guns)

E    Two French frigates in harbour, one of which was the *Melpomène*, now recovered from the pounding she had received from the *Agamemnon* the previous October. She was taken into British service.

many phantoms. We have lost many men from the season, very few from the enemy.' Nelson himself suffered from poor health and the heat, but managed to keep going: 'I am here the reed among the oaks: all the prevailing disorders have attacked me, but I have not strength for them to fasten upon. I bow before the storm, while the sturdy oak is laid low.'

There were, of course, some casualties inflicted by the French. Among the first was a friend of Nelson's, Commander Serocold, who was hit 'by grape-shot passing through his head as he cheered the people who were dragging the gun'. The military plan was to mask Fort Monteciesco while another battery was constructed further down the ridge leading to Calvi. On 6 July, Stuart led a feint night attack on this fort while setting up this new gun position

(B2 on Map 13). It was built to breach the walls of Fort Mozzello from a range of about 700 metres, the fort from which Nelson was wounded in the eye. By 19 July the breach in the walls was considered sufficient to warrant an assault. Stuart assembled a force of three battalions for the operation. In reserve was the 51st Foot (West Riding); the 50th Foot (West Kent) built a feint battery (B3 on Map 13) during the night, while the actual storming was assigned to the 18th Foot (Royal Irish) and the light companies (six) from each battalion. Lieutenant-Colonel Moore led the light companies against Fort Mozzello and Lieutenant-Colonel Wemyss led his battalion against Fountain Battery. Both works were carried in the first rush with little loss, although Moore received a slight head wound.

Calvi, however, refused to give in. As the range was too great, yet another battery (B4) had to be constructed nearer the town. More heavy guns were brought forward and this battery opened fire on 31 July. The garrison's guns responded with a salvo that killed Lieutenant William Byron of the 18th Foot, the great-uncle of Lord Byron the poet. These shots were virtually the last the French fired, as Stuart then summonsed the town to surrender. After negotiations it was agreed that the garrison would capitulate on 10 August, unless relieved before then by an expedition from France. None arrived.

The end came none too soon for the British. Lord Hood was unwell, Stuart was sick, Nelson was half blind as well as ill with malaria, while the soldiers and sailors were dropping like flies from fever, fatigue and the heat. The loss of British troops during the siege did not exceed ninety, with a dozen seamen killed or wounded. However, two-thirds of the besiegers had collapsed sick, the remainder being utterly exhausted by the severity of their labours and the climate. Moore was to write in his diary a phrase in which modern readers may recognize a slight Churchillian ring: 'Perhaps there was never so much work done by so few men in the same space of time.'

Corsica was allied to Britain. Nelson went for a medical examination on board the *Victory* by the Physician of the Fleet, Dr Harness. He reported that there was 'a wound of the iris of the right eye, which has occasioned an unnatural dilation of the pupil, and a material defect of sight'. Nelson, writing to Lord Hood, stated, 'As to all purposes of use', his eye was gone. 'I feel the Want of it but such is the chance of War, it was within a hair's breadth of taking off my head.' A month later, to his wife Fanny, he made light of the damage: 'The blemish is nothing, not to be perceived unless told.' Nelson's name never appeared in the Calvi casualty list.

## THE ÇA IRA ACTION

On 8 March 1795 the elderly Admiral Sir William Hotham, flying his flag in the *Britannia*, who had taken over from Lord Hood the previous October, received news that the French Admiral Pierre Martin had sailed from Toulon with fifteen ships-of-the-line heading for Corsica. Martin's task was to protect a convoy of troop transports carrying an invasion force to try to retake the island. Hotham set sail with fourteen British and one Neapolitan ship-of-the-line. On the morning of 12 March French were sighted and the signal for general chase was hoisted. The French crammed on all sail to escape, with their enemy frantically trying to catch up on a parallel line. With only a feeble breeze, progress was agonizingly slow for both sides. The *Agamemnon*, being a fast sailer despite, as Nelson put it, 'only having 344 [out of 525] at quarters, myself included', was able to keep up with the leading British frigates. Early on 13 March, some twenty miles south-west of Genoa, the foremost British ships, helped by a much improved but squally wind, gradually closed with the enemy.

Not all French seamanship was up to the excitement of the chase. At about 8.00 a.m. the 80-gun *Ça Ira* managed to run on board (collide with) the ship ahead of her, the 74-gun *Jean Bart*, in the process losing her fore- and maintopmasts. Not only was she slowed by the drag of the tangled spars, ropes and canvas in the water, but the masts had fallen on her larboard (lee) side and blocked most of her gun ports there. The first British ship to

come within range of the damaged *Ça Ira* as she dropped astern of the French fleet was the 36-gun frigate *Inconstant* commanded by Captain Thomas Freemantle (he was to be captain of the 98-gun first-rate *Neptune* at Trafalgar). Despite the discrepancy in firepower, Freemantle immediately opened fire. Nelson was to describe the *Ça Ira* as being 'absolutely large enough to take *Agamemnon* in her hold'. Freemantle was heavily punished for his daring by the Frenchman's far more powerful broadsides, and compelled to hold back. By 10.45 a.m., when the *Agamemnon* came up to take over the fight, the *Ça Ira* had been taken in tow by a frigate.

As the *Agamemnon* approached, with decks cleared for action, one regrettable sacrifice had to be made – the captain's fresh meat supply of seven live bullocks was hove overboard, seemingly alive and kicking when they hit the water. Although the *Ça Ira* was under tow and so incapable of manoeuvring, the next two hours were an education in British seamanship and gunnery in what was very much a nimble David against a wounded Goliath affair. The encounter is best described in Nelson's own words in his journal:

> As we drew up with the enemy, so true did she fire her stern guns that not a shot missed some part of the ship, and latterly the masts were struck every shot, which obliged me to open our fire a few minutes sooner than I intended; for it was my intention to have touched her stern before a shot was fired. But seeing plainly, from the situation of the two fleets, the impossibility of being supported ... I resolved to fire as soon as I thought we had a certainty of hitting. At a quarter before eleven, a.m., being within a hundred yards of the *Ca Ira*'s stern, I ordered the helm to be put a-starboard and the driver and after sails to be braced up and shivered, and as the ship fell off, gave her our whole broadside, each gun double-shotted. Scarcely a shot appeared to miss. The instant all were fired, braced up our after yards, put the helm a-port, and stood after her again.

For the next two hours Nelson continued to zig-zag across the unfortunate Frenchman's stern, raking her alternately with the starboard and larboard batteries. Nelson was to comment that 'the ship [the *Agamemnon*] was worked with such an exactness as if she had been turning into Spithead'. The only response came from the *Ça Ira*'s stern chaser guns – but even that quickly fell away as the crews were cut down. By this time:

> the *Ca Ira* was a perfect wreck, her sails hanging in tatters, mizzen topmast, mizzen-topsail, and cross-jack yards shot away. At one p.m. the [towing] frigate hove in stays, and got the *Ca Ira* round. As the frigate first, and then the *Ca Ira*, got their guns to bear, each opened her fire, and we passed within half pistol-shot [about twenty yards]. ... I observed the guns of the *Ca Ira* to be much elevated, doubtless laid for our rigging and distant shots; and when she opened her fire in passing, the elevation not being altered, almost every shot passed over us ...

By this time the 120-gun *Sans Culottes* ('without breeches', the slang term for revolutionaries) was approaching, so Hotham signalled for his leading ships to join him. The *Agamemnon* bore away and the action ceased. The *Sans Culottes*, renamed *L'Orient*,

## The *Agamemnon* Engages the *Ça Ira*, 13 March 1795

- *Ça Ira*, having been damaged in collision with the *Jean Bart*, is taken in tow by a frigate after driving away the British frigate *Inconstant*.
- Nelson, in *Agamemnon* well ahead of the main fleet, comes up to renew the fight.
- With *Agamemnon* astern, *Ça Ira* can only fire her stern chasers.

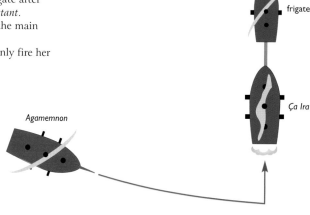

- At about 11.00 a.m. *Agamemnon* begins a series of tacks astern of the French ship so that it is raked by a full broadside.

- *Ça Ira*, unable to manoeuvre, can only reply with stern chasers.
- For around two hours Nelson skilfully completes a series of tacks so that the progressively more damaged and helpless *Ça Ira* is raked repeatedly.

- In the course of these manoeuvres *Ça Ira* becomes 'a perfect wreck', although she does not strike her colours.

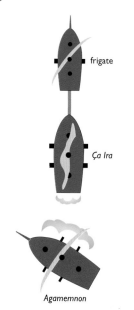

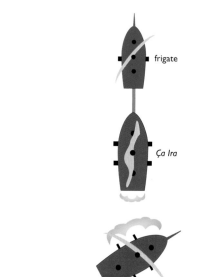

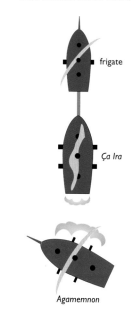

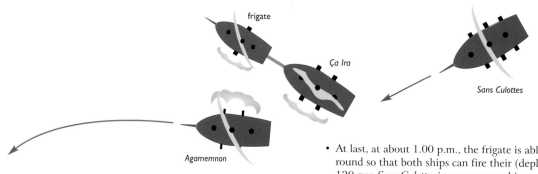

- At last, at about 1.00 p.m., the frigate is able to bring *Ça Ira* round so that both ships can fire their (depleted) broadsides. The 120-gun *Sans Culottes* is seen approaching.
- At this moment Hotham signals for Nelson to rejoin the main fleet, so *Agamemnon* disengages.

## Old Agamemnons

Those that served with Nelson on the *Agamemnon* rated very high in his affection – and he in theirs. 'On board ship,' as an officer wrote, 'he was almost adored; he had a kind word for everyone: even the powder-monkeys did not escape his pleasant smile.'

When the time came for the long-overdue major refit of the *Agamemnon* and Nelson was finally to accept command of the 74-gun *Captain*, almost the entire crew, officers and ratings, clamoured to go with him. He could have had command of a more prestigious 74 much earlier, but he had refused. 'Though I have been offered every 74 which has fallen vacant, yet I could not bring myself to part with a ship's company with whom I have gone through such a series of hard service, as has never before, I believe, fallen to the lot of any one ship.'

The fact that so many of his men desperately wanted to follow their captain speaks volumes for Nelson's leadership, competence and integrity. In fact, naval regulations allowed a captain to take a limited number of his officers and crew with him to a new command. In the case of a 64, the limit was only twenty, including seven petty officers plus his coxswain, clerk, steward and cook, but fortunately the *Captain* had many more vacancies, so in the event some forty petty officers and seamen were able to transfer. In addition, some fifty of the 69th Foot (which eventually became the Welsh Regiment) who had been serving as marines, along with their commander, Lieutenant Charles Pierson, left the *Agamemnon* for the *Captain*. They were to fight at the Battle of St Vincent against the Spanish in 1797 – an exploit that entitled them to have the naval battle honour 'St Vincent' emblazoned on their Colours, the only regiment in the British Army to gain this distinction.

Among the officers who turned over to the *Captain* were Lieutenants Edward Berry (first lieutenant), Peter Spicer, James Summers, James Noble, Henry Compton and Midshipman William Hoste. All fought with great courage at St Vincent. Berry was with Nelson as his flag captain on the *Vanguard* at the Nile and had the honour to command his beloved *Agamemnon* at Trafalgar. He later became a rear-admiral with three gold medals to his name (the only other naval officer of his time to equal this was Lord Collingwood). In addition to being with Nelson at St Vincent, Compton was with him in the boats of the 74-gun *Theseus* at Tenerife and on board the *Vanguard* at the Nile. Berry and Compton were the last 'Old Agamemnons' to do duty in the same ship as Nelson.

Of the warrant or petty officers joining the *Captain*, two stand out. One was the boatswain Joseph King, described by Nelson as 'one of the best boatswains I have seen in His Majesty's service'. Nelson had known King for a long time, as they had originally served together on the frigate *Boreas* in the West Indies some ten years earlier. He fought at St Vincent, as did the second man, the coxswain John Sykes. Sykes probably saved Nelson's life twice during the hand-to-hand fighting in the ship's boats off Cadiz in July 1797, by parrying blows intended for his captain with his cutlass, and on the second occasion with his head! Although wounded, Sykes recovered, and Nelson proposed to get him a lieutenant's commission as soon as he had served sufficient time. Nelson wrote of him, 'His manners and conduct are so entirely above his station that Nature certainly intended him for a gentleman.' Unfortunately this was impossible, as Sykes was accidentally killed by the bursting of a cannon while supervising the firing of a salute as his ship was entering Gibraltar harbour.

It was another 'Old Agamemnon', John Lovell, whose shirt was torn up to bind Nelson's wound when he was hit in the arm during the night attack at Tenerife in 1797. Regrettably perhaps, there were none of Nelson's *Agamemnon* shipmates with him on the *Victory* at Trafalgar. One man who should have been was his old servant and valet Tom Allen. Allen was recruited for the *Agamemnon* from Burnham Thorpe and remained faithfully at Nelson's side, afloat or ashore, for seven years. He was at St Vincent, the Nile and Copenhagen. To his lifelong regret Allen just missed Trafalgar. He was at home at Burnham Thorpe when Nelson received (at Merton) the news that sent him to Trafalgar. Allen was instructed to join Nelson immediately, but he had just married and was enjoying his honeymoon. He delayed his departure and arrived at Portsmouth just twenty-four hours after the *Victory* had sailed. Afterwards he stoutly maintained that he would never have allowed Nelson to wear a coat covered with decorations on the quarterdeck in the heat of battle – he claimed he prevented Nelson from doing just that at the Nile.

Allen knew his job and was devoted to his master but was something of a rogue who took advantage of his privileged position so close to Nelson. When selected to be the captain's valet, he proudly called himself a 'wally-de-sham' (*valet de chambre*). Nelson's biographer Carola Oman describes Allen as 'black haired, stunted, uncouth, entirely illiterate, and never wrong ... Nelson endured him for seven years'. One cannot help but wonder how he got appointed in the first place. In later years Allen, perhaps not unexpectedly, became a pauper. Luckily for him his plight came to the attention of *Victory*'s old captain and Nelson's great friend, Hardy. Hardy secured him a place as a pensioner at Greenwich Hospital, where he ended his days with his wife in some comfort. Hardy erected a memorial stone to his memory when he became Governor at Greenwich.

---

became the ill-fated French flagship at the Battle of the Nile, while a part of her mainmast would eventually provide the wood for Nelson's coffin.

The next day, 14 March, the action continued. During the night the *Ça Ira* had been taken in tow again, this time by the French 74, *Le Censeur*. Along with other ships, the *Agamemnon* was engaged. Nelson recorded, 'At twenty-five minutes past nine the *Ça Ira* lost all her masts, and fired very little. At ten *Le Censeur* lost her mainmast. At five minutes past ten they both struck. Sent Lieutenant George Andrews to board them, who hoisted the English colours ...'. Meanwhile, two English 74s, *Bedford* and *Captain* (soon to hoist Commodore Nelson's broad pennant), had been badly damaged, and Hotham, despite Nelson's pleas, called off the engagement.

The cost to the *Ça Ira* had been over 350 dead or wounded, to *Le Censeur* 250 and to the *Agamemnon* a mere thirteen.

## The End of the *Agamemnon*

Nelson's favourite ship came to a somewhat ignominious end in June 1809, some twenty-eight years after her launching at Buckler's Hard. Within a year of first putting to sea the *Agamemnon* was engaging the French at the Battle of the Saints in the West Indies; her three years under Nelson saw her on blockade duty off Toulon, the capture of Corsica (Bastia and Calvi) and the fight with the *Ça Ira*. Other highlights included involvement in the Nore mutiny in 1797, Calder's action off Cape Finisterre in July 1805 and the crowning triumph in Nelson's column at Trafalgar three months later. More duty in the Caribbean followed, then she participated in the expedition to Copenhagen in 1807 and blockaded the mouth of the Tagus in the Peninsular War before finally joining Rear-Admiral de Courcy's squadron off South America.

On 16 June 1809 Captain Jonas Rose, an elderly officer who had commanded the *Agamemnon* for three years, stepped out onto his quarterdeck at two bells in the early morning watch. It was dark and cold, with a light wind from the east-north-east. He had come to oversee the ship's approach to her anchorage in Maldonado Bay, eighty miles east of Montevideo in what is now Uruguay. Also on deck was the first lieutenant, Lieutenant A.F. Parr who had been the junior midshipman on the *Agamemnon* at Trafalgar. The ship sailed past Lobos Island and Punta del Este on a broad reach until she neared the northern entrance to Maldonado Bay. Rose, who had used the anchorage before, gave the order to tack, head up into the wind so that the launch could be lowered. The master, Thomas Webb, was to take the launch and place a flag-buoy off the shoal where the 74-gun *Monarch* had grounded the year before. Thus for the final approach to the anchorage, the officer primarily responsible for navigation would not be on board. Rose then got the admiral's permission to proceed. It was getting light as the *Agamemnon* worked her way south-east between Gorriti islet and the shore. Ahead was the *Bedford* (74) and astern, just rounding the *Monarch* shoal buoy, was the 80-gun flagship *Foudroyant*. As the *Agamemnon* slid slowly and silently along, the only voice heard was that of the leadsmen in the chains calling out the soundings as they heaved the lead. Rose heard the shouts, 'By the mark five ... and a quarter four.' The bottom was not much more than 25 feet below the hull – and it was shelving fast. As Rose well knew, the *Agamemnon*'s after draft was 22 feet 7 inches when victualled – the ship had a mere 3 feet of water under her.

Rose knew he was in trouble. He needed to turn windward (larboard), further into the centre of the channel, as the shoals around Gorriti were close to lee. Orders were shouted and the crew worked the jib in order to bring her head round into the wind with enough steerage way to veer (tack) the ship into deeper water. It did not work. Her bow fell off, her jib shivered and she began to make leeway. Rose shouted, 'Stream the buoy!' and the anchor buoy was thrown over the bow. 'Let go anchor!' The best bower splashed down. For a minute or two the anchor held the bow into the wind. Then it lost its grip, the ship drifted to starboard and with a slight lurch took ground (went around) by the stern before swinging around until she lay, listing slightly, with her starboard side on the shoal. She was stuck fast and holed below water. Attempts were made to haul her off by kedging but the hawser snapped with the strain. Other ships came to her assistance. It was discovered that the hole had been made by the fluke of her starboard anchor piercing her bottom when she listed. By sunset the *Agamemnon* was listing badly, with water above the lower-deck ports and the orlop deck flooded, the pumps having long ago been abandoned as unequal to the struggle.

*Agamemnon* Founders, 16 June 1809        Map 14

For two days the squadron helped off-load stores and remove everything of value possible from the doomed ship. On the afternoon of 18 June a sorrowful Captain Rose assembled his crew on the sloping deck. Edward Fraser, in his book *The Sailors Whom Nelson Led*, quotes an officer's account of the final moments before the old ship was abandoned:

> The dead silence was broken only by the moaning of the wind and the mournful splash of the waters in the hold, with the groaning of the vessel as she swayed with the swell. The rats, squeaking and gibbering, could be seen struggling through the water in black patches, swimming for life away from the ship to Goretta [Gorriti] Beach. Poor Rose, with a voice trembling with emotion and faltering, tried to bid his crew farewell. ... [when, almost inaudible, he began again] to allude to 'this old ship that we must now quit' he broke down altogether. The poor old officer was only able to add, in a choking voice, 'Goodbye, Agamemnons. May God bless you all! Agamemnons, goodbye!'

Over the side they went into waiting boats. The last man off was Captain Rose.

Shortly afterwards Rose faced an automatic court martial held on board the *Bedford*. The court found:

> *Agamemnon* was run upon the shoal owing to the incorrectness of the Chart or a Bank [sandbank] recently strewn up, and that no blame attaches to Captain Jonas Rose; that he, the Officers and Ships Company appear to have done their utmost to get the Ship off, and afterwards save her Stores. In consequence thereof the Court has acquitted Captain Rose, the Officers and company for the loss of the said Ship.

However, Rose did not get another command and died on half pay of ten shillings a day in 1820. One of the ships helping to take off stores from the *Agamemnon* was the brig *Nancy*. The salvaging operation continued through until November. On 16 November the *Nancy*'s log records, 'Heavy gales with squalls of rain ... observed the *Agamemnon* to have parted in two.' The next day, 'No part of the wreck of HM the late Ship *Agamemnon* to be seen.'

# Officers and Warrant Officers

## THE OFFICERS

It is British ranks that are discussed in detail here, but those of the French and Spanish navies were little different in title or duties. The ships of each nation that fought at Trafalgar were interchangeable, and the system of command, skills of seamanship and gunnery drills were much the same no matter what the language of the crew. A lieutenant, boatswain or carpenter in the French or Spanish service had virtually the same responsibilities as in the Royal Navy. Minor differences in the detail of drills and dress existed, but if you put a French armourer on a Spanish or British ship he would quickly adapt to familiar tasks.

The difference between officers and warrant officers needs to be made clear. In the Royal Navy sea officers, as they were called, were commissioned by the Admiralty, whereas warrant officers received their warrants from the Navy Board – a subordinate organization. Commissioned sea officers were ranked from lieutenant to admiral, while warrant officers included such men as the master (the most senior warrant officer), the surgeon, the purser, the boatswain, the gunner and the carpenter. The sea officers were the generalists, the executive officers, the commanders who controlled and fought the ships and, with the exception of the captain who dined in his own cabin, messed in the wardroom. The warrant officers were the technicians and specialists whose command functions were limited to their departments. Some of them (master, purser, surgeon and chaplain) were of sufficient social status to use the wardroom. The commissioned sea officers could rise to command ships, squadrons or even fleets, sometimes at a remarkably young age (Nelson was a post captain at twenty). They received their appointment to a specific ship, usually limited to the time that ship was at sea. They then agitated for a post on another ship or ashore, or, if nothing was available, joined the large body of officers without any job on half pay. Warrant officers had much lower horizons, and usually spent many years aboard a single ship.

### A Commission

The word 'commission' comes from the Latin word *committere*, meaning 'to entrust'. In the Royal Navy it could be used in connection with either a sea officer or a ship. In the former case it was a document specifying the status of the officer in a particular naval warship. When a newly appointed captain took over, one of his first duties was to assemble the crew to listen to the captain 'read himself in'. The men were mustered aft and the captain read his commission out in front of all the officers and men. This gave concrete proof of the new captain's authority to be there and to act in the name of the sovereign.

When a ship is assigned a particular duty or to sail to a particular part of the world, she is said to be 'in commission'. She remains in commission until such time as she returns to her home port to pay off, at which time she may be 'recommissioned' or 'decommissioned'. From this we get the expression that something 'has been commissioned' or equally that a person could be put 'out of commission' by a severe hangover.

A typical example of a commissioned officer was Lieutenant Samuel Burgess, fifth lieutenant on the 98-gun *Prince* at Trafalgar. He had served as a midshipman in the 98-gun *Impregnable,* the 32-gun frigate *Unicorn,* the 36-gun frigate *Dryad* and then the 50-gun *Isis* before becoming a lieutenant on the 18-gun *Sylph*. After Trafalgar he commanded the brig *Pincher,* still as a lieutenant. In 1816 he was flag lieutenant on the 110-gun *Queen Charlotte,* after which he finally made commander. In contrast, Thomas Tait (purser), Thomas Hawkins (gunner), Samuel Simpson (boatswain), William Johnson (carpenter) and the cook, as 'standing officers', were expected, in theory, to remain (stand) with the *Prince* from building onwards, whether she was at sea or in 'ordinary' (dockyard reserve), until they, or she, finally perished.

### SOCIAL BACKGROUNDS
**British officers**
It would be quite wrong to suppose that the majority of commissioned British sea officers came from the aristocracy. Far more often, their background was respectable middle to upper middle class. Many were following in their father's or another close relative's footsteps. Nelson's family, with his father a village vicar and his uncle a naval captain, was far closer to the norm than that of Lieutenant the Honourable Michael de Courcy, a supernumerary lieutenant on the 74-gun *Spartiate* at Trafalgar, who was the third son of Lord Kingsale and Susan, daughter of Conway Blennerhasset of Castle Conway, Co. Kerry. It was more usual for a man of his pedigree to join the Army than the Navy, largely because commissions could be bought for cash in the Army. A particularly infamous example is that of the young Lord Brudenell (later the Earl of Cardigan) who in 1832 purchased the colonelcy of the 15th Hussars for almost £40,000 (many millions of pounds in today's money).

## *HMS Victory*'s Officers and Senior Warrant Officers at Trafalgar

### Captain

*Great friend of Nelson, whom he served with at the Nile and Copenhagen. Was with Nelson when he was hit and frequently in attendance while he lay dying. Later rose to be First Sea Lord at Admiralty, Governor of Greenwich Hospital and Vice-Admiral. Died 1839 aged 70.*

**Thomas Hardy**

### First Lieutenant

*Although not the senior lieutenant he was first lieutenant at Trafalgar. This guaranteed immediate promotion to captain. He was not promoted further and died 1839.*

**John Quilliam**

### Lieutenants

**Edward Williams**
*Gundeck officer at Trafalgar. Carried a bannerol of lineage at Nelson's funeral. He was promoted commander after the battle but received no further promotion. Died 1843.*

**John Pasco** *Although the senior lieutenant on Victory he was the signals officer during the battle. He was wounded and later promoted commander. Captain 1811. Retired as Rear-Admiral 1847. Died 1853 aged 78.*

**Andrew King**
*Fourth lieutenant at Trafalgar and gundeck officer. Had been in action at Glorious First of June 1794 and Copenhagen 1801. Commander 1806 and Captain 1807. Ended his service as Supt of Packet Establishment. Died 1835.*

**John Yule**
*Gundeck officer at Trafalgar. Had served as first lieutenant of Alexander at the Nile. Promoted commander after the battle. Died 1840.*

**Alexander Hills**
*Aged 25 at Trafalgar, he had previously been a master's mate. Newly promoted lieutenant at the battle, where he was a gundeck officer. No trace after 1809.*

**William Ram**
*Son of army officer. Newly promoted lieutenant. Gundeck officer. Badly wounded; when he knew he was dying, he ripped off his own bandages to hasten his end.*

**George Bligh**
*Son of an admiral; no relation to Capt. Bligh of Bounty fame. Officer in command on forecastle at Trafalgar. Severely wounded in head. Promoted commander. Captain 1808. Died 1834.*

**George Brown**
*Initially assisted Pasco, a signals officer at Trafalgar; later a gun officer. Flag lieutenant Lord Collingwood when the latter died aboard Ville de Paris 1810. Commander 1810. Called to Bar 1821. Retired as Captain 1840. Died 1856.*

### Master

*Had been a master for 10 years. Very experienced, having been in action at Tenerife in 1797, the Nile, Siege of Acre (wounded), and Nelson's master on the Elephant at Copenhagen 1801. Held in great respect by Nelson who was godfather to his son Horatio Nelson Atkinson, who became a lieutenant. Master-Attendant Portsmouth. Died 1836 aged 69.*

**Thomas Atkinson**

### Captain RM

*Son of a Lt-Col. RM he was 29 at Trafalgar. His father ensured him a good start in his career by using his patronage to get him commissioned as a 2nd Lieut. aged six. He was killed by a musket ball in the neck while gallantly repelling a French boarding party from the* Redoutable.

**Charles Adair**

### Lieutenant RM

*Had been nine years in the Royal Marines at Trafalgar. Wounded in the battle and became a captain in 1808. Drowned in 1809 when a ship's boat capsized off Bermuda.*

**James Peake**

### 2nd Lieutenant RM

*Aged 19 at Trafalgar where he was badly wounded. Recovered sufficiently to serve another 12 years. Retired 1817. Died Douglas, Isle of Man 1861.*

**Lewis Reeves**

### 2nd Lieutenant RM

*Aged 20 and newly commissioned. Lieutenant 1809. At the capture of Martinique and Guadaloupe 1809, where he saved four people from drowning. Died 1861. RN School Eltham has a Rotely scholarship.*

**Lewis Rotely**

### Surgeon

*Attended Nelson as he lay dying in cockpit and published detailed account of Nelson's death in 1807. Promoted to Fleet Physician in 1806 and FRS in 1818. Knighted 1831. Died in London in 1842 aged 69.*

**William Beatty**

### Chaplain

*Chaplain on London at Copenhagen. Linguist. Acted as Nelson's private secretary and translated captured documents. Comforted dying Nelson. Died 1840 aged 70.*

**Rev. Alexander Scott**

### Purser

*Aged 67. Supported Nelson as he lay dying. Lost both his sons in the Navy: Comd. Henry Burke was lost in the Seagull in 1805 and Lieut. Walter Burke killed in 1801. Burke died 1815 aged 77.*

**Walter Burke**

### Gunner

*Born in London. Aged 50 at the battle at which his son served as a midshipman on the quarterdeck.*

**William Rivers**

### Boatswain

*Appointed bosun by warrant dated March 1803. Was severely wounded in the thigh but refused to leave his post. Granted £30 from Patriotic Fund.*

**William Willmet**

### Carpenter

*Aged 25 at Trafalgar.*

**William Bunce**

In the Royal Navy this was unthinkable. An officer first had to earn his commission by training and experience at sea, then pass a stiff examination before he could qualify (he might still have to await a vacancy) for a commission as a lieutenant at the bottom of the ladder. Thereafter, his subsequent promotion depended on ability, patronage and luck – but never money. Of the 172 lieutenants in Nelson's fleet at Trafalgar, less than 10 per cent were obviously upper class, the majority, perhaps 80 per cent, were middle class, with the balance having worked their way up from seaman through petty officer to the quarterdeck.

The average Army officer considered himself the social superior of his naval counterpart. Even if lacking in impeccably noble origins, he could point to his actual commission – a parchment document that was signed and sealed by the Sovereign personally, rather than by three admirals as was the case for the Navy. The Army officer held his King's (or Queen's) commission; his fellow naval officer an Admiralty one. The Army commission started (and still does) with the words, 'To Our Trusty and well beloved … Greetings. We reposing especial Trust and Confidence in your Loyalty, Courage and good Conduct', which sounded more impressive than, 'By Virtue of the Power and Authority to us given We do hereby constitute and appoint you Lieutenant of His Majesty's Ship the …'. But it was the ending of the Admiralty's commission that was perhaps needlessly blunt. After stressing the importance of obeying orders, the commission ended with the words, 'you will answer to the contrary at your peril'.

## French officers

The Seven Years War (1756–63) had been a disaster for France and her navy. She lost many of her colonial possessions, including Canada and those in India. King Louis XV, preoccupied with an endless succession of mistresses, paid scant attention to his shattered navy. At the Treaty of Paris in 1763 France had even accepted a British representative stationed in Dunkirk to oversee the dismantling of its port facilities and to see they remained that way – and the French paid him! The morale of the officers and seamen had been destroyed. However, Louis XVI and the American War of Independence (1775–83), in which France sided with the rebelling British American colonists, combined to produce a dramatic revival of French sea power as cities and provinces funded the construction of fine new ships. Although France's fleet had been defeated at the Battle of the Saints in 1782, she could claim to have been on the winning side in the war. The next ten years leading up to the Revolution saw the growing strength and confidence of the French navy and its officer corps.

The bulk of its officers, however, in contrast to those of Britain, were aristocrats. All important posts, along with promotion, invariably went to officers of the Grand Corps de la Marine. They were the '*officiers rouge*' who, before they could join the 'Corps', had to prove they were born with 'four quarterings of nobility'. Mostly they came from Provence or Brittany, districts that have been described as 'still lingering in the twilight of the Middle Ages'. Class-conscious, rigid, conservative, personally brave but inclined to be timid and defensive in battle – these are all characteristics that can be applied to the traditional officer corps of the French navy in the years preceding the Revolution. An attempt was made to loosen the stiff hierarchy in the early 1780s by commissioning a number of successful privateer captains. Known as '*officiers bleus*' – a term of disparagement – they were scorned, insulted and mostly relegated to unpopular or unimportant assignments. Unsurprisingly, they did not last.

The Revolution changed all this within months, if not weeks. Resistant to social reform or change, their arrogance and behaviour detested by many in their crews, the *officiers rouge* faced mutiny and the threat of violence. Some were mobbed, some killed, many fled. By early 1792, out of 640 officers based on ships or ashore in Brest, nineteen were in jail, twenty-eight were trying to resign and 361 had gone missing – they had emigrated without bothering with the formality of resignation, as it was much quicker and safer. Into the yawning gaps their departure created came a ragtag of 'citizens'. Dockyard functionaries, merchant marine officers, pilots, junior officers, petty officers – virtually anybody who had some passing acquaintance with the sea could gain a naval command. Members of the trained corps of *cannoniers matelots* (naval gunners) were decreed petty aristocrats and converted into soldiers to fight royalist resistance in the Vendée. Their replacements were mostly peasants who had never seen the sea, but whose ignorance was of little import in comparison with their revolutionary credentials. They formed 'clubs' on board to ensure their ship was run with proper revolutionary rules, and the clubs could, and did, countermand the officers. Long cruises were cut short, seasick crews surrendered. It is said that one officer was killed when he seized the helm and tried to steer towards the enemy. Amateur captains and green crews could not handle a large warship. They collided, ran aground or just sat at anchor. Even when at sea, French ships often failed to set their topgallant sails – the new 'seamen' being too frightened to go so far aloft.

By 1805, however, things were improving, even if slowly. Napoleon wanted a competent navy and had been unimpressed by its sorry performance at the Nile in 1801. The state of the French Fleet at Trafalgar is discussed in detail in Section Six, but it should be noted here that the officer corps was a decidedly more competent body than it had been ten years earlier. Émigré naval officers had been pardoned and had returned, aspiring officers had to complete three years' training aboard ship for their ensign's commission, more money was poured into the Navy, administration had been overhauled and many new ships built. If some French captains at Trafalgar seemed less than professional, this (as we shall see) was no longer due to the chaos and incompetence of the Revolution.

## Spanish officers

Much like the pre-Revolutionary French, Spanish naval officers were invariably aristocrats. Fortunately for them, the cry of '*liberté, egalité, fraternité*' was not taken up in Madrid, and the naval officer corps remained ardent royalists, intensely proud of being officers in a 'royal' (as in Britain) or 'king's' navy. Despite this, the royal Bourbon coat-of-arms naval flag was replaced in 1785 by the new red-gold-red national flag. The navy became *La Armada Espanola* – the Navy of the Spanish Nation. Britain had her Royal Navy, France her Imperial Navy but Spain, perhaps surprisingly, just the Spanish Navy; not that this name change affected the social background of the officers or their loyalty to the king.

## OFFICER RANKS: A COMPARISON

All three navies engaged at Trafalgar had a very similar rank structure. The table opposite includes the non-commissioned ranks that would be expected to lead to officer status, with examples of officers who fought in the battle and their primary duties. In the British table the approximate equivalent Army rank is shown.

# BRITISH

| Rank | Examples at Trafalgar | Duties | Army equivalent |
|---|---|---|---|
| Volunteer Class 1 | Henry Spence, *Leviathan* | general seaman duties | – |
| Midshipman | Edward Knapman, *Spartiate* | command of six guns | – |
| Sub-Lieutenant | John Kingdon, *Pickle* | 2nd in command of a schooner | ensign |
| Lieutenant | Andrew King, *Victory* | command of 16 guns (middle deck) | captain |
| First Lieutenant | William Cumby, *Bellerophon* | 2nd in command of ship (took command when captain killed) | captain |
| Commander | none at Trafalgar | command of sloop of about 18 guns | major |
| Post captain | Richard King, *Achille* | command of 3rd rate | colonel* |
| | William Prowse, *Sirius* | command of 5th rate | colonel |
| Commodore | none at Trafalgar | command of an independent squadron of up to 10 ships | brigadier |
| Rear-Admiral blue/white/red** | William, Earl of Northesk (white) | 3rd in command of Fleet, flag in *Britannia* | major-general |
| Vice-Admiral blue/white/red | Cuthbert Collingwood (blue) | 2nd in command of Fleet, flag in *Royal Sovereign* | lieutenant-general |
| | Horatio Nelson (white), | commander-in-chief of fleet, flag in *Victory* | |
| Admiral (blue/white) | none at Trafalgar | member of Admiralty Board/commander-in-chief of fleet | general |

# FRENCH

| Rank | Examples at Trafalgar | Duties | British Navy equivalent |
|---|---|---|---|
| *Aspirant* | Antoine Donadieu, *Bucentaure* | protection of the ship's Colours | midshipman |
| | Alphonse Cachard, *Formidable* | captain's aide | |
| *Ensigne de Vaisseau* | Pierre Juan, *Achille* | command of 36-pdr battery | sub-lieutenant |
| | Claude Rigodit, *Duguay-Trouin* | signals officer | |
| *Lieutenant* | Yves Langelade, *Algéciras* | command of 18-pdr gundeck | lieutenant |
| | Jean Silhouette, *Formidable* | navigating officer | |
| *Lieutenant en pied* | Felix Jacon, *Scipion* | 2nd in command of 3rd rate | first lieutenant |
| *Capitain de Corvette* | Francois Taillard, *Argus* | command of 16-gun brig | modern lieutenant-commander |
| *Capitain de Fregate* | Francois Bazin, *Fougueux* | command of 3rd rate | commander |
| | Mathieu Prigny, *Bucentaure* | chief-of-staff to commander-in-chief | |
| *Capitain de Vaisseau* | Jean Hubert, *Indomptable* | command of 3rd rate | post captain |
| | Jean Le Tellier, *Formidable* | flag captain | |
| *Contre-Amiral* | Charles Magon, *Algéciras* | command of 2nd squadron of the squadron of observation | rear-admiral |
| *Vice-Amiral* | Pierre Villeneuve, *Bucentaure* | commander in chief | vice-admiral |
| *Amiral* (admiral) | none at Trafalgar | a temporary grade seldom used | |

# SPANISH

| Rank | Examples at Trafalgar | Duties | British Navy equivalent |
|---|---|---|---|
| *Aspirante* | not known | general | volunteer Class 1 |
| *Guardia Marina* | Don Antonio Bobadilla | protection of Colours *Santisima Trinidad* | midshipman |
| *Alferez de Fragata* | not known | gundeck and signals aide | senior warrant officer |
| *Alferez de Navio* | Don Joaquin Falcon | gundeck, eventually took command of *San Juan Nepomuceno* | sub-lieutenant |
| | Don Teodorimo Lope | flag lieutenant *Principe de Asturias* | |
| *Teniente de Navio* | Don Alejo de Rubaclava | first lieutenant *Montañés* | lieutenant |
| *Capitan de Corbeta* | Tomas de Ramery, *Bahama* | 2nd in command of ship | modern lieutenant-commander |
| *Capitan de Fragata* | Don Josef Quevedo, *San Leandro* | command of a 4th rate | commander |
| *Capitan de Navio* | Don Dionisio Galiano, *Bahama* | command of a 3rd rate | captain |
| *Capitan de Bandera* | Don Joseph Guardoqui, *Santa Ana* | flag captain | brigadier |
| | Don Cayetano Valdes, *Neptuno* | command of 1st or 2nd rate | commodore |
| *Jefe de Escuadra* | Don Baltasar Hidalgo de Cisneros | command of 1st squadron *Santisima Trinidad* | rear-admiral |
| *Teniente General* | Don Ignacio Maria de Alava | command of 2nd squadron *Santa Ana* | vice-admiral |
| *Almirante* | Don Federico Carlos Gravina | command of Spanish Fleet *Principe de Asturias* 2nd in command to Villeneuve | admiral |
| *Capitan General de la Amada* | none at Trafalgar | | Admiral of the Fleet |

Although British ranks do not always precisely correspond to those in the French and Spanish navies, the former will be used throughout this book to avoid confusion.

* A post captain of less than three years' seniority in the rank equated with a lieutenant-colonel, but there were no junior captains at Trafalgar.

** All grades of admiral were ranked from 'blue', the most junior, through 'white' to 'red' (see below under 'Admirals').

## THE COMMISSIONED OFFICER'S PROMOTION LADDER

All commissioned officers on board the ships of the British fleet at Trafalgar owed their promotion to a combination of ability, patronage and good fortune. The significance of each factor varied between individuals: a strong combination of all three often resulted in accelerated promotion, at least to the rank of captain – again Nelson is the most obvious example. The promotion system described here is the British one.

For the young man aspiring to an officer's career there were two major hurdles to overcome. The first was getting a lieutenant's commission, the second was being promoted to post captain. After that it was seniority that counted: if you lived long

enough you would make it to admiral, although whether you were employed in that capacity was another matter. With the exception of the importance of seniority, today's Royal Navy has two similar hurdles – obtaining a commission as a sub-lieutenant and getting promotion beyond lieutenant-commander. The great majority of Nelson's officers at Trafalgar had gained their commission by one of four routes. These were:

*Going to sea as an officer's servant*
A boy would start off as a servant (normally the captain's) and serve the required time on a ship (minimum six years), gaining experience of seamanship. Of the six years, at least two would have to be as a midshipman or master's mate before he became eligible to take the oral examination for lieutenant. This was the

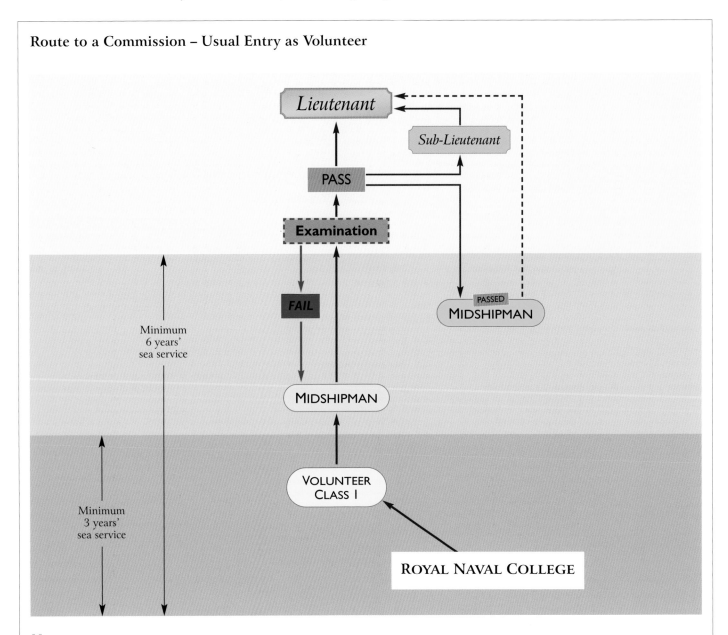

**Route to a Commission – Usual Entry as Volunteer**

### Notes
• The Royal Naval College produced very few candidates for a commission at this time.
• It was common for midshipmen to fail the examination many times and remain midshipmen for years.

• There were far fewer lieutenant's vacancies than passed midshipmen waiting for them, so even passing the examination did not guarantee quick promotion.

## Route to a Commission – the Usual Lower Deck Routes

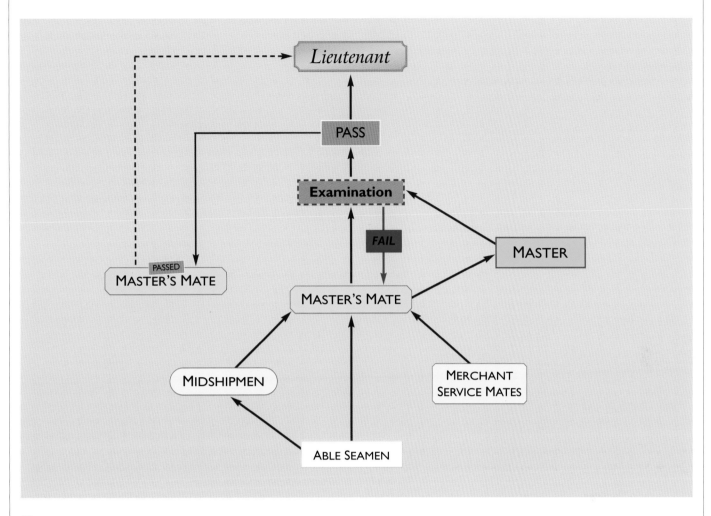

**Notes**
• An able seaman might have to have worked his way to midshipman or master's mate through several petty officer rates.
• The system of allowing masters to take the examination for lieutenant only started in 1805; prior to that a master had reached his ceiling.

• It was unusual, but certainly not unknown, for midshipmen to become master's mates and then master.
• As with passed midshipmen, there could be a substantial wait for passed master's mates before they were commissioned.

route taken by most young gentlemen from respectable families, who might or might not have a close relative as a ship's captain. Most commissioned sea officers had risen by this route.

At the time Nelson joined his uncle's ship, the *Raisonnable*, in 1771 it was not too difficult to circumvent the requirements for three years' sea service before being rated midshipman or master's mate. It was possible with the right kind of patronage to be borne on the muster book of a ship while still at school, or even in the nursery. The most notorious example was Thomas Lord Cochrane (1775–1860), whose most obliging post captain uncle entered him on his ship's books at five and continued to carry him on a number of ships until 1793, when the eighteen-year-old Cochrane actually turned up for duty. In this case, what would appear to be a corrupt system worked remarkably well – Cochrane rose to be one of the most courageous, if controversial, admirals of his day, most famously taking commmand of the revolutionary Chilean navy and thus helping Chile and Peru to gain their independence.

*Promotion from the lower deck*
A boy or seaman could rise by merit through the petty officer ranks and be appointed a midshipman or master's mate. Once he had served two years in either of these positions, he was eligible to take the lieutenant's exam. If they got promotion, these officers were normally considerably older than most of their equals in rank. A number who tried this route became midshipmen but never rose further. An example at Trafalgar was Robert Atwell, who was serving on the *Prince* as a midshipman during the battle but was rated as yeoman of signals. Atwell had considerable battle experience. He had been in action in 1795 as an ordinary seaman on the *Irresistible*, as an able seaman in the *Russell* at Camperdown two years later, and as yeoman of the sheets in *Ramillies* at Copenhagen. Despite serving at Trafalgar (an enormous plus on anyone's service record), the unfortunate Atwell never made it to lieutenant. Forty-three years later, however, he received the Naval General Service Medal with three battle clasps.

*From the Merchant Service*
Although the pay and conditions in the Merchant Service were better (and the discipline laxer) than those in the Royal Navy, if a seaman rose to the rank of mate it might be worth his considering a transfer. Mate was probably the highest rank he was likely to achieve, as to be a master of a merchant vessel you normally needed capital to invest in your ship, thus becoming a part owner. A transfer into the Royal Navy meant he could count on becoming a master's mate either immediately or within a short time. Within two years he could then take the exam. Even if he failed, he had a fair chance of making up for lower pay in prize money. Some, but not many, officers had taken this route.

*From the Royal Naval College, Portsmouth*
This was founded in 1729 to take young lads of between thirteen and sixteen for three years' training in such subjects as mathematics, seamanship, physics, navigation, astronomy and gunnery before going to sea – all of which sounds impressive. However, it was not deemed a success, and few officers chose this path to the quarterdeck. Some knowledge of Latin was required for entry to the college, three years' academic study was worth little in comparison to practical experience on a ship, there was no possibility of making vital personal contacts with future senior officers and, finally, the college boys acquired a reputation for vice and indiscipline. As the naval historian N.A.M. Rodger so aptly put it, 'In practice, few successful officers came from it, and not many of any kind.'

Each rung of the ladder from volunteer Class 1 to admiral is discussed below with, wherever possible, examples from Nelson's fleet at Trafalgar. Also included, where relevant, are statistics and comments concerning each rank and officer casualties during the battle. Although the following paragraphs are concerned with British officers, some reference is made to corresponding French and Spanish equivalents where detail is available. The full-dress (ceremonial) and undress (normal daily wear) uniforms for each rank for the distinctions are shown on pp. 197–212.

**Volunteer Class 1** (French no equivalent, Spanish *Aspirante*)
A recent Order in Council had abolished the 'captain's servant' route, replacing it with 'Volunteers Class 1'. They were mostly young boys who had to be at least eleven years old; by Trafalgar this had been changed so that only the sons of officers could enter at eleven and everybody else had to be thirteen. Like their predecessors, however, the volunteers still had to serve as midshipmen or master's mates and take the exam before qualifying for a lieutenant's commission. The parents of those youngsters who were not directly related to the captain were generally acquainted with him, as personal connections were still a key factor in most boys being able to secure a berth on a warship. The system of selection of these 'young gentlemen' who would provide the fleet's future captains and admirals did not involve the Admiralty – it was a somewhat haphazard arrangement.

Volunteers wore no particular uniform, but were of sufficient social status to be kept apart from the other boys. They were therefore berthed in the gunroom, under the care of the gunner. Prior to Trafalgar the gunner moved forward out of this gunroom accommodation – but the volunteers remained. The gunroom was merely the aftermost part of the (lowest) gundeck screened from the remainder of the deck by a canvas bulkhead. Volunteers had to sling their hammocks along the sides. If this proved impossible, then they had to do so in the cable tiers. The gunroom's only advantage was that in reasonable weather it could be ventilated by opening the gunports. The volunteers' other 'perk' was that as potential officers they were allowed on the quarterdeck – but only for occasional recreation purposes.

Volunteers were aboard doing their sea time, gaining experience and learning the duties of a seaman. After a minimum of three years, they could start to think of securing a midshipman's slot. This was the first step up on the long ladder of a career that could perhaps see them with their own flag – as an admiral. Until they obtained a midshipman's berth, their pay would, according to the Admiralty Regulations and Instructions of 1806, remain at £9 a year. If their ship was fortunate enough to capture an enemy vessel or rich merchantman, then they could expect to share equally with the rest of the crew (excluding petty officers and above) two-eighths of the prize money – usually a disappointingly insignificant sum for each individual.

There was no maximum or minimum number of volunteers permitted on a warship. At Trafalgar there were in total 131 in the British Fleet. The *Victory* had the most with ten, and the 74-gun *Conqueror* had nine, as did the *Mars*, but the 80-gun *Tonnant*, 74-gun *Spartiate*, 64-gun *Polyphemus* and 36-gun frigate *Euryalus* had none. The average number per ship (including the four frigates) was about four. Of these none were killed in the battle and only nine wounded (5 per cent). Perhaps the eight volunteers on the 98-gun *Téméraire*, the second ship in the weather line at Trafalgar, provides a not untypical cross-section of how these youngsters fared in their future careers. One thing they had in common after the battle was that all escaped untouched in a ship that was at the centre of the fight, suffering forty-seven dead and seventy-six wounded. They were, in ascending order of seniority:

*William Shepheard*
Aged twelve at Trafalgar, his first time in action. Midshipman the following year but he took another nine years before he made lieutenant. It was to be another sixteen years after that before he was promoted commander and nine more before he could relax somewhat, having become a post captain at forty-seven (compared with Nelson at twenty). Shepheard retired at sixty after service with the coastguard and then sat waiting to rise to the top of the captain's seniority list. At sixty-five he was made a rear-admiral and seven years later, in 1865, just as the American Civil War was ending, he came within two rungs of the top of the ladder as a half-pay vice-admiral, after rising slowly but surely for exactly sixty years. He enjoyed this dizzy height for another seven years before his death at the age of seventy-nine.

*Henry Gordon*
Nothing known.

*Henry Walker*
Fifteen years old at Trafalgar, which was his first time in battle. It is uncertain when he became a midshipman or master's mate but he must have done the qualifying time in one of these posts and passed the exam as he was promoted to lieutenant in 1813, aged twenty-three. That, however, appears to be the end of his naval career. He retired in that rank and died in 1854.

*Francis Harris*

Age at Trafalgar uncertain, but possibly as young as nine. He had only just joined the navy that year, so it was assuredly his first time at sea, certainly the first time he had responded to the 'beat to quarters' for real. He continued to serve, almost certainly as a midshipman, after the battle and saw action several times between then and his promotion to lieutenant in 1815 – by which time he was probably in his early twenties. He rose no further until his retirement, at which point he was made a commander – which slightly boosted his half-pay (pension). As he had failed to become a post captain, he was stuck at commander for the remainder of his life. He died in 1883, having seen out the Napoleonic Wars, the Indian Mutiny, Crimean War, American Civil War, the Zulu War and the first Boer War, at the splendid age of eighty-seven. He must surely have been one of the last survivors of Trafalgar – an old man with memories of that unforgettable day in battle on the decks of the 'Fighting' *Téméraire.*

*John Hearle*

Another young lad of thirteen who had joined as a volunteer that same year. After Trafalgar, however, there appears to be no further trace of him – he certainly never made lieutenant.

*Henry Douglas*

Age uncertain but he had only just joined prior to the battle. His subsequent career was similar to that of his young comrade Francis Harris in that he had only reached commander when he retired in 1860, despite seeing more action on board the 74-gun *Belleisle* the year following Trafalgar and on the 36-gun frigate *Astrea* in 1811. He secured promotion to lieutenant while serving on the Canadian Lakes in 1815. Like Harris he had a long life ahead of him. In fact, he outlived Harris by two years, dying in 1885.

*Benjamin Mainwaring*

Fifteen years old, and with a cousin serving as a lieutenant on the 38-gun frigate *Naiad* at Trafalgar. Although a Volunteer Class 1, Mainwaring was borne on the ship's books as an able seaman. This was merely a matter of convenience and was not unusual – it in no way altered his status or his duties. He seemingly made it to midshipman and passed his exam, as he became a lieutenant in 1814. As for so many of his contemporaries, the end of the Napoleonic Wars at Waterloo in 1815 saw the end of his promotion prospects. The naval officers' Thursday night toast, 'A bloody war or a sickly season', had lost its potency. So perhaps Mainwaring considered himself lucky to have five years with the coastguard from 1831 to 1836. Despite this he remained a lieutenant, dying aged fifty-eight in 1852.

*James Rivers*

He was also borne on the books as an able seaman at Trafalgar. But he ended up with a slightly different career from his fellow volunteers. His service in the battle won him quick promotion to midshipman but seven years later, in 1812, he secured promotion, not to lieutenant, but to master, transferring in that rank to the service of the Honourable East India Company. However, within two years he is recorded as dying of fever at Chowinghee (India) while a lieutenant on the H.E.I.C. ship the *Minto.*

Of the eight young lads on the *Téméraire,* two were in the muster books as able seamen, only one was promoted post captain before retirement (subsequently reaching vice-admiral), two made commander (but only on retirement), three made it to lieutenant (one via master and in the H.E.I.C. service) and of two there is no trace after the battle. Only one of these eight boys can be said to have later made a reasonable success of his naval career – but this was about par for the course, despite the fact that the war had another ten years to run.

**Midshipman** (French *Aspirant*, Spanish *Guardia Marina*)

Midshipmen were, in modern parlance, officer cadets, who were expected to learn sea officer's duties during at least two years on the job training at sea, usually following three or four years as a Volunteer Class 1, although a few were still rated as able seamen. Two examples of this at Trafalgar were James Dott on the *Defiance* and Thomas Leigh on the *Conqueror.*

A midshipman's ambition was to be commissioned as a lieutenant; some made it, some did not. But, promoted or not, as a 'gentleman' and potential officer he was entitled to be addressed as 'Sir' by his juniors. Midshipmen had worn an approved uniform since 1748. In full dress this was a single-breasted navy-blue cloth coat with a standing collar. On either side of the collar, at the front, was a white cloth patch with a brass button close to the back edge. To this day the white patch is still worn by all officer cadets of the three Services. The present writer recalls getting into serious trouble at the Royal Military Academy Sandhurst if the buttons were not gleaming and the cloth smoothly and immaculately whitened! The coat had nine brass buttons and three more around each cuff. Tradition has it that these buttons were to prevent young midshipmen (many just young boys) from wiping their noses on their cuffs. Most had continuous sniffles, some might shed a tear through homesickness, but it was seen as highly irregular for a young gentleman to be seen using his cuff as a handkerchief. Hence the naval slang for a midshipman – a 'snotty'. A white waistcoat was worn under the coat with grey breeches – although trousers were common for everyday use. A black cocked hat worn athwartships (sideways on) completed the picture. As another mark of his status the midshipman was armed with a long dirk slung over his shoulder on a black leather cross-belt. The newly appointed midshipman was mighty proud of his uniform and of the privilege of being seen in it on the quarterdeck. The downside was that he had to pay for all this finery together with books and navigation equipment – from his pay of a little over £33 a year if on a first rate, £28-16-0 if on a third.

## Some Midshipmen Lose Their Pigtails

As captain of the 44-gun frigate *Mediator,* Cuthbert Collingwood (Nelson's number two at Trafalgar) liked to check on his midshipmen's assimilation of the intricacies of navigation. One of them, Jeffry Raigersfield, never forgot one occasion, recalling 'at this time it was the fashion for your young bucks of the Navy to wear their hair in a pigtail behind, close up to their neck'. Collingwood liked to see the midshipmen calculate a noon sight in front of him on the quarterdeck. On one occasion only three or four out of a dozen or more came up with the right answer. Collingwood 'observed to them how remiss they were, and suddenly, imputing their remissness to their pigtails, he took his penknife out of his pocket and cut off their pigtails close to their heads above the tie, then presenting them to their owners, desired they would put them into their pockets and keep them until such time as they could do a day's work'.

# Royal Navy Officers' Rank Distinctions in 1805

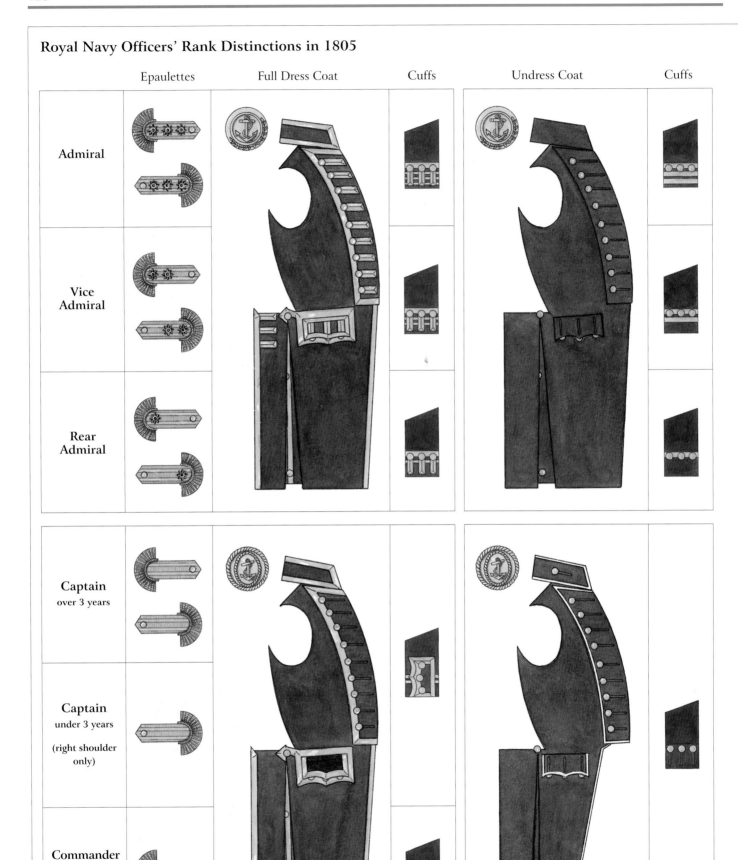

|  | Epaulettes | Full Dress Coat | Cuffs | Undress Coat | Cuffs |
|---|---|---|---|---|---|
| Admiral | | | | | |
| Vice Admiral | | | | | |
| Rear Admiral | | | | | |
| Captain over 3 years | | | | | |
| Captain under 3 years (right shoulder only) | | | | | |
| Commander (left shoulder only) | | | | | |

|  |  | Full Dress Coat | Cuffs | Undress Coat | Cuffs |
|---|---|---|---|---|---|
| **Lieutenant***<br><br>* After 1804 sub-lieutenants wore the undress uniforms of lieutenants but had no full dress. |  |  |  |  |  |
| **Midshipman** |  | none |  |  |  |

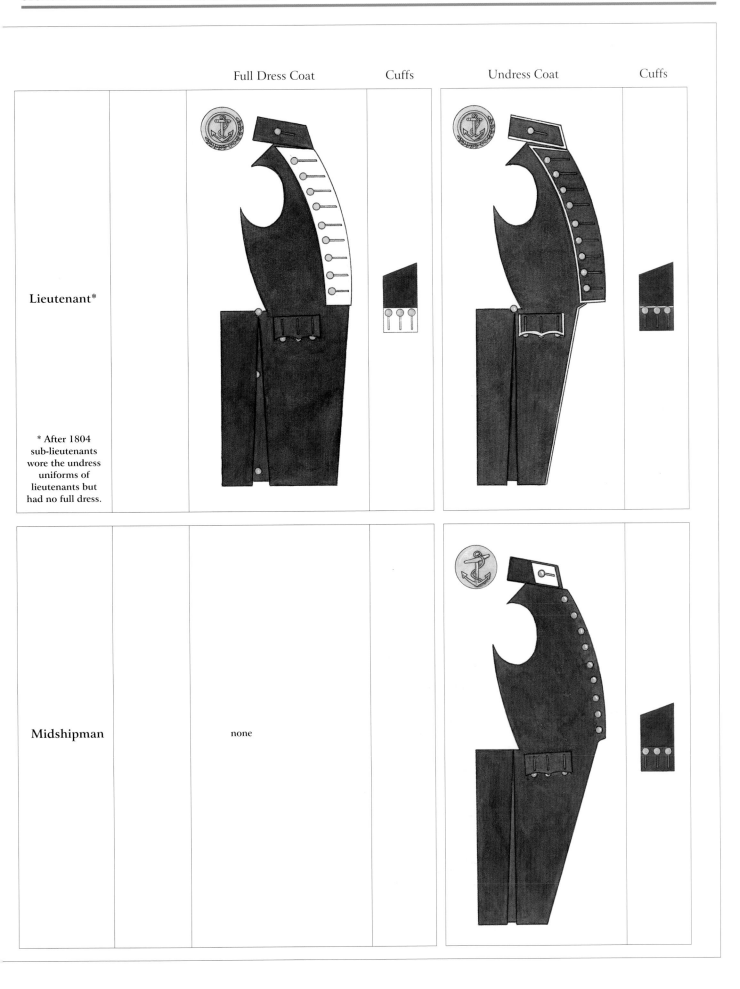

The age of midshipmen could vary enormously. The common perception is of lads in their mid teens but, although a handful might be fifteen or under, most (around 70 per cent) were between sixteen and twenty-five. The youngest on the *Victory* at the battle was sixteen-year-old James Poad, the oldest, at twenty-nine, was Daniel Harrington. The average age for the twenty-two aboard was eighteen years six months. The oldest known midshipman was the famous Billy Culmer, who was born in 1733, was a midshipman with Lord Howe in 1757 and was still at sea in that rating in 1790 aged fifty-seven. Thirty-three years as a midshipman was quite an achievement. Tough, hard drinking, hard swearing, Culmer must have terrified the younger lads in the midshipman's mess. Somehow, after all those years, he was persuaded to take the promotion exam again. Old enough to be the father of the captains seated in front of him, Culmer quickly lost patience with the questioning. When asked what he would do in a situation he considered impossible, he told the board it was humbug, and that if that really was the position then he would let the ship 'go ashore [founder] and be damned, and wish you were all aboard her'. He passed, dying as a lieutenant in 1802.

Midshipmen were accommodated in the cockpit on the orlop deck, below the waterline with the consequent lack of ventilation. Although cramped, dark and smelly, at least the space was not shared with the guns. However, their mess table was used as the surgeon's operating table in battle, as the cockpit (where Nelson died), probably the safest part of the ship, was converted into a makeshift hospital operating theatre. It was there that midshipmen ate, drank, studied, slung and took up their hammocks on a daily basis. In 1793 Midshipman Richard Parker was court-martialled and busted to seaman for refusing an order to take up his hammock. The effect on Parker was to make him more insubordinate – four years later he was executed for leading the Nore mutineers (see p. 33). For minor disciplinary infringements a midshipman could be banished to the topgallant crosstrees of the mainmast, over a hundred feet up, for several hours. In bad weather this was a grim experience; exposed to the worst of the elements, the victim had to lash himself to the mast to avoid being thrown off. But in calmer times it was not a particularly severe punishment – at least one admiral claimed he did most of his reading at the masthead when he was a boy. Midshipmen ate the normal seaman's rations, served by a few scruffy ships' boys. The food could be supplemented occasionally if they could afford extras or if serving under a generous captain – sometimes the leftovers from the wardroom or captain's table found their way down to the orlop deck.

Midshipmen's duties were intended to give them experience in all aspects of seamanship, navigation, fighting the ship and the general responsibilities of the sea officers they hoped to become. Examples are given below:

## A Midshipman's Berth

A young midshipman entering the gunroom of a frigate for the first time described what he saw:

> A dismal dungeon-like looking place, flanked on each side by a row of miserably cramped cribs, called cabins. Overhead there was certainly what, by some poetic-license, continued to be denominated a skylight; but as to any light afforded, it might as well have been underfoot .... At the head of the table sat a pale, calculating, anxious-looking, middle-aged man, whose sole pretension to anything like uniform consisted in wearing a cross-anchor button on a plain blue coat [a typical purser].

At the opposite end was the marine officer, 'whose easy contented air [he had little to do compared with the purser] and portly person formed a lively contrast to the meagre figure at the head'. The marine officer was waited on by a private, 'a bolt-upright, grim looking Jolly, whose head and the beams above were in perpetual collision'.

### When not at quarters (action unlikely)
*Understudying the officer of the watch*
Midshipmen were normally divided into three watches and deployed in various parts of the ship during each watch. Two or three would be on the quarterdeck, under a master's mate. One might be detailed to supervise the hoisting of signals, another would be on the poop deck. Those on the quarterdeck would be involved in learning how to tack the ship, what orders were required for sail changes, heaving the log, calculating the ship's position and marking up the log board. The officer of the watch (a lieutenant) would use them as messengers – their duties included waking up his relief. It was the practice for the senior midshipman on duty to be in charge on the forecastle, perhaps with another of his comrades. Each had to keep his own detailed personal log of events during the watch, which was supposed to be periodically checked by the master or captain.

*Commanding a sub-division of the ship's company*
The majority of the crew (excluding the marines) were divided into as many divisions as there were lieutenants (discounting the first lieutenant). The *Victory* at Trafalgar had some 600 eligible men, divided into eight divisions of about seventy-five men under a lieutenant, each division with two or three sub-divisions and a midshipman in charge of each. Under the lieutenant he was responsible for the discipline, welfare, cleanliness and administration of these men.

*Assisting and supervising procedures in port*
His duties could include supervising the stowing of supplies in the hold or the operation of the capstan, taking messages ashore or to other ships and, if experienced, taking charge of one of the ship's boats plying to and from the shore. He might also form part of a press gang from the ship if new recruits were needed. He did everything a lieutenant must do, but under instruction, gradually being given more responsibility leading up to his promotion exam.

### At quarters (in action)
Details given are for a first-rate ship (such as *Victory*) with up to twenty-four midshipmen.

*Assisting the captain or first lieutenant on the quarterdeck*
Up to five midshipmen would be available as messengers for any task that arose and to assist the signals officer with the hoists and with watching for, and recording, signals from other ships.

*Commanding six each of the twelve short 12-pounder guns on the quarterdeck*

*Commanding one of the medium 12-pounders on the forecastle*

*Commanding sections of guns under the lieutenants on all three gundecks*
A likely distribution would be, remembering that these duties were shared with some master's mates:

- upper deck four midshipmen, each in charge of six long 12-pounders (three from each of the starboard and larboard batteries)
- middle deck six, each in charge of six 24-pounders as above
- lower deck six, each in charge of four 32-pounders as above.

*Commanding a prize crew or a captured enemy* (more senior midshipmen)

*Commanding a ship's boat*
This would be with a landing party or as part of a cutting-out expedition (capturing an enemy ship in port by boarding at night).

After two years, the midshipman could attempt the lieutenant's exam provided he was at least twenty years old. He had to take with him his certificate of service, signed by his various captains, which set out his periods of time at sea – the board would check they added up to at least six years. Most boards were not so fussy over age. Birth certificates could be forged or were merely a chit signed by the applicant's vicar, so a promising candidate who looked on the young side was likely to be passed with the words 'appeared to be more than twenty years of age' written on the certificate. The main exam was a series of testing oral questions on navigation and seamanship. The candidate was asked what he would do and what orders he would give in various demanding hypothetical circumstances. Three captains comprised the board, which sat on the first Wednesday of every month at most major home ports. It could be a daunting experience for many, far more intimidating than the average modern job interview, but less so than the three days of interviews and leadership tests that today's officer candidates undergo. For a small minority, a board member who knew them, or was a friend of an important relative, smoothed their path. One such fortunate candidate later wrote, 'One of the Commissioners was an intimate friend of my father … Commissioner Hood, after a few questions had been put to me, said, "I think we need not ask you any more".' There was, however, one final question after which the examination quickly ended with a certificate, 'which ought to get me a commission without interest [patronage]'.

Nevertheless, a considerable number failed at their first attempt. Questions such as, 'Your ship being now under courses [probably just main sail, fore sail and mizzen], you are supposed to be in such a situation as to oblige you to wear; give the proper orders, and wear your ship' could floor the unprepared candidate. Those that did succeed had 'passed for lieutenant' but still had to await an actual commission, which depended on the availability of vacancies or influential friends or relatives. The problem was that there were far more midshipmen who had qualified for promotion than lieutenant's vacancies. Some waited years, some until the end of the Napoleonic Wars, when an understanding Admiralty promoted them all – on half pay.

There were 460 midshipmen in Nelson's fleet at Trafalgar, 425 of whom were in the ships-of-the-line. Of these, 237 were on board the sixteen 74s, giving an average of about fifteen each – one under the official complement for this type of ship. The 100-gun *Britannia* carried the most with twenty-six (*Victory* had twenty-two) and the 74-gun *Thunderer* the least with nine. By comparison, the Spanish 112-gun *Principe de Asturias* had only seven and the 74-gun *Bahama* three. Thirteen midshipmen were killed in the battle and forty-one wounded – a 12 per cent casualty rate. As to be expected, the two flagships first into the centre of the action, *Royal Sovereign* and *Victory*, suffered the most, the former with two killed and five wounded, the latter with two killed and four wounded.

If the twenty-two midshipmen on the *Victory* are taken as fairly typical, a look at their fates is revealing. Two became admirals (when retired), one a captain, six commanders, seven lieutenants, one a purser (most unusual), one remained a midshipman, two had an unknown future and two were killed. None was given a command at flag rank and only one as a post captain. Despite their having fought on the *Victory* at Trafalgar, lack of luck, ambition, ability or patronage took its inevitable toll.

**Master's Mate** (no precise French or Spanish equivalent)
A master's mate was another rating that could be classed in modern terminology as a senior officer cadet, as they held a higher rating than midshipmen. They, like their midshipman shipmates, were what were known as 'inferior officers', that is officers without either commission or warrant but superior to petty officers – a convoluted and complex system. Although a minority of young 'gentlemen', a prime example being Nelson's great friend and captain of the *Victory* Thomas Hardy, were master's mates at some time, most were not. Those who chose this path to a lieutenant's commission were more likely to have come up through several petty-officer ratings or been a mate on a merchant vessel first. For these reasons master's mates were often older than the average midshipman and had more sea time, and consequently the senior of them was to be found in charge of the midshipman's mess in the after cockpit. Another reason why most midshipmen missed this rating as a stepping stone to promotion was that a 74's complement of master's mates was only three (compared with sixteen midshipmen) – even the *Victory* only had six.

As their title implies, they were mates to the master, the senior warrant officer on any ship. It was therefore possible to seek promotion to master rather than lieutenant. Only a few took this route (none of those at Trafalgar seem to have done so), as it was a dead end. Until the autumn of 1805, masters could not be promoted directly to lieutenant. Like all rules, there were rare exceptions (see p. 145) but the ambitious master's mate set his sights on the lieutenant's exam and the far wider horizons a pass could bring.

A master's mate's full-dress uniform differed from that of a midshipman only in that it had a falling (flat rather than upright) collar without the white patches. Instead, it had white piping at the front edge of the coat, pocket and behind the cuff buttons. He wore a dirk or sword and his undress uniform was much the same. As was to be expected, his pay was a marginal improvement on that of a midshipman, being £46 per annum for those on first rates, £40 for those on third rates.

Their main duty in normal times was fine-tuning their understanding of the master's and a lieutenant's job. There was always a master's mate on watch acting as number two to the officer of the watch, and, in unrated ships or if casualties or sickness had taken their toll, he could take his turn in charge of a watch. Other things being equal (which they were often not), he was first in line for appointment as acting lieutenant or (after 1804) sub-lieutenant. Apart from this, he did much the same as a midshipman, although probably in more of a supervisory, as distinct from learning, role. He mustered the seamen petty officers' division of the crew (that is, the petty officers involved in seamanship duties), he supervised stowage in the hold, he navigated and he commanded a ship's boat. He was heavily involved in the fitting out of the ship, the checking of ropes, sails and rigging and overseeing the raising of the anchors. At quarters (on the *Victory*, for example) one was to be found with the signals officer, one commanding a forecastle gun and at least one on each gundeck commanding a section of the batteries. If the master was absent for any reason, the senior master's mate took over his duties.

There were ninety-seven master's mates at Trafalgar, of whom one was killed and fourteen wounded (about 15 per cent). This gave an average for ships-of-the-line of just over three each. The complement was six for the first rate, four for a second and three for a third. At the battle every ship had a minimum of one master's mate: the *Victory* had seven, the *Thunderer* one. Two examples from the battle are of interest.

James Spratt of the 74-gun *Defiance* entered the service somewhat late in 1796, when he was already twenty-five, as a Volunteer Class 1. He was a midshipman the following year and fought as such at Copenhagen in 1801. By 1805 he was a master's mate and took part in Calder's action in July three months before Trafalgar. His conduct during the battle, when he led a boarding party onto the French 74-gun *Aigle*, had to swim across and was then wounded, guaranteed him swift promotion to lieutenant, a pension for his wounds and a gratuity from the Patriotic Fund. He later invented the homograph, the predecessor of semaphore. He became a retired commander in 1838. His son followed him into the Navy, eventually becoming a vice-admiral.

The other was William Buchanan on the 74-gun *Defence*. He entered the Navy at eighteen in 1795 as an able seaman but within a year was medically discharged. Three year later he convinced the doctors to accept him again. He was twenty-eight at Trafalgar, still rated able seaman but holding the post of master's mate. Quick promotion to lieutenant followed the battle. In 1808 he was in the 74-gun *Audacious* off the north coast of Portugal watching the disembarkation of Sir John Moore's troops – the same Moore who had played a leading role in the taking of San Fiorenzo in Corsica fourteen years before. Within a year Buchanan was the beach master organizing the

hasty embarkation of the same troops after the Battle of Corunna. After promotion to commander, he retired as a post captain in 1846.

## Officers' Food and Drink

Officers normally dined together in the wardroom or gunroom. Only the captain ate alone in his cabin, although most were sociable enough to invite fellow officers or midshipmen to dine fairly regularly. Each officer had a boy (or marine private) to wait on him at table, and each mess had one or two cooks, rated as landsmen, who were usually decidedly more skilful than the ship's cook. Officers usually supplied their own rations, only eating the Navy's food to supplement their own or when their funds or stocks ran out. Fresh milk and eggs from the livestock made regular appearances on the officers' table. When the *Agamemnon* fitted out in 1793, Nelson wrote to his wife, 'I have got a keg of tongues which I suppose you ordered, and also a trunk from Wells, Norfolk, and a hamper of three hams, and a breast of bacon, and a [pig's] face, not very well packed.' A not untypical breakfast of a wealthy captain who liked his food might be 'a pair of ducks, a dish of kidneys, and a grilled turbot the size of a moderate cartwheel, as well as the usual hams, eggs, toast, marmalade, and coffee'. This standard could obviously not be sustained over a long commission.

The officers were drummed to dinner (lunch) to the tune of 'Hearts of Oak'. When dining with Captain Edward Pellew (who, to his everlasting regret, missed Trafalgar by a month) on the *Tonnant*, an important guest might expect something of a feast. Included might be steak and kidney pie in the shape of a castle, a ragout of pork, cauliflower, carrots, spring greens, puréed potatoes, truffled gelatine, pudding, jellies and cheeses. An altogether sumptuous affair – no doubt eminently suitable for senior officers. Supper was far less grand, perhaps 'soup, hot mutton chops, coffee and a wedge of solid duff [suet pudding]'.

The officers drank coffee, tea, cocoa, beer, spirits and wine. French wine was popular and was readily available either by capture or purchase. Claret was said to 'assist the memory, give fluency to speech, and animate the mind with real gaiety to enliven conversation'.

**Sub-Lieutenant** (French *Ensigne de Vaisseau*, Spanish *Alferez de Fragata*)
While for the French and Spanish a sub-lieutenant was a substantive commissioned rank, this was not so for the British – although it is today. The British instituted the rank in late 1804 as a temporary measure and it was abolished at the end of the war. The appointment was open to midshipmen or master's mates who had qualified for promotion to lieutenant but were waiting for a vacancy. The holder was regarded as a commissioned officer while in the rank. They were intended to fill vacancies on smaller vessels that needed a qualified second-in-command to a lieutenant, such as gun brigs.

On larger ships (fifth rates and above) acting lieutenants were appointed instead of sub-lieutenants, so there were no officers of this rank at Trafalgar. There were, however, eight acting lieutenants in the fleet, one each on the 74s *Spartiate*, *Minotaur*, *Achille*, *Colossus*, *Defence* and *Leviathan*, the 64-gun *Africa* and the 10-gun schooner *Pickle*. All were confirmed as lieutenants shortly after Trafalgar. Two were wounded, Mark Sweny on the *Colossus* severely. (Ten years later he was the first lieutenant on the 74-gun *Northumberland*, which conveyed Napoleon to exile on St Helena.)

**Lieutenant** (French *Lieutenant*, Spanish *Alferez de Navio*)
The man who finally received his lieutenant's commission had every reason to feel a mixture of relief and pride. He was at last a sea-service officer, he messed in the wardroom where he ate far better food, slept in his own cabin (albeit small and makeshift), had a personal servant and wore a smarter uniform and sword as he walked the quarterdeck. The only niggle lieutenants had was that, unlike the Royal Marine officers of the same rank, they were not entitled to wear epaulettes. Their pay, however, had more than doubled, to just over £100 a year. Along with the chaplain, a lieutenant was the only officer, warrant officer or petty officer whose pay was fixed no matter what the rate of the ship he served on. The senior lieutenant on the 102-gun flagship *Victory* (John Pasco) received precisely the same as the junior lieutenant on the 36-gun frigate *Sirius* (Richard Burton). All other officers and senior ratings could secure a small payrise by getting a transfer to a higher-rated ship.

## Acting First Lieutenant William Norman

Norman was one of four brothers in the Royal Navy, two of whom were killed in action. He had been a lieutenant for six years by Trafalgar and his appointment at the battle was as acting first lieutenant of the 74-gun *Thunderer*. The reason he was only acting was that the senior lieutenant, John Stockham, was commanding the ship as Captain Lechmere had gone home to attend Sir Robert Calder's court martial. Unfortunately for Norman, whereas Stockham received an automatic promotion to captain, a gold medal, the thanks of Parliament and a splendid sword from the Patriotic Fund, Norman got nothing. As with Lieutenant Jeremiah Brown of the *Ajax*, Norman found himself still a lieutenant after the battle.

Five years later he had still not been promoted. At that time he was first lieutenant of the 36-gun frigate *Sirius* at the capture of the island of Bourbon (now Reunion and a Department of France) in the Indian Ocean. Norman then sailed with the invasion force to attack the nearby island of Isle de France (Mauritius). He commanded the boats (the usual job of a first lieutenant) from the *Sirius* that led the assault on the tiny islet of

Isle de la Passe at the southern entrance to what was then Port Bourbon (now Mahebourg) on the south-east of the island. The present writer has visited Isle de la Passe, a tiny, granite rock inhabited by seabirds and only accessible if you can persuade a local fisherman to take you through the reef in a pirogue. Much of the French fortifications remain untouched except by time. Norman would have had a difficult landing, as there is little beach, only black rocks and heavy seas. As he scrambled ashore, he was shot through the heart by a musket ball, dying instantly. At that moment he was a commander, a promotion that had been long in coming and about which he knew nothing.

Isle de France fell to the British in 1810 and remained a British colony until 1969. On the walls of the old fort on Isle de la Passe, near where Norman fell, it is still possible to read the names of some of the British soldiers of subsequent garrisons scratched in the rock, including those of the 5th Foot (later Royal Northumberland Fusiliers). It could not have been a popular posting.

It was normal, though not universal, practice on a ship-of-the-line for the senior lieutenant to be the 'first luff' (first lieutenant). The second senior had overall charge of gunnery, the fifth signals, while traditionally the most junior had responsibility for supervising the crew's musketry training in addition to his normal work. A lieutenant's duties can be summarized as:

*Watch-keeping*
This was his primary function at sea. The lieutenants took it in turn to take charge of the starboard and larboard watches, which meant they were in command of the ship, unless the captain was on deck, and had total control and responsibility for everything that occurred during their watch. In every case the captain would have laid down exactly the circumstances in which he was to be called – these would vary from captain to captain depending on the degree of confidence he had in his officers' ability and judgement. In an unexpected emergency giving the right orders immediately was down to the officer-of-the-watch. Admiralty regulations stated:

> If during war, a strange sail be seen at night, he [the officer-of-the-watch] is to send a Midshipman to inform the captain, and is himself to get the Ship ready for action: he is to keep out of gunshot of the strange Ship until everything is ready [one would have thought the captain would have taken over by this time]; but, in doing this, he is to be careful not to remove to such a distance as to risk the losing sight of her.

*Commanding a division of the crew*
On a three-decker such as the *Victory* with eight lieutenants, this meant about sixty-five to seventy men. He was responsible for their welfare, discipline and administration.

*At quarters, in overall charge of the gun batteries*
One was on the forecastle with two on each of the upper, middle and lower decks. The exceptions were the first lieutenant, who was with the captain on the quarterdeck, and the signals officer.

The first lieutenant's duties differed from the others. In today's Royal Navy he would be called the 'Number One', in the US Navy the 'executive officer' (XO). Responsible to the captain for the day-to-day running of the ship, he was the second-in-command and, like William Hennah of the *Mars* and William Cumby of the *Bellerophon*, took command at the height of the battle if his captain was killed. Specifically, his duties included:

*Responsibility for the manning of the ship and the rating of the crew and petty officers*
As new men came aboard he, assisted by the master and boatswain, would interview them to ascertain their age and experience. The object was to decide on the new recruit's rating aboard, whether as a landsman, ordinary or able seaman, or petty officer. This information would be entered in the muster book.

*Ensuring the quarter bill was drawn up*
This was the list on which every man's duties aboard and in action were shown.

*Dividing the crew into watches (normally two)*
He did not take a turn at officer-of-the-watch.

*Presiding over the wardroom*
His position entitled him to the best cuts of meat and first glass of wine.

*In battle, assisting the captain on the quarterdeck*
He would be ready to take over should the captain fall.

One drawback for lieutenants and officers of all higher ranks was the lack of what we might call job security. His career became a series of separate commissions, often linked by varying periods on half pay. This was not so much of a problem during a war, but with a shrinking navy in peacetime and fewer dead men's shoes, half pay, although helpful, seldom kept a man or his family much above the poverty line – much like our modern state pension. If he wanted to be sure of reasonable financial security, he had to make post captain (commander, the next step up for most, was not sufficient). Then his pay would double, triple or quadruple depending on the rate of the ship he commanded. But, far more importantly, seniority would then carry him steadily upwards into the ranks of the admirals – he had only to stay alive long enough. The problem was to secure a foothold on what was probably the most difficult rung of the promotion ladder.

The answer lay in being noticed through political patronage, having the attention of his commander-in-chief or distinguishing himself in action. The Admiralty in London made the actual promotion, but commanders-in-chief on more distant overseas stations had the authority to promote officers temporarily. Although these promotions were subject to eventual Admiralty confirmation this was rarely, if ever, withheld. The system was not as unworkable as it might seem, as in most cases it was not in the best interests of a patron to put forward an incompetent candidate. Obviously, an appointment to a flagship was much sought after, as was that of first lieutenant – after a major battle such as Trafalgar these officers were almost, but not quite, automatically promoted. Of the twenty-seven first lieutenants of ships-of-the-line at Trafalgar, four did not receive promotion, twenty became commanders and three jumped straight to post captain (see box opposite). Nevertheless, for many officers, lieutenant was as far as they got. On average a lieutenant had about a one in five chance of making it to post captain. The award for the ultimate in patience, staying power or sheer doggedness must go to Lieutenant G.H. Fortye, who was promoted lieutenant in

1744. In 1799 he was still topping the lieutenants in the Navy List having been in the rank for fifty-five years – he did not make Trafalgar!

There were 172 British lieutenants at Trafalgar, all but fifteen of whom were serving on ships-of-the-line. The complement for a first and second rate was eight (including the first lieutenant). The *Victory* had nine, the *Royal Sovereign* six and the *Britannia* seven. Among the second rates, *Téméraire* and *Dreadnought* had eight, while *Neptune* and *Prince* were one short. Among the 74s the average was just over five out of a complement of six. Nine lieutenants died at Trafalgar and nineteen were wounded – an 18 per cent casualty rate among the ships-of-the-line.

> ## Royal Navy Toasts
>
> **Monday night** – 'Our ships at sea'
> **Tuesday night** – 'Our men'
> **Wednesday night** – 'Ourselves' (as no one else is likely to concern themselves with our welfare)
> **Thursday night** – 'A bloody war or a sickly season'
> **Friday night** – 'A willing foe and sea room'
> **Saturday night** – 'Sweethearts and wives – may they never meet'
> **Sunday night** – 'Absent friends'

## Commander

Originally 'master and commander', this rank had been established in 1747, although it existed prior to this, for captains of the increasing number of 10- to 18-gun sloops in the Navy (all commanders of ships of any size were called 'captain' on their own ship, no matter what their actual rank). These ships were too small to warrant both a captain and a master, so the posts were combined. In order to receive his promotion, the commander had to have spent two years as a lieutenant. He had the same duties and responsibilities on his ship as a post captain had on his, but he could never, other than in an emergency situation, command a ship larger than a sloop. He could, however, purchase a single eight-guinea gold-bullion epaulette for his left shoulder – impressive, though it gave him a somewhat lopsided look. His promotion to

---

### Lieutenant John Quilliam

Quilliam was something of a rarity in Nelson's fleet, a commissioned sea officer who had risen from the lower deck. Not only that, but he had got himself the plum job of first lieutenant on the fleet commander's flagship – an appointment many ambitious young officers would have done almost anything to secure. And we know that Quilliam was not the senior lieutenant on the *Victory*. This was John Pasco, Nelson's signals officer, who was some three years senior to Quilliam, who had been promoted lieutenant in 1798 aged twenty-seven.

Quilliam was born on the Isle of Man on 29 September 1771. As a young lad he worked as an apprentice stonemason and was said to have worked as a labourer on the construction of the Red Bridge in Douglas, which was started in 1793. However, this occupation lost its appeal and he ran away to join the merchant marine. It was while he was serving on a merchant vessel moored in Castletown harbour that the press gang pounced and dragged young Quilliam into the Royal Navy. Despite this inauspicious start to his new career, Quilliam, obviously a bright young man, made the most of his opportunities. In less than five years he had passed the necessary exam and was a lieutenant – a remarkable achievement for a man of little, if any, education. He was the third lieutenant of the 36-gun frigate *Ethalion* in 1799 when she captured the treasure ship *Thetis*.

This eventually netted him £5,000 in prize money – a sum that would take him fifty years as a lieutenant to earn from his pay.

Local Isle of Man tradition has it that Quilliam first came to Nelson's notice at the Battle of Copenhagen when he was serving as first lieutenant on the 38-gun frigate *Amazon*, and took over command after Captain Riou's death. The story goes that Nelson, when on board the badly damaged *Amazon*, asked Quilliam how he was getting on. To this Quilliam replied, in a typical non-committal Manx phrase, 'middlin'. This response is said to have amused the Admiral, and perhaps Nelson remembered the incident when he appointed him first lieutenant of the *Victory*.

As noted above, Quilliam was one of the three lieutenants promoted post captain after the battle, jumping the intermediate rank of commander. His naval success established his social position on his home island, and he married into the Stevenson family, one of the principal families on the island. Unfortunately for him, he was unable to hang on long enough to reach the top of the captain's seniority ladder and thus secure a rear-admiral's half pay in retirement. He died in 1839 aged sixty-eight. A Trafalgar Day service, attended by the Royal Naval Association and the Royal British Legion, is held annually at his graveside in Arbory (Isle of Man) Churchyard.

## First Lieutenants' Post-Trafalgar Promotions

| Name | Ship | Promotion | Rank at death |
|---|---|---|---|
| *Ships-of-the-line* | | | |
| John Quilliam | *Victory* | Post Captain | Post Captain |
| John Clavell | *Royal Sovereign* | Commander | Post Captain |
| Arthur Atchison | *Britannia* | Commander | Post Captain |
| Thomas Kennedy | *Téméraire* | Commander | Post Captain |
| George Acklom | *Neptune* | Commander | Commander |
| George Hewson | *Dreadnought* | – | Vice-Admiral |
| William Godfray | *Prince* | Commander | Post Captain |
| John Bedford | *Tonnant* | Commander | Post Captain |
| Thomas Fife | *Belleisle* | Commander | Post Captain |
| Lewis Hole | *Revenge* | Commander | Admiral |
| John McKerlie | *Spartiate* | Commander | Rear-Admiral |
| William Hennah | *Mars* | Post Captain | Post Captain |
| Thomas Simmons | *Defiance* | Killed | – |
| James Stuart | *Minotaur* | Commander | Post Captain |
| James Couch | *Conqueror* | – | Post Captain |
| William Daniell | *Achille* | Commander | Post Captain |
| Thomas Toker | *Colossus* | Commander | Post Captain |
| James Green | *Defence* | Commander | Post Captain |
| Eyles Mounsher | *Leviathan* | Commander | Post Captain |
| William Cumby | *Bellerophon* | Post Captain | Post Captain |
| John Croft | *Orion* | Commander | Commander |
| James Lilburne | *Swiftsure* | Commander | Commander |
| Jeremiah Brown (acting) | *Ajax* | – | Lieutenant |
| William Norman (acting) | *Thunderer* | – | Commander |
| George Moubray | *Polyphemus* | Commander | Post Captain |
| John Smith | *Africa* | Commander | Post Captain |
| Hugh Cook | *Agamemnon* | Commander | Post Captain |
| *Frigates* | | | |
| Kempthorne Quash | *Euryalus* | – | Post Captain |
| Thomas Perkins | *Phoebe* | – | Commander |
| John Maples | *Naiad* | – | Rear-Admiral |
| William Hepenstal | *Sirius* | – | Commander |

The expectation that a first lieutenant of a line-of-battle ship in a major battle would receive automatic and virtually immediate promotion was almost confirmed after Trafalgar – but not quite. Discounting the unfortunate Simmons who was killed on the *Defiance*, all but four were promoted. Twenty-two out of twenty-six is almost 85 per cent. Of these, three jumped straight to post captain. There were special circumstances in each case – see below.

One wonders why the first lieutenants of the *Dreadnought* and *Conqueror* were ignored. Hewson of the *Dreadnought* seems to have the most reason to have felt unjustly treated. He was first lieutenant of a three-decker 98-gun ship, a position of considerable responsibility. He had been a lieutenant for ten years, making him one of the most senior lieutenants present, and he had already proved himself in action (his promotion from midshipman to lieutenant was the result of his performance in battle). He does not seem to have been incompetent, as he eventually became a post captain and died a vice-admiral. There must be some explanation but the present writer has been unable to find it.

A similar puzzle exists with Couch, the first lieutenant of the *Conqueror*. He had held that position throughout the chase to the West Indies, and at Trafalgar the *Conqueror* had been in the thick of the fight, received the surrender of Villeneuve's flagship and been engaged with the huge *Santisima Trinidad*. One wonders what Couch had done wrong, or if he had seriously antagonized some senior officer, as it took him another twelve years to make commander, plus seven more to captain.

The explanation for neither Brown of the *Ajax* nor Norman of the *Thunderer* being promoted is clear – they were both only acting first lieutenants. Neither got any further, as Brown died in 1817 and Norman was killed in the attack on Isle de France (Mauritius) in 1810 (see box on p. 133) before the news of his promotion to commander reached him.

None of the four frigate first lieutenants received promotion. Promotions were for those on line-of-battle ships only, as it was not the job of frigates to close with the enemy and exchange broadsides. However, of the officers concerned, two eventually made commander, one a post captain and one lived long enough to retire a rear-admiral (Maples of the *Naiad*).

Of those that survived the wars, twenty-three had a reasonably comfortable retirement having reached post captain or higher. All those four who ultimately made flag rank received it on retirement. Hole of the *Revenge*, who was the only one to survive long enough to get almost to the top of the ladder, died an admiral aged ninety-one in 1870.

post captain was far from assured. As for a lieutenant, he depended on patronage or being noticed for gallant or otherwise distinguished service. It was just possible to jump the rank of commander, but it was rare and the circumstances had to be exceptional. Trafalgar produced such circumstances, with three examples.

The first was John Quilliam, first lieutenant of the *Victory*. To have such an appointment on Nelson's flagship at a battle of such magnitude virtually guaranteed accelerated promotion provided one survived. Survival on the *Victory*'s quarterdeck at Trafalgar was purely a matter of luck, with the odds no better than fifty-fifty. But Quilliam's luck held – he was unscathed and thus secured promotion straight to post captain. This caused considerable ill feeling, before and after the event, as Quilliam was not the senior lieutenant onboard – he was fourth! John Pasco had been a lieutenant for ten years, Quilliam only seven, so by naval convention Pasco should have been the first lieutenant – instead of which he was the senior signals officer.

The second to leapfrog over commander rank was Lieutenant William Hennah, first lieutenant of the *Mars,* with thirteen years in that rank. During the action his captain, George Duff, had his head removed by a cannonball so Hennah took command. The *Mars* suffered severely, became unmanageable and lost heavily under fire from at least five enemy ships during the intense engagement. Hennah fully merited his double promotion. He also collected a testimonial from the crew of the ship, together with a presentation vase from the Patriotic Fund.

The third was Lieutenant William Cumby, first lieutenant of the *Bellerophon*. This ship was likewise heavily engaged, with several enemy ships at close quarters that made three attempts at boarding. Her captain, John Cooke, was struck down on his quarterdeck by two musket balls in the chest (very similar to Nelson's mortal wound). As he lay dying, his last words were, 'Tell Lieutenant Cumby never to strike.' Cumby fought on. His well-deserved reward was promotion to post captain.

## Post Captain

A post captain commanded any sixth-rate ship or above, i.e. one with twenty or more guns. He must, other than in very exceptional circumstances, have served a year as a commander. To make post captain was to have succeeded in one's naval career. The younger you received the promotion, the more likely it was that you would eventually become an admiral. Nelson, having achieved the rank when he was still just nineteen, was exceptionally well placed to reach the very top, and would have done so had he not been killed. Because promotion thereafter was entirely by seniority, a post captain was waiting for old men to die, and at the same time hoping to survive himself. Slowly, over the years he climbed the ladder, crossing off his seniors as they fell off.

The post captain's seniority dated from his first appointment to command a rated ship. The Admiralty did not write promoting him to post captain, they wrote giving him a commission to command a rated ship. This first command would normally be a fifth- or sixth-rate frigate, but as there were about three times the number of commanders as frigates, the wait for promotion could be long and possibly fruitless. For the first three years he was equated to an Army lieutenant-colonel and continued to wear the single epaulette of a commander. Thereafter he was the equal of a colonel and proudly put up his second epaulette. Advancement within the rank of post captain came normally by being given a commission on a higher-rated ship, quite probably interspersed with varying periods (Nelson had one of five years) 'on the beach' on half pay.

As a captain's pay was dependent on the rate of his ship, not his seniority, there was much to be gained by commanding a 74 instead of a 36-gun frigate, for example. Captain Hardy, commanding the 102-gun *Victory* at Trafalgar, would have been paid

nearly double Captain Blackwood of the 36-gun *Euryalus* (£386-8-0 compared to £204-8-0 per annum). At Trafalgar, Hardy was a 'flag captain', i.e. the captain commanding a ship wearing an admiral's flag – in this case Nelson's. Captain Rotherham, commanding the *Royal Sovereign* (Vice-Admiral Collingwood's flagship) and Captain Bullen commanding the *Britannia* (Rear-Admiral Earl Northesk's flagship) were also flag captains – both also junior to Blackwood. However, it was common for comparatively junior captains who were admiral's protégés to be appointed flag captains. Many senior captains would have regarded it as insulting to have been offered a flag captain's post. The more adventurous, such as the thirty-five-year-old Blackwood, would have preferred the semi-independent nature of a frigate's command with the likelihood of a cruising commission in which a rich prize was the probable outcome.

A captain was king. On his own ship his authority was, for good or ill, little short of absolute. He lived, dined and slept in his cabin and could not visit the wardroom without invitation – a tradition that continues today. In a two- or three-decker he lived in a particularly grand style, with his accommodation divided into a 'day cabin' across the full width of the stern, a small 'sleeping cabin' and a 'dining cabin'. As he paid for all the furnishings, they could vary from modest to luxurious. Across the stern was a splendid sweep of windows and access to two quarter galleries – one a private toilet, the other for him to see the set of the sails. The only drawback was that he had to share his accommodation with at least four, possibly six, guns. As with all cabins, furnishings and partitions were removed when the ship prepared for battle. So the captain's accommodation became just like any other part of a gundeck – a particularly dangerous part if the ship was raked from the stern, as the shards of flying glass from the shattered windows became a deadly blast of shrapnel.

In return for all his privileges, status, high pay (up to four times that of a lieutenant) and the lion's share of any prize money, the captain had to accept final responsibility. He was ultimately held to account for everything that happened on his ship. Needless to say, most duties were delegated, but regulations spelled out in some detail his overall responsibility for stores, provisions, ship's books, accounts, muster rolls, discharges, discipline, cleanliness (of ship and crew), rating of the crew and the overall performance of his ship. The final regulation, No. 111, covers it neatly: 'Lastly, the Ship and every person in it being placed under the command of the Captain, he will be held responsible for every thing that shall be done on board.' If his ship foundered, struck another ship or rock, or did not perform satisfactorily in action, the captain was

### Captain John Perkins

Perkins' story is included here to illustrate that men of merit, no matter what their background, could reach post rank. This man, however, was exceptional, as he was of mixed race and may have once been a slave on a Jamaican sugar plantation. By 1775 he was a local master or mate in the merchant service. In that year he was taken on as an extra pilot on the flagship of the Jamaica Squadron. Within a few years he was commanding the *Punch* schooner tender with remarkable success. In 1782 he was commissioned as a lieutenant by Sir Peter Parker and put in command of the brig *Endeavour*. Again he did well. Within two years Rear-Admiral Rodney used his powers of patronage to promote Perkins to master and commander, while remaining in command of the same ship. However, Rodney's action was not confirmed, so Perkins had to wait another thirteen long years before he was confirmed as a commander. In 1800 he was advanced to post captain and commanded the 22-gun sixth rate *Arab* and then the 32-gun frigate *Tartar*. Perkins retired due to poor health in the year of Trafalgar. It was the end of an extraordinary career. He never visited England and spent his entire thirty years at sea in a single station, finally dying in Kingston, Jamaica, in 1812.

## Prize Money

Particularly for officers, the prospect of prize money was an important perk of naval service. In 1708 the British government enacted the 'Cruizer [sic] and Convoys Act'. One of its effects was to formalize the process of prize taking. It gave practically all the money gained by the sale of captured enemy vessels to the captors, 'for the better and more effectual encouragement of the Sea Service'. Every prize appeared before the High Court of Admiralty for 'condemnation'. The Act laid down exactly how the proceeds were to be divided. This distribution remained unchanged for a hundred years and even then it was only marginally altered. The distribution at the time of Trafalgar was:

| Rank | Share |
|---|---|
| Captain | $^3/_8$* |
| Marine captains, lieutenants, masters: equal shares in | $^1/_8$ |
| Marine lieutenants, admiral's secretary, principal warrant officers, master's mates, chaplain: equal shares in | $^1/_8$ |
| Midshipmen, inferior warrant officers, principal warrant officer's mates, marine sergeants: equal shares in | $^1/_8$ |
| The remainder: equal shares in | $^2/_8$ |

Appointment to one of the well-known prize money commands would mean an almost automatic fortune for a captain or flag officer. The latter could hope to gain sums well in excess of £1 million at today's values – Sir Hyde Parker received some £200,000 when in command in the West Indies. Nelson often bemoaned his lack of opportunity to gain prize money.

Agents handled prize money, and payment was often very late, sometimes taking years to filter down to the recipients. The agents made their fortune from their 5 per cent fee on the total value, the large number of prizes they handled and drawing interest on the money while they waited for it to be collected. In one notorious case a captain whose ship had made several captures in the period 1796–8 was drowned in 1805. This caused endless complications. In the event the agent did not pay the prize money due until 1826, by which time he had accumulated twenty-eight years' interest.

* Flag officers had one of the captain's shares. Thus an independent roving command with no admiral within hundreds of miles was popular.

## Life in an East Indiaman

Convoy protection was second only to blockade duty as a task of Nelson's navy. Many ships were assigned to escorting East Indiamen (merchant ships of the East India Company) to and from India. These ships were a combination of trader, passenger-carrier and warship. The captain of an Indiaman during the maritime supremacy of the Company was paid about £10 a month, but it was his perks that made him rich. A major one was the passage money paid by all the private passengers – minus the cost of their food and wine. The amounts received were so enormous that he could realize sufficient funds from five or six India or China voyages to make him independent for life. One captain made £30,000 on the round voyage from London to India and China and back. The other officers shared proportionately in a voyage. Even with these amazing profits some captains were not satisfied, and they smuggled and traded illicitly for further gain.

One such ship was the *Earl of Balcarres*, of 1,417 tons with a crew of the captain, six mates (officers), surgeon, six midshipmen, purser, gunner, boatswain, carpenter, sailmaker, master-at-arms, cooper, caulker, butcher, baker, two cooks, two stewards, eight junior rates, six quartermasters, seven officer's servants (one each) and seventy-eight seamen. Indiamen, built for cargo and passengers, were notoriously slow sailers. In a calm they 'drifted about more like logs of wood than anything else'. Their slowness

in convoy infuriated the Royal Navy escort commanders, one of whom described an Indiaman as 'a haystack of a vessel' whose progress was so slow that a fast sailing ship was directed to 'take her in tow and fairly lug her along'.

These lengthy voyages were usually hell for the passengers, except for senior officers who paid £250 for a small cabin. Soldiers, women, children and livestock were simply herded together; so-called cabins were merely canvas partitions that were removed in any emergency.

On the outward journey of one voyage the captain had two men flogged with three dozen lashes each, and the captain ordered the men doing the flogging to change after each twelve cuts so that 'new strength might be added'. Another man was put in irons for pilfering a little water under a hot tropical sun. A boy on his first voyage was ordered aloft onto the spanker boom on a rough day – not surprisingly, he fell off and was drowned. The captain also caused three men to be flogged for allegedly breaking into a Chinaman's house to steal liquor. The Chinaman came on board and picked out the men, but the captain did not ask them for their defence, 'being satisfied they could have offered none'. Ten seamen rebelled at this harshness. A court later found them guilty, not of mutiny as charged, the sentence for which would have been death, but of riotous assembly, for which they received two months in Newgate Prison and a fine of a shilling each.

automatically court-martialled. The detail to which the captain's regulations went is well illustrated by No. 83, which in part reads:

> He is strictly to forbid the sticking of candles against the beams, the sides or any other part of the Ship. He is strictly to enjoin the Officers not to read in bed by the light of either lamps or candles; nor to leave any light in their Cabins without having some person to attend it.

There were twenty-nine British post captains at Trafalgar. Of these, two were killed (Captains Duff of the *Mars* and Cooke of the *Bellerophon*) and three wounded (Captains Moorsom of *Revenge*, Durham of *Defiance* and Morris of *Colossus*). Twenty-one of these captains eventually made it to at least rear-admiral. So a high proportion (78 per cent) lived long enough to enjoy the benefit of greatly enhanced half pay.

## Commodores' Broad Pennants, 1806–26

Prior to 1806 all Commodores flew the broad pennant without the disks.

Commodore, with a captain of his
ship under him, red squadron

Commodore, with a captain of his
ship under him, white squadron

Commodore, with a captain of his
ship under him, blue squadron

Commodore, captain of his
own ship, red squadron

Commodore, captain of his
own ship, white squadron

Commodore, captain of his
own ship, blue squadron

After 1824, the red broad pennant was used by commodores with captains under them, now called commodores of the first class, while the blue broad pennant was used by commodores who were also captains of their own ships, now called commodores of the second class.

### Private Vessels

Most vessels had no admiral or commodore aboard, and the captain was their highest officer. They were called 'vessels' and flew ensigns and long pennants based on their admiral's colour. If a vessel was operating directly under the orders of the Admiralty, it flew the red ensign.

Private ship, red squadron

Private ship, white squadron

Private ship, blue squadron

## Commodore

A commodore was a post captain who had been given temporary command over a detached squadron. It was a post, not a rank. Because a captain's promotion was rigidly dependent on seniority, it gave the Admiralty some flexibility in that it allowed the temporary command of senior captains by their junior (but more competent) peers. A commodore's ship was called a pennant ship, as distinct from an admiral's flagship. As such it wore a broad pennant, red, white or blue according to the squadron of his admiral (see above). If his ship had her own captain, while the commodore commanded the squadron, he drew the pay of a rear-admiral. If he commanded his ship as well as the squadron, he drew no extra pay and carried a white ball below his pennant. However, in both instances the commodore wore the uniform of a rear-admiral and ranked with an Army brigadier-general. There were no commodores at Trafalgar.

## Admiral

By an extraordinary quirk of history there was only one grade of lieutenant and post captain but ten grades of admiral. The system was a relic from the mid-seventeenth century when the British Fleet was divided into three divisions, each distinguished by a different coloured (red, white and blue) ensign. Each division was composed of three squadrons commanded by an admiral, vice-admiral and a rear-admiral. By 1805 this system of organizing the fleet had long since been superseded, but the admiral's rank structure remained. Until 1805 there was no admiral of the red, this slot being taken by the admiral of the fleet. Therefore by the year of Trafalgar there were ten rungs on the admiral's promotion ladder. Starting with the bottom rung, the climb could progress from rear-admiral of the blue to rear-admiral of the white to rear-admiral of the red. Similarly, promotion to vice-admiral meant, theoretically, being a vice-admiral of first the blue, then white, then red. The next step up would be to admiral, with yet again progress from blue through white to red. Above them all was the solitary admiral of the fleet. The admiral's rank flags are shown below.

There were specific rules as to on which mast admirals were to wear (flags were always worn, never flown) their flags on their flagships. Admirals had theirs at the top of the mainmast, vice-admirals at the top of the foremast and rear-admirals the mizzenmast. All wore the appropriate coloured ensign, with a Union flag in the corner, at the stern of their ship (see following page). The admiral of the fleet wore the Union flag at the top of the mainmast. At Trafalgar, Nelson was a vice-admiral of the white, Collingwood a vice-admiral of the blue and Earl Northesk a rear-admiral of the white. However, Nelson had instructed that all ships were to wear the white ensign to facilitate recognition in the smoke and confusion of battle.

Having so many admiral ranks made the structure exceedingly top heavy. By the end of the war (barring Waterloo the following year) the 1814 Navy List showed 187 admirals of various colours and grades. They were:

Admiral of the Fleet – 1
Admirals – 61 (21 red, 20 white and 20 blue)
Vice-Admirals – 65 (22 red, 19 white and 24 blue)
Rear-Admirals – 60 (19 red, 17 white and 24 blue)

As noted above, most post captains could expect to reach admiral's rank if they lived long enough. However, strict adherence to this system could mean incompetent and doddering captains or admirals getting an important operational command – with predictable results. Two methods of circumventing the system for the good of the Service were used. The first was to promote poorly regarded captains to be 'rear-admiral without distinction of squadron', commonly referred to as an 'admiral of the yellow'. This was an appointment to be avoided, since it marked the captain out as an officer whose sea career was over and was, in effect, a retirement scheme for captains past their prime. Their compensation was the title and a rear-admiral's half pay. It was then possible to select the more junior but younger and more competent captains for promotion from those near the top of the list – those above having being sent to the 'yellow squadron'. If they needed to reach well down the captain's list for talent, the Admiralty made use of the temporary appoint-

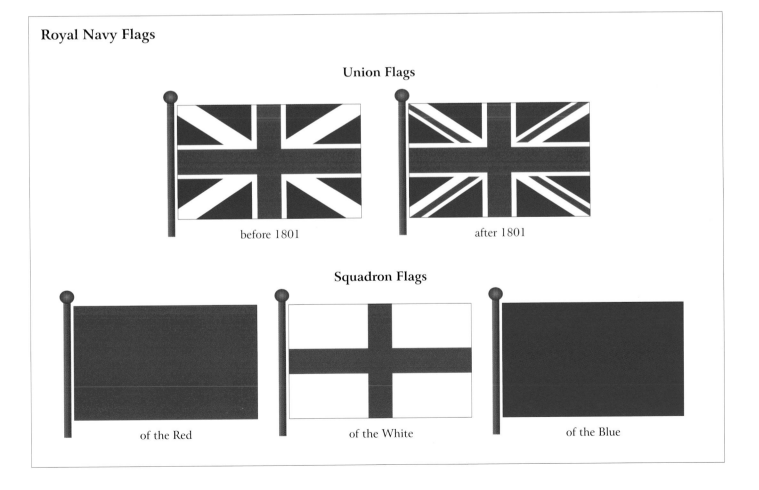

## Royal Navy Flags

### Union Flags

before 1801

after 1801

### Squadron Flags

of the Red

of the White

of the Blue

**Admirals' Flags, 1805**

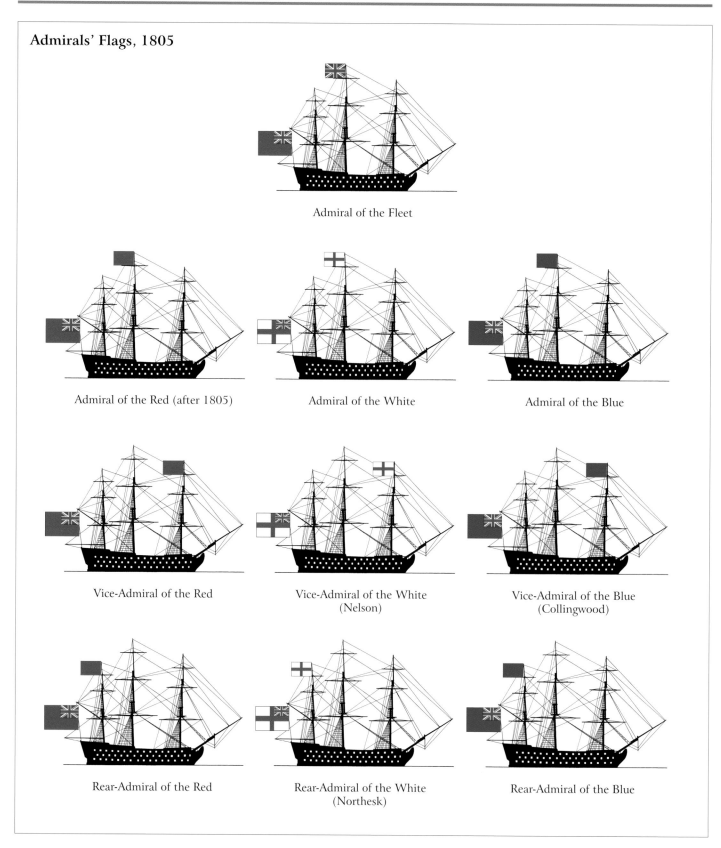

Admiral of the Fleet

Admiral of the Red (after 1805)

Admiral of the White

Admiral of the Blue

Vice-Admiral of the Red

Vice-Admiral of the White
(Nelson)

Vice-Admiral of the Blue
(Collingwood)

Rear-Admiral of the Red

Rear-Admiral of the White
(Northesk)

Rear-Admiral of the Blue

ment of commodore. They could also promote an admiral but leave him on half pay while giving the active command to his more go-ahead juniors.

There were no restrictions on how many admirals were permitted in each grade or squadron. Nor was it necessary to climb laboriously up the ladder rung by rung from blue to white and finally red; it was common to jump grades on the way up. Nelson came onto the admiral's ladder as rear-admiral of the blue in 1797 aged thirty-nine. Two years later he was rear-admiral of the red, having skipped white. He then became vice-admiral of the blue in 1801 and the white in 1804. Collingwood was promoted straight to rear-admiral of the white in 1799, then to rear-admiral of the red in 1801, and at Trafalgar he was one grade below Nelson as a vice-admiral of the blue. Earl Northesk had started his admiral's career in a similar manner by being appointed rear-admiral of the white in 1804.

Admirals normally wore their flag on a three-decker, as such ships were built to accommodate an admiral and his staff in addition to the captain. Nelson's retinue of eight was, for a fleet commander, quite modest and comfortably within his entitlement. They included his flag lieutenant (signals officer), Lieutenant Pasco; his secretary, John Scott, who was cut down by a roundshot at Nelson's side at the outset of the battle; his valet, Gaetano Spedillo from Naples; the secretary's clerk; Nelson's personal steward, Lewis Chevallier; and three able-seamen servants. The *Victory*, like other first-rate ships, accommodated the admiral in spacious quarters at the stern of the upper gundeck directly under the captain's quarters. This meant that the officer's wardroom was below on the middle gundeck.

Admirals' pay was generous but not excessively so. The annual rates were: admiral of the fleet £1,825, admiral £1,277-10-0, vice-admiral £912-10-0 and rear-admiral £638-15-0. Thus Nelson's salary was 2.4 times that of his flag captain, Hardy, and 4.5 times that of Captain Blackwood in the *Euryalus*. Interestingly, an admiral of the fleet received some 114 times the pay of an ordinary seaman; in today's Royal Navy the difference from the very top to the bottom is about twelve times.

However, it was not their pay that made many admirals super-rich. To be an admiral with an active command overseas carried with it enormous potential for making money, together with virtually unlimited scope for the use of patronage. The most lucrative, and therefore the most coveted, station was the Jamaica one, where, in close proximity to the wealthy Spanish possessions, potential fortunes in prize money abounded. An admiral was entitled to one-eighth of all the prize money secured by his captains, so it was hardly surprising to find his favourite frigate captains spending weeks out cruising the most likely areas for prizes. The temptation to put pocket before naval strategy in deploying the squadron was not always resisted. When the First Lord of the Admiralty, Earl Spencer, wrote recalling Sir Hyde Parker, later to be Nelson's superior at Copenhagen, from the Caribbean, he stated:

> I trust you will not look upon your recall in any other light than as is meant, namely, as a change of service, which may naturally be looked for after so long a term [four years] as you have enjoyed of the most lucrative station in the service ... I rejoice that your stay on the Jamaica Station has proved so advantageous.

## A Rich Spanish Prize

A prize to beat all prizes, a real lottery jackpot, was brought into Portsmouth at the end of April 1793. A French privateer, the 22-gun *Dumourier*, had captured a Spanish treasure ship called the *St Jago* sailing home from Lima in South America. Both these vessels were then taken by the British 36-gun frigate *Phaeton*. The *Britannic Magazine* of 1793 published the details of this amazing haul. One can imagine the fury and frustration of the French privateer captain being forced to surrender a once-in-a-lifetime haul to the hated English.

> The *St Jago* was registered by the Spanish Government for £800,000, so that she is doubtless worth a great deal more, and by far the richest prize carried into Britain ...
> May 10. This day between ten and eleven o'clock, the treasure taken out of the above prizes, and conveyed to the Gun-Wharf, was loaded into 21 wagons, provided by Messrs. Badger and Clarke, in order to be conveyed to London. The wagons were escorted by a party of the Life Guards, amidst acclamations of thousands of spectators of all descriptions. London. May 14. .... The above wagons loaded with Spanish treasure, and solid bars of silver weighing from 165 to 167 pounds each, occupied the streets of the metropolis on their way to the Tower. They were escorted by a detachment of horse, accompanied by some Naval officers and British tars. They were received at the Tower by the Governor, Officers and Garrison under arms, and conducted to the parade with drums beating, colours flying, and bands of music playing. The British flag flew triumphantly over the tri-coloured one of France upon every wagon ... The specie [coin] has since been removed to the Bullion office in the Bank ...

As an entire squadron had been present when the capture was made, every ship's company received a share. The ships involved were under the command of Rear-Admiral Gell, whose squadron consisted of the 98-gun *St George*, the 74s *Ganges*, *Edgar* and *Egmont*, plus the *Phaeton*. This meant that, in total, just short of 3,000 men were entitled to a share. *The Britannic Magazine* continued: 'It is reported that seven boxes of rough diamonds have been discovered, secreted in a private part of the *St Jago*, since the above treasure [the coinage] was sent to London: and the ship is in consequence ordered to be broken up and examined.'

Discounting the diamonds, a rough estimate of what would be due to the crews was given as:

| | |
|---|---|
| Amount of property removed into the privateer | £500,000 |
| Salvage for the *St Jago* | £62,500 |
| Head and gun money for the *Dumourier* | £1,220 |
| **Total** | **£563,720** |

**Subdivision into Shares**

| | |
|---|---|
| Admiral Gill | £70,465 |
| Captains, each | £28,186 |
| Captains of Marines, Sea Lieutenants, Sailing Masters | £2,072 |
| Lieutenants of Marines, Boatswains, Gunners, Pursers, Carpenters, Masters Mates', Surgeons, Pilots and Chaplains, each | £1,194 |
| Midshipmen, Captains' Clerks, Sail-makers, Carpenters', Boatswains' and Gunners' Mates, Masters at Arms, Corporals, coxswains, Quarter Masters, Surgeons' Mates, and Sergeants of Marines, each | £332 |
| Seamen and Marines, each | £35 |

The magazine was in error in claiming this was the richest prize ever seized up to that date. In 1744 another Spanish ship carrying £600,000 worth of gold was taken. No other ship being in sight at the time, the crew of her captor, the *Solebay*, did not have to share the loot; even the lowest ratings became entitled to £1,000 each.

While admirals had the power to make their captains rich, they also had the authority, on distant overseas stations, to promote officers to fill vacancies that occurred on station. Such promotions were always subject to eventual endorsement by the Admiralty, but it was rare indeed for this to be refused. In fact, the Admiralty themselves often wrote recommending individuals to the admiral on station for promotion. Spencer again, to Admiral Harvey on the Leeward Islands station, wrote: 'Give me leave to recommend to you for promotion on some future opportunity Lt Matthew St Clair of the *Lapwing* [a 28-gun frigate]. I should also be glad to hear of Captain Barton of that ship having a larger frigate ...'. Little wonder that lieutenants, commanders or captains were so keen to catch a favourable glance from an admiral's eye.

## Marine officers

The duties of marines in general will be discussed in the next section. In the French and Spanish fleets army officers commanded the troops that had been drafted in as marines on their ships. British marine officers were commissioned officers and as such they lived in the wardroom, had their own cabins and could walk on the quarterdeck. Their service uniform was a scarlet coat, crimson waist sash, white breeches, high black boots and sword. Perhaps most importantly for their self-esteem, lieutenants wore the cherished gold epaulette on the right shoulder, making them, in this respect, the equal of a junior naval post captain, who in turn equated to an Army lieutenant-colonel. Marine captains had two epaulettes – a dress distinction that caused considerable resentment. Their hats were black top hats with an upward curved brim, white band and white over red feather plume.

A captain commanded all marine detachments on first, second and third rates, with up to three lieutenants or second-lieutenants under him. For fourth and fifth rates the establishment allowed for two, and on sixth rates one. Sloops and smaller vessels had no officer. More senior marine officers (majors and lieutenant-colonels) were seldom seen at sea, being based ashore at the barracks or at the headquarters in London on administrative or staff duties. Unlike army officers, marine officers could not purchase their commissions. Promotion was based entirely on seniority and thus tended to be slow. As to duties on board ship, marine officers had an easy ride when not in action – another potential cause of friction with their naval comrades. They had no watch-keeping duties, and most of the musketry training and posting of sentries around ship could safely be left to the sergeants, so for much of the time they were fighting boredom. In action it was different, as there was plenty of excitement on the quarterdeck, which was their position at quarters. Their responsibility was the control of the marines deployed as sharpshooters on the quarterdeck or in the tops and either leading or repelling boarders. Even then their command was much reduced, as over half the marines were likely to be forming part of the gun crews on the lower decks under naval officers.

The Admiralty recognized that marine officers had the advantage of commissioned rank without a great deal of responsibility aboard ship. A marine captain had the equivalent status of a naval lieutenant, while the marine subaltern was very much his junior. The marine officer's somewhat anomalous position, particularly in comparison to that of the master, was further acknowledged by rules allowing marine lieutenants only the same share of prize money as warrant officers. Naval regulations endeavoured to clarify the dilemma:

> though lieutenants of marines share in prizes only with warrant officers of ships, upon consideration of their different sea duty, yet it is not intended to degrade their rank; and they are, while they do their duty, to be considered and treated in all respects as a commissioned officer should be.

At Trafalgar there were eighty-seven marine officers in Nelson's fleet, all except seven serving on the line-of-battle ships. Although two- and three-deckers were theoretically entitled to up to four officers, only the three first rates (*Victory*, *Royal Sovereign* and *Britannia*), two second rates (*Téméraire* and *Dreadnought*), and one third rate (*Bellerophon*) had their full complement. The 98-gun *Prince* and the 64-gun *Agamemnon* had only two marine officers each. Of the eighty officers on the line-of-battle ships, four were killed and twelve wounded. A 20 per cent chance of becoming a casualty was slightly higher than that of the naval officers, which undoubtedly reflected the fact that the duties of marine officers kept them exposed on the quarterdeck or upper deck throughout the action.

Of the four marine officers on the *Victory*, one was killed and two wounded. Captain Charles Adair was shot by a musket ball through the back of the neck. Like all others killed that day, he was tossed overboard and had the dreaded DD (Discharged Dead) written opposite his name in the muster book. Lieutenant James Peake was wounded, only to drown four years later when the boat he was in capsized off Bermuda. Nineteen-year-old Second Lieutenant Lewis Reeves was severely wounded but lived on until 1861. The only one to come through the battle unscathed was Lieutenant Lewis Rotely, who lived to be seventy-six, dying, like his fellow officer Reeves, in 1861. The marine officers on the *Royal Sovereign* and *Téméraire*, both ships that took a hard pounding, also suffered heavily. Out of four officers on the *Royal Sovereign*, one was killed and one wounded; on the *Téméraire* two were killed and one wounded. On no other ship was a marine officer killed.

Despite promotion being entirely by seniority and the overall smallness of the corps, a large proportion of those officers who survived Trafalgar got promoted – two to full general. Of the eighty-three that lived through the battle, forty-four were never subsequently promoted, twelve made captain, nine major, ten lieutenant-colonel, two colonel, one major-general, three lieutenant-general and two general. The latter were Second Lieutenant John Coryton of the *Spartiate* and Captain Elias Lawrence of the *Colossus*. The 98-gun *Dreadnought* had the most senior marine officer onboard. He was Captain Thomas Timmins who had been commissioned as a second lieutenant twenty-seven years earlier and fought in the American War of Independence, being present at the Siege of Charlestown. After Trafalgar he went on to become a lieutenant-colonel. All three of his fellow officers on the *Dreadnought* did well after the battle, two becoming lieutenant-colonels and one a colonel.

# WARRANT OFFICERS

Warrant officers received their warrant from the Navy Board, which was responsible for the financial and technical aspects of naval administration, including the granting of warrants to the technical, specialist officers. Warrant officers were heads of specialist departments responsible to the captain for their efficiency and administration. In the time-honoured British fashion (which still applies today) the technical experts were kept in their place; it was the commissioned officers, trained only as seamen, who retained overall command.

Warrant officers, like petty officers (see Section Four), were divided into seamen and specialist non-seamen, known as idlers. The crucial distinction between the two is that seamen (along with marines) stood watches and idlers did not; except in an emergency or in action they worked by day and slept by night. Wardroom warrant officers who were idlers included the surgeon, purser and chaplain, and lower down the scale came the carpenter, sailmaker, schoolmaster, armourer, master-at-arms, ropemaker, caulker and cook. In 1805 the word 'idler' had no derogatory connotations, but understandably the seaman on deck on a black night in the driving rain envied the idler swinging gently in his hammock below, and over the following century it developed its current meaning of someone who is work-shy and habitually avoids duty.

Naval ranks and ratings were complex and the dividing line between junior warrant officers and senior petty officers in terms of duties, pay and privileges is hard to distinguish. However, all had to be literate, and it is possible to group the warrant officers into four levels – wardroom warrant officers, gunroom warrant officers, 'standing' warrant officers and junior warrant officers, who equated with petty officers.

As with all seamen, and indeed officers, the temptations of the bottle and dishonesty relating to stores under their charge were not always successfully resisted. In the seven years 1807–14 most courts martial involving warrant officers were the results of drunkenness or theft of stores. Surprisingly, pursers, who perhaps had the best opportunities for peculation, did not head the list. Courts martial during this time had boatswains way out in front with fifty-five, followed by carpenters with thirty-seven, gunners twenty-four, pursers fourteen and a solitary surgeon.

## WARDROOM WARRANT OFFICERS

These were senior warrant officers entitled to walk the quarterdeck, have their own cabins, dine in the wardroom and, like all senior warrant officers, be addressed officially as 'Mr'. These privileges put them, in some respects, on a level with the commissioned sea officers – the lieutenants. In practice, however, in terms of social and professional status no warrant officer was the equal of a commissioned officer.

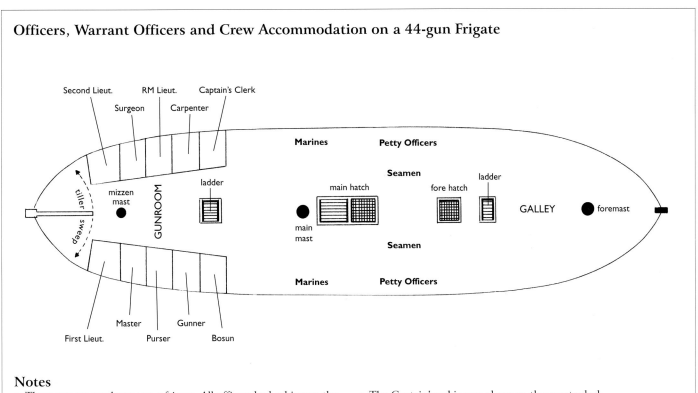

## Officers, Warrant Officers and Crew Accommodation on a 44-gun Frigate

### Notes
- There was no wardroom on a frigate. All officers had cabins on the gundeck but only those officers who had wardroom status ate in the gunroom.
- The Captain's cabin was above on the quarterdeck.
- The crew slept in hammocks amidships and foreward. Note that the marines slept between the officers and the seamen.

## Officers and Senior Warrant Officers' Accommodation on a 74-gun Ship

### Quarterdeck

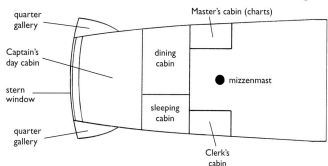

**Notes**
- The captain's accommodation was spacious with room to entertain or to hold meetings with his officers.
- He had sole use of the quarter gallery on the starboard side and the full benefit of the stern window for light.
- However, in action all the furniture and partitions were removed so that the two pairs of guns that were a permanent feature of his accommodation could be fired.

### Upper deck

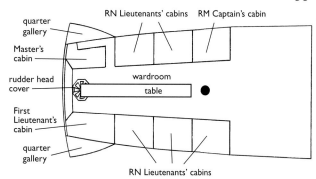

**Notes**
- The officers' cabins averaged about 8 square feet, usually with canvas sides.
- Each cabin was shared with a 24-pdr cannon. Cots were usually slung above the cannon.
- The First Lieutenant and Master had larger cabins and a stern window, and the First Lieutenant direct access to a quarter gallery.
- Dining, drinking and socializing took place in the wardroom. The large table there hid the rudder head, which stuck up through a hole in the floor.
- Cabins and wardroom were cleared for action.

### Lower deck

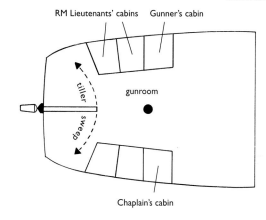

**Notes**
- The sweep of the tiller was somewhat disconcerting and took up considerable space.
- The Bosun and Carpenter had cabins forward near their respective stores and about this time the Gunner moved forward as well.
- Two cabins are shown empty. They could have been used by RM officers displaced by some higher-ranking civilian guest. Alternatively they may not have been erected.

### Orlop deck

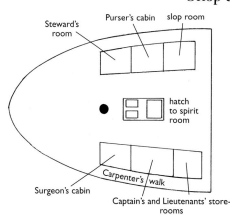

**Notes**
- Both the Purser and Surgeon had their cabins down below water level on this deck, as this was where they worked in battle and had their stores or medicines.
- It was always gloomy, usually foul smelling and cramped.
- Note the carpenter's walk, a narrow passageway that allowed him and his mates to inspect the hull and plug leaks or holes made in battle.

## Master

The master was the senior warrant officer on any ship. His primary responsibility at sea was navigation, and he had achieved his position either by working his way up from the lower deck, perhaps learning his navigational skills by many years at the wheel as a quartermaster, or by serving as a master's mate. Alternatively, he may have entered from the merchant marine or even been a midshipman who had chosen to limit his promotion prospects but get higher pay. However, as for the rank of lieutenant, there was an examination to pass. The prospective master had to appear before a board composed of a senior captain sitting with three well-qualified masters. If no vacancy existed for a man newly qualified as a master, he could be appointed second master to ships of third rate or above. He would then receive £63 per annum and be berthed with the midshipmen.

Prior to 1805 a master in the Royal Navy had hit his ceiling as regards promotion in rank. The only way he could improve his position was financially, by becoming the master of a larger ship. From 24 August 1805 a master of a first rate received £151-2-0 a year and that of a fifth rate £100-16-0, the latter amount being equal to that of a lieutenant. Also, of considerable significance, he was entitled to half pay when unemployed. The year 1805 was a good one for masters, as, in addition to their increased emoluments, the block on promotion to commissioned rank was lifted. The *Naval Chronicle* published just before Trafalgar stated:

> A former Order of Council, which prevented Masters in the Royal Navy from being made Lieutenants, is rescinded; and this regulation will, in the opinion of Officers of high distinction, be of material use in the Service. It is a fact that deserves to be noticed, that there is not, at this moment, a single instance of a Master who is bringing up his Son with a view to his being a Master.

Before this new order the best a master could expect was promotion ashore as Master-Superintendent at a dockyard or perhaps as a Queen's Harbourmaster, or even the prestigious appointment of Master of the Royal Yacht. An example is that of Mr F. Ruckert of the frigate *Euryalus*, who became Master-Superintendent, Sheerness, and later Master of the Royal Yacht *William and Mary*. After the battle only five of the thirty-one masters present were eventually commissioned. The second masters of the *Achille* and *Orion* became lieutenants, while the masters of the *Minotaur*, *Leviathan* and *Sirius* all retired as commanders.

Another niggling grievance of many masters was not addressed in 1805, and that concerned their uniform, indeed the uniforms of all the senior warrant officers. The problem was that the blue coat with its turn-down collar could be mistaken,

### A Master's Grievances

An entry in Volume 14 of the *Naval Chronicle* dated September 1805 indicates that a recent Order in Council had rectified a longstanding grievance of masters in the Royal Navy:

> It is with great pleasure we learn, that the long-expected increase of Pay is shortly to take place for the Lieutenants and Masters in the Royal Navy.
>
> The Master under a Third-rate has really not enough of Pay to support himself equal to the Society he is placed in – in a Sloop of War it is out of the question; it is a mere impossibility for him to pay his mess, and keep up the necessary appearance of an officer. ...
>
> ... he must ever remain a Master – there is no point for his views to rest on; there is no incitement to energy and emulation, where there is no hope of preferment. ...
>
> How it must mortify a Man who has been years in the Service to see young people put over his head, whom he himself had qualified for their Office, and who often, too often, are apt to forget the pains taken in their instruction! It must mortify a Man ... to feel himself excluded totally from that promotion which is open to every other individual in the Royal Navy but himself.

by those not versed in the detail of naval dress, for a civilian one – or at least not that of an officer. For the master this was particularly galling in view of his senior position in the ship's hierarchy. There were occasions when a master taken prisoner was not recognized as an officer and so not given the courtesies and privileges due to his status. However, when wearing his cocked hat, white waistcoat, breeches and stockings with his sword at his side with telescope or speaking trumpet in his hand, there was no mistaking that he was a man of authority. On a 74 he had, along with the first lieutenant, a permanent cabin at the stern and on the larboard side of the wardroom. It had stern windows and a passage behind it to the officers' quarter-gallery (toilets). Above, on the larboard side of the quarterdeck, adjoining the captain's dining cabin, was the master's 'office' where he kept his (privately purchased) navigational instruments, nautical books and charts. In here he kept the official logbook, plotted courses, marked positions or wrote up hydrographic information on uncharted coasts, shoals and reefs. In this small cabin, with its chart table, he instructed the young midshipmen in chart work and navigational calculations.

His duties were demanding. Admiralty Regulations and Instructions ran to thirty-eight paragraphs for masters but only twenty-six for lieutenants – which is presumably the reason why, apart from the captain, the master was the highest-paid officer on all ships-of-the-line. Apart from overall responsibility (under the captain) for navigation he would supervise pilotage and instruct his mates and the midshipmen in taking the noon sights of the sun to fix the ship's precise position. He had responsibility for the security and issue of beer and spirits. Every day he was required to report to the captain the quantity of beer and water consumed during the previous twenty-four hours. He was to regularly check the sails, rigging, anchors and cable tier. Every week he had to check the boatswain's and carpenter's accounts of stores issued and, most importantly, he had charge of the ship's official logbook. If necessary he could be a watch-keeping officer. In addition he was responsible for the stowage of the hold and the trim of the ship. Article IV of the master's regulations, which relates to taking on ballast, states: 'He is to examine every Vessel which carries ballast to the Ship, to see whether it be laden to its proper marks; he is to see that the ballast is sweet and clean, before he allows it to be taken into the Ship ...'. He had plenty of work to delegate to his master's mates and junior warrant officers.

Although most masters deserved their higher pay, there was sometimes resentment, indeed patronising arrogance, towards them from the lieutenants in the wardroom. W.H. Long's *Naval Yarns* of 1899 puts it thus: 'As the master, though only a Warrant Officer, from his being sometimes allowed to take watch, and put the ship about, is apt to give himself airs of consequence, and frequently has the astonishing impudence to think himself your equal.'

In action the master's position was on the quarterdeck with responsibility for 'conning' the ship in accordance with the captain's orders. Like all personnel on the poop, quarterdeck or upper deck, masters were very exposed in battle. At Trafalgar three British masters were killed (on the *Royal Sovereign*, *Colossus* and *Bellerophon*) and four wounded (on the *Britannia*, *Revenge*, *Mars* and *Africa*). This is 22 per cent of the thirty-two masters present, in percentage terms a substantially higher casualty rate than the 16 per cent suffered by lieutenants.

## Surgeon

Prior to 1805 surgeons had been paid miserably. A basic yearly salary of £60 was supplemented by an allowance of 2d per man on the ship – so the bigger the ship, the more their pay. The year of Trafalgar saw their pay more than triple to about £200 a year for junior surgeons – more for those with over ten years' service. The government agreed to provide medicines (previously the surgeon paid for them – an arrangement that must surely have worried his patients). The same year also saw an improvement in their status, with a better uniform, the privilege of wearing an officer's sword and their rank made equal to that of surgeons in the Army. These improvements were an attempt to attract more surgeons into the Navy, as there were longstanding shortages. They helped but did not eradicate the problem.

Surgeons remained 'technicians' who provided their own instruments, with the lower social status that implied. They did not require a medical degree to practise – their warrant was dependent on passing an oral exam at Surgeon's Hall in London. Although the surgeon dined in the wardroom, his cabin was down on the orlop deck alongside the dispensary and the cockpit, which was converted from midshipman's berth to makeshift operating theatre in battle. Here he lived and worked below the waterline in perpetual gloom, peering at his patients under the flickering light of candle lanterns. The main compensation for the surgeon, and all whose duty in battle kept them on the orlop deck, was its comparative safety. The enemy aimed largely at the upper deck, the masts and rigging (see Section Five), with very few shots coming through below the waterline. Not a single British surgeon or assistant was so much as scratched at Trafalgar.

Virtually every ship was entitled to one surgeon and from one to three assistant-surgeons. His duties were, as to be expected, checking the health of new men, charge of the sick and injured on board, prescribing medicines, advising the captain on matters of health, performing surgical operations as necessary and the mainte-

nance of a medical journal of his patients and the treatment he gave them. His superiors periodically inspected this. For most of his time the surgeon was concerned with flues and fever, hernias (common due to all the heavy lifting and heaving), fractures, toothache, seasickness and 'recreational' ailments acquired ashore – for which he prescribed his little 'blue pill'. Then, with the taller or recently joined crew members, there was the continual banging of heads on the low beams. It was not uncommon for men to knock themselves senseless. There were those who considered the above average level of lunacy in the Royal Navy (one madman per thousand, seven times that of the civilian population) was due to this frequent head-bashing.

It is true to say that naval surgeons generally had not acquired a good reputation during the eighteenth century. It had been assumed that the low pay and rough life was taken up only by those unable to secure better positions ashore. This was unfair to a large number of devoted men. Nevertheless, a number who 'from misfortune had taken refuge on board' had given their profession a poor reputation. Drunkenness was inevitably part of the problem. One wonders if the bottle had anything to do with the plight of Surgeon William McDonald of the *Colossus*. By Trafalgar he had already been a naval surgeon for twelve years but after the battle nothing of note is recorded of his career except his death eighteen years later. At the time he was still a surgeon, probably drunken, certainly embittered, on the insignificant sloop *Driver* off the west coast of Africa. Perhaps it was his liver that finally gave up the struggle.

The most famous surgeon at Trafalgar was William Beatty of the *Victory*. He attended Lord Nelson at his death, carried out the post-mortem and later published an account. He became a Royal Navy physician (an altogether more prestigious position than surgeon), a licentiate of the College of Physicians in 1817, Fellow of the Royal College of Surgeons and Physician of Greenwich Hospital, and was knighted in 1831.

Others with bright futures included William Burnett of the *Defiance* who had been present at the battles of St Vincent and the Nile as well as Calder's action prior to Trafalgar. He was knighted and rose to be Director-General of the Medical Department of the Navy. Peter Suther had just been appointed acting surgeon of the *Swiftsure* in time for Trafalgar but later rose to be surgeon on the Royal Yacht, *William and Mary* and, in 1855, Deputy-Inspector of Hospitals and Fleets. He died in 1877 – surely one of the last survivors of the battle. Lastly, John Jameson of the *Agamemnon* who became Physician to the Baltic Fleet in 1807, was knighted and later appointed Inspector of Hospitals and Fleets. He died in New South Wales, Australia, in 1844 – one wonders what he was doing there.

### The Royal Navy and Its Lunatics

Whether or not the comparatively high incidence of lunacy in the Royal Navy was due to the knocking of so many heads on the low beams must, I suppose, remain a matter of conjecture. What cannot be disputed was that the naval authorities went out of their way to look after these unfortunates, establishing their own mental hospital at Hoxton in London. In 1813, for example, there were 140 inmates listed with a fair mix of social backgrounds and ratings. Included in the total were one captain, four lieutenants, three Royal Marine lieutenants, one surgeon, one assistant surgeon, two carpenters, one gunner, one master's mate and a midshipman – 14 per cent of the inmates. This might suggest that the level of insanity among the senior ranks was relatively higher than that of their juniors, but it is more likely that the officers' relatives had greater influence on their treatment or the medical authorities were more inclined to persevere with them. Some men were discharged cured or into the care of their family, while some died in the hospital. Their fate was preferable to that of the remainder. If Hoxton gave up on them, they were likely to be discharged, still insane, to make room for others, and sent to the living hell of the nearby Bethlehem Hospital, or 'Bedlam' as it was better known. It was founded in 1247 by sisters and brethren of the order of the Star of Bethlehem, and eventually became infamous for the brutal ill-treatment meted out to the insane.

## Purser

The purser led a very stressful life, not during battle where he worked in the comparative safety of the cockpit with the surgeon, but every day, week after week without remit. He was the ship's storekeeper (for all non-war-related stores) and shopkeeper. As such, he was likely to be one of the most unpopular officers on board. This stemmed from the fact that he was invariably held by the crew to be cheating or overcharging them. The financial responsibility for his stores was an immense burden. If any disappeared, or if they were seen to be short, the purser paid, and he lived in terror of 'being brought into debt'. Consider a 38-gun frigate such as the *Naiad* at Trafalgar with a complement of around 300 men stocked up for a comparatively short voyage of three months. The purser, Mr Thomas Menzies, whose wage was a mere £39-6-0 a year, had to account for every ounce of 25,200 lbs of bread, 25,200 gallons of beer, 3,600 4-lb pieces of salted beef, 3,600 2-lb pieces of salted pork, 3,600 quarts of pease and 5,400 of oatmeal, 1,800 lbs of butter, 3,600 lbs of cheese and 6,300 quarts of rum (or 12,600 of wine). These supplies represented a huge amount of money, and were undoubtedly his most important responsibility. The purser was charged on his account with the value of them, and received credit for the standard ration multiplied by the number of men in the ship's complement, plus credit for the return of unused victuals. So Menzies, like all the other thirty pursers at Trafalgar, had to issue items out on a daily basis to every man in accordance with his regulation entitlement. The scope for fiddling was unlimited. At the end of a voyage the purser had to hand back to the Victualling Board what was left and get his ledgers that recorded his issues 'passed'. Getting his accounts passed could take anything from a few months (very fast) to years (common). In the previous century the shortest delay recorded was six months, the longest fifty-seven years! Little wonder that pursers with any experience were shrewd businessmen, miserly, watchful, suspicious and regarded by many as naturally dishonest. Woe betide the purser who did not know his regulations in every minute detail, whose mental arithmetic was anything but computer accurate or was confused by his accounts. To assist him he was given just one steward.

The wonder is that anybody wanted the job – but there is no evidence of a lack of applicants, despite the fact that they had to put up a bond to the Navy Board of £1,200 in a first rate and £400 in a sixth rate or smaller. The job's popularity derived from the fact that the Navy turned a blind eye to the purser taking one-eighth commission of the value of everything he issued by weight or measure. Officially, this was for unavoidable wastage, leakage or shrinkage. A man entitled to a pound (sixteen ounces) of bread, for example, would receive fourteen ounces – one of the Spithead mutineers' demands was for seamen to get a full pound. Thus came about the 'pursers' pound' of fourteen ounces; for every pound of provisions the purser issued, he made a profit of the value of two ounces. Nowhere was such a thing condoned in any regulation, but it was the custom, the practice and accepted on all ships – without it there would have been no pursers, or they would have to have been paid many times their rate. Given the amount of provisions, even on a frigate, there would seem to be plenty of scope for a purser to avoid debt, indeed to make a handsome profit. However, all was not as it seems.

The purser had many enemies. Among the most feared were rats, mice, weevils, cockroaches, time, heat, water, leaking casks and unscrupulous or uncooperative contractors. The last mentioned needed very careful watching. For example, they supplied the casks of salted beef and pork. Each cask was marked with its contents – the number of double (8-lb) and single (4-lb) pieces of beef or 4-lb and 2-lb pieces of pork. The contractor counted the pieces in and sealed the cask, which might not be opened until months later on the other side of the world. Fortunately for the purser the opening of these casks was governed by regulations. They had to be opened 'in public on the open deck, under the inspection, and in the presence of the master of the ship, or one of his mates, together with the purser's steward'. Every piece was counted out and deficiencies (a common occurrence) noted in the logbook. Later, many months later, the purser had to sort it out with the contractor – if he could be found. The Victualling Board bowed out smartly, claiming it was a private matter between the purser and contractor, although they still charged the purser if he was found to have been 'brought in debt of salt flesh' at the price of fresh meat, several times the cost of the salted variety!

If a purser was to make money, then it was likely to be through his role as private businessman. His role as shopkeeper, as distinct from storekeeper, involved the sale of 'slops' – the Navy's term for seamen's working clothes. The crew were issued with hammocks free but expected to buy their rough, everyday clothes. The Navy Board supplied the purser with bales of slops, on which he received £5 commission for every £100 sold. He also acted as auctioneer. When an officer or seaman died on board, his personal effects were auctioned off alongside the mainmast and the proceeds were eventually sent to his next-of-kin with the purser retaining some 10 per cent. The procedure, known as 'Dead Men's Cloaths', was conducted according to regulations, one of which stipulated that a seaman could not buy any clothing 'as are of a quality above his wear or station'. This, presumably, prevented the carpenter's mate strutting about in an officer's silk stockings.

Pursers could not receive their warrant unless they had served at least a year as a captain's clerk or eighteen months as secretary to a flag officer. The bigger the ship, the more their official pay, which was low for a wardroom officer. Their cabin was on the orlop deck next to the slop room. In action the purser remained on that deck in the cockpit helping with the wounded. Perhaps action was not unwelcome, as with luck deficiencies in supplies could probably be written off as battle damage by a helpful board of survey.

Not one purser was killed or wounded at Trafalgar, again reflecting the relative safety of the cockpit in battle. The best-known purser was William Burke of the *Victory*, who was related to the political philosopher Edmund Burke. At sixty-seven he was the oldest man in the British Fleet with over thirty years at sea. At the start of the action Burke had remained on the quarterdeck until Nelson noticed his presence and remarked, 'Mr Burke, I expect every man to be upon his station.' Burke went below, where he later supported Nelson as he lay dying. Burke had by then lost two sons to the Navy. Lieutenant Walter Burke had been killed in 1801 whilst cutting out a French corvette, while the purser's eldest son, Commander Henry Burke, had drowned with his entire crew only five months before Trafalgar when his ship, the 16-gun *Seagull*, foundered. Nelson's purser, surely a much-saddened old man, died quietly at Rochester, Kent, in 1815 aged seventy-seven.

It was unusual for a master's mate, the son of a horse artillery major, with a fair chance of making lieutenant, to seek and obtain a purser's warrant. Yet Thomas Goble, a master's mate on the *Victory*, did exactly that. He had entered the muster books as an able seaman on 5 October 1805; eight days later he was a master's mate assigned to serve as Captain Hardy's Secretary. When Nelson's Secretary, John Scott, was disembowelled by a cannonball, Goble became acting Secretary to the Fleet. The following year he was appointed purser, serving in that capacity until his retirement twenty years after the battle.

## Chaplain

> A clergyman, appointed Chaplain of one of His Majesty's Ships, must remember that it is his indispensable duty, that the morality of his conduct and the decency, sobriety, and regularity of his manners be such as become the sacred Office to which he is appointed, and such as may inspire the Ship's company with reverence for it, and respect to himself.

Thus reads Article 1 of the six articles governing the duties of the Anglican chaplain in the 1806 Regulations and Instructions relating to His Majesty's Service at Sea. The tone reflects the experiences of the previous century, when the majority of chaplains who went to sea came from the bottom of the ecclesiastical barrel. Because of his calling the chaplain was supposedly, as a man of God, upright, sober and a gentleman – characteristics that, by 1790, entitled him to a place in the wardroom. For many years, however, his wardroom status had been debatable and, of perhaps greater importance, he had not been permitted to use the officer's toilets – the quarter gallery. This meant, as a petition of the time complained, that the chaplain had to 'ease himself' in full view of the common seamen. What with this indignity and a basic pay rate of less than an ordinary seaman, to which was added an allowance of fourpence for every crew member, it was hardly surprising the Royal Navy failed to attract the best clergymen. At the time of Trafalgar a chaplain received nineteen shillings a month or £11-4-0 a year. To this, on a third-rate ship, he could add about £14 allowance a year, or slightly over £1 a month. This put him on about the same level as a marine corporal, a yeoman of the sheets or a caulker's mate. Not until 1812 were his pay and conditions properly reviewed, giving him the guarantee of wardroom status, pay of £150 a year (a huge rise) and half pay entitlement after eight years' service.

Although every ship of fifth rate or larger was supposed to carry a chaplain, they were rarely, if ever, to be found on frigates – none of the four British frigates at Trafalgar had one. In the French Revolutionary navy there was little use for clergymen, whereas in the Catholic Spanish navy the priest had a key role and was an officer of undisputed status. In 1804 a Reverend John Dunsterville joined the 74-gun *Culloden*. Seaman Robert Hay wrote of him:

> Mr Dunsterville, besides reading prayers on Sunday, would, when the weather permitted, deliver a sermon, but he was never under the necessity of composing any, for he brought aboard two or three dozen written ones, which were more than sufficient for the whole passage.

With so little to keep them occupied it is no wonder that boredom frequently led to the bottle, although in some ships the chaplain took on the duties of schoolmaster as a way of supplementing his meagre pay. In battle he was to be found in the cockpit ministering to the spiritual needs of the dying. Trafalgar is a good example of the unpopularity of a naval career for the clergy. Only twelve (44 per cent) of the British ships-of-the-line had chaplains onboard. They were *Victory*, *Royal Sovereign*, *Britannia*, *Téméraire*, *Neptune*, *Dreadnought*, *Revenge*, *Defiance*, *Achille*, *Orion*, *Swiftsure* and *Thunderer*. The only one wounded was the Reverend John Greenly of the *Revenge*, who later became canon of Salisbury Cathedral.

The best-known Trafalgar chaplain was the Reverend Alexander John Scott of the *Victory*, whose career is described on p. 17.

## GUNROOM WARRANT OFFICERS

Officers living in or using the gunroom were a mixed bunch. Firstly there were the master's mates, midshipmen and assistant-surgeons (of whom the first two were 'inferior' officers rather than warrant officers) who aspired to reach wardroom status. Then there was, sometimes on larger ships, a schoolmaster – who would never reach the wardroom. Finally there were the standing warrant officers: carpenter, gunner and boatswain.

### Assistant-surgeon

These gentlemen, formerly called surgeon's mates, were medically qualified and awaiting a slot as surgeon. There were supposed to be two on a two-decker and three on a three-decker. At Trafalgar six out of the seven first rates, including the *Victory*, had only two assistant-surgeons instead of three (the exception was the 98-gun *Dreadnought*). Eight of the remaining line-of-battle ships had only one instead of two. Of the fifty-one assistant-surgeons at the battle, all survived unharmed, having spent their time down in the gloom of the orlop deck helping to lop off limbs.

Assistant-Surgeon Robert Bolton of the *Orion* found naval life unsatisfactory and transferred to the Army two years after the battle, having to accept demotion to hospital assistant in order to do so. He was present at the early Peninsula battles of Rolica and Vimiero in 1808 and got his old rank of assistant-surgeon back two years later when serving with the 62nd Foot (Wiltshire) in Sicily. In 1813 he was a surgeon on the medical staff, again in the Peninsula, before becoming the surgeon of the 78th Foot (Rosshire Buffs) in India. He lived long enough to collect both the Naval General Service Medal, with clasp Trafalgar, and the Military General Service Medal with two clasps – surely a unique achievement. He lived on until after the American Civil War, dying in 1866 probably well into his eighties – a reassuring example for a medical man.

### Schoolmaster

This individual was never going to be anything but a schoolmaster. All rated ships were entitled to one, although many, probably most, went to sea without. There was not even one on the *Victory* at Trafalgar. When this happened, some of his duties were sometimes taken over by the chaplain – although why it was assumed the latter could teach mathematics is not clear. His basic pay was miserable at £24-6-0 on a sixth rate, rising to £31-6-0 on a first rate. This was the same rate as midshipmen, clerks, armourers and masters-at-arms. The schoolmaster, however, could supplement this with £20 at the end of each year provided his captain certified he deserved it. He also endeavoured, with variable success, to extract a little extra each month from his pupils. He was not allowed in the wardroom and had no cabin of his own, so was compelled to sling his hammock where he could find space in the gunroom. It was not unknown, as with schoolteachers worldwide, for his pupils to mock him and play practical jokes on him. 'We youngsters had a schoolmaster, a clever, seedy looking creature, whose besetting sin was love of grog; with very little trouble it floored him and then, I don't like to record it, we used to grease his head and flour it.' One's mind boggles to think of the consequences of such goings on in today's classroom!

The schoolmaster was required to be examined by the master, warden and assistants of Trinity House before he could receive his warrant. He was also required to produce certificates, not so much of his competence to instruct writing, navigation and mathematics, but as to his sobriety and moral virtues. His pupils were the boys, volunteers and midshipmen. Had there been a schoolmaster on the *Victory*, he would have had to cope with forty boys aged from under ten to eighteen, plus another twenty-one young midshipmen. All in all, the schoolmaster's lot does not appear to have been a particularly happy one, so it is little wonder that so many ships sailed without them.

## STANDING WARRANT OFFICERS

### Carpenter

The present damage-control officer on a modern warship is a descendent of the carpenter of Nelson's day. He was a craftsman who had served an apprenticeship ashore to a shipwright and then been to sea for at least six months as a carpenter's mate. Sometimes he had been a carpenter's mate on a merchant ship but had been pressed into naval service. His warrant appointed him to a specific ship and he remained with it, supposedly permanently. His overriding responsibility was to keep his ship afloat, and the importance of this task was reflected in his pay. Although this varied in accordance with the rate of ship, on two- and three-deckers he received a pound a month more than the other standing officers (boatswain and gunner). Thus on a 74 he was paid £57-6-0 and on a 100 £69-6-0. He had his cabin forward on the orlop deck next to his store where timber, tools and an abundance of nails were kept. Strangely, the carpenter does not seem to have been trusted with the keys to his own store; regulations stipulated they must be kept hanging outside the first lieutenant's cabin. If the carpenter needed them, he had to apply to the officer-of-the-watch, who then sent a midshipman to collect them.

In wooden ships a competent carpenter was crucial. He had two mates on first-, second- and the larger third-rate ships and one on smaller rates. He was allowed up to twelve crew on first rates, ten on second or large third rates, and eight on smaller ones. Most frigates had five. These comparatively high numbers reflect the importance of their duties and the volume of their daily work. Some of the carpenter's duties are listed below:

*Fitting out*
An extremely busy time involving such things as the making of tables and benches for the officers.

---

### A Midshipman 'Cobbed'

Midshipman Elliot of the *Goliath* was once convicted by an unofficial 'midshipman's court martial' of saving the schoolmaster's life. For this offence he was 'cobbed', which on this occasion meant being stretched over the gunroom table and his bare buttocks whacked with the leather sheath of a midshipman's dirk. The reason for this demeaning and painful punishment was that Captain Foley had become concerned at the lack of practical navigational knowledge among his midshipmen. On board the *Goliath* was a Volunteer Class 1 who had been educated at Christ's Hospital and was an excellent mathematician. Foley had appointed him as acting schoolmaster with special responsibility for giving extra instruction in navigation to a disgruntled group of midshipmen. One day the newly appointed schoolmaster, who could not swim, somehow fell overboard, usually a fatal accident. On this occasion, however, the gallant young Elliot leapt into the water and kept him afloat until a boat could be lowered to pick them up. His brother midshipmen were far from happy, so a 'court-martial' was convened. The punishment was awarded, 'As there was no denial of the fact, he was found guilty of the aggravated offence of saving a schoolmaster.'

---

*Routine maintenance of the woodwork of the entire ship*
The woodwork included the boats, gratings and ladders, and taking care of it required daily inspections, twice daily of the lower-deck ports, masts and spars. In bad weather or when carrying a heavy press of sail, the carpenter and his mates would inspect the masts and spars several times during a watch.

*Soundings of the pump well*
These had to be taken at set times and the result reported to the officer-of-the-watch to be recorded in the log.

*Maintaining a supply of shot plugs*
Every night everything must be ready for a beat to quarters and a report made to the officer-of-the-watch.

*In action, checking for damage to the hull from cannonballs*
Small holes were immediately plugged; larger ones had to have a heavy mat lowered over the side against the hole, where the force of the water and suction held it in place.

Once again the British casualty figures for Trafalgar bear out that it was safer below deck. Only one carpenter was killed, Mr Lewis Oades of the *Téméraire*, and none was wounded. On the *Victory*, which was in the heat of the action for several hours, the entire carpenter's crew of two mates and ten men escaped untouched.

### Gunner

Like the other standing warrant officers, the gunner stayed with the ship in and out of commission. He was invariably a lower-deck seaman who had worked his way up as a petty officer – probably as a quarter gunner and gunner's mate – before taking the gunner's examination before a 'mathematical master' and three senior gunners. In smaller ships with only one or two sea officers, the gunner often took his turn as officer-of-the-watch. By 1805 the gunner had left the gunroom and the supervision of the volunteers for a cabin forward near the powder room. He made his own messing arrangements and it was quite common for the gunner to have his wife on board – in which case she was usually 'mother hen' to the young boys. The gunner's pay on a third rate was £45-6-0 a year, on a first rate £57-6-0, some £12 below a carpenter.

The gunner had direct control over a substantial crew consisting of gunner's mates, quarter gunners (one for every four guns), two yeoman of the powder room, an armourer and his mates and, in first or second rates or large 74s, a gunsmith. They were his petty officers. The actual gun crews were composed of a mixture of seamen, landsmen and marines. Although he was responsible for training the gun crews, assisted by his petty officers, and the firing of salutes, the gunner did not control the firing of the guns in battle – lieutenants and midshipmen did this.

His was the crucial task of supervision of the flow of shot and cartridges from the magazine to the guns (see Section Five).

In peaceful times the gunner had particular responsibilities:

• When the ship was commissioned he had to apply to the Ordnance Storekeeper at the port for the established number of guns for his ship, together with the ammunition and gunner's stores. All had to be carefully checked and checked again as they were loaded on board.
• He had responsibility for the maintenance and equipment of all the guns and keeping the shot racks full.
• He had to supervise the armourer, who had responsibility for the storage, maintenance and repair of all muskets and pistols.
• His most important task was the proper control over the powder magazines. This entailed very strict enforcement of the safety regulations, essential for preventing a naked flame or spark sending the entire ship skywards. As part of the precautions, the keys were held by the captain and a marine sentry was posted outside the magazine.

The gunner's duties at quarters and how he prepared the powder room for action are described in detail in Section Five.

All the British gunners were fortunate at Trafalgar as none was killed or wounded.

## Boatswain (Bosun)

The bosun was probably the most important man on the ship as far as the seamen's everyday work, routine and discipline were concerned. In some ways he can be equated with the regimental sergeant major in the Army. With the assistance of his mates with their 'starters' (a rattan cane or a rope's end), used to encourage the laggards, the bosun supervised all activity on deck and aloft. It was his mates who rousted the men from their hammocks, ensured the prompt changeover of the watches and supervised the daily routine of the ship's company. They were responsible for the hoisting of yards, the trimming of sails, the securing of anchors and boats, the lowering of boats and the regular, daily inspections of the rigging and ropes.

The bosun and his mates communicated their instructions by the use of their 'call', an instrument whose shrill notes were the summons to a variety of duties, followed by the occasional shouted order. The call was a symbol of office in much the same way as a modern Army warrant officer's pace stick is. British seamen were invariably sufficiently well trained that a lot of yelling and bellowing was unnecessary; the silence with which they carried out their duties was later admired by Napoleon on his way to exile on St Helena on board the *Northumberland*. A skilled man could produce about eight different sounds, known as 'pipes', by blowing into the call and 'throttling' with his hands. There were distinctive 'calls' or 'pipes' that everyone understood, such as 'haul', 'hoist', 'call all hands' and 'pipe down', when all hands not on duty were to turn in – the origin of today's 'pipe down' meaning to be quiet. One call drew the seamen's attention to the bosun or his mate who would shout the order when he finished his 'pipe', and a shrill, steady high note continuing for about five seconds meant 'pipe still' or stand at attention as a salute, perhaps to a passing ship. It could also be a warning to avoid an accident. All these calls and pipes earned the bosun's mates the nickname of 'Spithead Nightingales'.

The bosun had usually risen up through the ranks and would have served at least a year as a petty officer, often as a bosun's mate. He had to be literate but needed no specific qualifications. Like the other standing warrant officers, he had probably reached his career ceiling and so could only improve his position by being transferred to a larger ship. He drew the same annual pay as a gunner, £45-6-0 on a third rate and £57-6-0 on a first rate. The bosun had both the sailmaker and ropemaker under his direct command, as the condition of the rigging and sails was his most vital responsibility. As such, he had control over a large store adjoining his cabin forward on the larboard side of the orlop deck – locked with another key that hung outside the first lieutenant's cabin. With so much canvas in his care, there was a temptation to sell off small pieces of the lighter variety to seamen wanting to make or mend clothes. To do so was risky, however, as regulations unmistakably forbade the cutting up of 'any cordage or canvas without an order in writing from the captain and under the inspection of the master'.

The bosun spent much of his time during the day on deck. When all hands were called at any time (for instance, tacking or wearing at night) the bosun was required to be present. In action his quarter was on the upper deck, controlling the crew sailing the ship as distinct from those fighting. This was a highly dangerous position as is shown by the casualties amongst bosuns at Trafalgar. Two were killed (William Forster of the *Defiance* and Thomas Robinson of the *Bellerophon*, who died of his wounds) while those on the *Victory*, *Téméraire*, *Tonnant*, *Spartiate*, *Minotaur* and *Colossus* were wounded. Eight casualties out of twenty-seven is almost 30 per cent – the highest proportion of losses suffered by any British rate at the battle.

## OTHER WARRANT OFFICERS

These crew members were appointed by warrants but were, in practice, equated with, and paid as, senior petty officers. They were subject to the captain's powers of discipline and appointment and were not members of the gunroom. They were the armourer, master-at-arms, caulker, sailmaker, ropemaker and cook.

### Armourer

He was under the control of the gunner and was assisted by two mates on line-of-battle ships, while on ships of eighty guns or more a gunsmith was added to his crew. His task was the care and repair of all the ship's small arms. On a 74 there were 130 black-metalled muskets for the use of seamen, 120 India-pattern muskets and bayonets for the marines, 70 pairs of pistols, 200 hand grenades, 60 poleaxes, 230 swords, 100 pikes and 60 tomahawks. This gives the impressive total of well over a thousand weapons, most of which required cleaning, oiling, repairing or sharpening – in the damp, salt-laden air a major headache.

The armourer was an artificer, not a seaman. He could not be pressed into service, while his warrant from the Navy Board gave him immunity from the more menial tasks of seamen or landsmen. He was also the ship's blacksmith, complete with tools, including a portable forge that could be set up ashore if required. These were very necessary, as he had responsibility for the repair of all the ship's metalwork of the hull, rigging and armament. His annual pay was that of a midshipman, schoolmaster or master-at-arms (£31-6-0 on a first rate). Surprisingly, a gunsmith was rated below an armourer's mate, receiving the same pay as a sailmaker's crew or steward.

On Nelson's flagship at Trafalgar the senior armourer was an American, James Morrison from New York. His number two, James Cepell from London, was also rated as armourer. The two mates, John Melebury and Hugh Stevens, came from Sweden and London respectively. The gunsmith, William Barnett, was from Glasgow. Four countries represented within a crew of five must have been exceptional.

## Master-at-arms

Every rated ship had a master-at-arms. Article 1 of the regulations concerning their duties reads:

> No person is to be rated Master at Arms, unless he be appointed by a warrant from the Lord High Admiral, or the Lords Commissioners of the Admiralty. Captains are never to recommend to this situation any man who is not perfectly sober, orderly, respectful and obedient; who has not served a considerable time in His Majesty's Navy, is well acquainted with its discipline, and so far Master of Military manoeuvres as to be able to instruct the seamen in the use of the musket.

To the present writer, who spent many years in the infantry, this sounds much like the naval equivalent of the provost sergeant in charge of the regimental police. The master-at-arms, assisted by two ship's corporals (one for each watch), was responsible for enforcing the general rules and regulations of shipboard life. In particular he had to be vigilant with regard to fire hazards:

> He is to see the fire [in the galley], and all lights (except those which the Captain shall expressly allow) extinguished at the time the Captain shall direct. And no Officer of any rank or description is in any way to interfere with, or on any pretence to prevent, his perfectly executing this duty.

He was also 'to prevent, or put an end to, all improper drinking, all quarrelling, rioting, or other disturbances'. Powerful stuff. If he found anyone infringing regulations, he was to report them to the officer-of-the-watch – which meant a logbook entry and retribution to follow. His description by a contemporary writer as a man who had 'great power and is what is called a great man among the little ones' seems to say it all. His annual pay was £31-6-0 on a first rate and £24-6-0 on a sixth rate. This put him below a master's mate but above a carpenter's mate.

The *Victory*'s master-at-arms at Trafalgar was William Elliott from Birmingham, who had been on board for two and a half years by the time of the battle.

## Caulker

The caulker worked under the direction of the carpenter. There was one on every rated ship, with fourth rates and larger having one caulker's mate as well. As his title implies, the caulker's responsibility was to keep the ship watertight by caulking the ship's sides and decks. This was a never-ending task, particularly on a large three-decker – rather like the proverbial painting of the Forth Bridge. In addition to checking that no seams had started in the hull or deck, his duties included the inspection, care and maintenance of the pumps, gunports, scuppers, hauseholes and

all other openings. At quarters his station was in the cable tier, where he prepared balls of oakham and tallow to assist the carpenter in plugging leaks.

Before he could receive his pay of £30-6-0 a year he had to produce a certificate from his captain that 'he had been attentive to his duty'. Caulkers received the same pay no matter what rate the ship they served on, which considering the difference in size between a small frigate and a 100-gun flagship must have been the cause of some justifiable grumbling.

## Sailmaker

The sailmaker, working under the bosun, held a key position on any sailing ship. On a first-rate ship there were thirty-seven sails that could be set with a total sail area of 5,568 square yards of canvas. In addition she had to have up to twenty-two spares. Every sail was subjected to close inspection when brought on board during fitting out. The secret of a sailmaker's success aboard lay in keeping the sails dry and preventing them from providing an everlasting meal for rats and mice. To do this a system of continuous checks had to be maintained, with damp sails being brought up on deck to dry in fine weather. The sails not in use were stowed together with the spares, providing great scope for chaos if they became jumbled up. If extra sails had to be set, they had to be found quickly, so they were stored with wooden tallies attached for speedy identification.

Repair was another endless chore for the sailmaker and his solitary mate – there was only one mate for all ships-of-the-line. This workforce was obviously inadequate for the size of the task, so the sailmaker supplemented his crew with two seamen in fourth rates and above, and one in smaller ships and sloops. As all able seamen had to be able to 'sew a seam', more men could be drafted in if there was a backlog of repair work.

The regulations of 1806 stated that, 'No person is to be rated as sail-maker, who is not appointed by a Warrant from the Commissioners of the Navy.' There were only five regulations for him, the fifth stating that he could not receive his wages until the captain had signed a certificate as to his 'sobriety, obedience, and attention to his duty'. Provided the captain obliged, he received £27-6-0 a year on line-of-battle ships. The sailmaker on the *Victory* at Trafalgar was assisted by a mate and two crew – all older men, at thirty-six, thirty-three and forty-one respectively. None became a casualty.

## Ropemaker

The ropemaker also worked under the bosun. As his title implies, he spent his days making rope from spun-yarn. As a first rate had some 26 miles (42km) of rope in her standing and running rigging alone, all of which was subject to constant stress and chafing, the ropemaker was invariably a busy man. He had no official mates to help but seamen could be, and were, drafted in to make or splice rope. Regulations stated that all the rope he made was to be handed to the bosun when completed and he was to make a daily report to the master of the amount of rope made that day. He received slightly more pay (£30-6-0 per annum) than the sailmaker but the same as the caulker. Like the sailmaker, he required a captain's certificate before he got it. The ropemaker on the *Victory* during the battle was the twenty-nine-year-old James Hartnell. He lived long enough to receive the Naval General Service Medal, which was not issued until 1847.

# Cook

Virtually every ship, large or small, was entitled to a cook. He was always an old seaman of many years' experience, and the naval regulations also required him to have been a Greenwich pensioner. He was frequently a cripple, having lost an arm, a leg or an eye in some past action or accident. A cook's warrant was therefore something of a reward for long service or compensation for his afflictions. There was no real need for him to have any culinary skills. A contemporary opinion on his skills states: 'All his science is contained within the cover of a sea-kettle. The composing of a Minc'd-py, is Metaphysicks to him; and the roasting of a pig as puzzling as the squaring of a Circle.' These remarks were mostly justified, as his 'cooking' was, as often as not, merely watching water boil. It was rare for the cook to do any 'cooking' himself; he contented himself with supervising his mates and serving the food to the individual mess cooks.

The galley was forward on the upper deck under the forecastle, and by 1805 had in most ships-of-the-line been equipped with a Brodie stove (like the one on the *Victory*). At the fore end were two large coppers for boiling, capable of taking 400 gallons between both of them. In the centre were two ovens in which up to 80 lbs of bread could be baked; there was also a grill, spits that were automatically rotated by a chain, and a distiller that produced small quantities of fresh water. It was fuelled by coal, supplemented by large amounts of wood – for Nelson's day, a fairly modern piece of kit. Whether the crew always received the benefits of its capabilities is, however, doubtful, as the bulk of the roasting and baking was done for the officers.

As mentioned above, the ship's meat supply was mostly heavily salted in casks, with the number of pieces therein written on the outside. When taken out it was totally inedible in any form until most of the salt had been removed. The cook's regulations stated that he should 'see that the salt meat is properly watered, and that all provisions are carefully and cleanly boiled'. This was normally done by putting the pieces to soak (steep) for twenty-four hours in the steep-tub – the one thing all cooks were scrupulous about was counting the pieces in and counting them out

again. They were then placed in the coppers for boiling. Boiling was the only way to make salted meat in any way chewable. It also reduced still further the amount of salt impregnated in it over the weeks, months or years of stowage.

A cook's pay was poor. At £21-6-0 a year on a line-of-battle ship it was only marginally better than an able seaman's. However, the job had its perks apart from the obvious one of a full stomach. He made extra money in flagrant breach of Article VI of his regulations, which stated:

> He is not, on any account, to give the skimmings of the coppers in which salt meat has been boiled to the men, either to mix with their puddings or to use in any other manner, as scarcely any thing more unwholesome, or more likely to produce scurvy, can be eaten.

During the boiling process the fat floated to the surface and formed unsavoury lumps of yellowish sludge. But the crew did not regard it as unwholesome; in fact, many were prepared to pay the cook for the luxury of spreading it on their bread (biscuits). And eating it did not cause scurvy. It had alternative uses such as greasing the rigging or it could sometimes be sold to merchants for tallow. From this slush, the ship's cook was often given the nickname 'slushy' and the modern expression 'slush fund' came into our everyday language.

As often as possible, fresh meat (from live animals) was available either from contractors in an overseas port or from the livestock taken on board when the ship first sailed. They included cattle, sheep, pigs, goats, chickens, geese and ducks, all corralled in pens or coops. Up to twelve cattle and thirty sheep was not uncommon. The pens were normally on the upper deck, the coops on the forecastle, in the ship's boats or on the quarterdeck. The cook usually delegated the plucking and butchery to his assistants – men told off to help him (he had no official mates).

The cook on the *Victory* was a Charles Carroll of uncertain age and disability. His place at quarters was at his galley, his particular duty being to ensure the stove was out.

# THE BATTLE OF ST VINCENT, 14 FEBRUARY 1797

The year 1797 was both a good and a bad one for Nelson. It was bad in that he was wounded twice, the second time resulting in the agonizing amputation of his right arm; good in the sense that his outstanding initiative and courage at St Vincent secured him copious honours ('my chains and medals and ribbons'). But, far more significantly, it confirmed him in the eyes of the Admiralty as what today's Services would call a 'high flyer'. His performance at St Vincent secured him independent command in the Mediterranean, victory at the Nile and, eventually, command at Trafalgar.

Scope for him to excel seemed, at the outset, decidedly limited. By February 1797 he had been a post captain for eighteen years, and he had never taken part in a major sea battle. He had missed the Battle of the Saints, which took place near the cluster of tiny islets known as 'The Saints' between the much larger Caribbean islands of Guadeloupe and Dominica in 1782. There, Admiral Rodney shattered the French by turning conventional naval tactics on their head and bursting through the French line. Later, in 1794, Nelson was fighting in Corsica when Admiral Howe took his fleet into a 'pell mell' engagement with the French some 400 miles west of Ushant on 1 June (a victory known in British history books as 'The Glorious First of June').

Less than a year before St Vincent, in 1796, Nelson had been made a commodore and thus entitled, albeit temporarily, to fly his own broad pennant. Now, on 14 February 1797, off Cape St Vincent on the southern tip of Portugal, Commodore Nelson was to be given a chance, a fleeting one, to play a crucial role in securing another resounding victory. Little wonder Nelson was delighted at the prospect of a worthwhile clash with an elusive enemy, even though he was to fight as the commander of a 74-gun ship, the *Captain*, with no fewer than four admirals outranking him. When the *Captain*'s Royal Marine drummers beat 'to quarters' that morning, Nelson climbed the ladder to his quarterdeck in ignorance of the fact that he was then the fifth admiral in the fleet – he had risen to the top of the captains' list and been promoted on 2 February to Rear-Admiral of the Blue. He was not to be informed officially until 1 April. Some accounts of St Vincent imply this promotion was among the rewards for his actions that day – it was not.

## THE STRATEGIC SITUATION AT THE END OF 1796

In July 1796 Spain signed an alliance with France. Three months later, terrified about the security of her rich Caribbean possessions, she declared war on Britain. At a stroke France virtually doubled her naval power, in terms of quantity if not in quality. On land the young Napoleon Bonaparte was making a reputation as a general at the head of the Army of Italy. Milan fell in May, Leghorn in June. It was but a short step from there to Corsica, his birthplace, an island that was not only allied to Britain but often served as a convenient forward base for the British Mediterranean Squadron, then under Admiral Sir John Jervis. In Paris the idea of attacking England through its backdoor, rebellious Ireland, was now considered entirely practical – an attempted landing in Bantry Bay failed in December 1796 due to dreadful weather.

From the British point of view the Mediterranean was fast becoming untenable. There were French squadrons at Brest, Rochefort and Toulon, now supported by Spanish ones in Cadiz and Cartagena. On land only Gibraltar and a friendly Portugal could be relied on to offer shelter and supplies to British ships. Jervis was isolated with sizeable enemy forces threatening his lines of communication through the Straits. In September the British decided to withdraw from the Mediterranean, abandoning it to become a French/Spanish lake.

In October, Jervis's fleet, with the newly promoted Commodore Nelson flying his swallowtail broad pennant in the 74-gun *Captain*, was in San Fiorenzo Bay in north-west Corsica. With a French invasion imminent from Leghorn, the priority was to evacuate the British troops, stores and equipment, along with the British Viceroy, Sir Gilbert Elliot, from the base at Bastia on the opposite side of the island. This task was given to Nelson. It was a task impossible to keep secret, as it involved the assembly of transports and much feverish activity ashore. The Corsicans, understandably, sought to please their probable new masters and actually invited the French in Leghorn to send troops. By mid-October, just when Elliot had resigned himself to capture, Nelson literally walked up the garden path to his house, having appeared, as if by magic, from nowhere. He had arrived early that morning (14 October) on the frigate *La Minerve* to oversee the evacuation. On 19 October the French landed in the north and the next day appeared on the outskirts of Bastia just as Nelson was being rowed out to his ship in the last boat to leave the harbour. They sailed for Elba – a British possession.

Having deposited Sir Gilbert on Elba, Nelson rejoined Jervis, whereupon, on 2 November, the British Fleet sailed. While Nelson was away, no fewer than nineteen Spanish ships-of-the-line had been sighted to the north, but Jervis was reluctant to leave before the return of the seven of his ships under Rear-Admiral Man that had gone to Gibraltar for supplies. Man never rejoined, as, fearful of running the gauntlet of the Spanish and French fleets between him and Jervis, he sailed for England, where on arrival at the end of December he was removed from

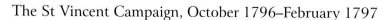

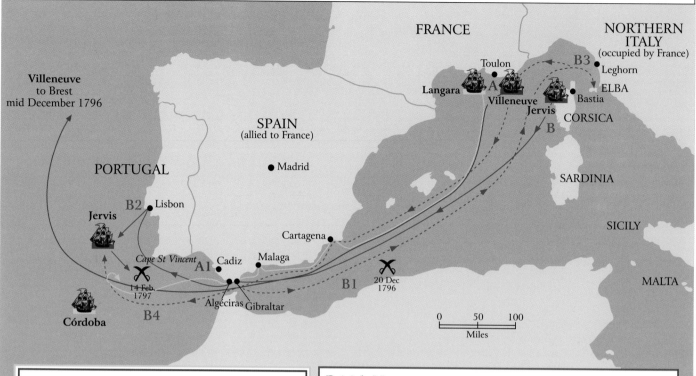

The St Vincent Campaign, October 1796–February 1797                                          Map 15

### French & Spanish Notes

➤ French fleet under Villeneuve

➤ Spanish fleet under Langara then Córdoba

A • Oct. 1796 Langara joins Villeneuve at Toulon to form a combined fleet of 34 ships.

• End Nov. Combined fleet ordered into Atlantic to support French invasion of Ireland.

• 6 Dec. Langara insists on putting into Cartagena for repairs and supplies. French continue through Straits and north to Brest, but too late to invade Ireland.

• Langara is replaced by Córdoba, who is ordered to escort convoy from Malaga to Cadiz.

A1 • Spanish fleet and convoy blown westward by gales. On 14 Feb. it is attacked by Jervis while trying to get back to Cadiz: the Battle of St Vincent.

### British Notes

➤ British fleet under Jervis

- - ➤ Nelson's independent voyages

B • Sep. 1796 British decide to withdraw from Mediterranean and their base in Corsica. Nelson is sent to evacuate British from Bastia to Elba.

• 2 Nov. Jervis sails for Gibraltar with Nelson.

• 1 Dec. Jervis arrives in Gibraltar and is ordered to Lisbon.

B1 • 12 Dec. Nelson with 2 frigates is sent to evacuate Elba. On 20 Dec. he has successful fight with 2 French frigates.

B2 • 19 Jan. 1797 Jervis with 10 ships sails for a position off Cape St Vincent. On arrival he finds 5 ships under R-Adm. Parker waiting.

B3 • End Jan. Nelson sails from Elba, calling at Toulon and Cartagena to check for enemy presence – none.

B4 • 12 Feb. Nelson sails through Spanish fleet undiscovered during night and joins the British fleet the next day.

---

his command. By 2 November Jervis could wait no longer. He set sail for Gibraltar, still hopeful of finding the enemy fleet at sea. But he was to be disappointed. On arrival at Gibraltar on 1 December, Jervis found instructions awaiting him to proceed to Lisbon, to the more secure mouth of the River Tagus.

## NELSON RETURNS TO ELBA

A move to the Tagus, however, would leave the tiny British garrison and Sir Gilbert Elliot marooned on Elba (as Napoleon would be seventeen years later). Jervis sent two frigates, the 42-gun *La Minerve* (originally French) and the 36-gun *Blanche*, to extract them. The obvious choice to lead such a risky mission was Nelson, who transferred his pennant from the *Captain* to the *Minerve* before setting sail on 12 December. During the darkness of the early hours of 20 December they sighted and chased two Spanish frigates (*Santa Sabina* and *Ceres*). Nelson rather let his enthusiasm get the better of him, taking over personal control of

the ship from her captain, James Cockburn. *Minerve* closed the distance with Nelson skilfully positioning his ship across the stern of the *Santa Sabina*, threatening the most deadly of rakes, before hailing the Spaniard to demand surrender. In excellent English the Spanish captain refused. A furious exchange of broadsides began in a typical single-ship action. In the blackness neither ship's gun captains could see much as they peered through the gun ports, so they fired at the flashes of the enemy's guns.

Gradually, superior gunnery won the day. After refusing to surrender several times and suffering 164 casualties, the *Santa Sabina* struck her colours and her captain was rowed across to surrender his sword. It then became clear why he spoke English so fluently. He introduced himself as Don Jacobo Stuart, the great-grandson of King James II of England, Scotland and Ireland – the Catholic monarch who lost the Battle of the Boyne in 1690 to the Protestant William III (a victory still celebrated during 'the marching season' by Protestant Ulstermen). The *Ceres* had also surrendered to the

*Blanche*, so Nelson now had two prizes. Prize crews were put onboard, including the first lieutenant of the *Minerve*, John Culverhouse, and a young lieutenant by the name of Thomas Hardy. However, Nelson's triumph did not last. Out of the darkness loomed another Spanish frigate that fired into the *Santa Sabina*, forcing Nelson to cut her adrift in order to engage this new enemy. When the approaching dawn revealed two more Spanish ships-of-the-line with yet another frigate, Nelson could do little but abandon his prizes and flee. But the *Minerve* could only limp away with masts shot through and shrouds and rigging badly cut. She was saved by the gallant prize crew of the *Santa Sabina* who hoisted English colours over Spanish ones and thus distracted her pursuers. Nelson's two frigates reached Elba on Christmas Day 1796.

Nelson had arrived in the morning, in time to attend a colourful ball that evening hosted by Lieutenant-General John de Burgh, the commander of all forces on Elba. News of his recent success had spread and Nelson was agreeably surprised when his entry was announced by the band playing 'See the conquering hero comes', followed by 'Rule Britannia'. To his brother he wrote, 'I am loaded with compliments.' But his mission to evacuate Elba ran into difficulties. General de Burgh had heard nothing about it and seemed reluctant to act on Nelson's word alone. He would be persuaded if the former viceroy of Corsica, Elliot, would put it in writing, but Elliot was away in Naples on a diplomatic mission. It was to be over a month before Nelson sailed. When Elliot finally returned on 22 January, he did not favour evacuation, as his reception in Naples and Rome had been decidedly friendly. With the general and the viceroy determined to stay, Nelson suggested a compromise. The troops would remain, with several transports just in case, but Nelson would evacuate the naval element and their stores. He would also take Elliot to Lisbon so he could report the situation in Italy first-hand. On 29 January 1797 the ex-viceroy and his ADC, Colonel John Drinkwater, boarded the *Minerve* and the small convoy finally left Elba escorted by two more frigates, the 36-gun *Romulus* and 32-gun *Southampton*.

The presence of these two ships allowed Nelson to leave the convoy, which was heading first for Gibraltar, to make a dash for Toulon. He was desperate to know the whereabouts of the Spanish fleet. They were not there, nor were they at Cartagena. He pressed on. On 9 February he reached the Rock, where he learnt that the Spaniards had passed through the Straits five days earlier. Nelson stopped just long enough to take on water and welcome back on board Lieutenants Culverhouse and Hardy, together with their seamen, who had been released in an exchange deal with the Spanish, and for Elliot to make his report. On 11 February he sailed again to join Jervis off Cape St Vincent. However, as he left, two Spanish ships-of-the-line that had been waiting close by in Algéciras Bay gave chase. It was to be an eventful day. Colonel Drinkwater, who was on the quarterdeck with Nelson watching the Spaniards, asked if an engagement was likely. Nelson thought it quite possible. Looking aloft at his pennant, he added, 'But before the Don get hold of that bit of bunting I will have a struggle with them and sooner than give up the frigate I'll run her shore.' Shortly afterwards they went to dinner. The officers had barely started the meal when it was interrupted by the cry of 'Man overboard!'

The captain, George Cockburn, thinking the Spanish ships sufficiently far astern, immediately ordered a boat lowered. Lieutenant Hardy clambered aboard to take charge. The search took some time, as there was no sign of the unfortunate seaman. Meanwhile, not only was the *Minerve* still making headway under full sail against the strong west–east current, but the boat was drifting far astern and the Spaniards were fast closing the gap. Hardy was in grave danger of being taken prisoner a second time in less than two months. Seeing this, Nelson exclaimed, 'By God I'll not lose Hardy!' According to Drinkwater, Nelson turned to Cockburn to order 'Back the mizzen topsail!' (More likely the order was to 'back the topsails', as with just the mizzen backed the reduction of speed would have been slight; the current was pushing both the ship and the boat eastwards equally.) Hardy and the boat's crew were retrieved almost under the guns of the nearest enemy, the 74-gun *Terrible*. For reasons best known to her captain, when the *Minerve* slowed the Spaniard similarly backed her topsails, thus allowing her quarry to escape. Intervening to save Hardy and his men at the risk of losing his ship was typical Nelson. He put at risk, not only the *Minerve* and all in her, but also his primary duty of transmitting vital news and intelligence to his admiral. When he ordered the topsails backed he had no idea the Spanish ship would do the same. Fortune, as they say, favours the brave.

On the night of 12 February the *Minerve* found herself in far greater danger. On either side of the frigate were the flickering lights and occasional looming hulks of ships-of-the-line – Nelson had found the Spanish fleet. He kept track of them until they turned about and then followed, but on a course that would intercept them if they turned west. They did not, so the likelihood was that they were headed for Cadiz. On the morning of 13 February, Nelson, Elliot, Drinkwater, Culverhouse and Hardy scrabbled up the side of *Victory* to report to Jervis. Not only was Nelson able to pinpoint the Spanish position and destination, but Culverhouse and Hardy, having spent several weeks in Spanish hands, were able to supply critical information on the numbers and state of morale of the enemy fleet.

## ST VINCENT: SPANISH PROBLEMS AND PLANS

Teniente General (Vice-Admiral) Jose Córdoba y Ramos was the third commander of the Spanish fleet in Cartagena in six weeks. In early December the first, Langara, had insisted on leaving his French allies while en route from Toulon to Brest to put into Cartagena for repairs and supplies. The French pressed on without him, and Madrid immediately replaced him with one of the most outstanding Spanish admirals of the age, Teniente General José de Mazarredo. However, Mazarredo agreed with his predecessor – the fleet was grossly undermanned and poorly supplied. As there was little likelihood of these deficiencies being made good, Mazarredo refused the poisoned chalice. Thus Córdoba got the job.

There was nothing wrong with Spanish ships in terms of design, construction or general sailing abilities. Some of the best ships in the Spanish Navy, like the 74-gun *San Ildefonso* and *Bahama*, were built during the last twenty years of the eighteenth century. Mazarredo had commented that the *San Ildefonso* 'sailed to windward like the frigates and tacked like a boat; she has a specious [sound] battery ... stable in all positions, instances and circumstances'. The problems lay more in the lack of funding, initiative and political will to keep these fine ships in repair or properly manned. Two years earlier a senior naval staff officer had written:

> ... it has come to my notice that all the ships, with few
> exceptions, are in a bad state of repair and without the

means to change the situation. Even the weakest of enemies could destroy them with ease ... If we have to enter battle this [Mediterranean] squadron will bring this nation into mourning, digging the grave of the person who has the misfortune to command it.

It was an uncannily accurate forecast of events.

Despite a gallant officer corps, few Spanish commanders had battle experience at sea. Worse was the acute shortage of trained seamen and the reliance thus placed on levies of landsmen. Spain had established a Sea Register of the Merchant Navy but even this system could not cope with the demands of a huge merchant fleet as well as the needs of the fighting ships. At St Vincent, for example, Córdoba's flagship, the majestic four-decker 136-gun *Santisima Trinidad*, with a crew of over 900, could only muster 60 men that the British would rate as 'able seamen' – a sobering statistic. In other words, all Córdoba's ships were packed with a preponderance of landsmen and soldiers, all of whom lacked the training or experience to perform well in the demanding and dangerous environment of the sea. By 1797 the capable Navy minister Antonio Valdes (a former commodore) had been replaced and his role taken over by Chief Minister Manuel de Godoy, who exercised dictatorial political control. A former Guards officer, Godoy's interest in matters nautical was limited. The navy was neglected. Money for stores, equipment and repairs was reduced to a trickle; those who protested, like Langara and Mazarredo, were dismissed. When Córdoba sailed from Cartagena on 1 February 1797 he was two weeks away from disaster. An observer watching the fleet would have been impressed by the sight of 27 ships-of-the-line, 8 frigates and 28 gunboats (to supplement the bombardment of Gibraltar) leaving port under press of sail. Only those on board could know that the fleet's seeming strength and beauty was illusory.

At the last moment Córdoba had been given an additional complication. Four urcas (merchant ships) carrying mercury, essential for the process of refining silver, were waiting at Malaga for an escort to Cadiz. With the merchantmen was the 74-gun *Santo Domingo*. Córdoba was ordered to deliver these ships to Cadiz, thus delaying the fleet. Córdoba's intentions as he headed westwards were, firstly, to collect his merchant convoy from Malaga; next, to deliver the gunboats to Algéciras (across the bay from Gibraltar); then to convey his charges to Cadiz. Finally, he would sail for Brest for the long-delayed link up with the French. With reasonable winds he should be in sight of Cadiz by 6 February, and could then decide in safety when he should continue his voyage. It was to be done in easy stages. There was no hurry – after all, his ships had ridden at anchor for two months ever since Langara had abandoned Villeneuve when the combined fleet had been making for Brest in early December.

Córdoba's voyage went well initially. He collected his merchantmen (and the *Santo Domingo*, which was to be with him at St Vincent) and by 5 February was sailing through the Straits. There he detached three 74s, the *Bahama*, *Neptuno* and *Terrible*, to escort the gunboats into Algéciras. The first two remained at Algéciras while, as described above, the *Terrible* nearly captured Hardy on 11 February before going on to rejoin Córdoba. By 6 February, Cadiz was in sight. Unfortunately for the Spanish, fate chose the moment the urcas were preparing to enter harbour to wreck the proceedings. Suddenly, the wind changed dramatically.

A violent easterly gale, a Levanter, began to thrust all Córdoba's ships westward away from Cadiz. Short of seamen, crammed with seasick soldiers and landsmen, with huge seas threatening to broach many ships, there was nothing their captains could do but run before the storm with virtually bare masts. For nearly a week the gale continued, driving the Spanish ever further westwards. Not until 12 February did the wind suddenly reverse its direction, allowing the exhausted crews to turn back towards Cadiz. With him, supposedly in three divisions but now somewhat scattered and out of formation, were 25 ships-of-the-line, including seven first rates, upwards of eight frigates plus the four urcas carrying the mercury. Córdoba flew his flag on the *Santisima Trinidad*. In the early hours of 14 February his fleet was sailing east-south-east, the wind was westerly, and ahead with the van was Teniente General Joaquin Moreno (on the 112-gun *Principe de Asturias*) with the urcas.

## ST VINCENT: BRITISH PROBLEMS AND PLANS

Jervis had anchored off Gibraltar on 1 December 1796, bringing with him fifteen ships-of-the-line, five frigates and three sloops. Awaiting him were orders to use the Tagus (Lisbon) as his base. The British, with the exception of the garrison on Elba, had abandoned the Mediterranean. Now Jervis's primary function was to ensure that no enemy squadron escaped through the Straits unchallenged. He was in effect to blockade the Straits, but not so closely as to prevent a battle.

Jervis's difficulties were twofold. First, the weather allied to poor pilotage cost him five 74-gun ships-of-the-line. On 10 December an easterly gale swept three ships from their moorings and drove them ashore on the North African coast. The *Courageux* struck rocks, sinking rapidly with the loss of three-quarters of her crew, while the *Gibraltar*, although refloated, had to be sent to England for docking. Fortunately the *Culloden* was not badly damaged and was able to rejoin the fleet. A few days later the *Zealous* was crippled when she hit a rock in Tangier Bay. Then, on 21 December, as Jervis was leading his ships into the Tagus estuary, the *Bombay Castle* went aground on a sandbank, forcing her abandonment. A similar fate befell the *St George*, and although she was refloated she had to go to Lisbon for repairs. All the captains of these ships would (or should) have faced court martial for these losses. To have his command cut by a third with not an enemy in sight was a grievous blow for Jervis, and boded ill for any encounter with an enemy twice or even three times his number.

Jervis's second problem was to do with intelligence, or rather lack of it. The same gales that had blown away his fleet in early December had blown Villeneuve through the Straits and on towards Brest, so the French were out of the bottle and had escaped north – something Jervis was supposed to prevent or at least delay. The French, however, had been on their own, so where were the Spanish? They must surely be following their allies shortly. As we know, they failed to appear, as they were sitting safely in Cartagena while their commanders bemoaned their fleet's deficiencies. By mid-January, Jervis was also concerned about Nelson. Not knowing that his commodore had been forced to wait a month in Elba, he was worried that Nelson and his convoy might have been intercepted by the Spanish on his return journey. On 18 January, Jervis led his ten remaining battleships out from Lisbon to a position off Cape St Vincent. He chose that location because it would 'enable me to go speedily to his

[Nelson's] assistance in case the fleet of Spain should attempt to interrupt his passage through the Gut [Straits]'. He only had a hundred miles, two hundred at the most, to sail but it took him almost three weeks to get there – another example of how adverse winds can play havoc with war at sea. Jervis finally arrived in position on 6 February, the day the Levanter began to blow his enemy towards him.

On arrival Jervis was delighted to discover a reinforcement of five ships-of-the-line waiting for him under Rear-Admiral William Parker, with his flag on the 98-gun *Prince George*. The other four were the 90-gun *Namur*, and the 74s *Colossus*, *Irresistible* and *Orion*. Still anxious for news, Jervis sent ashore for information. On 9 February a frigate brought word that the Spanish had passed through the Straits on the 6th, almost certainly headed for Cadiz. This was disappointing. Jervis wanted them at sea: with fifteen battleships he was confident he could defeat them. Yet the disappointment was short-lived. The next day news came that Córdoba was still at sea and well out into the Atlantic. On 11 February the Elba convoy arrived, reporting that the Spaniards were close and 'in a good deal of disorder'. The following day Jervis signalled his ships to clear for action. Midshipman George Parsons on the *Barfleur* has described some of what this involved:

> Grinding cutlasses, sharpening pikes, flinting pistols, among the boarders; filling powder, and fitting well-oiled gunlocks to our immense artillery by the gunners, sling our lower yards with chains; and, in short, preparing a well-organised first rate for this most important battle.

The course was south-west towards the enemy. On 13 February, Nelson appeared with more precise details of Córdoba's position. Tomorrow would be St Valentine's Day.

## THE BATTLE: OPENING MOVES

By 14 February, Córdoba and his captains had had enough. A week of riding out the easterly gales had exhausted the meagre crews, crippled hundreds of landsmen and soldiers with the horrors of seasickness and scattered his ships. With the favourable wind change all the Spanish admiral wanted was to gather his ships and head for Cadiz. If he had to fight to get there, so be it – according to an American neutral the British had only nine ships-of-the-line against his twenty-three so he was confident his enemy posed no serious threat. During the night of 13/14 February there had been much firing of signal cannons and hoisting of lights as the Spaniards struggled to regroup. The fleet was on a bearing of east-south-east about 35 miles south-west of Cape St Vincent. Dawn on the 14th was fine but with a mist

### Captain-of-the-Fleet

The captain-of-the-fleet at St Vincent was Captain Robert Calder, who was to be court-martialled for alleged cowardice during the clash with the French off Cape Finisterre three months prior to Trafalgar. His position at St Vincent was that of chief-of-staff to Admiral Jervis. A captain-of-the-fleet was allowed for a fleet of fifteen or more ships, and often held the rank of rear-admiral. Calder was a captain but ranked above all other captains present and was in receipt of the pay and privileges of a rear-admiral. As captain-of-the-fleet, he was the admiral's adviser (though Jervis did not think much of Calder's suggestions) and could issue orders in his name. A commander-in-chief who trusted his captain-of-the-fleet could delegate a considerable workload onto him. The relevant Admiralty Regulations and Instructions stipulated that an admiral could require a captain-of-the-fleet to assist 'in regulating the details of the fleet, in making the necessary distribution of men, stores, provisions, and in such other duties as he shall think fit to direct'. As noted above, Jervis was none too happy with Calder's performance at St Vincent. He was later to write:

> I hope Sir Robert Calder will have more confidence than when he served with me; his dread of approaching the shore was at the time truly ridiculous, and I was under the necessity of directing the master not to pay the smallest regard to his influence.

It seems neither tactics nor navigation were among Calder's strong points.

over the water. Córdoba's command was still disorganized, sailing in three irregular divisions. In the van was Teniente General Joaquin Moreno with his flag on the 112-gun three-decker *Principe de Asturias*; under his protection were the four mercury-carrying urcas. Behind, forming the centre division, was Córdoba in the world's largest battleship, the giant 136-gun *Santisima Trinidad*. The rear division was under Teniente General Morales de los Rios in the 112-gun *Concepcion*.

At 8.00 a.m. signal guns were heard to the north, and rightly recognized as British frigates reporting a sighting through the thinning mist. Córdoba ordered the 74s *Infanta de Pelayo* and *San Pablo* to investigate – he was to fight the battle without them. At 10.00 a.m. Córdoba could count the opposition. To his dismay, heading towards him in two lines of battle were fifteen, not nine, battleships, which appeared to be closing on the rear division. Perhaps they intended to attack his rear and at the same time secure the weather gauge. It was decision time for the Spanish. Córdoba signalled for all ships to wear onto the larboard tack – complete a 180-degree turn, thus reversing the fleet's order of sailing. His aim was admirable – to form a line of battle on the larboard tack and keep the weather gauge while protecting his precious urcas at the rear – but the implementation was poor. Such a manoeuvre was beyond the indifferent Spanish seamanship, and the result was that the fleet slowed, lost time and failed to form a recognizable line of battle. Instead, the rear division (Morales) became merged with the centre (Córdoba) in a straggling bunch, with many ships masking the fire of the others. Worse, a sizeable gap had opened up between Moreno's division (with the urcas) and the main body. The Spaniards still had the advantage of numbers (although much reduced) and had kept the weather gauge but were heading away from their destination with the enemy now between them and Cadiz. They would almost certainly have to fight.

Shortly after 10 a.m. with the mist clearing fast, Captain Robert Calder, on board the 102-gun *Victory*, began to count the Spanish ships as they sailed slowly into view on the starboard quarter.

'There are eight sail-of-the-line, Sir John.'

'Very well, sir.'

'There are twenty sail-of-the-line, Sir John.'

'Very well, sir.'

'There are twenty-five sail-of-the-line, Sir John.'

'Very well, sir.'

'There are twenty-seven sail-of-the-line, Sir John, near twice our own number.'

By this time Jervis had had enough of Calder's increasingly agitated tone. 'Enough sir!' he snapped. 'The die is cast and if there are fifty sail I will go through them!'

## St Vincent: Spanish Situation, dawn to about 10.00 a.m.

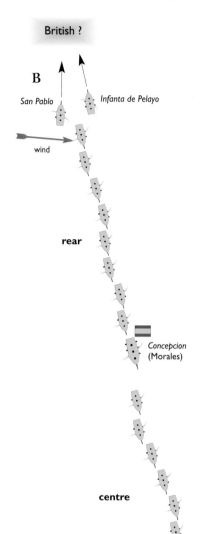

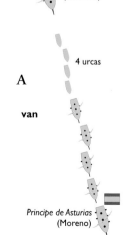

### Spanish Notes

**A** Córdoba in 3 divisions sailing ESE. The mercury transports (urcas) are in the van escorted by Moreno and 5 battleships.

**B** At around 8.00 a.m. signal shots are heard, thought to indicate ships to the north (rear). Two 74s (*Pelayo* and *San Pablo*) are sent to investigate. They do not return until after the battle.

From 8.00 a.m. the Spanish fleet consists of 23 battleships (including the mercury-carrying *Santo Domingo*) and 4 urcas.

### Orders of Battle/Casualties (Spanish)

| Ship | Guns | Admiral | K* | W* |
|---|---|---|---|---|
| *Santisima Trinidad* | 136 | V-Adm. Don José de Cordoba y Ramos | | |
| *Principe de Asturias* | 112 | V-Adm. Don Joaquin Moreno | | |
| *Conde de Regla* | 112 | | | |
| *San Josef* | 112 | R-Adm. Don Xavier Winthuysen | 40 | 90 |
| *Mexicano* | 112 | | | |
| *Concepcion* | 112 | V-Adm. Count Morales de los Rios | | |
| *Salvador del Mundo* | 112 | | 42 | 124 |
| *San Nicolas* | 84 | Commodore Don Tomas Geraldino | 114 | 90 |
| *Oriente* | 74 | | | |
| *Atlante* | 74 | | | |
| *Soberano* | 74 | | | |
| *San Ildefonso* | 74 | | | |
| *San Ysidro* | 74 | | 29 | 68 |
| *San Domingo* | 74 | (joined fleet with 4 urcas from Malaga) | | |
| *Terrible* | 74 | | | |
| *Glorioso* | 74 | | | |
| *Conquestador* | 74 | | | |
| *Firme* | 74 | | | |
| *San Genaro* | 74 | | | |
| *San Francisco de Paula* | 74 | | | |
| *San Antonio* | 74 | | | |
| *San Fermin* | 74 | | | |
| *San Juan Nepomuceno* | 74 | | | |
| *Brigada* | 34 | | | |
| *Casilda* | 34 | | | |
| *Perla* | 34 | | | |
| *Paz* | 34 | | | |
| *Dorotea* | 34 | | | |
| *Guadalupe* | 34 | | | |
| *Santa Teresa* | 34 | | | |
| *Matilda* | 34 | | | |
| *Diana* | 34 | | | |
| *Atocha* | 34 | | | |
| *Ceres* | 34 | | | |
| *Vigilante* (brig) | 12 | | | |

### Comments

• The above order of battle does not include the two 74s (*Infante de Pelayo* and *San Pablo*) that were detached early on 14 February and took no part in the battle, nor the *Neptuna* and *Bahama*, sent to Algéciras.

• *Santisima Trinidad*, *Principe de Asturias*, *San Ildefonso* and *San Juan Nepomuceno* later took part at Trafalgar.

• The battleships carried 1,596 cannons distributed over seven first rates, one second rate and eight third rates. They had only 354 more guns than the British, who had eight fewer ships. Also present were eleven frigates and a brig. Overall the Spanish had the theoretical advantage in ships-of-the-line of 23:15. The Spanish were also superior in frigate numbers by 11:4. The Spanish casualties amounted to 200 killed and 1,284 wounded, together with more than 1,500 prisoners. Assuming an approximate total strength of 12,600 all ranks in their battleships, this gives a loss of nearly 24 per cent.

*K = killled, W = wounded

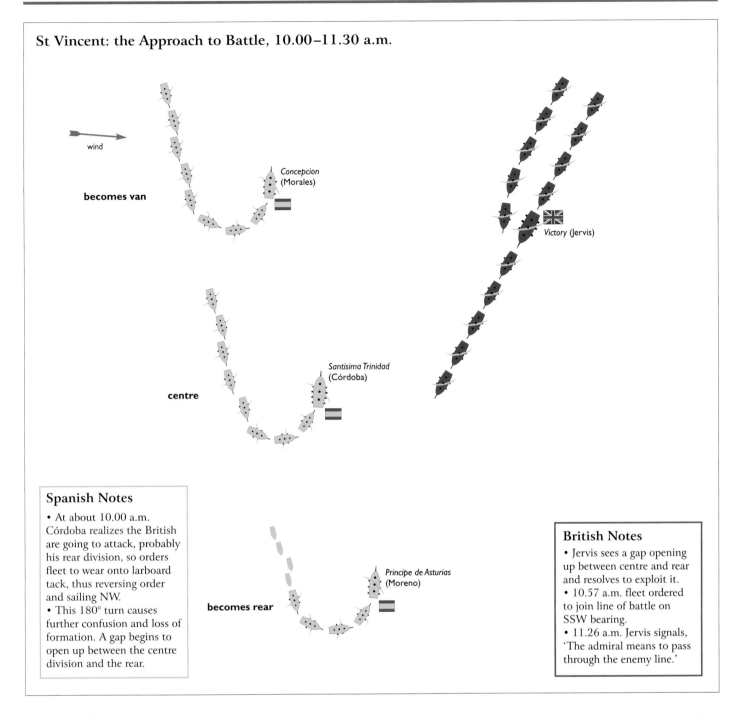

## St Vincent: the Approach to Battle, 10.00–11.30 a.m.

wind

becomes van

*Concepcion*
(Morales)

centre

*Santisima Trinidad*
(Córdoba)

*Victory* (Jervis)

becomes rear

*Principe de Asturias*
(Moreno)

### Spanish Notes

• At about 10.00 a.m. Córdoba realizes the British are going to attack, probably his rear division, so orders fleet to wear onto larboard tack, thus reversing order and sailing NW.
• This 180° turn causes further confusion and loss of formation. A gap begins to open up between the centre division and the rear.

### British Notes

• Jervis sees a gap opening up between centre and rear and resolves to exploit it.
• 10.57 a.m. fleet ordered to join line of battle on SSW bearing.
• 11.26 a.m. Jervis signals, 'The admiral means to pass through the enemy line.'

'That's right, Sir John!' exclaimed the Canadian-born Captain Ben Hallowell, slapping his admiral on the back. 'That's right, and by God we'll give them a damned good licking!' Hallowell, who had been ashore attending a court martial when his ship the *Courageux* was lost on the Barbary Coast four days earlier, was then a passenger on the *Victory*. According to one of Vice-Admiral the Honourable William Waldegrave's midshipmen, the fourteen-year-old George Parsons, on the quarterdeck of the 98-gun *Barfleur,* the view that morning was 'the grandest sight I ever witnessed. The Spanish fleet, close on our weather bow … looked a complete forest huddled together; their commander-in-chief covered with signals'. Córdoba was desperately, and seemingly unsuccessfully, trying to get his gaggle of ships into some order.

Jervis's plan was bold and simple – to sail for the gap in the Spanish line, cut off the rear division of nine ships and then turn on the main fleet. At 10.57 a.m. he made the necessary signal to the fleet, until then sailing in two columns, to form line of battle 'as most convenient'. This meant each ship formed in a single line either ahead or astern of the flagship. No time was to be wasted in getting into the regular order of sailing with each division centred on its own subordinate admiral. The result was the unconventional line shown above with the 74-gun *Culloden* in the lead and Nelson's *Captain* fourth from the rear, all sailing south-south-west. In regular order or not, the fleet looked impressive, 'so beautifully close was our order of sailing, that the flying jib-boom of the ship astern projected over the taffrail of her leader'. Twenty-nine minutes later, to make sure all understood his intention, the signal, 'The admiral means to pass through the enemy's line' was hoisted. The race was on. Jervis sought to reach the gap before Moreno could close it, and he just made it.

## Orders of Battle/Casualties (British)

| Ship | Guns | Admiral/Captain | K* | W* |
|---|---|---|---|---|
| Culloden | 74 | Capt. T. Troubridge | 10 | 47 |
| Blenheim | 98 | Capt. T. Frederick | 12 | 49 |
| Prince George | 98 | R-Adm. W. Parker Capt. J. Irwin | 8 | 7 |
| Orion | 74 | Capt. Sir James Saumarez | 0 | 9 |
| Colossus | 74 | Capt. G. Murray | 0 | 5 |
| Irresistible | 74 | Capt. G. Martin | 5 | 14 |
| Victory | 102 | Adm. Sir John Jervis Capt. R. Calder | 1 | 5 |
| Egmont | 74 | Capt. J. Sutton | 0 | 0 |
| Goliath | 74 | Capt. Sir Charles Knowles | 0 | 8 |
| Barfleur | 98 | V-Adm. W. Waldegrave Capt. R. Dacre | 0 | 7 |
| Britannia | 100 | V-Adm. C. Thompson Capt. T. Foley | 0 | 1 |
| Namur | 90 | Capt. J. Whitshed | 2 | 5 |
| Captain | 74 | Commodore H. Nelson Capt. R. Miller | 24 | 56 |
| Diadem | 64 | Capt. G. Towry | 0 | 2 |
| Excellent | 74 | Capt. C. Collingwood | 11 | 12 |
| **Totals** | | | **73** | **227** |
| Minerve | 38 | Capt. G. Cockburn | | |
| Southampton | 32 | Capt. J. Macnamara | | |
| Lively | 32 | Capt. Lord Garliesc | | |
| Niger | 32 | Capt. E. Foote | | |
| Bonne Citoyenne | 20 | Cdr C. Lindsay | | |
| Raven | 18 | Cdr W. Prowse | | |
| Fox | 14 | Lt. J. Gibson | | |

### Comments

• The 15 battleships carried a total of 1,242 guns divided between two first rates, four second rates and nine third rates. There were also four frigates and three sloops present, but they were not involved in the action and consequently suffered no losses.

• Of the battleships, four would later take part in the battle of Trafalgar (*Victory*, *Britannia*, *Colossus* and *Orion*). Apart from Nelson, only two ship's captains were at Trafalgar. They were Captain Cuthbert Collingwood of the *Excellent*, who rose to vice-admiral and took command of the fleet when Nelson died, and Commander William Prowse of the sloop *Raven*. At Trafalgar, Captain Prowse commanded the 36-gun frigate *Sirius*. He had started his naval service as an able seaman, rising eventually to rear-admiral and colonel of the Royal Marines.

• British casualties were extraordinarily light – primarily a reflection of the poor gunnery of the Spanish. Out of a line-of-battle total of around 8,000 all ranks, a loss of 300 represents a mere 3.75 per cent. Seven ships had nobody killed and one, *Egmont*, had no casualties at all. For obvious reasons Nelson's *Captain* suffered the worst, with the most killed (24) and wounded (56). The only other ships whose losses rose into double figures were the *Culloden*, *Blenheim* and *Excellent*, all of whom were heavily engaged at some time during the battle. Surprisingly, the *Colossus*, driven out of the line early on by damage to masts and yards, had only five wounded – evidence perhaps that the Spanish aimed high.

*K = killled, W = wounded

## BATTLE IS JOINED

To the first lieutenant of the *Culloden* a collision with Moreno's three-decker seemed inevitable. His shouted warning to Captain Thomas Troubridge drew the unfazed response, 'Can't help it Griffiths, let the weakest fend off.' At the last moment the *Principe de Asturias* gave way. As the *Culloden* swept past, she fired the first shots of the battle, a massive, double-shotted broadside from her larboard battery at a range of a few metres. Fourteen lower-deck 32-pounders and fifteen upper-deck 24-pounders roared out in rapid succession. Most of the 58 iron balls slammed into the Spaniard's hull. She shuddered and fell away. Troubridge was followed by the rest of the British van – *Blenheim*, *Prince George*, *Orion*, *Colossus* and *Irresistible*. The Spanish fleet had been decisively cut in two.

At 12.08 p.m. Jervis, convinced he had isolated the enemy's rear, signalled for the second stage of his plan – the attack on the main body. Beginning with the *Culloden*, all ships were to tack in succession as they arrived at the spot where the *Culloden* had tacked, thus maintaining the same line of battle. The problem was that while the British had been sailing south-west, the distance between them and the Spanish main body to the north had widened. With this new British manoeuvre it might take a considerable time to catch up with the enemy. It was possible the Spanish could avoid a major battle, even turn east for Cadiz and sail round the rear of the British. (Jervis could have ordered the fleet to tack together. Each ship would have tacked immediately and made straight for the enemy, thus ensuring a speedy attack and frustrating any attempt the Spanish might have of avoiding a fight.)

### Nancy Perriam

One of a number of women present at St Vincent, Nancy Perriam served in the *Orion* with her husband, whose station at quarters was in the ship's magazine. Nancy normally performed domestic tasks for the captain and other officers – laundry, sewing, and the like. In battle she went down to the cockpit to help the surgeon amputate limbs and remove splinters. As *Orion* tacked in her turn at the start of the action, she recalled that, 'she had just begun mending a shirt for our dear captain [Sir James Saumarez]'.

Considerable credit belongs to Moreno at this stage. Not only had he been sorely hurt by *Culloden*'s gunnery, he was also completely cut off from the main fleet and heavily outnumbered, having only five warships with which to face the entire British fleet. Yet daunting though the situation was, he determined to attack. The vulnerable moment for the British was as each ship started to turn in order to tack. If Moreno could position several ships close to the point where each of his enemy changed course, he might be able to inflict serious damage not only to each ship as they turned, but to Jervis's entire battle plan. Moreno signalled his intention to attack. The *Blenheim*, *Prince George* and *Orion* tacked perfectly one after another as though in a review. By the time *Colossus*'s turn came the *Principe de Asturias* was waiting for her. With her foreyard shot down, *Colossus* missed stays (failed to tack) and began to drift northwards out of the line. The *Orion* slowed to help her with a broadside. Over the next few minutes a general mêlée developed as *Irresistible*, *Victory*, *Egmont* and *Goliath* came up on the British side and the 112-gun

## St Vincent: Opening Phase, 12 noon to 12.30 p.m.

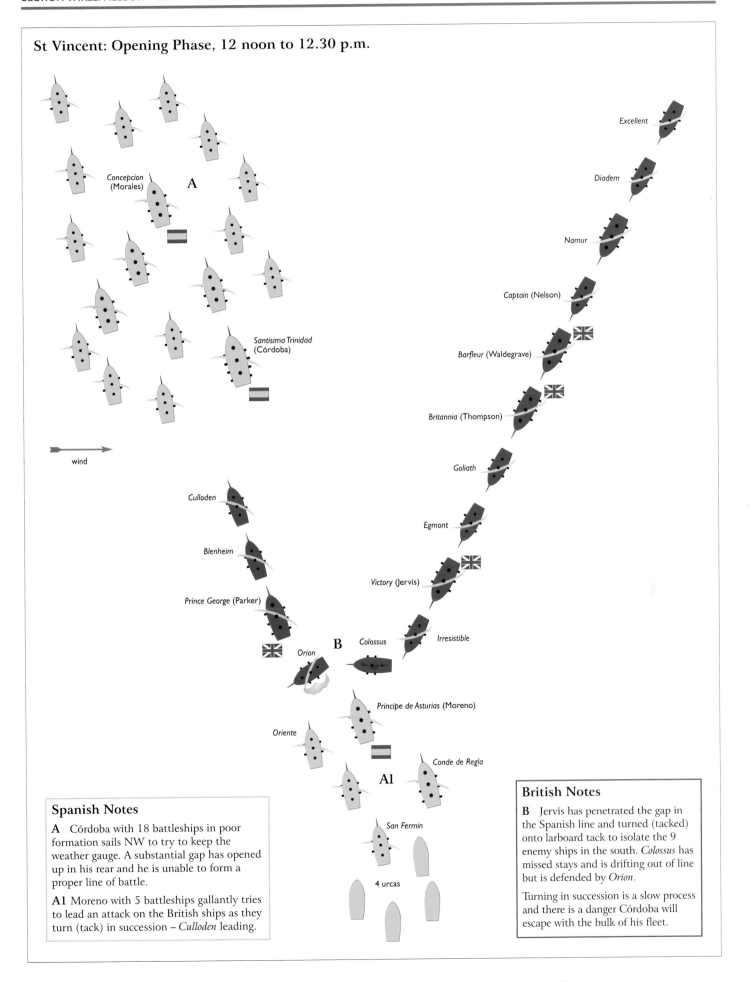

Concepcion
(Morales)

A

Santisima Trinidad
(Córdoba)

wind

Excellent

Diadem

Namur

Captain (Nelson)

Barfleur (Waldegrave)

Britannia (Thompson)

Goliath

Egmont

Culloden

Blenheim

Victory (Jervis)

Prince George (Parker)

Orion    B    Colossus    Irresistible

Principe de Asturias (Moreno)

Oriente

Conde de Regla

A1

San Fermin

4 urcas

### Spanish Notes

**A**  Córdoba with 18 battleships in poor formation sails NW to try to keep the weather gauge. A substantial gap has opened up in his rear and he is unable to form a proper line of battle.

**A1**  Moreno with 5 battleships gallantly tries to lead an attack on the British ships as they turn (tack) in succession – *Culloden* leading.

### British Notes

**B**  Jervis has penetrated the gap in the Spanish line and turned (tacked) onto larboard tack to isolate the 9 enemy ships in the south. *Colossus* has missed stays and is drifting out of line but is defended by *Orion*.

Turning in succession is a slow process and there is a danger Córdoba will escape with the bulk of his fleet.

*Conde de Regla* on the Spanish. By about 12.45 p.m. the British fleet was divided into three. The van of five ships had tacked and, headed by the *Culloden*, was closing on the rear of the Spanish main body. The centre four ships, including the *Victory*, had been forced to stop and become embroiled in a running fight with the Spanish rear. A gap was opening up between Parker's van and Jervis's centre. The remaining six ships were still in line heading for the original tacking point. It was time for the British admiral to re-exert control.

As Jervis climbed up onto the *Victory*'s poop he was nearly decapitated by a cannonball. Instead, the victim was an unfortunate sailor (the only fatality on the *Victory*) standing close by, whose blood and brains were splashed all over the admiral. A shocked Captain Grey leapt across to support him. Jervis, however, was untouched. Wiping the mess from his mouth and face with his handkerchief, he calmly remarked, 'I am not at all hurt, but do, George, try to get me an orange.' A midshipman produced one. After rinsing his mouth, Jervis, seemingly unperturbed, gave three new orders to the fleet. The first was to the master of the *Victory* to change onto a more northwesterly course, probably in order to get to windward of the enemy, the second to *Britannia* (Vice-Admiral Thompson): 'leading ship [*Britannia*] to tack and others in succession'. The third was to all ships in Thompson's division, 'to take up stations for mutual support and engage the enemy as arriving up in succession'. Jervis wanted each ship of the rear division to tack immediately and join the van in an all-out attack on Córdoba before he could get away while he brought up the centre against the Spanish rear. But there was no response, no acknowledgement, from the 100-gun *Britannia*. For whatever reason, be it smoke or a misunderstanding of the flags, Thompson sailed serenely on towards the original turning point with *Barfleur*, *Captain*, *Namur*, *Diadem* and *Excellent* sailing in her wake waiting for their admiral to tack. There was now a real danger of either the Spanish escaping or the British van (the *Culloden* had caught up with Córdoba's rear) being overwhelmed by the sheer number of the enemy. At this moment Nelson acted.

## NELSON INTERVENES

At about 12.50 p.m. Nelson made the most monumental decision of his career so far. Entirely on his own initiative he took his ship out of the line, wore round 270 degrees and sailed his single ship straight at the enemy. He was going to place the *Captain* just ahead of the *Culloden*, the leading ship of the British van, which had been engaging the enemy for some fifteen minutes. Captain Calder, standing alongside his commander-in-chief on the *Victory*'s quarterdeck, saw what was happening and anxiously suggested to Jervis, 'Sir, the *Captain* and *Culloden* are separated from the fleet. Shall I recall them?' For the second time that morning Jervis slapped him down: 'I will not have them recalled. I put my faith in those ships. It is a disgrace they are not supported and [are] separated.'

### Oranges for Officers

A useful task in battle for young midshipmen seems to have been keeping the officers, at least the senior ones, supplied with oranges. It was a midshipman who handed Admiral Jervis an orange to suck after his face had been spattered with blood and brains. Similarly, on Vice-Admiral Waldegrave's flagship, the *Barfleur*, oranges loomed large in the life of the fourteen-year-old midshipman George Parsons. As he himself said:

> I was certainly very young, but felt so elated as to walk on my toes, by way of appearing taller, as I bore oranges to the admiral and captain, selecting some for myself, which I stored in a snug corner of the stern-galley, as a corps de reserve.

Again, shortly after watching the *Captain* disappear into the enemy line:

> just as I had applied one of my select store of oranges to my mouth, she [a Spanish warship] opened an ill-directed fire, apparently into the admirals' stern-galley, that I was viewing her from. The first bang caused a cessation of my labours, the second made me drop a remarkably fine Maltese orange, which rolled away and was no more seen, and the third made me close my commanders on the quarterdeck, bearing to each an orange.

It is not difficult to see why Nelson made his historic move. It was entirely within the spirit of Jervis's intentions and was not, as many have alleged, disobedience to orders. His thought process was probably along these lines:

- The flagship has signalled to the *Britannia* to tack towards the enemy and we, the following five ships, will do so in succession. Jervis wants us to attack. However, turning in succession will take some time, as will the tacking itself.

- In the meantime the Spanish fleet has turned eastwards, which seems to indicate they are trying to get round behind us and head for Cadiz. They are only about a mile away now but if we continue south and tack in succession the main enemy body may succeed in getting away. I wonder why Jervis did not signal to tack together? Although he intends to attack, he seems to want to do so in a conventional line ahead formation.

- The *Britannia* has failed to tack – it looks as though she is heading for the original tacking point further south where the current firing is taking place. If this happens, and we follow, Córdoba with the bulk of his fleet will escape round our rear. Why does Thompson not tack?

Nelson made his decision. Turning to the master he ordered, 'Hard a larboard. Wear ship.' The *Captain* completed her turn and steered between the *Diadem* and *Excellent*, from whose quarterdeck Captain Cuthbert Collingwood (destined to be Nelson's second-in-command at Trafalgar) must have watched this extraordinary manoeuvre with a mixture of astonishment and admiration. The *Captain* sailed straight for the Spanish line. Such a move was fraught with risk, as she would be exposed to the fire of several enemy ships as the distance closed. Contrary to popular belief, however, Nelson did not have to fight alone for an hour before the rest of the fleet arrived. She joined the battle just ahead of the *Culloden*, her action forcing the leading Spanish ships to turn back to windward and to slow down, with the result that the British ships caught up more quickly and the action soon became more general. Within a matter of fifteen minutes, but unseen by Nelson through the smoke, the *Orion*, *Blenheim* and *Prince George* joined the fight from the south.

Nelson had left the line at around 12.50 p.m. and within twenty minutes was hotly engaged. By 1.19 p.m. Jervis realized Thompson in the *Britannia*, for whatever reason, was not going to turn, so he signalled for all the rear division to come onto the larboard tack. Every ship joined the fight at her own best speed. Some tacked, others, like the *Barfleur*, wore, the slower sailers such as *Britannia* and *Namur* took a long time, eventually coming up at the rear hardly in time to open fire. By 1.45 p.m. a thunderous mêlée was taking place as more and more British ships arrived, forcing the Spanish to fight and abandon their attempt to turn east. Jervis had got his big battle – thanks to Nelson's initiative.

## St Vincent: Nelson Makes His Move, 12.30–1.00 p.m.

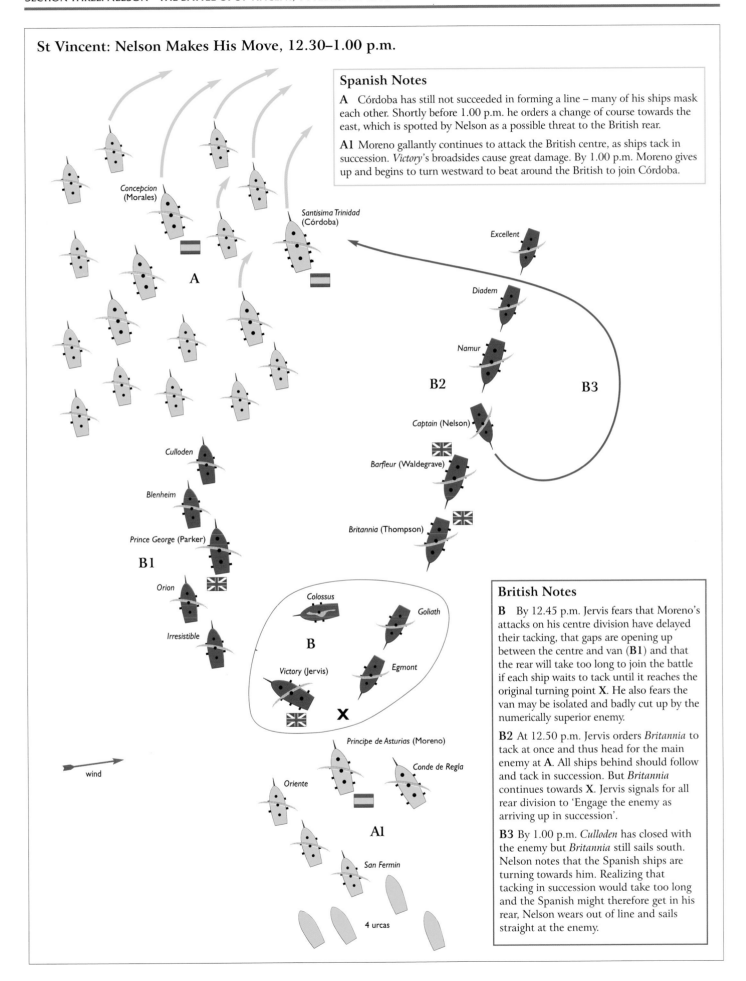

### Spanish Notes

**A** Córdoba has still not succeeded in forming a line – many of his ships mask each other. Shortly before 1.00 p.m. he orders a change of course towards the east, which is spotted by Nelson as a possible threat to the British rear.

**A1** Moreno gallantly continues to attack the British centre, as ships tack in succession. *Victory*'s broadsides cause great damage. By 1.00 p.m. Moreno gives up and begins to turn westward to beat around the British to join Córdoba.

### British Notes

**B** By 12.45 p.m. Jervis fears that Moreno's attacks on his centre division have delayed their tacking, that gaps are opening up between the centre and van (**B1**) and that the rear will take too long to join the battle if each ship waits to tack until it reaches the original turning point **X**. He also fears the van may be isolated and badly cut up by the numerically superior enemy.

**B2** At 12.50 p.m. Jervis orders *Britannia* to tack at once and thus head for the main enemy at **A**. All ships behind should follow and tack in succession. But *Britannia* continues towards **X**. Jervis signals for all rear division to 'Engage the enemy as arriving up in succession'.

**B3** By 1.00 p.m. *Culloden* has closed with the enemy but *Britannia* still sails south. Nelson notes that the Spanish ships are turning towards him. Realizing that tacking in succession would take too long and the Spanish might therefore get in his rear, Nelson wears out of line and sails straight at the enemy.

## St Vincent: The Battle Is Joined, 1.00–3.00 p.m.

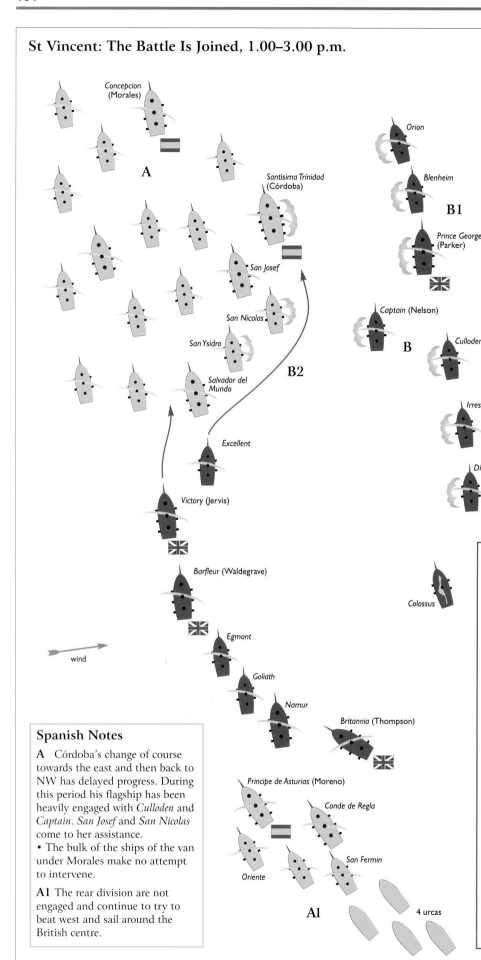

Concepcion
(Morales)

**A**

Santisima Trinidad
(Córdoba)

San Josef

San Nicolas

San Ysidro

Salvador del
Mundo

**B2**

Excellent

Victory (Jervis)

Barfleur (Waldegrave)

→ wind →

Egmont

Goliath

Namur

Britannia (Thompson)

Principe de Asturias (Moreno)

Conde de Regla

San Fermin

Oriente

**A1**                                                    4 urcas

Orion

Blenheim

**B1**

Prince George
(Parker)

Captain (Nelson)

Culloden

**B**

Irresistible

Diadem

Colossus

### Spanish Notes

**A**  Córdoba's change of course towards the east and then back to NW has delayed progress. During this period his flagship has been heavily engaged with *Culloden* and *Captain*. *San Josef* and *San Nicolas* come to her assistance.

• The bulk of the ships of the van under Morales make no attempt to intervene.

**A1** The rear division are not engaged and continue to try to beat west and sail around the British centre.

### British Notes

• About 1.20 p.m. Jervis signals to all rear divisions to turn onto larboard tack individually and attack.

• By 1.45 p.m. the battle is joined in earnest as ship after ship closes with the enemy.

**B**  Nelson takes station just ahead of *Culloden* and they are both heavily engaged for almost an hour before other ships are able to complete their delayed turn and catch up.

**B1** As Parker's ships begin to arrive there is confusion around *Culloden* and Captain Parker orders his ships to 'fill and stand on' – keep going. Intense fighting has developed around *Santisima Trinidad* and those escorting her. *Orion*, *Blenheim* and *Prince George* pull ahead. As *Irresistible* and *Diadem* come up, Jervis orders them to cease fire, as they are endangering *Excellent* and *Victory*.

• At 2.15 p.m. Jervis signals to *Excellent* 'Pass through the enemy line' to assist *Captain* and *Culloden*. En route *Excellent* fights first the 112-gun *Salvador del Mundo* and *San Ysidro* (who surrenders).

**B2** At around 3.00 p.m. *Excellent* passes between *Captain* and *San Nicolas*.

## St Vincent: Nelson's Patent Bridge for Boarding First Rates

### Phase 1 – Broadsides exchanged

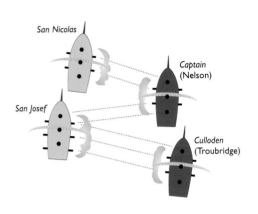

**Notes**
- The *Captain* and *Culloden* (both 74s) are heavily engaged against the 112-gun *San Josef* and the 84-gun *San Nicolas*.
- The range is very short and both sides suffer considerably.

### Phase 2 – *Excellent* arriving

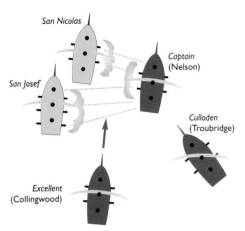

**Notes**
- *Captain*, now seriously outgunned, continues to swap broadsides while *Culloden* falls away disabled.
- *Excellent*, sent by Jervis to assist, sails directly for the gap between *Captain* and her enemies.

### Phase 3 – *Excellent* sails between *San Josef* and *Captain*

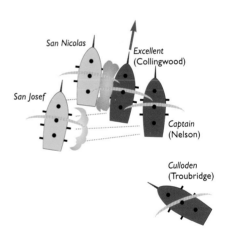

**Notes**
- In Collingwood's words: 'we did not touch sides, but you could not put a bodkin between us so that our shot passed through both ships, and in attempting to extricate themselves they got on board of each other'.

### Phase 4 – Nelson's patent bridge

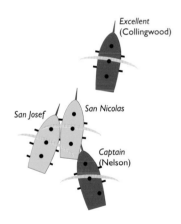

**Notes**
- As *Excellent* passes she fires into both enemy ships, whereupon they crash into each other and become entangled.
- Nelson sails deliberately into the starboard quarter of *San Nicolas*. *Captain*'s cathead locks into the stern gallery of the Spaniard and Nelson leads a boarding party and takes the ship.
- Using *San Nicolas* as a bridge, Nelson leads another boarding party up the chains of *San Josef*, whose captain surrenders to him.

## NELSON'S PATENT BRIDGE

By 1.45 p.m. the *Victory* had hoisted the signal, later to become famous as the last signal she flew at Trafalgar, 'Engage the enemy more closely.' At one stage the fire of the leeward line British ships *Irresistible* and *Diadem* was in danger of hitting the *Victory* and *Excellent* to windward. As British ships came looming up through the smoke, Parker signalled for his division, 'Fill and stand on' – get underway to the north to make more space. At 2.15 p.m. Jervis signalled to Captain Collingwood in the *Excellent* to 'pass through the enemy line'. She put on more sail and was soon engaged at close range by the 112-gun *Salvador del Mundo*. The *Excellent*'s broadsides were so devastating that the Spanish ship lowered her Colours – only to raise them again as the British ship sailed on. Next, Collingwood fought a deadly duel with the 74-gun *San Ysidro*. The battering she received induced the Spaniard to strike her Colours. Still pressing forward, the *Excellent* joined the one-sided battle around the *Captain* and *Culloden*.

By about 3.00 p.m. the *Culloden* and *Captain*, although heavily outgunned, had been exchanging broadsides with the *Santisima Trinidad*, the 112-gun *San Josef* and the 84-gun *San Nicolas* for about an hour. Unsurprisingly, both sides were seriously damaged. The *Captain* had her wheel smashed and had lost her foretopmast, which made steering problematic. Through the clouds of smoke Collingwood saw four ships ahead of him. On his starboard quarter the *Culloden*, seemingly disabled, was falling away; on the starboard bow was the *Captain*, rigging shot away, sails shredded and foretopmast gone, but still trading shots with two more powerful enemies. Almost directly ahead was the *San Nicolas*, with the huge bulk of the *San Josef* on the larboard bow. Both these ships appeared crippled but were still firing. Collingwood could not know that Nelson had earlier been hit in the side by a flying splinter from a rigging block that would have knocked him down had Captain Ralph Miller not caught him. Nor did he know that on the *San Josef* Rear-Admiral Don Francisco Xavier Winthusen had lost both his legs or that 150 of his men had been killed or wounded. Collingwood ordered the master to take the *Excellent* between the two Spanish ships. As she passed between, she fired both broadsides. Many of the balls went clean through the Spaniards: 'we did not touch sides, but you could not put a bodkin between us, so that our shot passed through both ships'. The effect was to render both Spanish ships virtually unmanageable hulks. They crashed together and became entangled, locked in an embrace that rendered them stationary and helpless.

If Nelson had illustrated his tactical insight and initiative when he took his ship out of the line, he was now about to demonstrate, yet again, his personal courage and leadership. Despite the *Captain* having 'not a sail, shroud or rope left', Nelson told Miller to lay aboard the *San Nicolas* and summon the boarding party. The helm was put down and the two ships came together, with the *Captain*'s bow ramming into the Spaniard's starboard quarter, and her spritsail yard passing over the *San Nicolas*'s poop and becoming conveniently entangled with her mizzen shrouds. Two boarding parties had assembled. One, under Lieutenant Charles Pierson, consisted of soldiers of the 69th Foot, serving as marines; the second was mainly of seamen under Captain Edward Berry (a passenger at this time). The *Captain*'s cathead was jammed into the stern gallery of the *San Nicolas* and this provided a route across.

---

### Private Matthew Stevens

Eighteen years later, Stevens was still serving with the 69th. A Scotsman with a wry sense of humour, at Waterloo he was the quartermaster of the 2/69th. When a soldier was struck down at his side by a long shot at the start of the battle, he quietly remarked, 'Aweel, it is time for a respectable non-combatant to gang awa!' He died, still quartermaster of the 69th, in India in 1821 – a rare old soldier who no doubt downed a good few free beers while regaling his audience with tales of fighting under both Nelson and Wellington.

---

### Nelson's Injury at St Vincent

In 1803 Nelson jotted his wounds down on a piece of paper. Second on the list was 'his belly off Cape St Vincent'. That he was blinded in one eye and lost his right arm are common knowledge today, but the fact that a piece of flying wood from a block hit him in the side at St Vincent, causing a lasting abdominal weakness, is much less well known. He was listed in the official report as 'bruised but not obliged to quit the deck'. Indeed, after being hit he was able to lead the boarding party and later to scramble aboard the *Victory*. He himself dismissed it with the comment, 'On my return on board the *Irresistible* my bruises were looked at, and found but trifling, and a few days made me as well as ever.' He was understating the problem. The 'contusion of no consequence' was giving him considerable pain. Ten weeks after the battle he wrote to the Duke of Clarence, 'My health is getting so indifferent from want of a few months' repose, and the pains I suffer in my inside, that I cannot serve, unless it is absolutely necessary, longer than this summer.'

A few days after the injury he developed what he himself called 'a suppression of urine', probably caused by a blood clot in the bladder cavity that blocked his urethra. This affliction was temporary, but the weakness of the bowel wall, or hernia, was permanent. Coughing exacerbated it and could, at times, result in an extremely painful lump the size of a fist.

---

Private Matthew Stevens of the 69th smashed the upper quarter-gallery window with the butt of his musket and scrambled through into the captain's cabin, closely followed by Nelson with drawn sword. Some twenty soldiers and seamen with muskets, pikes and cutlasses followed Nelson as best they could but found themselves unable to get out – the doors were locked and Spanish officers started firing pistols at them through the window. There was much banging of marine muskets in response, followed by a splintering of wood as the door gave way under a torrent of axe blows. At the head of his boarders Nelson burst out onto the quarterdeck. Commodore Don Thomas Geraldino was cut down in the rush. Nelson's party discovered that Berry's party had clambered across the bowsprit and taken the quarterdeck. Almost 130 Spaniards were casualties, and the Spanish ensign was being hauled down and the ship was in British hands. Nelson accepted the swords of the surviving officers – the *San Nicolas* made a handsome prize.

Still entangled with the *San Nicolas* on the larboard quarter was the much larger three-decker 112-gun *San Josef*. As Nelson was regrouping, getting more soldiers across from the *Captain*, securing prisoners and organizing a prize crew, the Spaniards on the *San Josef* started firing down from the rear-admiral's stern gallery. Nelson was now to do something no other British captain had done before (or was to do afterwards) – he used a captured ship as a bridge to board and take another even larger one. At the head of another boarding party, Nelson scrambled up into the chains, from where he leapt over the bulwark onto the *San Josef*'s quarterdeck. There was no resistance. Instead the Spanish captain came forward to offer his sword, explaining that he was surrendering and that his admiral was dying. However, the *San Josef*'s capture, although seemingly easily accomplished, came only at the end of a desperate and gallant fight. For over an hour she had been pounded by at least four British ships (*Captain*, *Culloden*, *Blenheim* and *Prince George*) before the *Excellent* arrived to add her broadsides. She had absorbed an enormous weight of shot and lost her admiral, a third of her crew and the ability to sail or fire all but a handful of her guns.

Now came the famous formal surrender scene on the quarterdeck of the *San Josef* that has been immortalized so many times by imaginative painters. Every uninjured Spanish officer came forward in succession in strict order of seniority to hand his sword to Nelson. As he accepted them, he 'gave [them] to William Fearney [ex-*Agamemnon*], one of my bargemen, who put them with the greatest sang-froid under his arm. I was surrounded by Captain Berry, Lieutenant Pierson, 69th Regiment, John Sykes, John Thomson, Francis Cook, all Old Agamemnons'. Francis Cook pushed his way forward to shake Nelson's hand. The cost to the *Captain* had been high, with 24 killed and 56 wounded, about a third of the British fleet's casualties.

The closing stages of the battle saw British ships closing in around the *Santisima Trinidad*, like jackals around a wounded lion. She had been putting up a most gallant fight against the *Excellent*, *Blenheim* and *Orion* but by this time was so badly battered, with her fore- and mizzenmasts down and close to 200 casualties, that she was prepared to strike her Colours. Officers on the British ships attacking her saw first a white flag, then when that went unheeded, an English flag was hoisted above her own. She had had enough. Unfortunately, at that precise moment (4.22 p.m.) Jervis signalled the end of the action with an order to wear and come onto the starboard tack. The most precious prize of all was abandoned and rehoisted her colours. The British would not meet her again until Trafalgar. They had, however, secured the *Salvador del Mundo* and *San Josef*, each of 112 guns, the *San Nicolas* of 84 and the *San Ysidro* of 74 – no mean achievement.

## THE AFTERMATH

Jervis's fulsome commendation of his actions was all that Nelson could wish for. As Nelson went aboard the admiral's flagship, *Victory*, Jervis embraced him and 'said he could not sufficiently

> ### Nelson's Account of the Boarding of the *San Josef*
>
> Commodore Nelson's 'Account of Proceedings' includes the following description of how the *San Josef* was taken.
>
> A fire of pistols, or muskets, opening from the stern gallery of the San Josef, I directed soldiers to fire into her stern; calling Captain Miller, ordered him to send more men into the *San Nicolas* [which he had just taken]; and directed my people to board the first-rate, which was done in an instant, Captain Berry assisting me into the main chains.
>
> At this moment a Spanish officer looked over the quarterdeck rail, and said they surrendered. From this most welcome intelligence, it was not long before I was on the quarterdeck, where the captain, with a bow, presented me his sword, and said the admiral was dying of his wounds. I asked him on his honour if the ship was surrendered. He declared she was: on which I gave him my hand, and desired him to call on his officers and the ship's company and tell them of it: which he did.

thank me, and used every expression to make me happy'. Jervis went so far as to publicly set down his captain-of-the-fleet Captain Robert Calder when he suggested that Nelson's action had been in contravention of the Navy's tactical bible, the *Fighting Instructions*. Jervis replied, 'It certainly was so, and if ever you commit such a breach ... I will forgive you also.' The next day the 32-gun frigate *Lively* was sent to England with the admiral's official dispatch on the battle, in which Nelson was confident that his name would feature prominently. Aboard the *Lively* was Sir Gilbert Elliot (former Viceroy in Corsica and a great friend of Nelson's) who had witnessed the battle, along with his ADC, Colonel John Drinkwater.

Nelson missed no opportunity to ensure that he received his due reward. To make certain the Admiralty and others in England knew what he wanted, he came aboard the *Lively* in order to speak to Sir Gilbert and appeared irritated when told the latter had just left to visit Jervis on the *Victory*. Instead he made his feelings plain to Drinkwater. When Drinkwater suggested that Nelson was sure to get a baronetcy, he was immediately contradicted. Nelson wanted something much more distinctive – nothing less than the splendid star and ribbon of the Order of the Bath. Drinkwater later wrote:

> The word [baronet] was scarcely uttered, when placing his hand on my arm, and looking me most expressively in the face, he said, 'No, no: if they want to mark my services, it must not be in that manner.' 'Oh', said I, interrupting him, 'you wish to be made a Knight of the Bath.' ... 'Yes, if my services have been of any value let them be noticed in a way that the public will know me.'

---

### A Chaplain's Experiences

The chaplain of the *Prince George* wrote to the *Edinburgh Herald* to relate his experiences and feelings during the battle:

> With regard to my own feelings during the action, which lasted five hours and a half, they were various. The cockpit is my appropriate station – a station, which in my opinion, demands more fortitude than any other in the ship. When the firing commenced, my sensations, I will acknowledge, were somewhat unpleasant; there was a solemnity which awed, if it did not frighten. We waited with anxious suspense, unknowing what was passing above, except the tremendous and incessant roar of the cannon, which stunned and deafened us. Our attention was soon called away to other objects. A seaman whose thigh had been dangerously wounded by a

splinter was brought down to us, and he was shortly succeeded by others, wounded and dying. It was a scene I can never forget; but it is the most painful I have to remember. During the intervals I could be spared from the amputations, I went upon deck, but there the scene was altogether different. Our seamen were in their element ... when any of the enemy's ships struck [surrendered], enthusiasm resounded through the whole fleet, and the cheers were repeated even by the wounded in the cockpit.

It is worth noting that the chaplain would have had a number of opportunities to leave the cockpit, as the *Prince George* only had seven seamen wounded – eight seamen and one marine were killed.

## Rewards and Punishments

### British

To the victor go the spoils. In addition to the eventual payment of prize money for the four captured ships, all senior officers received more immediate awards. Nelson, as noted above, got his Order of the Bath, Jervis was created Earl St Vincent with a pension of £3,000 a year, Vice-Admiral Waldegrave eventually became Lord Radstock, and Rear-Admiral Parker and Vice-Admiral Thompson were made baronets, though Jervis was unimpressed with Thompson's conduct during the battle and got rid of him as soon as possible afterwards. All flag officers and captains received a gold medal specially struck for the battle.

### Spanish

To the vanquished go the penalties. In July 1799 a Spanish Council of War handed out punishments to those senior officers it found guilty of failing in their duty at the battle. Cordoba was guilty of incompetence and sentenced to 'loss of employment with no right to any other'. He was banished from court and the high spheres of government – not very fairly, as he had several critical problems not of his making and he could not control the weather, which pushed him inexorably towards the enemy guns he had sought to avoid. However, his heroic and prolonged defence of his flagship eventually earned him a pardon. The document rehabilitating him recorded that his action 'showed true military spirit and it is generally known that he demonstrated great moments of bravery despite his lack of choice of means in the manoeuvres'. Morales was, probably rightly, found guilty of failing to bring the van to the aid of his commander-in-chief – of avoiding a fight. He received the same sentence as Cordoba. The captains of five ships (*San Francisco de Paula*, *San Ildefonso*, *San Juan Nepomuceno*, *Conquistador* and *San Antonio*) were suspended for between one and six years, while their seconds-in-command were reprimanded.

In other words, he wanted a medal he could wear. As he told his brother, 'Chains and medals are what no fortune or connection in England can obtain; and I shall feel prouder of those than all the titles in the King's power to obtain.'

Had Nelson seen his admiral's confidential dispatch, he would have been appalled. The only person to be mentioned by name was Calder, whose 'able assistance has greatly contributed to the public service during my command'. When this was made public, Nelson's friends at home raised an outcry. What was not known was that Jervis had written a covering letter with the dispatch in which several captains were praised, including Nelson, 'who contributed very much to the fortune of the day'. In the end Nelson got what he wanted, becoming Rear-Admiral Sir Horatio Nelson KB. The letter informing him of his knighthood referred to 'your very distinguished conduct in the brilliant Victory obtained over the Fleet of Spain'. St Vincent also netted Nelson a gold medal and the Freedom of London (in a gold box worth a hundred guineas), Norwich and Bath.

But, most importantly, it was St Vincent that first made Nelson famous. Before it he was largely unknown outside the Navy and his circle of family friends. He had certainly proved both his courage and his talent on the *Agamemnon* and elsewhere, but there was nothing to distinguish him from a dozen or more able captains waiting for their seniors to retire or die. After St Vincent, England, indeed much of Europe, rang with his name.

## Nelson and St Vincent

This battle proved to be a critical turning point in Nelson's career. It is worthwhile to highlight the reasons for this (not in order of importance).

*His physical courage under fire*
He seemed to thrive on the dangers of battle and made light of personal injury or pain. He appeared inspired by action and this in turn inspired his men. Accounts of his exploits and example spread throughout the fleet and his actions at St Vincent laid the foundation for his legendary reputation within the Royal Navy, which was to reach its peak at Trafalgar – and afterwards.

*His ability to grasp and act on a tactical situation*
His realization that only immediate action could bring about the close battle his admiral wanted, and his seizing the moment to wear out of the line entirely on his own initiative, were outstanding examples of Nelson's tactical leadership.

*His ability to grasp and act upon a fleeting opportunity*
This was demonstrated by his quick regrouping on the *San Nicolas* and assault up the side of the *San Josef*.

*The cementing of the relationship between Nelson and Jervis*
Jervis had already shown a high regard for Nelson's ability by assigning him duties (e.g. Corsica and Elba) in command of detached squadrons. St Vincent confirmed Jervis's faith in him.

*Nelson's ability to make use of his exploits to gain public acclaim*
He undoubtedly had a powerful hunger for glory, something evident in his character from the earliest stages of his career. He had an instinctive understanding of the importance of public opinion and he made sure through his writings and his friends that his doings were public knowledge in England. Nelson became the hero of the hour – much to the fury of Calder, who resented his success.

# Petty Officers, Seamen and Marines

## PETTY OFFICERS

As with the officers, there was little difference between the duties and specialist skills of petty officers of the different European navies in the early nineteenth century. In many cases the titles could be translated almost literally. A French gunner's mate was a premier cannonier, while a gun captain (in command of one gun) was an aide cannonier or chef de piece. So although it is the British petty officers and seamen who are discussed in this book, the French and Spanish ships at Trafalgar had their almost exact equivalents. As in armed services the world over, it is only the names that are different, not the ranks or duties that go with them.

The word 'petty' is derived from the French word *petit*, meaning small. Quite how the Royal Navy came to adopt it as a general term for their senior NCOs is less certain. Today it is used for a specific rank equivalent to an Army sergeant, but at the time of Trafalgar it referred to all those members of the crew of a warship who held ratings above that of able seamen or were specialists – known as idlers (see p. 143). These men received higher pay and a higher share of prize money but did not hold a warrant. In Army terminology they were NCOs, from lance-corporal to staff-sergeant. Their appointment, unlike that of warrant officers, was dependent on the captain of their ship, who could rate or disrate a man without reference to higher authority.

### TYPES OF PETTY OFFICER

On the *Victory* at Trafalgar the numbers of petty officers on board were as follows (most figures are taken from *The Muster Roll of HMS Victory* by John D. Clarke).

*Seamen Petty Officers*
The following POs were officially recognized and received the appropriate pay for their rate:

Quartermasters 8
Quartermaster's mates 4
Boatswain's mates 4
Yeomen of the sheets 3
Coxswain 1
Quarter gunners 13

There were also a number of unofficial junior petty officers who were not recognized for extra pay until 1806 (and not even then in the case of gun-captains). Nevertheless, they all had responsible positions and charge over a number of seamen. They could perhaps be likened to that much-maligned Army junior NCO of bygone years – the local, acting, unpaid lance-corporal. At Trafalgar they were:

Captains of the forecastle 3
Captains of the afterguard 3
Captains of the foretop 3
Captains of the maintop 3
Captains of the waist 3
Gun captains 104 (estimated)

Note that the muster roll of the *Victory* shows only three captains of the tops for each position, when four were required.

This gives a total of 33 seamen petty officers drawing extra pay for their rate; 15 unpaid but who were recognized as junior petty officers a year or so later; plus 104 who continued to have responsibilities but were not given additional pay above that of able seaman in the new Regulations and Instructions Relating to His Majesty's Service at Sea published in 1808.

*Idler Petty Officers*
Clerks 3
Carpenter's mates 2
Gunner's mates 3
Yeomen of the powder room 2
Armourer's mates 2
Ship's corporals 2
Caulker's mates 2
Trumpeter 1
Sailmaker's mate 1
Carpenter's crew 10
Gunsmith 1
Stewards 5

This gives a total of 34 idler POs, virtually the same number as seamen POs.

Judging by these figures, the British fleet at Trafalgar had almost a full complement at the battle. *Victory*'s only deficiencies were one yeoman of the sheets (who was responsible for the ropes), twelve quarter gunners and perhaps two from the carpenter's crew. It is difficult to explain why quarter gunners were so few, barely

---
### Crew of a Typical French 74
---

The numbers indicate the war establishment of a French 74-gun ship such as the *Intrépide*. They show the naval officers, warrant officers, petty officers and crew, but not the soldiers doing duty as marines. The French ships at Trafalgar, however, did not carry full complements.

**Officers (14)**
1 captain
1 second captain
5 lieutenants
5 ensigns
1 surgeon
1 chaplain

**Officer cadets (16)**
12 midshipmen, 4 volunteers

**Warrant and petty officers (92)**
*Boatswain and crew*
1 boatswain
2 boatswain's mates
3 yeoman of the sheets
2 yeomen of the anchors
15 quartermasters

1 coxswain of the longboat
1 coxswain of the barge
1 coxswain of the cutter

*Pilot and crew*
1 pilot
2 pilot's mates
4 second pilot's mates

*Carpenter and crew*
1 carpenter
1 carpenter's mate
4 second carpenter's mates

*Gunner and crew*
3 gunners
3 gunner's mates
37 gun captains
  (1 for every 2 guns)

*Sailmaker and crew*
1 sailmaker
1 sailmaker's mate
2 second sailmaker's mates

*Caulker and crew*
1 caulker
1 caulker's mate
4 second caulker's mates

**Seamen (492)**
23 topmen
134 able seamen
136 ordinary seamen
134 landsmen
65 boys/apprentices

**Supernumeraries (28)**
2 assistant surgeons
2 surgeon's mates
1 apothecary
1 secretary
1 armourer
1 armourer's mate
1 purser
1 purser's mate
2 senior stewards
1 cooper
1 cook
1 butcher
1 baker
12 servants
  (plus those of the captain)

The total number of crew including officers but excluding all army personnel was 642. This compares approximately with the complement of a British third rate of 80 guns. A British 74 had a full complement of 640, but of these some 100 would be marines. A French 74 would expect to have around 100 soldiers (a company) on board doing duty as marines.

The French did not have a direct equivalent of the British master, but the 'pilote', as his title implies, had some responsibility for navigation.

---

half the entitlement, as they were important individuals, each having charge of four guns during action. Almost certainly seamen had been nominated by the captain to act in this capacity, but they were not shown as such on the muster roll. The ship had virtually 100 per cent of its complement of idler petty officers – the extra clerks and stewards being those of the admiral's (Nelson's) retinue.

Discounting the quarter gunners, for whom the statistics are incomplete, the seamen petty officers had three killed and four wounded out of 20 – which represents a very high 35 per cent casualty rate, reflecting the fact that their duties kept them above the water line. In comparison, the 34 idler petty officers, with the exception of the admiral's and captain's clerks on the quarterdeck, had remarkably safe billets in battle, and only a 9 per cent casualty rate. The captain's clerk was killed, and two slightly wounded, the yeoman of the powder room and the agent victualler's clerk. One wonders what the circumstances of their injuries were, as neither had obvious reasons to visit danger spots.

The different types of petty officer are discussed below, in order of their 1808 pay rates on first-rate ships, with, where possible, particular reference to an individual who fought on the *Victory* at Trafalgar.

### Captain's clerk (£2-15-6 per month)

Thomas Whipple was Captain Hardy's clerk. Born in Dorset, at the time of the battle he was a young man of twenty, of good education. He had the same rate of pay as a midshipman or master-at-arms – the highest of any petty officer without a warrant – so was rated as one of the senior petty officers and probably lived with the midshipmen on the orlop deck. His duties were the maintenance of the large numbers of ledgers and forms (over twenty-five in number)

that the captain had to present to higher authority during or at the end of his commission. There was a lot of copying involved – for example, two copies of the muster book and log book had to be sent to the Admiralty. Whipple had to prepare these documents and copy out all his captain's other official correspondence, which could include instructions to the officers and letters to other ships, merchantmen, the Navy Board or the Admiralty. It was an exacting, laborious and, one suspects, rather tedious job, as everything had to be copied by hand. To carry out his duties the clerk had the privilege of a small office on the quarterdeck just forward of the captain's cabin. He worked in close co-operation with Walter Burke, the purser; indeed, to become a purser required several years' service as a captain's clerk, so that would probably have been young Whipple's ambition if he intended to make his career in the Navy.

Unfortunately Whipple became the only idler petty officer fatality on the *Victory*. He was out on the quarterdeck close to his captain, taking notes of events, when a cannonball passed within an inch of his head and he fell to the deck. Midshipman George Wesphal, who had been walking with him, was astounded to find his friend dead but without a mark on his body. He had been killed by the intense pressure – something that remained a mystery to his contemporaries.

### Carpenter's mate (£2-10-6 per month)

There were two carpenter's mates on the *Victory*: John Kidd, a young man of twenty-five from Scotland, and John Leakey from Devon, who, at thirty-eight, was well above the average age for the crew. We do not know much about either, but it is quite possible that Leakey had previous service, perhaps as a shipwright or as a carpenter on merchant ships. Both were on the maximum pay rate for their position, as they were serving on a first rate. Transfer to a frigate on promotion to carpenter would have given them the princely rise of £0-15-6 per month, and if either were to become a carpenter on a first rate they would receive well over double their Trafalgar pay. As with all mates, they were understudies. During the battle they would both have been working below the waterline, inspecting the hull for shot holes and carrying out emergency repairs. It was not a dangerous job, and neither Kidd nor Leakey was injured that day.

### Caulker's mate (£2-6-6 per month)
Although this individual (there was only one, on fourth rates and above) had a crucial job keeping the ship watertight, it is a little strange that he was the only person on board on this pay scale – a shilling a month more than quartermasters and boatswain's mates seems somewhat pointless. William Biggs. aged thirty-two, carried out these duties at Trafalgar, no doubt as part of the carpenter's team touring the bowels of the ship looking for damage.

### Quartermaster (£2-5-6 per month)
There were eight quartermasters on the *Victory* at Trafalgar, a full complement for a first rate; there were six on a 74 and three on a frigate. Their job was extremely skilful and demanding. For every hour of every day there had to be a quartermaster on the wheel, usually accompanied by one of his mates or an experienced able seaman. At Trafalgar there were four on the wheel of the *Victory* until it was smashed. Not only did the quartermaster have to understand and obey all orders for the sailing of the ship that might be passed to him by the master or officer of the watch, but he also had to have a feel for the ship. He needed to be able to read the wind in the sails, and know just how much rudder was needed in a wide variety of circumstances. He was constantly on the alert, as the safety of the ship was, literally, in his hands. In foul weather it was a physically as well as mentally exhausting task, so he would have perhaps two or more other hands to help hold the great double wheel. Four could be on duty during an eight-hour watch, each being relieved after two hours if necessary. Of the eight on the *Victory*, John King, at fifty-four, was the third oldest man on the ship – the oldest being the sixty-seven-year-old purser and the next an able seaman of fifty-six called William Mitchell. Perhaps not so strong as he used to be, King was also rated as the yeoman of signals, and as such he had responsibility for the stowing and maintenance of the flags. Henry Ford, next oldest of the quartermasters, was the same age as Nelson, forty-five, and his shipmate John Thorling was only a year younger. Their combined experience of conning those great sailing warships must have been unsurpassed. Regrettably, Thomas Johnson, who at twenty-one was unusually young for the rate, was killed that day.

### Boatswain's mate (£2-5-6 per month)
The boatswain's (bosun's) mates were probably the most unpopular petty officers on most ships, as they enforced discipline, which included administering on-the-spot punishments with their rope's end (starters) to slackers on the order 'start that man'. It was usually a bosun's mate that carried out a flogging – in fact, he actually made the cat-o'-nine-tails, as one was never supposed to be used twice. They were also the 'Spithead Nightingales' with their calls. They roused men from their hammocks, cutting them down if they were slow getting up. They checked that hammocks were folded correctly for stowing by putting them through a hoop – hence the expression

'to be put through the hoop'. They worked directly under the boatswain, and as such they trained the seamen in their duties. They had their eye on eventual promotion to boatswain, a key warrant officer position with a wage of almost double theirs. In action they were deployed on the forecastle and upper deck, not fighting but supervising the sailors whose job it was to sail the ship. At Trafalgar the *Victory* had her full complement of four boatswain's mates, two to each watch. The youngest was twenty-four-year-old John Cormick from Ireland. Above him in seniority came John Hunniford, aged twenty-six and from Devon, James Wright, aged twenty-eight from London, who was slightly wounded, and John Welsted, a Dorset man, who at thirty-six had probably been passed over for promotion. None of the four lived long enough to receive the Naval General Service Medal (NGSM) in 1848.

### Gunner's mate (£2-5-6 per month)
Captain Hardy had three out of the four gunner's mates he was allowed on the flagship. They were John Ebbs, aged twenty-six from Dorset (who lived long enough to wear his NGSM), John Browne, aged thirty, from Ireland and Thomas Bailey, thirty-two, an American. During the battle Bailey was helping serve a gun on the quarterdeck – unusually, as gunners' duties normally kept them in or near the powder rooms. A shot smashed seventeen-year-old Midshipman William Rivers' left leg and he fell writhing in agony beside Bailey. Bailey knew Rivers well, as he was the son of his boss, the gunner, and he carried the wounded man down to the cockpit where his leg was amputated. Rivers survived, was promoted to lieutenant and died in Greenwich Hospital in 1856. When Bailey returned to his gun, Nelson approached and ordered him to fire at the fore rigging of the *Redoutable* – possibly the last order Nelson gave, as he was struck down a few moments later.

### Yeoman of the powder room (£2-5-6 per month)
Yeomen were storemen on third rates or above. The *Victory* had two of the powder room, William Spencer aged twenty-six and Launcelot Brown aged forty-three. Their primary task was 'to attend the fore and after magazines, and to receive and to deliver the powder when wanted for action, or otherwise'. Brown was extraordinarily unlucky to be wounded, albeit slightly, as this duty should have kept him down below the waterline in the safest part of the ship. There were other yeomen for the boatswain's, carpenter's and gunner's stores, plus a yeoman of the sheets (ropes attached to sails) and a yeoman of signals. Their duties, however, were not as critical, for obvious safety reasons, as those in the powder room, and this was reflected in their wages: only the yeoman of the sheets was rated above able seaman for pay.

### Armourer's mate (£2-5-6 per month)
Assisting the armourer maintain all the small arms on board were two armourer's mates, Hugh Stevens aged twenty-five from London and John Melebury aged thirty-five from Sweden – one wonders how he managed to end up fighting for the British so far from home.

### Ship's corporal (£2-5-6 per month)
On the *Victory* the ship's corporals were Michael Clements, aged twenty-nine, who lived to get his NGSM, and Daniel Henley, thirty-five, who did not. Their task was to assist the master-at-arms in his inspections. On the 74-gun *Mars* the Captain's (Standing)

Order Book specified that the master-at-arms and his corporals were to remain on duty until midnight every day. They were required 'to go frequently about the Ship, particularly about the cable tiers, the cock-pit, and the storerooms to see that there are no lights burning at improper times; nor at any improper time in improper places; and if he find any such lights, he is to put them out, and inform the Officer of the Watch of the persons who were using them'.

The corporals also trained both seamen and landsmen to use the muskets, pistols and side arms carried on board. They were regarded as important individuals whose duties with regard to safety and lights were taken very seriously: they could report persons much senior to themselves who had failed to comply with regulations. At Trafalgar they would have continually toured the ship to check no fires were developing.

### Junior petty officers

Yeoman of the sheets (£2-2-6 per month)
Coxswain (£2-2-6 per month)
Trumpeter (£2-0-6 per month)
Sailmaker's mate (£1-18-6 per month)
Quarter gunner (£1-16-6 per month)
Carpenter's crew (£1-16-6 per month)
Gunsmith (£1-15-6 per month)
Steward (£1-15-6 per month)

The coxswain with Captain Hardy at Trafalgar was Robert Bookless, a twenty-seven-year-old from Newcastle. He had charge of the captain's barge but was also his trusted servant, a mixture of butler (not valet, which was the steward's job), bodyguard and major-domo. All rated ships were officially allowed one trumpeter, in this case twenty-one-year-old Phineas Board. Presumably he originally made signals to the ship's company but by Trafalgar the purpose of his role had lapsed, and no account of the battle records any use of his trumpet. The large number of stewards (the establishment allowed one) includes valets and servants for the admiral, captain and purser.

Casualties among this group of petty officers on the flagship amounted to one killed and three wounded. The dead man was the yeoman of the sheets, Andrew Sack, a thirty-three-year-old from Switzerland. All the wounded were quarter gunners hit while serving their guns. They were George Quinton, William Honnor (a pressed man) and William Tarrant. Tarrant recovered and eventually became a boatswain, living long enough to receive his NGSM in 1848 (in 1977 the medal was still in the possession of his descendants). Another quarter gunner worthy of a mention was Peter Reynolds, who had volunteered for the Navy in 1794, seen service under Admiral Cornwallis and fought at the Gut of Gibraltar in 1801. He was discharged after nineteen years' service and admitted to Greenwich Hospital in 1826 under the name Peter Moser. In 1831 he was promoted boatswain for duty in the hospital wards, dying there in 1856 at the grand old age of eighty-four.

# SEAMEN

When a new man came on board, whether volunteer or pressed, he was interviewed by the first lieutenant and probably the boatswain before being given a rating in accordance with his previous experience – or lack of it. The rating he was given affected his duties, pay, prize money and promotion prospects. If he had absolutely no seamanship experience he would be rated as a landsman. Some experience at sea would lead to a rating of ordinary seaman, while a man with two years' service on another warship or on a merchant ship would almost certainly get rated able seaman. His claims were likely to be tested by questioning from the officer and boatswain, and if he could produce a previous captain's or master's report to substantiate his skills so much the better. If the new recruit had some skill such as carpentry, could write, worked as a sailmaker or had some other relevant trade, then he might be rated as a specialist and therefore an idler. These rates were not set in stone. The captain would confirm them and they would be entered in the ship's muster book, but if they were found inappropriate or if the man misbehaved, the captain could move him as necessary. Similarly, good work, aptitude and the learning of new skills could earn promotion. Some men were content to serve many years without rising above able seaman. One such was Isaac Copeland, who joined the Navy as an able seaman in 1759 and survived four wars before finally being promoted quarter gunner in 1804, only to be invalided out within a few months – he must have regretted missing Trafalgar.

Many men, even if pressed or rated landsman, made it to able seaman, thus increasing their pay from £1-2-6 to £1-13-6 a month. Of the twenty-five men listed in the *Victory*'s muster roll at Trafalgar as having been pressed some two years earlier, one was

then a quarter gunner, most were able seamen and fewer than five were landsmen. One man, twenty-two-year-old Frederick Bush, whose home country was Prussia, was pressed in Gibraltar as an ordinary seaman to fight at Trafalgar – no doubt he felt fate had dealt him a strange hand, although it is likely he had previously been to sea on a merchantman. The record for both promotions and demotions must surely go to Robert Satchell. He entered the Navy as an able seamen in 1793, and being a man of ability was soon promoted to boatswain's mate. By 1801 he was a boatswain but lost his position following a court martial for fighting and drunkenness. Within six years he was once again a boatswain but this time was caught selling his stores and again lost his rank. The extraordinary thing about this seaman's career was that during those six years he had been a quartermaster's mate, a boatswain's mate three times, a yeoman of the sheets twice, a sailmaker's mate, a gunner's mate and a quartermaster twice. What a character!

## RECRUITMENT

Like all major conflicts, the Revolutionary and Napoleonic Wars created a growing and insatiable demand for manpower in every country involved. The ever-increasing requirements of the Navy and the Army placed huge demands on a country of nine million people. As Britain was an island dependent on trade and control of the seas for survival, priority went to the Navy. However, it took far longer to train a sailor than a soldier, and this, coupled with the increasing size of the fleets and the unavoidable wastage due to sickness, injuries and battle, meant the need for seamen could never be satisfactorily met. At the start of the war Parliament voted an increase in the size of the Navy to 45,000, then in 1794 to

85,000 (including 12,000 marines). By 1799 the figure had leapt to a peak of 120,000 (20,000 marines). The Peace of Amiens in 1802 saw a reckless reduction in the strength of the Navy in terms of ships laid up and men laid off. Fourteen months later, when war resumed, the manpower mountain had to be climbed again. In reality it could never be conquered in terms of sufficient experienced seamen, as distinct from untrained landsmen.

Captains were responsible for manning their ships. Naturally they wanted men with sea time, men who had experience and skills, as there was little time or inclination to train ignorant recruits. The next best alternative was a volunteer, hence the expression 'one volunteer is worth three pressed men'. In peacetime a captain would send recruiting parties ashore (and round the countryside) to tempt, persuade or bribe young men, preferably seamen, to join his ship. It could be a costly business for him, with the hire of a band, printing of posters and accommodation for the recruiting officer and his men all coming from his pocket. In wartime things changed dramatically. The captain still had to find a crew, but used other methods in the attempt to make up the continuous shortfall.

## Volunteers

The nucleus of the Navy, the best seamen that every captain sought were volunteers, most of whom were either being 'turned over' (transferring from one ship that was being decommissioned to a new ship) or merchant seamen. A volunteer received a bounty (varying according to experience) and two months' pay in advance from which to buy 'slops' from the purser. There were many reasons for volunteering – one of which was to avoid being 'pressed' (see below). Once caught by the press gang, it was better to agree to come as a 'volunteer' and thus qualify for the bounty than to be dragged forcibly on board. This also meant having the letter V after one's name in the muster book instead of the stigma of a P.

## The Impress Service

Yet another common expression used today, that of something being 'pressed into service', originates from the Navy of the eighteenth and nineteenth centuries. The Impress Service was a permanent organization based in the main ports around the coast. It was staffed by naval officers who would otherwise be on half pay – mostly men who were elderly, idle or desperate for a shore job. As one source put it, 'none, generally speaking, but worn out lieutenants were appointed to that service'. Captains were appointed as 'Regulating Officers' who controlled the 'press gangs' (usually led by a lieutenant with a midshipman or warrant officer) and inspected the recruits with the assistance of a surgeon. A regulating captain based in London might have seven gangs under his control, each gang consisting of seven or eight toughs, not seamen. Their incentive was the £1 paid to the gang leader for every recruit and, equally lucrative, the chance of a bribe of up to £10 or more to let a man who had been caught run. In 1795 there were 1,000 officers and men operating in 85 gangs around the English coast.

### An Over-enthusiastic Press Gang

Poole. Nov. 30th.
This morning arrived in Steedland Bay, the *Maria* [merchant ship], from Newfoundland, having some passengers on board, besides the crew; the officers of the impress service expecting some resistance, had called for military assistance, and 20 soldiers, armed, went on board the tender, which went down the harbour to meet the vessel; when coming alongside, and finding the people obstinate, orders were given to the soldiers to fire, which they did; the pilot (then at the helm), and two other men were killed on the spot, and seven others dangerously wounded, one of whom is since dead.

Lieutenants Philips and Glover, with all who were on board the tender, are taken into custody, and the whole town is in the greatest commotion.
*The Times*, 3 December, 1794.

There was a second type of press gang. This was a temporary, ad hoc band of seaman from a particular ship sent ashore by the captain, who in wartime held a 'press warrant' to grab recruits. Press gangs were supposed, by the wording of their Admiralty Warrant, only to take seamen – a word sometimes given a very broad interpretation. Parts of the warrant make interesting reading:

We do hereby Impower and Direct you to impress, or cause to be impressed, so many Seamen, Seafaring Men and Persons whose Occupations and Callings are to work in Vessels and Boats upon Rivers, as shall be necessary either to Man His Majesty's Ship under your Command ... giving unto each Man so impressed One Shilling for Prest Money. And, in the execution thereof, you are to take care that neither yourself nor any Officer authorised by you to demand or receive any Money, Gratuity, Reward or other Consideration whatsoever, for the sparing, Exchanging, or Discharging, any Person or Persons impressed or to be impressed, as you will answer it at your Peril.

The procedure for finding suitable recruits usually followed a familiar pattern. The lieutenant would select an inn as his gang's 'rendezvous'. This was their base from which they sallied forth to scour the back streets, brothels and taverns, often with guidance from a local man. The gang would stop and question likely-looking men. Well aware of the risk of impressment, few sailors would go ashore in seamen's clothes, but suspicious answers or traces of tar on the hands would give the press gang sufficient 'evidence' to seize them. At this stage a judicious offer of a bribe might get the gang to move on. Another alternative for the unlucky captive was to come quietly as a 'volunteer' and thus claim a bounty. Often, however, they resisted strongly. The struggle could turn ugly and it was not uncommon for sympathetic relatives or friends to attempt a rescue; there are records of women pelting the gang with missiles. These raids were often carried out the night before sailing so that there would be no repercussions if the gang took somebody with immunity from impressment. Foreigners, particularly Americans, sometimes ended up at sea in a strange ship in this way.

Those men who were pressed were taken to the rendezvous, where they were held in a large room under guard. This was just the first stage of what could be a lengthy and miserable journey to their final berth on board one of His Majesty's warships. Next came their transfer to a 'pressing tender'. This was a small vessel moored nearby that was in reality a floating jail in which those 'pressed' (together with volunteers) were held until such time as the gang had got their quota. Conditions on these rotting, decrepit craft were usually appalling. One man recalled, 'Upon getting on board this vessel, we were ordered down in the hold, and a grating put over us; as well as a guard of marines placed round the hatchway, with their muskets loaded and bayonets fixed ... In this place we spent the day and the following night huddled together, for there was no room to sit or stand separate.' This man was lucky if he only had one night in a pressing tender – some unfortunates spent several weeks there.

Even at the end of this depressing introduction to the Navy, most recruits went next to a receiving hulk, normally an old warship moored in the harbour. It was larger, but the hold was just as foul smelling, wet and uncomfortable. There they would wait until finally assigned to a warship. Although the figures below are for an eighteen-month period some fifty years before Trafalgar they give an inkling as to the sort of success a press gang could expect in an English port, in this case Hull.

|  | Able | Ordinary | Landsmen | Total |
|---|---|---|---|---|
| Volunteered ashore | 41 | 35 | 32 | 108 |
| Pressed ashore | 90 | 46 | 2 | 138 |
| Totals | 131 | 81 | 34 | 246 |

### Notes
• Only two landsmen were pressed, so it seems this gang kept to the instructions in its warrant quite rigidly.
• Overall only 34 (14 per cent) out of 246 recruits were landsmen.
• There is no way of knowing how many of the 108 volunteers offered their services after the gang had caught them in order to get a bounty.
• On the *Victory* at Trafalgar, out of 500 seamen only 28 (5.6 per cent) had been pressed – a tiny proportion, only six of whom were landsmen.

Perhaps one of the most hated aspects of press gangs was what was called 'impressment afloat'. This allowed the captain of a warship to stop a merchant vessel at sea, send a boarding party over and press any seaman he wished, subject to leaving the master, mates, apprentices and sufficient men to sail her home. If the ship was returning from a voyage and just outside a port, only a handful of seamen were needed to man her. Many merchant ships built special hiding places where a few key men could conceal themselves to evade the press gang, members of which were not averse to thrusting a cutlass between stacks of cargo.

Those exempt from impressment included pilots, fishermen, apprentices, officers of merchant ships and foreigners. Such individuals carried (they failed to do so at their peril) a 'protection' issued by the Admiralty. This was a form of identity document that described the man and stated his occupation. The system was far from watertight; a protection could easily be sold, forged or borrowed, as the description of the holder was extremely vague. Foreigners could volunteer but they could not be pressed into service. However, many Americans were taken. They could obtain their protections just by going in front of a notary and swearing to their American birth. Since there was no simple way of distinguishing a British from an American accent at the time, it was easy for a British citizen to obtain a protection by deception, and equally easy for a press gang to question a protection's validity. One wonders how Ordinary Seaman William Sweet from New York found himself the only pressed man among the twenty-two Americans aboard the British flagship at Trafalgar, who included a midshipman and the armourer. Altogether there were 72 foreigners on board (9 per cent of the complement).

In national emergencies, such as in early 1803, when the government was desperate for manpower for the Navy, authority was given for a 'press from protections'. Certificates of exemption were no longer valid and anybody with a remote connection to the sea who was unlucky enough to be grabbed could be pressed. This was called a 'hot press', and it could net all sorts. A John Wetherell described one at Harwich:

> They commenced their man plunder as I term it. The market house was to be their prison, where a lieutenant was stationed with a guard of marines and before daylight next morning their prison was full of all denominations, from the parish priest to the farmer in his frock and wooden shoes. Even the poor blacksmith, cobbler, tailor, barber, fisherman and doctor were all dragged from their homes that night.

### Quota men
There were times, and 1795 was one of them, when even press gangs and allowing a 'hot press' could not provide enough men. In that year Parliament passed two Quota Acts, which laid down that each county had to provide a quota of men for service at sea, the number depending on its population and number of sea ports. London had to produce 5,704; Yorkshire, the largest county, 1,081; and Rutland, the smallest, 23. Parishes did not find the system popular, especially as they could be fined for not producing their quota. Volunteers from the poor were encouraged, petty criminals persuaded and sometimes money raised so that a more generous bounty could be used as an inducement. Stockton excelled itself with a poster proclaiming 'the largest bounties ever given' – £31-5-0 for an able seaman, over one and a half times his annual pay. In meeting their quotas counties could count an able and ordinary seaman as worth two landsmen. Many areas came near to hitting their targets, London, for example, which raised the equivalent of 5,264 (1,371 seamen and 2,522 landsmen). In 1796 the prime minister, William Pitt, was able to inform Parliament that the Acts had succeeded. It is impossible to tell how many quota men were on the *Victory* in 1805.

### Prisoners
Those convicted of minor crimes (robbery and more serious offences were generally excluded) were often allowed to enlist rather than serve their sentences. Debtors could sometimes get out of Newgate by using their bounty to pay off their debt. Some prisoners who had completed their sentence but could not be released until they had paid their upkeep fees had them paid by the Impress Service in exchange for their joining the Navy. For obvious reasons, smugglers were regarded as worth having – in 1805 a regulating captain at Whitehaven requested the Revenue Service (Customs) to let him have anybody caught smuggling instead of prosecuting them. Prisoners of war could also enlist. The hulks where most of them lived were trawled for recruits, which resulted in a few French royalists coming forward and a fair number from other nations – anything was better than rotting in the rat-infested prison ships for years awaiting peace or a prisoner exchange.

---

### Foreign Seamen on the *Victory* at Trafalgar

Of the 823 men on board the *Victory* at the battle, 63 were not British nationals. These were:
1 African, 22 Americans, 1 Brazilian, 2 Canadians, 7 Danes, 2 Dutch, 4 French, 2 Germans, 2 Indians, 1 Jamaican, 6 Maltese, 2 Norwegians, 1 Portuguese, 4 Swedes, 2 Swiss and 4 West Indians.

## SEAMEN RATINGS AND DUTIES

To gain better pay and promotion, the raw recruit had to acquire certain basic skills. If he did not do so, through idleness or inability, he was likely to remain a landsman – an unskilled crew member. All seamen of whatever rating were divided into two equal watches for the sailing of the ship in normal times in fair weather. In battle all had additional duties. The four seamen rates were:

### Boys

There were three categories of boys in 1805, namely boys 1st, 2nd and 3rd class. Boys under fifteen were rated as 3rd class, those from fifteen to seventeen as 2nd class. The boys 1st class, also known as 'volunteers Class 1', were training as officers, destined to be midshipmen at least, and probably lieutenants in due course (see p. 126 for further details). On a first-rate ship, regulations allowed eight boys 1st class, thirteen 2nd class and nineteen 3rd class. On a 74 there would be six, ten and fourteen respectively, on a large frigate four, six and ten. The 2nd and 3rd class boys were almost certainly set for a life on the lower deck. In the eighteenth century it was common for boys of eleven or twelve to seek and obtain some sort of employment. For young lads living near the coast or in one of the naval towns, going to sea had the allure of adventure and seeing exotic foreign places. It offered higher pay than an agricultural worker (plus a small share of prize money) with the added bonus of a career, if they made good. However, mothers were understandably not always happy to lose their sons at such a tender age. As Adam Smith wrote in *The Wealth of Nations* in 1812, 'A tender mother, among the inferior ranks of people, is often afraid to send her son to school in a seaport town, lest the sight of the ships and the conversation and adventures should entice him to go to sea.'

If these enticements were not enough, there was a charitable organization whose primary purpose was to help and encourage boys to join the Navy. This was the Marine Society, founded in 1756 and dedicated to recruiting orphans and boys of impoverished parents from the streets and giving them clothes and a minimum amount of training for sea service. Ten years before Trafalgar it was sending 500 to 600 boys a year to the fleet. On joining their pay per year (from 1807) was 1st class £9, 2nd class £8 and 3rd class £7, irrespective of the rate of ship they served on. As a secondary undertaking the society also provided sea clothes to about 1,000 landsmen a year.

Those boys rated as 3rd class were almost invariably employed as officers' servants until they reached the age of fifteen. Occasionally this custom was deliberately ignored, as happened on the *Swiftsure* in the early 1800s, where they were employed in the tops, quickly becoming expert seamen. The 2nd class boys were divided between the two watches to learn to be seamen, although a number had to become landsmen before being rated as ordinary or able. In battle both classes of boys were usually combined with landsmen and stationed at the hatchways, with the task of keeping the deck well swabbed with water to dampen down spilt powder, or of handing cartridges to the nearest gun as they were passed up from below. On the *Victory* at Trafalgar an estimated 83 boys and landsmen were employed on these duties at the fore, main and after hatchways and along the decks. It was a dangerous task, but vital if the guns were to be kept firing. There were three boys killed on the *Victory*

during the battle, one 2nd and two 3rd class, of whom one was a thirteen-year-old lad called Stephen Sabine, a Marine Society recruit from the back streets of London. Only two boys were wounded (both 2nd class). Of the thirty-one 2nd and 3rd class boys on the flagship, the five casualties represent 16 per cent.

### Landsmen

As noted above, in peacetime most captains avoided recruiting landsmen, as their ignorance could prove a great liability on board a ship at sea. As one captain put it, 'Boys soon become good seamen; landsmen rarely do, for they are confirmed in other habits.' In wartime, however, shortages of experienced seamen and the need to commission many more ships combined to make the recruitment of landsmen essential. A number were pressed men but the majority came in fulfilment of the Quota Acts of 1795. All a landsman needed to do his duties was brawn; he was given the menial tasks and expected to gradually absorb some seaman's skills with the passage of time. Thus landsmen would be found hauling, hoisting and lifting, manning the pumps, pushing on the capstan to raise anchors, shifting ballast or stores (under supervision) in the hold and scrubbing, cleaning and painting. They were generally known as 'waisters', men who did most of their menial, unskilled duties of swabbing and hauling in the waist of the ship. The 'waist' was the area of the upper deck between the forecastle and quarterdeck, and today's derogatory term 'waster' owes its origin to the average seaman's contempt for these men.

In action some landsmen might be part of a gun crew (purely to provide more muscle on the gun tackles), but many would be grouped at the hatchways and along the passageways, passing cartridges up from the magazines to the guns or helping to carry wounded below. Of the 500 seamen rated from landsman to able seaman on the flagship at Trafalgar, 89 (18 per cent) were landsmen. This would be roughly the percentage for the whole fleet. On the *Victory* five were killed and nine wounded, a 16 per cent casualty rate.

### Ordinary seamen

This was the first rung on the ladder. An ordinary seaman drew £0-2-6 a month more than a landsman – almost precisely a penny a day. There were 201 with Nelson on the *Victory*, men who had begun to learn the appropriate skills but still required supervision. In action some would be found on the weather deck but most were likely to be in the gun crews. One of the more interesting was Joseph Burgin, who had enlisted as a landsman in 1798 under the name of Joseph Coxhead. After promotion to ordinary seaman, he fought at the Nile on Nelson's flagship, the 74-gun *Vanguard*. At Trafalgar he was desperately wounded serving No. 13 gun on the middle deck. A round shot shredded his left leg, necessitating amputation high up on the thigh. It is impossible to comprehend the agony he must have suffered as the surgeon cut and sawed, but he survived, was discharged from the Navy and in April 1806 was admitted to Greenwich Hospital. One would have thought his life expectancy would be low. Far from it. He was resident at the Hospital for an incredible fifty-six years, dying in July 1862 aged eighty-four. Also of interest is an Army deserter, Ordinary Seaman Samuel Martin, who fought at Trafalgar, only to be returned to his regiment afterwards! Casualties among this rate on the *Victory* amounted to 11 killed and 19 wounded, some 15 per cent.

## Able seamen

These men were competent sailors. They had served at sea for at least two years, either in the Navy or merchant service, and drew £1-13-6 a month, putting them on the same level as cook's mates, coxswain's mates and captain's cooks. The ambitious able seaman could look forward to promotion to petty officer and ultimately, perhaps, to warrant officer; a tiny proportion made it to commissioned rank as lieutenants. A high percentage had come from the merchant service, as, despite its lower pay, the Royal Navy had several distinct advantages. One of these was the likelihood of an easier life. Merchantmen had comparatively small crews (the profit motive being uppermost in the owner's mind), and so their members had to work much harder, particularly in wartime when as many seamen as possible were diverted to man warships. Just how hard life could be on a merchant ship in wartime is made crystal clear by a description of the *Blandford* coming into St Mary's Road, Sicily in 1758:

> A ship came in from Malaga, which had been out so long that her bottom was quite green and her sails and rigging bleached white. The crew was so emaciated with continual fatigue and their strength so much exhausted that they could scarcely hold themselves on the yards, and one of them was so weak that he fell from the mainyard as the ship came into the Sound.

When looked at in terms of ship's tonnage per man of crew, the differences in workload become clear. A West Indiaman would have between 10 and 15 tons per man, but in coasting trades up to 30 tons was acceptable. On a line-of-battle ship 3 tons per man was the ratio. The food was generally worse on a merchantman – again, the bigger the economies, the bigger the profits. Discipline was slacker and medical treatment or compensation for injuries poorer or non-existent. Finally, and perhaps most importantly, the Navy held out better prospects of promotion. Even the lower pay was more than outweighed by the bounty paid on joining and the chance of prize money.

The able seaman was competent in all the basic skills of sailing. These included rope work (knots and splicing) and lifting heavy weights with the use of blocks and tackle. He had to be able to raise and lower yards, 'sew a seam', bend sails (hoist sails to a yard and attach them), set, furl (take them in completely) and reef them (reduce the area of sail). Much of this work required going aloft. The topmen, those seamen who raced up the ratlines to the yards some 150 feet above the deck, were the best of the younger able seamen. Captains took pride in their topmen's skill and speed at going aloft and getting down. It was not unknown for the boatswain's mates to be told 'start the last man down' – a stupid order, since it meant men on the higher tops took unnecessary risks getting down. There were 210 able seamen on Nelson's flagship, of whom 35 were casualties, 10 killed and 25 wounded. This represents 17 per cent of these men.

## CONDITIONS OF SERVICE

*HMS Victory* was caught up in the scramble to get her crew up to strength at the renewed outbreak of war in May 1803. After fourteen months of peace, the Navy was a shadow of its previous wartime strength. On 11 May 1803 Lieutenant John Quilliam, *Victory*'s first lieutenant, assisted by Boatswain William Willmet, placed 351 seaman onto the muster books. These men all found themselves in the Mediterranean for the Toulon blockade, then took part in the fruitless chase to Egypt and the West Indies, before finally fighting at Trafalgar. Quilliam interviewed and rated them all. He was forced to accept a higher proportion of landsmen (21 per cent) than he would have wished. Of the 74 men, 29 came from London, many grabbed by the press gangs that were doing brisk business along the Thames' wharves and in the dark alleyways or dingy riverside taverns that stretched from Wapping to Greenwich and beyond.

Among those picked up was twenty-three-year-old John Roome. He had been born in Battersea and was working the Thames as a lighterman, a lighter being a flat-bottomed boat used to load or offload cargoes. On the basis of this dubious seafaring experience, the press had seized Roome weeks earlier, so he had been compelled to endure the horrors of 'pressing tender' and 'receiving hulk' before arriving aboard the *Victory*. Lieutenant Quilliam had no choice but to rate him landsman – rowing a riverboat and humping cargoes did not make him a seaman. However, there must have been something about him, perhaps his intelligence or self-confidence, that made the first lieutenant place him with the signals section of the crew. Some two and a half years later he was to be the man who actually hoisted Nelson's famous signal, 'England expects ...' just before the start of battle. His divisional officer was Lieutenant John Pasco, the signals officer, while his immediate superior, whose duty it would be to train him in the recognition and use of the flags, was the elderly (fifty-six-year-old) quartermaster and yeoman of signals John King. One of Roome's messmates would have been a young man two years his junior, who also came from London, Able Seaman Alfred Taylor, who was similarly with the signals section. Unfortunately, while Roome would survive the battle, Taylor would not.

The following sections reconstruct Roome's likely experiences during his first few weeks on the *Victory*, to give an insight into conditions of service in Nelson's Navy.

## Berths and belongings

One of the first things Roome and his new shipmates would have done was to report to the boatswain or one of his mates for the issue of their two hammocks each. It has been said that his hammock was a seaman's best friend (a soldier's was his rifle). However, he did not have to pay for them as he did for his mattress, bolster (pillow), two blankets and slops (seamen's clothes), the costs of which were deducted from his wages. The issue of two was a comparatively recent improvement. The word hammock came from the Carib word *hammorca*, a native bed suspended between two poles or trees. It was not made of netting but rather from 'a piece of hempen cloth, six feet long and three feet wide' and was numbered. Roome would have gone down to the lower gundeck to find his berth and sling his hammock from the appropriately numbered nails in the bulkhead. He would have been forcibly struck by the virulent stench coming up from the bilge water rising through the orlop deck from the hatches down to the hold. Even with the gunports open it could never be completely dispersed, though seamen soon got used to it.

Another shock awaiting him was the cheerlessness of the gundeck, the lack of headroom – he had probably cracked his head already – and the fact that he shared his berth with around 460 other men and thirty 32-pounder guns. Not only must he get into the habit of moving around in a permanent crouch, but the hammock nails were also only 14 inches apart, thereby imposing horizontal restrictions as well as vertical. If the ship was in port, when all hammocks could be occupied at the same time, Roome would bump his neighbours on either side every time he turned and the hammock moved. With the ship at sea, however, it was not quite so claustrophobic, as the berthing arrangements were carefully planned so that his immediate neighbour would be on a different watch from himself. In many ships this meant that the man next to Roome had the same hammock number and the same job, but on the other watch. When he was on watch, a seaman's hammock had to be lashed up to the beams, thus giving a little more space for those resting.

One of the first lessons Roome and his new fellow landsmen had to learn was how to roll up their hammocks. The boatswain's mates would have demonstrated this daily chore, surely accompanied by much cursing and dire threats. Early every morning the hammock had to be rolled into a sausage-shaped bundle, with the bedding inside, of the exact size to pass through the mate's metal hoop; woe betide the man who put clothes inside the bundle or allowed any bedding to poke out. The hammocks were taken up to the weather deck and stowed in nets or racks around the sides in order to give some protection from musket fire – if properly rolled up, it is said they could support a man in the water for up to twenty-four hours.

## Sanitary arrangements
Very quickly Roome had to learn the sanitary arrangements available. They were crude and uncomfortable, but certainly better than those he was used to ashore – disposing of human waste into the sea was infinitely more hygienic than the puddles of raw sewage found in so many cobbled back streets in London and other cities. On the *Victory* he went to the 'heads', which was, and still is, the naval name for toilets. It referred to the forward section of the forecastle which was provided with gratings (so waves could wash the area) and 'seats of easement' in what Dr Johnson in his *Dictionary* called a 'place of retirement'. The boxes with holes, for that is all they were, were supposedly positioned so that waste fell into the water. This was fine if a seaman sat, as he was intended to, on the lee-side head, otherwise the ship's side would be fouled due to the wind or heeling of the ship; in the early seventeenth century cleaning up such a mess was a punishment for liars! Either way, weather or lee side, the heads was not a place to dally in heavy seas. Another problem was the totally inadequate number of seats. The *Victory* had six for some 800 men – the senior officers had similar arrangements but in the privacy of the quarter galleries, while those berthed in the gunroom used chamber pots. In addition there were two small 'round houses' on

### Slops
These were a seaman's working clothes – not an official uniform, although they did provide some degree of uniformity. They were purchased from the purser. Regulations stated that every newly joined man was to be checked as to his clothing needs. Only those essential items that he lacked in his personal clothing were issued (sold) to him.

> When any new raised men, either volunteers or pressed appear … examination is to be made how they are furnished with clothing and bedding, and the Captain is to cause such as appear in want thereof to be supplied according to their necessities, but not exceeding in the whole, to any one person, the amount of two month's wages. And he is to take care not to let the pressed man have anything more than shall be absolutely necessary to kept [*sic*] them clean and protected from the whether [*sic*].

Items available for issue were:
jackets – short, blue with pearl buttons
waistcoats – yellow, red or striped
breeches – voluminous, knee length, worn with stockings and generally unpopular
trousers – white or blue, cut above the ankles and wide bottomed so easily rolled up
stockings – wool or silk
shirts – linen or jersey, red or blue checkered pattern or white
headgear – round straw hats, often tarred for cold climate, and worsted Dutch caps with ear flaps
apron – long felt or leather, worn as a protective garment
shoes – black with silver buckles
belt – leather with sheath for a knife
foul-weather coat.

the foremost bulkhead of the upper deck, one for the use of junior warrant officers, the other for seamen in the sick berth. Roome would have been in serious trouble if he ventured into these.

Naturally, the need to urinate came far more frequently than the need to go to the heads. Roome would have been introduced to the narrow channels (platforms) that extended from the sides of the ship, intended to spread the lower shrouds of the masts. The hardware used to secure the shrouds were called the 'chains'. To stand in the chains meant climbing over the side to stand on the platform, where the leadsman stood to heave the lead to determine water depth. To perform a call of nature from this position necessitated clinging on tightly with at least one hand. Failure to do so could result in loss of life. As one seamen described it:

> I narrowly escaped drowning, for going into the main [mainmast] chains to exonerate nature, the ship yared [*sic*] to port and heeled so deep to starboard, the side whereon I was, that I were dipped head and ears, the affright of which, together with the surface motion of the sea, almost forced me from my hold. If it had I could not have escaped.

Whether the importance of using the lee chains, to avoid performing into the wind, was explained to Roome and other newcomers is perhaps doubtful – some things are best learnt from experience. Some ships had 'piss-dales', which looked rather like modern urinals on the side of the ship, each with a pipe leading out through the side; these were decidedly more convenient and a lot safer than the lee chains. The *Victory* did not have these modern conveniences, so reliance was placed on the old-fashioned bucket for the messes. Despite all these possibilities men such as Roome were not averse to urinating elsewhere if they could get away with it. Admiralty instructions even went so far as to state that sentries be posted over gratings to stop men 'easing themselves' down into the hold! The French were equally distrustful. Their regulations stated that care should be taken that men do not urinate over the sills of the gunports, while in harbour the men were not allowed to use the 'seats of ease', so as not to soil the ship's sides, latrine buckets being placed in the heads instead.

## Messes
Just about the only choice Roome had on joining the ship's company was that of whom he messed (ate) with. A mess was a group of shipmates who ate together, drank together, played together and, on the rare occasions when they were allowed, went ashore together. Understandably, there often developed a far stronger bond between 'old messmates' than 'old shipmates'. The group would normally

consist of from four to eight men. The men could choose their mess-mates (provided the others accepted him), although seamen and marines were discouraged from messing together (the first lieutenant would almost certainly have vetoed it). Apart from this, there were no restrictions as to rating or job. It was possible for men to change their mess but this was only possible on a certain date (perhaps monthly) and with the permission of the first lieutenant. The mess was centred on the table at which they ate, which was suspended between the guns on the lower deck and lashed up to the deck above during action. On a three-decker like the *Victory* more mess tables were located on the middle deck. There were benches on each side of the table, which could accommodate four men on a line-of-battle ship. One would expect Roome to have chosen to mess with fellow Londoners, as the large new draft would have had to sort themselves out into messes almost immediately after coming aboard. Whoever he joined, he would have had to take his turn as mess cook. This entailed collecting the rations for the mess from the purser's steward's room in the after part of the orlop deck, putting them in a bag and taking those that required cooking to the galley for the cook's mates to boil; the cook himself (Charles Carroll) supervised. Finally he would bring the bag of cooked food to the mess table. Roome might be required to do this duty for a week or perhaps only for a day at a time – ships varied. Another chore for the mess cook was to keep the wooden eating utensils clean. Kept in a rack above the mess table, they included square wooden plates, from which we get the expression 'three square meals a day'.

## Food and drink

Roome would probably have been surprised at the quantity and quality of the food and drink aboard. It was certainly as good as, if not better than, what he could expect ashore in Battersea, and most importantly it was always there, every day, on the mess table. The quality of the food on the *Victory* when Roome joined was high, as she had just been provisioned for several months for duty in the Mediterranean. A list from her log book of some of the provisions loaded into her hold in 1803 makes impressive reading and goes a long way to dispelling the myth that the food on Royal Navy ships was invariably rotten, crawling with maggots and weevils. Among the stocks lowered down the hatchways were live bullocks, cows, calves and chickens (for fresh meat, milk and eggs), butter (useful for greasing guns when rancid), bread, rice, salted beef and pork, cheese, oatmeal, flour, raisins, sugar, suet, cabbage, peas, onions and lemons. Drink included water, wine, rum and small beer (a watered-down variety with only 1.3 per cent alcohol). While the cooks could, and often did, succeed in making good food unappetizing, there is no doubt that these stocks represented a reasonable and balanced diet. It is known that some barrels of pork salted in 1815 were used in the Crimean War forty years later – the comments of those who had to eat it can be imagined, but as long as it was thor-

### Provisions and Stores Carried by the *Victory*

When fully loaded at the start of a commission expected to last six months, the *Victory*'s hold carried about 900 tons of food, water, fuel, shot and powder, in addition to specialist stores or equipment and the fresh provisions that would be used to supplement the diet as frequently as possible. The approximate distribution of this load was as follows (figures in tons):

| | |
|---|---:|
| Fuel (coal) for galley stove | 50 |
| Spare timber (for carpenter) | 20 |
| Fresh water | 300 |
| Solid shot | 120 |
| Gunpowder | 35 |
| Beer | 50 |
| Salted beef and pork | 30 |
| Biscuit or bread | 45 |
| Flour | 10 |
| Butter | 2 |
| Dried peas | 15 |
| Sand, pitch, tar | 20 |
| Cheese | 2 |
| Ballast (pig iron and shingle) | 200* |
| **Total** | **899 tons** |

*This would vary according to the amount of cargo carried.

oughly steeped (soaked) to remove the salt before boiling it would have been edible. As has been mentioned earlier, Nelson went to great lengths during the two years prior to Trafalgar to ensure his ships were restocked with fresh food and water at every possible opportunity, from supply ships or sending ships to Gibraltar, Corsica, Malta and the Barbary Coast (North Africa).

The standard allocation of food for Roome and his messmates for a week was: 4 lbs of salt beef, 2 lbs of salt pork, 2 pints of peas, 3 pints of oatmeal, 6 oz of butter, and 12 oz of cheese. There was also a daily ration of 1 lb of bread (biscuit), fresh vegetables (as available) and a gallon of beer. These were basic entitlements, which would vary as the voyage lengthened. If some stocks dwindled, substitutes were used, for example instead of meat more cheese or stock-fish (fish such as cod, cured by being split open and dried in the air without salt), watered-down wine for beer, rice for oatmeal. Days when meat was not served were called 'banyan days', a reference to an East Indian sect whose adherents were forbidden to eat meat.

Although the food was not normally as revolting as some historians have maintained, there were times when both the quality and quantity suffered. During a lengthy commission or months at sea on blockade, the fleet relied on transport ships bringing supplies or ships going to port to restock. The weather, pirates, privateers and unforeseen events could interrupt the movement of both transports and warships. Sometimes food was contaminated when it reached the fleet. A survey on the transport *Sovereign* held in Palermo in June 1799 found that the flour, raisins and peas she carried had been destroyed by rats, whose corpses had been found inside the casks, which were riddled with rat holes. A year before Trafalgar, poor stowage in the *Victory*'s hold caused 399 gallons to be lost due to the pressure of the casks on top causing leaks in those at the bottom. Returns and surveys on provisions often contained reports of food that was 'rotten, maggoty, stinking and unfit for men to eat'. It was thrown overboard, as was the bread on the 20-gun *La Bonne Citoyenne* in 1799, when it had disintegrated into 'a clod of mould and dirt and a nuisance to the ship'.

For Roome and his messmates, drink was one of the few pleasures on board. It was usually issued twice a day, once between noon and 1 p.m. and again between 4 and 5 p.m., to coincide with dinner and supper respectively. These were the high points of the day for most. A variety of alcoholic drinks could be issued as alternatives to each other. Thus Roome would normally drink a gallon of beer a day, the staple issue. Only when beer ran out would wine, rum (in the West Indies), arrack (in the East Indies) or brandy be substituted. All drink was diluted with water. There were two types of beer available – small beer and strong beer. Small beer was often not much more than water with hops floating in it, which went sour very quickly, so was more commonly used for shorter voyages. Some

## The Agent Victualler

The agent victualler was a key individual in any fleet, though seldom mentioned in naval histories and certainly not in the account of the great naval battles of the age. As a civilian on the admiral's staff, his rank equated approximately with that of a senior warrant officer. At Trafalgar Richard Ford held this appointment, with an assistant, John Geoghehan, who was wounded. Ford had been with Nelson since 1803, entrusted with the task of ensuring a ready supply of provisions for the fleet from the various friendly ports in the fleet's area of operations. It was he who went ashore to find and negotiate with the local contractors. When Spain entered the war as France's ally in December 1804, Ford found that many good sources of supply were abruptly closed to him. His search for new sources in the Mediterranean was extensive and time consuming but eventually rewarding. Supplies of cattle were increased from the Maddalena Islands (off northern Sardinia). Naples brandy, Ford reported, was as good as that from Spain and cheaper. Cheap Portuguese wine mixed well with the brandy, making a substitute for the loss of the popular strong Spanish wine. Ford looked as far afield as southern Russia, although his efforts there were only partially successful. Russian pork proved 'nauseous and stinking', but the peas, when boiled, were as good as the English variety. The wheat, although somewhat dark in colour, made acceptable biscuits. Ford did a lot of wholesale buying after haggling over quantities and price with the contractors, although it was often necessary for pursers to buy fresh supplies, as the opportunity arose directly from merchants. Between 1 January and 31 March 1804, the *Goliath*'s purser spent £2,207 on four live oxen (with fodder), 54,610 lbs of fresh beef, 43,971 lbs of bread, 3,746 lbs of rice, 7,380 gallons of wine, 11,000 onions, 4,320 bundles of leeks, 2,184 cabbages and 14 pumpkins. The daily wine ration per man in the Mediterranean was one pint (instead of a gallon of beer), so with a complement of around 600 men the wine supply would have lasted almost exactly three months – nice calculating on the part of the purser.

More staggering statistics: the agent victualler for Nelson's fleet in the Mediterranean during a period of eight months in 1804 arranged the purchase for the fleet of 505,047 pieces of fresh beef, 379 sheep, 21,300 oranges, 81,685 onions, 119,015 gallons of wine and 30,326 gallons of brandy.

---

wines were popular in the Mediterranean: Spanish Mistela (known as Miss Taylor) was a favourite, whereas the red wine 'Black Strap' was not. Being sent to the Mediterranean was sometimes referred to as being black-strapped.

Rum started to be issued after Jamaica was captured in 1655. It was very powerful and had the great advantage of not going bad no matter how long it was stored. The watered-down version (two parts water to one of rum) issued to seamen in the Caribbean (where it was very cheap) had been called 'grog' since the 1740s, when it was instituted by Admiral Vernon, nicknamed 'Old Grogram' after the material from which his cloak was made. Kenneth Fenwick in *Far off Ships* paints the scene nicely:

> the Monkey's Orphan [a young sailor too inexperienced to go aloft] struck up *Drops of Brandy* on the quarterdeck, and there was a rush of mess cooks for the ceremony of serving out the first half of the day's grog ration, in which was a dash of lemon juice and sugar. The master's mate on watch did the actual measuring out, aided by the Master-at Arms, the petty officer of the day, and a sergeant of marines.

Roome's ration, in place of beer, would be half a pint of grog or a pint of (watered-down) wine. The watering down of rum was done on deck, where the two ingredients were mixed in a tub by the quartermasters of the off-duty watch under close supervision. Drunkenness on board was rightly regarded as a flogging offence, as a man intoxicated on duty could put the ship and his comrades at serious risk. Officers and warrant officers drank as much, or more than, the seamen, but a court martial awaited those drunk on watch. Stories of prodigious quantities being consumed by individuals abound. After the *Monarch* had captured a prize laden with wine, the purser ended up selling claret at a shilling a gallon. A mess of four warrant officers took two gallons a day.

Despite all this talk of alcoholic drinks, it was fresh water that was the most in demand for drinking. It was kept in large casks called leaguers in the bottom of the hold. The *Victory* could take 300 tons – this equates to 675,000 gallons. However, it did not keep well. Within a month it was often unfit to drink, so fresh water was taken on board at every opportunity. During the day seamen were normally allowed to get a drink from the 'scuttle butt' – a leaguer placed on deck, sometimes under a marine guard to prevent wastage. Another non-alcoholic beverage was coffee, often served at breakfast. It was certainly not coffee as we would recognize it today. Rather, it was made from burnt ship's biscuit, crushed and boiled in water with a touch of sugar added. Roome would have called it 'Scotch coffee'.

Apart from food and drink, Roome would have been agreeably surprised to find that – although no smoking was permitted, except on the forecastle, because of the fire risk – pipe tobacco was issued free, mostly for chewing.

### French Smoking Restrictions

Smoking on board warships of all nationalities was always the subject of rigid rules, which is why in the Royal Navy tobacco was almost universally chewed rather than smoked. In the French Navy, certainly in the days prior to the Revolution, some smoking was permitted. Seamen were issued with three pounds of tobacco (in sticks) for the duration of a commission. Pipe smokers could only light up from the match kept burning in the galley and all pipes had to have a lid. Smoking was allowed on the forecastle, but only on the lee side. In bad weather a man could smoke on the gangways, but again only on the lee side. A high proportion of seamen chewed rather than smoked their allowance. Pipes, however, were sometimes put to a novel use: the resuscitation of a half-drowned man. It was believed (by the French) that a man pulled from the sea could be revived if the stem of a pipe was pushed up his anus like an enema tube. Then by blowing on the bowl, smoke would be introduced into the lower intestine, thus causing the man to vomit up the seawater he had swallowed! Perhaps it worked.

## Watch-keeping and time-keeping

As Roome soon found out, shipboard life followed a mundane routine with little daily variety for the vast majority of his time at sea. Excitement, when it came, did so in the shape of mishaps, foul weather or, even rarer, action against an enemy. Different captains would organize the days and weeks with slightly different emphasis, but the overall patterns were very similar. Being a landsman, Roome was allocated to a watch (larboard or starboard) and from day one at sea the watch system governed every minute of every day. To understand how Roome's day was organized means understanding the watches.

Each watch had an equal number of men in it and was divided into groups under petty officers with specific duties. The most experienced seamen – also known as 'the most elderly and corpulent' – were stationed on the forecastle; they were called sheet-anchor or forecastle men. Then came the topmen for working the sails on the fore-, main- and mizzenmasts, all young able seamen whose duties required them aloft, above the lower yards; the youngest usually climbed the highest. Next came the afterguard, mostly ordinary seamen or landsmen, who worked the after-braces, main, mizzen and lower staysails from the quarterdeck. These men never went aloft except to furl the mainsail, a rare occurrence. There would also be a smaller poop afterguard, which would include men in the signals section such as Roome. Last came the 'waisters', landsmen (and some ordinary seamen) stationed in the waist of the ship to heave and haul on the main and fore sheets (ropes) and do all the dirty, unskilled jobs going. Roome had been unusually lucky to escape this fate during his first time at sea. The approximate numbers in each group on each watch on the *Victory* during the run up to Trafalgar are given below, calculated on the basis of half the seamen (able and ordinary) and half the landsmen. The figures do not include officers, petty officers, marines or boys.

| Foretop | 40 | Afterguard | 35 |
|---|---|---|---|
| Maintop | 45 | Poop afterguard | 10 |
| Mizzentop | 25 | Waisters | 50 |
| Forecastle | 40 | **Total** | **245** |

The diagram on the right sets out a normal 24-hour watch system. The 24 hours are shown as starting at midnight, though in fact the Navy's day started at midday, when the master, his mates and midshipmen checked the sun's position and reported noon; by tradition, the first watch was immediately after hammocks had been taken below at about 8.00 p.m. The two watches, larboard and starboard, alternated throughout the period, doing four-hour stints, except for the two dog watches, which only lasted two hours each, and were designed to ensure the same crew members were not always on duty at the same time day after day. Let us assume Roome was in the larboard watch and look at the main daily activities during each watch.

*Middle watch (midnight to 4.00 a.m.)*
Sometimes known as the graveyard watch. Shortly before 4.00 a.m. the quartermasters on duty would wake the lieutenant, mates and midshipmen of the next watch, as was the routine at the end of every watch.

*Morning watch (4.00 a.m. to 8.00 a.m.)*
This was the only time during this 24-hour period when Roome could snatch a few hours' sleep. At about 4.30 a.m. the boatswain and carpenter would come on deck to begin repair work. The

cook lit his galley fires and began preparations for breakfast, usually an unappetizing oatmeal gruel called 'burgoo', sometimes made more palatable by the addition of molasses. Around 5.00 a.m. members of the duty watch began to wash the decks and scrub the planks with heavy 'holystones' and the nooks and crannies with smaller 'prayerbooks'. Following them were other landsmen with brooms, swabs and buckets to dry the decks, while others polished the brass fittings. By 7.00 a.m. this work was finished and the first lieutenant, Quilliam, who did not do officer-of-the-watch duties, would come onto the quarterdeck to supervise the day's work. At about the same time the men whose duty it was brought up the casks of food and drink from the hold for that day's use and took them to the steward's (purser's assistant) room for issue. Whoever was Roome's mess cook would collect his mess's rations between 7.00 a.m. and 7.30 a.m., take what had to be cooked to the galley and be responsible for having all the food at his mess table ready for eating at meal times.

About ten minutes before 8.00 a.m. Roome would have been rousted out by the yells of the boatswain's mates – 'Up all hammocks!', 'Out or down! Out or down!' This meant that if he were not out of his hammock quickly enough, a mate would cut the cord at the head end, bringing it and Roome crashing to the deck. He would have to roll up his bedding inside his hammock before taking the bundle up on deck (provided it passed through the mate's hoop) to its correct place in the racks around the side. Roome then mustered on deck with his watch before reporting to his duty station at 8.00 a.m. At this time it was the custom for Captain Hardy to appear on the quarterdeck and authorize breakfast to be piped. Roome would be able to go below to join his mess, provided he was not required as part of the skeleton crew that remained on watch.

*Forenoon watch (8.00 a.m. to noon)*
During this time the men would have practised exercises, boarding, fire and gun drills. Roome would also have been involved with learning the signal flags, practising hoists and, occasionally, musket or cutlass training under the master-at-arms or his corporals. At 11.00 a.m. it was usual to have 'divisions', when hands paraded on the gundecks for inspection by their divisional officers (lieutenants). At the end of divisions all hands (except key crew) might be piped to witness punishments. Just before noon Roome would see the young midshipmen come to the quarterdeck to be tested on their navigation by Mr Atkinson, the master. At noon all hands were piped to dinner and Roome's watch was stood down.

*Afternoon watch (noon to 4.00 p.m.)*
This watch included the hour's break for the main meal of the day, dinner. As with breakfast, all except the bare minimum of essential crewmen (officer of the watch, quartermaster, helmsmen, lookouts, etc.) messed together. At one bell (12.30 p.m.) after the meal had been eaten, the fifer on the main deck began to play 'Nancy Dawson' or some other tune that meant grog was ready. The mess cooks darted up the ladder with small tubs to the butt, where the master's mate had publicly mixed the alcohol with water and lemon juice. The rum was drawn from a cask on the open deck because of the fire risk (the 20-gun *Glasgow* caught fire when the cask was opened in the hold in Montego Bay, Jamaica in 1779). Half a day's ration was measured out with great care and the mess cooks carried it down to a reception of cheering and banging of plates. It was shared out in tots (if it was spirits) slightly smaller than the one

# The 24-Hour Watch System at Sea

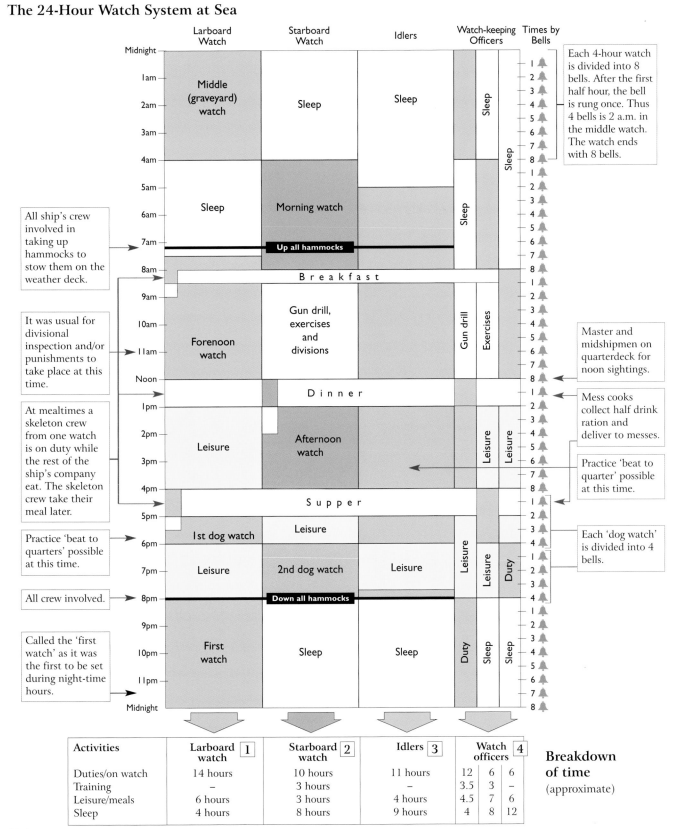

All ship's crew involved in taking up hammocks to stow them on the weather deck.

It was usual for divisional inspection and/or punishments to take place at this time.

At mealtimes a skeleton crew from one watch is on duty while the rest of the ship's company eat. The skeleton crew take their meal later.

Practice 'beat to quarters' possible at this time.

All crew involved.

Called the 'first watch' as it was the first to be set during night-time hours.

Each 4-hour watch is divided into 8 bells. After the first half hour, the bell is rung once. Thus 4 bells is 2 a.m. in the middle watch. The watch ends with 8 bells.

Master and midshipmen on quarterdeck for noon sightings.

Mess cooks collect half drink ration and deliver to messes.

Practice 'beat to quarter' possible at this time.

Each 'dog watch' is divided into 4 bells.

| Activities | Larboard watch | 1 | Starboard watch | 2 | Idlers | 3 | Watch officers | | 4 |
|---|---|---|---|---|---|---|---|---|---|
| Duties/on watch | 14 hours | | 10 hours | | 11 hours | | 12 | 6 | 6 |
| Training | – | | 3 hours | | – | | 3.5 | 3 | – |
| Leisure/meals | 6 hours | | 3 hours | | 4 hours | | 4.5 | 7 | 6 |
| Sleep | 4 hours | | 8 hours | | 9 hours | | 4 | 8 | 12 |

**Breakdown of time** (approximate)

## Notes

1. During the 24-hour period this watch has a long period on duty and only 4 hours sleep at best.

2. This watch will follow the same timings as today's larboard watch during the next 24 hours. This way the duties are fairly distributed.

3. In theory the idlers are well named, as they get every night in their hammocks.

4. It is difficult to be precise with watch-keeping officer's timings, as the watches were divided between a variable number of officers. While on duty their responsibilities were heavy but their periods off duty were much longer than those of most seamen.

used by the mate, so that a little was left over. This remnant was called the 'cook's plush', and he drank it as a reward for his trouble. This was the highlight of the day. Some men would save their half ration until supper so as to combine it with the second issue, while others might use it to pay off a debt. After dinner, although off watch, Roome could not go below to rest – he had no hammock to go to anyway – but he could take some leisure time to doze, play cards, chat, wash or mend his clothes, provided there were no more exercises, gun drills or cleaning to keep idle hands busy. Depending on the captain's wishes the entire crew might practise going to their battle stations, or quarters (see pp. 240–1), in the second half of this watch or the second part of the first dog watch, as during these times nobody's sleep was disrupted.

*First dog watch (4.00 p.m. to 6.00 p.m.)*
Roome was back on watch. This short watch also included men being piped to supper and the second issue of drink.

*Second dog watch (6.00 p.m. to 8.00 p.m.)*
During these two hours, unless all hands were required for some reason, Roome was free of all duties – it was genuine leisure time. Shortly before 8.00 p.m. 'down all hammocks' was piped. The entire crew collected their hammocks and slung them in their berths, a task which took some fifteen minutes.

*First watch (8.00 p.m. to midnight)*
Roome's last watch in the 24-hour period. The next day he would still be in the larboard watch but following the timings of today's starboard watch. He would undoubtedly be tired, having managed under four hours in his hammock out of the entire day.

From the above it is clear that Roome's days (and nights) were ruled by the clock. On board everything was regulated, duties done and meals taken at or within certain fixed time frames. To survive Roome would have quickly had to master the confusing (to a landsman) way the Navy told the time. Unlike in civilian (and Army) life, the system was based on the 24-hour clock and 'bells'. The actual measuring of time during a watch was by the hourglass, different sizes of which were used to measure periods from a minute to four hours. A watch of four hours was divided into eight half-hour intervals. To start the watch the officer of the watch told the quartermaster on duty to turn both a half-hour glass and a four-hour glass so that the sand started to fall. When the half-hour emptied, the quar-

## Funerals at Sea

All bodies of persons who died of natural causes at sea were first sewn up in a shroud of old sailcloth with one or two shot at the feet end. The shrouded body was lain on a long, broad plank, which in turn was rested on the lower sill of one of the gundeck or upper gundeck ports ready for tilting, the gun having been run in and secured. Then it was committed to the sea from the starboard side – the honourable side; dead animals, tainted carcasses and rubbish were thrown over the larboard side. However, the ceremonial prior to sliding the corpse into its watery grave varied; here rank was important.

If the dead man was a seaman, the chaplain assembled a few of his shipmates, and the funeral service was read with a boy present holding a lighted candle. A petty officer's funeral had more men attending and the ship's bell was tolled. For a captain the rites were far more impressive. The chaplain would hold a funeral service (mass on a French ship) to the accompaniment of full military honours, including a full marine guard, muffled drums and a nine-gun salute.

## Seamen's Diseases in 1780

Admissions to the Royal Naval hospital at Haslar in 1780 totalled 10,839 individuals. Of these, 1,670 were either undiagnosed or with comparatively rare illnesses. The remaining 9,161 cases fell into the following categories:

| | |
|---|---:|
| Continued fevers | 5,539 |
| Intermittent fevers | 33 |
| Scurvy | 1,457 |
| Ulcers/abscesses | 979 |
| Rheumatism | 337 |
| Flux (dysentery/diarrhoea) | 240 |
| Consumption (TB) | 218 |
| Venereal disease | 183 |
| Contusions (bruising) | 133 |
| Smallpox | 42 |

termaster informed the officer, who authorized the ship's bell to be struck once and the glass turned. If it was the morning watch then the time was 'one bell in the morning watch' or 0430 or 4.30 a.m. Eight bells (when the four-hour glass emptied) signalled the end of a watch, so 'bells' started again after half an hour into the next watch. The short, two-hour, dog watches ended at four bells.

## Health

During the ten years of naval warfare culminating at Trafalgar, the Royal Navy suffered some 1,500 deaths in action plus around 4,250 wounded. This was a mere 6 per cent of the Navy's total losses. Of the remaining 94 per cent, 82 were due to sickness and 12 per cent to accidents. A ship's surgeon and his staff spent most of their time caring for the sick in the sick berth on the starboard side of the upper gundeck underneath the forecastle. This was quite distinct from the cockpit on the orlop deck, which was used as the makeshift operating theatre in battle. The sick berth had fresh air and access to hot water (from the galley below) and the nearby heads. It also had access to some fresh distilled water from the Brodie stove in the galley, which was capable of producing six to seven pints a day. The sick berth was partitioned off from the rest of the deck by canvas screens and the sick lay in canvas cots slung from the overhead beams.

If Roome reported sick, and in the many months on board prior to Trafalgar the chances were high that he would, then the procedure was as follows. If he felt badly ill or was injured, he could report to see the surgeon, William Beatty, at any time. However, it was normal for the surgeon and his assistant, Neil Smith (who was promoted surgeon after his sterling work at Trafalgar), to take a sick parade each morning at the mainmast, where they examined those who presented themselves. If Roome was undergoing some daily treatment for an injury or illness, then he had to attend the sick berth at 8.00 a.m. There he would be seen by the surgeon's mate, William Westenburgh, who reported to the sick berth before breakfast to attend to patients' needs. Later in the morning the surgeon would make his rounds and the loblolly boys (orderlies) would wash, shave and feed the bedridden seamen. Westenburgh would then spend most of the day preparing and administering medicines, dressing wounds or ulcers, maintaining the surgical instruments, keeping records of medicines used and supervising the loblolly boys. The surgeon, who had overall responsibility for the health of the crew and cleanliness of the ship, was supposed to visit each patient twice a day and keep accurate records of his treatment and condition.

There is no doubt that Nelson's fleet at Trafalgar was a very healthy one in comparison with Gravina's command. When Nelson returned to Gibraltar after his futile chase to the West Indies, he was able to thank God for not having lost an officer or man from sickness since he left the Mediterranean. In contrast, the Spanish hospitalized 691 men (of whom 26 died) in Martinique, and on their return voyage 21 died and 95 were sick. After the action with Calder in July 1805, 200 men were disembarked sick from Gravina's remaining four ships, and 1,500 from Villeneuve's fourteen.

Shipboard afflictions generally fell into three main categories:

*Respiratory ailments*
Colds, influenza, tuberculosis and pneumonia. These illnesses were mostly associated with the seas surrounding Britain, so were unlikely to have caused much of a problem during the months preceding Trafalgar, which the *Victory* spent in warm waters.

*Fevers*
Usually divided into 'continual' and 'intermittent' (recurring) fevers, malaria being a good example of the latter. Some of these fevers would be accompanied by dysentery, diarrhoea or the 'bloody flux', as it was then called. Typhus, also known as ship or gaol fever, could be a serious problem. Malaria was a killer in the East Indies, although nothing like as deadly as yellow fever. Because Nelson's fleet was continuously at sea – nobody went ashore in the West Indies, for example – his crews were able to escape the worst ravages of this latter illness. An example of just how devastating it could be came from the 74-gun *Hannibal*, which lost over 200 men to yellow fever (nearly four times the number killed on any British ship at Trafalgar) in the Caribbean during the mid-1790s.

*Accidents*
These could include falls from aloft, burns from guns misfired in practice, limbs or feet crushed by falling barrels or sudden tightening of ropes or chains and, probably most common of all, hernias, the inevitable result of the frequent lifting of heavy casks and barrels.

*'Lifestyle' diseases*
It has been calculated that an average of between 8 and 10 per cent of the average ship's crew had contracted either syphilis or gonorrhoea, though the doctors and ship's surgeon were expected to examine new recruits for signs of these diseases at their initial medical examination. On this basis perhaps some 65 of Nelson's crew at Trafalgar were infected. Another common complaint was night blindness of varying degrees of severity. It was due to lack of vitamins; in its early stages it could easily be feigned, particularly by topmen who did not want to work aloft.

Once the greatest scourge of a seafaring life, scurvy had by 1805 largely been beaten within the Royal Navy, though this does not mean it was completely eliminated. French surgeons have described the disease in horrific terms. Men's bodies were 'covered with ulcers and corruption, swollen in all their parts, the ulcers filled with fluid, the gums swollen, rotten and disintegrating in shreds, bleeding at the mouth and nose, and dying in a bloody flux'. By far the worst example of what this awful disease could do occurred some sixty years before Trafalgar when Commodore George Anson took eight ships around the world between 1740 and 1744. He set sail with a total complement of 1,955 men, of whom nearly 1,300 were to die of scurvy.

In 1776, on a prison ship in Halifax harbour during the American War of Independence, Colonel Ethan Allen witnessed how scurvy could be almost miraculously cured. A man he considered virtually dead from the disease spent his last remaining money on 'two quarts of strawberries'. Just this one meal brought about an astounding improvement, but unfortunately the cause of the cure was not understood, so the man eventually died. Not until 1795 did the Admiralty accept that fresh fruit prevented scurvy. In that year the First Lord, Earl Spencer, issued regulations that lemon or lime juice was to be issued regularly on every ship in the Royal Navy – hence the reference (by Americans) to a British sailor (or soldier) as a 'limey'.

However, despite the best endeavours, this horrible disease was not entirely eradicated. Between November 1804 and April 1805 quite a serious outbreak of scurvy developed in Nelson's Mediterranean fleet. During that period there were some 250 sufferers of this disease spread over fifteen ships, peaking with 260 cases in April 1805. The cause was the closure of Spanish provision markets to naval victuallers on Spain's entry into the war against Britain. Until new sources of supply could be found, the disease could not be prevented. Dr Snipe, Nelson's fleet physician, was eventually able to arrange with a Mr Broadbent, an English merchant in Messina, for the supply of 10,000 gallons of freshly pressed Sicilian lemon juice for the Mediterranean fleet and another 20,000 gallons for the Channel fleet at 8d. a gallon.

---

## A Cure for Yellow Fever?

The *Naval Chronicle* for 1805 contains the following possible cure for yellow fever.

### CURE OF THE YELLOW FEVER

A CASE of the yellow fever has been recently cured in Jamaica by sweating in the steam of hot sugar. The Lad upon whom this experiment was made was placed close to the steams of the coppers, which had an instantaneous and happy effect. The pulse fell from 100 to 70 in a few minutes; the sweat poured off in streams; this head was immediately relived; and he did not complain of being too hot, notwithstanding a breath of air could not enter the room, and he was surrounded with the steam of sugar from all the coppers. The process was repeated the next day, after which the Patient put on his clothes, came down stairs, said he was quite well, and eagerly called for food.

---

## Accidents Will Happen

Midshipman Thomas Huskisson, who served aboard the 74-gun *Defence* at Trafalgar, has left a gruesome account of an accident he witnessed:

One day in fitting out topgallant masts which had been struck in bad weather the main topgallant mast rope gave way, by which accident a young man named Dalton who was on the main topsail yard was killed. The heel of the mast struck him on the head and knocked his brains out. On the following morning at breakfast, something was discovered in the tea kettle of our mess, which led to examination of the scuttle butt from which the water had been taken; and in it a quantity of the brains of the unfortunate man were found, which must have fallen in when the accident occurred. The scuttle butt was placed just before the main mast, and by chance had been left uncovered.

## Discipline

Strict discipline had to be maintained on all ships. Men's lives depended on each crew member following orders and understanding their duties. Slackness, drunkenness, disobedience and anything else that might be detrimental to the safe and efficient running of the ship could not be tolerated. Efficiency, order and professionalism by all on board were rightly regarded as all-important, not only in battle but during the long months or years during which the ship's company fought the weather, disease and boredom. Good discipline and good morale were invariably the result of good leadership from the captain. He and his officers had the backing of the Articles of War, the bible of naval law, which had been drawn up in the 1650s and amended in 1757 for the edition that was in use in the British fleet at Trafalgar. However, rigid enforcement of the maximum punishment allowed under these Articles was seldom the best way to have a happy, well-disciplined ship. Punishments, sometimes very severe punishments, were necessary, and the seamen themselves accepted this, but the severity and frequency of their application varied between individual captains. Interestingly, overzealous or unfair punishments were not among the list of grievances of the Nore and Spithead mutineers in 1797. A copy of the ship's log, with all the punishments entered into it, had to be sent to the Admiralty every three months.

Shortly after Roome had been taken on board the *Victory* in May 1803, Captain Hardy would have read out all thirty-six Articles of War to the entire crew, as all captains were required to do at the start of a ship's commission and thereafter at least once a month. They took twenty to thirty minutes to read. By Trafalgar, Roome would have heard them at least twenty-eight times, so by the time he jumped ship at Chatham on the *Victory's* return he would have known the precise Article (No. 16) that he was contravening. This states, 'Every person in or belonging to the fleet, who shall desert or entice others so to do, shall suffer death, or such other punishment as the circumstances of the offense shall deserve, and a court martial shall judge fit.' As we shall see later, Roome escaped such retribution.

Out of the thirty-six Articles nineteen carry death as the most severe sentence, and death is mandatory for nine of these: cowardice, failure to pursue an enemy or come to the assistance of a friendly ship, deserting with a ship, setting fire to a ship or powder magazine, murder and 'the unnatural and detestable sin of buggery and sodomy with man or beast'. Perhaps unexpectedly, death was not mandatory for taking part in a mutiny but only for organizing one ('shall make or endeavor to make any mutinous assembly'). Any offence for which a death sentence could be awarded had automatically to be tried by a court martial.

This left the captain to deal with the comparatively minor crimes of drunkenness, uncleanness, theft in all its forms, fighting, insolence, using profane oaths, neglect of duty, sleeping on duty, skulking and the like. He had a number of possible punishments of varying degrees of severity available, up to and including flogging. Although officially the maximum sentence a captain could award without authorization from higher authority was a dozen lashes, this provision was accepted as being widely ignored as courts martial were often difficult to organize. (In 1806 the upper limit of a dozen lashes was removed from Regulations and Instructions.) The captain could not, however, deal with charges against officers or warrant officers for which the punishments included cashiering, dismissal, demotion or loss of seniority.

To supplement the Articles, all captains drew up their own rules and regulations as to how they wanted their ships to be run, what today we would call 'Standing Orders'. They might include detailed orders as to when the captain was to be called to the quarterdeck, the responsibilities of the officer-of-the-watch and departmental officers or warrant officers, together with those covering the daily and weekly routine of his ship.

---

### On Watch at Sea

Captain George Duff of the 74-gun *Mars*, who was killed at Trafalgar, set out exactly how he wanted his ship run in his General Order Book. The contents contained what today we would expect in any unit's or ship's Standing Orders: detailed regulations on daily routine, who does what and when. Captain Duff's orders were operative at Trafalgar and may be regarded as typical of how most of Nelson's warships would have been run. Those covering alertness and lookouts are quoted below:

the Ship should be constantly in readiness for Action ... On any surprise or sudden incident happening in the night, the Lieutenant of the Watch is to send a Midshipman to acquaint the Captain with the particular circumstances thereof ... the Lieutenants are therefore particularly enjoined not to suffer any person whatsoever to be off the Deck in his Watch, upon any consideration; nor allow the people to lay about the Decks, but to make them Walk the Decks in their respective stations; and to cause the Watch to be mustered at least every two hours. Whoever is absent at the time of muster is to be reported to the Captain the next morning by the Lieutenant in whose Watch such neglect was discovered. And for the better discovery of objects in the night, independent of the general look out of the Watch on deck, the following stations are to be occupied solely for that purpose; and the look out men relieved every half hour, are to call the stations they are at, except in foggy Weather:

| | |
|---|---|
| Starboard Cat head | A Forecastle man |
| Larboard      do | A Fore Topman |
| Starboard gangway | A Main Topman |
| Larboard      do | A Waister |
| Starboard side the Poop | Seaman Afterguard |
| Larboard      do | Mizen Topman |

... A Man is to be kept constantly at the Fore and Main topmast heads from sunrise to sunset, except in rainy or foggy Weather, and to be relieved every half hour. A Midshipman is to be on the Forecastle and one on the Poop ...

At Night when a sail is seen, the Captain is to be made acquainted with it; and the First and Signal Lieutenants, Master, Boatswain and Carpenter to be sent for, who are to see everything in their departments clear; some guns to be got ready and preparation for making sail.

Whenever a strange sail is seen by Day the Captain is to be acquainted with it and a Midshipman of the Watch is immediately to go to the Masthead with a Spy glass to endeavour to ascertain the course of the Vessel seen &c. which is to be reported to the Captain.

The punishments could be divided into informal ones awarded on the spot by the captain or officers and senior warrant officers with the captain's sanction and formal ones meted out by the captain at a formal hearing or a court martial. The informal ones included:

*Starting*

This involved being hit over the back or shoulders with a cane or rope's end by a boatswain's mate for some perceived slackness, usually on the orders of an exasperated officer to 'start that man'. If it was common practice in a ship then morale would suffer. In 1809 the Admiralty forbade it after the court martial of Captain William Corbett, who had allowed starting to become an everyday occurrence applied in an unjust and excessive manner. The infamous Captain Hugh Pigot of the 32-gun frigate *Hermione,* who was eventually chopped up and thrown overboard by his mutinous crew in 1797, was a great believer in indiscriminate 'starting'. He once ordered the starting of the master of an American merchant ship that had run on board (collided with) his ship, thereby creating an international incident.

*Gagging*

Meted out for persistent blasphemy or insolence. The offender would be placed in a sitting position, hands tied behind his back, his mouth forced open and an iron pump bolt put across it and secured behind his head. Another method was the use of a 'cangue', a wooden collar made of two planks with a 12-lb shot attached, which the man had to wear while performing his duties. One captain was known to make the culprit walk on the lee side of the quarterdeck until he heard another man swear. The unfortunate man was sometimes driven to standing on a nearby seaman's toes hoping to provoke an oath, whereupon he would cry 'Sir, such a man swears!' The collar would then be transferred to the new offender.

*Drinking salt water*

A minor offence of being late on watch might be punished by being made to drink half a gallon of sea water. If the offender failed, he might be given another punishment such as being 'seized up'.

*Being seized up*

The offender was tied up in the shrouds, spread-eagled on the weather side (preferably in inclement weather) for as long as the officer considered appropriate. It was not uncommon to punish errant midshipmen in this way or to send them to the masthead for a long time.

*Scrubbing*

Reserved for dirty seamen who refused to wash themselves or their clothes. The offender was put in a large tub of seawater and scrubbed with stiff brooms by those of the crew who had been forced to eat or sleep near him. The present author can remember similar regimental scrubbings in the Army in much more recent times – they were most effective.

*'Kissing the gunner's daughter'*

A punishment reserved for boys, which saw the victim being tied to a gun and caned on his backside (see box on p. 187).

*Being put in irons*

There was no cell in a warship so conventional confinement was not possible. A seamen in irons would have either one or both legs in shackles, completely immobilized, and be sitting or lying on the lower deck near the gunroom.

*Other*

These might involve any extra or unpleasant duties such as cleaning the heads, forfeiture of grog ration or, for an officer for example, extra watch-keeping duties.

Formal punishments awarded by the captain for less serious or first offences or by a court martial included loss of rating for a seaman or petty officer, flogging, running the gauntlet, loss of seniority for an officer, being dismissed from the service and hanging.

*Running the gauntlet*

This punishment was one of those reserved for theft. According to H. Baynham in *From the Lower Deck* (1969), it was not as straightforward as the title implies. The culprit was seated on a tub and then dragged around the deck with the crew taking cuts at him with three knotted rope yarns called a knittle:

> The cavalcade starts from the break of the quarterdeck, after the boatswain has given the prisoner a dozen lashes, and the ship's crew are ranged round the decks in two rows, so that the prisoner passes between them, and each man is provided with a three yarn knittle ... With this, each man must cut him, or be thought to be implicated in the theft.

The Admiralty abolished this punishment the year following Trafalgar. It was certainly open to abuse and does not appear to have been used anything like as frequently as flogging.

*Flogging*

According to the records, flogging was the most common punishment awarded by captains, for a wide variety of offences. The number of lashes given depended on the seriousness of the offence, whether it was a first offence and the whim of the captain. A man might get six for sleeping on duty but twelve for having wet clothes below deck. Drunkenness usually merited twelve on the first occasion or for quiet and private inebriation but could be more for a persistent drunkard. One man was awarded eighteen for filthiness, although one suspects either that his captain was something of a disciplinarian or that other lesser punishments had failed to have the desired effect. For flagrant disobedience twenty-four was not thought unfair. However, of the everyday common crimes on board ship, theft was always regarded as the most heinous (seamen had nowhere to lock up belongings), and thirty-six lashes was not considered excessive.

Midshipmen could be flogged, and a number were, including a young Jeffrey Raigersfeld who later rose to rear-admiral (see box on p. 186). The lash was in frequent use in other navies. The Spanish used it for virtually any comparatively minor offence, while something as serious as attempted desertion brought at least fifty strokes. For repeated attempts at 'running', the offender was likely to be sent for several years as a galley slave. This was a brutal and much feared sentence, a hangover from mediaeval times, which would break if not kill most men.

## Midshipmen Flogged

Although being sent to the masthead was the most common punishment for a midshipman, they were not exempt from being flogged, even when still boys of under nineteen. Rear-Admiral Jeffrey Raigersfeld records in *The Life of a Sea Officer* how as a midshipman on board the 44-gun frigate *Mediator* under Captain Cuthbert Collingwood (later Nelson's second in command at Trafalgar) he and his fellow midshipmen suffered this extremely painful punishment:

> midshipmen were ... always open to the caprice of their commanding officers, punishments awarded to them during their apprenticeship, such as mast-heading, disrating, being turned before the mast, being flogged, and in fact being turned out of the service, all of which are severe punishments ... are ultimately for advantage of the individual ... On board the *Mediator* ... while at anchor in St John's Road, Antigua, all the midshipmen were sent for into the Captain's cabin, and four of us were tied up one after the other to the breech of one of the guns, and flogged across our bare bottoms with a cat-o-nine-tails, by the boatswain ... some received six lashes, some seven, and myself three. No doubt we all deserved it, and were thankful that we were punished in the cabin instead of upon deck ...

An entry in the log of the 36-gun frigate *Trent* dated 23 August 1801 reads: 'Punished Geo. Duval, Midshipman, with 21 lashes.' The father of this sixteen-year-old boy wrote an anguished letter of complaint to the captain, Sir Edward Hamilton (a notoriously brutal but brave commander), claiming his boy had been cruelly treated by being 'flogged ... in a most Public and unmerciful Manner'. Not only that, but afterwards Captain Hamilton had young Duval unceremoniously put ashore in Jersey without friends or money.

The captain's response was as amusing as it was honest. He had caught the boy in the act of peeping through the captain's cabin window while the captain was 'going to embrace a lady', and he had had the boatswain administer the lashes 'in the usual way'. Still unhappy, Mr Duval senior wrote to the Admiralty. He need not have bothered. They pointed out that Captain Hamilton could have brought the boy before a court martial – although perhaps the captain would not have relished that idea – in which case the punishment would have been more severe. Their lordships, however, assured Mr Duval that the incident would not be held against his son in 'his future prospects in the Service'.

---

As far as we know, Roome was not flogged, but he would have witnessed a number of floggings being inflicted in his short stay in the Navy. The instrument used was the cat-o'-nine-tails, made and wielded by a brawny boatswain's mate. It was said, by a contemporary source, that twelve lashes from a Navy cat laid on with enthusiasm by a muscular mate was the equivalent of fifty from the Army cat administered by a young drummer. Certainly 500 or even 1,000 lashes were not unusual in the Army. A new cat was often made for each flogging. It consisted of a rope handle about two feet long, to which the nine tails of cord were attached. Once made it was put in a red baize bag until needed. At this stage readers may have guessed the origin of no fewer than three common expressions derived from this punishment: that 'a cat has nine lives', 'letting the cat out of the bag' and 'no room to swing a cat'. If the crime was theft, the mate put a knot in each tail (a 'thieves' cat') so that the wounds and pain would be more severe. It was said that you could always tell a thief because of the terrible scarring on his back – he had become 'a marked man'. Another witness claimed that after two dozen lashes a man's back 'looks inhuman; it resembles roasted meat burnt nearly black before a scorching fire'.

Usually a certain day of the week was set aside for flogging. The carpenter was ordered to 'rig the gratings', i.e. to secure two gratings, one upright to the break of the poop, the other flat on the quarterdeck. At six or seven bells in the forenoon watch (11.00 or 11.30 a.m.) the boatswain's mates piped 'All hands to witness pun-

### French Galley Slaves

Much of the hard labour and dirty work around major French ports was supposedly done by *forçats* – galley slaves or prisoners. They were accommodated in special prison hulks and were chained together in pairs, known charitably as 'companions'. The length of sentence of these unfortunates was instantly apparent from the colour of their caps. Lifers had green, long-term prisoners green with a red band, short timers all red. They were the responsibility of an organization called the *Service de Surveillance des Bagnes* (which, roughly translated, means Penal Guard Service), the officers of which were *argousins* (wardens) and the NCOs *gardes de chaines*. A chain gang of five pairs had one guard, who was usually careful not to antagonize his charges too much as they had a fearsome reputation of arranging 'accidents'. If real trouble occurred, as it did from time to time, troops were called out from the local garrison to encourage better behaviour and more work at the point of a bayonet.

ishment'. The men mustered aft on the weather deck, with most of the marines with loaded muskets and fixed bayonets paraded on the poop, looking down onto the quarterdeck. All the officers were present on the starboard side of the quarterdeck in formal dress wearing swords. Near the gratings stood the culprit escorted by the master-at-arms with his sword drawn, the boatswain and his mates. One of the mates held the red bag containing the cat. When all was ready the first lieutenant reported to the captain. At this point the captain usually addressed the crew, concluding with the order to strip. The seaman's shirt was removed. 'Seize him up' was the next order. The quartermasters spread-eagled him against the upright grating and tied his wrists to it and his feet to the one on which he stood. Then the captain read out the relevant Article of War that covered the offence, he and all officers removing their hats as he did so. His final order was 'Do your duty.'

The boatswain's mate would then take the cat from the bag and start the punishment. The master-at-arms (in some cases the sergeant of marines) counted the strokes out loud and timed each stroke with a quarter of a minute hourglass. If more than twelve strokes were involved, a second or third mate took his turn. Some captains made use (if they had one) of a left-handed mate so that the wounds would be crisscrossed. After each stroke it was customary for the mate to run his fingers through the thongs to prevent blood congealing on them. According to one witness, 'When a poor fellow is being punished, his agonising cries pierce your soul.'

The scene is awful! Hot boiling lead poured on a criminal's back would be but nothing in comparison to the suffering of those who come under the lash of the unrelenting boatswain's mates.' Pigot, probably the most brutal captain in the Navy's recorded history, ordered eighty-five separate floggings in thirty-eight weeks with a total of 1,392 lashes. There was much wisdom in the saying that after a flogging, 'a bad man was very little better; a good man very much worse'. It was certainly true in Pigot's case, as his crew murdered him in a bloody and gruesome manner.

Even a man such as Nelson, who inspired great loyalty, devotion and respect from his men and whose courage and professional ability were acknowledged to be of the highest order, was not particularly sparing in the use of the cat. In the eighteen months that he commanded the 28-gun frigate *Boreas* as a young captain, he had 54 of the 122 seamen flogged and 12 of the 20 marines – virtually half the entire crew. Just after the bombardment of Cadiz in July 1797, Earl St Vincent ordered the hanging of four mutineers on the day following their trial, a Sunday. The condemned men pleaded for a few days to prepare themselves for death and St Vincent's second-in-command, Vice-Admiral Thompson, spoke in favour of a slight delay. St Vincent would have none of it. The men, who had confessed they had plotted a mutiny for six months and had conspirators on other ships, were hanged on the Sabbath. Nelson approved, commenting, 'Had it been Christmas Day, instead of Sunday, I would have executed them.' St Vincent demanded the Admiralty remove Thompson from his command.

Captain Hardy, Nelson's longstanding friend and his flag captain at Trafalgar, was far fonder of the lash than many captains. During the first three weeks of October 1805 he had twenty-three men flogged for drunkenness, every one receiving thirty-six lashes – a total of 828. These were all seamen except for three cook's mates and, surprisingly, a boatswain's mate called John

McCormick, who would have been more used to inflicting punishment than receiving it! No fewer than ten of these men received their punishment on 19 October, two days before the battle. In contrast, Collingwood, Nelson's second-in-command at the battle, hated awarding a flogging. During one period of five months he only had a dozen men bare their backs and then usually only to receive minimum sentences such as seven lashes. He gave nine for stealing half a guinea where other captains would probably have awarded at least four times as many.

*Flogging through the fleet*
This was the ultimate flogging punishment in terms of disgrace, number of lashes inflicted and the spectacle it provided *pour encourager les autres*. Only a court martial whose sentence had been confirmed by the Admiralty could award this punishment, usually given in place of execution. It entailed 200 to 600 lashes, awarded in turn by each ship-of-the-line in the harbour. A flogging round the fleet was designed to impress those who saw it and deter future offenders. It was an occasion never to be forgotten, not just by the unfortunate recipient but by every man who watched. The procedure was as follows.

The prisoner would be held on the flagship under the control of the naval provost marshal. The admiral instructed the flagship captain, 'You are hereby required and directed to hoist a yellow flag at the foretopmasthead of His Majesty's ship under your command, and fire a gun at nine o'clock tomorrow morning [the dreaded "one gun salute"], as a signal for the boats of the fleet to assemble alongside of His Majesty's ship ——, to attend said punishment.' The captains of the other ships-of-the-line in harbour were ordered, 'When the signal for punishment is made tomorrow morning, you are to send a lieutenant with a boat manned and armed from the ship under your command to His Majesty's ship ——, in order to

## Boys' Punishments

There were three categories of beatings, of increasing severity, which could be given to boys. They were on-the-spot caning, summary flogging and a flogging awarded by a court martial. Whenever a boy was beaten or flogged, it was on his bare bottom rather than across the back and shoulders, as endured by men.

*Caning*
All boys under nineteen could be caned instantly for any minor offence by any officer or the boatswain; the punishment was not recorded in the ship's log. As with a flogging, the boy was made to 'kiss the gunner's daughter'. He was tied over a gun, his body stretched lengthways along the barrel, his wrists tied together underneath so that he was embracing the barrel, while his stomach rested on a folded mattress or hammock. Six cuts could be administered to his hands, although this was rarely done as it could prevent him climbing the rigging.

*Summary flogging*
For more serious or repeated offences a boy could be flogged with a reduced cat (with only five tails rather than nine and no knots), sometimes called a 'boy's cat' or a 'pussy cat'. As with caning, the lash was applied to the bare buttocks. The punishment was carried out on the weather deck in front of the assembled boys but supposedly cleared of seamen, although this was seldom enforced, and there are reports of seamen climbing the rigging to watch. As

it was a flogging rather than a caning, the boy was permitted to bite on a piece of hide or wrapped cloth and be given a drink of water after every dozen strokes. The punishment had to be recorded in the log.

*Court-martial flogging*
This rare punishment involved a flogging with a cat-o'-nine-tails. The offence committed had to be very serious, such as that of seventeen-year-old Valentine Woods, who in 1813 was awarded 60 lashes for stabbing a crewmate. In another case that caused something of a stir, in 1822, Marine Private William Osborne was accused of having sex with a fourteen-year-old boy, William Webber, on board their sloop *Shamrock*. The evidence records that Osborne seduced Webber in an empty cabin, where they were found 'in a very indecent and unclean attitude'. However, the capital offence of sodomy could not be proved. The sentences were for 'the said William Osborne to receive fifty lashes on his bare back with a CatO'nine Tails and the said William Webber to receive thirty six Lashes in the usual Way of punishing boys, on board ... and both to be mulcted of all wages due and to be dismissed the service'. The *Shamrock*'s log entry reads: 'Thursday 14 November 1822: 9.30 a.m. Punished Wm Osborne (Marine) with fifty lashes in pursuance of the Sentence of the Court Martial on the 11th inst. Also Wm Webber (Boy) with thirty-six lashes on his posteriors, after which they were both discharged from the Service.'

attend the punishment.' The captain of the prisoner's ship was also instructed to send his surgeon with the lieutenant. It was this lieutenant's task to see that the requisite number of lashes was given, while the surgeon was to intervene to stop or postpone the punishment if the man appeared close to death.

On the day the signal gun was fired, the yellow flag was hoisted and the ship's boats pulled away to converge on the flagship, whose own boat had been prepared with a grating rigged up in the form of a tripod. At the appropriate moment a detachment of red-coated marines with muskets climbed down into the boat. A drummer followed them with his drum muffled by a piece of black cloth. The lieutenant and surgeon from the offender's own ship had gone aboard the flagship and, accompanied by the provost marshal and a boatswain's mate from the flagship carrying the cat in its red bag, they now escorted the prisoner down into the boat, where he was tied to the grating. The flagship's captain shouted to the provost marshal to read out the sentence before giving the order for the punishment to start.

After the first set of lashes the boat, with the marine drummer in the bow thumping out the solemn, slow beat of the 'Rogue's March', would begin the pull to the next ship, while the other boats followed in line astern. At the next ship, which could be as much as a thirty-minute row away, the crew would be lining the sides or hanging in the rigging to get a good view of what was happening. When the flagship's boat came alongside, it was secured and the provost marshal again read out the sentence. The captain sent down one of his mates to lay on his ship's share of the sentence. Then the provost marshal moved off towards the third ship and so on until all ships had been visited or the punishment was halted for the day. Given the high number of lashes, the time taken to row round the fleet and the deteriorating condition of the prisoner, the sentence would probably not be completed in one day. For example, it is recorded that a seaman sentenced to 600 lashes received 200 at a time, once a fortnight, representing several weeks of agony and awful anticipation.

Flogging was undoubtedly a cruel punishment, but it was a cruel age and naval punishments were by no means more drastic than those awarded in civilian life, where a man could be hung for stealing a sheep. The seamen generally felt that it was a necessary evil. As Captain Francis Liardet wrote, 'The best conducted seamen in the Navy will now candidly tell you that in ships where the cat is not used on proper occasions, that they are the most uncomfortable vessels to sail in, as the willing and hard-working men do the work of the lazy ones.' Captain Chamier added, 'I have known a man faint before he was seized up; but, although I have seen four hundred lashes applied, and at each dozen a fresh boatswain's mate, yet I never knew a man who died of the punishment in my life.'

## Admiral John Byng (1704–57)

During the Seven Years War, in 1756, Byng was ordered to take a squadron to secure the island of Minorca, a British possession under attack by the French. He tried to establish communications with the garrison, but before he could land his troops a French squadron of about equal size appeared. Byng mishandled the approach to battle and the French got away with little damage. After four days Byng sailed for Gibraltar, leaving the island to be captured by the French. There was a public outcry, and Byng was brought home and court-martialled. He was found not guilty of cowardice or disaffection, but condemned for not doing his utmost against the enemy in battle or pursuit. The sentence was death – mandatory under the Articles of War. Although the court recommended mercy the government, anxious to find a scapegoat for its own mismanagement, insisted on the ultimate penalty and Byng was shot on the quarterdeck of his own flagship, HMS *Monarch*. The French writer Voltaire, who sought to have Byng's sentence commuted, commented afterwards, 'In this country [England] it is as well to put an admiral to death now and then, to encourage the others (*pour encourager les autres*)', coining a phrase that is still in use today.

### Hanging

This was the method of execution used for any seaman convicted by a court martial and sentenced to death. Officers so convicted were shot – the most famous senior officer to suffer this fate being Admiral John Byng in 1757 (see box). The Articles of War stipulated that death was mandatory for any officer or seaman convicted of cowardice, murder, arson of a ship or magazine, or sodomy. Officers would also be executed for failure to pursue an enemy through cowardice or deserting to the enemy with a ship. Another ten offences, including mutiny, desertion, disobedience in battle and striking a superior officer, carried the death sentence in certain circumstances. But in fact death sentences were actually carried out comparatively rarely, particularly in comparison to civilian life. One reason for this was the difficulty in assembling courts martial and another the general leniency of naval justice; even when the death sentence was pronounced on an offender he was often pardoned before it was carried out. Figures from the earlier period of the Seven Years' War are illuminating. Of 254 men convicted of desertion, only a fifth were sentenced to hang and only thirteen were actually executed, almost all for desertion aggravated by murder, assisting the enemy or repeated offences. Certainly there were no executions in Nelson's fleet during the period of Roome's service from May 1803 to Trafalgar.

If possible, a hanging took place on the offender's own ship. As with a flogging round the fleet, it was carried out in harbour and a gun was fired to summon a boat with an officer and full crew from every warship to witness the event. The condemned man stood on the cathead with a bag over his head. The rope was passed through a block attached to the fore yardarm and the noose was placed round his neck. When the boatswain was given the nod, 'hoist away' was piped and a group of seamen from all ships on station hauled the squirming and kicking body into the air. If his executioners were feeling sympathetic, they might jerk him up quickly and suddenly enough to break his neck. One such occasion has been described by a witness thus: 'the executioners ran with all speed towards the poop; and the unfortunate culprit, hurried aloft with the rapidity of thought, died in an instant … it seemed to me the most humane execution I had ever witnessed'. Otherwise the victim was in for a slow, gurgling death by strangulation. It was not unknown for a condemned man, given the chance, to leap into the sea at the last moment to drown himself.

Desertion, or 'running' as the Navy called it, was one of the more common crimes. This is understandable in view of the comparatively high percentage of men who were on board unwillingly and the fact that after a long commissioning most of the crew were not allowed ashore, instead being 'turned over' immediately to serve on another ship. Rough statistics have shown that the peak time for desertion was during the first six months of service, with up to 18 per cent of offences by the crew occurring in the first month. Although desertion potentially carried the death sentence, executions were rare. Article 16 stated deserters 'shall suffer death, or such other punishment as the circumstances of the offense shall deserve'. Courts made maximum use of this let-out clause – understandably considering the acute shortage of manpower.

Perhaps most surprising of all was the fact that a seaman could, and many did, take part in a mutiny without suffering death. It was the ringleaders, those found guilty of 'mak[ing] or endeavour[ing] to make any mutinous assembly upon any pretence whatsoever ... shall suffer death', who invariably paid the ultimate price. If you merely took a passive part and did not offer violence to anybody, then your chances of being hung from the yardarm were slight. But mutiny during the Napoleonic Wars was widespread. Brian Lavery in his book *Nelson's Navy* estimates that there were over a thousand during the period 1793–1815, there being twelve courts martial for this offence in 1805. The 'Great Mutinies' of the Nore and Spithead in 1797 are the best known. However, the aftermath of the mutiny on the 74-gun *Marlborough* later the same year gives us a revealing insight into just how ruthlessly an execution could be enforced, in this case by Earl St Vincent (formerly Admiral Jervis), a ferocious disciplinarian. Nelson once said of him, 'Where I would take a penknife, Lord St Vincent takes a hatchet.'

Some of the crew of the *Marlborough* had mutinied to prevent the execution of one of their number, sentenced for an earlier violent mutiny while the ship had been at Beerhaven. The officers had crushed these mutinies with great difficulty. When the *Marlborough* joined Lord St Vincent's fleet off Cadiz, a court martial was immediately assembled. When the first man was sentenced to death (a ringleader who had wanted to seize the ship and sail her to Ireland), Lord St Vincent ordered that he be hanged the next morning by the men of the *Marlborough*; contrary to normal practice, no other ship's crews were to have a hand on the rope. The *Marlborough*'s captain, Ellison, was convinced his crew would refuse to carry out the execution and went aboard Lord St Vincent's flagship, the 110-gun *Ville de Paris*, to tell him so.

The admiral was not impressed. 'What do you mean to tell me, Captain Ellison, that you cannot command His Majesty's ship the *Marlborough*? For if that is the case, sir, I will immediately send on board an officer who can.' Ellison tried again, stressing that he was fearful his men would refuse and that it would be better if crews from other ships participated.

Lord St Vincent would have none of it. 'That man shall be hanged, at eight o'clock tomorrow morning, and by his own ship's company: for not a hand from any other ship in the fleet shall touch the rope. You will now return on board, sir; and lest you should not prove able to command your ship, an officer will be at hand to you who can.' A worried Ellison returned to his ship to have all the gunports closed and the guns rolled back and secured.

That evening Captain Campbell of the 74-gun *Blenheim* received written instructions from the admiral that he was to command all the fleet's launches the next morning to ensure the execution was carried out. Each launch was to be commanded by a lieutenant and armed with carronades and twelve rounds of ammunition, with a gunner's mate and four quarter gunners in addition to the crew. Campbell was told that if there were any signs of mutiny on the *Marlborough*, an attempt to open her ports or any resistance to the hanging, he was to close to within touching distance of the ship's sides and order all his launches to open fire, continuing until all resistance ceased. If absolutely necessary, Campbell was to sink the *Marlborough*. It was a situation unique in British naval history.

By 7.30 a.m. next day all hands throughout the fleet had been mustered to witness punishment while Campbell had assembled his flotilla of launches within a pistol shot (20 yards) of the *Marlborough*. He gave the order to load the carronades. All eyes were on the heavily armed boat carrying the provost marshal and the condemned man as it left the side of the flagship. The crisis point had arrived – would the *Marlborough*'s crew hang their shipmate? The final drama is best described in J. S. Tucker's *Memoirs of Earl St Vincent*, published in 1844:

> The ship [*Marlborough*] being in the centre between the two lines of the fleet, the boat was soon alongside, and the man was speedily placed on the cathead and haltered. A few awful minutes of universal silence followed, which was at last broken by the watch-bells of the fleet striking eight o'clock. Instantly the flagship's gun fired, and at the sound the man was lifted well off; but then, visibly to all, he dropped back again; and the sensation throughout the fleet was intense. For at this dreadful moment, when the eyes of every man in every ship were straining upon this execution, as the decisive struggle between authority and mutiny, as if it were destined that the whole fleet should see the hesitating unwillingness of the *Marlborough*'s crew to hang their rebel, and the efficacy of the means taken to enforce discipline, by an accident on board the ship the men at the yard-rope unintentionally let it slip [or perhaps deliberately, to break his neck quickly], and the turn of the balance seemed calamitously lost; but then they hauled him up to the yard-arm with a run ... Lord St Vincent remarked 'Discipline is preserved, sir!'

## Benefits of service

*Pay*

The men's pay was credited and debited while at sea but no payment was made until the crew was turned over at the end of a commission, which meant pay was always months, if not years, in arrears. Even then the seamen seldom saw cash. Payment was often made with 'tickets' that could only be cashed at the port from which the ship had been commissioned. Wives or parents who had been sent tickets had to travel to that port to collect their money. Many men, at the wrong port and desperate for cash, sold their tickets at up to half their face value to 'dockside dealers' to get hold of actual coins. Debts acquired during the voyage (mostly for items from the purser's store) were deducted from pay or bounty due, and it was not unknown for debts to be larger than the man's credit. Regulations stated that payments due were to be made by the ship a seaman was leaving before he was mustered on his new ship, although sometimes this was not possible, which caused something of an administrative headache and outraged complaints from those concerned.

*Prize money*

This was probably the greatest inducement for naval service, even for seamen who got a miserly share. The object was to capture an enemy warship or merchantman, which would later be sold and the value divided between the ship's complement. The majority of the proceeds were earmarked for the admiral of the fleet and the ship's commissioned and warrant officers, but an eighth was kept to be divided between the midshipmen and petty officers, and a further quarter between the remaining crew and marines.

Following the capture of the French frigate *Beta* by the British fifth rate *Alpha* in 1801, the *Beta* was valued at a total of £16,000, of which the *Alpha*'s captain received £4,000, the junior warrant and petty officers £77 each and the remaining crew and marines £17 each. The difference between the highest and lowest amounts received is staggering. The captain's prize money was over twenty times his annual salary whereas that of a landsman barely equalled a year's pay. However, the lowest-rated seamen would do proportionally much better with 'head money'. This was paid out following the capture of a warship, at a rate of £5 for every member of the enemy crew at the start of the action. This would have given a substantial boost to a landsman's prize money but meant nothing to the captain.

After Trafalgar, Parliament voted a special grant (in addition to prize money for captured ships) of £300,000, to be shared among all who served in the fleet that day. For details see p. 539. Captain Hardy's prize money was £973 and a Government Grant of £2,389-7-6, totalling £3,362-7-6 (more than nine years' pay). At the other end of the hierarchy, all seamen from boy 3rd class to captain of the forecastle received £1-17-6 and £4-12-6, totalling £6-10-0 (less than four months' pay). Put another way, the captain of the flagship got over 500 times as much as an able seaman.

For a longer discussion of prize money, see p. 137.

*Promotion*

There was a reasonable prospect of promotion for any seaman who was ambitious and willing to work. A few pressed men and landsmen made good, but it was mostly volunteers who possessed the necessary drive. Most seamen with ambition would initially be looking no higher than boatswain's mate, a rate of considerable importance, prestige and authority, especially as it involved carrying the 'starter' and wielding the cat. It was a position that could be attained at a relatively young age. Of the four boatswain's mates on the *Victory* at Trafalgar three were in their twenties, the youngest being twenty-four.

*Shore leave and women*

Although shore leave was permitted, many captains were fearful of granting it, especially for pressed men. The risk of them doing a 'runner' was considerable, particularly when a ship came into a home port. The Admiralty, faced with endless demands for manpower, did everything it could to retain experienced men. In wartime it was not uncommon for the crew of a returning ship to be 'turned over', that is transferred immediately to another ship, or ships, that were about to start their commission. This was, understandably, desperately unpopular. After many months at sea, the last thing a seaman wanted was to be forced to sail again more or less at once on a different ship. It was a major grievance.

Petty officers could lose their rating if there was no appropriate vacancy, friends would be split up and morale damaged. In these circumstances all in authority realized that the temptation to disappear, not only among pressed men and lower rates but also for more senior men, could be almost irresistible. Our friend Roome is a good example, as he went into hiding in 1806 and so missed another nine years of war service. Prolonged shore leave in England, therefore, was the exception rather than the rule. So, if the men of a ship in port were not allowed to join the ladies, the ladies were invited to join them.

Providing ladies of pleasure for ships in a large port such as Portsmouth or Plymouth was a well-organized business. The crew had (they hoped) been paid and a fleet of fifteen to twenty ships in port meant a market of thousands of thirsty and licentious seamen, representing a lot of money. The prostitutes were taken to the ships in bumboats. The boatmen charged each woman about a shilling to take them out, but they only paid if they got chosen by the seamen, who were leering and cheering over the side as the bumboats closed in. This meant the boatmen tended to be fussy about who they took. On the ship the master-at-arms and his corporals were supposed to keep order and prevent liquor being smuggled on board. They were largely unsuccessful – short of lifting a lot of skirts, there was no way to check. Admiralty regulations only allowed wives of the crew to come on board. To get round this the seamen claimed their 'guests' were their wives – hence the saying that sailors have a wife in every port! Another expression associated with this entertainment is telling somebody to 'show a leg' when reminding them it is time to get up. The seamen's 'wives' could remain on board overnight and were allowed to sleep in the hammocks for longer than the men. When in port it was the custom of the boatswain's mates to roust out the crew with yells of 'show a leg'. If the limb was hairy, the seaman was tipped out or cut down, if smooth then it was left alone. Allowing 'wives' on board was a long-established custom. When the 74-gun *Magnanime* docked in 1756, nobody was allowed ashore on leave but wives were permitted to visit. Out of a crew of 750, 492 produced 'wives', who 'all declared themselves married women, and were acknowledged by the sailors as their wives. Where or when they were married was never enquired, the simple declaration was considered sufficient to constitute a nautical and temporary union'.

Nevertheless, some women (apart from genuine passengers) went to sea. The Admiralty turned a blind eye. It was not uncommon for the captain, perhaps the first lieutenant and the senior standing warrant officers (boatswain, gunner and carpenter) to have their wives on board, and sometimes a few other petty officers managed it as well. Seldom mentioned in accounts of life aboard ship, these women were never borne on the ship's books and made their own arrangements with the purser for victualling. They were therefore shadowy figures, usually accommodated in the cockpit on the after part of the orlop deck – which supposedly got its name because the noise of the wives squabbling and shrieking was reminiscent of the fights in a cockpit ashore. Earl St Vincent complained that women on a ship used too much water with their washing. They were normally given certain duties such as washing, sewing, attending the sick berth and helping the surgeon with the wounded in battle or perhaps passing up cartridges. When the 44-gun *Horatio* struck a rock in 1815 and all hands were called to the pumps, five women

## Landsman John Roome, 'R'

Roome deserted the *Victory* at Chatham in 1806. He disappeared into his old London haunts and nothing was heard of him again for forty years. By 1846 the man who had hoisted Nelson's famous signal was a down and out, selling watercress and red herrings in Blackfriars, London. One winter afternoon a doctor, the son of Dr Forbes Chevers, who had been the surgeon on the 80-gun *Tonnant* at Trafalgar, stopped to talk to him and discovered that the old man had served with Nelson at the battle, and even hoisted the famous signal 'England expects that every man will do his duty.' Intrigued, but somewhat sceptical, Chevers made more enquiries and eventually called Roome into his house in Upper Stamford Street to test his story with some questioning. He satisfied himself that Roome was genuine and determined to try to improve his lot. He brought the situation to the notice of Captain Pasco, who had been the signals officer on *Victory* at Trafalgar and was now actually commanding the ship, then laid up in reserve at Portsmouth but serving as the flagship of the Port Admiral.

It was Pasco's efforts on behalf of 'his old shipmate' that persuaded the Admiralty to agree that Roome had been 'whitewashed' of his offence by the Naval Deserters' Amnesty Act of 1813 and that he be admitted to Greenwich Hospital as an in-pensioner. Roome was an old rascal who made the most of his thirteen years at Greenwich, doing well out of the tips he received from visiting naval officers and their friends. He became actively disliked by his fellow pensioners, not just for his cantankerous behaviour, but also because he spoiled one of their lucrative little sidelines. For many years country visitors to the Hospital had been asking to be introduced to the man who had hoisted Nelson's signal. The response had always been to point out a man known by the pensioners as a 'Greenwich Canary'. This was any pensioner who instead of the normal blue coat was walking around in the 'punishment dress' of a yellow coat with red sleeves, worn by pensioners who had been drunk the previous Sunday. The delighted visitors were usually very generous with their shillings – which the 'canary' was obliged to share with his co-conspirators later. To get round the problem of several canaries wandering around the hospital grounds, the story was put about that pensioners in such dress were all Trafalgar veterans.

Roome's arrival put a stop to all this, making his presence anything but popular. He died in the Hospital aged seventy-eight in December 1860, the same month as the launch of *HMS Warrior*, the world's first ocean-going iron-hulled battleship. Like *Victory*, it is today a popular tourist attraction at Portsmouth.

appeared to help. In 1800 the old store ship the 54-gun *Tromp* was due to sail to the West Indies and the gunner, William Richardson, was persuaded against his better judgement to take his wife. What convinced him was 'the captain's, the master's and boatswain's were going with them; the serjeant of marines and six other men's wives had leave to go; a person would have thought they were all insane, wishing to go to such a sickly country'. He was right to be pessimistic. Yellow fever accounted for virtually the entire wardroom, most midshipmen, the assistant surgeon, the master and his pregnant wife, the marine officer, boatswain, master-at-arms, armourer, gunner's mate, captain's steward, cook, tailor and captain's wife's maid. Richardson's wife caught the fever but survived.

Occasionally women got caught up in a battle. John Nicol, who served in the powder magazine of the 74-gun *Goliath*, the leading British ship at the Nile, was kept informed of what was happening above by asking the boys and women who carried the cartridges:

> Any information we got was from the boys and the women who carried the powder. The women behaved as well as the men ... I was much indebted to the Gunner's wife who gave her husband and me a drink of wine every now and then ... some of the women were wounded and one woman belonging to Leith died of her wounds.

She was buried on Aboukir Island.

## More Ladies of the Sea

The book *Old Times Afloat* by Colonel C. Field RMLI, published in 1932, contains some fascinating snippets of information on women who, dressed as men, served as seamen or, in one case, tried but failed to do so:

> 1782. Died at Poplar, Mrs Coles, who during the last war [American War of Independence] served on board several men-of-war as a sailor. After her discharge, upon a small fortune devolving to her, she resumed the female character, and was from that time considered as a very polite and elegant woman. *The Annual Register*

> 30th March. On Wednesday last, a young girl, about sixteen years of age, in boy's attire, went on board the *Valiant*, in Cawsand Bay, to offer herself as a servant, and requested to see the Commanding Officer. On being introduced to the officers in the wardroom, she unfortunately dropped a courtesy instead of making a bow, which, causing a general laugh, so discomposed her that she was nearly fainting; but on being encouraged and assisted by the officers, she soon recovered herself; and informed them her desire to be a sailor. On learning her abode, a messenger was sent to her brother, who immediately came with her clothes, thanked the officers for their polite treatment, and returned with her the same evening to Millbrook. *The Edinburgh Annual Register*

> 1807. In the public prints of this year it was stated that an old woman named Tom Bowling was brought before the magistrates charged with some trivial offence. She told the magistrate that she had served as a boatswain's mate on board a man-of-war for upwards of twenty years [she must have wielded the cat a good few times], and had a pension from the Chatham Chest. She always dressed as a man. *The Mariner's Mirror 1913*

Inevitably, children were sometimes born on board. It was not always certain who the father was so it was common to record a male child whose father could not be identified as 'a son of a gun' – yet another expression derived from the old sailing Navy. It was rare, but not unknown, for a child to be born during a battle. A woman supposedly gave birth on 74-gun *Tremendous* during the battle of the Glorious First of June in 1794, to a boy named Daniel Tremendous McKenzie. Many years later he had the nerve to apply for the Naval General Service Medal, which was refused. There is no record of a birth in the master's log and the surgeon's log has been destroyed, but the muster book for that time shows a Daniel McKenzie aged twenty-seven and rated AB whose medal claim was allowed, presumably the baby's father. There is no record of the number of women present at Trafalgar, although some certainly were. Jane Townsend of the 74-gun *Defiance* applied (unsuccessfully) for a medal, backed up by 'strong and highly satisfactory certificates of her useful services during the combat'. There is no reference to any women on the *Victory* at the battle, but that does not rule out the possibility.

*Pensions, gratuities and 'widow's men'*
Officers 'on the beach' between commissions or retired lived on half pay, which was effectively their pension. A widow of an officer killed in the service received a full year's pay, orphans a third of that. If the officer was not married, then a widowed mother over fifty could claim. Admiralty regulations also specified pensions for warrant officers in circumstances where they were in some way physically or mentally incapacitated. The regulations stated:

ARTICLE I

WARRANT Officers serving in the Navy, who by age and long service shall be worn out, or rendered incapable of discharging their duty, shall be superannuated [retired], and maintained during the rest of their lives, under the following regulations:

II

Gunners, Boatswains, Carpenters, Pursers and Cooks, (whose employments are constant) must have served full fifteen years before they shall be entitled to apply for superannuation; and shall then, if their claims are admitted, receive an annual pension equal to their pay in the Ship of the highest rate they have served in.

The above was subject to a medical examination by a senior physician 'in conjunction with the Master, Wardens and assistants of the Royal College of Surgeons in London', who were required to 'inspect into, and make judgement of, the state of his body and mind, and of his unfitness to serve His Majesty'. It sounds a fairly rigorous procedure.

This meant that Walter Burke, for example, the *Victory's* purser at Trafalgar, who at sixty-seven would probably have been able to convince the medical board that he was at least 'worn out', would have received a pension of £4-16-0 a month. Similar payments were made to any petty officer or seaman who was 'hurt, maimed or disabled' during his service. A certificate 'expressing the nature of the hurt', signed by the captain, senior lieutenant, master and surgeon, was a requirement of qualification for this benefit. The money for these payouts came from the Chatham Chest ('for the relief of hurt and wounded seamen in His Majesty's Service'), a fund to which all seamen contributed, or rather had contributions deducted from their pay. The reality was that, apart from the commissioned officers on half pay, everybody else had to be injured, 'hurt' or 'worn out' to qualify for any payment after leaving the Service.

Only a small proportion of petty officers or seamen could expect to be given a place at Greenwich Hospital. Here deserving but destitute men who had a good record of service could be accommodated, fed and looked after into their old age as in-pensioners. Out-pensioners were much more numerous but only received a small pension from the Hospital. Today's reader will be familiar with the Army's red-coated pensioners who reside in the Chelsea Hospital; the Greenwich Hospital performed the same role for old sailors at the time.

Then there were 'widows' men'. Every captain was required 'to enter on the Books of the Ship or Vessel he commands, as part of her complement, one or two (as the Clerk of the Cheque shall inform him that circumstances require) fictitious names in every hundred Men of her complement, which are to be borne as able seamen, under the appellation of Widows' Men'. Not only their pay but also the value of their rations was to be kept for 'the relief of poor widows of Commission and Warrant Officers of the Royal Navy'. As these non-existent men were all given names and entered in the muster books as able seamen, it is not possible to say with certainty how many widows' men were carried by the British fleet at Trafalgar. However, assuming one per hundred, an approximation would be 200. An able seaman's pay rate plus the value of victuals multiplied by 200 would put at least £500 per month or £6,000 a year into this fund. Multiply this by ten or twelve times to include all ships of the Navy from fourth rate upwards and a very considerable sum is reached – solely for the benefit of officers' and warrant officers' widows.

*The Lloyd's Patriotic Fund*
This fund was established to reward personnel of the Army or Navy who performed gallant deeds. The money was raised by contributions from commerce and appeals to the patriotic public, to be disbursed after consideration by the Fund Committee. It presented special rewards of decorated swords or vases to officers and money to all those wounded in the Service and to the widows of those killed. For Trafalgar the Committee agreed the following scales:

| Rate | dangerously wounded | slightly wounded |
|---|---|---|
| Lieuts and capts RM, masters | £100 | £50 |
| Pursers, gunners, surgeons, etc. | £50 | £30 |
| Midshipmen, clerks, gunners mates, etc. | £40 | £25 |
| Seamen and marines | £20 | £10 |

Admirals got vases and captains swords. Special gratuities were given to men of any rank whose wounds permanently disabled them, seamen and marines receiving £40. Those dangerously wounded from the *Victory's* crew included Lieutenant Pasco (who received £100) and Second Lieutenant Reeves RM (£50); Midshipman Rivers (£80), Ordinary Seaman Burgin (£40) and Private Wells RM (£40) were all disabled. Slightly wounded men included Lieutenant Peake RM (£30), Boatswain Willmet (£30), Midshipman Bulkeley (£25) and Able Seaman Gibson (£10).

# THE ROYAL MARINES

Since 1802 the marines had become the Royal Marines (RM) and thus entitled to 'royal' blue facings (cuffs, collars and lapels) to replace the white ones on their uniforms. This had long been the custom for any royal regiment in the Army. As the author and RM historian Colonel Field has written, the marines were Britain's 'sea soldiers'. They date their formation back to 1664 with the raising of the Duke of York and Albany's Maritime Regiment of Foot. However, it was not until 1755, on the eve of the outbreak of the Seven Years' War, that the marines became a permanent corps under the Admiralty, as distinct from Horse Guards. Although they had extensive barracks ashore, a Royal Marine could expect to serve the great majority of his time at sea. Every warship with twelve guns or more had a marine detachment on board, and the more guns she carried, the more marines she was permitted – very approximately, one marine per gun.

Although a part of the Navy, the marines retained Army ranks. Starting with the lowest, the ranks were boy marines (allowed from 1804), privates (divided into those with under seven years' service, from seven to fourteen and over fourteen), drummers (always senior to privates), corporals and sergeants. The marines were some years behind the Army in having colour-sergeants, but there are a number of references to the senior sergeant in a large detachment being nominated as the sergeant-major. In 1796 the orders for the marines on the 74-gun Blenheim stated that 'The sergeant who is appointed sergeant-major of the detachment … is to be answerable for the appearance of all guards.' Seemingly at Trafalgar it was still an unofficial appointment, as the rank does not appear in the marine pay scales. Sergeants and corporals were distinguishable by having white shoulder knots on their right shoulders. Sergeants were armed with halberds while corporals carried muskets. Officers started as second lieutenants, rising to first lieutenant, captain, major, lieutenant-colonel and colonel. Normally only officers up to captain served at sea.

Marines were basically seagoing infantrymen. They wore smart red jackets, had pipe-clayed white belts, white trousers, black shoes and black 'round hats' (top hats with brims) and carried muskets and bayonets. Paraded on deck, their disciplined ranks made a colourful contrast to the somewhat drab, work-worn clothes of their seamen comrades. Marines were in no way seamen. Regulations stated they were 'not to be obliged to go aloft', although some did so voluntarily and a few became seamen, which gave them higher pay. The rise was worth having, as

marines were (boys excepted) the worst-paid men on board a warship. A marine with under seven years' service received £0-19-3 a month; in the Navy even the lowest of the low, a pressed landsman, got £1-2-6. If a marine was still a private after fourteen years his pay rose by the minuscule sum of £0-4-1 a month.

Ninety-three RM officers and 2,610 of other ranks fought at Trafalgar. This total of 2,703 represents some 14 per cent of the overall complement of the British fleet at the battle and is close to the total number of guns in the fleet, estimated at 2,780. As with seamen, most ships were down on their marine manpower entitlement. A careful examination of the muster rolls shows that numbers varied considerably, even among ships of the same rating. For example, on the 74s Belleisle and Bellerophon there were 128 marines of all ranks on the former but only 72 on the latter – a difference of 56. Nevertheless, the sixteen 74s at Trafalgar carried 1,447 marines, including officers, giving an average of 90 (a typical 74, the Colossus, carried 92 guns, including carronades).

As with soldiers and seamen, the number of marines fluctuated considerably between war and peace. The overall strength in 1797 was 22,700, in 1802 it was 30,000; the following year (after the Peace of Amiens) it fell to 12,000, only to shoot up again after much scraping of the barrel in 1804/05 to 31,000. Just under 9 per cent of the Royal Marines were in the fleet at Trafalgar (in comparison, about 16 per cent of the Royal Navy's membership was present). Marines were recruited much like soldiers, by recruiting parties travelling around with much drumming and drinking to the inns, taverns and market squares of many towns. The country was divided into five large recruiting districts, posters were stuck up, bounties were offered (up to £26 by 1801), while recruiting sergeants extolled the virtues of travel, adventure, pay and prize money (apart from the prize money, not a lot has changed!). Despite enthusiastic sergeants and much liquid inducement, there were never enough marines in times of major conflict, partly because they could not be pressed into service. The solution was to draft in infantry regiments to supplement numbers. As we saw in Section Three, it was a soldier, not a marine, who smashed a hole in the stern window of the San Nicolas at St Vincent so that Captain Nelson could clamber through. At some time or other at least twelve British Army regiments served as marines. Because of this some, like the author's old regiment the 16th Foot (Bedfordshire and Hertfordshire), were allowed to play 'Rule Britannia' as a regi-

## Royal Marine Shore Organization

By Trafalgar the Royal Marines as a corps numbered some 31,000 all ranks. Ashore the corps was divided into four 'divisions' numbered 1 to 4 but more often known by the name of their headquarters and barracks: Chatham (which supplied the marines on Victory), Portsmouth, Plymouth and Woolwich. Each division was commanded by a commandant with the rank of either major-general or colonel. Initially each division had, like Army regiments, two elite companies designated as the Grenadier and Light Companies, but these were abolished in 1804. There were extensive barracks at each divisional location – the one for Portsmouth was at Southsea and now houses the splendid Royal Marine Museum. Divisions consisted of a large number of companies – in 1805 Chatham had 47, Portsmouth 48, Plymouth 48 and Woolwich 30. At this time the official establishment for a company was one captain, two first lieutenants, two second lieutenants, eight sergeants, eight corporals, five drummers and 130 privates, giving 156 all ranks. These companies were administrative and training sub-units. Marine detachments on board ships bore no relation to the companies, as officers, NCOs and men were sent where needed in the numbers required.

mental tune. However, no soldiers fought at Trafalgar in the British Fleet, whereas the Combined Fleet relied entirely on soldiers to carry out marine duties.

On board the *Victory* the marines were accommodated on the middle gundeck. The detachment was divided into watches like seamen and came on duty with their watch. Their duties can be conveniently divided into those performed when out of action and those when at quarters during a battle.

## Duties out of action

### Guard duties

On a large warship up to thirty marines would be employed on guard duty. That does not mean that thirty men were actually standing guard throughout one watch, but that thirty were required to man the various positions, allowing for each post being relieved after two hours. A marine on guard would wear full uniform with loaded musket and fixed bayonet. They were doing what the Army would describe as sentry duty, mostly at semi-static posts. It was the custom for marines on duty with fixed bayonets on the weather deck to unfix them when topmen went aloft and to fix them again when they came down, so that if a man fell from the rigging he would not land on an upturned bayonet! Guard duty must have been a soul-destroying way of spending so much time, though life could become a little more interesting if a drunken seaman tried to barge his way into a storeroom or if the sentry could hear what was going on in the captain's cabin. The captain would lay down exactly where he wanted marine guards in his Order Book; they would certainly be stationed outside the captain's cabin, the powder magazines, the spirit room, the bread room and the boatswain's, carpenter's, purser's, captain's and lieutenant's stores, and on the hatchways leading to the magazines. A typical standing order enjoined the sentries 'to walk brisk on their posts [it could only have been a pace or two in many places], backwards and forwards, never to sit down, read or sing, smoke, eat or drink, but be continually alert and attentive to the execution of their orders, nor ever to quit their arms on any pretence whatsoever'.

What were they guarding against? The obvious answer is theft and unauthorized entrance. They had also to keep a sharp eye out for fire hazards, particularly in the vicinity of the magazines. In extreme circumstances they were to prevent or suppress mutiny. Marines were not encouraged to mix with seamen. They slung their hammocks separately, and at punishments they were usually drawn up on the poop overlooking the proceedings, able to fire down if the seamen became mutinous. In other words, they formed a barrier – physically if necessary – between the ship's officers and warrant officers and the seamen. In this capacity they were not always successful. The marines did not prevent the famous mutinies at the Nore and Spithead in 1797, indeed some of them even joined in. In the same year marines failed to stop murder and mutiny on the *Hermione* – the rush of vengeful

---

## The Royal Marine Artillery

In 1805 the Royal Marine Artillery was only a year old. Prior to this the specialized task of manning the mortars in the Navy's bomb vessels (used to bombard shore establishments, harbours and towns) had been given to the Royal Artillery. As with infantry soldiers deployed on ships, there had been an undercurrent of carping and arguing as to how far naval authority extended over soldiers, which came to a head when artillerymen in bomb vessels off Havre de Grace 'refused to do any other duty other than simply that of attending mortars in time of action, and keeping them prepared for service'. A exasperated Admiralty formed the Royal Marine Artillery and put it firmly under Navy control. An artillery company was formed for each of the four Royal Marine Divisions, composed of one captain, three first lieutenants, five second lieutenants, eight sergeants, five corporals, eight bombardiers (lance-corporals), three drummers and 62 gunners. This gave a very high ratio of officers (1:8) and NCOs (1:3) to gunners, which reflected the technical nature of firing the mortars.

---

seamen yelling for blood easily knocked down the marine guard on Captain Pigot's door.

When in port Captain Duff's (*Mars*) orders stated:

They are always in port to mount guard with their Uniforms cleaned dressed and properly accoutred. Two Centinels [sic] to be posted on the Poop, one on each Gangway, and one on each side of the Forecastle; they are to be regularly relieved every two hours, and after the Watch the Centinels are to give the Word 'All's Well' every quarter of an hour beginning with the one on the Starboard side of the Poop, repeating it forward and round again on the Larboard side. The Centinels are to challenge all boats coming to, or passing near the Ship in the night, and are not to permit any to come on board, or any person to go or enter or go from the Ship after sunset and before sunrise, without leave first obtained from the Officer of the Watch.

It was also quite common for some marines to be employed as sentries within naval dockyards. Sometimes they would be used as semi-skilled labour, fitting out ships under supervision until the crew arrived. Additionally it was commonplace to see the red-coated marines in the rough and tumble of press-gang work or perhaps two men and a corporal sent ashore to collect and escort a deserter back to the ship.

### General duties

Marine muscle was used to supplement that of the seamen in various unskilled chores around the ship. If more men were needed at the pumps or straining on the capstan bars to bring in an anchor or shifting ballast and casks in the hold, then marines were available. They could not be ordered into the rigging but they were not exempt from hard physical work in addition to the time spent cleaning their muskets, equipment, uniforms or whitening their belts. Like their soldier comrades ashore, 'bull' took up much of their time.

### Training

Those marines on watch but not on guard would be required to spend some part of the day on drill and musketry on the weather deck. Additionally, marines had to learn the drills with the great guns on the gundecks. Again, the Order Book of the *Mars* makes this clear: 'The Seamen and Marines are to be exercised at the Great Guns and Small Arms [which included grenades] as much as possible. To this end the Commanding Officer on board is to direct a convenient proportion in rotation to be exercised during one hour at least every day.' At dusk it was customary for the marines (certainly on the *Belleisle*) to unload their muskets by discharging them into the air. They were then carefully reloaded so that should they be needed during the night there would be no misfires.

## Private David Newton RM (c.1780–1878)

A Mrs K. Rogers supplied the following information, published in the *Journal of the Nelson Society* in January 2000.

David Newton who died aged 98 was almost certainly the oldest survivor of the Corps who fought at Trafalgar. He was serving on the recently built 74-gun *Revenge* under Captain Robert Moorsom whose first shots were simultaneous broadsides from both starboard and larboard batteries, the former into the Spanish 74-gun *San Ildefonso*, the latter into the French 74, *Achille*. When Newton died the *North Devon Journal* ran the following obituary:

'A Trafalgar Veteran David Newton of Cholesbury, who died a few days ago, at the residence of his son James Newton of Cholesbury (near Tring, Herts), was engaged as a marine at the Battle of Trafalgar and was wounded in that action [he was one of nine wounded]. He enlisted when 18 years of age but left the service about 60 years ago. He was in his 99th year and for the last three years had been in receipt of a pension of 10s 6d per week.'

There is a memorial stone in Cholesbury, Buckinghamshire which states:

David Newton. In his youth a Royal Marine who
Fought in the ship Revenge at the Battle of Trafalgar.
In his old age a faithful soldier and servant of Jesus Christ.
He departed this life July 31st 1878 in his 99th year.
Exchanging an earthly pension for a crown of glory
That fadeth not.

## Duties at quarters

### General deployment

When the marine drummers (there were two on all ships with over 64 guns) 'beat to quarters' (usually to the tune of 'Hearts of Oak'), the entire ship's company including all marines raced to their action stations. This was not the same as clearing the ship for action, which always preceded the 'beat to quarters' and is explained in Section Five. A man at quarters was in his battle position ready to fight. Marines had two main functions in action: to fight on the poop, quarterdeck and forecastle as infantrymen and to form part of a gun crew as marine artillerymen. The proportion of a marine detachment assigned to each role varied with the rate of the ship (and therefore the size of the detachment), the type of action envisaged, the orders of the admiral and, to a lesser extent in a fleet action, the captain. In a small sixth-rate frigate of 28 guns with a maximum of 34 marines including one officer the priority was usually musketry, leaving the guns to be crewed entirely by seamen. An example was the *Enterprise* in action in 1776. She had 24 men, including the officer, on the quarterdeck and 10 on the forecastle.

At Trafalgar, however, the marines were deployed differently. Nelson was no great believer in putting marksmen in the tops to fire down onto enemy decks at close range. The swinging masts made for bad aiming, firing could not be controlled, they got in the way of the topmen, they were lost for the rest of the battle and if the mast came down (as many did), so would a number of marines. They were, he considered, better employed down on deck. It was rare to have a line-of-battle ship with a full crew, gun crews were seldom up to strength and it was never possible to man all guns on both sides of a gundeck simultaneously. Fourteen men were needed for a full crew on a single 32-pounder on the lower deck, a battle led to casualties and the primary function of a battleship in action was to keep her guns firing. It is no surprise, therefore, to find the bulk of the marines among the gun crews. The evidence is that about two-thirds of a marine detachment would be employed with the great guns – probably with more on the lower deck with the heaviest guns that needed the largest crews – and one-third on the top decks as musketeers. On the *Victory* at Trafalgar that meant around thirty-five to forty fought as infantrymen and the remainder as gunners.

### Fighting on the top decks

These marines were divided into groups (platoons) to fight from the poop, forecastle and, to a lesser extent, the quarterdeck. The marine captain would normally be close to the ship's captain on the quarterdeck, with a subordinate marine officer on the poop and another on the forecastle. Assuming some 40 marines were under Captain Charles Adair as musketeers on the *Victory*, it is likely that around 20 were aft and the balance forward. Their primary task at Trafalgar was to sweep the decks of any enemy ship that came close alongside and their secondary one to help repel boarders. These duties they performed with controlled firing in groups under their officers or NCOs.

Marines' musket-firing tactics differed markedly from those employed by soldiers. Instead of standing upright in a steady line, the marines were expected to take cover while reloading and occupy alternative firing positions. This involved 'springing sideways with Life and Spirit', halting of their own accord at the point directed, 'so that … a Detachment will occupy any Part of the Deck in a Moment, without being troubled by tedious Movements [formal drill]'.

A marine officer needed to understand something of seamanship so that he could anticipate where his men would be most needed to bring effective fire onto the enemy decks. The ship's sides were used to give protection, with marines ducking down to reload. Perhaps the most difficult technique to master was the need to synchronize firing with the roll of the ship. They learnt 'never to give Fire but when the Ship is rising with the Wave: If you fire when she pitches, you hit nothing but Salt-Water'. Allowances had also to be made for the constant need to change positions, so that one moment firing might be into the wind, the next to leeward. A ship heeling over in the wind gave a clear view to leeward but exposed the deck, so it was safer to fire to windward. The problem then was that the roll exaggerated the height of the bulwark and thus obstructed the firer. Different drills were employed to counter some of these difficulties. Two ranks were formed to fire to leeward and three to windward. The two ranks kept as close in behind the bulwark as possible and endeavoured to fire rolling volleys starting from either flank. When in three ranks, one whole rank fired at a time while the other two reloaded. This was the theory, but in battle things tended to get a bit ragged.

## Royal Marines at Trafalgar and Casualties Suffered

The actual numbers of Royal Marines present on each ship at the battle taken from the muster rolls are as shown below, together with the casualties.

| Ship | Officers | | | Other Ranks | | |
|---|---|---|---|---|---|---|
| | *Present* | *Killed* | *Wounded* | *Present* | *Killed* | *Wounded* |
| *Victory* | 4 | 1 | 2 | 142 | 18 | 9 |
| *Téméraire* | 4 | 2 | 1 | 126 | 8 | 12 |
| *Neptune* | 3 | – | – | 113 | – | 3 |
| *Leviathan* | 3 | – | – | 80 | 2 | 4 |
| *Britannia* | 4 | – | – | 74 | 1 | 7 |
| *Spartiate* | 3 | – | – | 77 | – | 1 |
| *Minotaur* | 3 | – | – | 72 | – | 3 |
| *Ajax* | 3 | – | – | 109 | – | – |
| *Agamemnon* | 3 | – | – | 67 | – | – |
| *Conqueror* | 4 | – | 1 | 79 | – | – |
| *Belleisle* | 3 | – | 1 | 125 | 8 | 19 |
| *Mars* | 3 | – | 1 | 75 | 8 | 16 |
| *Royal Sovereign* | 4 | 1 | 1 | 125 | 13 | 16 |
| *Africa* | 2 | – | 1 | 76 | 6 | 7 |
| *Orion* | 3 | – | – | 88 | – | 4 |
| *Achille* | 3 | – | 2 | 76 | 6 | 14 |
| *Colossus* | 3 | – | 1 | 78 | 8 | 31 |
| *Tonnant* | 3 | – | – | 85 | 9 | 16 |
| *Bellerophon* | 4 | – | 1 | 68 | 4 | 20 |
| *Dreadnought* | 4 | – | – | 96 | 1 | 4 |
| *Polyphemus* | 3 | – | – | 61 | – | – |
| *Revenge* | 3 | – | 1 | 105 | 8 | 9 |
| *Swiftsure* | 3 | – | – | 77 | 2 | 1 |
| *Defiance* | 3 | – | – | 75 | 6 | 9 |
| *Thunderer* | 3 | – | – | 108 | 2 | 1 |
| *Defence* | 3 | – | – | 106 | 3 | 6 |
| *Prince* | 3 | – | – | 107 | – | – |
| *Phoebe* | 1 | – | – | 30 | – | – |
| *Euryalus* | 2 | – | – | 36 | – | – |
| *Naiad* | 2 | – | – | 37 | – | – |
| *Sirius* | 2 | – | – | 37 | – | – |
| **Totals** | **94** | **4** | **13** | **2,610** | **113** | **212** |

2,704 RMs were present at Trafalgar, of whom 117 were killed and 225 wounded, a total of 342 casualties (12.6 per cent).

From these casualties it is easy to identify those ships of both British columns that were heavily engaged at close range for a considerable time. In Nelson's column only the *Victory* and *Téméraire* had high marine casualties – the former 30 (20 per cent) the latter 23 (17.5 per cent). Collingwood's column suffered much worse. The most devastating losses occurred on the *Colossus*, where 40 out of 81 (50 per cent) of all ranks were down. The *Bellerophon* was next with 25 (35 per cent), then the *Mars,* also with 25 (32 per cent), *Tonnant* 26 (29 per cent), *Royal Sovereign* 31 (24 per cent) and *Belleisle* 28 (22 per cent).

Of the 93 Royal Marine officers at Trafalgar 17 (18 per cent) were killed or wounded compared with 325 (12 per cent) other ranks.

A third method used by well-trained marines was what was termed 'Marine Firing'. This allowed individuals to fire when they had a target, then duck down to kneel for reloading. The object was to sweep the enemy decks with continuous blasts of musketry. It was not easy to achieve in the smoke and confusion, with bursting eardrums and on heaving decks encumbered with bodies, tangled ropes and rigging all amongst leaping guns and sweating crews. Even against small targets, marines were trained to fire whenever possible as a body, however small. Enemy gunports were such a target. Instructions stated: 'A platoon of the best Marksmen should be picked out, and ordered to take Aim, and fire at the Port-Holes: Two or Three expert Men killed at a Gun may silence it for half an Hour.' There is no better example of this than the action between the 36-gun British frigate *Phoenix* and the French 40-gun *Le Didon* some two months before Trafalgar. *Le Didon* ran on board (rammed) the starboard quarter of the *Phoenix*. With the ships locked together only the French were able to bring a gun to bear, and that was a brass 32-pounder on *Le Didon*'s forecastle. However, as fast as the Frenchmen tried to fire it, the marines, firing in volleys, knocked them down.

### Boarding

Marines were more often used to repel boarders than as boarders themselves. Not only were marines far less agile than seamen when it came to clambering up ropes or balancing along fallen yards or masts, they were also not best armed for boarding. Muskets were cumbersome weapons, especially with bayonets fixed, often impossible to wield effectively in a confused, confined close-quarter mêlée on a cluttered enemy deck. Seamen with cutlasses, tomahawks and pistols were far more effective. If a British ship was to launch a boarding party, the best role for marines was to clear the way with effective musketry. After an initial assault, marines were more useful in reinforcing success, helping secure the enemy ship and guarding prisoners.

The situation was different with regard to repelling enemy boarders. The marines could use their fire to great effect, inflicting heavy losses as they gathered to attack on the enemy deck or in the rigging. At Trafalgar the British 74-gun *Revenge* had three officers and 105 marines on board. At one stage a Spanish three-decker ran her bowsprit over her poop, the Spaniard's fore rigging and forecastle crowded with sailors and soldiers ready to board. However, 'they caught a Tartar, for their design was discovered and our Marines with their small arms, and the carronades on the poop, loaded with canister shot, swept them off so fast that they were glad to sheer off'. A rush with fixed bayonets was also helpful in seeing off boarders who managed to scramble on board.

### With the 'great guns'

Royal Marines helped serve the guns at Trafalgar. Up to two-thirds of the detachments on each ship-of-the-line joined with the seamen as gun crew members. The majority helped serve the 32-pounders on the lower decks. This is borne out by the quarter bills for the 74-gun *Goliath* (not at Trafalgar), which clearly show up to three marines in the crews on the lower gundeck. Unlike most of the seamen gun crew, the marines had no other duties and would remain with the guns until after the action, whereas a seaman might be called away to man the pumps, fight a fire or join a boarding party.

### Landing parties

Marines formed an essential part of any landing party, going ashore in the ship's boats to carry out an attack or raid. If a large assault was envisaged, all the marine detachments from the fleet or squadron involved could combine for the operation.

# UNIFORMS OF THE BRITISH NAVY AND COMBINED FLEET

## ROYAL NAVY

### ◄ Rear-Admiral (Earl of Northesk)

Northesk wears the undress uniform prescribed for flag officers in 1795. The regulations contained no details of cut or measurement, so officers could still retain an amount of individuality. Rank was distinguished by gold lace on the cuffs and epaulettes, which had been unofficially worn for some years. The Royal Navy had adopted them because foreign troops often failed to recognize British naval personnel as officers; they were already widely used by Britain's land forces.

### ➤ Post captain

This captain has removed his epaulettes prior to battle. Two plain gold epaulettes would have indicated that he was a captain of 'three years' post', while a more junior captain would have worn a single epaulette on the right shoulder only. Although not specified in the 1795 regulations the undress coat is shown with stand-and-fall collar as in many contemporary illustrations. The captain has a bicorn hat worn 'fore-and-aft' as was usual for officers below flag rank, and he has adopted black Hessian boots in place of shoes and stockings.

### ▲ Vice-Admiral (Lord Nelson)

Lord Nelson's undress coat bears four embroidered stars: the Order of the Bath (top), the Sicilian Order of St Ferdinand and Merit (centre right), the Ottoman Order of the Crescent bestowed by the Sultan of Turkey after the victory at the Nile (centre left), and the German equestrian Order of St Ferdinand and St Joachim of Leiningen (bottom). Nelson wears a plain hat with a green eye shield that could be folded up or down to protect his damaged eye. At Trafalgar Nelson was unarmed. He had two swords on the *Victory*; it is said that one was a dress sword of 1795 pattern and the other a fighting sword of the new 1805 pattern with shortened blade, possibly purchased from his cutler on his last visit to London. It is likely that prior to action the swords were put out ready for use, but that he forgot to put either on, and they remained lying on his cabin table throughout the battle.

# ROYAL NAVY

### ◄ Midshipman

Midshipmen were at the first stage of the officers' promotion ladder; contrary to popular impression, they were more likely to be in their 20s or even 30s than they were to be young boys. The 1787 regulations confirmed the dress that had been in use for some time before this date, and this illustration shows the grey breeches worn for everyday use. The dirk is usually associated with midshipmen, but was also carried by officers, and in this instance is suspended from a black leather shoulder belt, although by this period a sword belt worn around the waist was more common.

### ► Lieutenant

Regulations specified white breeches and stockings for undress uniform, but this junior officer has opted for the more fashionable blue pantaloons and black Hessian boots. Prior to the battle Vice-Admiral Collingwood noticed one of his lieutenants wearing boots, and advised him to put on silk stockings: 'if one should get a shot in the leg, they would be so much more manageable for the surgeon'. In 1804, the new commissioned rank of sub-lieutenant was introduced, and these officers wore the undress uniform of lieutenants for all occasions.

### ▲ Surgeon

This illustration is based upon Dr Beatty as shown in Arthur Devis' painting 'The Death of Nelson', and shows the prescribed uniform of May 1805 issued to surgeons. In this painting the chain embroidery lace on the collar of his dress coat is set so as to reveal the blue lining between the two rows, and buff breeches worn with Hessian boots have replaced the regulation white breeches. There were two grades of medical officer, those of physician and surgeon, and prior to these regulations both grades had been dressed as warrant officers. According to the new regulations the surgeon's uniform was similar to that of the physician but had a plain collar. If he was surgeon of a hospital he was entitled to have two embroidered buttonholes on the collar, of intertwined gold braid, whilst those serving on board ships were allowed only one. For undress, the coat had a falling collar, no lace and three buttons on the cuffs and pockets. The design of the gilt buttons was a plain anchor within an oval, with the letters 'H.S.' for hospital staff serving ashore. Assistant surgeons and hospital mates were given a single uniform for use on all occasions of plain blue without lapels, with white waistcoats and white or blue breeches. Dispensers wore the same uniform but with lapels.

## ROYAL NAVY

### ➤ Boatswain

Although ranked as a warrant officer, the
boatswain was not of 'wardroom rank' and
therefore he did not share the officers'
quarters, nor the warrant officers'
uniform, which was not extended to
lower-ranking personnel until
1807. Instead he wears a
distinctive blue coat and tails
with buttoned back lapels. The
low top hat, with a cockade on one side,
could, as in this case, be decorated with the
ship's crest. His unofficial badge of office
was the 'boatswain's call' or whistle by
which he sent orders around the ship,
often worn on a chain or cord around the
neck. Under his arm he also carries a
cane, the end of which was waxed and
tipped with a twine thread.

### ▲ Purser

The purser, a warrant officer appointed by the Victualling Office, was
financially responsible for the clothing and victuals on his ship.
Pursers were usually educated men of some personal wealth, and
though poorly paid, they were unofficially permitted
to make a profit from their financial
dealings. In this illustration the purser is
in the sick bay administering rum, the
only form of anaesthetic available to
the wounded. His uniform is that
accorded to warrant officers in the Dress
Regulations of November 1787.

### ➤ Master

The senior warrant officer
was the master, who was
responsible for all matters of
navigation and the instruction of
junior officers in that art. This
figure illustrates the uniform of
the warrant officer, regulated in
1787 and worn until 1807. The
blue coat had a falling collar
without ornamentation; the
lapels were blue and fastened by
brass buttons bearing a fouled
anchor design as worn by
captains. There were three
buttons on the cuff and also on
the back pockets. The coat was
lined in white but not edged,
and worn with a white
waistcoat and
breeches. The
cocked hat was
presumably plain, as
it is not mentioned
in the regulations.

### ➤ Seaman

This seaman is depicted as a
'topman', who was required to work
the three masts above the lower
yards. During this period seamen had
no prescribed uniform, but there were distinct nautical
styles favoured among particular ship's crews. Clothing could be purchased ashore or
more commonly via the 'slops' system operated by the ship's purser. This comprised
ready-made garments or bolts of cloth cut and sewn by tailors within the crew in
exchange for 'grog', and inadvertently produced considerable uniformity in clothing
amongst crews. Checked shirts were very popular, as were large handkerchiefs worn
around the neck. Straw hats covered with lacquer or tarred in northern climates were also
common, as were round hats, which occasionally had the ship's name adorning the front.

# ROYAL NAVY

### ◄ Boatswain's mate

One of the most feared men in the crew, the boatswain's mate was a petty officer promoted from within the ranks by the ship's captain and responsible for enforcing discipline. In this illustration he carries a 'starter' or 'rope's end' with which to 'persuade' the men to work harder. Boatswain's mates wore no uniform, but the additional pay they received enabled them to afford neater clothes than the seaman.

### ➤ Seaman

Select members of the crew could wear a standardized form of dress, paid for out of the captain's pocket. This seaman belongs to the captain's gig or barge. Since there was no standard uniform for seamen, only the captain's imagination and budget served as limits to his choice of dress. The waistcoat worn in this illustration is of the popular type of the period, scarlet kerseymere cut very low and very long. There are recorded instances of some captains dressing these crews in scarlet frocks, white hats and black handkerchiefs; or white and blue 'Guernseys', with white jackets and smallclothes. Even more extreme examples include the harlequin dress of the gig crew of *HMS Harlequin*, and kilts and Scottish bonnets with worsted thistles on their jackets.

### ▲ Master's mate

This member of the second tier of warrant officers wears the specified uniform of blue coat with white edging, no lapels, blue falling collar, blue round cuffs with three buttons, and three buttons on each pocket. These buttons were of the same pattern as warrant officers. The coat was lined in white with white waistcoat and breeches, although here more practical pantaloons have replaced the breeches.

# ROYAL NAVY

### ➤ Gunner's mate

The gunner's mate was stationed in the powder room during action. He had no distinctive uniform, and is illustrated wearing felt slippers to avoid sparks from static electricity whilst working. In the background a lantern glows behind a heavy glass window to provide light without risk of fire.

### ▲ Ship's cook

This figure is based on a watercolour by Thomas Rowlandson. There was no prescribed uniform for the ship's cook, but the traditional voluminous breeches worn with stockings survived at least until the late 1790s, by which time trousers had become increasingly common. The Commissioners of the Navy appointed these warrant officers from the Greenwich Pensioners, or from ex-petty officers who had lost limbs on service. Their only duty was to soak the salt meat to remove the salt, and then to boil it before serving it out to the different messes.

### ➤ Ship's carpenter

Each ship had a carpenter who was a warrant officer, assisted by one or two mates and a number of semi-skilled assistants. The carpenter had to have served his indentures with a shipwright and to have served at sea as a carpenter's mate, before taking an examination at Shipwright's Hall before a quorum of master shipwrights. This figure wears a typical working dress with an apron to protect his clothing and a 'thrum cap', which was a headdress made of 'thrums', fabric off-cuts woven to give a shaggy appearance.

# ROYAL NAVY

## ◀ Seaman

Foreigners made up a considerable proportion of the Navy, and this Jamaican seaman wears trousers cut well above the ankle, with legs that allowed them to be rolled up; plain, light colours and stripes were especially popular. The flexible rammer had a length of cable instead of a shaft, which meant that the gun did not have to be run so far inboard, and the gunner did not have to lean out of the gunport.

## ◀ Ship's boy

Ship's boys were usually aged between 12 and 16, and invariably came from poor backgrounds or had been recommended by magistrates after conviction for petty crimes or vagrancy. The number of boys employed on board ship was limited by Admiralty regulations, from 16 on a large frigate to 32 on a first rate. Intended to act as officer's servants whilst learning seamanship, they were invariably put to seaman's duties immediately.

## ➤ Gun captain

Prior to going into action gun captains were issued with powder tubes or quills, for insertion in the touch-holes, and the flinted gunlocks with which to fire the guns. This sailor has improved the appearance of his jacket by edging it with white tape. He carries a black leather pouch across his shoulder containing the quills, and a powder horn with which to prime his gun.

## ▲ Seaman

This seaman belongs to the after-guard, which was composed of poor seamen and landsmen. Their duties were to work the after braces, the spanker, mainsail and lower staysails. At quarters they were stationed on the gundeck (as here), or as sail-trimmers or small-arms men. Most men in the gun crews would be stripped to the waist with a handkerchief tied tightly round their ears to deaden the noise of the cannon.

# ROYAL NAVY

### ◀ Captain, Royal Marines

Contemporary sources show marine officers wearing cocked hats with gold loops and tassels and white over red feathers, but the distinctive 'round hat' was also worn on active service. Although the stand-and-fall collar was more common in undress, this illustration shows the unlaced coat worn on active service, with ten buttons on each lapel, one at each end of the collar, and four on each cuff and pocket flap. These gilt buttons, placed in pairs, bore raised anchors in sprays of laurel with 'ROYAL MARINES' above. The coat also had two buttons on each back skirt at waist level, with an additional button set in the pleats. The skirts were hooked back revealing the white lining, each turnback being ornamented with an embroidered badge in the shape of a heart. Lapels were buttoned over on active service, but otherwise worn with the upper buttons unfastened, revealing the blue facing colour. Marine officers carried infantry-pattern swords with a gold and crimson sword knot, carried on a white shoulder belt with a gilt plate bearing the royal crest.

### ▼ Private, Royal Marines

Marines are shown in various sources as assisting the gun crews; this private wears typical shipboard undress clothing.

### ▼ Private, Royal Marines

The Marine other ranks' jacket was single breasted and decorated with buttonhole loops. Privates wore white pipe-clayed bayonet and cartridge-pouch belts crosswise over the shoulders. Attached to the bayonet belt was a rectangular brass plate with the crown and anchor and a scroll inscribed 'ROYAL MARINES', with laurel sprays below. The cartridge pouch flap was decorated with a brass eight-pointed star plate bearing the motto 'PER MARE PER TERRAM' on the circlet and the royal cipher in the centre.

### ► Drummer, Royal Marines

Based on a painting by Bernard Drummond in the National Maritime Museum, this figure illustrates the blue shoulder 'wings', and the cuffs and sleeves with V-shaped lace pattern as worn by some infantry drummers of the period. There are some later references to white lace, but it is likely that marine drummers wore the ordinary regimental pattern (white with red and blue stripes), like most infantry drummers.

## FRENCH NAVY

### ◄ Vice-Admiral (Villeneuve)

Villeneuve wears an undress version of the new uniform ordered for general officers and admirals in September 1803, in this case the same as that of a *général de division*, except for the buttons, which had an anchor design. The undress coat was the same as that of the full-dress version except in the width of embroidery used. The waistcoat was plain white cloth with gilt brass buttons. Villeneuve was described on his surrender as wearing green corduroy pantaloons and sharp-toed half boots, in place of the regulation white breeches. Sky-blue lines woven into the gold sash showed that the wearer was a vice-admiral. The optional epaulettes consisted of gold twisted fringes lined with blue cloth, with three silver stars on each.

### ▲ Rear-Admiral (Magon)

This figure of Magon shows one of the undress versions of uniform assigned to admirals, in this case the corresponding army rank of a *général de brigade*, with a single row of oak-leaf embroidery indicative of rank confined to the collar and cuffs. The double-breasted frock coat of national blue cloth had a stand-and-fall collar, and gauntlet cuffs. Two stars are worn on the epaulettes, which were of the same pattern as the vice-admiral's, above left.

### ➤ Commodore (Cosmao-Kerjulien)

As a commodore (*chef de division*) Cosmao-Kerjulien ranked between captain and admiral. He wears the common campaign uniform with simplified embroidery on the collar and cuffs only. Epaulettes were worn with this coat.

# FRENCH NAVY

### ◄ Captain, ship-of-the-line

This captain wears his full-dress coat as decreed in May 1804. It consisted of a single-breasted dark-blue coat and lining, with scarlet collar and cuffs and two fringed gold epaulettes. The nine buttonholes down its front were embroidered with gold lace with an anchor design, as were the pockets and cuffs, the collar and the hips and skirt slits on the tails. The undress coat was dark-blue cloth, with stand-up collar, cuffs and lining of the same. The cuff openings underneath were fastened, as was the sleeve, by two small buttons; the pockets were in the tails. This coat was decorated like the full-dress coat with two gold-laced buttonholes on the collar and three laced buttonholes on each cuff. The waistcoat was of white cloth. Dark-blue breeches were worn but could be replaced during summer months with white. The belt buckle was gilt and engraved with a relief design of a 'trophee of arms' crossed with an anchor. The sabre waist belt had two pockets on the inside for pistols. Black boots with turndowns were worn when on duty on board ship.

### ➤ Lieutenant, aide to vice-admiral

Naval officers attached to a staff function wore plumes on their hats and a coloured brassard. This was edged and fringed in gold, and worn on the left upper arm. The brassard was white for an admiral's aide or adjutant, scarlet for a vice admiral's and blue for a rear admiral's. A good deal of latitude was tolerated in the dress of aides; this officer wears the dress coat of a lieutenant, and white pantaloons instead of breaches, and is armed with a gilt-hilted sabre.

### ◄ Lieutenant

The 1804 full-dress coat was single breasted, of dark-blue cloth and lining, with scarlet collar and cuffs. Lace was restricted to the collar in the form of two gold embroidered anchors. The 1804 regulation undress coat of lieutenants was specified as all dark blue, with the same embroidery as the full-dress coat. The officer in this illustration wears a non-regulation round hat and pantaloons, both popular with many naval officers. His rank is further distinguished by his two narrow-fringed epaulettes.

# FRENCH NAVY

## ◄ Surgeon, 2nd Class

There were three different branches of medical officer in the French navy: doctors, surgeons and pharmacists, each with their own uniforms as decreed in 1804. The coat was medium blue, without lapels and lined medium blue. The collar and cuffs were of black velvet for doctors, scarlet for surgeons and dark green for pharmacists. The waistcoat for doctors was medium blue, but of the distinguishing collar and cuff colour for the other branches. Within each branch there were three classes, identified by a complicated lacing system. This officer's full-dress coat would have had two gold-laced buttonholes on the collar, three on the cuffs and three on the pocket flaps, whereas the undress coat as shown here has two buttonholes on the collar only.

## ◄ Gunnery master

From May 1804 all petty officers were issued a dark-blue *paletot* (tail-less jacket). The black glazed hat was common to all French sailors and was decorated at the side with a rosette of the national colours, held by a strap of gold lace and a brass button. The front of the hat was often decorated with an anchor design. Quartermasters had two yellow chevrons above the cuff, and other non-commissioned officers were identifiable by the colour of their collars and of the laced chevrons on their sleeves; gunnery masters wore red ones.

## ◄ Ensign

The ensign's order of dress was the same as that of lieutenants, the only distinguishing feature between the ranks being the use of a single counter epaulette worn on the right shoulder and a fringed epaulette on the left. The prescribed uniforms for junior officers were not necessarily adhered to and there are references to full-dress uniforms with dark-blue cuffs instead of scarlet, of turnbacks being added to the tails and pantaloons being worn instead of breeches. On board ship all officers wore a gilt-hilted sabre, with gold sword knot, with a black scabbard trimmed with gilt furnishings carried on a black waist-belt trimmed with more or less gold according to rank. This young officer has substituted a dirk instead of his cumbersome sabre, despite the practice being forbidden. He is using a speaking trumpet, made from copper with a silver mouthpiece.

# FRENCH NAVY

### ◄ Officer, Marine Artillery

In May 1803 the seven demi-brigades of marine artillery were abolished and reconstituted into four regiments. On 9 November 1804 they were granted the title *Corps Imperial de l'Artillerie de la Marine*. This officer wears basically the same uniform as that issued to the other ranks, but of a finer quality and cut. The buttons are of gilt, and he would have worn a gorget as a sign of his rank. The boots with yellow-buff turndown were the preferred choice of footwear for most officers.

### ➤ French seaman

In 1804 French sailors of all ranks wore a dark-blue jacket with turned-down collar and lapels, with two rows of brass buttons down its front, the cuffs having three buttons, trousers with horn buttons and a red waistcoat. The sailor illustrated is stripped to the waist for action and wears a tricolour on his cap to identify his nationality. French sailors often wore their hair long in a queue tied with a black bow.

### ▼ Chef de Bataillon, 67th (Line) Regiment

This figure depicts Chef de Bataillon Jacquemet of the 67th Regiment, who was wounded whilst saving the Colours of his regiment. The undress uniform illustrated is of the type often worn by infantry officers whilst on active service, consisting of a single-breasted blue *surtout* without lapels; it frequently featured a red collar with red piping on the cuffs.

### ➤ Private, Marine Artillery

From 1803 marine artillerymen were ordered to wear a dark-blue coat with dark-blue cuffs, lapels, scarlet piped turnbacks and brass buttons; the red collar was piped with white and red cuff flaps. Regulations specified a dark-blue waistcoat and breeches and black gaiters but this illustration shows no gaiters and a non-regulation white waistcoat, as depicted in some contemporary illustrations.

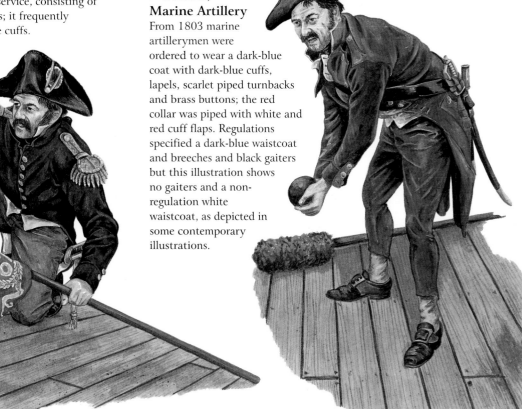

# FRENCH NAVY

◄ **French seaman**
Unlike the British Royal Navy, the French had abandoned a separate marine infantry corps in January 1794, and French sailors took over their duties. This seaman has retained his dark-blue *paletot* from the July 1803 regulations with scarlet collar and cuff flaps. The hat is also non-regulation, of a pattern widely in use during the 1790s. This seaman is in a 'top' and about to light a grenade with his slow match. Note the haversack with grenades on his left leg.

▲ **Grenadier, 1st Swiss Regiment**
In 1803 the four Swiss demi-brigades had regained the traditional red coats worn by Swiss troops in French service. In March 1805 they were amalgamated into the 1st Swiss Regiment, but it is unlikely that they would have received the new uniforms assigned to the new 1st Regiment, so this illustration depicts a grenadier in the uniform of the 1st Demi-brigade, with coat and collar of garance, white lapels and cuffs, and blue trim. The brigade had spent a lot of time on the Atlantic coast, where several of its companies came to be pressed into service as marines on board *Algéciras* and *Achille*. They first sailed to the Caribbean, where 100 men were added to the garrison of Guadeloupe, then returned to Europe to participate in the Battle of Trafalgar.

◄ **Chasseur, Chasseurs d'Orient**
The chasseur illustrated here wears the original shako authorized in October 1801, with the popular drooping side-plume. These shakos are sometimes depicted with both plume and cockade fixed to the front, which gave regiments some degree of individuality because the peak was detachable and could be affixed wherever desired. The coatee was dark blue, with scarlet collar and cuff flaps. Piping was white, with turn-back badges of a white or red hunting horn. Buttons were of white metal. Blue shoulder straps piped white should have been worn, but these were often replaced by green epaulettes with or without red 'crescents'. The blue waistcoat was often substituted for white during summer, and loose trousers were frequently worn on campaign instead of blue breeches.

# SPANISH NAVY

### ◄ Admiral (Gravina)

The dress of Spanish naval officers followed that of army general officers in colouring, but their undress had lace on the cuffs and lapels but not on the collar, which was plain red. Admirals had three embroidered bands of gold on each cuff. The scarlet waistcoat was edged with gold embroidery, and the scarlet sash with three rows of gold embroidery; the breeches were also scarlet and the bicorn laced gold. It was usual to wear a buff waistcoat and breeches in undress. Gravina's straight-bladed sword has a hilt of solid gilded brass with a square grip, with fluting down the front and back of the oval pommel, but the knuckle bow and quillion are plain. His scabbard is made of black fishskin with gilt mountings. This small sword was introduced into the Spanish navy in 1717 and is based on the swords used by the Spanish guard regiment. This had a silver hilt, and in order to make the distinction the naval sword was ordered to be of gilt brass. Contemporary illustrations of Gravina show an embroidered red silk cross on the chest, the insignia of the Order of Calatrava.

### ▲ Brigadier (Galiano)

The rank of brigadier, equivalent to commodore, was peculiar to the Spanish navy and the illustration is based on the uniform worn by Galiano in his circa 1800 portrait in the Museo Naval, Madrid. It shows him wearing the 1793 uniform, which is of a similar pattern to that of a captain of a ship-of-the-line, but with broad silver embroidered lace on the cuffs, worn above the three narrow gold laces.

### ► Rear-Admiral (Cisneros)

The rank of rear-admiral equated to the army rank of *mariscale de campo* or major-general, and on the uniform this was distinguished by the use of one embroidered band of lace on the cuff and on the scarlet sash worn around the waist. The edge of the bicorn was laced gold and decorated with a red cockade and gold loop. Cisneros' sword has an urn-shaped pommel with grips and quillions decorated with intertwined beads. The flat shell is pieced with an intertwined pattern, as is the grip, and it had a triangular hollow-ground blade.

# SPANISH NAVY

### ➤ Captain, frigate

The double-breasted full-dress coat had a red collar edged with gold lace; the pockets were also laced all round. The coat tails were square ended but were not folded back to reveal any of the red lining. The round cuffs were red with the top edge bound with a single row of gold lace, and a frigate captain had two narrow bands of lace (the captain of a ship-of-the-line had three). The double-breasted undress blue cloth coat was cut with tails, with a plain collar and red lining. The laced waistcoat of this figure is just visible, and is of the same pattern worn by flag officers. The red breeches were officially worn with white stockings and buckled shoes, but this captain has replaced these with fashionable boots common in other navies. The bicorn hat, worn with both full and undress, is edged with gold lace, and decorated with the national red cockade.

### ▲ Lieutenant

Lieutenants of ships-of-the-line were identified by one narrow gold lace band on the cuff; those of frigates had no cuff lace but instead wore a gold epaulette on each shoulder.

### ◄ Vice-Admiral (Alava)

The full-dress coat of a vice-admiral differed from that of an admiral by having no embroidery at the seams. The cuffs had two embroidered bands of gold lace on both the full and undress versions.

# SPANISH NAVY

### ◄ Midshipman

This figure wears a practical double-breasted blue coat, with plain red cuffs and standing collar. The top buttons have been left undone to reveal the coat's red lining. On board ship officers could wear an alternative form of dress consisting of a blue single-breasted coat with gold buttons, worn with a red waistcoat, blue pantaloons and unlaced hat.

### ▲ Ensign

Ensigns (*alferes*) of ships-of-the-line wore a gold epaulette on their right shoulder whilst those of frigates wore an epaulette on the left shoulder. The long-tailed coat has squared closed lapels with seven buttons on each, and three buttons positioned below the right-hand lapel. The coat is lined red with red collar, cuffs and lapels edged with gold lace. The sword belt had a brass buckle ornamented with a crown and anchor design. This figure is shown with the blue trousers sometimes worn by these junior ranks.

### ➤ Private, Marine Artillery Brigade

Troops of the *Real Cuerpo de Artilleria de Marina* (marine artillery) were issued with a long-tailed dark-blue coat with false turnbacks revealing the red lining, red collar and cuffs. The collar had a yellow embroidered badge depicting a 'flaming' bomb over an anchor badge. The lapels were blue piped red and fastened by six brass buttons. It is uncertain from contemporary illustrations whether the cuff flaps were red or blue, and in this illustration they are blue with red piping. Sergeants wore gold and crimson silk epaulettes.

# SPANISH NAVY

### ◄ Private, 2nd Voluntarios de Cataluna

The 1802 regulations stipulated that light infantry regiments wore a green hussar-styled jacket with red collar, cuffs and shoulder straps with yellow lace and braid. This was replaced in April 1805 with a dark-blue coatee of infantry cut; dark-blue collar piped yellow, yellow lapels, cuffs, cuff-flaps, pocket piping and brass buttons. This speculative illustration shows a mixture of the old and new uniforms, with the 1802 red girdle with leather cartridge-box worn round the waist, and white breeches with tasselled garters. The bicorn hat was decorated with a green plume, red cockade and loop in the same colour as the button.

### ◄ Private, Burgos Regiment

Again it can only be speculated which uniform was worn by the infantry regiments engaged at Trafalgar. The figure shown illustrates the uniform of the April 1805 regulations. This consisted of a black bicorn hat with red cockade and plume. The white short-tailed coatee had closed lapels, with white turnbacks and regimentally coloured lapels and piping on the pockets and turnbacks. White breeches and black gaiters completed the regulation dress.

### ▲ Grenadier, Marine Infantry Brigade

The *Infanteria de Marina* wore an all-blue short-tailed coatee first issued in 1802 with scarlet lapels, collar (with a yellow anchor motif), turnbacks and cuffs, with blue cuff-flaps. A white waistcoat was worn with white breeches and black half gaiters, and buttons were of brass. The ordinary marine infantry wore a plain bicorn hat with a yellow cockade loop while grenadiers wore tall bearskin caps as illustrated, with a long and richly embroidered bag at the back of the cap. Grenadiers (unlike the other infantry) had pointed lace loops on their cuffs, and were armed with a short sabre with its scabbard slung below the bayonet.

NELSON: PART FOUR

# CADIZ AND SANTA CRUZ, JULY 1797

## CADIZ

In May 1797 Admiral Sir John Jervis's fleet of 20 ships-of-the-line, with his flag in the 110-gun *Ville de Paris* (a ship 'which feels like a rock after the trembling, leaky *Victory*'), was blockading the Spanish port of Cadiz. The blockade was a close one, following information that the Spaniards, under their new commander Admiral Josef de Mazarredo, would soon put to sea. It was poor intelligence. The defeat at Cape St Vincent and Cordoba's dismissal, coupled with rock-bottom morale among the Spanish fleet, ensured it remained tucked up safely in Cadiz harbour. The blockade was extremely tight, with the inshore squadron under Nelson so close that he wrote to a friend, 'We are looking at the ladies walking the walls and Mall of Cadiz.' Its object was to exercise economic pressure on the Spanish and force them to venture out to break the blockade, thus allowing the rich Havana convoys in and merchant ships to come and go. Without commerce, without their gold from the West Indies, Jervis was hopeful the merchants of the city would squeal loudly enough to be heard in Madrid – and the Navy would be ordered out. It was wishful thinking. The weeks passed and still the Spanish sat at anchor. By July, Jervis had decided that a direct bombardment of the city might provoke the necessary reaction.

In late May, Nelson had transferred his flag from the crippled *Captain* to the 74-gun *Theseus*. With him went Captain Ralph Miller and a number of other favoured crew members, including some 'old Agamemnons'. Jervis had called the *Theseus* 'an abomination'. She had suffered under a weak captain and a bullying first lieutenant and had been one of the disaffected ships in the recent, politically motivated Nore mutiny. For this reason she had been sent from the Channel to the Mediterranean Fleet. Jervis reasoned, rightly, that if anybody could sort out the *Theseus* it would be a combination of Nelson and Miller. Once on board his new flagship, Nelson discovered that the ship, although fitted out for foreign service in March, had not a single item of spares in her stores. The carpenter had no timber or nails, the boatswain no blocks or ropes. The *Theseus* had lacked leadership, and this is what Nelson, Miller and their officers provided. Stores were stocked, the carpenter got his timber and nails and, among other things, was put to work making scaling ladders – something that caused considerable curiosity and comment. Within two weeks a piece of paper was picked up on the quarterdeck and handed to Nelson. It read:

Success attend Admiral Nelson! God bless Captain Miller! We thank them for the Officers they have placed over us. We are happy and comfortable, and will shed every drop of blood in our veins, and the name of the *Theseus* shall be immortalized as high as the *Captain*'s.
SHIP'S COMPANY

Although Nelson was not averse to the use of the lash, he was above all a fair man. He would earn the respect of his men by his courage and professionalism and their devotion (like Napoleon) by acts of kindness and generosity. He put the welfare of his men first. He understood that a well-disciplined ship could have high morale and be an efficient fighting unit. An example of his personal intervention on behalf of men under his command occurred while blockading Cadiz, when he personally visited the *Swiftsure* to see two men in irons accused of shamming madness to secure a discharge. He wrote to Jervis asking that the fleet physician, Dr Weir, visit them, and offered £50 from his own pocket for the younger of the two to get proper treatment, then recommended that both be discharged. Such an act was quickly common knowledge on every ship.

Nelson, in command of the inshore squadron, had the task of bombarding Cadiz. He needed to land explosive shells in the town to set fire to buildings, kill civilians and generally cause chaos. No actual landing was contemplated. The defences were strong, with over 70 guns in various shore batteries, and the only vessel Nelson had capable of lobbing shells, as distinct from firing direct, was a converted Dutch galliot (fishing vessel) named the *Thunder*, armed with a mortar and a howitzer. It was commanded by a Lieutenant John Gowerley, who had an artillery officer, Lieutenant Baines, to supervise the firing. It was not exactly an overwhelming force. The *Thunder* would need careful positioning so that it could hit its target whilst eluding the attacks of the Spanish batteries. The operation would be carried out at night, the range to the town would be about 2,500 yards and a flotilla of ship's boats would accompany the bomb vessel for close protection.

On 3 July Nelson had instructed that all the squadron's launches (with carronades), barges and pinnaces, fully manned with armed seamen, should assemble by 8.30 p.m. All of the 25 to 30 boats could be either rowed or sailed. With the bomb vessel and these boats, he hoped to 'make it a warm night at Cadiz'. In support would be the 74-gun *Goliath*, the 32-gun frigate *Terpsichore* and the 10-gun cutter *Fox*. At around 9.00 p.m. Captain Miller clambered down into his barge to begin the task of guiding the *Thunder* into its

## A British Cutter

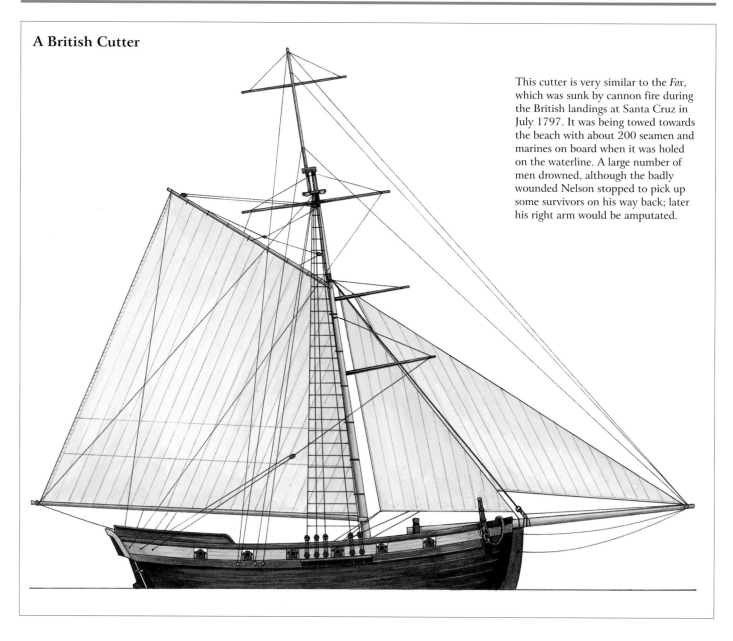

This cutter is very similar to the *Fox*, which was sunk by cannon fire during the British landings at Santa Cruz in July 1797. It was being towed towards the beach with about 200 seamen and marines on board when it was holed on the waterline. A large number of men drowned, although the badly wounded Nelson stopped to pick up some survivors on his way back; later his right arm would be amputated.

firing position. It was far from easy. Despite Miller leading the way, the bomb vessel seemed unable to steer the correct course. It was during the inevitable shouting of orders and counter-orders that an astonished Miller came to realize that Nelson was himself on the *Thunder* directing operations. Miller was not best pleased. There was delay and confusion, the moon rose on a clear night and the chances of securing the element of surprise dwindled accordingly.

Before the boom of the *Thunder*'s first shell rolled across the water to the sleeping citizens of Cadiz, the Spanish defenders had been alerted. They had assembled a flotilla of gunboats under the command of Captain Miguel Tyrason, and within minutes he had launched a spirited attack – heading straight for the *Thunder*. The approaching Spaniards were clearly visible to Nelson, and he shouted to Miller to organize a force of boats to intercept them – a task easier ordered than done. With the noise of the *Thunder*'s firing and the boats bobbing up and down all around, it was almost impossible to hear shouted commands. Even when bellowing through a speaking trumpet, it was difficult to make instructions understood. There was delay and hesitation. Seeing the situation,

Nelson leapt into his own barge to lead the counter-attack personally. The shout went up: 'Follow the admiral!'

It was a simple and effective order. Nelson's and Miller's boats led the charge into the head of the Spanish flotilla. It was a naval battle in miniature but with swivel guns, carronades, pistols and cutlasses instead of great guns doing the damage. Nelson's boat had only ten men on board under his coxswain John Sykes. It closed with a far larger Spanish vessel manned by at least 30 men and a desperate hand-to-hand fight ensued with pistols flashing in the darkness, men screaming and the rasp and clash of steel on steel. Heavily outnumbered, Nelson and his men were soon in serious difficulty. Heavy blows were aimed at Nelson, only to be parried by Sykes who fought alongside his admiral. Later, a seaman recalled that Sykes 'seemed more concerned with the Admiral's life than with his own: he hardly ever struck a blow but to save his gallant officer'. Finally, Sykes, unable to parry a vicious sweep by a cutlass aimed at Nelson's head with his own weapon, blocked it with his hand. This certainly saved Nelson's life but his coxswain was down. At about this time assistance arrived in the form of Miller's men, who boarded the

Spanish boat from the other side. After a few moments of brutal brawling that saw 18 Spaniards killed, the remainder surrendered. Among the prisoners was the Spanish commander Miguel Tyrason.

By this time the bulk of the British boats had arrived and the Spanish flotilla had turned back towards the harbour pursued by Miller. Nelson was left holding and comforting his wounded coxswain, saying, 'Sykes, I cannot forget this.' Nor did he. Sykes was 'mentioned in dispatches' – an extremely rare honour for a rating. Nelson also recommended his coxswain for promotion to lieutenant, but Sykes had not been a petty officer long enough, so had to be content with a gunner's warrant. Regrettably, this was to be his undoing, as within two years the accidental explosion of a great gun killed him.

The events of that night in early July had once again demonstrated Nelson's personal courage and his belief in the 'come on' as distinct from the 'go on' style of leadership that so endeared him to his men. In a letter to Nelson, Jervis wrote, 'Every service you are engaged in adds fresh lustre to the British arms and to your character.' However, the night's activities had not achieved the desired results. Only a few shells had hit the town. Nelson reported that 'a shell fell in a Convent and destroyed several priests (that no harm, they will never be missed)', although how he knew this is not clear. Further bombardments took place two days later and again on 10 July. Although fires were started, buildings hit and people killed, there was no sign of the Spanish fleet putting to sea. On 14 July the inshore squadron rejoined the main fleet. Nelson clambered aboard the *Ville de Paris* for a meeting with Jervis to plan the next move.

## SANTA CRUZ

Admiral Jervis was an unhappy and angry man, exasperated that nothing he did could prise the Spanish Fleet out of Cadiz. Always a disciplinarian, mostly short-tempered, he had been a man to avoid during those long weeks of blockade. He vented much of his dissatisfaction on his officers, famously remarking at this time, 'I dread not the seamen [referring to recent mutinies]. It is the indiscreet, licentious conversations of the officers which produce all our ills, and the presumptuous discussion of the orders they receive.' When a plump lieutenant came on board the *Ville de Paris* one morning, Jervis exclaimed to his flag captain, 'Calder, all the lieutenants are running to belly. They have been too long at anchor. Block up the entering port except for admirals and captains, and make them climb over the hammocks.' The one senior officer who remained in his favour was Nelson, who had proved courageous both mentally and physically and could be trusted with an independent command. As a clear-thinking admiral with initiative he was something of a rarity, and the obvious man to command an attack on Santa Cruz.

The principal port of Tenerife, one of the larger Spanish Canary Islands, Santa Cruz in 1797 was a valuable stopping-off place for Spanish ships en route to or from the West Indies. Treasure ships called there for provisions, water and sanctuary before the final dash for mainland Spain. As early as April 1797, Nelson had put forward a plan to attack Santa Cruz in co-operation with the Army, but the military had declined the invitation. Now Jervis asked Nelson if he could attack with the Navy alone to seize the town and, more especially, the *San José*, a ship supposedly carrying cargo valued at £30,000 that was sheltering in the harbour. It was not a mission Nelson would ever refuse. Jervis' actual orders to his rear-admiral were 'for taking possession of the Town of Santa Cruz by a

sudden and vigorous assault'. Nelson's squadron consisted of three 74s, *Theseus* (his flagship under Miller), *Culloden* (Troubridge) and *Zealous* (Hood); three frigates, the 38-gun *Seahorse* (Fremantle), the 36-gun *Emerald* (Waller) and the 32-gun *Terpsichore* (Bowen), the 10-gun cutter *Fox* (Gibson) and the mortar vessel *Terror*.

Santa Cruz posed problems for an attacker. It was flanked by steep mountains and there were few beaches but many stretches of rocky coast that made landings exceedingly dangerous, if not impossible. The three forts and nine gun batteries (of three or four guns each) spread along the three-mile shoreline fronting the town had a perfect shoot out to sea. A stone wall running along the line of the shore linked the batteries. This much was known to Nelson and his captains when they planned the attack in detail at three meetings held on the *Theseus* as they sailed towards their objective. What they did not know for sure was the strength, state of training or deployment of the garrison. The Spaniards were commanded by the resourceful and energetic Commandant General of the Canary Islands, Don Antonio Gutierrez. However, he did not command an impressive force. There were only 400 regular soldiers, 110 French sailors (who had been stranded on the island when they lost their ship to a cutting-out expedition led by Lieutenant Thomas Hardy two months earlier) and a militia force mostly without muskets. In the event the militia raised 700 men, who performed very creditably considering their poor training and equipment. The gun batteries and forts were manned by under 400 artillerymen, less than half those needed to keep all guns in action. At no time could Gutierrez count on more than 1,700 men, and as with all defenders, they had to be spread thinly until they knew where the enemy would strike.

Nelson had the initiative. He could choose the point of attack, he could concentrate at that point and, above all, he had the opportunity of achieving surprise – probably the biggest single factor for success in any battle, large or small. An amphibious landing has always been one of the most risky operations of war, from Caesar's landings near Deal to the British at San Carlos Bay in the Falkland Islands two thousand years later. If the landing is opposed, the risks to the attackers are multiplied fivefold. For these reasons Nelson wisely rejected a frontal attack straight at the harbour. Instead, he decided, after detailed consultations with his captains, that the objective of the landings would be Castillo de Paso Alto, a fort about a mile to the north-east of the port that defended the extreme left flank of the enemy where precipitous hills plunged into the sea. From there a bombardment of the town would be the next step. The planning and preparation were meticulous. The banging of carpenters' hammers never ceased as scaling ladders and wooden sledges for dragging 18-pounders were hastily constructed. Iron ramrods were made to replace the easily broken wooden ones used by the marines (they were wooden because iron rusted so quickly at sea). A number of the sailors in the landing party were to wear red marine jackets to impress the enemy with the number of 'soldiers' attacking them. Every day men of the landing party could be seen at musketry drill and firing practice over the ship's side.

The plan itself was something of a masterpiece that would have scored high marks at a modern military staff college. To achieve surprise the approach to the small beach south-west of the castle would be during darkness, the actual landing at dawn, followed by an immediate assault with scaling ladders – to carry the place by 'escalade' as the Army called it. Overall command rested with Nelson but, uncharacteristically, he would not join the landing. Instead, the attackers would be under 'General' Troubridge of the

*Culloden*, who had gallantly led the attack at Cape St Vincent five months before. He would have almost 1,000 men, a mixture of seamen and marines, with whom to storm the fort and subdue the town. The assault force was divided into three divisions or companies, each under a lieutenant with a master's mate or midshipman as second-in-command. Each had a strong complement of warrant and petty officers, including a master-at-arms, carpenter and armourer with their tools. It was the job of the three frigates to carry the landing parties, towing the ship's boats (the 1797 equivalent of assault craft) behind them. The intention was to sail the frigates to within a mile of the shore, disembark the attackers into the boats, tie the boats together one behind the other and row for the beach. Once ashore, the boats would return for ammunition, stores and several 18-pounders, this task being co-ordinated by a naval captain ashore – a forerunner of the 'beachmasters' of the 1944 D-Day landings. Once the operation was underway, the three ships-of-the-line would close in to bring their broadsides to bear on the shore defences.

Throughout the daylight hours of 21 July, with the squadron hove to well below the horizon, every ship hummed with frenetic activity. A major part of the day was spent in transferring seamen and marines onto the frigates and then getting the boats linked up behind. About 200 men went from the *Theseus* to the *Seahorse*, 270 from the *Zealous* to the *Emerald* and 150 from the *Culloden* to the *Terpsichore*. An almost identical exercise, called 'cross-decking', was carried out by soldiers and marines of the British Task Force prior to the landings in the Falklands almost two centuries later. If there is any truth in the polite version of the old Army instructor's saying 'Preparation and planning prevents poor performance', Nelson's attack on Santa Cruz should have proved it. It did not – the operation was a total failure.

When Nelson arrived with his battleships within sight of the town just after dawn on 22 July, he was not prepared for what he saw. The frigates had released their boats but these little black blobs were bobbing about still over a mile from the shore. Through his glass he could make out the rise and fall of the sweeps, but he could also discern that progress towards the landing place was desperately slow: the crucial factor of surprise had gone. The reason was an adverse wind blowing strongly offshore. Between May and September the sea north of Santa Cruz becomes what the locals call 'the white sheet'. The surface of the water is whipped up by trade winds funnelled down the deep valleys and gullies of the steep volcanic range of hills north of the town. They blow offshore with considerable force, creating the choppy waves and sudden eddies that had reduced the progress of the struggling ship's boat to a crawl. As Nelson watched in dismay, three cannon shots from the fort in the centre of the harbour announced that the Spaniards had been alerted.

This depressing setback was then compounded by a totally uncharacteristic decision taken by Troubridge. He ordered all the boats back to the frigates while he, Captain Bowen of the *Terpsichore* and the commander of the marines, Captain Oldfield, were rowed out to the *Theseus* to ask what to do next. The attack had stalled before it had even started. However, the Spanish would take some time to summon reinforcements, call out the militia and rush men to the threatened landing place. Had Troubridge continued, he would have come ashore late but still before Gutierrez could intervene. His rash decision had wasted several critical hours and jeopardized, if not ruined, the entire operation. According to Captain Miller Troubridge was unwell, and had been so for some

days, something that may have affected his judgement, although he was still able to carry on in command, and later climb a precipitous mountain in the broiling sun.

Nelson and Troubridge conferred, and decided that the landing should now take place further up the coast, just north of Paso Alto at the mouth of the Barranco del Bufadero. From there the force would climb a ridge that seemingly led to a position on the hill overlooking the castle, their objective. This was an alternative plan that had been considered earlier, so Nelson quickly agreed to it, although its implementation could not begin until around 10.30 a.m. As the boats struggled to make their new landing place, the battleships' attempts to move in close to fire on the castle were thwarted by offshore winds and current. Even the small *Terror* was unable to lob her bombs accurately. Troubridge's force was on its own.

Not long before noon the force began to climb. Anyone who has been to the Canary Islands in July will find it easy to imagine the suffering of those men. They were painfully unfit after so long on board ship, many in heavy jackets, with little water as they sweated and panted their way laboriously uphill. The midday sun was a killer, the hill was a killer. Captain Miller later described the climb as being up 'a tremendous hill without a path and full of rocks and loose stones'. When the leading group staggered to the summit, chests heaving, drenched in sweat, they realized that the ridge they thought connected them to the hill overlooking Paso Alto did no such thing. They were separated from it by a deep valley, the Valleseco. On the far side they could see Spanish positions on the hill behind a stone wall, but to attack them would mean descending into the valley and advancing uphill again to confront an enemy able to bring plunging fire down onto slow-moving, exhausted targets. Troubridge was appalled. What from sea level appeared a continuous ridge was two quite separate features. The whole day had been a disaster. There was no way he could get his force to attempt an attack. Men would be dropping of heatstroke long before they reached the Spanish. A Spanish officer later wrote, 'they were dying of thirst … in those mountains there were no areas where they could take shelter from the blazing sun'. Driven by their maddening thirst, a handful of seamen tried to get down to the valley stream. Two were shot and another died of heat exhaustion as he tried to climb back. Troubridge made the only decision possible: retreat. Not until 10 that night were all the dejected and exhausted men back on their ships.

Nelson was now about to make his one and only serious error of judgement as a senior commander, turning an ignominious failure into a disastrous one and losing his right arm in the process. He had doubts about making a second attempt (he later called it a 'forlorn hope') but nevertheless launched one on the night of 24 July. The doubts were dispelled, or at least lessened, by unforeseen intelligence, which coincided with Nelson's own thinking but turned out to be completely false. During the retreat on 22 July a German deserter had been taken on board the *Seahorse* by the marine commander Captain Oldfield. Captain Fremantle's wife Betsey, who was on board the *Seahorse*, spoke excellent German and was thus able to act as interpreter during the deserter's interrogation. According to her, the German said, 'the Spaniards have no force, are in the greatest alarm, all crying and trembling, and that nothing could be easier than to take the place, only 300 men of regular troops, the rest are peasants who are frightened to death'. Nelson summoned his captains to a conference. They urged action and Nelson agreed: another attack would be launched. Any misgivings Nelson had entertained were suppressed by a combination of circumstances. First and fore-most was the German's information that Spanish morale was low, that they had very few reliable troops and that with one more push they would collapse. This coincided with Nelson's own less than positive opinion of the Spanish as fighters – although his experience had been gained against Spain's Navy, not her Army, and there was perhaps a touch of over-confidence in his thinking. Moreover, he did not relish the prospect of sailing away empty handed, the expedition a failure, without having properly crossed swords with the enemy. Knowing what Nelson was aware of at the time, knowing him to be a bold, aggressive commander, knowing he had the backing of his captains, it was really inconceivable for him not to try again. This time, however, he intended to lead the assault personally.

Again the planning was thorough. However, the Spanish hor-nets' nest had been seriously disturbed, so achieving surprise was going to tax the planners' ingenuity. Nelson tried. He intended to anchor his squadron off Barranco del Bufadero again and bombard Castillo de Paso Alto from the *Terror*, in the hope that Gutierrez would be deceived into thinking the British were going to reinforce a former failure. A dummy 18-pounder of wood and canvas was to be placed in a boat to add authenticity to the deception. In the event, continued squally weather prevented the feint being launched. The attack had to rely on darkness, speed, concentration and aggression against a supposedly demoralized and weaker enemy. The actual attack had the benefit of simplicity. Over 1,000 men, who included more marines from the recently arrived 50-gun *Leander* under Captain Thompson, would go ashore at the mole in the centre of the harbour. They had to land there, as most of the shoreline was rocky – decidedly unsuitable for beaching boats under fire. After landing they would regroup in the town square (immedi-ately behind the mole), before storming over the walls of the adja-cent citadel, the Castillo de San Cristóbal, using scaling ladders.

---

## Nelson's Second Attempt to Take Santa Cruz Phase 1: The Landings                Map 16

**Key**

- **B** Spanish infantry positions behind walls
- Spanish artillery fire, with interlocking arcs
- Short-range musket fire

---

### British Notes

**A** Three frigates bring the attackers to within 2 miles of the shore then disembark about 1,000 seamen and marines into the ships' boats.

**B** The flotilla of boats in 6 divisions heads for mole with Nelson in the lead. The cutter *Fox* is towed behind with reserve force of 200.

**C** Here a Spanish sentry on mole and ships in harbour spot the approaching boats. All shore batteries open fire. British boats cut the ropes and row for the mole individually.

**D** Enemy fire, the swell, darkness and confusion lead to most boats being swept south of the mole. Some boats broken up, Nelson wounded in arm. Landings made by Bowen, Fremantle, Troubridge, Waller, Miller and Hood. The mole battery taken with heavy losses.

### Spanish Notes

**A** Spanish headquarters in Castillo de San Cristóbal

**B** Rosario Battery

**C** Concepción Battery

**D** San Telmo Battery

**E** Mole Battery

**F** Field artillery positioned to fire down mole after the British had landed and taken Mole Battery

This was essentially the frontal assault that had been discarded as too risky when the squadron had first arrived off the island. Frontal attacks against an alerted enemy behind fortifications are very much a last-resort tactic, seldom successful without overwhelming fire support and rarely recommended in military manuals. Night attacks too are notorious for encountering unpleasant surprises. Success depended on the reliability of the German deserter, who was to be taken along as a 'guide' and must have been desperately praying he had not exaggerated the state of Spanish morale. The plan envisaged an assault by six 'divisions' in the ships' boats, led by Nelson (together with his stepson Lieutenant Josiah Nisbet, Captain Fremantle and the German) in the *Seahorse*'s barge. Also in Nelson's division was the boat carrying Captain Bowen. Following close behind, coming in successive waves, would be the other five divisions under Captains Troubridge, Miller, Waller, Hood and Thompson. Each division's boats would be roped together. They were to rendezvous at an assembly point around the *Zealous* at 10.30 p.m. and from there they had a two-mile row to the mole. Close behind them in support would be the cutter *Fox*, under Lieutenant Gibson, with a reserve of about 200 men. By this time the *Terror* had been lobbing shells at Paso Alto for over two hours, hoping to draw Spanish troops away from Santa Cruz itself.

It was a long row. The night was starry but not particularly clear, with a light wind and heavy swell breaking over the beach and rocks. By midnight the little invasion flotilla had not been discovered. As 1.00 a.m. approached, with the boats within a few hundred yards of the mole, most men were now confident they could arrive undetected. However, the sentry in the battery at the end of the mole spotted them, as did seamen on some of the ships moored nearby. Alarm bells rang – literally. Within moments a hail of gunfire swept the water from the shore defences. Midshipman William Hoste, watching from the quarterdeck of the *Theseus*, described it thus: 'At one a.m. commenced one of the heaviest cannonading I ever was witness to from the town upon our boats, likewise a heavy fire of musketry.' In the boats ropes were cut and each crew strained on the sweeps as they pulled for the mole. Nelson later estimated he was opposed to around 30 to 40 cannons and 400 to 500 men. The reality, according to Spanish sources, was about 20 guns and 100 men – Nelson had achieved a huge superiority in terms of manpower, but not firepower, at the point of attack.

They say that few military plans survive the first shots and Nelson's attack on the mole at Santa Cruz was not one of them. Gutierrez, whose headquarters was in the Castillo de San Cristóbal, reacted swiftly, deploying a battery of field guns to fire straight down the mole to enhance the already formidable defences. A veritable whirlwind of canister and musket balls swept the British boats as they approached the landing. Bowen's boat grounded just north of the mole and he led a rush at the battery on its seaward end. His men took it and spiked the guns, but could make no further progress against the furious firing coming from the castle and the guns blocking the landward end of the mole – for the defenders it was difficult to miss. The next to land was Fremantle's barge with Nelson, the 'guide' and over 60 men. As Nelson clambered forward, still in the barge, and in the act of drawing his sword, his right arm was struck a hammer blow. A musket ball had hit him just above the elbow, smashing the bone and severing a main artery. Nelson collapsed into the bottom of the boat crying 'I am a dead man', blood pumping from his wound. If the bleeding had

continued at that rate, he would have been right. However, the prompt and effective action of his stepson saved him. Josiah gripped Nelson's arm above the wound and, using two neckerchiefs, bound the wound tightly. Later Nelson readily acknowledged he owed his life to this action.

As Fremantle's men scrambled ashore or onto the mole to join Bowen, their commander was also hit in the arm. Then Thompson's boat hit the beach, but he had only time to tell his crew to take the wounded back to the *Seahorse* before he himself was hit. By this time the mole had become a killing ground. The Spanish guns at the town end had come into action, blasting straight down the mole into the darkness, cutting down attackers as a reaper does corn. One of the first to fall to these guns was Captain Bowen along with George Thorpe, his first lieutenant, and six of his men. The German deserter whose information had justified the attack was killed soon after. Many more fell wounded. Within a matter of a few minutes the attack on the mole had collapsed in a welter of casualties and chaos, with the admiral, three captains and a lieutenant down. In these circumstances it was just as well that most boats were swept south of the mole by the swell. Some made landings as much as 200 yards to the south, while others, appalled by the deadly fire and fearful of being smashed onto the rocks, turned away and headed back out to sea.

Captain Troubridge came ashore on a small beach just south of the mole and under the walls of Gutierrez' headquarters in Castillo de San Cristóbal. Following behind were one or two of Waller's boats. Soaked, with muskets useless due to wet powder, they charged forward, drove aside some militiamen and made their way towards the flashes and noise coming from the town square. They emerged onto the square at its northern end but were unable to attack the castle, as they had lost their scaling ladders in the landing and could not fire their muskets. Hopeful that Nelson and the other groups would soon arrive, they sheltered in a warehouse fronting onto a street now called Calle Cruz Verde. With an optimistic show of initiative, Troubridge summoned a sergeant of marines, grabbed two Spanish civilians and sent them under a flag of truce to the citadel to demand its surrender. Gutierrez detained the delegation and did not bother to reply.

Captain Miller, in the *Theseus*' pinnace, and Captain Oldfield RM, in her launch, grounded their boats in heavy surf 30 yards from the shore and had to abandon them. They managed to make the shore at the mouth of a stream called the Barranquillo del Aciete some 200 yards south of the mole, but their powder was rendered useless by the soaking and a number of men also managed to lose their muskets. Miller managed to get enough men together to rush the nearest enemy positions and drive them away. Within a few minutes Captain Hood's party joined them, and although they were still under fire they attempted to regroup in order to assault the citadel. Miller soon realized this was a hopeless undertaking, as not only had they lost their ladders, but the seamen (some marines were willing to make the effort) were obviously disinclined to move, particularly as they had virtually no weapons capable of firing and had suffered severe losses. Afterwards Miller was frank about his men's waning morale, writing, 'as a body [they] behaved indifferently through the night'.

Another small group of boats eventually approached the shore even further south, at the mouth of the Barranco (River) de Santos that runs through Santa Cruz. Here, over 200 men of the Canaries Infantry Regiment supported by 120 militiamen gave them a hot

## Nelson's Second Attempt to Take Santa Cruz Phase 2: The Fighting in Town          Map 17

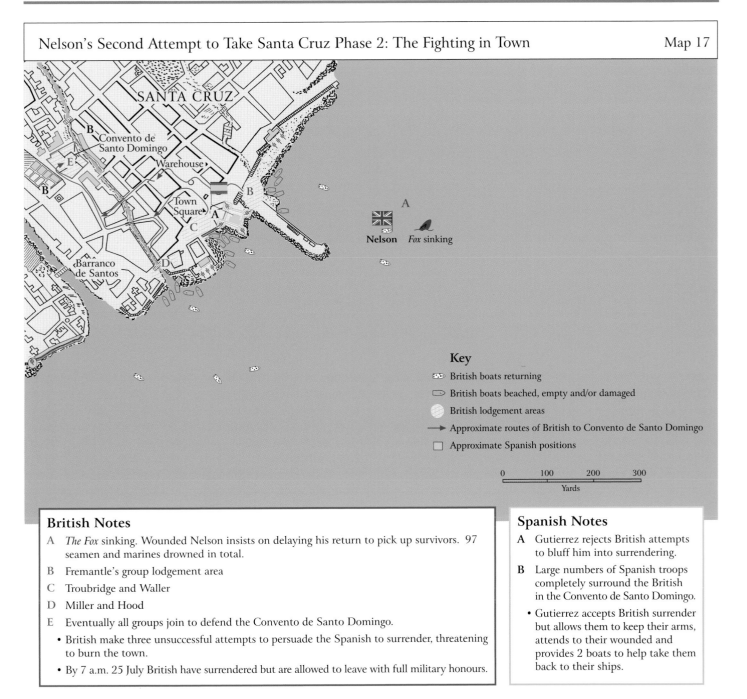

**Key**

🛶 British boats returning

🛶 British boats beached, empty and/or damaged

🔵 British lodgement areas

➤ Approximate routes of British to Convento de Santo Domingo

☐ Approximate Spanish positions

```
0        100       200       300
|————————|—————————|—————————|
              Yards
```

**British Notes**

A   *The Fox* sinking. Wounded Nelson insists on delaying his return to pick up survivors. 97 seamen and marines drowned in total.

B   Fremantle's group lodgement area

C   Troubridge and Waller

D   Miller and Hood

E   Eventually all groups join to defend the Convento de Santo Domingo.

• British make three unsuccessful attempts to persuade the Spanish to surrender, threatening to burn the town.

• By 7 a.m. 25 July British have surrendered but are allowed to leave with full military honours.

**Spanish Notes**

A   Gutierrez rejects British attempts to bluff him into surrendering.

B   Large numbers of Spanish troops completely surround the British in the Convento de Santo Domingo.

• Gutierrez accepts British surrender but allows them to keep their arms, attends to their wounded and provides 2 boats to help take them back to their ships.

reception. Some 300 muskets blazing away at close range as fast as the firers could reload was too much – the boats turned back. At least 200 men from the assault force never landed.

Meanwhile, Miller and Hood tried to find their way to the main square. However, with the darkness, their unfamiliarity with the maze of streets and the enemy harassing them at every corner, they were soon hopelessly lost. Eventually, still taking casualties, this group blundered into a square in front of the Church of the Concepción (now a cathedral). They were a quarter of a mile east of Troubridge, the senior officer in command at the town square, and south of the river. In the end it was Troubridge, realizing his position was untenable, unable to attack the citadel, still suffering casualties and with no other group nearby, who fought his way to join Miller. The combined force of around 400 men took over the large, square convent building (Convento de Santo Domingo),

which provided an excellent defensive position without windows on the ground floor. Using ammunition and powder captured from Spanish positions overrun earlier, they were able to keep the surrounding Spaniards at bay.

Nevertheless, the position of the British in the town was hopeless. Cut off, with dwindling ammunition and completely encircled, their only possible way out was bluff, coupled with the threat to burn the town. Incendiary devices were prepared and Captain Oldfield sent a delegation to the citadel demanding that the *San José* be surrendered or the town would be torched. Gutierrez rejected the offer. The British tried again, this time sending two friars who had watched the bonfire preparations. The Spanish commandant was unmoved. A resolute enemy under an able commander had fought well, far better than Nelson or anybody else had thought possible. The British had been deci-

## The Amputation of Nelson's Right Arm

The surgeon of the *Theseus*, Eshelby, recorded Nelson's injury in his log: 'Compound fracture of the right arm by a musket ball passing through a little above the elbow, an artery divided; The arm was immediately amputated and opium afterwards given.' The best reconstruction of the operation is that by Professor L. P. Le Quesne, which appeared in the *Journal of the Royal Naval Medical Service* in 2000:

> In an hospital on shore the operation would have been performed with the patient sitting on a chair, firmly held by two assistants, with the surgeon standing by his side. In the cockpit of the *Theseus* Nelson may well have sat on a chest, and probably beside Eshelby there were two further assistants holding lanterns. The operation performed was a standard, circular amputation, rather closer to the shoulder joint than normal because of the site of the injury. Initially the bleeding was controlled by the use of a screw tourniquet; after the main brachial artery had been ligated this was

released, so that the smaller vessels could be identified and secured. This was done by passing under the vessel a curved needle, with a thread or silk ligature, in such a way that a portion of muscle was incorporated in the tissue. These ligatures were left long, protruding from the wound. The wound itself was not sutured. The whole procedure probably took five minutes.

It seems that Royal Naval surgeons charged a fee for treating officers – certainly senior ones – as Nelson submitted a list of expenses incurred due to his wound to the Court of Examiners of the Company of Surgeons. The first refers to Assistant Surgeon Remonier, who received 24 guineas for 'assisting in amputating my arm and for attendance from July, 1797, to the 14th August following during which time he sat up 14 nights'. The second item reads: 'Paid Thomas Eshelby for amputating my arm, quitting the "*Theseus*" and attending me to England in the "*Seahorse*" frigate from 25 July to 3rd September ... £36.'

---

sively defeated. The German deserter, lying dead near the mole, could not be brought to account for his exaggerations. Troubridge sent Hood to negotiate an honourable withdrawal. Gutierrez was exceedingly generous. By 7.00 a.m. on 25 July Hood had signed a truce which Troubridge accepted. The British left with full military honours with their arms and marched down from the convent to the town square where an impressive parade of Spanish (and French seamen) troops were drawn up. Gutierrez arranged for two Spanish vessels to assist in taking the British back to their ships, but only after they had been given bread and wine. The officers refused a full breakfast and were given cake and lemonade instead. Arrangements were made for the British wounded to be cared for in the local hospital.

While the British had been receiving a thorough beating ashore, what had been happening at sea? As soon as Nelson's arm was bound, his barge turned round and headed back to get him to a surgeon. At about the same time the cutter *Fox* was hit by a cannonball that went clean through her at the waterline. Within moments she began to sink, forcing the crew and the 200 men of the reserve into the water, where a number drowned. Nelson, despite his pain and shock, insisted his boat diverted to pick up several of the struggling men. He was now about to demonstrate, yet again, his truly remarkable stoicism, his ability to bear intense pain or endure prolonged periods of sickness and yet still function as a capable commander. When his boat drew alongside the *Seahorse*, Nelson refused to go aboard for fear his wound would alarm Betsey Fremantle. This meant a second, much longer, delay in getting his wound seen by a surgeon. It was about an hour after being hit that he finally arrived at the *Theseus*. With the boat rising and falling from the swell, Nelson insisted on climbing on board without assistance, exclaiming, 'Let me alone, I have yet my legs left and one arm.' Midshipman Hoste watched in amazement as his admiral clambered aboard. He later wrote to his father, 'his right arm dangling by his side while with the other he helped himself jump up the ship's side, and with great spirit which astonished every one, told the surgeon to get his instruments ready'. The surgeon, Thomas

Eshelby, was assisted by a French royalist refugee, Louis Remonier from the hospital at Toulon. Nelson, seated on a chest, submitted to having his arm cut off above the elbow with a saw – without anaesthetic. Instead of complaining of the awful agony of the amputation, he was more concerned that the surgeon's instruments felt cold. How he was able to notice such a thing in the circumstances is almost beyond comprehension, but it was important to him and forever afterwards he would insist his surgeons warmed their instruments before use. Within half an hour of losing his arm he was issuing orders and signing a copy of a surrender ultimatum to be sent ashore, though it was never sent as the extent of the defeat ashore became clear.

Santa Cruz was a serious setback and a blow to British morale. It cost the lives of 146 all ranks (killed, drowned or missing) and 105 wounded. The breakdown was as follows:

| Killed (in *Fox* or boat landing) | Drowned | Missing | Wounded |
|---|---|---|---|
| 1 capt. | 97 seamen | 5 seamen | 1 R-Adm. |
| 4 lieuts | & marines | | 2 capts |
| 2 RM lieuts | | | 1 lieut. |
| 23 seamen | | | 1 mid. |
| 14 RMs | | | 85 seamen |
| | | | 15 RMs |
| **Totals** 44 | 97 | 5 | 105 |

The *Fox* was sunk, and a considerable number of ship's boats destroyed. The above figures represent a 25 per cent casualty rate, well in excess of that of the British fleet at Trafalgar. Nelson, typically, accepted responsibility and dictated a letter of thanks to his Spanish opponent for his chivalrous conduct as the victor. The letter offered, 'my sincerest thanks for your attention to Myself and your humanity to those of our wounded who were in your possession or under your care as well as your generosity to all that were landed'. With the letter, signed with a hesitant, left-handed signature, went English beer and cheese. Gutierrez responded in kind with another letter and Malmsey wine, where-

## Two Letters from Nelson to Jervis

The last letter written by Nelson with his right hand, dated 24 July 1797, was addressed to Sir John Jervis, who, unbeknown to Nelson, had been gazetted to an earldom on 16 July, the king choosing for him the title St Vincent.

*Theseus* off Santa Cruz
July 24th 8 p.m.

My Dear Sir,
I shall not enter on the Subject why we are not in possession of Santa Cruz. Your partiality will give me credit that all has hitherto been done which was possible, but without effect. This night I humble as I am, command the whole, destined to land under the batteries of the Town and tomorrow my head will probably be crowned with either Laurel or Cypress. I have only to recommend Josiah Nisbet to You and my Country. With every affectionate wish for your health and every blessing in the world believe me your most faithful

Horatio Nelson

The Duke of Clarence should I fall in the service of my King and Country, will I am confident take a lively interest in my Son in Law on his name being mentioned.

Feeling himself a failure after the Santa Cruz disaster, Nelson wrote a private letter to Jervis on 27 July. Considering the pain he was in and that he was using his left hand, the writing itself is reasonably legible.

*Theseus* July 27th 1797

My Dear Sir,
I have become a burden to my friends and useless to my Country but by my letter wrote the 24th you will perceive my anxiety for the promotion of my son in law Josiah Nisbet, when I leave your command; I become dead to the World I go hence and am no more seen. If from poor Bowen's loss, you think it proper to oblige me I rest confident you will do it, the Boy is under obligations to me but he repaid me by bringing me from the Mole of Santa Cruz. I hope you will be able to give me a frigate to convey the remains of my carcass to England. God Bless You, My Dear Sir & Believe me your most obliged and faithful

Horatio Nelson

You will excuse my scrawl considering it is my first attempt.

## Nelson's Wounds

Before he was struck down with a mortal injury Nelson had been wounded five times – more than any other admiral in the Royal Navy during the Napoleonic Wars. His injuries were:

• April 1794 – a 'sharp cut in the back' at the siege of Bastia. A light wound with no after effects.

• 12 July 1794 – a badly cut right eye at the siege of Calvi caused by a roundshot landing nearby and driving sand and stones into his face. He lost the sight of the eye although it healed well and looked almost normal.

• 14 February 1797 – at the Battle of St Vincent, he was struck a violent blow in the abdomen by a flying splinter from a rigging block. He suffered very severe bruising and possible abdominal trauma which left him with a weakness that caused problems for the rest of his life.

• 24 July 1797 – while he was leading a landing party during the attack on Santa Cruz, Tenerife, a musket ball hit him on the upper right arm, which had to be amputated. It took some four months to heal properly and left him with another permanent disablement.

• 1 August 1798 – at the Battle of the Nile he was struck on the forehead by a piece of flying metal. Blood loss and the location of the wound led to it being initially thought very serious, even fatal. However, this was not the case and although it caused nausea and awful headaches for some months afterwards there was no lasting damage.

upon Nelson offered to carry dispatches to Cadiz for him. Such were the courtesies of a bygone age.

On 20 August, Nelson sailed for England on the *Seahorse*, one of the many sick or wounded men transferred to the frigate for the journey home. Betsey Fremantle was somewhat distressed by his appearance. Her diary records, 'Admiral Nelson came on board at twelve o'clock, he is quite stout but I find it looks shocking to be without one arm.' A later entry gives a clear indication that the voyage was far from pleasant: 'from morning to night you hear nothing but these unfortunate people groan'.

This was a real low point in Nelson's life. Not only had he lost his arm, which was giving him considerable pain, but he had also lost a battle. The thought that he had failed professionally made him doubly despondent, and he considered his career was over, as is shown by his letter of 27 July to Jervis (see box p. 221).

After his return home his wound did not heal properly; six weeks after the operation, one ligature could not be withdrawn from the stump. Daily dressings were needed, while the pain was such that he required doses of opium to help him sleep. Weeks of worry lay ahead. He visited London for more medical advice, seeing several eminent physicians and surgeons. It was even suggested he might have to submit to another operation, a course of action that was, fortunately, not pursued. Then, on 30 November, he awoke suddenly free of pain. The dressing was removed and the offending ligature came away. A few days later he left a message for the parson of St George's church in Hanover Square to be read out at the next Sunday service: 'An officer desires to return thanks to Almighty God for his perfect recovery from a severe wound and also for many mercies bestowed on him.'

# Guns, Gunnery and Tactics

It is virtually impossible for us today to visualize the horror, blood, butchery, shrieks, uproar, smoke and general pandemonium of a gundeck in battle. The nearest we can get to such a horrendous experience is to read accounts by those who were there, who somehow lived through it. So, before describing the weapons that caused this terror and destruction, here are three quotations from men at the receiving end:

> it was like some awfully tremendous thunderstorm, whose deafening roar is attended by incessant streaks of lightening, carrying death in every flash and strewing the ground with victims of its wrath; only in our case the scene was rendered more horrible than that by the presence of torrents of blood which dyed our decks ...
> I was busily supplying powder when I saw blood suddenly fly from the arm of a man stationed at our gun. I saw nothing strike him; the effect alone was visible ...
> The cries of the wounded now rang through all parts of the ship. These were carried to the cockpit as fast as they fell, while those more fortunate who were killed outright were thrown overboard ... A man named Alderich had one of his hands cut off by a shot and almost at the same moment he received another shot which tore open his bowels in a terrible manner. As he fell two or three men caught him in their arms, and as he could not live, threw him overboard ...

And:

> smoke bursting forth from the many black iron mouths and whirling rapidly in thick rings till it swells into hills and mountains, through which the sharp, red tongue of death darts, flash after flash, and mingling fire and smoke slowly rolls upwards like a curtain in awful beauty ... And ever and anon, amid the breaks of the cannon's peal and shrieks and cries of the wounded mingling with the deep roar of the outpoured and constantly reiterated 'hurra, hurra, hurra!' sweep over the sea ...

For obvious reasons, the middle deck was the worst. According to a Royal Marine at Trafalgar:

> A man should witness a battle in a three decker from the middle deck for it beggars all description it bewilders the senses and hearing, there was fire from above, and fire from below besides the fire from the deck I was upon the Guns recoiling with violence, reports louder than thunder the decks heaving. I fancied myself in the infernal regions where every man appeared a devil. Lips might move but orders and hearing were out of the question.

Burst eardrums and deafness – temporary, partial or, for some, permanent – were a common outcome for survivors. Modern psychiatrists and post-traumatic stress counsellors would have had a real bonanza. However, although conditions in battle were appalling on all decks above the waterline, the real bloodbath usually occurred on the upper decks – the poop, quarterdeck and forecastle, which were almost completely exposed. The Reverend Scott, Nelson's chaplain on the *Victory* at Trafalgar, wrote a few days afterwards, 'On the quarter-deck, poop and forecastle the slaughter was immense; on the other decks comparatively nothing; on the lower deck only two wounded, and, strange to tell, by musket-balls.' The musket balls were almost certainly fired through open ports when the *Victory* was entangled with the *Redoutable.*

## THE GUNS

Napoleonic naval warfare (indeed all naval warfare) was about guns. The whole object of any captain in action was to bring his guns to bear. In battle two-thirds of the crew abandoned other tasks for duty with the guns, firing them or supplying them with ammunition. It was the crew that fired the fastest and most accurately that won. This Section will look at these guns under six interrelated headings – Ordnance; Ammunition; Gunpowder; Equipment; Gunnery; and Tactics. Any important differences between the British, French and Spanish ordnance or gunnery will be highlighted. However, the guns themselves, the methods of firing and the problems involved were virtually identical whatever the nationality of the man behind the piece. For this reason the description below is based primarily on the British system in use at Trafalgar.

## ORDNANCE

Under the overall control of the Ordnance Board, naval guns were manufactured at iron works in Scotland and Northern England. Before being accepted into service, however, they had to be shipped to Woolwich for testing. These tests were arbitrary, always dramatic and sometimes dangerous. Each gun was stuffed with gunpowder, well in excess of a normal charge, and then fired. If the gun survived, it was inspected for cracks. If none was found, it had passed and could be sent to one of the naval ordnance depots near Chatham, Portsmouth or Plymouth. From there they were issued to ships as part of the gunner's stores.

All muzzle-loading guns were of the same basic design. They were cast in a mould and then bored, or tubed, by the insertion of a powerful cylindrical gouge. They were generally cast in two lengths: the 'long' and 'short' varieties. Both had approximately the same range but the long gun was more accurate and could be laid 'point blank' – level or horizontal – to hit any target up to 400 yards away, whereas the short gun would have to be slightly elevated to hit the same target. Each gun consisted of an iron tube (brass guns were expensive and therefore quite rare) closed at one end, the breach, where the metal was thickest, as it had to withstand the force of the propellant powder. A glance at the diagram below will clarify the different parts of the gun. The aftermost part, behind the base ring, was the 'cascable', with a ball, called a 'button', and a loop on top termed a 'thimble'. Forward of the base ring were the two sections known as the first and second 'reinforce', separated by two 'reinforce rings' around the gun. Forward of the second reinforce was the 'chase' part of the barrel, which narrowed down to the 'neck' of the muzzle before widening again at the 'swell' of the muzzle. The bore was round with parallel sides. The chamber, in which the powder for firing was placed, was the aftermost part of the bore. A touchhole was drilled down to connect the top of the breach with the chamber. On the outside of the gun were two 'trunnions', protruding cylindrical lugs situated just aft of the second reinforce ring. They supported the gun on its carriage and allowed it to be elevated or lowered for aiming. It was usual for the manufacturer to mark his initials on the left trunnion and the gun's number on the right.

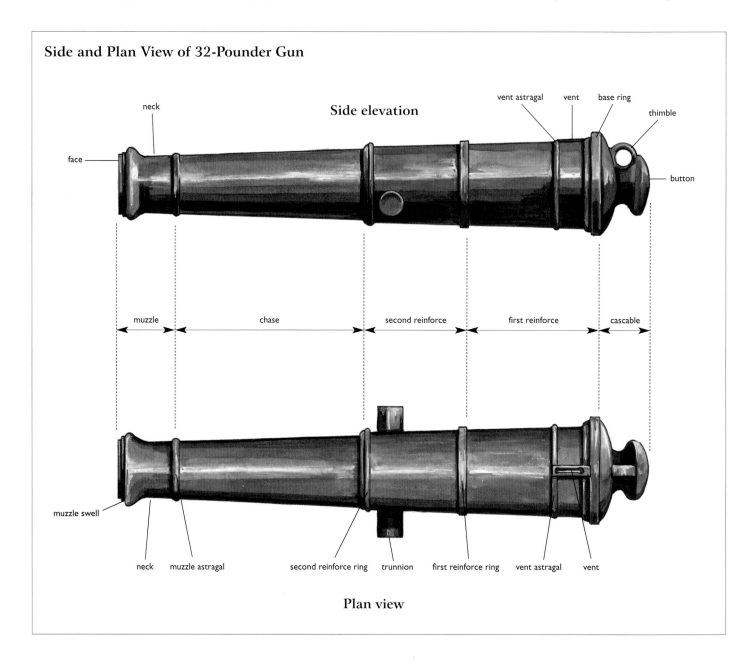

**Side and Plan View of 32-Pounder Gun**

Side elevation

Plan view

The guns were painted black, though the ingredients of the 'paint' used were somewhat unusual. The original recipe was:

To one gallon of vinegar add a quarter of a pound of iron rust, let it stand for one week; then add a pound of lamp black and three quarters of a pound of copperas; stir it up at intervals for a couple of days. Lay five to six coats on the gun with a sponge, allowing it to dry well between each application; polish with linseed oil and soft woollen rag; it will look like ebony.

## Cannons

There were two types of gun on the ships of both fleets at Trafalgar: cannons and carronades (although a few Spanish also carried some howitzers). Naval cannons of every weight or size were referred to by the British as 'great guns' to distinguish them from 'small arms' – muskets and pistols. When a ship was referred to as a 100- or 74-gun ship it meant she carried 100 or 74 great guns; the British in 1805 did not count carronades, as naval bureaucracy could not cope with the variations this would cause in regulations for rating and manning. The great guns were classified by the weight of the ball they fired in pounds. At Trafalgar the British Fleet was armed with 32-, 24-, 18-, 12-, 9- and 6-pounders, the French had 36-, 24-, 12- and 8-pounders and the Spanish 36-, 24-, 18-, 12-, and 8-pounders. For the technical details of the *Victory*'s guns, including weight, range and charge weight, refer to the box below right.

## Carronades

These were short-barrelled and lightweight – the 68-pounders on the *Victory* only weighed 1.8 tons each, compared with a 32-pounder great gun at 2.75 tons. They fired a heavy shot with a low velocity over a short range (up to 400 yards). The 68-pounder was justly nicknamed the 'smasher' by the British or the 'devil gun' by the French; when loaded with grapeshot the damage it could do to flesh and bone was horrendous. The boatswain of the *Victory*, William Willmet, was in charge of the larboard carronade on the forecastle (not the normal job of a boatswain) and had the honour of firing her first shot of the battle. He had loaded with one roundshot and a keg of 500 musket balls, and his target was the vulnerable stern windows of Villeneuve's flagship, the 80-gun *Bucentaure* – a perfect raking shot. When almost at touching distance, five yards at most, he jerked the lanyard. The French gunners were cut down in swathes.

Carronades (they were named after the Carron Company, which developed them) were eminently suited to smashing enemy ships and men at close range. Even the 68-pounder was light enough to be mounted on a quarterdeck, forecastle or poop. It could be oper-

### Accuracy of French 24- and 36-Pounders

Like the British, the French tended to test-fire their guns on land initially, where conditions were far better than those at sea. Using a 24-pounder, the French recorded that out of 100 shots at a one-metre-square target at 200 metres, 37 would hit. At 400 this figure dropped to 13, at 600 to eight. The charge was a third the weight of the ball. At this range the maximum lateral deviation of the shots was 4 metres. Considering the smallness of the target, indeed the difficulty of seeing much of it at 600 metres, the accuracy was relatively good. Certainly, if a warship had been the target the number of hits would have shown a steep increase. At 600 metres the ball took 1.5 seconds to reach the target. Guns could fire out to considerable ranges, although to hit and damage even a large ship at over 1,500 yards would be something of a minor miracle. The 36-pounder elevated to 16 degrees would reach 3,300 metres with a charge of 36 lbs – but it took 18 seconds to get there!

### Weight and Ranges of *Victory*'s Guns

| Gun | Weight (tons) | Point-blank range (yds) | Maximum range (yds) |
|---|---|---|---|
| 32-pdr | 2.75 | 400 | 2,640 |
| 24-pdr | 2.5 | 400 | 1,980 |
| 12-pdr long | 1.7 | 375 | 1,320 |
| 12-pdr medium | 1.6 | | |
| 12-pdr short | 1.4 | | |
| 68-pdr carronade | 1.75 | 450 | 1,280 |
| 18-pdr carronade (used in launch) | 0.5 | 270 | 1,000 |

ated by a crew of four or five, as it was mounted on a sliding carriage that absorbed most of the recoil and did not require the same muscle power to haul it forward after firing. It needed less powder in the charge than the great guns did, while the carriage was fitted with castors rather than trucks (wheels), which meant it could be trained quickly over a wider angle. Its sole defect was its inability to compete with the great gun in a stand-off duel at long range, since a 68-pounder cannonade had roughly half the effective range of a 32-pounder great gun. A ship armed only with carronades that could not close with her opponent was obliged to sit and suffer without being able to strike back. It was in the judicious combination of carronades with cannons that a ship-of-the-line had the potential to become a really formidable gun platform.

The secret of producing a gun that was light and short-barrelled but could throw shot accurately with high velocity at close ranges lay in reducing the windage – the gap between the inside of the bore and the ball. Windage was necessary so that a ball could be muzzle-loaded; if it were too tight a fit, trapped air would prevent ramming. The windage for a 32-pounder great gun was 0.6in, cut to 0.1in with the 68-pound carronade – a very substantial reduction. In order to obtain the highest velocity from the short carronade, hollow shot was developed. Strangely, perhaps, this process was not taken a step further by filling the shot with powder to make a shell – a common enough projectile for armies. One reason for this was that solid shot were seen as better for destroying wooden ships, whereas shells were more suited to 'soft' land targets such as humans and horses. Secondly, the stowage of powder-filled shells in the restricted space of ships' magazines was thought to increase the chances of an explosion (either accidental or during a battle) that would destroy her and her crew in a matter of seconds, as happened to the French flagship *L'Orient* at the Nile.

The Navy Board was enthusiastic about equipping ships with at least some carronades but the Admiralty dragged its feet. It was first proposed that they be part of the armament on the upper works of ships, where there was space to fit them in, as early as 1779 – a year after the first one was manufactured. However, it was far from compulsory to carry them, and often they only came on board if the captain requested them. A report from Plymouth in 1780 said, 'most captains at that port disapprove of carronades, and do not intend to take any'. Nevertheless, in 1794 the guidelines changed and carronades began to be carried in all classes of ship, including frigates. By the end of the century 20-gun ships even had carronades as their main armament.

## 68-Pounder Carronade

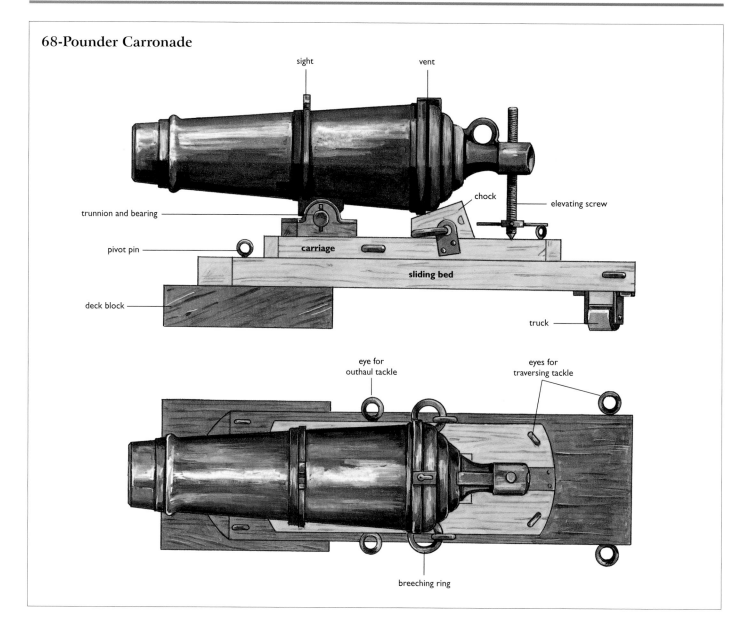

At Trafalgar British ships had 68-, 32-, 24- and 18-pounder carronades, although at least ten had none at all. The French had only 36-pounders, while the Spanish carried howitzers, guns that fired at a higher angle of trajectory, instead. In Nelson's fleet they were mounted on the quarterdeck, forecastle and poop but with no degree of uniformity – another reason why the British never counted them in a ship's rating. The 102-gun *Victory* had only two 68s on her forecastle, whereas the 74-gun *Belleisle* was crammed with carronades: fourteen 32-pounders on her quarterdeck (plus two 9-pounder guns), two 24s on her forecastle (again with two 9-pounder guns) and six 24s on her poop. As noted before, the *Belleisle* was formerly French so had a marginally larger quarterdeck than British 74s. The 74-gun *Conqueror* had only guns (fourteen 9-pounders) on her quarterdeck but two 32s on her forecastle and six 18-pounder carronades on her poop.

There was uniformity on the French ships in that all carried carronades of the same size (36-pounders) on the poop deck, with second rates having six and third rates four. Despite this, like the British (and the Spanish with howitzers), they did not count carronades in the rating of a ship.

### Distribution

The guns were distributed on either side of the gundecks on a line-of-battle ship, and all the guns on one side of a ship constituted a broadside. On each gundeck they were divided into the larboard battery and the starboard battery – the 'lower-deck starboard battery' meant the fifteen 32-pounders on the starboard side of the lower deck. The heaviest guns were always located on the lower deck to ensure the overall centre of gravity was as low as possible. Thus a three-decker such as the *Victory* would have 32-pounders on the lower deck, 24s on the middle deck and 12s on the upper deck. On the British ships at Trafalgar the guns on the quarterdeck and forecastle varied considerably both in weight and number (no British ship carried guns, as distinct from carronades, on her poop). The *Victory* had twelve 12-pounders on her quarterdeck but only two on her forecastle, together with two 68-pounder carronades. In contrast the 74-gun *Colossus* had four 24-pounders on her quarterdeck and two more on the forecastle. Much depended on the whim of the captain, particularly on the weather deck. The bigger the gun, the more space and crew it required. There were a number of permutations and combinations of guns, crew numbers and space on the weather deck. Captain Hardy on the *Victory* found room to mount twelve 12-pounders on her quarterdeck but no carronades, whereas Captain Morris on the *Colossus* had space, on a slightly smaller quarterdeck, to pack in four 24s and ten 32-pounder carronades. The 12-pounders were divided into three versions: the 'long' (9ft 6in), 'medium' (9ft) and 'short' (8ft 6in). On the *Victory* and elsewhere, long 12-pounders were usually carried on an upper gundeck, the medium variety on the forecastle and the short ones on the quarterdeck.

Every gun had a ship's number allocated to it and a quarter bill was drawn up listing the crew of that gun. According to regulations, No. 1 gun was the foremost gun on the larboard side of each deck and No. 2 the foremost on the starboard side. In addition to this official numbering, many guns were given nicknames, painted on above their port. They could be named after a well-respected captain – examples included 'Admiral Nelson', 'Captain Berry' and 'Billy Blue' (Admiral Cornwallis) – or, more likely, a lady of the night who had entertained the seamen enthusiastically on the ship's last visit to a home port. When giving fire orders a quarter gunner might shout, 'Untampion "Billy Blue"! Shot and wad her!' – always referring to the gun as 'her', despite the masculine name.

Guns were distributed more uniformly on the gundecks than on the quarterdeck or forecastle. Space was still the overriding factor in determining how many were carried where: the longer the ship the more guns. Only the slightly longer ships captured from the French (*Belleisle* and *Tonnant* at Trafalgar, for example) could accommodate 32. The middle decks of three-deckers had either 28 or 30 guns and upper decks from 26 to 30. The 38-gun frigate *Naiad* had 28 short 18-pounders on her single gundeck, eight 9-pounders on her quarterdeck and two on her forecastle. The three 36s (*Euryalus*, *Phoebe* and *Sirius*) had 26 on the gundeck, eight on their quarterdecks and two on their forecastles.

## Napoleon's Views on Carronades

We know that many French ships at Trafalgar had carronades in addition to their normal armament. However, they had only recently been so equipped and only because of the pressure applied to the Minister of Marine (Decrès) by Napoleon personally – being an artillerist he knew what he was talking about. The difficulty lay in procuring enough carronades and getting them distributed among the fleet. Throughout the year (1804 and into 1805) he kept pressing his minister, saying, in early June 1805, 'It was with carronades that the English set *L'Orient* on fire [at the Nile in 1798 and not necessarily true] and in them they have an immense advantage over us.'

Two weeks later, replying to Decrès' list of difficulties, Napoleon's anger was obvious. 'The least that can be asked of the administrative branch is that soldiers [why not seamen?] shall fight with equal terms. It is the first duty of a minister, and nothing can excuse his fulfilling it. Have we not disadvantage enough without that of armament? Your "ifs" and "buts" – that is no justification.' A week later, his exasperation boiling over, he begged, 'But, for God's sake ship me some carronades ...'.

There is still controversy and conflicting evidence as to how many French ships managed to secure this armament before the battle.

All the British first and second rates had exactly the number of guns they were supposed to carry and none carried any carronades, except for the *Victory*, which carried 102 guns plus two large, 68-pounder carronades. The same was not true of the 74s. Of the 16 at Trafalgar, only nine had 74 great guns. These exceptions were:

*Achille* – 66 plus 18 carronades. Her design was copied from a former French ship of the same name that had been captured and broken up before Trafalgar.

*Belleisle* – 66 plus 22 carronades. A captured French ship, she was particularly heavily armed, with thirty-two 32-pounders on her lower deck, 30 on the upper deck, two 9-pounders on her quarterdeck and another two on her forecastle.

*Colossus* – 64 plus 18 carronades

*Defiance* – 62 plus 18 carronades

*Revenge* – 76 and no carronades. A new ship, she had 30 guns on each gundeck plus fourteen 9-pounders on her quarterdeck and two on her forecastle.

*Spartiate* – 62 plus 20 carronades. She was a captured French ship with a slightly longer hull, enabling her to have 30 guns on her upper deck instead of the more usual 28.

*Swiftsure* – 62 plus 18 carronades.

If the *Victory* fired every gun of one of her broadsides, including carronades, the weight of iron discharged at the enemy was 1,136 lbs. Her opening broadside at Trafalgar was from her larboard side, with all guns except the carronade treble-shotted as the range was so close – a total of some 3,272 lbs, or almost 1.5 tons of metal. By way of comparison the *Mars*, an average 74 with no carronades, had a normal (single-shot) broadside of 880 lbs, and the 36-gun frigate *Euryalus* a mere 266 lbs – making it obvious why frigates had no business in the line of battle.

---

## A Nasty Accident

Midshipman Parsons on the *Barfleur* has left an account of an unintentional firing of a gun on the day following Trafalgar. At the moment of firing the gun was 'housed', i.e. secured with tackle with the muzzle raised and the breech end lowered to rest on the rear of the carriage. The gunport would be closed. Parsons describes what happened:

At this moment a violent explosion from our lower deck, with the hasty flight of the port, part of the side, and a round shot of thirty-two pounds, through the air, caused great excitement; and the cry of fire ensuing, caused some confusion in the *Barfleur*. This was speedily got under [control], and our captain [Dacres] made his appearance on the quarterdeck completely drenched [no explanation of how this had happened], and proceeded to inquire

into the late alarming occurrence. The men had slept at quarters, and one of them was soundly sleeping on the breech of a lower deck gun, that was housed. A waister [ignorant landsman] from the sister-kingdom [Ireland], rather raw in the service, possessed of an inquiring mind, was at a loss to determine how pulling a string affixed to the lock could cause such a thundering noise; in his philosophical experiment he had placed the lock on full cock, gave a gentle pull with the aforesaid string, fired the gun, killed the sleeper, smashed his foot to pieces by the recoil, and stood transfixed with horror and pain at the success of his experiment. The loss of his foot saved his back [he escaped a flogging], and the carpenters soon repaired the damage.

## The Inside of a Gun Port

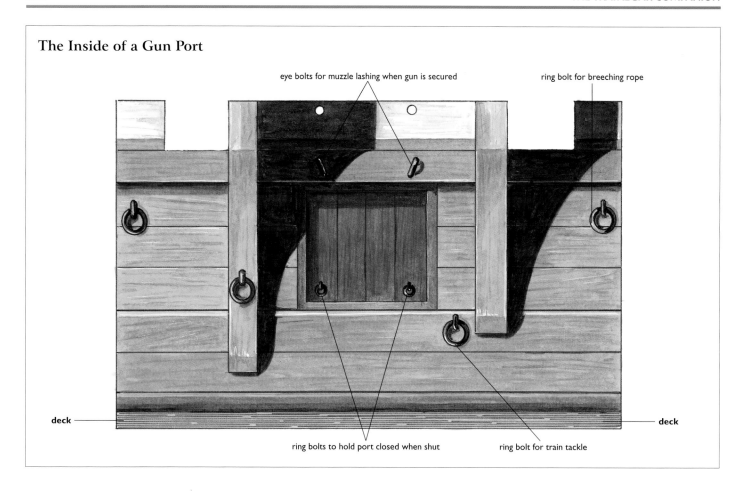

eye bolts for muzzle lashing when gun is secured

ring bolt for breeching rope

deck

deck

ring bolts to hold port closed when shut

ring bolt for train tackle

## Gunports

Gunports were simply holes, almost square, on the side of a ship, with an outward-opening heavy flap hinged at the top that could be raised or lowered by means of a rope called a 'port tackle'. When closed it was hooked to an iron bar to prevent it swinging open as the ship rolled. When a gun was pointed (aimed), it was 'run out' so that the muzzle protruded through the port. When it recoiled, the muzzle came inboard again. Discounting the quarterdeck, poop and forecastle, the *Leviathan*, another typical British 74 at the battle, had 28 such ports on each side, the *Victory* 44. The largest were those on the lower deck, which had to accommodate the biggest guns. On the *Victory* these measured about 3.5 feet square.

The importance of gunports is often overlooked. Quite apart from their primary function, of allowing a ship to fire her broadsides, they had a significant impact on the day-to-day life of seamen accommodated on the gundecks. This was because the ports also served as the ship's windows, letting in air and light. With the ports shut, in heavy rain or rough weather, the decks would be unbearably dark, damp and airless. In hot weather the humidity, stink of stale air and sweat from hundreds of bodies became nauseating. Even with the ports open, it was dingy and dank; with them shut for any length of time, it became not only unpleasant but also unhealthy below decks. Conversely, in winter or stormy weather having them shut was essential to keep out cold air and water. By 1805 all ports had had a small scuttle with a sliding lid cut in it to permit some ventilation and light when the weather prevented the whole port being left open. Some also had a 'bull's eye' of glass to let in a little light when the ports were shut. Fussy captains liked open port flaps to be at exactly the same angle.

However, what was crucial for the guns was the height above the waterline of the sill of the lower-deck ports. For most ships this was about 5ft 7in, which was normally, but not always, sufficient to allow the ports on the lower gundeck to be open to permit firing in any reasonable weather. A ship rolling heavily with lower ports open was a ship with fourteen large holes in her side through which huge quantities of seawater could pour, putting her in danger of foundering. With the ports 5ft 7in above the water a roll through 120 degrees was needed before water came in. With the ports shut, 28 guns could not fire, a situation that reduced a first- or second-rate ship to a third rate, or a third rate to a large frigate. An example of this difficulty was Lord Howe's flagship, the 110-gun *Queen Charlotte*, at the battle of 'The Glorious First of June'. Her lower-deck ports had only 4ft 6in of clearance, so in order to keep her guns firing from this flooded deck, all pumps had to be manned throughout the action – a huge drain on manpower, which reduced her rate of fire.

Counting the number of gunports was a quick way of estimating a ship's firepower. At the Battle of the Nile, Captain Ralph Miller of the 74-gun *Theseus* endeavoured to convince the French that his ship was a three-decker by painting black gunports on the outside of the hammock-cloths that were in the hammock netting around the upper deck. Whether this ruse deceived anybody is not clear.

With opposing ships close alongside each other, open gunports became useful targets for musketry fire. When two ships were locked together, men could sometimes scramble through in order to board an enemy ship. In these circumstances, with the ships' sides grinding together, the guns could not be run out through the ports and would be fired from within the ship – if necessary, in extremis, through a closed port.

## Gun construction

The diagram shows what a gun looked like. It rested on a wooden truck carriage, mounted on four wheels called 'trucks'. By Trafalgar the truck carriage had been in use, almost unchanged, for over 150 years. Its merits were its simplicity, its ease of maintenance and repair (both jobs were well within the capacity of a ship's carpenter) and its cheapness. It consisted of a platform, known as the 'bed', with two side pieces (cheeks) or brackets that had top edges stepped down from the front of the gun to the rear.

The gun rested on top of the brackets, with its trunnions fitting into two recesses. It was raised or lowered when aiming by a large wooden quoin (wedge) with a handle on the rear face, which was jammed under the breech of the gun. The quoin was pulled back to elevate the muzzle and pushed further under the breech to lower it – both heavy tasks carried out by seamen levering with handspikes under the breech. Even more levering was needed to move the muzzle to either side. In practice it was often easier to alter the ship's course than to move the guns.

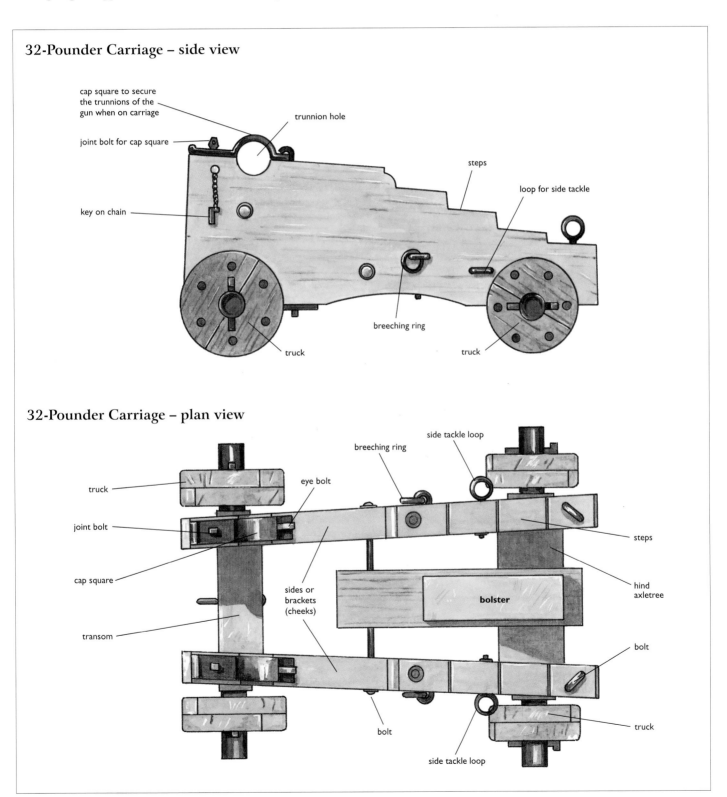

### 32-Pounder Carriage – side view

cap square to secure the trunnions of the gun when on carriage

trunnion hole

joint bolt for cap square

steps

loop for side tackle

key on chain

truck

breeching ring

truck

### 32-Pounder Carriage – plan view

truck

eye bolt

breeching ring

side tackle loop

joint bolt

steps

cap square

sides or brackets (cheeks)

bolster

hind axletree

transom

bolt

bolt

truck

side tackle loop

## Range and penetration

It is not generally known that the three-mile territorial limit around a nation's coasts was originally decreed because this was twice the effective range of a warship's guns. Essentially, the degree to which shot penetrated an enemy vessel depended on the range, which depended on the velocity, which depended on the size of the charge. A long-range shot (over 1,000 yards) with the maximum possible charge might do little damage to the hull, possibly not even penetrate. A shot fired at shorter range with a normal velocity and charge (one-third the weight of the shot) could, probably would, pierce an enemy ship through, penetrating both sides and leaving a few splinters and comparatively small holes, certainly not large enough to give the carpenter any problems. Conversely, at close range a lower-velocity shot using a charge of one-quarter of its weight would smash its way through the timber of one side only and cause dozens of lethal splinters to be hurled around the gundeck.

Then there was the question of the effect of elevation on the range. The expression to fire at 'point blank' range is well known and in common use today. To most people it means to shoot at extremely close range, only a few feet (or even inches) from the target, such that a miss is virtually impossible. There was a lot of this type of point-blank firing at Trafalgar once the ships became engaged in the mêlée stage of the battle. However, 'point blank' is a gunner's technical term that involved careful calculation. If a great gun was fired with the barrel in a true horizontal position, the trajectory of the shot was a parabola. When the ball left the barrel it was forced very slightly above the line of sight (this being a straight line from the muzzle to the target). This occurred just as the shot left the barrel, and was called the 'first point blank primitive'. The 'second point blank primitive' was the point at which gravity pushed the shot below the line of sight. Thus firing at any target between these two extremes was technically firing point blank. Using the normal charge of one-third the weight of the shot (see below) for 32-, 24- and 18-pounder great guns, point-blank fire was, according to Lieutenant Beauchant's *Naval Gunner*, anything up to 400 yards.

To increase the range, the barrel had to be elevated by pulling out the quoin. The range tables given by Beauchant indicate that every quarter degree raised, up to one degree, added 100 yards to the range. From then on, up to ten degrees, each degree of elevation produced a gradually reducing range increase. With ten degrees the range of these guns was 2,900 yards. However, few, if any, captains would open fire at such an extreme range – at Trafalgar the French 74 *Fougueux* fired her first ranging shots at the *Royal Sovereign* at something over 2,000 yards, and they fell short.

The introduction of shorter guns such as the carronade permitted ships that could not carry the heavy long guns to throw a heavy broadside, provided they engaged their enemy at closer than 1,000 yards. However, when it came to firing double-shotted, the long gun had the advantage in that its superior weight gave it the stability to resist the discharge of two balls with 8 lbs of powder (a third of the weight of a 24-pounder). Short versions had to use 4 lbs, giving a velocity of 645ft per second against 950ft and a penetration of solid elm of only 7in instead of 13.5in. Double-shotted guns threw one shot 100 to 150 yards beyond the other and had a range of about half that when firing a single shot with the same amount of powder. Grapeshot had around two-thirds the range of a single ball.

Calculating the penetration capability of different guns, with different charges at different ranges and single or double shot, was a complicated procedure and the subject of extensive experimentation ashore. The *Naval Gunner* set out a number of tables showing the thickness of ships' sides and the penetration achieved by various guns and sizes of charge against solid elm. Ships were constructed of oak but, according to the author, 'though it [oak] is a harder wood than elm, it is found from experiment not to resist a cannon ball so much, which may proceed from the oak splitting'. Simplified extracts from two tables are shown below:

### Thickness of ships' sides (oak) in inches

| First rate | at the load line | 30 |
| | at the upper deck | 21 |
| Second rate | at the load line | 26 |
| | at the upper deck | 20 |
| Third rate | at the load line | 24 |
| | at the upper deck | 18 |

Note that shots needed greater force to penetrate the lower decks than the upper deck. This was of particular importance for the British, as their primary target in battle was the enemy's hull. No account is taken in this extract of the fact that a shot hitting a closed port would have less than half the thickness to penetrate.

### Penetration of long 32-pounder (single shot) against solid elm

| Charge | Velocity per second (feet) | Penetration (inches) |
| --- | --- | --- |
| 16 lbs | 1,600 | 45 |
| 11 lbs ($^1/_3$ shot weight) | 1,300 | 29.6 |
| 8 lbs ($^1/_4$ shot weight) | 1,130 | 22.5 |
| 5 lbs 4 oz | 925 | 15 |
| 2 lbs 10 oz | 650 | 7.3 |

To ensure penetration wherever a shot hit, a 32-pounder needed to have at least an 11-lb charge – a third of shot weight being the most common charge for all guns. Even a 9-pounder mounted on a quarterdeck using a 3-lb charge would penetrate the upper deck of a 74. It should be noted, however, that the above figures assume a strike at right angles. If the shot hit the hull at a 45-degree slant, it had to penetrate a quarter as much hull thickness again. What all these complex tables were saying was that the best way to do serious damage was to get in close and use as much powder as possible; in practice, one-third the weight of the shot, as one-half would use up powder at too great a rate. As we shall see below, these were precisely the British tactics.

## AMMUNITION

### Solid shot

The spherical cannonball or roundshot was by far the most important and commonly used projectile for all navies and armies. This solid iron ball was cast in clay moulds and had replaced the stone shot that had been in use up to the sixteenth century. Some 70 to 80 per cent of the ammunition carried onboard all ships at Trafalgar was roundshot. It was so common for hundreds of years that today ammunition for guns and small arms is still counted in 'rounds', although none of the multitudinous types resembles that shape. The cannonball was a projectile capable of punching holes in hard targets such as ships' hulls and knocking down masts. It also made a fearsome mess of soft targets – seamen or marines – not just because

## Types of Shot Used at Trafalgar

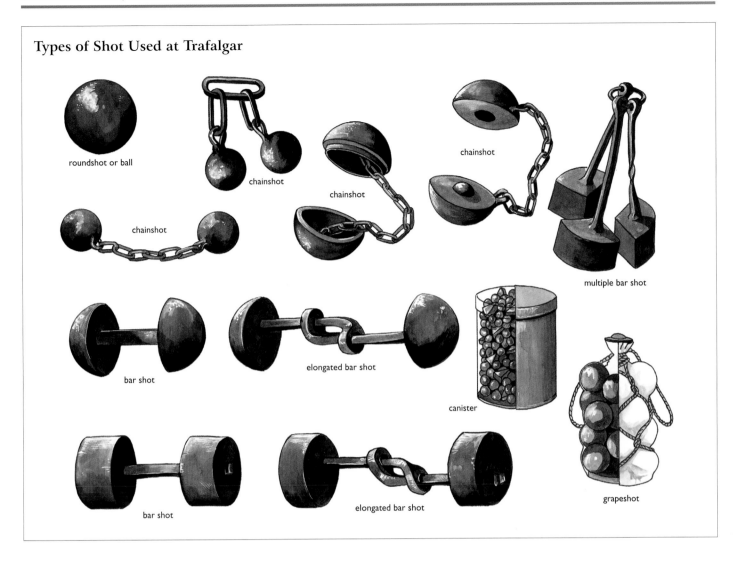

roundshot or ball

chainshot

chainshot

chainshot

chainshot

chainshot

multiple bar shot

bar shot

elongated bar shot

canister

bar shot

elongated bar shot

grapeshot

a direct hit could cut a man in two, but also because when it hit woodwork it caused dozens of lethal splinters to fly around.

Despite these useful properties, roundshot seldom sank a ship, and certainly not at Trafalgar. Holes below the waterline were rare, while those on the waterline were often comparatively small and could be plugged effectively by the carpenter and his crew. So roundshot was mostly used to batter an enemy into submission. This took time. In order to keep up a heavy weight of fire for prolonged periods (some ships at Trafalgar were in close action for five hours), a warship had to carry lots of guns and lots of roundshot. According to Peter Goodwin's excellent book *Countdown to Victory*, Nelson's flagship carried 120 tons of shot (of all types) at Trafalgar and fired off 2,669 rounds – just over 28 tons. The usual holding of roundshot for a 74 was 60 per gun. An immediate supply of roundshot was available from the shot racks, which were round holes cut in the coamings along the sides of hatchways and companionways. For bulk storage see p. 232.

### Dismantling shot

The intended targets for these double-headed projectiles were ropes, rigging, shrouds and stays; hitting any men who got in the way was a bonus. Dismantling shot was specialist ammunition designed to cripple a ship's ability to sail, manoeuvre and reduce her speed. It consisted of two shots joined together by a bar or chain or of elongated shot, joined by bars that extended when

fired. The shot itself varied from the simple spherical cannonballs to iron cylinders or hemispheres. Because of its irregular shape and the consequent high level of air resistance, dismantling shot could not be used at long ranges. The French and Spanish carried a higher percentage of this type of ammunition than the British, as they tended to favour crippling an enemy's sailing rather than fighting ability, certainly at the outset. At Trafalgar the *Victory* fired only 35 double-headed shots – the equivalent of one gun in three firing one each. For a British 74 three dismantling shot per gun was the usual holding.

### Anti-personnel shot

There were two types of anti-personnel shot in use at Trafalgar – grapeshot and canister. Both were effectively large shotgun ammunition, filled with small roundshot that spread out when fired into a deadly cone. Against solid objects it was more or less useless but against men it was lethal, and fired at close range it rarely missed. Grape was simply a tarred canvas bag filled with large iron balls and then tied up with cord – hence the name grapeshot. The weight, size and number of shot in the bag varied with the size of the gun that was to fire it. Tiered grapeshot that did away with the bag was not in use at Trafalgar, as it was not invented until much later. Grapeshot was effective up to about 600 yards but most destructive if fired at a much shorter range and able to sweep the deck of the target ship. As opposing ships closed, it became increasingly difficult, and eventually impossible, for lower-deck guns to be elevated sufficiently to fire at the open top decks, so most grapeshot was allocated to the guns on the quarterdeck, poop and forecastle. Again, *Countdown to Victory* gives us some interesting statistics for grapeshot fired by the *Victory* at Trafalgar. In total 186 rounds were fired. Of these, only 10 were from the lower-deck 32-pounders, 20 from the 24s (middle deck) and 156 from the 12s on the upper, quarter and forecastle decks. Even this amount was comparatively small – on average each of the forty-four 12-pounders would have fired grapeshot a mere 3.5 times in four hours of close-quarter battle. A 74 would carry some five rounds of grape per gun – perhaps 400, including some for carronades. There were normally nine shot ('grapes') in each grapeshot of all British great guns. Each shot used in a 32-pounder weighed 3 lbs (the equivalent of a hefty cricket ball), in a 24-pounder 2 lbs, in an 18-pounder 1.5 lbs and in a 12-pounder 1 lb (a hefty golf ball).

The 'official' quantities of grapeshot supposedly carried by the various rates are given below, although in practice the amounts would vary. Note that no grapeshot was allocated to 32-pounder guns on first rates, although we know that *Victory* carried some and fired a few at Trafalgar.

| Rate | 32-pdr | 24-pdr | 18-pdr | 12-pdr | 9-pdr | 6-pdr |
|------|--------|--------|--------|--------|-------|-------|
| 1st | – | 112 | – | 140 | – | – |
| 2nd | 78 | – | 104 | 130 | – | 84 |
| 3rd (74 guns) | 78 | – | 130 | – | 168 | 28 |
| 3rd (64 guns) | 132 | – | 182 | – | 84 | – |
| 5th | – | 132 | – | 154 | – | 48 |

Canister (also known as case) was, as its name implies, a thin tin canister filled with musket balls or other smaller shot than grape (up to 1 lb when fired from a 32-pounder). Again, it was very effective as anti-personnel ammunition at ranges of up to about 350 yards, and particularly suited to carronades. It is doubtful if any was used (or carried) at Trafalgar.

### Storage of shot

On the gundecks some roundshot was kept readily to hand in the holes cut in the hatchways coamings. On clearing for action, shot garlands beside the guns were filled from these. Bulk storage was in shot lockers – wooden, rectangular boxes with angles and hinged lids. The *Victory* had three, each of which was divided vertically into compartments for different weights or type of shot. There was one fore and aft of the pump well in the hold, with another aft of the grand magazine.

### GUNPOWDER

Nobody who witnessed the obliteration of the 124-gun French flagship *L'Orient* at the Nile in 1798, in two vast eruptions heard some 15 miles away in Alexandria, would ever need reminding of the virtually instant oblivion that awaited the crew of a ship whose powder magazine exploded. Fire on board a wooden warship was dreaded more than enemy guns. The precautions taken to prevent it – the rules restricting smoking, use of candles and the galley fire and the elaborate safeguards built

into the construction of a ship's magazines – were all designed to keep the powder safe. It was the gunner who had the day-to-day responsibility for the stowage and care of the powder in the magazines, and Admiralty regulations governing his conduct were specific and uncompromising. When taking on board gunpowder (in barrels) he was:

> V
>
> … to inform the Captain when the powder will be ready to be sent on board, that the fire in the Galley may be put out, before the Vessel which carries it is suffered to go alongside. While the powder is taking into the Ship, no candles are to be kept lighted, except those in the light-room; nor is any man to be allowed to smoke tobacco. As soon as the whole is stowed in the Magazine, the Gunner is to see the doors, the light-room and the scuttle carefully secured, and is to deliver the keys to the Captain, or to such other Officer as he shall appoint to take charge of them.

> VII
>
> He is never to go to the Magazine without being ordered to go there. He is never to allow the doors of the Magazine to be opened but by himself; he is not to open them until the proper Officer [on the *Victory* at Trafalgar this was the master-at-arms] is in the light-room … he must take care that no Person enters the Magazine without wearing the leather slippers supplied by the Ordnance.

Gunpowder was made from a mixture of saltpetre (75 per cent), sulphur (10 per cent) and charcoal (15 per cent). There were powder mills at Faversham, Waltham Abbey and Dartford. Faversham produced almost exactly a ton a day throughout the year (364 tons). Waltham Abbey was the site of the Royal Gunpowder Mills, which is now open to the public. The best-quality powder was the 'cylinder' powder that in 1805 had just started to be issued regularly to the Navy. It was made with charcoal charred in cylinders (ovens) rather than kilns, which burned more uniformly, thus giving the powder greater efficiency. Because it was more powerful than the older type (which was still in use), the barrels, which came in weights of 100 lbs, 50 lbs and 25 lbs, were labelled with red lettering and kept separately to avoid overloading the cartridges and thus the guns. Barrels were made of wood with wooden or copper bands, with those containing the old powder labelled in blue and those containing recycled powder in white. After manufacture the powder was sent, in the barrels, to the Grand Magazine at Purfleet, on the Thames estuary, for testing.

The best method of testing was to place a small amount ('a drachm or two') on a piece of clean writing paper and fire it by means of a red-hot iron wire. If there was an immediate flash and 'a good report' that left the paper free from white specks and did not burn holes in it, then the powder was properly made. The quality of cylinder powder was such that a mere 2 oz of the best quality could

---

### The Royal Gunpowder Mills, Waltham Abbey

This historic site, set in 75 acres of parkland and boasting 21 historic buildings, was the home to gunpowder and explosives production and research from 1660 to the 1990s. It is now open to the public for the first time in 300 years, and the whole area can be explored, with its mix of fascinating history, exciting science and lovely surroundings, much of which can be viewed from an observation tower. There is an introductory film, hands-on and photographic displays and history trails, all of which combine to show the visitor how the powder fired by the fleet at Trafalgar was made and transported.

project a 64-lb ball from a mortar 180ft: 30ft further than the older pit-charcoal powder could achieve. Powder that had been recycled, i.e. taken out of filled cartridges and re-barrelled, would only project the ball about 112ft. These tests indicate clearly how important the quality of the powder was. However, it was not just the process of manufacture that affected the gunpowder's efficiency; it had another enemy – damp. Almost as many precautions had to be taken against damp as against fire. Wet powder was useless; damp powder was unreliable, and therefore dangerous. The continuously damp atmosphere on board ship made the special construction of the powder rooms and magazines of critical importance. The test to see if powder had absorbed too much water was to weigh it. Good powder, even if exposed for two or three weeks to the atmosphere, should not become significantly heavier. Specifically, a barrel of powder originally weighing 100 lbs should not increase by more than 12 oz. If the increase was greater, the powder was condemned.

The barrels of powder were stored in the magazine, also known as the powder room. Frigates and smaller ships had one magazine but two-deckers had two and a three-decker such as the *Victory* had three, all located amidships, away from the ship's sides and as low down as possible in the safest part of the ship. First there was the grand magazine, well forward in the hold, which held the stock of barrels. Then there were two hanging magazines (forward and aft), suspended between the orlop deck and hold so that the cartridges (powder) were well clear of bilge water but still below the gundeck and the danger of fire. All three magazines were needed for a ship of *Victory*'s size to ensure sufficient storage capacity for both barrels and made-up cartridges but, equally importantly, to facilitate the speedy distribution of cartridges to the guns on all decks in action. Adjoining the main magazine, but not the hanging magazines, was a smaller filling room in which cartridges were made up and stored in small wooden cases ready for use on racks round three sides of

## The Main and Hanging Magazines

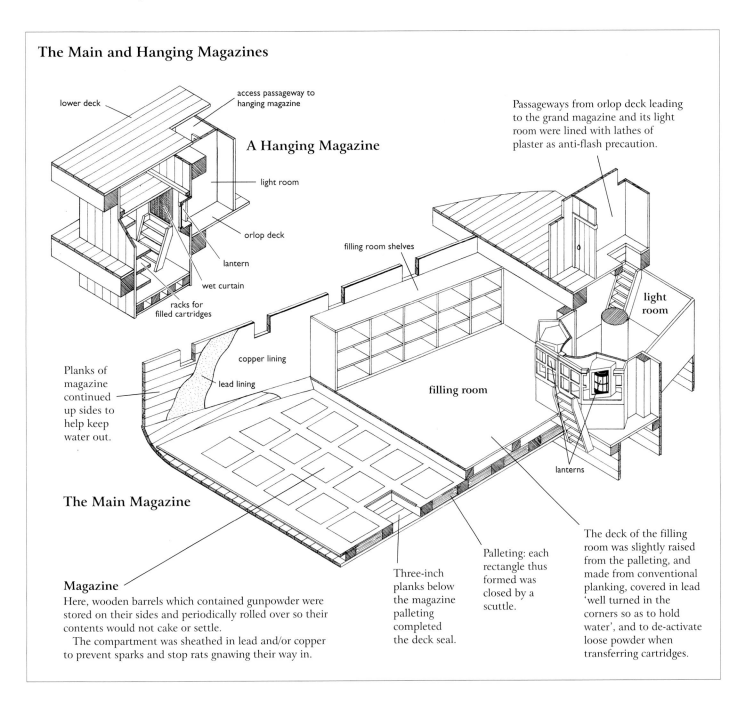

lower deck

access passageway to hanging magazine

### A Hanging Magazine

light room

orlop deck

lantern

wet curtain

racks for filled cartridges

Passageways from orlop deck leading to the grand magazine and its light room were lined with lathes of plaster as anti-flash precaution.

filling room shelves

**light room**

copper lining

lead lining

**filling room**

lanterns

Planks of magazine continued up sides to help keep water out.

### The Main Magazine

**Magazine**
Here, wooden barrels which contained gunpowder were stored on their sides and periodically rolled over so their contents would not cake or settle.
  The compartment was sheathed in lead and/or copper to prevent sparks and stop rats gnawing their way in.

Three-inch planks below the magazine palleting completed the deck seal.

Palleting: each rectangle thus formed was closed by a scuttle.

The deck of the filling room was slightly raised from the palleting, and made from conventional planking, covered in lead 'well turned in the corners so as to hold water', and to de-activate loose powder when transferring cartridges.

the room. This work required good light, so each magazine had a tiny adjoining light room, more a compartment or box for the hanging magazines, with candle lanterns behind thick glass. Magazines in the hold, such as the grand magazine on the *Victory*, had specially constructed panels filled with charcoal to absorb moisture. The hanging magazines on the *Victory* were not powder rooms but rather for the storage of the wooden cases, each containing one made-up cartridge, as once firing started, it was not possible to fill bags quickly enough to meet the demand and they were far safer in boxes.

It was the gunner, Mr William Rivers on the *Victory*, who had to regularly check the condition of the powder and its stowage in the grand magazine. Every three months he had to ensure all the barrels were turned to prevent the nitrate separating from the other ingredients – a mammoth undertaking, as the *Victory* sailed for Trafalgar carrying 35 tons in some 780 barrels (including half-barrels). Empty barrels were not allowed to be broken up or used for any other purpose, but they were returnable: for every empty barrel the gunner returned to the Ordnance storekeeper at the end of a commission, he received a shilling – a reasonable incentive. *The Practical Sea-Gunner's Companion* of 1781 stated, 'After an Engagement, he is to procure a Survey to be made of the Powder in general.'

A final word on gunpowder: the amount used by the *Victory* during the battle was 17,100 lbs – about 7.6 tons or 22 per cent of her stock. This represented 150 barrels and 80 half-barrels. She also used two barrels of priming powder. The 'empties' would have entitled Rivers to about £9-10-0, virtually two months' pay. All this powder was used to discharge 2,669 rounds – an average of just over 25 shots per gun and carronade.

## Cartridges

The gunner and his mates were responsible for the making up of cartridges on board, using wooden ladles to measure the powder. This was a crucial task. The made-up bags had to be filled with precisely the correct amount of powder and they had to be used in the right weight of gun, firing at the appropriate range. Particular care had to be taken with the more powerful cylinder powder, as there was a danger of an overload in a gun. Cartridges intended for single-shot firing at a distance with the new powder were a third the weight of the shot. Thus a 32-pounder loaded with one ball and firing at a target over 600 yards away would use a cartridge weighing 10 lbs 11 oz. At closer range the cartridge used would be a quarter the weight of the shot – in this case about 8 lbs. If the gun was double-shotted at very close range, then again the rule of thumb was a quarter the weight of a single shot. Each cartridge had to be clearly labelled with the gun it was intended for and the weight of the powder in it. Reduced charges were also required for short guns or for guns that had heated up due to continuous firing. Admiralty regulations emphasized this point: 'It is also suggested that the rule which Captains of Men of War have hitherto practised in reducing the charges of powder for carronades as well as for cannon, when the pieces become warm in a long engagement, may be rigidly attended to.'

### Quantities of Gunpowder Used with Different Shots (British)

| Gun | Powder weight (lbs) | |
| --- | --- | --- |
| | single-shotted | double-shotted |
| 32-pdr | 10.6 | 8 |
| 24-pdr | 8 | 6 |
| 18-pdr | 6 | 4.5 |
| 12-pdr | 4 | 3 |
| 9-pdr | 3 | 2.25 |
| 6-pdr | 2 | 1.5 |

These figures are those issued by the Admiralty in 1806 and show that guns loaded with one shot used cartridges a third of their weight, a quarter for double-shotted. All were for firing at point-blank range.

In the bedlam of battle, gun captains had to keep their wits about them to ensure the proper cartridge was being loaded for the task in hand. A Board of Admiralty memorandum dated 20 August 1801 stated that cartridges containing cylinder powder for carronades should only weigh one-twelfth of the shot. For the *Victory*'s 68-lb carronades this would be a very small bag of some 5.5 lbs. This was also the size used as 'blanks' for gun salutes.

The cartridge bags used at Trafalgar by the *Victory* were made of thick paper, according to the *Gunner's Expense Book – Ammunition Expended on 21 October 1805*, which lists a total of 3,970 paper cartridges as having been used. The 32-pounders had required 937, the 24-pounders 1,234 and the 12-pounders 1,799. The problem with paper was that, although it was cheap, there was more of a risk that small burning embers would remain in the breach of the gun after firing, so any slipshod sponging of the barrel could bring instant disaster. It was also more difficult to keep dry in store. Flannel cartridges had been in service for some time, and were recognized as more effective as they were entirely consumed by the explosion as the gun fired – although the gun was still sponged. However, they do not seem to have been in use, at least by the British flagship at the battle, probably because of the extra cost.

The actual filling was done in the filling room adjoining the magazine, lit by the lanterns in the light room, with all concerned wearing leather slippers and using wooden ladles. The room was normally lined with a fire-resistant material, with the ready-for-use cartridges placed on racks to be passed up through the hatches in wooden cases, each containing one cartridge, to the gundecks during battle. In action it was the practice to have only three cartridges available at any time for each gun – one in the gun and two in the salt box. At quarters the gunner's location was normally in the main filling room. Here regulations required him, among other duties, to 'take all opportunities of filling powder [cartridges], that there may be no cessation of firing for want of ammunition; and he is to be attentive to send out cartridges with the quantity of powder reduced or increased as the Captain shall, from time to time, send him directions'.

Mr Rivers and his like had the vital responsibility of ammunition supply during battle, not only with regards to maintaining a steady flow, but also to ensuring the correct cartridges were available as needed. Undoubtedly a good gunner earned his none too generous pay of £4-16-0 a month.

## Gunlocks and priming tubes

The method of actually exploding the cartridge requires explanation. Soldiers had fired their handguns or muskets from as far back as the fifteenth century using first matchlocks, then wheel-locks and finally flintlocks – in the last two cases where a spark was made by a flint flying forward and striking metal (the cock). Sailors had mostly stuck to using the slow match to ignite the powder in the touchhole of their guns, until compelled to adopt the flintlock for all guns in the late 1770s. Having to pour loose fine-grained powder into the touchhole on a heaving deck in all the confusion

## Gun Salutes (British)

Regulations stated all salutes were to be fired (cartridge only) from upper-deck guns. A much reduced amount of powder was used – for example, a 2-lb charge for a 24-pounder gun and 1 lb for a 12-pounder. Five seconds seems to have been the most popular interval, though the regulations strangely omit to mention this important detail.

Gun salutes were a complex business in Nelson's navy. They had to be exactly right in order not to cause offence – or even an international incident. There were twenty-eight regulations governing who was entitled to be saluted, when and by how many guns. All the complex permutations were laid down, requiring careful thought by ship's captains and watch-keeping officers. All salutes had to be returned – failure to acknowledge a salute was a serious breach of etiquette. The occasions when saluting was mandatory included the following:

• When a ship or ships joined a fleet or squadron commanded by a flag officer. If several ships arrived at the same time, all would fire the required salute but the flagship would not return the salute until all had ceased firing. When two squadrons met, only the flagships saluted.
• When a flag officer hoisted his flag on taking command, all ships saluted. It must have sounded as though a full-scale battle was in progress!
• Flagships had to return the salutes of foreign ships-of-war, as did captains if they were so saluted. However, Regulation XXIV made it clear that Royal Navy ships were not to initiate saluting foreign ships.
• Merchant ships were required to salute British warships by striking their topsails. If they neglected to do so, their name, master, port of origin, together with an account of the incident, was to be sent to no lesser personage than the Secretary of the Admiralty 'in order to their being proceeded against in the Admiralty Court'.
• When ambassadors, noblemen and envoys embarked on any British warship – the former got 15, the latter two 13. They received the same again when disembarking.

• A ship entering a foreign port or roadstead might salute the fort, but only if he was certain his salute would be returned by an equal number of guns. It is unclear how he was expected to know this in advance.
• Salutes were fired by ships in port to celebrate certain anniversaries. The number of guns fired was not to exceed twenty-one by each ship. In 1805 they were, with the number of guns in parentheses:
  • birth (21), accession and coronation (17 each) of the king
  • birth of the queen (21)
  • restoration of King Charles II (17)
  • defeat of the Gunpowder Plot (17).

The entitlement of flag officers was as follows:
• Admiral and commander-in-chief of the fleet: 17. He had to return 15 to all flag officers and 13 to captains.
• Admirals: 15. He returned two fewer guns to a vice- or rear-admiral, four fewer to a captain. The *Victory*'s log for 16 August 1805 reads, 'At 3 saw Ushant bearing EbE 8 or 9 leagues [24 to 27 miles]. At 6 moderate and clear. Saluted Adm. Cornwallis in HM Ship *Ville de Paris* with 15 guns.'
• Vice-admirals and rear-admirals: 13. The former returned two fewer guns to a rear-admiral and four fewer to a captain, the latter two fewer to a captain.
• Commodores were to salute and be saluted as rear-admirals.

There were some tricky decisions to be made, even if you knew you had to salute and the number of guns to fire. The important thing was to be noticed! Lieutenant Fordyce in his treatise mentions the right moment for saluting on going into harbour or joining the admiral at sea. He recommended: 'firing the salute the moment before shortening sail, so that while the smoke is still curling around, the ship is seen steadily shortening sail and picking up her berth. The salute then cannot escape the notice of all the vessels assembled in the roadstead … The same applies at sea.'

He gave a final word of warning – if using carronades, ensure the cartridge was steadily pushed home, since there was a tendency for it to slew the wrong way when rammed: 'your salute otherwise may be vexatiously spoiled. Be sure the colours are up.'

of a battle with a continuously burning match to hand meant some spillage was inevitable and potentially dire. A considerable improvement had been the temporary adoption of a priming tube made of tin in the mid-1750s. A piece of saltpetre-permeated cord was rolled in fine gunpowder before being allowed to dry. This ensured a very rapid burning time. It was then cut into short lengths and inserted into a thin tin tube that was inserted into the gun's vent and pushed home into the chamber. The top was 'bushed' out, primed with a mixture of gunpowder paste and wine and allowed to dry hard. When lit with the slow match it worked well, cutting down spillage dramatically. However, after the Battle of Quiberon Bay in 1759, Admiral Hawke complained that these tin tubes flew out of the vent on firing and caused injuries. They also were hot and sharp to step on in bare feet!

Not until goose-quill tubes were tried out in conjunction with musket flintlocks by Sir Charles Douglas in 1778 – at his own expense in the 90-gun *Duke* – was the final solution found. However, it was another four years before the gunnery of the *Duke* and *Formidable* (of which Douglas was flag captain) at the Battle of the Saints in the West Indies convinced the sceptical.

The performance of these two ships had been so obviously superior to the rest of the fleet that Britain finally adopted the flint-lock (as a gunlock) to be used in conjunction with a goose quill. Even so, at Trafalgar slow matches were available just in case!

It was normal practice for the guns to be kept loaded at all times, but the gun captains did not attach the locks until the marine drummers beat 'to quarters'. The body of the gunlock was made of brass with steel hammer and frizzen plate (priming pan cover). The lock was fitted on the right side of the vent by means of two bolts secured by butterfly nuts. A steel trigger eye, attached by a wooden toggle to the firing lanyard (needed so that the gun captain could stand back to avoid the recoil), was fitted at the rear of the lock. When the pan was primed, the frizzen closed, the hammer with its flint cocked and the lanyard pulled, the flint flew forward, struck the frizzen and made a spark. The spark lit the powder in the pan, the flash passed through the flash hole to the entrance of the vent and ignited the top of the quill which fired the cartridge that propelled the ball out of the muzzle at around 1,600 feet per second. This was a seemingly lengthy chain reaction but one that, in reality, was all but instantaneous.

## Accidents at the Guns

Accidents with unpleasant consequences for those nearby were not uncommon. The main causes were:

• Shipping large quantities of water through the lower-deck ports, which put the ship in danger of sinking, or at least made it difficult to continue the action. The crew had to take great caution in a heavy sea, opening lower-deck ports a few at a time or not at all.
• The tremendous recoil of an overheated gun, which saw the gun leaping back and the recoil being taken unequally by the breeching ropes. This could cause a rope to snap and the gun to run loose, crushing anybody at the rear. To prevent this, care had to be taken to reduce the charge of overheated guns and check that the breeching ropes were taking the recoil equally.
• The bursting of a gun, which could be caused by the muzzle having dipped into the water at the moment of firing or by one

load of powder and shot being accidentally put on top of another. Loading too many different types of shot over one cartridge, particularly putting odd pieces of iron bars and bolts on top of a roundshot, could also jam the barrel, with the same result. Constant vigilance by the gun captain was essential.
• Minor explosion of powder on the gundeck. For this reason spare cartridges were always held as far away from the gun as possible, on the disengaged side or, if both sides were firing, amidships. The number of cartridges at the gun position was strictly limited to three and loose powder was mopped up regularly with wet swabs.
• The breaking of the iron rings to which the breechings were attached, or their being weakened and finally pulled out of the hull by continuous recoils.

## EQUIPMENT

### Tackle

Guns were secured by four ropes and five blocks, collectively called tackle, which played an essential role. If a gun broke loose, it became an uncontrolled mass of metal and wood careering wildly about with the ship's movement, crushing men or objects unlucky enough to get in its path – the origin of the modern description of someone dangerously unpredictable as a 'loose cannon'. It could be recaptured by having a heavy canvas sail thrown over it, but this was a hazardous process. A gun could be secured in three main ways. Firstly, it could be housed or stowed, that is lashed securely when not in use, with the muzzle tied firmly to a pair of eyebolts above the port. Secondly, it could be run in board for loading, and thirdly run out, with the muzzle protruding through the port, for firing. The four ropes involved were as follows:

#### Breeching rope

This thick hemp rope (7in circumference for a 32-pounder) was used to check the massive recoil, allowing the muzzle to recoil inboard enough that the sponge and rammer could be used. This put a huge strain both on the rope and on the ring bolts that secured the rope to the ship's side. One end was fixed to a ring bolt on the larboard side of the port. The rope then passed through a ring bolt on the side of the carriage, through the thimble above the button, and back through another ring bolt on the other side of the carriage to the fourth ring bolt on the starboard side of the port. After continuous firing the guns became extremely hot and their recoil increasingly violent – sometimes so great as to lift the carriage from the deck to touch the beams above. With well over three tons of gun and carriage hurtling backwards with this force, it was not unknown for the breeching ropes to snap like twine. This was more of a danger on the lower deck where ropes were often wet and thus subject to rot, and these guns were sometimes fitted with double breeching ropes to prevent rupture. Spare breeching ropes were always to hand in action.

#### Gun (or side) tackle (2)

These two tackles were used to haul the gun back to the run-out position after firing. A gun crew needed so many men (14 for the 32-pounder) not for the loading and firing process so much as for the heaving and hauling to get the muzzle back out through the

port. There was one tackle for each side of the gun, and the rope was threaded through one double and one single block to make a pulley arrangement. One block hooked into a ring bolt on the side of the carriage, the other to a ring bolt on the ship's side.

#### Train tackle

This was the same as the gun tackle, but its purpose was to prevent the gun rolling forward when the ship heeled during reloading. To this end it was attached to an eyebolt at the rear of the carriage and to another fixed to the deck near the centre line.

### Gunner's tools

A considerable number of tools and accessories had to be to hand at every gun position in battle; without them the guns could not be fired. The tools for loading and cleaning were kept hooked to the beams above the gun and were taken down and laid by the gun when required for a gun drill or at 'beat to quarters' prior to action. Each is briefly described below.

#### Sponge

This was made of sheepskin and fitted to a wooden head on the end of a stave by copper nails. The stave was 9ft to 11ft in length so that it projected out of the barrel when pushed home. Kept wet from a bucket of water beside the gun, the sponge was used to swab out the barrel after every shot to extinguish any smouldering embers from the cartridge bag after firing.

#### Gun ladle

This was a long-handled wooden or copper ladle used for inserting the cartridge down the bore if this was not done by hand.

#### Rammer

This was a flat-headed wooden stave about 9ft long, used to load the cartridge, shot and wad by pushing them down the bore to the bottom. Many were marked off on the side so that the man using it could tell when the ball was fully home.

#### Flexible rammer

This was a piece of thick rope fitted with a sponge at one end and a rammer at the other. As it could be slightly bent, it was used to load when the weather was rough and the gunports closed, when there was insufficient room to get the long wooden staves into the muzzle. It was also used (as at Trafalgar) when an enemy ship was close alongside, in order to avoid exposing the crew to musket fire while sponging or ramming at the port.

### Worm or wad hook

This was a corkscrew-shaped piece of iron attached to a 9ft stave, used after every four or five shots to remove any accumulation of flannel cartridge bases at the bottom of the bore. If this was not done frequently, the accumulation of cartridge material could cover the lower part of the vent hole and prevent the pricking of the cartridge or the flash from the quill entering the cartridge. With some cartridges it was necessary to worm after every shot – a serious disadvantage as it slowed the rate of fire considerably. The worm was also used when a gun had to be unloaded: with the guns kept loaded at sea, the cartridge had to be checked periodically to ensure it had not become damp. Sometimes worms were attached to the other end of the sponge, as this speeded up the drill and allowed the same man to do both tasks.

### Vent reamer or bit

This was an iron pike made from a square cross-section rod with a corkscrew twist at one end and a handle at the other – similar to a gimlet. It was used to clear the vent hole of carbon deposits.

### Thumb stall

This was a piece of leather made to fit over a thumb with a strap, intended to protect the thumb of the gunner whose job it was to cover the vent hole during sponging and loading. If the hole was not sealed, the air forced down by the sponge could ignite any embers in the bore – in other words, the gunner's thumb over the vent prevented a through draught. When the sponge was withdrawn it created a partial vacuum that also helped to ensure no smouldering debris remained. Covering the vent hole was an absolutely critical job, and one that could easily be forgotten in the stress and turmoil of battle.

### Vent pricker

This was a copper wire about a foot long with a point at one end and a handle at the other, used to make a small hole in the cartridge by pushing it down the vent hole. This ensured easy ignition of the charge by the flash from the quill. If there was no resistance to the pricker, then the order 'ram again' was shouted to ensure the cartridge was pushed to the bottom of the bore.

### Apron

This was a thin sheet of lead about a foot square, placed over the vent when the guns were not in use, known as the 'apron' because it was held in place by two white cords. It kept water or dampness out of the vent.

## 32-Pounder Gun with Equipment

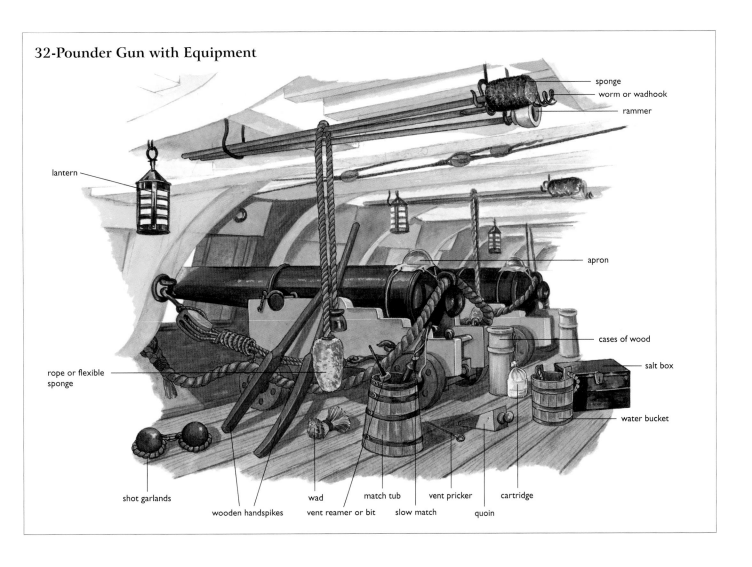

sponge
worm or wadhook
rammer
lantern
apron
cases of wood
salt box
rope or flexible sponge
water bucket
shot garlands
wooden handspikes
wad
vent reamer or bit
match tub
slow match
vent pricker
quoin
cartridge

*Lantern*
This was used during firing at night and sometimes by day due to the clouds of smoke. The General Orders Book for the 74-gun *Mars* at Trafalgar reads, 'Upon coming to action in the night, the Lanthorn Man at each Gun must immediately upon the Drum beating to Arms, go for his Lanthorn and place it securely hung up in the Midships at the place appointed.'

*Match tubs*
These were small, cone-shaped, wooden kegs partially filled with water, used to hold the slow match. They were lit from the lantern at the start of the action and kept burning to the rear of each gun in case the gunlock failed or was damaged. The match was made from hemp boiled in a mixture of spirits of wine and saltpetre and burned at the rate of one foot in three hours.

*Shot garlands*
These were circlets of rope, capable of holding several balls piled in a pyramid and placed on the deck by the gun ready for immediate use.

*Salt boxes*
These were wooden boxes, each able to hold two cartridges, which were kept by the powder men well to the rear of the gun when firing. It was from these boxes that cartridges were handed to the loader. They were called salt boxes because they were lined with a layer of salt to prevent cartridges getting damp. To prevent sparks accidentally getting into the box during firing, the lid was hinged by leather held in place by copper fittings. Despite this, things could, and did, go wrong. During the Battle of Camperdown in 1797 against the Dutch, Surgeon Young of the 64-gun *Ardent* witnessed a salt box accident: 'An explosion of a salt box with several cartridges abreast of the cockpit hatchway filled the hatchway with flame and in a moment 14 or 15 wretches tumbled down upon each other, their faces black as a cinder, their clothes blown to shatters and their hats afire.'

*Cases of wood*
Lightweight cylindrical wooden cases made of poplar with an elm lid and a cord carrying strap, these were made in various sizes to carry the different weights of cartridge. It was in these wooden cases that the cartridges were passed up by hand from the filling room to the gundecks and to the powdermen.

*Wooden handspikes*
Two were allocated to each pair of opposite guns, e.g. to the No. 1 gun starboard and the No. 1 gun larboard. They were used to lever up the breech so that the gun captain could move the quoin when adjusting the elevation or move the carriage when pointing the gun. It was usual for one to have an iron claw – making it into a crowbar less likely to break when levering to raise the base of the barrel.

*Water buckets*
A wooden or leather bucket was placed by every gun to wet the sponge or the deck swab, used by the boys to extinguish any glowing embers that might fall on the deck. The French were supposed to use a mixture of five parts seawater to one of vinegar for swabbing out the guns. Contrary to received tradition, the ship's boys were not always employed dashing up and down bringing cartridges (powder) for the guns. To start with there were not enough boys (thirty-one on the *Victory*) and some ships' orders expressly forbade their employment in this way. Called 'powder monkeys', their task was mainly to use swabs and the water bucket to damp down loose powder on the deck. Captain George Duff's orders for the *Mars* at Trafalgar made this point abundantly clear: 'The Officers are to suffer no Boys to hold Powder, but the Boys will be made useful in attending with wet hand swabs to damp any loose powder on the Deck.'

*Powder horn*
This was a cow horn fitted with a spring-loaded tip and a wooden bung with a central filling hole at the wide end. The bung was closed with a wooden screw stopper and the horn carried by a sling over the shoulder of the gun captain. It was filled with small-grain pistol powder for filling the priming pan of the gunlock.

*Belt pouches*
These leather pouches were usually worn by certain gun crew members, for instance the gun captain, the second captain or the primer. They contained items such as quill tubes, gunlock flints and spare lanyards.

*Quarter bolts*
In addition to the ring bolts on either side of each gun port to which the side tackles were normally hooked, there was another bolt, the quarter bolt, on the ship's side between each gun position. It was shared by two guns and enabled them to be trained far to the left or right.

*Wads*
Wads were plugs rammed down the bore to keep powder and shot in position. Two were required for each firing, one to separate the cartridge from the ball, the other on top of the shot to keep it from rolling out when the ship heeled. They were made up on board under the instructions of the gunner, who was given pieces of old rope or cable, known as 'junk' – another old naval word still in common use. This material was beaten into shape in a 'wad former', then bound with worsted to keep its shape. For a 32-pounder they needed to be about 2.5in thick and slightly larger than the bore for a good fit. In battle the wads were kept in a net hung close to the shot garlands.

*Tompion (usually pronounced 'tompkin')*
This was a wooden bung placed in the muzzle of the gun when not in use to keep out rain, seawater and dirt, made in different sizes to fit each calibre.

*Speaking trumpets*
Although the General Orders of the *Mars* stated, 'The strictest silence [is] to be observed by the Men at their Guns, and Officers are directed to prevent any unnecessary noise', once firing started the din became almost unbearable. The use of the speaking trumpet, made of copper, was an indispensable piece of equipment for all officers, master's mates or midshipmen on the gun decks, but even then orders had to be screamed repeatedly.

# GUNNERY

The previous paragraphs have described and discussed the ordnance and the ammunition. Those that follow look at how these guns were used – gunnery. It was good gunnery that won battles. Ships were rated by the number of guns they carried, and, other things being equal, the ship with the most and heaviest guns was likely to win an engagement, provided – crucially – that her gunnery was effective. Gunnery should not be confused with tactics, which are discussed below. Gunnery was all about the firing of the gun, the speed of firing, good aiming, and a steady supply of the right ammunition to the right gun. It was about a well-organized gundeck, individual crew members, their training and how smoothly they performed their drills under great stress and danger. Tactics concerned manoeuvring a ship, a squadron or a fleet so that its gunnery could be applied most effectively. In the end, once battle was joined, the result invariably depended on gunnery, and this was certainly true at Trafalgar.

## CLEAR FOR ACTION

The first order given on any warship that anticipated the possibility of battle was 'clear for action'. Practised frequently to ensure thoroughness and speed, this meant ensuring all departments of the ship were ready for battle, in particular preparing the gundecks for firing and to counter or minimize the effect of enemy fire. This involved all hands in activities that had been reduced to a drill, so that every man knew exactly what to do, when and in what order. To clear for action involved considerable effort by the entire crew. They acted as a team, as there was much to be done quickly – and simultaneously. A well-trained crew could have their ship cleared for action in 15 minutes in almost complete silence, and she could remain in that state for hours or even several days, depending on the threat. Living conditions at sea were always hard, but when the gundecks were stripped of everything except

the guns, including the admiral's and captain's furniture, in order to give an unobstructed view from one end to the other, they became extremely austere. When exactly to clear for action at Trafalgar seems to have been for the captains to decide. Timings for the same event shown in ships' logs vary considerably. That of the *Euryalus* indicated the *Victory* hoisted No. 13 'Prepare for Battle' at 7.00 a.m. on 21 October. However, according to Midshipman Richard Roberts of the *Victory*, the flagship had cleared for action at mid-morning on 19 October and remained in that state of readiness until 'beat to quarters' at 10.00 a.m. on the 21st – about 48 hours. The log of the *Dreadnought* indicates she cleared at 'daylight' on 21 October, while that of the *Spartiate* specifies 6.40 a.m. and many ships' logs make no mention of it at all. The details of the tasks to be done provide a summary of the work involved, which might vary slightly from captain to captain – the details would be set out in the ship's general orders.

- All hammocks/bedding rolls were stowed in the net racks around the poop, quarterdeck, waist and forecastle and then covered with wetted canvas. They acted as a protective parapet against musket balls.
- The decks were wetted and sanded to prevent slipping. The leather fire buckets containing sand were distributed to the gun positions on all decks, the galley fire was extinguished, the lower courses (sails) were wetted, wet screens were hung around hatchways and passageways to the magazines and water was put on the floor of each. The master-at-arms and cook both reported for duty in the grand magazine light room, though why that was their battle location is something of a mystery.
- Each gun captain was issued with spare flints, a slow match, powder horn, pouch containing quill firing tubes and cartridge prickers and reamers.

---

## An Admiral's Inspection

In the 1830s a Lieutenant A. D. Fordyce wrote a comprehensive manuscript detailing all matters pertaining to the running of a ship-of-the-line of Nelson's day. In it he gives the timings of a practice 'clear for action' and 'beat to quarters' for an admiral's inspection. The drummers beat to quarters at 17.5 minutes past 10 in the morning. The captain reported 'All ready' to the admiral 9 minutes and 10 seconds later – the ship having cleared for action and the men being ready at quarters. This was a remarkably good performance, provided it was an unannounced inspection! For the next two hours and more the admiral put the crew through its paces with a thorough inspection of different aspects of seamanship and gun handling. Among the activities and battle eventualities the admiral ordered and watched were:

- Inspected upper deck quarters.
- 1st, 2nd, and 3rd Division of boarders and 1st and 2nd Division of pikemen called.
- Exercised main deck quarters.

- Shifted breechings of main-deck guns.
- Dismounted main-deck gun, larbd. Side and transported aft.
- Firemen called.
- General fire [alarm].
- Dismounted and transported two guns on main-deck, one supposed to have burst.
- Ship would not wear.
- Cut away the mizzen-mast.
- Starboard quarters to clear wreck.
- A racking [raking] shot took away fore rigging.
- Wore ship.
- Whole of main rigging gone.
- Admiral inspected lower-deck quarters.
- Bowsprit carried away.
- Manned both sides of each deck at quarters …

Altogether it was a series of tough, practical tests. One hopes, for the captain's sake, that all went well.

- Arms chests containing muskets, pistols and cutlasses were taken to the gundecks for distribution to the crews.
- A salt box containing two cartridges was placed by each gun. Junk (old rope) wads were placed in nets hung from the beams.
- Casks of fresh water were placed at intervals amidships on each deck – battle was thirsty work.
- The stern windows were removed and (sometimes) a position prepared for a stern chaser gun.
- All cabin partitions and bulkheads (wooden or canvas) were taken down on the gundecks (including those of the captain, or admiral on a flagship). Loose furniture (chests, cots, tables, chairs, etc.) was stowed in the hold.
- If speed was critical, loose gear could be thrown overboard instead of stowed below. The 74-gun *Ajax* jettisoned numerous items, including ten cot frames, six wooden ladders, six stanchions, a grinding stone, four weather sails and 30ft of copper funnelling for the galley stove. All this helped make room for the gun crews and reduce the number of splinters likely to fly around.
- The sick berth was dismantled from under the forecastle on the upper deck. The cockpit was cleared on the orlop deck and the surgeon set out his instruments and medicines; canvas or mattresses were placed on the cockpit deck and the area well lit with hanging lanterns. Fresh bandages were torn up and buckets or casks set out for amputated limbs. Vinegar mixed with oil of turpentine was made ready for sealing stumps.
- The two ladders on either side of the quarterdeck leading up to the poop remained, despite the fact that they made life awkward for the closest quarterdeck gun crews; in 1808 Admiralty instructions had them centralized amidships. Some ladders were dismantled and replaced with scrambling nets, although the main companionways would remain, to allow the wounded to be carried below.
- Most of the timber supports (pillars) fitted between decks were knocked out with heavy mallets to permit more room for gun crews.
- Netting, called 'sauve tet' (save head), was stretched over the quarterdeck and forecastle to give some protection from falling debris.
- The spare tiller and relieving tackles were made ready in case the tiller was damaged, as happened on the *Victory* during her approach to the enemy line at Trafalgar.
- The ship's boats were either left stowed on the skid beams fitted across the waist of the ship or lowered and towed astern – sometimes with some of the livestock in them. On the *Victory* at Trafalgar the admiral's barge, pinnace and launch remained onboard, while the two cutters, normally slung on the davits on either side of the poop, were towed.
- The carpenter and his crew assembled and checked their tools and equipment before inspecting the wings or 'carpenter's walk', the narrow passageway around the ship's sides below the waterline on the orlop deck, for obstructions. During battle he and his men would patrol this walk looking to repair leaks or holes. Part of the equipment to be prepared were the slings used to lower one of his crew if work was required on the outside of the hull.
- The boatswain had to make sure he had stores to hand for immediate repairs to rigging and shrouds. The ship had to be able to sail, steer and manoeuvre for as long as possible in battle. Rigging, sails and possibly masts were highly vulnerable (particularly to French or Spanish gunners who tended to aim at

them), so it was extremely important to strengthen them before the action. Among the more important tasks for the boatswain to supervise was the 'stoppering' of the topsail sheets. This involved these sails being hoisted and made fast lightly with spunyarn so that they could be brought into use instantly. 'Preventer shrouds' (also used in bad weather) were put in place to reinforce the normal shrouds that supported the masts. The main, fore and mizzen stays were duplicated. Finally, the lower yards were slung with chains to prevent them crashing to the deck if the ropes were severed. Grappling hooks were suspended from the ends of the lower yards to snag with the enemy's rigging.

- Additional shot was carried up to the gundecks and distributed in shot garlands by the guns. Midshipman Roberts stated that he was involved in supervising bringing up 1,000 shot for each deck of the *Victory* during the morning of 19 October as part of clearing for action.
- The lanterns in the magazine light rooms were lit and battle lanterns hung on the beams aft of the guns.
- What to do with live animals before a battle was often something of a dilemma. The general rule was that they were to be slaughtered, but this took time and was messy. Alternatively, they could be thrown overboard alive – a lengthy and difficult, not to mention distressing, task, as they did not remain docile during their disposal. A better option for the smaller livestock, such as chickens, was to cage them and place them in the boats that were towed astern – with luck they would survive and continue to lay. It was hard to decide when to dispose of them. If it was done during 'clear for action' and then there was no battle, all the ship's fresh meat had gone uselessly. If left until 'beat to quarters' when all hands were required at their battle stations, it might be too late. During Trafalgar at least one French pig escaped both slaughter and drowning, only to be 'rescued' and quickly consumed by its ravenous 'saviours'.

When all was ready, the first lieutenant reported the fact to the captain. It was likely he would then go on a tour of inspection to satisfy himself all was well. When the enemy actually came in sight, and as the distance closed, his next executive order would probably be 'beat to quarters'.

## 'BEAT TO QUARTERS'

This was the order for all hands to muster at their battle stations and prepare for immediate action. The ship had already been cleared, so all that really remained were last-minute preparations to enable the guns to be fired. Many ships at sea in wartime kept their guns loaded and almost ready to fire during the normal watch system. The orders of Captain George Duff of the 74-gun *Mars*, who was to die at Trafalgar, were unambiguous on this matter:

> It being highly proper that the Ship should be kept constantly in readiness for Action and particularly so as to prevent any surprise during the night, the Lieutenants are therefore directed to see their respective Quarters clear every evening by sunset; that each Gun is provided with a Crow[bar], Rammer, Spunge [sic], Powder horn &., Shot and Wads; upon no consideration to suffer any Lumber between the Guns. They are also to see that the Water Casks for the men during the Action are properly disposed, well lashed and constantly full; and the Officers to see the Lanthorns at the respective Quarters are properly Matched …

With the enemy in sight the captain gave the order 'Beat to quarters!' The Royal Marine drummers paraded on the quarterdeck and repeatedly tapped out the tune 'Heart of Oak'. Boatswain's mates' pipes shrilled and yells of 'All hands to quarters! All hands to quarters!' and 'Rouse out! Rouse out!' were repeated throughout the ship. On a warship in today's Royal Navy 'Action Stations' is announced over the tannoy, accompanied by the urgent sounding of a klaxon or bell. The US Navy still sounds 'General Quarters'. The drums' continued rattle heralded a rush up companionways, along passages and decks as every man ran to his quarter. There were two main 'bills' (duty lists) on a warship, the 'watch bill' to specify the exact duties of each man in normal times and the 'quarter bill' their duties in action. On the *Victory* on the morning of Trafalgar (again according to Midshipman Roberts), although the enemy had been sighted at daylight, it was not until 10.00 a.m. that Captain Hardy ordered 'beat to quarters'. An hour later, satisfied that all was ready and the enemy still some way off, he authorized 'dinner and grog'.

At quarters the entire crew was deployed ready to fight the ship, leaving a skeleton crew in charge of the actual sailing. If the ships were involved in a close-range mêlée, it was common to reduce sail to topsails only. The following paragraphs, describing quarters on the *Victory* as she sailed for the enemy line, are best read in conjunction with the deck diagrams on the following pages. They do not claim to portray the exact deployment of every man – an impossibility – but rather a realistic reconstruction of how the 823 men on Nelson's flagship went into battle. The gun crews are shown manning guns on both batteries on each deck, which is how they might initially have mustered when it was uncertain which broadside would open fire. Once this decision had been made, the men on the guns that were not to fire joined those on the opposite gun to make up a full crew.

## The poop deck (pp. 244–5)

The *Victory*, like several other British ships at the battle, had no guns on the poop. As it was the highest deck in the ship, it was likely that both Nelson and Hardy moved between it and the quarterdeck as necessary. The precise number of seamen on the poop is uncertain, but they would have combined the duties of signallers hoisting flags (the flag locker was across the stern) with adjusting the mizzen sails. The diagram shows six seamen under the signals lieutenant, Pasco, assisted by the master's mate and midshipman, and also Lieutenant George Brown, who appears to have been acting as an assistant signals officer at the outset. However, at the start of the battle he was sent below to the middle gundeck.

The Royal Marines were divided into two groups at quarters. The majority formed part of the gun crews on the gundecks, the remainder – 40 men and the officers – assembled on the poop deck, whose height enabled the marines to fire down on the enemy. However, this made the poop very overcrowded and once battled started we know some were deployed on the quarterdeck and further forward. Of the two sergeants shown on the diagram, one was probably James Seckar. Seckar was on the quarterdeck when Nelson was shot and helped carry the wounded admiral below to the cockpit.

An estimated 56 men are shown on the poop at quarters.

## The quarterdeck (pp. 246–7)

When not in action, the quarterdeck was almost exclusively the place from which the ship was commanded. Only officers, and those seamen whose duties required their presence, were allowed on this deck. However, at quarters it became a fighting as well as a command deck, with, in this case, twelve short 12-pounders to be manned. The nine-strong gun crews shown are, like all gun crews, responsible for a pair of opposite guns. The crews include six powdermen (not normally boys) who at quarters positioned themselves as near amidships as possible with their salt boxes. Also shown are the captains of the main- and mizzentops, each with six topmen, who would be in the tops ready to work the sails as necessary. On deck would be the riggers, probably under a boatswain's mate, together with four helmsmen at the wheel.

A total of 78 seamen are shown at the gun crews, in the tops and as riggers. They would have been commanded by one or two of the midshipmen – we know Midshipman Rivers, the seventeen-year-old son of the gunner, was on the quarterdeck.

Decisions about the conning of the ship would have been made by Captain Hardy (although he did refer to Nelson on occasion) who passed them to Mr Thomas Atkinson, the master. He in turn translated the captain's instructions into specific orders to the four quartermasters at the helm, or passed them forward to his mate on the forecastle.

The naval command element on the quarterdeck consisted of Nelson, Hardy, Lieutenant Quilliam (first lieutenant) and Atkinson (master), supported by their staff John Scott (admiral's secretary), Thomas Whipple (captain's clerk), George Andrews (secretary's clerk), Richard Ford (agent victualler) and his clerk John Geoghehan. There were also at least three midshipmen to carry messages, relay orders or take charge of an unexpected task as it arose. Captain Adair RM and the other two marine officers were on the poop deck initially, as were the two marine drummers who beat to quarters. The estimated number of personnel present was 91.

## The waist

This was a narrow part of deck on either side of the ship's boats, which seemingly remained amidships throughout the Trafalgar action, although normal practice was to tow them astern to minimize the number of splinters flying around. There were no men in the waist at quarters.

## The forecastle

In battle this became primarily a gun platform for the two 68-pounder carronades and two medium 12-pounder guns. Each pair is shown with a crew of nine. They were commanded by Lieutenant George Bligh, although the forecastle was usually given to the junior (in this case the ninth) lieutenant. A master's mate, midshipman and the boatswain, Mr William Willmet, assisted him. The foretop would have been occupied by its captain with his topmen, while on deck were more riggers under one or two boatswain's mates. Some 36 men are depicted on the forecastle.

Thus the weather decks of the *Victory*, including the poop, would have had about 183 men at quarters – some 22 per cent of the men on board. These men were by far the most exposed and they consequently suffered a disproportionate number of casualties.

*HMS Victory*: a Cross-section

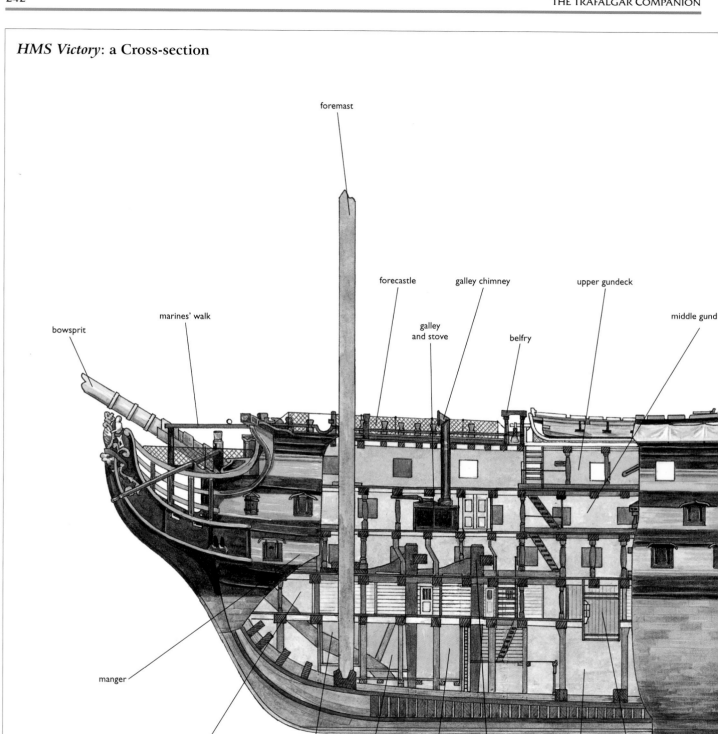

foremast

bowsprit

marines' walk

forecastle

galley chimney

galley
and stove

belfry

upper gundeck

middle gund

manger

orlop deck

filling room

mooring bits

main hold

light room

main magazine

forward hanging
magazine

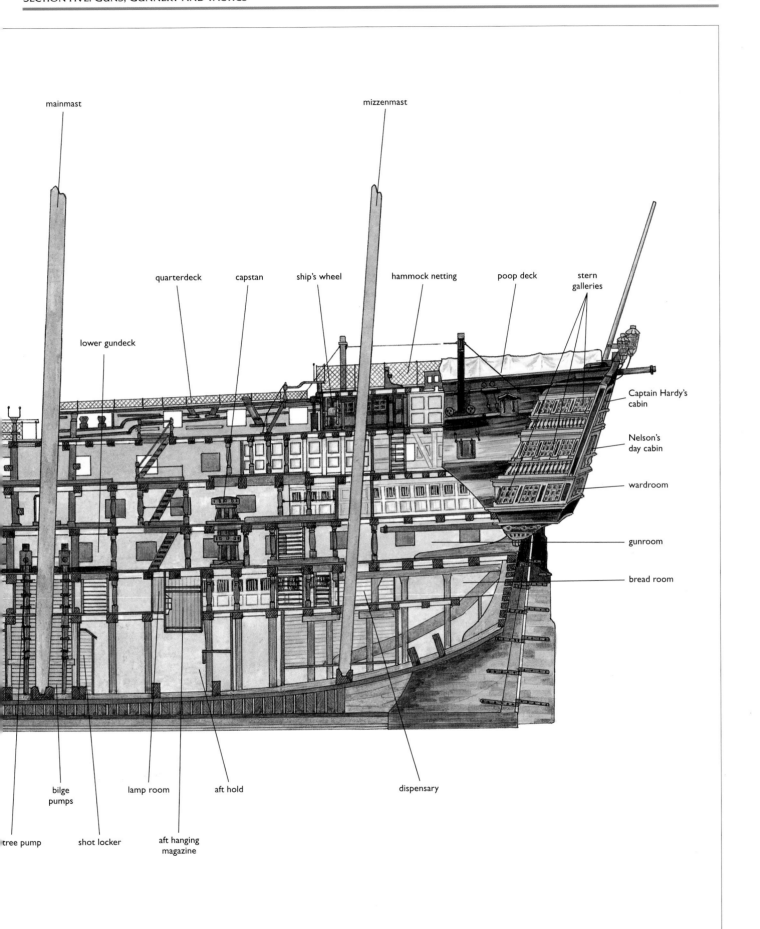

mainmast

mizzenmast

quarterdeck

capstan

ship's wheel

hammock netting

poop deck

stern galleries

lower gundeck

Captain Hardy's cabin

Nelson's day cabin

wardroom

gunroom

bread room

bilge pumps

lamp room

aft hold

dispensary

tree pump

shot locker

aft hanging magazine

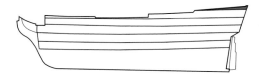

*HMS Victory*'s Poop Deck at Quarters prior to Trafalgar

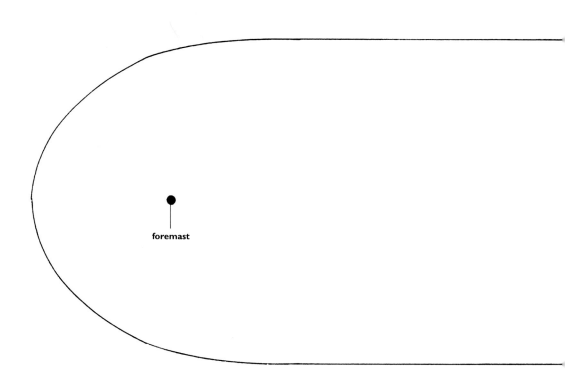

foremast

### Key

 Lieutenant

 Master's mate

 Midshipman

 Seaman

 Captain RM

 Lieutenant RM

 Sergeant RM

 Drummer RM

 Private RM

### Known Personalities
1.  Lieut. J. Pasco (signals lieutenant)
2.  Lieut. G. Brown (assistant signals officer initially)
3.  Capt. C. W. Adair RM
4.  Lieut. J. G. Peake RM
5.  2nd Lieut. L.B. Reeves RM
6.  2nd Lieut. L. Rotely RM
7.  Mr T. L. Robins
8.  Midshipman J. Pollard
9.  Sgt Seckar RM (he was later on the quarterdeck and helped carry the mortally wounded Nelson below)
10. Landsman J. Roome (probably working on the hoists)

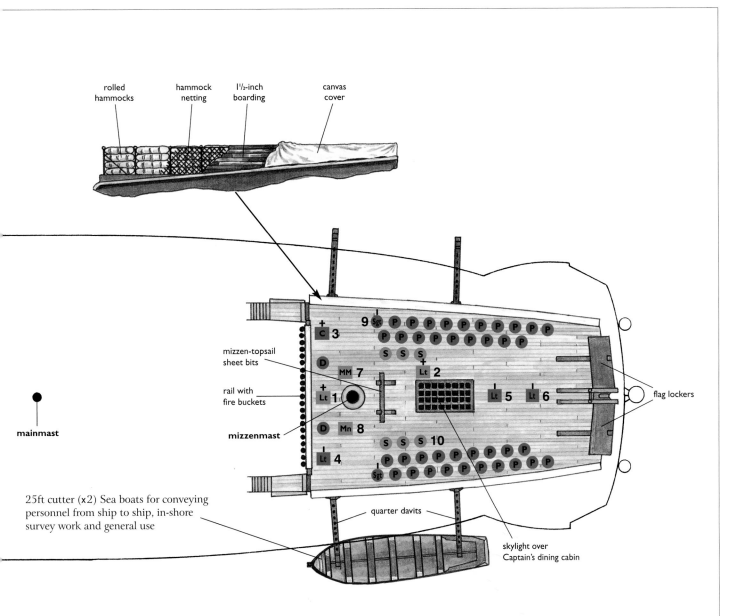

rolled hammocks

hammock netting

1½-inch boarding

canvas cover

mizzen-topsail sheet bits

rail with fire buckets

mainmast

mizzenmast

flag lockers

25ft cutter (x2) Sea boats for conveying personnel from ship to ship, in-shore survey work and general use

quarter davits

skylight over Captain's dining cabin

## Notes

- There were no guns on the *Victory*'s poop at Trafalgar. Personnel totalled around 56 at any one time.
- The signals officer and midshipman would have moved between the poop and quarterdeck as required. The poop was the highest point on the ship's deck and therefore better for observing signals and hoists. It was also the location of the flag locker.
- Some seamen were needed on the poop to assist with signals or handling the mizzen course (sail) and doing duty as riggers.
- 40 marines plus all their officers packed onto the poop made a tempting target. According to Rotely it soon became a 'slaughterhouse'. However, we know that Captain Adair RM, possibly also with 2nd Lieut. Reeves, later moved to the quarterdeck with some of his men.

**HMS *Victory*'s Quarterdeck and Forecastle at Quarters prior to Trafalgar** (12 short 12-pounders on quarterdeck, 2 medium 12-pounders and 2 × 68-pounder carronades on forecastle)

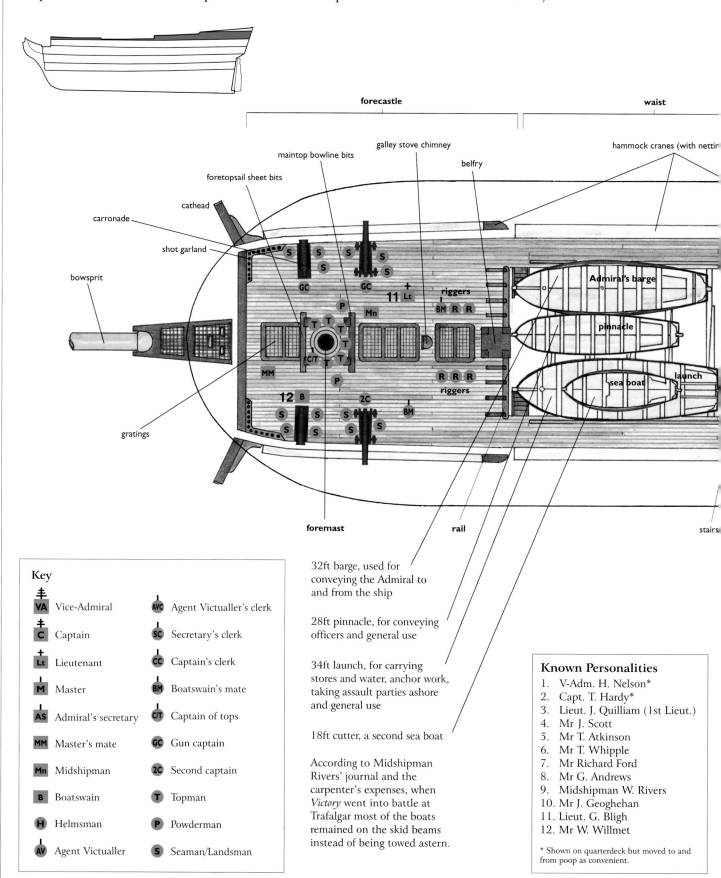

32ft barge, used for conveying the Admiral to and from the ship

28ft pinnacle, for conveying officers and general use

34ft launch, for carrying stores and water, anchor work, taking assault parties ashore and general use

18ft cutter, a second sea boat

According to Midshipman Rivers' journal and the carpenter's expenses, when *Victory* went into battle at Trafalgar most of the boats remained on the skid beams instead of being towed astern.

**Key**

| | | | |
|---|---|---|---|
| **VA** | Vice-Admiral | **AVC** | Agent Victualler's clerk |
| **C** | Captain | **SC** | Secretary's clerk |
| **Lt** | Lieutenant | **CC** | Captain's clerk |
| **M** | Master | **BM** | Boatswain's mate |
| **AS** | Admiral's secretary | **C/T** | Captain of tops |
| **MM** | Master's mate | **GC** | Gun captain |
| **Mn** | Midshipman | **2C** | Second captain |
| **B** | Boatswain | **T** | Topman |
| **H** | Helmsman | **P** | Powderman |
| **AV** | Agent Victualler | **S** | Seaman/Landsman |

**Known Personalities**
1. V-Adm. H. Nelson*
2. Capt. T. Hardy*
3. Lieut. J. Quilliam (1st Lieut.)
4. Mr J. Scott
5. Mr T. Atkinson
6. Mr T. Whipple
7. Mr Richard Ford
8. Mr G. Andrews
9. Midshipman W. Rivers
10. Mr J. Geoghehan
11. Lieut. G. Bligh
12. Mr W. Willmet

* Shown on quarterdeck but moved to and from poop as convenient.

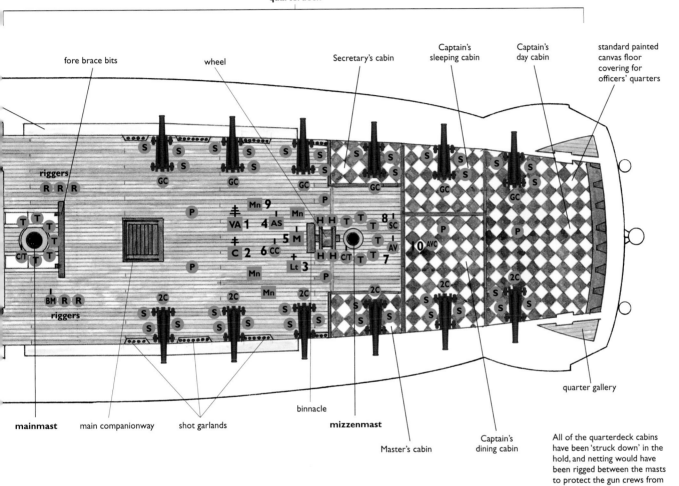

**quarterdeck**

fore brace bits

wheel

Secretary's cabin

Captain's sleeping cabin

Captain's day cabin

standard painted canvas floor covering for officers' quarters

riggers

quarter gallery

binnacle

**mainmast**  main companionway  shot garlands

**mizzenmast**

Master's cabin

Captain's dining cabin

All of the quarterdeck cabins have been 'struck down' in the hold, and netting would have been rigged between the masts to protect the gun crews from falling rigging and splinters.

## Notes

- This deck (and the poop) was the command centre of the fleet. From here were issued all orders to the fleet, to the ship and to the guns. Hence the quarterdeck was overcrowded with senior personnel. Along with the poop, it was the most dangerous part of the ship.
- **Forecastle** Under the command of a lieutenant supported by a master's mate, midshipman and the boatswain. There were 18 gun crew (plus the boatswain, Mr Willmet, on a carronade), riggers under a boatswain's mate and topmen under the captain of the foretop. Approximate total 36.
- **Waist** No seamen would normally be at quarters in the waist.
- **Quarterdeck** From here the admiral commanded the fleet and the captain the ship. The former had his own staff, the captain, the 1st lieutenant, master and signals officer (shown on poop). There were also 54 gun crew, 4 helmsmen, captains of the tops and topmen for the main and mizzenmasts and riggers. Approximate total 91.
- Estimated total on quarterdeck and forecastle 127.

## *HMS Victory*'s Upper Gundeck at Quarters prior to Trafalgar (30 long 12-pounder guns)

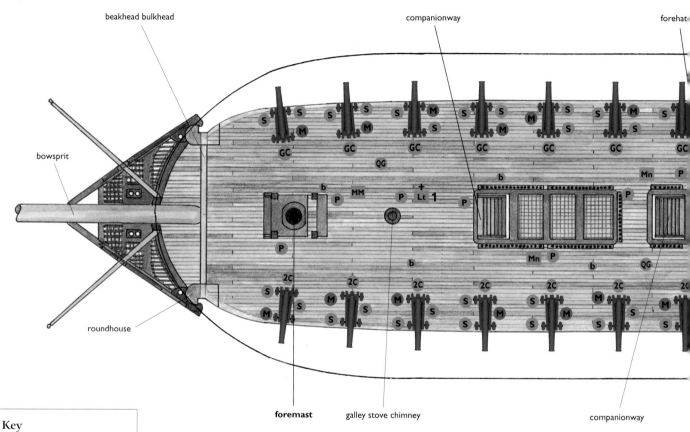

beakhead bulkhead

companionway

forehat

bowsprit

roundhouse

**foremast**

galley stove chimney

companionway

### Key

+
**Lt**  Lieutenant

**MM**  Master's mate

**Mn**  Midshipman

**QG**  Quarter gunner

**GC**  Gun captain

**2C**  Second captain

**P**  Powderman

**S**  Seaman/Landsman

**b**  Boy

**M**  Marine

▪▪▪▪  Shot racks

**Known Personalities**
1.  Lieut. J. Yule
2.  Lieut. W. A. Ram

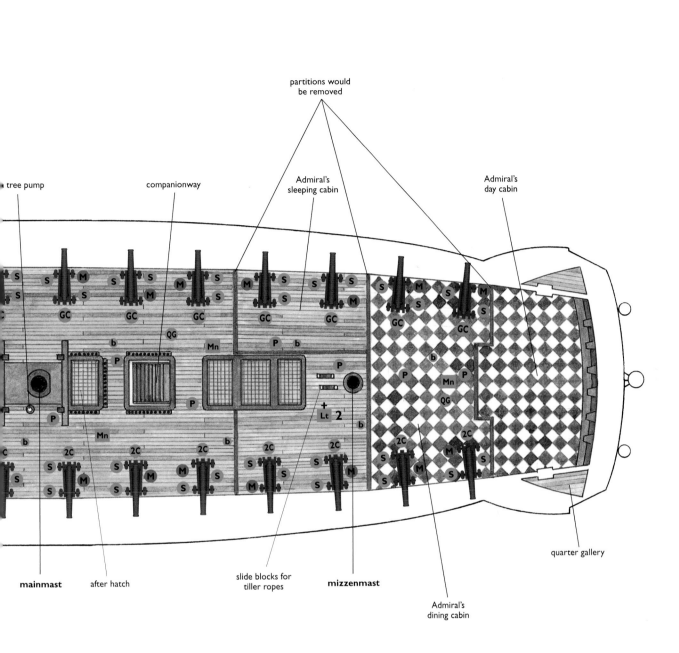

partitions would
be removed

tree pump

companionway

Admiral's
sleeping cabin

Admiral's
day cabin

S S M S S S M S S S M S S S M S S
S M S S S M S S M S S S M S S
GC          GC          GC          GC          GC          GC          GC
b                                          P    b          b
QG                                    P
Mn                                                    Mn
P                                                              P
P                                                        QG
P                                              +
Mn                                        Lt 2
b                                                    b
b          2C          2C          2C          2C          2C                    2C          2C
S S M S S S M S S M S S S M S S S
S M S S M S S M S S

mainmast        after hatch                slide blocks for        mizzenmast                    quarter gallery
                                          tiller ropes

                                                                        Admiral's
                                                                        dining cabin

## Notes
- This deck had 30 of the lightest great guns – the long 12-pounders.
  In each gun crew were 9 men including the powderman. In action
  they would all work one gun at a time.
- The 11 boys were spread out along the deck with the primary duty
  of using wet swabs to damp down spilt powder.
- Numbers on the deck were approximately 2 lieutenants, 1 master's
  mate, 5 midshipmen, 4 quarter gunners, 105 seamen, 30 marines
  (in the gun crews) and 11 boys. Total 158.

## *HMS Victory*'s Middle Deck at Quarters prior to Trafalgar (28 x 24-pounder guns)

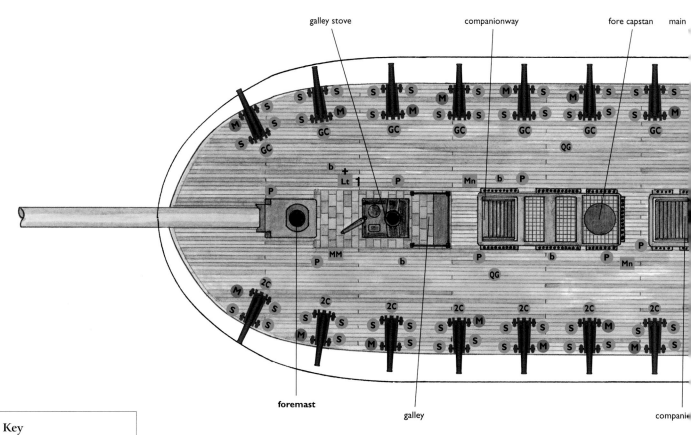

galley stove

companionway

fore capstan    main

GC        GC        GC        GC        GC        GC

QG

Lt 1

b        P        Mn        b    P

MM

b                                P
P                                        P    Mn
QG                                    b

2C        2C        2C        2C        2C        2C

foremast

galley

companio

### Key

| | |
|---|---|
| **Lt** | Lieutenant |
| **MM** | Master's mate |
| **Mn** | Midshipman |
| **QG** | Quarter gunner |
| **GC** | Gun captain |
| **2C** | Second captain |
| **P** | Powderman |
| **S** | Seaman/Landsman |
| **b** | Boy |
| **M** | Marine |
| ▬▬▬ | Shot racks |

### Known Personalities
1. Lieut. A. King
2. Lieut. G. Brown

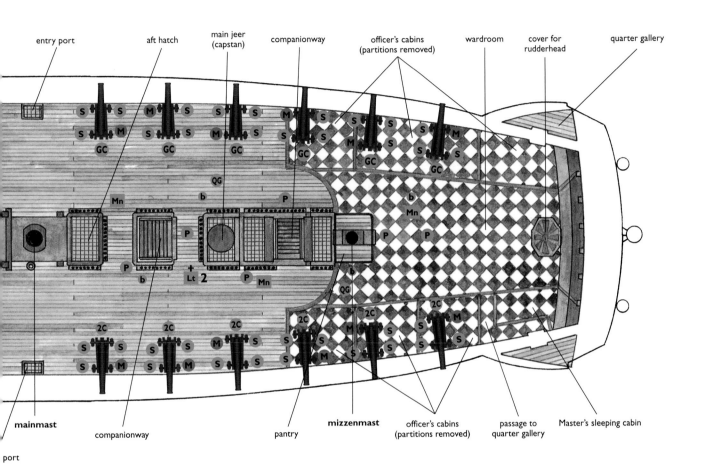

entry port

aft hatch

main jeer (capstan)

companionway

officer's cabins (partitions removed)

wardroom

cover for rudderhead

quarter gallery

mainmast

companionway

pantry

mizzenmast

officer's cabins (partitions removed)

passage to quarter gallery

Master's sleeping cabin

port

## Notes
- This deck had 28 24-pounders with a probable crew of 11 including a powderman for each pair of guns.
- Each gun crew is shown as having 1 marine, but it may be that some guns had 2 and others none.
- This deck was commanded by the 3rd lieutenant, who directly controlled the forward guns 1–8 and their opposites. The 7th lieutenant commanded the after guns (9–14).
- Numbers (approximate) were 2 lieutenants, 1 master's mate, 5 midshipmen, 4 quarter gunners, 126 seamen, 28 marines and 9 boys. Total 175.

*HMS Victory*'s **Lower Gundeck at Quarters prior to Trafalgar** (30 x 32-pounder guns)

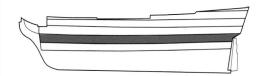

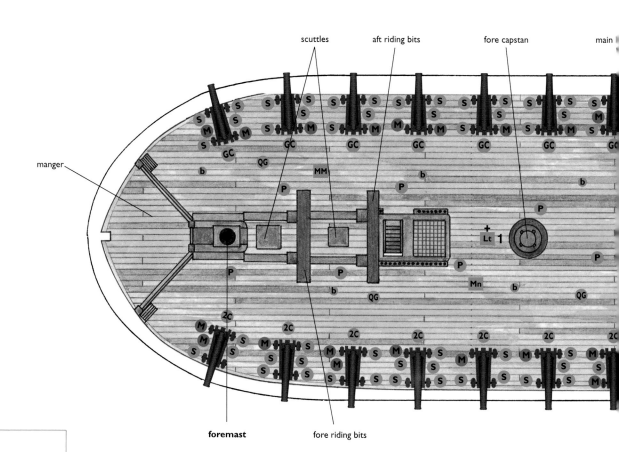

**Key**

+
Lt  Lieutenant

MM  Master's mate

Mn  Midshipman

QG  Quarter gunner

GC  Gun captain

2C  Second captain

P  Powderman

S  Seaman/Landsman

b  Boy

M  Marine

▪▪▪▪  Shot racks

**Known Personalities**
1. Lieut. E. Williams
2. Lieut. A. Hills

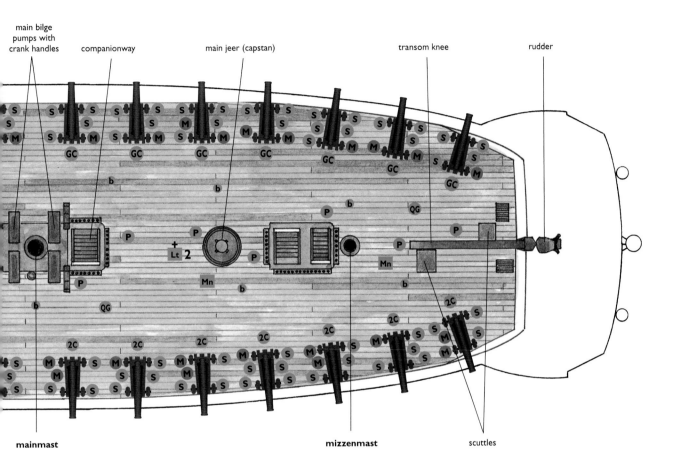

main bilge pumps with crank handles

companionway

main jeer (capstan)

transom knee

rudder

mainmast

mizzenmast

scuttles

## Notes

- This gundeck had the heaviest guns with the largest crews. The 14 men in a full crew included one powderman. As with the crews on other decks, once firing started then the crew for each pair of guns would join forces on the one in use. As the *Victory* was some 30 men under complement only 13 men are shown in each crew.
- The exact positioning of the officers and petty officers is approximate. As always powdermen stood at quarters as near midships as possible.
- The estimated number of men on this deck is 2 lieutenants, 1 master's mate, 5 midshipmen, 5 quarter gunners, 44 marines, 11 boys and 158 seamen (including 15 powdermen). Total 226.
- When mustering at quarters gun captains took charge of the starboard battery, second captains the larboard.

## HMS *Victory*'s Orlop Deck at Quarters prior to Trafalgar

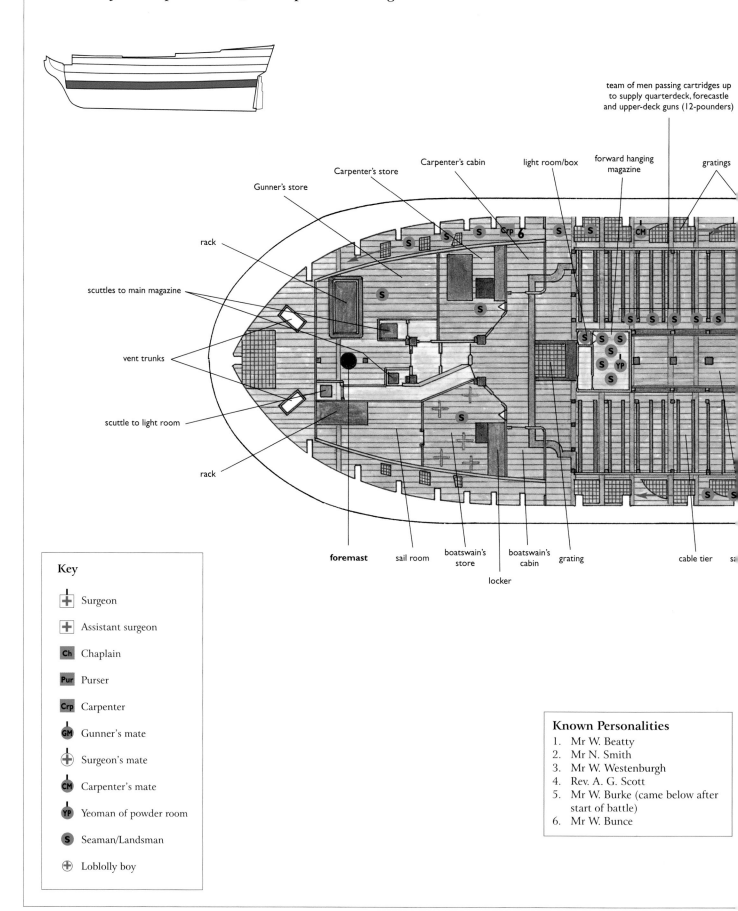

team of men passing cartridges up
to supply quarterdeck, forecastle
and upper-deck guns (12-pounders)

Carpenter's cabin

light room/box

forward hanging
magazine

gratings

Carpenter's store

Gunner's store

rack

scuttles to main magazine

vent trunks

scuttle to light room

rack

foremast    sail room    boatswain's
store    boatswain's
cabin    grating    cable tier

locker

**Key**

+ Surgeon

+ Assistant surgeon

Ch Chaplain

Pur Purser

Crp Carpenter

GM Gunner's mate

+ Surgeon's mate

CM Carpenter's mate

YP Yeoman of powder room

S Seaman/Landsman

+ Loblolly boy

**Known Personalities**
1. Mr W. Beatty
2. Mr N. Smith
3. Mr W. Westenburgh
4. Rev. A. G. Scott
5. Mr W. Burke (came below after start of battle)
6. Mr W. Bunce

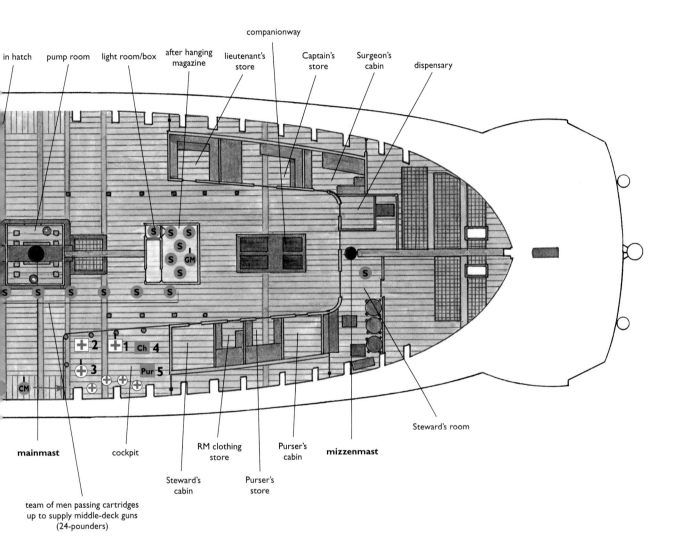

companionway

in hatch  pump room  light room/box  after hanging  lieutenant's  Captain's  Surgeon's  dispensary
                                      magazine       store        store      cabin

S S S
S S I
S S GM
S S

S S S S S

S

+2  +1  Ch 4

+3       Pur 5

CM

Steward's room

mainmast              cockpit         RM clothing    Purser's    mizzenmast
                                      store          cabin

                      Steward's       Purser's
                      cabin           store

team of men passing cartridges
up to supply middle-deck guns
(24-pounders)

## Notes
- There were no guns on this deck as it was below the waterline. In the after cockpit the surgeon set up his operating table using the midshipmen's mess table. The carpenter and his crew moved around the 'carpenter's walls' looking for leaks or holes and plugging them.
- Here the two hanging magazines provided cartridges for the 24- and 12-pdrs. They were passed up through hatches and along passageways by a human chain of landsmen and idlers.
- Approximate numbers were: carpenter's crew 13, storemen 4, in light rooms 2, in hanging magazines 12, passing cartridges 14 and in after cockpit 9. Total 54.

## *HMS Victory*'s Hold at Quarters prior to Trafalgar

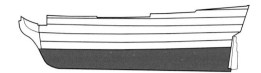

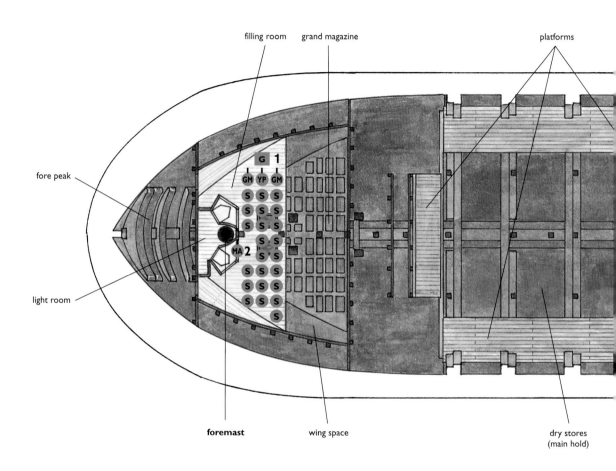

filling room     grand magazine                          platforms

fore peak

light room

foremast          wing space                              dry stores
                                                          (main hold)

**Key**

**G**  Gunner

**GM**  Gunner's mate

**MA**  Master-at-arms

**YP**  Yeoman of powder room

**S**  Seaman

**Known Personalities**
1.  Mr W. Rivers
2.  Mr W. Elliott

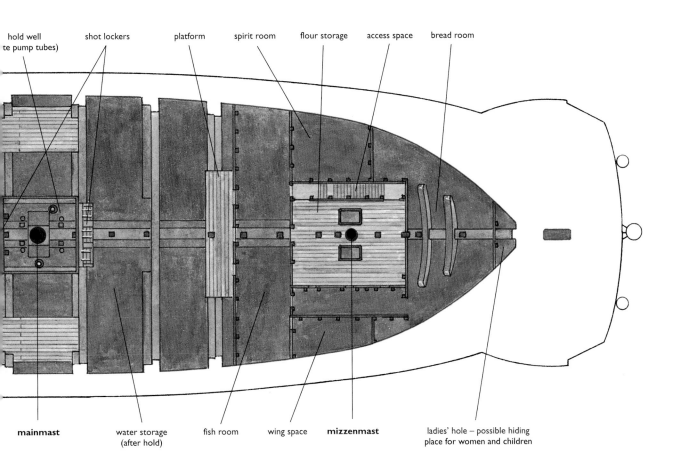

hold well
(te pump tubes)    shot lockers    platform    spirit room    flour storage    access space    bread room

**mainmast**    water storage    fish room    wing space    **mizzenmast**    ladies' hole – possible hiding
    (after hold)                                   place for women and children

### Notes
- The only place manned in the hold at quarters was the grand magazine, which included a light room and filling room.
- This magazine supplied cartridges for the 32-pounders on the lower deck and the two carronades, and provided the reserve.
- The gunner was in charge. His crew (23 shown) with 2 mates supervised the filling of additional cartridges as required and provided the human chain to pass cartridges up and along the lower gundeck for the 32-pounders.

## The upper gundeck (pp. 248–9)

Here were thirty of the lightest great guns – the long 12-pounders – in a larboard and starboard battery of 15 each. In overall command of the deck was the fourth lieutenant (Lieutenant John Yule) positioned forward directly in charge of guns 1–8 and those opposite. His number two was the eighth lieutenant (Lieutenant William Ram), whose position at quarters was aft, directly commanding guns 9–15 and their opposites. Assisting were a master's mate and four midshipmen (a fifth is shown doing duty as a messenger). This was a full complement of junior officers for this deck, so they presumably followed normal practice with regard to command of specific guns. This being so, the master's mate would have been responsible for guns 1–3 and opposites, with a midshipman directing guns 4–6, 7–9, 10–12, 13–15 and their opposites. There were only 13 quarter gunners on the muster roll (there should have been 25), so only four are shown on this deck.

Each gun crew had nine men responsible for a pair of opposite guns. They were not expected to fire all guns of both broadsides simultaneously on any deck – there was never sufficient manpower anyway. With opposing ships sailing in parallel line astern, all firing would be from one side or the other. Problems arose in a confused mêlée such as Trafalgar, when it was highly likely that enemy ships would appear on both sides at close range. In this case the captain (or lieutenant on a gundeck) had to decide whether to split the crews and try to man all guns (not normally a practical solution) or fire alternate guns with full crews on both sides. If there had also been heavy losses, the situation became something of a nightmare, with the number and frequency of shots fired falling off dramatically from both broadsides.

The gun captains took command of the starboard guns at quarters, with the second captain in each crew opposite on the larboard broadside. The great majority of marines were in the gun crews, mostly without their hot, red jackets, so it was impossible in the smoke and confusion to tell them from the seamen. In the diagram two marines are shown in each gun crew, although the distribution could have varied. At quarters the 11 boys (there were only 31 in total) were usually spread out around the deck. Their primary duty (as powder monkeys) was dousing any embers on the deck with wet swabs.

The complement on this deck is shown as 158.

## The middle gundeck (pp. 250–1)

The middle gundeck had slightly less space than the other two, as there was an entry port on each side where otherwise a gun could have been. Both batteries therefore had fourteen 24-pounders. The senior officer on this deck was the third lieutenant, Lieutenant Andrew King, who was forward commanding guns 1–8 and their opposites. Aft, when he had come down from the poop, was his second-in-command, seventh lieutenant George Brown, responsible for guns 9–14 and their opposites. With the larger guns went a larger crew, 11 men, again responsible for an opposite pair. Like the upper deck, this one had its full complement of one master's mate and five midshipmen, but only four quarter gunners. The master's mate had responsibility for guns 1–3 and their opposites, and the midshipmen were in charge respectively of numbers 4–6, 7–8, 9–10, 11–12 and 13–14 and their opposites.

According to the *Mars'* standing orders, at quarters 'the first Captains of the Guns [are] to go for their Locks and place them

on the Starboard Guns; the second Captains in the same manner are to place their Locks on the Larboard Guns'. One seaman or marine in each gun crew was designated for fire duties. The orders for him at quarters were, 'the Fire Bucket man is to bring his Fire Bucket opposite his Gun, upon coming into action, and he is to be in readiness to break off from his Gun to supply Water at whatever part of the Ship it is called for'.

This deck had an estimated 175 men present, of whom 28 were marines and nine were boys.

## The lower gundeck (pp. 252–3)

Here were the heaviest guns with the largest crews. The thirty 32-pounders had crews of 14 (for two opposite guns), but because the *Victory* at Trafalgar was some 30 men below full complement, the crews are shown with three or four marines in each. As this was the most powerful gundeck, it had the second most senior lieutenant in command; he was also the ship's gunnery officer. This was Lieutenant Edward Williams, who was that morning commanding guns 1–8 and their opposites on the forward half of the deck. Lieutenant Alexander Hills, the ninth lieutenant, commanded guns 9–15 and their opposites. Whereas master's mates and midshipmen on the other decks commanded up to six guns here, on the lower deck they were normally responsible for four (two pairs). However, the *Victory* on this occasion was three short of her entitlement of 24, so they commanded up to six.

This deck is shown as having a total of 226 men, including 158 seamen, 44 marines and 11 boys.

## The orlop deck (pp. 254–5)

Down below the waterline, this was obviously not a place to find guns. However, beat to quarters saw a number of key personnel mustering here to carry out last-minute preparations for battle. They were men concerned with repairing the ship, caring for the wounded and replenishing the guns. The orlop deck housed the stores of the carpenter, gunner, boatswain, purser, captain and lieutenants, not to mention the sail room and dispensary. Then there were the two hanging magazines full of filled cartridges. There was a lot of valuable kit and dangerous gunpowder on the orlop deck, most of which merited a marine sentry with fixed bayonet in normal times. At quarters these marines were probably withdrawn to join either the musketeers on the weather deck or a gun crew; it is unlikely that during a battle anybody would have come below bent on breaking into locked storerooms, especially when the orlop deck was a hive of activity. A storeman is shown present in those stores (gunner's, carpenter's and boatswain's) from which additional items might be needed during the battle.

The diagram shows the carpenter, Mr William Bunce, with a crew of two mates and ten men (probably including the caulker) split into two groups along the carpenter's walk. With their repair equipment they would patrol the walk and patch up or plug leaks or holes in the hull. At quarters the surgeon (William Beatty) with his assistants (Neil Smith and William Westenburgh) would set out his instruments, bandages, mattresses and medicines in the after cockpit. It was also the place for the chaplain (for obvious reasons) and the purser (for not so obvious ones), although we know that at Trafalgar Mr Walter Burke had to be told by Nelson to go below at the start of the action, where he spent much of his time comforting the dying admiral.

Of crucial importance to gunnery on the *Victory*, indeed on any warship in any battle, was an organized and smooth flow of shot and cartridges to the guns. There was a huge potential for chaos. The right cartridges had to go to the right guns on the right deck in the right amount at the right time. Ammunition, particularly cartridges (in their wooden boxes), had to be carried or passed from the magazines up to the powdermen on the decks. This involved handing the boxes up through scuttles (small hatches with copper covers that were normally secured by padlocks) and along passages – in the case of some 12-pounders as far as the quarterdeck and forecastle. A shipboard scuttle (from the Spanish *escotilla*, a hatchway) was really a hole in the deck. Hence the expression 'to scuttle a ship' meant to sink it by deliberately making holes in the hull below the waterline.

Because of the danger of fire and accidental explosion, no more than three cartridges per gun were allowed on the gundecks at any one time and, until the moment of loading, they had to remain in a container. Cartridge boxes were passed up and along from hand to hand in a human chain; in order to regulate the flow the man below waited until the man next in line was empty-handed before passing him another box. Overall responsibility for co-ordinating, controlling and supervising this vital operation was entrusted to Mr William Rivers, the gunner (father of the midshipman of that name) – perhaps surprisingly no commissioned officer was involved directly. The gunner's location at quarters was in the grand magazine in the hold (see below), so these duties had to be delegated on the orlop deck to his mates, probably one in each hanging magazine, although we know one was on the quarterdeck.

These petty officers had, at quarters, to ensure the lantern was lit in the light room/box – the small chamber built just forward of the magazine and separated from it by double windows of thick glass. A vital duty was to check that all fire precautions had been observed. The floor and walls were covered with felt or with a rough frieze known as 'fearnaught', all of which had to be wetted. No man could enter the magazines without putting on leather slippers and emptying his pockets of any metal objects. The petty officers had to be certain that they identified the differing weights of cartridge on the shelves. They then ensured their men (mostly idlers and landsmen) were posted at the scuttles (hatchways) and at intervals between them. Once battle began, the forward hanging magazine replenished the 12-pounder guns on the upper, forecastle and quarterdecks, while the after one supplied the 24-pounders on the middle deck. The diagram shows a gunner's mate with six men in each hanging magazine, with another eight men for passing cartridges, to give a total of 30 men. This number is not set in stone but rather a tentative minimum estimate. The mate in charge could use virtually all his team to pass the cartridges if needed rather than having six in the magazine itself as shown, as no filling of cartridges took place in these magazines.

About 54 men were mustered on this deck.

### The hold (pp. 256–7)

The only place manned at quarters in the hold was the 'grand magazine'. This consisted of the actual magazine in which was stored the powder barrels, the filling room for filling cartridges and the light room. It supplied cartridges for the lower gundeck's 32-pounders and the carronades, and acted as a reserve if more cartridges needed to be filled. By way of comparison, French 74s had two magazines. The main powder room was aft and was responsible for supplying cartridges to all guns abaft the mainmast on all decks. The forward magazine was similar to a hanging magazine on the *Victory* in that it only contained filled cartridges. These went to guns forward of the mainmast.

The *Victory*'s grand magazine floor was wetted down, as were the curtains of flame-resistant material hung across the entrance. The gunner, Mr Rivers, was to be found here at quarters, along with two of his mates. He had overall responsibility for ammunition supply, so during battle would certainly have moved around checking the situation at all magazines and on the functioning of the chains of men passing cartridges up to the gundecks. The diagram shows him having 24 men (including the yeoman of the powder room) for duties in the grand magazine and for passing up the powder.

## GUN CREWS

Gun crews varied in number depending on the size of the gun. On the deck diagrams of the *Victory* the crews of the 32-pounders are shown with 14 men, the 24-pounders with 11 and the 12-pounders with nine. The notes that follow refer to the crew of a British 32-pounder gun with the 14 men; a French 36-pounder had 15, 24-pounder 13, 18-pounder 11, 12-pounder nine, 8-pounder nine, and 6- and 4-pounders five. All crews were responsible for a pair of opposite guns. When firing on one side only, 14 men were quite enough for the heaviest gun, with eight of them having clearly defined functions; the others mostly added muscle power when hauling on the tackles. One of the 14 was a powderman who did not get involved with handling the gun or the tackles. Before firing started, it was common to see the powdermen sitting quietly on their salt boxes near the centre line of the decks. These crews could divide in order to fire their two guns simultaneously, but to do so meant a dramatically reduced rate of firing. They are shown divided in this way on the diagrams, as this was the 'at quarters' position, when it was not known which side would open fire first. The crews got both their guns ready for firing by loading and running out first one gun, then the other on the opposite side.

Casualties might reduce the numbers available. However, even without battle losses, sheer fatigue during a lengthy engagement such as Trafalgar would render a crew of six or seven virtually incapable of handling a 32-pounder for more than the occasional shot. It was running the gun out that was the problem, especially when hauling 'uphill' as the ship heeled. With a reduced crew they would wait for a favourable roll so the deck dipped down on the firing side. Yet another drain on a crew in battle was the need to call away men for other urgent duties. Although they were allocated to a gun on the quarter bill, opposite the names of some seamen would be a letter indicating their other duty in battle if required. Examples were 'P' meaning 'pump', 'B' for 'boarder', 'S' for 'sail trimmer' and 'F' for 'fireman'. If a 32-pounder was lucky enough to start a battle with a crew of 14, the likelihood was that by the end of a major engagement this would have dwindled to ten or eleven utterly exhausted men.

When broadsides were to be fired on both sides, a more practical option was to use a full crew on alternate guns. Another possibility was to fire all guns on one broadside and then for all crews to rush to man their gun on the opposite side. The exact permutation of which guns would be crewed on a confused, smoke-filled gundeck in a heavy action was for the lieutenant in command to decide. Only he knew the situation and what was possible.

## Gun Positions – Crew Deployment (the example shown is a 32-pounder on *HMS Victory* at Trafalgar)

### A  Housed

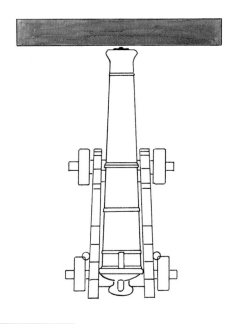

**Key**

- **GC**  Gun captain
- **2C**  Second captain
- **Ldr**  Loader
- **Spg**  Sponger
- **A/Ldr**  Assistant loader
- **A/Spg**  Assistant sponger
- **HSpk**  Handspike man (2)
- **Aux**  Auxiliary (5)
- **Pdr**  Powderman

**Notes**
- Guns were housed when not in use. So this gun is shown secured with no crew present.
- While in this state the 32-pounders would have been loaded with a single shot, but the gunlocks would not have been attached.

### B  Cast Loose

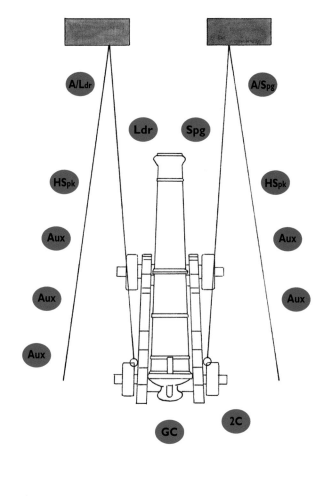

**Notes**
- Only the gun (side) tackles are shown.
- This gun has been 'cast loose' and pulled back to the full extent of the breeching rope for loading with a second shot to make it double-shotted.
- A full crew of 14 are shown, having taken up the gun tackles in preparation for running out the gun. The tompion has been removed prior to loading and the gun captain will now attach the lock.
- The second captain checks the train tackle runs out smoothly.

The members of a typical gun crew were as follows. Numbers 1 and 2 were the only crew members who were not involved in running out. Numbers 3 to 8 had specific functions in addition to hauling on the gun tackle, numbers 9 to 13 provided extra brawn (and were reserves to replace casualties), and number 14 was the powderman.

| | | | |
|---|---|---|---|
| No. 1 | Gun captain | No. 6 | Assistant sponger |
| No. 2 | Second captain | No. 7 | Handspike man |
| No. 3 | Loader | No. 8 | Handspike man |
| No. 4 | Sponger | Nos. 9–13 | Auxiliaries |
| No. 5 | Assistant loader | No. 14 | Powderman |

## C  Just Fired

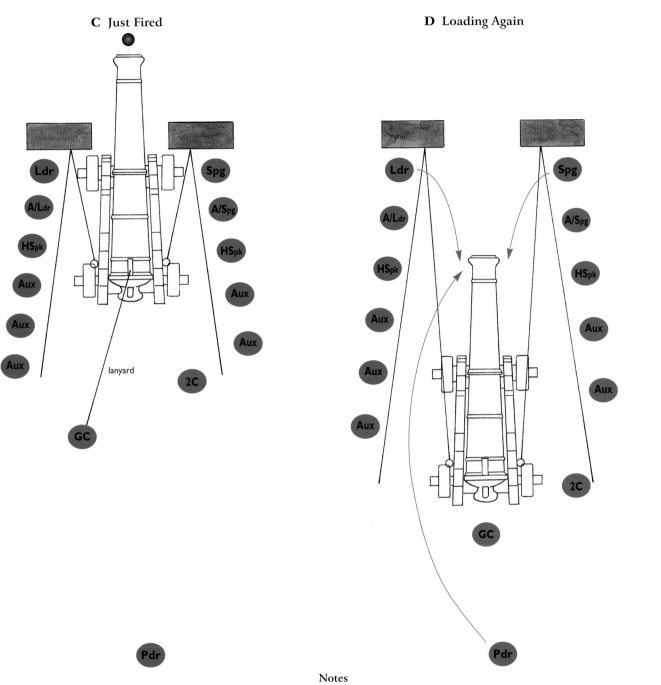

lanyard

## D  Loading Again

**Notes**
- The crew members have been taking the strain on the tackles to keep the gun carriage tight against the ship's side while it was pointed (aimed) and lateral and elevation adjustments made. It was then primed.
- The second captain cocks the lock while the gun captain waits for the gun to bear.
- The first shot is fired by the gun captain jerking the lanyard.
- At the moment of firing the crew drop the tackles.

**Notes**
- This shows the gun fully recoiled and being reloaded.
- The loader and sponger move to either side of the muzzle and the powderman comes forward with his salt box containing 2 cartridges.
- The gun captain 'serves' his vent and the gun is sponged, a cartridge and wad are rammed home, the gun is then loaded with shot and another wad and rammed down prior to being run out again.

The sequence of orders for a first shot from a 32-pounder on *Victory*'s lower deck at Trafalgar is described on the following pages. In 1805 there were (strangely) no official gun drills laid down, so small variations in who did what occurred. What is described is only one way of serving the gun in action. It is assumed all guns were initially housed (secured) and loaded with a single shot. The text should be read in conjunction with the diagrams above and on p. 263.

## FIRE ORDERS

Below is a typical sequence of orders given for firing and reloading a gun. The initial order to cast loose the guns would have come from the captain, along with instructions as to the type of shot to be used. This message was taken and/or shouted down to the gundecks, usually by midshipmen. The initial orders, when all was calm and quiet, would be shouted out to the whole gundeck by the lieutenants. After that the gundeck lieutenants might decide changes on type of shot, but instructions to switch fire from one broadside to another or to fire both simultaneously would normally come from the quarterdeck. The officers would initiate and supervise the changeover. The gundeck master's mates and midshipmen would shout the orders relating to what shot to use or which guns were to fire to the quarter gunners or, if necessary, direct to gun captains. Once battle was joined in earnest, with guns firing at will at close range, the din, smoke and confusion meant that the gun drill orders were given (if needed) by quarter gunners or gun captains.

### Sequence of firing orders

Silence!
Cast loose your gun!
Take out your tompion!
Level your gun!
Shot and wad your gun!
Run out your gun!
Prime!
Point your gun!
Fire!
Serve your vent!
Worm [about every fourth shot] and sponge!
Load with cartridge!
Shot and wad your gun!
(The sequence was completed and the gun loaded again.)

At any naval battle of the period, the drills, techniques and problems of gunnery were virtually identical no matter what the rate of ship or nationality of the crew serving the guns. The only significant difference between British gunnery at Trafalgar and that of the French or Spanish was that generally the former aimed at the enemy's hull while the latter two concentrated on masts and rigging. This is explained in detail below. Small variations existed in drills, but the actions and difficulties described here were generally common to all gunnery. Space prohibits detailing every movement of every crew member, but the basic actions, considerations and decisions that took place on the receipt of each of the above orders are explained.

### Silence!

On a gundeck in action, silence was clearly impossible, but every effort was made to minimize noise so that orders could be heard. As the *Mars'* general orders said: 'The strictest silence to be observed by the Men at their guns.' Unnecessary shouting was forbidden, as it was vital that the midshipmen and quarter gunners heard key orders as to what shot was to be loaded, which guns were to fire and when. Officers and petty officers on the gundecks had speaking trumpets and orders were relayed and repeated as required. As the *Victory*, and the other ships, sailed towards the Combined Fleet with the men at quarters, the gundecks would have been quiet. The quarterdeck midshipmen's shouting down the hatchways to 'cast loose the guns' was audible to every seaman and marine.

### Cast loose your gun!

This order told the gun crews to release the guns from the lashings that held them secure. The men nearest the muzzle, Nos. 3 and 4 (loader and sponger), did this. The two gun tackles had to be freed and the rope passed to the crew members on each side of the gun so they were ready to pull the gun further inboard. At the same time the port was opened outwards, letting in a welcome stream of light. The gun captain fixed his gunlock to the gun. Sponges, handspikes, rammers and all implements were taken from the hooks above and laid beside the gun. As there was still plenty of time at Trafalgar before the battle, each crew of 14 probably got one broadside run out and ready to fire and then moved across and did the same with the other.

### Take out your tompion!

The tompion was taken from the muzzle by either the loader or sponger and left hanging from the muzzle by a lanyard. The No. 1 or No. 2 (gun captain or second captain) hooked the train tackle to the rear of the carriage and to the ring bolt fixed to the deck amidships. Because the guns had just been released from their secure position, they had to be pulled back a short distance to the limit of the breeching rope. Then, with the train tackle preventing forward movement and the breeching rope backward movement, the guns were ready for loading.

### Level your gun!

The handspike men raised the breech of the gun so that the gun captain or second captain could insert the quoin under it to level the gun so it was horizontal to the deck.

### Shot and wad your gun!

As the *Victory*'s guns were already loaded with a cartridge and one ball, the full loading procedure was not necessary. However, the orders were now for all guns to be double-shotted, so there were differences to the usual drill. The choice was either to load another shot (or grapeshot) on top of the one already in the gun, or to remove that ball and cartridge and reload with a lower weight of cartridge for close-range firing; we don't know which happened on the *Victory*, but as the enemy were still a long way off and there was no certainty as to the range at which fire would need to be opened, the guns were probably loaded with a second shot without changing the cartridge.

In this case, the assistant loader (No. 5) would have picked up a ball (it was not recommended that 32-pounders on the lower deck fired grape) from the shot garland and handed it to the loader (No. 3). The loader placed the ball in the muzzle, holding his left hand over it (to prevent it rolling out if the ship heeled) and then took a wad from the assistant loader in his right hand, and inserted it after the ball. While this was happening, the assistant sponger (No. 6) handed a rammer to the sponge man (No. 4) who was standing to the right of the muzzle. As soon as the wad had been inserted, he rammed down the wad and shot. Meanwhile, the gun captain had inserted his vent pricker down the vent at the breech and when he felt the cartridge fully down shouted 'Home!' The rammer was withdrawn and handed to the assistant sponger who laid it on the deck.

The crew of the *Victory* went to quarters at 10.00 a.m. on the morning of Trafalgar and at around 11.00, as the enemy were still some way off, dinner and grog were piped. One watch would have

# Gun Positions – Housed, Cast Loose, Loading and Firing

## Notes

- In this position the gun was housed or secured when not likely to be used. It was, however, kept loaded with the vent covered and no gunlock in place.
- The first order to get the gun into action was 'Cast loose your gun'.

### A Gun housed

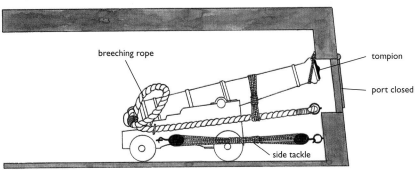

- The gun has just been cast loose. It cannot be loaded in this position as it has not been immobilized.
- The tompion is removed, the train tackle attached and the gun hauled inboard until checked by the breeching rope. The gun is then in position C for loading.

### B Gun just cast loose

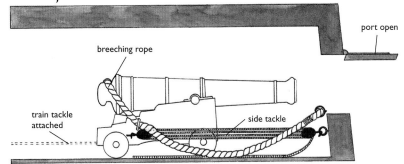

- The gun has been hauled inboard (or recoiled) for loading (or swabbing) and is held stationary by the breeching rope and train tackle.
- The gun is horizontal to the deck and all the crew except the gun captain would be forward of the breech.
- After loading the gun was run out to the position at D.

### C Gun having just recoiled

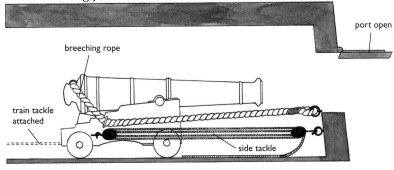

- This shows the gun in the firing position. When in this position the gun was pointed (aimed).
- When the recoil was expected to be particularly rapid or violent (notably if the deck was on the upward roll when the gun fired) the train tackle would be unhooked, otherwise the blocks might be broken under the carriage and the tackle entangled.

### D Gun at the instant of firing

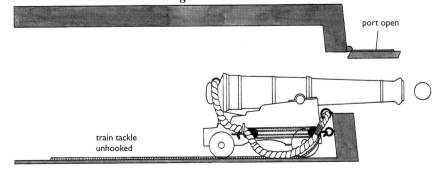

gone for a hasty meal and drink before returning to relieve the watch still at quarters. This meant that the guns were left loaded and run in, held stationary by their breeching and train tackles. It is highly unlikely that any guns would have been run out until the order to fire was imminent, with a suitable target close or clearly in sight. After they returned to their guns, fortified with grog and food, the next order would almost certainly have been Captain Hardy's.

*Run out your gun!*

With the gun tackles hooked onto the rings in the side of the carriage, the gun captain called 'Heave!' and all crew on each side hauled the gun forward. Care had to be taken that the slack of the breeching rope did not foul the trucks (wheels). The gun was run out until the muzzle protruded through the port and the front of the carriage was hard up against the ship's side. During this running out the gun captain may have had to give instructions to ensure the gun was properly positioned in the centre of the port. Once run out, the gun had to be held in position so that it did not roll back with the heel of the ship. The French did this by making a couple of turns of the breeching rope around the cascable, while two crew continued to take the strain on the gun tackle; it was essential not to forget to release the breeching rope before firing. It is not certain whether British crews copied this or if all the men on the gun tackles continued to hold the gun tight against the side. During this time the second captain unhooked the train tackle and pulled it back out of the way of the recoil.

It is worth re-emphasizing here how important it was to have sufficient men on the gun tackles. They had not only to run out the 3.5-ton monster, but perhaps also to hold it firm in position, possibly for some minutes, until the gun was actually fired – good reason not to run out the guns too soon.

*Prime!*

The gun captain thrust his vent pricker several times down the vent to pierce the cartridge bag in the chamber. If he could not feel the cartridge, he shouted for the sponge man to ram again, although with the guns already loaded, this would not have been the case that morning at Trafalgar. If in doubt, he would wipe the vent pricker across the palm of his left hand to check it left a black smear of powder. Next he inserted a quill tube (the fuse) in the vent before pouring a small amount of fine powder from his powder horn into the pan of the gunlock and closing it.

*Point your gun!*

In layman's language this meant aim the gun, making all necessary adjustments for lateral movement and elevation. Aiming was, in practice, an art rather than a science. Range tables set out point blank distances (400 yards for the 32-, 24- and 18-pounders), angles of elevation required to shorten or increase the range, and the correct weight of powder for the cartridge. Nevertheless, on the day it was the gun captain's judgement, experience, knowledge of his gun's idiosyncrasies, ability to judge ranges and good timing in the jerking of the firing lanyard that decided whether a shot hit anything much above 400 yards. Once a target was in sight, a decision was required as to the range – usually estimated by knowing the type of ship and what it looked like to the gunner crouched behind his gun. The diagram opposite shows approximately what the *Victory* would have looked like at certain ranges when seen by a gun captain on Villeneuve's flagship, the 80-gun *Bucentaure*.

The next decision was what part of the ship you wanted to hit. If the enemy were still some way off, beyond point-blank range, then probably the shot would be intended as a dismantling one, with the aim of knocking down the tops, hitting yards or masts and cutting stays or shrouds so that your enemy lost way – lost the ability to manoeuvre. If this happened, then the ship became vulnerable to being outmanoeuvred and raked or, if it was more powerful than its attacker, was slowed sufficiently that it could not pursue. The problem was that there was lots of scope for missing. Gaps in the rigging were large, many shots went high and holes in sails were hardly crippling. Unless the firer was very lucky, many hits were needed to do serious damage. Both the French and Spanish gunners tended to favour this type of aiming, and used it on the approaching British at the start of Trafalgar.

Aiming to hit 'between wind and water' was another option. This was plunging fire, intended to strike the hull well below the water line and fill the ship with holes so that she began to sink, or at least had to divert many of her crew to the pumps. Very few wooden warships, of any nationality, were sunk by gunfire. They were battered into surrender, boarded, blew up, were crippled by fallen masts and yards or caught fire, but they seldom sank. The reasons were that plunging fire was only practical with heavy guns (24-pounders and above) at short range, as only their shot had the velocity to penetrate several feet of water and then the hull. Shots hitting at an angle had a greater thickness to penetrate, and even if they did so the wood fibres of oak tended to go back into place afterwards, thus limiting the damage and facilitating temporary repairs. There is no convincing evidence that any ships of either side at Trafalgar deliberately aimed 'between wind and water'.

The third tactic, and the most common for British gunners, was to aim at the enemy's hull above the water line – anywhere from the lower gunports to the quarterdeck – the object being to kill or maim men and disable guns. This was accomplished by ball, grape and sprays of splinters. The closer the action, the less the need to aim. At Trafalgar, once the two British columns had broken the enemy line, the battle broke up into a series of mêlées at extremely close range. Gunners on both sides had little need to aim, instead just ran out their guns and fired. Fights between individual ships became deadly slugging matches, with some ships, such as the *Victory* and *Redoutable*, locked together and still firing – but certainly not aiming. The British approach to battle was painfully slow at Trafalgar, so their gunners had an excessively long wait before the enemy line was cut and they could bring their guns to bear on a worthwhile target. This meant that aiming was seldom a problem throughout the day.

Assuming some aiming, even if only rough alignment, was required, the procedure was as follows. During the actual running out the gun captain would have tried to get the gun pointing generally in the right direction. This was not easy, as it was difficult to co-ordinate the exertions of the men heaving on the gun tackles. Once the guns were run out, some lateral adjustment was invariably needed. This was achieved by the two handspike men (Nos. 7 and 8) using their spikes to lever the carriage in the right direction. They were assisted by the men on the gun tackles who heaved to pull the gun towards whichever side the gun captain indicated, either angling the gun slightly or straightening it in the port. With little help from the trucks (which did not turn), not to mention the pitching motion of the deck and the weight of the

# French Gun Captain's View of *Victory* during Her Approach to Battle

- First ranging shot falls short.
- Second shot falls alongside.

**A**
11.45am

All timings are approximate

**A**
2,200 yards

Many misses
Little damage
No casualties

- More shots going over. Large hole in maintop-gallant sail.
- Capt. Blackwood leaves *Victory*.
- Several more enemy ships open fire.
- Adm.'s secretary (Scott) killed, as are 8 marines on poop.

**B**
12.05pm

**B**
1,200 yards

- Firing much more effective as range closer.
- Wheel smashed.
- Mizzen-topmast down.
- Ship's boats damaged.
- 200ft of foresail shredded.

**C**
12.18pm

**C**
600 yards
(just under point-blank range for a 36-pdr)

Progressively more serious damage and losses

- Both studding sails ripped from booms.
- By the time *Victory* cut the line at 12.30pm some 50 casualties had been inflicted.

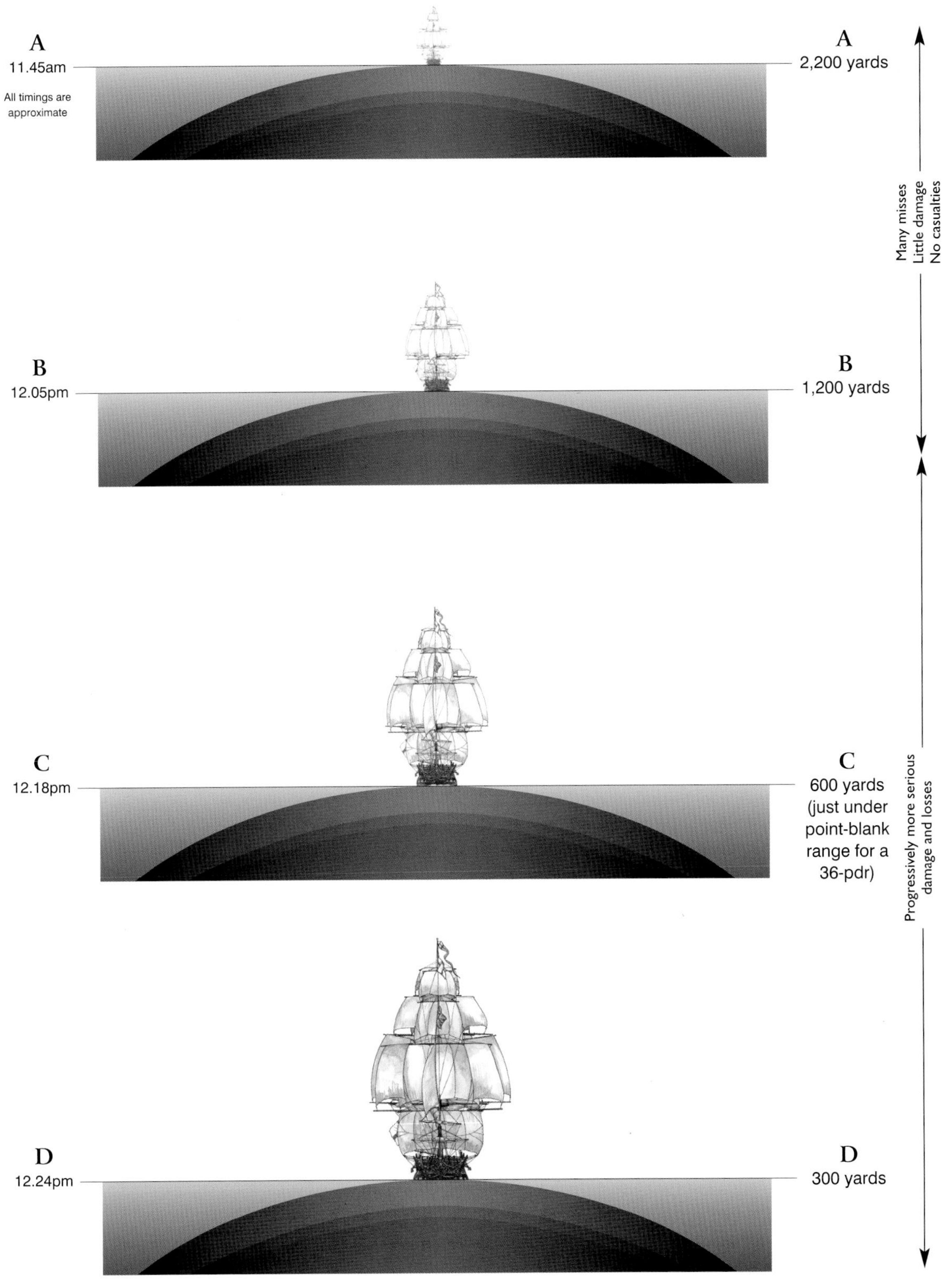

**D**
12.24pm

**D**
300 yards

## Notes

- A, B, C and D show the view of the *Victory* seen by a gun captain of Villeneuve's flagship, *Bucentaure*, as she slowly sailed into range and eventually, after about 45 minutes under increasingly effective fire, cut the Combined Fleet's line.
- The drawings of the *Victory* give a clear picture of the size of the target at various ranges and the difficulty in hitting anything much more than 1,500 yards away.
- Because of the very light wind the *Victory* approached at a speed of about 1.5 knots or around 45 yards every minute.
- The arc corresponds to the base ring of a 36-pounder with the gun captain looking along the top of the barrel from behind the base ring.

gun, pointing could be a difficult and slow business. Once the gun was pointing in the right direction, the next adjustment had to be for elevation. Bearing in mind all the considerations as to range, type of fire, point of aim and so on discussed above, the gun captain knelt on one knee behind the gun and closed one eye. He squinted along the top of the barrel, with his left hand on the base ring and his right grasping the quoin (sometimes the No. 2 may have adjusted the quoin). To his right and left the handspike men had taken up a crowbar and handspike and inserted them under the breech. Their task was to lever up the breech slightly – for which considerable strength was needed – so that the quoin could be either pushed further in or pulled further out. As there were no sights, the gun captain had to use the centre line and the top of the muzzle to aim. He may have been aiming above the target, at the rigging, at the hull or lower, depending on the range. In all circumstances he would have been telling the handspike men, 'Up a bit!', 'Up a bit!', 'Hold it!', 'Down a bit!' while he or his second captain slid the quoin in or out. Again this could take some time to get right and certainly required considerable muscle. When satisfied, the gun captain took hold of the firing lanyard and moved back beyond the recoil of the gun. When he was in position, the second captain (No. 2) cocked the gun-lock. The breeching rope was checked to ensure it could not foul the trucks on recoil. The gun was ready for the next order.

At close range it was merely a matter of fire, reload, run out and fire again, and the ship that did this fastest was likely to win. At the start of an action a British crew averaged around 90 seconds per shot or three in five minutes, whereas many French or Spanish crews barely managed one shot in the same time. The huge physical strain, even without casualties, could rapidly reduce the rate of fire, no matter how well trained the crew. As far as basic gunnery was concerned at Trafalgar, victory went to the ships that fired the fastest for the longest. And Nelson knew full well from the outset which they were likely to be.

### Fire!

When a gun was to be fired at point-blank distance, it could be aimed directly at the object. Beyond this distance the gun had to be fired with the point of aim higher than the intended target, and at closer ranges it was best to aim slightly below the target. If two projectiles were fired, the aim must be higher to compensate for the reduction in range due to the double weight. Firing round-

shot double-shotted was ineffective above 800 yards, and bar and grapeshot lost much of their effectiveness over 400 yards. If the gun captain was ordered to fire while either the ship or the target was moving rapidly, rather than traversing the gun to cover the target it was better to leave the gun square in the port and wait until the target crossed his line of sight.

Nevertheless, no gun captain could expect to fire the instant he heard the order from his superior unless the target was so close as to be almost touching. In most circumstances the actual moment he yanked his lanyard was entirely his decision, because he was the only man able to judge the precise moment to fire, from looking down the line of the gun and watching for the target to appear at the right spot. It was far from easy. The gun captain had to understand the movement of the ship under his feet. He had to know whether the ship was between waves or swells, whether he was firing from the lee or weather side and whether his side of the ship was coming up or going down as it heeled. Although there were other factors, the basic choice was whether to fire with a rising or falling side. Whenever possible, British gunners were trained to fire with a rising side because a small misjudgement could still gain a hit on masts or rigging, while a similar error while firing on the down could result in the shot missing the hull and plunging uselessly into the water – ricochets were possible but uncommon unless the sea was exceptionally calm. The only problem with firing on the rise was that the deck would be sloping away from the side firing, so the force of the recoil would be greatly increased, with the consequent risk of the ring bolts or breeching rope breaking. At all events the gun captain, who was kneeling on one knee well back behind the gun, had a tricky task in jerking the lanyard just a fraction of a second before his line of sight crossed the aiming point on the target.

While waiting for the shot to be fired, the crew were still holding the gun tackles and bracing the gun against the ship's side. At the moment of firing they dropped the tackle for the recoil. The gun captain then immediately hooked on the train tackle and pulled it taut. At the same time the handspike man on the right chocked the trucks with his crowbar. These manoeuvres prevented the gun rolling forward again.

### Serve your vent!

This was a critical order. It meant that the gun captain must stop the vent by placing the thumb of his left hand (protected by a

---

### Some Gunnery Techniques

Hitting the hull was always likely to bring decisive results. Although it was difficult to aim at with any sea running, as it kept partially disappearing from view, the chances of a hit through the ports or below the waterline increased in proportion to the decreasing range. Guns would be disabled, crews became casualties, leaks required men to leave their positions to man the pumps, and shots deep inside the hull could crack the base of a mast. The ensuing chaos on the gundecks also slowed the supply of cartridges. One of the most damaging techniques at close quarters was to alternately depress and elevate the guns, firing with reduced charges. This caused the maximum splintering in the target ship. A first-hand account of this method was written by a lieutenant on the 74-gun *Brunswick* at the Battle of the Glorious First of June:

> All her masts [of the French *Le Vengeur*] went soon after, but from the weight of shot thrown into her, viz 3 rounds shot of 32 lb., i.e. 96 lb. of ball from each gun, driving home our quoins at one time, watching their rising, to fire beneath the water line, next withdrawing the quoins to elevate the muzzles and rip up her decks, this alternative mode of firing for two hours and a half alongside, we rather think it may probably happen her masts were cut by our shot from within board. The silence of their fire for the last two hours, shews [sic] the people were employed at their pumps, but all their efforts could not preserve their ship from sinking.

This was a rare example of gunnery actually sinking a ship.

leather thumb-stall filled with horsehair) over it. This had to be done before the gun was sponged to prevent a rush of air escaping through the vent when the sponge was thrust down the bore. This draught had the effect of fanning any smouldering fragments of cartridge and forcing them back into the end of the bore. The unfortunate loader, as he thrust home the next cartridge, could become the victim of a premature detonation, resulting in death or the loss of an arm. If the vent was properly blocked, the sponge extinguished the glowing embers. A thumb-stall was needed if the gun captain was not to lift his thumb involuntarily as the sponge forced hot gases out of the vent.

*Worm and sponge!*
This involved using the worm (see p. 237) to remove any build up of cartridge material that might cover the lower end of the vent and prevent pricking the cartridge or the flash from the quill reaching the powder. Worming was done when necessary – normally after about every fourth shot – by the sponge man standing on the right of the muzzle. It was immediately followed by sponging, after the sponge had been dipped in the water bucket.

*Load with cartridge!*
By this time the powderman would have come forward on the left of the gun with his salt box containing two cartridges. The lid was removed and one cartridge handed to the loader (No. 3). He placed the cartridge in the muzzle, seam downwards, and then took a wad from the assistant loader (No. 5) and inserted it on top of the cartridge. Immediately, the sponger (No. 4) rammed both down the bore, giving it several thrusts to ensure it had reached the chamber. This fact was checked by the gun captain, who felt for the cartridge with his vent pricker. Meanwhile, the powderman closed the lid of his salt box and returned amidships to await the next loading and (if necessary) replenish his cartridge(s) from the men passing up charges in wooden cases from the magazines, in this case the grand magazine.

*Shot and wad your gun!*
The sequence starts again.

## TYPES OF FIRING

To get the best results, firing had to be controlled for as long as possible in terms of choice of timing, targets, guns and shot. Initially instructions would come from the captain on the quarterdeck, but once the range had closed to under 600 metres, decisions often had to be left to the discretion of the gundeck officers. When ships were engaging each other within musket shot (150 yards), gun captains were often left to 'fire as you bare', or, as the Army would say, 'fire at will'. As a general rule the British lighter guns on the quarterdeck, poop and forecastle would fire more grape- and chainshot, targeting the men, rigging and shrouds on the enemy's open decks. Gun captains were trained to fire as the enemy's deck dipped towards them, thus exposing more men. The heavier guns would fire more shot and concentrated on hitting the hull and killing gun crews.

Individual guns were numbered, while gundecks were divided into quarters and divisions as well as into larboard and starboard batteries. A full broadside would include all the guns on one side of the ship – 52 guns (including carronades) on the *Victory*, 40 on the French *Bucentaure* and 56 on the Spanish *Santa Ana*. In

practice a full broadside was seldom, if ever, fired simultaneously. The shock of such a recoil would put too severe a strain on joints and decking, while the likelihood of every gun having a worthwhile target at precisely the same moment was remote. More common was to fire a battery from one deck only, or to fire all the larboard or starboard batteries in succession. Even then, the firing was likely (at least at the start of the action) to be 'ripple' fire, with each gun firing in succession as it came to bear. On the gundecks it was possible to fire by divisions, for example the larboard or starboard forward division. Things became more complex when alternate guns were fired or certain numbers of guns on both sides had to be manned. On occasion crews would have to dash from one side to the other. Sometimes firing on both sides, but only with alternate guns, was an option. The theoretical permutations were numerous but the key to avoiding chaos was simplicity and regular training. During the bulk of the battle at Trafalgar, gundeck officers and their subordinates spent their time deciding what guns were to fire on which side, moving crews and checking ammunition supply. The gun captains decided when exactly to fire.

As discussed earlier, the French and Spanish favoured dismantling fire. To be effective against masts, yards or rigging at long range required precision firing. Rather than blazing away with whole broadsides, it was recommended that one gun on either side of the quarterdeck and forecastle, each with skilled gun captains, be given responsibility for dismantling fire. This type of fire was most effective in a fresh wind, since the stronger the wind, the more likely a damaged mast would collapse, sail split or yard fall. In lighter winds it was the masts and spars that presented the more rewarding target. At Trafalgar, where there was only a whisper of wind, the *Victory*'s foretopsail, some 320 square yards in area, was riddled with some 90 holes but continued to function. (It still exists today and at the time of writing is being restored so it can be displayed in public.) Dismantling fire was common in a chase situation, when the pursuer would try to bring down a mast or some critical rigging in order to slow the enemy ship while the pursued did the same in order to escape. Again, a well-aimed bow or stern chaser would probably be more successful than trying to bring a broadside to bear.

At Trafalgar the first shots of the Combined Fleet at the *Victory* were fired at a range of about a mile and a quarter. These were ranging shots, intended more to warm up the guns than to do serious damage. Apart from the first 20 to 30 minutes of the action, virtually all firing was at short range, much at extremely short range, some less than pistol shot (20 yards). As soon as a ship joined the mêlée, the gundecks quickly became a hellish combination of noise, smoke and varying degrees of carnage. In these circumstances most crews fired at will as soon as they had reloaded and struggled to run out their gun – the target was obvious.

### Rapidity of fire

The single most important factor in the British victory at Trafalgar was rapidity of fire, a skill that came only with constant practice and rigorous attention to every minute detail of the drills. British ships spent month after month at sea on blockade, cruising or escorting convoys, during which time captains constantly exercised their men at the guns, whereas the French and Spanish, many of whose ships were bottled up in port, seldom got down to the serious practice of gunnery. With a fresh, well-trained crew a British gun would expect to fire three shots in five minutes – less than two minutes per shot, compared with the French average timings of eight minutes for firing a 36-pounder, five for an 18-pounder and four for an 8-pounder. The average Spanish crew could do no better. This gave the British Fleet a huge, battle-winning advantage. For both sides rapidity suffered as casualties, confusion and exhaustion took their toll, but inevitably the slower fleet suffered most.

Second in importance to speed was the ability to hit with the first broadside. If this was raking fire, the results would be decisive, with the enemy ship never able to properly recover or reply effectively. Follow it by a rapid second broadside and the fight was won almost before it had started. This is what happened when the *Victory* cut the line at Trafalgar and fired her first broadside into the flimsy stern of Villeneuve's flagship *Bucentaure*, less than five yards away. Mr Willmet waited to fire his carronade until he could almost touch the French Tricolour. His barrel of musket balls was followed by a continuous series of thunderous crashes as all 51 guns on the *Victory*'s port side came to bear. Many French guns were smashed and several hundred men went down in a matter of moments. Villeneuve's after-action report to the Minister of Marine said of these first broadsides: 'the lightness of the wind, which made all movements slow and difficult, did not prevent this ship [the *Victory*], which was athwart the *Bucentaure*'s stern, from pouring in several triple-shotted broadsides, which were exceedingly deadly and destructive'.

Because of the huge advantage at close range of getting in the first two or three broadsides in rapid succession, it was sometimes worth taking the odd shortcut with the firing drills. One possibility was to ram home the cartridge, shot and wad together, and use a wad that did not fit too tightly – wads sometimes required several hard thrusts to drive down the bore. Whether this technique was adopted at Trafalgar is not known.

A final point of gunnery needs emphasis: the human factor. In a close mêlée that lasted perhaps for hours, the physical effort required of the crews was enormous. An excellent, but possibly apocryphal, example occurred at the Nile. Towards the end of an exceptionally long action, the first lieutenant of the 74-gun

*Alexander* reported to the appropriately named Captain Sir Alexander Ball. According to the English poet and philosopher Samuel Taylor Coleridge, who for a period worked as Ball's secretary when he was governor of Malta in 1804:

> the first lieutenant came to Captain Ball and informed him that the hearts of the men were as good as ever, but that they were so completely exhausted, that they were scarcely capable of lifting an arm. He asked therefore, as the enemy had now ceased firing, the men be permitted to lie down between their guns for a short time. After some reflection, Sir Alexander acceded to the proposal ... Accordingly, with the exception of himself, his officers and the appointed watch, the ship's crew lay down, each in the place to which he was stationed, and slept for twenty minutes. They were then roused, and started up, as Sir Alexander expressed it, more like men out of an ambush than from sleep ... They recommended their fire ... and it was soon discovered that during the interval ... the French had sunk down by their guns, and there slept, almost side by side, as it were, of their sleeping enemy.

### Drinks to Quench Thirst in Battle

There were two types of drink that could be given to French gun crews to slake their thirst in action. The first, 'breuvage', was wine diluted with water, and the second, 'hipsy', was composed of 30 quarts of water to one of good vinegar and one of brandy. It was also used to quench the thirst of seamen on watch in less stressful times. In British ships wine was substituted for vinegar. The drink issued to men in action was sometimes known as 'fighting water', but like all diluted drinks it was regarded with some contempt by most seamen, who described it as 'water-bewitched'. One hopes that, in the heat and confusion of battle, no one drank the water used to sponge out the guns by mistake – it was seawater with vinegar added.

It was not unknown for men to be ordered to lie down to avoid the worst effect of enemy fire before they were required to fire. This was certainly a well-known technique and may have been employed at Trafalgar. Lord Howe had used it in 1794 as his fleet approached the enemy. The newspaper *The True Briton* of 7 August 1794 had this to say:

> When Lord Howe was bringing up his Ship in the late Engagement [The Glorious First of June] into action, he ordered all his men to lie upon their backs on the deck, til they came almost close to the enemy; the Officers standing all the time. This manoeuvre which we hear is his Lordship's constant practice, saves a number of men from random shots, and gives them an additional energy in action.

But if gunnery was all about smashing an enemy, battle tactics were all about getting a ship (or fleet) into the most advantageous position to do so.

# TACTICS

Put simply, tactics is the art of fighting battles, operations the art of conducting campaigns and strategy that of fighting wars. In Napoleonic naval terms, tactics were all about securing an advantage of position over an enemy so that when the guns fired they inflicted the maximum damage and casualties. Conversely, a captain sought to place his ship where his opponent's fire would be the least effective. The fleet commander's overriding aim would always be to concentrate more ships and more guns than the enemy could

muster at a given place and time. Naval tactics could also be divided into those manoeuvres adopted by individual ships and those by the admiral commanding the squadron or fleet. However, good tactics could be negated by poor gunnery and vice versa. In the end, decisive results were the product of individual ships overwhelming their opponent so that its fire slackened and the damage inflicted became increasingly one-sided. This could not happen until both ships were exchanging broadsides at close range – at distances of 200 yards or less, often much less. The British 'Fighting Instructions', the tactical manual of the day, had this to say on the subject:

> XX
> Not to fire within point blank
> Every commander is to take care that his guns are not fired till he is sure he can reach the enemy upon a point blank; and by no means to suffer his guns to be fired over any of our own ships.

Virtually all the elements of naval tactics of the time are illustrated at Trafalgar. They are discussed below under key headings.

## Single ships

### Arcs of fire

The fire of all ships was heaviest at right angles to the hull. So a ship would try to manoeuvre to bring either the larboard or starboard broadside to bear, while at the same time avoiding the full weight of the enemy's guns. Firing directly ahead or astern was not possible unless bow or stern chasers were mounted, which they were not on most if not all of the ships-of-the-line at Trafalgar. The adoption of the wider-spaced hull ring bolts for the gun (side) tackles between the ports by British ships in 1780 allowed guns to be trained to a maximum of 45 degrees each side of the beam. Nevertheless, as the diagram below makes clear, there was still a large area forward and astern of a ship in which an enemy was almost invulnerable. One problem with the right-angle arc of fire was that firing full broadsides did not bring a ship any closer to its enemy. If a captain wanted to close the range, he had to turn, thus temporarily reducing or abandoning firing. This was always the dilemma for single ships involved in a chase. There was little point in pursuing a ship of equal sailing ability, as, barring poor seamanship or accidents, she would never be caught. To catch an enemy you pointed your bow at the fleeing ship, crammed on maximum sail (having regard to the strength of the wind) and abandoned all thought of firing a broadside until the range was close. Perhaps you brought a bow gun into action in an attempt to damage a mast, yard or rigging, thus slowing the enemy. Similarly, the pursued might use a stern chaser to try to ensure escape. If the distance closed sufficiently, either ship might risk luffing up into the wind or wearing away in order to bring some guns to bear, fire a broadside (probably at the masts or rigging) and then resume her original course. The point here was that captains had to manoeuvre their ships in order to use the arcs of fire of their guns to best effect. Having done that, it was the actual gunnery that counted.

### 'Bow and 'quarter' positions

Good tactics for the single ship lay in the art of knowing how to manoeuvre for the most advantageous position – and keeping it. With the possible exception of the rake (see below), the best position was 'on the bow' (Ship B2 in the diagram below). The

---

## Firing Positions

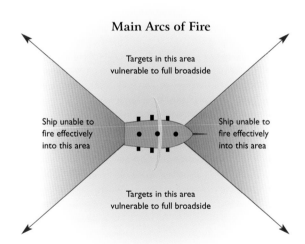

**Main Arcs of Fire**

Targets in this area vulnerable to full broadside

Ship unable to fire effectively into this area

Ship unable to fire effectively into this area

Targets in this area vulnerable to full broadside

### Notes
- Ships were only able to fire full broadsides effectively at right angles to the direction of sailing.
- The maximum angle at which guns could fire was about 45° from the vertical.
- Enemy ships in the shaded areas could not be hit except with bow or stern chasers – the least effective guns.

- The weakest point of a ship was always the bow or stern.
- Therefore it was almost impossible for a pursuing ship to inflict damage on the pursued unless the range was very short and she was able to change course to bring at least some broadside guns into action.

---

**'Bow' and 'Quarter' Positions**

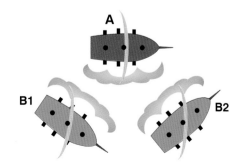

### Notes
- Ship **B1** has positioned herself on the starboard quarter of Ship **A**. Her entire larboard broadside can fire into **A**, whereas **A** can respond with only slightly over half of her starboard guns. Additionally, **B1**'s guns can half rake **A**, whose fire will hit nearly at right angles.

- Ship **B2**, on the starboard bow, has the further advantage of firing down **A**'s poop/quarterdeck into the exposed forecastle of **A**. **B2**'s position can be held, with skilful seamanship, for some time.

## Firing Positions

### Notes
- There was no more devastating way of inflicting casualties or damage than raking an enemy. Each gun fires as it comes in line with the target and the shots can travel the entire length of the ship. The only disadvantage is that only one broadside is possible as the ship passes the enemy's bow or stern.

### The Rake

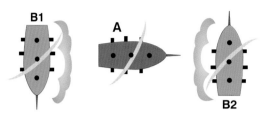

- An effective rake was often sufficient to cripple the fighting capability of an opponent.
- Here **B1** is raking the stern, the weakest part of **A**. **B2** is raking the bow – slightly less vulnerable than the stern.

attacking ship positioned itself on the weather (larboard or starboard) bow to fire down onto the exposed forecastle with the poop/quarterdeck guns, while at the same time the broadside guns could half rake the enemy. All the major lines were handled and belayed (secured) on the forecastle, while the foremast itself was also very vulnerable; it was a perfect area to target. With skill this position could be maintained until the adversary had suffered sufficient damage aloft to prevent her tacking. The attacker then endeavoured to bear away, rake the enemy and take up a similar position on the lee bow. That was the theory, but putting it into practice required considerable skill and judgement on the part of the captain, who had to match every enemy move, and expert seamanship from his crew. Not every ship would attempt complex manoeuvres, many preferring simply to swap broadsides.

### Raking
What was the weakest part on any ship? The stern. Here were rows of glass windows, here the timber was thinner, here were the wardroom, captain's and perhaps admiral's living quarters. It was the softest, most vulnerable part of a sailing warship. An enemy passing across the stern, firing shot after shot at close range, had achieved the perfect rake. For the unfortunate recipient it frequently lost her the action. Thousands of shards of jagged glass and flying splinters joined the grapeshot and ball in scouring the decks from end to end. When the French flagship *Bucentaure*

struck her colours at Trafalgar, Captain James Atcherley RM was sent onboard to accept Villeneuve's sword. He later described the effects of raking fire thus:

> The dead, thrown back as they fell, lay along the middle of the decks in heaps, and the shot, passing through these, had frightfully mangled the bodies. … More than four hundred had been killed and wounded, of whom an extraordinary proportion had lost their heads. A raking shot, which entered in the lower deck, had glanced along the beams and through the thickest of the people, and a French officer declared this shot alone had killed or disabled nearly forty men.

A ship that had been badly raked tended to drift rather than sail, with her ability to return fire dramatically reduced, both largely the result of an instantaneous shortage of men for the tasks involved. The only drawback for the attacker was that a rake was all over within a matter of seconds – there was no stopping for a second broadside without further manoeuvres. An excellent example of a ship repeatedly raking the stern of an enemy was Nelson's pursuit in the *Agamemnon* of the *Ça Ira* in March 1795 – see p. 116.

A rake could also be fired into a ship's bow. This could also be potentially crippling but was less likely to be so, as the bow was a narrower target with curved surfaces, more solidly built than the stern and backed by a strong bulkhead.

---

### Judging the Strength and Range of an Enemy Ship

In fine, clear weather it was possible to see a ship over the horizon from the topgallant crosstrees at a distance of about 18 miles. A rough way of estimating its size and therefore its likely strength in terms of guns had been established through experience. If the distant ship's maintopgallant could be seen from the deck, with the topgallant resting on the line of the horizon, a seaman was sent aloft to the same height. If from that position he could see the enemy's deck, the adversary was of about the same strength (rate). If part of the upper works were visible, then it was a ship of lesser strength. If the deck could not

be seen then the strange ship was larger. As the vessel approached, it was usually possible to recognize the nationality even if it was not flying an appropriate flag, by looking at the build of the ship, the position and proportions of the masts (their spacing) and the cut of the sails.

One method of judging the closer ranges for the purpose of gunnery was to note the movement of personnel. At around 800 yards the general movement of men could be distinguished, at 700 yards heads could be made out, and at 400 yards they could be seen clearly.

## The Weather Gauge

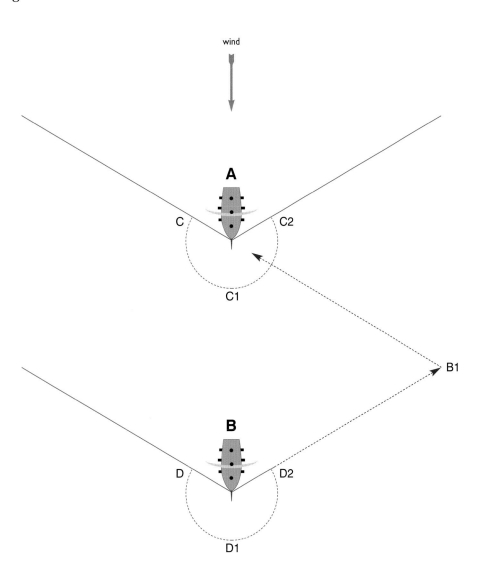

### Notes

Ship **A** holds the weather gauge to windward of **B**. She has a choice of all courses within the angle **C**, **C1**, **C2**. **A** can bear down on **B** directly. **B** has a similar choice of courses **D**, **D1**, **D2**, but no way of moving directly on **A**. The shortest route by which she could do so is **B–B1–A** – wearing, which takes much longer.

The above example is the extreme position, with **A** directly astern of **B** with a following wind. Nevertheless, any ship to windward of another holds the weather gauge and has the advantage in terms of manoeuvre and initiative in attacking.

## The weather and lee gauges

A ship or group of ships that had the weather gauge – was to windward of its opponent – had the better position to manoeuvre for an attack. In Nelson's fleet at Trafalgar every ship had (and held) the weather gauge until it joined the mêlée. British captains normally sought the weather gauge, manoeuvring to get it if necessary, before action was joined.

The diagram above shows an extreme example of how being to windward of an enemy puts an attacker in a powerful, dominating position. By the same token, the ship downwind has the lee gauge and therefore suffers from having much more restricted room for manoeuvre.

The weather gauge gave an admiral or captain who sought a tactical victory the advantage of the choice of whether, when and how to attack. As an attack developed, it could also open up the opportunity of doubling the enemy's line (see p. 276), while the smoke from firing cleared sooner and tended to drift downwind to obscure the lee ship's view. There were, however, disadvantages. Firstly, disabled ships had problems withdrawing from the action, as they tended to drift down towards the enemy (lee) line with further unpleasant consequences. Secondly, in heavy weather, ships in the windward position were less likely to be able to open their lower gunports as the ship heeled. At close range, however, those in the lee line were more likely to be holed below the waterline.

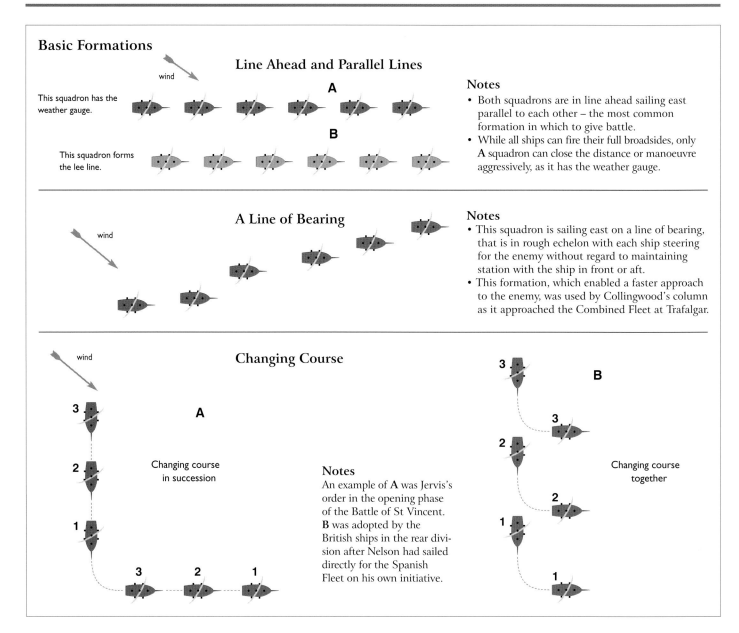

**Basic Formations**

### Line Ahead and Parallel Lines

This squadron has the weather gauge.

**A**

This squadron forms the lee line.

**B**

**Notes**
- Both squadrons are in line ahead sailing east parallel to each other – the most common formation in which to give battle.
- While all ships can fire their full broadsides, only **A** squadron can close the distance or manoeuvre aggressively, as it has the weather gauge.

### A Line of Bearing

wind

**Notes**
- This squadron is sailing east on a line of bearing, that is in rough echelon with each ship steering for the enemy without regard to maintaining station with the ship in front or aft.
- This formation, which enabled a faster approach to the enemy, was used by Collingwood's column as it approached the Combined Fleet at Trafalgar.

### Changing Course

wind

**A**

Changing course in succession

**B**

Changing course together

**Notes**
An example of **A** was Jervis's order in the opening phase of the Battle of St Vincent. **B** was adopted by the British ships in the rear division after Nelson had sailed directly for the Spanish Fleet on his own initiative.

## SQUADRON AND FLEET FORMATIONS

The formations adopted had all to do with the approach to battle rather than the battle itself. Once a general mêlée ensued, lines were broken and ships intermingled and slogged it out, as at Trafalgar. Although perhaps an oversimplification, there is considerable truth in the view that admirals controlled the tactics of the approach but captains the tactics of fighting.

### Line ahead

This was the normal formation adopted by all navies for the approach to battle by ships-of-the-line. A common distance between ships was one to two cables (200 to 400 yards). A fleet of thirteen ships would cover a distance of 2,750 to 5,500 yards. Nelson's weather column at Trafalgar of the same number was in line ahead formation, though bunching by the better sailers and serious straggling by the laggards meant it stretched over a much greater distance. Nevertheless, line ahead facilitated control. With frigates deployed in front and to the flanks, signals could be seen and relayed more easily. A variation was to approach on a

line of bearing, as Collingwood's column did at Trafalgar. This was sometimes adopted when the need was for speed of attack, when captains singled out their opposite numbers in the enemy formation and sailed directly for them. The order to form a line of bearing frequently resulted in a ragged echelon formation.

An admiral wanting to change the direction of his line had a choice between doing so 'in succession' or 'together'. With the former the leading ship changed course but those following did not do so until they reached the spot where the first ship turned. A line ahead formation was thus maintained, but the process of getting all ships onto the new bearing could be lengthy. A good example was Jervis' initial order to turn against the Spanish at St Vincent (see pp. 162–3). To change course 'together' entailed every ship turning at the same time so that line ahead became a line abreast or in echelon. In the face of the enemy this was an extremely aggressive move. It could also be used, if later followed by another turn together, to bring the ships back into line ahead on the original bearing but some distance from the original line. Again, the Battle of St Vincent provides an example when a number of ships followed Nelson turning, more or less together, to attack the enemy directly.

## The tactics of the approach

### The end-on approach

In this scenario, opposing fleets approach each other on opposite tacks in line ahead. No firing is possible until the fleets start to pass each other sailing in opposite directions. If the leading ships pass within effective range, they have the option of exchanging broadsides and continuing to do so with the next enemy ship they pass, as soon as they have reloaded. The same happens as each of the following ships comes level with an opponent. Although full broadsides were fired, the chance of this type of action being decisive was remote, since the fleets were unlikely to be engaged for any length of time. Unless one admiral was inclined to be bold and unorthodox and turn on his enemy, little lasting damage would be inflicted on most ships. This was very far from Nelson's idea of good tactics.

### The oblique approach

Again, two fleets approach on opposite tacks but this time at a slightly oblique angle. In this case, however, the angle is not great enough for the ships to open fire on each other due to the restricted arc of fire of the guns (maximum 45 degrees). The dia-gram shows a different, much greater oblique angle approach. Here all ships can fire effectively as the range closes. The likely outcome is a running battle, broadside to broadside, with the fleets in parallel lines sailing in the same direction. Unless one admiral turned away, this type of engagement, which was the most common until the end of the eighteenth century, could result in a prolonged firefight, some seriously damaged ships and, just occasionally, a decisive result.

### Crossing the T – a head-on approach

In this situation both fleets are in line ahead but one has sailed across the head of the other at right angles and 'crossed its T'. In the late nineteenth and much of the twentieth centuries, with modern battleships and guns of vastly superior range, to have crossed an enemy's T was considered to be an excellent tactic. This was because it allowed a number of ships to concentrate their fire on the leading enemy for some considerable time without that enemy being able to reply effectively. The theory was sound but in practice, particularly in the days of sail and shorter-range guns, it was not necessarily so advantageous.

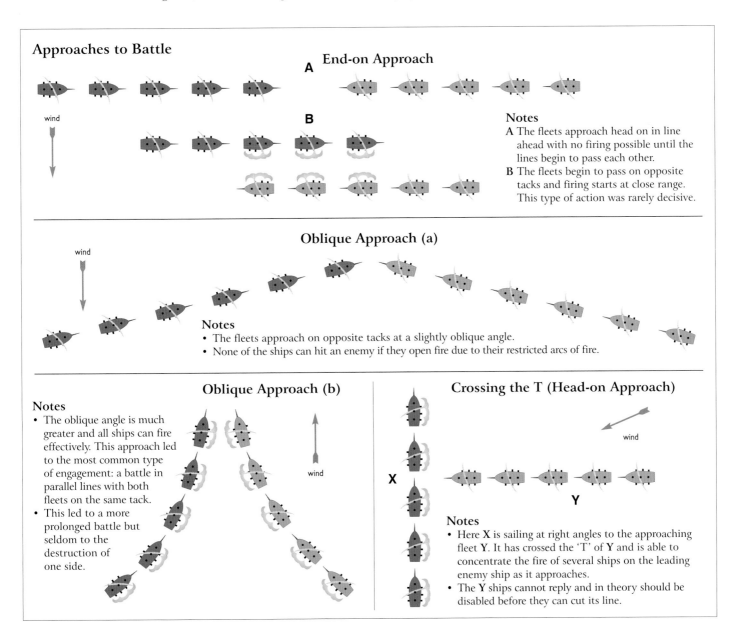

**Approaches to Battle**

**End-on Approach**

wind

**Notes**
A The fleets approach head on in line ahead with no firing possible until the lines begin to pass each other.
B The fleets begin to pass on opposite tacks and firing starts at close range. This type of action was rarely decisive.

**Oblique Approach (a)**

wind

**Notes**
• The fleets approach on opposite tacks at a slightly oblique angle.
• None of the ships can hit an enemy if they open fire due to their restricted arcs of fire.

**Oblique Approach (b)**

**Notes**
• The oblique angle is much greater and all ships can fire effectively. This approach led to the most common type of engagement: a battle in parallel lines with both fleets on the same tack.
• This led to a more prolonged battle but seldom to the destruction of one side.

wind

**Crossing the T (Head-on Approach)**

wind

**Notes**
• Here X is sailing at right angles to the approaching fleet Y. It has crossed the 'T' of Y and is able to concentrate the fire of several ships on the leading enemy ship as it approaches.
• The Y ships cannot reply and in theory should be disabled before they can cut its line.

## Crossing an Enemy's T – the Theory

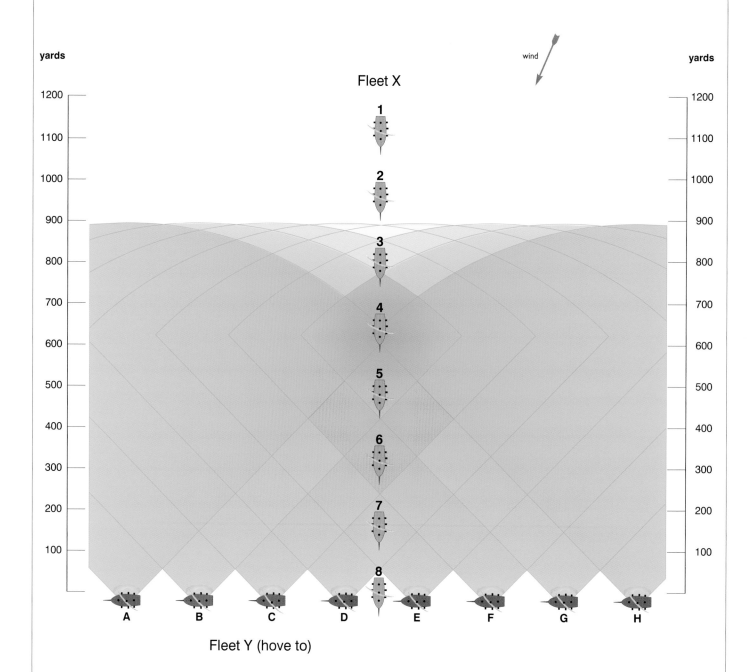

**yards**                                                                    wind                              **yards**

Fleet X

Fleet Y (hove to)

## Notes

- Fleet Y has hove to in order to cross the T of Fleet X as it attempts to break the line. Numbers **1–8** show the positions of X's leading ship as it approaches Y's line.
- At **1** and **2** the range is too great and the visible target too small for it to be worth opening fire.
- At **3** ranging shots are expected.
- At **4** all Y's eight ships open fire.
- At **5** ships A and H cannot hit, assuming their arc of fire is 45°.
- At **6** A, B, G and H cannot hit.
- At **7** only D and E can hit, but the range is close – under 200 yards.

- At **8** none of Y's ships can hit and X's leading ship is about to cut the line and rake D and E.
- Assuming the speed of X's leading ship is very slow, say 1.5 knots (as at Trafalgar), it would take about one minute to sail 50 yards.
- If all Fleet Y opened fire at 700 yards (position 4) and took about 4 minutes to reload and fire again, then A, B, G and H would only fire once, C and F twice and D and E three times before X reached position 8.
- Assuming full broadsides were fired, some 500-plus shots would have been fired.

At Trafalgar, Nelson's weather column had its T crossed by the Combined Fleet as the British admiral sought to break through his enemy's line. The *Victory* was hit frequently as the range closed, indeed her wheel was smashed and plenty of holes appeared in her sails but she, and the ships following, cut Villeneuve's line before going on to win a decisive victory. Why was she not hammered to the point of disablement during those last fifteen minutes as she crawled towards the enemy? In simple terms, Nelson knew his enemy, knew his own ships' strengths and knew the inherent weaknesses of the Combined Fleet's tactical position. He knew that, given the comparatively short effective range of the guns, enemy fire was only likely to hit from about 700 yards. Any fire from much beyond that range would miss such a small target as a ship bow on to the firer. He knew that Villeneuve's command was in places bunched and at others scattered, so the number of ships able to bring their guns to bear was limited. He knew that French and Spanish gunnery was not of a high standard in terms of accuracy or speed of firing. Nelson knew he had every chance of get-

ting through the real danger zone of a depth of 600 to 700 yards in 12 to 15 minutes (the wind being about the pace of a walking toddler) without crippling damage. He knew that only perhaps two or three ships would be able to fire at him twice, or at most three times, during those critical minutes, as their reloading time (about four minutes) was decidedly sluggish. Events proved him right.

*Breaking the line*
The diagram below shows two possible ways of breaking an enemy's line of battle, and there were several others. The object of this tactic was to bring the battle to the enemy, to attack decisively and fight at close range. It was used to facilitate raking, to concentrate against a particular part of the enemy's line, as a preliminary to doubling some defender's ships, and to bring on a mêlée battle. In such a battle, gunnery, seamanship, training and morale combined to destroy the enemy's ability and will to continue. It was primarily a tactic favoured by Nelson rather than Villeneuve or Gravina.

## Common Battle Tactics

### Breaking the Line (a)

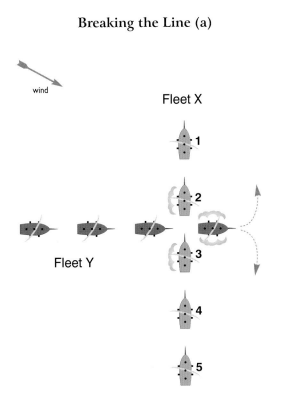

wind

Fleet X

1

2

3

4

5

Fleet Y

### Breaking the Line (b)

wind

Fleet Y    Fleet X

**Notes**
- Fleet **Y** has the weather gauge and more freedom of manoeuvre.
- Fleet **Y** breaks line in line ahead. The leading ship rakes ships **2** and **3** of Fleet **X** as it passes through the gap and can then turn north or south to continue the action.
- The following ships would probably break the line between **3** and **4**.

**Notes**
- Parallel line of battle. Y again has the weather gauge and individual ships can therefore turn and break X's line.
- Both lines are likely to break up, with the battle turning into a mêlée.

## Common Battle Tactics

### Doubling the Line

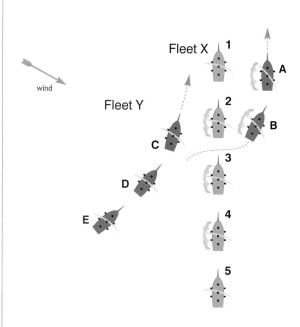

### The Mêlée (Trafalgar, 2.00 p.m.)

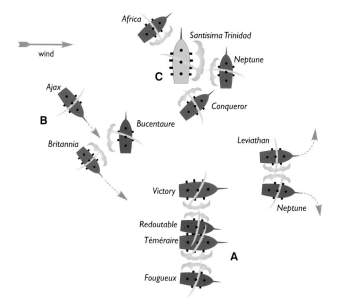

**Notes**
• Here Fleet Y is in the process of doubling the line on ships 1 and 2 of Fleet X, having broken through between 2 and 3. In this process 2 and 3 may well have been raked by **A** and **B**, reducing their speed and thus facilitating the double by **C** and **D**.
• A ship that has been doubled is in a desperate situation. In this case, though, Fleet **Y**'s ships must take care that shots from **C** and **D** do not hit **A** or **B**.
• Note this is only one of several ways in which this doubling could be carried out.

**Notes**
• Here is a segment of the battle at Trafalgar where the mêlée is at its height. Five French/Spanish ships struggle to survive against eight British ships within a very small area. These approximate positions clearly show what a tangle the situation has become.
**A** The two British ships and two French ships are locked into exchanging fire at almost touching distance, with the opportunity of boarding action.
**B** The *Ajax* cannot yet fire effectively, whereas *Britannia* is able to fire a devastating broadside as she passes the *Bucentaure*'s larboard quarter.
**C** The *Santisima Trinidad* looks (and is) doomed, being fired on at close range from three sides, including being raked by the *Conqueror*.

*Doubling the line*
The classic example of the devastating consequences of doubling an enemy's line was at the Battle of the Nile (see pp. 286–93), when the French fleet, stationary at anchor, was pounded almost to destruction by British ships on either side. The problems for the ship sandwiched between two enemies were usually insurmountable. Not only was the ship hopelessly outgunned, but in order to reply it had to man both larboard and starboard broadsides simultaneously. Even if this was possible, the weight of fire delivered was dramatically reduced. At the Nile only two of the French ships-of-the-line escaped.

*The mêlée*
The mêlée – which he called the 'pell mell' battle – was normally Nelson's objective in the approach to battle, as in a fight at close quarters British gunnery could be relied on to overcome the enemy. The mêlée was a free-for-all with individual ships manoeuvring to bring their guns to bear on the nearest target looming through the smoke. Sometimes its focus was a duel between two ships; sometimes two or even three ships would combine against one. Control by the admiral was tenuous if not non-existent – the battle was mostly in the hands of the captains of the ships and

the captains of the guns. In a mêlée such as that at Trafalgar, ships came onboard each other (crashed together, became entangled and locked together), fired their guns within touching distance of their target and attempted to board or repel boarders. The diagram illustrates such a situation at the height of the mêlée of Nelson's column at Trafalgar.

### BOARDING

Ships of both sides boarded, or attempted to board, at Trafalgar. It was something of a speciality for Captain Lucas of the 74 *Redoutable*, the ship from which the sharpshooter mortally wounded Nelson. This being so, the next few paragraphs are mainly concerned with boarding as carried out by the French – although the principles, methods and weaponry differed little, no matter what nationality the boarding party.

The first requisite for a captain determined to board was getting his ship physically attached to his opponent, in such a way that the boarding parties could scramble across from one ship to the other. This was by no means easy. The main problem was the 'tumble-home' of both ships – the inward inclination of the ship's upper sides, which caused the upper deck to be narrower than the middle or lower decks. With two ships alongside each other, there

## The *Royal Sovereign*'s Fire at Trafalgar

The 100-gun *Royal Sovereign*, the flagship of Vice-Admiral Collingwood at the battle, is an outstanding example of how a ship could endure the most awful pounding and still remain a fighting ship. Equally, she demonstrated how well-led and rigorously trained gun crews with high morale could deal out crippling punishment to their enemies for hours. Training had ensured that her gunners could fire at least three times in five minutes at the start of the action. During the four hours of fighting she was engaged with no less than six enemy ships, including a duel with the 112-gun *Santa Ana*, the huge, black hulk flying the flag of Vice-Admiral Alava.

Collingwood personally checked some of the guns to see they were well laid. The *Royal Sovereign* cut the line and swung alongside the *Santa Ana* to begin swapping broadsides.

Collingwood left the poop and stood among the guns on the quarterdeck, every now and then bending down to check the alignment of a gun. No fewer than five other ships had opened fire on the *Royal Sovereign*: the French 84-gun *Neptune*, 80-gun *Indomptable*, 74-gun *Fougueux*, the Spanish 74-gun *San Justo* and the 64-gun *San Leandro*. Ships carrying a total of 488 guns were, for a while, engaging one with only 100, a potential advantage of nearly 5:1. It was a miracle Collingwood survived. He was slightly wounded, but not before he had congratulated a black gun captain whom he had watched fire ten times at virtually touching distance into the *Santa Ana*. So amazed was Captain Tyler of the nearby 80-gun British *Tonnant* at the *Royal Sovereign*'s gunnery that he later admitted pausing during the first few moments to watch and admire.

was a gap of several feet between the two upper decks, even if the lower decks were grinding together. This gap, plus both ship's bulwarks, presented serious obstacles to a boarding party, with the danger of falling into the tumble-home to a nasty death by crushing and drowning a considerable deterrent to an attacker. One way of overcoming the problem was to lower the main- or foreyard so that it formed a bridge. Boarding from alongside was, however, avoided if possible unless the enemy's decks had been swept clear of defenders by guns, grapeshot, grenades and musketry, it being accepted that, other things being equal, one defender was usually able to see off three attackers without much trouble.

A far better bet was for the boarding ship to get her opponent's bowsprit skewered in the fore or main shrouds and rigging. This was a doubly good position from which to board, as not only was the enemy's bowsprit a bridge, but she would also be on the receiving end of a devastating rake from bow to stern before the boarders clambered across to finish the job. Nevertheless, it required some very skilful seamanship to get this manoeuvre exactly right. When boarding from the weather side (as in the diagram below), the attacking ship must be the faster. As soon as it was very close to the weather quarter, fire was opened with every gun that could be brought to bear. Under cover of the

## Boarding Positions

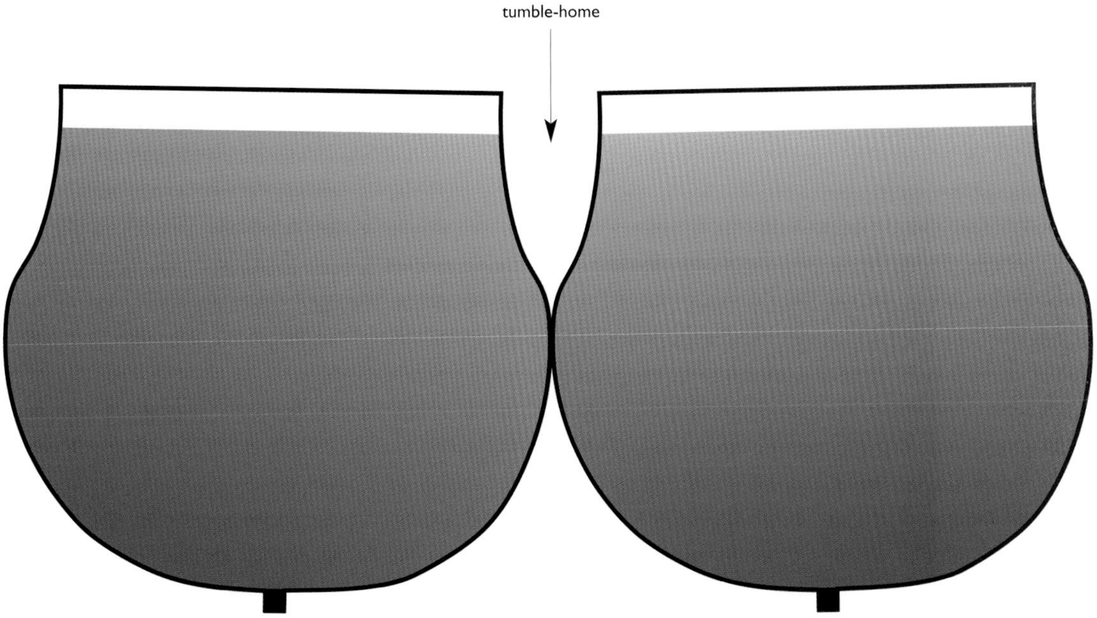

tumble-home

### Notes
• Note how boarding is made difficult by the tumble-home gap when two ships are alongside and touching at the lower decks.

• This problem was sometimes overcome by one ship lowering her foreyard or mainyard to form a bridge.

smoke, speed was increased to bring the enemy abreast, then to pull ahead and turn across her bow, fixing her opponent's bowsprit in the shrouds. This was instantly followed up with a shower of grappling hooks to reinforce success. However, if the enemy captain had his wits about him, he would see what was coming as his opponent began his turn. With some quick orders and a nimble crew, he might slow his ship by backing his sails, so instead of ramming his bowsprit into a mass of rigging, he just avoided the collision and came close astern of his enemy. He could then make his attacker pay a painful price for his audacity by raking him up the stern.

Boarding could, and did, take place from other positions. From the quarter was practicable, as was from the stern, though the latter was difficult as long as the enemy was able to make the opposite of the movements of the attacking ship. A prime example of British boarders clambering through the stern of a ship was Nelson's attack on the Spanish *San Josef* at St Vincent (see p. 166–7). In this case the *Captain* was laid aboard the starboard quarter of the *San Josef*, which hooked her spritsail yard in the Spaniard's mizzen shrouds. Nelson and his boarding party smashed their way in through the window of the quarter gallery.

In his after-action report (written in Reading, England, where he was a prisoner of war), Captain Lucas of the *Redoutable* wrote:

> Ever since the *Redoutable* was fitted out, no measures had been neglected on board to train the crew in every sort of drill; my ideas were always directed towards fighting by boarding. I so counted upon its success that everything had been prepared to undertake it with advantage: I had had canvas pouches to hold two grenades made for all captains of guns, the cross-belts of these pouches carried a tin tube containing a small match. In all our drills I made them throw a great number of paste-board grenades and I often landed the grenadiers in order to have them explode iron grenades; they had so acquired the habit of hurling them that on the day of the battle our topmen were throwing two at a time. I had 100 carbines fitted with long bayonets on board; the men to whom these were served out were so well accustomed to their use that they climbed halfway up the shrouds to open a musketry fire. All the men armed with swords were instructed in broadsword practice every day and pistols had become familiar arms to them. The grapnels were thrown aboard so skilfully that they succeeded in hooking a ship even though she were not exactly touching us.
>
> When the drum beat to quarters, each went to his station ready armed and with his weapon loaded; he placed them near his gun in nettings nailed between each beam.
>
> Finally the crew had themselves such confidence in this manner of fighting that they often urged me to board the first ship with which we should engage.

Like the British, the French nominated boarders on the station bill (quarter bill). Normally, up to about a quarter of the crew of a French 74 might expect to form boarding parties. The men were taken from the gun crews – two from each gun on the gundecks and one from the quarterdeck and forecastle guns. They were divided into two groups: grenade men and musketeers, whose pri-

mary function was to clear the enemy's upper decks with a sustained, close-range fusillade, and the actual boarding party, mostly armed with cutlasses, tomahawks and pistols. If a reserve was needed to meet an unexpected threat or reinforce the boarders, the grenade men were used.

As a rule, French junior and petty officers all had pistols as well as swords. Seamen were armed with a boarding axe or tomahawk and cutlass. Some sure-footed men were detailed off to try to get onto the wales of the enemy ship and shuffle along cutting the ropes holding open the gunport lids. Wales were an extra thickness of timber fixed along the sides of a ship between each row of gunports to prevent the port lids being damaged when going alongside for boarding. They also provided a precarious path along which a man with an axe or cutlass could inconvenience the enemy gunners. With these slammed shut and no quick way of raising them, gunnery would prove difficult if the ships drew apart. Another trick was for some carpenter's mates to go on board the enemy ship after the boarding party had cleared a space to smash holes in the quarterdeck and forecastle through which grenades could be dropped – not unlike Army house-clearing techniques today.

## Boarding weapons

Boarding weapons were virtually identical for all ships at Trafalgar. Brief notes on each type are given below.

### Musket and bayonet

The problem with most patterns of musket was that they were too long for boarders. The French sea-service musket, for example, was over 5ft 6in long; add a bayonet and you had a pike well in excess of 6ft in length. For close-quarter fighting on a narrow, heaving deck cluttered with guns, fallen spars, masts, shrouds and rigging, a musket was virtually useless after the first shot. A musketeer had no time to reload and could neither wield his weapon as a club nor effectively indulge in bayonet fighting in the confined and obstructed space on the enemy's deck. For these reasons musketeers (including the British Royal Marines) were far better employed firing their muskets from their own poop, quarterdeck, forecastle or tops in order to clear the way for the boarding party of seamen. Alternatively, musketeers could be extremely effective in repelling enemy boarders. Controlled musket fire could knock over attackers with comparative ease as they scrambled along yards or over the gunwales. Similarly, it was not too difficult to impale an enemy on your bayonet as he heaved himself over your ship's side, unable, for a few moments, to defend himself. On British ships the Royal Marines' detachment on the upper decks was primarily used either to prepare the way for the seamen to board or in a defensive action against enemy attackers. However, once a part of the enemy ship's deck had been taken, marines were a useful reinforcement.

The British flintlock musket was a version of the Army's 'Brown Bess', being slightly shorter in length. Two types were issued by the Ordnance Board. The 'bright sea-service' musket had a bright metal barrel and fittings and was used mostly for parades and guard duties – keeping it rust free must have been a pain. The other, the 'black sea-service', had a blacked barrel and was meant to be used for fighting, particularly when the flash of sunlight on metal might give away a position.

# French 18th-Century Naval Weapons

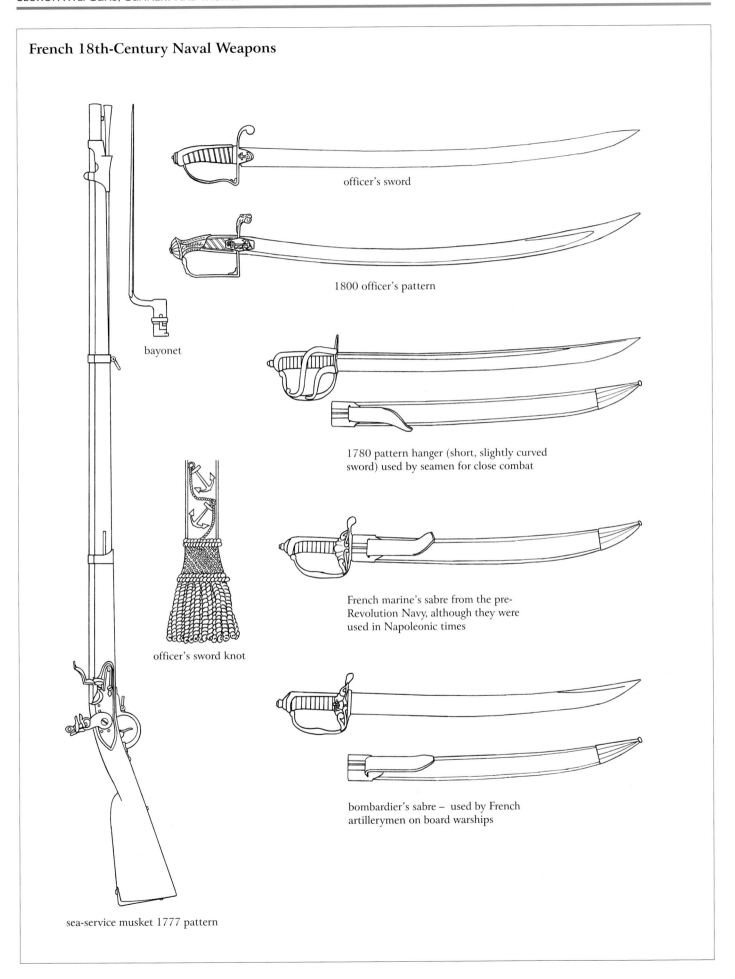

officer's sword

1800 officer's pattern

bayonet

1780 pattern hanger (short, slightly curved sword) used by seamen for close combat

officer's sword knot

French marine's sabre from the pre-Revolution Navy, although they were used in Napoleonic times

bombardier's sabre – used by French artillerymen on board warships

sea-service musket 1777 pattern

## British Naval Weapons

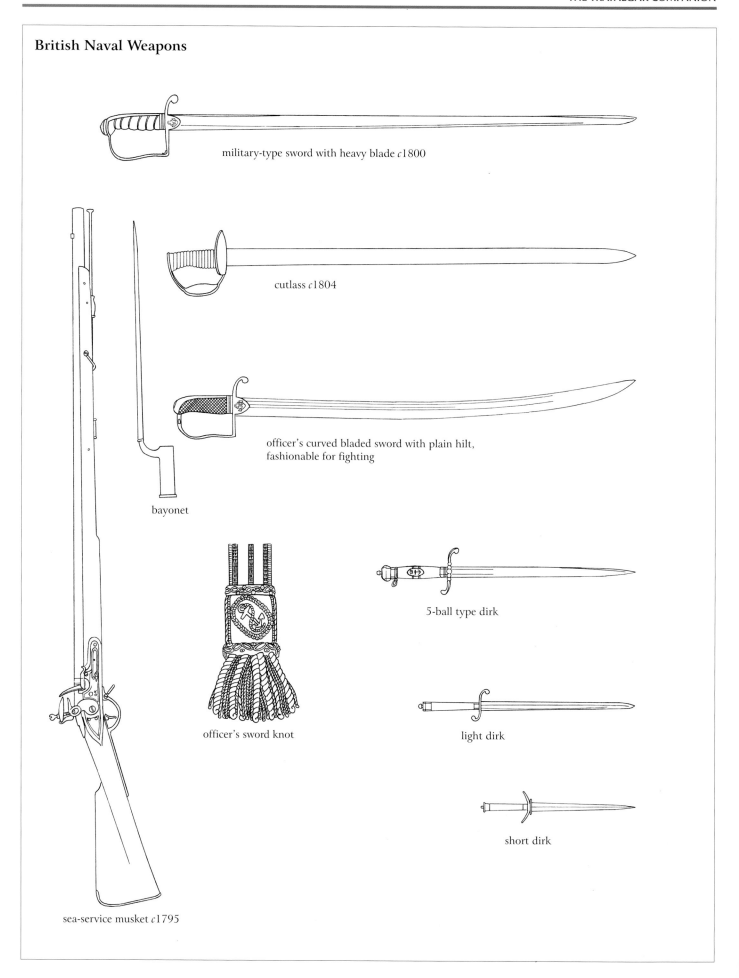

military-type sword with heavy blade *c*1800

cutlass *c*1804

officer's curved bladed sword with plain hilt,
fashionable for fighting

bayonet

5-ball type dirk

officer's sword knot

light dirk

short dirk

sea-service musket *c*1795

## Pike

The French used full-length pikes and 'half-pikes'. The former were unwieldy weapons with the point on an 11ft 6in ash pole, and only useful as a defensive weapon to repel would-be boarders. The half-pike had a 7ft 6in shaft. It was a little more handy in length, but once a thrust was parried and the assailant inside your guard, your chances of surviving uninjured were small. The British stored their pikes in racks around the masts where they could be grabbed quickly to push back enemy boarders. No sensible seaman would attempt the difficult business of getting onto an enemy ship armed with a pike.

## Pistol

These were mostly, but not entirely, carried by officers and petty officers, who often had two tucked into or hooked onto a waist belt. They were very effective at the sort of close-quarter fighting that ensued with boarding where pointing the pistol rather than aiming at a man perhaps only a few feet, or even inches away, was all that was needed. The only problem was the time it took to reload, so a pistol was never the only weapon carried. Special sea-service pistols with brass fittings and a steel belt-hook were issued. British pistols usually had heavy, brass butt plates so that they could quickly be turned into a useful club for hand-to-hand encounters.

## Blunderbuss

A number of these somewhat crude and antiquated weapons were carried on French ships for the use of boarders or, more often, in defence against them. The word is a corruption of the Dutch word *donder*, meaning 'thunder', and the German word *buchse*, meaning 'tube' – literally 'thunder-tube'. It was a muzzle-loading firearm with a bell-shaped muzzle with a large calibre so that it could be loaded with many balls – an early version of the shotgun. It was useful at close range, as the scattering of the balls made it hard to miss. Several opponents could be felled with one shot, so it was handy to have when clearing a passageway.

## Cutlass

The French version was a type of short sword with a flat, very wide, slightly curved blade just over 19 inches long. It looked more like a machete or meat chopper than a sword, or like the parang issued to British troops for use in the jungle. It had a dark wooden handgrip protected by a collar and guard of iron. The British had longer, straight blades (28–30 inches), which were rather somewhat cumbersome. The cutlass was the favoured (and intimidating) boarding weapon, with the French version being the better of the two. This was because of its shortness, which ensured it could be swung in restricted spaces, its heavy, curved blade making it an excellent cutting and hacking weapon. It could easily be thrust into a belt when both hands were needed

for scrambling about or hauling oneself over a bulwark, and it was not unknown for it to be held between the teeth. When issued to boarders, it was always without a scabbard – an unnecessary encumbrance.

## Hanger

The French hanger was a slightly different type of cutlass. Its blade was some three inches longer, its guard was cast in brass and it came in a sheath of blackened calf leather. It got its name from its iron belt-hook. Hangers were seldom seen in the Royal Navy but were sometimes used in the merchant service.

## Swords and dirks

The slim, straight swords carried by officers were almost as much status symbols as weapons. The British certainly disliked them for fighting, as the blades were too thin and weak for cutting, and only the point was any use. Many officers armed themselves with cutlasses for battle or had privately made swords with curved blades. The dirks (long daggers) that British and Spanish midshipmen wore were used in a mêlée but often as a secondary weapon.

## Tomahawk/boarding axe

A very useful weapon and tool carried by a proportion of boarders of all nationalities, the boarding axe consisted of a head with a spike on the poll that curved backwards at the point. The blade had a curved cutting edge, and the shaft had a belt-hook just below the head. This could be a deadly weapon in a hand-to-hand brawl but was more often used to cut away debris such as fallen spars and sever grappling irons or cables.

## Hand grenades

Grenades were used by all navies for lobbing or dropping onto enemy decks to clear the way for boarders. The French were particularly keen on them and in battle invariably armed their topmen with a good supply carried in a pouch or canvas haversack holding three or four grenades. The fuse was lit by a slow match contained in a tin match tube worn on the outside of the hat and secured by a stopper and chain. The grenade was a hollow iron ball filled with powder. The French version weighed over 3 lbs with a fuse-burning time of six seconds. Having lit the fuse, the French grenadier was supposed to whirl his arm round three times before releasing – although it is unlikely he went through this performance in the tops. The whirling round was to ensure the fuse was well alight and to delay the throwing for two or three seconds so that it was close to exploding when it landed. To ensure that they would not be thrown back before exploding, most grenades had paper soaked in water in which saltpetre had been dissolved, pasted to them with a combustible mixture. A strong arm could hurl a grenade 25 to 35 yards.

# THE BATTLE OF THE NILE, 1 AUGUST 1798

In March 1798 Rear-Admiral Nelson hoisted his flag at Spithead on the 74-gun *Vanguard*, commanded by the handsome and gallant Captain Edward Berry, who had served under Nelson on the *Agamemnon* (the ship Berry would command at Trafalgar) and as his first lieutenant on the *Captain* at Cape St Vincent. Nelson was to join Jervis' fleet off Cadiz. For two years the Mediterranean had been a French lake. But by April 1798 persistent rumours of France's build up and fitting out of a large flotilla of transports at Toulon and bases elsewhere could be ignored no longer. An attack of considerable magnitude was obviously being planned. Its objective, however, remained a mystery, despite the activities of numerous spies. The Royal Navy must re-enter the Mediterranean. Nelson was despatched from Gibraltar on 9 May with a small squadron to position himself off Toulon.

Nelson's squadron consisted of the 74s *Vanguard*, *Orion* (under Captain Saumarez), *Alexander* (Captain Ball), the 36s *Caroline*, *Emerald* and *Flora*, the 32-gun *Terpsichore* and the 20-gun *Bonne Citoyenne*. It was the start of twelve exasperating weeks criss-crossing 1,500 miles of the Mediterranean, chasing an evasive enemy. The first major setback came as he entered the Gulf of Lyon on 20 May. A violent gale scattered the squadron, with the *Vanguard* suffering the worst. All sails were furled but at 2.00 a.m. on 23 May the maintopmast disappeared over the side 'with the topsail yard full of men'. Two men died – one lost overboard, the other killed when he struck the booms. Next, the mizzen-topmast went over the side, then the foremast collapsed. The storm did not abate. So much water was shipped that the lower deck had to be scuttled (have holes cut in it) to allow the water to drain into the bottom part of the ship. With the ship dismasted the wind was driving the *Vanguard* remorselessly onto a lee shore – the rocky coast of eastern Sardinia. Only the brilliant efforts of Captain Ball in the *Alexander*, who managed to get the flagship under tow, saved Nelson from being hurled on the rocks. They came so close to disaster that he 'could easily distinguish the surf breaking on the rocky shore' before they eventually found shelter to windward of the little island of San Pietro. It was a close call. At one stage Nelson told Ball to cut the *Vanguard* loose, but with great courage and determination the latter refused. Forever afterwards Nelson rightly regarded himself in Ball's debt. Writing of the incident to his wife, Fanny, on 24 May, he imagined the consequences if Ball had obeyed him: 'Figure to yourself this proud conceited man [himself; it was a well-established failing], when the sun rose on Sunday morning, his fleet dispersed and himself in such peril that the meanest frigate out of France would have been a very unwelcome guest.'

Within two days *Vanguard* had been repaired – itself a notable achievement – and set sail north-west. Meanwhile Jervis had sent a much larger force under Captain Troubridge in the *Culloden* to rendezvous with Nelson off Toulon. On 7 June the combined squadrons made up one of the finest fleets of 74s Britain ever assembled. In addition to the *Vanguard*, *Orion*, *Alexander* and *Culloden*, there were the *Bellerophon* (Darby), *Minotaur* (Louis), *Defence* (Peyton), *Zealous* (Hood), *Audacious* (Gould), *Goliath* (Foley), *Theseus* (Miller), *Majestic* (Westcott), *Swiftsure* (Hallowell), the 50-gun *Leander* (Thompson) and the 18-gun brig-sloop *Mutine* (Hardy): thirteen ships-of-the-line, a 50 and a brig-sloop.

But Toulon was empty. Some three weeks earlier, the French fleet had sailed eastwards to rendezvous with some 300 transports from Genoa and Corsica. It was the opening part of the French plan to occupy Egypt, which they saw as the link joining Africa, Europe and Asia, milk its wealth and, they hoped, use it as a springboard to India and a blow to Britain's Asian trade. Commander-in-chief of the expedition was the twenty-eight-year-old General Napoleon Bonaparte, who had recently made his name conquering northern Italy. Bonaparte headed south to pick up two divisions commanded by General Desaix off Civitavecchia, which did not arrive. It was with considerable relief that he found this large contingent off neutral Malta.

Bonaparte stopped off there to water the fleet. Malta's ruler, the Grand Master of the Knights of St John, agreed to let them – but only two ships at a time. A contemptuous Bonaparte proceeded to capture the island and its tiny neighbour, Gozo. Despite their formidable defences (three forts, 900 cannons and several miles of battlements), the Knights, once the scourge of Islam, had long since grown sleek and soft, and they had no stomach for anything but a perfunctory defence. The days following the island's surrender on 12 June saw a systematic plundering of the treasury and stripping of valuables, the accumulated wealth of 500 years, from all of Malta's rich churches and palaces. Much of the haul was stuffed into the hold of *L'Orient*. Mixed with mundane casks of wine, water and shingle ballast were gold and silver plate, artworks, bejewelled cups, crucifixes, statues and ornate weapons, models of ships in silver and rich silk altar clothes from China. It was a treasure trove that Bonaparte told Paris was worth a million francs – about a seventh of its true value. The fleet was also carrying another three million francs from French-occupied Switzerland.

Nelson followed the French down the west coast of Italy, calling for information at Naples on 15 June at the same time his

## Nelson's 'Band of Brothers'

Nelson knew his Shakespeare, in particular the words he put into the mouth of King Henry V before the battle of Agincourt: 'We few, we happy few, we band of brothers.' After the Nile, Nelson wrote of his captains, 'I had the happiness to command a Band of Brothers.' He rightly felt that these men were among the elite of the senior officers in the Navy. Nelson trusted them, imbued them with his tactical ideas and was confident they would do what was necessary with the minimum of signalling. At the Nile they fully vindicated that trust. They in turn had complete faith in Nelson as a commander, they were delighted to be serving under him and they gave him their loyalty. Many, but not all, had served with him before. Several were with him again at Trafalgar. Later 'the band of brothers' came to mean any captain who was close to Nelson; however, the original band, in order of seniority, were:

### Sir James Saumarez (Orion)
Two years older than Nelson, from a Channel Islands naval family, Saumarez was a formal, somewhat severe commander who was given respect rather than devotion by his men. Not a close friend of Nelson, although he had commanded the Orion at Cape St Vincent. Not present at Trafalgar.

### Thomas Troubridge (Culloden)
Son of a London baker, Troubridge had first gone to sea as a cabin boy on a merchantman. He became a close friend of Nelson, having fought at Cape St Vincent and as his second-in-command in the abortive attack on Tenerife. Nelson once called him 'the very best sea officer in His Majesty's Service'. Troubridge was not at Trafalgar and by then had fallen out with Nelson, as he openly criticized the latter's infidelity with Emma Hamilton.

### Henry D'Esterre Darby (Bellerophon)
An Irishman, who before the Nile was something of an unknown quantity. At that battle, at which he was wounded, he distinguished himself by single-handedly taking on L'Orient and slugging it out for an hour before being driven off. Not at Trafalgar.

### Thomas Louis (Minotaur)
Not well known to Nelson. He had served in the American War of Independence and then for some time as an officer in charge of the Impress Service in Ireland. Fought well at the Nile but was not present at Trafalgar.

### John Peyton (Defence)
Served in the American War of Independence and on frigates in the Mediterranean. Although ill at the Nile, he continued to command. Not at Trafalgar.

### Alexander John Ball (Alexander)
Son of a Gloucestershire landowner, Ball was an intelligent and charming man. Nelson was forever grateful to him for saving the Vanguard off Sardinia by his great courage and superb seamanship. Not at Trafalgar. In later years he became Governor of Malta.

### Samuel Hood (Zealous)
He came from a well-known naval family, two of his cousins being admirals, and studied a wide variety of subjects related to his profession, including navigation, astronomy, geography and shipbuilding as well as languages. Not at Trafalgar.

### Davidge Gould (Audacious)
Perhaps the least distinguished of the 'brothers', although he handled his ship well enough at the battle. Not at Trafalgar.

### Thomas Foley (Goliath)
A Welshman who had fought at Cape St Vincent. He led the attack at the Nile and it was his decision to anchor on the inside of the enemy line. It was a battle-winning move, followed by others and exploited by Nelson. Not at Trafalgar.

### George Blagden Westcott (Majestic)
Another baker's son, this time from Devon. He was in his thirties before promotion to lieutenant and forty-five when he made post captain. At fifty-three he was the oldest captain at the Nile and the only one to lose his life.

### Benjamin Hallowell (Swiftsure)
Born American, he had served with Nelson on Corsica and at Cape St Vincent. A good friend of Nelson and had the coffin made for Nelson from the mast of L'Orient (see box p. 293). Not at Trafalgar.

### Ralph Willet Miller (Theseus)
Another American-born officer, but one who joined the Royal Navy to fight the rebellious American colonists. In action with Nelson in Corsica, served as his flag captain at Cape St Vincent on the Captain. He was also with Nelson on the Theseus, taking part in the disastrous attack on Tenerife. Nelson called him 'the only truly virtuous man I ever knew'. Killed in 1799 in action off Acre.

### Thomas Boulden Thompson (Leander)
He had been with Nelson leading a landing party in the assault on Santa Cruz. He knew Tenerife well and was involved in planning the attack. Not at Trafalgar.

### Thomas Masterman Hardy (brig-sloop Mutine)
Of all the band of brothers, Hardy is the most famous for his long association with Nelson and the fact he was with him at his death at Trafalgar. Their friendship had started on the frigate Minerve when Hardy was a young lieutenant. Hardy served with Nelson in all his great fleet actions, Cape St Vincent, Nile, Copenhagen and finally Trafalgar.

### Edward Berry (Vanguard)
Another old friend of Nelson's who had served as his first lieutenant on his beloved Agamemnon, the ship Berry would command at Trafalgar. He was also first lieutenant on the Captain at Cape St Vincent.

---

opponents were enriching themselves in Malta. Sailing at almost twice the speed of his prey, Nelson took the short cut through the Straits of Messina and by 22 June he had caught them up.

As darkness fell on the night of 22 June 1798, the French fleet of 13 ships-of-the-line, seven 40-gun frigates, eight corvettes and nearly 300 transports, along with two Venetian 64s and eight smaller Venetian frigates (Venice belonged to France at this time),

was about 40 miles south-east of the southern tip of Sicily (Map 18). It was a floating forest of ghost ships that slid silently through the banks of fog that covered that part of the Ionian Sea. Stern and masthead lanterns flickered and bobbed, now visible, now not. Hundreds of pairs of eyes peered anxiously into the grey darkness as officers on watch tried to keep the ships ahead and abeam in sight. Inevitably there was muddle and confusion in the order of sailing.

Some ships closed up, others slipped back as they wallowed through the water and swirling mist. This huge gaggle was spread over several square miles. Ahead and to the flanks were the frigates.

These ships carried some 55,000 men. Of these, 36,500 were soldiers and over 1,000 civilians (astronomers, architects, engineers, artists and mathematicians), with the balance being seamen; there were also about 300 women. Crammed in with the humans were 1,200 horses and an indeterminate number of other livestock. Also onboard were 60 field and 40 siege guns, 45,000 tons of gunpowder, 12,000 tons of lead, rations for 100 days and fresh water for 40 days. The warships were tasked with escorting this unwieldy mass of transports to Egypt.

Every French ship was short of competent sailors but full of miserable, seasick soldiers. Most men had not wanted to join the expedition and desertion had been rampant before departure, with some units losing a quarter of their strength. Even General Bonaparte had not relished the prospect of weeks at sea. His message to Vice-Admiral Brueys, the fleet commander, reflected his misgivings: in it he demanded good food and a comfortable bed, 'for someone who will be ill throughout the whole journey'. Bonaparte's embarkation promise to reward his soldiers (sailors were not mentioned) with enough loot to buy six acres of land had failed to raise spirits. In any case, it was unfulfilled.

Vice-Admiral François Brueys d'Aigallers was a forty-five-year-old aristocrat who had somehow survived 'The Terror' to be appointed commander of a squadron based in Corfu, which had successfully supported Bonaparte's Italian campaign. This success had resulted in Brueys being given command of the naval element of Bonaparte's Egyptian expedition. It was an appointment fraught with problems. The voyage had been something of a nightmare with such a huge, slow-moving fleet of transports to protect. Most ships were ill prepared, all were grossly overloaded, many were desperately short of experienced seamen and Bonaparte had installed himself with his staff on the flagship, so there was no avoiding the general's daily interference in matters nautical.

The French flagship *L'Orient* was sailing under yet another new name. She had begun life as the *Dauphin Royal*, but following the Revolution this became the *Sans Culottes* ('without breeches' – the nickname for working-class revolutionaries, as aristocrats wore breeches, commoners trousers). Finally, she had been renamed *L'Orient* – 'the East', where she was heading. She was a towering three-decker carrying 124 guns, and the weight of fire from one of her broadsides was almost 1,400 pounds (the *Victory*'s equivalent was 1,148). The quarterdeck and forecastle carried eighteen 8-pounders and six 36-pounder sea howitzers (the French forerunner of the carronade). The upper gundeck had thirty-four 12-pounders, the middle thirty-four 24-pounders and the lower thirty-two 36-pounders – a massive armoury. She was

grossly overloaded, even for her size – 200ft long, 50ft at the beam and displacing 3,500 tons. She carried a crew of 1,100 but this was doubled by hundreds of troops and civilians, together with naval and military staff whose equipment and bulging baggage cluttered the decks, in addition to the enormous haul of treasure plundered from Malta.

As the night of 23 June merged into the morning of the 24th, officers on the quarterdeck of the flagship heard the thump of gunfire as distant ships signalled each other to keep direction through the patches of fog. Sound travels far and fast over water at night and the guns could have been 20 or more miles away. Any alarmist thoughts within the French flotilla were dismissed as the sounds slowly died away with approaching daylight. What nobody could know was that a moment of destiny had passed. In those few hours before dawn the whole bloodstained story of Europe for the next seventeen years was decided. The French fleet, creeping slowly through the darkness at the pace of the slowest transport, had been overtaken by the British. They missed each other by a few miles. Had they clashed, Nelson would surely have wreaked havoc on his vulnerable quarry, Egypt would never have been invaded, Bonaparte perhaps killed or captured – the possibilities are endless. As it was, Nelson's faster ships pulled away, taking him to Alexandria two days ahead of the French. On 28 June he gazed with understandable frustration at an empty harbour. Desperately disappointed, he turned north to renew his search. It would be another month before he returned for a victory that in its scale would eclipse even that of Trafalgar.

That the British and French should both be making for Alexandria but the pursuer should arrive before the pursued was another extraordinary quirk of fate. It enabled Bonaparte to disembark, bringing ashore much of the Malta millions, and begin his successful campaign of conquest against the Mamelukes of Egypt, a military order that had survived since the Crusades. Had Nelson waited just twenty-four hours, he would have had the battle he sought. His plan to divide the fleet into three squadrons, two to attack the French warships, the other to tackle the helpless transports, would have been put into effect. The slaughter and the loot would probably have been unsurpassed.

It was not to be. Nelson spent a month chasing rumours and shadows as far afield as Syracuse in Sicily before finally returning to Alexandria. At dusk on 31 July the fleet came in sight of the Pharos and Pompey's Tower. Early next morning the *Alexander* and *Swiftsure* were detached to look into Alexandria's roadstead. There they spied a mass of masts with French flags flapping in the breeze. Initial elation soon turned to dismay. They were transports – not a ship-of-the-line amongst them. Captain Saumarez of the *Orion* later recalled that he had never felt more hopeless than when he sat down to eat that day: 'Judge what a change took place when,

### Midshipman the Hon. George Elliot Sights the Enemy

Midshipman Elliot always disputed that the *Zealous*, who first signalled the enemy had been found, did in fact spot them first. He claimed this honour for himself. His account reads:

I, as signal-midshipman, was sweeping round the horizon ahead with my glass from the royal-yard when I discovered the French fleet at anchor in Aboukir Bay. The *Zealous* was so close to us that, had I hailed the deck, they must have heard me. I therefore slid down by the backstay and reported what I had seen. We instantly made the signal, but the under-toggle of the upper flag at the main came off, breaking the stop, and the lower flag came down. The compass-signal, however, was clear at the peak; but before we could recover our flag, *Zealous* made the signal for the enemy's fleet; whether from seeing our compass-signal or not I never heard. But we thus lost the little credit of first signalling the enemy which, as signal-midshipman, rather affected me.

It was a small incident that rankled and was remembered.

## The Battle of the Nile, 1–2 August 1798: The Campaign                          Map 18

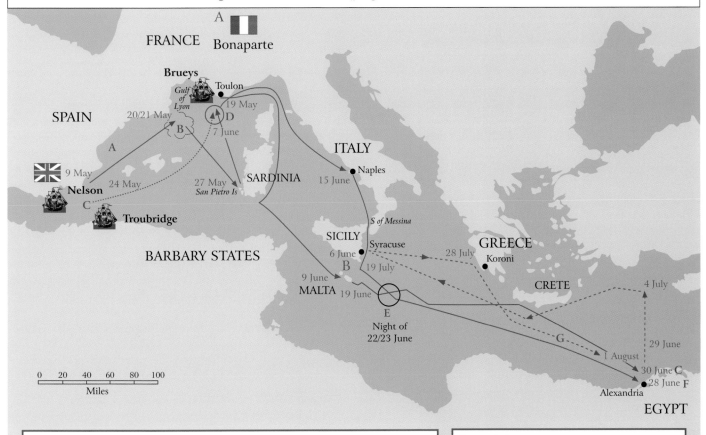

**British Key/Notes**

→ Nelson's first route (2 May–28 June)

····► Troubridge's route reinforcing Nelson

- -► Nelson's second route searching for French fleet (29 June–1 August)

A   Nelson sent (in *Vanguard*) with three 74s and five frigates/sloops to locate French fleet.

B   *Vanguard* badly damaged in violent storm and towed to small island of San Pietro to refit before sailing for Toulon again.

C   Troubridge with ten 74s, one 50 and one frigate sent to reinforce Nelson off Toulon.

D   Nelson and Troubridge join forces and sail in search of French.

E   British and French fleets almost clash during night of 22/23 June.

F   Nelson arrives at Alexandria two days before the French and leaves again.

G   After over a month of fruitless searching, Nelson arrives back at Alexandria to find French fleet in Aboukir Bay.

**French Notes**

→ Bonaparte/Brueys' route

A   Bonaparte assembles an invasion force of 36,500 troops plus 13 ships-of-the-line, 31 frigates and sloops and 280 transports to invade Egypt. The huge fleet leaves Toulon 19 May 1798.

B   Bonaparte captures Malta after token resistance (9–17 June) and sails for Alexandria.

C   French army lands at Alexandria on 30 June – two days after Nelson's departure. By the time the British fleet returned on 1 August Bonaparte had taken Alexandria, won the Battle of the Pyramids and occupied Cairo.

as the cloth was being removed, the Officer of the Watch came running in saying, "Sir, it is now just made that the enemy is in Aboukir Bay and moored in line of battle."'

After the landings Brueys, who knew the coast lacked sheltered anchorages, had wanted to return to Corfu. Napoleon would have none of it; he did not want his fleet hundreds of miles away and out of contact. Grudgingly, Brueys lined his fleet up at anchor in the western part of the 16-mile wide-open Aboukir Bay 15 miles east of Alexandria. The French fleet's position was seriously flawed. Brueys had wanted to shelter his ships by having the van as close to the shoals around Aboukir (Nelson's) Island as possible, and all of them close to the shallower water marked on Map 19 at the four-fathom line. Because he considered the northern part of the line could not

be outflanked, he put his weaker ships (74s) in the van. The centre had three of the four more powerful ships (*Franklin*, *L'Orient* and *Tonnant*) while the 80-gun *Guillaume Tell* (William Tell) bolstered the rear (southern end). However, while a 74 needed 30ft of water under her hull, the bigger ships needed more, so the fleet could not be as close to the four-fathom line as Brueys would have liked. All the ships were anchored at the bow. In order to hold a ship in position, the anchor cable had to be as near horizontal as possible, otherwise it would easily lose its grip on the bottom, particularly in sand or mud. This in turn meant long cables of four or five times the depth of the water. Anchored with a single anchor, the ships would swing with the wind (there is no tide in the Mediterranean), so allowance had to be made to ensure the ship would not swing into the shallower water. Moreover, there had to be large gaps – of about 160 yards at the Nile – between the ships so the lengthy cables did not get entangled as the ships moved. Thus the line of battle was at least a mile and a half long.

The wind caused another problem. On that day (1 August 1798) it was blowing from the north-west, straight down the line of the fleet, making it impossible for ships at the rear to move quickly to support the centre or van if they were attacked from that direction. To reinforce the van would entail weighing anchor, then moving out into the bay until on the larboard tack before turning onto the starboard tack and sailing back towards the action – a lengthy process that in the event no French ship attempted. Brueys was under the misguided belief that an attack from the north was not practical due to the proximity of the shoals. He also hoped he would have to fight only with his starboard broadsides, confident that the huge weight of fire he could bring to bear on an approaching enemy would prevent them breaking or outflanking his line. A difficulty he could not have foreseen was that the British fleet appeared when he had many men ashore fetching fresh water – four miles away. Nelson attacked at once, in the late afternoon, so Brueys was unable to get his men back during the night and this depleted the already under-strength gun crews.

Even the battery on Nelson's Island, intended to support the van of the fleet, was, in the event, impotent (although it did open fire, initially with the two mortars) due to the excessive range (over a mile), the weight of the guns (mere 6-pounders) and the approaching darkness. Guns in the fort and Aboukir Castle, despite some accounts, could never have been part of the equation.

## THE BATTLE

Nelson's captains were familiar with (and enthusiastic about) his intention of fighting at close quarters and concentrating on a particular part of the enemy line. As the fleet advanced, the only general signals he needed to launch his attack were No. 53, 'Prepare for battle', and No. 54, 'Prepare for battle and for anchoring with springs, sheet cable to be taken in at stern port'. Nelson had seen the French were themselves anchored, so he intended his ships to select their enemy, choose the most advantageous position, anchor by the stern and commence firing. In the Royal Navy this meant making fast a stream-cable to the mizzenmast and passing it out of one of the gunroom ports, carrying it along the side and bending to an anchor at the bow. Once the anchor was let go, it was possible, by slackening one cable and hauling on the other, to swing the broadsides in any direction.

When hoisting this signal Nelson had no intention of doubling the French line. He intended to anchor close to leeward of the enemy, for a broadside-to-broadside slogging match between stationary ships at close range. His subsequent signals were as follows:

### Nos. 45 and 46 together – 'Engage the enemy's centre', 'Engage the enemy's van'
This confirmed to his captains which part of the line was to be attacked. Nelson intended to position all his 13 ships for a decisive gunnery duel against seven or eight of the French.

### No. 31 – 'Form line of battle astern or ahead of the admiral as most convenient'
There was no set order to the approach – captains were to make their best speed and course and not to worry if they were ahead or astern of the flagship.

### No. 66 – 'Make all sail, the leading ship first'
Attack!

### No. 5, with a red pennant – 'Engage the enemy more closely'
This was Nelson's last signal as the action joined. It remained flying throughout the battle, as it did at Trafalgar.

Because there were no reliable charts of Aboukir Bay, the British approach was tempered by a degree of caution, with the leadsmen standing in the chains hurling their leads and singing out the decreasing depths to anxious captains and masters. The plan at this stage was still to attack the leeward side of the enemy, so it was a safe assumption that there was a sufficient depth of water. Nevertheless, the Culloden, to the infinite chagrin of Captain Troubridge, came too close to a reef when wearing to turn into the bay and went aground. Modern maps still show this as 'Culloden Reef'.

At about 6.00 p.m. Captain Foley in Goliath was leading the attack as the British ships approached the northern end of the French line, which because of the angle could not bring much effective fire to bear. As the ship came within gunshot of the French 74 Guerrier, Foley made a far-reaching decision. He decided to take the Goliath round onto the shore side of the enemy – to double his line. Made on the initiative of a single captain, this was an act of outstanding seamanship that led to an outstanding victory. Midshipman the Honourable George Elliot has provided the details:

> When we were nearly within gunshot, standing as A.D.C. close to Captain Foley, I heard him say to the Master that he wished to get inside the leading ship of the enemy's line (the Guerrier). I immediately looked for the buoy on her anchor, and saw it apparently at the usual distance of a cable's length – i.e., 200 yards – which I reported. They both looked at it, and agreed there was room to pass between the ship and her anchor [over the cable] (the danger was the ship being close up to the shoal), and it was decided to do it. The Master then had orders to go forward and drop the anchor the moment it was a ship's breadth inside the French ship, so that we should not actually swing on board her. All this was exactly executed.
>
> I also heard Foley say he would not be surprised to find the Frenchman unprepared for action on the inner side; and as we passed her bow I saw he was right. Her lower-deck guns were not run out, and there was lumber, such as bags and boxes, on the upper-deck ports, which I reported with no small pleasure. We fired the first broadside into the bow. Not a shot could miss at that distance. The Zealous did the same, and in less than a quarter of an hour this ship was a perfect wreck, without a mast or broadside gun to fire. By this time, having no after-bitts to check the cable by (which came in at the stern port), it kept slowly surging – i.e., slipping – and at last the remaining stoppers broke (our sails had flown loose by the gear being shot away – we had not time to fold them), and it ran to the clinch, and placing us a little past the second ship of the French line, so as to engage her and the third ship. We were just in this position when the leading ships of the body of our fleet came in.

## The Battle of the Nile, 1–2 August 1798: Tactical Features                 Map 19

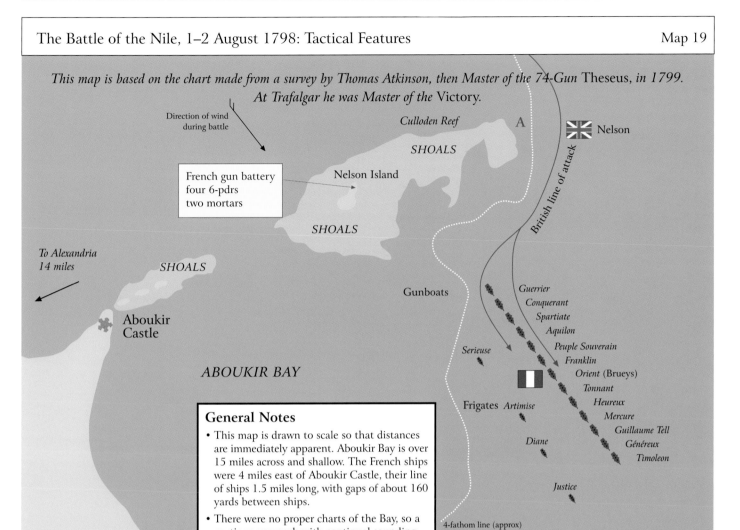

*This map is based on the chart made from a survey by Thomas Atkinson, then Master of the 74-Gun* Theseus, *in 1799. At Trafalgar he was Master of the* Victory.

Direction of wind during battle

Culloden Reef

A

Nelson

SHOALS

French gun battery four 6-pdrs two mortars

Nelson Island

SHOALS

British line of attack

SHOALS

To Alexandria 14 miles

Aboukir Castle

Gunboats

Guerrier
Conquerant
Spartiate
Aquilon
Peuple Souverain
Franklin
Orient (Brueys)
Tonnant
Heureux
Mercure
Guillaume Tell
Généreux
Timoleon

*ABOUKIR BAY*

Serieuse

Frigates  Artimise

Diane

Justice

**General Notes**

- This map is drawn to scale so that distances are immediately apparent. Aboukir Bay is over 15 miles across and shallow. The French ships were 4 miles east of Aboukir Castle, their line of ships 1.5 miles long, with gaps of about 160 yards between ships.

- There were no proper charts of the Bay, so a cautious approach with continual sounding with the lead was essential. No ships-of-the-line could get closer inshore than the 4-fathom line.

4-fathom line (approx)

To Rosetta, 12 miles across bay, at mouth of the Nile

*LAKE ETKO (very shallow)*  ★ Fort

0        1        2        3
Miles

**British Notes**

- The British attack achieved the huge advantage of concentration and doubling the French van. The initiative of Capt. Foley in *Goliath* in finding and making use of the gap between the *Guerrier* and the 4-fathom line was decisive.

A The *Culloden* cut the corner round the reef that now bears its name, and went aground here, thus missing the battle.

- Nelson deliberately doubled (surrounded) the French line and then anchored his ships so that he outnumbered and outgunned the enemy he was attacking. His ships had the advantage of the weather gauge, and could move down either side of the French line at will.

**French Notes**

- Brueys was confident he had his fleet in a strong defensive position, well able to see off an attack from the east. But he had not got his ships near enough to the 4-fathom line, particularly in the NW towards Nelson Island. Also, with his ships anchored and joined by cables, his arc of fire was restricted to the east and from his starboard broadsides only.

- With the ships being so far apart and the wind direction unfavourable, if the van or centre was attacked, the rear ships could not assist and were left out of the battle.

- Many ships' boats were ashore collecting water when the British fleet appeared – with over 4 miles to sail/row to return, many French ships started the battle with significant numbers of absentees.

- The gun battery on Nelson Island was virtually useless, as it was dark for most of the battle and the range around 2 miles.

- Note the NW wind blowing straight down the line of French ships, rendering it impossible for the rear division to move up to join the battle.

## The Battle of the Nile: the British Double the French Van and Centre

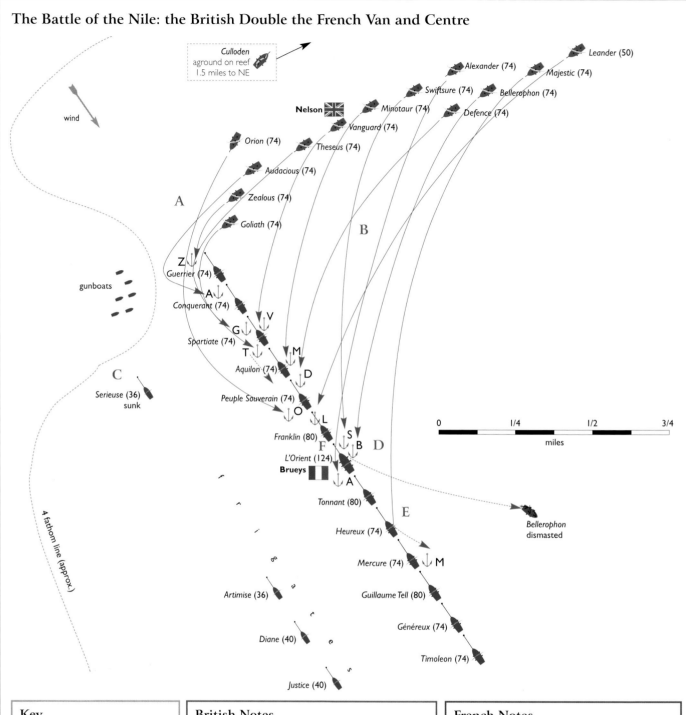

### Key

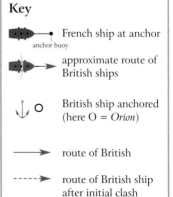

French ship at anchor
anchor buoy

approximate route of British ships

British ship anchored (here O = Orion)

route of British

route of British ship after initial clash

### British Notes

**A** The *Goliath*, *Zealous*, *Audacious*, *Orion* and *Theseus* navigate the narrow gap between the *Guerrier* and the shallow water to double the French van. All anchor and open fire.
**B** Nelson in *Vanguard* leads remaining ships to attack the French from the seaward side.
**C** The frigate *Serieuse* fires on *Orion* and is sunk.
**D** *Bellerophon* loses an unequal duel with *L'Orient*, is dismasted and drifts away.
**E** *Majestic*'s bowsprit gets entangled with the rigging of *Heureux*. After suffering severely, she breaks free to engage the *Mercure*.
**F** *Swiftsure* and *Alexander* replace Bellerophon and double the French flagships.

### French Notes

• Seven ships from the centre and van found themselves attacked by 12 British ships. Not only were they outnumbered and outgunned, but they also had to man both broadsides, frequently simultaneously with numerically weak crews. The doubling of their line was totally unexpected and demoralizing.
• The ships in the rear were not engaged but made no attempt to support the van and centre due to the difficulty of having to weigh anchor and then beat into the wind in darkness.
• As the ships were anchored in line ahead with large gaps between them, once engaged no ship could fire in support of those ahead or astern.

## The *Vanguard*

The *Vanguard* was eleven years old when she became Nelson's flagship in the spring of 1798. Although she had not played any part in the major naval battles of the previous decade, she had had considerable service in the Channel and West Indies. She was a typical two-deck 74 of the time, 168 feet long with a complement of 640 – she was under strength at the Nile. Her armament consisted of twenty-eight 32-pounders on the lower deck, twenty-eight 18-pounders on the upper deck, fourteen 9-pounders on the quarterdeck and four 9-pounders on the forecastle.

Nelson, in the *Vanguard*, realized that Foley, in taking the leading ship onto the shore side, had opened up a momentous opportunity to double the line. He took it. The *Zealous*, second in line, followed the *Goliath*'s lead round to the shore side of the French line while the *Vanguard* hove to, allowing the *Orion*, *Audacious* and *Theseus* to overtake her, then came up on the outside, supported by the *Minotaur* and *Defence*. Nelson had achieved the decisive concentration he wanted – initially eight ships against five. *Zealous* anchored on the weather bow of the *Guerrier* where the *Goliath* had been. Her first lieutenant, William Webley, summarized the fight in these words, 'Captain Hood ... placed the *Zealous* so well that in seven minutes her [the *Guerrier*'s] fore mast was shot away, and in twenty she was totally dismasted, and about eight o'clock I took possession of her without the *Zealous* having lost one man.' The fact that the *Guerrier* continued to fight for at least two hours after so much initial slaughter speaks volumes for the courage of her crew. Captain Hood of the *Zealous* later wrote, 'I could not get *Le Guerrier*'s commander to strike though I hailed him twenty times, and seeing he was totally cut up and only firing a stern gun ...'.

As the *Orion* came down behind the line, the French frigate *Serieuse* had foolhardily opened fire on the 74. The convention was that frigates were left alone if they did not provoke their more powerful enemies and events proved the wisdom of following this custom: the answering fire shattered and holed *Serieuse* so badly that she sank – a rare fate for wooden ships.

The Frenchmen struggled vainly with drastically depleted crews and mounting losses to, in several cases, fire both broadsides simultaneously. The *Majestic* went on to run on board the *Heureux* before breaking away to engage the *Mercure*. The three rear French ships were without opponents, while the *Bellerophon* took on the giant *L'Orient*.

### The *Vanguard* at the Nile

Meanwhile, the *Vanguard* headed for the French third ship, the *Spartiate*, aiming for her starboard, seaward side. She reached this position around 6.40 p.m., anchoring by the stern in some eight fathoms (48ft) of water and about 60 yards from the *Spartiate*. At that stage the French ship had been doubled, as she was already heavily engaged on the shore side by the *Theseus* under Captain Miller. However, Miller, thinking perhaps that the admiral would want the honour of dealing with the enemy without assistance and fearful that some of his shots might strike the flagship, gave orders to continue down the line. About 150 yards further on he anchored with the *Aquilon* 50 yards on his larboard beam to start another furious exchange.

The move of the *Theseus* took some time (the raising of the anchor was a slow process) and the *Vanguard* soon found herself

at a serious disadvantage fighting two ships. Two determined 74s exchanging broadsides at 60 yards was a murderous business, as it was difficult to miss, even in the dark. With all guns firing, both ships were able to send at least 700 lbs of hot metal smashing into their adversary with each broadside. The next French ship down the line, only 150 yards away, was the *Aquilon*. Her

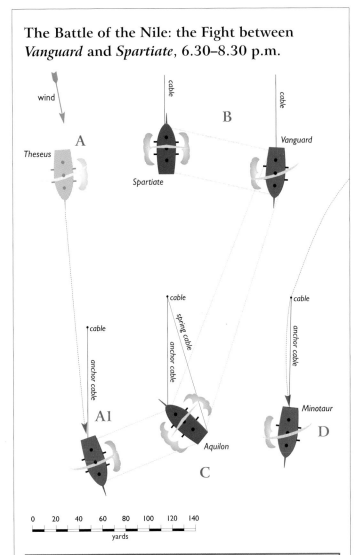

## The Battle of the Nile: the Fight between *Vanguard* and *Spartiate*, 6.30–8.30 p.m.

### Notes

**A** Initially the *Theseus* anchors inside the *Spartiate* and they exchange broadsides. On the arrival of the *Vanguard* on the other side, she moves down to **A1**, fearful of her shots striking Nelson's flagship.

**A1** The second position of *Theseus*: she anchors by the stern and opens fire on the *Aquilon*.

**B** The *Vanguard* anchors about 60 yards from the *Spartiate* (3rd in French line) and a deadly duel at close range ensues.

**C** The *Aquilon* has hauled on the cable and brought her starboard broadside to bear on the *Vanguard*, at the same time engaging the *Theseus* on the larboard side. The *Vanguard* is effectively raked and is fired on by two ships, suffering numerous losses in her forward gun crews.

**D** The arrival of the *Minotaur* forces *Aquilon* to cease firing into the flagship, undoubtedly saving the *Vanguard* from serious consequences.

captain hauled on his anchor cable to pull the ship slightly out of line so that his starboard broadside was able to fire into the bow of the *Vanguard*. It was raking fire, and disastrous for the forward guns and their crews. In all, some seven gun crews were cut down again and again as fresh men replaced them. Even when the *Theseus* came into action on her larboard side, the gallant *Aquilon* kept her starboard guns firing at Nelson's ship. With men absent ashore from an already depleted crew and with mounting losses, that she was able to keep both broadsides firing at all was a remarkable achievement. Only when the *Minotaur* arrived and she was sandwiched between two enemies both pounding her to pieces did she strike her colours (to the *Minotaur*).

At the height of the struggle with the *Spartiate*, at around 8.00 p.m., Nelson was on his quarterdeck when he was suddenly struck violently on the right side of his forehead by a piece of flying langrage (pieces of iron, nails, bolts, etc. used by the French as canister). The blow knocked him into the arms of Captain Berry. As he fell he cried out, 'I am killed! Remember me to my wife.' Blood poured down his face and a three-inch long flap of skin fell over his right eye, blinding him. The pain was intense, the bleeding profuse, so the wound appeared far more serious than it actually was. Nelson seemingly did not lose consciousness and he was half carried, half supported down three companionways to the cockpit on the orlop deck. There he was seen by the ship's surgeon, Michael Jefferson. Jefferson had known Nelson for some time. He had signed a certificate concerning his eye injury at Calvi and had more recently been involved in dressing the stump of his right arm. Nelson's confidence in him is illustrated by the fact that he personally requested his appointment to the flagship. Jefferson described the injury as, 'Wound in the forehead over the right eye. The cranium bared for more than an inch, the wound 3 in long.' He cleaned and dressed the wound using strips of adhesive plaster to close it before bandaging his head. Nelson was then given a medicine containing a small quantity of opium before being led to a nearby compartment to rest. Although still in pain, Nelson called for his secretary in order to start on his despatch, but he was too nervous to write anything. After a short while a seaman appeared to say the French flagship *L'Orient* had caught fire and Nelson immediately returned to the quarterdeck.

While Nelson had been below the *Spartiate* had surrendered. Two hours of brutal exchange had severely damaged the *Vanguard* but beaten the *Spartiate* into submission. *Vanguard*'s master, Wales Clodd, recorded events with the minimum of words and plentiful abbreviations typical of log entries: '31 mins past [six] Opend our Fire on the *Spartiate* which was continued witht Intermission until $^{1}/_{2}$ past 8 when she Struck to Us. Sent Lieut. Galway wth. a Party of Marines to take Possession of her.' By the end of the battle at noon next day the *Vanguard* had suffered 105 casualties. They consisted of 30 killed (3 officers, 20 seamen and 7 marines) and 75 wounded (7 officers, 60 seamen and 8 marines).

### *L'Orient*'s fight to the death

*L'Orient* was a first-rate, three-deck floating fortress, over 200ft long with 124 guns and a crew of over a thousand, including soldiers of the 69th Demi-Brigade. She flew the flag of the French commander-in-chief, Vice-Admiral Brueys, and was commanded by his flag captain, Commodore Casa Bianca. Also on board was Rear-Admiral Ganteaume. Anchored in Aboukir Bay, she was in the centre of the French line, seventh from the ship in the van and six from the rear.

It was pure chance that when the *Bellerophon* came up the next unengaged enemy ship was *L'Orient*. Undeterred by her size, Captain Darby brought his ship to within a ship's length off the French flagship's starboard bow before dropping his anchor. His aim was to anchor in such a position to be able to rake, or almost rake, his huge adversary while she could not bring a full broadside to bear. But the anchor failed to hold. It dragged on the sandy bottom so that by the time her forward movement was checked she was abeam of the *L'Orient* in precisely the position Darby had sought to avoid, with her upper deck 12 feet lower than the *L'Orient*'s. Then the Frenchman fired first. Before the British ship could recover and reply, her guns roared again. The consequences were instant and dire. Down went between 60 and 70 men killed or wounded. Down went Captain Darby stunned and bleeding from a head wound. Down went another nine officers and warrant officers, including Lieutenants Daniell (first lieutenant), Launder, Hadawell and Jolliffe, Captain Hopkins RM, the master Mr Kirby, master's mate Mr Ellison, midshipman Mr Botham and the

---

### The Effects of Nelson's Wound

In 2000 Volume 86 of the *Journal of the Royal Naval Medical Service* carried a fascinating article by Professor L. P. Le Quesne, part of which discussed the possible effects on Nelson's health of the head wound he received at the Nile. The relevant part reads:

On August 31st Jefferson [his surgeon] recorded in his log that the wound on Nelson's forehead was healed perfectly, but there was still some swelling of the neighbouring tissues ...

The wound on his forehead may have healed well, but in the weeks following his injury Nelson himself was not well. He had a variety of symptoms – he could not sleep, at times he thought that he would die, he complained constantly of headaches. As he wrote to St Vincent 'My head is splitting, splitting, splitting at this moment ...'. The question clearly arises as to whether these symptoms were the consequence of a significant head injury – as we would say today a post-concussional syndrome. His symptoms were certainly compatible with this diagnosis of it, but they are not necessarily diagnostic of it, and there are two salient features which are of great importance in this context. First, there is no evidence that Nelson lost consciousness at the time of the injury, and there is no mention of him experiencing a very significant symptom, retrograde amnesia – that is to say loss of memory of events prior to the injury, often extending back for 12 hours or more. In the absence of these two symptoms it is very difficult to describe his head injury as being serious ... When he reached Naples he was indeed an exhausted man; but it is hard to account for this as a consequence, at least solely, of his head injury.

boatswain Mr Chapman. In just a few moments a huge hole had been made in the command structure. Fortunately, of those hit, only Jolliffe was killed outright. Daniell was able to take command after his wound was bound up and Launder managed to remain upright on his gundeck. In addition to the human losses, eight guns had been dismounted or disabled.

The two ships had swung together almost to touching distance. Amazingly, the British gun crews began to return fire, broadside for broadside into the enemy's ports, as fast as the guns could be reloaded. Within half an hour Daniell had a leg taken off by a cannonball before being killed outright by a grapeshot as he was being carried below. Lieutenant Launder was summoned from his gundeck to take command. The upper decks had become a death trap. The unequal struggle had not lasted much more than 30 minutes when the mizzenmast, shot through close to the deck, came crashing down. Shortly afterwards it was the turn of the mainmast, which snapped without warning, bringing an enormous tangle of spars, sails and rigging down on top of the men below. Crushed among the wreckage of splintered wood and heavy canvas, just as he was yelling through his speaking trumpet, was Launder. The third commander of the *Bellerophon*, Lieutenant Cathcart, was fetched from his gundeck.

Fires broke out on both the *Bellerophon* and *L'Orient*, but although most were put out, one particularly fierce blaze on the French ship appeared in danger of spreading to the British ship. At that moment Cathcart had gone below, leaving a fourteen-year-old midshipman, John Hindmarsh, in charge. This young lad instantly gave the order to sheer off. He gathered some men, cut the anchor cable, had the spritsail set and gradually the *Bellerophon* drifted free from nearly two hours of torment. He had almost certainly saved his ship from total destruction, if not from burning then from being smashed to pieces. Captain Darby, who came back on deck soon afterwards, immediately endorsed the lad's decision. The *Bellerophon* took no further part in the battle with *L'Orient*. As she came away from the line of battle, her foremast collapsed – she was then completely dismasted. She drifted away into the night to lick her wounds, which in human terms amounted to 197 (49 killed and 148 wounded) out of a complement of 571 (almost 35 per cent) – the highest casualties of any British ship at the Nile.

*L'Orient* now had to face fire first from one direction, then from two and finally from three sides. Trailing some distance behind the British fleet were two 74s, the *Swiftsure* (Captain Hallowell) and *Alexander* (Captain Ball), followed by the much smaller 50-gun *Leander* (Captain Thompson). The 74s had been delayed, as they had had to catch up after a reconnaissance of Alexandria harbour. By the time they were negotiating the shoals around Nelson's Island, it was dark. Only the frantic waving of lanterns by the *Culloden,* aground on a treacherous reef (according to Troubridge, her captain, the leadsman had been calling eleven fathoms when she struck), saved the *Swiftsure* from the same fate. Shortly after 8.00 p.m. the *Swiftsure* closed on the French centre (almost firing on the battered *Bellerophon* as she slipped away) and positioned herself on *L'Orient*'s starboard quarter at a distance of about 20 yards. From there she engaged the enemy flagship with all her starboard batteries. A few minutes later the *Alexander* approached. Her captain took his ship astern of *L'Orient* and came up into the wind to anchor some 40 yards off her larboard quarter. The flagship was subjected to heavy punishment on both sides and was forced to man both broadsides simultaneously. In the centre the *Peuple*

## The Battle of the Nile: the Concentration against *L'Orient*, 8.00–9.00 p.m.

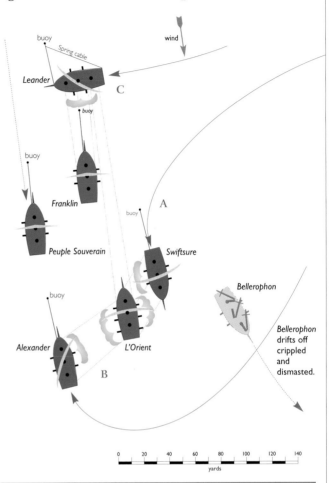

### British Notes

A The first to arrive to replace the *Bellerophon* is the *Swiftsure*. Captain Hallowell anchors very close on *L'Orient*'s starboard bow. She is so close that when *L'Orient* catches fire, the intense heat melts the pitch in *Swiftsure*'s seams.

B The *Alexander* (Captain Ball) follows *Swiftsure*, cuts the French line, bears up into the wind and anchors in a position where she is able to deliver her fire into *L'Orient*'s larboard quarter.

C The last of the 3 British ships to arrive is the *Leander* (Captain Thompson). She makes for the gap left by the *Peuple Souverain* and positions herself so that she can rake both the *Franklin* and *L'Orient*.

• It is the concentrated fire from these ships that eventually causes the fire and blowing up of *L'Orient* at around 9.00 p.m.

### French Notes

• The French flagship, having driven off the *Bellerophon*, now has to face the fire of two 74s and a 50-gun ship. All the British ships are anchored in places that enable them to fire raking or similar shots at close range.

• *L'Orient* is unable to reply to *Leander*'s raking shots and must man both broadsides while receiving fire from 3 ships from 3 directions.

• The *P. Souverain*, after having her cable cut by gunfire, has drifted into a difficult position, unable to offer much assistance to *L'Orient*.

• The *Franklin* is receiving raking fire into her bow to which she is unable to reply.

*Souverain*, after being trapped between the *Orion* and *Defence* (both of whom were concerned their fire would hit each other), was dismasted and driven out of the line. The little *Leander* bravely moved into the gap to anchor. She swung on her cable to position herself perfectly to rake the bows of both the *Franklin* and *L'Orient*, while at the same time avoiding any effective return fire from either of her two adversaries. By this stage, with the mêlée fully developed and British ships on either side of the French line, it had become desperately difficult for the gunners to avoid firing on their own ships. Each British ship had been ordered to display four lanterns on a horizontal pole at the mizzen peak, but these were often shot away. This, coupled with the darkness, the banks of swirling smoke and the effect of the flashes of the gunfire on night vision, undoubtedly resulted in some shots hitting unintended targets.

By 9.00 p.m. *L'Orient* was in a desperate plight. Midshipman John Lee, then an eleven-year-old on the *Swiftsure*, years later recalled how as an ADC to Captain Hallowell he had been employed fetching bottles of ginger beer from the cabin locker round the mizzenmast for the refreshment of the officers (and himself). He went on to describe seeing *L'Orient* catch fire:

> Captain Hallowell, observing an appearance of fire in the mizzen chains of *L'Orient*, ordered me to run below and desire Lieutenants Waters, the Hon. F. Aylmer, Davis and Mudge to point every gun that would bear upon this spot, to which also the musketry of the marines stationed upon the poop, under Captain Allen, was directed, with a view to preventing the enemy from extinguishing the conflagration ... The conflagration soon began to rage with a dreadful fury.

On board the flagship Vice-Admiral Brueys had displayed almost unbelievable personal gallantry and stoicism. Early in the battle he had received a head wound that he ignored. Then a cannon ball removed both his legs. He refused to be taken below, saying that a French admiral must die on his quarterdeck, and had a tourniquet bound round both stumps before being propped up in a chair to continue in command. But Brueys was not to suffer long – shortly afterwards his head was removed by another roundshot, and he was thus spared witnessing the final catastrophic spectacular that finished his flagship.

The uncontrollable spread of the fire, the frantic efforts of many of *L'Orient*'s crew to escape and the attempts by *Swiftsure* to rescue enemy seamen are best described by the chaplain of the *Swiftsure* at the time, the Reverend Cooper Willyams:

> Several of the officers and men [of *L'Orient*] seeing the impracticability of extinguishing the fire, which had now extended itself along the upper-decks and was flaming up the masts, jumped overboard, some supporting themselves on spars and pieces of wreck, others swimming with all their might to escape the dreaded catastrophe. Shot flying in all directions dashed many of them to pieces, others were picked up by boats of the fleet, or dragged into the lower ports of the nearest ships. The British sailors humanely stretched forth their hands to save a fallen enemy, though the battle at that moment raged with uncontrolled fury. The *Swiftsure*, that was anchored within half a pistol shot of the bow of *L'Orient* saved the lives of the Commissary, First-Lieutenant, and ten men, who were drawn out of the water into the lower-deck ports ...

On board the *Swiftsure* and *Alexander* and other nearby ships, desperate measures were taken to try to nullify the effects of the explosion all knew was inevitable. Magazines were closed down, everything on decks doused with water, shrouds and sails not required for sailing were wetted and rolled up, hatches were closed and crew with fire buckets stood by on all decks. The *Swiftsure* was so close and the heat so intense that pitch melted in her seams and ran in streams down her sides. On the French flagship the fire raced up the rigging and along the yards and decks, obliging many gun crews to abandon their guns. Hallowell calculated that the *Swiftsure*, being virtually alongside *L'Orient*, would escape the worst effects of the blast, as it would be mainly upwards and over her. He posted sentries to prevent any man from cutting her cable. It could only be a matter of minutes before the flames reached one or both of the magazines. Incredibly, according to the Reverend Willyams, the lower-deck guns of the *L'Orient* continued to fire up to the moment they were blown to oblivion. Those men on the upper decks, however, some naked as the flames had seared away their clothes, were hurling themselves into the water. Willyams described the volcanic eruption when the fire reached the gunpowder:

> At thirty-seven minutes past nine [timings differ, the log of *Culloden* recording 9.55] the fatal explosion happened ... *L'Orient* blew up with a crashing sound that deafened all around her. The tremendous motion, felt to the very bottom of each ship, was like that of an earthquake; the fragments were driven such a vast height into the air that some moments elapsed before they could descend ...

Although contemporary accounts tell of a single massive explosion, recent French surveys of the wreckage on the bottom of the bay have concluded that there were two. The first was in her main magazine and blew off her stern, followed within seconds by that in the forward magazine. A rain of flaming debris and bodies was scattered over the fleets. For perhaps ten minutes afterwards there was a stunned silence. No guns fired and battle ceased as all contemplated what they had witnessed. Such was the power of the explosion that in recent times divers have found a cannon weighing two tons some 400 yards from the wreck. Over a thousand men perished in the eruption; only about sixty lived to tell the tale, one of whom was Rear-Admiral Ganteaume.

In the aftermath one survivor presented himself on the quarterdeck of the *Swiftsure* stark naked except for a cocked hat. 'Who the deuce are you, sir?' snapped Captain Hallowell. *'Je suis de*

---

### The Boy Stood on the Burning Deck

Some readers may be familiar with the poem 'Casabianca', by the Victorian writer Felicia Hemans (or perhaps may recall the more vulgar Army version). The poem begins:

> The boy stood on the burning deck
> Whence all but he had fled;
> The flame that lit the battle's wreck
> Shone round him o'er the dead.

It goes on to describe how the boy obediently waits for his father's order before escaping from the ship, but his father is lying unconscious below deck, so the order does not come and the boy perishes in the explosion.

The poem is based on the fate (according to legend) of the young son of Commodore Casa Bianca, the captain of *L'Orient*, who is known to have died at the Nile.

L'Orient, *monsieur.*' He was Lieutenant Berthelot, and explained that he had been on the lower gundeck until the planking on the deck above was ablaze. He had removed his clothes before leaping into the sea. Then a dreadful thought struck him – he could not be recognized as an officer. He clambered back through a gunport, scrabbled through the flames and smoke to where he had left his clothes, donned his hat and flung himself back into the water!

## THE END OF THE BATTLE

The *Franklin* struck her colours at midnight. The *Tonnant* was then the only French ship still firing, although she was dismasted by 3.00 a.m. An hour later the *Heureux* and *Mercure* eventually ran aground but continued to fire sporadically. At this stage scores of men on both sides were collapsing of fatigue rather than wounds. At dawn firing was resumed. Of the French, the *Timoleon* could still be counted as a fighting ship, while the *Heureux* and *Mercure*, although crippled, had their colours still flying and the *Guillaume Tell* and *Généreux* were comparatively unscathed. Aground on the shoals, *Heureux* and *Mercure* soon surrendered. At around noon those French ships still capable of getting under way did so – with the object of escaping rather than attacking. The first away was the *Guillaume Tell* flying the flag of Rear-Admiral Villeneuve, the man destined to have another catastrophic encounter with Nelson seven years later. The *Généreux*, *Timoleon* and the two frigates *Diane* and *Justice* followed him. But the *Timoleon* failed to make it. After an ineffectual attempt to wear, she ran aground, her foremast going over the side as she struck. The crew escaped ashore while her captain set his ship on fire with the colours still flying. Such was the end of the greatest disaster suffered by the French Navy since La Hogue (Barfleur) almost a hundred years before.

### The 'Powder Monkey' Pub

A new pub called The Powder Monkey was opened in Exmouth, Devon in September 2000. It is named after Nancy Perriam, the wife of a seaman on the *Orion* at the battles of Cape St Vincent and the Nile, whose unofficial duties included passing the powder from the magazines to the guns. When her husband was later killed, she returned to Exmouth where she lived to be sixty-seven, and is buried in the same churchyard at Littleham as Fanny, Lady Nelson and her son, Nelson's stepson Josiah. The *Exmouth Journal* reported that the pub was opened by the eighty-year-old Mrs Peggy Eyres, a great-niece of Nancy Perriam.

The Nile was the longest naval battle of the era, lasting as it did for some 18 hours from first to last shot. It was also a naval disaster of monumental proportions for the French. Of the 17 ships-of-the-line and frigates present, only four escaped capture or destruction. Nelson's report of the casualties shows 5,225 French killed or wounded out of 11,230 men in the fleet, losses of 46 per cent. The British losses, mostly on the *Bellerophon*, *Majestic* and *Minotaur* (*Culloden* had nil and *Zealous* only eight), amounted to 218 killed and 677 wounded. With a fleet complement of about 8,068, this represented only 11 per cent. At a stroke the British had regained control in the Mediterranean, cutting off Bonaparte in Egypt. Another year was to pass before he abandoned his army and slipped on board a frigate with his staff to dodge the British fleet en route back to Europe, and his demoralized soldiers had two more years to wait before survivors were repatriated. This defeat at the Nile persuaded Turkey to declare war on France and her traditional enemy Imperial Russia to do the same. France's dreams of attacking the British in India evaporated.

It was Nelson's first victory as a fleet commander, and a spectacular triumph. It was won by his tactics of concentration, of isolating a part of the enemy line, of explaining to his captains in advance that so long as they used their initiative to these ends and closed with the enemy, he was content. How appropriate these tactics were and how well his captains understood them were exemplified that summer evening by Captain Foley risking taking his ship round onto the inside of the French, something not originally considered. Nelson was well rewarded for his brilliant victory – though not as well as he wanted. He was created Baron of the Nile and of Burnham

---

## Nelson's Coffin

The coffin in which Nelson was eventually buried after Trafalgar was made from a piece of timber from the shattered mainmast of *L'Orient*. A large section of the mast was picked up by a boat from the *Swiftsure* a day or two after the battle, and from this Captain Hallowell had the carpenter construct the coffin. Not only were the planks were made from the mast, but all other fittings were also made with materials from *L'Orient*. Hallowell certified the authenticity by pasting a paper on the bottom of the coffin on which he wrote: 'I do hereby certify that every part of this coffin is made of the wood and iron of *L'Orient*, most of which was picked up by His Majesty's ship under my command in the Bay of Aboukir. – *Swiftsure*, May 23rd. 1799 - BEN HALLOWELL.'

Seemingly this idea did not occur to Hallowell until some considerable time after the battle, as this strange gift was not given to Nelson, as we see from the above date, until some ten months later. Perhaps he thought it an appropriate way of reminding his friend of his mortality at a time when Nelson was the object of universal flattery and adulation. After signing the certification Hallowell penned a short note to Nelson to accompany the gift.

The Right Hon. Lord Nelson K.B.
My Lord
Herewith I send you a coffin made of part of l'Orient's main mast, that when you are tired of this life you may be buried in one of your own trophies but may that period be far distant, is the sincere wish of your obedient and much obliged servant. Ben Hallowell.

The task of making the presentation fell to a fourteen-year-old midshipman called Henry Masterman Marshall. He must surely have wondered, as the boat containing the coffin was rowed across to the admiral's flagship, what his reception was likely to be. Fortunately, Nelson had a sense of humour. He thanked the nervous young midshipman and sent his compliments to Captain Hallowell. Nelson was both amused and pleased with this remarkable gift, and for some time insisted on it being placed behind his chair at the dining table in the great cabin. Eventually it was relegated to the hold but Nelson made sure it went with him when he transferred his flag to the 80-gun *Foudroyant* in June 1799.

## Nelson's Island

Nelson's Island, formerly Aboukir Island, stands about 13 miles east of Alexandria and guards the northern entrance to Aboukir Bay. Although now only some 400 yards long north–south and 140 yards wide at the southern end, in past centuries it was substantially larger. At the time of writing considerable archaeological digging is taking place, which has revealed faint outlines of walls and potsherds. Of even greater interest, a number of graves have been uncovered. It was used after the battle as a suitable place to bury some of the British dead who were not thrown overboard; John Nichol, a seaman on the *Goliath*, tells us that the gunner's wife from the *Goliath* was buried there after the island's capture by several boatloads of seamen and marines a few days after the battle. Its tiny garrison of gunners had been unable to fire effectively during the action and had little option but to surrender. The Reverend Cooper Willyams from the *Swiftsure* also confirmed taking part in burial services there. According to Willyams, it was afterwards garrisoned by British troops until 1801 and ship's crew were allowed ashore in the knowledge that there was no 'danger of hurting their constitution in ale-houses'.

There are currently plans for the British seamen and marines whose graves are discovered to be reburied with full military honours in a Commonwealth War Graves cemetery at Alexandria.

---

Thorpe – he wanted to be a viscount. Parliament voted him a pension of £2,000, and again he considered himself hard done by: 'They cut me off £1,000 a year less than St Vincent [for Cape St Vincent] or Duncan [for Camperdown].' The Irish Parliament proposed, but did not agree, to give him another £1,000, but the East India Company gave him the handsome sum of £10,000. The City of London presented him with a sword. But the gift he really admired was the gaudy Turkish Order of the Crescent, created for non-Mohammedans. 'A superb aigrette ... or plume of triumph ... being a blaze of bril-liants crowned with a vibrating plumage, and a radiant star in the middle.' He wore it in his hat like some enormous cap-badge.

Both Houses of Parliament voted their thanks to the fleet. Alexander Davison, Nelson's friend and prize agent, struck special commemorative medals at a personal cost of £2,000. They were cast in gold for admirals and captains (even Troubridge got one), silver for commanders (only Hardy) and lieutenants, copper for warrant officers and bronze for everybody else. Hardy and all the first lieutenants were promoted.

## British Casualties at the Nile

Nelson received casualty returns from all his ships after the action and on 3 August compiled the following list:

| Ship | Killed | | | Wounded | | | Total |
|---|---|---|---|---|---|---|---|
| | Officers | Seamen | Marines | Officer | Seamen | Marines | |
| *Theseus* | | 5 | | 1 | 24 | 5 | 35 |
| *Alexander* | 1 | 13 | | 5 | 48 | 5 | 72 |
| *Vanguard* | 3 | 20 | 7 | 7 | 60 | 8 | 105 |
| *Minotaur* | 2 | 18 | 3 | 4 | 54 | 6 | 87 |
| *Swiftsure* | | 7 | | 1 | 19 | 2 | 29 |
| *Audacious* | | 1 | | 2 | 31 | 2 | 36 |
| *Defence* | | 3 | 1 | | 9 | 2 | 15 |
| *Zealous* | | 1 | | | | 7 | 8 |
| *Orion* | 1 | 11 | 1 | 5 | 18 | 6 | 42 |
| *Goliath* | 2 | 12 | 7 | 4 | 28 | 9 | 62 |
| *Majestic* | 3 | 33 | 14 | 3 | 124 | 16 | 193 |
| *Bellerophon* | 4 | 32 | 13 | 5 | 126 | 17 | 197 |
| *Leander* | | | | | | 14 | 14 |
| **Total** | **16** | **156** | **46** | **37** | **555** | **85** | **895** |

**Notes**
- 55 per cent of all casualties occurred in three ships (*Vanguard* 105, *Majestic* 193 and *Bellerophon* 197).
- Of the 218 killed, 7 per cent were officers, 72 per cent seamen and 21 per cent marines. About six seamen became casualties for every marine.
- *L'Orient* acquitted herself well before being blown up. The three ships with which she was primarily engaged (*Bellerophon*, *Swiftsure* and *Alexander*) suffered some 300 casualties; a high proportion would have been inflicted by the French flagship.

# A Fleet Comparison

## THE BRITISH

The Peace of Amiens in March 1802 did not do the Royal Navy much good. The following months saw government funds dramatically cut back, ships mothballed, officers in their hundreds (including Nelson) forced into semi-retirement on half pay and thousands of experienced seamen discharged. When war resumed in May 1803 there was a frenetic scramble to undo the damage. The Navy once again had priority for money and men. Without her 'wooden walls' constantly positioned in 'The Ditch', as Napoleon scornfully called the Channel, Britain was vulnerable to both invasion and a crippling loss of trade.

The dismantling of a large part of the Navy had been accomplished while Earl St Vincent was First Lord of the Admiralty. When he assumed that professional pinnacle in early 1801 the Navy estimates stood at £14 million for the year with 135,000 men mustered. In January 1803, with St Vincent and a complacent government still in office, the estimates had shrunk to £9.5 million and the manpower to 95,000 – a 32 per cent reduction in money, 30 per cent in men. Not until the start of 1805, when hostilities had been resumed for nearly two years, did the government budget for virtually the same amount of expenditure and slightly less manpower as four years earlier. By this time St Vincent had gone and Viscount Melville had been the First Lord for eight months. As he and his political masters soon discovered it is much quicker and easier to dismantle than to construct – no matter what the activity. Rebuilding is rarely just a matter of throwing cash at the problem.

Let us look at Nelson's navy in early 1805, and in particular at the ships that really counted in the run up to Trafalgar – ships-of-the-line of 64 guns or more (first, second and third rates) and frigates (fifth and sixth rates). There were 181 ships-of-the-line on the books together with 188 frigates – slightly more of both categories than before the peace treaty. So why

did Nelson only have 27 of the former (15 per cent) and sometimes as few as four of the latter (a minute 2 per cent) to chase, find, and finally corner his enemy? There are several strands to the answer.

• The first and most important reason is that the above figures, although correct in themselves, give a wholly false picture of the effective size of the Royal Navy. They represent the projected paper strength, not the actual operational strength. The 181 ships-of-the-line include 26 ships 'building or ordered', 39 earmarked as fit only for harbour service and 33 in ordinary – requiring a thorough, and consequently lengthy, refit. That left only 83 two- and three-deckers in commission, fit for service at sea. Nelson had virtually a third of them at Trafalgar.

• Even the above does not tell the whole truth. 'Fit for service' had a wide interpretation. Many ships were worn out with being constantly at sea patrolling, blockading and escorting. Long periods away from port meant a squadron's ships would be constantly in need of repair. This was especially so in winter. Nelson's letters best illustrate the problem. Writing to the Prime Minister on 24 August 1803, when he was off Toulon as the commander-in-chief in the Mediterranean, Nelson complained, 'The Admiralty knows the state of the others ... it is not a store ship a week which could keep them in repair.' To his close friend Alexander Davison he wrote, 'I never saw a fleet altogether so well officered and manned. Would to God the ships were half as good, but they are what we call crazy.' Finally, to the Admiralty in May 1804, 'the *Kent* will be ordered to England in July ... and, fearful of any accident happening to her, I shall direct a transport to accompany her. ... the *Renown* ought to proceed to England before the winter, and the *Superb* also ... nothing but the great exertions of Captain Keats has kept her at sea this last season.' Neither the French nor Spanish suffered so severely in this way as seven-tenths of their time was spent sitting peacefully at anchor.

### Wastage Rate of Ships 1793–1802

Ship losses during the first ten years of the Revolutionary Wars make interesting reading. The figures refer to all naval ships including small, unrated ones such as sloops, bombs and cutters.

|  | British | French | Spanish | Dutch | Danish |
|---|---|---|---|---|---|
| Taken | 51 | 279 | 57 | 93 | 1 |
| Mutinied | 5 | – | – | 1 | – |
| Expended | 7 | – | – | – | – |
| Wrecked | 135 | 9 | – | – | – |
| Destroyed in action | 5 | 99 | 19 | 4 | 14 |
| **Total** | **203** | **387** | **76** | **98** | **15** |

In ten years of war the British lost only five ships in action but 135 were wrecked – proof indeed of just how much time her ships spent at sea in all weathers and all seasons. By contrast, the other nations' navies spent most of their time in port, usually penned in by a British blockade.

Losses to enemy action (in one way or another) are also revealing, when one remembers that the other four nations were all enemies of Britain at some stage during this period. The British suffered 56, the French 378, the Spanish 76, the Dutch 97 and the Danish 15. Thus Britain inflicted about ten losses on her opponents for every one she sustained.

- Building new ships and repairing old ones takes time. A total of 88 ships were ordered in 1804, but of these only ten were 74s, and there was little chance of any being available the following year. While ships are being built other ships at sea are being lost (captured or wrecked), damaged or worn out. The wastage during 1804 was three ships-of-the-line ('sold or taken to pieces') and eight frigates (seven 'captured, destroyed or wrecked'). Despite the priority now given to the Navy, despite the vigorous exertions of the Admiralty under Melville, during that year only six ships-of-the-line and twelve frigates were brought into service (built and launched, purchased or captured). 1804 saw a net gain of three ships-of-the-line and an overall loss of two frigates.

- The balance between battleships and frigates was seldom right. Frigates were the workhorses of the navy, and there were never enough of them. They cruised, patrolled, escorted, reconnoitred, passed signals, carried dispatches, carried troops and acted as flagships, guardships and receiving ships as well as hunting for enemy frigates, privateers and merchantmen. The only duty not required of a frigate was to fight in the line of battle. Of the 188 frigates on the books in January 1805, only 83 were actually available. They were scattered in bases from Newfoundland to Capetown, from the Caribbean to Calcutta, with no fewer than 36 on the West Indies and North America stations. As described in Section One, Nelson was forever bemoaning his lack of frigates. This was particularly apparent during the Trafalgar campaign and was largely responsible for his inability to make and maintain contact with the Combined Fleet in the Mediterranean, and for his fruitless and frustrating chase to the Caribbean and back. Map 2 on pp. 26–7 shows the deployment in early 1805 of 79 of the ships in commission. The ships not shown were either being used for special duties or sailing between stations.

In summary, then, the Royal Navy in 1805 had barely recovered from the 'peace dividend' reductions of the years 1802–3. It took many months to put new ships to sea and fill them with something near a full complement of officers and crew. Considering Britain's global commitments and the drain of normal wastage Nelson, with a third of the Navy's operational battleships at Trafalgar, had little ground for complaint. Indeed, if he had not been forced to send six ships to Gibraltar to provision and water, Nelson's fleet would have equalled that of Villeneuve.

## THE FRENCH

In 1789 France had a navy second in strength and competence only to that of Britain. It was centred on three main seaports – Brest and Rochefort on the Atlantic and Toulon on the Mediterranean. There were the bulk of the ships, the shipbuild-

### Royal Navy Expenditure Estimates 1805

| Item | Cost (£) |
|---|---|
| Pay and maintenance – 90,000 seamen + 30,000 RM | 5,850,000 |
| Maintenance for ships in service | 4,680,000 |
| Ordinary expenses (maintenance for ships in reserve) including half-pay for officers | 1,394,940 |
| 'Extraordinaries' including building and repair of ships and 'extra' or unforeseen work | 1,553,690 |
| Transport service and 'maintenance of prisoners of war in health and sickness' | 1,557,000 |
| **Total** | **15,035,630** |

ing industry, dockyards, bases and barracks for marine units, the headquarters of the senior admirals and many thousands of skilled shipyard workers (*ouvriers*). Coordinating the building, repairing, fitting out, recruiting, replenishing and provisioning – a vast administrative task – was the French naval civil service of specialists, technicians and administrators run by the appropriately entitled *officiers de plume* (officers of the pen). Naturally they were regarded as useless bureaucrats, very inferior beings, by the *officiers de l'épée* (officers of the sword) – sea-going naval officers. While many of these were competent officers with considerable experience they all had one thing in common – they were aristocrats. The officer corps was filled by the sons of the nobility. The first requirement for becoming an *élève de la marine* (midshipman) was a certified copy of the family genealogy proving that the would-be officer had sufficient 'blue blood'.

The storming of the Bastille in Paris on 14 July 1789 and the subsequent French Revolution put an end to most of this. The cry went up for social reform, equality and the end of the nobility. Many, including the King and Queen, were forced to bow to 'Madame Guillotine'. Everybody was equal, everybody was addressed as 'citizen'. The executioner sat at the admiral's table. Unsurprisingly, the officer corps had little interest in social reform but were desperately anxious to save their necks. Discipline in the Navy disintegrated. Senior officers were denounced and hauled before 'Committees of Public Safety'; the ranks of authority were purged. Numerous officers were mobbed and driven away into exile, some killed. By early 1792, of the 640 naval officers supposedly based at Brest 19 had been jailed, 28 were trying to resign and 361 had fled. In Toulon several were strung up from lamp-posts.

The vacancies were filled by very junior officers, merchant marine officers, petty officers, dockyard functionaries, pilots and even ordinary seamen. Some could barely read or write. The names of the ships were changed, the old emblems of the fleet were burned, and the cap of 'liberty' was placed with pomp and circumstance on the quarterdeck. The effect on the Navy was catastrophic. Amateur captains commanded green crews by committee. Ships ran aground, collided or declined to sail. Many crewmen were too frightened to climb aloft to set the topgallant sails. When Vice-Admiral Morand de Galles, in command at Brest in 1793, took his fleet to sea in early spring, it ran into bad weather. Several ships collided with each other or were dismasted as the incompetence of his officers and crew was exposed. One captain was killed by accident as he tried to do a seaman's job. The flagship could not wear as the headsails blew away, because the captain could not muster more than thirty men on deck. Shortly after this fiasco Morand de Galles was cashiered and imprisoned for over a year, not for his ships' dreadful performance at sea, but because he was suspected of being a nobleman.

The following year, when Vice-Admiral Villaret-Joyeuse took another French fleet to sea, the extent of the culling of the officer corps was obvious. The admiral and another flag officer had been lieutenants three years earlier, the third flag officer had been a sub-lieutenant, nine out of twenty-six captains were from the merchant service, one a lower-deck rating and another a merchantman's boatswain.

Another casualty of the Revolution was the Marine Artillery Corps (*Corps Royal des Cannonniers-Matelots*), well-trained gunner-sailors who were now regarded as elitist. They had supervised gunnery on board ship and provided the gun captains for many of the guns. A typical French 74 would have had about 52. Servicing the guns was now entrusted to politically reliable 'citizens', with lamentable results. The 1790s were not good years for the French Navy. Their main battle fleets sought, understandably, to avoid action. On the two occasions that they were forced to fight, the 'Glorious First of June' in 1794 and in Aboukir Bay four years later, they went down in dismal defeats.

By 1800 Napoleon, then First Consul, had had enough. His background and interests lay in soldiering and artillery, but he needed an effective navy if his troops were ever to cross the Channel, and he set about the reformation in his customary dictatorial and detailed manner. A new Minister of Marine was appointed, Vice-Admiral Denis Decrès (an able administrator if not much of a naval strategist), while a start was made on purging the officer corps of its more obvious incompetents. A naval career was opened up to former royalist officers who wished to return, together with educated young men of all classes. Two floating naval schools were set up at Brest and Toulon with cadets completing a three-year course. In an effort to improve discipline the old pre-1789 naval regulations were restored. Large funds were made available to rebuild the fleet, which had shrunk from 83 ships-of-the-line in 1792 to 46 ten years later, while the number of frigates had gone from 74 to 37. Additional large naval seaports were developed at Cherbourg and Antwerp – the latter regarded by the British, rightly, as 'a pistol aimed at the head of England'. 'Flotillas' of gunboats were instituted and achieved some successes in the Channel. In 1803 four regiments of Marine Artillery were established (increased to five in 1805) along with companies of *ouvriers* (specialist artisans). The maximum establishment was 14,400.

A year before Trafalgar these regiments were granted the title *Corps Imperial de l'Artillerie de la Marine*.

Nevertheless, despite the First Consul's drive, despite the extra millions of francs, nothing could compensate for the lack of time, and by May 1803 France was at war again. Reform took time, ships took time to build, training took time, much of it wasted by complacency, corruption and resistance to change. Never was Napoleon's own saying, 'Ask of me anything but time', so apt. France needed a prolonged peace to put her fleet in order – all she got were the fourteen months following the Peace of Amiens in March 1802. By Trafalgar the desperate plight into which the Revolution had plunged the French Navy was far from over. There were not enough men for the ships, for the dockyard establishments or the forts. Batteries had a quarter of their establishments, gun mountings were rotten and desertion endemic. Napoleon, on visiting Brest, did not exaggerate when he exclaimed, '*Il manque de tout!*' ('It lacks everything!') Toulon was another example of how negligence combined effectively with incompetence to frustrate and delay efforts to rebuild the fleet. New ships were to be laid down but the wood for their construction was missing – at one stage there was not a piece of solid oak in the dockyard. Three of the building slips needed to be reconstructed while two more required extensive repairs. Then it transpired there were only 200 carpenters available. A levy on carpenters was made on the surrounding district, which produced more tradesmen but led to violent demands for more pay. When Admiral Latouche-Tréville hoisted his flag on the newly built *Bucentaure* in January 1804 he found there was no proper system of supplying her or other ships as they became available.

Map 3 on p. 31 shows that by March 1805 the French had 21 ships-of-the-line operational at Brest and perhaps four more at Rochefort and at Ferrol, plus another at Cadiz. Another eleven rode at anchor at Toulon. In total this was a mere 41 ships, whose crews had still not recovered from the damage inflicted by the Revolution of some fifteen years earlier. Confronting them were about 56 well-manned British battleships out of some 83 operational. Not only were the French squadrons separated, they were also bottled up in port by the blockading British. To have any hope of successfully confronting his enemy at sea Napoleon would need to rely on his allies – the Spanish. Only a combined fleet would have a chance of redressing at least the numerical balance.

## The Revolution Undermines the French Navy

It became virtually impossible for French officers to maintain discipline after the Revolution. They were insulted with impunity, gallows were erected outside their homes and any seamen given even a mild punishment by his captain could complain with certain success to his commune. Lists of naval officers were posted in their home towns encouraging anyone who wanted to report them to their local commune or council for lack of *civisme* (revolutionary enthusiasm). The council and the seamen of the district would then vote on whether the officer should be dismissed. Many were denounced, dismissed or even imprisoned.

A typical example of the impossibility of exercising proper command occurred in 1789 in Toulon. Vice-Admiral d'Albert de Rions, who had fought with great courage at the Battle of the Saints and was held to be one of the most capable flag officers in the service, was in command at the port. He and a party of officers went to deal with a dockyard disturbance caused by the dismissal of two petty officers for inciting a mutiny. D'Albert and his companions were beaten up and thrown into jail. Later the Revolutionary Assembly released them and declared there had been a 'misunderstanding and nobody was to blame'. D'Albert left his command. The following year at Brest he again attempted to discipline a coxswain and again mutiny threatened, so d'Albert de Rions resigned. His successor lasted a week before he did the same.

## THE SPANISH

In 1793 Nelson, as captain of the *Agamemnon*, had the opportunity of visiting Cadiz (see pp. 108–9) while Spain was allied to Britain. He was shown around the dockyard, later writing to his wife that the Spanish Navy had 'very fine ships but shockingly manned'. Coincidentally, in the same year Admiral Gravina travelled to England on a supposedly clandestine intelligence mission. However he and his companion Captain Valdés (commanding the 80-gun *Neptuno* at Trafalgar) were welcomed in a very open, hospitable manner. As Nelson toured Cadiz so Gravina inspected Portsmouth. In his report to Madrid, while somewhat critical of the British ship design and lack of conformity in construction, he was full of praise of the superior gunnery – in particular how the fitting of gunlocks had speeded up the rate and reliability of firing. So while Nelson considered the Spanish ships excellent and the crews poor, Gravina by and large drew the opposite conclusion about the Royal Navy. They were both right, and twelve years later not much had changed.

In the latter half of the eighteenth century the Spaniards had four main shipbuilding bases – Havana (which built 197 ships in less than 100 years), Ferrol, Guarnizo (near Santander) and Cartagena. Spain had a powerful navy (third largest in the world after Britain and France). The fleets were based at Ferrol, Cadiz and Cartagena in Spain and Havana in Cuba. The Spaniards were renowned for the excellence of their ships' design and construction. In 1785 Vice-Admiral José de Mazarredo, probably the best Spanish admiral of that century, wrote of the 74-gun *San Ildefonso* that 'she sailed to windward like the frigates; she managed and tacked like a boat; she has a spacious battery ... stable in all positions, instances and circumstances'. The earlier problem of excessive pitching in heavy seas in ships such as the *Montañés*, *Neptuno* and *Argonauta* had been remedied by adjusting the distribution of ballast. Nelson considered that he 'never saw finer men-of-war' than the Spanish ships at Cadiz in 1793. He was delighted eight years later to hoist his flag on the 120-gun *San Josef* (the former *San José*, which he had captured at St Vincent), though its size and draught were too large for the shallow waters of the Baltic. Collingwood backed up his commander's opinion when he described the *Santa Ana,* the three-decker he fought at Trafalgar designed by the outstanding Spanish naval architect of the age, Romero y Landa, as a 'Spanish perfection'. Even Villeneuve, who was bitterly critical of his fleet's readiness for battle, praised his Spanish ships as being 'so beautiful, so strong'. Probably the finest ship in the Spanish Navy, and arguably the best ship at Trafalgar (another contender was the 80-gun *Argonauta*), was the 112-gun *Principe de Asturias*.

In 1796 Spain had 47 ships-of-the-line, but although their quality was unquestioned no new ships were built after the following year due to mounting economic problems. This, added to the fact that she lost ten ships in the period 1796 to 1802 (four captured at St Vincent, another at Trinidad and five destroyed on operations or burnt/blown up by accident), meant that by 1805 it was unlikely Spain could arm and provision the 30 ships required by her convention with France. At Trafalgar only half this number were present.

The British line-of-battle ships at Trafalgar had an average age of 17 years, with the oldest being the 43-year-old 100-gun *Britannia* and the newest, only launched in April 1805, the 74-gun *Revenge*. Most French ships had been built within the previous decade in order to replace heavy losses sustained at the Nile and elsewhere. The Spanish, however, had more older ships, with an average age of

24 years, their oldest being the positively ancient 100-gun *Rayo* built in 1749 (at 56 the oldest ship at the battle), and even their newest, the 74-gun *Argonauta*, was seven years old.

For over a decade prior to Trafalgar Spain had had difficulties manning her fleet with competent seamen. The years 1778–88 had seen a huge increase in Spanish trade with her overseas possessions in the Indies. This had led to the expansion of the merchant fleet. According to a review of seamen in 1787 Spain could muster 53,147 sailors of whom all but 5,800 were either fishermen or coastal craft sailors – but she needed 89,350 to man her fleet. In 1796 that fleet had almost 150 ships, including 47 of the line and 52 frigates, but their crews were predominantly landsmen and soldiers. On top of the manpower shortage came severe financial restrictions on repairing, building and supplying ships.

During the years immediately prior to Trafalgar a yellow-fever epidemic had struck along Spain's southern coastal regions. In February 1805 one in four of the 35,500 inhabitants of Malaga died of the disease. Then, despite the fact that Gravina had been introduced to the scurvy-repelling properties of lemon juice on his visit to England in 1793, Spain failed to introduce it even after the Royal Navy had done so in 1797. As Dr Julian de Zulueta wrote in his essay 'Trafalgar – The Spanish View':

> many were the Spanish officers and doctors ... made prisoners in a naval engagement and ... taken on board an English man-of-war, who must have witnessed the daily issue of grog with lemon juice. Yet none of them seems to have realised that lemon juice was one of the main ingredients in the English recipe for success in naval warfare.

In 1801 Admiral Mazarredo recalled in a letter to the King how in 1794 he had had only 60 trained seamen out of a complement of 500 – a mere 12 per cent; the other 440 'were without training or any understanding whatsoever of a ship's rigging or routine on board such as securing a topgallant sail from the yardarm or taking in a reef'. Gravina's report on 19 October 1805, the day he left Cadiz en route to Trafalgar, recorded only a marginal improvement. On board the 112-gun *Principe de Asturias* there were only 184 competent seamen out of a total complement of 1,113 – 16 per cent. Overall, of the 11,947 men on board the Spanish ships at the battle only some 18 per cent were mustered as trained seamen.

The officers were all royalists (the French Revolution had horrified, if not terrified, them), honourable men and staunch Roman Catholics. They were also aristocrats born to positions of authority. While degrees of professionalism varied, virtually all were personally courageous and a number of senior commanders skilled navigators. Religion played a crucial part in the life of all ranks on a Spanish ship, just as it did ashore throughout Spain. Of the fifteen ships at Trafalgar one was named for the 'Most Sacred Trinity' and another seven after saints. The priest on every ship was an officer of great importance. Before battle he would administer the Sacrament to all hands, prayers would be said and the captain would invariably make a supposedly morale-boosting speech. On the 74-gun *San Juan Nepomuceno* at Trafalgar Captain Churruca kept his message of encouragement short but hardly sweet. 'In God's name,' he is quoted as saying, 'I promise eternal blessedness to all who do their duty.' He then announced that those who failed in any way would be instantly shot, or, if they escaped the eyes of himself or his officers, would live their lives in a permanent state of wretchedness. Churruca, along with 103 others of his crew, died that day.

# THE TRAFALGAR FLEETS: A BALANCE SHEET

## THE SHIPS

The British under Nelson had 27 ships-of-the-line, four frigates, a schooner and a cutter. In the Combined Fleet under Villeneuve the French fielded 18 ships-of-the-line, five frigates and two brigs. The Spanish (with Gravina as second-in-command of the Combined Fleet) had 15 ships-of-the-line but nothing smaller.

Thus in the line of battle Nelson could count on 27 ships against Villeneuve's 33. An advantage of six battleships was a substantial one on paper but overall numbers were but a small part of the complex equation. The tables below provide a closer look at the statistics.

### British Fleet

| Rate | Guns | Ships | No. |
|------|------|-------|-----|
| 1st | 100+ | *Victory, Royal Sovereign, Britannia* | 3 |
| 2nd | 98 | *Dreadnought, Neptune, Prince, Téméraire* | 4 |
| 3rd | 80 | *Tonnant* | 1 |
| 3rd | 74 | *Achille, Ajax, Belleisle, Bellerophon, Colossus, Conqueror, Defence, Defiance, Leviathan, Mars, Minotaur, Orion, Revenge, Spartiate, Swiftsure, Thunderer* | 16 |
| 3rd | 64 | *Africa, Agamemnon, Polyphemus* | 3 |
| 5th | 38 | *Naiad* | 1 |
| 5th | 36 | *Euryalus, Phoebe, Sirius* | 3 |
| Schooner | 10 | *Pickle* | 1 |
| Cutter | 8 | *Entreprenante* | 1 |
| **Total** | | | **33** |

### Combined Fleet

#### French

| Rate | Guns | Ships | No. |
|------|------|-------|-----|
| 3rd | 80 | *Bucentaure, Formidable, Indomptable, Neptune* | 4 |
| 3rd | 74 | *Achille, Aigle, Algéciras, Argonaute, Berwick, Duguay-Trouin, Fougueux, Héros, Intrépide, Mont Blanc, Pluton, Redoutable, Scipion, Swiftsure* | 14 |
| 5th | 40 | *Cornélie, Hermione, Hortense, Rhin* | 4 |
| 5th | 36 | *Thémis* | 1 |
| Brig | 18 | *Furet* | 1 |
| Brig | 16 | *Argus* | 1 |
| **Total** | | | **25** |

#### Spanish

| Rate | Guns | Ships | No. |
|------|------|-------|-----|
| 1st | 136 | *Santisima Trinidad* | 1 |
| 1st | 112 | *Principe de Asturias, Santa Ana* | 2 |
| 1st | 100 | *Rayo* | 1 |
| 3rd | 80 | *Argonauta, Neptuno* | 2 |
| 3rd | 74 | *Bahama, Monarca, Montañés, San Augustin, San Francisco, San Ildefonso, San Juan Nepomuceno, San Justo* | 8 |
| 3rd | 64 | *San Leandro* | 1 |
| **Total** | | | **15** |
| **Combined Fleet Total** | | | **40** |

*Notes*

• The proportion of first-rate ships in the two fleets was about equal, comprising as they did 11 per cent of the British Fleet and 12 per cent of the Combined Fleet. This was due to the French (unusually) having no ship larger than a third rate. The three largest ships in the battle belonged to the Spanish. The *Santisima Trinidad* with 136 guns and four decks was the largest ship-of-the-line in the world. Both the *Principe de Asturias* and *Santa Ana*, with 112 guns each, were larger than the three British first rates (*Victory, Royal Sovereign* and *Britannia*).

• In size and number of guns on first rates the Combined Fleet had the advantage, but this is not the case when second rates are also taken into account. Both first and second rates were three-deckers, so the British had the considerable advantage of having seven three-deckers against four of the enemy. In a close action, a ship with three batteries had a very substantial edge over one with only two. This might be negated by heavy weather, which could force a three-decker to close her lower-deck ports, but at Trafalgar the wind was barely above a whisper.

• Apart from weight of fire (see below), a three-decker dominated ships of lower rates in a mêlée battle in other ways. Since the larger ships had higher decks, the marines firing their muskets could shoot down at their adversaries on smaller vessels, while it was exceedingly difficult for sharpshooters on the quarterdeck or forecastle of a two-decker to find a worthwhile target on a three-decker looming above them.

• The Combined Fleet had a superiority of 11 third-rate 80s and 74s (28 against 17), of which no fewer than six were the excellent 80-gun ships as against one British. Nelson was at a considerable disadvantage here, and having three of the much weaker 64s to his opponents' one compounded it. However, this was at least partially overcome by his comparatively large proportion of three-deckers, and this comparison of numbers and rates is only one factor, and not necessarily a critical one, when assessing the merits of each fleet at start of the battle.

## THE GUNS

It is the great, or long, guns of line-of-battle ships of each fleet that are compared here, discounting, initially, the carronades, which are discussed separately below. The figures below give a theoretical estimate of the potential firepower of each fleet in terms of the numbers of guns and the weight of metal they could throw. Frigates or smaller ships are not included as they played no part in the fighting.

### British Fleet

| | | | | | Type of gun (-pdr) | | | | | |
|---|---|---|---|---|---|---|---|---|---|---|
| Ships (-gun) | 36 | 32 | 24 | 18 | 12 | 9 | 8 | 6 | 4 | Total weight of both broadsides (lbs) |
| 1 x 102 | – | 30 | 28 | – | 44 | – | – | – | – | 2,160 |
| 1 x 100 | – | 28 | 28 | – | 44 | – | – | – | – | 2,096 |
| 1 x 100 | – | 28 | 28 | – | 28 | – | – | 16 | – | 2,000 |
| 3 x 98 | – | 84 | – | 180 | 30 | – | – | – | – | 6,288 |
| 1 x 98 | – | 28 | – | 30 | 30 | – | – | 10 | – | 1,806 |
| 1 x 80(66)* | – | 32 | – | 34 | – | – | – | – | – | 1,636 |
| 7 x 74 | – | 196 | – | 196 | – | 126 | – | – | – | 10,934 |
| 2 x 74 | – | 56 | – | 60 | – | 32 | – | – | – | 3,160 |
| 1 x 74 | – | – | 56 | – | – | 18 | – | – | – | 1,506 |
| 2 x 74(62)* | – | 28 | – | 34 | – | – | – | – | – | 1,508 |
| 1 x 74(66)* | – | 32 | 30 | – | – | 4 | – | – | – | 1,780 |
| 1 x 74 | – | 28 | 30 | – | – | 16 | – | – | – | 1,760 |
| 1 x 74(66)* | – | 30 | 36 | – | – | – | – | – | – | 1,824 |
| 1 x 74(66)* | – | 30 | – | 36 | – | – | – | – | – | 1,608 |
| 3 x 64 | – | – | 78 | 78 | – | 36 | – | – | – | 3,600 |
| **Total** | – | 630 | 314 | 648 | 176 | 232 | – | 26 | – | **43,666** |
| | | | | | | | | | | **(19.5 tons)** |

*Indicates the six ships that did not have the number of great guns for their rate – the balance being made up, or exceeded, by carronades. They were *Tonnant* (80) and *Achille, Belleisle, Colossus, Spartiate* and *Swiftsure*, all supposedly 74s.

*Notes*
• The largest gun in the British Fleet was the 32-pounder on the lower decks of all ships except one 74 (*Ajax*) and the 64s, although all the French and some Spanish ships had 36-pounders. These 32-pounders accounted for 31 per cent of the total of 2,026 guns carried by the British line of battle at Trafalgar. If 32-pounders and 24-pounders are counted as heavy guns then the British line-of-battle had 944 heavy guns, comprising 46 per cent of total gun armament.
• Perhaps the most remarkable thing is the almost complete lack of uniformity among every rate of ship – except for the three 64s. The 80 and five 74s carried fewer guns than their type indicates, for the reason that there was no uniformity as to the number or type of carronades that the various rates were supposed to carry. The gunnery arrangements on the poop, quarterdeck and forecastle were still left very much to the whim of the captains. Some substituted carronades for guns, some added them and some did not. In addition, three of the fleet were formerly French ships (*Tonnant, Spartiate* and *Belleisle*), with different dimensions and deck space from the British-built ships and different numbers and types of guns on the various decks. One 74, the *Ajax*, carried 24-pounders on both her gundecks, while the *Belleisle, Mars* and *Colossus* had 24-pounders on their upper deck rather than the more usual 18-pounders. All somewhat confusing.

### French Fleet

| | | | | | Type of gun (-pdr) | | | | | |
|---|---|---|---|---|---|---|---|---|---|---|
| Ships (-gun) | 36 | 32 | 24 | 18 | 12 | 9 | 8 | 6 | 4 | Total weight of both broadsides (lbs) |
| 4 x 80 | 120 | – | 128 | – | 72 | – | – | – | – | 8,256 |
| 14 x 74 | 392 | – | 420 | – | – | – | 224 | – | – | 25,984 |
| **Total** | 512 | – | 548 | – | 72 | – | 224 | – | – | **34,240** |
| | | | | | | | | | | **(15 tons)** |

*Notes*
• The most important difference between the French and British ships at Trafalgar was that the French had 36- rather than 32-pounders on the lower decks. This immediately gave them heavier broadsides than Nelson's ships of the same rate. It is this factor that gave the total weight of fire of the 18 French ships: 34,240 lbs or 78 per cent of the British weight of fire.

• These heavier guns in the French ships compensated to some extent for their lack of any three-deckers. If we count the 24- to 36-pounder guns as heavy then the French carried 1,060 heavy guns – a very high proportion (78 per cent) of their total armaments, and one that far exceeded the equivalent figure for the British and Spanish fleets.

## Spanish Fleet

| | Type of gun (-pdr) | | | | | | | | | |
|---|---|---|---|---|---|---|---|---|---|---|
| Ships (-gun) | 36 | 32 | 24 | 18 | 12 | 9 | 8 | 6 | 4 | Total weight of both broadsides (lbs) |
| 1 x 136* | 34 | – | 34 | 34 | – | – | 18 | – | 6 | 2,820 |
| 2 x 112 | 60 | – | 64 | – | 64 | – | 36 | – | – | 5,112 |
| 1 x 100 | 30 | – | 32 | 30 | – | – | 10 | – | – | 2,468 |
| 2 x 80* | – | 60 | – | 64 | 20 | – | – | – | – | 3,312 |
| 8 x 74 | – | 224 | 28 | 240 | – | – | 128 | – | – | 13,184 |
| 1 x 64 | – | – | 28 | 30 | – | – | 6 | – | – | 1,274 |
| Total | 124 | 284 | 186 | 398 | 84 | – | 198 | – | 6 | 28,170 |
| | | | | | | | | | | 12.5 tons |

• Indicates ships whose number of guns do not equal that for their rate. The *Santisima Trinidad* had an additional ten obusiers (howitzers) making up her 136. Similarly the *Argonauta* and *Neptuno* had up to 18 howitzers on their quarterdecks and forecastles.

*Notes*
• Only the first-rate Spanish ships carried 36-pounders and had 24-pounders on their middle decks.
• The Spanish 80s and 74s were comparatively lightly armed with 18-pounders on their upper decks rather than the much heavier 24s carried by the French. In this respect they were the same as the 80 and 13 of the British 74s. They carried 594 heavy guns (24- to 36-pounders) which, at 46 per cent, exactly matched the British figure.

## CARRONADES

Comparing the fleets solely on the basis of their guns does not give an accurate picture of their firepower, as additional carronades and/or howitzers were mounted on the poop, quarterdeck and forecastle of many of the ships of both fleets at Trafalgar. Carronades were particularly effective at close range, where they could sweep the upper decks of an enemy with a more powerful and deadly blast of metal while utilizing less manpower or space than a gun. As has been noted, in 1805 carronades and howitzers were still not officially counted when rating a ship. Our sources as to precisely how many and what calibre carronades were carried by each ship are vague, reflecting the general uncertainty at the time. The notes below are best estimates.

## British Fleet

In 1794 the Admiralty had laid down an official complement of carronades, but it was to be implemented only for new ships or for old ones that came in for a complete refit. Initially the carronades were intended to be in addition to the complement of guns but by 1797 they had begun to replace some of them. However, by the early 1800s the situation was still confused. In his book *Nelson's Navy* Brian Lavery quotes a source as stating that carronades were 'so unequally [carried] on board ships of the same class, that it is not possible to give [a] general statement of the ordnance now in use'. This was certainly the case of the ships at Trafalgar. On the right is a list of the British line-of-battle ships known with some degree of certainty to have carried carronades at the battle. There are likely to have been others, such as the *Royal Sovereign*.

| Ship | Carronades carried (-pdr) | | |
|---|---|---|---|
| | poop | quarterdeck | forecastle |
| *Victory* | – | – | 2 x 68 |
| *Tonnant* | – | 14 x 32 | 4 x 32 |
| *Achille* | 6 x 18 | 10 x 32 | 2 x 32 |
| *Ajax* | – | 8 x 32 | – |
| *Belleisle* | 2 x 24 | 14 x 32 | 2 x 24 |
| *Bellerophon* | 8 x 18 | – | 2 x 32 |
| *Colossus* | 6 x 18 | 10 x 32 | 2 x 24 |
| *Conqueror* | 6 x 18 | – | 2 x 32 |
| *Revenge* | 6 x 18 | – | 2 x 32 |
| *Spartiate* | – | 14 x 32 | 6 x 32 |
| *Swiftsure* | 6 x 18 | 10 x 32 | 2 x 32 |

*Notes*
• Only about 41 per cent of Nelson's ships can be confirmed as having carronades. Those that did thereby massively increased their broadsides. As an example the ship carrying the most, the former French *Belleisle*, had a guns-only single-broadside weight of 890 lbs. Her 18 carronades added another 272 lbs, giving a total of 1,162 lbs for each of her broadsides. However, the partial replacement of lighter guns by carronades made a mockery of the classification of ships by the number of great guns carried. At Trafalgar the so-called 74-gun *Belleisle* had 66 great guns and 18 carronades, making her an 84. The *Colossus*, another so-called 74, had only 64 guns plus 18 carronades, making her an 82.
• There was some uniformity with the recently built 74s *Achille* (1798), *Colossus* (1803), *Swiftsure* (1804) and *Revenge* (1805), which had carronades distributed between the poop, quarterdeck and forecastle.

## The Guns at Trafalgar Compared to Those at Waterloo

Compared to the firepower of the three fleets at Trafalgar, that available to the three armies at Waterloo was strikingly little. **Numbers** At Waterloo the British fielded 141 guns, their allies the Prussians 134 and the French 222 – a total of 497 guns on the battlefield. At Trafalgar the British had 2,026 and the Combined Fleet 2,636 – a total of 4,662 guns, more than nine times the Waterloo figure.
**Calibre** The guns at Waterloo ranged from 6-pounders through to the maximum 12-pounders; at Trafalgar the smallest guns were 4-pounders but they ranged right up to 36-pounders.

**Weight of fire** If all the artillery at Waterloo fired simultaneously they would have fired 1.5 tons of metal. If the fleets at Trafalgar had done the same they would have fired 47 tons – 31 times more! The French at Waterloo amassed 80 guns into what was termed their 'Grand Battery' to soften up the British position for half an hour prior to launching their main infantry assault. One volley from these guns threw 0.25 tons. This was exceeded by the total broadsides of a single 74 such as the *Mars*, which alone could fire 0.75 tons of shot.

### French Fleet

Villeneuve's fleet at Trafalgar had some carronades but it is unlikely that every ship had procured a full complement of them before the battle. Their value was recognized by Napoleon himself, and he was the driving force behind arming every French ship with these and larger-calibre guns. His intention was to abolish all guns from 12-pounders downwards on all ships (including frigates), along with the six obusiers (howitzers) carried on the quarterdeck/forecastle of all line-of-battle ships. He envisaged his fleet being armed solely with 36-pounder guns and 36-pounder carronades. As late as March 1805 he was writing to Decrès (Minister of Marine), 'I have spoken several times of my project of arming ships of the line with guns of the same calibre. ... I think this carronade will have greater power than an ordinary 18-pounder.'

As the weeks went by with seemingly little action to this end Napoleon's letters to Decrès became increasingly insistent, if not desperate.

*13 March*
In this war the English have been the first to use carronades, and everywhere they have done us great harm. We must hasten to perfect their system, for the argument is all on one side for sea service in favour of the system of large calibres, and we ought to put calibres higher than 36 if it were not for the difficulty of handling the shot. I specially desire that you will not lose sight of an object so important.

The difficulty lay in actually procuring enough carronades and getting them onto the ships. Unfortunately, Napoleon's Minister of Marine seemed unable to instil the necessary urgency into his rambling and inefficient departments.

*2 June*
It was with carronades the English set the *L'Orient* on fire [at the Nile] and in them they have an immense advantage over us ...

*13 June*
The least that can be asked of the administrative branch is that soldiers shall fight with equal arms, it is the first duty of a minister, and nothing can excuse his not fulfilling it. Have we not disadvantage enough without that of armament? Your 'ifs' and 'buts' – that is no justification.

*22 June*
But for God's sake ship me some carronades. It is only with guns you can arm ships of the line, and for ships of the line there is nothing but guns of heavy calibre.

*5 July*
The English, without saying a word, have practised this method [mounting carronades]. Here's ten years we are behind their Admiralty ... I see no attention being paid to it.

However, Napoleon's insistence on having heavier guns clearly had some results. All the French ships at Trafalgar had 36-pounders on the lower gundeck and 24-pounders on the upper deck – considerably out-gunning all British ships of similar rates. Decrès's efforts with carronades were less convincing. There is some evidence that Villeneuve's line-of-battle ships had 36-pounder carronades on the poop but not elsewhere. The distribution was, seemingly, uniform – six for 80-gun ships and four for 74s. Again these were much heavier than any British carronades except for the two on the *Victory*. The five French frigates all appear to have had two 36-pounder carronades on both quarterdeck and forecastle. Nevertheless, a hint that the French were probably not fully equipped with carronades comes from Major-General Contamine, commanding the embarked army expeditionary force, who in his after-action report commented:

... the enormous height of their ships [British three-deckers] gave them great command over ours, and made the effect of the musketry and of the fire of the 32-pounder – and sometimes 64-pounder – [reference to *Victory*'s 68-pounder] carronades with which their poops were armed very deadly.

### Spanish Fleet

The evidence as to whether any Spanish ships at Trafalgar carried carronades is fragmentary and inconclusive. Napoleon makes no mention of his allies having them, and in view of his opinions on the subject he would surely have used Spanish possession of carronades as another stick with which to beat his Minister of Marine. It is more likely that Gravina's ships had howitzers (obusiers) augmenting the lighter guns on the quarterdeck and forecastle. The *Santisima Trinidad*'s complement of 136 guns consisted of 126 great guns and 10 howitzers, and the two newest 80s (*Argonauta* and *Neptuno*) carried 18 howitzers each and the *Principe de Asturias* 16.

## Summary

| British Fleet | | Combined Fleet | |
|---|---|---|---|
| Three-deckers (98–102) | 7 | Three-deckers (100–136) | 4 |
| Two-deckers (80) | 1 | Two-deckers (80) | 6 |
| Two-deckers (74) | 16 | Two-deckers (74) | 22 |
| Two-deckers (64) | 3 | Two-deckers (64) | 1 |
| Single deckers (36–38) | 4 | Single-deckers (40) | 5 |
| Unrated ships (10) | 2 | Unrated ships (16–18) | 2 |
| Total guns | 2,026 | Total guns | 2,636 |
| Total weight of broadside | 19.5 tons | Total weight of broadside | 27.5 tons |
| Proportion of 24- to 32-pdrs | 46% | Proportion of 24- to 26-pdrs | 63% |

## PERSONNEL

### British Fleet

The approximate total number of British personnel on the ships at Trafalgar is 18,438, including four frigates and the two smaller ships. (For a more detailed breakdown, see Section Four.) On ships-of-the-line that participated in the battle the total was approximately 17,237. This was divided as follows:

| | |
|---|---|
| Naval personnel | 14,684 |
| Royal Marines | 2,553 |

*Notes*

• Only eight ships carried crews that were up to strength or slightly over. However, the proportion of trained naval warrant officers, petty officers and seamen to landsmen and boys was high, with approximately five of the former ratings to one of the latter.

• There were 2,700 Royal Marines (including officers) at Trafalgar. Of these 2,553 were on line-of-battle ships – 15 per cent of total manpower. As will be seen below, this was markedly less than the equivalent French figure and dramatically less than the Spanish.

• The average number of marines on a British 74 at Trafalgar was 90, which if carronades are counted gives a rough figure of just over one per gun.

The officers in the British Fleet were exceptionally experienced professionals. Strictly speaking Nelson's trusted 'band of brothers' were the captains who had served under him at the Nile, and only two of them were at Trafalgar (Hardy and Berry). Nevertheless, when handed the Navy List by Lord Barham, the First Lord of the Admiralty, in September and told he could select his own officers Nelson replied, 'Choose yourself, my lord, the same spirit actuates the whole profession; you cannot choose wrong.' His confidence was entirely justified by his officers' performance during the battle, and by the fact

### Sickness in Nelson's Fleet

In a report to Nelson, dated *Victory* at Spithead 18 August 1805, Leonard Gillespie, the physician of the fleet, certified the number of sick in the ships just returned from the West Indies. They were as follows: *Victory* 14; *Canopus* 36; *Superb* 20; *Spencer* 15; *Swiftsure* 29; *Belleisle* 15; *Conqueror* 10; *Tigre* 11; *Leviathan* 26 and *Donegal* 19; a total of 195 out of 5,500–6,000 men, or 3 or 4 per cent. This is very low compared to the equivalent French and Spanish figures.

Gillespie added that of these sick only 23 were cases of scurvy, alongside 9 fluxes, 10 fever, 32 ulcers, 45 wounds and accidents, 10 rheumatism, 23 'pulmonic inflammations', 2 venereal disease (on *Donegal*) and 60 other complaints. These total 214, which does not correspond with the number listed sick. However he goes on to elaborate on the subject of scorbutics (those showing early signs of scurvy but who have not yet developed the disease): 'The number of scorbutics has considerably decreased in the Fleet, in consequence of the refreshments procured at Tetuan and Gibraltar. *Spencer* and *Tigre* have 40 scorbutics each; *Belleisle* 160 scorbutics; *Conqueror* 36 scorbutics.' It appears that these were not included on the sick list as they presumably remained on duty.

that of the 29 captains (of ships-of-the-line and frigates) who survived no fewer than 22 became admirals.

The roles of seamen and marines have been discussed in some detail in previous sections so all that is necessary here is to summarize how their morale and training gave Nelson a battle-winning edge over his enemy at Trafalgar.

• Although many ships were slightly under full complement (*Victory* was almost 30 men short), most crew members were volunteers, with a comparatively small proportion of landsmen. Again, most had been placed on the muster books in 1803, which meant they had around two years' sea experience prior to the battle. In this time a large number of the landsmen had become useful sailors.

• British sailors' morale was high and they desperately wanted a fight; they were delighted to be serving under their beloved Nelson and they knew that, given a chance, they were more than a match for any enemy, no matter how many ships he had. When the Combined Fleet was sighted early on 21 October off watch, crews stampeded up the hatchways cheering and yelling. There at last was the elusive foe they had chased for so many months.

• This supreme confidence in their admiral's and their own ability came from the knowledge that they knew their job. They could tack or wear in a matter of minutes, they could fire their great guns every 90 seconds (their opponents took from four to five minutes). They understood the tactics of their admiral and their captains. Their ships would make every endeavour to close with the enemy so they could hit and smash hulls.

• Finally, and very importantly, the British crews were healthy, far more so than their French and Spanish counterparts. Sickness levels were low due to Nelson and his captains' dedication to ensuring that ships were clean and as much fresh food and citrus fruit as possible was provided during the previous long months at sea, which included the slog to the West Indies. On Nelson's return to Spithead on 18 August 1805 he referred to the crews of *Victory* and *Superb* as being 'in perfect health'. Some illuminating statistics underline the huge improvements made in British fleets in the twenty years prior to Trafalgar. In the Caribbean, that notoriously unhealthy station, in 1781 Admiral Rodney lost 1,516 men out of about 12,000 (one man in eight) from sickness. Nelson, in the two years 1803–5, lost 110 dead and 141 hospitalized out of 6,500 (one man in 26). Health had become a battle-winning, indeed a war-winning, factor.

## Combined Fleet

The French Fleet was in a sorry state when it returned from the West Indies, with worn-out ships and some 1,500 sick seamen. The Minister of Marine summarized the situation and what needed to be done in his letter of 23 August to Napoleon.

> Here I will consider the present state of affairs. Admirals full of honour but depressed by the difficulties which they have encountered; crews to be heartened; ships of every description in part ill-equipped, ill-manned, ill-commanded, of differing sailing qualities and whose very number daunts and disconcerts those entrusted to command them, who have never had such a burden to bear ... It is a question of restoring the confidence of men disheartened, who will certainly be beaten by the enemy if a better opinion of themselves and of the service which they are called upon to perform cannot be instilled into them.

That was two months before Trafalgar. Ten days later, sitting in Cadiz, Vice-Admiral Villeneuve continued to bombard the same Minister of Marine with letters bemoaning his problems and lack of improvement in the state of his ships and crews, both French and Spanish. Southern Spain having recently been ravaged by yellow fever, manpower, any manpower, was at a premium and the Spanish authorities were themselves short of funds and in no mood to supply their own let alone the French ships with anything that was not paid for in cash up front. To quote General Beurnonville, France's Ambassador in Madrid, 'We lack everything at this present time, the magazines and arsenals are drained, the public treasuries are empty, and the Treasury Redemption Office – the only bank which was paying – has somehow just suspended payment.' That was as late as 9 September.

The French Agent in Cadiz, whose thankless daily task was to try to squeeze blood from the Spanish stone, was the Commissioner for Commercial Affairs, a Monsieur Le Roy. Seemingly he was not equal to the task. Villeneuve's letter of 2 September to Decrès is illuminating.

> The lack of funds, the poverty of the port, the great requirements of the ships, and those of the crews, increase in proportion to the time that is passing ... M. Le Roy is to write to you, giving in detail the expenditure to which he is pledged. An ill-equipped Squadron has not been able to pass nearly five months at sea, without having requirements of every description; there are ships which have scarcely a set of sails in good condition. I am urging M. Le Roy to procure supplies; I have known him a long while, I know that he is full of zeal, of honesty, that he is animated by the keenest desire to do right, but unfortunately he is not gifted with the disposition that gains him the attachment of the men with whom he has to do business; also his credit is practically nil, and our stores and re-victualling suffer from it accordingly. I am writing to the Ambassador and am appealing for his assistance.

Monsieur Le Roy was obviously an abrasive character not well suited to the delicate task of extracting supplies and support from reluctant allies. Even the Inspector of Artillery refused to supply shot or powder unless paid in cash, until given a direct order from Madrid. Villeneuve's letter makes two other relevant points.

> The Spanish Squadron is improving appreciably by the exchange of bad ships for better ones; nevertheless, it will only number 15 of the line for want of seamen ...

and

> The sickness continuing in the *Achille* and *Algéciras*, I have ordered these ships to shift their stores to the ground tier, to scour and to lime-wash everywhere.

Two weeks after this letter he sent a detailed report on each French ship that would fight at Trafalgar to Decrès. Six ships are listed as having 'weak crews' and to be suffering from excessive 'sickness'. Seven are described as 'poor sailers', 'crank', in a 'bad condition', 'an indifferent sailer', 'making six inches of water an hour', 'foremast badly wounded by shot' or 'bottom bad'. Only five ships (*Bucentaure*, *Argonaute*, *Neptune*, *Duguay-Trouin* and *Redoutable*) come out unscathed.

On 24 September, while praising the quality of the Spanish ships Villeneuve deplored the state of the crews.

> What is essentially lacking in this [Spanish] Squadron is seamen and the funds to supply them with clothing; it is very distressing to see such fine and powerful ships manned by herdsmen and beggars and having such a small number of seamen.

Four days later he was to write:

> Your Excellency will observe that the shortage of the crews amounts to 2,207 men; we have 649 men in the hospitals at Cadiz of whom perhaps a third may be fit to embark at the moment of setting sail.

Pessimist though he undoubtedly was it is difficult not to feel some sympathy for the Combined Fleet's commander as he struggled to get his ships and crews ready for sea. Not only did many ships and most seamen give rise to much anxiety, but the quality and quantity of provisions for the three-month voyage ordered were also worrisome. In yet another letter on 24 September he stated:

> The bad quality of some of these stores has doubtless contributed to the deterioration which they have suffered but one of the principal causes is the length of time they have been on board. Amongst the ships fitted out at Toulon there are some which have biscuit and flour eighteen months old ... all the *Redoutable*'s biscuit has been condemned as unfit to be taken on a cruise, it has been made close to two years. ... This kind of loss adds greatly to the difficulty I experience in provisioning for a three months' cruise. About 2,000 quintals (one quintal equals 100 kg) of biscuit and 250 kegs of lard are still wanting ... the Spanish Navy were pledged to provide me with this and they have not been able to deliver it.

Villeneuve's pessimism continued into October. On 8 October he held a Council of War with fourteen of his senior commanders on his flagship the 80-gun *Bucentaure*. An extract of the minutes records:

> The ships of the two Allied nations are for the most part badly manned from the weakness of the crews; that several of the ships have never yet been able to exercise their people at sea in any way and that the three-deckers

*Santa Ana* and *Rayo,* and the *San Justo* 74, fitted out in haste and barely out of the dockyard, can in extreme necessity put to sea with the Fleet but that they are by no means in a state to render the service in action of which they will be capable when they are completely organized.

He is referring primarily to the crewing problems here as Spanish ships such as the *Santa Ana* were of excellent design.

## French Fleet

On 1 October Villeneuve wrote to his minister:

My Lord,
I have the honour to inform your Excellency that General Lauriston left here yesterday, and also General Reille. General Lauriston was saluted with 11 guns on leaving the *Bucentaure,* agreeably to the Imperial decree concerning military honours.

The expeditionary troops embarked the same day [4,000 men destined to be landed at Naples according to Napoleon's orders]; they are commanded by Adjutant-Commandant [Major-General] Contamine, appointed by General Lauriston, as you gave orders.

Personnel on board the French Fleet at Trafalgar were divided into three broad categories – naval, marine artillery and army expeditionary troops. When there were no army personnel on board the marine artillery (*Corps Imperial de l'Artillerie de la Marine*), who were armed with muskets, bayonets and swords, were required to act as infantry if necessary. The approximate breakdown (including officers) for French ships-of-the-line is as follows:

| | |
|---|---|
| Naval personnel | 9,173 |
| Marine artillery | 900 |
| Army troops | 4,000 |
| **Total** | **14,073** |

*Notes*
• Marine artillery personnel on board usually comprised around 10 per cent of the total. The number of purely infantry troops could be boosted by drafting in Army soldiers. On many occasions these extra men were troops in transit intended primarily for land operations, examples being Villeneuve's expedition to the West Indies earlier in 1805 – and the soldiers destined for Naples at Trafalgar. Elements, possibly a company or two from each of the 1st, 2nd, 3rd and 4th Marine Artillery Regiments were present, primarily as gun captains, on French ships at the battle.
• The 4,000-strong Army expeditionary force that fought at Trafalgar was made up of battalions (or detachments) from the 2nd, 16th, 67th, 70th, 79th and 93rd Ligne (Line). They were supported by detachments from the 1st Swiss and 6th Depot Colonial Regiments, two companies (batteries) of foot artillery and two troops of dismounted Chasseurs d'Orient. All these men were supposed to disembark at Naples for land operations. They comprised some 28 per cent of the men sailing on French ships. Villeneuve intended them to be used to make up crew deficiencies – if only for muscle power and musketry. On 28 September he wrote, 'The expeditionary troops will be able to make up this shortage but they cannot supplement the small number of seamen that are left to us.'

• On the same day (28 September) General Lauriston, then still the commander of the troops, reported to the Minister of Marine as follows:

The troops are beginning to recover well [from their miserable voyage to and from the Caribbean]; they are drilled daily. The morale of the two corps, the 16th and 67th is excellent, they are commanded by very good officers. I wish most sincerely that they may not have to go on a long cruise; they would then be in the same condition as the 2nd Regiment, which will be a very long time before it recovers from the dispersion which it has suffered.

These two corps have few sick in Cadiz; they will, at least at the time of landing, be fit to serve a campaign. The 16th will have 1400 men, not including the 350 sick left in Vigo; the 67th form one battalion of 650 men, not including 120 left in Vigo. ...

I have induced Admiral Villeneuve to distribute them equally to each [French] ship, so that they may only have to perform supplementary duties on board. Several ships lack a large number of seamen; it was desired to make up for them with the troops, which would by no means have achieved the object and would have fatigued and exhausted men neither clad for, nor accustomed to, the working of a ship.

These soldiers suffered approximately 224 casualties at Trafalgar. The commanding officer of the 67th, Chef de Bataillon (major) Jacquemet, distinguished himself by saving the Eagle of his regiment despite serious wounds.

## Spanish Fleet

The Spanish Navy suffered from identical personnel problems as the French, with the possible exception of her officers, many of whom were experienced seamen and navigators. At Trafalgar Gravina brought the following estimated manpower to the battle – all figures include officers:

| | |
|---|---|
| Naval (including naval artillery) | 6,881 * |
| Army – infantry | 4,135 |
| Artillery | 931 |
| **Total** | **11,947** |

* only about 1,240, 18 per cent, trained seamen

*Notes*
• Although Spanish ships sailed with more than their overall complement this was due to the large Army contingent (infantry and artillery), which in no way made up for the acute shortage of seamen. Much of the problem was due to the large numbers of sick. In 1793 Nelson had written of this problem on Spanish ships: 'The Captain of the (Spanish) frigate said, "It was no wonder they were sickly, for they had been sixty days at sea." By then a British crew would be in fine condition.' 713 Spaniards were left behind in hospitals in Cadiz when the fleet sailed.
• Some 42 per cent of all personnel on Spanish ships were soldiers, compared with 28 per cent for the French and 15 for the British. The 15 ships carried some 5,066 soldiers giving an average of over 330 on each ship-of-the-line. Many (particularly the infantrymen) would have been put to work hauling, heaving, lifting and cleaning – the *Santa Ana* needed 250 men on her capstans to raise her five anchors.

According to Gravina's report (now in the Naval Museum, Madrid), on 19 October of the 5,066 military personnel 4,135 were infantrymen and 931 army gunners.

• Units providing the infantry were the Regimento de Africa, de Burgos, de Cordoba, de Corona and de Soria. Detachments from the Regimento de America and the Voluntarios de Cataluna were also present. Probably between two and three companies were on every Spanish ship.

• It is a reasonable estimate that one man in three in the Combined Fleet was military as distinct from naval – less than one in five could be accurately described as a seaman.

## SUMMARY OF EACH FLEET'S ADVANTAGES

| **British** | **French/Spanish** |
|---|---|
| Four more three-deckers | Six more line-of-battle ships |
| More experienced and professional officers | More heavy guns |
| More trained and very experienced seamen | Overall heavier broadsides |
| More skilled gunners | |
| Higher morale and confidence | |
| More effective battle tactics | |

**Manpower comparison (line-of-battle ships)**

|  | Naval | Military | Total | Military as % of total |
|---|---|---|---|---|
| British | 14,684 | 2,553 | 17,237 | 15 |
| Combined | 16,954 | 9,066 | 26,020 | 35 |
| French | 10,073 | 4,000 | 14,073 | 28 |
| Spanish | 6,881 | 5,066 | 11,947 | 42 |

Quite apart from command, which is discussed in Section Seven, the British had an overwhelming advantage in all aspects of personnel training, experience and morale. Against these the Combined Fleet's slight numerical and material advantages were to prove, unsurprisingly, of modest value.

The following part of this section gives details of the ships in each fleet at the battle, including rate, age, armament, complement, sailing ability and condition. There are notes on the captain (admirals are discussed under Section Seven), the ship's role at Trafalgar, the casualties and damage she suffered and her subsequent fate. The British Fleet was divided into two divisions but their order of sailing did not exactly correspond to the two columns Nelson eventually led into action; here they are shown in the weather (Nelson) and lee (Collingwood) columns as near as possible to the order in which they came into action. The Combined Fleet was initially divided into five divisions (van, centre, rear, and an observation division of two squadrons). However, by the time the battle was joined the fleet had come about so the van had become the rear and the squadron of observation part of the line at the rear. Because of this confusion the Combined Fleet's ships are listed as near as possible to the order of battle starting in the north, at about noon on 21 October – just as the action opened.

## Ships of the Same Name

The fact that nine ships of three different nationalities shared four names can be confusing for the reader. They were:

| **British** | **French** | **Spanish** |
|---|---|---|
| *Neptune* | *Neptune* | *Neptuno* |
| | *Argonaute* | *Argonauta* |
| *Achille* | *Achille* | |
| *Swiftsure* | *Swiftsure* | |

# THE BRITISH FLEET

# *Victory*

## Officers

| | |
|---|---|
| Flag Officer | Vice-Admiral Viscount H. Nelson (k) |
| Admiral's Sec. | J. Scott (k) |
| Agent Victualler | R. Ford |
| Captain | T.M. Hardy |
| Lieuts | |
| J. Quilliam (1st) | J. Pasco (w) |
| E. Williams | G. Brown |
| A. King | W.A. Ram (k) |
| J. Yule | A. Hills |
| G.M. Bligh (w) | |
| Captain RM | C.W. Adair (k) |
| 1st Lieut. RM | J.G. Peake (w) |
| 2nd Lieuts RM | L. Rotely |
| | L.B.Reeves (w) |

## Warrant Officers

| | |
|---|---|
| Master | T. Atkinson |
| Surgeon | W. Beatty |
| Chaplain | Rev. A.J. Scott |
| Carpenter | W. Bunce |
| Boatswain | W. Willmet (w) |
| Gunner | W. Rivers |
| Purser | W. Burke |

(w) = wounded; (k) = killed

## History/Characteristics

- The flagship of Vice-Admiral Nelson, a first-rate three-decker built at Chatham and launched in 1765, making her the second oldest British ship at Trafalgar. She had been Sir John Jervis's flagship at St Vincent in 1797, but later that year was declared unfit for service and ordered to be converted to a hospital ship. However, she was refitted as a three-decker in 1799 and became Nelson's flagship in the Mediterranean in 1803. Despite her age she sailed well, although she was not the fastest ship in the fleet.

- Armament 102 guns:
  lower deck 30 x 32-pdrs
  middle deck 28 x 24-pdrs
  upper deck 30 x 12-pdrs
  quarterdeck 12 x 12-pdrs
  forecastle 2 x 12-pdrs + 2 x 68-pdr carronades
  + 1 x 18-pdr carronade for launch
- Crew 823 (naval 677, RM 146)

## Commanded by

Captain Thomas Masterman Hardy, the only captain to have served with Nelson at all of his four fleet actions. He was a tall, heavily built man of a reserved and unemotional nature – quite the reverse of Nelson. Born in 1769, he was entered on the muster book for service as a twelve-year-old in 1781 but continued to attend school. After a period in the merchant service he re-entered the Royal Navy as a midshipman in 1790 and served in the Mediterranean. In 1793 he became a lieutenant on the 38-gun frigate *Minerve* with Nelson, the start of a long friendship. On one occasion Nelson risked losing his ship to save Hardy from capture by the Spanish (see p. 155).

Hardy was present at St Vincent in 1797 and appointed to command the French 18-gun brig-sloop *Mutine* after leading a cutting-out expedition to capture her at Santa Cruz the same year. He served in her throughout the Nile campaign. Promoted captain in 1798, he was given command of Nelson's flagship the 74-gun *Vanguard*. In 1801 Nelson asked for him as his flag captain on the *San Josef and St George*, and Hardy took soundings in a small boat of the approaches to Copenhagen before the battle. Finally, in 1803, he became once more flag captain to Nelson in the *Victory* for the Trafalgar campaign and battle.

Hardy was beside Nelson when the admiral was mortally wounded and visited him twice as he lay dying in the cockpit, bidding him farewell with his famous kiss. He brought Nelson's body home and participated in the funeral ceremonies. He received a gold medal, the thanks of parliament, a Patriotic Fund £100 sword of honour and £500 silver vase (the only officer to receive both Fund awards). He spent the rest of the war commanding the 74-gun *Triumph* on the North America station, and lived to become a Vice-Admiral and First Sea Lord before becoming governor of Greenwich Hospital. He died, and was buried there aged seventy, in 1839.

## At the battle

*Victory* led the weather (northernmost) column and came under fire at about 12.15 p.m. before breaking the enemy line at about 12.30. She raked and severely damaged Villeneuve's flagship, the *Bucentaure*, before running aboard the *Redoutable*, which ultimately struck to the *Victory*; it was while they were locked together that Nelson was shot. *Victory* suffered 159 casualties (57 killed, 102 wounded) and disabling damage, necessitating her being placed under tow. The master's log is somewhat cursory in describing her condition – 'At 5, the mizzen mast fell about 10 feet above the poop. The lower masts, yards and bowsprit all crippled. Rigging and sails very much cut.' Nevertheless, despite being in continuous action for over four hours and heavily battered, she was still capable of firing her guns to the end.

## After the battle

She was towed to Gibraltar by *Polyphemus*, repaired at Chatham in 1806 and recommissioned in 1808 as a second-rate 98. In 1809 she acted as troopship during the evacuation of British troops from Corunna before being laid up in 1812 to undergo extensive repairs at Portsmouth. In 1824 she became the flagship of the Port Admiral, and in 1889 became the flagship of the commander-in-chief, Naval Home Command. *Victory* currently acts as flagship of the Second Sea Lord, thus being the oldest commissioned warship in the world.

*Victory*
jury-rigged, under tow en route
to Gibraltar with Nelson's body

# *Téméraire*

## Officers

Captain      E. Harvey
Lieuts
    T.F. Kennedy (1st)    W. Smith
    H.C. Coxen         J. Wallace
    B. Vallack          A. Davidson
    J. Mould (w)       T. Coakley (acting)
Captain RM         S. Busigny (k)
2nd Lieuts RM     S.J. Payne (w)
    J. Kingston (k)    W.N. Roe

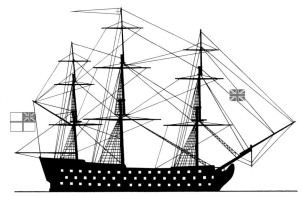

## Warrant Officers

Master      T. Price
Surgeon    T. Caird
Chaplain    Rev. J. Sherer
Carpenter   L. Oades (k)
Boatswain   J. Brooks (w)
Gunner      F. Harris
Purser       W. Ballingall

---

## History/Characteristics

- Built 1798 at Chatham, a comparatively new three-decked second-rate which had done nothing very exciting before Trafalgar. A good sailer, she was named the 'Fighting *Téméraire*' by Turner in his 1838 painting, although seamen called her the 'Saucy *Téméraire*'. When her crew were ordered to the West Indies after several years at sea they plotted mutiny, but the officers quickly put it down. Eighteen were hanged at Spithead in January 1802.

- Armament 98 guns:
  lower deck 28 x 32-pdrs
  middle deck 30 x 18-pdrs
  upper deck 30 x 18-pdrs
  quarterdeck 8 x 12-pdrs
  forecastle 2 x 12-pdrs
- Crew 755 (naval 625, RM 130).
  Of the total ship's company 220 were Irish.

---

## Commanded by

Captain Eliab Harvey. Born like Nelson in 1758, he was a long-serving naval officer, MP and enthusiastic gambler, with a violent temper. Harvey had been a captain for twenty-two years in 1805 (making him the senior British captain at Trafalgar) but had yet to command a ship in a general action. His first service was as a midshipman under Lord Howe on the North American station during the American War of Independence. He was MP for Maldon, Essex, 1780–1, then commanded the *Santa Margaritta* at the reduction of Martinique and Guadeloupe in 1794. He became MP for Essex again in 1802 until 1812 and commander of the *Téméraire* on the recommencement of the war in 1803. He greatly distinguished himself at Trafalgar and was well rewarded with the thanks of parliament, promotion to rear-admiral and a gold medal (but not a sword of honour, which he declined in favour of another unspecified award), and was a pall-bearer at Nelson's funeral. In 1809 he was insubordinate to Lord Gambier (he declared he had never seen a man so unfit to command) and was dismissed by a court martial, despite apologizing profusely. Within a year all was forgiven and he became a vice-admiral, being promoted to admiral in 1819. He was an MP (again for Essex) from 1820 until his death in 1830 aged seventy-two.

## At the battle

The second ship in the weather column, close behind the *Victory*, *Téméraire* broke the enemy line at around 12.30 p.m. and was heavily engaged throughout the battle. Collingwood would later write, 'Nothing could be finer than her conduct in the fight – I have no words in which I can sufficiently express my admiration of it.' When the *Victory* engaged the *Redoutable* the *Téméraire* came up alongside on the French ship's starboard side. One of the dozens of grenades and fireballs thrown down found its way into the magazine and the *Téméraire* was saved from catastrophe by the quick actions of the master-at-arms. Later she was fired on by the *Neptune* and then ran onboard the *Fougueux*, which she captured by boarding. She suffered 123 casualties (47 dead, 76 wounded), second only to the *Victory* in the weather column. As the smoke of battle drifted away she was seen dismasted, temporarily helpless with a French prize on each side of her (*Redoutable* and *Fougueux*), and signalled for a frigate to come and take her in tow; the *Sirius* obeyed.

## After the battle

Towed by the *Sirius*, she lost another 43 men who were prize crew on the *Fougueux* when she was wrecked in the storm after the battle. From 1820 to 1836 she was a receiving and victualling ship. Her last commission was from 1836 to 1838 when her captain was Thomas Kennedy, who as her first lieutenant at Trafalgar had led the boarders onto the *Fougueux*. Forty years after launching, in 1838, she was sold to the breakers for firewood for £5,530. Turner's painting, exhibited at the Royal Academy in 1839, shows her being towed away to be broken up.

# Neptune

## Officers
Captain      T.F. Freemantle
Lieuts
   J. Acklom (1st)    W. Mowat
   A.F. Westropp    Hon. G.L. Proby
   G.W. Hooper    A.P. Green
   I. Shaw
1st Lieut. RM    G. Kendall
2nd Lieuts RM    W. Burton
            L. Rooke

## Warrant Officers
Master    J. Keith
Surgeon    L.F. Nagle
Chaplain    Rev. C. Burne
Carpenter    J. Hiatt
Boatswain    J. Scott
Gunner    uncertain
Purser    S. Hodgson

## History/Characteristics

- Built at Deptford in 1797, she was comparatively new at Trafalgar, a fine second-rate three-decker with 98 guns but already with a reputation as being an indifferent sailer. In 1797 she was held in readiness to attack the Nore mutineers (which proved unnecessary) before being sent to the Channel Fleet for the long grind of blockade duties. She joined the British Fleet off Cadiz in May 1805.

- Armament 98 guns:
  - lower deck 28 x 32-pdrs
  - middle deck 30 x 18-pdrs
  - upper deck 30 x 18-pdrs
  - quarterdeck 8 x 12-pdrs
  - forecastle 2 x 12-pdrs
- Crew 741 (naval 625, RM 116)

## Commanded by

Captain Thomas Francis Freemantle, a short, stocky man with round features and black eyes. Born in 1765, he entered the service as a thirteen-year-old midshipman in 1778 and was lucky to survive when his ship was lost off Cuba when he was fifteen. He became a lieutenant at the unusually young age of eighteen (Nelson was nineteen) and was promoted captain in 1793 and appointed commander of the 28-gun frigate *Tartar*. In 1794 he was employed blockading Toulon and under Nelson at the reduction of Bastia, Corsica. Freemantle's 36-gun frigate *Inconstant* slowed down the French battleship *Ça Ira*, allowing Nelson in the *Agamemnon* to catch up and cripple her. Freemantle was in action (mentioned in despatches) off Leghorn two years later and in the leading boats to hit the mole at Santa Cruz in Nelson's abortive attempt to capture the town in 1797; he was badly wounded. He missed St Vincent and the Nile and thus was not among the original 'band of brothers' but he nevertheless served under Nelson on more occasions than most, becoming one of his closest friends. After a long period recovering from his wound he commanded the 74-gun *Ganges* in Nelson's squadron at Copenhagen in 1801. For his services at Trafalgar he received a gold medal and sword of honour but was not promoted rear-admiral until 1810. He commanded squadrons in the Mediterranean and Adriatic, capturing several towns, during the years 1812 to 1814. He was promoted vice-admiral and commander-in-chief in the Mediterranean in 1818 but died suddenly at Naples the following year, aged fifty-four.

## At the battle

The third ship in the weather column to pass through the enemy line at around 12.45 p.m., *Neptune* raked the stern of the *Bucentaure* and then luffed up in the lee of the huge *Santisima Trinidad*; the two ships slugged it out until the Spaniard became unmanageable. Later *Neptune* sailed north and became briefly engaged with the *Intrépide*. Her masts, although damaged, did not fall, but much of her rigging was cut to pieces and she received nine holes between wind and water that kept the carpenter, John Hiatt, occupied. Casualties amounted to 10 killed and 44 wounded – amazingly, among the 39 officers, midshipmen and warrant officers only the captain's clerk was wounded. The captain's log is not very informative as to damage, the only reference being 'At 6, wore per signal and unbent [lowered] the foresail and fore topsail, being shot to pieces. Bent [raised] others.' Seventeen-year-old Midshipman William Baddock later wrote, 'The old *Neptune*, which never was a good sailer, took it into her head to sail better that morning than I ever remember to have seen her do before.'

## After the battle

The following day *Neptune* took the *Royal Sovereign* in tow but after the gale switched to the *Victory* and brought her to Gibraltar. She was involved in the bombardment and capture of Martinique in 1809. Her career ended nine years later when she was broken up at Plymouth.

# Leviathan

## Officers

| | |
|---|---|
| Captain | H.W. Baynton |
| Lieuts | E. Mounsher (1st) |
| | J. Harding |
| | J. Baldwin |
| | A.B. Howe |
| | F. Baker |
| | J. Carter (acting) |
| Captain RM | G.P. Wingrove |
| 1st Lieuts RM | N. Cole |
| | T.J. Waldegrove |

## Warrant Officers

| | |
|---|---|
| Master | J.W. Trotter |
| Surgeon | W. Shoveller |
| Carpenter | J. Avory |
| Boatswain | A. Bowbray |
| Gunner | J. Wells |
| Purser | S. Rickards |

## History/Characteristics

• Built at Chatham in 1789, a good two-decker whose first service was off Toulon. While in the Channel Fleet under Lord Howe in 1794 she was heavily engaged in the run up to, and battle of, the Glorious First of June. On 28 and 29 May she faced the 110-gun French ships *Revolutionaire* and *Queen Charlotte*. During the battle itself she reduced the enemy 74-gun *America* to a floating hulk after an hour of furious exchanges of fire, losing 43 killed and wounded. Two years later in the West Indies *Leviathan* suffered another 24 casualties, this time from shore batteries at Leogane guarding the approaches to Port-au-Prince, Haiti. She continued to live dangerously. 1798 saw her delivering troops to Minorca and covering the capture of the island. The next year she captured the Spanish frigate *Santa*

*Teresa* near Majorca, and in 1800 she attacked a Spanish convoy off Cadiz and took a brig, then two days later assisted in the capture of two Spanish frigates, the 32-gun *Carmen* and 34-gun *Florentina* – it would have been a lucrative time for her captain (James Carpenter) in terms of prize money.

• Armament 74 guns:
  lower deck 28 x 32-pdrs
  upper deck 28 x 18-pdrs
  quarterdeck 14 x 9-pdrs
  forecastle 4 x 9-pdrs
She may have replaced some 9-pounders with carronades.

• Crew 623 (naval 540, RM 83)

## Commanded by

Captain Henry William Baynton, another Trafalgar captain who lived to become an admiral. Born in 1766, the son of the British Consul-General in Algiers, he entered the service as a young boy and was promoted lieutenant in 1783 at sixteen – an incredibly young age; one wonders how he managed to get round the promotion board. He had an exciting time in the West Indies during the period 1794–7, when he fought ashore during the capture of Martinique; assisted in the boarding and capture of the 32-gun French frigate *Bienvenue* in Port Royal; was present at the taking of Guadeloupe, survived the wreck of his own ship the 36-gun *Reunion,* and was involved in the taking of Trinidad. His leadership and daring on these occasions earned him promotion from commander to captain in four months. As commander of the 74-gun *Cumberland* off San Domingo in 1803 he captured the 40-gun French frigate *Creole* along with four smaller vessels. The following year he got command of the *Leviathan* and was employed on blockade off Toulon. He shared in the pursuit of Villeneuve to the Caribbean and back prior to Trafalgar. His actions that day earned him a gold medal, the thanks of parliament and a Patriotic Fund sword of honour. He carried the Guidon on the barge at Nelson's funeral procession along the Thames from Greenwich. In 1807 he participated in the expedition to Buenos Aires. From 1811 to 1812 he commanded the royal yacht, *Royal Sovereign*, at the end of which time he was promoted rear-admiral. He became a vice-admiral in 1821 and admiral in 1839, dying in Bath a year later aged seventy-four.

## At the battle

*Leviathan* was the fourth ship to follow the *Victory* through the enemy line at around 1.00 p.m. She had to search for a ship to attack as the *Bucentaure* and *Santisima Trinidad* were already virtually surrounded by British ships and invisible in the smoke, and found the French 80-gun *Neptune* with which she exchanged broadsides. Later, heading north, she tackled the Spanish 74-gun *San Augustin*, coming alongside, boarding and capturing her. Although in the battle for at least three hours her losses were light – 4 killed and 22 wounded. This was remarkable, as she had not escaped a heavy pounding from enemy gunfire. The mainpiece of her head was shot through, all three masts, bowsprit and most of her lower and topsail yards damaged, her mizzen-topsail shot away and a great part of her rigging shredded. In addition she received eight hits between wind and water and had three guns disabled.

## After the battle

She was mostly involved in operations against merchant convoys, chasing privateers and attacking shore batteries in the Mediterranean. Her last commission was 1814–16. Thereafter she performed the ignominious duty of convict hulk for twenty-eight years. Worse was to follow. For the next four years she became a target ship in Portsmouth, her wooden walls smashed by British gunfire until she was no further use even for that painful duty. In 1848 the breaker's yard took her splintered timber as firewood. What a long, drawn-out, undignified death for a Trafalgar veteran!

# Conqueror

## Officers

| | |
|---|---|
| Captain | I. Pellew |
| Lieuts | J. Couch (1st) |
| | R. Spear |
| | H.F. Senhouse |
| | G. FitzMaurice |
| | W.M. St George (k) |
| | R. Lloyd (k) |
| Captain RM | J. Atcherley |
| 2nd Lieuts RM | J.N. Fischer |
| | T. Wearing (w) |

## Warrant Officers

| | |
|---|---|
| Master | J. Seymour |
| Surgeon | W. Standbridge |
| Carpenter | J. McFarlane |
| Boatswain | J. Capie |
| Gunner | J. Pearson |
| Purser | F. Beaty |

## History/Characteristics

- Having been built at Harwich in 1800, and only commissioned as recently as 1803, the *Conqueror* was one of the two newest British ships at the battle, the other being the *Colossus*. As such she was in generally fine condition and a good sailer. Apart from a brief clash with a French sloop off Brest she did not have much opportunity to show her mettle until the Trafalgar campaign, when she took part in the pursuit of the French to the Caribbean.

- Armament 74 guns:
  - lower deck 28 x 32-pdrs
  - upper deck 30 x 18-pdrs
  - quarterdeck 14 x 9-pdrs
  - forecastle 2 x 9-pdrs

  She had also placed six 18-pdr carronades on her poop and two 32-pdrs on her forecastle.
- Crew 573 (naval 490, RM 83).

  This meant she was well below her full complement of 640.

## Commanded by

Captain Israel Pellew. Born in 1758 in Cornwall, he was later to be described as one of the finest sailors that county ever produced. Pellew entered the service as a thirteen-year-old in 1771, in time to participate in the American War of Independence, and was in the *Flora* when she was scuttled off Rhode Island to prevent her capture in 1778. After promotion to lieutenant in 1779 he was in command of the armed cutter *Resolution* when she took a notorious Dutch privateer, *Flushinger*, in 1783. Ten years later he was serving in the 36-gun frigate *Nymphe*, commanded by his elder brother, Edward Pellew (Hornblower's admiral in the popular TV series), when she captured the French frigate *Cleopatre*.

His career as a captain did not start well. In 1796 he was in command of the 32-gun frigate *Amphion* when there was a fire in her fore magazine that blew off the whole of the fore part of the ship, which sank immediately in ten fathoms of water in Portsmouth harbour. The explosion was so violent that wreckage and bodies were hurled as high as the main topgallant masthead. The wife of a seaman was blown up with her baby; her body was later recovered with the child still alive locked in her arms. Captain Pellew was dining with guests in his cabin. On hearing the first rumblings he rushed out onto the quarter gallery only to be thrown through the air to crash down on the deck on a nearby hulk, injuring his head and chest. Leaving the cabin probably saved his life as there were only 40 survivors out of some 200 on board. It was believed the gunner had been stealing powder and dropped a light – if so one wonders what the marine sentry was doing! Pellew was acquitted by a court martial, only to encounter more trouble when the crew of his next command, the 32-gun *Greyhound*, were among those involved in the Nore mutiny of 1797 – the mutineers expelled him from his ship.

He did not get another command until the *Conqueror* in 1804. For his leadership and skill at Trafalgar he received the gold medal, thanks of parliament and a sword of honour. He continued in command of the *Conqueror* with the Rochefort squadron until 1808. As a rear-admiral he served as Lord Exmouth's Fleet Captain in the Mediterranean from 1811 to 1815. Made an admiral in 1830, he died two years later aged seventy-four.

## At the battle

*Conqueror* was the fifth ship to cut through the same gap in the enemy line shortly after 1.00 p.m., following astern of the *Leviathan*. She engaged the *Bucentaure* and her broadsides brought down the French flagship's mizzenmast and then mainmast. The *Bucentaure* had by then received the fire of at least four British ships and suffered accordingly. *Conqueror* went on to attack the *Santisima Trinidad* with the *Neptune*. Later Pellew sailed north and was briefly engaged with the *Intrépide*. Her casualties were amazingly light (only four other British ships received less) at three killed (two were lieutenants) and nine wounded. She had been substantially cut up by enemy shot, although was still able to sail. Her mizzen-topmast and maintopgallant mast had been shot away; her fore- and mainmasts were badly wounded; her tiller destroyed, her rigging in tatters and several shots had hit between wind and water on the larboard side. Her figurehead had been decapitated.

## After the battle

She was able to tow the *Africa* to Gibraltar after the gale. When she returned to Plymouth her crew's request to replace her figurehead with a bust of Nelson was granted. It was ornamented at the crew's expense and placed with some ceremony on her bow. Her duties until the end of the war involved blockade duty off Rochefort and the mouth of the Tagus. In 1816 she was sent to St Helena for service guarding Napoleon in his exile. She remained there until 1820, was paid off at Chatham and broken up there in 1821.

# *Britannia*

## Officers

Flag officer    Rear-Admiral the Earl of Northesk
Captain    C. Bullen
Lieuts    A. Atchison (1st)
   J.H. Marshall    R. Lasham
   F. Roskruge (k)    W. Blight
   C. Anthony    J. Barclay (acting)
Captains RM    A. Watson
    W. Jackson

1st Lieuts RM
   L.B.J. Halloran (son of the chaplain)
   J. Cooke

## Warrant Officers

Master    S. Trounce (w)
Surgeon    A. Cornfoot
Chaplain    Rev. L.H. Halloran
Carpenter    J. Simpson
Boatswain    uncertain
Gunner    M. Aylward
Purser    J. Hiatt

## History/Characteristics

- *Britannia* was built at Portsmouth in 1762, making her forty-three years old at Trafalgar – the oldest ship of either fleet. Prior to the French Revolutionary Wars her service had been as a flagship in the Channel and at the second relief of Gibraltar in 1781, followed by action against the French fleet of Ushant and in the final relief of Gibraltar. In 1793 she was in the Mediterranean off Toulon. She saw action against the French off Genoa in 1795 and was present, carrying the flag of Rear-Admiral Thompson, at the battle of St Vincent. In 1803 she was stationed at St Helens guarding the Isle of Wight from invasion. The following year saw her on blockade duty off Brest and then in 1805 Cadiz.

- Armament 100 guns:
    lower deck 28 x 32-pdrs
    middle deck 28 x 24-pdrs
    upper deck 28 x 12-pdrs
    quarterdeck 12 x 6-pdrs
    forecastle 4 x 6-pdrs
- Crew 788 (naval 710, RM 78).
Like most British ships she was a number of men short, particularly marines. A number of 74s had more, such as the *Belleisle* with 128 and *Orion* with 91, and even the 64-gun *Agamemnon* had 70.

## Commanded by

Captain Charles Bullen, who was also flag captain to Rear-Admiral the Earl of Northesk who flew his flag on the *Britannia* as third in command at Trafalgar (admirals are discussed in Section Seven). As such he was the most junior post captain at Trafalgar, having been promoted as recently as 1802. Bullen was born in Dorset (one of three Dorset captains at the battle, the others being Hardy and Digby) in 1768, entering the service at eleven. Within a year he was in action as a midshipman on the *Loyalist* at the reduction of Charlestown harbour during the American War of Independence and then as a lieutenant on the 74-gun *Ramillies* at the Glorious First of June in 1794. Excitement of a different sort followed when he was under Lord Northesk on the 64-gun *Monmouth*; he narrowly escaped death when her crew mutinied at the Nore. He particularly distinguished himself as first lieutenant of the *Monmouth* at the Battle of Camperdown in 1797, taking possession of the Dutch ship *Delft* and displaying great gallantry in saving many of the crew, being himself nearly drowned. His actions earned quick promotion to commander and he was a captain by 1802. His services at Trafalgar brought him the usual gold medal, thanks of parliament and sword of honour. In contrast to the huge 100-gun *Britannia*, Bullen's next command was four years (1807–11) commanding frigates in the Mediterranean and off the coast of Spain – first the *Volontaire*, then the 40-gun *Cambrian*. Perhaps it was a relief to get an independent command with a better prospect of prize money after all those years with an admiral at his shoulder.

From the end of the Napoleonic Wars in 1815 Bullen had another twenty-eight years' service before he finally drew his pension in 1843. However, his days of real excitement had long gone. During that time he commanded the 50-gun *Akbar* off North America, was superintendent of Pembroke dockyard (twice), commissioner of Chatham dockyard and captain of the yacht *Royal Sovereign*. He retired as a rear-admiral, but his longevity ensured he made admiral in 1852. He only enjoyed his exalted rank for a year as he died in 1853 aged eighty-six – the last of the Trafalgar captains.

## At the battle

At about 1.00 p.m., following in the wake of the *Conqueror*, the *Britannia* sailed majestically through the enemy line, the sixth ship in the weather column to do so. She managed to fire at least one broadside into the unfortunate *Bucentaure* before that ship surrendered. She then continued north, firing into the *Santisima Trinidad* as she passed the Spanish giant. Royal Marine 1st Lieutenant Lawrence Halloran described how this broadside 'shattered the rich display of sculpture, figures, ornaments and inscriptions with which she was adorned'. She later engaged the *Intrépide*, one of whose lieutenants, the Marquis Gicquel des Touches, recalled, 'Then I dashed off to the quarterdeck myself. On the way I found my midshipman lying flat on the deck, terrified at the sight of the *Britannia*, which ship had come abreast of us within pistol shot and was thundering into us from her lofty batteries. I treated my emissary as he deserved – I gave him a hearty kick.' The *Britannia* suffered 10 killed and 42 wounded. Among the former was the signal officer Lieutenant Francis Roskruge, who was hit by a double-headed shot. She had comparatively light damage to masts and hull and lost her main- and mizzen-topsails.

## After the battle

Escorting three of the prizes home (and towing the French *Berwick*) was to be *Britannia*'s last active duty. She was renamed *St George* in 1812 and *Barfleur* in 1819 before being finally broken up in Plymouth in 1826 after sixty-four years' service.

# *Africa*

## Officers

| | |
|---|---|
| Captain | H. Digby |
| Lieuts | J. Smith (1st) |
| | G. Macrae |
| | G.W. Bourn |
| | J.S. Pearce |
| | M. Hay (acting; w) |
| Captain RM | J. Fynmore (w) |
| 1st Lieut RM | T.N. Brattle |

## Warrant Officers

| | |
|---|---|
| Master | W. Ottey |
| Surgeon | D. Gardner |
| Chaplain | Rev. W. Williams |
| Carpenter | T. Coats |
| Boatswain | W. Sarth |
| Gunner | W. Shepherd |
| Purser | W. Holman |

## History/Characteristics

*Africa*, a small 64-gun two-decked third-rate, was built on the Thames in 1781. She was sent to the East Indies and became part of the squadron under Vice-Admiral Sir Edward Hughes. In 1783 she was involved with supporting the British in the siege of Cuddalore, south of Madras, on the east coast of India. This was followed by a naval action against perhaps the finest French admiral of the eighteenth century, André de Suffren, an extremely corpulent officer who was killed in a pistol duel five years later, no doubt not helped by the fact that he provided such a large target. *Africa* did nothing further of interest until the French Revolutionary Wars. In 1796 we find her participating in another bombardment, this time of Fort Leogane, Santo Domingo (Haiti) in 1796. She appears to have come off second best in her duel with the shore batteries, as immediately afterwards she was sent to Jamaica for a refit with damaged masts and eight casualties. Her next appearance worthy of notice was at Trafalgar.

- Armament 64 guns:
    lower deck 26 x 24-pdrs
    upper deck 26 x 18-pdrs
    quarterdeck 10 x 9-pdrs
    forecastle 2 x 9-pdrs

Note how a ship of her size was, long before 1805, badly out-gunned by a 74 not only in terms of numbers of guns but also in their weight. Strictly speaking ships of her class were now too lightly armed for a line of battle. Nevertheless, she did well at Trafalgar.

- Crew 498 (naval 420, RM 78).

Marines constituted 18 per cent of her crew, well above average for most British ships.

## Commanded by

Captain Henry Digby. He was born in 1770 and entered the service at thirteen. He was a lieutenant five years later and while serving on the 32-gun frigate *Pallas* was commended for his behaviour when the 98-gun *Boyne* exploded in harbour nearby. In 1795 he was promoted commander. The following year while in command of the sloop *Incendiary*, and then as a captain commanding the frigate *Aurora*, he made numerous valuable captures. In 1796 his prizes included a Spanish frigate, a French corvette, a privateer and seven others from a fleet of 48 merchantmen. After a spell commanding the 74-gun *Leviathan* in 1798 he managed to get back in command of a cruising frigate, the *Alcmene*, stationed off Portugal, and made several important captures including the 28-gun French privateer *Courageux*. However his biggest windfall came, as the story goes, by following a dream. Three times he was awakened from sleep by thinking he heard somebody calling his name and telling him to change course. So vivid was the dream that Digby altered course and thereby intercepted the Spanish treasure ship the 36-gun *Santa Brigada* which he then helped to capture. Its hold was stuffed with 1,400,000 specie (coins) and other valuable cargo.

After Trafalgar Digby received the customary rewards of a captain – gold medal, parliamentary thanks and a sword of honour. He was promoted rear-admiral in 1819, waited eleven years for his next step up, and another eleven before he got to the top of the seniority ladder and became an admiral. He was by then in the sinecure position of commander-in-chief at Sheerness. He died quietly at home in Dorset the following year aged seventy-two.

## At the battle

*Africa* played a prominent role at Trafalgar, although perhaps not quite that envisaged by Nelson. During the night before the battle she became separated from the fleet (she had missed the earlier signal to come south) so, before the firing started, found herself well to the north of the *Victory* sailing south close to the van of the Combined Fleet. She continued south to join the weather column and en route exchanged broadsides with six or seven enemy ships as they passed in opposite directions. According to her log she commenced firing on the leading ship of the enemy van at 11.20 a.m. By about 1.30 p.m. *Africa* had entered the fray and joined the *Neptune* and *Conqueror* in tackling the massive *Santisima Trinidad*. After seeing the enemy fleet's van returning towards the fight the *Africa*, along with *Leviathan*, *Conqueror*, *Britannia* and *Neptune*, sailed to meet them and she became engaged in the fight with *Intrépide*. She suffered 18 killed and 44 wounded and lost her maintopsail yard; all her masts and bowsprit were severely damaged, her rigging and sails cut to pieces and her hull suffered several hits between wind and water.

## After the battle

She was towed in under jury rig by the *Conqueror*. In 1808 she was in the Baltic on blockade duty off the port of Roggersvick when, in a flat calm, she was attacked by some 25 Danish gun and mortar boats, losing exactly the same number of men (62 killed and wounded) as at Trafalgar. The Danes damaged her badly and came within a whisker of capturing her, but she was spared by the enemy withdrawing during the night. Two years later saw her on the Halifax station wearing the flag of Vice-Admiral Sawyer and taking part in the chase of the famous American frigate the 44-gun *Constitution* ('Old Ironsides'). In March 1813 she was broken up at Portsmouth after thirty-three years of invaluable service.

# *Ajax*

## Officers

| | |
|---|---|
| Captain | Lieut. J. Pilford (acting) |
| Lieuts | J. Brown (acting 1st) |
| | T. Prowse |
| | P. Mitchell |
| | T.D. Barker |
| | C. Wood |
| | H.N. Rowe |
| Captain RM | D. Boyd |
| 2nd Lieuts | S.B. Ellis |
| | J. Cinnamond |

## Warrant Officers

| | |
|---|---|
| Master | D. Donaldson |
| Surgeon | W. Mustard |
| Carpenter | T. Prior |
| Boatswain | J. Turner |
| Gunner | J. Dunnett |
| Purser | W. Bundock |

---

### History/Characteristics

• *Ajax*, a second-rate two-decker, had only been in service for seven years by Trafalgar, having been launched from Randall's Yard, Rotherhithe in 1798. She joined the blockading force off Brest and then Rochefort and in 1800 captured the French privateer *Avantageur*. The following year she went with the British expeditionary force to Egypt to support the landing of troops in Aboukir Bay. In July 1805 she was with Sir Robert Calder in his action with Villeneuve off Cape Finisterre. There, under Captain William Brown, she was in the thick of the action, suffering 18 killed and wounded – almost twice as many as at Trafalgar. In October 1805 she had recently been refitted following the damage she sustained in the July engagement.

• Armament 74 guns:
  lower deck 28 x 24-pdrs
  upper deck 28 x 24-pdrs
  quarterdeck 14 x 9-pdrs
  forecastle 4 x 9-pdrs

She was heavily armed with 24-pdrs on her upper deck instead of the usual 18s. Also she carried 8 x 32-pdr carronades, supposedly on her quarterdeck, in which case it is likely they replaced most of the 9-pdrs on that deck.

• Crew 702 (naval 590, RM 112).

Overall she was well over her usual complement of 640, mostly due to her large contingent of marines – 16 per cent of her crew, above the average for British ships at the battle and more appropriate for a first-rate three-decker.

---

## Commanded by

Lieutenant John Pilford. Pilford (normally the first lieutenant) was acting as captain as Captain William Brown had returned to England to be a witness at Vice-Admiral Calder's court martial. Pilford was one of only two lieutenants (the other being Lieutenant Stockham of the *Thunderer*) commanding a line-of-battle ship at the battle. He had entered the service in 1788 and had been a master's mate on the 74-gun *Brunswick* at the battle of the Glorious First of June in 1794. He had passed for lieutenant and his action during the battle secured his promotion to that rank. Thereafter he continued to see plenty of action, first on the 74-gun *Russell* in the engagement off Groix in 1795 then the following year on the 18-gun sloop *Kingfisher*, in which he captured several privateers and successfully, with considerable gallantry, helped suppress a mutiny. In 1800 he was a lieutenant on the only 78-gun ship in the Royal Navy, the former French *Impetueux* assisting French royalists in Morbihan (a Department of France). He commanded a boat in an impressive cutting-out expedition that captured and destroyed the 18-gun corvette *Insolante*, took several smaller craft and prisoners, destroyed some guns and blew up a magazine. Next came the action under Calder in which the *Ajax* was heavily involved. Thus, by Trafalgar, Pilford was an officer of proven capability and courage. Nevertheless, on the morning of 21 October 1805 he must surely have felt somewhat overawed with the sudden responsibility of commanding a line-of-battle ship in what was obviously developing into a major clash between large fleets. He did well, and his reward was immediate promotion to captain, a gold medal, the thanks of parliament and a sword of honour. Despite his success at Trafalgar Pilford's career thereafter was decidedly dull, with the highlight being his appointment of Captain of the Ordinary at Plymouth – the officer in command of all the ships 'in ordinary' (in reserve) from 1828 to 1831. He did not live long enough to be promoted to admiral and died in 1834 at Stonehouse, Devon.

## At the battle

The *Ajax* was well back in the centre of the weather line so did not arrive at the enemy line until (according to her master's log) 1.12 p.m. She was briefly engaged with the *Intrépide* before sailing north in pursuit of several fleeing enemy ships. She was not heavily engaged for any length of time, so suffered only light casualties – two killed and nine wounded. Not a single officer or warrant officer was hit. Only three ships had fewer casualties. The master, Mr David Donaldson, recorded the damage in his log as: 'The standing and running rigging much cut by shot, and the sails much damaged, the gangway netting and hammocks completely shot to pieces, and all the boats damaged by shot. The jolly boat towing astern was sunk and cut adrift.' This confirms that only one of the ship's boats was normally towed astern during a battle, and the value of the hammocks as protection from musket balls.

## After the battle

*Ajax* did not survive the battle for long. While under Captain the Hon. Henry Blackwood (captain of the frigate *Euryalus* at Trafalgar) she caught fire while with Sir John Duckworth's squadron in the Dardanelles. The fire broke out in the night in the after part of the ship and roared up through the main hatch. The thick smoke and darkness hampered efforts to control the blaze, the smoke so dense that officers and men on the upper deck could only distinguish each other by shouting or touch. It became impossible to launch any boat except the jollyboat, and some 250 crew out of 633 were lost. Most men jumped into the water. Blackwood spent half an hour in the sea, having leapt from the spritsail yard, before being picked up by a boat from the *Canopus*. He was cleared of blame at the inevitable court martial. *Ajax* was the shortest lived of any British Trafalgar ship.

# *Agamemnon*

## Officers

| | |
|---|---|
| Captain | Sir E. Berry |
| Lieuts | H. Cook (1st) |
| | S. Clark |
| | W. Coote |
| | T. Pinto |
| | S. Blacker |
| Captain RM | H.B. Downing |
| 2nd Lieuts RM | H. Raban |
| | D. Campbell |

## Warrant Officers

| | |
|---|---|
| Master | T. Webb |
| Surgeon | J. Jameson |
| Carpenter | G. Robins |
| Boatswain | T. Needham |
| Gunner | A. Freeburne |
| Purser | C. Ross |

## History/Characteristics

• Built at Buckler's Hard and launched in 1781, *Agamemnon* had seen twenty-four years' service by Trafalgar. She was a two-decker, third-rate warship but was lighter and faster than the 74s – Nelson considered her 'without exception the finest 64 in the service'. *Agamemnon* was in action in the Battle of Ushant in 1781 and the following year in the Caribbean in Admiral Rodney's victory over the French at the Battle of the Saintes, during which she suffered 28 killed and wounded. She became Nelson's favourite ship and details of her actions under his command from 1793 to 1796 have been described in Section Two pp. 108–18. She was with Nelson again as part of his squadron participating in the attack on Copenhagen in 1801, although due to navigational difficulties among the shoals she was unable to play a fighting role.

• Armament 64 guns:
    lower deck 26 x 24-pdrs
    upper deck 26 x 18-pdrs
    quarterdeck 10 x 9-pdrs
    forecastle 2 x 9-pdrs
Her broadsides weighed a total of 1,200 lbs compared with the 1,562 lbs of some 74s.

• Crew 490 (naval 420, RM 70).

## Commanded by

Captain Sir Edward Berry. An original member of the 'band of brothers', Berry was slightly built with startlingly blue eyes and fair hair. He became renowned for his reckless daring and impulsiveness – but not so much for his administration or seamanship skills. He became one of Nelson's closest service friends – until Emma Hamilton entered the admiral's life.

Born in 1768, the son of a London merchant, Berry entered the service as an eleven-year-old volunteer in 1779, and served on the *Burford* during the American War of Independence as both a volunteer and midshipman. During the period 1782–3 he took part in no fewer than five fleet actions against the French Admiral Suffren. His gallantry in leading a boarding party onto a French ship in the West Indies in 1794 confirmed his promotion to lieutenant, and he also did well during Lord Howe's victory on the Glorious First of June in 1794. The following year he became the first lieutenant on the *Agamemnon* under Nelson. Again he performed well and was mentioned in despatches. When Nelson transferred to the *Captain* he took Berry with him and secured his promotion to commander. He was present at the Battle of St Vincent in 1797 as a passenger, and during the action accompanied Nelson in the boarding of the Spanish ships *San Nicolas* and *San Josef* (see pp. 166–7). Promoted post captain in 1798, his next appointment was as flag captain (at Nelson's request) on his flagship, the 74-gun *Vanguard*. As such he was standing alongside Nelson when the admiral was wounded in the head at the Battle of the Nile in 1798. Given the honour of carrying the victory despatches home, Berry was captured and severely wounded when his ship, the *Leander*, was taken by the French *Généreux*. Berry was exchanged within three months. He arrived in England in December 1798 to be knighted and given the freedom of the City of London and his first gold medal. In 1799 as captain of the 74-gun *Foudroyant* he was present at the taking of Malta from the French.

Berry and the *Agamemnon* joined Nelson on 13 October 1805, just in time for Trafalgar – provoking Nelson to remark, 'Here comes Berry! Now we will have a battle!', a reference to Berry's having been in more fleet actions than any other captain. Berry received a gold medal (the small variety, admirals got the bigger one), the thanks of parliament and from the Patriotic Fund not a sword, but a silver vase!

In 1806 Berry, still commanding the *Agamemnon*, was in action yet again, this time at the Battle of Santo Domingo where Sir John Duckworth's squadron destroyed the French West Indian squadron. Berry became a baronet and was presented with his third gold medal. He is thought to be the only naval officer of his time except for Admiral Collingwood to have been awarded three gold medals – but then he had been in eight general actions and numerous minor engagements. After 1806, however, his life became dull by comparison and he was not destined for battle again. After commanding the royal yachts *Royal Sovereign* and *Royal George* from 1813 to 1815, Berry was not actively employed. He died at Bath in 1831 aged sixty-three.

## At the battle

The *Agamemnon* followed the *Ajax* into the action and fired a broadside into the by then floating hulk of the *Bucentaure* before sailing north to engage Rear-Admiral Dumanoir's returning ships. She briefly engaged the *Intrépide*. Her losses were two killed and eight wounded and she was hit below the water line, which kept her pumps going throughout the afternoon. According to the master, she was making '3 feet water per hour'.

## After the battle

She initially took the *Colossus* in tow. In 1806 she was present at the Battle of Santo Domingo in the West Indies, at which she suffered more casualties (14) than at Trafalgar. Later the same year she, in conjunction with the *Heureux*, captured the notorious French privateer *Dame Ernouf* off Barbados. The next year she took the *Lutine* and joined the squadron off Martinique before finally leaving the Caribbean to escort a large convoy home. In 1807 she was part of Admiral Gambier's fleet bombarding Copenhagen. She sailed in 1808 for South America, where her captain (Jonas Rose) was over confident in seeking his anchorage in Maldonado Bay. She struck a sandbank and foundered (see box on p. 118).

## Agamemnon

Nelson's favourite ship. She did not
enter the action until late so her
casualties and damage were light.

# *Orion*

## Officers

| | |
|---|---|
| Captain | E. Codrington |
| Lieuts | J. Croft (1st) |
| | J. Julian |
| | E. Elers |
| | J. Roberts |
| Captain RM | H.W. Creswell |
| 2nd Lieuts RM | S. Collins |
| | S. Bridgeman |

## Warrant Officers

| | |
|---|---|
| Master | C. Halliday |
| Surgeon | T. Johnston |
| Chaplain | Rev. G. Outhwaite |
| Carpenter | J. Mills |
| Boatswain | J. Marshall |
| Gunner | J. Filmore |
| Purser | W.B. Murray |

---

### History/Characteristics

- Built on the Thames in 1787 the *Orion*, a two-decker, third-rate 74, was destined for an eventful career. It started while in the Channel Fleet in 1794 under Lord Howe at the Battle of the Glorious First of June where she suffered substantial material damage and had 5 men killed and 24 wounded (more than she would suffer at Trafalgar). The next year, under Captain Sir James Saumarez, she engaged the French in the action off Isle Groix, suffering 24 casualties. In 1797 she played a prominent part in the British victory at St Vincent, exchanging broadsides with three Spanish ships including the four-decker *Santisima Trinidad*. She then joined Nelson in the Mediterranean in time to participate in his stunning success in Aboukir Bay (the Nile).

Her losses at this battle were the heaviest she was to sustain in her 26 years' service – 13 killed and 29 wounded, almost double those at Trafalgar. She then sailed to Gibraltar, then Malta and finally home to Plymouth to be paid off and repaired. Her next commission was not until 1805.

- Armament 74 guns:
  lower deck 28 x 32-pdrs
  upper deck 28 x 18-pdrs
  quarterdeck 14 x 9-pdrs
  forecastle 4 x 9-pdrs
- Crew 541 (naval 450, RM 91).

## Commanded by

Captain Edward Codrington. Born in 1770 and educated at Harrow, he entered the service as a young midshipman in 1783. It took him ten years to make lieutenant. The following year he served on Lord Howe's flagship, the 110-gun *Queen Charlotte*, at the Glorious First of June. He was then appointed commander and captain of the fireship *Comet*. In 1795 he was promoted captain and took command of the frigate *La Babet* (yet another French capture) and took part in Lord Bridport's action with the French off Isle Groix, for which he received the thanks of parliament. His next success was while in command of the 32-gun frigate *Druid*. With two other frigates, he captured the *Ville de l'Orient* packed with troops bound for an abortive invasion of Ireland. For his services at Trafalgar he received the gold medal, his second thanks of parliament and some unknown alternative to the sword of honour or silver vase.

His next action was as the captain of the 74-gun *Blake* in 1809. While participating in the forcing of the Scheldt his ship was twice set on fire and spent three hours aground under sustained fire from shore batteries. Codrington's actions earned him a mention in despatches. In 1811–13 he commanded a squadron off the coast of Portugal and Spain, performing valuable service at the defence of Tarragona and the defeat of the French near Villa Suca. As captain of the 80-gun *Tonnant* and Captain of the Fleet under Sir Alexander Cochrane he was present at most important naval actions of the American War, 1812–14. Promoted rear-admiral at forty-four, Codrington still had a lot of active service in front of him, including the capture of Washington, the defeat of the American Fleet in the Penobscot Bay, the capture of Alexandria, the expedition against Baltimore and the attack on New Orleans. He was rewarded with another mention, another thanks of parliament and a KCB (Knight Commander of the Order of the Bath). He was made vice-admiral in 1821 and served as commander-in-chief in the Mediterranean from 1826 to 1828. As such he commanded British, French and Russian squadrons in the pacification of Greece and at the Battle of Navarino almost twenty-two years to the day (20 October 1827) after Trafalgar. He commanded the Evolutionary (Training) Channel Squadron in 1831, was promoted admiral in 1837 and appointed Commander-in-Chief Portsmouth from 1839 to 1842, while also serving as MP for Devonport 1832–40. He died aged eighty-one in Eaton Square, London, in 1851. He had three sons. One was drowned at sea while still a midshipman, another (Sir William) became a general and the last an admiral of the fleet (Sir Henry John).

## At the battle

The *Orion* arrived in the battle at about 1.30 p.m. (the master's log states, 'passed the *Santa Anna* dismasted at 1.30, and had struck') and was involved in the ferocious fight with the French 74-gun *Intrépide*, forcing her to lower her colours. Damage to her rigging and spars was light but she received 24 casualties (1 killed, 23 wounded) in the comparatively short time she was closely engaged.

## After the battle

She took the Spanish ship *Bahama* in tow until 24 October. In 1807 she took part in the bombardment of Copenhagen and the capture, intact, of the Danish Fleet. There followed the expedition to the Baltic in 1808–9, which was her last service before being broken up in 1814. Her career had been both long and distinguished.

# *Minotaur*

## Officers

| | |
|---|---|
| Captain | C.J.M. Mansfield |
| Lieuts | J. Stuart (1st) |
| | A. McVicar |
| | N. Bell |
| | J. Morgan |
| | C. Giddy |
| | R. McLeod (acting) |
| Captain RM | P. Hunt |
| 2nd Lieuts RM | N.B. Grigg |
| | T. Reeves |

## Warrant Officers

| | |
|---|---|
| Master | R. Duncan |
| Surgeon | R. Crichton |
| Carpenter | C. Peake |
| Boatswain | J. Robinson (w) |
| Gunner | F. Graham |
| Purser | G. Jackson |

## History/Characteristics

- A third-rate, two-decker 74 built at Woolwich in 1793 and commissioned the following year when she was sent to the Mediterranean. In 1797 her crew joined the mutiny at Spithead but she redeemed herself at the Nile where she was able to support Nelson in the *Vanguard* in the thick of the battle. The fierceness of the fighting is illustrated by her casualties – 23 killed and 64 wounded. Despite Nelson's wound he sent for the *Minotaur*'s captain, Thomas Louis, and thanked him with the words, 'Your support has prevented me from being obliged to haul out of the line.' In 1800 she participated in the siege and capture of Genoa. Her crew was involved in the successful cutting-out expeditions that year at Genoa and Barcelona, taking the galley *Prima* at the former and two 22-gun corvettes, *Esmeralda* and *Paz*, at the latter. In 1801 she was present at the landings of British forces at Aboukir Bay, Egypt. Two years later, in conjunction with the *Thunderer* and *Albion* she chased and captured the 40-gun French frigate *Franchise*.

- Armament 74 guns:
    lower deck 28 x 32-pdrs
    upper deck 28 x 18-pdrs
    quarterdeck 14 x 9-pdrs
    forecastle 4 x 9-pdrs
- Crew 615 (naval 540, RM 75).
Naval personnel slightly under strength.

## Commanded by

Captain Charles John Moore Mansfield, whose date of birth is uncertain. He was promoted to lieutenant in 1778, commander in 1793 and captain the following year. In 1796–7 he commanded the small 32-gun frigate *Andromache* in the Mediterranean. During this time he captured an Algerine corsair, inflicting 64 killed and 40 wounded at a cost of a mere 2 killed and 4 wounded. In 1803, in command of the *Minotaur*, he assisted in the Channel chase and capture of the French 40-gun frigate *Franchise*. For his Trafalgar services he was awarded the gold medal, received the thanks of parliament and a sword of honour. In 1807 he was present at the bombardment of Copenhagen and the seizure of the Danish Fleet. He died in 1813.

## At the battle

It was about two hours after firing opened around noon that the *Minotaur* joined the action, as she was almost the last ship in the weather division (the rear ship being the *Spartiate*). The master's log records, 'At 2.10 observed four French and one Spanish ships bearing down towards the *Victory*. Hauled towards them …'. She engaged the 80-gun French *Formidable* and later ended the battle by forcing the Spanish *Neptuno* to surrender. Her losses were light – 3 killed and 22 wounded – reflecting her late arrival into the fight. Mr Duncan (the master) recorded the damage as, 'fore topsail yard shot away, fore topmast head wounded, several sails damaged three shots between wind and water and most braces shot away'.

## After the battle

In 1809, off Finland, her boats took part in a hard fight with, and capture of, four Russian gunboats and a brig in Frederickshamm harbour. In December 1810, when part of a convoy escort, she became separated from the other ships in a violent storm and was wrecked on the Haak Sands at the mouth of the Texel. Some 370 lives were lost including that of her captain. There is a legend that the ship's pet, a tame wolf, and one of her lieutenants both tried to save themselves by clinging to the mainmast together, but that eventually both drowned when exhaustion and cold overcame them.

# *Spartiate*

## Officers

| | |
|---|---|
| Captain | Sir F. Laforey |
| Lieuts | J. McKerlie (1st) |
| | J. Clephan |
| | G. Bignell |
| | J.J. Ridge |
| | F.J. Thomas (acting) |
| 1st Lieut. RM | S.H. Hawkins |
| 2nd Lieuts RM | J.R. Coryton |
| | G.D. Hawkins |

## Warrant Officers

| | |
|---|---|
| Master | F. Whitney (acting) |
| Surgeon | J.P. O'Berne |
| Carpenter | T. Murray |
| Boatswain | J. Clark (w) |
| Gunner | L. Baxter |
| Purser | D. Forrest |

## History/Characteristics

- The *Spartiate* was built by the French at Toulon in 1793. She was a third-rate two-decker, well designed, larger than most British 74s and a good sailer. At the Battle of the Nile in 1798 she was dismasted and forced to strike her colours by the combined efforts of the *Theseus, Vanguard, Minotaur* and *Audacious*. The British kept her name and she was stationed in the West Indies until 1805 when she joined Nelson's fleet.

- Armament 74 guns:
   lower deck 28 x 32-pdrs
   upper deck 30 x 18-pdrs
   quarterdeck 2 x 18-pdrs + 14 x 32 pdr carronades
   forecastle 2 x 18-pdrs + 6 x 32-pdr carronades
She only carried 62 guns at Trafalgar, having replaced most guns on the weather decks with heavy carronades. This made her effectively an 82-gun ship.
- Crew 620 (naval 540, RM 80). Slightly under strength.

## Commanded by

Captain Sir Francis Laforey. The son of an admiral, Laforey was born in America (Virginia) in 1767, entering the service at thirteen in 1780. Nine years later he was a lieutenant, and the following year he became a commander and captain of the 16-gun cutter *Fairy*. He participated in the capture of Tobago in 1793 and was sent home with the despatches – for which he received the traditional reward of promotion to captain. In 1794, while commanding the 28-gun frigate *Carysfoot*, he recaptured the 32-gun frigate *Castor*, which had been lost only three weeks earlier. He commanded the 64-gun *Scipio* in the West Indies under his father and assisted in the capture of the Dutch possessions of Demerara, Essequibo and Berbice in 1796. In 1798 he commanded the 38-gun frigate *Hydra*, taking part in the chase and destruction of the French frigate *Confiante* off Le Havre. For his services at Trafalgar he received the usual rewards of a gold medal, parliamentary thanks and sword of honour. He carried the standard in the leading barge of Nelson's funeral flotilla as it sailed up the Thames from Greenwich. He was still the captain of *Spartiate* blockading Rochefort in 1807 and was present at the capture of the Neapolitan islands of Ischia and Procida (off Naples) two years later. As a rear-admiral he was commander-in-chief of the Leeward Islands from 1811 to 1814. He became vice-admiral in 1819 and admiral in 1830, and died in Brighton in 1835 aged sixty-eight.

## At the battle

The *Spartiate* was the rearmost ship of the weather column, following close astern of the *Minotaur* (they fought together as a pair). Shortly after 3.00 p.m. she, along with the *Minotaur*, engaged the *Formidable* as the latter led five of Dumanoir's van southwards. According to Mr Whitney (the master) both British ships 'commenced close action with these headmost ships, receiving and returning the fire of the five ships in passing'. *Spartiate* (and *Minotaur*) then wore and engaged the Spanish *Neptuno*. The *Spartiate* had 23 casualties – 3 killed and 20 wounded. The master's log records damage as follows – 'fore mast and bowsprit badly wounded in two places, one shot through the heel of the main topmast which splintered it very much, two shot between wind and water, and a number do. [ditto] in our sides'. Her rigging and sails were also badly cut up.

## After the battle

She took the *Tonnant* in tow during the gales over the next three days. In 1807 she was with the blockading squadron off Rochefort and in 1809 participated in the capture of the islands of Ischia and Procida. She returned to Sheerness after the war, blockaded the ports in Holland in 1832 and was on the South American station until 1835. She became a hulk at Plymouth in 1842 but was not finally broken up until 1857, when she was sixty-four years old.

# *Royal Sovereign*

## Officers

| | |
|---|---|
| Flag officer | Vice-Admiral Lord Collingwood (second-in-command to Nelson) |
| Captain (and flag captain) | E. Rotherham |
| Lieuts | |
| J. Clavell (1st; w) | F.B. Gibbes |
| J. Simmonds | E. Barker |
| J. Bashford (w) | B. Gilliland (k) |
| Captain RM | J. Vallack |
| 2nd Lieuts RM | |
| R. Green (k) | J. Le Vesconte (w) |
| A.W. Hubbard | |

## Warrant Officers

| | |
|---|---|
| Master | W. Chalmers (k) |
| Surgeon | R. Lloyd |
| Chaplain | Rev. J. Rudall |
| Carpenter | G. Clines |
| Boatswain | I. Williamson |
| Gunner | uncertain |
| Purser | B.S. Oliver |

## History/Characteristics

• A first-rate, 100-gun three-decker built at Plymouth in 1787, making her eighteen years old at Trafalgar. She looked impressive with an appropriate figurehead for her name – a full-length effigy of King George III dressed as a Roman emperor with sword and scarlet cloak, on either side the figures of Fame and Fortune blowing trumpets. Nevertheless, she was noted for her sluggish sailing qualities, thus acquiring the nickname the 'West Country Wagon'. She carried the flag of the Channel Fleet from 1790 to 1794 and fought in Lord Howe's famous victory at the Glorious First of June in 1794, losing 58 killed and wounded as well as sustaining heavy damage to masts and spars. Bearing the flag of Vice-Admiral Cornwallis, she was present in the action against the French off Brest in June 1795. For the next four years the *Royal Sovereign* was the flagship of the Channel Fleet. Her crew was heavily implicated in that fleet's mutiny in 1797, when two mutineers were hanged from her yardarm. She remained with the same fleet until 1803 when she was sent to carry the flag of Rear-Admiral Bickerton off Toulon.

• Armament 100 guns:
>    lower deck 28 x 32-pdrs
>    middle deck 28 x 24-pdrs
>    upper deck 30 x 12-pdrs
>    quarterdeck 10 x 12-pdrs
>    forecastle 4 x 12-pdrs

When firing both broadsides she used 2,096 lbs of shot. It is clear that she carried carronades at Trafalgar as Lieutenant Simmonds' journal states, 'October 25th … Lost overboard one of the poop carronades by the violent rolling of the ship.' They were probably 18-pdrs, perhaps six on the poop and others replacing some of the guns on the quarterdeck and forecastle.

• Crew 826 (naval 697, RM 129).

## Commanded by

Captain Edward Rotherham. The son of a doctor, he was born at Hexham, Northumberland in 1753 – making him, at fifty-two, five years older than Nelson and the oldest British captain in the fleet. He entered the service later than most officers at twenty-two (having previously been to sea in a collier) and served as a midshipman and master's mate for two years. He was an acting lieutenant on the *Monarch* under Lord Howe in 1780 and lieutenant in 1783. Howe must have thought well of him as he was first lieutenant on the *Culloden* at the admiral's great triumph of the Glorious First of June in 1794 which secured his promotion to commander. Six years later he was a post captain.

At Trafalgar he sailed into action wearing a cocked hat covered in decorations and several sizes too large. When told he looked ridiculous (one wonders who dared) and advised to take it off he replied, 'I have always fought in a cocked hat, and I always will.' His services during the battle secured for him a gold medal, the thanks of parliament and a silver vase instead of a sword. As captain of the *Bellerophon* he escorted the *Victory*, with Nelson's body on board, back to England, and carried the guidon at Nelson's funeral. He continued as captain of the *Bellerophon* in the Channel and Baltic during 1806–9. He was captain of Greenwich Hospital for the two years 1828–30 and died in 1830 aged seventy-seven. He was one of only five captains who survived the battle who did not make it to flag rank, even in retirement. Considering his age when he died this is somewhat strange.

## At the battle

*Royal Sovereign* led the lee column into battle. She was the first British ship to come under fire shortly before noon and the first British ship to open fire shortly thereafter. During her approach to the enemy line no fewer than seven ships opened fire on her. She cut the line well ahead of the next British ship, the *Belleisle*, between the *Fougueux* to starboard and the *Santa Ana* to larboard. She came under fire from the *Indomptable* as she swung to larboard to come alongside the *Santa Ana*. From then on their battle was a desperate slugging match, an exchange of thunderous broadsides at a range of a few yards until the Spaniard struck his colours. This seemingly endless gunnery duel between giants cost the *Royal Sovereign* 141 casualties – 47 killed and 94 wounded. Only three British ships suffered more (*Victory*, *Colossus* and *Bellerophon*). By the time the *Santa Ana* struck the *Royal Sovereign* was almost unmanageable, having lost her main- and mizzenmasts and had her foremast damaged, with all rigging shot away.

## After the battle

On 21 October she was taken in tow by the *Euryalus* after Collingwood transferred his flag to that frigate. The next day towing duties were taken over by the *Neptune* followed on the 23rd by the *Mars*. Lieutenant Simmonds' journal for that day records, 'At noon read the articles of war and punished [flogged] two seamen for drunkenness and disobedience of orders.' Captain Rotherham must have been something of a disciplinarian that he could not wait for calmer times. After Trafalgar the *Royal Sovereign* spent most of the remaining ten years of the war as a flagship in the Mediterranean or the Channel. In April 1814 she carried the returning exiled King Louis XVIII from Dover to Calais – in less than a year he was on the run again when Napoleon escaped from Elba. Her name was changed to *Captain* in 1825. She was used as a receiving ship until 1841 when she was finally broken up aged fifty-four.

**Royal Sovereign**
about to stern rake *Santa
Ana* with her larboard
batteries as she breaks the
enemy line between
*Santa Ana* and *Fougueux*

# *Belleisle*

## Officers

| | |
|---|---|
| Captain | W. Hargood |
| Lieuts | T. Fife (1st) |
| | T. Coleman |
| | W. Ferrie (w) |
| | R. Bastin |
| | E. Geale (k) |
| | J. Woodin (k) |
| 1st Lieut. RM | J. Owen (w) |
| 2nd Lieuts RM | P.H. Nicolas |
| | J. Weaver |

## Warrant Officers

| | |
|---|---|
| Master | W. Hudson |
| Surgeon | W. Clapperton |
| Carpenter | J. Hicks |
| Boatswain | A. Gibson (w) |
| Gunner | B. Kinsley |
| Purser | J. MacFarlane |

## History/Characteristics

- The *Belleisle* was initially the French *Formidable*, a third-rate, two-decker 74 built in 1793, well designed and somewhat larger than the usual British 74. She was captured in an action off the Isle Groix (off southern Brittany) in 1795 and renamed *Belleisle* by the British (who already had a *Formidable*) in the mistaken belief she had been taken near the Belle Isle, an island some distance to the south of Groix. During the period 1803–4 she was employed blockading Toulon and the following year accompanied Nelson during his chase to the Caribbean and back.

- Armament 74 guns:
  - lower deck 30 x 32-pdrs    upper deck 30 x 24-pdrs
  - quarterdeck 2 x 9-pdrs + 14 x 32-pdr carronades
  - forecastle 2 x 9-pdrs + 2 x 24-pdr carronades
  - poop 2 x 24-pdr carronades

  She was a heavily armed ship for her rate. Because she had a slightly longer hull than most 74s she could accommodate 30 x 24-pounders on her upper deck, as could *Mars* and *Colossus*. Her guns total 64 not 74 as a number of 9-pounders had been replaced by carronades. In total she was armed with 82 guns/carronades.
- Crew 728 (naval 600, RM 128).

  One of the few British ships that had slightly over her complement.

## Commanded by

Captain William Hargood, a slightly built, well-respected officer of considerable experience. The son of a purser, Hargood was born in 1762, entering the service at eleven. He first saw action as a midshipman in the 50-gun *Bristol* in the attack on Sullivan's Island, North America in 1776. Promoted lieutenant in 1780, he was with Nelson during the disastrous expedition to Nicaragua and was on the *Port Royal* when she was captured by the Spaniards in the unsuccessful defence of Pensacola the following year. He saw action again in the 74-gun *Magnificent* in Lord Rodney's engagements off Dominica in 1782 and was made commander in 1789 and captain in 1790. When he was commanding the small 24-gun frigate *Hyaena* in 1793 she was captured by a French squadron of two 74s and several frigates. Hargood again became a prisoner but escaped. He was court-martialled for failing to resist for long enough but acquitted. In 1797 he was captain of the 50-gun *Leopard* at Yarmouth when the Nore mutiny began. Hargood instantly suppressed a half-hearted attempt by his crew to join the mutineers. Two weeks later, after the *Leopard* had set sail, and just as the watches had changed, the crew rushed aft and overpowered the marines and officers. They left only Hargood at liberty. As the ship headed back for Yarmouth he attempted to seize the wheel. He was overpowered and carried struggling to his cabin. The story goes that the seaman pushed him into the cabin with the words, 'Steady-ho, baby lamb-kin!' This became a nickname that stuck. After Trafalgar he received the usual awards – gold medal, thanks of parliament and a silver vase.

Hargood continued in command of the *Belleisle* until he transferred to another 74, the *Northumberland*, in 1808. His remaining service was mundane, consisting of blockade duties and co-operating with the Austrians in the Adriatic until he was made rear-admiral in 1810. He became second-in-command at Portsmouth followed by the command of a squadron in the Channel in 1811. Promoted vice-admiral in 1814, he was Commander-in-Chief Plymouth from 1833 to 1836. In old age he became a chronic invalid, dying at Bath in 1839 aged seventy-seven.

## At the battle

The *Belleisle* cut into the enemy line just behind, and to the starboard of, the *Royal Sovereign* at around 12.05 p.m. She exchanged shots with the Spanish *Santa Ana* and the French *Indomptable* before coming under fire from the *San Juan Nepomuceno*. At about 1.00 p.m. the *Fougueux* ran aboard the *Belleisle* and they became locked in a brutal embrace. The *Mars* joined in the action and after an hour of slogging it out the *Fougueux* dropped astern. By 1.30 p.m. the French *Aigle*, the Spanish *San Leandro* and *San Justo* were firing into the crippled *Belleisle*. She was now surrounded, a floating – but still firing – wreck, her masts gone, her rigging reduced to shreds. This desperate situation was made worse by the arrival of the *Principe de Asturias* followed by the French *Neptune*. Incredibly, still firing a few starboard guns, Hargood held on. Not until well past 3.00 p.m. did other British ships (*Polyphemus*, *Defiance* and *Swiftsure*) begin to arrive to take some of the pressure off. By 3.30 *Belleisle* was defenceless, and dismasted – a seaman waved a Union flag on a pike! At 3.25 her log records, 'Ceased firing, and turned the hands up to clear the wreck.' The cost was 126 casualties – 33 killed and 93 wounded. Considering she had been hammered for over three hours, mostly at close range from different directions, losses of 17 per cent were light.

## After the battle

She was taken in tow by the frigate *Naiad*. In 1806 she was on the North America station and with two other ships, chased and destroyed the French 74-gun *Impeteux*. She was the flagship of Rear-Admiral Cochrane in the West Indies in 1807, where she was present at the capture of the island of Thomas, and served in the Walcheron expedition in 1809. Her last active service was at the capture of Martinique in 1809. She was sold out of the Navy in 1814.

# *Mars*

## Officers

| | |
|---|---|
| Captain | G. Duff (k) |
| Lieuts | W. Hennah (1st) |
| | J. Black (w) |
| | B. Patey* |
| | E.W. Garrett (w) |
| | G.L. Decoeurdoux |
| | W.H.T. Boyce |
| Captain RM | T. Norman |
| 2nd Lieuts RM | C. Holmes |
| | R. Guthrie |

## Warrant Officers

| | |
|---|---|
| Master | T. Cooke (w) |
| Surgeon | J. Torkington |
| Carpenter | W. Cook |
| Boatswain | J. Bunt |
| Gunner | A. Collis |
| Purser | E. Hatfull |

*Patey was one of ten sons of a gunner, nine of whom joined the Navy. He also had his fifteen-year-old nephew George on board, serving as a midshipman.

---

## History/Characteristics

- Built at Deptford in 1794 and named after the Roman god of war, *Mars* was something of a 'lazy' sailer – she could not keep her place at the head of the lee column at Trafalgar. In June 1795 she played a gallant part in the action of Admiral Cornwallis off Brest when she was surrounded by several enemy ships but continued to resist until other ships came to her aid. Afterwards she was with the Channel Fleet. Her crew was implicated in the Nore mutiny of 1797 and her officers compelled to leave their ship. In 1798 she took part in the action with, and capture of, the French 74-gun *Hercules*. Her losses were severe, over 70 killed and wounded – her captain (Alexander Hood) being among the former. From then until Trafalgar she was flagship of the squadrons blockading Rochefort and Brest.

- Armament 74 guns:
  lower deck 28 x 32-pdrs
  upper deck 30 x 24-pdrs
  quarterdeck 12 x 9-pdrs
  forecastle 4 x 9-pdrs
- Crew 615 (naval 540, RM 75). Slightly under strength.

---

## Commanded by

Captain George Duff, a large, imposing man with fair hair, well respected by his crew and a devoted husband and father. He was one of only two captains killed at Trafalgar – the other being his close friend Captain Cooke of the *Bellerophon*. Duff was the grand-nephew to Vice-Admiral Robert Duff and had his thirteen-year-old son, Norwich, serving as a volunteer in the *Mars* during the battle. George Duff was born in 1764, in Banff, Scotland, and stowed away on a merchant vessel when only nine. He entered naval service at thirteen in 1777. He was supposedly promoted lieutenant in 1779, though this makes him a lieutenant at fifteen having a mere two years' service. In 1780 he was serving on the *Panther* and was present at the capture of the Spanish Admiral Don Juan Langara. He was also present on the 74-gun *Montague* at Lord Rodney's action off Martinique, the attack on St Kitts and the capture of the French Admiral de Grasse in 1782. He was promoted commander in 1790 and captain in 1793 (by which time Nelson, who became a lieutenant the same year as Duff, had been a captain for fourteen years). Duff commanded the 98-gun *Duke* in the unsuccessful operations off Martinique in 1793, the 74-gun *Vengeance* during the mutiny in Bantry Bay in 1797, and the 36-gun frigate *Glenmore* when she recaptured the East Indiaman (East India Company merchantman) in 1799. He was killed early in the Trafalgar action, virtually cut in two by a cannonball hitting him in the chest, his mangled body lying on the deck covered with the Union flag for some three hours. He was buried at sea the next day. A monument to him was erected in St Paul's Cathedral and his family received his posthumously awarded gold medal and silver vase from the Patriotic Fund.

## At the battle

The *Mars* took heavy punishment both materially and among her crew at Trafalgar. She came into action astern and to starboard of the *Belleisle* at about 12.10 p.m. She was fired on by the *Fougueux*, and in the course of finding a gap through the line she was raked in the stern by the French 74-gun *Pluton*. To avoid running on board the *Santa Ana*, she luffed up into the wind and again exposed her stern to two more 74s, the Spanish *Monarca* and French *Algéciras*. She was severely mauled until the arrival of the *Tonnant* took some of the pressure off her. Nevertheless, she was damaged again by the *Pluton*. By then Duff was dead and his ship unmanageable. The master's log reads:

> At 1.15 Captain Duff was killed, and the poop and quarterdeck almost left destitute, the carnage was so great; having every one of our braces and running rigging shot away, which made the ship entirely ungovernable, and was frequently raked by different ships of the enemy ... there not being one shroud standing in either fore, main or mizzen rigging. The fore mast and main mast badly wounded. Mizzen mast cut half asunder, main top mast cut half in two, and not a sail in state of setting.

Of the crew 98 were hit – 29 dead and 69 wounded. There were 14 naval officer casualties (including master's mates and midshipmen) out of 31 – 45 per cent. The *Mars* had no fewer than four Duffs among the officers. In addition to the captain and his son Norwich, there was Master's Mate Alexander Duff, who was also hit and died in the arms of his younger brother Thomas Duff, a Volunteer Class 1. Lieutenant Hennah (first lieutenant) became the senior uninjured officer on the *Mars* and as such received Villeneuve's sword when the admiral came on board to surrender.

## After the battle

*Mars* was employed on blockade duties of Rochefort the following year capturing the 40-gun French frigate *Rhin*, which had survived Trafalgar. Later the same year, operating with a squadron, she assisted in the capture of four more French frigates. She was present at the bombardment of Copenhagen and taking of the Danish Fleet in 1807 and served in the expedition to the Baltic and in the Channel in 1808–13. After the war she was a receiving hulk at Portsmouth where she was finally broken up in 1823 after some thirty years' service.

## Belleisle

Dismasted and wallowing after the battle. Note the numerous shot holes in her hull.

# *Tonnant*

**Officers**

| | |
|---|---|
| Captain | C. Tyler (w) |
| Lieuts | J. Bedford (1st) |
| | C. Bennett |
| | F. Hoffman (w) |
| | B. Clement |
| | H.B. White |
| | W.S. Millett |
| Captain RM | A.H. Ball |
| 2nd Lieuts RM | J. Cottell |
| | W. Magin |

**Warrant Officers**

| | |
|---|---|
| Master | E. Soper |
| Surgeon | F. McB. Chevers |
| Carpenter | J. Chapman |
| Boatswain | R. Little (w) |
| Gunner | R. Rose |
| Purser | G. Booth |

## History/Characteristics

- A French 80-gun third-rate, two-decker built at Toulon in 1792. She was a splendid ship, well-designed, roomy and a fair sailer. However, she was devastated at the Battle of the Nile in 1798 and after losing all her masts and being pounded into a hulk was forced to capitulate. The British did not change her name. In 1803 she was detached with a squadron blockading Ferrol.

- Armament 80 guns:
    lower deck 32 x 32-pdrs
    upper deck 32 x 18-pdrs
    quarterdeck 2 x 18-pdrs + 14 x 32-pdr carronades
    forecastle 4 x 32-pdr carronades
She had only 66 guns, having replaced guns with carronades on the quarterdeck and armed the forecastle entirely with them. This gave a total armament of 84 pieces.
- Crew 688 (naval 600, RM 88).
She was quite seriously under strength in naval personnel.

## Commanded by

Captain Charles Tyler. The son of an Army officer, Tyler was born in 1760, entering the service in 1771 at the youngest possible age of eleven. He became a lieutenant in 1779, commander in 1782 and captain in 1790. He was commanding the 32-gun frigate *Meleager* at the reduction of Calvi, Corsica, in 1794, where Nelson lost his right eye. He then spent two years as captain of the 38-gun frigate *Aigle*, mostly chasing privateers, followed in 1801 by command of the 74-gun *Warrior* at Copenhagen – for which he received the thanks of parliament (although his ship played no real part in the battle). He was badly wounded at Trafalgar by a musket ball in his right thigh. For his gallant services Tyler received all the usual awards – gold medal, another thanks from parliament and a sword. For his wound he was given a pension of £250 a year – very generous for that time, being only slightly less than the annual salary of a captain of a third-rate. He was present at the surrender of the Russian fleet at Lisbon in 1808 and was made rear-admiral in 1808 and vice-admiral in 1813. Between 1812 and 1815 he was commander-in-chief, Cape of Good Hope. He died at Spa in 1835 aged seventy-five. Both his sons went into the Navy, one becoming a captain and the other a vice-admiral.

## At the battle

The *Tonnant* was fourth in the lee column. She came under fire as she approached the enemy line and had two of her band struck down as they played 'Britons, strike home'. She cut the line between two 74s, the Spanish *Monarca* and the French *Algéciras*, in the process raking the nearby French 74-gun *Pluton.* She was then closely engaged with the *Monarca* and *Algéciras,* the former of which struck her colours to her but raised them again as the *Tonnant* became locked together with the *Algéciras.* Though the *Algéciras* attempted to board she was repulsed and after a long and deadly struggle struck to the *Tonnant* after being herself successfully boarded. *Tonnant* then became engaged with exchanging broadsides with the Spanish 74, *San Juan Nepomuceno,* which soon also surrendered. She suffered 76 casualties – 26 killed and 50 wounded – and severe damage to the ship. All three topmasts and mainyard were shot away, her hull and rudder were hit and a large part of her starboard quarter galley and rails had disappeared.

## After the battle

She was towed to Gibraltar by the *Spartiate.* She spent the years 1806 to 1809 with the Channel Fleet, and in 1814 was on the North American station and engaged in the capture of Bladensburg and Washington. She also participated in the expedition against New Orleans and the attack and capture of six American gunboats and a sloop. In 1818 she carried the flag of Rear-Admiral Hallowell on the Irish station. She was broken up in 1821, aged twenty-nine.

# *Bellerophon*

## Officers

| | |
|---|---|
| Captain | J. Cooke (k) |
| Lieuts | W.P. Cumby (1st) |
| | E.F. Thomas |
| | D. Scott (w) |
| | J.A. Douglas |
| | G.L. Saunders |
| Captain RM | J. Wemyss (w) |
| 1st Lieut. RM | P. Connolly |
| 2nd Lieuts RM | L. Higgins |
| | J. Wilson |

## Warrant Officers

| | |
|---|---|
| Master | E. Overton (k) |
| Surgeon | A. White |
| Carpenter | R. Mart |
| Boatswain | T. Robinson (k) |
| Gunner | J. Stevenson |
| Purser | T. Jewell |

## History/Characteristics

- The *Bellerophon*, invariably referred to as the *Billy Ruff'n* by the seamen, was one of the smaller (common) class of third-rate, two-decker 74s. Built in a private yard near Rochester and launched in 1786, she was named after the hero of Greek mythology who rode into battle on the winged horse Pegasus – the badge of the modern British Airborne Forces. Like most 74s she was a responsive sailer with a reasonable turn of speed. However, *Bellerophon*'s commission in 1793 failed to get off to an auspicious start – she collided with the *Monarch* and had to return to port. In October she joined the Channel Fleet. She put up a tremendous fight at the Glorious First of June. Shortly before the battle she attacked the French 100-gun *Revolutionnaire,* sustaining the unequal duel for an hour and a half until three other British ships arrived. It is said she inflicted over 400 casualties. She was also in the thick of the fight on 1 June 1794, sustaining severe damage and losing 31 dead and wounded. She witnessed the loss of the 98-gun *Boyne,* which blew up at Spithead on 1 May 1795, and was with the squadron that captured eight merchantmen off Belle Isle in June of that year. In 1798 she was in the British line attacking the French at the Nile. There she took on another giant,

the 124-gun *L'Orient*. She was dismasted with 15 of her guns put out of action when Captain Darby cut his cable and drifted out of the line. Her losses totalled 193 killed and wounded – more than any British ship except the *Colossus* suffered at Trafalgar. She later served in the Mediterranean and with Nelson off Sicily. In 1801 she was with the Channel Fleet. 1802–3 saw her in the West Indies and Channel Fleet, during which she made several captures including a French 74, the *Duquesne.* In the period 1793–1815 *Bellerophon* saw more action than any other ship.

- Armament 74 guns:
    - lower deck 28 x 32-pdrs
    - upper deck 28 x 18-pdrs
    - quarterdeck 14 x 9-pdrs
    - forecastle 4 x 9-pdrs + 2 x 32-pdr carronades
    - poop 6 x 18-pdr carronades

Note that her gundeck broadsides had only 14 guns and those on the upper deck were only 18-pounders.

- Crew 522 (naval 450, RM 72). A smaller 74, her complement was 590 all ranks, so she was seriously under strength in seamen.

## Commanded by

Captain John Cooke – an officer with a reputation as a strict but fair disciplinarian. Born in 1763, he entered the service in 1776 as a thirteen-year-old boy. He was a midshipman during the American War of Independence and was present on the 74-gun *Eagle* at the attack on Rhode Island in 1776. Promoted lieutenant in 1779, he served in the 90-gun *Duke* at Lord Rodney's defeat of the French off Dominica in 1782. He was made commander in 1793 and commanded the fireship *Incendiary* at Lord Howe's victory on 1 June 1794. Promoted captain, he commanded the *Nymphe* at the capture of the French frigates *Resistance* and *Constance* in 1797, and the same year was expelled from his ship by mutineers during the Nore mutiny. He commanded the 38-gun frigate *Amethyst* in the expedition to Holland in 1799 and to Ferrol the following year. In 1801 Cooke was involved in the taking of several small French ships including the French corvette *Vaillante,* the frigate *La Dedaigneuse* and the Spanish *General Brune.* Immediately prior to Trafalgar he had commanded the guardship at Plymouth. He was killed at the battle while reloading his pistols, struck down, like Nelson, by musket shots, conspicuous on his quarterdeck while wearing his gold epaulettes. There is a tablet to his memory in St Paul's Cathedral. His widow received the gold medal and the commemorative silver vase.

## At the battle

The *Bellerophon* broke the enemy line at around 12.30 p.m. As she did so she was under fire from four ships (*Bahama, Aigle, Swiftsure* and *Montañés*) although she was able to rake both the *Bahama* and *Montañés* with her larboard and starboard broadsides respectively. She become locked together with the French 74 *Aigle* and repelled three attempts by the French to board her that saw the *Aigle*'s captain being cut down by Royal Marine musketry. Eventually the crippled *Aigle* was cut loose and drifted away. This enabled the *Bellerophon* to compel the nearby shattered hulk of the Spanish *Monarca* to surrender to her. Her gallant fight had cost the second highest casualty list of the British Fleet at Trafalgar – 150 (27 dead and 123 wounded). Among the dead and dying were the captain, master and boatswain. Physical damage included the loss of her main- and mizzen-topmasts, all her lower yards badly broken, her hull holed in several places and most of her shrouds and rigging cut.

## After the battle

From 1806 to 1809 the *Bellerophon* was stationed in the Channel and the Baltic but her only excitement was the capture of some Russian gunboats and a convoy in 1809. Her real claim to fame after the battle came when, under Captain Frederick Maitland, she accepted the surrender of Napoleon in person off Rochefort. As the ex-emperor climbed aboard a Royal Marine guard saluted him. Afterwards there was nothing but anti-climax, being paid off, and the ignominy of ten years as a convict hulk, first for boy convicts then for some 480 adults at Sheerness. At last, in 1834, at the age of forty-eight, she was towed to the breaker's yard at Plymouth. Her figurehead is still preserved at Portsmouth dockyard.

# *Colossus*

## Officers

| | |
|---|---|
| Captain | J.N. Morris (w) |
| Lieuts | T.R. Toker (1st) |
| | G. Huish |
| | G. Bulley (w) |
| | W.G. Nash |
| | G. Bague (w) |
| | W. Forster (acting; k) |
| | M.H. Sweny (acting; w) |
| Captain RM | E. Lawrence |
| 2nd Lieuts RM | W. Laurie |
| | J. Benson (w) |

## Warrant Officers

| | |
|---|---|
| Master | T. Scriven (k) |
| Surgeon | W. McDonald |
| Carpenter | G. Alderson |
| Boatswain | W. Adamson (w) |
| Gunner | W. Storar |
| Purser | J. Ault |

## History/Characteristics

• Virtually a brand-new ship at Trafalgar, she was built at Deptford in 1803 and named after the gigantic ancient Greek bronze lighthouse statue that stood at the entrance to Rhodes harbour, one of the seven wonders of the world. *Colossus* was a third-rate two-decker belonging to the 'Larger Class' of 74s. Not until 1804 was she commissioned and sent to join the blockade off Brest. In September 1805, as part of Collingwood's squadron watching Cadiz, she joined Nelson for the clash at Trafalgar.

• Armament 74 guns:
  lower deck 28 x 32-pdrs
  upper deck 30 x 24-pdrs
  quarterdeck 4 x 24 pdrs + 10 x 32-pdr carronades
  forecastle 2 x 24-pdrs + 2 x 24-pdr carronades
  poop 6 x 18-pdr carronades
She had only 64 guns, but her carronades more than compensated for the small number of guns on the quarterdeck and forecastle, giving her a total armament of 82 pieces. She was the only British ship at Trafalgar to have 24-pounder guns on her quarterdeck and forecastle. On these two decks plus the poop she carried two broadsides that, together, could deliver 620 lbs of shot – over twice that of the *Victory*. *Colossus* was aptly named in terms of firepower – her problem was a shortage of men to crew the guns adequately.
• Crew 571 (naval 490, RM 81).
She was substantially under manned.

## Commanded by

Captain James Nicoll Morris, the son of a naval officer who was killed in the attack on Charlestown in the American War of Independence. Born in 1763, he entered the service as a twelve-year-old in 1775. He first saw action when serving on the 98-gun *Prince of Wales* in the attack on St Lucia and Grenada in 1779 and became a lieutenant in 1780 at the impressively young age of seventeen. While on the Newfoundland station in command of the sloop *Plato* he was present at the capture of the French ship *Lutine*. He was promoted captain in 1793. When commanding the frigate *Lively* off Cadiz in 1798 he went aground on Rota Point and lost his ship. He served in the Mediterranean 1799–1800 before becoming captain of the *Colossus* at the blockade of Brest and watching Cadiz 1804–5. At Trafalgar he was badly wounded in the thigh and was only prevented from dying from loss of blood by the prompt application of a tourniquet – he remained in command on the poop. His gallantry and services were rewarded with the gold medal, thanks of parliament and a sliver vase. He was appointed a colonel of marines in 1810 and rear-admiral the following year and was third-in-command in the Baltic in 1812. He was made vice-admiral in 1819 and died in 1830 aged sixty-seven.

## At the battle

The *Colossus* was the sixth ship of the lee column to reach the enemy line at around 12.35 p.m., having suffered from 'a galling fire from the enemy's rear' for the previous ten minutes. The first enemy she engaged was the French *Swiftsure*, then, after passing through a dense bank of smoke, she crashed onboard the French *Argonaute*. A murderous exchange of broadsides began, with the two ships' gunports almost touching. According to the British captain's log it was ten minutes before the *Argonaute* drifted clear, according to the French captain half an hour. During this time Captain Morris was wounded. There is a splendid story that a hen-coop was smashed, allowing the cockerel to fly out and alight on the captain's shoulder, much to the amusement of all who saw it. Next the Spanish *Bahama* and the *Swiftsure* (again) opened fire on the *Colossus*. However, she gave back far more than she received and after a period of intense mutual slaughter the *Bahama* struck. The *Colossus* had the highest casualty toll of any British ship at Trafalgar – 200, of whom 40 were killed and 160 wounded. A lieutenant and the master died, while the captain, three lieutenants, a RM 2nd lieutenant and the boatswain were among the wounded. *Colossus* suffered severe material damage. Her mainmast was hit many times and had to be cut away, her foremast was shot through, two anchors and three boats destroyed. Her sails and rigging 'were very much cut, and quite unmanageable', and four of her starboard lower-deck ports had been smashed when she crashed into the *Argonaute*.

## After the battle

She was taken in tow by the *Agamemnon*. In 1807, still under Captain Morris, *Colossus* was with the squadron watching Rochefort. In 1811 she lost two of her boats in an attack on an enemy convoy in the Basque Roads when 45 officers and men were captured. She performed no other service of consequence and was broken up at Chatham in 1827 aged twenty-four.

# Achille

## Officers

| | |
|---|---|
| Captain | R. King |
| Lieuts | W.W. Daniell (1st) |
| | P. Prynn (w) |
| | G. Canning |
| | J. Bray (w) |
| | W. Hill |
| | E. Barnard (acting) |
| Captain RM | P. Westropp (w) |
| 2nd Lieuts RM | W. Liddon (w) |
| | F. Whalley |

## Warrant Officers

| | |
|---|---|
| Master | T. Watson |
| Surgeon | W. Gray |
| Chaplain | Rev. J.C. Whicher |
| Carpenter | J. Wallis |
| Boatswain | P. Johnson |
| Gunner | R. Hills |
| Purser | J. Lamport |

## History/Characteristics

- Sometimes incorrectly (for example in the Trafalgar Roll) called *Achilles*. Although she was never a French ship, having been built at Gravesend in 1798, she was named after the French *Achille*, which was captured at the Glorious First of June and later destroyed. A third-rate two-decker 74, she had very little, if any, action prior to the battle, having spent much of the time on blockade duties off Rochefort. The autumn of 1805 found her in Collingwood's small squadron off Cadiz.

- Armament 74 guns:
   lower deck 30 x 32-pdrs
   upper deck 30 x 18-pdrs
   quarterdeck 4 x 18-pdrs + 10 x 32-pdr carronades
   forecastle 2 x 18-pdrs + 2 x 24-pdr carronades
   poop 6 x 18-pdr carronades
There were 66 guns, with carronades replacing some 18-pounders on the quarterdeck, forecastle and poop: a total armament of 84 pieces.
- Crew 619 (naval 540, RM 79). Slightly under complement.

## Commanded by

Captain Richard King. The son of an admiral, he was born in 1774, entering the service as a fourteen-year-old in 1788. He rose quickly up the promotion ladder, to lieutenant in 1791 and post captain three years later at twenty-one, putting him on a par with Nelson and making an exceptionally good start to a naval career, particularly as his service until then had been mundane. He was a member of the court martial that convicted Richard Parker, the leader of the Nore mutineers, in 1797, and thereafter his career came alive. When captain of the 36-gun frigate *Sirius* between 1797 and 1802 he captured two Dutch ships, the 36-gun *Furie* and the 26-gun *Waakzamheid*, together with 253 men. Next he took the 6-gun *La Favorie* plus a Spanish brig. Then, in company with the *L'Oiseau,* he added the French frigate of 36 guns *La Dedaigneuse* to his impressive haul. Within a few years he had made himself a wealthy man. Trafalgar earned him the gold medal, parliamentary thanks and a sword of honour from the Patriotic Fund. For the rest of the war he was employed on blockade duties off Ferrol, Cadiz and in the Mediterranean. In 1812 he became a rear-admiral and had his flag in the 110-gun *San Josef* off Toulon. He was then appointed commander-in-chief East Indies, a post he retained until 1820. He was made vice-admiral in 1821 and served as commander-in-chief at the Nore from 1833 to 1834 when, very unusually for an admiral, he died of cholera aged sixty. His son also became an admiral.

## At the battle

*Achille* broke the line astern of the *Colossus* at around 12.45 p.m. She was immediately in the thick of the fight, firing a raking broadside into the stern of the Spanish *Montañés* before luffing up, coming alongside and beginning a brutal engagement at pistol-shot range, which lasted about twelve minutes before the *Montañés* sheered away. Next she fell in with another Spanish ship, the *Argonauta*. Coming in on his enemy's larboard beam Captain King fought it out for nearly an hour, by which time the Spaniard had ceased firing and closed her lower-deck ports. However, before *Achille* could take possession, she first fired into the French *Achille* before becoming locked into another hour of close-range exchanges with the French *Berwick*, which ended with the *Berwick* hauling down her colours.
Considering the length, range and intensity of the fighting the *Achille* came off comparatively lightly with the loss of her topmasts and 72 casualties – 13 dead and 59 wounded. Only one senior rank was killed – Midshipman Francis Mugg.

## After the battle

In 1809 she took part in the ill-fated expedition to Walcheron island, off Holland, which saw 4,000 soldiers die of malaria. In 1810, while blockading Cadiz, she witnessed the destruction of seven Spanish and one Portuguese warships together with twenty-four merchantmen that were all driven ashore in a gale and then set on fire to prevent them being pulled off and salvaged by the enemy. In 1811 she was on blockade duty off Toulon, defending Sicily and in the Adriatic blockading Venice. After a refit in 1813 she went first to the blockading squadron off Cherbourg, then escorted a convoy to the Cape of Good Hope before finally sailing for the South America station. She was taken out of commission in 1815 but was given no further duties, although officially still in service, until she was broken up at Sheerness fifty years later in 1865. At sixty-seven she was indeed a very old lady.

# Revenge

## Officers

| | |
|---|---|
| Captain | R. Moorsom (w) |
| Lieuts | L. Hole (1st) |
| | P.G. Pickernell |
| | F. Wills |
| | E.J. Holcombe |
| | W. Wright |
| | J. Berry (w) |
| Captain RM | P. Lely (w) |
| 2nd Lieuts RM | H.B. Fairlough |
| | A. Copperthwaite |

## Warrant Officers

| | |
|---|---|
| Master | L. Brokenshaw (w) |
| Surgeon | W. Dykar |
| Chaplain | Rev. J. Greenly (w)* |
| Carpenter | W. Russell |
| Boatswain | G. Forster |
| Gunner | J. Tucker |
| Purser | J. Buckingham |

*The only chaplain to be injured at Trafalgar.

## History/Characteristics

- A brand-new 74-gun, third-rate two-decker, built and launched in 1805. She was also one of the first ships to be painted following Nelson's preference with a black hull, a yellow strake along each tier of ports and black port beds. This pattern of chequered painting distinguished most of the British ships at the battle, and they became known as 'Nelson's chequer players'. *Revenge* joined the squadron off Cadiz and witnessed Nelson's arrival there in September 1805.

- Armament 74 guns:
   lower deck 30 x 32-pdrs
   upper deck 30 x 18-pdrs
   quarterdeck 12 x 9-pdrs
   forecastle 2 x 9-pdrs + 2 x 32-pdr carronades
   poop 6 x 18-pdr carronades
The carronades had been added to her armament rather than replacing 9-pounders.
- Crew 598 (naval 490, RM 108).
Overall she was under manned, particularly as regards naval personnel, although she had more marines than was strictly necessary.

## Commanded by

Captain Robert Moorsom. A Yorkshireman, he was born in 1760 and entered the service as a fourteen-year-old midshipman in 1774. He served in the Channel, at the relief of Gibraltar in 1781 and again the following year, and he took part in several minor actions including the capture of a convoy bound for the West Indies in 1782. In 1790 he was taken seriously ill while commanding the 16-gun sloop *Ariel* in the East Indies. He was sent home, arriving in England in May 1791 to find he had been promoted captain. He recovered, married and was appointed to command first the 32-gun frigate *Astrea*, then the *Niger*, another 32, and later the 50-gun *Hindustan*. From 1803 to 1804 Moorsom commanded the 74-gun *Majestic* before joining the *Revenge* in the blockading squadron off Cadiz in 1805. By Trafalgar he had been in the Royal Navy for over thirty years but, almost exceptionally among the captains, he had not seen a fleet action or been engaged in a serious fight. Trafalgar, during which he was wounded, was to be the only real highlight of his career at sea. Nevertheless, Moorsom had always been an enthusiastic trainer and something of a gunnery expert – both of which attributes paid enormous dividends during his one and only battle. For his services he received the usual awards – gold medal, the thanks of parliament and a sword. He carried the 'great banner with the augmentations' at Nelson's funeral but his career after Trafalgar, while not lacking in promotion, was anything but exciting. He became private secretary to the First Lord of the Admiralty in 1807, then a Lord Commissioner of the Admiralty, Surveyor General of the Ordnance, while still a captain. Promoted rear-admiral in 1810, he also became MP for Queenborough, Sheerness and was made a vice-admiral in 1814. He was Commander-in-Chief Chatham from 1824 to 1827 before being promoted admiral in 1830. He died five years later aged seventy-five.

## At the battle

The *Revenge* was the eighth ship in the lee column to break the enemy line at about 12.50 p.m. She quickly became involved in a fearsome mêlée and at one time was in the centre of a triangle of three enemy ships including the 112-gun *Principe de Asturias*. She was heavily engaged with the Spanish *San Ildefonso* and *Principe de Asturias* and the French *Achille* and *Aigle*. Her gunnery was magnificent but had it not been for the intervention of other British ships she would probably have been destroyed. The battle cost her 79 casualties – 28 killed and 51 wounded, the proportion of dead (35 per cent) to wounded unusually high. Her bowsprit, three lower masts (masts being divided into sections), maintopmast and gaff were badly damaged, and she received nine hits below the waterline. Her stern, transoms, beams and knees were severely splintered, several lower-deck ports were destroyed and three guns dismounted. She had absorbed an enormous amount of shot, much of which had smashed through her gundecks. Considering her structural damage she was fortunate not to have many more casualties.

## After the battle

Her first captain after a refit on return to Portsmouth was the Hon. Charles Fleming, who became instantly unpopular by having the Nelson chequers painted out and a single stripe substituted. However he lasted only a few months and to the crew's delight the new captain gave orders for the *Revenge* to be once again one of the 'Nelson chequer-players'. In 1806 she was at the mouth of the Gironde when her boats were involved in the cutting out of the French corvette *Caesar*. Later, off Rochefort, she took part in the pursuit of more French corvettes and frigates. In 1807 she was off Cadiz and then in the Channel. In 1809 she participated in the action off the Basque Roads and in the destruction of several ships, at the cost to her of 18 casualties. From then until the end of the war she was deployed in the Channel and Mediterranean on minor operations. She was in the Mediterranean between 1823 and 1832 and again a few years later. Still active in 1840, *Revenge* took part in operations along the coast of Syria, including the bombardment of Acre. She was finally broken up in Sheerness in 1851 after forty-six years' service.

# Defiance

## Officers

| | |
|---|---|
| Captain | P.C. Durham (w) |
| Lieuts | T. Simons (1st; killed) |
| | W. Hellard |
| | J.U. Purches |
| | A.B. Pidgley |
| | H.J.S. Hargrave |
| Captain RM | B. Alves |
| 1st Lieut. RM | G.I. Bristow |

## Warrant Officers

| | |
|---|---|
| Master | J. Osman |
| Surgeon | W. Burnett |
| Chaplain | Rev. R.H. Barker |
| Carpenter | W. Caught |
| Boatswain | W. Forster (k) |
| Gunner | A. Jacks |
| Purser | G. Jackson |

## History/Characteristics

• Another 74-gun third-rate two-decker, designed by Sir Thomas Slade and built in a private yard on the Thames in 1783. However, she was not commissioned until 1794 (one wonders why) and her first four years were anything but auspicious. She was deeply involved in three consecutive mutinies. The first, in 1794, resulted in five of her crew being hanged. The second was the 1797 mutiny at Spithead, which resulted in a number of grievances being rectified. The third was in the following year, when ten of her crew were hanged and ten transported for life for being involved in what was known as the conspiracy of the 'United Irishmen'. Wearing the flag of Rear-Admiral Sir Thomas Graves, she was present at Nelson's victory at Copenhagen in 1801, during which she was several times set on fire by red-hot shot from the shore batteries. Her next engagement was Sir Robert Calder's clash with Villeneuve on the latter's way back from the West Indies in July 1805.

• Armament 74 guns:
 lower deck 28 x 32-pdrs
 upper deck 28 x 18-pdrs
 quarterdeck 14 x 9-pdrs
 forecastle 4 x 9-pdrs
• Crew 577 (naval 500, RM 77). Considerably under strength in seamen.

## Commanded by

Captain Philip Charles Durham. He was born in 1763 in Fifeshire, Scotland, entering the service at fourteen in 1777, and was present in the *Elgar* at the relief of Gibraltar in 1781. He had the misfortune the following year, when acting as a lieutenant, to be officer of the watch on the *Royal George* when she sank at Spithead, and spent several hours in the water before being rescued. This disaster so early in his career had no effect on his promotion as he was made substantive lieutenant the same year. He was in the *Union* late in the year during Lord Howe's relief of Gibraltar and in the action with the combined fleets off Cape Spartel (Tangier). Promoted commander in 1790 and captain in 1793, he commanded the 44-gun frigate *Anson* in the action off Isle Groix and Lorient and in the expedition to Quiberon Bay in 1795. In 1798 he received the thanks of parliament for his capture of the French 74-gun *Hoche* and two frigates off Tory Island (Northern Ireland). He was commanding the *Defiance* in Calder's action off Cape Finisterre three months before Trafalgar (he refused to go home to attend Calder's court martial, as did the captains of *Ajax* and *Thunderer*). Durham was wounded at Trafalgar and received the customary gold medal, parliamentary thanks and sword of honour. He bore Nelson's banner at his funeral. He later served as a commodore in the Mediterranean and assisted in the destruction of two French ships near Cette (Gabon, West Africa). He was made rear-admiral in 1810 and Commander-in-Chief Windward Islands 1813–16, being present at the reduction of the French islands of Martinique and Guadeloupe in 1815. He was promoted vice-admiral in 1819 and admiral in 1830 and became MP for Queenborough, then Devizes in 1835, serving as Commander-in-Chief Portsmouth 1836–9. He was also an equerry to HRH the Duke of Cambridge. He died aged eighty-two in Naples in 1845 as Admiral Sir P.C. Henderson-Calderwell-Durham, having acquired the additional names in 1817 and 1840 respectively.

## At the battle

*Defiance* joined the battle at about 1.30 p.m. after exchanging shots with the third ship from the rear of the enemy line (*Principe de Asturias*). Later she ran onboard the French *Aigle*, which she lashed herself to and boarded. After a stiff fight the British colours were hoisted and the ship seemingly captured. However, the enemy rallied, counter-attacked and drove the British back. Captain Durham had the lashings cut, sheered off a short distance and opened up a heavy fire – within half an hour the *Aigle* surrendered, this time permanently. The cost to *Defiance* was 70 casualties, made up of 17 dead and 53 wounded, with the first lieutenant among the former and the captain the latter. Her bowsprit, fore- and mainmasts (i.e. the lower of the three sections to each mast) were shot through, her mizzenmast, three topmasts (i.e. the middle sections), jib and gaff damaged. Her rigging and sails were badly shredded and her hull hit several times.

## After the battle

She tried unsuccessfully to take in tow the *Aigle*. Between 1806 and 1809 *Defiance* assisted at the blockade of Lorient and in the landing of British troops in northern Spain. In 1809 she took part in a successful action with three 40-gun French frigates. Similarly she was with the squadron that took five Spanish sail-of-the-line, five frigates and five sloops lying in the harbour at Ferrol during the period 1809–10. She was paid off at Chatham in 1813 and then used as a prison ship until 1816, when she was broken up aged thirty-three.

# *Swiftsure*

## Officers

| | |
|---|---|
| Captain | W.G. Rutherford |
| Lieuts | J. Lilburne (1st) |
| | T. Sykes |
| | R. Carter |
| | T. Reed |
| | R.H. Barclay |
| 2nd Lieuts RM* | W. Gibbons |
| | R. Gordon |
| | H. Miller |

## Warrant Officers

| | |
|---|---|
| Master | G. Forbes |
| Surgeon | P. Suther (acting) |
| Carpenter | T. Evans |
| Boatswain | A. Bell |
| Gunner | J. McPhail |
| Purser | J. Robinson |

*The only line-of-battle ship to have no RM officer above the rank of second lieutenant.

## History/Characteristics

• A third-rate, two-decker 74 built at Buckler's Hard and launched in 1804, making her one of the newest ships at the battle. Initially sent to cruise off the north coast of Spain, she joined Nelson on Christmas Day 1804 off Toulon and participated in the search for Villeneuve's fleet in the Mediterranean and the fruitless chase to the West Indies prior to Trafalgar. This *Swiftsure* is often confused with the ship of the same name that fought with Nelson at the Nile, which was later captured by the French and fought against the British at Trafalgar.

• Armament 74 guns:
  lower deck 28 x 32-pdrs
  upper deck 28 x 18-pdrs
  quarterdeck 4 x 18-pdrs + 10 x 32-pdr carronades
  forecastle 2 x 18-pdrs + 2 x 32-pdr carronades
  poop 6 x 18-pdr carronades
In total there were only 62 guns as a number of 18-pounders had been replaced by carronades; the total armament was 80 pieces of ordnance.

• Crew 570 (naval 490, RM 80).
Another ship seriously short of her proper complement of seamen.

## Commanded by

Captain William Gordon Rutherford. The son of a Scottish father and American mother, Rutherford was born in North Carolina in 1764 but educated in Edinburgh. He entered the service as a fourteen-year-old boy in 1778. By 1793 he was an acting lieutenant on the 98-gun *Boyne* in the West Indies. As a lieutenant in 1794 he distinguished himself ashore with a detachment of seamen in the capture of Martinique, being mentioned in despatches and made commander. Promoted captain in 1796, he took part in the capture of Curaçao in 1800. He had command of a series of frigates including the 36-gun *Decade* at the blockade of Cherbourg in 1804. In 1805 he was appointed to the *Swiftsure*. For Trafalgar he received the usual captains' awards – gold medal, thanks of parliament and a sword. After the battle his career seems to have stagnated. Although the war had ten years to run Rutherford does not appear to have played any active role in it. He was made Captain of Greenwich Hospital in 1814 – perhaps an appropriate appointment as he may have been in poor health and died there four years later aged fifty-four. He had not lived long enough to make rear-admiral, even in retirement.

## At the battle

The *Swiftsure* did not reach the action until some two hours after the first shots were fired as she was well to the rear of the lee column. She did, however, have a long and deadly struggle with the French 74 *Achille*. After some forty minutes the French ship was seen to be on fire. At around 4.30 p.m. the *Prince* arrived and fired her massive broadside into the stricken ship, bringing down the flaming upper half of the *Achille*'s mainmast. Within minutes she exploded. The *Swiftsure* suffered lightly, her losses being consistent with her comparatively late arrival. Of her total casualties of 17, 9 were killed and 8 wounded. Of all the officers and warrant officers only one midshipman was wounded. Structural damage was negligible.

## After the battle

She took in tow the French 74-gun *Redoutable*; when the latter was found to be sinking the *Swiftsure* was compelled to cut her loose but, despite the violent gale, was able to use her boats to rescue 170 Frenchmen. The next few years were uneventful and it was not until 1813 that her boats captured a French privateer, the 8-gun *Charlemagne*, off Cape Rousée, Corsica. In 1814 she was in the Mediterranean followed by two years in the Caribbean. In 1816 she became a receiving ship at Portsmouth until 1845. The old lady was then shot to pieces as a target ship for a few months before what was left was sold as firewood for £1,050. She was forty-one.

# *Dreadnought*

## Officers

| | |
|---|---|
| Captain | J. Conn |
| Lieuts | |
| R. Morris (1st) | G. Stone |
| G. Hewson | N. Palmer |
| W. Landless | C.W. Betty (w) |
| J.L. Lloyd (w) | J. Neale |
| Captain RM | T. Timins |
| 1st Lieuts RM | J. McCallam |
| | T. Lemon |
| 2nd Lieut. RM | D. Marlay |

## Warrant Officers

| | |
|---|---|
| Master | R. Burstal |
| Surgeon | M. Felix |
| Chaplain | Rev. T. Hardwick |
| Carpenter | W. Haswell |
| Boatswain | E. Burr |
| Gunner | J.M. Watkins |
| Purser | J. Hopper |

## History/Characteristics

- *Dreadnought* was a 98-gun, second-rate three-decker, and 'sister' ship to the *Téméraire*. Her birth was a long and difficult one as she sat on the stocks in Portsmouth dockyard for thirteen years before she was finally launched in 1801. She was the first line-of-battle ship launched after the union of Great Britain and Ireland, and her figurehead carried a lion couchant on a scroll containing the royal arms as emblazoned on the standard. She was considered a slow ship. In 1803 she carried the flag of Admiral Cornwallis with the Channel Fleet off Brest, and then that of Vice-Admiral Collingwood off Cadiz in 1805. Collingwood only transferred his flag to the *Royal Sovereign* ten days before Trafalgar, one of the reasons being, as Collingwood put it, 'The *Dreadnought* certainly sails very ill …'.

- Armament 98 guns:
  - lower deck 28 x 32-pdrs
  - middle deck 30 x 18-pdrs
  - upper deck 30 x 18-pdrs
  - quarterdeck 8 x 12-pdrs
  - forecastle 2 x 12-pdrs

  Exactly the same firepower and distribution of guns as the *Téméraire*.
- Crew 725 (naval 625, RM 100).
  Only a few naval personnel short of her complement.

## Commanded by

Captain John Conn. Born in Waterford, Ireland in 1764, he entered the service as a fourteen-year-old boy in 1778. He was a lieutenant on the *Royal Sovereign* at Lord Howe's famous victory at the battle of the Glorious First of June, 1794. Made commander in 1800, he commanded the bomb vessel *Discovery* at Copenhagen in 1801. Later the same year he commanded a division of four mortar boats in an attack on the French invasion flotilla assembling at Boulogne. He was promoted captain in 1802 and commanded the 80-gun *Canopus*, flagship of Rear-Admiral Campbell, with Nelson's force blockading Toulon from 1803 to 1805. For services at Trafalgar he received the gold medal, the thanks of parliament and the sword of honour. While in command of the 74-gun *Swiftsure* off Bermuda in 1810, he was afflicted by mental illness and jumped overboard, drowning before he could be rescued.

## At the battle

*Dreadnought* was one of the rearmost ships in the lee column and thus arrived late to the action. She came alongside the Spanish 74-gun *San Juan Nepomuceno* and brought her three heavy batteries to bear. Within ten minutes the Spaniard had had enough and Captain Conn took his prize. The *Dreadnought* then pursued the *Principe de Asturias*. Her losses for her comparatively short time in action totalled 33 – 7 killed and 26 wounded. Her damage was also slight, just her masts cut and her maintopsail yard shot away – yet another example of how many enemy shots went high, even at quite close ranges.

## After the battle

She bore the flag of Rear-Admiral Sotheby with the Channel Fleet from 1808 to 1810, during which time her boats lost heavily in an attempt to cut out a French ship off Ushant. She had no further active sea service, ending her days as a hospital ship at Milford and then from 1831 to 1857 (dates which include the Crimean War) as a seamen's hospital at Greenwich. She was broken up in 1857 aged fifty-six.

# *Polyphemus*

## Officers

| | |
|---|---|
| Captain | R. Redmill |
| Lieuts | G. Moubray (1st) |
| | W. Sandey |
| | C. Squarey |
| | J. Medlicott |
| | R. Mayne |
| Captain RM | M. Perceval |
| 2nd Lieuts RM | J. Mackintosh |
| | C.A. Trusson |

## Warrant Officers

| | |
|---|---|
| Master | R. Louthean |
| Surgeon | J. Corbet |
| Carpenter | J. Roaf |
| Boatswain | G. Bruce |
| Gunner | uncertain |
| Purser | J. Stewart |

## History/Characteristics

• A third-rate two-decker with 64 guns, *Polyphemus* was something of an elderly lightweight in any line of battle in 1805. Having been launched in 1782 she was twenty-three years old at Trafalgar, although her first active service had not started until the French Revolutionary Wars. She did exceptionally well in 1795 by taking the Dutch 74-gun *Overijssel*. Two years later she captured the 40-gun French frigate *Tortue* and in 1801 was part of Nelson's squadron in the attack on the Danes at Copenhagen in which she lost 31 dead and wounded in a tough gunnery duel with the far more powerful floating battery the *Provestenen*. At the recommencement of the war in 1803 she took part in the capture of the Spanish frigate, the 36-gun *Santa Gertrudis*.

• Armament 64 guns:
   lower deck 26 x 24-pdrs
   upper deck 26 x 18-pdrs
   quarterdeck 10 x 9-pdrs
   forecastle 2 x 9-pdrs
• Crew 484 (naval 420, RM 64).
She was only about ten men short overall and, unusually, had exactly one marine for each gun carried.

## Commanded by

Captain Robert Redmill. His date of birth is uncertain but he entered the Navy as a boy. He was a lieutenant in 1783 and had command of the 14-gun fireship *Comet* in action against the French in 1795. Promoted captain in 1796, he commanded the 64-gun *Deft* in operations along the coast of Egypt and in supporting the British landings in Aboukir Bay in 1801 – for which he received a Turkish gold medal. After Trafalgar he was awarded another gold medal, the thanks of parliament and a sword. However, his career was cut short by ill health in 1806 and he died in 1819.

## At the battle

One of the later arrivals into the mêlée, she became engaged with the French *Neptune* and the French *Achille* before the latter blew up, after which the *Polyphemus*, along with other ships, became involved with picking up survivors. Her casualties were very light – two killed and four wounded – reflecting that by the time she came into action many of the enemy had been heavily pounded and some had already struck. Similarly, damage was confined to the 'main mast and main topmast wounded'.

## After the battle

She took the Spanish *Argonauta* in tow despite the severe gales on the days following the battle. She later towed *Victory*, with the body of Nelson on board, to the Straits of Gibraltar. In 1806 she was involved with the cutting out of the 16-gun corvette *Cesar*. Later the same year she was on the South America station and witnessed the disastrous British attack on Buenos Aires. She then became the flagship of the commander-in-chief of the Jamaica station. While on that station she was involved in several minor actions as well as the bombardment and capture of San Domingo. She was paid off in 1812. From 1816 to 1832 she was used as a powder ship at Chatham and later that year was broken up, aged fifty.

# *Thunderer*

## Officers

| | |
|---|---|
| Captain | J. Stockham (acting)* |
| Lieuts | W. Norman (acting 1st) |
| | J. Clark |
| | T. Carter |
| | T. Colby |
| Captain RM | G. Elliot |
| 2nd Lieuts RM | W. Hockley |
| | J. Lister |

## Warrant Officers

| | |
|---|---|
| Master | R. Cock |
| Surgeon | J. Stokoe |
| Chaplain | Rev. J. Holmes |
| Carpenter | E. Trego |
| Boatswain | R. Keefe |
| Gunner | W. Watt |
| Purser | H. Wells |

*Stockham was normally the first lieutenant, but was acting captain as Captain Lechmere was absent attending Calder's court martial.

## History/Characteristics

• A third-rate, two-decker 74 built on the Thames in 1783, making her twenty-two years old at Trafalgar. While with the Channel Fleet under Lord Howe in 1794 she was in action with the rear ships of the French Fleet on 28 May. She then participated in the British victory of the Glorious First of June. A year later she took part in the capture of three French ships-of-the-line, then accompanied the expedition to Quiberon Bay. In 1797 she was on the Jamaica station and assisted in the destruction of the French 44-gun frigate *Harmoine* off San Domingo. In 1803 she was with the Channel Fleet and participated in the chase and capture of the 40-gun *Franchise*. In July she pursued and captured the French 16-gun privateer *Venus*. After a period on the Ireland station she was present in Sir Robert Calder's fleet in its clash with Villeneuve off Cape Finisterre in July 1805, at which she suffered 19 casualties – more than at Trafalgar. She joined Nelson at Plymouth on 18 September.

• Armament 74 guns:
    lower deck 28 x 32-pdrs
    upper deck 28 x 18-pdrs
    quarterdeck 14 x 9-pdrs
    forecastle 4 x 9-pdrs
• Crew 611 (naval 500, RM 111).
Somewhat under complement for seamen and over strength with marines. She was under strength in naval officers, having only four lieutenants instead of six.

## Commanded by

Lieutenant, acting captain John Stockham. He had been promoted lieutenant in 1797 and served as first lieutenant on the *Thunderer* at Calder's action off Cape Finisterre three months earlier. For his successful command at Trafalgar he received immediate promotion to substantive captain together with a gold medal, the thanks of parliament and a sword of honour. His subsequent career was curtailed by his death, at Exeter, in 1814.

## At the battle

As she was the second to last ship in the lee column the fiercest fighting was over by the time the *Thunderer* joined the battle. She was of some assistance to the *Revenge,* and subsequently engaged the Spanish *Principe de Asturias* and French *Neptune.* Her casualties were light – four killed and twelve wounded. Similarly, although her main- and mizzenmasts and bowsprit had been hit the damage was superficial and she was able to take the *Santa Ana* in tow.

## After the battle

1806 found her with Lord Cornwallis off Cadiz. The following year she did well when participating in the destruction of a Turkish squadron at the Dardanelles. In 1808 she was on blockade duty off Rochefort. She performed no other important service and was broken up at Chatham in 1814 aged thirty-one.

# *Defence*

## Officers

| | |
|---|---|
| Captain | G.J. Hope |
| Lieuts | J. Green (1st) |
| | W. Hosie |
| | T. Janverin |
| | G. Kippen |
| | J. Cooke |
| | J.H. Plumridge (acting) |
| Captain RM | H. Cox |
| 1st Lieut. RM | J. Wilson |
| 2nd Lieut. RM | A. Burton |

## Warrant Officers

| | |
|---|---|
| Master | R. Turner |
| Surgeon | J. Gillies |
| Carpenter | P. Crusoe |
| Boatswain | J. Phillips |
| Gunner | A. Goldie |
| Purser | J.F. Bushell |

## History/Characteristics

- She was launched at Plymouth in 1763, two years before the *Victory* and only one year after the *Britannia*. This made her, at forty-two, the second oldest ship at the battle. She had probably seen more action than any ship in either fleet at Trafalgar. Having just missed the Seven Years' War (1756–63) she spent her time on routine cruising until 1780, when she was involved in the heavy fighting for the relief of Gibraltar under Admiral Rodney. In January of that year the *Defence* and several other ships chased and captured a Spanish convoy and seven ships-of-war. The following month she was again involved in a fierce running action against a Spanish squadron of 14 ships-of-the-line. *Defence* played a key role in scattering the enemy at a cost of 10 dead and 21 wounded. In 1783 she was in the East Indies in Vice-Admiral Hughes' squadron. She participated in his final battle with the French under Admiral Suffren off Pondicherry when her casualties were even heavier – 45 killed and wounded. She fought under Howe at the Glorious First of June when she was the first ship to break the enemy line. Her captain at that battle, Gambier, was something of a religious fanatic and the *Defence* acquired the nickname 'The Praying Ship'. As in most of her battles she suffered heavily, losing 54 dead and wounded while her commander received a gold medal. In 1795, during an indecisive chase of the enemy near Toulon she lost another seven men. 1798 found her in Nelson's fleet when he destroyed the French at the Nile. Yet another battle, yet another 15 casualties. Her crew, who had been involved in the Spithead mutiny the previous year, again mutinied in September 1798, and 19 seamen were sentenced to death. In 1799 she was engaged in operations against lightly armed ships and merchantmen off St Croix and coastal batteries on the French coast. *Defence* was present at the Battle of Copenhagen in 1801, although not in the squadron under Nelson that attacked the Danish Fleet and batteries.

- Armament 74 guns:
    lower deck 28 x 32-pdrs
    upper deck 28 x 18-pdrs
    quarterdeck 14 x 9-pdrs
    forecastle 4 x 9-pdrs
- Crew 599 (naval 490, RM 109).
She was under strength in seamen at Trafalgar.

## Commanded by

Captain George Johnstone Hope. Born in 1867, he entered the service at fifteen in 1782 and was promoted lieutenant in 1788, commander in 1790 and captain three years later. He commanded the 36-gun frigate *Romulus* in Vice-Admiral Hotham's action off Genoa in 1795. In 1798 he chased and captured the French gunboat *Legere* off the Egyptian coast. She was carrying despatches for Napoleon and her captain threw them overboard at the moment of capture, but two seamen leapt into the sea and recovered them. His services as a Trafalgar captain earned him the usual reward of a gold medal, thanks of parliament and sword. He was captain of the *Victory*, bearing the flag of Vice-Admiral Saumarez (one of Nelson's original band of brothers) in the Baltic in 1808. Promoted rear-admiral in 1811, he was a Lord of the Admiralty from 1812 to 1813, then became MP for East Grinstead and major-general, Royal Marines in 1818 – the year he died at the comparatively young age of fifty-one. One of his sons, James, became admiral of the fleet.

## At the battle

Being the last ship in the lee column, *Defence* was not able to join the battle until about two and a half hours after the first shots. Nevertheless, she was in time to engage the French *Berwick* and then the Spanish *San Ildefonso* for about an hour until she struck. The exchange of broadsides cost her 36 casualties – 7 killed and 29 wounded. Much of her lower and topmast rigging was shot away, her gaff cut in two and her mainmast slightly damaged.

## After the battle

She took the *San Ildefonso* in tow as a prize and managed to keep her under tow despite the gales of the next few days. *Defence* was present at the bombardment of Copenhagen in 1807 – her second time attacking the Danes. In 1809 she was back in the Baltic bombarding a Russian battery at Porcola Point. On Christmas Eve 1811, she was driven onto a lee shore in a violent storm and wrecked. Of her crew of about 530 only about 6 survived. Among the dead was her captain, David Atkins. It was a sad end to forty-eight years of active service in which she had participated in four major fleet actions and countless smaller engagements – something of a record.

# *Prince*

## Officers

| | |
|---|---|
| Captain | R. Grindall |
| Lieuts | W. Godfray (1st) |
| | W. Kelly |
| | J. Edwards |
| | A. Ferris |
| | S. Burgess |
| | A. Baldwin |
| | J. Hall |
| Captain RM | F. Williams |
| Lieut. RM | E. Pengelly |

## Warrant Officers

| | |
|---|---|
| Master | R. Anderson |
| Surgeon | J. Fullarton |
| Carpenter | W. Johnson |
| Boatswain | S. Simpson |
| Gunner | T. Hawkins |
| Purser | T. Tait |

## History/Characteristics

- A second-rate, three-decker of 98 guns built at Chatham in 1788, she was known as a sluggish sailer. She wore the flag of Rear-Admiral Bowyer in the Channel Fleet in 1793 and was present with Lord Bridport's fleet in his successful action against the French off Lorient in 1795. She was in the Mediterranean with Lord St Vincent in 1798. Her armed launch attended the execution of the ringleaders of the mutiny in the *Marlborough*. In 1799 she wore the flag of Rear-Admiral Sir Charles Cotton as third-in-command of the Channel Fleet. In 1803 she was employed on blockade duties off Brest and Cadiz.

- Armament 98 guns:
  - lower deck 28 x 32-pdrs
  - middle deck 30 x 18-pdrs
  - upper deck 30 x 12-pdrs
  - quarterdeck 10 x 6-pdrs
  - forecastle 2 x 6-pdrs

This gave her exactly 100 guns – she appears to have had ten 6-pounders on her quarterdeck instead of the more usual (as with the *Dreadnought*) eight 12-pounders.
- Crew 735 (naval 625, RM 110).

One of the few British ships at Trafalgar to have virtually a full complement.

## Commanded by

Captain Richard Grindall. Born in 1750, making him eight years older than Nelson, he was the oldest, and second most senior, British captain at the battle. He became a lieutenant in 1776, commander in 1781 and captain in 1783. When in command of the 36-gun frigate *Thalia* in 1795 he captured the 12-gun French cutter *Requin* off Dunkirk. In 1795 he commanded the 74-gun *Irresistible* in Lord Bridport's successful action against the French off Isle Groix, in which he was wounded. As captain of the 74-gun *Ramillies* off Rochefort in 1799 he operated in support of the French Royalist insurgents in the Morbihan. For Trafalgar he received the customary gold medal, thanks of parliament and sword. After Trafalgar he rose quite rapidly in rank, becoming a rear-admiral in 1805 and vice-admiral in 1810. However, his service record does not indicate active commands for the remainder of the war. He died in 1820 aged seventy.

## At the battle

Because she was a slow sailer *Prince* was allowed to depart from the order of sailing in the weather column and steer obliquely between the two columns so that she got more of her sails to draw. As her master's log puts it, she approached the enemy 'steering down between the lines with all sail set'. This meant she joined the battle quite late in the afternoon (shortly after 3.00 p.m.) and fought with the ships of the lee column rather than those of the weather. She engaged the Spanish 112-gun *Principe de Asturias* ('discharged two broadsides into a Spanish three-decker'). She then 'came alongside of a French two-decker [*Achille*]. Gave her three broadsides which cut away her masts and set her on fire.' She used her boats to save about 140 men from the *Achille*, which had blown up. She was the only British ship-of-the-line to suffer no casualties at the battle, though she received slight damage to her bowsprit, fore- and mizzenmasts. When the signal was made to take possession of prizes the *Prince* sent a prize crew over to the *Santisima Trinidad*.

## After the battle

Trafalgar saw the end of the *Prince*'s active career. After the peace in 1815 she became a receiving hulk at Portsmouth until in 1837, at the age of forty-nine, she was broken up.

# *Euryalus*

## Officers

| | |
|---|---|
| Captain | Hon. H. Blackwood |
| Lieuts | K.C. Quash (1st) |
| | J.P. Williams |
| | W. Pike |
| 1st Lieut. RM | J. Sandford |
| 2nd Lieut. RM | W.T. Paschoud |

## Warrant Officers

| | |
|---|---|
| Master | F. Ruckert |
| Surgeon | E. Owen |
| Carpenter | T. Parrott |
| Boatswain | W. Phillips |
| Gunner | P. Richards |
| Purser | J. Toby |

## History/Characteristics

- A fifth-rate, single-deck 36-gun frigate. She was a new ship at Trafalgar, having been launched from Buckler's Hard in 1803 and initially deployed on the coast of Ireland and then watching Boulogne. In 1805 she was with Lord Collingwood, and when Villeneuve's fleet arrived at Cadiz in August she was sent to England with the news. On 15 September she accompanied the *Victory* when she sailed from Spithead, joining the blockading fleet off Cadiz. Her duties prior to the battle were keeping watch on the harbour and reporting the movements of the Combined Fleet.

- Armament 36 guns:
  upper deck 26 x 18-pdrs
  quarterdeck 6 x 9-pdrs + 6 x 32-pdr carronades
  forecastle 2 x 9-pdrs + 2 x 32-pdr carronades
- Crew 262 (naval 224, RM 38).
She was carrying virtually her full complement.

## Commanded by

Captain the Hon. Henry Blackwood. Born in Ireland in 1770, he entered the service as a boy, though the exact date is in some doubt. He was signal midshipman on the 110-gun *Queen Charlotte* in 1790 and was promoted lieutenant the same year, serving as first lieutenant on the 74-gun *Invincible* at the Glorious First of June. He was mentioned in despatches and promoted commander, then captain in 1795. This was the start of a long career as a highly successful frigate captain. In 1796 Blackwood was in command of the 28-gun *Brilliant* when she captured the 64-gun French *Nonsuch*. The following year he was compelled by the Nore mutineers to moor his ship across the river to obstruct passage. Perhaps his most successful exploit occurred in 1800; he was commanding the 36-gun *Penelope* when he sighted the French 80-gun *Guillaume Tell* leaving Malta. He closed with her and opened fire, shooting away her main- and mizzen-topsails and slowing her down until two British battleships came up and captured her. He was present during the British landing operations in Aboukir Bay in 1801. In 1803 he was appointed to command the *Euryalus*. He was in command of the inshore squadron watching Cadiz, performing invaluable service in reporting every move of Villeneuve's fleet in the weeks prior to Trafalgar. On the morning of the battle Nelson invited him on board the *Victory* to thank him for his services and to get him to witness a codicil to his will. Blackwood did not leave the flagship until the enemy had opened fire. For his services Blackwood received the sword of honour from the Patriotic Fund but not the gold medal, which was reserved for captains of line-of-battle ships. In 1806 he left his beloved frigates to command the 80-gun *Ajax* in the expedition to the Dardanelles in 1807. Unfortunately, his ship was destroyed by fire and Blackwood nearly drowned; he was acquitted of blame by the court martial. He commanded the 74-gun *Warspite* from 1807 to 1813, which included two years blockading Toulon. At the end of the war he was Captain of the Fleet to the Duke of Clarence (later King William IV) at the Spithead fleet review to celebrate the ending of the war. Promoted rear-admiral in 1814 and vice-admiral in 1821, he was Commander-in-Chief at the Nore from 1827 to 1830 before dying in Ireland two years later, aged sixty-two. He married three times, and two of his sons became naval captains.

## At the battle

According to her log the *Euryalus* 'took our station on the *Victory*'s larboard quarter and repeated the Admiral's signals'. Throughout the battle she observed the action. Her log is by far the most comprehensive of all the logs in describing the battle and the immediate events leading to it. She was not involved in the fighting; she was fired upon but suffered no casualties and only very superficial damage. She sustained far more damage when the *Royal Sovereign* fell on board her due to the heavy swell after the battle.

## After the battle

Collingwood shifted his flag to *Euryalus* at about 6.00 p.m. and from her signalled for many of the prizes to be abandoned during the subsequent storm. She took part in the ill-fated Walcheron expedition in 1809 and captured the 14-gun French corvette *Etoile* in the same year. In 1810 she was once again under Captain Blackwood, and during the pursuit of a French convoy exchanged broadsides with an enemy 74. 1813 saw her off Toulon and involved in the capture of a schooner, 20 merchant vessels and a store ship. In the war with America she took part in the destruction of Fort Washington and the capture of Alexandria in 1814. She was commissioned for a tour in the West Indies from 1818 to 1821 and then in the Mediterranean for another four years. She was paid off at Chatham in 1825. This was followed by thirty-two years as a convict ship (surely a record), first at Chatham then Gibraltar, before being sold to a Mr Recano for £337-6-8 in 1859, aged fifty-six.

# Sirius

## Officers

| | |
|---|---|
| Captain | W. Prowse |
| Lieuts | W. Hepenstal (1st) |
| | D. Anderson |
| | R. Burton |
| 1st Lieuts RM | T. Moore |
| | W. Murray |

## Warrant Officers

| | |
|---|---|
| Master | W. Wilkinson |
| Surgeon | T. Robertson |
| Carpenter | W. Mitchell |
| Boatswain | M. Pope |
| Gunner | H. Perry |
| Purser | R. Williams |

## History/Characteristics

- A single-decked, fifth-rate frigate with 36 guns built at Deptford in 1797. When in the North Sea the following year she made her first captures – two Dutch ships, the 36-gun *Furies*, which put up a stiff fight, and the smaller 28-gun *Waakzaamheid,* which did not. In 1801 in another long chase she, in conjunction with another frigate, took the 36-gun French frigate *Dedaigneuse*. From 1802 to 1805 she was with the fleet off Brest and gave good service to Vice-Admiral Calder in his action with Villeneuve off Cape Finisterre three months before Trafalgar.

- Armament 36 guns:
  upper deck 26 x 18-pdrs
  quarterdeck 8 x 9-pdrs
  forecastle 2 x 9-pdrs
- Crew 273 (naval 234, RM 39).
A full complement.

## Commanded by

Captain William Prowse, born in Devon in 1753, making him fifty-two at Trafalgar. Unusually he entered the Navy as a boy, then served for seven years as an able seaman. In 1778 he was promoted midshipman. He saw active service throughout the American War of Independence. He was a master's mate in the *Albion* at the action off Grenada in 1879 and Martinique in 1782 – the year in which he was promoted lieutenant. He served on Lord Howe's flagship, the 98-gun *Barfleur*, at the Glorious First of June, in 1794 but was so severely wounded that he had a leg amputated. Within two years he was a commander and captain of the brig *Raven* at the battle of St Vincent and was promoted captain. As captain of the *Sirius* he took part in Vice-Admiral Calder's action off Cape Finisterre in July 1805. His services at Trafalgar gained him the Patriotic Fund sword of honour. In 1806 he performed a gallant service in the Mediterranean by attacking a French flotilla at Civita Vecchia, capturing a corvette and driving the other ships to seek shelter. Promoted rear-admiral in 1821, he died five years later aged seventy-three.

## At the battle

She was with the reconnoitring frigate squadron under Captain Blackwood in the days prior to and during the battle. She did not become engaged in the mêlée and thus suffered no casualties or damage.

## After the battle

She took the badly damaged *Téméraire* in tow. From 1806 to 1808 she was in the Mediterranean, still under Captain Prowse. In 1809 she was in the Indian Ocean cruising off Isle de France (Mauritius) and Bourbon (Réunion). She took part in the attack on St Paul (capital of Bourbon), which included the taking of the 40-gun French frigate *Caroline*, and the next year she participated in the combined operations that resulted in the taking of Bourbon. She also played a prominent part in the capture of Isle de la Passe (Isle de France) in August 1810 and later seized a 26-gun Indiaman. Her last service was in the unsuccessful attack on Grand Port (Bourbon) when she ran aground on a coral reef and had to be set on fire by her captain (Samuel Pym). Her crew removed all possible stores and she blew up at 11.00 a.m. on 25 August 1810. She was only a youngster of thirteen.

## Euryalus

Captain Blackwood's ship. She performed
the vital duty of watching and reporting the
enemy fleet's movements before the battle.
Here she is shown closing on the enemy line,
but well to windward of Nelson's column.
She was not engaged in the action.

# *Naiad*

## Officers

| | |
|---|---|
| Captain | T. Dundas |
| Lieuts | J.F. Maples (1st) |
| | T.F.C. Mainwaring |
| | H. Le Vesconte |
| 1st Lieuts RM | E. Jones |
| | T.S. Perkins |

## Warrant Officers

| | |
|---|---|
| Master | H. Andrews |
| Surgeon | J. Macansh |
| Carpenter | T. Webb |
| Boatswain | J. Smith |
| Gunner | R. Gallon |
| Purser | T. Menzies |

## History/Characteristics

- A fifth-rate, single-decked 38-gun frigate launched in 1797. She was sent to the Channel for three years where she had several successes including the capture of a French gunboat and, in conjunction with another frigate and after a stiff fight, the 44-gun *Decade*, whose commander was a certain Captain Villeneuve. The following year, 1798, she participated in the chase and capture by three British frigates of two Spanish frigates. It proved a very rewarding operation. The Spanish ships were carrying £600,000 worth of treasure, which eventually entitled each British captain to nearly £50,000. In 1801 she had several more typical frigate successes in small-scale cutting-out operations and in seizing a corvette and schooner. She joined Nelson in August 1805.

- Armament 38 guns:
    upper deck 28 x 18-pdrs
    quarterdeck 8 x 9-pdrs + 6 x 32-pdr carronades
    forecastle 2 x 9-pdrs + 4 x 32-pdr carronades
- Crew 333 (naval 294, RM 39).
She was over strength compared with the other frigates in the squadron, perhaps due to her having 38 guns instead of 36 and 10 carronades all needing crews.

## Commanded by

Captain Thomas Dundas. He entered the service in 1778, in time to serve in the American War of Independence, and was promoted lieutenant in 1793, commander 1795 and captain in 1798. When in command of the West Indiaman *La Prompte* in 1799 he captured the Spanish vessel *Urca Cargadora*. His career until Trafalgar had been somewhat lacking in battles, although he did make a few minor captures. In command of the *Naiad* at Trafalgar he performed his role well as part of Nelson's frigate squadron and received a sword of honour from the Patriotic Fund for his services. He remained with *Naiad* and in 1808 was part of the blockading force off Rochefort. His subsequent service was uneventful. However, he lived long enough to see his seniority take him first to rear-admiral in 1825 followed by vice-admiral in 1837. He died in 1841 in his late seventies.

## At the battle

In the days before the battle *Naiad*, along with the other frigates, was trailing the Combined Fleet and reporting its strength and course. She spent much of her time repeating signals by day and night. A typical log entry was on 19 October, 'Employed variously, and repeating various signals from the *Euryalus* to the *Phoebe*.' She remained, as was her duty, out of the mêlée. At about 4.00 p.m. she took the badly damaged *Belleisle* in tow. She suffered no casualties or damage, and she did not open fire.

## After the battle

She towed *Belleisle* off the shoals to which she was drifting. In 1808 she was with the squadron blockading Rochefort. Three years later off Boulogne she had her final excitement of the war: while lying at anchor off the roads she was attacked by a swarm of 18 French gunboats, gun brigs and a bomb vessel. For two days the attacks continued but failed to capture her or drive her away. During this small, but bitter, action the *Naiad*'s crew boarded and secured the 12-gun *Ville de Lyons*; her losses were 16 killed and wounded. In 1813 she was paid off and remained in ordinary (reserve) until 1823. She was then sent to the Mediterranean and employed in operations against the Bey of Algiers, during which time her boats took part in the destruction of an Algerian brig. Paid off again in Portsmouth in 1826, she remained there in ordinary for twenty years. Then, in 1846, she set sail (in an age of steam) for the Pacific as a depot ship. She was a store ship at Valparaiso (Chile) and Callao (Peru) until the end of the American Civil War in 1865. However, even at sixty-eight, she still had value as she was purchased by the Pacific Steam Navigation Company and continued as a store ship (hulk) at Callao until 1898! When she was finally broken up the gallant old lady was 101, the longest lived of the British Trafalgar ships except for the *Victory*.

# *Phoebe*

## Officers

| | |
|---|---|
| Captain | Hon. T.B. Capel |
| Lieuts | T.P. Perkins (1st) |
| | J. Hindmarsh |
| | A. Dixie |
| | D. O'Hea |
| 1st Lieut. RM | M. Timpson |

## Warrant Officers

| | |
|---|---|
| Master | J. Burton |
| Surgeon | G. Makie |
| Carpenter | S. Lovenewton |
| Boatswain | T. Evans |
| Gunner | J. White |
| Purser | H.C. Bradford |

## History/Characteristics

• A fifth-rate, single-decker 36-gun frigate built in Deptford in 1795. In 1797 she had a long duel with the French 36-gun frigate *Nereide*. They were both perfectly matched in size and guns and their fight included a long chase, tacking, coming about, the use of bow and stern chasers and even, at one stage, the *Nereide* coming on board the *Phoebe*. The final round was fought with broadsides at 300 yards for 45 minutes in the dark. At 10.45 p.m. the French ship struck her colours, having suffered 75 dead and wounded to the *Phoebe*'s 13. Four years later off the North African coast *Phoebe* did the same again in another individual action against the 40-gun *Africaine*. The French ship was heavily laden and had 400 troops, six field artillery pieces and much ammunition for delivery to the French Army in Egypt. The *Phoebe* quickly overhauled her opponent, and the resultant exchange of broadsides, during which the French soldiers remained on deck, caused havoc on the *Africaine*. For two hours the firing continued until the French ship was on fire, had a foot of water in her hold, many guns dismantled and 344 casualties. Only then did she surrender. Once again the *Phoebe*'s losses amounted to 13 killed and wounded. In 1802 Captain Capel took command and for the next three years the *Phoebe* patrolled the Mediterranean. In 1805 she was with Nelson in his fruitless dash to and from the West Indies.

• Armament 36 guns:
    upper deck 26 x 18-pdrs
    quarterdeck 8 x 9-pdrs
    forecastle 2 x 9-pdrs
• Crew 256 (naval 225, RM 31).
She was up to strength.

## Commanded by

Captain the Hon. T. B. Capel. He was born in 1776 and entered on the muster roll of the frigate *Phaeton* as the captain's servant at the age of six, though he did not join until sixteen. He was a midshipman in 1793 and saw his first action in that capacity on the 80-gun *Sans Pareil* in Lord Bridport's engagement off Lorient in 1795. Promoted lieutenant in 1797, he served as Nelson's signals lieutenant on the *Vanguard* at the Nile and was made acting commander by Nelson and put in command of the brig *Mutine*. He was sent home with duplicate despatches which, due to the capture of the *Leander*, brought the first news of the victory to England. His reward, traditional for the officer bringing home news of a great victory, was confirmation as a commander and promotion to captain – two promotions simultaneously was exceedingly rare. From 1799 to 1802 he was in the West Indies, initially commanding the 22-gun *Arab* and then, until she was wrecked, the 32-gun *Meleager*. In August 1802 he took command of the *Phoebe*, remaining with her until Trafalgar. His services at the battle were rewarded with a silver vase from the Patriotic Fund. John D. Clarke, in his thoroughly researched *The Men of HMS Victory at Trafalgar*, shows that of the fifteen vases presented by the Fund all were silver except Capel's, which is described as gilt! On his return to England Capel sat on the court martial of Sir Robert Calder. He commanded the 40-gun *Endymion* during the forcing of the passage of the Dardanelles in 1807 and served in the American War 1812–14, followed by four years commanding the royal yacht, *Royal George*. He was promoted rear-admiral in 1825 and vice-admiral in 1832. He was Commander-in-Chief in the East Indies 1834–7, made admiral in 1847 and Commander-in-Chief Portsmouth the following year. He died in London in 1853 aged seventy-seven.

## At the battle

During the approach of the fleet on the morning of 21 October the *Phoebe* was to the north of the weather column and 'repeated several signals from the flagship'. Like the other frigates she was not engaged in the mêlée and therefore suffered no casualties or damage. She did, however, repeat a number of signals during the afternoon.

## After the battle

She spent much time and effort trying to assist damaged British ships and get prizes under control. This included sending her carpenter and some marines on board prizes. She spent that night 'giving assistance to ships in distress'. On 23 October she took the French *Swiftsure* in tow. Her next important duty was participating in the capture of Isle de France (Mauritius) in 1810. She was then involved in action against French ships off Madagascar before joining Rear-Admiral Stopford in the attack and capture of Java in 1811. In 1814 she was sent, in company with the 20-gun sloop *Cherub*, to the Pacific to break up the American whaling trade and attack her fur stations. These duties involved them both in a hard fight with the American 32-gun frigate, *Essex*. The duel continued for two hours before the *Essex* struck – not surprisingly as she had by then received 124 casualties, 58 crew killed and 66 wounded (another 30 were later found to have drowned). The cost to the *Phoebe* was ten killed and wounded and the *Cherub* four. The *Phoebe* had a remarkable career as six gold medals were awarded to her captains. When the Naval General Service Medal was very belatedly introduced in 1848 one of her old crew, Stephen Laurie, received the medal with six clasps – a record that few men could equal. *Phoebe* became a depot ship in 1822 before being broken up in 1841 aged forty-six.

# *Pickle*

## Officers

| | |
|---|---|
| Captain | Lieut. R.J. Lapenotiere |
| Sub-Lieut. | J. Kingdon |
| Midshipman | C. Hawkins |
| Second Master | G. Almy (acting) |
| Assistant Surgeon | L.G. Britton |

## History/Characteristics

- A schooner with eight carronades brought into the Royal Navy in 1800 as the *Sting* but renamed *Pickle* two years later, she was primarily a fast dispatch vessel and was used as such and for cruising in the Channel for much of 1802 and 1803, including a voyage to Malta. She did good service in assisting with the rescue of the crew of the 74-gun *Magnificent* when she was wrecked off Brest in 1804. In the same year one of her crew was flogged around the fleet for mutiny.

- Armament: 8 x 12-pdr carronades
- Crew 42 – no RMs, but carried some extra seamen instead.

## Commanded by

Lieutenant John Richard Lapenotiere. The La Penotiere family had come to England in the revolution of 1688 with 'Dutch William' and John Lapenotiere's brother, father and grandfather served in the Navy. John was born in Devonshire (Ilfracombe) in 1770, and entered the service as a eleven-year-old boy. From 1785 to 1788 he served in the merchant marine, employed in the Pacific with the King George's Sound Company, and he participated in a similar expedition from 1791 to 1793. On the outbreak of war he rejoined the Royal Navy and was on the 98-gun flagship *Boyne* in the West Indies during operations against French-controlled islands. Promoted lieutenant in 1794 and given command of the hired cutter *Joseph* in the Mediterranean, he was frequently in action. For his services at Trafalgar he received immediate promotion to commander and later a sword of honour from the Patriotic Fund. He commanded the 16-gun *Orestes* at Copenhagen in 1807. While chasing an English vessel that had been captured by the Danes he was fired on, and engaged a shore battery at Helsingor (Elsinore). The flash from one of his guns caused a minor explosion that stripped the skin off his face, ears and neck and burnt his hair. For the next few years he was based at Plymouth patrolling off the Lizard and the Scilly Islands, where he captured several enemy privateers including the 10-gun *Dorade* and the 16-gun *Loup Garou*. He was promoted captain in 1811 and died in Cornwall in 1834 aged sixty-four.

## At the battle

She was positioned north of the weather column and did not participate in the battle so suffered no loss or damage. She assisted in the rescue of French seamen (and two women) after the *Achille* blew up.

## After the battle

She had the honour of carrying Collingwood's victory dispatch to England. In 1807 while in the Channel she captured the 14-gun French privateer *La Favorite*. On 27 July 1808 she was wrecked on a shoal off the entrance to Cadiz, although her crew was saved. 6 November, the day Lapenotiere arrived in London with the Trafalgar despatch, is still celebrated as 'Pickle Night', usually with a special dinner on board *HMS Victory*.

# *Entreprenante*

## Officers

| | |
|---|---|
| Captain | Lieut. R.B. Young |
| Midshipmen | T. Mitchell |
| | A. Wade |
| Surgeon | M. Martin |
| Second Master | W. Adeane |

## History/Characteristics

- She was a cutter captured from the French in 1801, replacing a ship of the same name that had been captured in 1793. A fast sailer, she was used to carry orders and dispatches between ships and stations.

- Armament: 10 x 12-pdr carronades
- Crew 41 (no RM). Slightly under full complement.

## Commanded by

Lieutenant Robert Benjamin Young. He was the son and grandson of naval officers, born in Douglas, Isle of Man in 1773. In 1795, as an acting lieutenant commanding the 16-gun *Thorn*, he was present at the capture of the French corvette *Le Courier National*. He served ashore in the operations against the Caribs at St Vincent in the West Indies and as a lieutenant on the 20-gun *Bonne Citoyenne* at St Vincent in 1797. The following year he was wrecked in the *Colossus* off Sicily. He was in the *Savage* in the expedition to Holland in 1799 and first lieutenant of the 74-gun *Goliath* at the capture of *La Mignonne* near San Domingo, 1803. For his services at Trafalgar he received the Patriotic Fund sword but did not receive promotion. He continued in command of the *Entreprenante* for a further two years blockading Brest. As first lieutenant of the 44-gun *Ulysses* he took part in the Walcheron expedition of 1809. He was promoted commander in 1810, awarded a Greenwich Hospital pension in 1839 and died at Exeter in 1846 aged seventy-three.

## At the battle

She was not engaged, other than picking up survivors of the French *Achille* after she blew up, and thus suffered no losses or damage.

## After the battle

Not until 1810 was she engaged in another major action. While off the coast of Spain she became becalmed near Malaga and was fired on by four French privateers which had virtually surrounded her. By noon the *Entreprenante* had her topmast shot away and two of her starboard guns disabled. She fought off three attempts to board her until finally, after some four hours' fighting, the French withdrew with an estimated loss of 80 casualties. The *Entreprenante*'s losses were one killed and ten wounded. At Gibraltar the officers and crew received the public commendation of the commodore of the station. By 1813 she had disappeared from the Navy list, so her eventual fate is uncertain.

# THE COMBINED FLEET

The ships of the Combined Fleet are listed in order according to their position (north–south) at the start of the battle.

• Virtually all ships show complements over the official numbers for that rate, because the fleet was carrying many more soldiers than normal. The French had at least 4,000 extra troops forming the expeditionary force to be landed at Naples. Some 28 per cent of the men on French ships belonged to the military. In the absence of detailed strengths for the French ships the crew numbers have been estimated on the basis of the normal official complement, on the assumption that the extra troops were evenly divided between ships.

• The Spanish too had packed their ships with soldiers and pressed landsmen to make up for shortages in trained crews. Approximately 42 per cent of personnel on Spanish ships were soldiers of one sort or another. This gave an average for the Combined Fleet of 35 per cent military personnel – the British had 15 per cent. The complements of each Spanish ship are based on Admiral Gravina's report on the manning of his fleet dated 19 October 1805.

• The Spanish captains were among the best of the senior officers at the end of a century that had seen a Spanish naval revival, although economic problems had prevented Spain building any new ships after 1797. All Spanish captains except for Valdés (*Neptuno*) and Argumosa (*Monarca*) had received their Trafalgar commands in early 1805. All surviving captains were promoted on 9 November 1805.

• The French 74s carried broadsides of 36-pounders on their lower decks (compared to the Spanish and British 32-pounders). Similarly their upper-deck guns were 24-pounders whereas all Spanish and many British 74s carried 18s. Each French ship is shown as having the official number of carronades, but as noted above (p. 302) these may not be accurate; their exact numbers and distribution are not known. Finally, the French pound weighed slightly more than the British.

# *Neptuno*

## History/Characteristics

• A Spanish 80-gun ship, the larger version of a third-rate two-decker. Built at Ferrol in 1795, she nearly fought at St Vincent in 1797 but was detached shortly before the action. She had been the rearmost ship of the fleet early that morning as Villeneuve headed for the Straits of Gibraltar. However, when the fleet wore round 180 degrees at about 8.00 a.m. to head back for Cadiz she became the leading ship of the van.

• Armament 72 guns:
  lower deck 30 x 32-pdrs    quarterdeck 8 x 12-pdrs
  upper deck 32 x 18-pdrs    forecastle 2 x 12-pdrs

This gave a total of 72 guns but she also carried 18 howitzers (obusiers), making an armament of 90 pieces.

• Crew 800 (naval 445, infantry 285, marine artillery 70). She was over strength with some 44 per cent soldiers.

## Commanded by

Commodore Don Cayetano de Valdés y Flores Bezan, a skilled officer and accomplished navigator. Born in 1767, he entered the Navy as a cadet aged fourteen. He commanded the research ship *Atrevida*, part of Admiral Malaspina's expedition round the world, from 1789 to 1794 and the 74-gun *Pelayo* at St Vincent. He participated in the blockade of Cadiz and was then involved in an expedition to crush a rebellion in Santo Domingo and the taking of Guarico and Port Dolphin in 1802. Seriously wounded at Trafalgar, he was promoted to rear-admiral immediately afterwards. When France invaded Spain in 1808 he fought against the French on land throughout the Peninsular War, initially as a major-general and later as a lieutenant-general. In 1823 he was condemned to death for plotting against the government and he fled to England where he remained in exile until the change of regime in 1833. Under Queen Isabella II he became Governor of Cadiz, Captain General, Minister of Marine and President of the Cortes in rapid succession. He died in 1835 aged sixty-eight.

## At the battle

At around 2.00 p.m. *Neptuno* turned back with the rest of the van. As she arrived to join the mêlée, the *Minotaur* and *Spartiate* engaged her heavily on either side. She continued this unequal fight for a considerable time, becoming the last ship of the Combined Fleet that fought to the end to surrender. She was dismasted and lost 89 casualties – 42 dead and 47 wounded.

## After the battle

The *Neptuno* was taken as a prize and put under tow by *Minotaur* but was recaptured on 23 October, only to be wrecked on the coast in the violent gales after the battle.

# *Scipion*

## History/Characteristics

- A French 74-gun third-rate, two-decker built in Lorient in 1799 and launched in 1801. She had formed part of Villeneuve's fleet that went to the West Indies in May/June 1805 and was involved in the clash with the British under Rear-Admiral Calder off Cape Finisterre in July. Her condition on her return to Cadiz was reported by Villeneuve as 'Ship is very good; average sailer, stowage space very old-fashioned, sheathing very old.'

- Armament 74 guns:
  lower deck 28 x 36-pdrs
  upper deck 30 x 24-pdrs
  quarterdeck 12 x 8-pdrs
  forecastle 4 x 8-pdrs
  poop 4 x 36-pdr carronades
- Crew 755 (naval 490, infantry 215, marine artillery 50). Slightly over complement.

## Commanded by

Captain Charles Berrenger, a competent although not particularly well-known officer who had commanded the *Scipion* during the expedition to the West Indies and during the action against the British in July. His handling of his ship at Trafalgar was somewhat timid.

## At the battle

She was part of Dumanoir's van squadron, which sailed away from the action for about two hours before turning back in response to desperate signals. Along with three other ships, led by Dumanoir's flagship the *Formidable*, she was briefly engaged with the *Minotaur* and *Spartiate*. She failed to play a positive part in the battle and was able to sail away to the southwest before ultimately turning north again to head for Rochefort. The cost was 17 killed and 22 wounded and some light damage to her rigging and masts.

## After the battle

*Scipion* escaped after Trafalgar but was captured by Sir Richard Strachan's squadron on 4 November after a much stiffer struggle lasting several hours. It is likely that most of the 39 casualties noted above were incurred during this later action. She was taken into Royal Navy service under the same name, becoming the flagship of Rear-Admiral Stopford at the capture of Java in 1811. She was out of commission at Portsmouth in 1816 and broken up three years later.

# *Intrépide*

## History/Characteristics

- A French 74-gun, third-rate two-decker. She was originally Spanish, having been built at Ferrol of the same design as the *Montañés* and *Monarca* and launched in 1799 as the *Intrepido*, then given to the French who kept the name. She took part in Villeneuve's expedition to the West Indies in May/June 1805 and in his action with Calder on the way home in July. On her return Villeneuve was none too happy with her condition, which he described as 'Sails very badly, the bottom is very bad', and complained, 'the Spaniards, to whom this ship formerly belonged, assure us she sailed very well...'.

- Armament 74 guns:
  - lower deck 28 x 36-pdrs
  - upper deck 30 x 24-pdrs
  - quarterdeck 12 x 8-pdrs
  - forecastle 4 x 8-pdrs
  - poop 4 x 36-pdr carronades
- Crew 745 (naval 480, infantry 215, marine artillery 50). Well over manned.

## Commanded by

Captain Louis Antoine Cyprian Infernet, a tough, uneducated, rough-spoken but long-serving and experienced Provençal officer. He was a large man, five feet ten inches tall and beefy. An officer who knew him said, '*Infernet parle mal, mais il se bat tres bien*' – 'Infernet speaks badly, but he is very well built.' He had served, initially as a cabin boy, in the 'old navy' of the monarchy, where his experiences included surviving the blowing up of his ship, the *Cesar*, in the battle against the British under Lord Rodney off Dominica in 1782. At one time he had been a prisoner of war until exchanged. He was a cousin of the equally tough, self-made soldier of the French Empire, Marshal Massena. He took command of the *Intrépide* after her return from the West Indies in August 1805 and at Trafalgar he was to fight one of the most gallant actions of the battle. During some two hours of intense fighting he engaged, or was engaged by, seven or eight British ships – on one occasion he was under fire from four or five simultaneously. Exposed as he was, it is extraordinary that he came through unscathed. Lieutenant Senhouse of the *Conqueror* afterwards commented that Infernet's actions and eventual surrender were, 'one of the most gallant defences I have ever witnessed'. Infernet was repatriated for a second time six months after Trafalgar in one of the frequent exchanges of prisoners. On his return Napoleon decorated him with the Grand Cross of the Legion of Honour. Perhaps inevitably he became known as '*L'Intrépide Infernet*'. Like many of the better officers of Napoleon's navy, he was pensioned off without promotion on the restoration of the Bourbon monarchy. Nevertheless, he is one of the very few French naval captains to have his name inscribed on the Arc de Triomphe in Paris.

## At the battle

The *Intrépide* was initially part of the centre division but had been unable to get into her correct position in the line. At the start of the battle she was therefore part of Dumanoir's van division, which eventually turned back to assist the hard-pressed centre under Villeneuve. However, the *Intrépide* was the only one out of the ten ships that turned back to sail straight for the mêlée of the main action. She put up the most heroic fight, at times exchanging broadsides with *Britannia*, *Ajax*, *Agamemnon*, *Leviathan*, *Neptune* and *Orion* as well as having a prolonged duel with the *Africa*. She finally surrendered to *Orion*. The battle had cost her 242 casualties, although the breakdown into killed and wounded is uncertain. She was completely dismasted, had her tiller and wheel smashed and numerous guns dismounted. As Infernet was to say, 'I was obliged to yield.'

## After the battle

She was towed by the *Ajax*. However, during the severe gales on the days following the battle it became impossible for the British to retain all their prizes. *Intrépide* was one of the ships burnt on Collingwood's orders.

# *Formidable*

Rear-Admiral P.R.M.E. Dumanoir le Pelley

## History/Characteristics

- A French 80-gun third-rate two-decker, built in 1794 at Toulon. At Trafalgar she was the flagship of Rear-Admiral Dumanoir, commanding the van division. She had carried Dumanoir's flag to the West Indies under Villeneuve in the early summer of 1805 and taken part in the action against Calder in July. Villeneuve was scathing about her condition on her return, describing her in his September report as 'a very bad sailer; old-fashioned stowage space [making stability difficult]; poor coppering covered in barnacles like a wooden ship'.

- Armament 80 guns:
    lower deck 30 x 36-pdrs
    upper deck 32 x 24-pdrs
    quarterdeck 12 x 12-pdrs
    forecastle 6 x 12-pdrs
    poop 6 x 36-pdr carronades
- Crew 840 (naval 550, infantry 235, marine artillery 55). Over strength.

## Commanded by

Captain Jean Marie Letellier, who was also flag captain to Dumanoir. He had been flag captain during the voyage to the Caribbean and at the action off Cape Finisterre in July 1805. At Trafalgar he commanded his ship commendably, particularly after his admiral was wounded. He was eventually court-martialled for striking his colours in the action against Sir Richard Strachan on 4 November. However, the court was of the opinion that, 'the Captain conducted the defence of the ship committed to his care in the most honourable manner; they clear him of all censure and request the President to hand him back his sword'.

## At the battle

The *Formidable* led four ships of the van (out of ten that turned back) in an attempt to come to the assistance of the centre in mid-afternoon. Due to the very light wind *Formidable* (and others) had difficulty in tacking to come south and had to use her boats to tow her bows through the wind. She came south to windward of the main mêlée and clashed with the two late arrivals of Nelson's column – the *Minotaur* and *Spartiate*. The engagement was indecisive and *Formidable*, on Dumanoir's orders, sailed initially south-west to clear the action before ultimately turning north again towards Rochefort. Her casualties amounted to 67 – 22 killed and 45 wounded. A later report by her second-in-command, Commander Donnadieu, stated she fired 1,090 rounds – 430 36-pounder, 620 24-pounder and 40 12-pounder. The accuracy of this is perhaps doubtful as her firing at Trafalgar had hardly been extensive; perhaps he included expenditure on 4 November, when she was badly damaged and captured by Sir Richard Strachan's forces.

## After the battle

She escaped from Trafalgar only to fight what was for her a much fiercer action on 4 November against Sir Richard Strachan's ships, at which she was severely damaged and captured. She was taken into the Royal Navy and renamed *Brave*. However, in 1808 she was not considered worth commissioning and became a prison hulk at Portsmouth. She was broken up in 1816.

# *Mont Blanc*

## History/Characteristics

- A French 74-gun third-rate two-decker built in 1789 and launched two years later. She went with Villeneuve to the West Indies and took part in the action against the British under Calder in July 1805 on her return voyage. In September Villeneuve commented bluntly, 'This ship ought to be one of the first to go into dock; her bottom is believed to be in a bad condition; her crew is weak, having lost many through sickness; indifferent sailer.'

- Armament 74 guns:
    - lower deck 28 x 36-pdrs
    - upper deck 30 x 24-pdrs
    - quarterdeck 12 x 8-pdrs
    - forecastle 4 x 8-pdrs
    - poop 4 x 36-pdr carronades
- Crew 755 (naval 495, infantry 215, marine artillery 45). The heavy losses due to sickness had been made up with large numbers of pressed men and soldiers, with the result that she sailed to Trafalgar above her complement.

## Commanded by

Capitaine de Vaisseau Jean Noel de Lavillegris, who had commanded the *Mont Blanc* in the West Indies and in the indecisive action against Calder. He did not play a prominent role at Trafalgar. He was heavily engaged with Sir Richard Strachan's ships on 4 November and was forced to order, after consulting his senior officers, the surrender of his ship. He died before Dumanoir's court martial into the loss of his four ships.

## At the battle

*Mont Blanc* was part of Dumanoir's van squadron; these ships had continued to sail away from the mêlée until about 2.00 p.m. and as such did not join the battle until around 3.00 p.m. As it was she was the last of the four ships that followed the *Formidable* south and therefore was engaged only briefly and at a distance before sailing away to the south-west. Her losses amounted to some 20 killed and 20 wounded.

## After the battle

She was caught up in the fight on 4 November with the British ships under Strachan. Like the others she was captured after suffering extensive damage. As an illustration of the sort of damage close-range broadsides could inflict it is worth quoting from Lavillegris' report to the French Minister of Marine dated 6 November 1805.

> Our masts wounded in various places, not a shroud left to secure them; all our sails unserviceable, absolutely stripped of braces, sheets and bowlines ... the ship threatening to founder, having seven feet of water in the hold, the powder magazine having several tiers of barrels already awash ... the master caulker and the carpenter having also reported that they could not manage to stop up the shot-holes below water; two enemy ships engaging us at point blank and killing numbers of our people ...

The *Mont Blanc* had had enough. After she was taken over by a British prize crew the efforts of every man on the pumps were needed to save the ship. Lavillegris again:

> ... by eleven o'clock the same evening it [the water] had risen to eleven feet [in the hold] in spite of the fact that a chain pump had been working since 5.30 ... carpenters, both French and English, were constantly occupied in stopping the leaks ...

Some 41 shot had penetrated at or below the water-line. She was eventually taken into Royal Navy service and saw out the war as a prison hulk. She was broken up in 1819.

# Duguay-Trouin

## History/Characteristics

- Another French 74-gun, third-rate two-decker. She was built in Rochefort in 1796 but not launched until 1800. She had not been with Villeneuve during his sortie to the Caribbean and back, so had also missed the action with Calder in July 1805. Perhaps for this reason Villeneuve was able to report her being (in September) 'a fine ship; fit for any employment'.

- Armament 74 guns:
    lower deck 28 x 36-pdrs
    upper deck 30 x 24-pdrs
    quarterdeck 12 x 8-pdrs
    forecastle 4 x 8-pdrs
    poop 4 x 36-pdr carronades
- Crew 755 (naval 490, infantry 215, marine artillery 50). Over strength.

## Commanded by

Capitaine de Vaissau Claude Touffet. He had not been with Villeneuve in the recent expedition to the West Indies or at the clash with Calder off Cape Finisterre in July 1805. His participation in the action at Trafalgar was comparatively short and indecisive. However, he was forced to surrender to the British under Sir Richard Strachan on 4 November after a far fiercer fight. Touffet himself was shot and killed early in the action, and the officer losses were so heavy that at one stage the senior officer on the quarterdeck was the French equivalent of a sub-lieutenant.

## At the battle

As Nelson's weather column approached on her larboard side she fired briefly on the *Victory* and *Téméraire* and was one of several ships to fire at the *Africa* as she headed south to join the battle. *Duguay-Trouin* was part of Dumanoir's van squadron and followed astern of the *Formidable* when Dumanoir eventually returned to the main action at around 3.00 p.m. She was, however, well to windward of the mêlée and only clashed briefly with the *Minotaur* and *Spartiate*, the last two ships of Nelson's weather column to join the action. Her losses were 36 – 12 killed and 24 wounded along with minor damage to rigging and spars.

## After the battle

She escaped to the south-west, but after surviving the gales of the next few days and making for Rochefort Dumanoir's four ships clashed with Sir Richard Strachan's squadron. After a hard fight the *Duguay-Trouin* was the last to surrender, having at the end to face three British ships. She was taken into British service and renamed *Implacable*, and participated in the evacuation of British troops from Corunna in 1809. Many years later she was renamed the *Lion* before serving as a training ship from 1855. However, it was not until after the Second World War that the grand old warrior, again under the name *Implacable*, was towed out into the Channel to be scuttled, the last but *Victory* of the wooden warships of Trafalgar.

# *Rayo*

## History/Characteristics

- A Spanish 100-gun first-rate three-decker built in Havana in 1749 – making her, at fifty-six, the oldest ship at Trafalgar. Most of her life had been as an 80-gun two-decker called *San Pedro*, and not until 1803 was she rebuilt as a first rate with 100 guns. On 8 October 1805 the *Rayo* was one of three ships described in the minutes of the Council of War held on the *Bucentaure* as 'fitted out in haste and barely out of the dockyard, can in extreme necessity put to sea with the Fleet but that they are by no means in a state to render the service in action of which they will be capable when they are completely organized'.

- Armament 100 guns:
   lower deck 30 x 36-pdrs
   middle deck 32 x 24-pdrs
   upper deck 30 x 18-pdrs
   quarterdeck 6 x 8-pdrs
   forecastle 2 x 8-pdrs
She may have also carried some howitzers.
- Crew 830 (naval 407, infantry 362, marine artillery 61). Overall she was slightly under strength but with 51 per cent soldiers she had an excessively high proportion of military to naval personnel.

## Commanded by

Commodore Don Enrique (Henry) Macdonell, an Irishman who had left his home country at eighteen to fight against the English, following in the footsteps of countless generations of his compatriots. He joined the Spanish Army and became an officer in the Regimento de Hibernia. He was present at the Siege of Gibraltar, but then transferred to the Navy. At one time he also served in the Swedish Navy. He had been called out of retirement for his Trafalgar command at the request of Vice-Admiral Gravina. With his eight previous active commands he was probably the most experienced of any of the Spanish captains present. However, his contribution to the action during the battle was negligible. In 1817 he was appointed to the Spanish Supreme Council of Admiralty – the climax of a brilliant career. Sadly, Macdonell was to end his life forgotten, laid low with sickness and in poverty.

## At the battle

The only first rate in Dumanoir's van division, *Rayo* sailed away from the action for about two hours after the first shots were fired. At about 2.00 p.m. she turned with the van to go to the assistance of the centre. However *Rayo*, along with several other ships, turned away to the east without having any serious engagement with the enemy. The lightness of her casualties – 4 killed and 14 wounded (2 per cent) – is proof of the insignificance of her contribution. Some sources allege that she was the only ship at Trafalgar not to fire a single shot.

## After the battle

Having escaped virtually unscathed from Trafalgar *Rayo* redeemed herself somewhat by participating, in the middle of a gale, in the sortie on 23 October under Commodore Cosmao in the *Pluton* to recover some captured ships. Mountainous seas and the presence of ten British ships thwarted this attempt, and the *Rayo* narrowly avoided being wrecked on a lee shore by dropping all her anchors and rolling her masts over the side. It gave her but a short respite. The next day Macdonell was forced to surrender to the 74-gun British *Donegal*, which had missed Trafalgar as she had been sent to Gibraltar for water. Even that was not the end as two days later *Rayo* was driven ashore in the continuing storm and was one of the prizes burnt on Collingwood's orders.

# San Francisco de Asis

## History/Characteristics

- A Spanish 74-gun, third-rate two-decker built at Guarnizo (near Santander) in 1767, making her, at thirty-eight, one of the older ships at the battle. She was not present at St Vincent in 1797, nor had she participated in the recent voyage to the West Indies.

- Armament 74 guns:
    lower deck 28 x 32-pdrs
    upper deck 30 x 18-pdrs
    quarterdeck 12 x 8-pdrs
    forecastle 4 x 8-pdrs
- Crew 657 (naval 370, infantry 234, marine artillery 53). Over strength with a very high proportion of soldiers (45 per cent).

## Commanded by
Captain de Navio
Don Luis Antonio
de Flores

## At the battle
Opened fire briefly on the *Victory* and *Téméraire* as they approached the Combined Fleet just before noon. As part of Dumanoir's van she sailed north away from the action until about 2.00 p.m. when the van tacked or wore round. However she kept well to leeward of the mêlée and soon turned away from the action with little contact with any British ship. Her losses were negligible – 5 killed and 12 wounded – as was her damage. She easily escaped to Cadiz.

## After the battle
She participated in the sortie under Commodore Cosmao on 23 October but was wrecked in Cadiz Bay the next day.

# San Augustin

## History/Characteristics

- A Spanish 74-gun third-rate two-decker built at Guarnizo (near Santander) in 1768, making her, at thirty-seven, one of the older ships at Trafalgar. She had been captured by the Portuguese off Rio de la Plata in 1776 but returned to Spain by the peace treaty the next year. She was not with the Spanish Fleet at St Vincent.

- Armament 74 guns:
  lower deck 28 x 32-pdrs
  upper deck 30 x 18-pdrs
  quarterdeck 12 x 8-pdrs
  forecastle 4 x 8-pdrs
- Crew 711 (naval 413, infantry 243, marine artillery 55). Over strength with soldiers.

## Commanded by

Commodore Don Felipe Jado Cajigal, a Basque, born near Santander into a military family. By 1805 he had had more sea-time than the majority of his contemporaries, been wounded in action and served in several command roles in Cuba and during the American War of Independence. He did, however, miss St Vincent. He handled his ship well at Trafalgar, being one of only two ships that made any real attempt to come to the assistance of the centre. During the action he was wounded.

## At the battle

*San Augustin* was the leading ship of Villeneuve's centre division, according to her captain 'next ahead of the *Trinidad*'. She opened fire on the *Victory* and the other leading ships of Nelson's weather column as they approached. In his report Cajigal states, 'I gave orders to open fire and in fact it was opened from all the gun-decks with cool promptitude, rapidity and, so it seemed to me, with great accuracy.' As we now know the firing at the weather column was largely ineffective. *San Augustin* continued to sail north following the van after the general mêlée had developed in the centre. She turned back in response to the signals at the same time as the van at around 2.00 p.m. However, instead of avoiding the mêlée she sailed straight for the nearest British ship, the *Leviathan*, and fought a long duel with *Leviathan* and several other ships. The third attempt to board by the *Leviathan*'s crew was successful and the *San Augustin* struck her colours. She lost her fore- and mizzenmasts while suffering a very large number of casualties. Losses of 385 (killed 184, wounded 201) represented 54 per cent of her crew. They were the highest of any Spanish ship at Trafalgar – only four French ships had more.

## After the battle

She was taken as a prize, towed by *Leviathan,* but was burnt on Collingwood's orders on 26 October.

# Héros

## History/Characteristics

- A French 74-gun, third-rate two-decker built in 1795 but not launched until five years later. She had not been involved in the expedition to the West Indies or therefore the fight with Calder off Cape Finisterre. Villeneuve called her a 'bad sailer'.

- Armament 74 guns:
  lower deck 28 x 36-pdrs
  upper deck 30 x 24-pdrs
  quarterdeck 12 x 8-pdrs
  forecastle 4 x 8-pdrs
  poop 4 x 36-pdr carronades
- Crew 690 (naval 425, infantry 215, marine artillery 50).

## Commanded by
Capitaine de Vaisseau Jean Baptiste Remy Poulain. He was killed at Trafalgar by a broadside fired into the stern of the *Héros*.

## At the battle
The *Héros* belonged to the centre division and when she first opened fire on the approaching British weather column with her larboard broadsides she was slightly to windward and just ahead of the *Santisima Trinidad*. Her part in the action was negligible as she continued to sail north away from the mêlée in the centre until around 2.30 p.m. After eventually coming about she soon turned away south-east to the lee of the line of battle and ultimately escaped with some damage to her rudder and rigging together with 12 killed and 24 wounded.

## After the battle
She escaped to Cadiz but was among those French ships captured in Cadiz harbour by the Spanish in 1808 after France had invaded Spain. She was finally broken up at Ferrol in 1860.

# *Santisima Trinidad*

Rear-Admiral B.H. de Cisneros

## History/Characteristics

- The 'Most Holy Trinity' was, at Trafalgar, a Spanish 136-gun first-rate four-decker, carrying the flag of Rear-Admiral Cisneros. She had been built in 1769 as a 116-gun three-decker, but a refit shortly before the Battle of St Vincent had added a fourth gundeck by connecting the quarterdeck to the forecastle, thus creating a complete fourth tier of guns. Nearly 200 feet long and weighing 3,410 tons, she looked a magnificent giant. She was made from cedar wood and painted with four distinct lines of red with narrow white lines between, with her bows adorned with a huge white figurehead representing the 'Most Holy Trinity'. Recent research has revealed that she was not, as had been thought, the longest warship in the world at that time – several French three-deckers were longer. Her size brought several disadvantages. She had always suffered from stability problems, even after a height reduction in 1778, and Admiral Mazarredo even suggested she be used solely for harbour defence at Cadiz! Her design was also faulty in that she constantly veered leeward

and heeled too much in any sort of sea. This meant the slope of the gundecks was such that pointing and firing was often problematic, with barrels sometimes striking the top of the ports. She fought hard at St Vincent, only narrowly avoiding capture.

- Armament 136 guns:
    lower deck 34 x 36-pdrs
    middle deck 34 x 24-pdrs
    upper deck 34 x 12-pdrs
    quarterdeck 18 x 8-pdrs
    forecastle 6 x 4-pdrs

This makes 126 guns, which were augmented by ten 24-pdr obusiers (howitzers), making the total 136. Single shotted she could fire a total weight of 2,856 lbs of metal or 1.43 tons.
- Crew 1,048 (naval 604, infantry 382, marine artillery 62). Her crew was 42 per cent military but overall, and unusually for a Spanish ship at Trafalgar, slightly under full complement.

## Commanded by

Commodore Don Francisco Javia de Uriate y Borja. He was born into a noble family in 1753 near Cadiz where he was destined to spend most of his forty-nine years of naval service. He was wounded and captured at Trafalgar and taken to Gibraltar. In 1806 he was promoted rear-admiral. Then in 1808 the French invaded Spain and Napoleon put his brother Joseph on the throne. This tested the loyalty of all Spaniards, particularly those in positions of authority. Uriate refused to take the new oath of loyalty with the words, 'Neither my honour nor my conscience permits me to change my oath of allegiance to my legitimate sovereign', instead fleeing to Seville to join the resistance. In 1816, after Napoleon's fall, he became vice-admiral and governor of Cartagena. In 1836 he was appointed Captain-General of the Navy and two years later wrote a vivid account of the last fight of the *Santisima Trinidad*. He died in 1842 aged eighty-nine – the longest lived of any of the Spanish Trafalgar captains.

## At the battle

*Santisima Trinidad* was in the centre division just astern of the *Héros* as the Combined Fleet sailed north at noon on 21 October. Along with several other ships, she opened fire on the *Victory* as the latter approached at the head of the weather column. She was also in a position to fire at the *Téméraire* and *Leviathan* as they closed with the line between 12.45 and 1.00 p.m. From then on she was in the centre of the mêlée, exchanging broadsides with the *Neptune*, *Britannia*, *Africa* and *Conqueror*, and put up one of the most gallant fights of the battle despite seeing huge numbers of her men cut down by the shots from all directions that smashed into her hull. At one stage a party from the *Africa* sent aboard to accept a perceived surrender was sent back. Eventually she struck to the *Prince* and was taken in tow by her. The cost of such a battering was appalling. Some 30 per cent of her crew had been hit – 205 killed and 108 wounded, among the latter Rear-Admiral Cisneros and Captain Uriate. Although she was completely dismasted, it was the damage below that had crippled her. Most fit men were manning the one working pump, battling water rising at 18 inches an hour.

## After the battle

Her fate is best described by her captain, writing many years later:

The English three-decked ship *Prince* took possession of the *Trinidad* and towed her with great difficulty, but it not being possible to keep the water under – it mounting to 15 feet in the hold and the people being exhausted after manning the pumps day and night without cessation – at midday on the 24th of the same month the English suddenly resolved to leave her to founder, three or four ships of their nation [principally *Neptune*, *Ajax* and *Prince*] taking the people off between them … they were obliged to abandon in this great extremity a large number of wounded and disabled, who went down in the *Trinidad* at dawn, at a distance of 7 or 8 leagues [21–24 miles] south of Cadiz.

### Santisima Trinidad

with *Bucentaure* astern, both firing at *Victory* as the
latter slowly approaches the Combined Fleet line

# Bucentaure

Combined Fleet Commander-in-Chief
Vice-Admiral P.C.J.B.S de Villeneuve

Commander, Army expeditionary force
Major-General T. de Contamine

Chief-of-Staff to the admiral
Commander M.P.L.A. Prigny

## History/Characteristics

• The flagship of Vice-Admiral Villeneuve, the commander-in-chief of the Combined Fleet, she was a French 80-gun third-rate two-decker, built at Toulon in 1803 but not launched until the following year. She was Villeneuve's flagship in the expedition to the West Indies in 1805 and the action against the British under Calder off Cape Finisterre in July of that year. On his return to Cadiz Villeneuve spoke highly of the *Bucentaure*: 'This ship is suitable for any kind of employment; she sails well, and her crew, although much weakened by the losses that have been sustained, is one of the best in the squadron.'

• Armament 80 guns:
    lower deck 30 x 36-pdrs
    upper deck 32 x 24-pdrs
    quarterdeck 12 x 6-pdrs
    forecastle 6 x 12-pdrs
    poop 6 x 36-pdr carronades
Note how the longer 80-gun two-deckers have room for one gun more than on a 74 on each battery on each of the gundecks.
• Crew 888 (naval 580, infantry 248, marine artillery 60). Above complement.

## Commanded by

Captain Jean Jacques Magendie. He was described by Midshipman Robinson of the *Euryalus*, who saw him as a prisoner of war, as 'a short fat jocular sailor, who found a cure for all ills in the Frenchman's philosophy, *fortune de guerre*'. This was the third time Magendie had been captured. He had been captain during the recent voyage to the Caribbean and the fight against Calder in July. He had a hard time at Trafalgar and around 2.00 p.m. was wounded in the mouth. He was taken to England on the *Euryalus* (along with Villeneuve) and stayed for a while in Reading. In January 1806 he was sent to France to arrange the exchange of prisoners. Villeneuve held him in high regard for his 'intelligence and capacity', on the basis of which he secured the appointment of aide de camp to Vice-Admiral Decrès, Minister of Marine – a post he held until 1815.

## At the battle

*Bucentaure* was in the centre division, astern of the *Santisima Trinidad*, at the start of the action. She opened fire on the *Victory* as she led the approach of the British weather column. The *Victory* broke through the line at about 12.30 p.m. just astern of the *Bucentaure*. At that moment Nelson's flagship raked the stern of Villeneuve's flagship – it was a blow from which she never had a chance to fully recover. The same punishment was inflicted in succession by the *Neptune*, *Leviathan* and *Conqueror*, and later the *Britannia* joined the unequal struggle. All the *Bucentaure*'s masts fell, her colours were secured to the stump of the mainmast and the 24-pounder battery on her upper deck almost totally dismounted. She eventually struck to the *Conqueror* but she sailed on, so the boat taking Villeneuve and his senior officers ended up going to the *Mars* where Villeneuve handed his sword to the first lieutenant. The cost in casualties was 282 – 197 killed and 85 wounded (32 per cent).

## After the battle

*Bucentaure* was put under tow by the *Conqueror*. On 23 October a slight lull in the storm encouraged several French ships under Commodore Cosmao to sail from Cadiz to attempt to recover some of the prizes. The *Conqueror* was obliged to cast the *Bucentaure* loose, thus causing her to be wrecked on the Puercos rocks at the entrance to Cadiz harbour.

# *Redoutable*

## History/Characteristics

- A French 74-gun, third-rate two-decker built in 1790 at Brest and launched a year later. She did not participate in the expedition to the Caribbean or the action against Calder off Cape Finisterre during the months preceding Trafalgar.

- Armament 74 guns:
  lower deck 28 x 36-pdrs
  upper deck 30 x 24-pdrs
  quarterdeck 12 x 8-pdrs
  forecastle 4 x 8-pdrs
  poop 4 x 36-pdr carronades
- Crew 643 (naval 403, infantry 200, marine artillery 40). A full complement in terms of total numbers.

## Commanded by

Captain Jean Jacques Etienne Lucas. A man of humble origins, Lucas became probably the most famous of the French captains to survive the battle. Unlike the other French hero, Infernet of the *Intrépide* who was a huge man, Lucas was four feet nine inches and slightly built, the smallest officer in the French Fleet. His incredible courage, however, ensured that he became known throughout the French Navy as 'le Redoutable Lucas'. He was beloved by his men and one of the few French naval officers to really devote himself to training his crew in musketry, hurling grenades and taking enemy ships by boarding. At Trafalgar he fought his ship to destruction and was himself severely wounded. Lucas spent some months in England as a prisoner of war although as an officer on parole he had plenty of freedom and rather a grand social life in Reading. On his return to France in 1806 the Emperor summoned him to St Cloud. He promoted Lucas rear-admiral and personally pinned the Gold Cross of the Legion of Honour on his chest with the words, 'Had all my officers behaved as you did, the battle would have been a very different story.' After the restoration of the monarchy Lucas left the Navy, living until 1819, when he died at Brest, disillusioned and disappointed at never having been recalled to the fleet by the royalist authorities.

## At the battle

The *Redoutable* was in the centre division just astern of the flagship *Bucentaure* at noon on 21 October. She opened fire on the *Victory* as she approached at the head of the British weather column and was raked in the bows at close range by the *Victory*'s starboard broadside as Nelson broke through the line. Thereafter she quickly became locked together with the *Victory* on her larboard side, and then the *Téméraire* to starboard. Sandwiched between these two huge three-deckers, with gunports almost touching, she endured probably the most devastating and unequal exchange of broadsides in the entire battle. Lucas later wrote, 'Our ship was so riddled that she seemed to be no more than a mass of wreckage.' Nevertheless, it was a sharpshooter from the mizzentop of the *Redoutable* that inflicted on Britain her most grievous loss – the mortal wounding of Nelson. *Redoutable* eventually struck to *Victory*, with heavy losses. The exact casualty figures for the battle are unknown; she sank in the storm the following day, and her total losses for the battle and storm together were the highest of any ship at Trafalgar at 568 – an extraordinary 487 dead and 81 wounded. Some 88 per cent of her crew had become casualties, and 75 per cent killed or drowned. Of the 29 officers of all ranks 12 were killed and 10 wounded. As to material damage that is best described by Lucas:

> All the stern was absolutely stove in, the rudder stock, the tiller, the two tiller-sweeps, the stern post, the helm port and wing transoms, the transom knees were in general shot to pieces; the decks were all torn open by the fire of the *Victory* and *Téméraire*; all guns were shattered or dismounted by the shots or from these two ships having run us aboard.

Her only mast to remain upright was her weakened foremast.

## After the battle

She was towed away as a prize by the *Swiftsure*, but on 22 October the gale soon put her in danger of foundering. The crew of the *Swiftsure* made a huge effort, at risk to their own lives, to save the Frenchmen trapped on the doomed ship. George Forbes, master of the *Swiftsure*, put these terrifying and dramatic rescue efforts succinctly in his log.

> At 5, the prize made the signal of distress to us. Hove to, and out boats, and brought the prize officer and his people on board, and a great many of the prisoners. At a quarter past, the boats returned the last time with very few in them, the weather so bad and sea running high that rendered it impossible for the boat to pass. Got in the boats. At quarter past 10, the *Redoutable* sank by the stern. Cut the tow, and lost two cables of eight and a half inch, and a cable of five inches, with the prize.

# *Bucentaure*

*Bucentaure* after she struck. Captain Atcherley RM from *Conqueror*
is bringing Vice-Admiral Villeneuve, General Contamine and
Captain Magendie back to his ship. Atcherley found *Conqueror* had
sailed on, so was forced to take his prisoners to the *Mars*.

*Redoutable*
firing her larboard broadside into
the *Victory* as Nelson's flagship
rakes the stern of *Bucentaure*

# San Justo

## History/Characteristics

- A Spanish 74-gun, third-rate two-decker built in 1779 at Cartagena. On 8 October Villeneuve commented on the *San Justo* as one of three Spanish ships that 'were barely out of the dockyard – were not in a position to engage'.

- Armament 74 guns:
  lower deck 28 x 32-pdrs
  upper deck 30 x 18-pdrs
  quarterdeck 12 x 8-pdrs
  forecastle 4 x 8-pdrs
- Crew 694 (naval 427, infantry 207, marine artillery 60). Above complement.

## Commanded by

Captain Don Miguel Gastón, who was born in 1776 in Cartagena de Indias (Columbia), the son of a senior naval officer. He studied naval hydrographics at Cadiz with another Spanish Trafalgar captain, Churruca. In the early 1790s he served on the 74-gun *San Isidro* as part of a squadron under his father's command. After Trafalgar he was particularly outspoken in criticizing the crew's lack of training. He never returned to his birthplace as wars of independence broke out from 1812 to 1825 and the Spanish South American empire broke up, leaving Cartagena de Indias to become the Republic of Columbia. He was, however, appointed military commander at Havana as a rear-admiral. In 1828 he returned to Cadiz and was promoted to vice-admiral. Ill health led to his retirement to Havana, where he died in 1839 aged seventy-three.

## At the battle

The *San Justo* was in the centre division, initially astern and to leeward of the *Redoutable*. She opened fire on the *Téméraire* as she approached the line. However, she managed to avoid being heavily engaged throughout the battle. She fired on the *Royal Sovereign* and the *Belleisle* during the course of the afternoon but the minor part she played, despite her central position in the line at the outset, is reflected in her receiving the lowest number of casualties of any ship in the Combined Fleet – seven wounded. Only two ships in the British Fleet (*Polyphemus* and *Prince*) had fewer. Her hull and masts were slightly damaged.

## After the battle

She escaped to Cadiz and was broken up in 1824.

# *Neptune*

## History/Characteristics

- A French 80-gun, third-rate two-decker built at Toulon in 1801 but not launched until 1803. She had participated in Villeneuve's expedition to the West Indies in the early summer of 1805 and fought against the British under Calder off Cape Finisterre in the July. On her return to Cadiz Villeneuve had reported that she was, 'In every respect one of the finest and most sea-worthy ships in the Fleet.'

- Armament 80 guns:
  lower deck 30 x 36-pdrs
  upper deck 32 x 24-pdrs
  quarterdeck 12 x 12-pdrs
  forecastle 6 x 12-pdrs
  poop 6 x 36-pdr carronades
- Crew 888 (naval 580, infantry 248, marine artillery 60). Over complement.

## Commanded by

Commodore Esprit Tranquille Maistral, an experienced officer of the pre-Revolutionary navy who had seen action on numerous occasions while still a young man. He was captain of the *Neptune* during Villeneuve's voyage to the Caribbean and at the action against Calder's fleet off Cape Finisterre in July 1805. Villeneuve described Maistral in a letter to the Minister of Marine as deserving, 'his high merited reputation, [the] smartness of his ship is a pattern to the Fleet'. His performance at Trafalgar is best described as competent rather than outstanding.

## At the battle

*Neptune* was part of the centre division. At around noon, according to Captain Maistral's report, his ship was, 'a little to leeward of the wake of the *Bucentaure,* but within hail; the *San Justo* ... was to windward of me on my larboard quarter within hail'. As the *Victory* cut the line the *Neptune* fired a broadside into her and another into the *Téméraire* as she followed the *Victory*. *Neptune* declined a one-to-one clash with the smaller *Leviathan* and turned away to the southeast. She was subsequently one of the ships that fired on the *Royal Sovereign.* Her losses amounted to 54 – 15 killed and 39 wounded.

## After the battle

She escaped to Cadiz and participated in the sortie led by Captain Cosmao on 23 October to try to recapture some ships taken by the British at the battle. It was not as successful as hoped and the *Neptune* ended up being towed back into Cadiz harbour. She was one of 11 of the 33 ships in the Combined Fleet that survived the hazards of the battle, the storm and Sir Richard Strachan's squadron on 4 November.

# San Leandro

## History/Characteristics

- A Spanish 64-gun, third-rate two-decker built in 1787. As a third-rate ship she compared unfavourably with most other ships of her rate in either fleet in that she was comparatively old (eighteen years), of the smaller class and lightly armed.

- Armament 64 guns:
  lower deck 28 x 24-pdrs
  upper deck 30 x 18-pdrs
  quarterdeck 4 x 8-pdrs
  forecastle 2 x 8-pdrs

  With her heaviest guns being 24-pounders she was decidedly under-gunned to sustain a close-range mêlée in a line of battle – as were 64s of any nation.

- Crew 606 (naval 347, infantry 202, marine artillery 57). She was over strength but 43 per cent of her crew were soldiers, which failed to compensate for a shortage of trained seamen.

## Commanded by

Captain Don José de Quevedo y Cheza, who commanded his ship with honour at Trafalgar. In 1808, after the French occupation of Madrid, he joined the rebels and took part in the seizure of the French ships that were still sitting in Cadiz harbour. He commanded the naval units that carried French prisoners of war to the Canary Islands. In 1812 he was rear-admiral and military governor of Vera Cruz (Mexico). After the war he was promoted vice-admiral and made captain general of Cadiz.

## At the battle

She was the rearmost ship in Villeneuve's centre division at the start of the action, sailing astern and to the lee of the *Neptune*. She opened fire briefly on the approaching lee column and after the *Royal Sovereign* had cut through the line and engaged the *Santa Ana* the *San Leandro* turned back to join the attack on the *Royal Sovereign*, firing into her bow. By about 1.30 p.m. she had joined the *San Justo* in engaging the *Belleisle*. Her casualties were light, amounting to 30 – 8 killed and 22 wounded. According to Captain Quevedo's report her material damage included main- and foremasts 'tottering', all sails shot through and rigging cut away as well as 'seven shot on the water-line and others in the side'. He considered it 'good fortune' his losses were so small.

## After the battle

She escaped to Cadiz and was taken out of service in 1812.

# *Indomptable*

## History/Characteristics

- A French 80-gun, third-rate two-decker built in 1789 at Brest and launched the following year. She was part of Villeneuve's fleet that led Nelson such a frustrating chase around the West Indian islands in the early summer of 1805. She was involved in the action against Calder's fleet off Cape Finisterre in the July. In September Villeneuve was to report, 'Fine ship, sailing well but having a very bad crew and very weak [through sickness and lack of good seamen].'

- Armament 80 guns:
  lower deck 30 x 36-pdrs
  upper deck 32 x 24-pdrs
  quarterdeck 12 x 12-pdrs
  forecastle 6 x 12-pdrs
  poop 6 x 36-pdr carronades
- Crew 887 (naval 580, infantry 247, marine artillery 60). Over strength in numbers, under strength in seamen.

## Commanded by

Captain Jean Joseph Hubert, born in 1765. He was wounded at Trafalgar and drowned with most of his crew when his ship was wrecked in Cadiz harbour on 24 October.

## At the battle

She was in the centre of the fleet when firing started, sailing just ahead but well to the lee of the *Santa Ana*. From there she fired on the *Royal Sovereign* as the latter led the British lee column into the attack. She continued to engage the *Royal Sovereign* after she broke through the line and went alongside the *Santa Ana*. Next she raked the *Belleisle* as she came through the gap after the *Royal Sovereign*, after which she drifted away, later to exchange broadsides with the *Revenge*. She suffered damage to her hull and masts, spars and rigging although she was able to sail away without a tow in the late afternoon. It is impossible to know how many battle casualties she suffered as most of her crew (and many survivors of the *Bucentaure*) were drowned when she was wrecked in Cadiz harbour on 24 October.

## After the battle

She escaped but was wrecked in the violent storm on 24 October. Only 2 officers and 178 seamen and soldiers survived. Among the missing was the wounded Captain Hubert.

# *Santa Ana*

Vice-Admiral Don I.M. de Alava

## History/Characteristics

- A Spanish 112-gun, first-rate three-decker built at Ferrol in 1784, she carried the flag of Vice-Admiral Don Ignatio Maria de Alava at Trafalgar. She did not join Villeneuve's expedition to the West Indies as she was in Cadiz, docked for the renewal of the copper sheathing of her hull. This had been completed by October, but even then Villeneuve was far from happy with her overall fitness, describing her as 'barely out of the dockyard – not in a condition to engage'. Despite this scathing assessment, from the outside she was sufficiently impressive for Vice-Admiral Collingwood to describe her as that 'Spanish perfection'.

- Armament 112 guns:
  lower deck 30 x 36-pdrs
  middle deck 32 x 24-pdrs
  upper deck 32 x 12-pdrs
  quarterdeck 12 x 8-pdrs
  forecastle 6 x 8-pdrs + 6 x 24-pdr howitzers (obusiers)
- Crew 1,189 (naval 720, infantry 383, marine artillery 86). Over strength – but she needed 250 men on the capstans to lift her anchors.

## Commanded by

Captain Don José Gardoqui, born 1755. He was held in high esteem by the Spanish naval authorities as an excellent seaman with long experience, which went back to his taking part in the capture of the British 64-gun *Ardent* in 1779. He was the only Spanish captain to have commanded three of the big 112-gun three-deckers (*Mejicano*, *Reina Luisa* and *Santa Ana*). He was wounded at Trafalgar where he was locked alongside the *Royal Sovereign* throughout the battle. He became the only Trafalgar captain to command a surviving Trafalgar ship, namely the *Santa Ana* to which he was reassigned in 1809. He was promoted rear-admiral and later held appointments in Cuba and the Philippines, where he died in 1814 aged fifty-nine.

## At the battle

She was the leading ship of the rear division and as such was able to open fire on the leading ships of the British lee column as they approached, led by the *Royal Sovereign*. The *Royal Sovereign* broke through astern of the *Santa Ana* shortly after noon and delivered a devastating, raking broadside from which the Spanish ship never really recovered. Collingwood's flagship then luffed up alongside her and an exchange of broadsides began with the yardarms of the ships touching. The next British ship to come through the line astern was the *Belleisle*, which delivered another raking broadside into *Santa Ana*'s stern. At about the time Collingwood heard of Nelson's injury the *Santa Ana* struck and was put under tow, initially by the *Euryalus*. She was by then a crippled, dismasted hulk unable to sail, her gundecks smashed and her hull holed. Her casualties amounted to 238 – 97 dead and 141 wounded, which was surprisingly light (20 per cent) considering the unmerciful pounding she had received at such close range.

## After the battle

Towed by *Euryalus* and then *Thunderer*, she was recaptured by the sortie from Cadiz on 23 October led by Captain Cosmao and continued to serve until 1812.

# Fougueux

## History/Characteristics

- A French 74-gun, third-rate two-decker built at Lorient in 1784 and launched the following year. This made her, at twenty-one, the oldest French ship at Trafalgar. Villeneuve considered she was 'in a bad condition; requires overhauling in dock'.

- Armament 74 guns:
  lower deck 28 x 36-pdrs
  upper deck 30 x 24-pdrs
  quarterdeck 12 x 8-pdrs
  forecastle 4 x 8-pdrs
  poop 4 x 36-pdr carronades
- Crew 755 (naval 495, infantry 215, marine artillery 45). Over strength, but deficient in seamen. Morale may not have been at its highest among the older crew members as they were owed 16 months' pay.

## Commanded by

Captain Louis Albin Baudouin, who was killed at Trafalgar.

## At the battle

The *Fougueux* was in the rear division, sailing immediately astern of the *Santa Ana* at the start of the battle. Commander Bazin, the second-in-command, always claimed the *Fougueux* was the first ship in the Combined Fleet to fire the first broadside of the battle, which was directed at the approaching *Royal Sovereign* a few minutes before noon. The *Royal Sovereign* broke the line through the gap between the stern of the *Santa Ana* and the bows of the *Fougueux*. The *Fougueux* next exchanged broadsides with the *Belleisle* as she came through the same gap and then collided with her. By about 1.15 p.m. she had drifted clear of the *Belleisle* and fired on the *Mars* before ultimately going on board the *Téméraire*, which was then sandwiched between the *Fougueux* on her starboard side and the *Redoutable* on her larboard. *Fougueux* struck her colours. She was wrecked on 22 October and her losses were exceedingly high, with only about 18 officers and 100 other men surviving. If these figures are approximately correct the *Fougueux* lost over 600 men killed or drowned.

## After the battle

*Fougueux* was taken in tow by the frigate *Phoebe* but by midnight she had broken adrift in the storm and heavy seas. Pierre Servaux, the master-at-arms, who escaped by jumping overboard, later gave a grim account of the appalling scenes as the ship was driven ever nearer to the rocks on shore:

> The water had risen almost to the orlop deck. Everywhere one heard the cries of the wounded and the dying, as well as the noise and shouts of insubordinate men who refused to man the pumps and only thought of themselves. The scenes of horror on board the ship that night were really the most awful and fearful that imagination can call up.

**Santa Ana**
at anchor and receiving supplies
in Cadiz harbour before the battle

# *Monarca*

---
## History/Characteristics
---

- A Spanish 74-gun, third-rate two-decker built at Ferrol in 1794.

- Armament 74 guns:
  lower deck 28 x 24-pdrs
  upper deck 30 x 18-pdrs
  quarterdeck 12 x 8-pdrs
  forecastle 4 x 8-pdrs
- Crew 667 (naval 370, infantry 243, marine artillery 54). Over strength, particularly with soldiers, who provided 45 per cent of the men on board.

## Commanded by
Captain Don Teodoro de Argumosa, an experienced officer who had commanded the 74-gun *San Isidro* at the Battle of St Vincent in 1797. By a strange quirk of fate, at that action he had exchanged fire with Nelson in the *Captain* and Collingwood in the *Excellent*. He was wounded at Trafalgar.

## At the battle
*Monarca* formed part of the rear division and at the start of the battle was sailing astern of the *Fougueux*. She opened fire on the approaching *Belleisle* and then the *Mars* as they neared the line. In the mêlée she was closely engaged by the larger 80-gun *Tonnant*, which fired a double-shotted broadside that brought down the *Monarca*'s mizzenmast. After two more crippling broadsides the *Monarca*, unable to reply effectively, drifted away and struck her colours. When she found herself alone she re-hoisted her colours for a while but she was a shattered hulk and eventually surrendered. She had suffered extensive damage and very severe casualties – 101 dead and 154 wounded, among the highest death rates of any Combined Fleet ship at the battle.

## After the battle
She was taken as a prize but deliberately wrecked and burnt on 26 October on Collingwood's orders.

# *Pluton*

## History/Characteristics

- A French 74-gun, third-rate two-decker built at Toulon and launched in 1805, making her virtually brand new and certainly the newest ship at Trafalgar. She had had her first taste of active service with Villeneuve's dash to the West Indies and fired her first shots in anger at the British off Cape Finisterre in July. However, this voyage seemed to have exposed some shortcomings, as on her return Villeneuve reported, 'This ship is crank, making much leeway when close hauled, [but] nucleus of crew very good.'

- Armament 74 guns:
  lower deck 28 x 36-pdrs
  upper deck 30 x 24-pdrs
  quarterdeck 12 x 8-pdrs
  forecastle 4 x 8-pdrs
  poop 4 x 36-pdr carronades
- Crew 755 (naval 495, infantry 215, marine artillery 45). Over strength.

## Commanded by

Commodore Julien Marie Cosmao-Kerjulien, born in 1761. He was a strong, burly Breton man who had run away to sea as a boy of twelve, and before he reached twenty he had been in action on numerous occasions and had become a competent, practical seaman. A highlight of his career was when he commanded the successful attack on Diamond Rock (an islet off the south-western point of Martinique) in May 1805 (see pp. 49–51). He again proved his worth in the action against Calder's fleet off Cape Finisterre when he brought his ship to the rescue of the 74-gun *Atlas*. On 16 September 1805 Villeneuve told the Minister of Marine in a letter that he placed Cosmao 'in the foremost rank' of his officers, and by Trafalgar Cosmao was one of Villeneuve's senior captains. He fought his ship unflinchingly at Trafalgar and was promoted rear-admiral after the battle. In 1809 he sat on the court martial of Rear-Admiral Dumanoir (who had been a prisoner since the battle) when the latter was charged with failing to do his duty at Trafalgar. According to Napoleon's account (given to the captain of the *Northumberland* on his way to exile on St Helena), when Dumanoir was acquitted, and so had his sword returned, a disgusted Cosmao stood up and broke his own. Napoleon approved of the gesture as much as he disapproved of the verdict. Cosmao died in 1825 aged sixty-four. His name is inscribed on the Arc de Triomphe in Paris.

## At the battle

The *Pluton* was in the rear division astern of the *Monarca* when the opening shots were fired just before noon. After the leading ships of the British lee column broke through the gap astern of the *Santa Ana*, *Pluton* strove to overtake the *Monarca* and plug the hole. In doing so she succeeded in heading off the *Mars* and engaging her with several broadsides. She then exchanged fire with the *Tonnant* before turning again on the by now seriously damaged *Mars* into which she fired broadside after broadside. The *Mars* moved away but by 3.00 p.m. *Pluton* was so full of holes between wind and water that with all her pumps manned she was still making several feet of water an hour. She drifted away and was able, along with four other ships (*Indomptable*, *Montañés*, *Argonaute* and *Principe de Asturias*), to escape to leeward and then head north for Cadiz. She suffered 192 casualties – 60 killed and 132 wounded.

## After the battle

On 23 October a slight lull in the atrocious weather allowed Commodore Cosmao in the *Pluton* to lead five ships-of-the-line, five frigates and two brigs out from Cadiz to try to retake some of the ships lost as prizes. It was a bold sortie. He succeeded in retaking the *Neptuno* and *Santa Ana* but in the process lost the *Indomptable*, *Rayo* and *San Francisco de Asis*, all wrecked. *Pluton* was among those French ships seized in Cadiz harbour in 1808 when France invaded Spain.

# *Algéciras*

Rear-Admiral C. de Magon de Clos-Dore

---
## History/Characteristics
---

- A French 74-gun, third-rate two-decker built at Lorient in 1801 but not launched until 1804 – so she was one of the newest ships at Trafalgar. She carried the flag of Rear-Admiral Charles de Magon de Clos-Dore at the battle. *Algéciras* had joined Villeneuve in the West Indies in June 1805 and therefore participated in the action against Calder when Villeneuve was intercepted off Cape Finisterre on his way home in July. Villeneuve's opinion of her in September was, 'A fine ship, sailing well; there are complaints of her being crazy [? slips to leeward too easily]. Her crew is very weakly and always reports many sick.'

- Armament 74 guns:
     lower deck 28 x 36-pdrs
     upper deck 30 x 24-pdrs
     quarterdeck 12 x 8-pdrs
     forecastle 4 x 8-pdrs
     poop 4 x 36-pdr carronades
- Crew 755 (naval 490, infantry 215, marine artillery 50). Over strength.

## Commanded by

Commander Laurent Le Tourneur. He was the junior French ship's captain of a ship-of-the-line in the Combined Fleet, with the rank of *capitaine de fregata* or commander. He also acted as flag captain to Rear-Admiral Magon. He was mortally wounded at the battle.

## At the battle

She was part of the so-called squadron of observation that by noon was at the rear, due to the light wind, shaky seamanship and Villeneuve's order to wear the fleet. *Algéciras* was sailing ahead of the *Bahama* and astern of the *Pluton* when the first shots were fired. The mêlée saw her heavily engaged with the 80-gun *Tonnant*, whose first double-shotted broadside brought down *Algéciras'* mizzenmast. An attempt by the *Algéciras* to rake the *Tonnant* was thwarted by more skilful seamanship and the French ship's bows went aboard the *Tonnant* amidships, fixing her on the receiving end of raking broadsides she could not avoid. As Le Tourneur later remarked, it 'totally stripped us of our rigging'. An attempt to board the *Tonnant* was driven back by carronades firing grapeshot. This deadly embrace continued for an hour during which time Rear-Admiral Magon was wounded and Le Tourneur mortally so. Eventually the *Algéciras* surrendered to a British boarding party. It was one of the bloodiest and most hard-fought one-on-one encounters of the battle. The cost was 219 casualties – 77 dead and 142 wounded.

## After the battle

*Algéciras* was taken as a prize, but recaptured by the sortie of the ships from Cadiz under Captain Cosmao on 23 October. She was taken out of service in 1826.

# *Bahama*

## History/Characteristics

- A Spanish 74-gun, third-rate two-decker built in Havana in 1784. She should have been at St Vincent but was detached shortly before the battle.

- Armament 74 guns:
    lower deck 28 x 32-pdrs
    upper deck 30 x 18-pdrs
    quarterdeck 12 x 8-pdrs + 8 x 32-pdr howitzers
    forecastle 4 x 8-pdrs + 2 x 32-pdr howitzers
- Crew 690 (naval 418, infantry 222, marine artillery 50). Over strength.

## Commanded by

Commodore Don Dionisio Alcala Galiano, nicknamed the 'learned sailor' for his intellectual ability and the publication of several works on exploration, navigation, astronomy and charting. Born in 1760, he entered the navy as a fifteen-year-old cadet. He made his name as an explorer and skilful navigator rather than a fighting sailor, having commanded the naval research vessel *Desaibierta* built for the round-the-world expedition of Admiral Malaspina, 1789–94. He also participated in hydrographic surveys around the Spanish peninsular and the Straits of Magellan. At Trafalgar he was to display quite exceptional gallantry up to the time he was struck down with half his head blown away. A street in Madrid was named after him.

## At the battle

*Bahama* formed part of the squadron of observation at the rear of the line, sailing astern of the *Algéciras* and ahead of the *Aigle*. She opened fire on the *Bellerophon* at around 12.20 p.m. as she approached the line. As *Bellerophon* came through the gap she raked the *Bahama* in the stern. She hauled clear but returned to attack the *Bellerophon*, who was then engaged with the *Aigle*. Within a short time the *Colossus* appeared on the scene and poured devastating broadsides into the *Bahama*. Galiano was wounded, his ship holed, his rigging in shreds but he refused to surrender. Shortly afterwards he was killed, the mizzenmast fell and a hurried council of war between surviving officers agreed to strike their colours to the *Colossus*, although the latter was too heavily pressed to send over a prize crew at that time. Her losses amounted to 142 – 75 killed and 67 wounded.

## After the battle

She was towed by the *Orion* to Gibraltar and in 1806 was taken into Royal Navy service as a prison hulk. She was broken up in 1814.

# *Aigle*

## History/Characteristics

- A French 74-gun, third-rate two-decker built at Rochefort in 1798 and launched two years later. She had participated in the expedition to the West Indies and the action against the British under Calder off Cape Finisterre in July 1805. She was then commanded by Captain Hubert. By Trafalgar he had exchanged ships with Captain Gourrège of the *Indomptable*. Villeneuve's comments on her condition in September were: 'In fairly good condition; an indifferent sailer, which is attributed to her old-fashioned stowage-space and the age of her [copper] sheathing; her crew is fairly good.'

- Armament 74 guns:
  lower deck 28 x 36-pdrs
  upper deck 30 x 24-pdrs
  quarterdeck 12 x 8-pdrs
  forecastle 4 x 8-pdrs
  poop 4 x 36-pdr carronades
- Crew 755 (naval 495, infantry 215, marine artillery 45). Over strength.

## Commanded by

Captain Pierre Paulin Gourrège, born in 1762. He was a rough and ready old Breton merchant skipper brought into the navy at the Revolution to replace royalist officers who had fled, been imprisoned or worse. He proved himself a thoroughly competent and reliable captain. At Trafalgar he put up one of the finest fights of the battle but unfortunately was mortally wounded in the process.

## At the battle

*Aigle* was part of the squadron of observation at the rear of the fleet, sailing astern and to the lee of the *Bahama*. She opened fire on the *Bellerophon* as she approached and came through the gap astern of the *Bahama*. The *Aigle* was unable to avoid going on board the *Bellerophon* and the two ships became locked together. *Bellerophon* was then under fire from four enemy ships but concentrated on keeping her starboard batteries firing into the *Aigle* only feet away. On the upper decks a furious exchange of musketry was taking place by which Captain Gourrège and then Captain Cooke were fatally hit. Twice the French attempted to board and twice they were beaten back. *Aigle* managed to drag herself clear in time for a brief engagement with the *Revenge*, but even this was not enough to force a surrender: the *Defiance* had to come alongside and send over a boarding party that after a stiff fight seized possession of their prize at around 3.00 p.m. Casualties had been high – some 270 were hit during the battle and many more drowned when she was wrecked on 26 October. In all some two-thirds of her crew perished. Among the dead were the captain, second-in-command, three lieutenants and nine junior officers.

## After the battle

She was taken under tow but was wrecked ashore during the storm on 26 October.

# *Montañés*

## History/Characteristics

- A Spanish 74-gun, third-rate two-decker built at Ferrol in 1794.

- Armament 74 guns:
    lower deck 28 x 32-pdrs
    upper deck 30 x 18-pdrs
    quarterdeck 12 x 8-pdrs
    forecastle 4 x 8-pdrs
- Crew 715 (naval 407, infantry 255, marine artillery 53). Over strength, particularly with troops who represented 43 per cent of the men on board.

## Commanded by

Captain Don José Francisco Alcedo. He had entered the navy in 1774 and by Trafalgar had become an experienced captain with considerable sea time and active service to his credit. He had taken part in an expedition against Algeria in 1775 and become a frigate commander in the West Indies during operations in Pensacola Bay (Florida). He took part in further operations in the Channel and at the blockading of Gibraltar in 1782, when he was wounded. Back in the Caribbean in the 1790s he took part in the capture of Port Dolphin (Santo Domingo) in 1794. He was killed at Trafalgar.

## At the battle

At noon *Montañés* was in the van part of the squadron of observation sailing to windward of the *Swiftsure*, which was astern of the *Aigle*. Like other ships in the fleet she opened fire on the approaching enemy ships of Collingwood's lee column. The *Bellerophon* broke the line ahead of the *Montañés*, raking her with her starboard batteries. Then the British *Achilles* broke the line astern of the *Montañés*, raking her then ranging alongside to engage for some 40 minutes. During this duel Captain Alcedo was killed. The *Montañés* then drifted away to the lee of the mêlée and joined the frigates and did not rejoin the action. Her loses were a foremast and 49 casualties, 20 dead and 29 wounded (at 7 per cent she had suffered lightly).

## After the battle

She escaped to Cadiz.

Clive Farmer

*Aigle*
giving *Bellerophon* a hard time,
assisted by *Bahama*

# Swiftsure

## History/Characteristics

- A French 74-gun, third-rate two-decker built in 1787, making her the second oldest French ship at Trafalgar. She had taken part in the recent expedition to the West Indies and the clash with Calder's ships off Cape Finisterre in July. On her return Villeneuve warned, 'This ship takes six inches of water an hour; she could not stand a winter cruise ...'.

- Armament 74 guns:
  lower deck 28 x 36-pdrs
  upper deck 30 x 24-pdrs
  quarterdeck 12 x 8-pdrs
  forecastle 4 x 8-pdrs
  poop 4 x 36-pdr carronades
- Crew 755 (naval 495, infantry 215, marine artillery 45). Over strength.

## Commanded by

Captain Charles l'Hospitalier-Villemandrin. He had commanded the *Swiftsure* in the Caribbean and off Cape Finisterre. At Trafalgar he handled his ship with competence and courage in the mêlée that developed between the British lee column and the Combined Fleet's centre and rear.

## At the battle

Villemandrin's comment on the situation with the rear of the Combined Fleet at the start of the action is illuminating: 'The Squadron of Observation, of which I made one, formed the rear in the reverse order, but of the twelve ships composing it, at the time of the engagement I only counted nine of them in fairly correct formation ... the three others were probably either to leeward or merged in the *corps de bataille* (centre division).' At around 12.30 p.m. *Swiftsure* clashed with the *Colossus*. This developed into a duel that according to Villemandrin lasted for an hour and a half, during which she lost first her mizzen- and maintopmast then mainmast, taffrail, wheel and foremast, with numerous guns dismounted. *Swiftsure* had become an unmanageable hulk with five feet of water in her hold. She struck to the *Colossus* at around 3.30 p.m. Casualties amounted to 191 – 68 killed, 123 wounded.

## After the battle

The *Dreadnought* towed her to Gibraltar in a sinking condition. *Swiftsure* was taken into Royal Navy service, renamed the *Irresistible* and employed as a prison hulk in the Medway.

# *Argonaute*

## History/Characteristics

- A French 74-gun, third-rate two-decker built at Lorient in 1794 but not launched until four years later. She did not accompany Villeneuve to the West Indies and thus missed his engagement with Calder.

- Armament 74 guns:
  lower deck 28 x 36-pdrs
  upper deck 30 x 24-pdrs
  quarterdeck 12 x 8-pdrs
  forecastle 4 x 8-pdrs
  poop 3 x 36-pdr carronades
- Crew 755 (naval 490, infantry 215, marine artillery 50). Over strength. From her captain's report we know that detachments of the 3rd Regiment of Marine Artillery and the 16th and 79th Ligne were on board.

## Commanded by

Captain Jacques Épron. Little is known of him apart from the controversy over his actions at Trafalgar. He was accused by Captain Mahé of the frigate *Hermione* of quitting his station with the ship's rigging undamaged, a charge instantly denied by both Épron and his officers in a flurry of correspondence with the Minister of Marine.

## At the battle

*Argonaute* was part of the squadron of observation sailing at the start of the battle astern of the *Swiftsure* and ahead of the *Argonauta* and *San Ildefonso*. She clashed with the *Colossus* shortly before 1.00 p.m. and they ran aboard each other and exchanged broadsides while locked together. According to Épron this murderous slugging match continued for half an hour before they broke loose from each other. The *Argonaute* then drifted away to leeward and was possibly engaged briefly by the *Revenge* before quitting the fight. Her captain stated the damage as, 'shrouds cut to pieces … as well as our back-stays, all the rigging cut up, and the spars in a most shattered state, especially the main and mizzen masts, the fore topmast, the jib-boom, courses, hull, boats and spare spars. In this condition we fell off to leeward …'. His casualty report lists 187 – 55 dead and 132 wounded.

## After the battle

She escaped and anchored to sit out the storm at the entrance to Cadiz on 22 October. She signalled for the *Hermione* to take her in tow but this was seemingly ignored by Captain Mahé. Then began the exchange of accusations and counter claims, the outcome of which the present writer has been unable to fathom. The *Argonaute* was taken by the Spanish in Cadiz harbour in 1808 after the French occupation of Madrid.

# *Argonauta*

## History/Characteristics

•   A Spanish 80-gun, third-rate two-decker built at Ferrol in 1798, she claimed to be 'the most perfect man-of-war in both fleets'. Even Villeneuve, forever the pessimist, called her 'excellent'. She led the Franco-Spanish line flying the flag of Admiral Gravina in the action against Calder off Cape Finisterre in July 1805. In this position she engaged and badly damaged the British 74-gun *Hero*.

•   Armament 80 guns:
      lower deck 30 x 32-pdrs
      upper deck 32 x 18-pdrs
      quarterdeck 8 x 12-pdrs
      forecastle 2 x 12-pdrs
To these 72 guns eight 32-pdr howitzers (some on the poop) should be added, to give 80 pieces.
•   Crew 798 (naval 458, infantry 279, marine artillery 61). With 43 per cent soldiers she was over complement.

## Commanded by
Captain Don Antonio de Pareja, an experienced, gallant captain who had commanded the frigate *Perla* at St Vincent in 1797. He was wounded at Trafalgar but survived.

## At the battle
Part of the squadron of observation, the *Argonauta* was sailing astern of the *Argonaute* and to the lee of the *San Ildefonso*. She opened fire at the approaching ships of the British lee column and in the subsequent mêlée was engaged at pistol-shot range for about an hour with the British *Achille*. It was a duel from which the *Argonauta* never really recovered. According to Pareja's after-action report, she had all the guns on the poop and quarterdeck dismounted, a number of guns in the batteries out of action, rigging destroyed, masts tottering, holed below the water and rudder useless. At around 3.30 p.m. the wounded captain gave his consent to strike his colours. She was taken over by 1st Lieutenant Owen RM of the *Belleisle*.

## After the battle
She was towed by *Polyphemus* as a prize but sunk on 26 October on the orders of Collingwood.

# San Ildefonso

## History/Characteristics

- A Spanish 74-gun, third-rate two-decker built at Cartagena in 1785 and originally named the *San Cristobal*. According to Admiral Mazarredo 'she sailed to windward like a frigate' – that is, could make good progress when close hauled to the wind without making too much leeway. She had fought at St Vincent in 1797.

- Armament 74 guns:
  - lower deck 28 x 32-pdrs
  - upper deck 30 x 18-pdrs
  - quarterdeck 12 x 18-pdrs + 8 x 32-pdr obusiers
  - forecastle 4 x 18 pdrs + 4 x 32-pdr obusiers

Like all Spanish 74s she was lightly armed compared with the French 74s.

- Crew 716 (naval 420, infantry 244, marine artillery 52). Over complement.

## Commanded by

Commodore Don José de Vargas y Varáez. He was wounded early in the action and obliged to hand over to his second-in-command Anselmo Gomendio. In 1808 he was even more unfortunate, being murdered by a disgruntled seaman.

## At the battle

The leading ship of a group of five at the rear of the fleet, she opened fire on the approach of the British lee column, in particular at the *Revenge*, which broke the line ahead of her. By 1.00 p.m. she was closely engaged by the *Revenge*, who raked her stern. Later in the afternoon she was obliged to surrender to the *Defence*. Of the circumstances at the time Vargas wrote: 'At 4.30 ... the second captain informed me that the ship had lost all her masts save the foremast which was about to fall also, there were many dead and wounded, and many shot between wind and water ... and not having people able to serve the guns ...'. Her casualties were listed as 160 – 34 killed and 126 wounded, which at 22 per cent was not excessive – about average for Spanish ships.

## After the battle

She remained a prize and was taken, dismasted, to Gibraltar. Her future was as a British prison hulk from 1808 and to be broken up in 1816.

## Argonauta

sailing near the rear of the
Combined Fleet before the
action started

# Achille

## History/Characteristics

- A French 74-gun, third-rate two-decker launched from Rochefort in 1803, making her one of the newest of Villeneuve's ships. She arrived in the West Indies in early June having sailed from Rochefort (along with the *Algéciras*) on 1 May with nearly 900 troop reinforcements. She took part in the action against Calder in July. By the time she returned to Vigo she had 200 men sick. Villeneuve was to comment, 'Very good condition [the Caribbean adventure had been her first voyage], sails fairly well, lost many men through sickness.'

- Armament 74 guns:
  lower deck 28 x 36-pdrs
  upper deck 30 x 24-pdrs
  quarterdeck 12 x 8-pdrs
  forecastle 4 x 8-pdrs
  poop 4 x 36-pdr carronades
- Crew 755 (naval 490, infantry 215, marine artillery 50). Most of her sick had been replaced by pressed men. Among the soldiers were men from the 67th and 93rd Ligne.

## Commanded by

Captain Louis Gabrielle Denieport, who was killed at Trafalgar.

## At the battle

She was sailing fourth from the rear of the Combined Fleet at noon, immediately ahead of the *Principe de Asturias*. During the prolonged mêlée that started at around 12.45 p.m. the *Achille* was heavily engaged by the British *Achille*, the *Revenge* and finally the massive 98-gun *Prince* that arrived late but in time to deliver the death blow to the

*Achille*, which caught fire and soon afterwards exploded. The *Prince* and other British ships lowered boats to pick up survivors but the final casualty toll was about 480, of whom it is thought 30–35 drowned. Among the dead was the captain, Denieport. Some 158 survivors ultimately returned to Cadiz and others were taken prisoner.

# *Principe de Asturias*

Admiral Don F. Gravina
Rear-Admiral Don A. de Escaño

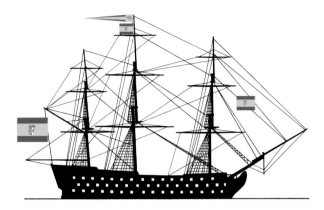

## History/Characteristics

• A Spanish 112-gun, first-rate three-decker, built in Havana of the finest tropical timbers in 1794. Some claim she was the best ship overall at Trafalgar. She had fought under Cordoba at St Vincent in 1797, where then she carried the flag of Rear-Admiral Moreno leading the rear of the Spanish Fleet and gallantly led the attack on the British centre as it tacked in succession to engage the main body.

• Armament 112 guns:
    lower deck 30 x 36-pdrs
    middle deck 32 x 24-pdrs
    upper deck 32 x 12-pdrs
    quarterdeck 12 x 8-pdrs
    forecastle 6 x 8-pdrs
She also carried 6 x 24-pdr howitzers.
• Crew 1,113 (naval 624, infantry 382, marine artillery 107). She carried more than her complement and 44 per cent were soldiers.

## Commanded by

Commodore Don Rafael de Hore. She also flew the flag of Admiral Don Frederico Gravina, the second-in-command to Villeneuve and the commander of the Spanish ships and the squadron of observation. On board also was Rear-Admiral Don Antonio de Escaño, chief-of-staff and flag captain to Gravina.

## At the battle

The *Principe de Asturias* was sailing third from the rear at around noon, coming into action to rake the *Revenge* at about 1.00 p.m. By 3.00 p.m. she was engaged by several British ships and was the only ship in Gravina's squadron that had not drifted away to leeward and out of the main mêlée. When the *Prince* arrived she was able to deliver a crushing broadside. As Escaño described it, 'She [*Prince*] discharged all her guns at grape-shot range into our stern.' This broadside severely wounded Gravina in the leg, and by 4.30 p.m. Gravina ordered the ships that could do so to withdraw. *Principe de Asturias* had suffered comparatively lightly with 162 casualties (14 per cent) – 52 dead and 110 wounded.

## After the battle

She eventually made it to Cadiz and remained in service until 1812.

# Berwick

## History/Characteristics

- French 74-gun, third-rate two-decker. Originally an English ship built at Portsmouth in 1775, she did duty with the Royal Navy, including flying the flag of Sir Hyde Parker in his clash with the Dutch squadron under Admiral Zoutmann in 1781. This action cost her 16 dead and 58 wounded. In 1795 she was captured by three French frigates and taken into French service. She took part in Villeneuve's voyage to the West Indies in the early summer of 1805 and was one of the two warships (the other was *Pluton*) employed in the taking of Diamond Rock (Martinique) in June. She was also engaged in the clash with Calder off Cape Finisterre in July. On her return to Europe Villeneuve described her as a 'Fine ship, does not sail very badly as in previous cruises. Her foremast is badly wounded ... weak in crew.'

- Armament 74 guns:
    lower deck 28 x 36-pdrs
    upper deck 30 x 24-pdrs
    quarterdeck 12 x 8-pdrs
    forecastle 4 x 8-pdrs
    poop 4 x 36-pdr carronades
- Crew 755 (naval 495, infantry 215, marine artillery 45). Over strength.

## Commanded by

Captain Jean Gilles Filhol Camas, an experienced officer who had commanded the *Berwick* throughout the recent months in the Caribbean. He was killed at Trafalgar.

## At the battle

*Berwick* was the last but one of the squadron of observation. Early on in the mêlée she ran aboard the *Defiance* and lost her bowsprit. She then clashed in a more prolonged struggle with the British *Achille* and by about 3.15 p.m. she was unmanageable and compelled to strike to *Achille*. Casualties in the battle are unknown as so many crew were drowned when she foundered.

## After the battle

She was initially towed as a prize by the *Britannia* but cast off on 23 October during the severe gale and wrecked, driven ashore on 26 October. According to Spanish records in Cadiz only 61 of her 'seamen and troops' were saved from the wreck.

# San Juan Nepomuceno

## History/Characteristics

- Spanish 74-gun, third-rate two-decker built at Guarnizo (Santander) in 1766, making her at thirty-nine one of the oldest ships at Trafalgar. She had not participated in the voyage to the West Indies or in the clash with Calder off Cape Finisterre.

- Armament 74 guns:
  - lower deck 28 x 32-pdrs
  - upper deck 30 x 18-pdrs
  - quarterdeck 12 x 8-pdrs
  - forecastle 4 x 8-pdrs
- Crew 693 (naval 431, infantry 212, marine artillery 50). Slightly over her complement but her proportion of soldiers (38 per cent) was below average.

## Commanded by

Commodore Don Cosme Damian Churruca. Born in 1761 he had risen from cadet to commodore by the age of forty-five, which spoke well of his ability. He fought during the long blockade of Gibraltar (1779–82) and then studied advanced mathematics and navigation at Cadiz, followed by a period at the naval school at Ferrol then further study including astronomy and mechanics until 1788. After this he spent several years exploring the Straits of Magellan and along the coasts of Chile and Patagonia (Argentina). He was a tough-minded professional officer who had a low opinion of French admirals. When Villeneuve wore his fleet through 180 degrees at Trafalgar Churruca raged, 'The Fleet is doomed. The French Admiral does not understand his business. He has compromised us all!' He sailed from Cadiz in October 1805 still owed several years' pay, heavily in debt and a bridegroom of five months. At the battle he died in agony, his leg almost torn from his body by a cannonball. A pension and back pay was eventually paid to his widow. His portrait hangs in the Naval Museum in Madrid, a street was named after him and he has two statues, one in Ferrol, the other at his birthplace, the little town of Motrico near San Sebastian in northern Spain.

## At the battle

*San Juan Nepomuceno* was the last ship in the Combined Fleet's line. During the mêlée she became heavily engaged with the *Bellerophon*, the 98-gun *Dreadnought* (an encounter that crippled her) and the 80-gun *Tonnant*. These larger ships smashed her into an unmanageable hulk and she was forced to surrender after a magnificent fight. Her casualties were high at 234 (34 per cent) – 103 killed (including Churruca) and 131 wounded.

## After the battle

She was taken as a prize to Gibraltar and afterwards taken into Royal Navy service as the *San Juan*. She became a receiving ship in 1808 and was broken up in 1818.

## French frigates

There were five frigates and two brigs with the Combined Fleet at Trafalgar, all French. They were not involved with the fighting during the battle but were positioned to the lee of the fleet in order to repeat and relay signals. Their logs give a reasonable picture of the battle from the limited viewpoint of a spectator – that of the *Thémis* being particularly detailed.

The frigates were 40-gun ships with twenty-eight 18-pounders on the upper deck, ten 8-pounders on the quarterdeck and two 8-pounders on the forecastle. Two 36-pounder carronades were mounted on the quarterdeck and forecastle. Crews were a round 330. All escaped to Cadiz.

Ships and captains were:

| | |
|---|---|
| *Rhin* | Commander Michel Chesneau |
| *Hortense* | Captain La Marre la Meillerie |
| *Cornélie* | Captain Jules François Martinencq |
| *Thémis* | Captain Nicolas Jugan |
| *Hermione* | Commander Jean Michel Mahé |

The brigs were:

| | |
|---|---|
| *Argus* (16 guns) | Lieut. Yves Francois Taillard |
| *Furet* (18 guns) | Lieut. Pierre Antoine Toussaint Demay |

## Thémis

This French frigate was employed on reconnaissance duties before the battle, and reported the 'enemy deploying into two columns to commence the attack'. She was not involved in the battle and was able to tow *Principe de Asturias* to Cadiz.

# NAPLES AND EMMA HAMILTON, 1798–1800

The two years following his victory at the Nile were the most controversial of Nelson's career. His activities, which included neglect of his professional duties, eventually resulted in his recall to England, the final break up of his marriage and the loss of the close friendship of men like Captain Thomas Troubridge, whom he had known since they had been fifteen-year-old midshipmen together. It was a period in which Nelson's vanity, infidelity and a cruel, ruthless streak in his character were exposed to the public gaze, and many did not like what they saw. Three interrelated areas of Nelson's life attracted particular criticism:

- his too close involvement in Neapolitan politics
- his blatant love affair with a married woman, Emma, Lady Hamilton
- his three-and-a-half-month triumphal journey home across Europe – made in the middle of a war.

## NEAPOLITAN POLITICS

In 1798 Naples was part of the Kingdom of the Two Sicilies, comprising the southernmost part of Italy and the island of Sicily. Its monarch was King Ferdinand IV, who was also King Ferdinand III of Sicily proper. Naples was allied with Austria and Russia against the French, who controlled northern Italy. In September 1798 preparations were in hand to assemble an army under the Austrian General Mack to confront the French. Captains Troubridge and Ball, both commanding ships in the Mediterranean station, reached Naples ahead of Nelson on 16 September and informed the British ambassador, Sir William Hamilton, that their illustrious admiral expected to stay only a few days as 'these times are not for idleness'. Nelson preferred to use Syracuse on Sicily as his main base for the blockade of Malta and from which to control future operations in the Mediterranean.

On 22 September Nelson arrived on the badly damaged *Vanguard* (he called it 'the wreck') still a sick man, not yet recovered from his head wound at the Nile. His fame had spread, and when he actually stepped ashore scores of fishermen opened their baskets to release hundreds of pigeons that rose up in a whirring, fluttering salute. The ambassador's barge came alongside with Sir William and Lady Hamilton, whom Nelson had met briefly in 1793. In writing to his wife describing the event, he enthused, 'I hope some day to have the pleasure of introducing you to Lady Hamilton, she is one of the very best women in this world. ... She is an honour to her sex'. One wonders what Fanny felt on reading such fulsome praise. Shortly afterwards the *Vanguard*'s

guns boomed twenty-one times in salute to the King of the Two Sicilies who, in an extraordinary reversal of diplomatic courtesies, was rowed out to the British flagship in a gilded galley. Among the illustrious guests who sat down to breakfast on the *Culloden* that morning was Commodore Francesco Caracciolo, the commander of the Neapolitan Navy – a man Nelson would unhesitatingly send to a degrading death nine months later.

However, the king was not accompanied by his forty-five-year-old Austrian-born queen, Maria Carolina (the sister of Marie Antoinette) as she was indisposed. This was not surprising, as she had recently lost her youngest child – the tenth infant death out of the eighteen children she had borne. Nevertheless, she was a formidable lady in more ways than one, ambitious, vain and domineering but above all a woman who abhorred all things French. According to Napoleon she was 'the only man in Naples' and to Nelson, 'a great king', and she was certainly the real ruler of Naples rather than her weak husband.

Nelson stayed for three weeks. Naples was assembling an army under the Austrian General Mack – who was to surrender a much larger army to Napoleon on the Ulm on the same day Nelson won his victory at Trafalgar. On 9 October Nelson, accompanied by Sir William and Emma Hamilton, met Mack at Caserta. Although Nelson had a reasonable first impression of the general, conversation was slow and frustrating, as Mack could speak no Italian or English and Nelson only English. Business was done in French with Sir William interpreting for Nelson.

On 14 October Nelson sailed with his squadron (less *Culloden*) for Malta, where the French were occupying the huge fortifications in Valletta but blockaded by ships under Captain Ball. After sending Ball to accept the surrender of the French garrison on the small island of Gozo he turned back to Naples after only six days, wrongly assuming Valletta would soon capitulate. On 5 November Nelson put forward a plan for Mack's army to advance north, take Rome and attack the French while he transported some infantry to Leghorn to be landed behind French lines, thus cutting their communications. The naval part of the plan succeeded admirably with Leghorn surrendering without a fight on 28 November. The land operations started well, with Mack (and King Ferdinand) marching into Rome on the 29th. However, on meeting a much inferior force of French troops at Castellana the Neapolitan army executed a smart about-turn before fleeing in disgraceful panic, led by the King disguised in civilian clothes. He arrived back in Naples drawn and dishevelled on 14 December.

## Nelson at Naples and Palermo, September 1798–July 1800                                      Map 20

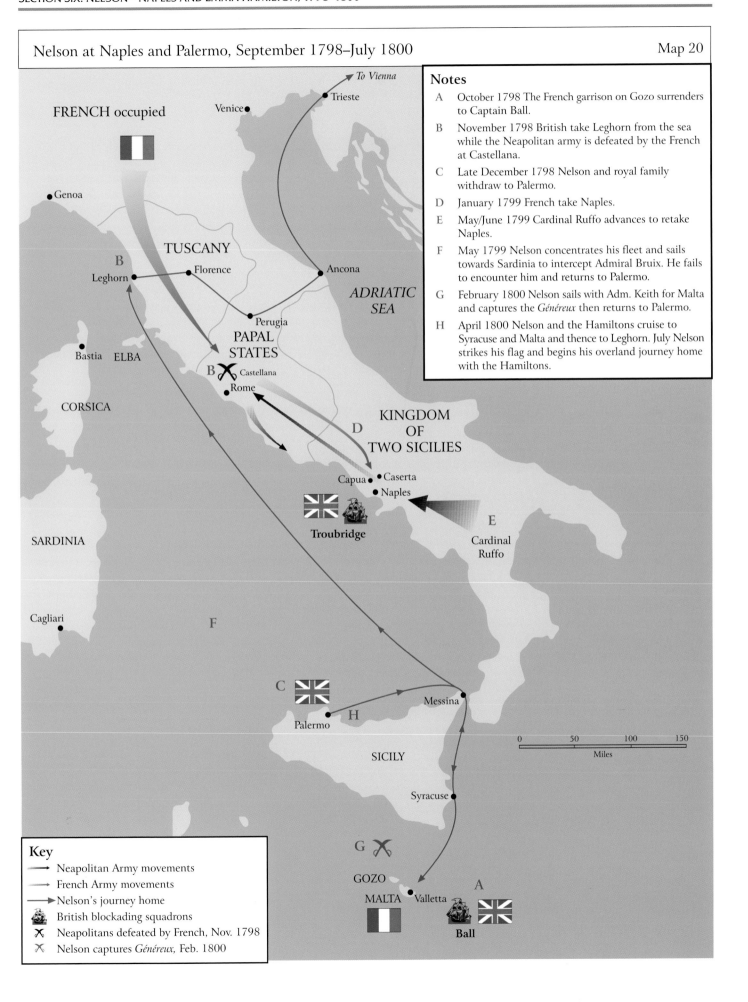

FRENCH occupied

Genoa

TUSCANY

B
Leghorn ●——— Florence ●

Bastia ● ELBA

CORSICA

SARDINIA

Cagliari ●

F

Venice ●

To Vienna
Trieste ●

Ancona ●

ADRIATIC
SEA

Perugia ●
PAPAL
STATES
B ✗ Castellana
● Rome

KINGDOM
OF
TWO SICILIES

D

Capua ● ● Caserta
● Naples

Troubridge

E
Cardinal
Ruffo

C

Palermo ●

H

Messina ●

SICILY

Syracuse ●

G ✗

GOZO
MALTA  Valletta

A

Ball

**Notes**

A  October 1798 The French garrison on Gozo surrenders to Captain Ball.

B  November 1798 British take Leghorn from the sea while the Neapolitan army is defeated by the French at Castellana.

C  Late December 1798 Nelson and royal family withdraw to Palermo.

D  January 1799 French take Naples.

E  May/June 1799 Cardinal Ruffo advances to retake Naples.

F  May 1799 Nelson concentrates his fleet and sails towards Sardinia to intercept Admiral Bruix. He fails to encounter him and returns to Palermo.

G  February 1800 Nelson sails with Adm. Keith for Malta and captures the *Généreux* then returns to Palermo.

H  April 1800 Nelson and the Hamiltons cruise to Syracuse and Malta and thence to Leghorn. July Nelson strikes his flag and begins his overland journey home with the Hamiltons.

0    50    100    150
Miles

**Key**

→ Neapolitan Army movements

→ French Army movements

→ Nelson's journey home

🚢 British blockading squadrons

✗ Neapolitans defeated by French, Nov. 1798

✗ Nelson captures *Généreux*, Feb. 1800

Having lost their opportunity to defeat their enemy away from Neapolitan soil, the Neapolitans now expected the French to invade any day. The following week was spent organizing the embarkation of the royal family, their relatives, retainers and an ever-growing assortment of Neapolitan nobility onto British and Portuguese warships, transports and some twenty merchantmen anchored in the bay, ready to escape to Palermo if necessary. Nelson masterminded the preparations from the British embassy. Lady Hamilton was at the centre of these activities, staying up night after night as the Queen delivered the royal treasures for packing and transfer to the *Vanguard*. An astonishing miscellany arrived – family jewels, thirty-six casks containing gold ducats, boxes of linen for the children, furniture, pictures, sculptures and plate. The total value was thought to be £2.5 million. It was, somehow, crated up, with many of the boxes being labelled 'stores for Nelson'. Captain Hardy was having an equally desperate time on the *Vanguard*. Not only was he trying to get ready to sail, but many of his crew were ashore on working parties fetching the royal belongings, while his sail-makers were frantically sewing cots for the royal family. It was a hugely overcrowded *Vanguard* that prepared to sail on 21 December, only to be prevented by a violent gale. The winds lessened and they left Naples on the 23rd, only to be hit by a storm that Nelson claimed 'blew harder than I have ever experienced since I have been at sea'. Amidst the terror, screaming, praying and the nauseating stench of vomit, Emma struggled to comfort and assist the royal family. At one stage Sir William, it was claimed, had retired with two loaded pistols vowing he would not die with the 'guggle-guggle-guggle' of sea water in his throat. The 200-mile nightmare lasted over three days, while France established a republic in Naples, with the support of many liberal Neapolitans who had rebelled against the monarchy – including Commodore Caracciolo, the former commander of the Neapolitan Navy.

For the next six months Nelson exercised his command from the Hamiltons' house in Palermo rather than from the quarterdeck of the *Vanguard* while he fell passionately in love with Emma, an emotional entanglement that was fully reciprocated. Seduced by the temptations ashore, Nelson showed an uncharacteristic reluctance to go to sea. A letter written by Lady Minto (wife of the British minister in Vienna) to her sister in July 1800 relaying information from two friends in Palermo relates how Nelson spent much of his time gambling:

> Nelson and the Hamiltons all lived together in a house of which he bore the expense, which was enormous, and every sort of gambling went on half the night. Nelson used to sit with large parcels of gold before him, and generally go to sleep, Lady Hamilton taking from the heap without counting, and playing with his money to the amount of £500 a night. Her rage is play, and Sir William says when he is dead she will be a beggar. However, she has about £30,000 worth of diamonds from the royal family in presents …

Nelson had positioned a blockading squadron off Malta under Ball and another off Naples under Troubridge. However, the Queen (and the King) soon became bored with the British blockade of Naples as a means of recovering their mainland kingdom. Instead, they determined to appeal to the conservative instincts of many of their subjects. One Cardinal Fabrizio Ruffo (described by Nelson as 'a swelled-up priest') was sent to stir up a counter-

revolution. He was remarkably successful, gathering about him a 'Christian Army of the Holy Faith'. It was a grotesque misnomer, numbering nearly 20,000 peasants and brigands reinforced by some Turks and Russians; Ruffo's second-in-command was a notorious bandit called Michelle Peza, nicknamed 'Fra Diavolo', translated by Nelson as 'The Great Devil'. This rabble marched up from the foot of Italy driving all opposition before it, eventually reaching Naples and shutting up the French in the Castle of St Elmo and the local insurgents in the castles of Uovo and Nuovo. Their majesties insisted that it would not be safe for them to return to Naples until it had been 'entirely cleansed' of all French and supporters of the French, and that British warships and troops would best support the process.

Just as Nelson was getting ready to oblige, a brig arrived with the news that the French Admiral Bruix with nineteen warships had left Brest for the Mediterranean, intending to join with a Spanish fleet off Cartagena. Nelson abandoned plans for Naples and set about assembling his fleet, withdrawing all Troubridge's squadron except for a frigate from the Bay of Naples. On 19 May Nelson, in the *Vanguard*, set sail to intercept the enemy. He left with more than a tinge of regret, as a note to Emma made clear.

> To tell you how dreary and uncomfortable the *Vanguard* appears, is only telling you what it is to go from the pleasantest society to a solitary cell, or from the dearest friends to no friends … You, and good Sir William, have spoiled me for any place but with you.

The French threat proved an idle one; Bruix soon sought sanctuary in Toulon and Nelson returned to Palermo and the machinations on the mainland.

Nelson, having been joined by Ball with the *Alexander* and *Goliath* and with his flag now on the 80-gun *Foudroyant*, limited his stay at Palermo to two and a half hours – just enough time to take on board Sir William and 'my dear Lady Hamilton, my faithful interpreter on all occasions'. He arrived in the Bay of Naples on 24 June to find flags of truce flying from the enemy-occupied forts and from Captain Foote's frigate *Seahorse*. Cardinal Ruffo had signed a three-week armistice and the French had withdrawn. The terms for the revolutionaries were generous, including the keeping of all their property and safe passage to Toulon for those that wished it. Nelson would have none of it; only the King could sanction the conditions of any surrender. The *Seahorse* and a cutter were sent to Palermo begging the King and Queen to come at once. On 28 June the rebels were given an ultimatum to surrender unconditionally and they complied. Those from the castles of Uovo and Nuovo were permitted to embark on a number of merchantmen in the harbour but not allowed to sail. On the 29th letters arrived from the King confirming that only unconditional surrender was acceptable. Queen Maria Carolina's advice, given to Nelson via Emma, was to act 'as if it [Naples] were a rebellious Irish town' and to proceed with 'the greatest firmness, vigour and severity'.

And so the city of Naples was subjected to a 'White Terror' that used royalist courts to hand down a horrific series of executions to revolutionaries and to settle private feuds and vendettas. On 25 June Commodore Caracciolo had been discovered hiding down a well, disguised as a peasant, and handed over to Nelson for court martial. This took place in the wardroom of the *Foudroyant* on 27 June, the court being composed of Neapolitan officers under a Count Thurn, the commodore's former flag captain. The verdict of guilty was seemingly a foregone conclusion as Caracciolo had fought against his King – thus committing treason. Nevertheless, the prisoner put up a spirited defence, claiming that it was the King who had betrayed his people by running away to Palermo with all the treasure and leaving behind an unpaid army. By a vote of four to two the court sentenced him to be hanged. Nelson, in a rare display of ruthlessness, ordered Caracciolo to be executed at five o'clock that same afternoon from the yardarm of the Neapolitan frigate *La Minerva*. He was deaf to the plea of the condemned man that he be shot 'as becomes my rank, and not hung up like a felon and a dog' and to a suggestion (by Thurn and Sir William) that he be given twenty-four hours to make peace with his maker. Midshipman George Parsons later described the event in words that made clear his sympathy for Caracciolo:

> ... the veteran, with a firm step, walked into Lord
> Nelson's barge, and with a party of thirty of our seamen,
> under one of our lieutenants, was taken to his flagship [*La
> Minerva*], the gun fired, and the brave old man launched
> into eternity ... The seamen of our fleet, who clustered on
> the rigging like bees, consoled themselves that it was only
> an Italian prince, and the admiral of Naples, that was
> hanging – a person of very light estimation compared with
> the lowest man in a British ship.

On 10 July the King arrived in Naples. Three days later the French, still bottled up in St Elmo, capitulated to Captain Troubridge's besiegers. On 14 July Troubridge marched to attack a rebel outpost at Capua with 1,000 of the best men from the squadron – thus seriously denuding it of seamen and marines. Nelson's flagship now became the seat of the government of Naples. The royal standard was hoisted, the King held his levées there and business of state was conducted in the admiral's cabin. Nelson had become so enamoured with Emma and entangled in Neapolitan affairs that his judgement was impaired to the extent he deliberately disobeyed his commander-in-chief, Lord Keith, three times. Keith's first order, which arrived the day before Nelson sent Troubridge against Capua, stated 'you are hereby required and directed to send such ships as you can spare ... [to] the island of Minorca to await my orders'. Nothing could be clearer; Nelson had been given discretion as to the number of ships but not as to the immediacy of his compliance. But he responded, 'As soon as the safety of His Sicilian Majesty's Kingdom is secured, I shall not lose one moment in making the detachment ... At present ... the safety of His Sicilian Majesty, and his speedy restoration to his kingdom, depends on [my] fleet.' Neapolitan affairs were accorded priority over British, and instead of sending ships to Minorca Nelson sent seamen and marines against Capua.

On 19 July an order reinforcing the first arrived, stating:

> I judge it necessary that all, or the greater part of [your]
> force ... should quit Sicily and repair to Minorca ... [to
> protect] that island during the necessary absence of ...
> [the] squadron under my command [searching for Bruix],
> or for cooperating with me against the combined [Franco-
> Spanish] force of the enemy.

In his second refusal Nelson acknowledged he was courting professional disaster.

> Your Lordship ... was not informed of the change of
> affairs in the Kingdom of Naples, and that all our marines
> and a body of seamen are landed in order to drive the
> French ... out of the Kingdom [Keith could not know
> these men had been sent *after* Nelson received the first
> order] ... Unless the French are at least drove from Capua,
> I think it right not to obey your Lordship's order ... I am
> perfectly aware of the consequence of disobeying the
> orders of my Commander-in-Chief.

Then, with astounding impertinence, he added, 'I have no scruple in deciding that it is better to save the Kingdom of Naples and risk Minorca, than to risk the Kingdom of Naples and save Minorca.'

On 22 July a third order arrived to the same effect as its predecessors: 'Your Lordship is ... directed to repair to Minorca, with the whole, or the greater part of your command, for the protection of that island, as I shall, in all probability, have left the Mediterranean.'

Nelson neither went himself nor sent the 'whole or greater part' of his force – instead he sent Captain Duckworth with a mere four ships. Such deliberate insubordination was a sacking offence, but Nelson escaped with a reprimand from the Admiralty. Sir Evan Nepean, Secretary to the Admiralty Board, wrote on 20 August:

> Their Lordships do not ... see sufficient reason to justify
> your having disobeyed the orders you had received from
> your Commanding Officer, or having left Minorca exposed
> to the risk of being attacked without having any naval
> force to protect it ... Their Lordships by no means approve
> of the seamen being landed [in Italy] to form a part of the
> army ... in operations at a distance from the coast where
> ... they might be prevented from returning to the ships,
> and the squadron be thereby ... no longer capable of
> performing the services required of it ... Your Lordship [is]
> not to employ the seamen in like manner in future.

Nelson never admitted being in the wrong. Fortunately Minorca was not attacked, and on 13 August 1799, in reward for his loyalty to Naples, King Ferdinand made him Duke of Bronte (meaning 'thunder'). The dukedom consisted of a 15,000-acre estate in the north-west of Sicily, on the slopes of Mount Etna. By 1799 it had been ruined by neglect and volcanic eruptions, but Nelson was delighted and afterwards always used the word 'Bronte' in his signature, in May 1800 signing himself as 'Bronte and Nelson of the Nile' and later on 'Nelson and Bronte'.

Nelson passed almost nine more months at Palermo before he was recalled to England. Most of that time was spent ashore with the Hamiltons. During those months Napoleon managed to escape from Egypt, arriving in France after a six-week voyage on 9 October 1799, and the French continued to hold out in Valletta. Napoleon's escape rankled with Nelson. He had often vowed that not a single Frenchman would return from Egypt and yet the most important one had managed to sail the length of his station undiscovered. During this period he made two personal sorties from Palermo. The first was a brief visit to Minorca in October 1799 to persuade General Erskine to release British troops to take Valletta. The second was in January/February 1800 when he accompanied Lord Keith to Malta, arriving with 1,500 Neapolitan troops to hasten the end of the siege. He went with some reluctance, writing to Emma, 'To say how much I miss your house and company would be saying little; but in truth you and Sir William have so spoiled me, that I am not happy anywhere else.' However, on 18 February the prospect of action boosted his spirits. Again to Emma, he wrote, 'I feel anxious to get up with these ships and shall be unhappy not to take them myself, for ... my greatest happiness is to serve ... my ... King and Country, and I am envious only of glory; for if it be a sin to covet glory, I am the most offending soul alive.' The encounter ended in a three-hour chase of the French flagship *Généreux* (one of only two ships to escape at the Nile) by Nelson in the *Foudroyant* accompanied by the 74-gun *Northumberland* and the 32-gun frigate *Success*. It was the frigate captain's skilful use of her greater speed and manoeuvrability to rake the stern of the *Généreux* again and again that slowed her sufficiently for the British 74s to catch up and force a surrender. Nelson could not resist a barbed comment when reporting his success to the Admiralty: 'The *Généreux* was taken by me, and my plan ... my quitting Lord Keith, was at my own risk ... The way he went the *Généreux* never could have been taken.'

After this success Nelson's sole ambition was to return to Emma; others could take Malta. He resorted to pleas of ill health, writing to Lord Keith, 'My Lord, my state of health is such that it is impossible I can remain much longer here ... I must ... request your permission to go to my friends at Palermo.' Keith, well aware of Nelson's real reason for wanting to quit the station, responded that the Malta squadron was forbidden even to visit Palermo for supplies but was to use Syracuse (Nelson's original preference) instead. Yet again Nelson flagrantly flouted his commander's instructions. On 10 March, despite pleas from Troubridge and Ball to remain, he sailed for Palermo. On arrival he sent *Foudroyant* back to the blockade and hoisted his flag, somewhat ignominiously, on a transport.

Lord Keith, with some justification, had had enough of Nelson. He wrote of: 'my extreme regret that your health should be such as to oblige you to quit your station off Malta, at a time when I should suppose there must be the finest prospect of its reduction. ... If ... [enemy ships] should come into the Mediterranean ... I should be much concerned to hear that you learned of their arrival ... either on shore or in a transport at Palermo.' The last sentence was intended to hurt. By May 1800 the First Lord of the Admiralty, Earl Spencer, told Keith that Nelson's 'further stay in the Mediterranean cannot ... contribute either to the public advantage or his own'. To Nelson, Spencer was slightly more tactful:

> ... having observed that you have been under the necessity of quitting your station off Malta, on account of your health ... it appeared ... much more advisable for you to come home at once, than to ... remain inactive at Palermo, while active service was going on in other parts of the station ... You will be more likely to recover your health and strength in England than ... inactive ... at a Foreign Court.

It would be interesting to know whether Nelson's health would have improved sufficiently to allow him to remain at Palermo had

---

### An Emma Anecdote

While in Palermo in 1799 a Mr Pryse Gordon dined with Nelson and the Hamiltons at their residence. While the details may be inaccurate the gist of the story has some credibility.

> He [Gordon] had been dining at the ambassador's, and after dinner a Turkish officer was introduced. In the course of the evening he boasted that he had put to death with his own sword a number of French prisoners. 'Look, there is their blood remaining on it!' The speech being translated, her Ladyship's eyes beamed with delight, and she said, 'Oh, let me see the sword that did the glorious deed!' It was presented to her; she took it in her fair hands, covered with rings, and, looking at the encrusted Jacobin [French revolutionary] blood, kissed it, and handed it to the hero of the Nile. Had I not been an eye-witness to this disgraceful act, I would not have ventured to relate it.

---

his journey home not been made so much more agreeable by the Hamiltons' company. Sir William was being recalled at the same time. On 24 April Nelson was back on board the *Foudroyant* along with Sir William, Emma and friends on what can best be described as a yachting cruise to Syracuse and Malta. At some stage between the dinners, parties and concerts Emma probably conceived Nelson's daughter, Horatia, who was born in late January 1801. On 12 May Nelson had the gall to write to Lord Keith saying he proposed to withdraw the *Foudroyant* and *Alexander* from the Malta blockade in order to take the Queen of Naples to Leghorn so that she might visit her daughter in Vienna, after which the *Foudroyant* would take Nelson and the Hamiltons to England. Keith's reaction on receiving this letter can be easily imagined, but Nelson took both ships without waiting for Keith's inevitable refusal. After calling at Palermo Nelson, the Hamiltons and the Queen with her entourage arrived at Leghorn on 14 June – the day Napoleon won one of his greatest victories at Marengo over the Austrians. This put paid to the Queen's continuing her holiday overland to Vienna.

Lord Keith himself arrived at Leghorn on 24 June to sort out the mess. He flatly refused permission for any ships-of-the-line to be used as cruise yachts and would only allow a frigate to take the Queen to Palermo. The British minister to Tuscany observed, 'the Queen wept ... [Lord Keith] remained unmoved and would grant nothing but a frigate ... He told her Lady Hamilton had had command of the fleet long enough ... Nelson does not intend going home till he has escorted [the Queen] back to Palermo. His zeal for the public service seems entirely lost in his love and vanity.'

Lord Keith finally cut the Gordian knot when he discovered that the Hamiltons were going with the Queen via Florence and Ancona. Nelson could strike his flag on 13 July 1800 and go overland with them to England. It was not just Lord Keith who disapproved of Nelson's behaviour. Lord St Vincent was to write, with bitter venom, 'Animal courage was the sole merit of Lord Nelson, his private character most disgraceful, in every sense of the word.'

## EMMA, LADY HAMILTON

Emma Hamilton, the wife of Sir William Hamilton the British envoy at Naples, became famous – more accurately notorious – as Nelson's mistress. Their affair, conducted with the knowledge, indeed the acquiescence, of the elderly Sir William, was the subject of endless gossip, newspaper articles and private correspondence. Nelson's behaviour eventually destroyed his wife and severely tested the friendship of several close naval friends, including Captain Troubridge. His craving for Emma embroiled him too deeply in Neapolitan affairs, leading him on occasion to neglect his naval duties. As described above, by the spring of 1800 he was even disobeying his commander-in-chief, hoisting his flag on a transport and exaggerating his health problems to justify quitting his station to return to his beloved Emma. Little wonder he was recalled.

Emma (born Emily) was the daughter of Henry Lyon, a blacksmith of Great Neston in Cheshire. Her precise date of birth is uncertain but is likely to have been in 1765, the year she was baptized. Her father died soon after her birth, forcing her mother to move to her home village in Flintshire, where she was dependent on parish relief. Little is known of Emma's childhood. As a teenager she was sent to work in London as a nursery maid, taking with her a developing asset that would ultimately bring her fame and social advancement – her beauty. From this humble start it was but a short step to becoming the mistress of a succession of gentlemen of means including, it is thought, a naval captain whose child she bore in 1780. The following year she was living with a country gentleman, Sir Harry Featherstonhaugh. Within twelve months he had lost interest, possibly due to an unwanted pregnancy. She then worked for a time as an 'attendant' at the 'Temple of Health' run by a disreputable quack called Dr Graham. Now a strikingly good-looking young woman, Emily Hart, as she called herself, was taken as a mistress by the Hon. Charles Greville, a gentleman with artistic tastes, with her mother (known as Mrs Cadogan) acting as housekeeper. This seems to have been a longer-lasting, more stable relationship during which she learned to sing, dance and act with some skill. Her beauty was such that Greville was able to arrange for her to sit for several fashionable painters, most notably George Romney.

Greville was the nephew of Sir William Hamilton, the British ambassador to Naples, and in 1786 an arrangement was made whereby 'Emma', as she was now known, was sent to visit the sixty-year-old Sir William in Naples. Greville was in debt and wanted to find a wife, while his uncle had met Emma briefly and, like most other men, found her not only attractive and willing but also bright and vivacious. The understanding was that in return for parting with his mistress Greville had his debts paid by his uncle. Emma was told she was going on holiday, but as the weeks passed it slowly dawned on her what the 'arrangement' was. Although initially horrified – there was an age difference of some forty years – she found Sir William considerate, kind and not too demanding, while she enjoyed the endless parties and social life of Naples. Perhaps more importantly, she began to form a friendship with Queen Maria Carolina. As the years passed Emma and Sir William established a genuine, loving relationship which resulted in their marriage, during a visit to England, in late 1791.

As Lady Hamilton there was now no bar to her acceptability in the highest circles of Neapolitan society and, more importantly, at court. Emma made the most of it. She became the indispensable link through whom the Queen frequently communicated with Sir William, and she also acquired a taste for the lavish diplomatic lifestyle, of being admired, of being the Queen's favourite – and of heavy gambling with others' money. Into this hotbed of gaiety, political intrigue and extravagance stepped Nelson, the hugely acclaimed hero of the Nile.

They had met briefly before in 1793 when Nelson was the captain of the *Agamemnon*. He had stayed in the Hamiltons' home and had been suitably impressed by Lady Hamilton's beauty and her 'attitudes'. These involved Emma posing in silence in the attitudes of the classical sculptures depicted on Sir William's collection of vases, sometimes concealing herself provocatively with the aid of a shawl while Sir William controlled the lighting. In the intervening years she and Nelson had corresponded in warm terms. As recently as 7 June 1798, just before the Nile, when he was anchored in Naples Bay, Nelson received a note from her revealing feelings that were surely more than platonic: 'God bless you, my dear Sir, I will not say how glad I shall be to see you. Indeed, I cannot describe to you my feelings on your being so near us. Ever, Ever dear Sir, your affte and gratefull [*sic*] Emma Hamilton.'

So when Nelson arrived in late September 1798, Emma had no inhibitions about instantly taking the injured admiral into her care. He was still suffering from his head wound, and Emma spent long hours nursing him and pandering to his vanity. Such physical closeness was strengthened by Emma's key role in Neapolitan affairs, in which Nelson soon became entangled. He admired her, not only for her voluptuousness and her vivacity but also for her ability (she spoke French and Italian) and her courage, as exemplified by her behaviour on board ship during the storm when the royal family was forced to flee to Palermo. The attraction was mutual and inevitably developed into a love affair. Emma quickly realized that Nelson thrived on adulation and praise and lost no opportunity in stoking his considerable vanity. As described above, his love for Emma affected his professional judgement to the extent that it eventually led to his (and Sir William's) recall. His leisurely overland journey home with Emma and Sir William did nothing to enhance his relationship with his Admiralty superiors.

## Horatia Nelson (1801–81)

Horatia was born at the end of January 1801 (along with a twin sister who died at birth) while Nelson was at sea. Nelson was ecstatic, and declared that she would grow into the most lovely woman as she was the daughter of 'the most beautiful woman of the age'. His love for his little daughter was unbounded although while Sir William lived it all had to be hushed up – Emma was indisposed with 'a stomach complaint' during confinement. Until Sir William's death when she was two Horatia was cared for by a wet nurse, Mrs Mary Gibson. Emma visited her often but Nelson much less frequently.

There had been problems with the christening as the birth details and names of the parents were required. Nelson's rather pathetic response was that they should say Horatia had been 'born at Portsmouth or at sea'. A better answer was that Nelson and

Emma should stand sponsors, telling the priest that the fictitious 'Mr and Mrs Thompson', Horatia's supposed parents, were 'out of the kingdom'. Nelson kept a watercolour painting of the little girl in his cabin alongside that of Emma. But his time with his beloved daughter was cruelly short. Before he left Merton to rejoin the fleet before Trafalgar he knelt quietly at prayer by her bed and in the codicil to his will written shortly before the battle he naively entrusted her to the care of the nation.

Horatia remained with Emma until her mother's death in 1815, then enjoyed a number of happy years with relatives. In 1822 she married Philip Ward, a clergyman, in a union that was to last thirty-seven years and produce ten children. She lived to the grand old age of eighty, dying at Pinner on 6 March 1881 – never admitting that her mother was Emma.

## Did Emma Really Look Like This?

If Emma had lived in modern times it is questionable if she would have been deemed much of a beauty. Certainly one suspects that by the age of thirty-five she had become somewhat blowsy – in 1799 Lady Elgin wrote, 'She is indeed a Whapper!' Most of the portraits show a woman who by today's standards is overweight and with a small rosebud mouth. Only George Romney's portrait of her as a young woman (reproduced right) shows her as strikingly lovely. One suspects the life she led in high society was not conducive to keeping the beauty of youth for long.

While in Dresden in October 1800 Nelson and the Hamiltons dined at the British Ambassador's house. Among the guests was a Mrs St George, who later wrote in her diary an amazingly detailed description of every facet of Emma's appearance.

It is plain that Nelson thinks of nothing but Lady Hamilton, who is totally occupied by the same object. She is bold, forward, coarse, assuming and vain. Her figure is colossal [she was, however, about five months pregnant with twins], but, excepting her feet, which are hideous, well shaped. Her bones are large, and she is exceedingly embonpoint [large]. She resembles the bust of Ariadne; the shape of all her features is fine, as is the form of her head, and particularly her ears; her teeth are a little irregular, but tolerably white; her eyes light blue, with a brown spot in one, which, though a defect, takes nothing away from her beauty of expression. Her eyebrows and hair are dark, and her complexion coarse. Her expression is strongly marked, variable, and interesting, her voice loud, yet not disagreeable.

Mrs St George did not think much of Emma's singing either, although it must be said her views were in a minority. 'Her voice is good, and very strong, but she is frequently out of tune; her expression strongly marked and variable; she has no shake [vibrato], no flexibility and no sweetness.'

## Did Nelson Really Look Like This?

A Thomas Kosegarten, an art expert, was part of Nelson's group that toured the Dresden Gallery in October 1800. He later published a book in which appears the following description of the admiral.

Nelson is one of the most insignificant-looking figures I ever saw in my life. His weight cannot be more than 70 lbs. A more miserable collection of bones and wizened frame I have never yet come across. His bold nose, the steady eye and the solid worth revealed in his whole face betray in some measure the great conqueror. He speaks little, and then only in English, and he hardly ever smiles. I have no doubt of his high ability, but one cannot look without astonishment at his slender body, although this can of course have no immediate connection with a great soul ... He was almost covered with orders and stars. His right arm is missing, the coat sleeve was fastened to the breast, as a rule Lady Hamilton wore his hat ... she behaved like a loving sister towards Nelson; led him, often took hold of his hand, whispered something onto his ear, and he twisted his mouth into the faint resemblance of a smile ...

*Sir William Beechey's portrait of Nelson, 1801*

What is extraordinary in this blossoming public relationship was the role of Sir William. He, Nelson and Emma lived together in a *ménage à trois* that seemed to be an amicable arrangement for each of them. Sir William was an old man and, seemingly wanting to keep both his wife and his friendship with Nelson, was content to let matters develop. It is entirely possible that Nelson and Emma did not consummate their love until spring 1800. In 1801 Nelson recalled that time in a letter, 'Ah! Those were happy times, days of ease and

nights of pleasure.' Sir William's reputation suffered too, but this was less important to him than a gentle, peaceful retirement. This 'Tria Juncta in Uno' (the motto of the Order of the Bath to which both men belonged) continued until Sir William's death in April 1803.

Nelson's homecoming and confrontation with his wife was less pleasant. Fanny Nelson had been cruelly treated and was infuriated by the constant admiring references to Lady Hamilton in her husband's letters. She exploded. 'I am sick of hearing of dear Lady

Hamilton and am resolved that you shall give up either her or me.' Within weeks Nelson left her for Emma, who was living with her husband in Piccadilly. Thereafter Fanny would often refer to Emma as 'the Lady of 23 Piccadilly'.

Nelson's daughter Horatia was born in January 1801. Nelson was overjoyed at being a father but the baby's parentage had to be concealed. The infant was handed over to a wet nurse while Nelson's and Emma's interest in the child was supposed to be on behalf of her real parents, a 'Mr and Mrs Thompson'. To Emma he wrote, 'I never had a dear pledge of love till you gave me one [Horatia], and you, thank my God, never gave one to any one else.' Emma had seemingly not told him of her other daughter by a lover of long ago – Sir William had known of this child and had helped support her financially. In September 1801 Nelson bought a house, Merton Place, just south of London. The trio moved in the following month and began again to build a social life with those of their friends who were prepared to ignore the delicate circumstances. After Sir William's death in 1803 it was at last possible to have Horatia with them at 'Paradise Merton'. Before Nelson left for the final time before Trafalgar he went through a quasi marriage with Emma, at which they exchanged rings and received a blessing from a priest.

Prepared to forgive him, Fanny did write making an attempt at reconciliation, but she was cruelly ignored. When writing his will on board the *Victory* Nelson added a codicil for Emma. After detailing her services to Britain while at Naples he continued:

> ... I leave Emma Lady Hamilton, therefore, a Legacy to my King and Country, that they will give her an ample provision to maintain her rank in life. I also leave to the beneficence of my Country my adopted daughter Horatia Nelson Thompson; and I desire she will use in future the name of Nelson only ...

Later, as he lay dying on the orlop deck, he whispered to Mr Scott, the chaplain, 'Remember that I leave Lady Hamilton and my daughter as a legacy to my country – never forget Horatia.' Perhaps unsurprisingly, the British government gave Emma nothing and ignored the existence of Horatia.

Sir William had left Emma comfortably off, while from Nelson she received Merton, an annuity of £500 and the controlling interest in £4,000 left for Horatia – more than enough to keep most widows comfortable. But Emma continued her old wild ways, resorting to drink, hosting parties and gambling to seek consolation for her loss. Eventually pressure from creditors forced her to sell Merton and live at various cheap addresses near Piccadilly. She resorted to selling a number of Nelson relics but could still not clear her debts. In 1813 she was imprisoned for a year, being released only through the pecuniary generosity of an Alderman Smith. Suffering from jaundice, weak and depressed, she fled to France to escape her remaining creditors. The decline in her health was rapid, and not helped by the 'baneful habit she had of taking wine and spirits to a fearful degree' (Horatia's words). On 15 January 1815 she died in poverty in Calais, aged about fifty. What would Nelson have thought?

## THE JOURNEY HOME, JULY TO NOVEMBER 1800

Nelson struck his flag in the Mediterranean on 13 July 1800 but did not set foot in England until 6 November. His journey soon developed into a leisurely, expensive holiday in which he was able to indulge his ego by appearing on countless occasions covered in his decorations, described by one observer as 'a perfect constellation of stars and orders'. He continued to enjoy the company, if not the bed, of his adorable Emma while she was able to demonstrate her 'attitudes' and singing ability to numerous admiring

---

### Frances (Fanny) Lady Nelson (1761–1831)

When Nelson returned home after losing his arm at Santa Cruz in 1797 Fanny tenderly nursed him during the months of pain that followed, and all through 1798 Nelson's letters to his wife appear as affectionate as ever. But in 1799 Lady Nelson seems to have become increasingly disquieted by rumours that reached her from Naples of Nelson's relationship with Emma Hamilton.

By the time Nelson returned home in November 1800 his adultery was public knowledge and unsurprisingly Fanny did not go to meet him and the Hamiltons. When Fanny and Nelson did meet they quarrelled, and after several weeks of altercations they finally separated in early 1801. It is alleged by some that this followed a particularly explosive row that left Nelson wandering the streets of London in a state of despair before ending up at the Hamiltons' house in Piccadilly. On 12 March Nelson sailed for the Baltic and Copenhagen. After that victory a letter to his agent Davison makes it clear the separation was final and acrimonious.

> You will, at a proper time, and before my arrival in England, signify to Lady N. that I expect, and for which I have made such a very liberal allowance for her [£400 a quarter, or nearly half his salary] to be left to myself, and without any inquiries from her; for sooner than live the unhappy life I did when I last came to England, I would stay abroad for ever. My mind is as fixed as fate ...

But Fanny never really stopped loving him. As late as Christmas 1801 she made one final attempt at reconciliation.

My dear Husband,
It is some time since I have written to you; the silence you have imposed is more than My affection will allow me and in this instance I hope you will forgive me in not obeying you. ... I now have to offer you for your accommodation, a comfortable warm House. Do, my Dear Husband, let us live together. I can never be happy till such an event takes place. I assure you again I have but one wish in the world, to please you. Let everything be buried in oblivion; it will pass away like a dream. I can only now intreat [*sic*] you to believe I am, most sincerely and affectionately,
         Your wife,
         Frances H. Nelson.

Nelson's vanity is not difficult to overlook, his cruelty to his wife much harder. The envelope to this sad letter is marked, 'Opened by mistake by Lord Nelson, but not read. [signed] A Davison'.

After Nelson's death Fanny, who had become Baroness and then Viscountess Nelson as he was himself honoured, received a generous pension and the Lloyd's Patriotic Fund silver vase. Although many of Nelson's friends failed to keep in touch there were exceptions such as Lord St Vincent and Thomas Hardy. She lived quietly, mostly in London, where her brother-in-law Earl Nelson often visited her. In her latter years her health began to fail and she never recovered from her son Josiah's death in August 1830. She died on 4 May 1831 in Harley Street, London aged seventy and was buried in the churchyard at Littleham, near Exmouth alongside Josiah.

audiences. A journey that should have been completed in three and a half weeks took three and a half months. England was still very much at war, so the Admiralty understandably regarded Nelson's prolonged public dalliance with his mistress, attended by ostentatious sightseeing and partying, as a neglect of his duties.

The coaches leaving Leghorn contained the eighty-five persons who comprised the Queen's and the Nelson/Hamilton entourage, who made an uncomfortable journey via Florence and Perugia to Ancona on the Adriatic coast – an indirect route to avoid the French threat from the north. The four-day sea voyage to Trieste on Russian warships was even more unpleasant, with bad weather, cramped conditions and Sir William, now seventy, depressed at leaving his beloved Naples where he had served for thirty-six years. On arrival most travellers collapsed into bed to recover before moving on to Vienna. This journey required over a hundred horses, fourteen coaches and three baggage wagons for the party, which had now shrunk to seventy people. The clattering cavalcade covered some 200 yards of road space. It arrived in Vienna on 17 August 1800.

The travellers' stay in that city was the highlight of the holiday and lasted five and a half weeks. The Queen and her four youngest children had reached their journey's end, and the Austrian court played host in the most lavish manner. Nelson and the Hamiltons, particularly Emma, made the most of it. Day after day, night after night an endless succession of entertainments was provided. There were court banquets, elegant balls, luncheon parties, tea parties, dinner parties, at least four concerts and theatre evenings. Then there were the sightseeing tours (including one into Hungary to visit Prince Esterhazy), the hunting parties and fishing trips – a favourite pastime of Sir William. Nelson was formally introduced to the Emperor (Queen Maria Carolina's son-in-law) and met Franz Thaller, a renowned sculptor who arranged for a plaster mask to be made of the admiral's face. He was also introduced to the distinguished musician Josef Haydn, and they got on so well that Haydn composed a 'Nelson Aria'. This so delighted the admiral that he exchanged the watch he had worn at the Nile for the pen Haydn had used to compose the music. Vienna went wild in welcoming its famous guests. Honours and invitations poured in; shops, taverns, dresses, even hats were named after Nelson. The farewell parties, vying to outdo the welcoming ones, included a huge firework display and an aquatic demonstration on the Danube.

A much reduced coach party of seventeen reluctantly left Vienna for Prague on 26 September. In a four-day stay in this beautiful city Nelson and his companions managed to make the most of yet more generous hospitality that included visiting Archduke Karl, one of the very few generals who had succeeded in defeating the French. He had already beaten two French generals – Jordan twice (in 1793 and 1796) and Massena at Zurich in 1799, and in 1809 was to inflict defeat on Napoleon himself at Aspern

and Essling. There was a visit to the theatre, and on Nelson's forty-second birthday the Archduke gave an 'Entertainment' during which the entire city was illuminated, including Nelson's hotel (for which he was annoyed to find the cost on his bill).

On 30 September the party left for Dresden. However, about 45 miles north of Prague they turned east, making for Litomerice (the modern name) on the River Elbe. For the remainder of their journey they would not have to endure endless jolting and jarring over rough, dangerous roads in coaches; instead they would sail smoothly down the river to Cuxhaven – a 350-mile river cruise. Although they stayed for ten days at Dresden there was no official welcoming hospitality on the scale of Vienna or even Prague. Much time was spent visiting the city sights, particularly the various porcelain factories. Nelson and the Hamiltons dined with a Mr Hugh Elliot, the British Ambassador; among the guests was a young Irish widow, Mrs Melesina St George, who left a less than flattering account of Emma's appearance in her diary. A Thomas Kosegarten who met him touring the famous Dresden Art Gallery paints an equally disagreeable word picture of the admiral (see box p. 402). The journey continued on 10 October aboard two specially equipped gondolas, which had covered areas for resting or sleeping plus reasonable toilet and cooking facilities.

The long journey north continued, with the party usually stopping to spend the night ashore. Progress was not fast as masts had to be lowered and raised again at a number of bridges, and there were numerous customs posts. Boredom was something of a problem – Sir William overcame it by fishing. They all went ashore at Magdeburg (in Prussia) before the final stage of the journey to Hamburg, which they reached on 21 October. Much to Nelson's annoyance there was no frigate waiting to take them home, and they were forced to stay for ten days until, frustrated by the Admiralty's failure to supply a frigate, Nelson hired a mail packet from Cuxhaven to Great Yarmouth. Nevertheless, their time in Hamburg was far from tedious. The huge dockyards impressed Nelson, and there were frequent luncheon and tea parties, more sightseeing, a visit to the theatre and invitations to dinner. Lady Hamilton hosted a dinner party at which she once more performed her 'attitudes' and sang. Perhaps the high spot of the stay was a reception organized by the English residents of Hamburg to which over a thousand guests were invited.

The five-day voyage on the mail boat *King George* was not pleasant. The winds reached gale-force strength and at one point the vessel went aground on a sandbank. All were mightily relieved to be stepping ashore at Great Yarmouth on 6 November 1800, where Nelson was given the Freedom of the Borough. Although the previous months had been a memorable experience – the cliché 'holiday of a lifetime' seems appropriate – one wonders what the bill was, and who paid.

## Lady Hamilton's Grave

In the *Nelson Dispatch* of October 1985 a Mr P.J. Pinkett quoted from an account of Emma's death and burial published in 1874. It reads:

Lady Hamilton died in a house in Calais, now No. 111 Rue Française, a street running parallel with the southern rampart of the town. When Emma fled to France, M. de Rheims, the English interpreter, gave her one of his small houses to live in – a house which was very badly furnished. On her death not a Protestant clergyman was to be found in Calais and the solemn service for the dead was read over her grave by an Irish half-pay officer. Emma sleeps in what was once the pleasure garden of a woman almost equally famous for her personal charms and strange adventures, the beautiful Elizabeth Chudleigh, better known as the Duchess of Kingstown.

The ground was consecrated and used as a cemetery until 1816, it was afterwards converted into a timber yard, and no trace remains of the woman whom Nelson, with his dying voice, bequeathed to the gratitude of his country. In the office of the *Juge de Paix* is an inventory of her effects to the value of 228 francs ... and pawn tickets for articles of plate and trinkets from *Mont de Piete*.

# Command and Control

## COMMAND

### THE BRITISH FLEET

On 18 August 1805 Nelson came ashore at Portsmouth, the first time he had set foot on dry land since he had hoisted his flag in the *Victory* as commander-in-chief in the Mediterranean in the summer of 1803. He had exactly four weeks, most of it spent at Merton, before setting sail again to resume command on the Mediterranean station – a command that extended into the Atlantic to include the waters off Cadiz.

Nelson's house at Merton was large – fifteen bedrooms – and for the few weeks Nelson spent there it was full with at least nine adults, seven children and a bevy of servants. It was also only an hour's coach ride from central London, and Nelson's time was divided between domestic happiness at home and an almost daily dash to Whitehall to catch up with news of the war. He attended meetings in Downing Street with the Prime Minister, William Pitt (who told him 'his services might be wanted'), and had to see Lord Castlereagh, the Secretary of State for War and the Colonies (an odd combination, except that so much effort was required to take or defend these overseas possessions), and George Canning at the Foreign Office. Nelson's opinions and advice were much sought after. Most of all he went to the Admiralty to see Lord Barham, the eighty-year-old First Lord. Despite his age Barham was far from senile and had a clear grasp of the essentials of British naval strategy. Additionally, he did not let his great seniority prevent him from listening to his juniors' opinions. He had great confidence in Nelson, whom he judged an outstanding admiral, and unlike others at the Admiralty he did not allow his opinion of Nelson to be clouded by the latter's private life.

At 5.00 a.m. on 2 September Nelson heard the clatter of carriage wheels and the snorting of hard-worked horses outside his door. His visitor wore the dusty, crumpled uniform of a post

---

### Captain Blackwood and the Capture of Vice-Admiral Decrès

Three years before Trafalgar, the famous frigate captain Henry Blackwood was commanding the 36-gun *Penelope* off Malta. One dark and stormy night he encountered Decrès' flagship, the 80-gun *Guillaume Tell*, and daringly engaged her, fighting single-handedly until daylight. Blackwood's tactics were bold to the point of being foolhardy but his consummate seamanship, combined with the bad weather and darkness, gave him the edge. He brought his ship up close under the stern of the Frenchman then brought his ship into the wind to fire his port broadside, then immediately wore and fired the starboard one. He managed to do this time after time throughout the night and so crippled his giant of an opponent that the English line-of-battle ships were able to catch up and, by morning, make an important capture. Blackwood and Decrès met and formed a mutual respect and liking for one another. The French admiral was released after the Peace of Amiens and became Minister of Marine.

---

captain. Nelson, who was already dressed, welcomed perhaps the most famous frigate captain of the age, Henry Blackwood of the *Euryalus*. Blackwood had travelled overnight, on his way to the Admiralty with exciting news. He had shadowed the French and Spanish ships from Corunna and Ferrol to Cadiz where they had arrived on 20 August, and now announced that Cadiz was crammed with enemy ships – there were 37 ships-of-the-line, and a host of smaller ones. Admirals Villeneuve and Gravina had joined forces – the Combined Fleet of Trafalgar fame was in existence.

The strategic significance of Blackwood's news was profound. Britain was still worried about the invasion threat from across the Channel. Boulogne was still bursting with soldiers and their transports, as were smaller ports along the French coast. A large enemy battle fleet was now at Cadiz, watched by eight ships of Vice-Admiral Collingwood – a tiny cork in a big bottle. For ten days from 20 August Collingwood was alone. The arrival of Vice-Admiral Calder with another 17 ships-of-the-line on 30 August did much to redress the balance, but not enough. The perceived danger during this period was that the Combined Fleet might either slip or force its way out of Cadiz and make for the Channel, joining up with the 21 French ships at Brest under Vice-Admiral Ganteaume and four more at sea under Commodore Allemand. The immediate need for the British was to get a fleet of sufficient strength built up outside Cadiz. What they did not appreciate (until rumours began to reach London in early September) was that Napoleon had abandoned his invasion plans, unable to ignore the military preparations of the Russian and Austrian armies. On 25 August the Emperor wrote to Foreign Minister Talleyrand, 'My mind is made up. My movement has begun. By September 17, I shall be with 200,000 men in

## The Opposing Commands Assemble, June–October 1805                              Map 21

Britannia (100)
Neptune (98)
Prince (98)
Téméraire (98)
Conqueror (74)
Defence (74)
Orion (74)
Revenge (74)
Spartiate (74)
Swiftsure (74)
Polyphemus (64)
•• Prince of Wales (98)
• Canopus (80)
• Donegal (74)
• Spencer (74)
• Tigre (74)
• Zealous (74)

Dreadnought (98)
Tonnant (80)
Achille (74)
Bellerophon (74)
Colossus (74)
Mars (74)
Minotaur (74)
Queen (98)

Principe de Asturias (112)
Neptuno (80)
Argonauta (74)
Monarca (74)
Montañés (74)
San Augustin (74)
San Francisco de Asis (74)
San Ildefonso (74)
San Juan Nepomuceno (74)
*Terrible (74)
*San Fulgencio (64)

SPAIN

• San Lucar

• Rota

• Cadiz

Bucentaure (80)
Formidable (80)
Indomptable (80)
Neptune (80)
Achille (74)
Aigle (74)
Algéciras (74)
Argonaute (74)
Berwick (74)
Duguay-Trouin (74)
Fougueux (74)
Héros (74)
Intrépide (74)
Mont Blanc (74)
Pluton (74)
Redoubtable (74)
Scipion (74)
Swiftsure (74)

A

B

C

Nelson's cruising station

Santisima Trinidad (136)
Santa Ana (112)
Rayo (100)
Bahama (74)
San Justo (74)
San Leandro (64)

Cape Trafalgar

Gibraltar

THE STRAITS

• Ceuta

Victory (102)
Ajax (74)
Thunderer (74)

Africa (64)
Agamemnon (64)

Cape Spartel

Belleisle (74)
Defiance (74)

Royal Sovereign (100)

Leviathan (74)

• Tangier

0   10   20   30   40   50
          Miles

### Key/Notes
A   French ships that assembled at Cadiz on 21 August from Corunna
B   Spanish ships that assembled at Cadiz from Ferrol on 21 August
C   Spanish ships already based in Cadiz
*   Ships under repair/left in Cadiz when the Combined Fleet sailed on 19 October
1   Vice Admiral Collingwood's squadron arrived off Cadiz 8 June and 22 August
2   Rear-Admiral Calder's squadron, joined 30 August
3   Vice-Admiral Nelson arrives to take command, 28 September
4   Arrived from England 3–10 October
5   Arrived from Gibraltar 8 October
6   Arrived from England 8 October. Collingwood transferred his flag from Dreadnought to Royal Sovereign
7   Arrived from England 13/14 October
•   To Gibraltar under Rear-Admiral Louis for replenishment 2–17 October and to escort the Malta convoy under Sir James Craig
••  Took Calder home to face his court martial 14 October

Germany.' L'Armée d'Angleterre was to become La Grande Armée and march away to victory on the Ulm (on 21 October) and Austerlitz. Napoleon lingered at Boulogne until 3 September to disguise his decision. So much for the myth that Trafalgar saved Britain from invasion.

Nelson swiftly followed Blackwood to the Admiralty, where Lord Barham informed him that he was to resume command of the Mediterranean Fleet. As many ships as possible would reinforce him as soon as they could be made available (he believed he would ultimately have 40 ships-of-the-line). His flagship, the Victory, would be ready in a week. In the event Nelson sailed with the Thunderer and Ajax and was later joined by the Belleisle,

Defiance, Agamemnon, Africa, Royal Sovereign and Leviathan, bringing his fleet to 34 ships-of-the-line by 13 October. Nelson's mission was to confront Villeneuve at Cadiz and prevent him from threatening either the Channel or the Mediterranean – preferably by destroying him. The Admiralty was convinced that acute food shortages at Cadiz meant that the Combined Fleet would eventually have to put to sea. Then, in Nelson's words, 'It is ... annihilation that the Country wants, and not merely a splendid victory ...'. Another important responsibility was the need to guard convoys and in particular protect General Craig and his expedition with 6,000 men to Naples. At this meeting Barham demonstrated his confidence in Nelson's ability by handing him the Navy List and telling him he could choose his captains. Nelson gave it back saying, 'Choose yourself my Lord, the same spirit actuates the whole profession; you cannot choose wrong.' Barham responded by insisting Nelson use Barham's secretary, Mr John Deas Thompson, to issue instructions for the ships he wanted as reinforcements: 'Have no scruple, Lord Nelson, there is my secretary. I will leave the room. Give your orders to him, and rely on it that they shall be implicitly obeyed by me.' Nelson began dictating.

On 12 September Nelson called at the Colonial Office to say farewell to the Secretary of State. He was shown into a small empty waiting room. After a while an Army major-general unknown to him entered – it was Sir Arthur Wellesley, the future Duke of Wellington, recently returned from India after a series of stunning victories over huge Mahratta armies. Wellesley instantly recognized the one-armed admiral; his first impression was far from complimentary (see box), but he had changed his mind by the time Nelson was called to see Lord Castlereagh. It was the only occasion on which the two greatest British commanders of the age met.

On the night of 13 September, the day before he went to Portsmouth to join the Victory, Nelson was in a sad, sombre mood. Sad because he was to part from his beloved Emma and little four-year-old Horatia – Emma had been exceptionally emotional and tearful in front of the guests at their final dinner party. According to Lord Minto she 'could not eat, and hardly drink, and near swooning, and all at table'. Sombre because of his heavy responsibilities and the uncertainty of what the future might hold, together with the niggling doubt that he might not return. Before retiring to bed he prayed, writing his prayer in his diary:

> May the great God whom I adore, enable me to fulfill the expectations of my country; and if it is His good pleasure that I should return, my thanks will never cease being offered up to the throne of His mercy. If it is His good Providence to cut short my days upon earth, I bow with the greatest submission, relying that He will protect those so dear to me, that I may leave behind. His will be done. Amen. Amen. Amen.

Nelson got no more than a fitful doze during the jolting overnight coach journey down the Portsmouth road. At 6 a.m. on 14 September he stepped stiffly down outside the George Inn. After breakfast with several friends from London he planned to avoid the crowd of well-wishers that had gathered outside by slipping out of the back door and making his way to his barge at the bathing beach at Southsea about half a mile away. It did not work. His last walk in England was through a jostling crowd of the men and women of Portsmouth, some cheering, some weep-ing, many openly praying for his success and safe return. When Nelson reached the top of the steps leading to the beach he paused to wave farewell. The crowd surged forward and jostled with the soldiers who had escorted him, determined to watch his departure. As the barge pulled away, the sweeps dipping in perfect timing, Nelson acknowledged the cheers by raising his hat. Turning to Captain Hardy he said, 'I had their huzzas before – I have their hearts now.' His flag, the red cross of St George, was hoisted to the top of Victory's foremast at noon. On the same day in Paris the Emperor issued orders for Villeneuve that would lead to the fleet action Nelson had sought for so long. That evening there were guests at dinner in the admiral's dining cabin. On Sunday 15 September at 8 a.m. Victory weighed and, accompanied by the frigate Euryalus, made sail to the south-south-east. Trafalgar was five weeks away.

## Nelson's command problems off Cadiz

Nelson joined his fleet off Cadiz on 28 September, the day before his forty-seventh birthday. He had sent instructions ahead via Blackwood in the Euryalus that the 17-gun salute to which he was entitled should not be fired, since he feared the enemy in Cadiz would correctly interpret the regular thudding of the guns as announcing his arrival, and in a postscript banned all salutes, even when the fleet was not in sight of Cadiz. Off Cadiz Nelson (who was a Vice-Admiral of the White) initially had four admirals under him: Vice-Admiral of the Blue Cuthbert Collingwood, Vice-Admiral of the Blue Sir Robert Calder, Rear-Admiral of the White William the Earl of Northesk and Rear-Admiral of the Blue Sir Thomas Louis.

Nelson faced a number of key command problems – tactical, personnel and administrative – that would require decisions and solutions in the coming weeks. They are summarized below.

### Relative strengths
The day Nelson arrived on station he had 28 ships-of-the-line of which eight (28 per cent) were three-deckers of 98 guns or more – a high proportion. So far as he knew the Combined Fleet could muster perhaps 46 but with only 3 three-deckers. The numerical balance was in favour of the enemy but he could expect further reinforcements in the coming weeks – and he knew that in terms of quality of crews he had a substantial advantage. Nevertheless, he needed to build up and then maintain his fleet at a strength of, he hoped, up to 40 battleships.

### Conflicting tasks
Nelson's primary aim was to bring on a decisive battle: he wanted another Nile, another annihilating victory. However, he had other

---

### Nelson Meets Sir Arthur Wellesley

Nelson was in a small waiting room in the Colonial Office when Sir Arthur was shown in, having just returned from his victories in India. Wellesley was later to describe the meeting as follows.

I found also waiting to see the Secretary of State, a gentleman who from his likeness to his pictures and the loss of an arm I immediately recognized as Lord Nelson. He could not know who I was, but he entered at once into conversation with me, if I can call it a conversation, for it was almost all on his side and all about himself, and in, really, a style so vain and so silly as to surprise and almost disgust me.

I suppose something that I happened to say may have made him guess that I was somebody, and he went out of the room for a moment, I have no doubt to ask the officekeeper who I was, for when he came back he was altogether a different man, both in manner and matter. All that I thought a charlatan style had vanished, and he talked of the state of this country and of the aspect and probabilities of affairs on the Continent with a good sense, and a knowledge of subjects both at home and abroad that surprised me equally and more agreeably than the first part of our interview had done; in fact he talked like an officer and a statesman.

## Vice-Admiral of the Blue Cuthbert Lord Collingwood

Although a lifelong close friend of Nelson despite the difference in their ages, Collingwood was a man of very different character. A typical north-countryman, he was never unduly elated by success or depressed by failure; quiet and retiring in his ways, he cared little for popular applause but was ever anxious to serve his country. He was a thoroughly professional officer possessing enormous experience and skill in seamanship. Although he could be a strict disciplinarian when necessary he was renowned for maintaining a high state of training and morale on his ships with a light hand. He kept careful records of the punishments he awarded, twelve lashes seeming to be the maximum. Often men of bad character were sent to him, and under his firm and just rule turned into fine seamen. He summed up his philosophy on discipline with the saying, 'I cannot for the life of me comprehend the religion of an officer who could pray all one day, and flog his men all the next.'

Cuthbert Collingwood was born in 1748, which made him at fifty-seven one of the oldest men at Trafalgar. Like Nelson and hundreds of other boys he joined the Navy as a forlorn lad of eleven in 1761 under the patronage of his maternal uncle, Captain Braithwaite. Collingwood had joined the frigate *Shannon* and he tells us that on his first day he sat unnoticed in a corner, weeping bitterly. He was found by a kindly lieutenant who, probably recalling his own experience, stopped to cheer him up. Collingwood was so grateful he opened his sea chest to offer a large slice of homemade cake to his new-found friend.

Collingwood attained commissioned rank as the fourth lieutenant on the 74-gun *Somerset* in 1775, two years before Nelson, after serving some fourteen years as a midshipman and then master's mate. His promotion came on the same day as the Battle of Bunker Hill in the American War of Independence, at which Collingwood was present with a party of seamen bringing supplies to the Army. While in the West Indies Collingwood followed in the footsteps of Nelson, like him being taken under the wing of the commander-in-chief, Sir Peter Parker. Collingwood succeeded Nelson in the 32-gun frigate *Lowestoffe*, then as commander of the armed brig the *Badger* and finally as a post captain in the 28-gun frigate *Hinchinbroke*.

Collingwood and Nelson were both in the disastrous Nicaraguan campaign with its horrendous losses due to sickness (see p. 62). As Collingwood said, 'I survived most of my ship's company, having buried in four months 180 of the 200 which composed it.' From there he took the *Hinchinbroke* back to Jamaica and was given the frigate *Pelican,* which was shipwrecked with all hands in a hurricane on Morant Keys. Collingwood and his men spent ten days on the beach with little food or water until they were rescued by the frigate *Diamond*. With the war over Collingwood spent four years (1786–90) at home, but when hostilities were renewed he became the flag captain on the 98-gun *Barfleur* at the battle of the Glorious First of June. When Rear-Admiral Bowyer was badly wounded Collingwood took control, handling the ship with great skill. He was furious that he was not among those awarded the King's gold medal. His next major action was as the captain of the 74-gun *Excellent* at the Battle of St Vincent in 1797. This time he was awarded his medal but refused it while one for the Glorious First of June was still withheld, arguing, 'I was then improperly passed over, and to receive such a

distinction now would be to acknowledge the propriety of that injustice.' The Admiralty agreed and a letter of apology accompanied by both medals arrived in due course.

He spent eight dreary, grinding years on blockade duties along the Atlantic ports of France and Spain before he once more served with Nelson, this time at Trafalgar when both were vice-admirals – Nelson was the senior as he was of the white squadron, Collingwood the blue. At the battle Collingwood commanded the fifteen ships of the lee column and his flagship, the 100-gun *Royal Sovereign*, was first to break the enemy line. With Nelson's death Collingwood assumed command and transferred his flag from his crippled flagship to the frigate *Euryalus*.

After Trafalgar Collingwood was rewarded with a peerage and the large Naval Gold Medal but his services at sea were still required off the coasts of Spain and in the Mediterranean. Collingwood had not been home since 1803 and was destined to die at sea in 1810 without ever seeing his family again. His only faithful companion throughout many of those years was his dog Bounce, who had served on many ships but remained terrified of the noise of gunfire. Bounce seemed to consider that as his master was an admiral he enjoyed enhanced status in the canine world. On one occasion Collingwood wrote to his wife: 'He [Bounce] considers it beneath his dignity to play with commoner's dogs, and truly thinks that he does them grace when he condescends to lift up his leg against them. This, I think, is carrying the insolence of rank to the extreme; but he is a dog that does it.' By 1809 poor Bounce had lost much of the springiness and energy that had been the hallmark of his youth. On a rough night off Toulon a wave washed him overboard to a sailor's grave from the quarterdeck of the 100-gun *Ville de Paris*.

Collingwood died on his flagship aged sixty-two on 7 March 1810. The combination of his failing health, weakened by endless years at sea, coupled with the heavy responsibilities of a wartime admiral, had finally proved too much. To Collingwood duty to his country always came before his love of family, however much he longed to be with them. Shortly before his death he wrote: 'Since the year 1793, I have been only one year at home. To my own children I am scarcely known; yet while I have health and strength to serve my country, I consider that health and strength due to it: and if I serve it successfully, as I have ever done faithfully, my children will not want friends.'

Collingwood was laid to rest in St Paul's close to Nelson. His body had been landed at Greenwich on 26 April and borne, with an escort of pensioners, to the vestibule of the Painted Hall where it lay in state until 9 May. On that day his coffin was carried from the Hall to the gates on the shoulders of twelve pensioners who had served with him. They walked slowly, reverently, between the lines of 500 pensioners drawn up on either side of the road, the coffin covered in Collingwood's flag from the *Ville de Paris*. Eight officers who had served under him walked alongside as pallbearers. The drummers and fifes of the hospital band playing the Dead March followed them. Then came the hospital staff and four captains and eight lieutenants, all of whom had been wounded in action. Finally, at the rear Lord Hood walked alongside the Lieutenant-Governor. At the gate on the London Road the body was placed on a hearse drawn by six horses. The procession followed by a long line of carriages then made its long mournful journey to St Paul's.

responsibilities that required ships-of-the-line and frigates. His orders required him to escort convoys and keep a watch on events in the Mediterranean. The *Royal Sovereign* arrived on 8 October with orders from Lord Castlereagh specifically requiring Nelson to support Craig's operations, which could involve landing Craig's troops, then at Malta, in southern Italy where in combination with Russian reinforcements from the Black Sea they would attack France's southern flank. If Villeneuve sailed while British ships were diverted on duties hundreds of miles away to the east through the Straits of Gibraltar, then the numerical balance might swing dramatically in the enemy's favour. In particular such duties would tie up additional frigates – ships of which Nelson did not have enough anyway.

### The enemy's intentions
What was Villeneuve going to do? Would he sit tight in Cadiz for weeks or even throughout the winter, or would the food shortages force him out? If he came out what would be his destination? He could head for the Atlantic, perhaps for Brest or even the Channel, or make a dash for the Straits and on to Toulon to support land operations. Would he seek a major fleet action or try to avoid it? Until he made his move Nelson could not be certain. He had to be able to follow their movements from the moment they weighed.

### Maintaining blockade
The prospect of another winter on blockade was unappealing. Nelson wanted his battle, but there was a delicate balance to be struck between too tight a blockade, which kept the enemy in harbour, and too loose a one, which allowed him to escape, avoiding a direct confrontation. Nelson did not want to deter Villeneuve from sailing by keeping a large and visible fleet on his doorstep. Rather he wanted to give the impression of weakness or at least of uncertainty, but while keeping the entrance of Cadiz under continuous observation. This required frigates.

### Securing timely information
As always Nelson was short of frigates, the eyes of any fleet. When he wrote on the subject to William Marsden, Secretary to the Board of Admiralty, on 5, 6 and 7 October he put his complaint clearly: 'I am most exceedingly anxious for more eyes and hope the Admiralty are hastening them to me. The last Fleet was lost to me for want of frigates.' He wanted eight frigates and three swift brigs with his fleet off Cadiz under Blackwood. By 11 October he had six: the *Euryalus*, *Phoebe*, *Amazon*, *Hydra*, *Naiad* and *Sirius* plus the schooner *Pickle* and brig *Weazle*. Nevertheless Nelson considered a total of 22 frigates and 16 sloops/brigs were needed to cover his area of responsibility, to be deployed between Cape St Mary (southern Portugal) and Cape Spartel, the Salvages (rocky islands north-west of the Canaries), Cape St Vincent, the Straits, off Cartagena, off Gibraltar, escorting Craig's transports and cruising the rest of the Mediterranean. A shortage of lookout ships had always haunted Nelson as both a squadron and a fleet commander. At Trafalgar he had four frigates, a schooner and a cutter available with the fleet.

### Wind and weather
When making plans Nelson had to take careful account of the unpredictable elements, especially the wind and its relationship with the nearby shoals and the coastline down to Cape Trafalgar. If Nelson kept his ships too close to Cadiz and a westerly gale sprang up then the fleet might be driven through the Straits while trying to avoid the lee shore. Then with a sudden shift of wind to the eastward the enemy would have a clear run to the Atlantic. In this situation Nelson was particularly concerned for his heavy three-deckers, which tended to make a lot of leeway. On the other hand, if Villeneuve was bound for the Mediterranean, he might come out at night when the land breeze served, catch the sea breeze at the mouth of the Straits and slip past them while the British ships were still becalmed. Any westerly wind would keep the Combined Fleet immobile at anchor in harbour. The wind most favourable for getting to sea was an easterly.

### Supply difficulties
Nelson had to be prepared for a long blockade. It was not what he wanted, but if Villeneuve was not enticed out or forced out by food shortages then the British Fleet might have to sit out the winter on station. This would entail detaching ships in turn to take on fresh water and victuals at Gibraltar and Tetuan. They would be absent for three weeks or more, and as soon as one detachment returned another group would have to leave. This unavoidable rotation would mean there were always ships away and unavailable for a fleet action. On 3 October Nelson sent a small squadron under Rear-Admiral Louis in the 80-gun *Canopus* to Gibraltar to revictual; it consisted of the 98-gun *Queen*, the 80-gun *Tigre*, the 74s *Spencer* and *Zealous* and the 50-gun *Endymion*. On the 17th he sent the 74-gun *Donegal*. None of them returned for the battle. On 19 October, the day Villeneuve came out of Cadiz, Louis, who was waiting for a suitable wind to bring him back, received orders to escort a valuable convoy past Cartagena. This unexpected loss of six or seven ships was to cause a last-minute change in Nelson's battle plan from an attack with three lines to one of two.

### Personnel problems
Although Nelson had expressed great confidence in the ability of his captains very few had served under him before – only two, Hardy and Berry, belonged to the original band of brothers. Of the 27 battleship captains who fought at Trafalgar only five belonged to Nelson's Mediterranean Fleet, all except one of the others coming from the Channel Fleet. Only five had commanded a ship-of-the-line in action, and only five had commanded their ships since 1803. As commander-in-chief Nelson needed to get to know the 19 who had not served with him before. He had to impress his leadership methods and tactical thinking on them, and they in turn had to know what he expected of them. He needed to train his fleet to function as he required in the confusion of battle with the minimum of orders and signals.

Then Vice-Admiral Sir Robert Calder had to return home to face a court martial following his engagement with Villeneuve on 22 July. Nelson also had to allow the three captains (Brown of the *Ajax*, Lechmere of the *Thunderer* and Durham of the *Defiance*) who had fought under Calder that day to return as witnesses. This would permanently deprive him of an admiral, three post captains and a battleship. Durham in particular was furious at the prospect of missing a battle. On board the *Prince of Wales* prior to departure, he insisted on seeing the relevant Admiralty order, which revealed that captains need only return if they were willing. Durham immediately turned on his heel, clambered down into his boat and was rowed back to his ship. Nelson's decision was made more difficult by Calder pleading to be allowed to sail back to Britain not on a smaller ship, as would seem logical, but on his flagship the *Prince of Wales* – a 98-gun three-decker Nelson did not want to lose.

Finally, as an example of the man-management problems that required the admiral's attention, the lieutenant of the frigate *Hydra* had deserted, running off in Italy with a Maltese ballet dancer and leaving behind several large debts. His father had written to Nelson for help saying that his son was 'very probably in prison'.

## Command decisions 28 September–18 October
*Maintaining blockade*
On arrival with the fleet Nelson immediately decided that he would withdraw the close inshore squadron. The main fleet would be stationed some 50 miles west of Cadiz, well out of sight over the horizon from any enemy ships that might attempt a reconnaissance from the harbour. He wanted to ensure Villeneuve remained uncertain as to whether or not the British fleet was in the vicinity and large enough to intercept him if he ventured out in strength. Nelson hoped that by maintaining a loose blockade he would tempt Villeneuve out. Fifty miles was rather further out than he would have preferred, as his lookout ships would have to be stretched over a long distance. Initially he could only spare the frigates *Euryalus* and *Hydra* to remain within sight of Cadiz. This meant the gap between them and the fleet had to be covered by 74s spread out at about ten-mile intervals to act as relaying ships for the frigates' signals. To begin with the *Mars*, *Defence* and *Colossus* formed this small ad-hoc observation squadron, over which Captain Duff (*Mars*) was given command – much to his delight. On 4 October Nelson instructed Duff, 'I have to desire that you will keep, with the *Mars*, *Defence* and *Colossus*, from three to four leagues [nine to twelve miles] between the fleet and Cadiz, in order that I may get information from the frigates stationed off that port.' On 19 October, when the Combined Fleet did start to come out, the frigates *Sirius*, *Euryalus*, *Phoebe* and *Naiad* along with the schooners *Pickle* and *Weazle* (not at Trafalgar) were on watch.

*Management and leadership*
On Sunday 29 September, Nelson's forty-seventh birthday, he held a combined birthday dinner and command briefing for the majority of his captains together with his two admirals, Collingwood and Northesk, which he repeated the following day for those captains not present. Most of these men knew their commander-in-chief by reputation rather than personally, and all were eager to meet him. This gathering, which took place in the admiral's spacious day cabin, was the only way Nelson could see, and be seen by, his senior commanders before the battle he hoped was imminent. He needed to impress his personality on them, give them confidence and make clear how he intended to fight the enemy – all things best done face to face. Nelson shrewdly combined a social occasion with all its attendant informality, and the protocol of his captains paying their respects to their new commander, with imparting his battle plan. His officers were delighted with his hospitality, flattered when their opinions were sought, and hugely impressed with the plan revealed to them – details of which (and the confirmatory written memorandum) are discussed below. Duff of the *Mars* was enthusiastic: 'He is so good and pleasant a man that we all wish to do what he likes, without any kind of orders. I have been myself very lucky with most of my admirals; but I really think the present pleasantest I have met with.'

The gathering on the *Victory* was a splendid example of the 'Nelson touch'. Nelson himself was exuberant: 'The officers who came on board to welcome my return forgot my rank as Commander-in-Chief in the enthusiasm with which they greeted me. As soon as these emotions were past I laid before them the plan I had previously arranged for attacking the enemy.' To Emma he was even more ecstatic, exclaiming emotionally, 'When I came to explain to them the Nelson Touch it was like an electric shock. Some shed tears, all approved – "It was new – it was singular – it was simple – it must succeed if ever they allow us to get at them!"'

With Calder Nelson's humanity got the better of his common sense. Sir Robert's passionate pleas that he not be forced to return on a smaller ship were granted, although Nelson knew full well (as did Calder) that he should retain the heavyweight *Prince of Wales*. Writing to explain his decision to Lord Barham, he finished with the words: 'I trust that I shall be considered to have done right as a man, and to a brother officer in affliction – my heart could not stand it, and so the thing must rest.'

Nelson could be equally generous to his junior officers, even those seriously at fault. With regard to the young lieutenant of the *Hydra* who had disappeared with the Maltese dancer he wrote to Captain Sotheran of the 74-gun *Excellent* in Naples harbour requesting that he contact the British embassy there with a view to locating the officer. His father had promised to pay his debts but Nelson volunteered to contribute any extra over £300 himself, writing, 'if a few more [pounds] are necessary to liberate the youth I will be answerable. All we want is to save him from perdition.' Considering the lieutenant had run off in wartime and the *Hydra* was one of Nelson's scarce, hard-worked frigates the admiral's action is quite exceptional, but a perfect example of the sort of act that so endeared him to his men.

*Supplies*
With the continual need for ships to replenish and restock, and Nelson's determination to keep his men healthy (an important factor in winning battles), there was no alternative to sending detachments of ships to Gibraltar and Tetuan. It had to be accepted their absence could coincide with a fleet action.

## The 'Nelson Touch'
The term 'Nelson Touch' originated, as described above, with Nelson himself. By it he meant his tactics for his hoped-for battle with the Combined Fleet. Nelson was, by 1805, an exceptionally experienced admiral. He had commanded a fleet in one outstanding victory (the Nile), been instrumental as second-in-command in achieving another (Copenhagen), and played a key role in defeating the Spanish at St Vincent. He had not commanded a fleet in an action at sea – both the Nile and Copenhagen had been against a stationary enemy close inshore – but he had given the tactics of such a battle considerable thought, particularly during his short leave prior to Trafalgar. Twice during that period he outlined his thoughts to others.

The first occasion was when chatting in the garden at Merton with his trusted friend Captain Richard Keats. Keats had commanded the 74-gun *Superb* during the long chase to the West Indies and his ship, like the *Victory*, was being refitted. To his lifelong regret Keats was to miss Trafalgar (he was replenishing as part of Louis's squadron at Gibraltar, which was then diverted to convoy duties), but he later vividly recalled the animated way Nelson had described his forthcoming battle tactics.

'No day,' said Nelson, 'can be long enough to arrange a couple of fleets and fight a decisive battle according to the old system [i.e. in two long parallel lines] ... I shall form the fleet into three divisions in three lines. One division will be composed of twelve or fourteen of the fastest two-decked ships, which I shall keep always to windward, or in a situation of advantage ... I consider it will always be in my power to throw it into the battle in any part I may choose ... With the remaining part of the fleet formed in two lines I shall go at them at once, if I can, about one third of their line from their leading ship ... I think it will surprise and confound the enemy. They won't know what I am about. It will bring on a pell-mell battle, and that is what I want.'

The second time Nelson expounded his plan was to Lord Sidmouth at the latter's home in Richmond Park. There he outlined the same tactics described to Keats, only this time drawing an imaginary sketch with his finger on a nearby table – a table that Sidmouth kept and had inscribed. 'Rodney,' Nelson said, 'broke the line in one point; I will break it in two.' Sidmouth's inscription on the table stated that Nelson said he would 'attack them in two lines, led by himself and Admiral Collingwood; and felt confident that he would capture either their van and centre; or centre and rear'.

A recent spectacular discovery by perhaps today's foremost Nelson scholar, Colin White, in the archives of the National Maritime Museum is a hitherto unknown rough sketch made by Nelson in September 1805 showing the tactics he intended to use if he caught the enemy fleet at sea. Almost certainly it was virtually the same as the one he drew with his finger on Sidmouth's table. White published his find in the *Journal of Maritime Research,* while the sketch is displayed in the Nelson Gallery of the National Maritime Museum at Greenwich. The sketch is reproduced below and the likely interpretation is based on that suggested by Colin White. On the reverse of the paper is a hurried note by Nelson reminding himself of things he must do, probably on his next visit to the Admiralty (see p. 412). This is a real gem, revealing as it does how Nelson took every opportunity to reward and further the careers of trusted subordinates. It is yet another example of why men were so eager to serve under him.

The Nelson Touch has often been described by historians as startling in its newness, solely the product of his tactical genius. Nelson himself claimed, 'It was new – it was singular – it was simple!' He exaggerated. That the tactics involved were entirely new was incorrect. The supposed innovations were his attacking in separate divisions, breaking the line in more than one place and seeking a close-range mêlée instead of exchanging broadsides while keeping formation. The first tactic formed the basis of Admiral Duncan's defeat of the Dutch at Camperdown in 1797; the second Rodney's great success at the Saints in 1782, when he broke the French line into four divisions; and the third was Admiral Hawke's close-quarter, pell-mell fight in Quiberon Bay as long ago as 1759. To this may be added Nelson's own triumphs at the Nile and Copenhagen, both of which quickly became close-range brawls. Nelson's genius was not so much that as a commander he generated new tactical ideas. Rather, he was the first admiral to combine these successful tactical manoeuvres, and to bring all his captains into the planning process, seeking their views and ensuring they fully understood what was required of them. Thus they went into battle inspired by his leadership, his confident enthusiasm, knowing their commander's plan and what they must do even in the thick of battle when signals were often invisible. This was the true 'Nelson Touch', rather than the introduction of new naval tactics.

## Nelson's Tactics Sketch – September 1805

Nelson's sketch is a rough doodle, drawn on a scrap of paper to demonstrate to a person or persons unknown how he intended to fight his next battle. The notes represent an informed, logical interpretation rather than a definitive one.

The sketch consists of two drawings, **A** and **B**, divided by the wavy, broken line in the centre.
• **A** probably shows a fleet (**A1**) sailing in a single line north-east to attack an enemy line (**A2**) that is sailing east and may have crossed, or be about to cross, **A1**'s T. The danger for **A1** is that before it cuts the enemy line **A2** could turn at point **A3** and catch **A1** between two fires.
• The drawing at **B** is more complex and shows almost exactly what transpired at Trafalgar. **B1**, **B2** and **B3** represent the British Fleet divided into three divisions. **B1** is what became Nelson's van (weather column) at Trafalgar. **B2** is Collingwood's rear (lee column) and **B3** a small squadron of observation (for the actual battle this squadron merged with Collingwood's column).
**B4** is the enemy fleet in a long single line heading north-east. The sketch envisages **B1** cutting the enemy line at its centre at **B6** and the **B2** column doing the same a number of ships from the enemy's rear at **B5**. The **B3** ships seem intended to turn parallel to the enemy line at **B7**, possibly to keep their van engaged so that it can't come to the assistance of the centre and rear. The plan is designed to cut the enemy line in two places and force a

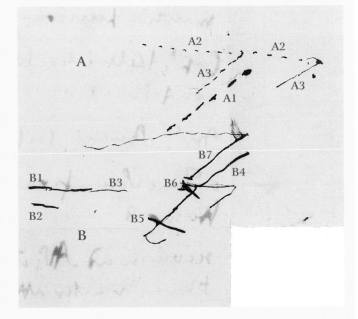

mêlée ('pell-mell battle') at close range. Nelson has emphasized the importance he attached to cutting the line in two places by scoring heavily with his pen at **B5** and **B6**.

## The Reverse of Nelson's Battle Plan Sketch

Interesting as the rough battle plan for Trafalgar undoubtedly is, the notes Nelson wrote on the reverse give us an equally fascinating insight into the character of the man and how he seldom forgot the men who served with him. The notes read:

> Ralph Dixon of the Doris Transport lost an arm in carrying my dispatches wants a pension. Capt: Kelwicks Son wants confirmation. Mr: Bunce Carpn: Victy: a Time Piece from Sir Aw: Hamond. Recommend Mr: Atkinson to be a Master attendt: Capt: Lydiard would be glad of a frigate

These notes were reminders Nelson had scribbled down in an odd moment so he would remember to bring them to the attention of the authorities while he was still in England prior to Trafalgar. According to Colin White, who is at the time of writing still researching for further information at the National Maritime Museum, 'Ralph Dixon' has yet to be identified. 'Captain Kelwick' is probably Captain Edward Killiwick, the officer commanding the 16-gun *Sardine* off Leghorn in 1796. He had died in 1802 and Nelson seems to be wanting to get this young man confirmed as a lieutenant. In this instance Nelson's

intervention was not successful as Killiwick had to wait until late 1807 for his promotion. 'Mr: Bunce' is William Bunce, the *Victory*'s carpenter, and 'Mr: Atkinson' the master who had served with Nelson throughout the 1803–5 campaign. Nelson was the godfather of Atkinson's son, who became Lieutenant Horatio Nelson Atkinson RN. He would have been happy to know that Atkinson was appointed Master Attendant of Halifax Dockyard, Canada, in 1806 and ended his service as Master Attendant at Portsmouth – the pinnacle of a master's career.

'Sir Aw: Hamond' is Sir Andrew Snape Hammond, then Comptroller of the Navy, who was a good friend of Nelson. 'Captain Lydiard' is Captain Charles Lydiard who had served under Nelson on the *Captain* in 1796. Nelson's intervention on his behalf appears to have been successful as he got his frigate, the 44-gun *Anson,* in December 1805. These notes reveal a great deal about the use of patronage and how Nelson was prepared to look after the interests of those who had served him well.

---

Not all the captains at Trafalgar were present at Nelson's briefings on 29 and 30 September. As more ships joined the fleet their commanders went to pay their respects to their commander-in-chief, where they were brought up to date with his tactical intentions.

### Nelson's Memorandum

Having given his subordinates verbal instructions at what today's armed forces would term the commander's 'O' (Orders) Group, Nelson followed them by writing confirmatory orders on 9 October. These were contained in his Secret Memorandum. Written laboriously with his left hand, the first draft was full of deletions and insertions. The procedure of following up verbal orders by confirmatory written ones to all subordinate commanders is still normal practice. A modern headquarters has numerous staff whose job it is to produce and distribute orders. On the *Victory* in 1805 the tedious, time-consuming task of producing and checking over thirty copies of the Memorandum fell on Nelson's secretary, Thomas Scott. Scott was the admiral's staff officer and in this instance felt it necessary to make several insertions to clarify the meaning as Nelson tended to ignore the need for punctuation. Scott then undoubtedly gave much of the copying to his clerk, Andrew George, and the captain's clerk Thomas Whipple. In case readers think this was a relatively safe desk job they are reminded that secretaries and clerks took their chances on the quarterdeck in action – both Scott and Whipple were killed at Trafalgar. Nelson was putting on paper for the first time his tactical thinking, the gist of what he had told his friends in England (Keats and Sidmouth) and elaborated to his captains some ten days earlier. It was his blueprint on how he wanted to fight his next battle. Because historians have seldom been able to agree either on their interpretation of the Memorandum or

on to what extent Nelson followed it at Trafalgar, it is worth examining it in some detail (see also the diagram on p. 416).

The Memorandum was written on the assumption that the enemy fleet had 46 ships-of-the-line and the British 40. At Trafalgar the actual numbers were 33 to 27 so the number of enemy ships to be cut off was reduced proportionately. The text below is taken from Corbett's *The Campaign of Trafalgar* published in 1910, which used the original document then held by the British Museum. The deletions made to the original text are shown as such and the additions in italics. It is likely that Scott read it back to Nelson and suggested improvements in grammar, sense or punctuation.

The comments do not address every aspect of the memorandum, but attempt to get as near to Nelson's thinking as possible.

Memo.
*Victory* off Cadiz 9 Octr. 1805
Thinking it almost impossible to bring a Fleet of forty Sail of the Line into a Line of Battle in variable winds thick weather and other circumstances which must occur, without such a loss of time that the opportunity would probably be lost of bringing the Enemy to Battle in such a manner as to make the business decisive —

I have *therefore* made up my mind to keep the fleet in that position of sailing (with the exception of the first and Second in Command) that the order of Sailing is to be the Order of Battle, placing the fleet in two Lines of Sixteen Ships each with an advanced Squadron of Eight of the fasting [*sic*; fastest] sailing Two decked ships *which* will always make if wanted a Line of Twenty four Sail, on which ever Line the Commander in Chief may direct …

# British Command Structure at Trafalgar

## THE ADMIRALTY

LORD BARHAM

### Notes

- The Admiralty flag was an administrative one rather than a combatant one such as the union jack or an admiral's flag. It showed a 'fouled' anchor, so called because an anchor thus weighed would come to the bows upside-down.

- The diagram shows the command structure on the day of the battle. Communication between Admiralty and Nelson was by packet boat and between Nelson and his ships by flag signals and personal contact.

**Ashore**

**At Sea**

## Commander-in-Chief Mediterranean

**Vice-Admiral Nelson**  — **Staff**

**Vice-Admiral Collingwood**

| **Weather Column** (12 ships-of-the-line) | **Lee Column** (15 ships-of-the-line) |
|---|---|

### Weather Column (12 ships-of-the-line)

Vice-Admiral Nelson Captain Hardy 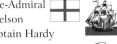 *Victory* (102)

Captain Harvey  *Téméraire* (98)

Captain Freemantle *Neptune* (98)

Captain Baynton *Leviathan* (74)

Rear-Admiral Northesk Captain Bullen *Britannia* (100)

Captain Pellew *Conqueror* (74)

Captain Digby *Africa* (64)

Lieut. Pilford *Ajax* (74)

Captain Berry *Agamemnon* (64)

Captain Codrington *Orion* (74)

Captain Mansfield *Minotaur* (74)

Captain Laforey *Spartiate* (74)

### Frigates

Captain Blackwood *Euryalus* (36)

Captain Capel *Phoebe* (36)

Captain Dundas *Naiad* (38)

Captain Prowse *Sirius* (36)

Lieut. Lapenotiere *Pickle* (10) (schooner)

Lieut. Young *Entreprenante* (8) (cutter)

### Lee Column (15 ships-of-the-line)

Vice-Admiral Collingwood Captain Rotherham  *Royal Sovereign* (100)

Captain Hargood  *Belleisle* (74)

Captain Duff  *Mars* (74)

Captain Tyler  *Tonnant* (80)

Captain Cooke  *Bellerophon* (74)

Captain Morris  *Colossus* (74)

Captain King  *Achille* (74)

Captain Moorsom  *Revenge* (74)

Captain Durham  *Defiance* (74)

Captain Rutherford  *Swiftsure* (74)

Captain Redmill  *Polyphemus* (64)

Captain Conn  *Dreadnought* (98)

Captain Grindall *Prince* (98)

Lieut. Stockham *Thunderer* (74)

Captain Hope *Defence* (74)

*Comments*

• Nelson was reiterating a well-known fact when stating it would take too long to get a fleet of this size deployed into line of battle and fight a battle in one day. A line of 46 ships at intervals of about 200 yards (one cable length) would stretch for over seven miles. Even if the distances between the ships were closed up to 100 yards the line would be over four miles. Manoeuvring such a line would take many hours, depending on wind strength and direction, and getting into position parallel to the enemy necessitated the enemy being willing to fight; Nelson had every reason to think the Combined Fleet wished to avoid battle.

• The order of sailing of the fleet was normally the prescribed order in which a fleet was disposed in two or more divisions for cruising. As the opposing fleets closed a formation change might be needed to get them into the correct order or line of battle to engage the enemy. If the ships were to fight in the order of sailing then less time would be wasted in signalling and preparatory manoeuvres immediately prior to opening fire. For Nelson speed into action was of the essence and he had no intention of fighting in a single line. On 10 October he drew up and distributed with the Memorandum the only order of sailing he is known to have issued, on the basis he would have 40 ships, including those of Louis. It is given below, with square brackets indicating those ships not present at Trafalgar. It is unclear why gaps were left – possibly for ships that might arrive later.

## Order of Sailing

**Van Squadron (1st Division)**
1. *Téméraire* (98)
2. [*Superb* (74; Keats' ship, with Louis)]
3. *Victory* (100, Nelson's flag)
4. *Neptune* (98)
5. –
6. [*Tigre* (74; with Louis)]
7. [*Canopus* (80; Louis' flag)]
8. *Conqueror* (74)
9. *Agamemnon* (64)
10. *Leviathan* (74)

**(2nd Division)**
11. [*Prince of Wales* (98; Calder's flag)]
12. *Ajax* (74)
13. *Orion* (74)
14. *Minotaur* (74)
15. –
16. [*Queen* (98; with Louis)]
17. [*Donegal* (74; at Gibraltar)]
18. [*Spencer* (74; with Louis)]
19. –-
20. *Spartiate* (74)

**Rear Squadron (1st Division)**
1. *Prince* (98)
2. *Mars* (74)

3. *Royal Sovereign* (100, Collingwood's flag)
4. *Tonnant* (80)
5. –
6. *Bellerophon* (74)
7. *Colossus* (74)
8. *Achille* (74)
9. *Polyphemus* (64)
10. *Revenge* (74)

**(2nd Division)**
11. *Britannia* (100, Northesk's flag)
12. *Swiftsure* (74)
13. *Defence* (74)
14. –
15. [*Kent* (74; did not arrive)]
16. [*Zealous* (74; with Louis)]
17. –
18. *Thunderer* (74)
19. *Defiance* (74)
20. *Dreadnought* (98)

The strange thing about this order of sailing is that no reference is made to an advanced or observation squadron although two are mentioned in the Memorandum. Nelson does, however, clearly mention its existence when writing to Ball on 11 October: 'I have an Advanced Squadron of fast sailing ships between me

and the frigates [Duff].' His aim was to have the heavier, bigger ships at the van of each squadron. When the *Prince of Wales* went home with Calder, the *Britannia* with Northesk was transferred to Nelson's division. Then, when Louis' squadron failed to return, the *Prince* came across, reinforcing his van squadron as well. Even then there were fewer ships in Nelson's line (12) than in Collingwood's (15).

• In the event the British Fleet consisted of 27 rather than 40 ships, so Nelson only formed one advanced squadron (consisting of *Mars, Defence, Colossus, Ajax* and *Agamemnon*) under Captain Duff – the *Agamemnon* and *Ajax* had been added to the original three after 4 October. However, by the time of the battle Nelson had seen seven ships disappear through the Straits, so to make up numbers Duff's ships were absorbed back into the two attacking columns – he took *Ajax* and *Agamemnon*, Collingwood *Mars, Colossus* and *Defence*. He also decided that the advanced squadron, hitherto employed as a link between the frigates and main fleet and intended to operate as a separate attacking force, was needed to bolster the strength of the main two divisions.

> The Second in Command will ~~in fact Command~~ *his line* ~~and~~ after my intentions are made know to him ~~will~~ have the entire direction of His Line to make the attack upon the Enemy and to follow up the Blow until they are Captured or destroy'd [*sic*].
>
> If the enemy's fleet should be seen to Windward in *Line of Battle* ~~but~~ *and* ~~in that position that~~ the Two Lines and the Advanced Squadron can fetch them (I ~~shall suppose them forty-Six Sail~~ *in* ~~of the Line of Battle~~) they will probably be so extended that their van could not succour their Rear.
>
> I should therefore probably make ~~your~~ the 2nd in Commands signal to Lead through about their Twelfth Ship from their Rear (or wherever ~~you~~ He could fetch if not able to get so far advanced). My line would lead through about their Centre and the Advanced Squadron to cut two or three or four Ships Ahead of their Centre, so as to ensure getting at their Commander In Chief on whom every Effort must be made to Capture. …

*Comments*

• Here Nelson envisages attacking from leeward, which is not what happened at Trafalgar.

• Once the enemy has been sighted and Nelson has made any final adjustments to the overall fleet plan of attack, he plans to give Collingwood subsequent command and control of the latter's line, allowing him to make his attack semi-independently with no (or minimal) interference from Nelson. In modern military terminology Nelson is employing 'mission command' – giving his subordinate his force and task and letting him get on with it.

• Nelson intends Collingwood's line to cut that of the enemy 12 ships from the rear. Thus with his 16 ships (in a 40-ship fleet) he will secure numerical superiority over the enemy rear squadron. If Collingwood is unable to cut off 12 ships from the rear then he is to cut off as many as possible.

• Nelson intends his column to break the enemy line about the centre where he expects the enemy commander-in-chief to be positioned. He does not indicate his flagship will be at the head of the line – 'My line would lead through,' not 'I would lead

## Rear-Admiral of the White William Earl of Northesk

Northesk was the third in command of the British Fleet at Trafalgar, with his flag on the 100-gun *Britannia*. His ancestors, who originated in Hungary, had settled in Angus, Scotland, and in the reign of Charles I his family was ennobled with the title of Northesk. William was born in 1760, the son of the sixth Earl of Northesk, and started his naval career aged eleven. He was promoted lieutenant in 1777 and served in the *Royal George* at the capture of the Caracan fleet off Cape Finisterre and a Spanish squadron under Don Juan de Langara. He was a lieutenant in the *Apollo* at the first relief of Gibraltar in 1780. He was then transferred to Lord Rodney's flagship the *Sandwich* and for his services at the battle with de Guichen that year earned promotion to commander.

The following year he had command of a hired ship, the *Eustatius*, at the reducing of the island of that name in the West Indies. From 1783 to 1793 he was on half pay. In 1792 he inherited the earldom at his father's death and in 1793 he took the 40-gun *Beaulieu* to the West Indies. In 1796 he was appointed to command the 64-gun *Monmouth* with the North Sea Fleet. She was one of the ships implicated in the Nore Mutiny, whose mutinous crew detained Northesk; the leader of the mutiny, Richard Parker, chose him to take a letter of their grievances to the King. After the trials he resigned his command. From 1800 to 1802 Northesk commanded the 98-gun *Prince* in the Channel. After a further period ashore he was given command of the 100-gun *Britannia*, joining the fleet blockading Brest under Cornwallis. On 23 April he finally received promotion to flag rank as rear-admiral of the white.

From Brest his squadron was detached under Calder to reinforce Collingwood off Cadiz. At Trafalgar the *Britannia* was fifth in Nelson's weather column and joined the mêlée early on, continuing in action until the end. Northesk had little to do during the action in his capacity as an admiral. His services were, however, amply rewarded. He was created a Knight of the Bath (KB) and received the thanks of parliament, a large gold medal, the Freedom of the City of London, a sword of honour and a vase valued at £300 from the Lloyds Patriotic Fund.

Northesk was a competent officer rather than an outstanding one who was never really required to test his ability as an admiral in battle. He has been described as:

> robust, well-made; with a manly open countenance, strongly indicative of his leading traits of character, great firmness, tempered by equal mildness and humanity. As an officer, he is scrupulously correct; and a warm supporter of the discipline of the service; though so averse from unnecessary rigour, that when a private Captain [a post captain], the writer has known him devote hours together to the patient investigation of truth, before he would consent to inflict punishment.

Some might feel he was being damned by faint praise, though his moderation with the lash probably helped ensure he was not too roughly handled by the mutineers at the Nore.

He was promoted vice-admiral in 1808, admiral in 1814 and held the position of Commander-in-Chief Plymouth from 1827 to 1830. He died in Albemarle Street, Piccadilly, aged seventy-one and was buried in the crypt of St Paul's Cathedral, not far from Nelson and Collingwood.

---

through', though at Trafalgar the *Victory* did lead the weather line. Nelson assumes there will be an advanced squadron (which in the event there was not) which will cut the line three or four ships ahead of the enemy flagship, thereby trapping Villeneuve between two groups of ships. He attaches great importance to concentrating his attack on the enemy flagship, thus destroying or neutralizing their commander early in the battle. In so far as Nelson's column cut through the Combined Fleet's centre, and quickly closed on the *Bucentaure*, this part of the plan was fulfilled at Trafalgar.

> The whole impression of the British *fleet* must be, to overpower from two or three Ships ahead of their Commander In Chief, supposed to be in the centre, to the Rear of their fleet. *I will suppose* twenty Sail of the *Enemys* Line to be untouched, it must be some time before they could perform a Manoeuvre to bring their force compact to attack any part of the British fleet engaged, or to succour their own ships which indeed would be impossible, without mixing with the ships engaged. Something must be left to chance, nothing is sure in a sea fight beyond all others, shot will carry away the masts and yards of friends as well as foes, but I look with confidence to a victory before the van of the Enemy could succour their ~~friends~~ *Rear* and then that the British Fleet would most of them be ready to receive their Twenty Sail of the Line or to pursue them should they endeavour to make off.

> If the Van of the Enemy tacks the Captured Ships must run to Leeward of the British fleet, if the enemy wears the British fleet must place themselves between the Enemy and the captured & disabled British Ships and should the Enemy close I have no fear as to the result.

*Comments*

- Again Nelson emphasizes the importance of decapitating the enemy high command. At the battle Villeneuve's flagship was ahead of the centre when the *Victory* cut the line, due to the Combined Fleet having worn through 180 degrees earlier – so instead of 20 ships being 'untouched', there were 13. As anticipated these 13 (under Dumanoir) did not get back into the action until it was too late for them to help the centre. Nelson believed, rightly, that by the time the enemy van returned (either by tacking or wearing) to the action, the enemy flagship and most of the centre and rear would have been disabled and enough British ships would be available to deal with them.

> The Second in Command will in all possible things direct the Movements of his Line by keeping them as compact as the nature of the circumstances will admit *and* Captains are to look to their particular Line as their rallying point. But in case signals can neither be seen or perfectly understood no Captain can do very wrong if he places his Ship alongside that of an Enemy.
>
> Of the intended attack from to Windward, the Enemy in Line of Battle ready to receive an attack ...

## Nelson's Memorandum

### The Memorandum as drawn

B

E

### Notes

• This diagram was part of the Memorandum. The enemy (E) is assumed to be 46 strong and the British (B) 40, about to attack from the windward.

• For the captains who had it explained verbally the lines are self-explanatory but there has been some confusion in later years, with some believing the British were in line abreast rather than line ahead.

### The Memorandum explained

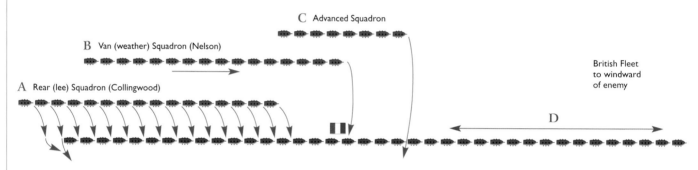

C  Advanced Squadron

B  Van (weather) Squadron (Nelson)

A  Rear (lee) Squadron (Collingwood)

British Fleet to windward of enemy

D

### Notes

A 'The Signal will most probably be made for the Lee Line to bear up together ... and to cut through beginning from the 12 ship from the Enemies rear ... if any are thrown round the Rear of the Enemy they will effectively compleat the business...'

B 'My line would lead through about their Centre ...'

C 'the Advanced Squadron to cut through two or three or four Ships Ahead of their Centre, so as to ensure getting at their Commander-in-Chief on whom every Effort must be made to Capture.'

D 'I look with confidence to a victory before the van of the Enemy could succour their rear ...'

The wording of the Memorandum is confusing in that it refers to a fleet of 'two Lines of Sixteen ships each with an advanced Squadron of Eight ...', whereas the line drawing only shows one advanced squadron.

### The Memorandum in practice

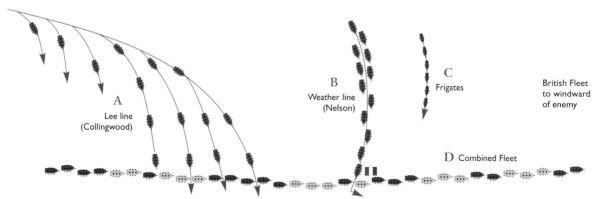

A
Lee line (Collingwood)

B
Weather line (Nelson)

C
Frigates

British Fleet to windward of enemy

D  Combined Fleet

### Notes

A Collingwood's column attacked as instructed on a line of bearing by individual ships. However, they hit the rear of the enemy fleet at considerable intervals rather than almost simultaneously as the Memorandum instructed.

B Nelson's weather column struck the centre in a somewhat ragged line ahead formation. The enemy flagship was quickly crippled as instructed.

C There was no advanced squadron, its ships having been absorbed into the lee line. Its position was taken by frigates that took no part in the action.

As Nelson had planned, the enemy van was unable to turn and reinforce the centre until too late.

There follows a diagram (copied opposite), which illustrates an attack from windward, which is what occurred at Trafalgar. It was roughly drawn, the lines being neither straight nor parallel, but their relative proportions and distances are preserved in the diagram here.

> The Division of the British fleet will be brought nearly within Gun Shot of the Enemy's Centre. The signal will most probably then be made for the Lee Line to bear up together to set all their sails even steering sails in order to get as quickly as possible to the Enemy's Line and to Cut through beginning from the 12 ship from the Enemy's rear [see diagram]. Some ships may not get through their exact place, but they will always be at hand to assist their friends and if are thrown round the Rear of the Enemy they will effectually compleat the business of Twelve Sail of the Enemy. Should the Enemy wear together or bear up and sail Large still the Twelve Ships composing in the first position the Enemy's rear are to be *the* Object of attack of the Lee Line unless otherwise directed from the Commander In Chief which is scarcely to be expected as the entire management of the Lee Line after the intentions of the Commander In Chief is *are* signified is intended to be left to the Judgement of the Admiral Commanding that Line.
>
> The Remainder of the Enemy's fleet 34 Sail are to be left to the Management of the Commander In Chief who will endeavour to take care that the Movements of the Second In Command are as little interrupted as possible.

*Comments*

• Again Nelson stresses the delegated authority given to Collingwood. He appreciates that once the mêlée, his 'pell mell' battle, starts nobody will have much time to watch for, or ability to see, signals. So he states his basic, and forever famous, tactical doctrine – '**no Captain can do very wrong if he places his Ship alongside that of an Enemy**'. At Trafalgar his captains' actions fully demonstrated their understanding of this simple order.

• It is only at this stage that Nelson makes clear that the lee line (Collingwood) is expected not to go through the enemy line in line ahead like his own line, but to bear up together after being signalled to that effect. The word 'together' is crucial as it meant each ship would bear up individually rather than in succession. Ships under Collingwood's command would make for the enemy line at best speed on their own line of bearing, cutting through between the enemy ships starting with Collingwood's flagship 12 ships from the rear. If that meant a few ships overlapped the enemy line so much the better as they could envelop it. At Trafalgar this was how Collingwood's column attacked although they reached the line over a far longer period of time than the plan envisaged.

• Should the enemy wear (turn away from the attackers), or bear up (turn towards them) then Collingwood should use his own initiative but still endeavour to take on the 12 ships at the enemy's rear.

• In the final sentence Nelson merely tells Collingwood, again, that he need only concern himself with the rear 12 enemy ships, leaving the rest to him.

*General comments*

• The Memorandum is a disjointed, poorly constructed piece of writing that is hard for the modern reader to understand on first reading – seemingly Scott also had problems, judging by the number of alterations. However, it cannot be compared with a modern operation order produced by a trained staff officer. Punctuation (or rather lack of it) and style in 1805 were quite different from today, and it was common practice to be far more long-winded. The important thing is that it appears to have got its message across. The recipients had all been briefed personally before so they should not have found it too difficult to understand.

• At Trafalgar the basic principles set out in the Memorandum were followed. The fleets may have been smaller than envisaged, there may not have been advanced squadrons but the enemy line was broken as intended. The British attacked the centre and rear of the Combined Fleet, the *Bucentaure* was crippled early on, while the enemy van was unable (or unwilling) to intervene until Villeneuve had been virtually defeated. Above all Nelson got his pell mell battle, his captains knew what was required and the result was the resounding victory he had sought for so long.

## THE COMBINED FLEET

Because of the reluctant alliance of Spain with France in 1803 the command arrangements for the Combined Fleet in 1805 were complex. Although France was the 'senior partner' the fleet was at anchor in a Spanish port, Cadiz, for two months prior to Trafalgar and thus relied on Spanish authorities sustaining it with victuals, stores and dockyard repairs. These were provided with much prevarication and delay, coupled with demands for cash payments for everything. There was considerable animosity between the two nationalities at senior level as well as between the French seamen and Spanish populace (including seamen), the causes of which will be explained below. The following paragraphs are concerned with the joint command as it was at Cadiz before the fleet weighed on 19 October two days prior to Trafalgar and should be read in conjunction with the diagram on page 419.

France's supreme commander was the Emperor Napoleon, who made all strategic and administrative decisions – naval, military and civil. He issued his orders through the Minister of Marine, Vice-Admiral Decrès. Both sat in Paris until Napoleon left on 23 September on his Austrian adventures; he was then immersed in soldiering and his interest in naval affairs waned considerably, although not entirely. The minister in Paris had direct command over the Combined Fleet in Cadiz. He communicated instructions to the fleet commander, Vice-Admiral Villeneuve, from whom he received reports. Spain acquiesced in this arrangement, although with misgivings at all levels of command. In Madrid King Charles IV was supposedly the supreme commander. However, he was sluggish and stupid to the point of imbecility, and totally under the influence of his wife Maria Louisa of Parma, who was the lover of the court favourite and Prime Minister, Manuel de Godoy, the so-called 'Prince of Peace'. Godoy was the point of contact in Madrid for Vice-Admiral Gravina, the commander of the Spanish ships at Cadiz and second-in-command to Villeneuve. Adding to the complexity of the system were two French generals. The first was the French ambassador to Spain, General Beurnonville, who was the link between Paris and Madrid. The second was General Lauriston, who not only commanded the French troops with the fleet but was also a personal ADC of the Emperor. As such he corresponded frequently and privately with Napoleon. He remained in that position until 28 September when he handed over command of the troops (but not his ADC role) to Adjutant-General (chief-of-staff) Contamine who fought at Trafalgar.

## Vice-Admiral Pierre Charles Jean Baptiste Sylvestre de Villeneuve

Born in 1763, Villeneuve was only forty-two at Trafalgar – remarkably young for such a large command. Courteous, quiet and reserved in manner, he came from a long line of gallant aristocrats; there was a Villeneuve fighting with Roland in the pass at Roncesvalles and another died at the side of the English King Richard I (the Lionheart) in the Crusades. The future vice-admiral entered Bourbon naval service (Les Gardes-Marine) in 1778 and served under de Grasse in the West Indies, taking part in the capture of Tobago. He was promoted to *capitaine de vaisseau* (line-of-battle ship captain) in 1793 and first met the future Emperor in the same year at the siege of Toulon, where Captain Bonaparte had taken charge of the artillery bombardment. Almost immediately afterwards the revolutionaries suspended him, but within two years, desperately short of competent officers, Villeneuve was reinstated and became naval chief of staff at Toulon. In September 1796 he raised his flag as *contre amiral* (rear-admiral) when still only thirty-three (Nelson was thirty-nine when promoted to the same rank). He commanded the right wing of the anchored French Fleet at the Nile – a catastrophic defeat from which he managed to escape with two ships-of-the-line and two frigates. In May 1804 he was promoted again to vice-admiral and in December given command of the fleet at Toulon. From there he sailed to the West Indies, chased unsuccessfully by Nelson, and on his return fought the indecisive action against Calder that ruined any chances of a secret combination of French fleets in the Channel.

Villeneuve fought with great gallantry at Trafalgar. He had laboured under grave disadvantages for several months and in the end had put to sea in order to avoid an ignominious dismissal. He was captured when forced to strike his colours and after the battle transferred to the *Euryalus,* which had become a temporary flagship for Collingwood. There he met Captain Durham (*Defiance*) who was visiting Collingwood. Villeneuve asked him, 'Sir, were you in Sir Robert Calder's action?' When Durham said he was Villeneuve sighed and said, 'I wish Sir Robert and I had fought it out that day. He would not be in his present position [awaiting a court martial], or I in mine.' Villeneuve lived in England on parole for about five months in Bishop's Waltham in Hampshire. During that time he and Captain Magendie (his flag captain at Trafalgar) were permitted to watch Nelson's funeral procession in London. In April 1806 he was exchanged for four British post captains.

He landed at Morlaix in Brittany, from where he wrote to Decrès reporting his arrival and asking for instructions, to be sent to Rennes where he intended to stay. At Rennes he put up in the Hotel de Patrie to await the expected courier. On hearing that Captains Lucas and Infernet had both been promoted to rear-admiral he wrote at once to Lucas to congratulate him and to pass his compliments to Infernet. He mentioned that he would demand a full inquiry into the battle (he was incensed by Dumanoir's behaviour) and wanted to call Lucas as a witness. In fact Villeneuve would undoubtedly have faced a court martial for losing his fleet at Trafalgar – it would have been automatic, as it was for any captain who lost his ship. No letter arrived from Decrès, plunging Villeneuve into deep depression. With no response from Paris, and knowing Napoleon's bitterness, even hatred, towards him, Villeneuve took a kitchen knife, lay on his bed and proceeded to stab himself in the chest and side. Five times he thrust the knife into his body. Still alive, in agony and covered with blood, he held the point of the knife over his heart, rolled over onto his stomach, and fell heavily on it, driving it home to the hilt.

There were inevitably rumours of murder but the inquiry found that the room had been locked from the inside. His servant testified that the admiral had appeared strange for several days and that he had thought it best to draw the charges from his pistols. Then there was his farewell letter to his wife and, in his baggage, Villeneuve's telescope, labelled '*A l'intrepide Infernet*' and his speaking trumpet, labelled '*Pour toi, brave Lucas.*' There could be little doubt he took his own life.

More than two years after Trafalgar Decrès plucked up the courage to suggest to Napoleon that a pension of 6,000 francs a year be granted to his widow, as was customary with officers' dependants of his rank. He put the case as strongly as he could, stressing that Villeneuve had been a gallant officer and worthy servant of the Empire. The Emperor, unsurprisingly, was reluctant to oblige. However, he finally yielded, though reducing the pension to 4,000 francs.

Villeneuve's name lives on, if not always in the most salubrious environments. As recently as 2001 an article appeared in a British newspaper describing the murder by knifing of a fifteen-year-old boy in a crime-ridden 'sink estate' called 'Villeneuve' in the otherwise picturesque town of Grenoble, near which Napoleon decisively fronted down the troops who were supposed to arrest him on his march to Paris after escaping from Elba in 1815.

In order to reach a fair judgement of Villeneuve's performance as commander-in-chief at the battle it is essential to understand how this tangled and divided command structure affected him. Some historians have dismissed him as incompetent, a pessimist who had been promoted above his ceiling, but an examination of the difficulties he encountered and the deliberate undermining of his authority suggest this is unduly harsh.

### Villeneuve under pressure

Vice-Admiral Villeneuve had been surprised, flattered and delighted to receive his appointment to command of the French Fleet at Toulon in late 1804. By that time Nelson had been blockading the port for a year. During this period French ships had scarcely put to sea. The Emperor, in his ignorance of naval affairs, considered this to be advantageous: British ships and crews would wear themselves out while the French conserved themselves in harbour. Any professional seaman of any national-

ity knew the reverse was true. To Villeneuve, who had been in the Navy twenty-six years and had seen how Nelson's fleet could fight at the Nile, such an argument was nonsense. Villeneuve spent the first part of 1805 evading Nelson and sailing to the West Indies as part of one of Napoleon's grand plans to disperse and confuse the British prior to an invasion (see pp. 44–54). But Calder spoiled things by intercepting the return voyage in July, destroying all hope of achieving Napoleon's planned secret rendezvous and descent on the Channel.

Villeneuve knew he had lost the Emperor's confidence. In early August while still at Corunna, Villeneuve had written to his minister, 'I am the arbiter of the greatest interests, but my despair is increased the more because no confidence is shown in me – because I can pretend to no success whatever I do.' Then, on 10 August he announced he would sail with Gravina's ships from Ferrol, 12 miles across the bay from Corunna – destination either Brest, and thence to Boulogne, or Cadiz. 'I am setting out. I shall proceed to Brest or to Cadiz according to circumstances. The enemy is observing us too closely for me to be able to disguise my route.' This attempt to get under way from Corunna and Ferrol collapsed in chaos when the wind failed before the fleets could clear the narrows. Efforts at anchoring were unimpressive as 'all the ships, French and Spanish, ran aboard each other'. This humiliation deepened Villeneuve's depression. He managed to get the fleet out on 13 August but by the 15th he had been compelled to make for Cadiz by contrary winds and a mistaken belief that ships sighted on the horizon were the enemy (they may have been Allemand's squadron, but were most likely merchantmen). He arrived in Cadiz on the 20th.

For Villeneuve the next two months were dogged by seemingly relentless strain, during part of which he was violently sick with colic. Under enormous pressure from unrealistic orders from

above, he also had to cope with preparing a fleet of two nations for operations while located in a reluctant ally's port with a disgruntled officer corps and an acute shortage of trained seamen.

## Villeneuve and Napoleon

Napoleon had developed a seething but generally unjustified contempt for Villeneuve, whom he blamed for the failure of his grandiose nautical schemes aimed at control of the Channel. Napoleon was a great soldier, but never a seaman, naval strategist or tactician. Unfortunately for his admirals he considered he could send fleets across the sea as easily as he could march armies across the land. Problems arising due to wind, weather, tides and the condition of ships tended to be glossed over in his complicated strategic plans, which often involved manoeuvring fleets across thousands of miles of ocean. As he once exclaimed angrily, 'The Navy is always

## Franco-Spanish Command Structure

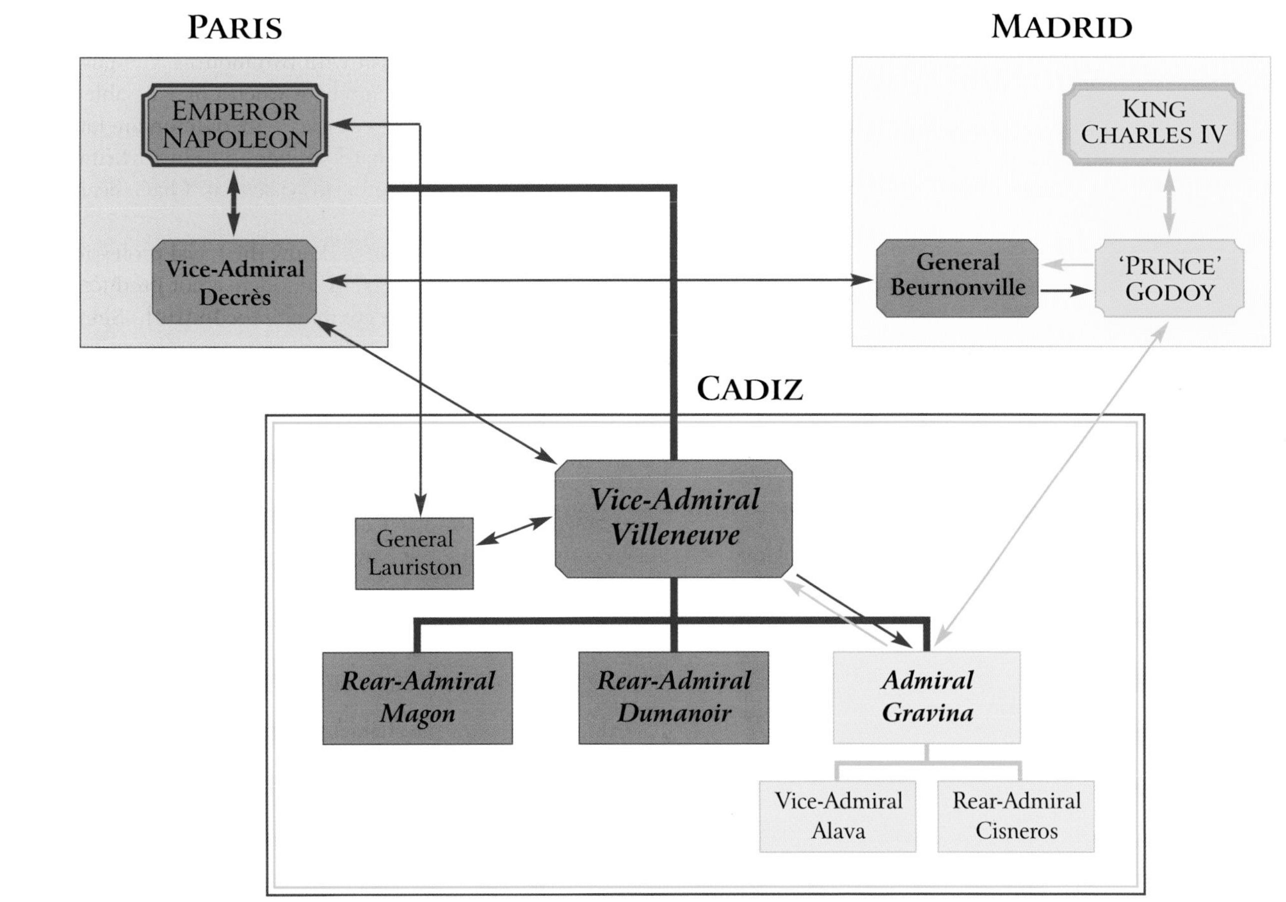

**PARIS**

EMPEROR NAPOLEON

Vice-Admiral Decrès

**MADRID**

KING CHARLES IV

General Beurnonville → 'PRINCE' GODOY

**CADIZ**

General Lauriston

*Vice-Admiral Villeneuve*

*Rear-Admiral Magon*

*Rear-Admiral Dumanoir*

*Admiral Gravina*

Vice-Admiral Alava

Rear-Admiral Cisneros

### Key/Notes

→ Main French direct line of communication
→ Main Spanish direct line of communication
━━ Chain of command

• This diagram shows the complicated system of communication between Paris, Madrid and Villeneuve at Cadiz before the Combined Fleet sailed on 19 October 1805.

• Admiral Gravina was the second-in-command to Villeneuve at the battle and had personal command of the squadron of observation.
• General Lauriston, as a personal ADC to the Emperor, communicated directly with Napoleon.

more willing to obey its barometers than my orders.' He refused to admit his own ignorance and resented professional advice.

Napoleon's view of Villeneuve was not improved by the despatches of General Lauriston. Lauriston was, by 1805, a *general de division* but more importantly a personal aide-de-camp of the Emperor. He had joined the flagship in Toulon in 1803 assuming command of the embarked troops, a duty additional to his role as an ADC. He was responsible directly to Napoleon, his reports and correspondence going straight to the Emperor, unseen by Villeneuve or Decrès. A former artilleryman like Napoleon, Lauriston went out of his way to undermine Villeneuve's authority and competence in the eyes of the Emperor.

On the voyage back from the West Indies that summer Lauriston had not been given the chance to grab some glory ashore on the islands with his soldiers, and as a result became even less enamoured with his admiral. He was not impressed by Villeneuve's performance against Calder off Cape Finisterre in July, or by his actions after reaching Cadiz. His report, written on 21 August, combined vitriol against Villeneuve with an attempt to ingratiate himself with the Emperor.

> Sire, I am only on board temporarily but I have the honour to be Your Majesty's aide-de-camp; I am truly humiliated at finding myself present at so many ignominious manoeuvres, powerless to do the slightest thing for the honour of Your Majesty's flag. We sail like a fleet of merchantmen who fear the attack of 4 or 5 of the line and it is a single man who is the cause of all this. ...
>
> The captains have no heart left to do well; attention is no longer paid to signals, which remain flying at the masthead for two or three hours. Discipline is utterly relaxed. ... this squadron needs a *man* and above all an admiral who commands confidence and attachment. The greatest resolution is required at this moment. Sire, this humiliating cruise has not disgusted me, I am ready to recommence a yet more trying one if only to be with a *man* and that I do not witness the discredit of the navy ...

Napoleon's contempt for Villeneuve caused serious problems for Decrès, who was not only Minister of Marine but also a professional naval officer of considerable experience and a contemporary and old friend of Villeneuve from the pre-Revolutionary navy. Decrès was in an invidious position, torn between loyalty to his Emperor and the need to shield his comrade and dissuade Napoleon from some of his more outlandish schemes.

Trying to co-ordinate and oversee Napoleon's elaborate plans was an immensely frustrating task. It involved daily dealings with the Emperor, submitting reports, receiving instructions and trying to moderate his more impractical proposals. His correspondence was voluminous: he wrote to Villeneuve, to the ambassador (General Beurnonville) in Madrid and to the Agent-General for Commercial Affairs of France (Monsieur Le Roy) in Cadiz. He had to remove and appoint senior commanders and after Trafalgar arrange and report on the court martial of Rear-Admiral Dumanoir.

Now Decrès endeavoured, ineffectually, to defend his old friend by telling the Emperor that, 'it was a distracting affair for him [Villeneuve]' and he believed 'it not to be cowardice but that he lost his head'. Napoleon responded with a furious broadside, this time directed at the minister himself. After reiterating his rage at Villeneuve's supposed treachery and Decrès' excuses he finished by

exclaiming, 'Until you have something plausible to say, I beg that you will say nothing at all to me about such a humiliating affair and will never recall such a dastard to my mind.'

Despite his anger, Napoleon insisted that even if Villeneuve had gone to Cadiz instead of the Channel he could combine with Spanish squadrons there and at Cartagena and still make a final bid for the Channel. Decrès responded in desperation:

> Sire,
> ... I lay myself at Your Majesty's feet to implore You not to associate the Spanish ships with Your Squadrons in their operations. ...
>
> Your Majesty desires that with such an assembly an operation should be undertaken which is very difficult in itself and which will become the more so from the elements composing the Fleet, from the inexperience of the leaders, from their being unaccustomed to command ...
>
> In this state of affairs, in which Your Majesty counts as naught my arguments and my experience, I know of no position more painful than my own ... I implore You on no account to order it to come round from Cadiz to the Channel ... Above all I implore You not to give orders that it is to attempt this transit with two months' victuals ...
>
> It is especially at this moment when I may be able to check the issue of orders, which in my opinion are fatal to Your Majesty's service that I am bound to insist firmly. May I be more fortunate in this case than I have been heretofore.
>
> But it is grievous to me to know the naval profession, since this knowledge wins no confidence nor produces any result on Your Majesty's combinations. In truth, Sire, my situation is becoming too painful ...

For once, Napoleon paid some attention to Decrès' advice. After years of dreaming about planning an invasion of England, he finally gave up hope. On 22 August he heard that Villeneuve had left Corunna. The following day, even before he knew for certain Villeneuve had made for Cadiz, Napoleon decided to turn his back on the Channel, the Navy and his useless admirals to march east with his Army.

His opinion of Villeneuve did not improve. For another week telescopes at Boulogne scanned the horizon for French topsails – nothing. The Emperor's anger erupted.

> I think he has not the character necessary for the command of a frigate. He is a man without resolution or moral courage. Two Spanish vessels have been in collision; some of his men have fallen sick; there had been contrary winds for two days; a ship of the enemy had been seen; it is rumoured that Nelson had joined Calder – and all his plans are changed, though these things by themselves are as nothing.

On 4 September, now in Paris, he wrote to Decrès:

> Admiral Villeneuve has filled the cup to overflowing; when he leaves Vigo [*sic*] he gives Captain Allemand [at Rochefort] orders to go to Brest and writes to you that it is his intention to go to Cadiz. It is treason beyond all doubt ... Villeneuve is a rascal who must be dismissed from the service in disgrace. He has no talents, no courage, no interests; he would sacrifice anything in order to save his skin.

## Admiral Gravina and the Spanish

It was as late as December 1804 that Spain became an unenthusiastic ally of France in the next round of the Napoleonic Wars. The Emperor's cajoling and the British attack on the Spanish treasure ships finally pushed Madrid over the edge. At this time Admiral Gravina was Spain's ambassador in Paris and in secret communication with Godoy. Gravina, who was a Neapolitan aristocrat by birth, had met Napoleon in 1801 and the two had got on surprisingly well considering their diametrically opposite backgrounds. Napoleon's priority then was a cross-Channel invasion. With Spanish ships now available and joined with the French at Brest the launching of his vast flotilla just might become practical.

However, unknown to Napoleon despite his spies in Madrid, Gravina had received secret instructions from his government. They began, 'It not being in the interests of Spain that her forces should go to Brest, this must be avoided with the double object of not leaving our coasts unprotected and of preventing our allies from succeeding in their much desired landing in England.' For Spain the naval arithmetic did not add up: England could still produce a fleet far superior in numbers and quality than any combination France and Spain could put together. Gravina therefore dutifully suggested alternative schemes to the French, each avoiding the commitment to Spanish ships assembling off Brest. The Emperor rejected them.

When Gravina arrived in Cadiz on 15 February 1805 to take command of the Spanish Fleet he was well aware of his government's wish to avoid being embroiled (via Brest) with the French invasion of England. Gravina commanded the Spanish squadron that accompanied Villeneuve to the West Indies that spring. He was therefore involved in the action off Cape Finisterre on 22 July at which his squadron lost two ships (*San Rafaël* and *Firme*); many Spanish claimed afterwards that they had been abandoned by the French and forced to strike their colours unnecessarily. Believing that the fate of his ships was a stain on his honour, when he returned to Madrid he spoke to Godoy offering to resign. Godoy was sympathetic and soothing. He succeeded in persuading Gravina that his duty lay in co-operating with the French and building up the fleet at Cadiz.

While Lauriston derided the efforts of Villeneuve he was forthright in his praise for Gravina. On being told by Gravina that he wished to resign over Godoy's supposed lack of confidence in him, Lauriston wrote to the Emperor on 22 August:

> I must inform your Majesty that Admiral Gravina confided to me that he had written yesterday to the Prince of Peace to ask permission to resign the command of the Squadron since it appears he did not possess the confidence of the Court. Your Majesty should be convinced that Admiral Gravina's retirement would cause the greatest harm to the Franco-Spanish Squadron; both have entire confidence in him … In general, Sire, we are not liked in Spain; but with a man full of honour and courage like Admiral Gravina, who is sincerely devoted to Your Majesty …

### The Prince of Peace

Manuel Godoy had gained his somewhat ridiculous title by negotiating Spain's leaving the First Coalition against France in 1795. He was also at various times the Duke of Alcudia, the President of the Council, Prime Minister and Generalissimo of the Spanish Navy. More importantly he was the lover of the Queen. From his beginnings as a private soldier in the Spanish *Gardes du Corp* he had done remarkably well. His role in the Trafalgar drama was limited to prodding the local Spanish authorities in Cadiz to provide the services necessary to get the French ships in a fit condition to sail. He had also to deal directly with Admiral Gravina to persuade him not to resign (see main text).

Lauriston was right about the attitude of the Spanish. The authorities in Cadiz outwardly complied with the orders from Madrid to co-operate with the French but actually raised difficulties, delayed deliveries and procrastinated. The daily drudgery endured by the French commanders was exceptionally wearing. Every piece of timber, every nail or cask of biscuits required constant haggling and hard cash to extract, grudgingly, from the Spanish authorities. They were not the only people antagonistic to their allies. Edward Fraser, writing in his book *The Enemy at Trafalgar* in 1910, put the problem succinctly:

> To add to Villeneuve's anxieties at the outset, the temper of both the officers and men of the Spanish Fleet and the populace of Cadiz showed itself openly hostile to the officers and men of the French Fleet. Letters from the Spanish Fleet sent from Ferrol three weeks before, detailing incidents of the fight with Calder and commenting in indignant terms on the conduct of their allies in letting the two Spanish ships be taken, were handed about at private gatherings and even in the wine shops. Colonel le Roy, the French Consul-General at Cadiz, had to make a protest to the Captain-General and Governor, the Marquis de la Solana, laying stress on the bad effect this sort of thing was having. A casual remark, attributed to one of the French captains, that the Spanish officers were 'a sorry lot' and that 'their gross incompetence and blundering had thrown the two ships away' was also reported all over Cadiz and did no good.
>
> … The ill feeling towards the French Fleet among the populace showed itself next in a very sinister way. Leave ashore, which had been granted on the fleet arrival to practically all officers, and certain of the men, had to be stopped owing to personal insults to various officers in places of public resort, and worse still in consequence of a number of assassinations of French seamen after dark.

## Discontent in the French Fleet

It was not only the Spanish who criticized their commander-in-chief. Villeneuve was not on particularly cordial terms with either of his two rear-admirals. Dumanoir still felt sore at having Villeneuve brought in over his head to take command at Toulon a year before, while Magon's hot temper did not always make for a rewarding relationship with his less volatile superior. After Villeneuve's failure to renew the action against Calder, Dumanoir is said, when the French flagship sailed past, to have given, 'vent to furious exclamations, and flung at him [Villeneuve] in his rage whatever happened to be at hand, including his field glass, and even his wig'. One wonders whether Dumanoir's long delay in complying with Villeneuve's signals to bring his van squadron back to assist the hard-pressed centre at Trafalgar (which resulted in his court martial) had anything to do with personal feelings.

There was also grumbling amongst some of the captains and more junior officers. While declining to admit their own deficien-

## Admiral Don Frederico Gravina

Born into an aristocratic family in Palermo, Gravina entered the Spanish Navy in 1768 at the age of twelve; Sicily like Spain was under the rule of the Bourbon family. It was the start of a distinguished career as a fighting commander, naval administrator and diplomat.

His operational experience went back to the days of the long blockade and siege of Gibraltar. From 1779 to 1782 he was off the waters of that great fortress on the Rock. In 1782 he commanded one of the numerous bomb vessels in the final, but unsuccessful, attack. He was promoted from his burnt-out vessel (destroyed by British red-hot shot) to serve on the prestigious *Santisima Trinidad*. As her captain he fought in the Franco-Spanish Fleet's duel with Lord Howe off Cape Spartel in 1782. In 1789 he took a year out from naval duties to study astronomy at Constantinople.

In that year he was promoted commodore and while in the frigate *Paz* achieved one of the fastest recorded passages from Cadiz to the Spanish colonies in South America. In 1793 he travelled to England (during the period England and Spain were allies) with Captain Valdés (captain of the *Neptuno* at Trafalgar). He was entertained and shown round the Portsmouth base, and compiled a secret report in which he praised the seeming superiority of British gunnery. The design of the gun carriages and the use of gunlocks particularly impressed him. Nevertheless, he felt, probably correctly, that Spain had the edge in ship design, strength and speed. Gravina was next sent to the Spanish part of San Domingo in 1800. After three years the King appointed him as ambassador in Paris – and as noted above he impressed the Emperor Napoleon, and got to know Decrès well. He was a guest at Josephine's coronation and played a major part in the negotiations leading to the signing of the Franco-Spanish pact in January 1805. For his services to Spain King Charles IV promoted him to Commander of the Spanish Navy, following which he went to Cadiz to organize the fleet.

He was forty-nine by the time of Trafalgar and had become a Spanish Grandee of the First Class – and thus allowed to wear his hat in the presence of the King! When Villeneuve appeared off Cadiz in April 1805 Gravina with six ships joined the Frenchman on his voyage to the West Indies and back. He was therefore involved in the action against Calder in July 1805 at which he lost two ships,

afterwards believing the Spanish had been badly let down and blaming Villeneuve for hanging back. As described in the main text Gravina's attempt to resign over this was prevented by Godoy.

At Trafalgar he commanded the squadron of observation (twelve ships-of-the-line, two frigates and a brig) as well as being Villeneuve's second. His flagship was the 112-gun *Principe de Asturias*, which survived the battle but only just, having to be towed away by the frigate *Thémis* and leaving Gravina with a shattered left elbow. Hospitalized on return to Cadiz, he lingered on for four and a half months in considerable pain before he died, almost certainly unnecessarily. There had been a prolonged argument between surgeons as to whether his arm should be amputated. If the operation had been carried out early before gangrene set in his chances of survival would have been good. An Englishman, Dr Fellowes, visited Gravina a few days before his death, later writing that Gravina had said to him, 'I am a dying man, but I die happy, I hope and trust, to join Nelson, the greatest hero that the world perhaps has produced.' He died in the arms of his brother, Archbishop Gravina of Nicea, his eyes fixed upon a crucifix.

In death Gravina was honoured almost as much as Nelson had been. He was embalmed and temporarily laid to rest in a chapel in Cadiz. On 29 March 1806 a requiem mass was held for him at the Church of the Convent of the Carmen, conducted by his brother. It was a formal state affair attended by Admirals Alava and Rosily, their staffs, the governor-general and a host of generals, colonels, navy officers of all ranks and senior civilians. Four years later his remains were removed to the Chapel of the Carmen. With him were buried his sword, hat, the shot-torn flag that had flown at the masthead of his flagship at Trafalgar, his baton as a Captain-General de la Armada and the banner of a Knight Grand Cross of the Order of Carlos III, the latter two honours having been conferred on his deathbed. Then, in 1869, he was transferred once again, this time to the Panteon Nacional in Madrid. His sword, hat, baton and flag were taken and put on display in the Museo Naval. Finally, in 1883, came another move to San Fernando, the naval port and arsenal near Cadiz, with another stately procession, headed by the Captain-General of Cadiz, which marched slowly from the railway station accompanied by the boom of minute guns to the Panteon de Marinos Illustres.

---

cies they made disparaging comments on Villeneuve's failure with 20 ships to defeat Calder with 15. And why had he not renewed the battle the next day when the weather had cleared and the wind was favourable? Then again why, when Villeneuve had arrived at Cadiz on 21 August with 29 ships when the British blockading squadron under Collingwood had only four (increased to eight the following day with Rear-Admiral Bickerton's arrival), did he not attack them? It was a window of opportunity only open for eight days. On 30 August it was slammed shut by Calder's arrival with another 17 ships-of-the-line.

As discussed in Section Six, neither the French nor the Spanish ships had fully recovered from debilitating losses of manpower due to sickness. Many ships were still in need of repairs; all needed revictualling for a voyage of four months. There was a dearth of trained seamen, crews were made up with pressed men and soldiers, and there was no chance to train or exercise anyone. On 28 September Villeneuve wrote to Decrès, 'Your Excellency will observe that the shortage of crews amounts to 2,207 men; we have

649 in the hospitals in Cadiz of whom perhaps a third may be fit to embark at the moment of setting sail.' Those weeks in Cadiz were a nightmare for Villeneuve.

### Villeneuve's orders

On 16 September Decrès sent the latest orders from the Emperor to Villeneuve. They had been composed on the erroneous belief that only 11 English ships were sitting outside Cadiz – in fact there were 29. Even when Napoleon was made aware of the true number five days later his instructions remained unchanged. Villeneuve was to enter the Mediterranean, join the Spanish squadron at Cartagena, proceed to Naples and disembark 4,000 troops to reinforce the French, after which he should make for Toulon. To the Emperor's orders Decrès added some of his own. The Combined Fleet was to attempt to capture an enemy convoy that was reported as proceeding in that direction. His ships were to carry three months' victuals and Villeneuve should 'seize the first favourable opportunity to effect [his] departure'.

When Villeneuve received his orders to break out of Cadiz and take troops to Naples Gravina again declined personal involvement. On 28 September he explained to Villeneuve that as he had been born in the Kingdom of Naples he could not take up arms against it. The following day in a letter to Godoy, he wrote that he had told Villeneuve:

> that we [the Spanish fleet] cannot, in any case, join you in hostilities against a brother of our King [Ferdinand IV of Naples was the brother of Charles IV of Spain]. Speaking once in Paris with the Minister of Marine, Decrès, I told him: I will follow you everywhere but I will not go against my country. If my King ordered me to do it, I would beg him graciously to confer on me the command of another force … to spare me the painful feeling of fighting against my country.

Villeneuve was being required to take his ill-prepared fleet on a mission that would inevitably entail a battle with a fleet of about equal size but manned by better crews – all for the sake of taking a few soldiers to Naples, something to which his Spanish co-commander expressly objected. His acknowledgement of these orders stated he would get the supplies on board, that the troops would embark and 'I shall make the signal to weigh as soon as the wind will allow of working out of the bay.' He then went on to explain that this might take some time.

> I am not aware if Your Excellency is acquainted with the local peculiarities of this harbour and how difficult it is to set in motion so numerous a Fleet, as they cannot be put to sea at the same time save only when the wind comes from north-east to south-east. … A steady easterly wind is absolutely essential to me in order to work out of the bay and I shall not be able to make the Straits until it has shifted and gone round to the west.

He neglected to mention the obvious, that an easterly wind would signal the English to be particularly alert. On the same day he wrote to his officers:

> The captains in command will realize from the position and strength the enemy before this port [Nelson's efforts at concealing his strength were to prove largely ineffective] that an engagement must take place the very same day that the Fleet puts to sea. … Our Allies will fight at our side, under the walls of Cadiz and in the sight of their fellow-citizens; the Emperor's gaze is fixed upon us.

Villeneuve knew a clash was inevitable the moment he put his nose out of harbour. Like so many nautical manoeuvres, when this happened depended on the wind.

## The Council of War

Villeneuve had received his orders to sail for the Mediterranean on 28 September (the same day Nelson arrived to assume command). First, he had to finish getting his ships repaired, victualled and crewed, embark the troops and await a favourable wind while seeking information as to the strength and whereabouts of the enemy fleet. On 30 September General Lauriston left, much to the admiral's relief, to the thump of an eleven-gun salute. General Reille accompanied him. Command of the troops then rested with Adjutant-Commandant Contamine. On 2 October Villeneuve reported the regiments had embarked. All the ships had three months' victuals –

except for biscuits. He had been told by Gravina, via the Spanish ambassador at Lisbon, that Nelson had hoisted his flag. The wind was variable but, 'I only await a favourable opportunity to order the Combined Fleet to weigh.' On 7 October he made the attempt. The signal to sail was hoisted. As he described to Decrès:

> In my impatience to carry out the Emperor's orders, heeding neither the strength of the enemy nor the condition of the greater number of the ships in the Combined Fleet, I desired yesterday [7 October] to take advantage of a north-east breeze on which the Fleet could work out, and I made the signal to prepare to set sail, but the wind having blown a gale from this quarter and being therefore diametrically opposed to the course that I was to shape, I was not able to carry out my design.
>
> Nevertheless, I could not turn a deaf ear to the observations which reached me from every side, as to the inferiority of our force in comparison with that of the enemy, which is at the present time from 31 to 33 line-of-battle-ships, of which 8 are three-deckers [a surprisingly accurate estimate – there were 29 of which 7 were three-deckers], … to put to sea in such circumstances has been termed an act of despair … an action on the very day of our leaving port was inevitable …
>
> I wished to have the opinions of all the flag officers and of the senior captains in the two Squadrons on this matter …

He failed to mention that the Council of War on the *Bucentaure* was called at the instigation of Admiral Gravina, who as early as 6 October had, according to Escaño's undated letter to Commodore Macdonell, 'considered it necessary, before weighing, to hold a council in which all of the commanding officers of both nations might be heard'.

Invitations went to those suggested by Gravina. It was a crowded admiral's cabin that morning. Representing Spain were Admiral Gravina, Vice-Admiral Alava, Rear-Admirals Escaño and Cisneros along with Commodores Hore, Galiano and Macdonell; for France were Rear-Admirals Dumanoir and Magon, Commodores Cosmao and Maistral, Captain Villegris plus the captain of the fleet (Villeneuve's chief-of-staff) Commander Prigny – in total, fourteen men.

Both commanders-in-chief held conferences before the battle but there were substantial differences in their methods of command. Nelson had called together all his admirals and captains to tell them what he intended to do and what he expected of them when action was joined. He was, albeit informally, giving his orders. Villeneuve, however, used his conference for a debate on whether, in difficult circumstances, to sail and offer battle. There was what today's politicians would call 'a frank exchange of views', a diplomatic way of describing a stand-up row.

There are two original sources as to what went on at the Council meeting – the official French minutes, and an undated letter from Gravina's chief-of-staff, Rear-Admiral Escaño, to Commodore Macdonell of the *Rayo*. The Spanish minutes mysteriously disappeared (see box on p. 424). The salient points are discussed below.

*French minutes*
Villeneuve described his orders from Paris to sail for the Mediterranean and Naples. The minutes record 'that the Combined Fleet should weigh at the first favourable opportunity and that wherever the enemy should be encountered in inferior strength, they must be attacked without hesitation …'.

## Vice-Admiral Don Ignatio Maria de Alava

Alava was the second-in-command of the Spanish ships at Trafalgar with his flag in the 112-gun *Santa Ana*. He also commanded the 2nd Squadron (in the original order of sailing) which formed the rear of the line at the battle, although in practice the squadron of observation was astern of his squadron. He was born in 1754, which made him fifty-one at Trafalgar. He entered service as a boy of twelve and within two years was participating in operations against pirates along the Barbary coast. In 1781 he commanded a small brig and then one of the floating batteries at the Siege of Gibraltar (at the same time as Gravina). He was also with Gravina in the action against Lord Howe off Cape Spartel in 1782. Thereafter he was promoted captain and given command of the frigate *Sabina*, followed by that of the ship-of-the-line *San Francisco de Paula*. He was sent, as a rear-admiral, to command a squadron in Manila in the Philippines, not returning to Cadiz until 1803 when he was promoted again to vice-admiral.

At Trafalgar the *Santa Ana* became locked in a duel with Collingwood's *Royal Sovereign* and was forced to strike her colours at around 2.30 p.m., by which time Alava had been taken below unconscious and bleeding from a head wound. Considerable confusion developed over his surrender. Collingwood, who had heard of Nelson's wounding, sent Captain Blackwood to convey the Spanish admiral on board the *Euryalus* (which was to become his

temporary flagship). Blackwood was told Alava was dying so returned instead with Captain Gardoqui who handed over a sword to Collingwood. Two days latter, during the storm, the *Santa Ana* was recaptured with Alava still on board. His wound was not serious and he began to make a good recovery. When Collingwood heard Alava was still alive and in Cadiz he considered that, as he had surrendered his ship and his sword, he was in honour bound to surrender himself again. He wrote to Alava accordingly on 30 October. Not until 23 December did Alava reply, arguing that as his ship had been recaptured he had been freed, and that he had not surrendered his sword – the one given to Collingwood apparently belonged to a Lieutenant Francisco Riquelme. Alava had no intention of giving himself up, and Collingwood had to be satisfied.

In 1810 Alava was commanding in Havana. Two years later he was Commander-in-Chief at Cadiz and in 1814 was appointed to the Supreme Council of the Admiralty. His final promotion was to admiral of the fleet in February 1817, and he died three months later aged sixty-three.

His nephew, Don Miguel Ricardo de Alava, was serving at Trafalgar on the *Principe de Asturias* as an ADC to Gravina. He went on to serve on the Duke of Wellington's staff as a colonel throughout the Peninsular War and became one of a handful of people to have fought at Trafalgar and Waterloo.

---

Villeneuve then explained the latest intelligence on the enemy received from the ambassador in Portugal, the Agent at Tangiers, coastal craft and lookouts: that Nelson had between 31 and 33 ships-of-the-line including 8 three-deckers plus a number of frigates. He then asked that, 'every person composing [the] council be so good as to give his opinion upon the situation'.

The minutes state that all present acknowledged that the ships of their fleet were badly manned. Several ships had not exercised their crews at sea and the *Santa Ana, Rayo* and *San Justo* had been fitted out in haste. They were only just out of the dock-yard and therefore 'by no means in a state to render the service in action of which they will be capable when they are completely organized'.

There was unanimous agreement that the enemy's fleet was 'far more powerful than our own', and that having to engage the enemy immedi-ately on leaving port would be disad-vantageous. All agreed that it would be better to await a more favourable opportunity 'which may arise from bad weather that would drive the enemy away from these waters, or from the necessity he will experience of dividing the force of his squadron in order to protect his trade in the Mediterranean and the convoys that may be threatened from Cartagena and from Toulon'.

### The Disappearance of the Spanish Minutes

In Volume I of Edouard Desbriere's *The Naval Campaign of 1805*, the loss of these minutes is described as follows.

It has been pointed out that Gravina's report to the Prince of Peace on the council of October 8th disappeared from the Archives of Madrid in suspicious circumstances. These last are questionable at the very least. The disappearance of the papers concerning Trafalgar from the Archives of the Marines at Madrid has been attributed successively to Murat, who in 1808 is supposed to have carried off these documents from the Admiralty (of whom the Prince of Peace was head) to send them to France. This version must be rejected in consequence of researches made in the French Archives de la Marine and in the Archives Nationales. Then a fire, which occurred at Madrid in 1808, has been mentioned. Finally, according to a certificate furnished by the present head [in 1933] of the Archives of the Ministry of Marine, Captain Ferrar, it would appear that on January 15th, 1847, the revolutionaries took possession of the papers of the Ministry of Marine.

Finally came the obligatory protestation: they all bore witness 'to the desire that they will always feel of going out to engage the enemy, whatever his force, as soon as His Majesty desires it, and they invited Admiral Villeneuve to be their spokesman to assure Him of their wholehearted devotion'. It all sounded very cordial.

*Escaño's letter*
Escaño was Gravina's chief-of-staff and it is clear from his letter that the views of the Spanish participants had been sought and a decision agreed upon prior to the meeting. Escaño, initially, was their spokesman. His letter records that Villeneuve in his opening remarks asked the council to consider whether,

as he had definite orders to leave Cadiz harbour with the entire Combined Squadron, it were possible to fulfil them by effecting this departure, or whether he should await an enemy attack on the Fleet at anchor ... The Spanish commanders stated, in the most decorous manner, that their opinion was in accordance with that expressed by their General [Gravina] through the Captain of theFleet [Escaño] since they had all discussed it among themselves beforehand ...

The Spanish opinion was that it would be foolish to attack in the current circumstances.

Some of the French officers, who had not debated the matter before, disagreed. As Escaño delicately put it: 'The French expressed various opinions with the warmth characteristic of their nation, some amongst them maintaining that there was no doubt about the proposal of leaving port, the result would be the rout of the opponent and the consequent ease of executing their orders [to go to Naples].'

Escaño had then attempted to sum up. He pointed out the huge disparity in seamanship between those (the British) 'who had been at sea with their squadrons without the least intermission since 1793 and those who had spent eight years without putting to sea'. He then tossed a match into the French gunpowder, concluding his summary of the Spanish position by saying 'that superior orders could not bind them to attempt the impossible, as nothing would serve as an excuse in the event of a disaster, which he saw to be inevitable if they weighed'.

The hot-tempered Magon reacted predictably: 'Magon refuted the Chief-of-Staff, and in his heated reply expressed himself with scant courtesy; the sensitive and punctilious Galiano sought to make him retract several expressions, tempers grew warm and General Gravina, rising, requested that the vote should be taken without further discussion. ... The result of the voting was that they should remain at anchor ...'.

How the votes were divided is not recorded here. Several historians have argued that it must have been unanimous because all present signed the minutes. This is unlikely in view of the heated dispute. It is more probable that the result was a majority verdict to do nothing at that time, and that those present signed that the minutes reflected that decision, not their own individual views.

It is not possible from these two primary sources to know precisely what insults were exchanged or by whom. Nevertheless, there was certainly a slanging match between the French and Spanish delegations. Honour was impugned. One secondary account says Galiano leapt to his feet facing Magon and put his hand on his sword hilt and had to be restrained from challenging him to duel. Another suggests that disparaging remarks concerning lack of courage at Cape Finisterre in July were bandied about. However, it seems likely that the Spanish spoke as one against weighing at that time, having discussed it before the meeting. Gravina had already said he could not fight against his king's brother in Naples. French opinion was probably divided, with the more impetuous officers demanding action.

Villeneuve – no doubt somewhat relieved – wrote immediately to Decrès, enclosing the signed minutes and explaining the Council of War's agreement to further delay. He promised that he would 'watch the weather and the movements of the enemy', adding at the end, 'I beg Your Excellency to assure the Emperor of the alacrity with which I shall seize the first available opportunity to carry out His orders.' The situation was about to change dramatically.

## Villeneuve's dismissal

On 15 September, when Napoleon dictated the order to send the Cadiz fleet to Naples, he had also decided to replace Villeneuve with Vice-Admiral Rosily de Mesros. This crucial and long-threatened decision, together with its lengthy delivery time to Villeneuve was a major cause of the battle off Cape Trafalgar. It was the primary reason why Villeneuve weighed anchor on 19 October, despite knowing that a British Fleet under the command of the redoubtable Nelson was waiting for him, and despite the fact that the fleet Council of War, signed by all the French

---

## Rear-Admiral Pierre René Marie Etienne Dumanoir le Pelley

Dumanoir was born in 1770 of an long-established noble family that owned large estates in the Cotentin area of France and had already provided the French Navy with two admirals. It was no surprise that young Pierre Dumanoir followed his forebears into the King's Navy at the age of seventeen. He rose steadily if inconspicuously up the lower rungs of the promotion ladder to frigate captain. Then, in 1799, he commanded the frigate in which Generals Marmont, Murat and Lannes escaped back to France in 1799 after Napoleon's campaign in Egypt and Syria. The little squadron also carried Napoleon himself as he abandoned his army and fled in secret. As a reward Dumanoir was one of several captains to receive immediate promotion to flag rank, aged only twenty-nine. He later gained some experience as a rear-admiral as second-in-command to Admiral Linois off Algéciras.

At Trafalgar he was the second-in-command of the French Fleet with his flag in the 80-gun *Formidable*. He commanded the 3rd Squadron, the rear in the order of sailing, which became the van when the Combined Fleet wore together that morning. After the battle was joined and the British had cut the allies' line Dumanoir's ships continued to sail away to the north-west for about an hour and a half before finally, in response to desperate signals, turning back to assist the stricken centre and rear. His arrival, with only half of his divided squadron, had little effect on the outcome and he led his four ships away in a wide swing to the west. On 4 November Sir Richard Strachan's squadron

intercepted them, and after a fight in which Dumanoir was wounded he and all his men went into captivity while his ships were absorbed into the Royal Navy.

Dumanoir was not exchanged until 1809, when he went home to face a court of enquiry into his actions at Trafalgar and for losing the four ships to Strachan. This court exonerated him as far as Trafalgar was concerned and recommended that he be placed on half pay for losing his ships. Napoleon would have none of it and ordered a court martial for Dumanoir and his captains who had struck their colours. Convening in January 1810, it found Dumanoir not guilty of professional misconduct and accordingly acquitted him and handed him back his sword. One member of the court, Rear-Admiral Cosmao, who had captained the *Pluton* at Trafalgar, seemingly voted for a guilty verdict. In 1816 Napoleon, on his way to exile in St Helena on board the *Northumberland*, told Rear-Admiral Sir George Cockburn that he had exerted all his influence to have Dumanoir shot or broken; to his pleasure Cosmao broke his own sword in disgust when Dumanoir got his returned.

Napoleon either quickly forgot or quickly forgave the unfortunate Dumanoir as within fifteen months of the court martial the latter was a vice-admiral and Governor of Danzig, which he held with great credit during the long siege until January 1814. At the restoration of the monarchy Dumanoir was made a count, and he died in 1829 in his sixtieth year.

## Rear-Admiral Charles Magon de Clos-Dore

Magon was acknowledged to be hot-tempered, daring, even reckless. It has been suggested that he would have made a better commander of the French Fleet than Villeneuve and that had he been in that position on the return from the West Indies the action off Cape Finisterre against Calder would have had a more decisive outcome. Perhaps even more relevantly, Magon might not have disappointed Napoleon at Boulogne as Villeneuve did.

Magon was born in 1763, which made him the same age as Villeneuve, forty-three, at Trafalgar. He came from a noble Breton family and entered the navy as a boy. He was first under fire at fourteen as an *aspirante* (midshipman) on Comte d'Orvillier's flagship in his battle with Admiral Keppel off Ushant. 1781 found him in the Caribbean where he participated in de Guichen's indecisive actions off Martinique against the British under Rodney. Magon's ship, the *Caton,* was badly damaged and was withdrawn from the fleet, which meant he missed Rodney's crushing defeat of de Grasse off Dominica in April 1782 (Rodney later boasted that in two years he captured four enemy admirals, two Spanish, one French and one Dutch). Nevertheless, the *Caton* was later captured and Magon became a prisoner of war.

As a captain he saw service in the Philippines. On his way home he safely escorted two Indiamen ships laden with valuable freight and was rewarded by a grateful Compagnie des Philippines with an ornamental belt, richly decorated with silver. At Trafalgar Magon displayed it on the quarterdeck, telling his crew that the first man to board an enemy ship could have it. In 1804, then a

rear-admiral, Magon was given command of the advanced guard of gunboats selected to lead the invasion flotilla across the Channel should an invasion ever get under way. From there he was sent to Rochefort.

In April 1805 he received orders to take troops and two ships-of-the-line (*Algéciras* and *Achille*) to reinforce Villeneuve in the West Indies. He arrived in early June off Martinique and was present at the engagement with Calder on 22 July on the fleet's return to Europe. When Villeneuve signalled to call off the fight Magon flew into a violent rage on his quarterdeck and, according to a witness, foamed at the mouth and yelled insults at Villeneuve's ship as it passed nearby – this was the occasion on which he threw his wig and telescope overboard as related in the main text.

At Trafalgar Magon was the third in command of the French Fleet with his flag on the 74-gun *Algéciras.* He commanded the second squadron of the Squadron of Observation under Gravina in the original order of sailing. It was towards the end of the afternoon that his ship became entangled with two British ships and was raked from end to end by the 80-gun *Tonnant.* While trying to organize boarders Magon was hit in quick succession by three musket balls. The first removed his hat and wig, the second hit his right arm and the third his shoulder. In great pain and bleeding profusely, Magon remained standing on his quarterdeck shouting orders for boarding. A few moments later he was struck again, in the stomach, by a piece of flying metal or a roundshot. He was killed instantly, dying as he would have wished.

---

and Spanish senior commanders, had agreed not to sail. The sequence of events was as follows.

On 16 September Napoleon decided to replace Villeneuve by Rosily and instructed Decrès to implement his decision: 'You will dispatch Admiral Rosily to take command of the fleet, giving him letters instructing Villeneuve to return to France and account to me for his conduct.' Napoleon was promoting Rosily to admiral. Although this was a temporary title conferred for the duration of a campaign on flag officers commanding at least 15 line-of-battle ships it had not been given to Villeneuve. The snub was undoubtedly deliberate.

On 18 September Decrès wrote to Rosily enclosing a copy of the orders the Emperor had sent to Villeneuve concerning the expedition to Naples, as they were now also his orders. In his covering letter he wrote:

> It is the Emperor's intention that you should proceed in all haste to the port of Cadiz; and I am informing Vice-Admiral Villeneuve that you are appointed to supersede him; I am also informing M. de Gravina, who commands His Catholic Majesty's naval forces.
>
> M. de Villeneuve is receiving orders to have you proclaimed as admiral, the rank which His Majesty is conferring on you. ...
>
> I repeat that the Emperor attaches the greatest importance to your discharging your mission without delay, but if circumstances should oppose insuperable obstacles His Majesty desires that at least you will cause either the whole Fleet or several divisions to leave port whenever the weather permits. These frequent sorties will maintain the crews in activity, they will drive off the enemy, will put an end to this blockade which is an insult to the flags of the two Powers ...

Although complying with Napoleon's instructions, Decrès endeavoured to give his old friend a last chance to redeem himself, to save himself the humiliation of being stripped of his command in front of the fleet before returning to Paris in disgrace. Decrès took two actions. First, he took the Emperor's words literally and did not write direct to Villeneuve telling him he was being replaced; instead he entrusted the letter to Rosily to deliver personally on his arrival in Cadiz. It would be several weeks, therefore, before Villeneuve knew (officially) of his dismissal – in the event Rosily took some five weeks on his journey. But Decrès had sent Villeneuve his orders to sail for the Mediterranean on 16 September (they arrived on the 28th) so he was giving Villeneuve time in which to sail while still in command. Second, Rosily was given instructions about what to do if faced by 'insuperable obstacles' and 'leaving port whenever the weather permits', and told to make 'frequent sorties' to 'maintain the crews in activity' that had not been in Villeneuve's orders. In other words Villeneuve had *not* been given a plausible reason to delay getting the whole fleet into the Mediterranean. To make sure there was no official leak of this forthcoming change of command Decrès also informed General Beurnonville in Madrid and Agent-General Le Roy in Cadiz via letters also carried by Rosily.

Rosily arrived in Madrid, via Bayonne, on 10 October – he was then 400 miles from Cadiz – and handed Decrès' letter to Beurnonville. But then he met an accident; the ambassador wrote, 'Vice-Admiral Rosily has broken one of the splinter-bar-stays of his carriage, which will oblige him to spend the whole of tomorrow in Madrid; but he will be on the road for *Cadiz* [emphasis in original] at a very early hour the day after ...'. He was not. Beurnonville wrote again on 14 October:

Rosily would have proceeded more rapidly to Cadiz, but that he had to become acquainted with the resources at his disposal and with our arrangements; it was also necessary for me to take some precautions respecting the brigand-infested roads through Andalusia … He left this morning … I have every reason to believe that Vice-Admiral Rosily will reach Cadiz before Vice-Admiral Villeneuve will be able to come to a decision.

Beurnonville neglected to mention that there was no mounted escort through Andalusia – Rosily would have to progress at the pace of his plodding militia escort. In a letter six days later, Beurnonville estimated Rosily's arrival date in Cadiz as 23 October.

Meanwhile, Villeneuve was continuing his waiting game at Cadiz. If he was hoping that Commodore Allemand's squadron from Rochefort and Rear-Admiral Salcedo from Cartagena would conduct operations to distract some of Nelson's ships away, he was disappointed. Allemand had been chasing a convoy off the Portuguese coast and successfully dodging the attempts of Calder and Collingwood to catch him. Although on 11 October Allemand was north-west of Lisbon he never came close to Cadiz. Salcedo got under way on 10 October with four ships, supposedly looking for Craig's convoy, but his was a feeble effort that petered out within forty-eight hours.

Then on 15 October Villeneuve got word of Rosily having been seen at Bayonne en route to Cadiz. It came as something of a shock. Why had he not been informed? And why was Rosily coming? He was much senior to Villeneuve, so perhaps the rumours that he was to be replaced could be correct. But Rosily was an elderly admiral who had not been to sea for many years – perhaps he was just coming to advise or report back to the Emperor on the situation. It was all very disconcerting. Three days later Villeneuve, hearing that Rosily had reached Madrid and with rumours about his replacement mounting, became convinced that his time in command was almost over. He decided to sail.

That same day, 18 October, he wrote to Decrès:

I am informed that Vice-Admiral Rosily has arrived at Madrid, the common report is that he is coming to take over the command of the Fleet; undoubtedly I should be delighted to yield him the foremost place if I am permitted to occupy the second; it is due to his seniority and to his abilities, but it would be too terrible to me to lose all hope of having an opportunity of showing that I am worthy of a better fate. I can only explain the silence that you have maintained on Admiral Rosily's mission by the hope that I should have been enabled to accomplish the mission with which I am entrusted at this moment, and whatever may be the obstacles, if the wind allows me to work out, I shall put to sea the first thing tomorrow.

## Villeneuve's Letter of Dismissal

Signed by Decrès as Minister of Marine, this letter was never received by Villeneuve.

Vice-Admiral Villeneuve.
The 3rd complementary day of Year XIII [20 September 1805].

M. le Vice-Admiral,

His Majesty the Emperor and King has just appointed Vice-Admiral Rosily to the command of the naval forces assembled at Cadiz and has given orders that you are to proceed to Paris in order to give an account of the campaign on which you have recently been employed.

You are therefore, as soon as Vice-Admiral Rosily hands you this dispatch, to make over to him the command of the Fleet and he will be proclaimed there as admiral.

You will at the same time hand over all the plans that I have forwarded to you and especially that of Naples, the memoranda and the papers, the knowledge of which is of consequence to the success of the operations with which he is entrusted, and you are to proceed to Paris without delay, agreeable to His Majesty's orders.

Accept, M. le Vice-Admiral, the assurance of my due consideration.

Villeneuve had understood Decrès' manoeuvrings, and realized that he had been given a chance to save his honour. He took it. He ordered Magon to get under way with seven ships to try to cut off the British frigates in a surprise sortie; the rest of the fleet was to follow him.

## Villeneuve's plan
### Fleet organization
The diagram overleaf shows how Villeneuve organized his Combined Fleet for sailing. He split the squadrons with due regard to the nationalities and sensitivities of his subordinate admirals. Gravina – who had voiced no dissent to the plan, possibly because he realized the fleet was very unlikely to reach Naples – was not only his deputy as commander-in-chief but also had overall command of the largest squadron, the squadron of observation with 12 ships-of-the line and two frigates. Gravina had direct command over this squadron's first squadron with his deputy, the fiery Magon, commanding the second squadron. As was normal practice Villeneuve took personal control over the Fleet's first squadron, which would be in the centre of the line. A Spanish admiral (Cisneros) sailed with him in the four-decker *Santisima Trinidad*. The second squadron, designated the van in the order of sailing, was under Spanish command (Alava) while the third squadron, under the Frenchman Dumanoir, was intended as the rear. In the event the fleet turned about, reversing the order of sailing and line of battle, during which a number of individual ships lost their proper places. The ships were mixed by nationality within the squadrons, none having fewer than three Spanish ships and the squadron of observation having alternating French and Spanish ships in the order of sailing. Villeneuve's intention was to avoid divisions; he had written to Napoleon from Corunna on 3 August, 'I think it desirable that in forming the line of battle we should intercalate the Spanish ships among the French; the circumstances of a naval action often place the fleet in extraordinary situations, and the glory or blame which might result should be shared by the two navies.'

### Fleet orders
In the main these orders were a re-issue of those Villeneuve had given to his fleet before it left Toulon, dated 21 December 1804. They are the equivalent of Nelson's Memorandum. The important instructions are quoted below with some general comments.

During the night I shall make no signals except those that are absolutely necessary … I by no means propose to seek out the enemy; I even wish to avoid him in order to proceed to my destination. But should we encounter him, let there be no ignominious manoeuvring; it would dishearten the crews and bring about our defeat.

## Combined Fleet Structure at Trafalgar

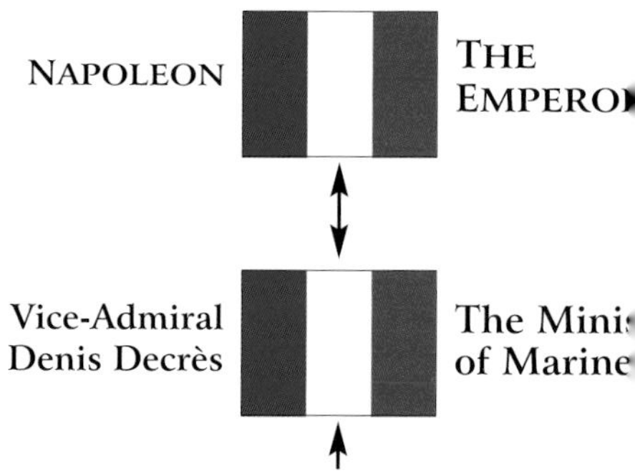

NAPOLEON — THE EMPEROR

### Notes
- Napoleon retained personal strategic control, Decrès acting mainly as a forwarding office.
- Overall command of the fleet belonged to the French (under Villeneuve) as they were the main prosecutors of the war and provided more ships (18).
- The second-in-command was the Spaniard Gravina, who also commanded the larger squadron.
- Each nation had three subordinate admirals present, with two squadrons under French and two under Spanish control. The ships were fairly evenly divided by nationality between squadrons.

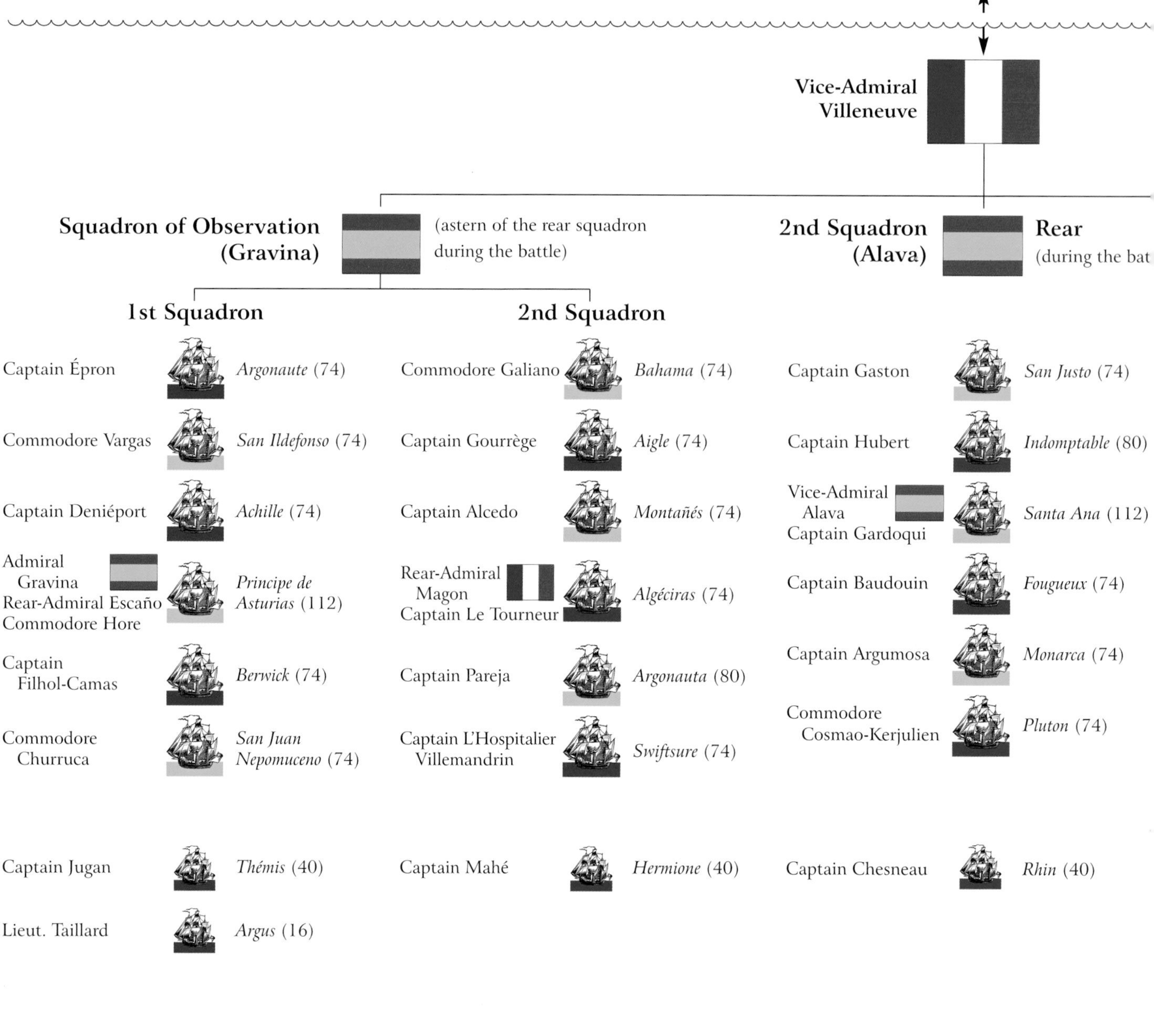

Vice-Admiral Denis Decrès — The Minister of Marine

Vice-Admiral Villeneuve

**Squadron of Observation (Gravina)** (astern of the rear squadron during the battle)

**2nd Squadron (Alava)** Rear (during the battle)

| 1st Squadron | | 2nd Squadron | |
|---|---|---|---|
| Captain Épron | Argonaute (74) | Commodore Galiano | Bahama (74) |
| Commodore Vargas | San Ildefonso (74) | Captain Gourrège | Aigle (74) |
| Captain Deniéport | Achille (74) | Captain Alcedo | Montañés (74) |
| Admiral Gravina / Rear-Admiral Escaño / Commodore Hore | Principe de Asturias (112) | Rear-Admiral Magon / Captain Le Tourneur | Algéciras (74) |
| Captain Filhol-Camas | Berwick (74) | Captain Pareja | Argonauta (80) |
| Commodore Churruca | San Juan Nepomuceno (74) | Captain L'Hospitalier Villemandrin | Swiftsure (74) |
| Captain Jugan | Thémis (40) | Captain Mahé | Hermione (40) |
| Lieut. Taillard | Argus (16) | | |

**2nd Squadron (Alava)**

| | |
|---|---|
| Captain Gaston | San Justo (74) |
| Captain Hubert | Indomptable (80) |
| Vice-Admiral Alava / Captain Gardoqui | Santa Ana (112) |
| Captain Baudouin | Fougueux (74) |
| Captain Argumosa | Monarca (74) |
| Commodore Cosmao-Kerjulien | Pluton (74) |
| Captain Chesneau | Rhin (40) |

*Comment*

Although Villeneuve states here that he would prefer to avoid a battle he is fully aware, as are his captains, that this is unlikely. His aim is to go through the Straits into the Mediterranean and on to Naples. The last sentence underlines how he appreciated the severe limitations under which his crews would sail and fight. 'No ignominious manoeuvring' put it neatly. Unfortunately for Villeneuve he felt compelled to order his fleet to make such a manoeuvre (wearing) prior to battle. The resultant loss of time and formation was disheartening to both crews and their commander.

**Notes**
- This was the command set-up at Cadiz prior to sailing. The order of sailing early on 21 October was squadron of observation, then the second, first and third squadrons. When the fleet wore at about 8.30 a.m. the order of sailing was reversed, the squadrons lost formation and command became more difficult.
- The squadrons were of unequal size, with the squadron of observation being the largest and then the first (centre) squadron.

**Ashore**

**At Sea**

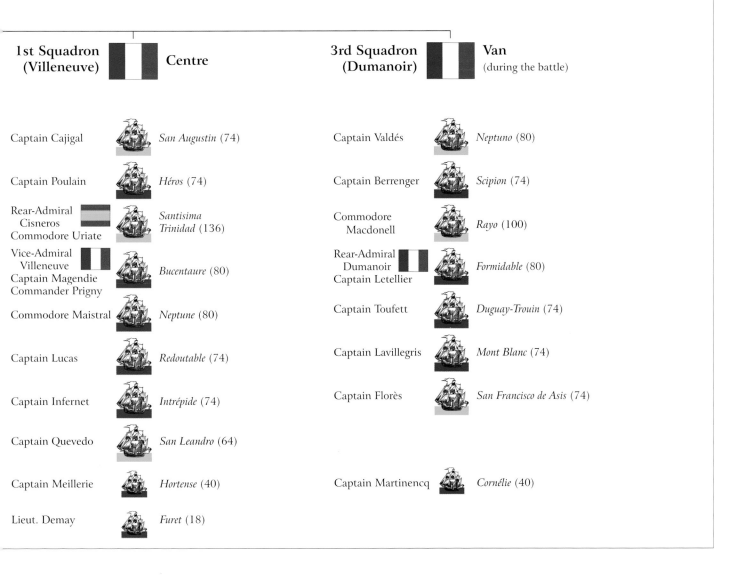

**1st Squadron (Villeneuve)** **Centre**

Captain Cajigal — San Augustin (74)

Captain Poulain — Héros (74)

Rear-Admiral Cisneros / Commodore Uriate — Santisima Trinidad (136)

Vice-Admiral Villeneuve / Captain Magendie / Commander Prigny — Bucentaure (80)

Commodore Maistral — Neptune (80)

Captain Lucas — Redoutable (74)

Captain Infernet — Intrépide (74)

Captain Quevedo — San Leandro (64)

Captain Meillerie — Hortense (40)

Lieut. Demay — Furet (18)

**3rd Squadron (Dumanoir)** **Van** (during the battle)

Captain Valdés — Neptuno (80)

Captain Berrenger — Scipion (74)

Commodore Macdonell — Rayo (100)

Rear-Admiral Dumanoir / Captain Letellier — Formidable (80)

Captain Toufett — Duguay-Trouin (74)

Captain Lavillegris — Mont Blanc (74)

Captain Florès — San Francisco de Asis (74)

Captain Martinencq — Cornélie (40)

If the enemy be to leeward [they were not], we, being free to manoeuvre, will form our line of battle; we shall bear down on him together; each of our ships will engage her opposite number in the enemy line and must not hesitate to board if the circumstances be favourable.

*Comments*
Villeneuve's intention, if the Combined Fleet found itself with the enemy to lee, was simple – it had to be. Each ship would, on his signal, turn together towards the enemy and sail directly at the enemy ship opposite – almost exactly what Collingwood's

ships did at Trafalgar. This would have the effect of bringing on a massive mêlée in which Villeneuve encouraged his captains to board. Knowing the lack of seamanship skills among his crews, he intended to cut Nelson's line in many places to give his ships the chance of raking the enemy at close range, and then make use of his advantage in troop and sharpshooter numbers to sweep the enemy's upper decks with musketry before boarding.

> Any captain commanding that is not under fire will not be at his post; any whose next ahead or next astern is closer than he to the enemy will not be doing his duty and a signal recalling him to his post will be a reflection on his honour.

*Comments*
Here we have Villeneuve giving almost identical instructions as Nelson – 'no Captain can do very wrong if he places his Ship along-side that of an Enemy'. Like Nelson he appreciated the problems of signalling in a battle and wanted his captains to know what was required of them in those circumstances. In the event Villeneuve was forced to make frantic signals for Dumanoir to join the battle.

> The frigates [he had five] are also to take part in the action; I have no need of them to repeat my signals; they must select a position where their co-operation may be of advantage in securing the defeat on an enemy ship, to support a French vessel over hard-pressed, to take her in tow or to render such other

assistance as may be necessary. What glorious opportunities present themselves to the young officers commanding frigates in such an action …

*Comments*
This instruction to frigates to abandon signalling and get involved in the exchange of broadsides is most unusual. A frigate's task in battle was to repeat signals, and the convention was that no ship-of-the-line would open fire on her unless she fired first. Villeneuve hopes that the frigates' joining the action against a hard-pressed ship will swing the balance – as indeed it might in some circumstances, though it might also invite disaster for the frigates.

> If on the other hand, the enemy appears to windward [as was the case] of us and exhibits the intention of attacking us, we shall await him in close-formed line of battle. It will be for the discretion and skill of the leading ship to make only such sail as is necessary and to keep to the wind only as needful to assist the formation of this order.

*Comments*
Here Villeneuve deals with the situation that occurred at Trafalgar. Being to the lee he accepts he must await an enemy attack and intends to do so in line. He stipulates a close line – that is one with gaps of perhaps 30 to 40 yards between ships. The leading ship is to reduce speed so that larger gaps do not appear. At the battle the Combined Fleet's line was ragged with large gaps, with some ships doubled up, concave in the middle, and the fleet spread over about four miles. This was the result of several factors, one of which was the van squadron initially sailing away from the action as it developed astern.

> The enemy will not confine himself to forming on a line of battle parallel with our own and engaging us in an artillery duel, in which success lies frequently with the more skilful but always with the more fortunate; he will endeavour to envelop our rear, to break through our line and to direct his ships in groups upon such of ours as he shall have cut off, so as to surround them and defeat them.
>
> In this case the captain in command must consult his own daring and love of honour far more than the signals of the Admiral, who perhaps being engaged himself and shrouded in smoke, may no longer have the power of making any. Here again it is a case of repeating that a captain who is not under fire is not at his post. The formation being broken, every effort must be exerted to go to the assistance of the ships assailed and to close on the flagship …

*Comments*
Ten months before Trafalgar, Villeneuve is predicting almost precisely how Nelson would attack if he was to windward of the Combined Fleet. He had foreseen, probably because of what he saw at the Nile, how such a battle would unfold. In these circumstances he foresaw a mêlée-type engagement where captains would be required to take their ships to the centre of the action without awaiting orders. A captain not under fire was not doing his duty.

On 18 October Villeneuve was informed that a signal had been received from the Spanish signal station at Algéciras, overlooking Gibraltar, that an English convoy of some 50 ships, escorted by four ships-of-the-line, had sailed – Craig's convoy escorted by Louis' squadron. This was encouraging news. Nelson's fleet must have been reduced in numbers. Now was the moment; Rosily had yet to arrive, the only problem was the wind. Early on 19 October it was clear but the wind was light and variable. Nevertheless, Villeneuve hoisted the signal for the ships to weigh.

---

## Rear-Admiral Don Baltazar Hidalgo Cisneros

Cisneros was the third in command of the Spanish ships at Trafalgar, wearing his flag on the giant *Santisima Trinidad*. He had joined the Navy in 1770, thus having thirty-five years' service at Trafalgar. He spent much of that time in the Mediterranean and the waters off America; he took part in the operations against Algiers in 1778 and was responsible for the capture of several British privateers including the *Rodney* and *Nimbre*. He commanded the 74-gun *San Pablo* at the Battle of St Vincent, being one of only four captains to come in for praise after what was a severe drubbing. During the next four years he commanded a squadron in the Mediterranean and from Cadiz.

He was wounded at Trafalgar and eventually forced to agree the surrender of his ship, which had by then suffered heavily and been completely dismasted by the combined broadsides of the *Conqueror*, *Africa* and 98-gun *Neptune*. Although the *Santisima Trinidad* eventually foundered Cisneros was saved and avoided becoming a prisoner in England. He contributed to the cost of the state funeral mass for the dead of Trafalgar that was held in the Church of the Convent of Carmen on 21 November.

He was promoted vice-admiral in November 1805 and transferred to Cartagena. He played a prominent role in the war of independence of the Spanish colonies in South America and in 1809 commanded in Buenos Aires until he was arrested by the revolutionaries. He was repatriated to Spain in 1810 and became head of the Department of Cadiz in 1813. Promoted Minister of Marine in 1818, Cisneros ended his service as commander-in-chief at Cartagena where he died in June 1829. His portrait still hangs in the Museo Naval in Madrid.

# CONTROL

There must be communication between all elements of an organization if it is to function, and no commander of any rank can exercise control if he cannot receive information and give orders. Although in 1805 naval commanders-in-chief at sea had no computers, satellite radio links or radar they had the benefit of a comprehensive system of communication that had steadily developed over the previous century. Key to the system was the signals lieutenant on each flagship, who supervised the signalling system that allowed messages to be passed throughout the fleet. After the first lieutenant he carried more responsibility than any other officer of his rank. Not that he was a specialist in the same way a signals officer is today; every officer, master's mate and midshipman had to understand signalling – especially those on frigates.

Communication was conducted at three levels – strategic, tactical and individual. The first involved communication between the Admiralty and the commander-in-chief either in a home port or at sea. At this level the medium was usually written instructions carried overland safe-hand of an officer travelling by coach, thence by fast sloop, brig, cutter or frigate. By day less lengthy messages could go in a matter of minutes from London to Portsmouth or Paris to the French dockyards (and eventually to Ferrol in Spain) via the shutter telegraph stations linking them. Strategic communication could take anything from a few minutes by land telegraph to many weeks by sloop to India or beyond.

Tactical communication was that between the admiral and his subordinate admirals and captains. At sea this was mostly carried out by flag or light signals, sometimes combined with gunfire; if ships were close enough together messages could also be hailed across. However, it was also commonplace to communicate via written instructions and personal contact. Ship's boats would ferry captains to the flagship, or junior officers might be sent to collect instructions – the signal 'for lieutenants' ordered a lieutenant from every ship in the squadron to climb down into a boat and make for the flagship. Individual communications were those carried out on board a ship. This was easy out of action but difficult, and sometimes almost impossible, in battle. Personal contact between the captain, his officers and crew was continuous and routinely facili-

tated by the use of the ship's bell, boatswain's pipes and speaking trumpets. Each ship's General Order Book would set down certain signals for use within the ship such as 'clear for action' or 'beat to quarters'. The Order Book for the *Mars,* for example, stipulated that the signal for boarding parties to assemble was a long roll on the drum.

The Boarders who may be called upon either to board the Enemy or to repel the Enemy who may attempt to board the Ship, are to be attentive to the Drum; and upon the call of the long Roll, they are immediately to assemble on both Gangways according to their station, from which place their officers will lead them over.

## Signal and Telegraph Stations in England

In 1795 coastal signal stations were established on prominent points around the English coast, predominantly in the south and east; there were sixty-two such stations on the coast between Plymouth and Yarmouth. They were responsible for observing the movement of ships, warning merchant ships of enemy in the area and alerting the militia to any likely threat from the sea. They were often under the command of an elderly, half-pay lieutenant assisted by a midshipman and two seamen, with two cavalrymen attached to carry messages to nearby units or garrisons. Each station had a tower and mast, and signals were made by a combination of flags and balls by day and lights at night. The invasion threat from France ensured that the manning of these stations was taken very seriously.

Telegraph signalling was invented by a clergyman, the Reverend Lord George Murray, who received £2,000 for it. It involved the opening and closing of six shutters in accordance with a code for letters and numbers. The stations themselves were far from expensive. The cost of one consisting of two accommodation rooms was only £215 – plus two twelve-guinea telescopes and an eight-guinea clock. In 1796 the first telegraph signalling stations were set up on prominent hills to link the Admiralty with the main naval bases at Chatham, Deal, Portsmouth and Plymouth (completed in 1806). A link to Yarmouth via Dunstable Downs was established in 1808. A signal station was set up on the roof of the Admiralty building in Whitehall and a short message could be sent to Portsmouth and a reply received within fifteen minutes via eight intermediate stations; from the Admiralty to Plymouth thirty intermediate stations were necessary.

Both in port and at sea it was the admiral who received and dispatched important letters and messages. The flagship was the communications centre of the fleet. When part of a squadron or fleet a ship-of-the-line rarely had to initiate a signal except in emergencies. Frigates, however, frequently had to impart information by signal and were often termed 'repeating ships', because they repeated signals from one to another in a chain back to the flagship. Frigates watched, shadowed and reported enemy strengths, locations and movement. In battle they mostly hovered on the flank of the fleet with the duty of repeating the admiral's signals.

While loosely blockading Cadiz in the weeks preceding Trafalgar Nelson augmented his communication chain, which stretched for some 50 miles west of Cadiz, with three ships-of-the-line. They were positioned between the fleet and the frigates that cruised back and forth across the entrance to the harbour, their officer's spyglasses constantly trained on the enemy as they counted masts and logged movement.

## THE BRITISH FLEET
### Identification friend or foe
Identification friend or foe (IFF) has been an operational problem on land or sea (and more recently in the air) since man first resorted to warfare to solve problems. Even with today's sophisticated IFF equipment, mistakes in action are far from infrequent and 'friendly fire' losses occur; the natural tendency to shoot first and ask questions later is not easy to overcome. In Nelson's time, and assuming daylight, difficulties arose

when two ships first sighted each other just over the horizon – perhaps at a distance of 20 miles – and again in the rolling smoke and roar of battle.

On hearing the cry of 'Sail-ho on the starboard bow!' in wartime the officer of the watch would instantly inform the captain. On a clear day it was quite possible for the seaman on lookout at the masthead to spot the tops of the masts of a ship over the horizon, while to those below it was invisible. At this distance, even as more of the masts became visible, it was often not possible to tell a friend from a foe. The first thing the captain would want to know was the size of the ship. At a distance of many miles, a 74 was hard to tell from a frigate, both being square rigged and carrying three masts. Sometimes it was impossible to be certain until the hull could be seen, revealing the number of gundecks. If the captain was still unsure at this stage he would clear for action. The next thing to establish was the ship's nationality. Telescopes would be trained on the stranger, who might or might not be wearing a national flag. During hostilities many ships carried and hoisted neutral, or even enemy, flags to dupe the unwary. As the ships closed the British ship would fire a shot and make a challenge by signalling the ship to identify herself. If British she would be able to respond by hoisting her ship's number under a union jack – every ship was issued with a number, which was recorded in the Signal Book carried on all warships. For example, the *Victory*'s number was 703 so up would go the union jack then the numeral pennant followed by No. 7 – No. 0 – No. 3 (see below under Flags). The *Africa* was No. 14, the *Defence* 200.

The problem was that with ships being lost and new ones launched there was no effective way of keeping the Signal Books up to date. To some extent the admiral on a station could obviate this by the use of a pennant board (opposite is Nelson's fleet board issued for Trafalgar). The commander-in-chief allocated single and double pennants to each ship in the fleet, however small, together with the position to which they should be hoisted. The board was kept on the quarterdeck or poop and updated as new ships joined the fleet or others left. This 'pennant code' was essential to identify the intended recipient of a signal. For example, if Nelson wanted to signal to the *Africa* 'Make all sail possible with safety to the masts', he would first hoist the *Africa*'s pennant(s). If there was no doubt *Africa* could see the signal then her single red and white

## Admiralty Numbers of British Trafalgar Ships

The numbers allocated to Nelson's line-of-battle ships are given below. These were their official identification numbers and could be used when answering a challenge from a British ship. For example the *Conqueror*'s number was 132 – she would hoist the blue and yellow chequered numeral pennant over 1 over 3 over 2.

| | | | |
|---|---|---|---|
| *Achille* | 7 | *Mars* | 397 |
| *Africa* | 14 | *Minotaur* | 398 |
| *Agamemnon* | 15 | *Neptune* | 436 |
| *Ajax* | 6 | *Orion* | 455 |
| *Belleisle* | 88 | *Revenge* | 529 |
| *Bellerophon* | 89 | *Royal Sovereign* | 522 |
| *Britannia* | 83 | *Spartiate* | 582 |
| *Colossus* | 142 | *Swiftsure* | 580 |
| *Conqueror* | 132 | *Téméraire* | 655 |
| *Defence* | 200 | *Thunderer* | 660 |
| *Defiance* | 201 | *Tonnant* | 656 |
| *Dreadnought* | 198 | *Victory* | 703 |
| *Leviathan* | 376 | | |

## Flags Worn on the *Tonnant* during the Battle

It is impossible to say with certainty exactly how many recognition flags were worn on any particular ship in either fleet. A officer on the *Tonnant* wrote:

We had hoisted our colours before the action in different places; at the ensign staff, peak, and in the fore and main topmast shrouds, so that if one was shot away the others might be flying. A number of our fleet had done the same, and several of the enemy had followed our example. The French Admiral's ship [Rear-Admiral Magon in the *Algéciras*], who so gallantly attempted to board us, had his hoisted in three places. One of our men, Fitzgerald, ran up his rigging and cut away one of them and placed it round his waist, and had nearly after this daring exploit reached his ship, when a rifleman shot him and he fell between the two ships and was no more seen.

pennant would be hoist to the maintopmast head; if visibility was thought to be a problem then her double pennant – red and white over yellow – would be hoisted where best seen. The *Africa* (and other ships) then knew the following signal was for her alone.

In battle, in the midst of a close-quarter mêlée with the chaos, casualties, drifting banks of smoke, and the certainty of rigging being shot away and the possibility of masts falling and dragging flags with them, recognition was particularly difficult. In these circumstances captains and lieutenants on the gundecks, who could only see out through the gunports, had to decide instantly whether to fire at a ship suddenly looming through the smoke, perhaps a mere pistol shot away. It was to lessen the likelihood of friendly fire that Nelson ordered every ship to wear the large white ensign over the stern at the peak of the gaff and the union jack from the foretopmast stay. Replacing these flags as necessary was a vital duty.

### Flags and pennants

During the day, flags and pennants in combination were used for signalling. Apart from the signalling pennants there were four long pennants (more like streamers), one of which was worn permanently at the maintopmast head by British warships at sea (other nations had their own versions). Since the union jack ceased to be worn at sea following changes in the rig in the 1720s the distinguishing mark of the warship had become the long pennant. Illustrated on p. 434 is the British common pennant (tricolour) and the red, white and blue squadron pennants. By 1805 the rigid tactical division of fleets into three squadrons (red, white and blue) had become obsolete. This, together with the fact that the two columns at Trafalgar did not entirely correspond with the order of sailing issued on 10 October, makes it uncertain which ships wore which pennant at Trafalgar.

Flags were no use if they could not be seen, but there were many obstacles to visibility, which often came in combination. Most obviously, flags could not be used at night or in mist or fog. Alternative methods of communication were lights, guns, bells, horns, drums and musket fire (see below pp. 442–3).

Distance frequently prevented flags being distinguishable. For this reason flags were large. A first rate such as *Victory* would have a white ensign 20 feet broad and 40 feet long and a white pennant at the mainmast head 72 feet long. On third rates the

## Nelson's Pennant Board at the Battle of Trafalgar

### Single and Double Pennants

| | | | | | | | | | | Where hoisted as Single Pennants |
|---|---|---|---|---|---|---|---|---|---|---|
| Neptune | Royal Sovereign | Queen | Victory | Superb | Defiance | Unité | Tonnant | Colossus | Melpomène | Main |
| Lively | Phoebe | Chiffonne | Prince | Rénommé | Decade | Kent | Amazon | Aimable | Agamemnon | Fore — Topmast Head |
| Belleisle | Aurora | Etna | Britannia | Ambuscade | Revenge | Seahorse | Mary | Spencer | | Mizen |
| Thunderer | Africa | | Téméraire | Prince of Wales | | Defence | Achille | | | Starb. — Main |
| | | Minotaur | Bellerophon | Dreadnought | | Polyphemus | | Orion | | Larb. |
| Canopus | | | Tigre | Donegal | Swiftsure | Sirius | | Leviathan | | Starb. — Fore |
| Ajax | Zealous | Hydra | Euryalus | Amphion | | Niger | Naiad | | Endymion | Larb. |
| Conqueror | Juno | | Beagle | Weazle | Nautilus | Merlin | Maryanne | Jalouse | | Starb. — Mizen |
| Spartiate | | Thunder | Bittern | Termangant | Childers | Eurydice | | Halcyon | | Larb. |
| | Nimble | | | Entreprenante | | | | | | Cross Jack Yard Arm |

*Left axis:* Distinguishing Pennants of the Mediterranean Fleet
*Right bracket:* Starb./Larb. (Main, Fore, Mizen) = Topsail Yard Arm

Memo  Where the double Pennants are used they will be hoisted where last seen

Nelson & Bronte

Given on Board the *Victory* off Cadiz the 29th Sept. 1805

### Notes
- These pennants were used to identify ships and to indicate individual ships for whom a message was intended.
- The pennant board was a permanent feature on the quarterdeck/poop. Ships leaving the station would be erased and new ones inserted in a blank space.
- In this case neither the *Mars* nor *Pickle* have yet been allocated their pennants.
- Ships in bold were at Trafalgar..

### Examples
*Victory* would have hoisted this pennant at the starboard topsail yardarm of the mainmast when she signalled the *Defence*: 'Make all sail possible with safety to the masts.'

Two pennants would be needed to indicate the signal was for the *Defence* if there was doubt it could be seen at the yardarm. Both identifying pennants would be hoisted where most visible.

ensign was marginally smaller but the pennant the same. Signal flags were not quite square, measuring about 12 by 14 feet. However, even with large flags, a clear day, a favourable wind and telescopes, three leagues (nine miles) was the absolute maximum distance at which a signal flag could be distinguished.

The difficulty could be overcome. Ships could use very limited gun signals and/or large black canvas balls hoisted over, or in combination with, flags. A good example of the use of distance signalling occurred on 19 October when the *Mars* hoisted No. 370 – 'The enemy's ships are coming out of port.' *Mars* was the last of the repeating ships between Cadiz and the main fleet but initially watchers on the nearest ship, the *Bellerophon*, could not distinguish the flag colours. The first lieutenant, William Cumby, stared long and hard and was convinced they were 370.

I immediately reported this to Captain Cooke and asked his permission to repeat it. The *Mars* at that time was so far from us that her top-gallant masts alone were visible above the horizon [see diagram overleaf]; consequently the distance was so great for the discovery of the colours of the flags that Captain Cooke said he was unwilling to repeat a signal of so much importance unless he could clearly distinguish the flags himself, which on looking through his glass he declared himself unable to do.

Others looked but could not commit themselves. Shortly afterwards the *Mars*, seeing her signal had not been repeated, made the distance signal for 370. She hoisted a ball, pendant, square flag and pendant at the main, and a ball at the foremast. The two balls indicated 300 and the flags 70. *Victory* immediately acknowledged it – much to the annoyance of Cumby.

## Principal British Flags and Pennants at Trafalgar (not to scale)

### White Ensign

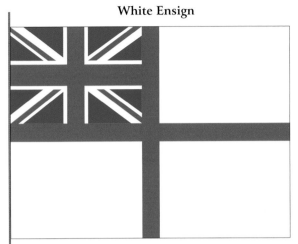

On Nelson's specific instructions all ships at the battle wore the White Ensign at the peak of the gaff (over the stern). The largest flag worn on the ships, at 20 feet wide it became established and recognized as the Colours of the Royal Navy.

### Union Jack

Much smaller than the Ensign, this ceased to be worn at sea following changes in the rig in the 1720s. To assist with identification Nelson ordered all ships to suspend the Jack from the foretopmast stays.

## Ordinary or Common Pennants

### Union Pennant

This pennant originated in 1661 and was known as the Union Pennant. It was worn at the maintopmast as a distinguishing mark of a British warship and kept flying at all times. It ceased to be used in 1864. It is uncertain which ships flew this pennant at Trafalgar rather than one of the squadron pennants below, as no fewer than 9 ships had left the fleet since Nelson's original order of sailing was issued on 10 October.

### Red Pennant

This was the pennant of the Red Squadron until 1864. It was worn at the maintopmast on all ships of that squadron when a fleet was divided into the 3 colour squadrons. There was no Admiral of the Red at Trafalgar so it is doubtful if this pennant was worn.

### White Pennant

Normally the pennant of the White Squadron.
At Trafalgar the fleet was not divided into colour squadrons so it is uncertain which ships flew this pennant, although as Nelson was a Vice-Admiral of the White it is possible that all, or most, ships in his column wore this pennant at the maintopmast.

### Blue Pennant

This belonged to ships of the Blue Squadron until 1864. There was no Blue Squadron at Trafalgar although Collingwood, commanding the lee column, was a Vice-Admiral of the Blue so it is possible the ships under his command wore this pennant (as shown on the individual ships in Section Six).

## Visibility over the Horizon

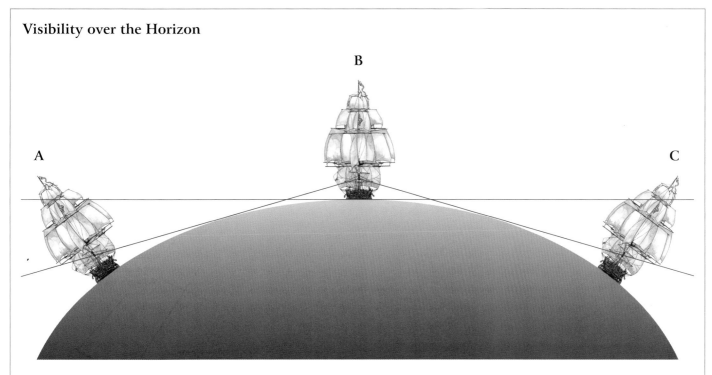

**B**

**A**

**C**

### Notes
The curvature of the earth's surface affects visibility from ships' decks. Ships **A** and **C** are hull down to **B** although she can see all their sails. **A** and **C** are entirely invisible to one another from the deck, though the topgallant of the one can be seen from the cross-trees of the other. In the diagram the curvature is intentionally much exaggerated, as are the sizes of the ships.

Other problems included:

*Distinguishing the colours*
Great care was taken not to use colours that did not contrast or show up clearly at a distance. For this reason green was never used, nor purple, brown or orange. Only five basic colours were used for all signal flags – black, white, red, yellow and blue – and blue and black, yellow and white, and blue and red were never used alongside one another. The colours had to contrast and the patterns kept bold and simple.

*Wind*
With no wind, or a very light breeze (as at Trafalgar), flags hung limply at a mast and were useless. This could be partially obviated by hoisting signal flags from halyards running at an angle from the mast or yard to the deck – rather like a slanting washing line. Also frustrating was a strong wind blowing directly from or towards the signalling ship, but by changing direction slightly the signalling ship could often overcome this.

*Obstructions*
Typical obstructions were the ship's sails or another ship. The problem was countered by the frigates being positioned to windward of the fleet (as at Trafalgar) and spread out some distance (perhaps half a mile) from the main line of battle. This ensured most, if not all, ships-of-the-line could see at least one frigate. They could also turn easily to make the most of the wind to stretch out the signal flags.

At least two sets of flags and pennants were kept on board, stowed in the flag locker that stretched across the stern of the poop deck near the mizzenmast on which most flags were hoisted. The locker was divided into compartments for each type of flag/pennant, often with a coloured picture (and/or number) of the flag it contained painted on the door to each compartment.

### Signal codes in use at Trafalgar
Most messages were signalled in a series of hoists of flags or pennants with the flags representing numbers, common sailing or tactical instructions (changing direction, anchoring, weighing, making more or less sail, preparing for battle, engaging the enemy, etc.) or specific words or letters. Once understood the system was not too complex, and although mistakes were not uncommon and signals were not always understood it was generally effective. If there was doubt as to whether a signal might go unnoticed then the ship originating it would fire a gun to attract attention. Sometimes a gun would be fired at intervals until the signal was acknowledged. A signal would be kept flying until repeated or acknowledged as being understood. It was the duty of all ships to repeat signals if necessary, while it was mandatory for all flagships of subordinate admirals to repeat general signals. The key was to make all the important signals before the action while the fleet was close together and the repeating frigates deployed and visible. Once battle started there were too many other pressing distractions, confusion and obstructed visibility to make any but the most urgent signals worthwhile attempting. There were three codes in use, *The Signal Book for the Ships of War 1799* (referred to here as the Admiralty Code), Popham's Telegraphic Code and the 'Private Signals' Code. These were additional to the admiral's Pennant Board described above. The first two were the most important.

## British Trafalgar Battle Flags and Pennants

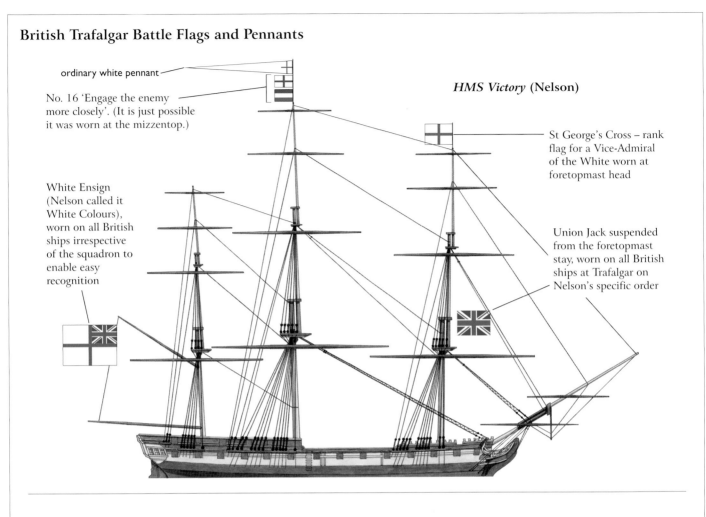

ordinary white pennant

No. 16 'Engage the enemy
more closely'. (It is just possible
it was worn at the mizzentop.)

*HMS Victory* (Nelson)

St George's Cross – rank
flag for a Vice-Admiral
of the White worn at
foretopmast head

White Ensign
(Nelson called it
White Colours),
worn on all British
ships irrespective
of the squadron to
enable easy
recognition

Union Jack suspended
from the foretopmast
stay, worn on all British
ships at Trafalgar on
Nelson's specific order

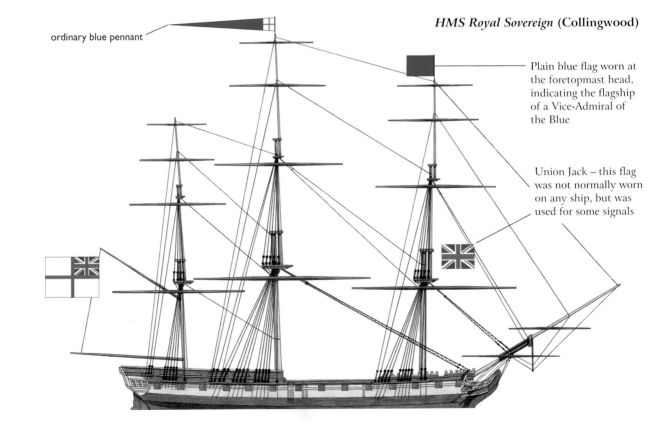

*HMS Royal Sovereign* (Collingwood)

ordinary blue pennant

Plain blue flag worn at
the foretopmast head,
indicating the flagship
of a Vice-Admiral of
the Blue

Union Jack – this flag
was not normally worn
on any ship, but was
used for some signals

## British Trafalgar Battle Flags and Pennants

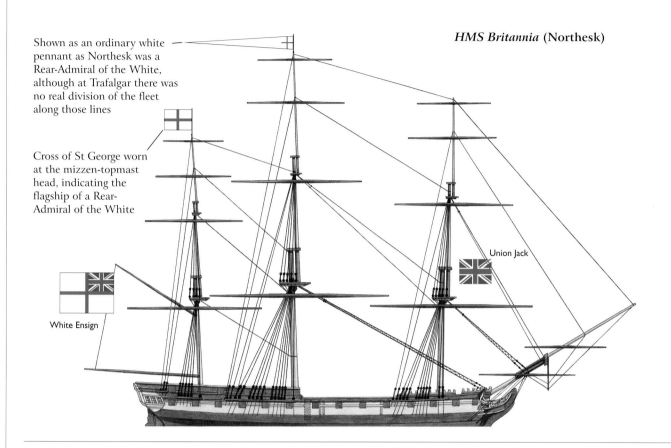

*HMS Britannia* (Northesk)

Shown as an ordinary white pennant as Northesk was a Rear-Admiral of the White, although at Trafalgar there was no real division of the fleet along those lines

Cross of St George worn at the mizzen-topmast head, indicating the flagship of a Rear-Admiral of the White

Union Jack

White Ensign

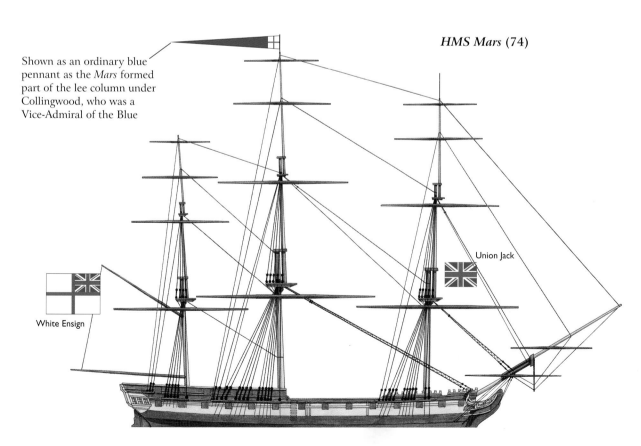

*HMS Mars* (74)

Shown as an ordinary blue pennant as the *Mars* formed part of the lee column under Collingwood, who was a Vice-Admiral of the Blue

Union Jack

White Ensign

## British Numeral Flags Used at Trafalgar (Admiralty and Popham codes)

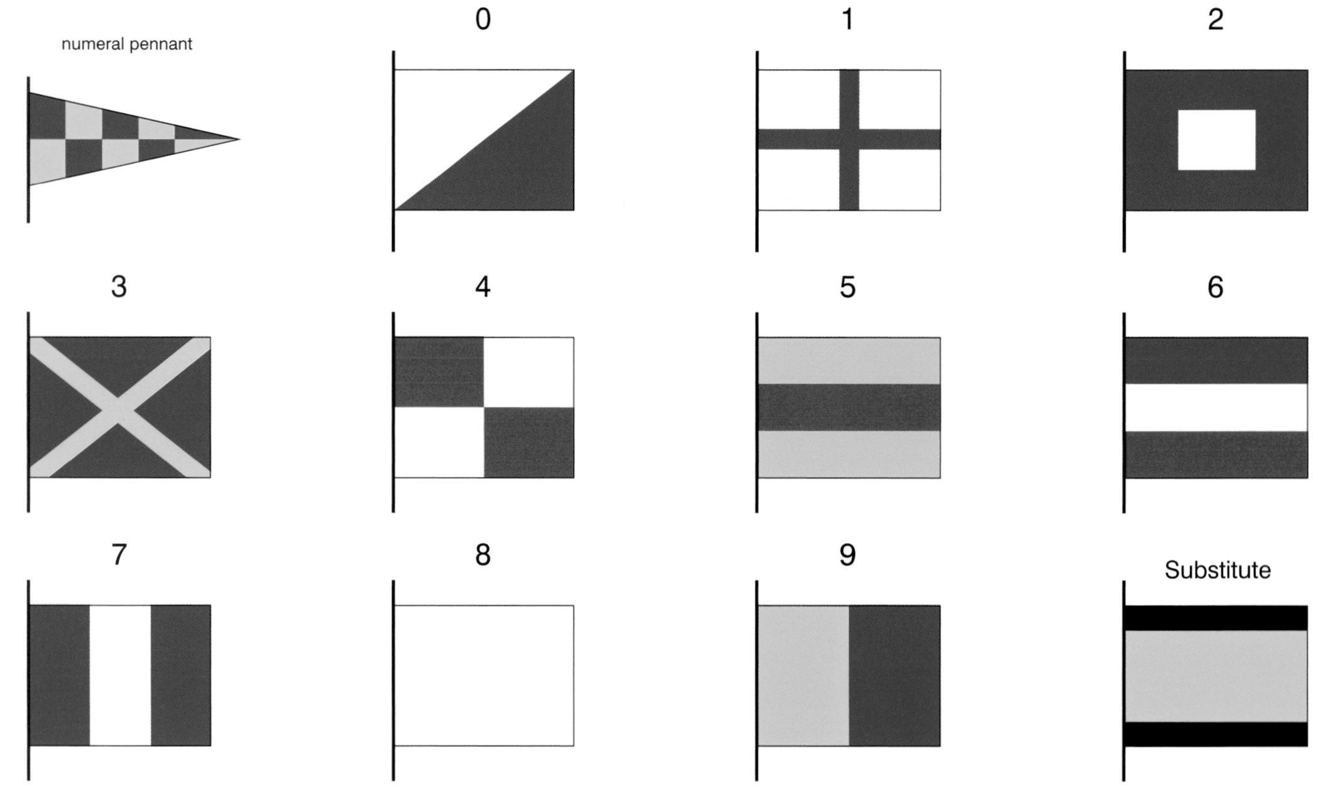

numeral pennant

0  1  2

3  4  5  6

7  8  9  Substitute

### Notes
- These basic numeral flags were common to both the Admiralty's *Signal Book for the Ships of War 1799* (as amended by Trafalgar) and Popham's Code.
- The fundamental principle behind both codes was the use of numbers to indicate messages or words in the codes. A single flag alone or under another flag indicated units. If there were two flags, the upper represented tens, the lower units. With three flags, the upper represented hundreds, the second tens and the third units. 1,000 was indicated by a ball (made of black canvas the same size as a flag) hoisted over the flags; hoisted below, the same ball meant 2,000.
- If the signal flags were to represent numbers only, as distinct from words from a code, then a blue/yellow chequered pennant would be hoisted above them.
- The Substitute flag was a 'ditto' flag repeating the flag above it.

### The Admiralty Code
This code was issued to every ship in the Navy and was signed by the Admiralty Board. It was a secret document so all captains were under orders to ensure it (along with other codes) was weighted down and thrown overboard if the ship was likely to be captured or lost by shipwreck. It contained the numerical signal flags (above), single flag signals (opposite) and a list of sailing or tactical instructions represented by a number. If a signal was purely numerical then the numerical pennant (blue/yellow chequered) would be hoisted above the numeral flags. A single flag meant units; when two flags were used the upper represented tens and lower units, and with three the upper hundreds, the middle tens and the lower units. To indicate the number was between 1,000 and 2,000 a ball would be hoisted above (the navy's term was 'superior') the numeral flags but below ('inferior') the pennant. For 2,000–3,000 the ball would be below – it was not thought necessary at that time to go beyond 2,999.

There were a number of single flags that had specific meanings, some examples of which are shown opposite. The Preparatory flag was important as it meant the signal below was not to be obeyed until it had been taken down and the signal itself left flying – critical with time-sensitive manoeuvres. If both the Preparatory flag and the signal itself were hauled down then the fleet was to prepare to comply but not actually do so until the signal was hoisted for a second time. A simpler method was to hoist a white flag below the signal, which indicated that the order was not to be complied with until the end of the day. An example from the Trafalgar signals was No. 63 – 'Prepare to anchor at the close of day'. This signal would have been hauled down with the Preparatory and a white flag, indicating it should be obeyed when it was hoisted a second time. (It never was, as after the battle Collingwood did not wish to anchor.) The master of the *Ajax* was one of the ships that recorded this signal in his log: '5 past 12, answered general signal 63 with preparative and a white flag [prepare to anchor as convenient].'

The Affirmative flag was hoisted to indicate a message was understood by the flagship – other ships used the white/red pennant. There was also a different 'negative /message not understood' flag for a flagship from that used by other ships. Some brief tactical orders such as 'Engage the enemy' or 'Chase the ships in view' could be indicated by a single flag. All ships to which signals were addressed were obliged to hoist the answering pennant as soon as they saw and understood it. The affirmative pennant was to be kept flying until the admiral (or other originator) had hauled the

# A Selection of Single Flag Signals, 1805

**Preparatory**

Hoisted above a signal giving a specific instruction, this flag ordered ships to prepare to obey that instruction as soon as the Preparatory flag was hauled down and the signal left flying. Always hoisted with signals directing the fleet to perform a manoeuvre together. Trafalgar example: Nelson to the fleet, 'Bear up and sail large on course East.'

**Telegraph**

Hoisted to indicate that the following signal was taken from the Popham Code, not the Admiralty one. Trafalgar example: the 'England expects…' signal.

**Finish**

This flag indicated the end of a message. If Popham's Code was being used, hauling down the Telegraph flag had the same meaning.

**Affirmative** (by flagship)

This flag was used by flagships only to indicate an affirmative response and that a signal had been understood. It was repeated by the last station.

**Affirmative** (by private/ individual ship)

Ships other than flagships responded in the affirmative by hoisting this pennant.

**Negative** (by flagship)

Negative, or message not understood.

**Negative** (by private/ individual ship)

Negative by ships other than flagships.

**Ship about to sail**

This was the 'Blue Peter'. When flying at the foremast head in port it indicated that the ship was due to sail and all crew ashore were to report onboard immediately.

**Engage the enemy**

With a red pennant over it, this flag meant 'engage closer'. It was also No. 4.

**An enemy in sight**



**Chase ships in view**

This flag was always followed by the bearing and if the whole fleet was involved 2 guns were fired. It was also No. 3.

**Union Jack**

Hoisted at the mizzen-topmast head together with the pennants of individual ships to order the captains of those ships to come aboard the flagship. At about 7.35 a.m. Nelson used this signal to summon the captains of the frigates (*Euryalus, Naiad, Phoebe* and *Sirius*) aboard the *Victory*.

**Truce**

On its own this flag indicated a truce or an order to discontinue the battle. The white flag today has the universal meaning of surrender or a truce. When hoisted below other flags it indicated the signal was not to be acted on until the end of the day – Nelson's signal 'Prepare to anchor after the close of day' would have required Preparatory – No. 6 – No. 3 – white flag.

signal down. As mentioned, it was rare for a ship other than the flagship to initiate a signal except in emergencies; extreme examples were No. 343 – 'The ship has sprung a leak' – and the even more alarming No. 344 – 'The ship has struck a shoal', a signal that required the captain to keep firing a gun until it was seen.

The bulk of the code (some 260 signals) listed two- or three-number signals with specific meanings. An example from Trafalgar is *Victory*'s general signal No. 72 – 'Form the order of sailing in two columns', which would have had the horizontal striped blue and white Preparatory flag hoisted over the No. 7 with the No. 2 below. By coincidence all three flags were blue and white. The Preparatory flag would have been hauled down with the signal left flying after acknowledgement, indicating the manoeuvre was to be carried out immediately. Quite complex instructions could be sent to specific ships. During the long morning approach to battle Nelson had occasion to tell the *Leviathan* to change her position. Up went the *Leviathan*'s pennants (blue/yellow over blue and yellow perpendicular stripes from the pennant-board code) followed by No. 269 ('Take station astern of the ships whose distinguishing signal will be shown after this signal has been answered'). *Leviathan* would respond with the 'affirmative/message understood' white/red pennant. Then, and only then, would the *Victory* hoist the pennants of the ship the *Leviathan* was sail astern of – in this case the *Téméraire*'s yellow over yellow pennants.

The union jack was normally used as a signalling flag, although it was also worn on all ships at Trafalgar as an aid to recognition. When hoisted at the mizzen-topmast head together with the pennant of the ships addressed, it indicated that those captains were to report to the flagship. Nelson summoned his frigate captains in this way at around 7.45 a.m. on 21 October. And, as mentioned above, a British ship could identify herself by hoisting the union jack over her Admiralty number.

The code included an elaborate system for points of the compass and bearings. It was based on four flags, each horizontally divided in half to represent one of the four quarters of the compass. The quarter from North to East was a flag red over white, North to West white over red, South to East blue over yellow and South to West yellow over blue. When indicating a direction the appropriate quarter flag was hoisted with the necessary combination of red, white, blue and Dutch pennants to indicate NNE or WNW or whatever compass point was required.

The Admiralty Code had its limitations and could be likened to a rather skimpy tourist's foreign-language phrasebook. To be able to carry out a reasonable conversation a dictionary was needed. Popham's Code provided it.

## The British Code Compromised

In July 1803 the 12-gun schooner *Redbridge* under the command of Lieutenant Lempriere was captured by the French. Lempriere had, like many of his peers, obtained an unofficial, small private copy of the 1799 Admiralty Code. Many junior officers did this, although they were not supposed to do so. However, Lempriere's much more serious mistake was in not disposing of the code by throwing it overboard when he realized capture was inevitable. The French found it, thus acquiring the operational code for the entire Royal Navy, and as Lempriere was a prisoner the Admiralty were unaware of what had happened. Not until several months later did London find out, when the captured *Redbridge*, now under French control, signalled using the British code to a British frigate off Toulon, instructing her to anchor. The frigate captain reported the incident to Nelson, who immediately changed his flags and informed the Admiralty. On 4 November 1804 a circular letter was sent to all commanders-in-chief instructing them to alter the numeral flags in accordance with the painted copy enclosed. These were the numeral flags in use at Trafalgar illustrated opposite.

*Popham's Telegraphic Signals (Code)*

Captain Sir Home Popham had invented his code five years before Trafalgar and revised it in 1803. Another updated version was issued to the Royal Navy in 1813 and Popham made final amendments in 1816. Using the same numeral flags as in the Admiralty Code, Popham devised a dictionary of words with corresponding numbers up to 2,994 (the word Zeal). Each letter was also allotted a number (see opposite) except that I and J were both represented by 9, and Popham's alphabet had V before U. This enabled any word not in the main code to be spelled out – as was DUTY in Nelson's famous signal. The words were arranged alphabetically under each letter in two columns, the words on the left being more common, those on the right less so and all starting with the number 1. By the use of basic words with their variations (and giving each the same number) it was possible for one number to have up to four or five meanings. For example under the letter E there were 64 numbers representing 195 words beginning with E – 259, say, could mean 'establish', 'established', 'establishing', or 'establishment' and was written in the vocabulary as '– 259 Establish-ing-ed-ment'. It was not difficult for the recipient to work out which meaning was intended from the general sense of the signal. So that it was clear which code was being used, a signal using Popham's code would always have the Telegraph flag (white over red triangles) hoisted above it (on a separate halyard). This was essential; otherwise, for example 329 could mean 'Enemy ships are coming out of port' (Admiralty Code) or 'his' (Popham's).

*Private Signal Codes*

These were separate codes drawn up by the commander-in-chief on a station for individual ships to use when making a challenge. They were, in effect, a series of prearranged passwords and responses using flags. Each involved a code that changed every ten days. The challenge consisted of a specific flag at the maintopmast head and another at the foretopmast head, and the correct response was indicated in the code. The day before Trafalgar Mr Ruckert, the master of the *Euryalus* off Cadiz, recorded in his log a good example of private signals being used for recognition purposes:

> At 8.20, perceived a line-of-battle ship with a brig in tow steering with all sail direct for the enemy within a very near distance. Made the private signal to her and proved to [be] *H.M.S. Agamemnon*. Made the signal to the *Agamemnon* for the enemy NE. Repeated it with many guns before it was noticed …

This code also contained the challenges and responses to be made at night using lights.

# Popham's Letter Code as Used at Trafalgar

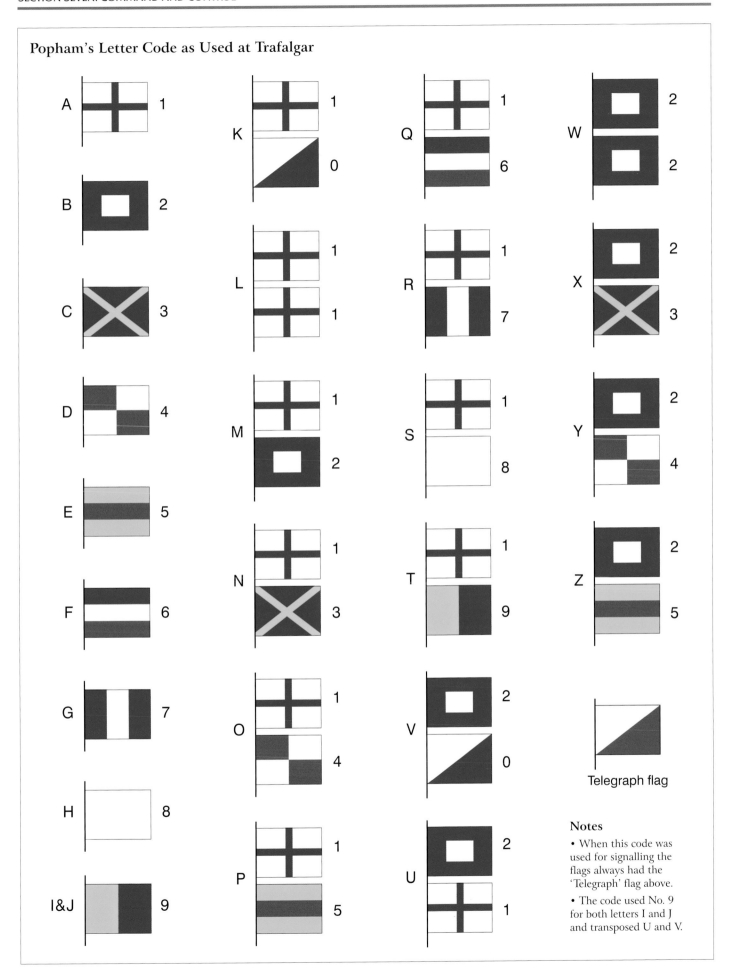

Telegraph flag

**Notes**
• When this code was used for signalling the flags always had the 'Telegraph' flag above.
• The code used No. 9 for both letters I and J and transposed U and V.

## Some Night (Light) Signals to Be Used in the Presence of the Enemy

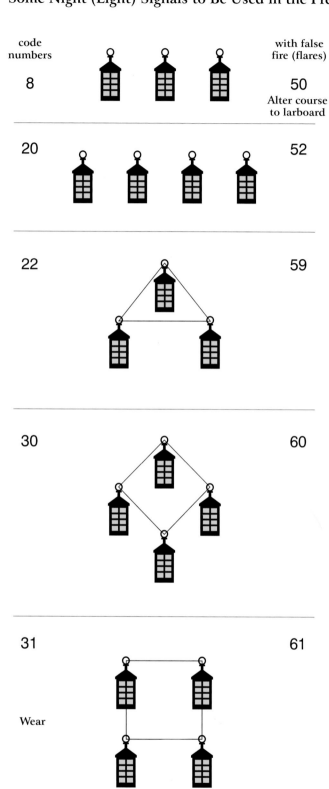

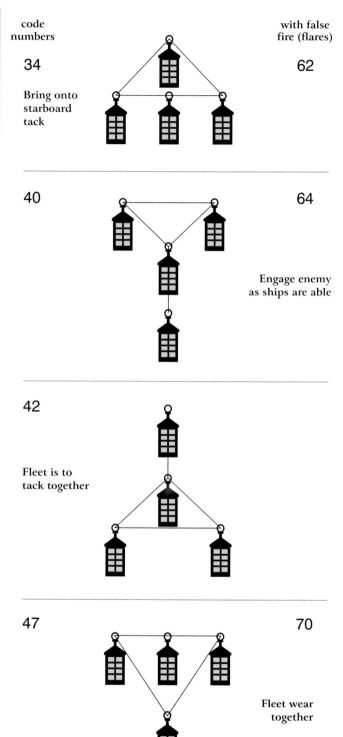

### Notes

- The lanterns, attached to a wooden frame, were shown at any part of the ship where best seen.
- This limited code was to be used in the presence of the enemy when guns could not be used.

- The lanterns were kept covered until placed in the form prescribed for the signal. This ensured all were shown at the same time. It was also important to cover them simultaneously to prevent the mistaking of the signal. Spare lights were kept in bags.

*Night signals*

Keeping in contact, passing information and signalling were always difficult at night and few fleet movements could be attempted. Night signals were made using lights (lanterns), rockets, false fires and guns in accordance with the Admiralty Code. False fires were made from gunpowder and wheat flour in the proportion 8:3. This mixture was contained in a paper tube made by rolling the paper thickly round a stick, which was then withdrawn and the contents hammered home. A match was used for lighting. A major problem, largely unavoidable, was that signalling at night gave a ship's approximate position away to friend and foe alike. Because lights were so easily obscured by sails they could be hoisted anywhere on the ship in order to be seen most clearly. In addition to signalling lanterns, in line of battle every ship was required to have one stern light and one at the bowsprit end permanently displayed. To ensure lights were shown at the same time and the signal not misunderstood, the lanterns were kept covered until in the position required for the signal, and covered simultaneously when they were no longer needed. Spare lanterns were kept ready in bags.

The code for night signalling equated lights with numbers that in turn represented messages in the signal book. When there was no enemy in range numerals were represented as follows:

| | |
|---|---|
| 1 | 2 lights at equal height |
| 2 | 2 lights one above the other |
| 3 | 3 lights at equal height |
| 4 | 4 lights at equal height |
| 5 | a false fire lit or a rocket fired |
| 10 | 1 gun (guns were always fired from the same side of a ship) |
| 20 | 2 guns (fired at 5-second intervals) |
| 30 | 3 guns (as above) |

Intermediate numbers were signalled by a combination of guns, lights, fires and rockets. For example, one gun with two lights at equal height meant 11; three guns followed by a false fire or rocket meant 35. To form line of battle in the dark (something to be avoided if at all possible) the flagship would fire five guns, hoist four lights and fire a rocket or light a false fire. Little wonder that when large fleets were trying to keep contact during darkness there was a constant booming and flash of rockets that could be heard or seen for miles around.

When the enemy was close, guns were not fired; instead a very limited code with lights and false fires was used. Some examples of this are shown opposite.

*Fog*

This was something of a nightmare as it meant that neither flags nor lights could be seen. Communication had to rely on sound, which included the use of guns, muskets, bells, drums, horns and voice (hailing). Guns were normally fired on the weather side and repeated only by flagships. The code was necessarily very limited. A gun fired every half hour meant the fleet or squadron was to continue on the same course under the same sail. The order to anchor was signalled by one preparatory gun followed by two guns after half a minute, and 'message understood' was a combination of drums and bells. If a ship struck a shoal or reef (not unlikely in a fog close inshore) the unfortunate captain signalled his plight by 'firing guns in quick succession with bells, drums, horns and muskets' – there could be no mistaking his distress!

## The French

The illustration overleaf shows only the three basic identification flags used by the French at Trafalgar. The large Tricolour Ensign was a ship's national colours and was hoisted over the stern. At Trafalgar some ships flew more than one ensign; we are told that both the *Pluton* and *Neptune* had three. The Tricolour had been adopted after the Revolution to replace the former royalist flag, which was predominately white – and easily confused with the British white ensign. Like other nations French ships carried the flags of other countries, it being a legitimate *ruse de guerre* to fly foreign colours to deceive an enemy. However, ships always fought under their own colours. It was the custom in the French Navy to 'enforce the colours' just prior to action, firing one or more guns to declare that the colours then flying were the true ones. As additional means of identification every French ship had a lozenge-shaped shield, painted blue over white over red and fixed to the stern. Like the British the French had command flags for the various commanders of the squadrons/divisions appropriate to their rank, but it is uncertain exactly which command flags were worn at Trafalgar.

The French signal code was based on that invented by the Chevalier du Pavillon (published in 1776). (*Pavillon* is also the French word for a nautical flag, and one wonders if it was named after the chevalier – the present writer remains uncertain.) It was a tabular code using two sets of ten flags hoisted where best seen. Each table had ten columns and ten rows and a number flag was depicted at the top of each column and left end of each row. By reading down and across the intersecting box could be located and the number in it cross-referenced to the signal of that number in the codebook. Tables in use were changed by the admiral with a specific flag signal.

## The Spanish

The two flags and pennant worn by Gravina's ships at Trafalgar are shown overleaf. Originally Spain's flags were, like the French and British versions, predominately white. In 1785 the king changed his naval flags by decree:

> In order to avoid the inconvenience and difficulties which experience has shown can be caused by the national flag used by my navy and other Spanish forces being mistaken ... for those of other nations, I have resolved that henceforth my warships shall use a flag divided lengthwise into three stripes, of which the top and bottom ones shall be red and each one quarter of the total width, the central stripe to be yellow bearing upon it my royal arms reduced to the two quarterings of Castile and Leon with the royal crown above; and the pennant with the same three stripes and the shield on a yellow square at the hoist.

A tabular signalling system, similar to that of the French, had been developed by Admiral José de Mazarredo, Nelson's opponent eight years before at Cadiz. A version of this system had been used for the combined Franco-Spanish Fleet in 1779 and undoubtedly another was devised for Trafalgar, as Villeneuve was able to signal to his entire fleet when necessary. On 20 September 1805 Admiral Decrès sent copies of the private signals in use in the French Fleet to Godoy in Madrid, who ordered them to be translated so that he could send them to all the officers commanding the Spanish vessels of war, but these translations would not have been available for Trafalgar.

All Spanish ships swung a large wooden cross that had been blessed by the priest from the boom-end over the taffrail before the start of a battle.

## French Flags and Pennant Worn at Trafalgar (not to scale)

### Tricolour Ensign

The 'Tricolour' Ensign or Colour adopted by Napoleon after the Revolution. It remains the French national flag today. The equivalent of the British White Ensign, it was hoisted over the stern of all French ships at Trafalgar.

### Tricolour Jack

The smaller French Tricolour jack was worn at the bow.

### Tricolour shield

This lozenge-shaped shield was fixed to the stern of French ships.

### Tricolour Pennant

This pennant was worn at the maintopmast head of all French ships at Trafalgar.

## SIGNALLING PROCEDURES

The following paragraphs relate to the British procedures but, apart from the different codes, both French and Spanish ships employed very similar methods. The main purpose of the signalling system was to allow the admiral to communicate with his captains. Within a fleet or squadron 90 per cent of all signals originated from the flagship. If he could the admiral either spoke personally to his captains (Nelson and Villeneuve both did this prior to Trafalgar) or summoned an officer to the flagship to collect instructions. It was a rule that any officer visiting a flagship had to take the 'orderly book' in which to write down verbal orders, and he would be required to sign for written papers. There were a number of general instructions – what today would be termed standing orders – designed to avoid unnecessary signalling. Examples were:

• Ships that could not maintain station for any reason were to quit the line, form astern and make every effort to keep up.

• If the admiral signalled to make more or less sail, repeating frigates were to take in or set sails as on the flagship.

• If the fleet was sailing into battle in two columns (as at Trafalgar), the columns were to be about one and a half miles apart, ships two cables (400 yards). The distance between the columns at the battle was something over a mile but some ships were closed right up while others were considerably more than two cables apart.

• In a line of battle, repeating frigates should deploy to windward unless ordered otherwise. British frigates at Trafalgar were to windward, French frigates (there were no Spanish frigates) to the lee.

• Ships were to conform with the admiral's movements unless ordered otherwise – there were special signals that indicated the flagship's movements were to be ignored.

• Subordinate flagships were required to repeat the commander-in-chief's signals. Other ships had a duty to repeat only if necessary.

## Spanish Flags and Pennant Worn at Trafalgar (not to scale)

### The Spanish Ensign

The Spanish Ensign, 33 feet wide, was worn at the battle over the stern of all her ships. The royal arms had been reduced to 'the two quarterings of Castile and Leon with the royal crown above'.

### Spanish Jack

Spanish Jack worn at the bow

### The Spanish Ensign in the National Maritime Museum

The Museum's biggest historic flag is the Spanish ensign, captured from the Spanish 74 *San Ildefonso* at Trafalgar. Made from narrow widths of red and yellow bunting hand sewn together with a linen hoist strip attached, it is about 33 feet wide and 45 feet long (British ensigns of the period were 20 feet wide). The ensign was hung in the crossing of St Paul's Cathedral during Nelson's funeral on 9 January 1806 and can be clearly recognized in contemporary engravings of the scene. There are plans to display it in the Queen's House for the bicentenary in 2005.

### Spanish Pennant

The pennant worn at the maintopmast head of all Spanish ships had the same three stripes, with the shield and crown on a yellow square at the hoist.

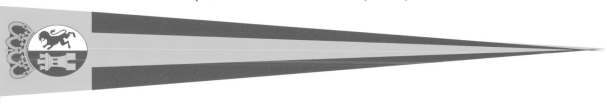

• Distant ships were required to 'stand towards the admiral if he indicates he has not understood' their signal.

The signals crew on a flagship was under command of the signals officer, usually a lieutenant of about middle seniority (fourth or fifth) – on other ships the duty often went to a midshipman. The signals officer was not a flag lieutenant, a modern term denoting an admiral's ADC with more responsibility for organizing social occasions than signalling. At Trafalgar Nelson's signals officer was Lieutenant Pasco, Northesk's was Lieutenant Roskruge and Collingwood's was Lieutenants Bashford and then Gilliard. It was an extremely vulnerable position in battle as the signals officer and all his staff remained exposed, mainly on the poop, throughout the action; at Trafalgar Roskruge and Gilliard were killed and Pasco and Bashford wounded. Under the signals officer would be perhaps a master's mate and one or two midshipmen, two or three petty officers or ABs, one of whom was likely to be rated a quartermaster or yeoman of signals. John King was such a man on the *Victory* – he

too was killed, as was AB Alfred Taylor. The remaining three or four men would be a mix of ordinary seamen or landsmen (such as John Roome who appears in Section Four) whose task was the actual hoisting and hauling down of the 'lifts' or groups of flags. For details of their various duties, see pp. 448–9.

Every signal sent and received had to be logged in the Signals Log, usually a chore given to a midshipman. The contents were supposed to be later transferred to the master's or captain's log, although judging from the masters' Trafalgar logs only a few key signals were copied across. Nelson's famous 'England expects …' signal is only mentioned in seven line-of-battle ships, but then it was hardly a crucial tactical message. The frigates repeated it, and we know it reached the *Spartiate*, the last ship in Nelson's column, where a diligent Acting Master Francis Whitney recorded, '11.59. The *Victory*, Vice Admiral Lord Nelson, made telegraph signals, the purport of which was: England expects every man will do his duty.'

Signals were hoisted on halyards in lifts of up to three flags (four was just possible) at a time. They were mostly hoisted at the mizzen where there were at least twelve halyards on each side of a flagship. Normally only flags that were kept permanently hoisted in battle were worn at other places. The *Victory* had Nelson's flag at the fore-topmast head and her long white pennant at the maintopmast head. This was also the location of signal 16 – 'Engage the enemy more closely.' Most short signals would be completed in a minute or so, only remaining hoisted until repeated or acknowledged. The 'England expects ...' signal was recorded at an average time of 11.50 in the logs of the seven ships that noted the time. *Victory*'s next signal ('Prepare to anchor ...') is recorded, again on average, as being received at 12.00 (noon). A reasonable estimate of the time taken for this signal of twelve lifts was about four minutes – fast work.

## British Trafalgar signals

The signals noted below are those significant ones made on 21 October between 6.00 a.m. and 12.25 p.m. This was the period of some six and a half hours during which the fleets slowly closed to give battle. All were made by either Nelson or Collingwood – the only other ship to initiate a signal during that time was the *Defence*, repeating a signal to the *Orion* to make more sail and change course slightly. The time shown is the average time taken from the logs that record it. The timings vary significantly; the 'England expects ...' signal is logged by seven ships at times varying from between 11.25 a.m. (*Orion*) to 12.10 p.m. (*Revenge*). Most ships put the time around noon. Some signals have been slightly shortened to save space.

| Signal | No. | By whom | To whom | Time logged |
|---|---|---|---|---|
| 1. Form the order of sailing in two columns | 72 | *Victory* | general | 6.00 a.m. |
| 2. Bear up and sail ENE | 76 | *Victory* | general | 6.14 a.m. |
| 3. Prepare for battle | 13 | *Victory* | general | 6.30 a.m.* |
| 4. Bear up and sail large on course E | 76 E flags | *Victory* | general | 6.50 a.m. |
| 5. Take station as convenient without regard to order of sailing | 265 | *Victory* | *Britannia Prince Dreadnought* | 7.24 a.m. |
| 6. Captain to come on board flagship | union flag over ship's pennants | *Victory* | *Euryalus Naiad Phoebe Sirius* | 7.50 a.m. |
| 7. Bear up and sail large on course steered by admiral | 76 | *Victory* | *Prince* | 8.30 a.m. |
| 8. Keep on larboard line of bearing though on starboard tack | 50 | *Royal Sovereign* | lee column | 8.45 a.m. |
| 9. Form larboard line of bearing, steering the course indicated | 42 (cancelled 50) | *Royal Sovereign* | lee column | 8.47 a.m. |
| 10. Make more sail | 88 | *Royal Sovereign* | lee column | 8.50 a.m. |
| 11. Interchange places in the line | 46 below *Belleisle*'s and *Tonnant*'s pennants | *Royal Sovereign* | *Belleisle Tonnant* | 9.22 a.m. |
| 12. Make more sail | 88 | *Royal Sovereign* | *Belleisle* | 9.25 a.m. |
| 13. Take station bearing SW from admiral | 267 SW flags below *Belleisle*'s pennants | *Royal Sovereign* | *Belleisle* | 9.30 a.m. |
| 14. Take station astern of *Téméraire* | *Leviathan*'s pennants 269 then *Téméraire*'s pennants | *Victory* | *Leviathan* | 9.36 a.m. |
| 15. Take station bearing from admiral as pointed out by compass signal | 267 below *Revenge*'s pennants | *Royal Sovereign* | *Revenge* | 9.40 a.m. |
| 16. Take station astern of *Royal Sovereign* | *Mars*' pennants 269 *Royal Sovereign*'s pennants | *Victory* | *Mars* | 9.41 a.m. |
| 17. Make more sail | 88 below *Revenge*'s pennants | *Royal Sovereign* | *Revenge* | 9.45 a.m. |
| 18. Alter course together one point to starboard | 81 below *Belleisle*'s and *Achille*'s pennants | *Royal Sovereign* | *Belleisle Achille* | 9.50 a.m. |
| 19. Lead the lee column | 97 below *Mars*' pennants | *Victory* | *Mars* | 9.55 a.m. |
| 20. Prepare for battle | 13 | *Victory* | general | 10.00 a.m. |
| 21. Lead the lee column | 97 below *Mars*' pennants | *Victory* | *Mars* | 10.45 a.m. |
| 22. Make all sail possible with safety to masts | 307 below *Defence*'s pennants | *Victory* | *Defence* | 11.02 a.m. |

| | | | | |
|---|---|---|---|---|
| 23. Make all sail possible with safety to masts | 307 below *Africa*'s pennants | *Victory* | *Africa* | 11.15 a.m. |
| 24. Make more sail | 88 | *Royal Sovereign* | lee column | 11.40 a.m. |
| 25. I intend to go through the end of enemy line to prevent them getting into Cadiz | Telegraph flag (Popham's Code) | *Victory* | *Royal Sovereign* | 11.40 a.m. |
| 26. Make all sail possible with safety to masts | 307 | *Victory* | general | 11.45 a.m. |
| 27. 'England expects …' | Telegraph flag (Popham's Code) | *Victory* | general | 11.50 a.m. |
| 28. Prepare to anchor after the close of day | 63 preparative 8 | *Victory* | general | 12.00 (noon) |
| 29. Take station astern of *Victory* | *Téméraire*'s pennants 269 *Victory*'s pennants | *Victory* | *Téméraire* | 12.05 p.m. |
| 30. Engage the enemy more closely | 16 | *Victory* | general | 12.15 p.m. |
| 31. Make all sail possible with safety to masts | 307 below *Africa*'s pennants | *Victory* | *Africa* | 12.25 p.m. |

*This signal was not made twice. However, there is confusion as to when Nelson made it. The problem arises because only one ship (*Pickle*) actually logged the time this signal was received. According to her log, 'At 10, the Commander-in-Chief made the signal to prepare for action …'. This was only about two hours before the first shots were fired and it seems unlikely that Nelson would have waited that long. Other ships record acknowledging the signal or clearing for action but mention no time. However, read in context their logs suggest this signal was made much earlier. The *Dreadnought* recorded, 'At daylight, observed a strange fleet to the eastward. Out 2nd reefs, and made sail and bore up. Cleared for action. At 8, light airs.' This seemingly indicates that she prepared for battle before 8.00 a.m. – but not necessarily in response to a signal to do so. The *Tonnant* is even briefer. The entry for the entire morning reads, 'A.M. – Fresh breezes with rain. Saw enemy's fleet ESE. Bore up and prepared for battle. At 11.40, the enemy fired on the *Royal Sovereign*. At noon, near the enemy.' Again, perhaps this indicates an early preparation for battle. The *Minotaur* is hardly more helpful. 'At 6.30, saw the French and Spanish fleets east. Bore up. Light airs. Fleet in company. French and Spanish fleets east. Set fore topgallant and topmast steering sails. Answered the signal to prepare for battle.' Even the *Britannia*, a flagship, is unhelpful: 'At daylight the enemy's fleet ESE 4 leagues [12 miles], consisting of 33 line-of-battle ships and several frigates. Bore up and made all sail to close with them. Cleared for action, the enemy forming the line and awaiting our attack.' All these ships-of-the-line mention bearing up and next clearing for action/preparing for battle. Nelson first signalled to the fleet to bear up at about 6.14 a.m. so a 'prepare for battle' signal fifteen minutes later looks likely; it was a signal that would normally be hoisted soon after sighting an enemy. It is also quite possible that captains exercised some discretion as to when they cleared for action or beat to quarters.

## Comments

• In the six hours between sighting the enemy and the first shot being fired at Trafalgar Nelson sent twenty signals, Collingwood ten, Northesk none and the *Defence* two (asking the *Orion* to make more sail and then to change course slightly). Of the *Victory*'s signals eight went to the whole fleet, one to Collingwood and eleven to individual ships. The *Royal Sovereign* signalled four times to the lee column and six times to particular captains. The signals crews on the other ships would have spent their time acknowledging signals, informing the captain of the message and, occasionally, repeating a signal.

• The 'light breezes' described in so many logs during the approach to action mean that the wind, such as it was, was almost a following one and would be expected to make flags difficult to read. But the ships were fairly close together and telescopes unable to see the flagships were trained on the frigates sailing well to windward, so there don't seem to have been any problems with seeing signals.

• Because Nelson had explained his tactics well in advance before the battle he only needed to make three general tactical signals during the entire morning. At 6.00 a.m. up went No. 72 ordering the fleet to form the order of sailing in two columns. Fifteen minutes later came No. 76 instructing all ships to bear up and sail east-north-east and, finally, the penultimate signal of the morning, kept flying throughout the battle: No. 16, 'Engage the enemy more closely'. Nelson's other signals were mostly concerned with making minor adjustments to the columns and urging individual ships to increase sail. He had to use the Popham Code twice for long signals. The first, at about 11.40 a.m. with the enemy line almost within effective range, told Collingwood that he intended to break through the enemy line to prevent them escaping to Cadiz. The second was the 'England expects …' signal, intended as a last-minute encouragement to the fleet. Nelson did his utmost not to interfere with Collingwood's command of the lee column. After the early general signals, sent before 7.00 a.m., he only once endeavoured, unsuccessfully in the end, to make a change, when he signalled (twice) in an attempt to get the *Mars* to lead the lee column.

• Collingwood's key signal to his command (9 above), hoisted at around 8.47 a.m., told them to form larboard line of bearing and steer straight for the enemy rather than follow immediately astern of the ship in front. Then, like Nelson, he was really only concerned with urging more speed and shepherding one or two ships into the correct place.

• The *Britannia*, flagship of Rear-Admiral Northesk, would appear from the master's brief log to have had a relaxed morning, certainly as far as the signals crew was concerned. Six and a half lines were devoted to the approach to battle, none of which contained the mention of any signals received, sent or repeated. According to the Admiralty Code subordinate flagships were to repeat the commander-in-chief's signals automatically. However, it seems the *Britannia* did not do this at Trafalgar, presumably because there was no need as she was sailing quite close astern of the *Victory*.

• The shortest master's log covering the morning was that of Mr Cocks of the *Thunderer*. Not only was there no mention of any signals but the happenings of those six tense hours were condensed to nineteen words: 'A.M. – Fresh breezes with rain [this was surely in the early hours of the morning while still dark]. Down topgallant yards and reefed the topsails. More moderate. Out reefs, and up topgallant yards.' Admittedly *Thunderer* was a slow sailer and did not arrive at the action until the battle was virtually over, thus only receiving sixteen casualties, but one would have thought her actions merited more than 'At 8, took the *Santa Ana* in tow.'

## 'England Expects that Every Man Will Do His Duty'

This famous signal, which is still hoisted every 21 October on the *Victory* at Portsmouth, merits a closer look than it is normally given in accounts of the battle. It was not the last signal made by Nelson before he came into action; it was hoisted at about 11.50 a.m., took about four minutes to make and was followed, according to ship's logs, by no fewer than four more signals (see p. 447). Nor was it a key tactical signal; instead it was intended as a final word of encouragement to the crews of the fleet just moments before they came under fire.

*Victory's signals crew*

We know the names and backgrounds of a number of the crew who handled this and other signals on the *Victory* at Trafalgar. The signals officer in charge was thirty-one-year-old Lieutenant John Pasco, who although the senior lieutenant was not acting as first lieutenant. Along with the rest of his signals crew his place of duty was the poop deck, and it was there that that morning he was severely wounded in the side and arm. His gallantry earned him immediate promotion to commander, while his wounds entitled him to a grant from the Patriotic Fund plus an Admiralty pension of £250 a year. He continued to serve but was not promoted to captain until 1811. He was granted a 'good service' pension in 1842 and five years later found himself captain of the *Victory* just before he finally retired as a rear-admiral. He died, aged seventy-eight, in 1853.

There was also another officer on the poop prior to the battle. This was a young twenty-year-old lieutenant named George Brown who was, in effect, second-in-command to Pasco. Years later he, and later still his grandsons, claimed that it was he, not Pasco, who suggested the alteration of the famous signal to Nelson. There is no evidence to substantiate this (see also below p. 449) and as it was hoisted before Pasco was wounded it is highly unlikely Nelson would have gone up to the poop, as he did, to discuss his signal with the junior, inexperienced officer while Pasco stood beside him. Once the action started Captain Hardy felt Brown would be of more use with the guns on the middle deck and sent him below. Brown did, however, later become the signals officer on Collingwood's flagship the *Ville de Paris*, and was serving in that capacity in 1810 when Collingwood died. Brown was promoted commander that year. He went onto half pay and was called to the bar in 1821, was appointed JP for Somerset and Bridgewater, promoted captain in retirement in 1840 and died in 1856.

The master's mate was Thomas Robins, eighteen years old, a young man who had joined the Navy as a Volunteer Class 1 when he was eleven. He would take command if the signals officer was hit (assuming Brown had gone below), and was required to do just that when Pasco was severely wounded. His gallantry earned him immediate promotion to lieutenant. There were also at least two midshipmen on the poop that morning. Their duties, apart

from the obvious one of supervising and checking the hoists, included maintaining the signals log, writing up the signals slate with the flag numbers and constantly watching for the acknowledgement of signals or for signals from other ships (particularly the frigates). They would also be employed taking signals and/or messages to the admiral down on the quarterdeck.

The next senior person we know who was present was rated as a quartermaster/yeoman of signals. This was John King, who was killed on the poop that afternoon. He was a petty officer with a pay rate the same as that of a corporal, boatswain's or gunner's mate, sailmaker and yeoman of the powder room. Yeomen were essentially storemen and as such King had the vital responsibility of the care, maintenance and stowage of the flags in the lockers across the stern of the poop. At fifty-four he was something of an old salt with only three men on board older than he was, and a man of considerable experience who would know his flags better than any man on the ship.

Then there was the young twenty-year-old Able Seaman Alfred Taylor who came from London. He had joined the *Victory* in May 1803, in time to see something of the Mediterranean and the Caribbean islands before his early death that afternoon. Landsman Roome, the man who we know helped haul on the halyards to hoist the signal, became well known in later years when he turned the story into something of a money-spinner (see p. 191). To make up the complement there were at least another three seamen to help haul on the halyards.

### An Error in Nelson's Famous Signal

If any reader cares to look carefully at the south façade of the plinth of Nelson's Column in Trafalgar Square he will read 'England expects every man will do his duty' – the word 'that' is missing after 'expects'. It is by no means the only time this mistake has been made. It occurs again in the stone inscription outside the Royal Exchange in Liverpool, and even the scroll on the covers of the seven volumes of Nicolas' *Dispatches and Letters of Lord Nelson* omits the word. Lieutenant Pasco's telescope, used at Trafalgar and later presented to Prince Alfred, was engraved with the words of the signal but with the same error.

A considerable number of commemorative Trafalgar medals were produced after the battle at private expense to be given to survivors. Where the words of the signal occur on such medals they are invariably wrong. A good example is Mr Boulton's Trafalgar Medal, produced in gold for admirals, silver for officers and pewter for ratings. On the reverse, around the top edge, are the words 'England expects every man will do his duty'; at least one medal was inscribed 'England expects every man to do his duty.' In case readers might think that 'that' was not in the original signal they are referred to the ship's logs.

*The signal*

It was probably around 11.35 a.m. when Nelson left the quarterdeck and climbed the steps leading to the poop. He had several signals he wanted to send including two long ones that he would need to explain personally to Pasco. At that time the enemy line was getting close, perhaps a mile and a half away at most. Everyone was expecting to see the puffs of white smoke and hear the boom of guns at any moment. At 11.40 up went the signal telling Collingwood that Nelson intended to go through the end of the Combined Fleet's line to prevent escape to Cadiz. Five minutes later came the general signal to make all sail possible with safety to the masts (No. 307).

While that short signal was still up Nelson would have turned again to Pasco, who was still probably holding the Popham signal code, to dictate his signal of encouragement to the fleet. Pasco's own words best describe what happened.

> His Lordship came to me on the poop, and after ordering certain signals to be made, about a quarter to noon, he said: 'Mr Pasco, I wish

to say to the Fleet, ENGLAND CONFIDES THAT EVERY MAN WILL DO HIS DUTY'; and he added, 'You must be quick, for I have one more to make, which is for Close Action.' I replied, 'If your Lordship will permit me to substitute the (word) *expects* for *confides* the signal will soon be completed, because the word expects is in the vocabulary, and confides must be spelt.' His Lordship replied in haste, and with seeming satisfaction, 'That will do Pasco, make it directly.' When it had been answered by a few ships in the Van, he ordered me to make the signal for Close Action, and *to keep it up*; accordingly I hoisted No. 16 at the topgallant mast-head, and there it remained until shot away.

The signal was hoisted below that of the 'telegraph' flag indicating Popham's code was being used.

The sequence of actions to get this signal hoisted would have been roughly as follows. Pasco would have checked the numbers for each word in Popham's code and either written them on a slate and handed it to Robins or a midshipman or, more likely, called out the numbers while the master's mate wrote them on the signal slate. It is quite possible that Lieutenant Brown carried out these duties or assisted. Whoever did it would have probably checked the slate was correct. Robins would have shouted for the telegraph flag to be hoisted – it was probably already attached to its own separate halyard. Whoever had the slate would then shout the numbers for the first lift of three flags 2 – 5 – 3 (ENGLAND). Another midshipman and Quartermaster King would be picking up the appropriate flags (which were already out and on the deck by then). They then checked they were fastened to the halyard in the correct order. Pasco himself may have looked to satisfy himself all was well before shouting 'hoist'. While 253 was up the next number 269 (EXPECTS) would be got ready on another halyard – there were sufficient halyards for all, or most, of the twelve lifts of this signal to have separate ones. As one lift came down another went up. There was no need for each lift (word or letter) to remain aloft for long, as all those watching had to do was quickly record the number on their slate. Every signals seaman knew the ten number flags like he knew his own name so there was no need to look them up. This signal was completed in about four minutes. As it was being hoisted a midshipman would record the signal and time in his signal log.

*Comments*

There are several points concerning this signal worth looking at.
• From time to time it has been suggested, initially by Brown's grandson in 1883, that Nelson had wanted the message to start with 'Nelson confides …' but that it was Brown who suggested 'England' and Pasco 'expects'. Pasco never mentioned this but an element of doubt must remain. The signal 'Nelson confides that every man will do his duty' rings true of the admiral. The entire fleet knew him well, men were delighted to serve under him and Nelson, knowing this, wanted to remind his men of his confidence in them. The word 'confides' certainly suggests a personal message and that the sender knows everyone will do his best. Substitute 'England expects' and you get an altogether harsher tone, almost as though the sender has his doubts that the fleet will give of their best, and is therefore reminding them of their duty. England meant very little to many seamen at Trafalgar. Some 10 per cent of those present were foreigners. Of the rest, they would fight for their shipmates and they would fight for Nelson. Nelson knew this, so it is uncharacteristic that he chose the word 'England'. Perhaps it was suggested to him by Brown while Pasco persuaded him to use

'expects' for the sake of speed. Whatever the truth, 'expects' was not a good word either. It conveyed the sense of doubt, whereas Nelson knew there was none. A better word would have been 'knows', which had a number in the code and so would have been just as quick, but Pasco quickly spotted the alternative 'expects' as it was only a few lines down from 'England' on the same page. Nelson was in a rush ('agreed it in haste') and responded 'that will do' – there was no time to start thumbing through the codebook.
• Then there is the question of how many ships actually received the signal and, if so, whether it was passed to all the crews. Pasco himself states clearly that after it was acknowledged by 'a few ships in the Van' Nelson ordered the next signal hoisted immediately. The *Euryalus* records repeating it at 11.56 (as does the *Naiad*) but only five ships-of-the-line logged it in their master's or captain's logs. As Collingwood saw the flags starting to go up he commented testily, 'I wish Nelson would stop signalling – we know well enough what we have to do!' This reaction is hardly surprising as by this time, according to his log and journal, his ship was only ten minutes from breaking the enemy line, was already under fire and about to reply. However, when shown the decoded message he changed his tune, exclaiming, 'Great Man, I forgive him!'

When the signal was received, how would it have been passed down to the gundecks? The answer is in the same way that any orders were relayed to the men below. Probably the captain or first lieutenant would have gone to the poop. Using a speaking trumpet he would have shouted something along the lines: 'Message from Lord Nelson – to be passed on by all repeating officers. England … expects … that … every … man … will … do … his … duty!' The repeating officers were the midshipmen posted at the hatchways and those on the gundecks who used their speaking trumpets to communicate. Another method, adopted on the *Ajax*, was to send a Royal Marine officer.
• How was the message received by the crews? Did it inspire them? Stories of universal wild cheering are almost certainly exaggerated. Second Lieutenant Samuel Ellis RM on the *Ajax* had this to say on the subject:

> These words were requested to be delivered to the men, and I was desired to inform them on the main deck of the Admiral's signal. Upon acquainting one of the quarter-masters of the order, he assembled the men with, 'Avast there, lads, come and hear the Admiral's words.' When the men were mustered, I delivered, with becoming dignity, the sentence, rather anticipating that the effect on the men would be to awe them by its grandeur. Jack, however, did not appreciate it, for there were murmurs from some, whilst others in an audible whisper muttered, 'Do our duty! Of course we'll do our duty. I've always done mine, haven't you? Let us come alongside of 'em, and we will show whether we will do our duty!' Still, the men cheered vociferously – more, I believe, from love and admiration of their admirals and leaders, than from a full appreciation of this well-known signal.

• Pasco's letter was written many years after the battle, which probably accounts for the fact that he states the signal immediately following 'England expects …' was No. 16, 'Engage the enemy more closely'. This was not so. The next signal told the fleet to prepare to anchor after the battle as Nelson realized from the huge swell developing that a storm was coming, and there was a danger of damaged ships being driven onto a lee shore. After this came a

## Three Trafalgar Signals

### *Sirius* to *Euryalus*, 7 a.m. 19 October: 'Enemy's ships are coming out of port'

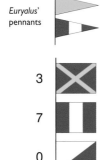

*Euryalus'* pennants

*Sirius* off Cadiz signals to *Euryalus* using Nelson's Pennant Board identification.

3

7          'Enemy's ships are coming out of port'
           (No. 370 in Admiralty Code).

0

### *Victory* to fleet, 11.50 a.m. 21 October: 'England expects that every man will do his duty'

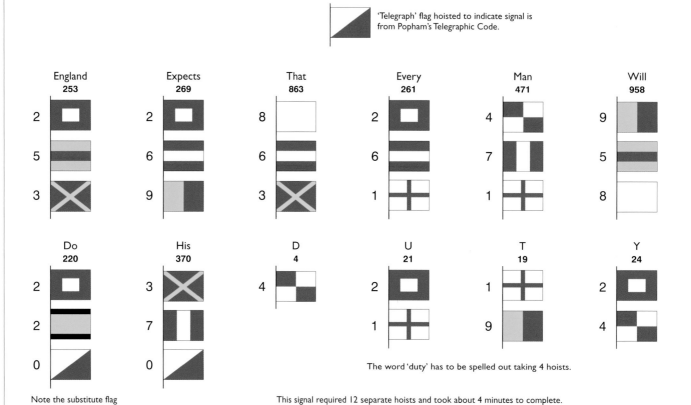

'Telegraph' flag hoisted to indicate signal is from Popham's Telegraphic Code.

| England 253 | Expects 269 | That 863 | Every 261 | Man 471 | Will 958 |

| Do 220 | His 370 | D 4 | U 21 | T 19 | Y 24 |

The word 'duty' has to be spelled out taking 4 hoists.

Note the substitute flag is used to indicate the second '2' in 220.

This signal required 12 separate hoists and took about 4 minutes to complete.

Care had to be taken that flags such as Nos 0, 4 and the telegraph flag were not hoisted upside down.

### *Victory* to fleet, 12.15 p.m. 21 October: 'Engage the enemy more closely'

1

6          This signal (No. 16 in the Admiralty Code) stayed hoisted throughout the action.

signal to the *Téméraire*, who looked like overtaking the *Victory*, to take station astern of her. Then came No. 16 and finally, at about 12.25 p.m., the *Africa* was signalled to make all sail possible.

• Finally, Pasco makes no mention as to which topgallant masthead he hoisted No. 16. All signals were normally hoisted on halyards on the mizzen but it is likely that this signal, which was to be kept flying throughout the battle, was hoisted at the main. This is where most artists have shown it, although there would have been the long St George's cross white pennant already in that position. It is possible Pasco hoisted it to the top of the mizzen, which had no flag. It was by then 12.15 p.m., and the enemy had opened fire, so instead of moving to the mainmast, which would have taken more time (and he had another signal to hoist) the quickest solution would have been to use the mizzen; his letter makes no mention of the main. We shall probably never know for sure.

## Combined Fleet Trafalgar signals

The Combined Fleet had considerable problems with signalling as soon as they started to leave Cadiz, brought about by the fact that the national codebooks were different and written in different languages. As noted above, Godoy's translation of French codes was not distributed until after the battle. The fleet obviously had to come to some workable arrangement, and agreed to use the French *General Signals when under Sail*, which set out a code for numerous common nautical and tactical instructions.

Examples are Villeneuve's order for the fleet to 'Wear together' which was Article 24 in the code book, 'Leading ship to make more sail' (Article 266) and 'Open fire' (Article 242). There was another code entitled *Signals by Night when under Sail*, but unfortunately the present writer was unable to trace a copy of these codes so details of the flags used cannot be included in this work. Serious shortcomings were minimized because all the frigates (repeating ships) were French, signalling direct to the French flagship. Nevertheless, lack of training and experience was immediately obvious, particularly at night, when the fleet tried to leave Cadiz on 19 October. Captain Lucas of the *Redoutable* recorded:

> About nine o'clock at night the flagship made the general signal to form in the order of battle at once. To carry out this evolution, those ships most to leeward ought to have shown a light at each masthead, so as to mark their positions. Whether this was done I do not know: at any rate I was unable to see such lights. At that moment, indeed, we were all widely scattered. Another cause of confusion was this. Nearly all the ships had answered the admiral's signals with flares, which made it impossible to tell which was the flagship.

The important signals made by ships of the Combined Fleet prior to battle on 21 October are given below with necessary comments or explanation. Without access to the actual codes it is impossible to indicate the flags used.

| Signal | By whom | To whom | Time logged | Comment |
|---|---|---|---|---|
| 1. Enemy squadron sighted | *Hermione* | *Bucentaure* | 6.30 a.m. | |
| 2. Frigates to reconnoitre enemy | *Bucentaure* | *Hermione* | 6.45 a.m. | |
| 3. 26 line-of-battle ships sighted | *Hermione* | *Bucentaure* | 7.00 a.m. | |
| 4. Form line of battle on starboard tack | *Bucentaure* | general | 7.10 a.m. | Problems due to lack of wind, no steerage way |
| 5. Close to cable's length | *Bucentaure* | general | 7.20 a.m. | |
| 6. Wear together | *Bucentaure* | general | 8.00 a.m. | This manoeuvre reversed fleet's order and took almost two hours |
| 7. Make more sail | *Bucentaure* | leading ships | 8.30 a.m. | |
| 8. Make more sail | *Bucentaure* | *Scipion* | 9.10 a.m. | |
| 9. Keep to wind | *Bucentaure* | *San Augustin* | 9.30 a.m. | |
| 10. Leading ship keep to wind, others follow in succession | *Bucentaure* | general | 10.00 a.m. | |
| 11. Line of fleet is extending too much | *Thémis* | *P. de Asturias* | 10.30 a.m. | |
| 12. Rear is extending too much | *Thémis* | *P. de Asturias* | 10.40 a.m. | |
| 13. Keep cable's length between ships | *P. de Asturias* | rear ships | 10.45 a.m. | Ships struggling to establish a line of battle |
| 14. Leading ship to keep to wind, others follow in succession | *Bucentaure* | general | 11.00 a.m. | Villeneuve knew an attack was being made in two columns on his rear and centre |
| 15. Keep to the wind | *P. de Asturias* | squadron of observation | 11.30 a.m. | |
| 16. Keep to wind | *Bucentaure* | *Rayo* | 11.30 a.m. | Fleet badly formed, ships doubled, some hove to |
| 17. Open fire when enemy in range | *Bucentaure* | general | 11.35 a.m. | Battle starts |

*Comments*

• The overall number of pre-battle signals was 17 compared with the British 31. The difference is partly due to the Combined Fleet being on the defensive and also sailing as one fleet, not in two distinct divisions as were the British.

• In almost exactly the same time period Villeneuve made 11 signals or 65 per cent of the total and Nelson made 20, again exactly 65 per cent. Gravina, his second-in-command, only had to make two minor signals to his squadron of observation. Again

this was because he did not have a semi-independent role as did Collingwood.

• Note how concerned Villeneuve was with the way his fleet was formed and his struggle in the light wind to get back into some sort of line of battle after wearing. All ten signals made after this manoeuvre were to chivvy ships to keep to the wind, keep cable's length between them or make more sail. It proved a frustrating and impossible task.

# THE BATTLE OF COPENHAGEN, 2 APRIL 1801

The Danes, and their beautiful capital city, had the misfortune of being twice attacked and defeated by Britain within the space of six years. On both occasions (in 1801 and 1807) the Danes lost their fleet, and on the second Copenhagen was almost destroyed under bombardment as well. The genesis of the first attack lay in the signing in December 1800 of a Treaty of Armed Neutrality between Denmark, Sweden, Prussia and Russia, instigated by Napoleon, by which the Baltic would be closed to British trade – worth £3 million a year. Quite apart from any other goods, such a move would cut off vital supplies for the Royal Navy and merchant ships, since it was from the Baltic that the bulk of fir for spars, hemp for rope and flax for sails came. Without these items ships could not be maintained, without the ships the blockade of French ports would collapse and without an effective blockade invasion became a virtual certainty.

Even before the ink on the treaty was dry Russia had seized the 300 British merchantmen that were in her ports, and the pro-French Tsar suggested to Napoleon that Portugal might be induced to join – and what about America? If the treaty kept expanding the consequences for Britain could be calamitous. It had to be broken up, and diplomacy could only work if backed up by the credible threat of force – specifically, by a fleet visible off Copenhagen to make it quite clear what would happen to the Danes if they failed to resist Russian pressure. Speed was of the essence. A minister, Nicolas Vansittart MP, was appointed the special envoy of the British government, and arrived in Copenhagen on 9 March to argue for British interests, in conjunction with William Drummond, the British representative in the city. If they failed, a British Fleet would be waiting outside the harbour to put a more compelling argument.

## The British prepare to sail

In February the fleet began to assemble at Great Yarmouth. Nelson did not get command, having to be content as second-in-command to Vice-Admiral Sir Hyde Parker. Perhaps, after nearly three years, the authorities' memory of Nelson's triumph at the Nile was waning somewhat in comparison with his more recent disobedience. Perhaps his lack of seniority was a mark against him or Parker, at sixty-two, was thought better able to act the diplomat initially, with the firebrand Nelson at his shoulder if the guns began to shoot. Probably it was a combination of all these.

If the Admiralty had wanted the fleet off Copenhagen quickly to reinforce negotiations, Parker was not the man to pick. He had been an adequate captain but several years spent accumulating prize money as an admiral in the West Indies had not fostered any sense of urgency in him. But the most immediate cause of his lingering in London rather than hastening to confront the problems of assembling a fleet for war was his recent marriage to an eighteen-year-old girl. His mind and his energies were elsewhere. When he did arrive at Yarmouth he hoisted his flag on the 74-gun *Ardent* while awaiting the arrival of the 98-gun *London*, but since he had brought his young bride he remained cosily ashore at the Wrestler's Arms. Nelson arrived aboard his flagship, the other 98-gun *St George*, on 4 March. The fleet assembling would consist of two second rates, fifteen third rates, two fourth rates, four frigates and an assortment of sloops, brigs, bombs, luggers and fireships. It was a veritable armada, and the problems arising in getting it ready quickly were manifold. Nelson, anxious to be off although consumed with jealousy over leaving Emma, fretted at the slowness of decision-making and lack of urgency shown by his elderly commander. Parker fussed and fumed about obtaining only eleven of the twelve pilots (mostly mates from the merchant service) with Baltic knowledge, a new edition of the signal book and a growing obsession that Danish gunboats posed a disproportionate threat. His fixation with trivia – he wrote several times to the Admiralty complaining of the lack of suitable stationery – and his need to have every last lugger in position before departure was exasperating for Nelson. Then there was Parker's social life. His new wife had arranged a ball for Friday 13 March so the fleet must certainly wait for that.

---

### Nelson's Jealousy

If Parker was reluctant to leave the embraces of his young wife, Nelson was consumed with worry on leaving Emma behind, and all because she had a dinner date with the Prince of Wales. On receiving the news in a letter from Sir William Hamilton that the notoriously lecherous prince would be coming on 22 February, Nelson wrote hysterically to Emma:

> I am so agitated that I can write nothing. I knew it would be so, and you can't help it. Why did you not tell Sir William? Your character will be gone. Good God he will be next to you, and telling you soft things. If he does, tell it out at table, and turn him out of the house. Do not sit long. If you sing a song, I know you cannot help it, do not let him sit next to you, but at dinner he will hob glasses with you … O, God that I was dead! But I do not, my dearest Emma, blame you, nor do I fear your inconstancy. I tremble, and God knows how I write. Can nothing be thought of? I am gone almost mad but you cannot help it. It will be in all the newspapers with hints. Recollect what the villain said to Mr Nisbet, *how you hit his fancy …*

The Admiralty had little time for Parker's procrastination. His full orders, which stressed the reasons for speed, had been sent to him on 23 February. These were followed by written orders two days later to leave London – a sure sign the Lords at the Admiralty were becoming agitated. Three days later Parker had arrived in Great Yarmouth complete with bride and baggage. On 9 March the authorities tried again with a direct order to sail. Parker either could not, or would not, see any urgency. He responded on Tuesday (10 March) saying the delay was due to an unfavourable wind coming from the south-east. Friday's ball remained in his (and most officers') diary – perhaps the wind would be better on the Saturday! St Vincent, the recently appointed First Lord, had had enough. He wrote privately in uncompromising terms.

> I have heard by a side wind that you have the intention of continuing at Yarmouth until Friday, on account of some trifling circumstance [the ball]. I really know not what they are, nor did I give myself the trouble of inquiring into them … .
>
> I have, however, upon consideration of the effect of your continuance at Yarmouth an hour after the wind would admit of your sailing would produce, sent down a messenger purposely to convey to you my opinion, as a private friend, that any delay in your sailing would do you irreparable injury …

In other words, sail or be sacked. It was enough. The ball was cancelled, the wind changed and the fleet sailed on Thursday 12 March.

## The Fleet sails

With only a few hours' notice to sail, there was a desperate scramble to get ready – the fleet had assumed they would stay at anchor at least until Saturday. Midshipman Millard on the *Monarch* wrote:

> all was hurry and confusion; the officers ignorant of the day, or even the week, that we were to sail, and had laid in no stock of provisions for the voyage. … Besides the provisions of all sorts which hurries down to the boats, a considerable body of troops … were embarking with their baggage and stores … When it is considered that each vessel, of about fifty, stood in need of these preparations, that they were all to be furnished from this pier, and in the space of a very few hours, any one may conclude that the picture did not want for life. I never witnessed such a complete buzz.

The Army contingent was under the command of Lieutenant-Colonel the Honourable William Stewart of the newly formed Corps of Riflemen, which supplied two companies under Captain Sydney Beckwith. The bulk of the 900 soldiers, however, came from the 49th Foot (Hertfordshire). For his contingent Stewart had requested no fewer than 99,000 musket cartridges, 4,000 carbine cartridges and 10,000 cartridge papers for carbines, entrenching tools and spikes for spiking guns – it was to be the job of his troops (and the Royal Marines) to assault and capture the enemy's gun batteries after the bombardment.

It came as no surprise to anybody that the fleet sailed without a number of ships that were not ready or had not even arrived at Yarmouth. Among them were the 74-gun *Elephant* (Nelson's flagship for the battle), which weighed four days later, and the 74-gun *Edgar*, which caught up after a matter of hours. More worrying was that Parker left without two of his subordinate admirals.

Rear-Admirals Thomas Graves and Thomas Totty had not yet arrived at Yarmouth, where they had been instructed to call to pick up their official orders before following the fleet. Graves, in the 74-gun *Defiance*, caught up on 18 March but Totty never got further than the sandbank in Yarmouth Roads. His ship, a 74 inappropriately named *Invincible*, went aground and sank with the loss of 400 lives – far more than were to die at Copenhagen.

Nelson was far from pleased with Parker's order of sailing instructions. Domett (captain of the fleet) prepared the drafts for the admiral's approval. Nelson's division, the starboard, consisted of eight ships-of-the-line but Parker had changed Domett's draft so that Nelson had two 64s and a 50 (*Agamemnon*, *Ardent* and *Isis*) – hardly a balanced force. He wrote: 'It was never my desire to serve under this man … For me to serve on in this way is to laugh at me, and to think me a greater fool than I am. If this goes on, I hope to be allowed to return the moment the fighting business is over.' Apart from a brief meeting with Parker in the Wrestler's Arms on 7 March, at which formal pleasantries had been exchanged, Nelson had not been shown his admiral's orders. Even as they sailed Midshipman Millard noted: 'Even at this time we did not know the place of our destination: the course given out by signal was NE by N, this being a course due for the Naze of Norway; this was the first assurance we had of being bound towards the Baltic.'

The Naze was some 500 miles away, marking the entrance to the Skagerrak, the arm of the North Sea that gives access to the Kattegat and so to the Baltic (see Map 22). After the Naze the next major landmark was the Skaw – the promontory on the north-eastern tip of Jutland. From there, southwards, another 160 miles would put the fleet outside Copenhagen. The voyage to the Skaw was not a pleasant one. The North Sea is seldom friendly for long, and rarely in March. But the worst suffering came not so much from the high seas that battered the ships for most of the next week as from the icy, arctic wind and sleet, which cut through the seamen's coats like a knife. The mixture of squalls and strong breezes had the topmen scrambling aloft and down again to reef and let out topsails, often in the dark. These men had to hang on to freezing ropes and go out along slippery frozen yards in tearing winds to haul in canvas that was encrusted with ice. The least they could suffer was raw cracked hands and salt-water boils, the worst a fall that meant instant death on the deck, or after two or three minutes in the freezing sea. However, there was a slight thaw in the relationship between the commander-in-chief and his second-in-command during this disagreeable voyage. The initiative came from Nelson. As they passed the Dogger Bank, knowing his admiral was fond of a good table, he ordered a fishing net be lowered. The area was known for its turbot and within a short time a splendid specimen was hauled in. Despite the dreadful weather Nelson had the fish sent across to the *London* and received a polite note of thanks from Parker in return.

By 17 March Parker was not where he should have been. Visibility was low due to mist and drizzle and by using dead reckoning the navigators estimated the fleet's position at the entrance to the Skagerrak (see Map 22). In fact it was, as reported by the sloop *Cruizer*, some 65 miles to the south, off Bovbjerg. Parker tacked north-west and hove to for the night, and by amazing luck aided by good navigation he was joined by the *Defiance* with one of his missing admirals, Graves. By the 19th, after some slow sailing and much tacking and wearing, the fleet reached the Skaw, exactly a week after leaving Yarmouth. That morning Nelson visited the *London*, uninvited, for his first meeting with his com-

## The British Fleet's Approach to Copenhagen, 12–30 March 1801                   Map 22

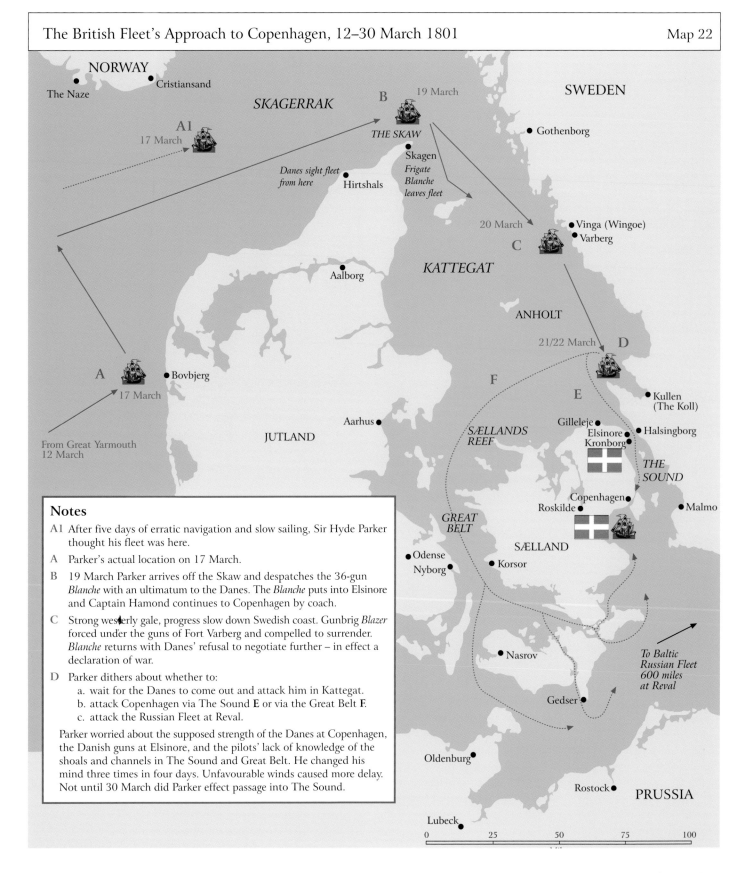

NORWAY

The Naze • • Cristiansand

SKAGERRAK

SWEDEN

**A1** 17 March

**B** 19 March

THE SKAW

• Gothenborg

Danes sight fleet from here • Hirtshals

Skagen
Frigate
Blanche
leaves fleet

20 March

**C** • Vinga (Wingoe)
• Varberg

KATTEGAT

• Aalborg

ANHOLT

21/22 March **D**

**A** • Bovbjerg
17 March

**F**

**E** • Kullen (The Koll)

From Great Yarmouth
12 March

• Aarhus

JUTLAND

SÆLLANDS
REEF

Gilleleje •
Elsinore • • Halsingborg
Kronborg •

THE
SOUND

Copenhagen •
Roskilde •                      • Malmo

GREAT
BELT

SÆLLAND

### Notes

**A1** After five days of erratic navigation and slow sailing, Sir Hyde Parker thought his fleet was here.

**A** Parker's actual location on 17 March.

**B** 19 March Parker arrives off the Skaw and despatches the 36-gun *Blanche* with an ultimatum to the Danes. The *Blanche* puts into Elsinore and Captain Hamond continues to Copenhagen by coach.

**C** Strong westerly gale, progress slow down Swedish coast. Gunbrig *Blazer* forced under the guns of Fort Varberg and compelled to surrender. *Blanche* returns with Danes' refusal to negotiate further – in effect a declaration of war.

**D** Parker dithers about whether to:
    a. wait for the Danes to come out and attack him in Kattegat.
    b. attack Copenhagen via The Sound **E** or via the Great Belt **F**.
    c. attack the Russian Fleet at Reval.

Parker worried about the supposed strength of the Danes at Copenhagen, the Danish guns at Elsinore, and the pilots' lack of knowledge of the shoals and channels in The Sound and Great Belt. He changed his mind three times in four days. Unfavourable winds caused more delay. Not until 30 March did Parker effect passage into The Sound.

• Odense
Nyborg •                • Korsor

• Nasrov

To Baltic
Russian Fleet
600 miles
at Reval

Gedser •

Oldenburg •

Rostock • PRUSSIA

Lubeck •

0        25        50        75        100

mander since exchanging greetings in the Wrestler's Arms. At last Parker disclosed his intentions, and on his return to his ship Nelson summarized his hour-long meeting in a letter to his friend Troubridge: 'I was glad to find that he [Parker] was determined to pass Cronborg [Castle] and go off Copenhagen in order to give

weight to our negotiator [Vansittart], and I believe this conduct will give us peace with Denmark.'

Nelson had also pressed Parker to go into the Baltic to confront the major danger, the Russian Fleet at Revel, before the thawing ice released them to join hostilities. The idea did not appeal to his commander-in-chief. 'Sir Hyde told me, on my anxiety for going forward with all expedition, that we were going to go no further without fresh orders. I hope this is alright …'.

Parker had not explained that his orders were specific, nor that he was sending Captain Hamond with the frigate *Blanche* that afternoon with a forty-eight-hour ultimatum to the Danes. If they failed to abandon the Armed Neutrality, Parker's orders stated he was to 'immediately proceed to vigorous hostilities' which would include 'destroy[ing] the Arsenal … with the whole of the shipping in that port'.

Nelson's hope that everything would be 'alright' was soon dashed. There now began a week of delay, dithering and indecision in which Parker changed his mind as to what course of action to take three times in four days. It would be eleven days before the fleet anchored just north of Copenhagen, and a full two weeks before the first shots of the battle for that city were fired – two weeks which the Danes put to good use with frantic efforts to bolster their defences. Instead of sailing down the Kattegat and into The Sound to lend a visible threat to back up the ultimatum, Parker only managed to reach an anchorage off Vinga on 20 March. That night was a wild one with a gale-force wind and heavy seas threatening to drive the fleet onto a lee (eastern) shore. According to the Reverend Scott, Parker's private secretary, who fulfilled the same role for Nelson at Trafalgar, 'The *London* was nearly lost yesterday [20 March] on a shoal with only 19 feet of water on it.'

On 21 March, a Saturday, the scattered fleet managed another few miles and took shelter in the lee of the Koll (Map 22). The next day as they weighed to approach The Sound the *Blanche* returned. On board were not only special envoy Vansittart and diplomat Drummond but also a large gaggle of British diplomatic staff and their families. They had been told to leave immediately, the ultimatum rejected – the Danes' decision was war.

The British Fleet anchored for the night of 22/23 March some 15 miles north-west of the entrance to The Sound. Late that night Mr Drummond was rowed across to the *London* to brief Parker on the Danish defences. Drummond was a diplomat who, although residing in Copenhagen for some considerable time, had no professional knowledge of military or naval affairs. He could count cannons but his judgements as to their range, siting, state of repair, weight of fire or the efficiency of their crews were, to say the least, suspect. Drummond had counted lots of cannons as well as witnessing the feverish activity in the city as the authorities began to organize their defences. The picture he painted was gloomy from the British viewpoint and Parker was alarmed by what he heard. He got little sleep that night. He was worried and uncertain what to do, recording in his journal that Drummond had 'informed me of the great preparations made by the Danes, both at Cronenbourg [sic] Castle [guarding the entrance to The Sound] and in their line of defence &. &. at Copenhagen'.

Early on 23 March he wrote a pessimistic despatch to the Admiralty – without consulting Nelson, Graves or Domett.

> From a rough sketch these gentlemen [he had yet to speak with Vansittart] have been able to furnish me with the mode of Defence the Danes have adopted for the preservation of the Arsenal, it appears to be a very strong one, and from the shoalness of the water, it will be very difficult for us to dislodge them without vessels of force, of a less draught of water than the ships of the line.

However, Parker had made up his mind to get on with his task, although he seemed anxious to cast doubt on the outcome; he continued:

> … as soon as the wind shifts to the northwards I shall proceed to put the remainder of my instructions into execution, in doing which their Lordships may depend upon every exertion in my power that the force under my command will admit of, in the peculiar navigation in which we are to be engaged …

He had seemingly decided to make straight for Copenhagen via The Sound, though the tone of his letter was hardly reassuring.

## Four days of dithering

Two fundamentals were essential for a prompt prosecution of operations. The first was that Parker stuck to his decision and the second that he had a favourable wind coming from a northerly direction to take him into The Sound. That morning (23 March) Parker discussed matters with the pilots on board the *London*. They were merchant seamen supposedly with experience of the narrow passages, shoals, channels and currents that abounded around the islands and promontories off Saelland. In reality they knew little, the charts were inaccurate and the Danes were hardly likely to leave their marker buoys in place. They were unenthusiastic about the venture and dwelt on the difficulties in their conversation with the admiral. Meanwhile he had, at long last, invited Nelson to come aboard, along with Vansittart from the *Blanche*.

Nelson was dismayed by the mood of his meeting with Parker and Vansittart. Lieutenant Layman, the officer in charge of the barge that had brought Nelson to the *London*, later described what he saw and heard.

> The Captain of the Fleet [Domett] said [to Layman] that the Danes were too strong to attack, and a torpor verging to [sic] despondency prevailed in the councils. While others were dismayed, however, Lord Nelson questioned those just arrived from Copenhagen, not only as to the force, but as to the position of the enemy.

Parker had changed his mind despite the fact that his orders to attack Copenhagen were unambiguous. He had announced to Nelson that his intention was to await the Danish Fleet in the Kattegat, where, in the deep open water, he would give battle. Vansittart's description of the defences, added to Drummond's views and combined with the pilots' pessimism, confirmed Parker's conviction that venturing into The Sound was far too risky. Vansittart put emphasis on the strength of the Trekroner (Three Crowns) and Lynetton forts, which were said to be heavily fortified and 'presented 100 pieces of ordinance'. He also added that the Swedes had promised more gunboats and had heard the Russians were busy cutting the melting ice at Reval to release their fleet early. Nelson subjected the British envoy to a detailed questioning as to the Danish defences' strengths and locations.

Nelson then had his say. He argued that the worst possible course was to sit in the Kattegat and await events, as this would give the Danes yet more time to improve the defences of the city. The Swedes would be emboldened and, above all, the Russians would gain time to get clear of the ice and sail to reinforce the Danes – who would be unlikely to come out into the open to confront the British on their own. As Nelson later put it:

The difficulty was to get our Commander-in-Chief either to go past Cronenbourg or through the Belt, because, what Sir Hyde thought best, and what I believe was settled before I came on board the London was to stay in the Cattegat, and there wait the time when the whole naval force of the Baltic might choose to come out and fight – a measure, in my opinion, disgraceful to our Country.

The strategic options available according to Nelson were:
1. To sail into The Sound, pass in front of the guns of Kronborg Castle and attack Copenhagen. The fleet could approach either from the north or from the south. The former would involve being heavily engaged with the Trekroner Fort and the ships in the Kronlobet Channel, the strongest part of the enemy's line, whereas approach from the south would mean sailing down the Holland Deep and attacking the weaker southern end of the Danish line up the King's Deep (Map 24 on p. 461).
2. To approach Copenhagen from the south via the Great Belt to the west of Saelland. This would take several days and would be vulnerable to delays by sudden shifts in wind direction but would mean the fleet was placing itself between the Danes and the Russians if they were to emerge from the Baltic.
3. To attack the Russians first. They were surely the main enemy, so the best tactic might be to sail into the Baltic, leaving a small squadron to mask Copenhagen, and deal with the Tsar's fleet as it emerged from winter hibernation.

Speed was essential for all these options. Every day's delay meant stronger Danish defences and more melting of ice at Reval. Nelson's preference was No. 3 above but with an approach to the Baltic via the Great Belt. He was suggesting to his commander not only that the latter's plan of sitting still and awaiting attack was unthinkable but that they disobey the Admiralty's orders and divert the fleet to attack the Russians first. Nelson's powers of persuasion and logic must have been remarkable because he succeeded in convincing Parker to change his plan. Now he would take his fleet through the Great Belt and let the wind decide the next move – the Russians at Reval or the Danes at Copenhagen. Nelson was rowed back to the *St George* late in the afternoon reasonably satisfied that the lengthy meeting had been worthwhile – at least Sir Hyde had agreed to do something other than sit on his hands and wait.

Nelson had not been shown Parker's orders. Simple and explicit, they required a speedy attack on Copenhagen. Once the Danes had been dealt with there would still be time to sail against the Russians. But Parker was convinced the enemy's defences were too strong, worried about running the gauntlet of guns firing red-hot shot from Kronborg Castle and alarmed by the pilots' warnings of navigational hazards. However, the choice of sailing via the Belt was a dubious compromise. It avoided the Castle guns but added some 240 miles to the voyage before Copenhagen could be reached. Even with helpful winds to permit tacking and wearing through the narrow channels (unlikely) and knowledgeable pilots (non-existent) this would take a week at least, giving the Danes that much more time to prepare. They would also know precisely what their enemy intended, giving them time to strengthen the southern defences of Copenhagen accordingly. It is surprising that Nelson accepted this lengthy indirect approach, although he probably felt it the only way he could get the fleet moving.

As soon as the conference ended Parker penned another despatch to London to explain why he was not intending to fol-low the Admiralty's orders – always a tricky business. Parker resorted to spreading the blame by including Nelson and Vansittart for his decision.

I have had recourse to a consultation with Vice-Admiral Lord Nelson and Mr Vansittart on the very formidable defence the Danes have made ... not only by many additional batteries to Cronenbourg Castle but also the number of hulks and batteries which have lately been placed and erected for the defence of the Arsenal at Copenhagen, and renders an attack so hazardous, join'd to the difficulty of navigation of the passage of the Sound [h]as led us to agree in opinion that it will be more beneficial for His Majesty's service to attempt the passage of the Great Belt which having passed and the wind favourable for going up the Baltic is, to attempt the destruction of the Russian ships at Reval ...

At 4.00 a.m. on Tuesday 24 March Parker ordered the fleet to weigh. By 7.00 a.m. the course was set to the west and for the first time it became obvious to all that the fleet was headed for the Belt, not The Sound. This caused surprise and consternation. Both the captain of the fleet, Domett, and the flag captain on the *London*, Otway, tackled their admiral on the grave disadvantages of using the Great Belt. Parker hesitated. Was he doing the right thing? Maybe he should attack via The Sound after all. Then a bomb ketch ran aground, a pointed reminder of the navigational difficulties ahead. The fleet hove to and Otway was sent to the *St George* to inform Nelson, whose comment was, 'I don't give a damn by which passage we go, so that we fight them.'

Nelson went across to see his commander-in-chief. He read out to Parker the 'appreciation of the situation' that he had prepared, setting out the options available and ending with the opinion that 'the boldest measures are the safest, and our country demands a most vigorous exertion of her force directed with judgement'. Sir Hyde agreed to pass the Kronborg guns, sail south down The Sound and down the Holland Deep to attack Copenhagen from the south up the King's Deep. The fleet turned back and anchored in approximately the same position as the night before. That same night, 24/25 March, the main instigator of the Armed Neutrality was throttled in his bed in St Petersburg. With Tsar Paul dead the battle of Copenhagen was almost certainly an unnecessary one – but news travelled slowly in 1801.

All the British needed was a wind with plenty of north in it to take them into The Sound. There was no such wind – not for another three days, and even then it was not until 30 March that the fleet finally braved the batteries at Kronborg.

## Into The Sound – at last

So why was Parker so worried about getting into The Sound? It was narrow, about 4,000 yards wide at its narrowest point and guarded by guns on either side. The most serious threat was from the batteries in Kronborg Castle. They were 36-pounders with an effective range of about a mile but they would be firing at moving targets and the likelihood of the gunners being well practised in that or indeed in any other type of firing was almost zero. On the eastern side were the Swedes in Halsingborg. They too had guns but Parker had no idea of the type, or whether they were manned. Even supposing they were, and could fire out to 1,700 yards like the Danes, nobody, including Nelson, seems to have done the simple arithmetic that showed there was a gap of at least 600 yards down the middle of the channel that neither Danish nor Swedish guns could reach effectively.

On Thursday 26 March the lack of the right wind did not prevent Parker finalizing a plan of attack. He allocated additional ships to Nelson, who would command the actual attack. In the event Nelson had de facto command of the entire fleet bar five ships-of-the-line, one of which was the *St George*, as Nelson transferred his flag to the 74-gun *Elephant*, under the captaincy of his old comrade-in-arms from the Nile Thomas Foley, since it had a shallower draft. Nelson planned to lead with his division into The Sound and anchor just north of the shoal known as the Middle Ground (Map 24). He would then carry out a detailed reconnaissance before leading his division down the Holland Deep to attack the southern end of the Danish line of blockships in the King's Deep. Parker's ships would remain in the north and endeavour to threaten the enemy in the Kronlobet Channel and Trekroner Fort. This plan would allow the maximum concentration against the weakest part of the Danish line. Once the King's Deep blockships and floating batteries had been subdued, he would send the fireships against the ships in the Kronlobet Channel. At about the same time some 25 ships' boats, each armed with a 24-pounder and packed with marines and soldiers, would carry out an amphibious assault on the Trekroner and Lynetton Forts. Difficulties looming were the navigational hazards among the unmarked shoals and mud banks in the Holland and King's Deeps and the fickle behaviour of the wind. A northerly wind was needed to take the fleet down the Holland, followed by a southerly one for the attack up the King's. That might be asking a lot of providence.

On 27 March the weather was calm with a light breeze from the south. The crews were exercised with gun drills and in the boats. Parker went on board the *Elephant* to discuss plans with Nelson. The commander-in-chief was still edgy about Kronborg Castle, and worried that when he took his fleet into The Sound the Danes would fire first. That evening he sent the brig *Cruizer* with a letter to Colonel Stricker, the commandant at Kronborg, asking precisely that. Stricker did not get the message until the morning of the 28th and had to consult Copenhagen, so Parker did not get a response until late that night when a Danish officer was escorted aboard the *London*, and confirmed the Danes would open fire.

On 29 March Parker finalized his plan for the passage into The Sound and, with a favourable wind, moved his fleet to within three or four miles of the entrance before anchoring for the night. Early on Monday 30 March the sentries on the castle walls sounded the alarm – signal flags were fluttering, the British Fleet was on the move. Danish gunners rushed to man their cannons in great excitement. It was the first time in their lifetime that they would be firing in anger. The 74-gun *Monarch* led the way and, in her eagerness, was soon well ahead. It must have been a splendid sight, so many ships forming a long curving arc as they headed south-east and then south through the entrance to the cold grey waters of The Sound. The plan was for the fleet to sail in line astern through the narrows, covered by the fire of several bomb ships under the control of the 74-gun *Edgar*. As the *Monarch* came abreast of the castle, in the centre of the channel, she hoisted her colours. As if this was the signal they had been waiting for, the Danish guns instantly opened up. All shots fell short. The *Monarch* responded with a rippling thunder as every gun of her starboard broadside fired in

quick succession. It was also the signal for British bombs to come into action. Midshipman Millard noted:

> not one of their shot reached us ... We expected to be 'saluted' from both shores, and were prepared accordingly [both broadsides manned]; but when the succeeding ships found that the batteries on the Swedish side were silent, they hauled over to that shore; and many of them, finding that the [Danish] shot fell short, would not condescend to fire at all.

There were, however, as Millard explained, two unnecessary casualties.

> The Captain of Marines, observing from the poop that none of our shot reached the shore, came down to my quarters in the cabin and took the bed [quoin] entirely out, that he might see the effect [raise the muzzle to maximum elevation]. Not being much used to the great guns he kept the lanyard in his hand while the gun was run out, which pulled the lock before the muzzle was out at the port [thus firing it early]. The man [a crewman] being priming at the time, the fire communicated with the contents in the powderhorn, and it burst in the man's hand, carrying away the tips of his fingers. One man, being green, contrived to have his leg in the way of the tackle when the gun recoiled, by which means the leg was broken.

These were the only casualties in the entire fleet as it passed into The Sound.

By 8.30 a.m. the fleet was safely through the entrance. When Nelson's van division dropped anchor it was off the town of Taarboek, five miles from their objective. There seemed to be no obstacles between the fleet and the walls of the citadel or the spires of Copenhagen's churches except the ships and floating batteries lined up to defend the city. It was an illusion. The flat sheet of water, with its lumps of floating ice, held hidden dangers. The Danes had removed all marker buoys so the British could not tell where exactly were the Holland and King's Deep. Where were the boundaries of the Saltholm Flats, the Middle Ground and the Refshale Shoal? Was the line of blockships in King's Deep in deep water, shallow water or even sitting on the muddy bottom? The rudimentary charts were useless without the buoys and the pilots had no idea. A 74 needed a minimum of four fathoms under her keel; where was the four-fathom line, where were the mudbanks and shoals? Nelson had to have answers to most of these questions before he could launch any attack. The only way to get them was a detailed reconnaissance and the laborious process of taking soundings and laying out makeshift buoys. Nelson gave instructions for Captain Foley to make four buoys from wooden water barrels. The master, Mr Fothergill, recorded in his log: 'Expended four breakers, 12 double-headed shot to buoy the Middle Ground.' It was a start, but many more than four would be needed.

## The Danish defences

The Danes had to face some serious long-standing difficulties when the need came to defend their capital, its harbour and arsenal in early 1801. Eighty years of peace had meant eighty years of neglected defences of probably the most vulnerable capital in Europe. Their problems are listed below and should be read in conjunction with Map 23 on which are shown the final defensive lines that faced Nelson.

## Copenhagen: The Danish Defence Lines, 2 April 1801                    Map 23

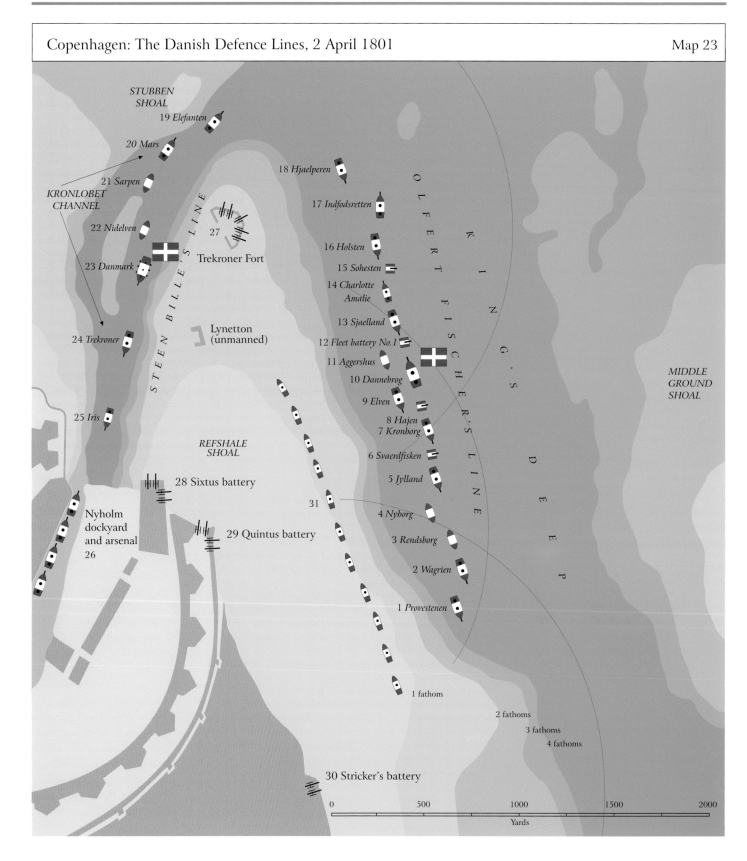

STUBBEN
SHOAL

19 Elefanten

20 Mars

21 Sarpen

KRONLOBET
CHANNEL

22 Nidelven

27

23 Danmark

Trekroner Fort

STEEN BILLE'S LINE

Lynetton
(unmanned)

24 Trekroner

18 Hjaelperen

17 Indfodsretten

16 Holsten

15 Sohesten

14 Charlotte
Amalie

13 Sjaelland

12 Fleet battery No.1

11 Aggershus

10 Dannebrog

9 Elven

8 Hajen
7 Kronborg

6 Svaerdfisken

5 Jylland

4 Nyborg

3 Rendsborg

2 Wagrien

1 Provestenen

OLFERT FISCHER'S LINE

KING'S DEEP

MIDDLE
GROUND
SHOAL

25 Iris

REFSHALE
SHOAL

28 Sixtus battery

31

29 Quintus battery

Nyholm
dockyard
and arsenal
26

1 fathom

2 fathoms

3 fathoms

4 fathoms

30 Stricker's battery

0            500            1000            1500            2000
                          Yards

• There was only one entrance or exit from the harbour, the very narrow Kronlobet Channel. Inside the harbour was the Danish operational fleet (no. 26 on map). There was no way Denmark could risk these ships, the cornerstone of national security, in a slogging match in open water. And if an enemy sank one or two old ships in the entrance to the channel – about

where no. 19, the *Elefanten*, is shown on the map – the entire fleet would be trapped and useless. It was therefore essential that this channel be heavily defended.

• Guarding the entrance to the Kronlobet Channel had always been the primary task of the Trekroner (Three Crowns) Fort. However, its defences had suffered from many years of neglect,

## Commodore Fischer's Defence Line

1. Blockship 30 x 36-pdrs, 28 x 24-pdrs. Stump mast.
2. Blockship 52 x 24-pdrs. Stump mast.
3. Cavalry transport 22 x 24-pdrs. Masts and sails.
4. Cavalry transport 22 x 24-pdrs. Masts and sails.
5. Blockship 26 x 24-pdrs, 26 x 18-pdrs, 18 x 8-pdrs.
6. Gun barge/floating bty 18 x 24-pdrs. No masts.
7. Frigate 22 x 24-pdrs. No masts.
8. Gun barge/floating bty 20 x 18-pdrs. No masts.
9. Signal corvette 10 x 24-pdrs.
10. Blockship (flagship) 24 x 24-pdrs, 24 x 12-pdrs, 12 x 8-pdrs. Stump mast.
11. Cavalry transport 20 x 24-pdrs. Masts and sails.
12. Floating bty 24 x 24-pdrs. No masts.
13. Blockship 30 x 24-pdrs, 30 x 18-pdrs, 14 x 8-pdrs.
14. Small blockship 26 x 24-pdrs.
15. Gun barge/floating bty 20 x 24-pdrs. No masts.
16. Blockship 24 x 24-pdrs, 24 x 12-pdrs, 12 x 8-pdrs.
17. Blockship 26 x 24-pdrs, 26 x 12-pdrs, 12 x 8-pdrs.
18. Frigate 16 x 36-pdrs, 2 x 12-pdrs, 4 x 150-pdr mortar (fully rigged).

## Captain Steen Bille's Squadron

19. Blockship 74 x 24-pdrs. Stump mast.
20. Blockship 26 x 24-pdrs, 26 x 12-pdrs, 8 x 8-pdrs.
21. Brig 18 x 18-pdrs.
22. Brig 18 x 8-pdrs.
23. Flagship 28 x 36-pdrs, 28 x 18-pdrs, 14 x 8-pdrs.
24. Line of battleship 28 x 24-pdrs, 28 x 18-pdrs, 18 x 8-pdrs.
25. Frigate 40 x 18-pdrs.

## Other Defences

26. Main fleet, unmanned and kept secure in dockyard.
27. Fort 66 x 24-pdrs, 3 mortars.
28. Shore bty 25 x 18-pdrs, 2 mortars.
29. Shore bty 26 x 18-pdrs, 9 mortars.
30. Shore bty 6 x 36-pdrs, 2 mortars.
31. Gunboat flotilla (11), each 2 x 18-pdr bow chasers.

## Notes

• With the exception of a frigate, all defences were fixed and anchored. The essential Danish defence requirement was to defend/control the King's Deep and Kronlobet channels and prevent the British from bombarding Copenhagen and the naval dockyard/arsenal.

• Commodore Fischer commanded the King's Deep line and Captain Steen Bille the Kronlobet (second) line.

Approximate strengths were:

|  | Guns | Mortars | Total Pieces | Men |
|---|---|---|---|---|
| Fischer's line | 670 | 4 | 674 | 5000 |
| Gunboat flotilla | 22 | – | 22 | 750 |
| Fort and shore batteries | 123 | 16 | 139 | 1200 |
| Steen Bille's line | 170 | – | 170 | 1200 |
|  | **985** | **20** | **1005** | **8150** |

## Key

⬤▸ Gunboat – moved by sail or oar

◗ Moveable artillery barge/cavalry transport

▣▸ Frigate/corvette/brig

▣▸ Blockship/ship-of-the-line

⚏ Gun barge

╱ 1500-yd arc – maximum effective range of shore battery guns and Trekroner Fort

with the ten-foot-high ramparts having fortifications only of wood and earth – very primitive protection. The six sides formed a small harbour but the garrison had no accommodation so had to live in tents erected on the narrow walls. At the time of the battle the fort had 66 24-pounders and three mortars with a hotch-potch of troops from the Marine Corps, Navy, Artillery Corps and Prince Frederick's Regiment manning the guns. It was far from being the formidable fortification the Danes wanted or the British imagined.

• If enemy bomb vessels lined up in the King's Deep they could, with their superior range, lob incendiary bombs into the harbour, arsenal and much of the city, while remaining out of effective range of the shore batteries. This would be a catastrophe. The answer lay in forming a forward line of defences out in the channel. The eventual line was as shown on the map. There were 18 separate ships (frigates, corvettes or brigs), blockships (hulks), moveable converted artillery and cavalry transport barges, and four fixed gun barges.

• This forward line of defences was essential but in itself caused difficulties. Its southern end was particularly vulnerable to raking fire, and even exposed to being doubled (as had happened to the French at the Nile) if there was enough deep water immediately west of the line. It also masked the fire of the Sixtus and Quintus shore batteries – in the event neither of these batteries played any significant role in the defence. Then none of Fischer's gun platforms could fire on an enemy approaching from north or south until the enemy came into their arc of fire. Finally, if the enemy concentrated overwhelming fire power against the southern end there was nothing any other part of the line could do to support it. It was partly due to these weaknesses that the Danes established the second line of shallow-draught gunboats shown on the map.

• Time was against the Danes. The British Fleet arrived off Kullen on 22 March. As late as the 24th only seven of the blockships were in position; three artillery barges were still in the dockyard, as was the Fleet Battery No. 1. The line lacked a third of its manpower and crews had not had time to practise gun drills. Parker's indecision and wavering gave the Danes another eight days' grace, which they put to good use.

• The Danes lacked manpower. The Danish authorities estimated the required number of men for the line of defences in the King's Deep as about 5,500. As late as 31 March press gangs were still roaming the streets of Copenhagen, desperately scraping the barrel of potential recruits. Quite apart from the numbers problem, the quality both of officers and ratings was questionable. A factor that enabled the defensive line to function was that seamen were not essential. The blockships and barges were fixed defences so once they were in position there was no requirement for seamanship. There were three broad categories of men making up the gun crews: regulars and reservists, soldiers, and volunteers and pressed men. Additionally there were the troops manning the guns on the Trekroner Fort (600) and a lesser number at Stricker's battery. The Lynetton battery was unmanned and the Sixtus and Quintus Batteries were unable to fire. Commodore Olfert Fischer (flagship the *Dannebrog*) was the overall commander-in-chief with particular command over the King's Deep defences with Captain Steen Bille (flagship the *Danmark*) commanding in the Kronlobet Channel. On the day of the battle Fischer had a mere 62 officers on the King's Deep vessels, of whom only 18 were regulars. Among this diverse mixture of men there was no uniformity of gunnery training – the men on the artillery barge *Hajen* were soldiers and craftsmen and had their first training in manning a naval gun early on the morning of the battle.

Map 23 shows the Danish defences on 2 April. Fischer's line was well out into the King's Deep with deep water on the city side before the Refshale Shoal, though Nelson had no way of knowing this. To try to counter any attempt to double the Danish line, sufficient men were put on board to man both starboard and larboard guns. Scores of barges and small boats had been ferrying frantically backwards and forwards, taking guns, equipment, supplies and ammunition to the line up to the last moment. Five of the blockships had left the dockyard without enough gun carriages – they would be sent out when ready. In the event the ships fought without them.

**Nelson prepares**

Immediately the British Fleet dropped anchor on 30 March Parker and Nelson went to take a much closer look at the defences. They took with them Rear-Admiral Graves and Lieutenant-Colonel Stewart along with Captains Domett, Otway, Foley, Freemantle and Riou. Parker records in his journal: 'Went with Lord Nelson &c. on board the *Amazon* [frigate] and reconoitred [*sic*] the enemy's line, which was found

## Crown Prince Frederick Visits the *Dannebrog*

The Crown Prince was the overall commander-in-chief of the Danish forces on land and sea. On 26 March, the day Nelson transferred his flag to the *Elephant*, the *Dannebrog*'s crew were standing smartly on deck as her guns fired a 21-gun salute; the Crown Prince was arriving in his barge at the start of an inspection. The prince was a popular man, particularly since an announcement he had made the day before in consequence of the Danes' worry about fireships (unnecessary, as it turned out).

His Majesty has most graciously proclaimed that any man who diverts or destroys a fireship will receive in reward 100 rigsdaler if an officer or petty officer and 50 rigsdaler if a rating. He has also declared that any battery that succeeds in setting an enemy ship on fire will be rewarded with 100 rigsdaler, for every mast shot away 50 rigsdaler and for every shot below the waterline 50 rigsdaler.

Quite how they were to keep the score was not explained.

to be far more formidable than we had reason to expect.' He neglected to mention that the *Cruizer* (sloop) and *Lark* (lugger) accompanied the *Amazon* and that they were fired on as they tacked back and forth to the northeast of the Middle Ground, sometimes within a mile of the Trekroner guns. No hits were recorded, which was fortunate considering the amount of gold braid on show.

Nelson gave orders for the sounding and marking of the Holland Deep to begin that day while it was still light. Captain Brisbane (*Cruizer*), Mr Fothergill and two pilots set off in a boat with the four buoys to begin the task. *Cruizer*'s log records, 'Sent the Master to buoy the Middle Passage.' On their return from the reconnaissance Parker, Nelson, Graves and several others had a discussion on the *London* as to what they had seen. As noted above Parker thought the defences stronger than anticipated. Stewart seemed to agree, writing: 'We soon perceived that our delay had been of important advantage to the enemy, who had lined the northern edge of the shoals near the Crown Batteries [Trekroner], and the front of the harbour and arsenal [the King's Deep] with a formidable flotilla.'

Nelson, however, was almost dismissive, writing to Emma: 'I have just been reconnoitring [*sic*] the Danish line of defence. It

## Captain Riou Encounters an Iceberg

A firm but fair disciplinarian and something of a perfectionist, Captain Edward Riou was a highly respected seaman and competent commander, who like Blackwood became renowned as a successful frigate captain. In late 1789 he was given command of the former frigate *Guardian*, packed with convicts and £70,000 worth of stores, livestock and seeds bound for New South Wales. While ashore at the Cape of Good Hope he met Captain Bligh on his way home after the mutiny and his epic voyage in the open boat. Almost two weeks after leaving the Cape of Good Hope, Riou sighted a huge iceberg and, because his ship was overloaded with men and animals, decided to send over boats to fill casks with fresh water. This was done but shortly after sailing the *Guardian* ran into fog as night was falling. Then the ship struck the submerged ice, and in the process of getting her off a large hole was torn in her bottom and icy water rushed into the hold. By midnight a gale had sprung up and the *Guardian* had six feet of water in her and was sinking fast.

The following day, Christmas Eve, all seamen and convicts took turns on the pumps. By Christmas Day, with the men on the point of collapse and the water still rising, Riou had to make a decision. He had five boats and 300 men on board, so he decided that all who desired could take the boats and try to make

the 1,200 miles back to the Cape. The first boat was swamped and all its occupants drowned quickly in the freezing sea. However, the others got away without mishap. One was picked up after two weeks by a French merchantman; the others just disappeared.

Riou remained on his ship along with three midshipmen, the boatswain, carpenter and twenty seamen. The boatswain later wrote: 'After the boats left us we had two choices, either pump or sink.' They pumped. 'Sometimes our upper deck scuppers was under water outside, and the ship lying like a log in the water ... Sixteen feet of water was the common run for the nine weeks in the hold.'

For nine weeks the *Guardian* moved slowly through the water. For nine weeks these twenty-six men toiled at the pumps in shifts throughout every twenty-four hours. Unbelievably they made it to Table Bay, where while at anchor a storm blew up and she sank. As an outstanding example of leadership Riou's would be hard to beat, as demonstrated by the fact that even the convicts manned the pumps, there was no rush for the boats and over twenty men volunteered to stay with their captain to await what must have seemed certain death. It is a striking contrast with Bligh's treatment of his men.

## The British Fleet Arrives off Copenhagen and Prepares to Attack                Map 24

Taarbœk

British Fleet arrives
a.m. 30 March

Parker, Nelson,
Graves, Foley
and others make
recce from
*Amazon* on
30 March and
again on
31 March.

A

B

E

Parker with 8
ships-of-line
a.m. 2 April

*Cruizer*
1 April

STUBBEN
SHOAL

KRONLOBET
CHANNEL

HOLLAND DEEP

C

These four ships acted as
additional markers for
the passage down the
Holland Deep on 1 April.

Trekroner

*Harpy* (sloop)

MIDDLE
GROUND
SHOAL

SALTHOLM FLAT

Citadel

Lynetton

KING'S DEEP

Copenhagen

REFSHALE SHOAL

*Fox* (cutter)

*Lark* (lugger)

Stricker's battery

DRACO
POINT
*Cruizer*
2 April

D

Nelson's intended
attack on 2 April.

Nelson anchors for night
1/2 April with:
12 ships-of-line
7 frigates
2 sloops
6 brigs
7 bombs
2 fire ships

SALTHOLM
ISLAND

AMAGER ISLAND

Dragor

### Key/Notes

▣▶  Danish line of defensive blockships

○  Nelson's improvised buoys along eastern edge of Middle
Ground shoal and western edge of Saltholm Flat.

A  30 March a.m. British Fleet arrives off Copenhagen roads,
having come under the guns of Kronborg Castle earlier as
they entered The Sound.

B  30 March p.m. Commanders recce the Danish defences
from north of King's Deep in *Amazon*, *Cruizer* and *Lark*.

C  Nelson's squadron, heavily reinforced, negotiates the Holland
Deep after makeshift buoys placed to mark the shallows of
the Middle Ground shoal.

D  Nelson anchors for the night 1/2 April before launching his
attack northwards up the King's Deep a.m. 2 April.

E  Parker, with the remainder of the fleet, moves to the northern
entrance to King's Deep to support the main attack by
Nelson.

0   1   2   3   4   5
Miles

## Nelson's Exhaustion before the Battle

Lieutenant-Colonel Stewart left a memorable account of an exhausted Nelson dictating his written orders before the battle. It gives a revealing insight into the pressures of high command and the burden of staff work in those distant days.

From the previous fatigue of this day [1 April], and the two preceding, Lord Nelson was so much exhausted while dictating his instructions, that it was recommended to him by us all, and indeed insisted upon by his old servant Allen, who assumed much command on these occasions, that he should go to his cot. It was placed on the floor, but from it he still continued to dictate. The orders were completed about one o'clock, when half a dozen Clerks in the foremost cabin proceeded to transcribe them. Lord Nelson's impatience again showed itself; for instead of sleeping undisturbedly, as he might have done, he was every half hour calling from his cot to these Clerks to hasten their work, for that the wind was becoming fair: he was constantly receiving a report of this during the night. The work being finished about six in the morning, his Lordship, who was previously up and dressed, breakfasted, and about seven made the Signal for all captains. The instructions were delivered to each by eight o'clock ...

---

looks formidable to those who are children at war, but to my judgement, with ten sail of the line I think I can annihilate them ...'

After the discussion Parker sat down in his cabin to write his orders, not the detailed ones for the attack – those would be for Nelson to decide later – but those establishing the broad principles of the attack, how the fleet would be divided and who was to command each part. He split the fleet into two very unequal parts, retaining control over eight ships-of-the-line, two 98s (*London* and *St George*), four 74s (*Warrior*, *Defence*, *Saturn* and *Ramillies*), and two 64s (*Raisonnable* and *Veteran*) and giving Nelson command of the rest. Parker recorded in his journal:

Lord Nelson to take the ships [ten, plus two more added the next day], frigates, bomb-vessels, fire-ships and gun-vessels therein mentioned under his command for the purpose of attacking the enemy's line, &c. &c. Issued several instructions on this occasion: Captain Rose of the *Jamaica* [frigate] to command the gun-brigs [6]; Lieutenant Hancock of the *London* to command one division of the boats for boarding, a lieutenant of the *St George* to command the other division.

Parker then went into considerable detail as to how the two divisions of flat boats, to be commanded by Captain Freemantle, were to be organized, each with a carronade and 30 soldiers. Barges and pinnaces were to have four marines and boarding parties were to be 'armed only' with cutlasses, poleaxes and pikes, with a broad-axe in each boat. Once his clerks had copied these orders and they had been collected, Parker's role in the battle, with the exception of one crucial signal, was over, although the following day (Tuesday 31 March) he insisted on a second reconnaissance. This time the seven artillery officers from the bomb vessels accompanied the expedition, which was followed by a council of war on the *London*. Its outcome was that the attack was

### Nelson's Ships Fired on the Night before the Battle

In his excellent book *The Battle of Copenhagen 1801*, Professor Ole Feldbaek describes an incident that no British historian seems ever to have mentioned. This was that Stricker's Battery in the south fired three mortar shells at Nelson's ships as they sat at anchor south of the Middle Ground on the night of the 1/2 April. Lieutenant Stricker (one wonders if he was the son of Colonel Stricker, commandant of Kronborg Castle) noticed the enemy was in range of his mortars and requested permission to fire. His request went all the way up the chain of command to the commander-in-chief, Crown Prince Frederick, who gave permission and eventually three shells were fired. Colonel Mecklenburg (commander of the Artillery Corps), peering into the darkness, thought they fell short and ordered firing to cease. However, Sub-Lieutenant Muller on the *Hajen* considered they fell in the middle of the British ships. One wonders what would have happened if the battery had continued firing throughout the night.

to go ahead, the only change being the addition of Captain Murray's *Edgar* and Freemantle's *Ganges* to Nelson's force.

The night of 30/31 March had been a grim one for the men in the small boats taking soundings and setting out buoys to mark the western side of the Holland Channel. With muffled oars, lead lines, boat compasses and shielded lanterns and led by Captains Hardy and Riou they slowly groped their way down the channel. It was bitterly cold, with slabs of floating ice grinding periodically against the sides of the boats while the men peered anxiously into the inky blackness. The leadsmen suffered most as they were quickly drenched and chilled to the bone. Sandbanks were identified, bearings taken and buoys positioned. By dawn the job was done, but it had to be repeated the next night for the eastern side. On 1 April, under Nelson's personal supervision, the markers along the edge of the Saltholm flat were reinforced by anchoring the *Cruizer*, *Harpy*, *Fox* and *Lark* at key points (see Map 24). Surgeon Ferguson of the *Elephant* was impressed: 'I could only admire when I saw the first man in all the world spend the whole of the day and night in the boats ...'. It was a job brilliantly done, and would today have earned several decorations. Without the successful marking of this passage an attack from the south would have been too risky.

At last, on Wednesday 1 April, the wind and current were from the north and the Holland Deep was buoyed – the operation could start. The first phase would be to get the whole of Nelson's division (80 per cent of the fleet) down the passage to what the Army would call an 'assembly area', in naval terms an anchorage off the southern end of the Middle Ground Shoal. Shortly after dawn the *Elephant* signalled for all masters and pilots to report to Nelson's flagship. The *Cruizer* anchored at the entrance to the channel and the other small ships went to their final positions as markers. After a final visit to Parker, Nelson personally hailed each one as he passed en route back to his ship to weigh. Midshipman Millard described the moment he saw a boat being rowed towards the *Monarch*.

> On directing my spy-glass towards her, I observed several officers in her, but at the end of the boat was a cocked hat put on square, with a peculiar slouch, so as to be at right angles to the boat's keel. I immediately ran to the officer of the watch and assured him Lord Nelson was coming on board, for I had seen his hat. My information did not receive much credit, till in the process of time the old checked surtout was discovered; and soon after a squeaking little voice hailed the *Monarch*, and desired us, in true Norfolk drawl, to prepare to weigh.

By 5.00 p.m. the fleet had been led down the Holland Deep by the *Amazon* and anchored for the night south of the Middle Ground. Although exhausted physically Nelson was eager and excited at dinner that night. According to Stewart, 'He was in the highest spirits, and drank to a leading wind, and to the success of the ensuing day.'

## THE BATTLE

### The plan

During the night, as if responding to Nelson's toast, the wind swung round to the south-east – perfect for a passage up the channel. During the night Captain Hardy, who was a 'volunteer' (a supernumerary officer without a specific command), took a boat into the southern end of the King's Deep to sound the depths of water in the approach to the enemy line; he used a long pole instead of the lead, which would make a loud splash when it entered the water. Hardy got so close to the *Provestenen* that he heard snatches of conversation. But his really important discovery was that the deeper water was towards the enemy line, the shallower on the Middle Ground (eastern side). On his return Hardy was, however, unable to convince the pilots, who insisted the opposite. In the event Nelson could not be sure the Danes had not moored close to the edge of the deep water so could not take the risk of doubling the enemy line as at the Nile. His ships followed the pilots and kept near the centre of the channel – with unfortunate consequences for several.

Nelson planned to concentrate on the centre and southern end of the enemy line first. He would overwhelm this part of the line and then move north with his ships divided into two attacking groups. The first wave would consist of the five line-of-battle ships *Edgar* (74), *Ardent* (64), *Glatton* (56 carronades), *Isis* (50) and *Agamemnon* (64), which would sail in succession. The *Edgar* would anchor opposite the *Jylland*, the *Ardent* opposite the *Kronborg* and gun barge *Svaedfisken*, the *Glatton* opposite the *Dannebrog*, the *Isis* opposite the *Wagrien* and the *Agamemnon* opposite the *Provestenen*. To reinforce the attack on the southern end of the enemy line the 36-gun frigate *Désirée* would position herself to the south of the *Provestenen* in order to rake her and the blockships and barges immediately to her north. Similarly the 28-gun *Jamaica* would lead the six gun brigs into the shallower water south-west of the line into positions from which they could fire into the southern enemy ships. Nelson did not know the names of the enemy vessels and so had numbered them in his orders, starting from the south – the *Provestenen* being No. 1.

The second wave was composed of the *Bellona* (74), *Russell* (74), *Elephant* (74), *Ganges* (74), *Monarch* (74) and Graves's flagship *Defiance* (74). As the enemy vessels in the south were pounded

---

## Nelson's Command at Copenhagen

Nelson had a very substantial part of the fleet under his command at the battle. As far as the fighting was concerned Parker played no part. The ships under Nelson and their captains were as follows:

| Ships-of-the-line | Frigates | Brig/Sloops | Gunboats | Bomb vessels | Fireships | Others |
|---|---|---|---|---|---|---|
| *Bellona* (74, Boulden) | *Amazon* (38, Riou) | *Cruizer* (18, Brisbane) | *Biter* (12) | *Discovery* | *Otter* | *Eling* (14 – schooner) |
| *Defiance* (74, Retalick, Graves' flagship) | *Blanche* (36, Hamond) | *Harpy* (18, Birchall) | *Bouncer* (12) | *Explosion* | *Zepher* | *Fox* (10 – cutter) |
| *Edgar* (74, Murray) | *Désirée* (36, Inman) | | *Force* (12) | *Hecla* | | *Lark* (lugger) |
| *Elephant* (74, Foley, Nelson's flagship) | *Alcmene* (32, Sutton) | | *Sparkler* (12) | *Sulphur* | | |
| *Ganges* (74, Freemantle) | *Arrow* (30, Bolton) | | *Teazer* (12) | *Terror* | | |
| *Monarch* (74, Mosse, then Yelland) | *Dart* (30, Devonshire) | | *Tigress* (12) | *Volcano* | | |
| *Russell* (74, Cuming) | *Jamaica* (28, Rose) | | | *Zebra* | | |
| *Glatton* (56 carronades, Bligh) | | | | | | |
| *Agamemnon* (64, Fancourt) | | | | | | |
| *Ardent* (64, Bertie) | | | | | | |
| *Polyphemus* (64, Lawford) | | | | | | |
| *Isis* (50, Walker) | | | | | | |

Of the above only the *Defiance*, *Polyphemus* and *Agamemnon* fought again at Trafalgar. The *Defence* was present at Copenhagen but was with Parker's division and took no part in the battle. Captains Hardy and Freemantle were captains at Trafalgar. *Defence*'s captain at Copenhagen is worthy of a postscript as he was a splendidly eccentric character. Captain Lord Harry Paulet, son of the Marquis of Winchester, once requested leave from his ship to visit London whilst in Portsmouth. His admiral refused permission, but said he could only go ashore as far as his barge could take him. Not to be outdone Paulet loaded his barge onto a large carriage and set off for the city. On another occasion, annoyed at the meagre amount of paint permitted by the Navy Board for ship maintenance, he wrote to the Board asking which side of his ship he should paint!

into submission these ships would sail up to the east of the battle line to take on the northern end. Two bomb vessels would throw shells into the Trekroner and the remaining five into the Nyholm arsenal. At the same time Parker was to approach from the north (wind permitting) to threaten the Trekroner Fort and the Danish line in the Kronlobet Channel. The final phase would be the storming of the Danish vessels and fort by the soldiers in the boats.

Nelson's plan ensured he out-gunned the Danes by concentrating his firepower. He also had the advantage of being able to manoeuvre against moored ships and fixed defences, and could switch his attack from one part of the line to another as required. However, his key battle-winning advantage lay in the superiority of his veteran crews, particularly his gun crews who were well trained and practised and able to fire at a far faster rate than their opponents.

### The battle begins

The wind might be strong and from a favourable direction but the water, or rather depth of it, continued to pose difficulties. At around 7.00 a.m. on 2 April Nelson summoned his captains for a final briefing. After they returned to their ships Nelson met the pilots and, to his exasperation, found them still reluctant to venture into the channel. Colonel Stewart later noted, 'The pilots … and several masters of the Navy, were ordered on board the *Elephant*. … A most unpleasant degree of hesitation prevailed among them all when they came to the point about … the exact line of deep water in the King's Channel.' Nelson was to be even more forthright, recalling later how he 'suffered the misery of having the honour of our Country entrusted to pilots who had no other thought than to keep the ships clear of danger, and their own silly heads clear of shot'.

The impasse was suddenly solved by a Mr Alexander Briarly, the master of the *Bellona*, who had been a master at the Nile and declared that he was prepared to lead the fleet. Where he led others followed and all repaired to their ships. Mr Briarly went back to the *Bellona* and promptly took a boat out to mark the southern end of the Middle Ground, on his return transferring to the *Edgar* to navigate for the fleet. He had taken on a huge responsibility.

According to Nelson's journal the blue and white horizontally stripped 'preparative' flag, followed by No. 68 – 'Weigh, outer or leeward ships first' – was hoisted at 9.30 a.m. Throughout the fleet all eyes were riveted on the 'preparative'. Within a matter of moments it came down, but with No. 68 remaining stretched out in the wind. They were off.

Midshipman Millard had left us the best description of Nelson's ships going into action that morning.

> The *Monarch* being the last but two or three in the line, we had a good opportunity of seeing the other ships approach the enemy to commence the action. A more beautiful and solemn spectacle I never witnessed.
>
> The *Edgar* led the van, and on her approach the battery on the island of Amak [Amager – Stricker's battery] and three or four of the southern-most vessels opened fire upon her.

---

### Practical Gunnery

Midshipman Millard was in charge of five of the quarterdeck guns on the *Monarch*; here is a final extract from his superb account of the battle.

> I pulled off my coat, helped to run out the guns, handed the powder, and literally worked as hard as a dray-horse. Every gun was supplied at first with a portion of shot, wadding etc. close by it; and when these were expended, we applied to a reserved place by the main-mast. It immediately occurred to me that I could not be more usefully employed than conveying this supply, which would enable the stronger ones to remain at their guns, for the men wanted no stimulus to keep them to their duty, nor any directions how to perform it. The only cautions I remember to have given were hinted to me by the gunner before the action – viz., to worm the guns frequently, that no fire might remain from the old cartridge, to fire two round-shot in each gun, and to use nothing else while round-shot was to be had.

---

### Captain William Bligh

Born in 1754, Bligh accompanied Captain Cook on his second expedition round the world (1772–4) on the *Resolution*. He was nicknamed 'Breadfruit Bligh' because of the discovery of the fruit on the voyage, and was sent, in 1787, in the *Bounty* to the Pacific to fetch breadfruit for introduction to the West Indies. On his return in 1789 a mutiny broke out and Bligh and eighteen others were set adrift. The mutineers settled on Pitcairn Island – where their descendants still live – and Bligh eventually landed in Timor, having made a voyage of about 4,000 miles in an open boat. He returned to England and ultimately succeeded in introducing the breadfruit tree into the West Indies. He became the governor of New South Wales from 1805 to 1808 but his rough manners and brutal behaviour caused yet another mutiny, this time by his soldiers, by whom he was imprisoned until 1810. Despite this he was promoted rear-admiral in 1811 and vice-admiral of the blue in 1817 – the year in which he died aged sixty-three.

His arrival on the *Monarch* before the Battle of Copenhagen was not well received. Although a brilliant navigator and good seaman, he relied on the lash for leadership and lacked common humanity. Midshipman Millard commented on his new captain:

> Captain Bligh was an excellent navigator, and I believe in every respect a good seaman, but his manners and disposition were not pleasant, and his appointment to the *Monarch* gave very general disgust to the officers.
>
> Some circumstances which occurred on our passage home served to increase the general disapprobation. On the 15th April we weighed … Captain Bligh … finding our pilots were not so scientific as himself, he liberally bestowed upon them the appellations of 'dolt' and 'blockhead', and pretending that the ship was not safe in their hands, he took charge of her himself. This was as unnecessary as it was unusual. These men had been accustomed to the Baltic trade the greater part of their lives, and were certainly as well able to conduct the ship from the Naze of Norway to Lowestoffe Point as Captain Bligh.

## Copenhagen: The Height of the Battle, Noon, 2 April 1801    Map 25

### Notes

**A** Both sides slug it out, broadside to broadside. Nelson's fear of running aground prevents a closer range.

**B** The *Agamemnon* goes aground and strong currents prevent the *Jamaica*, gunboats and 3 bomb vessels from joining battle.

**C** Parker's 8 ships approach slowly by tacking into the wind. At 1.30 p.m. Parker hoists signal 39 – 'Discontinue the action'.

**D** Riou and his frigates obey the signal to withdraw. Nelson 'turns a blind eye'.

### Key

**Danish**
- Blockship
- Frigate/corvette/brig
- Artillery barge/cavalry transport
- Gunboat
- Gun barge

**British**
- 3rd-rate 74
- Frigate
- Fireship
- Bomb vessel
- -------→ Route of Nelson's letter of truce

Map labels:

Defence — Ramillies — C — Sir Hyde Parker's 8 ships

STUBBEN SHOAL

Elefanten
Mars
Sarpen
Nidelven
Danmark — Steen Bille
Trekroner
Iris

Arrow (30) — D
Dart (30)
Alcmene (34) — Capt. Riou's frigate squadron
Blanche (36)
Hjaelperen
Amazon (38)
Indfodsretten

Trekroner Fort

Holsten — A — Defiance (74)
Sohesten — Monarch (74)
Charlotte Amalie — Ganges (74) — Otter (fireships)
Nelson — Zepher
Sjaelland
Fleet battery no.1 — Fischer — Elephant (74) — Explosion
Aggershus — Glatton (56) — Discovery
Dannebrog
Lynetton (unmanned)
Elven
Kronborg — A — Ardent (64)
Svaerdfisken
Jylland — Edgar (74)
Nyborg — Bellona (74) (aground)
Rendsborg
Wagrien — Isis (50) — Russell (74) (aground)
Volcano
Provestenen — Polyphemus (64)

MIDDLE GROUND SHOAL

REFSHALE SHOAL

Sixtus battery
Nyholm dockyard and arsenal
Quintus battery

*Rendsborg* forced to withdraw at 11.15 a.m.

Désirée (36)

1 fathom
2 fathoms
3 fathoms
4 fathoms
B —→

Stricker's battery

0   500   1000   1500   2000
Yards

A man of war under sail is at all times a beautiful object, but at such a time the scene is heightened beyond the powers of description. We saw her pressing on through the enemy's fire and manoeuvring in the midst of it to gain her station; our minds were deeply impressed with awe, and not a word was spoken throughout the ship but by the pilot and helmsman; and their communications being chanted very much in the same manner as in our cathedral service, and repeated at intervals, added very much to the solemnity.

Nevertheless, things had started to go wrong. First the *Agamemnon*, fifth in Nelson's order of battle, was making too much leeway and failed to get round the southern end of the Middle Ground. She was forced into the shallows. Despite desperate kedging, 'owing to the strength of the current and the hardness of the ground [she] made very little progress', as Captain Fancourt wrote later. She was out of the battle. Nelson had to change his plan, and the *Polyphemus* was signalled to take *Agamemnon*'s place.

Immediately astern of the *Edgar* came the *Ardent*, *Glatton*, *Isis* and *Désirée*. None condescended to fire until they came abreast of their allotted target. When the *Edgar* came opposite the blockship *Jylland* her log records, 'Came to anchor in seven fathoms water and opened fire on the enemy.' *Ardent* and *Glatton* followed in her lee to take their places without mishap, and Captain Bligh opened fire with a fearsome broadside of carronades on Fischer's flagship, whose colours were fixed to a mast stump. The *Isis* anchored by the stern (as did all British ships) abreast of the *Wagrien* and *Désirée* positioned herself at the southern end of the enemy line. But the *Bellona*, next in line astern, was in trouble. Coming a shade too close to the Middle Ground, she slid silently, almost imperceptibly, onto a protruding sandbank. A warning signal from the *Elephant* that she was running into danger came too late. Captain Sir Thomas Thompson was almost immediately struck by an unlucky shot that all but removed his left leg. First Lieutenant Delafons took command and hoisted signal 344 – 'Ship has struck on a shoal'. Although immobile and 800 yards from the enemy, *Bellona* remained in action for the duration of the battle. Astern of the *Bellona* the *Russell* made a similar error and came to a halt on the same shoal, almost aboard the *Bellona*. As so often in war, the plan had not survived the opening shots.

Nelson reacted immediately. He decided to replace the *Bellona* with his flagship and, crucially, to sail up King's Deep with the two grounded ships to starboard. The remaining ships would follow him. This decision undoubtedly saved the plan from collapsing completely. The crews of the *Bellona* and *Russell* cheered the *Elephant* as she passed them. She anchored just north of the *Glatton* and as the *Ganges*, *Monarch* and *Defiance* came up they placed themselves ahead of each other and began to fire. The British line was shorter than intended but as *Bellona* and *Russell* could keep firing the fleet managed to keep the overall concentration of fire on the southern end of the Danish line. As at Trafalgar Nelson's final signal to his ships was a general one, No. 16 – 'Engage the enemy more closely'.

## The height of the action

By 11.00 a.m. the whole of the King's Deep was filled with the continuous roar of gunfire and endless clouds of smoke that rolled across the water obscuring targets for both sides. Meanwhile the Middle Ground claimed more British victims. Due to a very strong southerly current, Captain Rose in his frigate *Jamaica* was having great difficulty leading his gun brigs and the bomb vessels round

the southern end of the Middle Ground. Despite valiant efforts, his ships arrived piecemeal and only three were able to play a part in the action. The bomb vessels *Explosion* and *Discovery*, the latter under Commander Conn who was to command the *Dreadnought* at Trafalgar, eventually took up position to the east and opposite the *Elephant* and began to lob their bombs into Nyholm. The *Volcano* was able to do the same but further to the south.

The other ships that had to change their plans were the five frigates under Captain Riou's control. Originally ordered to head north and support the attack on the most northerly blockships, Riou now realized that the enemy line north of the *Holsten* was not being engaged. On his own initiative he anchored the *Amazon* just north of the *Defiance* and ordered the ships astern of him to extend the line northwards in an arc. This meant his frigates took on the task of line-of-battle-ships and were directly engaged by the Trekroner guns. It was a remarkably bold decision.

The battle had now become a slogging match, though instead of the close-range duel at about 200 yards or less that Nelson had intended the distance between the opposing lines averaged about 500 yards. Nevertheless, British gunnery was both fast and accurate. At the height of the battle the situation looked approximately as shown on Map 25. For some three hours what Rear-Admiral Graves was to call 'the hottest action that has happened this war' continued. Gradually the superior gunnery and weight of fire began to break up the Danish line. First at about 11.15 a.m. the *Rendsborg* barge was forced to withdraw. Although she was able to anchor further back and open fire again, a gap had appeared in the line that exposed the *Nyborg*. At 11.30 Fischer was compelled to shift his flag to the *Holsten*. By 12.30 the *Nyborg* was forced to cut her mooring and drift north. She arrived in time to tow the crippled cavalry barge *Aggershus* with 214 killed and wounded on board to shelter west of the Trekroner Fort. At 1.00 p.m. the gallant seventeen-year old Sub-Lieutenant Willmoes, commanding the Fleet Battery No. 1, could continue no longer; one and a half hours of being pounded by both the *Elephant* and *Ganges* had inflicted 35 per cent losses. Willmoes cut his mooring and drifted north, colliding briefly with the *Sjaelland* en route. He later wrote to his parents:

I am, thank God, still with all my limbs, which I least expected to keep possession of. As I had about my small battery [twenty-four 24-pounders] Admiral Nelson and two British ships-of-the-line, who fired incessantly with grapeshot, round shot and bar shot, I did my duty and have been praised by the Crown Prince and the admirals, as well as all my colleagues, for standing firm. They told me they never believed I would escape with my life.

At around 2.30 the *Dannebrog* struck, having caught fire and with only three serviceable guns remaining. Fifteen minutes later the *Hajen* followed suit, after nearly four hours under a ceaseless hail of fire from the carronades of *Glatton* and the guns of *Elephant* and *Ardent*, much of it grapeshot. Had the *Glatton* not been firing too high the end would have come far sooner. The *Hajen*'s crew, who had had their first naval gun drill a few hours earlier, surrendered to a boarding party. Their young commander, Sub-Lieutenant Muller, who had spiked all serviceable guns and was attempting to build a raft to get his men away, was taken aboard the *Elephant*. There Colonel Stewart congratulated him on his great gallantry. He was presented to Nelson and, uniquely, allowed to keep his sword.

In case it seems that only the Danes were suffering, a look at the situation on the 74-gun *Monarch* is revealing. She was to suffer the highest losses of any British ship – 220, of which 57 were killed and 163 wounded, mainly in her duel with the blockship *Charlotte Amalie* and the gun barge *Søhesten*. Between the two of them they fielded forty-six 24-pounders but only suffered about a third of the casualties of their enemy – 72, of which 31 were killed. Put another way, the *Monarch*'s losses represented some 35 per cent of her complement, compared with losses of 20 per cent in her two opponents. Some extracts from Midshipman Millard's account best describe the experience of being on a British warship in action.

> I was on the quarterdeck and saw Captain Mosse on the poop. His card of instructions was in his left hand, and his right was raised to his mouth with the speaking trumpet, through which he gave the word, 'Cut away the anchor'. I returned to my station at the aftermost guns; and few minutes later the Captain was brought aft perfectly dead.

Command now devolved onto the first lieutenant, John Yelland.

> This brave veteran had taken care to have the decks swept, and everything clean and nice before we went into action. He had dressed himself in full uniform with his cocked hat set on square, his shirt-frill stiff starched, and his cravat tied tight under his chin as usual. ... How he escaped unhurt seems wonderful: several times I lost sight of him in a cloud of splinters: as they subsided I saw first his cocked hat emerging, then by degrees the rest of his person, his smiling face, so that altogether one might imagine him dressed for his wedding-day.

Sad to relate Yelland, who commanded *Monarch* brilliantly with superb gallantry, was turned down by Parker for immediate promotion to captain, despite Nelson's strong recommendation. The Admiralty later made him commander, but William Bligh of *Bounty* fame was sent over to take command. Millard continues:

> As I returned from the main mast and was abreast of the little binnacle, a shot came in at the port under the poop ladder and carried away the wheel; and three out of the four men stationed at it were either killed or wounded, besides one or two at the gun. ...
>
> Lt Dennis of the 49th Grenadiers had just come up the companion-ladder, and was going aft; the splinters shattered his sword, which was in the sheath, into three pieces, and tore off the finger ends of his left hand. This, however, he scarcely seemed aware of, for lifting up the sheath with his bloody fingers, he called out 'Look here Colonel!' [his commanding officer Lieutenant-Colonel Hutchinson]. ...
>
> This brave officer [Dennis] had, strictly speaking, no particular duty to do; those soldiers who were intended to assist in the projected assault were dressed in uniform and stationed on the poop and on the gangway, where they kept up a fire of musketry, till they were mowed down so fast that they were ordered below to await further orders. The remainder, in their working jackets without accoutrements, were attached to the great guns;

> so that some of the officers, being unacquainted with ship's duty, thought it prudent to retire. Dennis, though he could not act against the enemy, found means to make himself useful; he flew through every part of the ship, and when he found any of his men wounded carried him in his arms down to the cockpit. [Dennis became a major-general]

Eventually Millard received a minor wound.

> As I was returning with two shot in one hand and a cheese (or packet) in the other, I received a pretty smart blow on my right cheek. I dropped my shot, just as a monkey does a hot potato, and clapped my hand to the place, which I found rather bloody, and immediately ran aft to get my handkerchief out of the coat pocket. ...
>
> When I arrived on the main deck [gundeck], along which I had to pass, there was not a single man standing the whole way from the main mast forward, a district containing eight guns [each side], some of which were run out ready for firing; others lay dismounted; and others remained as they were after recoiling. ... I own I felt something like regret, if not fear, as I remounted the ladder on my return.

## Nelson turns a blind eye

Parker made one of the most controversial signals in naval history from the *London* at around 1.15 p.m. By 1.00 p.m. the situation looked alarming from his point of view. Nelson seemed to be getting as good as he was giving and Parker knew that several ships had gone aground. Fearing all was not well, he had hoisted signal No. 39 – 'Discontinue the engagement'. Parker's journal records, 'At 1 turning up to Copenhagen; $\frac{1}{2}$ past, made signal 39, and sent Captain Otway on board the *Elephant*.' There is no record by anyone on the *Elephant* of Otway arriving or what his mission was supposed to be. Some have suggested he went to check the situation with Nelson, or to give Nelson the commander-in-chief's authority to disregard the signal if he saw fit; the facts remains elusive.

The signal consisted of the firing of two guns to attract attention followed by a hoist of signal 39, a blue, white, blue vertically striped flag over a blue over white over red horizontally striped one. It was a general signal, that is made to the entire fleet, and it was the duty of other flagships (*London* and *Defiance*), frigates (*Amazon* certainly) and any other ships who considered it might not have been seen to repeat it. Colonel Stewart has left a graphic description of Nelson's reaction to this signal.

> When signal, No. 39, was made, the Signal-Lieutenant reported it to him. He continued his walk, and did not appear to take notice of it. The Lieutenant, meeting his Lordship at the next turn, asked, 'whether he should repeat it?' Lord Nelson answered, 'No acknowledge it.' On the officer returning to the poop, his Lordship called after him, 'Is No. 16 still hoisted?' The Lieutenant answered in the affirmative. Lord Nelson said, 'Mind you keep it so.' He now walked the deck considerably agitated, which was always known by his moving the stump of his right arm. After a turn or two, he said to me in a quick manner, 'Do you know what is shown on board

of the Commander-in-Chief – No. 39?' On asking what he meant, he answered, 'Why, to leave off action! Leave off action,' he repeated, and then with a shrug, 'Now damn me if I do.' He also observed, I believe to Captain Foley, 'You know, Foley, I have only one eye – I have a right to be blind sometimes'; and then, with an archness peculiar to his character, putting the glass to his blind eye, he exclaimed, 'I really do not see the signal.' This remarkable signal was, therefore, only acknowledged on board the *Elephant*, not repeated.

No fewer than thirteen ships noted this signal in their logs in some way or other. However, it was seemingly only repeated by four: the *Defiance*, *Agamemnon* (not involved in the battle) and the frigates *Désirée* and *Alcmene*. Rear-Admiral Graves was uncertain what to do. He saw the acknowledgement run up, and then hauled down, on the *Elephant*, but Nelson did not repeat the signal – not only that, but No. 16, 'Engage the enemy more closely', was kept flying. Graves had a duty to repeat it, but he hesitated. Then he ordered it hoisted, but in a position in which it could not be seen in the *Elephant* (the starboard maintopsail yardarm) – a compromise. It was not kept up for long and Graves made no attempt to obey it himself. The only ships to obey were the five frigates under Riou.

Riou, who had been wounded, was reluctant to withdraw but on seeing *Defiance* repeat the signal gave orders to sail, remarking bitterly, 'What will Nelson think of us?' Within a few minutes, as the *Amazon* turned to head towards Parker's approaching ships she was raked through her stern, and poor Riou was killed instantly by a shot that almost cut him in two. The first lieutenant – John Quilliam, who was to be Nelson's first lieutenant at Trafalgar – took over. That night Riou's body was committed to the deep.

Controversy has arisen over whether Parker's signal was discretionary – i.e. that Nelson was only expected to obey if he considered it necessary. But if that had been Parker's intention the signal would have been to the *Elephant* only, not a general one. Mr Atkinson, Nelson's master at Trafalgar, entered the signal in his log on the *St George* as:

| Time | From | Signal | To |
|------|------|--------|-----|
| 12.30* | London | 39 | general with two guns |

*The timing is probably too early.

There seems no doubt that Parker made the signal in order to end the action with immediate effect, and that Nelson deliberately disobeyed him, in the process adding a new phrase to the English language.

## The fighting ends

By 2.00 p.m. the Danish defences were on the point of collapse. Several hulks had struck, others had left the line but some continued to fire although their colours were not flying. Nelson was angry at this, believing it a violation of the conduct of war. The British ships and crews had also suffered severely, so entirely on his own initiative Nelson sent a letter of truce to the Danish authorities in Copenhagen.

> To the brothers of Englishmen the Danes
> Lord Nelson has directions to spare Denmark when no longer resisting but if the firing is continued on the part of Denmark Lord Nelson will be obliged to set on fire all the floating batteries he has taken, without having the power of saving the Brave Danes who have defended them.

In response General Lindholm, representing the Crown Prince, came on board the *Elephant*. He wanted to know the real reason for the truce. 'For humanity' was Nelson's reply. His intention was to allow the Danish prisoners and wounded to be removed from the prizes; for anything else Lindholm should consult with Parker. Lindholm resolved to do so and set out in his boat for the *London* but before he reached his destination the Crown Prince had ordered a cease-fire. The fighting was over – but not the deaths. Within a matter of minutes the fire raging on Fischer's former flagship, the *Dannebrog*, reached the magazine. Once again Midshipman Millard described what he saw.

> While I was thus employed [giving out biscuits and cheese], I heard a most tremendous explosion, and looking out of the port saw an immense mass of black smoke in the air, with sparks of fire and rafters scarce discernible from the thickness of the cloud. This proved to be the ship of the Danish Commodore ...

Copenhagen was Nelson's bloodiest battle. He later wrote, 'I have been in a hundred and five engagements and today is the most terrible of them all.' Stewart described the damage to the British ships and carnage below decks as dreadful. Freemantle agreed: 'the Nile ships are not to be compared to the massacre on board them'. As to the Danish prizes, one midshipman thought they resembled sieves, 'There not being a single plank in any of them but what has at least ten shot-holes in it.' In terms of human losses there was not a great disparity in numbers unless prisoners are taken into account, as the table below makes clear.

|            | Killed | Wounded | Missing | Prisoners | Total |
|------------|--------|---------|---------|-----------|-------|
| **British** | 254    | 689     | –       | –         | 943   |
| **Danish**  | 367    | 635     | 205     | 1,779     | 2,986 |

# The Battle

*May the Great God whom I adore grant me to fullfil [sic] the expectations of my Country; and
if it is His good pleasure that I shall return my thanks will never cease being offered up to the
Throne of His Mercy; if it is His good providence to cut short my days on earth, I bow with the
greatest submission, relying that He will protect those so dear to me that I may leave behind.
His will be done, Amen, Amen, Amen.*

Nelson's prayer, written on 14 September 1805 at Portsmouth
just before he set sail for Cadiz, Trafalgar and death in battle

## THE OPENING MOVES

### VILLENEUVE: 6.00 A.M. 19 OCTOBER TO 6.00 A.M. 21 OCTOBER

On Friday 18 October Villeneuve made up his mind to sail from Cadiz the following day. A message had been passed up the Spanish signal stations along the coast that six British ships-of-the-line had been sighted sailing through the Straits of Gibraltar, presumably detached from Nelson's fleet. These were Rear-Admiral Louis' ships, which had been sent for water and provisions over two weeks earlier; Villeneuve's information was well out of date, and his assumption that Nelson's strength had been reduced was wrong as six more British ships had arrived after Louis' departure. Nevertheless, Villeneuve's belief that his enemy had been weakened, combined with the certainty of his imminent dismissal, led to a flurry of signals fluttering from the *Bucentaure*'s masthead. He ordered the guns on the ships' long-boats, which had been patrolling the harbour entrance, to be hauled on board, and at dusk on 18 October signalled that the fleet was due to sail; all crew ashore were recalled to report on board immediately. An officer from each ship was summoned to attend the flagship to collect orders, and then, finally, the flags signalled 'Hoist in the boats'. According to Major-General Contamine, 'the whole Fleet [was] filled with the most ardent desire to give battle; our invalids, soldiers and sailors, forsook the hospitals; they rushed to the quay in crowds to embark; but the wind did not allow putting to sea that night …'.

Early on 19 October Villeneuve hoisted the signal to sail. There was only a light breeze but it was favourable for working out of harbour. Daylight revealed topsails being hoisted and boats being lowered to help tow ships through the mass of shipping. On board there was much chanting and heaving on capstans. A mile or so outside the harbour this activity had been spotted by the *Sirius*, causing intense excitement on board. Mr Ruckert, the master, recorded soberly and succinctly in his log Blackwood's reaction to events that morning.

At daylight observed the enemy's ships in Cadiz with topgallant yards across, and eight ships having their topsails hoisted to the mastheads. At 7, saw the northernmost ships under way. At 7.20 dispatched the *Phoebe* to repeat signals between us and the English fleet. At 8, saw 19 of the enemy under way. All the rest except the Spanish Rear-Admiral and another line-of-battle ship, with their topsails to the masthead. The *Defence* in sight from the masthead west. *Phoebe* WNW, firing three minute guns. At 8.10, came within hail of the *Naiad*, and ordered her to repeat as many signals as possible between us and the *Phoebe*. Made a telegraph [Popham Code] to the *Weazle*, intelligence to Gibraltar and Tetuan. At 9, ordered the *Pickle* to proceed with all dispatch off Cape Spartel [near Tangier], and inform all ships that the enemy is out [Blackwood was being slightly premature here], and cruise there 3 days and then return to this place. … At noon calm *Phoebe* and *Naiad* between us and the fleet …

It was lack of wind that finally frustrated Villeneuve's effort to leave Cadiz on the 19th. The harbour was crammed with ships and Cadiz was always a difficult harbour to get out of even with the right wind owing to cross-currents, reefs and the set of the tides. As Map 26 makes clear there was a lot of tacking (and in this case towing) needed to leave the harbour, a manoeuvre that had been known to take three days. The crews were inexperienced, the breeze dropped, the ships at the rear had to wait for those ahead and then the tide turned. These factors in combination halted the fleet by noon, and when the anchors splashed down Magon was the only admiral outside the harbour, with his flagship the *Algéciras*, the French *Neptune*, *Héros*, *Argonaute*, *Achille*, *Duguay-Trouin* and the Spanish *Bahama* together with the frigates *Hermione*, *Thémis* and *Rhin*; of these only *Algéciras*, *Bahama* and *Hermione* belonged to Magon's squadron. Neither the *Bucentaure*,

## Trafalgar: The Opening Moves                                                    Map 26

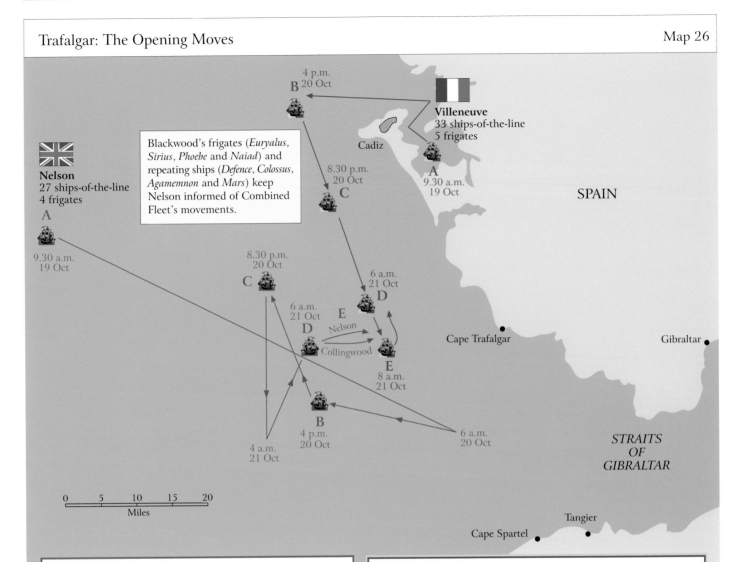

Blackwood's frigates (*Euryalus*, *Sirius*, *Phoebe* and *Naiad*) and repeating ships (*Defence*, *Colossus*, *Agamemnon* and *Mars*) keep Nelson informed of Combined Fleet's movements.

**Notes – Nelson**

A  Nelson positioned some 50 miles west of Cadiz with main fleet. Kept informed of enemy activity by frigates and repeating ships.

B  Having found the Straits empty Nelson is uncertain of Villeneuve's location and returns on WNW course. By 4 p.m. he is about 40 miles south of his enemy.

C  Nelson wishes to avoid a night battle and in order to lure the Combined Fleet further from Cadiz he wears his fleet and sails south until 4 a.m., when he again turns to confront his enemy.

D  Dawn reveals the enemy some 9–10 miles to leeward and Nelson forms the fleet into two attacking columns.

E  Nelson's weather column and Collingwood's lee column hit the enemy line about noon and the Battle of Trafalgar begins.

**Notes – Villeneuve**

A  Combined Fleet attempts to weigh but only Magon and six ships-of-the-line make the open sea.

B  Villeneuve's fleet is finally out of Cadiz but is in considerable disorder and forced westward before a wind change enables the fleet to wear and head for the Straits. More confusion.

C  Villeneuve continues on a southerly course through the night and the disorder in his fleet increases. The British Fleet is sighted to the SW and Villeneuve orders 'clear for action'.

D  Dawn on 21 Oct.: the Combined Fleet is still sailing south but in a long and somewhat disorganized line of battle. The British Fleet is sighted to windward.

E  Villeneuve wears the fleet and heads back towards Cadiz. This manoeuvre takes some two hours and results in a ragged line of battle.

the *Principe de Asturias* nor the lumbering *Santisima Trinidad* had moved. The Combined Fleet was starting to get into the tangle from which it never fully recovered.

One of the first out of Cadiz that morning had been Commander Mahé's *Hermione*, although it was her boats rather than the wind that had enabled her to make the open sea. Her task was to reconnoitre the enemy. Mahé's report records:

I got outside with the assistance of the boats. We sighted three frigates, a ship of the line and a brig-corvette. The ship and the brig made off west-south-west, with all sail set, making many signals and firing guns. One of the frigates stood south and the other two remained in observation in the offing ... all night I kept tacking about to windward of our division to observe the enemy.

The French commander had given a professional and accurate report of the activities of Blackwood's squadron. However, it was not a good day for Villeneuve. By nightfall on the 19th only a quarter of his fleet had got outside the harbour. Enemy frigates had seen and obviously reported what was happening to Nelson. The commander-in-chief, and indeed all his captains, knew that any chance of a surprise sailing had gone, as had the possibility of slipping away before the British could react. A full-scale battle appeared inevitable.

Sunday 20 October dawned dull and overcast but the wind was in the south. By 6.00 a.m. the *Bucentaure* had signalled to weigh. The last ship to get under way was the *Rayo* – her Irish captain, Macdonell, claimed his slowness was due to the number of anchors he had to raise! From early that morning the quaysides of Cadiz were packed with families of the Spanish crews, many in tears, who had come to say a final farewell to the fleet. In the church of the Iglesia de Carmen hundreds of people took the Sacrament and prayed for the safe return of their loved ones. The archbishop remained on his knees before the high altar for most of the day.

By mid-morning the weather had worsened. The wind veered to the south-south-west before rising almost to gale force, bringing heavy seas with rain squalls that lashed the ships and crew as they struggled to tie reef points while swinging wildly on the yards a hundred feet and more above the decks. It was a frightening business, and for most of the crew a new and unwelcome experience. Progress was slow, with many men more interested in hanging on than in struggling with the thrashing canvas. Only one man appears to have fallen – a topman from the *Bucentaure*, who lost his grip and went spinning into the sea. Up went the hoist 'man overboard' and the ship next astern, the *Redoutable*, hove to and lowered a boat on Captain Lucas' orders. Miraculously, the sailor was saved.

The Sunday had all the makings of another difficult day for Villeneuve. The weather and wind were both against him. The foul weather immediately exposed the indifferent seamanship of many crews. Just one man casting off the wrong sheet, a helmsman being slow to react or a misunderstood order was sufficient to frustrate a captain's intentions, and such errors were common. Collecting the fleet into some semblance of the intended order of sailing was almost impossible. At around noon Villeneuve signalled to the fleet, now clear of the narrows at the harbour entrance, to form in the three columns and a squadron of observation. The result was more confusion, with the clumsiness of the crews allowing several ships to fall away to leeward. A course on the larboard tack was adopted but without any real order. The other problem was the wind. Not only was it strong but it came from the south-south-west, forcing the fleet onto a course of west-north-west – the closest it could sail to the wind, and not the course to take it to the Straits. While the ships struggled to get into formation the wind changed again. This time it came from the west, which meant if it kept on the larboard tack the Combined Fleet would be pushed north-west – precisely the opposite direction from the one Villeneuve wanted. The French admiral hoisted, surely with considerable foreboding, the signal for the fleet to come about.

It took until around 4.00 p.m. for the Combined Fleet, then some ten miles out from Cadiz, to complete the change of course that would carry it to the Straits. But it was still in disorder. It was supposedly in five columns (three for the fleet and two for the squadron of observation) but from a seagull's eye view it must have resembled a scattered bunch of sheep. Just before dusk, sometime before 6.00 p.m., the French *Achille* sighted 18 ships to the south-south-west. This was critical news that had to be relayed to Villeneuve. However, the *Achille*'s attempts to make light signals were not understood; instead, she came within hailing distance of Magon's flagship and her captain shouted the news. Magon manoeuvred his ship to close with Admiral Gravina's *Principe de Asturias* and again the message was shouted across. Thus this vital news was passed from ship to ship. Gravina also sent the brig *Argus* to find the *Bucentaure*. Not until 8.30 p.m. did the news of the sighting reach the commander-in-chief – by which time it was over two and a half hours old. Villeneuve's report records his reaction.

> Night fell without my having perceived the enemy squadron, and I continued on the same course ... At 7.30 in the evening I had seen some signals ahead that I could not distinguish and at 8.30, the *Argus* came from Admiral Gravina to inform me that the line-of-battle ship *Achille* had observed at nightfall 18 enemy sail in the south-south-west. As the course which the Fleet was steering would bring us much closer to them, I signalled for the line of battle on the starboard tack, taking station as convenient, without regard to the established order of sailing, forming on the ships furthest to leeward. I held on thus throughout the night without altering course.

As Map 26 shows, at 8.30 p.m. the fleets were only 15 miles apart; for all Villeneuve knew a clash could be imminent. One cannot help but sympathize with his predicament. It was dark, his fleet was poorly trained in seamanship, his formation was muddled and unsuitable for a battle (only one of his columns could fire without risk to the others) and the enemy could sail into him at any moment. He made the only decision possible – to get his ships into a single line of battle on the leeward column immediately, never mind the order, and keep on the same course. This signal was immediately followed by 'Clear for action!', in French '*Branle bas de combat*' – literally, 'confusion under combat'. There was certainly confusion on Villeneuve's ships as they struggled to get into a new formation in the dark, trying to make sense of all the lights and lanterns to the sound of the desperate drumming of the *Generale* on the French ships; the sailors had put appropriate words to the drumbeats – '*Prend ton sac! – Prend ton sac! – Prend ton sac!*'

Something approaching chaos reigned as the ships endeavoured to comply. It became a night of alarm, of straining eyes, of shouting, of demanding identities, of misunderstood signals, of occasional gunfire, of lights and rockets and fires, some obviously the enemy's. All the while the French and Spanish ships sought to get into some sort of line. Captains clung to the stern lantern ahead in the hope that it formed part of the line. Progress was slow with a falling wind, a heavy swell developing and ships under shortened sail for fear of collision. The slowest sailers dropped astern. Captain Lucas of the *Redoutable* has left a vivid account of the night:

> The ships of this squadron, as the evening went on, made a great many signals, showing for their purpose quite a remarkable display of coloured fires.
>
> About nine o'clock at night the flagship made the general signal to form in the order of battle at once, without regard to the stations of individual ships. To carry out this evolution those ships most to leeward ought to have shown a light at each masthead, so as to mark their positions.

Whether this was done I do not know: at any rate I was unable to see such lights. At that moment indeed we were all widely scattered. The ships of the battle squadron and those of the squadron of observation were all mixed up. ... all I could do was to follow the motions of other ships near me which were closing on some to leeward.

Towards eleven I discovered myself close to Admiral Gravina, who, with four or five ships, was beginning to form his own line of battle. I was challenged and our name demanded, whereupon the Spanish admiral ordered me to take post in his line. I asked to lead it and he assented ... [in fact, the *Redoutable* should have been with Villeneuve in the centre division].

The whole fleet was at this time cleared for action, in accordance with orders signalled from the *Bucentaure* earlier in the night. ... With the certainty of a battle next day, I retained but a few men on deck during the night. I sent the greater number of the officers and crew to lie down, so that they might be as fresh as possible for the approaching fight.

## NELSON: 6.00 A.M. 19 OCTOBER TO 6.00 A.M. 21 OCTOBER

As dawn broke on 19 October sixteen-year-old Midshipman Hercules Robinson on the *Euryalus* was so close to Cadiz:

as to see the ripple on the beach; and then as the sun rose over the Trocadero with what joy we saw the fleet inside let fall and hoist their topsails ... and for two days there was not a moment we did not communicate, until I thought that Blackwood, who gave the orders, and Bruce, our signal Mid., [only thirteen and eventually to become an admiral] and Soper our signalman who executed them, must have died of it.

Robinson was right about the amount of signalling in store over the next forty-eight hours. The *Euryalus* hoisted many hundreds of flags in scores of signals describing the actions of the enemy fleet. Nevertheless, close as she was inshore, tacking backwards and forwards between Cadiz in the south and Rota across the bay in the north, *Euryalus* was not the first ship to hoist the signal that set in motion the events leading to the Battle of Trafalgar. That honour went to the frigate *Sirius* commanded by Captain William Prowse, who had spent his first seven years of sea service as an able seaman. His ship was even closer to Cadiz than the *Euryalus* and he, along with several of his officers, was scanning the forest of masts in the harbour. It was easy to tell if a ship was preparing to sail, even from a considerable distance, from the appearance of yards and then sails on previously barren masts. As Prowse peered through his eyeglass that morning he could see that yards were being hoisted. Other officers stared. There was a slight pause to confirm the momentous news before the captain ordered the signal that would set in train the battle. Up went the *Euryalus*' pennants over the 'telegraph' flag – Popham's Code was being used – '249 – 'Enemy' – 354 – 'have' – 684 – 'their' 875 – 'top' – 756 'sails' – 986 – 'yards' – 1374 – 'hoisted'. It was just after 6.00 a.m.

So the yards were going up on some ships but, encouraging though this was, it was not certain proof that the ships would sail. There was more waiting and watching, as the crew of the *Sirius* looked for the tiny figures of topmen climbing the ratlines

and sails being let fall as yards were hoisted from the deck. Time passed, sails began to appear on the northernmost ships and eventually it was possible to see the masts moving against the background. The enemy was getting under way! *Sirius*' next signal was No. 370 in the Admiralty Code – 'Enemy are coming out of port', anticipated for weeks and now passed along the chain of repeating ships from the *Sirius* to *Euryalus*, from *Euryalus* to *Phoebe*, from *Phoebe* to *Defence*, from *Defence* to *Agamemnon*, from *Agamemnon* to *Colossus*, from *Colossus* to *Mars* and finally from *Mars* to *Victory*, a journey of nearly 50 miles that took over two hours. While this was happening Blackwood had summoned his captains and despatched the sloop *Weazle* to Gibraltar to warn Louis. He then reorganized his repeating ships to include the *Naiad* between himself and the *Phoebe*.

The *Mars* had difficulty getting her message across the final expanse of sea to the flagship, so she sailed directly towards the fleet with signal 370 hoisted. Nelson had thought the bright sunshine heralded a beautiful day and signalled for Collingwood and several captains to come to dinner. One of these was Captain Cooke of the *Bellerophon*, who accepted and began to bring his ship closer to the *Victory* so there would be not too much rowing to be done later. On the poop of the *Bellerophon* that morning was her first lieutenant, William Cumby, a man who prided himself on his sharp eyesight. He could just see the topgallant masts of the *Mars* above the horizon and was positive they had flags hoisted. He looked hard and long and read them as No. 370. He informed his captain. Cooke was disbelieving. Even after a prolonged scrutiny through his telescope he failed to distinguish the colours. He would not pass it on to the *Victory* unless he was certain, but agreed to do so if anyone else could read it. Cumby kept insisting he was right and several officers and signallers trained their glasses on the *Mars*. Still nobody could be sure. Suddenly the flags disappeared. 'Now she will make the distant signal 370,' said Cumby. Sure enough the boom of a gun announced the same signal being hoisted but using a combination of flag, pennant and ball at different mastheads. However, before the *Bellerophon* could repeat it the *Victory* herself acknowledged. It was 9.30 a.m. More flags signalled dinner was cancelled, followed by 'General chase to south-east' – the fleet was headed for The Gut, as the Straits were known.

Nelson assumed that the whole fleet would be out that day and heading for the Mediterranean. The distance the enemy would have to sail was some 60 miles; with favourable light winds they could be slipping through the Straits within twenty hours. Nelson had to cut them off and also hoped that he would meet Louis and his six ships; he was unaware of the latter's delay. Speed was essential, and the instant he heard of the movement at Cadiz he signalled 'General chase' followed by the course. Nelson fretted at the lightness of the breeze and signalled for Captain Duff in the *Mars* to ensure he burned lights throughout the night and kept his position to the east of the main fleet so as to maintain contact with Blackwood's frigates. Slower first rates such as *Britannia*, *Dreadnought* and *Prince* were to 'take station as convenient' – they were being given authority to lag behind. The race was on, and the fleet became clothed in canvas as every possible sail was hoisted. It stretched out over several miles but only made a best speed of three knots as it headed south-east throughout 19 October.

As he stood on his quarterdeck that morning surveying his line Nelson noticed that two of his ships still had their iron mast hoops painted black instead of yellow. He knew that the enemy's ships had black hoops and wanted to ensure, so they could be recognized in the smoke and confusion of battle, that British ships were different. A signal was made to the *Polyphemus* and *Belleisle* and the boatswains, Mr George Bruce on the former and Mr Andrew Gibson on the latter, hurriedly issued yellow paint.

There was no news during the night of 19/20 October. As dawn came up on the Sunday the Combined Fleet was mostly still in Cadiz harbour while the British, having sailed some 60 miles in 20 hours, had the Straits in sight. The leading ship, the *Bellerophon*, was six miles further east still. It was immediately clear to all that the Straits were empty, not a strange sail in sight – the enemy had lost the race. Moreover, the wind had changed. It was now from the south-south-west, thus confirming to Nelson that the Combined Fleet could not have arrived before him. So where were they? They could be still beating towards him through the rain that was now falling; or they could have gone west; or they could have turned back to Cadiz. Whatever the truth was, Nelson had only one option – to wear the fleet and return the way he had come.

At 8.00 a.m. Nelson hove to and called Collingwood and several of his captains to the *Victory*. The frigates had reported only nine sail under weigh and in view of the thick weather and rising wind he was fearful the enemy would return to the shelter of the harbour. At 9.30 a.m. the *Agamemnon* signalled that all the Combined Fleet was out so Nelson continued on his west-north-west course until about 4.00 p.m. – approximately the same time that Villeneuve had begun to head south. Not long before this Blackwood had brought the *Euryalus* to within signalling distance of the *Victory* and hoisted a message confirming the whole enemy fleet was out but appeared determined to go westward. This was around the time that the wind veered to the west-north-west, thus taking the British Fleet aback. Some considerable time was required to re-form and head north. By then both fleets were heading towards each other on opposite courses. As darkness approached Blackwood was tasked with tracking the enemy throughout the night while *Defence*, *Colossus* and *Mars* were to keep up communications.

Some time that day Captain Blackwood found the time to write to his wife. His excitement comes through in every sentence.

> What think you, my own dearest love? At this moment the enemy are coming out and as if determined to have a fair fight; all night they have been making signals, and morning showed them to be getting under sail. ... I have let Lord Nelson know of their coming out, and have been enabled to send a vessel to Gibraltar, which will bring Admiral Louis and the ships there. At this moment (happy sight) we are within four miles of the enemy, and talking to Lord Nelson by means of Sir H. Popham's signals, though so distant, but reached along by the rest of the frigates of the squadron. ... It is odd how I have been dreaming all night of carrying home despatches. God send me such good luck! The day is fine, and the sight magnificently beautiful. I expect before this hour tomorrow to carry General [Admiral] Decrès on board the *Victory* in my barge, which I have just painted nicely for him.

It is clear from this letter that Blackwood (and presumably Nelson) thought as late as the day before the battle that the commander of the Combined Fleet was Decrès not Villeneuve; they had heard that Villeneuve was to be superseded and assumed that Decrès would take command.

At 8.30 p.m. Nelson again wore the fleet, this time to the south-south-west. By then the two fleets were a mere 12 miles apart but he did not want to bring on a battle during darkness, which would probably lead to an indecisive action, nor did he want to frighten Villeneuve back to Cadiz. It was better to let him keep coming south during the night and stay on a roughly similar and parallel course until nearly daylight. The *Africa* missed this signal and continued northwards until about midnight – at daybreak she would be about eight miles north of the *Victory*. At four o'clock in the morning of Monday 21 October Nelson wore once more and stood to the north-east. He was confident Villeneuve had continued to creep slowly south throughout the night. Nelson's new course was intended to bring about a decisive confrontation during the Monday morning. His trap had been perfectly sprung. Dawn was to reveal his enemy between nine and twelve miles to leeward.

## VILLENEUVE: THE APPROACH TO BATTLE, 6.00 A.M. TO NOON 21 OCTOBER

As the sun climbed slowly above the hills of Andalusia it silhouetted the ships of the Combined Fleet so that they were seen by their enemy some minutes before the lookouts on the frigate *Hermione* spotted the squadron of foreign sails on the horizon. Captain Mahé made the necessary signal to the flagship at 6.30 a.m. Villeneuve, indeed the entire fleet, knew it was Nelson. 'Frigates to reconnoitre the enemy' was the admiral's response. *Hermione* had a closer look. Mahé's report states:

> ... we sighted 33 sail to windward, amongst which we counted 26 of the line, 4 frigates and three corvettes or despatch craft [this is accurate; only the cutter *Entreprenante* was missed]. We signalled them at 7 o'clock and I enforced the signal with a gun in order to confirm it and to draw attention to it sooner. The enemy were advancing in groups and without formation; they were bearing down on the rear of our Squadron [fleet], which at 7 o'clock received orders to form the prescribed order of battle on the starboard tack. The wind was very faint from the west-north-westerly quarter.

Villeneuve was repeating the order he had made during the night when he had thought a battle imminent. It had been a false alarm. Now he could see a fight was inevitable and his fleet was certainly not in a proper line of battle to receive an attack. Captain Lucas of the *Redoutable* later wrote to the Minister of Marine:

> ... at daybreak, the enemy were sighted to windward ... The wind was very light and there was a heavy sea running. The Combined Fleet was spread out from south-east to north-west; the ships being much scattered and not forming any apparent order. The enemy also were not in any order, but their ships were fast manoeuvring to close. Their force was now reconnoitred and reported exactly. It comprised twenty-seven sail of the line, of which seven were three-deckers, besides four frigates and a schooner. At about seven in the morning the admiral again signalled the whole fleet to form in line of battle ... flag officers at the head of their divisions, on the starboard tack [still heading towards the Straits].

## Trafalgar: The Approach to Battle, 6.00 a.m., 21 October
The position of individual ships is approximate.

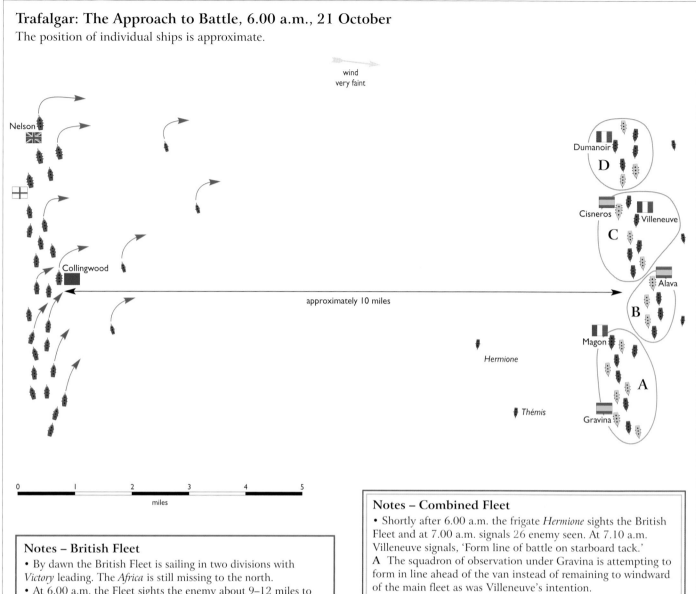

wind
very faint

Nelson

Collingwood

approximately 10 miles

Dumanoir

**D**

Cisneros

Villeneuve

**C**

Alava

**B**

Magon

Hermione

*Thémis*

Gravina

**A**

0    1    2    3    4    5
miles

### Notes – British Fleet
• By dawn the British Fleet is sailing in two divisions with *Victory* leading. The *Africa* is still missing to the north.
• At 6.00 a.m. the Fleet sights the enemy about 9–12 miles to the east and starts to form the order of sailing in two columns. Nelson then signals, 'Bear up and sail large on course E.'
• By about 7.15 a.m. Nelson realizes it will be impossible to maintain or achieve the correct order of sailing and signals, 'Take station as convenient without regard to order of sailing.'

### Notes – Combined Fleet
• Shortly after 6.00 a.m. the frigate *Hermione* sights the British Fleet and at 7.00 a.m. signals 26 enemy seen. At 7.10 a.m. Villeneuve signals, 'Form line of battle on starboard tack.'
**A** The squadron of observation under Gravina is attempting to form in line ahead of the van instead of remaining to windward of the main fleet as was Villeneuve's intention.
**B** Van squadron under Alava
**C** Centre squadron under Villeneuve
**D** Rear squadron under Dumanoir
Ships from all squadrons have become mixed so the order of sailing is a long way from that intended.

The Combined Fleet had become very mixed up during the night. The *Redoutable* belonged to the centre division but during darkness had found herself in the squadron of observation and Gravina had agreed she become his leading ship – of the entire fleet. With daylight and the order to form line of battle Lucas had to wear his ship and sail back in the opposite direction from all the other ships to find his correct position. Lucas continues.

I then left the place I had been in for the latter part of the night and put about to rejoin the chief and take post in the station assigned me in the line of battle [immediately ahead of the flagship *Bucentaure*]. I was, though, some distance from it [at least a mile and a half], and it was half-past eight before I succeeded in placing my ship in her station.

By this time the whole fleet was starting to come about so it is likely Lucas could continue sailing northwards or rather wallowing around while he waited for the fleet to come onto the new course.

At 7.10 a. m. Villeneuve made the signal 'Form line of battle on the starboard tack'. Ten minutes later he hoisted 'Close to cable's length [200 yards]'. If this order was to be followed by every ship the fleet would be over three and a half miles long. In the event, by the time the first shots were fired the Combined Fleet extended for some five miles. This was due to two factors: distances between ships varied from a few yards to half a mile after wearing the fleet, and the 12-ship squadron of observation became part of the main line of battle instead of forming a 'reserve' to windward.

At 8.00 a.m. Villeneuve made his most crucial decision of the battle – he hoisted the general signal 'Wear together'. Every ship was to put its stern through the wind and change course by 180 degrees to sail in the opposite direction back towards Cadiz, not south to the Straits as required by the Emperor's orders. The van, or rather in this case the squadron of observation, would become the rear and the rear the van. Villeneuve took the decision with the enemy bearing down on his fleet, with his ships still struggling to form a proper line of battle, in difficult weather conditions (very light breeze and heavy westerly swell) and in the knowledge of the poor seamanship of most of his crews. Surely he was aware that such a manoeuvre would take a long time, exhaust his crews and probably result in a battle with a fleet in a ragged, confused line of battle. He would be forced to fight off balance.

Before looking at the wisdom of this decision it is worth repeating the views of Captain Churruca of the *San Juan Nepomuceno*. Churruca and his second-in-command, Don Francisco Moyna, were both killed in the battle so what he allegedly said comes via Churruca's nephew, who was on board as a volunteer and supposedly overheard his uncle's remarks. In this account, Churruca had had his telescope alternatively trained on the enemy and the mizzen of the commander-in-chief's flagship for much of the time since the first sighting, and had been among the first to spot the 'wear together' signal. Turning to Moyna, he angrily exclaimed, 'The fleet is doomed. The French admiral does not understand his business. He has compromised us all!'

Churruca knew such an order would take all morning to comply with and that it would throw the fleet into confusion at the very moment when the enemy attack would develop. If Villeneuve had wanted to turn back then he should have made the signal two hours earlier as soon as the enemy had been sighted. By nine o'clock it was obvious to all that the British Fleet in two divisions intended to cut off the van (the former rear) and concentrate on the centre and rear. The agitated Spanish captain kept his eyeglass on the *Bucentaure* in the hope that Villeneuve would signal for the van (Dumanoir's squadron) to wear again, coming down to reinforce the rear and perhaps bring the enemy under two fires. Churruca waited in vain. Closing his telescope with a snap, he exclaimed, 'Our van will be cut away from the main body and our rear will be overwhelmed. Half the line will be compelled to remain inactive. The French admiral – will not – grasp it!' He strode off across the quarterdeck muttering, *'Perdidos! Perdidos! Perdidos!'* Events turned out remarkably similar to those Churruca predicted; even the order he wanted given was hoisted by Villeneuve, but not until after the battle had been in progress for over an hour. The failure of Dumanoir to bring his van about to succour the centre was to be the cause of one of that admiral's courts martial.

Villeneuve's decision was not as ill justified as Churruca's comments suggested. His orders were to get through the Straits and deliver the troops. At 8.00 a.m. he was some 40 miles off the entrance and 30 from Cadiz, with Cape Trafalgar 15 miles on his lee and some dangerous reefs and shoals in between. The enemy fleet, some six miles away to windward, was heading, seemingly, to cut him off from Cadiz. The wind was from the west, and very faint; if the two fleets turned south-east for the Straits it would give them both a speed of up to two knots. Villeneuve must have realized that with his ill-trained seamen and the heavy swell pushing his ships to leeward the odds were on Nelson catching his rear well before he got to the Straits. The fastest British ships would

probably reach Villeneuve quite quickly, especially as he would have to keep his fleet together or see the laggards cut off. If he continued his present course a battle was inevitable and was likely to take place with his fleet well strung out. Moreover, Villeneuve knew that at least six or seven British ships – Louis' detachment – had been seen passing through the Straits, and might intercept him. To be caught between two forces would undoubtedly be the end of the Combined Fleet. Although Villeneuve was resigned to a fight he wanted one without added complications. To keep on course seemed to present serious risks.

The alternative was to turn back. If he gave the signal immediately, even allowing for lack of wind, swell and indifferent seamanship his fleet should surely be in line of battle on the new course within two hours – well before Nelson was within gunshot range. Cadiz was closer than the Straits and could provide sanctuary for disabled ships, and with the swell indicating stormy weather it was surely prudent to have a safe harbour within reach to leeward.

All these thoughts must have been in Villeneuve's mind, but he tells us in his report that his overriding reason for reversing direction was to protect the rear of his fleet. At that time (see the diagram on p. 477) Nelson seemed headed for Dumanoir's squadron and if he continued Dumanoir would certainly be cut off and overwhelmed. Villeneuve wrote, 'I made the signal to wear together, and to form the line of battle on the larboard tack in reverse order; my sole object being to protect the rear from the projected attack of the entire enemy force.' One of the Spaniards who blamed the Frenchman for the loss of Spanish ships in July, Churruca was almost certainly eager to find fault. Nevertheless he was to be proved right in that once the fleet had reversed direction the best tactical move would have been to get the van to turn once more to support the centre.

Poor seamanship and the weather conditions meant that wearing the fleet took far longer than was intended. Every ship turned at more or less the same time but to come through 180 degrees and then find her correct position in the line proved an impossible undertaking for many. By 10.30 a.m. some ships were still struggling to come round and get into position. From 8.30 a.m. until just before opening fire over three hours later Villeneuve was continually chivvying and chasing his fleet and individual ships. He signalled, 'Make more sail', 'Keep to the wind', 'Leading ship to keep to wind others follow in succession', 'Line of fleet is extending too much', 'Rear is extending too much', 'Keep a cable's length between ships', and at 11.30 a.m. specifically to Gravina and his squadron of observation, 'Keep to the wind'. One can sense his mounting frustration as he watched his fleet's performance.

By 11.00 a.m. Villeneuve was still far from happy. The new line had taken on a ragged, concave shape that bulged eastwards in the centre. There were clumps of ships crowded together two or even three deep and more or less abreast of each other. In other parts of the line there were wide gaps with one or two ships straggling across. Some ships were virtually stationary, others barely making one knot as they strove to come to the wind. Not only was the swell pushing ships leeward, they had also lost the following wind. As they strove to obey their admiral's signals to keep to the wind it became impossible to maintain enough steerage way. Nelson's ships on the other hand, with a stern wind and press of sail, were able to take advantage of what little air was moving. This, combined with the westerly swell carrying them towards their enemy, ensured they were able to direct their attacks as planned at a speed of about two knots, at least double that of the disorganized Combined Fleet.

Villeneuve's most significant signal at this time was probably the last of those listed above, to Gravina. Villeneuve wanted the squadron of observation to keep to windward of the main line of battle as a reserve force, to intervene in the battle when required. Gravina, it will be recalled, had a semi-independent command of a strong squadron of twelve ships that included some of the better ships in the fleet (*Berwick, Montañés* and *Algéciras*, for example). It had always been Villeneuve's intention to keep this squadron to windward of the main fleet and since leaving Cadiz it had sailed as a separate formation. However, during the night of 20/21 October Gravina had endeavoured to bring his ships ahead of the van. By dawn on the 21st he had almost succeeded, thus lengthening the Combined Fleet line by at least one and a half miles. Villeneuve's attempt to get Gravina into his proper position failed; the Spanish admiral appeared to ignore the signal, and Villeneuve was thereby deprived of the means of making a counter move that might have made the British success more costly. Villeneuve reported it thus:

> At eleven o'clock [it was nearer 11.30] I signalled to the rear squadron [Gravina] to keep closer to the wind and support the centre, which appeared to be the point on which the enemy now appeared to be directing his main attack. The enemy meanwhile came steadily on, though the wind was very light. They had their most powerful ships at the head of the columns. That to the north had four three-deckers.

At about 11.40 a.m., with the nearest enemy column (Collingwood's) now barely a mile away, the Combined Fleet ran up their colours and the French or Spanish pennants. This symbolic act was carried out to the accompaniment of drums rolling and troops presenting arms. On every Spanish ship, a large wooden cross that had been blessed by a priest was suspended from the boom-end over the taffrail to protect the ship and crew from disaster. Captain Magendie on the flagship *Bucentaure* has left a detailed account of the proceedings.

> ... we ran up our admiral's flag, and our colours, which were greeted with shouts of '*Vive l'Empereur*' repeated throughout the fleet; the Imperial Eagle borne by MM Donadieu and Arman, midshipmen who were appointed to guard it throughout the engagement, was paraded round the decks by the Admiral, followed by the whole executive and by the Commander of the troops, M. Contamine; it is impossible, my Lord, to display greater enthusiasm and eagerness for the fray than was shown and evinced by all the officers, sailors and soldiers of the *Bucentaure*, each one of us putting our hands between the Admiral's and renewing our oath upon the Eagle entrusted to us by the Emperor ... the Eagle was displayed at the foot of the mainmast.

The Imperial Eagle was gilt, with outspread wings, affixed to a pole from which was hung a Tricolour flag. Napoleon presented one to every regiment in the French Army and line-of-battle ship in the Navy to be carried into action under the protection of specially selected junior officers.

Five minutes before the colours were run up signal No. 242 – 'Open fire' – had been hoisted. The *Fougueux* claimed to be the first to follow the order, with several ranging shots followed by a broadside at the *Royal Sovereign*. The guns of the *Santa Ana, Monarca* and *Pluton* quickly followed. Then every ship within range joined in. The flash of flame, thunderous crash of cannons and blankets of billowing smoke announced that the Battle of Trafalgar had begun.

## NELSON: THE APPROACH TO BATTLE, 6.00 A.M. TO NOON 21 OCTOBER

The morning of Monday 21 October broke slightly misty, yet bright. To midshipman Hercules Robinson on the *Euryalus* it was 'a beautiful misty, sun-shiny morning'. The sea was like glass, with the faintest of breezes coming from the west. A lazy Atlantic swell rolled at long intervals towards the Straits – a warning, of which the previous day's squalls were a foretaste, of a storm chasing them from the west.

According to William Beatty, the *Victory*'s surgeon:

> His Lordship came on deck soon after day-light: he was dressed as usual in his Admiral's frock-coat, bearing on the left breast four stars of different orders which he always wore with his common apparel. (His Lordship did not wear his sword: it was laid ready on his table but it is supposed he forgot to call for it. This is the only action in which he ever appeared without a sword.) He displayed excellent spirits, and expressed his pleasure at the prospect of giving a fatal blow to the naval power of France and Spain ... declaring to Hardy that 'he would not be contented with capturing less than twenty sail of the line.'

Some two miles to the south Nelson's second-in-command had also been up early. Collingwood's servant Smith had found his master up and dressing in his cabin at dawn. On informing the admiral that he had not yet seen the enemy Smith was told to take a look. He later explained, 'I then observed a crowd of ships to leeward; but I could not help looking with still greater interest at the Admiral, who during all this time was shaving himself with a composure that quite astonished me.' Collingwood was fussy about his dress in action. Soon after coming onto his quarterdeck he met his first lieutenant, John Clavell, and noted he was wearing boots. 'You had better put on silk stockings, as I have done,' said Collingwood, 'for if one should get a shot in the leg, they would be so much more manageable for the surgeon.' Clavell followed the admiral's advice and was indeed wounded later; it is not known where.

An officer on the *Belleisle* recorded:

> As the day dawned the horizon appeared covered with ships. The whole force of the enemy was discovered standing to the southward, distant about nine miles, between us and the coast near Trafalgar. I was awakened by the cheers of the crew and by their rushing up the hatchways to get a glimpse of the hostile fleet. The delight manifested exceeded anything I ever witnessed, surpassing even those gratulations [*sic*] when our cliffs are decried after a long period of distant service.

And on the *Neptune* Midshipman Badcock:

> It was my morning watch, I was midshipman of the forecastle, and at the first dawn of day a forest of strange masts was seen to leeward. I ran aft and informed the officer of the watch. The Captain (Captain Hargood) was on deck in a moment, and ere it was well light the signals were flying through the fleet to bear-up and form the order of sailing in two columns.

## Trafalgar: The Approach to Battle, 8.00 a.m.

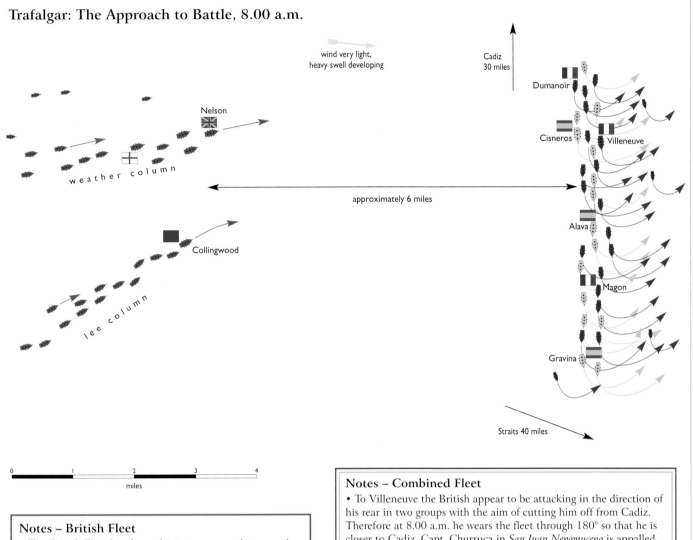

wind very light,
heavy swell developing

Cadiz
30 miles

Dumanoir

Cisneros          Villeneuve

approximately 6 miles

Nelson

weather column

Collingwood

lee column

Alava

Magon

Gravina

Straits 40 miles

0     1     2     3     4
miles

### Notes – Combined Fleet
• To Villeneuve the British appear to be attacking in the direction of his rear in two groups with the aim of cutting him off from Cadiz. Therefore at 8.00 a.m. he wears the fleet through 180° so that he is closer to Cadiz. Capt. Churruca in *San Juan Nepomuceno* is appalled at this decision, exclaiming, 'The fleet is doomed. The French admiral does not know his business. He has compromised us all.'
• Because of the heavy smell, very light breeze and indifferent seamanship many ships take up to two hours to finish wearing. The line becomes muddled.
• Gravina has formed his squadron of observation in the van of the line instead of remaining to windward. After wearing he will be at the rear of the fleet.

### Notes – British Fleet
• The British Fleet has formed into two somewhat ragged columns of attack, which have absorbed the former squadron of observation under Capt. Duff in *Mars*. Their speed is 2 knots at best and their distance from the enemy has closed to around 6 miles. *Africa* has not yet rejoined.
• At about 8.47 a.m. Collingwood signals his column to form on a larboard line of bearing and to make more sail. Individual ships then sail their own course to the enemy rather than following *Royal Sovereign* in line ahead.

As soon as Nelson saw the enemy, at about 6.00 a.m., he signalled No. 72 – 'Form the order of sailing in two columns'. Up went the answering pennants as each ship prepared to come round. This signal followed almost immediately by No. 76 – 'Bear up and sail east-north-east'. (The order to 'bear up' is defined as 'to change a ship's course in order to make her run before the wind after sailing for some time into the wind, or close hauled'.) These two quick signals were crucial, the start of Nelson's approach to the attack. However, there was still a long way to go. Given the light wind, it would take many hours before any clash could take place, but those flags were enough to get the fleet, which had been sailing in the opposite direction, turning towards the enemy and beginning to shake out into the two attacking columns astern (or nearly so) of the *Victory* and *Royal Sovereign*.

There has been some argument by historians as to whether the British Fleet bore up in succession or together. The evidence indicates the former. This is the meaning of No. 76 in the signal books of the time, and if Nelson had wanted ships to bear up together he would have made it clear in the signal. The master of the *Neptune*, James Keith, plainly states 'bore up in succession' (although other logs are silent on this issue) and fixes the time as before 6.30 a.m., and Lieutenant Humphrey Senhouse of the *Conqueror*, writing many years later, declared, 'The British Fleet bore up in succession at 6 in the morning.' Nevertheless, Nelson's ships were not in any precise order when the enemy was first sighted so it is likely that those ships in their station bore up in succession while those that were not probably did so together in order to cut corners to get into position.

For the next six hours and more the British Fleet sailed before the wind with every possible sail set. According to Mr Atkinson's log the *Victory* made three knots (though this seems too high bearing in mind the distance covered in the time), which would eventually leave the slower sailers well astern. Atkinson wrote, 'At 6, observed the enemy E by S, distance 10 or 12 miles. Bore up to the eastward. Out all reefs [of] topsails. Set steering sails and royals. Cleared for quarters …'. No. 13 – 'Prepare for battle' – was signalled at 6.30 a.m.

Several participants have left brief glimpses of how they readied themselves or watched others prepare for action during the long, painfully slow morning as they gradually closed on the enemy.

*Victory*, Surgeon William Beatty:

> His Lordship ascended the poop, to have a better view of both Lines of the British Fleet, and while there gave particular directions for taking down from his cabin the different fixtures, and for being very careful in removing the portrait of Lady Hamilton: 'Take care of my Guardian Angel!' said he, addressing himself to the persons to be employed in this business. Immediately after this he quitted the poop, and retired to his cabin for a few minutes …

*Belleisle*, 2nd Lieutenant Nicholas Harris RM:

> The officers now met at breakfast, and though each seemed to exult in the hope of a glorious termination to the contest so near at hand, a fearful presage was experienced that all would not again unite at that festive board. One was particularly impressed with a persuasion that he should not survive the day, but made the necessary disposal of his property in the event of his death. The sound of the drum, however, soon put an end to our meditations, and after a hasty and, alas! a final farewell to some, we repaired to our respective posts.

Of the ten naval and RM lieutenants on the *Belleisle* two were killed (Geale and Woodin) and two wounded. It is uncertain whether the officer who disposed of his property did so unnecessarily.

*Ajax*, 2nd Lieutenant Samuel Ellis RM:

> I was sent below with orders, and was much struck with the preparations made by the bluejackets, the majority of whom were stripped to the waist; a handkerchief was tightly bound round their heads and over the ears, to deaden the noise of the cannon, many men being deaf for days after an action. The men were variously occupied; some were sharpening their cutlasses, others polishing the guns, as though an inspection were about to take place instead of a mortal combat, whilst three or four, as if in mere bravado, were dancing a hornpipe; but all seemed deeply anxious to come to close quarters with the enemy. Occasionally they would look out of the ports, and speculate as to the various ships of the enemy, many of which had been on former occasions engaged by our vessels.

*Bellerophon,* Lieutenant William Cumby (first lieutenant):

> On going round the decks to see everything in its place and all in perfect order before I reported to the Captain the ship in readiness for action, the fifth or junior lieutenant [George Saunders], who commanded the seven foremost guns on each side of the lower deck, pointed out to me some of the guns at

his quarters, where the zeal of the seamen had led them to chalk in large letters on their guns the words 'Victory or Death'. Finding we should not be in action for an hour or more, we piped to dinner, thinking that Englishmen would fight all the better for having a comfortable meal, and at the same time Captain Cooke joined us in partaking of some cold meat etc., on the rudder head, all our bulkheads, tables etc., being necessarily taken down and carried below.

*Tonnant*, AB John Cash:

> Our good Captain called all hands and said: 'My lads, this will be a glorious day for us, and the groundwork of a speedy return to our homes for all.' He then ordered bread and cheese and butter and beer for every man at the guns. I was one of them, and, believe me, we ate and drank, and were as cheerful as ever we had been over a pot of beer.

*Revenge*, an AB:

> Some would be offering a guinea for a glass of grog, whilst others were making a sort of mutual verbal will, such as, 'If one of Johnnie Crapeau's shots knock my head off, you will take all my effects; and if you are killed and I am not, why, I will have all yours.'

*Britannia*, log:

> In clearing for action hove overboard 2 wine-pipes, 4 butts, 4 puncheons, 12 hogsheads, 12 barrels, and 64 half-hogsheads.

The 'clear for action' procedure was supervised by the gundeck officers, and while it was in progress the first lieutenant would visit each deck (as described by Cumby of the *Bellerophon*) before going to report to his captain that the ship was ready for battle. Some captains might accept the first lieutenant's word but most, and almost certainly all at Trafalgar, would then tour the decks themselves, not so much to check on readiness, but more to be seen by the crew, particularly the gun crews, and to talk to them and raise their spirits. On a flagship the admiral would normally take the opportunity to tour the decks and thus there would be a procession of gold braid climbing up and down hatchways, continually ducking low to avoid beams and walking up and down three or four decks. Depending on the inclination of the captain and the time available such an inspection could take up to an hour to complete. On the *Victory* the admiral's party on his rounds would have consisted of Nelson, Captain Hardy, Lieutenant Quilliam and Captain Adair RM. Others, such as the lieutenant in command on a gundeck, the boatswain, carpenter, gunner or surgeon, might join the party while their deck or area of responsibility was being visited. According to AB John Brown of the *Victory*, during Nelson's tour the admiral encouraged the men with remarks such as, 'My noble lads, this will be a glorious day for England, whoever lives to see it. I shan't be satisfied with twelve ships this day, as I took at the Nile.'

At about ten o'clock Captain Hardy called to his first lieutenant, 'Mr Quilliam, hands to quarters.' 'Mr Willmet!' he shouted, 'Hands to quarters!' Then, turning to the Royal Marine drummers James Berry (later killed) and James Long: 'Drummers – beat to quarters!' The red-jacketed marines, standing stiffly on the quarterdeck, began their staccato beat of the traditional tune for the occasion – 'Hearts of Oak'. At the same time the boatswain and his mates ran to the hatchways to sound their pipes. Within a matter of minutes every man was at his place. The first lieutenant received the reports of the officers before informing the captain that the ship was ready for battle.

It seems that on all ships there was time after clearing for action and then beating to quarters for the crews to have dinner – or at least something to eat and drink. On the *Victory* John Brown states the seamen had 'a bit of salt pork and half a pint of wine'. The mess cooks brought the food to them at their battle stations and they stood around their guns for this final refreshment. According to the 'remark book' of Midshipman Richard Roberts, also on the *Victory*, this meal was taken as late as eleven o'clock. The entry reads: 'At 10 A.M. – Beat to quarters. At 11. – Dinner and grog.' Before noon they were coming under fire.

### Stores Dumped Overboard from the *Belleisle*

Captain Hargood's journal goes into exact detail as to what stores were thrown overboard when the ship cleared for action. One can be fairly sure that it was the purser, James MacFarlane, who made sure all items were carefully noted down, as he would be held responsible for paying for losses if there was no official reason for their disappearance. The journal states:

Threw overboard unavoidably, in clearing for action, butts [half barrels] in packs 7. Do., [ditto butts] cut for grog and topsail halyard tubs, 2. Do, cut for cooks tubs, 3. Puncheons [small casks] and harness casks, 2; some beef and pork in harness tubs [meat ready for use by cook], iron hoops, 6 parcels, 10 in each; biscuit bags [empty] from the different births, 90 in number [they would be a fire hazard on the gundecks].

From the press of ships the *Victory* moved out with her consorts of the weather column into a wedge astern, of which she formed the apex – a wedge that as time passed gradually elongated itself into an irregular line. Individual differences in sailing, the fact that many ships had only worked together for a matter of days and the faintness of the wind revealed the problems the slower sailers had in holding their station. As the morning progressed the *Royal Sovereign* had difficulty keeping ahead of the lee column. At about 10.00 a.m. Nelson signalled the *Mars* to take the lead and Captain Duff hoisted studding sails in an effort to comply but the *Royal Sovereign*, refusing to concede her position of honour, did likewise. She slowly pulled ahead with a three-mile-long line of ships strung out astern.

Nelson had every reason to feel pleased. The battle he had sought for so long was now a virtual certainty. The enemy's numerical superiority was of little concern. Nelson's fleet was well trained; every captain knew his plan and his role and was as eager as himself to engage. He had the weather gauge, enabling him to manoeuvre and strike when and where he chose. The enemy was sailing south, obviously making for the Straits but still within reach of Cadiz. Nelson's early signals, including No. 76 indicating an easterly course, were intended not only to get his fleet into order of battle but also to ensure Villeneuve would be cut off if he should turn back to Cadiz. Nelson's confidence in his captains was made clear from the fact that after No. 76 was hoisted at 6.50 a.m. he made no other general fleet manoeuvre signal until six hours later when he made No. 16 – 'Engage the enemy more closely'. Over an hour passed while the two columns took shape, sliding gently over the sea, every minute or so rocked in succession by the western rollers. Nelson, who had been watching intently, realized that there would be delays if every ship was to reach her precise position in the order of sailing. What was important was speed. Turning to Lieutenant Pasco he ordered No. 265 to the masthead, addressed first to *Britannia* and shortly afterwards to the other two heavyweights *Prince* and *Dreadnought* – 'Take station as convenient without regard to order of sailing'. Within the next half hour his four frigate captains had been summoned on board the *Victory*, the *Euryalus'* log recording Blackwood as leaving his ship at 8.05 a.m.

About half past eight, while the frigate captains were arriving, lookouts watching the Combined Fleet some six miles off noticed a slow, almost imperceptible broadening of the sails while the masts were getting closer together: the enemy were turning away. Nelson and his officers trained their telescopes and gazed intently for some time. Then they saw the gaps between the masts of one or two ships begin widening again while the sails narrowed – Villeneuve was effecting an about turn, he was going to head back to Cadiz! Nelson had no need to change direction; he was still on course to intercept the enemy, who would take a long time to wear in this wind so he would be able to close the distance more quickly. His battle would now come earlier than anticipated. After signalling to the *Prince* 'Bear up and sail large on the course steered by the admiral', Nelson remained on the poop a while and spoke to his frigate captains – Blackwood recalled him saying, 'I mean today to bleed the Captains of the frigates, as I shall keep you on board until the very last minute.' Then, after a final look round, Nelson retired to his day cabin for a few minutes' private reflection. There he prayed:

May the great God whom I worship grant to my Country, and for the benefit of Europe in general, a great and glorious victory, and may no misconduct in any one tarnish it, and may humanity after victory be the predominant feature in the British Fleet! For myself individually, I commit my life to Him that made me, and may His blessing alight on my endeavours for serving my Country faithfully! To Him I resign myself, and the just cause which is entrusted to me to defend. Amen, Amen, Amen.

Nelson stood up to find his signals officer, Lieutenant Pasco, waiting at the doorway. This was around nine o'clock (not 11.00 a.m. as Pasco recollected). Pasco was not a happy man. He was the senior lieutenant on the *Victory* and, according to the usual custom should hold the appointment of first lieutenant, but Nelson had made him the signals officer – a vital position on a flagship, but one normally held by a far more junior lieutenant. The first lieutenant was Lieutenant Quilliam – to whom Pasco was three years senior – who by custom would be in line for immediate promotion to post captain after the battle; first lieutenants on ships other than the flagship would normally be made commanders. Pasco had every intention of raising the matter with Nelson that morning. But, as he later wrote:

On entering the cabin I discovered his Lordship on his knees writing [all furniture had been removed so Nelson's paper was either on the floor or on the bench seat across the stern windows]. He was then penning that beautiful prayer. I waited until he rose and communicated what I had to report, but could not at such a moment disturb his mind with any grievances of mine.

With Pasco's departure Nelson's thoughts then turned to Emma, Horatia and home. He had a nagging presentiment of his own death and wanted not only to make his peace with God but also to

---

### Nelson's Appointment of Quilliam as First Lieutenant on the *Victory*

The position of first lieutenant was an important and much-coveted one; in addition to the crucial duties it involved, the first lieutenant automatically assumed command if the captain became a casualty, and after taking part in a major victory was guaranteed immediate promotion. It was customary for the senior lieutenant on a ship to be appointed to the position, but the first lieutenant on the *Victory*, Quilliam, was some three years junior to the senior lieutenant, Pasco. According to John Clarke's carefully researched book *The Men of HMS Victory*, there were only two days difference in the dates they were mustered on the books of *Victory* – Quilliam on 10 April and Pasco 12 April 1803. Nelson presumably appointed Quilliam as first lieutenant on his reporting on board and made no change only two days later when the much senior lieutenant arrived. It is often forgotten that Quilliam was the *Victory*'s first lieutenant throughout Nelson's

chase of Villeneuve to the Caribbean and back. Perhaps Pasco felt confident that when Nelson arrived back with the fleet in September after his break in England he would get the appointment. It was not to be.

All sources indicate that it was Nelson who appointed Quilliam, though Captain Hardy as commander of the *Victory* would usually have been responsible. So why did Nelson insist on flouting normal, accepted procedures? We can only surmise, but a likely possibility is that Nelson was impressed by Quilliam's performance at the Battle of Copenhagen in 1801, when as first lieutenant on the 38-gun *Amazon* he took after Captain Riou's death (see p. 134). Additionally, Nelson knew Pasco's proven worth as a signals officer and probably wanted him in that post for the likely battle ahead. Had he lived he would no doubt have made certain Pasco was adequately rewarded.

---

ensure those he loved were cared for if he did not return. He was particularly concerned that his previously prepared will, which made proper provision for his wife and family, had not catered adequately for Emma and Horatia; he had agreed only that the house at Merton should go to 'the longest liver [*sic*]' of Sir William, Lady Hamilton and himself. The problem was that he was not rich, nor was he related to Emma, and he had not acknowledged Horatia as his own daughter, thus they would not benefit from any pension, prize money or award if he was killed. At this last moment Nelson sought to solve these difficulties by writing a codicil to his will. Although he could specify a legacy from his own purse or entitlements to both, he could only do so at the cost of depriving Lady Nelson and other family members. Perhaps feeling this to be unjust, he proceeded to write the rather pathetic and wholly unrealistic document quoted in the box on the right. Hardy and Blackwood witnessed it.

Nelson had been in his cabin for perhaps an hour, between around 8.30 a.m. to 9.30 a.m. During that time the *Victory* had initiated no signals, though Collingwood had been hoisting flags trying to get the lee column into some sort of order. Amongst the six signals made during this time to ships to make more sail or change positions one was of more consequence than the rest. At about 8.47 a.m. up went No. 42 – 'Form larboard line of bearing steering the course indicated' followed immediately by 'Make more sail'. Collingwood had realized that it would not be possible to get his column in a proper line ahead and to come up parallel to the enemy line before turning together, with the *Royal Sovereign* cut-

### Nelson's Codicil to His Will

Nelson wrote this codicil in his cabin during the approach to battle.

October the twenty-first, one thousand eight hundred and five, then in sight of the Combined Fleets of France and Spain, distant about ten miles.

Whereas the eminent services of Emma Hamilton, widow of the Right Honourable Sir William Hamilton, have been of the very greatest service to our King and Country, to my knowledge, without her having received any reward from either our King or Country:

Could I have rewarded these services, I would not now call upon my Country; but as that has not been in my power, I leave Emma Lady Hamilton, therefore, a legacy to my King and Country, that they will give her ample provision to maintain her rank in life.

I also leave to the beneficence of my Country my adopted daughter, Horatia Nelson Thompson; and desire she will use in future the name of Nelson only.

These are the only favours I ask of my King and Country at this moment when I am going to fight their Battle. May God Bless my King and Country, and all those who I hold dear. My relations it is needless to mention; they will of course be amply provided for.

Nelson Bronte

Poor naive Nelson. There was no way the government was going to acknowledge responsibility for Emma, let alone keep her in the extravagant lifestyle to which she was accustomed.

ting through at the twelfth ship to the rear. Instead he ordered each ship to advance at best speed on a line of bearing towards the enemy, so that the lee column would form a rough echelon astern and on the starboard quarter of the *Royal Sovereign*. This way the column would reach the enemy more quickly, and although the ships would not break their line simultaneously as Nelson's original plan envisaged, at least each British ship would cut through at several points – the essential objective of the lee column. It may have been, as one officer described it, 'scrambl[ing] into battle as best we could, each man to take his bird', but it proved an effective, if somewhat piecemeal, attack.

For some three hours, from 8.30 a.m. to after 11.30 a.m., the only signals hoisted by *Victory* and *Royal Sovereign* were concerned with positioning individual ships or making more sail. Nelson was content that all was going well, the main frustration being the lack of wind and the slow progress of some ships that began to fall astern as the morning progressed. Broadly speaking, his plan, as set out in the Memorandum, was being implemented. There were two distinct attacking squadrons; the third squadron of faster ships under Duff had had to be absorbed into the others, but this was not a serious problem. The *Ajax* and *Agamemnon* were with Nelson, the *Mars*, *Colossus* and *Defence* with Collingwood. It looked as though the weather column would be headed by the heavier ships with the bigger broadsides (*Victory*, *Téméraire* and *Neptune*). By mid-morning Nelson was not so certain on this score with the lee column, as although the *Royal Sovereign* was in the lead the *Dreadnought* and *Prince* were lagging. On a course east by north, he still intended to attack Villeneuve's flagship and cut off the van if possible, but as yet did not know where the enemy commander was. So his intention as the fleet slowly approached the enemy was to menace both the van and centre. If he hauled a point or two to the wind he might make a direct threat to the van, if he bore up a point or two he would threaten the centre.

What little wind there was seemed to be falling slightly. Log lines were recording only one and a half to two knots. According to 2nd Lieutenant Samuel Ellis RM on the *Ajax*, 'we approached the enemy at not more than a knot and a half an hour'. The small sprinkling of foam at the bows had sunk to mere ripples. The sea was oily, unbroken save for an eddy from a plunging fish or the splash of a gull diving for some drifting garbage from a galley chute. The sun was out and the sight of those two fleets closing for battle was something survivors would never forget, indeed it was something the world would never again witness – the final great clash of the 'wooden walls' before they disappeared into history. On board every ship the crews were at quarters, officers in full uniforms with hats, swords, silk stockings and silver buckled shoes gathered on the quarterdecks. The dark blue of their uniforms contrasted sharply with the vivid splash of scarlet jackets and white belts of the Royal Marines parading on the poops and forecastles. Also on the poops, signals officers and midshipmen busied themselves with telescopes and code books as they tried to interpret flags that mostly hung listlessly from mastheads. On the gundecks the officers' smart appearance contrasted with the seamen and marines, many stripped to the waist and barefooted, who stood or crouched by the guns. Every now and then someone would go to a port to peer out for a glimpse of the enemy, to judge how close they were. Gunners were ready in the main magazines, carpenters stood by with their men and wooden plugs while the masters-at-arms prowled the decks, unnecessarily fussing at trivial faults. Below on the orlop decks the surgeons had converted the midshipmen's dining tables to operating tables, instruments were set out, reams of bandages prepared and empty casks positioned to receive their gory load of severed limbs. For those below the hours of waiting were hard to bear.

On those ships that had them, bands (mostly drums, fiddles and fifes) struck lively patriotic tunes such as 'Rule Britannia', 'Britons Strike Home' and 'God Save the King', thumped out with varying degrees of skill but considerable enthusiasm. Crews on the forecastles of the leading ships cheered wildly at each other. Even the tiny *Pickle* was determined to live up to the occasion. Midshipman Hercules Robinson on the *Euryalus* has left a description of her.

> Even the saucy little schooner *Pickle* – a tiny thing, too small except to make herself useful to Blackwood's frigates – tried to look fierce and threatening, with a confident assumption ridiculous to witness. She took post between the stately lines of the towering three and two-deckers, cleared for action fore and aft in ludicrous imitation of them, with her small boarding-nettings triced up, and her 4-pounder popguns – about as large and as formidable as two pairs of jack-boots – double-shotted and run out.

The *Pickle*'s position on the diagram on p. 484 is to the windward of the fleet with the rest of Blackwood's squadron as Robinson's location is unlikely. He also got her armament wrong – she had eight 12-pounder carronades.

While the slow sailers fell astern in both columns the faster ones pulled slowly ahead. 'Make all sail with safety to the masts' and 'Make more sail' were hoisted no fewer than ten times during the chase that morning. It had begun to develop into a race – albeit a very long and laborious one. As the *Belleisle* crawled past the *Tonnant*, Lieutenant Paul Harris RM tells us, 'the captains greeted each other on the honourable prospect in view. Captain Tyler [*Tonnant*] exclaimed: "A glorious day for old England! We shall have one apiece before night!"' But as the distance between the fleets shortened the cheering eventually died away. On the quarterdeck just the voice of captain or master to the helmsmen could be heard, and below the endless creaking of timbers. The situation on the *Belleisle* was typical of most ships during the final half hour. Lieutenant Nicholas again:

> We were steering directly for them. The silence on board was almost awful, broken only by the firm voice of the captain [Hargood], 'Steady!' or 'Starboard a little! Steady so!' which was repeated by the master to the quartermaster at the helm, and occasionally by an officer called to the now impatient men: 'Lie down there, you, sir!'

The *Belleisle* was not the only ship to make the men, especially those exposed on the upper decks (but never the officers), lie down as the enemy line loomed closer. It was a common-sense precaution that would reduce casualties during the many broadsides to come during the final mile.

Midshipman William Badcock, on the *Neptune*, recounted how at ten o'clock his ship had come so close to the *Victory* that Nelson was concerned he would be overtaken. He did not need to signal. Picking up a speaking trumpet he shouted across, '*Neptune*, take in your stuns'ls [studding sails] and drop astern; I shall break the line myself.' The studding sails were small sails attached to the extremities of mainsails by means of small yards, thus prolonging the main yards. Later, with battle imminent and the *Neptune* still close on the larboard quarter of the *Victory*, Badcock had a splendid view of the Combined Fleet.

> At this period the enemy were forming their double line in the shape of a crescent. It was a beautiful sight when their line was completed: their broadsides turned towards us showing their iron teeth, and now and then trying the range of a shot [a likely occurrence but not mentioned elsewhere] to ascertain the distance, that they might, the moment we came within point-blank (about six hundred yards) open their fire upon our van ships – no doubt with the hope of dismasting some of our leading vessels before they could close and break their line.
>
> Some of the enemy's ships were painted like ourselves – with double yellow sides, some with a broad single red or yellow streak, others all black [e.g. *Santa Ana*], and the noble *Santisima Trinidad* with four distinct lines of red, with a white ribbon between them, made her seem to be a superb man-of-war ... She was lying under topsails, topgallant sails, royals, jib, and spanker; her courses were hauled up [normal battle practice as they obscured the view], and her lofty, towering sails looked beautiful, peering through the smoke as she awaited the onset. The flags of France and Spain, both handsome, chequered the line, waving defiance to that of Britain.

Meanwhile on *Victory* there had been concern among a number of the officers for the safety of their commander-in-chief. The flagship was leading the line and would be the first under fire and inevitably at the centre of the fight. Perhaps his lordship could be persuaded to hoist his flag on the *Euryalus* or another frigate. There were precedents for this, notably Admiral Rodney and the renowned fighting French Admiral de Suffren, for whom Nelson had great admiration. After witnessing Nelson's codicil Hardy and Blackwood had discussed this possibility and when Nelson reappeared on deck Blackwood broached the subject. He later recorded the incident and his efforts, when this failed, to get agreement for other ships to take the lead.

> I proposed hoisting his flag in the *Euryalus*, whence he could better see what was going on, as well as what to order in case of necessity, but he would not hear of it, and gave as his reason the force of example; and probably he was right.
>
> My next object, therefore, was to endeavour to induce his Lordship to allow the *Téméraire*, *Neptune* and *Leviathan* to lead into action before the *Victory* ... after much conversation, in which I ventured to give it as the joint opinion of Captain Hardy and myself, how advantageous it would be to the Fleet for his Lordship to keep as long as possible out of the Battle, he at last consented to allow the *Téméraire*, which was then sailing abreast of the *Victory*, to go ahead.

Blackwood's attempt to hail the *Téméraire* failed so he went across to her in a boat to convey the message but, on his return, found Nelson 'doing all he could to increase rather than diminish sail'. Blackwood suggested to Hardy that he try to get his lordship to reduce sail, but Hardy refused; he knew there was no way Nelson was going to let another ship take the lead. At about this time Lieutenant Bligh on the forecastle had the starboard lower studding sail lowered in order to reset it. Nelson noticed and, not knowing the reason, angrily remonstrated with the young officer for reducing sail without permission. Later, at around 12.15 p.m., some fifteen minutes before she broke the enemy line and just as she was coming under fire, Nelson hailed the *Téméraire* personally. Speaking as he always did with a slight nasal intonation, he said, 'I'll thank you Captain Harvey, to keep your proper station, which is astern of the *Victory*.'

Then there was the question of Nelson's decorations, which he insisted on wearing. The four great stars covering his left breast – sequin and wire replicas sown on his undress uniform jacket, and somewhat tarnished by sea air – nevertheless announced to the world who he was and provided a conspicuous target. *Victory*'s surgeon, Beatty, had suggested to Dr Scott the chaplain and Mr John Scott, Nelson's secretary, that the admiral be asked to cover his decorations with a handkerchief. Both felt it would be a waste of time. Beatty disagreed, and was resolved to make the suggestion. John Scott then warned, 'Take care, Doctor, what you are about. I would not be the man to mention such a matter to him.' Whether Beatty heeded this advice or was called away to his duties below before he had a chance remains uncertain; in any case he did not speak to Nelson on the matter.

By eleven o'clock Nelson was beginning to be concerned about two things. Firstly, the weather. The long Atlantic swell was a clear indication that storms were on the way, almost certainly within the next twenty-four hours, perhaps less. During that Monday afternoon a fierce battle was in prospect where many ships of both sides would be damaged, some dismasted and oth-

ers uncontrollable. Only 12 miles east was Cape Trafalgar, and the sea along the coast northwards to Cadiz was treacherous with reefs and rocks on the lee shore, perhaps posing as much danger to damaged ships as an enemy. There was little doubt in Nelson's mind that his fleet must be prepared to anchor after the battle to ride out the storm.

His second difficulty was not knowing exactly where in the curving line stretched across the middle distance was Villeneuve's flagship. He assumed it was in the centre, but until colours were hoisted he would not know for sure. Probably Villeneuve would be in a three-decker but the seemingly muddled enemy formation with bunching, gaps and the mix of French and Spanish ships added to the uncertainty. An important element in Nelson's plan had always been to concentrate on the enemy's commander-in-chief from the start – neutralize him early and the Combined Fleet would, he hoped, be rudderless. Equally important was ensuring that most of the enemy did not slip away back to Cadiz, and the only way to be sure of this was for Nelson to steer for the van rather than the centre. Writing to Decrès in mid-November, Rear-Admiral Dumanoir stated:

> ... in the van only the five leading ships were in line. The enemy fleet bore down in two columns, with all sail set, studding sails alow [*sic*] and aloft; the southern column was heading for the head of our rear division [i.e. *Santa Ana*] and the northern one, headed by the three-deckers, was standing for the centre of our van.

By 11.40 a.m. Nelson had made up his mind. Villeneuve had still not raised his colours, thus showing he accepted battle, so perhaps his intention was to run for home. If Nelson was to be certain of cutting off the bulk of the enemy he would have to attack the van – which would mean abandoning most of his original plan and relying on his captains, particularly those in Collingwood's line, to adapt to the change of circumstances and attack as soon as they were able. Up went a Popham Code signal for Collingwood. Mr Ruckert on the *Euryalus* logged it as, 'I intend to push or go through the end of the enemy's line to prevent them from getting into Cadiz.' At this stage the *Victory* was about a mile from the van.

About five minutes earlier Villeneuve had given the order to open fire and so his fleet had begun to hoist their colours. Until then every glass on the *Victory* had been trained on the centre of the enemy line as the officers desperately sought to locate Villeneuve's flagship. At the last possible moment a seemingly hesitant commander-in-chief's flag was spotted coming up to the masthead, not of a large three-decker, but of the 80-gun *Bucentaure*. Instantly Nelson reverted to his original plan and ordered Hardy to haul away to starboard. He was to head for the *Bucentaure*, but this meant he still had over a mile to sail before he could reach the enemy's line. Another thirty to forty minutes would pass before this happened, while a mile and a half to the south the *Royal Sovereign* would become the first British ship to breach the line.

Historians seldom discuss this last-minute change of course and the fact that the *Victory* was under fire from several ships of the enemy van, and others ahead of the *Bucentaure*. Nor do they mention that the *Victory* exchanged broadsides with them. These events are, however, well documented. The best source is Mr Atkinson's log; while his timings may not be absolutely accurate there is no reason to doubt the facts: 'Standing towards the enemy's van in passing down their line with all sail set. At 4 minutes past 12, opened our fire on the enemy's van in passing down their line.' The *Orion*'s log records, 'The *Victory*, after making a feint of attacking their van, hauled to starboard so as to reach their centre, and then wore round to pass under the lee of the *Bucentaure*.' Mr Halliday, the master of the *Orion*, was mistaken in thinking it was a deliberate feint on his admiral's part – he may have forgotten about 'going through the end of the enemy's line' signal. The final piece of evidence of the *Victory*'s actions prior to breaking the line comes from the enemy. Dumanoir wrote:

> At a quarter past noon the enemy's northern column engaged our van (which I commanded); a cannonade took place for forty minutes, but the enemy, probably finding that our line was in too close an order, came up to starboard and cut through the centre stern of our Admiral.

Dumanoir makes it clear that an exchange of fire took place between the *Victory* and several van ships prior to her closing with the *Bucentaure*. She would almost certainly have received some fire from the *Mont Blanc*, *Duguay-Trouin*, *San Francisco de Asis*, *San Augustin*, *Héros* and *Santisima Trinidad* during this time.

The next astern, the *Téméraire*, seems to have followed the course of the *Victory* and turned to starboard in her wake, as her log states: 'At 25 minutes past noon [questionable] the *Victory* opened her fire. Immediately put our helm to port [turned starboard] to steer clear of the *Victory* and opened our fire on the *Santisima Trinidad* and two ships ahead of her [*Héros* and *San Augustin* or *San Francisco de Asis*] when the action became general.' It is likely most of the following ships of Nelson's column made straight for the enemy and did not have to make a turn to starboard.

The final forty minutes or so from the time the first shots were fired at the *Royal Sovereign* some twenty minutes before noon until the *Victory* cut through the line astern of the *Bucentaure* were highly dramatic ones for the crews of the leading ships. Key events on the *Victory* and *Royal Sovereign* are reconstructed and summarized below in approximate chronological order, bearing in mind that the timings given in logs and participants accounts vary considerably. Those given are therefore best estimates.

## *Victory*

**11.35 a.m.**  Villeneuve gives authority for his fleet to open fire. Some ranging shots fired (particularly at the *Royal Sovereign*) which is closest (about a mile) to the enemy line, followed by the first broadside from the *Fougueux*.

**11.40 a.m.**  Nelson signals to Collingwood that he intends to attack the van to prevent the enemy escaping back to Cadiz. Also at this time, the *Africa*'s log states, 'the *Africa* engaged the headmost ship of the enemy's van [*Neptuno*] (the *Africa* then on the starboard tack), viz. A Spanish two-decker, bearing the flag of an admiral, and engaged the whole of the enemy's van line as we passed them ...'. The timing here is a little early and while the leading ship was a Spanish two-decker it did not carry an admiral. This ship certainly ran the gauntlet of at least eight ships on her way to join the central mêlée.

**11.45 a.m.**  Nelson instructs Pasco to hoist the 'England expects ...' signal (see pp 447–51). Afterwards, Captain Blackwood recorded, the admiral said, 'Now I can do no more. We must trust to the Great Disposer of all Events, and the justice of our cause. I thank God for this great opportunity of doing my duty.'

Looking towards where the *Royal Sovereign* was leading the lee line into battle, Nelson then exclaimed, 'See how that noble fellow Collingwood carries his ship into action.'

**11.50 a.m.**  At about this time the Combined Fleet hoist their colours and Nelson immediately turns to starboard to attack the *Bucentaure*.

**Noon**  Nelson has the signal 'Prepare to anchor at the close of day' hoisted.

**12.05 p.m.**  According to the *Victory*'s log she starts to exchange fire with some of the enemy van ships and those of the centre as she continues to sail slowly south-east towards the *Bucentaure*. The enemy shots at this stage mostly fall short; some shots whirr overhead and a hole appears in the maintopgallant sail. The *Téméraire* appears to be passing the *Victory* so Nelson hails her to 'Take station astern'.

**12.10 p.m.**  Up till about this time the poop and quarterdeck of the *Victory* were crowded with senior officers, making it a highly vulnerable target. Present with Nelson were Captain Hardy, Lieutenant Quilliam, Captain Adair RM, Mr Atkinson, Surgeon Beatty, Chaplain Alexander Scott, the admiral's secretary Mr John Scott and the visitors – Captain Blackwood and up to three other frigate captains, perhaps twelve in total. Shortly after the first enemy shots were fired Blackwood departed. He took Nelson's hand saying, 'I trust, my Lord, that on my return to the *Victory*, which will be as soon as possible, I shall find your Lordship well, and in possession of twenty prizes.' Nelson responded only too truthfully, 'God bless you Blackwood, I shall never speak to you again.' It is uncertain when the other frigate captains left. The log of the *Euryalus* records Blackwood returning 'after noon'. Prowse (*Sirius*) is shown as departing but no mention of the time or of his return; Capel (*Phoebe*) is recorded as leaving for the *Victory* at 9.30 a.m. but no time is given for his return. The log of *Naiad* has no entry for either Dundas' departure or his return.

**12.15 p.m.**  Nelson has 'Engage the enemy more closely' hoisted to the maintopgallant masthead. It was kept up until shot away later that afternoon.

**12.15 to 12.30 p.m.**  *Victory* is now receiving effective fire from several ships, which is returned by her larboard broadsides. Although some eight ships fired at the *Victory* during this time it was the four in a tight group in the centre that had the best shoot. Major-General Contamine wrote in his report: 'Four of ours, the *Héros*, *Santisima Trinidad*, *Bucentaure* and *Redoutable*, brought their broadsides to bear on her and concentrated a very vigorous fire on her bows.'

Nelson's secretary John Scott is smashed to the quarterdeck by a roundshot. Captain Adair RM with some assistance from a seaman attempted to drag the body from Nelson's sight but the admiral asked, 'Is that poor Scott that is gone?' Adair replied that it was. 'Poor fellow!' said Nelson. Most of the blood on Nelson's jacket when he was shot probably belonged to Scott.

Another shot ploughs into the Marines packed onto the poop, killing or wounding eight. Nelson immediately orders Adair to disperse his men round the ship. In doing so he may have unwittingly brought about his own death, as the role of the Royal Marines was to pick off enemy sharpshooters.

As Nelson and Hardy pace backwards and forwards across the quarterdeck a shot smashes through the ship's boat and strikes the fore-brace bitts on the quarterdeck. A splinter strikes Hardy on the

## Trafalgar: The British Fleet's Final Approach to the Enemy Line, about 11.45 a.m.

### Notes – British Fleet

• Unsure as to which is Villeneuve's ship, Nelson decides to attack the van to prevent the enemy from returning to Cadiz.
• Then Villeneuve's flag is hoisted on *Bucentaure*, so Nelson reverts to his original plan and changes course to head towards the enemy flagship.
• The Combined Fleet have now started firing and the British Fleet comes under fire from some 14 enemy ships while *Africa* exchanges fire with each ship of the van as she sails south to join the weather column.
• All the frigates go to windward to repeat signals as required.

Africa

Neptuno
Scipion
Intrépide (not originally in this squadron)
Formidable (Dumanoir)
Cornélie
Mont Blanc
Duguay-Trouin
Rayo
San Francisco de Asis

Van (originally rear)

Euryalus
Sirius
Naiad
Phoebe
Pickle
Entreprenante
Britannia
Neptune
Victory (Nelson)
Téméraire
Leviathan
Ajax
Conqueror
Agamemnon
Orion

Only when Nelson sees Villeneuve hoist his colours does he know his location and turns to attack him.

Héros
San Augustin
Hortense
Santisima Trinidad (Cisneros)
Furet
Bucentaure (Villeneuve)
Redoutable
San Justo
Neptuno
San Leandro

Centre

wind very light, heavy swell

Collingwood goes on to cut the line astern of *Santa Ana* at about 12.15 p.m.

Prince
Minotaur
Spartiate

Royal Sovereign (Collingwood)
Belleisle
Mars
Tonnant
Bellerophon
Colossus
Achille

Indomptable
Rhin
Santa Ana (Alava)
Fougueux
Argus
Monarca
Thémis
Pluton

Rear (originally van)

Dreadnought
Thunderer
Defiance
Revenge
Defence
Swiftsure
Polyphemus

0     1/2     1
miles

Algéciras (Magon)
Bahama
Aigle
Montañés
Swiftsure
Hermione
Argonaute
Argonauta
San Ildefonso
Achille
Berwick
Principe de Asturias (Gravina)
San Juan de Nepomuceno

Squadron of Observation

### Notes – Combined Fleet

• The Combined Fleet stretches in a concave arc some 5 miles in length. It has not been able to form a proper line of battle. There are gaps and many ships are doubled, even trebled, thus masking the fire of several.
• The line is disordered and the squadrons reversed after wearing, with *Intrépide* now in the van (instead of the centre) and *San Justo* in the centre (instead of the rear).
• Progress is extremely difficult with few ships able to make more than 1 knot – half the speed of Nelson's ships. This is because the wind is so light and Villeneuve's ships are struggling to bear up close to the wind and being pushed leeward by the heavy swell, whereas the British are sailing before the wind with every sail possible on the yards and stays.
• At 11.35 a.m. Villeneuve signals 'Open fire' and five minutes later the Combined Fleet run up their colours. The battle begins.

left shoe, tearing away the buckle but not injuring the foot. For a moment neither officer knew if the other had been hurt. Nelson commented, 'This is too warm work, Hardy, to last long.'

A shot smashes into and destroys the wheel. This was serious and might have caused real problems for the flagship had emergency steering arrangements had not been part of the 'clear for action' routine. The master, Mr Atkinson, went below to the gunroom where tackles had been hooked onto the tiller to get an alternative system working. It needed some 20 men – a large drain on manpower. Helm orders were probably shouted down a speaking tube as the noise of gunfire would have made instructions through a speaking trumpet hard to hear.

The enemy broadsides did substantial other damage apart from inflicting human casualties. The mizzen-topmast collapsed, most of the foresail was torn from the yardarm, rendering it useless, the studding sails were shot away and all the other sails were peppered with holes of varying sizes.

**12.30 p.m.** A final signal to the *Africa* – 'Make all sail possible with safety to the masts' – is made before the *Victory* is hauled to port to pass astern of the *Bucentaure*. Nelson's 'pell mell' battle starts.

## Royal Sovereign

**11.30 a.m.** Seeing the *Victory* setting her studding sails, and regarding the whole business as something of a race, John Clavell, the first lieutenant, requested permission from Collingwood to do the same. 'The ships of our line,' replied the admiral, 'are not yet sufficiently up for us to do so now; but you may be getting ready.' The studding sail and royal halyards were manned. Ten minutes later Collingwood gave him the nod so Clavell reported to Captain Rotherham that the admiral wanted more sail. Up went the extra canvas and the ship pulled gradually ahead.

**11.40 a.m.** The extra sail and her recently renewed copper bottom made the *Royal Sovereign* able to outstrip any of the British ships-of-the-line at Trafalgar. An earlier attempt by Nelson to get the *Mars* to lead had come to nothing and, as Collingwood's flagship neared the enemy, it was obvious that she would soon become the main target for the enemy guns. At about this time the first ranging shots were fired at the *Royal Sovereign*, closely followed by a broadside. There was concern that Captain Rotherham in his best uniform, gold-braid epaulettes and cocked hat would present too obvious a target, but efforts by his officers to get him to wear something less conspicuous proved fruitless: 'Let me alone! I've always fought in a cocked hat, and always will!' Collingwood signalled to his column to 'make more sail'.

**11.42 a.m.** The men on the exposed upper decks are ordered to lie down.

---

### Midshipman John Aikenhead (*Royal Sovereign*) Prepares for Death

John Aikenhead was the senior midshipman on Collingwood's flagship and thus pitched into the centre of the action from the start. As battle approached he wrote movingly to his father. His letter also contained his will and a list of the property stored in his sea chest.

We have just piped to breakfast; thirty-five sail, besides smaller vessels, are now on our beam, about three miles off. Should I, my dear parents, fall in defence of my King, let that thought console you. I feel not the least dread on my spirits. Oh my dearest parents, sisters, brother, dear grandfather, grandmother and aunt, believe me ever yours!

Accept perhaps for the last time your brother's love; be assured I feel for my friends, should I die in this glorious action – glorious no doubt it will be. Every British heart pants for glory. Our old Admiral [Collingwood] is quite young with the thoughts of it. If I survive nothing will give me greater pleasure than embracing my dearest relations. Do not, in case I fall, grieve – it will be to no purpose. Many brave fellows will no doubt fall with me on both sides. Oh! Betsey, with what ardour I shall, if permitted by with God's providence, come to England to embrace you all!

Aikenhead was killed in the battle, one of the many casualties on Collingwood's flagship.

---

**11.50 a.m.** Collingwood sees all the hoists for Nelson's 'England expects ...' signal going up and down the *Victory*'s mizzen and, frustrated by its length, grumbles that he wished Nelson would make no more signals as everyone was well aware of what was required. However, after being told the meaning he relents.

**Noon** Collingwood's journal states: 'About noon, the *Royal Sovereign* opened fire on the 12th, 13th, 14th and 15th ships from the enemy's rear, and stood on with all sail to break the enemy's line.' This relieved the tension of the starboard batteries and created a good cloud of smoke in which the ship could cover the final, most dangerous, half mile.

**12.15 p.m.** The ship altered course to larboard to pass close under the stern of the *Santa Ana*. Collingwood had reached the enemy some 15 to 20 minutes before Nelson, breaking through between the 15th and 16th ships from the rear of the enemy line, not the 12th as he later stated.

## THE FINAL APPROACH

*Royal Sovereign*, the first British ship to come under effective fire, did so at about 11.40 a.m. At roughly the same time, more than two miles to the north, the lonely *Africa* began her duel with the enemy van, followed some 20 minutes later by the *Victory*. Both these flagships led their divisions. The *Royal Sovereign* was under effective fire for some 35 minutes and the *Victory* for 25 – the time it took to cover the final three-quarters of a mile to the enemy line, when they were most vulnerable to heavy fire without being able to respond effectively. The enemy's objective was to cripple the approaching ships by cutting stays or rigging and bringing down yards or even masts, thus rendering the ships unmanageable before any mêlée took place. During these 20 minutes both leading British ships suffered damage and casualties, but their ability to reach the enemy and fight was not seriously impaired. Nelson knew from the start that these were the dangerous minutes, but he took the calculated risk in allowing his 'T' to be crossed. His confidence that he could 'run the gauntlet' successfully was vindicated that day. Three factors favoured the British:

• The French and Spanish crews' lack of training and live firing practice. This meant that, certainly for the heavier guns, crews required some four minutes between each broadside (or shot) and they were not skilled at judging distance and aiming at moving targets.

• The heavy swell hit the Combined Fleet beam on, causing a considerable roll that added to the aiming problems. Many shots fired 'at the gulls' with the aim of bringing masts down flew too high, while some aimed 'at the mackerel' to sink ships ploughed uselessly into the sea.

• Not every ship was able to fire at the approaching enemy for the whole period. In practice it is likely that individual ships firing at Nelson's column would have only been able to keep their target within the firing arcs of their guns for five to ten minutes.

The table below gives a very rough approximation of the number of the shots fired at the *Royal Sovereign* and *Victory* during this time, taking the above factors into account, plus the fact that the closer the two ships came the greater the chances of hits on them, but making no differentiation between calibres of guns firing,

### *Victory:* 12.05 to 12.30 p.m.

| Ship firing | Length of fire (mins) | Guns firing | Times fired | Shots fired |
|---|---|---|---|---|
| *Mont Blanc* (74) | 5 | 41 | 2 | 82 |
| *Duguay-Trouin* (74) | 5 | 39 | 2 | 78 |
| *San Francisco de Asis* (74) | 10 | 37 | 3 | 111 |
| *San Augustin* (74) | 5 | 39 | 2 | 78 |
| *Héros* (74) | 10 | 39 | 3 | 117 |
| *Santisima Trinidad* (136) | 10 | 72 | 3 | 216 |
| *Bucentaure* (80) | 5 | 43 | 2 | 86 |
| *Redoutable* (74) | 5 | 39 | 2 | 78 |
| **Totals** | | **349** | | **846** |

*Comments*

Some 350 guns from eight ships fired about 850 shots from their port broadsides. Taking into account the factors listed above that detracted from accurate firing, and the fact that we know that many shots missed completely at the longer ranges, it seems reasonable to assume about 15 per cent (say 130) hit the *Victory*. They were aimed primarily at the masts and rigging and perhaps some 70 per cent of these (90) hit their target, leaving another 40 or so shots that reached the hull or decks, causing Scott's death and the Royal Marines casualties and other damage like the smashed wheel.

### *Royal Sovereign:* 11.45 a.m. to 12.20 p.m.

| Ship firing | Length of fire (mins) | Guns firing | Times fired | Shots fired |
|---|---|---|---|---|
| *San Leandro* (64) | 10 | 32 | 3 | 96 |
| *Indomptable* (80) | 15 | 43 | 4 | 172 |
| *Santa Ana* (112) | 30 | 56 | 5 | 280 |
| *Fougueux* (74) | 30 | 39 | 5 | 195 |
| **Totals** | | **170** | | **743** |

*Comments*

Fewer ships were firing at the *Royal Sovereign* for most of the time as those such as the *Monarca* and *Pluton* were primarily aiming at the *Belleisle* and *Mars*. However, those that did concentrate on her were able to do so for most, if not all, of the time as the *Royal Sovereign* did not alter course and sail down part of the line as did the *Victory*. Assuming 170 guns fired about 740 shots and using the same calculations as above then about 111 shots (15 per cent) would have hit, with about 78 (70 per cent) going through sails and rigging and around 33 striking the hull and upper decks.

## The approach to battle: summary

• When Villeneuve wore at 8.00 a.m. Nelson understandably assumed his intention was to avoid battle and get back to safety in Cadiz harbour. His reaction was to order a chase to cut the Combined Fleet off, which developed into a race between the columns as to who would reach them first. There was mounting frustration with the lack of wind and the effect this had on the slower sailers. For most of the morning signals from both Nelson and Collingwood were primarily concerned with making more sail or changing the order of sailing.

• Because ships were making their own best speed irrespective of maintaining an order of sailing, both columns developed gaps and proper formation was largely lost. Captain Codrington of the *Orion* (in Nelson's column) recalled: 'We all scrambled into battle as best we could,' and Captain Moorsom in the *Revenge* (Collingwood's column) wrote: 'Admiral Collingwood dashed directly down, supported by such ships as could get up, and went directly through their line.'

• The large gaps in both columns meant that the fleet was not as concentrated as Nelson had intended. The ships following the leading flagships arrived piecemeal with a considerable time lag between groups. The *Royal Sovereign* cut the line at about 12.20 p.m. with the *Revenge* (the eighth ship in the column) 30 minutes behind, and the next ship to join the action was the *Defiance* 30 to 40 minutes later. The last ship, the 98-gun *Prince*, did not arrive until almost 3.00 p.m. The *Victory* broke through astern of the *Bucentaure* at about 12.30 p.m. but the *Orion* (ninth ship) did not join until almost an hour later and the *Spartiate*, the last ship of the weather column, not until nearly 3.00 p.m.

• As late as 11.40 a.m. Nelson was being forced to abandon his Memorandum plan and steer for the van. Only when, at the last moment, he identified Villeneuve's flagship was he able to revert to attacking the centre and the enemy commander-in-chief while the lee column took on the rear.

• Nelson had got his 'pell mell' battle: the basic principles of his original plan were in place, if not the detail. During the next four hours the issue would be decided by gunnery and guts.

# THE MÊLÉE

The Battle of Trafalgar lasted well over five hours, from the opening shots of the *Fougueux* to the surrender of the *Intrépide* at around 5.15 p.m. This was a long time for ships to be slugging it out at close range, reflected in the high casualty figures and crippling damage inflicted on the ships of both sides that were heavily engaged from the start. The most intense fighting occurred during the two hours after 12.30 p.m. Within the first 90 minutes Villeneuve had lost two ships (*Redoutable* and *Fougueux*) and Nelson was down (hit at about 1.15 p.m.). By 3.00 p.m. another nine of the Combined Fleet had struck (*Bucentaure, Santa Ana, Santisima Trinidad, Algéciras, San Juan Nepomuceno, Bahama, Monarca, Aigle* and *Swiftsure*), and a third of the fleet was out of action including three flagships (those of Villeneuve, Cisneros and Magon). By the time Nelson died at around 4.30 p.m. three more had surrendered (*San Augustin, San Ildefonso* and *Berwick*) while the *Achille* had caught fire and exploded; altogether 16 enemy ships had been captured or destroyed, another 11 were in full flight for Cadiz and Dumanoir was escaping westwards with four more. That left one Spanish ship, the *Neptuno,* and one French, the *Intrépide,* still battling on. When the *Intrépide* struck at 5.15 p.m., after a two-and-a-half-hour fight that was arguably the most gallant of the entire battle, she had been engaged by no fewer than seven British ships.

Within 30 minutes of 12.30 p.m. Collingwood had led eight of his ships into the rear of Villeneuve's line. Their arrival was a series of short sharp punches rather than one massive simultaneous blow. The *Royal Sovereign* hit home first, fighting on her own for ten minutes before receiving support from her next astern, the *Belleisle.* There was a gap of nearly half an hour between the arrival of the eighth ship (*Revenge*) and the leader of the next group of six (*Defiance*). To the north Nelson's initial thrust through the centre also consisted of eight ships led by *Victory,* although it took an hour for the last of them (*Agamemnon*) to arrive. The two 'tail enders', *Minotaur* and *Spartiate,* crawled in shortly before three o'clock.

The battle can be very roughly divided into three interrelated parts: Collingwood's and Nelson's almost simultaneous attacks, the subsequent confrontations between various combinations of individual ships, and the belated attempt of Dumanoir's van to return to assist the centre. No close-quarter mêlée involving up to 60 ships can ever be other than total confusion. A combination of dense smoke (with little wind to disperse it) and the proximity of the contestants cut visibility to under a hundred yards, sometimes to a hundred feet. Few, if any, logs recorded anything other than basic highlights and damage, and most masters had no clear idea of what enemy ships they were engaging – referring to their adversary as 'a French two-decker' or 'Spanish three-decker'. The logs are, understandably, silent as to movements or manoeuvres, once battle was joined, and subsequent recollections of timings and events vary wildly. The Trafalgar mêlée was a jumble of ship encounters, of enemy ships looming unexpectedly through the smoke, of one ship battling desperately against several enemy, of ships colliding and being locked together, of masts falling and of attempts at boarding. It was a twisted kaleidoscope of noise, chaos, fear and death. Above all it was a gunnery duel, with huge amounts of metal being thrown in all directions. It was the objective of every captain to manoeuvre

his ship so that his guns could get the best shot while presenting as difficult a target as possible. The objective of every man on the gundecks was to keep the broadsides firing. To rake an enemy was the ultimate success, to be raked the ultimate disaster.

## COLLINGWOOD'S COLUMN

### *Royal Sovereign*

The view from the bow of the *Royal Sovereign* at 11.45 a.m. was one that would never be seen again – a horizon covered by sailing ships of war. Captain Codrington on the *Orion,* still nearly three miles from the enemy, later remarked, 'I suppose no man ever saw such a sight as we did, for I called all my lieutenants up to see it.' From the leading ship of the British Fleet there was an uninterrupted view of the enemy. Straight ahead, perhaps a mile distant, there was a wide gap in the line plugged only by two ships wallowing along well to the lee of the rest of the fleet. If the *Royal Sovereign* kept her present course and speed she was destined to clash with an as yet unidentified three-decker. Looking to starboard revealed the rear of the Combined Fleet, much closer together with some ships seemingly doubled up. This was not a well-formed line but one of bunches of ships, the most distant being two miles to the south and almost abreast of Collingwood's flagship. To larboard the scene was similar. There Villeneuve's fleet extended for another two miles, again because of the concave nature of the line, the northernmost ship being abeam on the larboard side. Collingwood was headed for the centre of a shallow saucer.

The *Royal Sovereign* was supposed to cut the line at the 12th ship from the rear. However, Collingwood's angled view and the doubling of several enemy made counting difficult. A glance at the diagram on p. 488 shows that it is possible that four ships (*Aigle, Swiftsure, Argonaute* and *Argonauta*) could not be seen from the *Royal Sovereign*'s poop. If this was so then the *Santa Ana* was the 12th ship from the rear as far as Collingwood could tell. As he watched there was a sudden flash and puff of smoke from the ship astern of the three-decker. The first shot of the battle had been fired. Then, from the same ship, a flickering, darting flame from two lines of gunports, accompanied by a thick yellow-white cloud, heralded the first broadside. Within seconds the enemy three-decker had also fired. Others followed suit, and the thunderous rumble of guns became continuous. Then, dimly through the haze of smoke, the enemy's colours could be seen being run up. The *Royal Sovereign*'s target was the flagship of a Spanish admiral, 30 minutes away.

On the *Fougueux* the master-at-arms (on a French ship the officer in charge of gunnery) was Captain Pierre Servaux of the Marine Artillery. He has left a detailed account of the opening minutes of the action.

> At a quarter past twelve o'clock [it was 11.45 a.m.] the *Fougueux,* a man-of-war of seventy-four guns, fired the first gun in the fleet. As she did so she hoisted her colours. She continued her cannonade, firing on the English flagship, which was a greatly superior vessel in size, height, guns and the number of the crew. Her main-deck and upper-deck guns, in fact, could fire right down on to our decks, and in that way

## Trafalgar: Collingwood and Nelson Break the Line, 12.15 to 12.45 p.m.

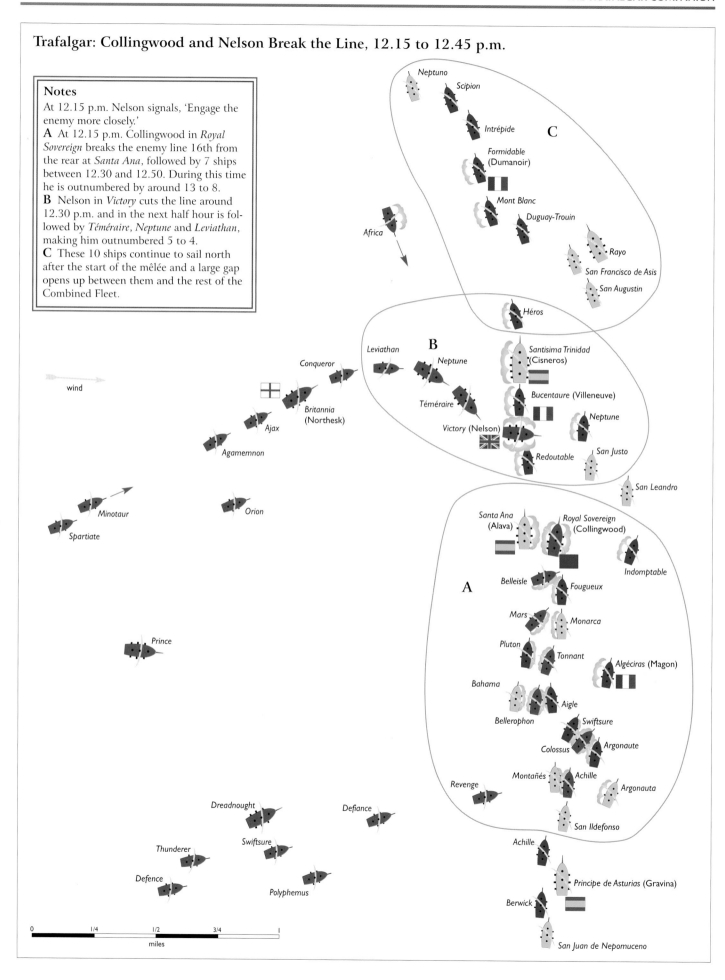

**Notes**

At 12.15 p.m. Nelson signals, 'Engage the enemy more closely.'

**A** At 12.15 p.m. Collingwood in *Royal Sovereign* breaks the enemy line 16th from the rear at *Santa Ana*, followed by 7 ships between 12.30 and 12.50. During this time he is outnumbered by around 13 to 8.

**B** Nelson in *Victory* cuts the line around 12.30 p.m. and in the next half hour is followed by *Téméraire*, *Neptune* and *Leviathan*, making him outnumbered 5 to 4.

**C** These 10 ships continue to sail north after the start of the mêlée and a large gap opens up between them and the rest of the Combined Fleet.

wind

Neptuno
Scipion
Intrépide
**C**
Formidable (Dumanoir)
Mont Blanc
Duguay-Trouin
Africa
Rayo
San Francisco de Asis
San Augustin
Héros

Leviathan
**B**
Neptune
Conqueror
Santisima Trinidad (Cisneros)
Britannia (Northesk)
Téméraire
Bucentaure (Villeneuve)
Ajax
Neptune
Agamemnon
Victory (Nelson)
Redoutable
San Justo
San Leandro

Minotaur
Orion
Spartiate

Santa Ana (Alava)
Royal Sovereign (Collingwood)
Indomptable
Belleisle
Fougueux
**A**
Mars
Monarca
Pluton
Tonnant
Algéciras (Magon)
Bahama
Aigle
Prince
Bellerophon
Swiftsure
Colossus
Argonaute
Montañés
Achille
Argonauta
Revenge
San Ildefonso
Achille

Dreadnought
Defiance
Thunderer
Swiftsure
Principe de Asturias (Gravina)
Defence
Berwick
Polyphemus
San Juan de Nepomuceno

0      1/4      1/2      3/4      1
miles

all our upper-deck men employed in working the ship, and the infantry marksmen posted on the gangways, were without cover and entirely exposed. We had also, according to our bad habit in the French Navy, fired away over a hundred rounds [it was probably nearer 200] at long range before the English ship had practically snapped a gun lock. It was, indeed, not until we found ourselves side by side and yardarm to yardarm with the English flagship that she fired at all.

The latter statement is inaccurate as the *Royal Sovereign* started firing before she reached the Combined Fleet's line. According to Commander Bazin, the second-in-command on the *Fougueux*, every time a broadside was fired it was greeted with a spontaneous roar of '*Vive l'Empereur!*' and '*Vive notre brave commandant!*'

By 12.15 p.m. the *Royal Sovereign* was within a few moments of breaking the line. Under effective fire by at least four ships for the last half hour, she was damaged, but not yet severely. A few casualties had been inflicted but most of the shots that hit had gone through ropes, rigging, spars and sails. Chunks of wood, pieces of rope and canvas had come raining down from aloft, only to be caught by the splinter net strung above the quarterdeck.

With the *Royal Sovereign* only 200 yards from the enemy the French ship astern was seen to be closing the gap between her and the Spanish flagship ahead. Up had gone the Frenchman's maintopgallant sail as Captain Baudouin strove to block the English admiral. Soon the bowsprit of the yellow-painted French 74 was almost touching the taffrail of the huge, black-bodied Spaniard. On the *Royal Sovereign* Captain Rotherham turned to Collingwood for a decision, which was made instantly: 'Steer for the Frenchman and carry away his bowsprit!'

Below on the *Royal Sovereign*'s gundecks every gun had been triple shotted, and both larboard and starboard batteries were manned. There was no need to aim; all the gun captain had to do was wait until a wooden bow (or stern) blocked his gunport – then jerk his lanyard. At least 50 guns of various calibres from 12 to 32 pounds would fire in rapid succession from the bow on either side. With all guns triple shotted, at least one and a half tons of assorted iron would be blasted into the Spaniard's stern and a similar weight into the French ship. At the last moment Baudouin ordered the maintopsail to be backed, thus slowing the *Fougueux* just enough to allow the *Royal Sovereign* to burst through the tiny gap. The awful rolling crash of her guns began.

## Trafalgar: Collingwood's First Four Ships Break the Line, 12.15 to 12.35 p.m.

### 12.15–12.20 p.m.

### 12.20–12.35 p.m.

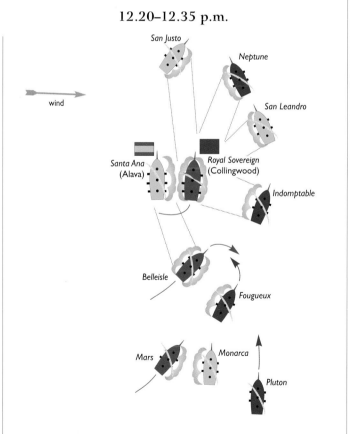

#### Notes
• *Royal Sovereign* is some 10 minutes ahead of the *Belleisle* and about to cut through the line between *Santa Ana* and *Fougueux*. All her guns are triple-shotted and both larboard and starboard batteries prepare to rake the Spanish and French ships. But she is under fire from 3 ships and very isolated.
• *Belleisle* and *Mars* are under fire from *Monarca* and *Pluton*.

#### Notes
• *Santa Ana* is raked by *Royal Sovereign* who then luffs alongside her. *Royal Sovereign* is for a time under effective fire from at least 5 ships.
• After some 10 minutes *Belleisle* arrives, rakes *Santa Ana* and then engages *Fougueux*.
• *Mars* is the next to arrive and engages *Monarca* while *Pluton* passes to the latter's lee.

On the *Santa Ana* the effect was so devastating that the ship was immediately crippled, only able to fight on with hugely reduced capacity. It is impossible to be sure of casualties but it is thought scores of men went down in a matter of moments and that perhaps 14 guns were disabled. The whole of her magnificent stern windows and transom disintegrated, and a hurricane of whirling metal, glass and splinters flew through the open decks, cutting down everyone in its path. It was the first British broadside of the battle and arguably the most effective – a perfect rake at virtual touching distance into the most vulnerable part of any ship's anatomy. Seconds later the starboard gunners had their turn. As the *Royal Sovereign* swung round to larboard to come alongside the *Santa Ana* she was able to fire into the larboard side of the *Fougueux* as the latter bore away to avoid a collision. Captain Servaux records the result:

> I thought the *Fougueux* was shattered to pieces – pulverized. The storm of projectiles that hurled themselves against and through the hull on the larboard side made the ship heel to starboard. Most of the sails and rigging were cut to pieces, while the upper deck was swept clear of the greater number of seamen working there, and of the soldier sharpshooters. Our gun-decks below had, however, suffered less severely. There not more than thirty men in all were put *hors de combat*.

For the next ten minutes the *Royal Sovereign* was isolated in the midst of her enemies. The *Santa Ana*'s uninjured starboard gunners fired into her as she came alongside and touched yardarms. Even allowing for the chaos and horror on the gundecks, and assuming her guns were at least double shotted, she would have been able to throw a ton of metal back into the *Royal Sovereign* – enough to make the British ship heel two feet out of the water. Then she shuddered again as the *Fougueux*'s broadside thudded into her starboard quarter. From about 400 yards off her starboard beam the 80-gun *Indomptable* joined in. Up ahead the *San Justo, Neptune* and *San Leandro* began to swing round to direct their guns too against the British flagship. A tremendous cannonade ensued; so incessant was the firing that several men on the *Royal Sovereign* claimed they saw shots strike each other in mid-air.

Collingwood set an impressive example of calm and control under fire. Midshipman Robinson watched him with profound admiration. Writing years afterwards, he said, 'I see before me dear old Cuddie (as we called Collingwood) walking the break of the poop, with his triangular gold-laced cocked hat, tights, silk stockings, and buckles, musing over the progress of the fight and munching an apple.' At one stage a studding sail was shot away to come crashing down across the hammocks stowed along the gangway. Never a man to see anything wasted, Collingwood immediately called over the first lieutenant to help him salvage it. With

## Collingwood Wounded

It is not generally known that Collingwood was wounded at Trafalgar. He would not allow his name to be included in the list of casualties sent to England, nor did he mention it in any of his letters at the time. Only some six months later, when his wife had heard rumours that he had been injured and wrote to ask him, did he acknowledge he had been hit. In a letter to his wife at the end of March 1806 he wrote:

> Did I not tell you how my leg was hurt? It was by a splinter – a pretty severe blow. I had many good thumps, one way or the other: one on the back, which, I think, was the wind of a great shot, for I never saw anything that did it. You know nearly all were killed or wounded on the quarterdeck or poop but myself, my Captain and secretary Mr. Cosway. ... The first inquiry of the Spaniards was about my wound, and exceedingly surprised they were when I made light of it, for when the Captain of the *Santa Anna* was brought on board, it was bleeding and swelled and tied up with a handkerchief.

the two giants locked together and swaying to and fro like wrestlers, shuddering and shaking as they delivered or received broadsides, there was little an admiral could do to influence events. Collingwood descended from the poop and walked across to the quarterdeck gunners. Bending low and shouting in their ears, he encouraged them not to waste a shot, occasionally peering along a barrel himself to check alignment. He stood for a time watching a crew on the larboard side, the gun captain of which was a black man who was later killed, and commended them as they fired some ten consecutive shots directly into the opposite gunport of the *Santa Ana*. That Collingwood was not struck down, as Nelson was to be less than an hour later, was miraculous, though he was slightly wounded (see box).

The master, Mr William Chalmers, was not so fortunate. He was mortally wounded only a few feet from Collingwood on the quarterdeck near the wheel. The admiral described how it happened:

> A great shot almost divided his body. He laid his head upon my shoulder, and told me he was slain. I supported him until two men carried him off. He could say nothing to me but to bless me; but as they carried him down, he wished he could but live to read the account of the action in a newspaper. He lay in the cockpit among the wounded until the *Santa Ana* struck, and, joining in the cheer which they gave her, expired with it on his lips.

These two three-deckers continued to fight their dreadful duel alongside each other until shortly after two o'clock. Midshipman George Castle has left an account of what it was like on a gundeck during that slugging match.

> I'm stationed at the heaviest guns of the ship [lower deck 32-pounders], and I stuck close to one gun and it poured into her [*Santa Ana*]; she was so close it was impossible to miss her. ... I looked once out of our stern ports; but I saw nothing but French and Spaniards round, firing at us in all directions. It was shocking to see the many brave seamen mangled so; some with their heads half shot away, others with their entrails mashed, lying panting on the deck. The greatest slaughter was on the quarterdeck and poop; we had seven ships on us at once [in fact, five or possibly six]. The *Belleisle* was next to us in the action, and she kept off a great deal of fire from us … likewise the *Tonnant*.

By 2.00 p.m. neither the *Santa Ana* nor the *Royal Sovereign* was capable of moving. They had beaten each other almost to death. That the Spanish flagship continued after the devastating first rake she received speaks volumes for the sheer guts of the crew and leadership of her officers. By this time she had lost her mizzenmast and her starboard side was 'almost entirely beaten in'; Admiral Alava lay wounded amid indescribable carnage, with almost 250 men dead or wounded. At about 2.15 p.m. she struck. The *Royal Sovereign* was by now a dismasted hulk, but she had suffered only 141 casualties, substantially fewer than her adversary. Shortly after the Spaniards lowered their colours a boat arrived from the *Victory* and Lieutenant Alexander Hill climbed on board to report that Nelson had been wounded. Collingwood later wrote, 'I asked the officer if his wound was dangerous. He hesitated; then said he hoped it was not; but I saw the fate of my friend in his eye; for his look told me what his tongue could not utter.' Although she had drifted apart from the *Santa Ana* the *Royal Sovereign* was unmanageable, and the *Euryalus* was instructed to take her in tow. When this had been achieved Collingwood picked up his speaking trumpet to shout across to Captain Blackwood to go aboard the *Santa Ana* and 'Bring me the admiral!' Blackwood found a badly wounded Alava unable to move so he took Captain Gardoqui back with him to surrender his sword instead.

## Belleisle

*Belleisle* was the next ship in the lee column coming up astern and to starboard of the *Royal Sovereign*. Captain Hargood had crowded on every stitch of canvas to close the gap ahead and come to the support of his admiral. *Belleisle* was ten minutes behind, and of all the ships approaching the enemy line that afternoon she suffered the most damage and losses before being able to reply. Hargood's orders to his officers had been short and clear. 'Gentlemen, I have only this to say: that I shall pass under the stern of that ship [*Santa Ana*]. Put in two round shot and then a grape and give her that. Now go to your quarters and mind not to fire until each gun will bear with effect.' The *Belleisle* intended to follow into the same gap as the *Royal Sovereign* but not to open fire until she was amongst the enemy.

It seemed to many on the *Belleisle* as she entered the zone of enemy fire that the French and Spanish gunners were far from being as useless as they had been told. A hail of shot whined and whirred through the sails and rigging and gouged dozens of splinters from bulwarks, masts and yards. There were screams and moans from men whose limbs were smashed by flying metal or chunks of wood. Apart from the officers, and Royal Marines on the poop and quarterdeck who declined to do so, most of the crew crouched or lay behind whatever cover they could find. The only sounds were the sickening crash of the enemy's gunfire striking the ship, the occasional scream of a wounded man and the captain's calm instructions to Mr Hudson (master) who repeated them exactly to the quartermaster at the helm, 'Starboard two points!' 'Starboard two points it is, sir!' 'Steady so!' 'Steady it is, sir!'

Hargood had positioned himself on the slide of the foremost carronade on the starboard side of the quarterdeck – in which position he was soon hit, but not seriously. Nearby was sixteen-year-old 2nd Lieutenant Paul Nicolas RM, who has left a vivid account of the scene as the *Belleisle* ran the gauntlet of the enemy guns – mostly those of the *Fougueux*, *Monarca* and *Pluton*.

> A shriek soon followed – a cry of agony was produced by the next shot – and the loss of the head of a poor recruit was the effect of the succeeding [one], and as we advanced, destruction rapidly increased. A severe contusion on the breast now prostrated our Captain, but he soon resumed his station. Those only who have been in a similar situation to the one I am attempting to describe can have a correct idea of such a scene. My eyes were horrorstruck at the bloody corpses around me, and my ears rang with the shrieks of the wounded and the moan of the dying.
>
> At this moment, seeing that almost every one was lying down, I was half disposed to follow the example and several times stooped for the purpose, but – and I remember the impression well – a certain monitor seemed to whisper, 'Stand up and do not shrink from your duty.' Turning round, my much esteemed and gallant senior [1st Lieutenant John Owen, who eventually became a lieutenant-general] fixed my attention; the serenity of his countenance and the composure with which he paced the deck, drove more than half my terrors away; and joining him I became somewhat infused with his spirit … . My experience is an instance of how much depends on the example of those in command when exposed to the fire of the enemy, more particularly in the trying situation in which we were placed for nearly thirty minutes from not having the power to retaliate.

By about 12.20 p.m. the *Belleisle* was approaching the same gap between the *Santa Ana* and *Fougueux* through which Collingwood's flagship had passed. However, she had suffered far more severely than the *Royal Sovereign*. Some 20 to 30 men were down when the order 'Stand to your guns!' was passed to the gundecks. Crews scrambled to their feet to man the guns of both broadsides as the moment arrived when, at last, they would get a chance to revenge themselves with a double rake – larboard at the *Santa Ana*, starboard at the *Fougueux*. The next order yelled from the quarterdeck, to be repeated by the midshipmen near the hatches and thus down to the officers on each gundeck, was 'Stand by both broadsides!' Nicolas continues:

> … when we reached their line. Our energies became aroused, and the mind diverted from its appalling condition, by the order of 'Stand to your guns!' which, as they successively came to bear were discharged into our opponents on either side; but as we passed close under the stern of the *Santa Ana*, of 112 guns, our attention was more strictly called to that ship. Although until that moment we had not fired a shot, our sails and rigging bore evident proofs of the manner in which we had been treated; our mizzen topmast was shot away and the ensign had been thrice rehoisted; numbers lay dead upon the decks, and eleven wounded were already in the surgeon's care. The firing was now tremendous and at intervals the dispersion of the smoke gave us a sight of the colours of our adversaries.

The *Belleisle* bounced and shuddered with each successive shock as the lanyards were jerked and each iron monster leapt amidships with recoil until snatched back by the breeching ropes. As one seaman described it:

> At every moment the smoke accumulated more and more thickly, stagnating on board between decks at times so densely as to blur over the nearest objects and often blot out the men at the guns from those close at hand on each side. … In fact the men were as much in the dark as to the external objects as if they had been blindfolded, and the only comfort to be derived from this serious inconvenience was that every man was so isolated from

his neighbour that he was not put in mind of his danger by seeing his messmates go down all round. All that he knew was that he heard the crash of the shot smashing through the rending timbers, and then followed at once the hoarse bellowings of the captains of the guns, as men were missed at their posts, calling out to the survivors: 'Close up there! Close up!'

As the *Belleisle* burst through the outline of a French 74 loomed suddenly through the smoke haze. She was under topsails and topgallants that towered up into clear air – the *Fougueux*. Nicolas again:

> At this critical period, while steering for the stern of the *L'Indomptable* (our masts and yards and sails hanging in the utmost confusion over our heads), which continued a most galling raking fire upon us, the *Fougueux* being on our starboard quarter, and the Spanish *San Justo* [? *San Leandro*] on our larboard bow, the Master earnestly addressed the Captain. 'Shall we go through, sir?' 'Go

through by ———' was his energetic reply. 'There's your ship, sir [*Indomptable*], place me close alongside her.' Our opponent defeated this manoeuvre by bearing away in a parallel course with us within pistol shot.

The *Indomptable* drifted away but not before firing a final broadside into the *Belleisle*. Within moments the bowsprit of the *Fougueux*, whether by design or accident is unclear, was plunged like an outstretched sword into the starboard side of the English ship. With a shuddering concussion her larboard bow struck the main channel and the ships ground together, still firing as best they could. According to Captain Servaux on the *Fougueux* the *Belleisle* appeared to be getting the worst of the exchange of fire. 'We soon saw the English vessel's mizzen-mast go by the board, and then her rudder and steering gear were damaged, making the ship unmanageable. Her sails flapped loose in the wind, and her sheets and running rigging were cut to pieces ...'. The *Belleisle*'s log records her mizzen cut through six feet above the deck at 1.10 p.m. Within another ten minutes both ships had drifted apart, badly bruised but still fighting.

## Trafalgar: Collingwood's First Four Ships Break the Line, 12.35 to 1.15 p.m.

### 12.35–12.45 p.m.

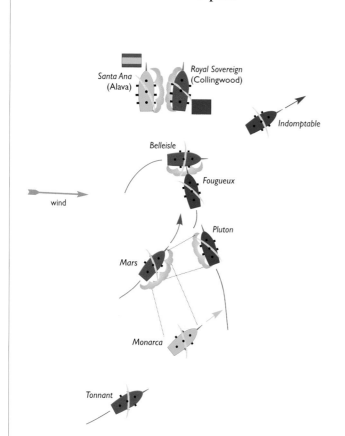

### 12.45–1.15 p.m.

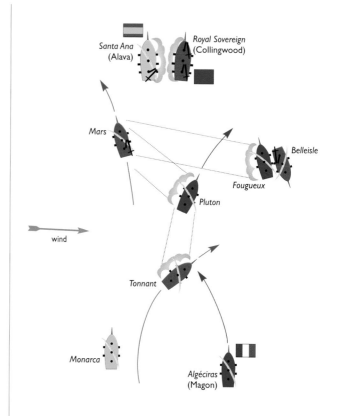

**Notes**
- *Mars* is heavily engaged with *Pluton* while *Belleisle* collides with *Fougueux*.
- *Monarca* bears away from *Mars'* fire. *Tonnant* is just approaching the line.

**Notes**
- *Santa Ana* and *Royal Sovereign* have inflicted serious damage on each other and continue to exchange point-blank broadsides.
- *Mars* luffs up to avoid colliding with *Santa Ana*, but in doing so is stern-raked by *Pluton*.
- *Fougueux* drifts clear of *Belleisle* and is also able to rake *Mars*.
- *Tonnant* overtakes *Monarca* to leeward but runs aboard *Algéciras*.

*Belleisle* was, from then on, a disabled ship, still able to fire spasmodically but wallowing helplessly in the swell. In this state she was further attacked by enemy ships that came close such as the *Principe de Asturias* and *Neptune*. At around 2.00 p.m. her mainmast, and shortly afterwards the foremast, collapsed – thus completely dismasting the ship. A witness described the incident.

> At about two o'clock the mainmast fell over the larboard side, and half an hour afterwards the foremast fell over the starboard bow. Thus was the *Belleisle* a total wreck, without the means of returning the fire of the enemy except from the very few guns still unencumbered by the wreckage of the masts and rigging [which had presumably blocked the gunports].

An officer present later stated:

> I was under the break of the poop, aiding in running out a carronade. A cry of 'Stand clear, there! Here it comes!' made me look up, and at that instant the mainmast fell over the bulwarks just above me. This ponderous mass made the ship's whole form shake; had it taken a central direction it would have gone through the poop, and added many to our list of sufferers. ... In this unmanageable state we were but seldom capable of annoying our antagonists, while they had the power of choosing their distance, and every shot from them did considerable execution. We had suffered severely, and those on the poop were now ordered to assist at the quarterdeck guns, where we continued until action ceased. ... We lay a mere hulk, covered in wreck and rolling in the swell.

Although some of the pressure was taken off her by the later arrival of the *Defiance*, *Polyphemus* and British *Swiftsure*, by 3.30 p.m. the *Belleisle* was a useless hulk with all masts gone, and eventually had to be put under tow by the frigate *Naiad*. At the end she suspended a union jack at the end of a pike and held it up to view, while an ensign was made fast to the stump of her mainmast. However, despite her prolonged battering, her casualties of 33 killed and 93 wounded were not exceptionally high and she was able to send her last remaining boat to accept the surrender of the Spanish *Argonauta*.

## Mars

*Mars* came into action a few minutes after the *Belleisle*, and on her starboard quarter. Earlier that morning she had been told to take the lead of the lee column, but despite crowding every yard with canvas the *Mars* was not sufficiently good a sailer to stay ahead of an admiral who was determined to be first into the enemy. She was also the one ship of the first eight in Collingwood's column that would fail to break through the line. The *Fougueux*, *Pluton*, *Monarca* and *Algéciras* all bombarded her at some time during her approach. Then Captain Duff spotted a gap that widened as the *Fougueux* went on to engage the *Royal Sovereign*, just ahead of the

### The Surrender of the *Argonauta*

Lieutenant John Owen of the *Belleisle* had the honour, as the senior Royal Marine officer on board, of being sent to accept the surrender of the *Argonauta*.

> A beaten Spanish 80-gun ship – the *Argonauta*, having about this time hoisted English colours, the Captain was good enough to give me the pinnace to take possession of her: the Master accompanied me with eight or ten seamen or marines who happened to be near us. On getting up the *Argonauta*'s side I found no living person on her deck, but on making my way, over numerous dead and a confusion of wreckage across the quarterdeck, was met by the second Captain at the cabin door, who gave me his sword, which I returned, desiring him to keep it for Captain Hargood, to whom I should soon introduce him. With him I accordingly returned to the *Belleisle*, leaving the Master in charge of the prize.

*Monarca* and ordered Mr Thomas Cooke, his master, to make for it. However, the sluggishness of the *Monarca* and the developing gap had also been noticed by Commodore Cosmao-Kerjulien in the *Pluton*. Setting every stitch of sail possible, Cosmao was able to pass the *Monarca* to lee and reach the gap just before the *Mars* arrived. As the *Mars* bore down on the line she fired a broadside into the *Monarca* who bore away. The *Mars* then found herself sailing straight into the guns of the *Pluton*.

The ships were close, and the Frenchman well positioned to rake the *Mars'* bow. To counter this Duff luffed up to windward bringing his ship onto a parallel course with his enemy – but not before receiving a broadside. The *Pluton* maintained a heavy fire as, to avoid going aboard on the *Royal Sovereign*, the *Mars* luffed again and then hove to. She had not penetrated the enemy formation and was now stationary with the *Pluton* on her starboard quarter – she had been out-manoeuvred and was now a sitting duck. Cosmao's gunners made the most of their advantage. Midshipman James Robinson later wrote, 'Captain Duff walked about with steady fortitude, and said: "My God, what shall we do? Here is a Spanish three-decker [*Santa Ana*] raking us ahead, and a French one [*Pluton*] under our stern!"'

By about one o'clock, the *Tonnant* appeared through the smoke to take some of the pressure off the by now unmanageable *Mars*, whose mizzen was about to fall. Unfortunately, at about this time, the *Fougueux* drifted clear of her embrace with the *Belleisle* and got into position to replace the *Pluton* in the unequal exchange with the *Mars*. The officer commanding the Royal Marines, Captain Thomas Norman, saw the critical situation developing and dashed up to Duff to warn him. With the wind so slack, with several enemy firing at her and having suffered heavy damage and losses, the *Mars* was in no position to manoeuvre. There was even doubt if she could bring her guns to bear on the new adversary – the *Fougueux*. When Norman spoke to his captain Duff responded, 'Do you think our guns would bear on her?' 'I think not, but I cannot see for smoke.' 'Then,' said Duff, 'we must point our guns on the ships on which they bear. I shall go and look, but the men below may see better, as there will be less smoke there.' He walked to the starboard side of the quarterdeck to peer over at the gunports. Then, turning to another sixteen-year-old midshipman, Alexander Arbuthnott, he told him to go below and get the guns pointed more aft, towards the *Fougueux*. As Arbuthnott left another broadside smashed into the ship. A ball decapitated poor Duff, who collapsed in a bloody heap at the foot of the poop-deck ladder. A Union flag was hastily found to cover his body, which was to remain there for the duration of the battle. The same shot also went on to kill two seamen nearby. Luckily Duff's thirteen-year-old son Norwich, an AB doing duty as a midshipman, was not on the quarterdeck to witness his father's horrific death.

Lieutenant William Hennah was now in command. It was about 1.15 p.m. and the *Mars*, although still firing and defiant, was little more than a floating wreck. Midshipman James Robinson was later to say, 'In a few minutes our poop was totally cleared, the quarter-deck and foc's'le nearly the same, and only the Boatswain [John Blunt] and myself and three men left alive.' The master, Thomas Cooke, who was among the wounded, later recorded in his log:

> At 1.15, Captain Duff was killed, and the poop and quarterdeck almost left destitute, the carnage was so great; every one of our braces and running rigging shot away, which made the ship entirely ungovernable, and was frequently raked by different ships of the enemy.

By the end of the battle the damage to the *Mars* was, again according to Cooke, exceptionally extensive: 'there being not one shroud standing in either fore, main or mizzen rigging. The fore mast and main mast badly wounded. Mizzen mast cut half asunder, main topmast cut half in two, and not a sail in a state of setting.' He might also have mentioned the spanker-boom shot away and a number of guns smashed or dismounted.

The *Mars* was now a mere hulk, still spitting fire, but used for target practice by passing enemy ships – the *Monarca* and *Algéciras* being examples. Considering the pounding she took, 29 killed and 69 wounded out of a complement of 615 was a relatively light butcher's bill. But the figures do illustrate how lethal it could be to be exposed on the upper decks of a ship in a mêlée.

### Tonnant

The *Tonnant* joined the action by cutting the line between the *Monarca* to larboard and the *Algéciras* (flagship of Rear-Admiral Magon) to starboard at around 12.30 p.m. Like the others she had come under heavy fire during her approach, during which Captain Tyler had his band playing 'Britons, Strike Home'. Two bandsmen were wounded along with another nine men during this period. According to Lieutenant Frederick Hoffman, the third lieutenant, the 80-gun *Tonnant* broke through with the enemy on either side 'so close that a biscuit could have been thrown on either of them. Our guns were double-shotted. The order was given to fire; being so close, every shot was poured into their hulls, and down came the Frenchman's [*Algéciras'*] mizzen-mast, and after our second broadside the Spaniard's [*Monarca's*] fore and crossjack yards.' A third broadside so crippled the Spaniard that she ceased firing and drifted away, hauling down her colours as she did so. She was the first ship of the Combined Fleet to surrender, albeit only briefly, doing so after only 10 to 15 minutes in action – a testimony to the accuracy and volume of the *Tonnant's* gunnery. However, as the *Tonnant* sailed on and no effort was made to send a party on board to accept her surrender Captain Argumosa had the colours raised again.

Through the banks of smoke Captain Tyler glimpsed the wallowing hulk of the *Mars* being pounded by the *Pluton*. He brought the *Tonnant* round to starboard and his broadside raked the *Pluton* through the starboard quarter. This move gave an alert Magon his chance to rake the stern of Tyler's ship. The main- and mizzen-topsails were braced round and the *Algéciras* forged ahead with her bows slowly coming into the wind. Tyler spotted the danger and brought his ship to starboard – but not in time to prevent being raked. Both ships were now so close that a collision was unavoidable, and the bowsprit of the *Algéciras* was thrust through the *Tonnant's* shrouds amidships. In his report Commander Le Toureur described what happened as he saw it:

> ... the *Algéciras* crowded on sail to prevent the English 90 [80]-gun ship breaking through ahead; this ship persisting in the attempt to cut the line at this point, we ran aboard her, entangling our bowsprit in her rigging; she then fired a whole volley of grape which totally stripped us of our rigging; but our well-sustained fire soon reduced her to the same state as ourselves. General Magon gave orders to board and all those told off for this service advanced most gallantly; we have to lament Lieutenant Verdreau who commanded the boarders as well as the greater part of the brave lads who followed him.

Lieutenant Hoffman wrote:

> A French ship of 80 guns [74], with an Admiral's flag, came up and poured a raking broadside into our stern, which killed or wounded forty petty officers and men, nearly cut the rudder in two, and shattered the whole of the stern, with the quarter galleries. She then in the most gallant manner [it is uncertain if it was deliberate], locked her bowsprit in our starboard main shrouds and attempted to board us with the greater part of her officers and ship's company. She had riflemen [in fact musketeers] in the tops who did great execution. Our poop was soon cleared, and our gallant Captain shot through the left thigh, and obliged to be carried below.
>
> During this time we were not idle. We gave it to her most gloriously with the starboard and main-deckers, and turned the forecastle guns, loaded with grape, on the gentlemen who wished to give us so fraternal a hug. The marines kept up a warm destructive fire on the boarders. Only one man made good his footing on the quarterdeck, when he was pinned through the calf of his right leg by one of the crew with his half-pike, whilst another was going to cut him down, which I prevented, and desired him to be taken to the cockpit. Our severe contest with the French Admiral lasted more than half an hour, our sides grinding so much against each other that we were obliged to fire the lower-deck guns without running then out.

By 1.15 p.m. both ships were still locked in their destructive embrace. They continued to fire into each other, although the better-trained and quicker gun crews of the *Tonnant* soon dominated the exchange. At one stage the seaman's most deadly enemy of all made its appearance, both ships catching fire when blazing wads started a blaze in the Frenchman's boatswain's store. Lieutenant Hoffman wrote, 'At length both ships caught fire before the chess-trees, and our firemen, with all the courage and coolness so inherent in British seamen, got the [fire] engine and played it on both ships, and finally extinguished the flames, although two of them were severely wounded in doing so.'

Down on the orlop deck Mr Forbes Chevers, a surgeon whose experience went back to the Battle of the Glorious First of June in 1794, was busy with knife and saw, lopping limbs. Among the wounded awaiting his attention was Captain Tyler, who lay in the purser's cot, as its usual occupant, Mr George Booth, a purser of ten year's standing, helped Chevers lift the wounded onto and off the surgeon's table. He in turn was helped by the wife of a petty officer, 'a very powerful and resolute woman'. At one time an officer went down to the cockpit to see the captain and recalled:

[I] found fourteen men awaiting amputation of either an arm or a leg. A marine who had sailed with me in a former ship, was standing up as I passed, with his left arm hanging down. 'What's the matter, Connelly?' 'Not much, sir,' he replied; 'I am only winged above my elbow, and I'm waiting my turn to be lopped.' His arm was dreadfully shattered by a grape-shot.

... One of the men, whose name was Smith, after his leg was taken off heard the cheering on deck in consequence of the enemy striking her colours [Algéciras], and cheered also. The exertion he made burst the blood vessels, and before they could be taken up he died.

This struggle continued well after 2.00 p.m., when a substantial boarding party led by lieutenant Charles Bennett was sent across to accept the Algéciras' surrender. Commander Le Tourneur's account cannot be bettered.

At 2.45, engaged by the same forces and continuing foul of [entangled with] the Tonnant, we lost the foremast which went by the board; the few men who remained on the upper works still defended them desperately. At 3 o'clock I was severely wounded in the shoulder; my officier de manoeuvre [navigating officer], M. Plassan, was hit by a bullet in the chest ... At 3.15, General Magon, who had already been wounded in the right arm and thigh by a splinter, received a bullet in the chest and fell dead on the spot. Our 18-pounder battery was at this time deserted and utterly silenced; we collected our men in the 36-pounder battery [lower gundeck], which continued to be served with the greatest activity. ... At 3.30, our main and mizzen masts fell and masked our guns. The enemy then pressed us closer than ever, we had several 36-pounders dismounted. ... we endeavoured to make a final effort by loading every gun that was still capable of being fired into the enemy and we had the satisfaction to see that lucky and well-aimed shots totally disabled the ships which were engaging us, and especially the Tonnant whom our guns forward – double-shotted and fired point blank – greatly damaged in her stern-frame and between wind and water aft. ... The final broadsides from the enemy so crippled us that they forced us to cease fire and 66 men from the Tonnant were sent on board, by whom we were taken in possession at 3.45.

However, this was not the end of the fight for the Tonnant. Out of the smoke to the south appeared a badly battered San Juan Nepomuceno, who had been heavily engaged with the Dreadnought (see below p. 515). There was an exchange of fire that brought

## An Attempt to Accept Surrender

Lieutenant Benjamin Clements of the Tonnant described his abortive attempt to accept the surrender of the San Juan Nepomuceno.

When at last down came her colours, I hailed a Spanish officer and asked if he had struck. When he said 'yes' I came aft and informed the First-Lieutenant [John Bedford]. He ordered me to board her. We had no boat but what was shot, but he told me I must try, so I went away in the jolly-boat with two men, but had not got above a quarter of the way when the boat was swampt [sic]. I cannot swim, but the two men who were with me could, one a black man the other a quartermaster; he was the last man in her, when a shot struck her and knocked her quarter off, and so she was turned bottom up. Macnamara, the black man, staid [sic] by me on one side, and Maclay, the quartermaster on the other, until I got hold of the jolly-boats fall [tackle for raising and lowering the boat], that was hanging overboard. I got my leg between the fall, and as the ship was lifted by the sea so was I, and as she descended, I was ducked. I found myself weak, and thought I was not long for this world. Macnamara swam to the ship and got a rope and [swam] to me again, and made it fast under my arms, when I [was] swung off and hauled into the stern port.

the Spaniard's foremast crashing down, snapped off some four feet from the deck, and a second broadside was sufficient to bring her colours down. Lieutenant Bedford, now commanding the Tonnant, sent another party to take her surrender but the attempt failed (see box); this honour fell to the Dreadnought shortly afterwards.

### Bellerophon

During the long, slow approach a midshipman on one of the Bellerophon's gundecks tripped over a gun captain's lanyard, accidentally firing the gun. No harm was done but the enemy ships opposite (Bahama, Aigle, Montañés and Swiftsure) took it as a challenge and opened fire. Cooke responded with his guns double shotted and steered for the gap opening up between the two Spanish 74s Bahama and Montañés astern. As Cooke brought his ship between his two enemies he loosed both broadsides, raking the Bahama in the stern and moments later the Montañés through the bow. Cooke had just ordered Mr Edward Overton, the master, to luff up and bring the ship alongside the Bahama when the topgallants of another ship appeared above the banks of smoke to leeward, so close that Cooke had to shout to the master to get the sails aback to check Bellerophon's way. There was, however, no time to avoid a collision, and the two ships ran aboard each other with a grinding crunch as the Bellerophon's bow smashed into the Aigle's larboard quarter. According to the Bellerophon's log her foreyard entangled with the Aigle's mainyard. They became bound together in one of the fiercest and most bloody engagements of the battle, which left both ships crippled, the 'Billy Ruff'n' with the third highest British casualty count of the action. The first lieutenant, William Cumby, has left us a detailed personal account of that afternoon. It is one of the best descriptions we have of what it was like on board a ship in the heat of the battle, and as such is quoted in full.

It had been Captain Cooke's original intention not to have a shot fired until we were in the act of passing through the enemy's line; but finding we were losing men as we approached their ships from the effects of their fire, also suffering in our masts and rigging, he determined to open our fire a few minutes sooner. ... At half-past twelve we were engaged on both sides, passing through their line under the stern of a Spanish seventy-four [Bahama], into whom ... we fired our carronades three times, and every long gun on the larboard side at least twice. Luckily for us, by this operation she had her hanging magazine blown up [the author is unable to verify this], and was completely

## Trafalgar: Collingwood's Second Four Ships Break the Line, 12.30 to 12.45 p.m.

### 12.30–12.40 p.m.

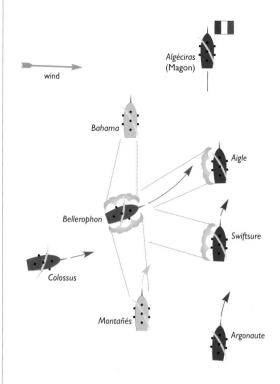

### 12.40–12.45 p.m.

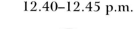
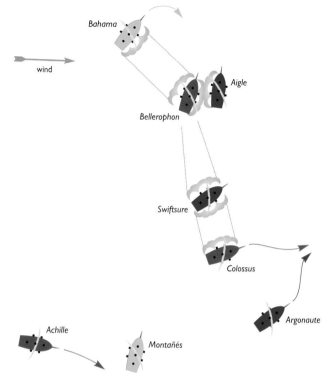

### Notes
• *Bellerophon* cuts the line and is able to rake both *Bahama* and *Montañés* in doing so. She is, however, under heavy fire from *Aigle* and *Swiftsure*.
• *Bellerophon* sees *Aigle* through the smoke and luffs up in an attempt to avoid colliding with her.

### Notes
• *Bellerophon* runs aboard *Aigle*.
• *Colossus* breaks the line and exchanges broadsides with *Swiftsure* before running aboard *Argonaute*.
• *Achille* steers to pass astern of *Montañés*.

beaten, for, in hauling up to settle her business to leeward [Cooke intended to come alongside the *Bahama* and finish her off] we saw over the smoke the top-gallant sails of another ship close under our starboard bow, which proved to be the French seventy-four, *L'Aigle,* as the name on her stern showed us. Although we hove back to avoid it, we could not sufficiently check our ship's way to prevent our running her on board with our starboard bow on her larboard quarter, our foreyard locking with her mainyard, which was squared.

By the Captain's directions I went down to explain to the officers on the main and lower decks the situation of the ship with respect to this new opponent, and to order them to direct their principal efforts against her. Having done so, as I was returning along the main deck, I met my poor messmate Overton, the Master, carried by two men, with his leg dreadfully shattered [he died of this wound]; and before I reached the quarter-deck ladder, having stopped to give some directions by the way, I was met by a quartermaster, who came to inform me that the Captain was very badly wounded and, as he believed, dead.

I went immediately on the quarter-deck and assumed the command of the ship – this would be about a quarter past one o'clock – when I found we were still engaged with

*L'Aigle* … . Our quarter-deck, poop, and forecastle were at this time almost cleared by musketry from troops on board *L'Aigle,* her poop and gangway completely commanding those decks, and the troops on board being very numerous. At this moment I ordered all the remaining men down from the poop, and, calling the boarders, had them mustered under the half-deck, and held them in readiness to repel any attempt that might be made by the enemy to board us; their position rendering it quite impracticable for us to board them in the face of such a fire of musketry so advantageously situated. [*Aigle,* although a 74 like the *Bellerophon,* was newer and bigger.] But whatever advantage they had over us on these upper-decks was greatly overbalanced by the superiority of our fire on the lower and main decks.

*L'Aigle* soon ceasing entirely to fire on us from her lower-deck, the ports of which were lowered down, whilst the fire from ours was vigorously maintained, the ports having, by my orders, been hauled up close against the side when we first fell on board her, to prevent their being torn from their hinges when the ships came in contact. While thus closely engaged and rubbing sides with *L'Aigle,* she threw many hand grenades on board us, both on our forecastle and gangway and in at the ports. Some of these exploded and dreadfully scorched several of our men; one of them I took up myself from our gangway where the fuse was burning, and threw it overboard.

One of these grenades had been thrown in at a lower-deck port and in its explosion had blown off the scuttle of the Gunner's storeroom, setting fire to the storeroom and forcing open the door into the magazine passage. ... the same blast which blew open the storeroom door shut-to the door of the magazine; otherwise we must all in both ships inevitably have been blown up together. The gunner [John Stevenson], who was in the storeroom at the time, went quietly up to Lieutenant [George] Saunders on the lower-deck and acquainted him that the storeroom was on fire, requested a few hands with water to extinguish it ....

At forty minutes past one *L'Aigle* hoisted her jib and dropped clear of us, under a tremendous raking fire as she paid off. Our ship at this time was totally unmanageable, the main and mizzen topmasts hanging over the side, the jib-boom spanker-boom and gaff shot away, and not a brace or bowline serviceable. We observed that *L'Aigle* was engaged by the *Defiance* [see below p. 514], and soon after two o'clock she struck. ...

Through the smoke haze Cumby could see that the nearby Spanish *Monarca* had struck. With her mizzen down, her hull smashed and holed and 255 casualties (101 dead) this was not surprising. Cumby sent across a boarding party to secure a prize. Then his account continues:

We were now without any opponent within reach of our guns, and our fire consequently ceasing, I had a message from the Surgeon stating that the cockpit was so crowded with wounded men that it was quite impossible for him to attempt some operations which were highly requisite, and begging I would allow him to bring some subjects up into the Captain's cabin for amputation if the fire was not likely to be renewed for a quarter of an hour. I gave him the requested permission ... .

Midshipman John Franklin was the signals midshipman on the *Bellerophon*, and of about 40 men on the poop at the start of the afternoon he was one of only eight who escaped unscathed. He has described an encounter with one of the group of French sharpshooters in the *Aigle's* foretop, a musketeer who was conspicuously, but foolishly, wearing a cocked hat. He had been firing for some time when he shot dead Franklin's friend Midshipman John Simmons while they were conversing together, then a few minutes later shot and killed a wounded seaman whom Franklin and a marine sergeant were about to carry below to the surgeon.

'He'll have you next!' Franklin exclaimed.

'Indeed he will not!' replied the sergeant, picking up a musket and going in search of a suitable spot from which to finish off the sharpshooter.

## The Death of Captain Cooke of the *Bellerophon*

Cooke was one of only two British captains to die at Trafalgar (the other was Captain Duff of the *Mars*). An eyewitness has described how it occurred.

He had discharged his pistols very frequently at the enemy, who as often attempted to board, and he had killed a French officer on his own [French] quarterdeck. He was in the act of reloading his pistols (and on the very same plank [spot] where Captain Pasley lost his leg on the 1st of June), when he received two musket balls in his breast. He immediately fell, and upon the Quarter-Master's going up and asking him if he should take him below, his answer was: 'No, let me lie quietly one minute. Tell Lieutenant Cumby never to strike!'

Cooke has a marble memorial slab on the wall of St Paul's crypt, close to Nelson's tomb.

## Midshipman John Franklin, later Arctic Explorer

Franklin had a remarkable career during which he alternated between operational naval appointments and voyages of arctic exploration, dying on an expedition to find the North-West Passage aged sixty-one.

Born in 1786, Franklin was a midshipman on the *Polyphemus* at Copenhagen in 1801. He served on the China station and was signals midshipman on the *Bellerophon* at Trafalgar. He was a lieutenant on the *Bedford* for the expedition to New Orleans during the American War in 1812, and was wounded and mentioned in despatches in 1814. 1818 saw him command the brig *Trent* in Captain Buchan's Arctic expedition, the start of his career as an explorer, and in 1819 he commanded an expedition overland from Hudson Bay to the shores of the Arctic Ocean. Promoted commander in 1821, he became a Fellow of the Royal Geographical Society the following year, and post captain in 1822. Early in 1825 he commanded another two-year expedition to the same area that, in combination with the work of another explorer, added some 1,200 miles to the known North American coastline. He was knighted in 1829, and commanded the frigate *Rainbow* off the coast of Greece from 1830 to 1833, being awarded the Order of the Redeemer of Greece for his services. For eight years from 1836 he was Lieutenant-Governor of Van Diemen's Land (Tasmania), which was then being populated mainly by convicts from England. He founded a college and established a scientific society in Hobart.

His final, and fatal, expedition was again to the Arctic area of North America in 1845, commanding the ships *Erebus* and *Terror* in search of the fabled North-West Passage. After July 1845 nothing more was heard of him or his men for fourteen years. An expedition to find them in 1857 ultimately discovered the skeletons of many of the men on King William's Island. Franklin had died on 11 June 1847 but his death was not, apparently, so dreadful as that of others in his party who, according to an Eskimo woman, 'fell down and died as they walked'.

Franklin had been promoted rear-admiral in October 1852 while officially missing rather than dead. A monument was erected to him and his wife in Westminster Abbey and a statue in Waterloo Place. There is also a Franklin Strait between the Prince of Wales Island and the Boothia Peninsular north of King William's Island, all now part of the North Western Territory of Canada.

Shortly afterwards Franklin spotted the man in the hat raising his musket and aiming in his direction again. He instantly dodged behind a mast so the shot hit the deck just behind him. This time, however, the sergeant fired and Franklin saw the Frenchman, whose features he vowed he would never forget as long as he lived, tumble head first into the sea. The marine sergeant later told Franklin it was his seventh shot.

Sharpshooters and grenade throwers were employed to clear the upper decks to facilitate boarding. Another midshipman later stated:

> Two actual attempts were made by the crew of *L'Aigle* to board us, while the French Captain was seen and heard vociferating, '*A l'abordage!*' On one of these occasions five of the enemy got on our starboard sprit-sail yard-arm, and were making their way to the bowsprit when a seaman named McFarlane let go the sprit-sail brace (a rope supporting that end of the yard), which suddenly canting with their weight, they all fell into the water.

The same writer has described another danger that almost caused another fire on the *Bellerophon*.

> Our main topmast being shot away, the sail, in falling between the ships (*L'Aigle* and *Bellerophon*), had been hooked, or held, by something in our main chains, and consequently hung like a curtain before the muzzles of our guns. It was soon in a blaze, but sail trimmers were immediately sent to clear the sail, etc., which dropped into the water. Shortly after this the First Lieutenant (Captain Cumby), being now in command, walked around the decks to encourage the men and stimulate their exertions at the guns, observing that, 'we had nothing else to trust to, as the ship aloft had become an unmanageable wreck'.

### *Colossus*

Commanded by Captain James Morris, *Colossus* was the sixth ship in Collingwood's column. She followed about five minutes astern of the *Bellerophon*, thus cutting the line around 12.35 p.m., and almost immediately became the fourth British ship to go aboard an enemy and become involved in a brutal exchange of broadsides gunport to gunport. Her 200 casualties that afternoon – almost 30 per cent of the crew – would be the highest of any British ship at Trafalgar, the result of close action with the French *Swiftsure*, the *Argonaute*, the *Bahama* and then the *Swiftsure* again. She was victorious on each occasion – but at a cost not only of human losses but of her mainmast, two anchors, three boats, several guns and a tottering foremast.

As the *Colossus* came through the smoke the first enemy that loomed large and close was the *Swiftsure*, which had thrown her sails aback to avoid *Bellerophon* and *Aigle*, locked together nearby. The French ship bore up to avoid the worst effects of the *Colossus'* broadside before disappearing into another bank of smoke, only to be replaced by the *Argonaute*. Both the British and French ships were close and steering convergent courses; there was nothing Captain Morris or Captain Épron could do to avoid yet another crashing collision, in which four of the

*Colossus'* starboard gunports were snapped off. In his report, Épron claimed to have deliberately brought about the collision: 'having hauled aboard the tacks on the courses we closed up the opening and obliged her to run us aboard to larboard'. There followed the usual hellish scenes on the gundecks as the ships exchanged deadly and destructive broadsides with muzzles a matter of feet apart. Within ten minutes the mutual battering and heavy swell combined to force the ships apart and the *Argonaute* dropped astern.

Morris's next opponent was the Spanish 74-gun *Bahama* under Commodore Galiano, whose resistance and death that day was to make him a national hero with his portrait in the Naval Museum in Madrid and a statue in the Plaza Mayor in his birthplace, Corunna. Earlier in the morning Galiano had toured the gundecks before summoning his officers to the quarterdeck. 'Gentlemen,' he said, 'you all know that our flag is nailed to the mast.' Then, turning to Don Alonso Butron, the captain of the marine infantry on board, 'I charge you to defend it. No Galiano ever surrenders, and no Butron should either.'

The battle between the *Bahama* and *Colossus* was prolonged, lasting well into the afternoon. The speed with which the British gunners could reload soon became decisive. Again and again, with not much more than a minute and a half between them, broadsides smashed into the Spaniard. A flying splinter struck Galiano on the foot and another tore open his scalp but he paid little notice and refused to go to the surgeon. He continued to give his orders and direct his guns 'as if the ship had been firing salutes at a review'. By two o'clock the *Bahama* had lost her mainmast but the fight was as intense as ever, with no sign of either ship giving way.

The resistance of the *Bahama*, which saw some of the most confused and furious fighting of the whole battle, highlighted Spanish courage as few other actions that day. It was not until past three o'clock, after some two and a half hours of almost continuous action and the loss of her captain, that she struck. Galiano's death was the beginning of the end. He was on the quarterdeck with his telescope in his hand when the wind of a passing shot made him stagger, and sent his glass spinning onto the deck. His coxswain, who was close by, picked it up and hastened to hand it back to his captain, at the same time asking respectfully if he had been hurt. Galiano had just assured him all was well when a roundshot flew between the two, cutting the unfortunate coxswain in two and covering the commodore in a spray of blood. Within a few seconds another shot struck Galiano, carrying away half his head.

An attempt was made to keep the news of their captain's death from the crew by covering his body with a flag, but the news soon reached the gundecks. Galiano's second-in-command was already lying wounded in the cockpit and command devolved onto the next senior lieutenant, Don Roque Guruceta. He held a hasty consultation with the other two uninjured officers and all agreed they could strike with honour. The nailed-up colours were torn down and a British union flag substituted. Shortly afterwards Roque was taken on board the *Colossus* to surrender his sword to Captain Morris.

### Yeoman of Signals Christopher Beatty

According to one source, of the 40 men initially stationed on the poop of the *Bellerophon* only eight escaped uninjured. One of these was Yeoman of Signals Beatty. When, in the thick of the fight, Beatty saw the white ensign shot away for the third time he snatched up the largest one he could find and began to climb hand over hand up the mizzen rigging with the flag wrapped round his shoulders. He was instantly spotted by the enemy sharpshooters who peppered away at him with their muskets. On reaching the top of the shrouds Beatty spread out the ensign and deliberately fixed it firmly by each corner to the shrouds. As if acknowledging his courage and honourable intentions the enemy stopped firing at him while he secured the flag. Beatty clambered down unhurt.

## Achille

The *Achille* was the seventh ship in Collingwood's column to reach the enemy line. At around 12.45 p.m. Captain Richard King steered to break through just astern of the Spanish *Montañés*. As he came down on the Spaniard's larboard side he was able to fire an effective broadside into her larboard quarter before luffing up and attacking her at pistol-shot range on her starboard side. Lieutenant Don Alejo Rubalcava, who became the commanding officer of the *Montañés* after the death of Captain Don José Alcedo and the wounding of the second-in-command, recounted the opening moves of the battle as he saw them.

> At 11.30 the General [Villeneuve] hoisted the signal to open fire as soon as they were within range, which we obeyed at noon [more probably 11.45], firing vigorously into a three-decker [*Royal Sovereign*] which was the leading ship of one of their lines. Nearly all our Squadron opened fire at the same time. At the half-hour we were firing intermittently as some of the ships had interposed themselves ... [and] the dense smoke in which we were enveloped on every side ... and with the calm it was difficult to distinguish the colours. At one o'clock [probably

a little earlier] a three-decker [in fact a two-decker] approached to place herself a pistol shot from us, pouring a terrible fire into our larboard quarter, which caused great havoc among the people, to the hull and to the rigging ...

The two ships hammered away at each other at point-blank range for about half an hour, during which time the Spanish captain was killed. Shortly after this Rubalcava took command.

> At this time [about 1.30 p.m.] the officer on the quarter-deck, Don Meliton Perez, informed me that I should have to take over command of the ship on account of the said losses and I observed in passing the main-deck that the crews of all the guns aft were out of action, many being stretched dead and dying on the deck. The same thing was apparent in the chief guns on the quarter-deck, but it did not detain me from going up on to the poop, where I instructed the midshipman entrusted with the charge of the colours that he should stand by them and on no account should he haul them down. Next I gave orders to the officers on the gun-decks to collect crews for all the guns capable of being employed and that they should fire on any enemy ship, keeping as close to the wind as possible ...

## Trafalgar: Collingwood's Second Four Ships Break the Line, 12.45 to 1.00 p.m.

### 12.45–12.55 p.m.

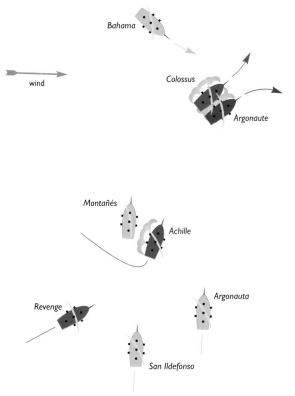

### 12.55–1.00 p.m.

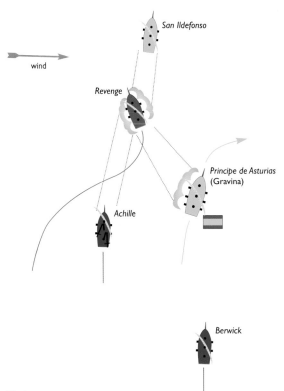

### Notes

• British *Achille* succeeds in stern-raking *Montañés* before luffing up alongside her to start a lengthy exchange of broadsides.
• *Colossus* breaks away from *Argonaute* who then bears away.

### Notes

• *Revenge* passes close to French *Achille* and her firing brings down the latter's mainmast, leaving only her foremast standing.
• *Revenge* then rakes French *Achille* through her bows before luffing up to engage *San Ildefonso* as well.
• *Principe de Asturias* bears away and is able to rake *Revenge* through her stern.

The *Montañés* was badly damaged and lost her foremast but Rubalcava appears to have exaggerated his casualties. She had only 20 killed and 29 wounded and was one of the few Combined Fleet ships to survive the battle and subsequent storm to escape to Cadiz.

Captain King turned away from the *Montañés* at around 1.30 p.m. in order to go to the assistance of the *Belleisle*, which was under severe attack. But before he could close the Spanish *Argonauta* appeared out of the smoke on his starboard side. King hove to on the *Argonauta*'s larboard bow and yet another prolonged exchange of broadsides began, lasting for over an hour. Captain Don Antonio de Pareja's report gives us an insight into the effects of being at the receiving end of such a lengthy cannonade.

> At this hour my ship had all the guns on the quarter-deck and the poop dismounted, a great number of the guns in the batteries were out of action, as much on account of the pieces [being injured] as from want of crews, the result of the numerous dead and wounded among them ... . The whole rigging was utterly destroyed, so that there were no shrouds left to the masts – save one to the main-mast – and they were threatening to fall at any minute, being shot through. In this situation it was very evident that this ship could make but slight and feeble resistance ... With these inexpressible feelings I was taken below to have my wounds dressed. ... my second having sent half an hour later to inform me that over and above the injuries we had already sustained, the ship was making much water ... and had lost her rudder ...

At that point Pareja gave his second-in-command authority to strike – she surrendered to another hulk, the *Belleisle*, at about 3.30 p.m.

The *Argonauta* had shut her lower-deck ports, ceased firing and was supposedly about to strike. However, before the British *Achille* could attempt to take possession the French *Achille* passed her namesake and distracted her attention by firing into her. Then the *Berwick*, which had been engaged with the *Defence*, interposed herself between the *Achille* and the *Argonauta*. The latter dropped to leeward (eventually surrendering to the *Belleisle*) while a hot action developed between the British *Achille* and the *Berwick*. This was the third major encounter that afternoon for the *Achille*, which had already virtually demolished the *Montañés* and *Argonauta*. Within 30 minutes the *Berwick* was disabled and her captain (Jean Camas) dead. When a lieutenant was sent aboard to claim the prize he counted 51 dead in her cockpit and piers. Her quarterdeck was said to have been swept clear of personnel three times, while her wounded amounted to 200. These figures are impossible to verify as most of her survivors of the battle were drowned when their ship was wrecked the following day.

## Revenge

The *Revenge*, under Captain Robert Moorsom (a gunnery expert), was the last of Collingwood's leading group of eight ships to reach the enemy line. There would be a gap of some 30 minutes before the next British ship (*Defiance*) would arrive at the head of Collingwood's second group. During the approach Moorsom had given orders that no firing was to take place until the enemy line was close: 'We shall want all our shot when we get in close; never mind their firing. When I fire a carronade from the quarter-deck, that will be the signal for you to begin ...'. The *Revenge* cut in just ahead of the French *Achille* before luffing up astern of the *San Ildefonso*, thus

being able to bring both broadsides to bear within a few moments to rake both enemy ships. While this was a smart piece of seamanship and enabled some effective initial gunnery, Moorsom had also exposed his own ship to being raked from Gravina's flagship, the three-decker 112-gun *Principe de Asturias*. What had seemed a skilful manoeuvre had placed the *Revenge* in the centre of a trio of enemy ships, all of which were able to bring fire to bear. That the *Revenge* was able to respond so well was, at least in part, due to the emphasis Moorsom had always placed on gunnery training.

When *Revenge* broke through ahead of the French *Achille* she cut it so fine that, as Moorsom wrote to his father:

> They closed so well together that a Frenchman's jib boom took my mizzen topsail as I passed and he was near jamming me between himself and his second ahead [*San Ildefonso*]. Perhaps it would have been better for me if he had done so; for a Spanish three-deck ship with Admiral Gravina's flag directly shot up on my lee quarter, the Frenchman [*Achille*] wore under my stern, and I was obliged to endure a raking fire for a considerable time without being able to help myself, for all our ropes were cut to pieces, and the wind was so light ...

While enduring this pounding from three different directions Lieutenant Peter Pickernell witnessed just how much mayhem one roundshot could produce.

> The shot entered the 3rd lower deck port from forward on the starboard side [probably from the *San Ildefonso*] and struck the gun (32-pounder) in which it made a large dint, then altering its direction, it struck the foremast in a vertical position and scooped out a large portion of the mast, which again altering its direction, it took a horizontal position and after decapitating a young midshipman by the name of Green, it struck the 7 men at the foremast tackle of the first gun forward on the starboard side who were running out after loading, and killed the whole of them by severing them nearly in two. It then stuck to the ship's side in a horizontal position, just above the waterway nearly under the breach of the gun, until the ship was in dock, when I cut it out by the Captain's desire.

*Revenge*'s battle went on throughout the afternoon, at various times involving the *San Ildefonso*, *Achille*, *Principe de Asturias* and the *Aigle*. She received support as more British ships arrived, headed by the *Defiance*. Nevertheless, she did not come off lightly. One seamen on the *Revenge* later wrote:

> After being engaged for about an hour two other ships fortunately came up and received some of the fire intended for us. We were now enabled to get at some of the shot-holes between wind and water and plug them up. This is a duty performed by the carpenter [William Russell] and his crew. We were unable to work the ship, our yards, sails and masts being disabled, and the braces completely shot away. In this condition we lay by the side of the enemy, firing away, and now and then we received a good raking from them, passing under our stern. ...
> Often during the battle we could not see for the smoke whether we were firing at friend or foe, and as to hearing orders, the noise of the guns so completely made us deaf we were obliged to look only to the motions that were made. In this manner we continued the battle until nearly five o'clock, when it ceased.

Orders were now given to fetch the dead bodies from the cockpit and throw them overboard. These were the bodies of the men who were taken down to the doctor during the battle badly wounded, and who, by the time the engagement was ended, were dead. Some of them, perhaps, could not have recovered, but others might had timely assistance been rendered. But it was impossible, for the rule is, as order is requisite, that every person shall be dressed in rotation as they are brought down wounded [there was no triage system at Trafalgar], and in many instances some have bled to death.

The next call was 'All hands to splice the main brace', which was the giving out of a gill of rum to each man, and indeed they much needed it, for they had not ate or drank from breakfast time.

By the time the surviving crew were downing their rum the *Revenge* was a mess, although considering the number of enemy that had flung shot into her casualties of 28 killed and 51 wounded cannot be considered heavy. Physical damage included bowsprit, three lower masts, maintopmast and gaff badly injured. She received nine shots through her hull. Her stern, transom, timbers, beams, knees, riders and iron standards were much damaged. Several chain plates were shot away, several lower-deck ports destroyed and three guns dismounted. She was destined for a long refitting and rebuilding in Gibraltar.

## Collingwood's column, 1.15 p.m.: comments

• By 1.15 p.m., an hour after the *Royal Sovereign* broke the line astern of the *Santa Ana*, Collingwood's first eight ships had been in action against 15 of the enemy. Most of these ships from both fleets had been closely and heavily engaged. The British ships were outnumbered during this period and therefore unable to achieve their desired concentration. Several British ships (*Royal Sovereign*, *Mars*, *Bellerophon*, *Colossus* and *Revenge* for example) had to deal with two or more enemy ships simultaneously. That they were able to do so and beat off multiple attacks was due in part to superior tactical ship-handling, but primarily to sustained and faster gunnery.

• The lack of wind, the damage done to yards, sails, masts and rigging, the needs of gunnery and increasing casualties had reduced the movement of ships dramatically, meaning that Collingwood's column and his opponents in the mêlée were virtually stationary for most of this time. Thus this part of the line had become compacted into a comparatively small area blanketed in smoke in which distinguishing friend from foe was difficult, signalling virtually impossible and collisions frequent.

• Within the first hour no fewer than five of the eight British

## Seaman Sam's Letter to His Father

Sam was a seaman on the *Royal Sovereign* who wrote to tell his father he had survived the battle.

Honoured Father,
This comes to tell you I am alive and hearty except three fingers; but that's not much, it might have been my head … Three of our mess were killed, and four more of us winged. But to tell you the truth of it, when the game began, I wished myself at Warnborough with my plough again … How my fingers got knocked overboard I don't know, but off they are, and I never missed them till I wanted them. You see, by my writing, it was my left hand, so I can write to you and fight for my king yet. We have taken a rare parcel of ships, but the wind is so rough we cannot bring them home, else I should roll in money, so we are busy sinking 'em and blowing 'em up wholesale

Our dear Admiral Nelson is killed! So we have paid pretty sharply for licking 'em. I never sat [sic] eyes on him, for which I am both sorry and glad; for to be sure I should like to have seen him – but then all the men in our ship who have seen him are such soft toads they have done nothing but blast their eyes, and cry, ever since he was killed. God bless you! chaps that fought like the devil sit down and cry like a wench. I am still in the *Royal Sovereign*, but the Admiral has left her, for she is like a horse without a bridle; so he is in a frigate … I saw his tears with my own eyes, when the boat hailed and said my lord was dead. So no more at present from your dutiful son. Sam

ships had at some stage collided with an enemy, been locked together and emptied broadsides into each other muzzle to muzzle. The ships involved thus far in these brutal exchanges were *Royal Sovereign/Santa Ana*, *Belleisle/Fougueux*, *Tonnant/Algéciras*, *Bellerophon/Aigle* and *Colossus/Argonaute*.

• Unsurprisingly, considering the intensity and closeness of the fighting, by 1.15 p.m. nine ships had become virtually unmanageable due to damage to masts, sails, rudders and so on: *Royal Sovereign*, *Belleisle*, *Mars* and *Bellerophon*, and in the Combined Fleet *Santa Ana*, *Fougueux*, *Monarca*, *Aigle* and *Montañés*.

• While the casualties inflicted by the British ships had been substantially higher than those caused by the French and Spanish, material damage appears to have been more equally inflicted. With ships firing at so close a range, and frequently alongside one another, it was difficult to miss. The winner was the ship that fired the fastest – the British. The other factor was that several British ships (*Royal Sovereign*, *Belleisle*, *Bellerophon* and *Revenge*) were able to fire devastating raking broadsides as they broke through the line. Guns were double or even treble shotted and the unfortunate recipients never fully recovered from these blows at the start of the mêlée.

• Both French and Spanish captains were anxious to board their adversaries as this was their declared best tactic. Their reliance on sharpshooters aloft and soldiers on the upper decks had been effective. A high proportion of British losses occurred on the exposed upper decks, where the heavy musketry, guns and showers of grenades were impossible to avoid. A good example of this problem was on board the *Bellerophon* where the upper decks were in danger of being swept clear and thus vulnerable to boarders. There the Royal Marines had to take shelter under cover to avoid the worst effects of the hail of grenades and musketry coming from the high decks of the *Aigle*. Nevertheless, no boarding attempt onto a British ship of Collingwood's column had so far succeeded.

• In summary, during the first hour Collingwood's first eight ships had achieved the mêlée they sought, and although outnumbered they had the edge in seamanship and gunnery, thus inflicting more losses than they received. During the next stage of the battle Collingwood's opponents could only realistically be reinforced by two so far uncommitted ships, the *Berwick* and *San Juan Nepomuceno*, whereas Collingwood could expect another six, headed by the *Defiance* (in the event he got the *Prince* as well). Their arrival is discussed below (pp. 511–6).

Now we turn north to Nelson's battle.

## NELSON'S COLUMN

### *Victory*

The master's log of the *Victory* records the moment she broke Villeneuve's line with the terse entry: 'At 20 minutes past 12, in attempting to pass through the enemy's line, fell on board of the 10th and 11th [it was the 12th and 13th] ships of the enemy's line, when the action became general.' The next entry reads: 'About 1.15, the Right Honourable Lord Viscount Nelson, K.B., and Commander-in-Chief was wounded in the shoulder.' A lot of exciting things happened in the intervening hour – but Mr Atkinson was in the gunroom trying to keep the emergency steering arrangements functioning, a duty that may well have saved his life as it kept him off the quarterdeck.

By 12.30 p.m., with the enemy line only 100 yards away, the *Victory* had lost her wheel and was on makeshift steering that required some 40 men taken from other duties. A lucky shot had brought her mizzen-topsail tumbling down, the foresail was in ribbons, studding sails torn away, all other sails were full of holes and the surgeon already had his hands full in the cockpit. Ahead there appeared to be a solid wall of ships from which came flickering flashes and the continuous booming thump of guns. Only the top half of masts jutting up above the banks of billowing smoke clearly showed the position of the enemy. Captain Hardy was heading for the supposed gap astern of the *Santisima Trinidad* and the bows of the *Bucentaure* but this gap had almost disappeared. The *Neptune* had fallen to leeward and the *Redoutable* had moved up to fill the space. Captain Lucas on the *Redoutable* explained his actions:

> The group led by Admiral Nelson was approaching our *corps de bataille*; the two three deckers [*Victory* and *Téméraire*] which were heading it were manoeuvring obviously to envelop the French flagship [*Bucentaure*]; one of them was endeavouring to pass her astern. Directly that I realised this intention ... I laid the *Redoutable*'s bowsprit against the *Bucentaure*'s stern, fully resolved to sacrifice my ship in defence of the Admiral's flag. ... I continued to close up on the *Bucentaure* so closely that I was hailed several times from her stern gallery that I was about to run her aboard; actually the *Redoutable*'s bowsprit did graze her taffrail, but I assured them they had nothing to fear.

On the *Victory*'s quarterdeck Hardy was uncertain where exactly he should steer. There were three ships lined up ahead, each slightly to windward of each other with a fourth in their lee. He pointed out to Nelson that he was almost certain to run aboard one of the enemy. The admiral was unconcerned, replying, 'I cannot help it. Go aboard which you please, take your choice.' The captain's orders were shouted down the speaking tube (probably by Lieutenant Quilliam) to the master below at the tiller to bring it hard to starboard. His men strained on the ropes and, painfully slowly, the *Victory*'s bows swung to larboard. Hardy had chosen to hit between the *Bucentaure* and *Redoutable*. As the bows began to line up the order 'Steady! Steady as she goes!' was yelled down and the great heavy tiller was hauled back to straighten the ship. Within moments the gundecks would get their target.

The first to fire would be the larboard 68-pounder carronade on the forecastle commanded by the boatswain, William Willmet. This was not the normal job of a boatswain in battle

but was obviously one he was determined to fulfil. As mentioned on p. 225 he had rammed first a roundshot then a keg of 500 musket balls down the barrel. Willmet crouched down with the taut trigger line in his hand, watching as the distance closed and the magnificent stern windows of the *Bucentaure* came into view. Fifty yards ... thirty ... ten. Now the details were clear, the lozenge-shaped blue, white and red escutcheon, the sun glinting off the glass of the captain's cabin on the upper deck and Villeneuve's immediately below.

The moment he jerked his lanyard, the *Bucentaure*'s stern disintegrated in a lethal blast of shattered glass and splinters. A cloud of dust and fragments fell onto the *Victory*'s forecastle as the cannon and musket balls swept down the Frenchman's decks, many from stern to bow. The shot had signalled to the gunners below that their turn had come. All 50 guns of the larboard broadside were double or treble shotted, the range was virtually zero, the target unmissable. A three-decker was delivering a point-blank stern rake into a two-decker: for the crew of the *Victory* it was a gunner's dream, for those on the *Bucentaure* a deadly nightmare. The guns fired in rapid succession. As the last shot crashed out there was comparative quiet. Those who were not deafened could hear the shrieks and cries from the scores of maimed and mutilated men inside the *Bucentaure*. About 120 shot had been flung the length of the decks in the space of perhaps 30 seconds. The balls smashed everything in their path. Guns were overturned, huge wooden splinters whirled through the air, shot ricocheted, gouged grooves in the decks, tore hunks from masts and ripped off men's limbs. It is said in some accounts that 20 guns were destroyed and 300 men killed or wounded, but this is an exaggeration, since when the *Bucentaure* eventually struck at around 2.00 p.m. she had 197 killed and 85 wounded. A more likely number of losses from this first broadside was 100 as she was able to continue the fight, albeit somewhat feebly, for another hour and a half, during which time a succession of up to eight British ships raked and battered her with increasing degrees of impunity. Nevertheless, it is true to say that Villeneuve's flagship never recovered from what was surely one of the most effective broadsides of the battle.

Villeneuve came through unscathed. His immediate reaction was to hoist an urgent and necessary signal, Article No. 5 in the code, which required only a single flag: 'All ships which from their present position are not engaging, to take any such as will bring them as promptly as possible into action', a long-winded way of saying 'Engage the enemy more closely', the signal permanently hoisted at the *Victory*'s maintopgallant. It was particularly intended for the van under Dumanoir who, as we shall see, did not comply until after his admiral had surrendered.

As the *Victory* came through her own smoke she was confronted, immediately ahead, by the French 74-gun *Neptune*, perfectly positioned to rake the British flagship in her turn, though fortunately only with a bow rake. The *Victory*'s bow was tougher than the *Bucentaure*'s stern so although the *Neptune*'s broadside did damage it was not catastrophic. Her figurehead, bowsprit, foremast, bow timbers and anchors all suffered but crew casualties were light. Meanwhile her starboard batteries had been presented with another fine target – the *Redoutable*. Once again came the thunderous roll of gunfire along the decks, the leaping recoils, the noise and the smoke as Captain Lucas's ship felt the weight of a 50-gun broadside. Hardy had the tiller dragged to larboard, thus bringing the *Victory*'s bows to crunch into the *Redoutable*.

## Trafalgar: The Clash of the Commanders-in-Chief, 12.15 to 1.00 p.m.

### 12.15–12.25 p.m.

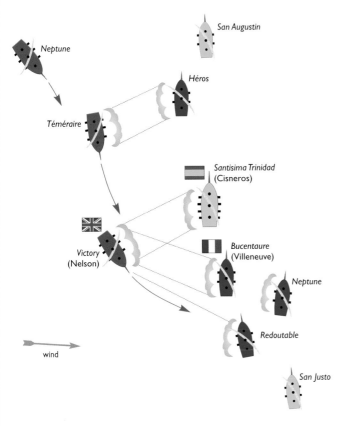

### 12.30–1.00 p.m.

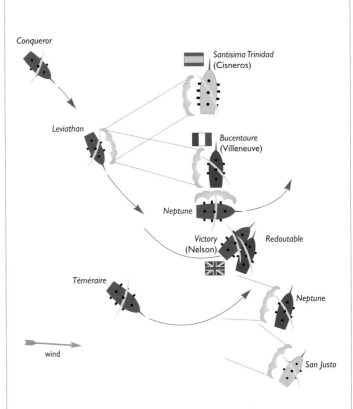

**Notes**

- As *Victory* makes her final approach to the enemy line she is under intense fire from *Santisima Trinidad* and *Bucentaure*.
- *Téméraire*, the next ship astern, exchanges fire with *Héros*.
- *Redoutable* and French *Neptune* open fire on *Victory* as she closes on the small gap between *Bucentaure* and *Redoutable*.

**Notes**

- *Victory* breaks the line at about 12.30 p.m. and delivers a devastating stern rake to *Bucentaure*. *Victory* then runs aboard *Redoutable*.
- British *Neptune* arrives next and also rakes *Bucentaure*.
- *Téméraire* breaks the line a little further south and exchanges broadsides with the French *Neptune* and *San Justo*.

---

The two ships came together. Lucas described the moment.

> ... to prove to the English Admiral that we did not fear his boarding us, I had the grapnels hoisted at every yard. In the end, the *Victory* not having succeeded in passing the stern of the French Admiral, ran aboard us alongside, overlapping us astern so that our poop was abeam of her quarterdeck. In this position the grapnels were flung aboard, those aft were cut loose but those forward held; our broadsides were fired muzzle to muzzle, there resulted in a horrible carnage.

According to Surgeon Beatty's account:

> On coming alongside [the *Redoutable*], and nearly on board of her, that ship fired her broadside into the *Victory*, and immediately let down her lower deck ports; which it has been learnt, was done to prevent her being boarded through them by the *Victory*'s crew.

Lucas has left us a colourful, if somewhat biased, account of how he fought his battle.

We continued our fire for some time, we managed to load several guns by means of sponges with rope handles [the British did the same]; several were fired at the full length of the breeching tackle, we not being able to bowse them to the ports which were blocked by the *Victory*'s side, and by the means of the firearms placed in our batteries we so prevented the enemy from loading his [guns] that he ceased to fire on us [in fact, *Victory*'s guns did not stop firing for this reason] ... I ordered the trumpet to sound, it was the recognized signal to summon the boarding parties in our exercises; they came up in such perfect order with the officers and midshipmen at the head of their divisions that one would have said it was only a sham fight. In less than a minute the upper works were covered with armed men who hurled themselves on the poop, on the nettings and into the shrouds ... Then there began a furious musketry fire in which Admiral Nelson was fighting at the head of his crew; our fire became so greatly superior that in less than fifteen minutes we had silenced that of the *Victory*; more than 200 grenades were thrown aboard her ...

## Midshipman William Rivers

William Rivers was a seventeen-year-old midshipman on the *Victory* at Trafalgar, and the son of the gunner of the same name. During the action the midshipman had the lower part of his left leg badly mangled by a shot and was carried down to the surgeon, William Beatty. As with any smashed limb the commonest remedy was to saw it off, and Beatty removed the young man's leg about four inches below the knee. Rivers remained stoically silent throughout the excruciating process. When the surgeon had finished his only remark was to ask the surgeon, 'What have you left me?' With the battle over Gunner Rivers, having heard his son was wounded, came down into the cockpit to see him. He stood there in the gloom wondering where among the rows of injured his son lay. Then, a voice called out, 'Here I am father, nothing is the matter with me, only lost my leg, and that in a good cause.' The Gunner was able to take

his son back to his own cabin. During the night young Rivers awoke to the sound of movement and of soft splashes. It was the loblolly men emptying the barrels of limbs into the sea. William's father admitted his son's left lower leg would be among them.

The loss of a leg did nothing to halt young Rivers' naval career. His conduct at Trafalgar won him promotion to lieutenant in January 1806, a grant from the Patriotic Fund of £40 and an Admiralty pension of £91-5-0 a year. Lieutenant Rivers saw service at the second Battle of Copenhagen in 1807. He was first lieutenant on the *Cretan* during the Walcheron expedition in 1809 but he did not receive further promotion. He became the warden at Woolwich Dockyard from 1824 to 1826 after which he was appointed a lieutenant of Greenwich Hospital, where he died thirty years later in 1856 aged sixty-eight.

---

Lucas was writing his report as a prisoner on parole in Reading in early January 1806. It was addressed to his Minister, Decrès, in Paris so he was naturally anxious to put the best gloss possible on his and his ship's performance. The first French attempt to board was, according to Beatty, largely beaten back by Mr Willmet swivelling round the starboard carronade on the forecastle. Another blast of a roundshot and 500 musket balls 'discharged ... right into the thick of the Frenchmen on deck at the critical moment, just as they were in the act of swarming up the hatchways' destroyed their enthusiasm. Lucas did, however, put up a magnificent fight and, as we shall see shortly, was soon sandwiched between two three-deckers – an impossible position for a 74. His report is only suspect when he speaks of his guns continuing to fire throughout. He is absolutely correct in emphasizing the damage his sharpshooters did – their greatest success being the mortal wounding of Nelson.

Beatty continues the story from *Victory*'s viewpoint.

The *Redoutable* commenced a heavy fire of musketry from the tops, which continued for a considerable time with destructive effect to the *Victory*'s crew; her great guns, however, being silent, it was supposed at different times that she had surrendered; and in consequence of this opinion, the *Victory* twice ceased firing on her, by orders submitted from the quarterdeck. At this period, scarcely a person in the *Victory* escaped unhurt who was exposed to the enemy's musketry.

The 98-gun *Téméraire* under Captain Eliab Harvey was next astern of the *Victory* as she fired into the *Bucentaure*. By 1.45 p.m. Harvey's ship had steered through the gap astern of the *Redoutable*, received fire from the French *Neptune* and then run aboard the starboard side of the *Redoutable* (see under *Téméraire*, below p. 508).

### Heroism of Two Royal Marines on the *Victory*

The *Naval Chronicle* of 1806 gives the following short account of the bravery and stoicism of two marines on Nelson's flagship.

A Corporal in the middle of the action, had his arm carried off by a cannon shot; he bound the stump with the sash of an officer, who had been killed, spirited up a party to board the enemy, and was himself at the head of that party, and the first that was on board the opposing ship. – A private marine was at the point of firing his musket, when his left arm was struck off by a ball; he afterwards fired off his piece, and went, unattended, to the cockpit, carrying his musket with him in his right hand.

It bears repeating that it was down on the gundecks that Trafalgar was won and lost. Beatty's account is the only one that gives us more than a brief glimpse of what was happening below on the *Victory*.

An incessant fire was kept up [initially] from both sides of the *Victory* ... the starboard guns of the middle and lower-decks were depressed, and fired with a diminished charge of powder, and three shot each, into the *Redoutable*. This mode of firing was adopted by Lieutenants Williams, King, Yule and Brown, to obviate the danger of the *Téméraire* suffering from the *Victory*'s shot passing through the *Redoutable*, which must have been the case if the usual quantity of powder and the common elevation had been given to the guns. ... When the guns on this deck [lower gundeck] were run out, their muzzles came in contact with the *Redoutable*'s side; and, consequently, at every discharge there was reason to fear that the enemy would take fire, and both the *Victory* and *Téméraire* be involved in her flames. Here there was seen the astonishing spectacle of the firemen of each gun standing ready with a bucket full of water, which as soon as his gun was discharged, he dashed into the enemy through the holes made in her side by the shot.

The likelihood of ships catching fire when locked together in battle was extremely high and officers were constantly alert to this danger. In these circumstances the fireman in each gun crew and the boys with their swabs became critical members of the crew. With ships' sides touching the red-hot blast of a gun could come straight through a port, scorching everyone and everything in its path. With hulls touching, guns could not be run out so the muzzle flashes became a real hazard inside the ship. When the *Victory* and *Redoutable* crunched together, their sides blocked out what little light came through the ports and with every discharge the resulting cloud of smoke hung stifling over the gundeck. On the *Victory*'s lower deck thirty 32-pounders were in action almost continuously. After a short time it was impossible to see anything beyond one's close comrades – and them only dimly. As the firing continued the smoke was made denser by lack of wind and the confined space of the gundecks with their low beams. With nowhere to disperse, it rolled heavily inboard, blurring out the feeble gleams of light emitted by the candle lanterns. Everything was enveloped in opaque blackness. Gunners choked and coughed as they groped for their tackle and served their guns almost as if deaf and blind. The loss of these senses had one blessing – the noise drowned out the worst of the shrieks and screams of the maimed, while the smoke obscured some of the horrors of the blood and butchery.

It says much for the high level of training, the value of drills repeated hundreds of times, that few serious mistakes were made. It says even more for the leadership of the officers and petty officers on the gundecks, many young boys in their teens, who had to exercise control, keep the guns firing, change the target as required, adjust the cartridge size, keep the ammunition coming, organize manpower changes to cope with casualties, find men for fire fighting and ensure boarders mustered when needed. To do all this they had to make themselves understood despite the appalling conditions and continuous loss of men. The words of 2nd Lieutenant Rotely, the only RM officer on the *Victory* to come through Trafalgar unscathed, bear repeating: 'A man should witness a battle in a three-decker from the middle deck, for it beggars description. ... I fancied myself in the infernal regions, where every man appeared a devil. Lips might move, but orders and hearing were out of the question; everything was done by signs.'

After some forty-five minutes tragedy struck on the *Victory*'s quarterdeck. A marksman in the mizzentop of the *Redoutable* shot Nelson through his left shoulder. He fell forward. 'They've done for me at last, Hardy.' 'I hope not,' replied Captain Hardy. 'Yes,' replied his Lordship, 'my backbone is shot through.' Lieutenant Alexander Hills was dispatched in a boat to inform Collingwood of the wounding. Details of Nelson's wounding and death over three hours later are described in the Prologue. It was at this stage that a strange misunderstanding of the situation on the *Victory* and *Bucentaure* occurred. Because the pummelling from both sides had reduced the gunfire from the *Redoutable* to only occasional shots, the *Victory*'s gunners stopped firing momentarily. On the *Redoutable* Lucas, noticing the pause and seeing that the *Victory*'s upper decks had been swept almost clear, assumed she was ripe for the taking. In his report he described his actions.

## 'Nelson's Revenge'

It was well known that Nelson was not generally in favour of posting seamen or marines in the tops to act as sharpshooters as was the French practice. Perhaps because he was killed by a shot fired from the mizzentop of the *Redoutable*, it became the custom in the Royal Navy by the mid-nineteenth century to mount guns on the deck specifically to deal with sharpshooters. Admiral Robert Hammick stated in 1893 that when he first went to sea there was a special gun mounted on the deck of his ship which was generally known as 'Nelson's Revenge', as it was so mounted that it could be fired at the enemy's tops even when close alongside. This type of gun may have been the 'gun and carriage for the purpose of dislodging marksmen from the enemy's tops in close action, and repelling boarders, etc.' for the invention of which Captain Thomas Bagnold RM received a silver medal from the Society of Arts in 1811.

I gave orders to cut away the slings of the main-yard and to lower it to serve as a bridge. M. Yon, midshipman, and four seamen succeeded in getting on board the *Victory* by means of the anchor and informed us that there was not a soul on her decks [an exaggeration]; but the moment that our brave lads were just hurling themselves after them [Yon and his men] the three decker *Téméraire* – who had doubtless perceived that the *Victory* had ceased fire and would inevitably be taken – ran foul of us on the starboard side and overwhelmed us with the pointblank fire of all her guns.

While it was certainly true that the *Victory*'s exposed upper decks had been denuded of many men (the French musketry had compelled Hardy to send the crews of the 12-pounders below to join those on the gundecks), there were some seamen and marines still on the quarterdeck and poop. When Hardy saw the French preparations for boarding Captain Adair RM was ordered to summon the *Victory*'s boarding parties from the middle deck to defend the ship. He sent 2nd Lieutenant Rotely RM. This was an extremely difficult task with the dreadful noise, leaping guns, dense smoke and the fact that many marines assisting the gun crews had discarded their red jackets and were thus unrecognizable as marines. Rotely tells us, 'With the assistance of two Sergeants and two Corporals (and in some cases by main force) I succeeded in separating about 25 men from the great guns and with this force I ascended to purer air.' The struggle to repel the boarders was successful but costly. Rotely recalled:

The poop became a slaughter-house, and soon the two senior lieutenants of marines [James Peake and Lewis Reeves] and half the original forty were placed hors de combat. Captain Adair's party was reduced to ten men, himself wounded in the forehead by splinters, yet still using his musket with effect [the situation was indeed dire if the RM commander found it necessary to pick up a musket]. One of his last orders to me was, 'Rotely, fire away as fast as you can!' when a ball struck him on the back of the neck and he was a corpse in a moment.

Surgeon Beatty's description of the fight to beat off boarders shortly after Nelson fell is worth recording.

To 'rush' the *Victory*, to get across onto her deck, was impossible; owing to the deep recurve [*sic*] of the two ships' hulls [the tumble-home], and the wide space of several feet that consequently separated the towering top-sides of the *Victory* from the bulwarks of the *Redoutable*. That brought the *Redoutable*'s men up, balked at the outset [Lucas attempted to form a bridge by lowering his main-yard to overcome this]. The next moment the *Victory*'s nettings were lined from end to end with seamen and marines who had rushed up hastily, tumbling up the hatchways from below on the call 'Repel boarders!'

## Dr Scott in *Victory*'s Cockpit

As described in the Prologue, Dr Alexander Scott, the chaplain on the *Victory*, spent most of the battle comforting Nelson as he lay dying. On first entering the cockpit he had been horrified by the awful sights and sounds that assailed him. The quotation below comes from Edward Fraser's *The Sailors Whom Nelson Led*.

> Dr. Scott's duties, of course, confined him to the cockpit, which was crowded with wounded and dying men, and such was the horror that filled his mind at this scene of suffering, that it haunted him like a shocking dream for years afterwards. He never talked of it. Indeed, the only record of a remark on the subject was one extorted from him by a friend soon after his return home. The expression that escaped him … was 'it was like a butcher's shambles'.
>
> His natural tenderness of feeling … quite disqualified him from being a calm spectator of death and pain, as there exhibited in their most appalling shapes. But he suppressed his aversion as well as he could, and had for some time been engaged in helping and consoling those who were suffering around him, when a fine young lieutenant (Lieutenant Ram) was brought down desperately wounded. This officer was not aware of the extent of his injury until the surgeon's examination, but, on discovering it, he tore off with his own hand the ligatures that were being applied, and bled to death. Almost frenzied by the sight of this, Scott hurried wildly to the deck for relief, perfectly regardless of his own safety. He rushed up the companion ladder – now slippery with gore – the scene above was all noise, confusion and smoke – but he had hardly time to breathe there, when Lord Nelson himself fell, and this event at once sobered his disordered mind. He followed his chief to the cockpit.

Opening with a brisk fire with small arms on Captain Lucas' boarders, they gave their opponents more than the Frenchmen expected. But at the same time they lost heavily themselves, mostly from French musketry in the tops and the hand-grenades, and from cannon shot from the *Redoutable*'s main-deck guns, fired with high angle elevation slantwise up through the decks. Within three minutes Captain Adair, with eighteen men had fallen dead, and a Lieutenant and a midshipman, with eighteen men, been struck down wounded, with many mortally [these numbers may not be accurate]. The Lieutenant got his death wound from a twenty-four pound ball that crashed up through the deck at his feet. The splinters from that one shot maimed five of the *Victory*'s seamen nearby.

Then the *Téméraire* came on the scene and took the Frenchman, so to speak, in rear.

The arrival of the *Téméraire* on the far side of the *Redoutable* put an end to any more boarding attempts. Lucas said of his new enemy's first broadside:

> It would be hard to describe the horrible carnage caused by the murderous broadside of this ship; more than 200 of our brave lads were killed or wounded, I was wounded at the same instant but not so seriously as to prevent me from remaining at my post.

It is impossible to tell whether Lucas' figure was an exaggeration, as *Redoutable*'s final casualty figures, the highest of any ship at Trafalgar at 487 killed and 81 wounded, include those men drowned when the ship sank during the subsequent storm. But the *Téméraire*'s onslaught clearly had catastrophic effects. Lucas continues with the most detailed catalogue of damage of any ship at the battle:

> … our ship was so riddled that she seemed to be no more than a mass of wreckage. In this state the *Téméraire* hailed us to strike and not to prolong a useless resistance; I ordered several soldiers who were near me to answer this summons with musket shots, which was performed with the greatest zeal. At very nearly the same minute the main-mast fell athwart the English ship *Téméraire* and that vessel's two topmasts fell on board the *Redoutable*; all the stern was absolutely stove-in, the rudder-stock, the helm-port, the tiller, the two tiller-sweeps, the stern-post, the helm-port and wing transoms, the transom knees, were in general shot to pieces; the decks were all torn open by the fire of the *Victory* and *Téméraire*; all the guns were either shattered or dismounted by the shots or from these two ships having run us aboard. An 18-pounder gun on the main-deck and a 36-pounder carronade on the forecastle having burst killed and wounded many of our people. The two sides of the ship, all the lids and bars of the ports were utterly cut to pieces; four of our six pumps were shattered, as well as all our ladders in general, in such a sort that communication between the decks and upper works was extremely difficult. All our decks were covered with dead, buried beneath the debris and the splinters from the different parts of the ship. A great number of wounded were killed on the orlop deck [a rare occurrence]. Of our ship's company of 643 men we had 522 disabled, 300 being killed and 222 wounded, amongst whom were almost the entire executive. … I do not know of anything on board that was not cut up by shot. … In this state of affairs the rudder-coat caught fire … we managed to extinguish it. … I only awaited the certain knowledge that the leaks which the ship had sprung were so considerable that it could not be long before she foundered, in order to strike.

By this time yet another ship had joined the fray. As Rotely neatly put it, 'Another French ship, the *Fougueux*, fell on board the *Téméraire* on her starboard side, so that four ships of the line were rubbing sides in the heat of the fight, with their heads all lying the same way, as if moored in harbour' – something never seen before or since.

The *Redoutable* had caught fire in more than one place during the action and men of the *Victory* assisted in putting the blazes out, hurling buckets of water from the gangway onto the burning forecastle. When a second fire was seen at the after end of the ship, Hardy sent Midshipmen David Ogilvie and AB (acting midshipman) Francis Collingwood (no relation to the admiral) with ten men in a boat across to help. They clambered in at the stern ports and were, according to Beatty's account, 'well received'. According to the *Victory*'s log the *Redoutable* surrendered at 1.30 p.m., although it was probably nearer 1.45 p.m.

## Trafalgar: The Clash of the Commanders-in-Chief, 1.00 to 2.00 p.m.

### 1.00–1.45 p.m.

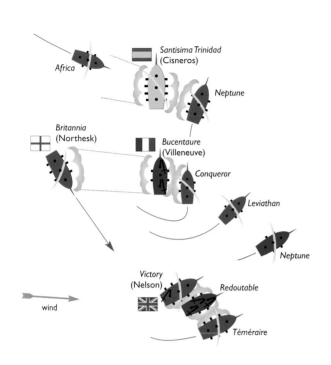

### 1.45–2.00 p.m.

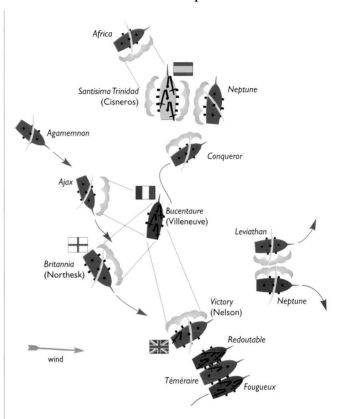

### Notes

• *Neptune* has luffed up and engaged *Santisima Trinidad*. *Leviathan* has broken through, raked *Bucentaure* and is about to engage French *Neptune*. *Redoutable* is sandwiched between *Victory* and *Téméraire*.

• *Conqueror* has also raked *Bucentaure* and come alongside to exchange muzzle-to-muzzle fire.

• *Britannia* then arrives and engages *Bucentaure* from windward.

• *Africa* joins the mêlée and bravely opens fire on the giant *Santisima Trinidad*.

### Notes

• *Fougueux* goes aboard *Téméraire* and *Victory* breaks clear of *Redoutable*.

• *Leviathan* and French *Neptune* exchange fire before the latter bears away.

• *Santisima Trinidad*, surrounded and crippled, is about to strike her colours; *Britannia*, *Ajax* and then *Agamemnon* arrive, putting *Bucentaure* in a similar situation.

---

## Officer Casualties on the *Redoutable*

The *Redoutable* struck to the *Victory* after a prolonged and deadly struggle and afterwards foundered in the storm, the result an estimated 568 casualties. Out of a complement of 29 officers only four survived the battle and storm unscathed. The official roll of the Navy and Army officers compiled from the archives of the Ministry of Marine in Paris is as follows.

Jean Lucas, captain: wounded
Henri Dupotet, lieutenant: wounded
Francois Pouloin, lieutenant: killed
Jean Maiol, acting lieutenant: wounded
Pierre Sergent, acting lieutenant: wounded
Alexandre Ducrest, acting lieutenant: wounded
Jean Laity, sub-lieutenant: wounded
Claude Tresse, lieutenant marine artillery: killed
Louis Guillaume, captain 79th regiment: wounded
Jean Medeau, sub-lieutenant 79th regiment: killed

Louis Auroche, captain 6th depot colonial regiment: wounded
Charles Neury, lieutenant 6th depot colonial regiment: killed
Charles Chafange, captain 16th regiment: killed
Savignac, sub-lieutenant 16th regiment: killed
Louis Hosteau, acting sub-lieutenant: wounded
Philippe Laferriere, acting sub-lieutenant: killed
Francois Lepeltier, acting sub-lieutenant: killed
Jacques Yon, acting sub-lieutenant: killed
Francois Perrin, acting sub-lieutenant: killed
Seraphin Maubrat, acting sub-lieutenant: killed
Henri La Fortelle, acting sub-lieutenant: wounded
Lemesle, acting sub-lieutenant: wounded
Theodore Le Ferec, acting sub-lieutenant: wounded

The only four officers who were not casualties were Jean Pean, paymaster, Allain Bohan, surgeon, Pierre Chauvin, lieutenant 79th regiment and Quentin Blondel, captain marine artillery.

By 2.00 p.m. the *Victory* had managed to push herself away from the hulk of the *Redoutable*, leaving her prize to Captain Harvey in the *Téméraire*. Apart from exchanging distant shots with some of the enemy van squadron when it returned some time later, there was little more the *Victory* could do that day.

## Téméraire

Captain Harvey did not bring the *Téméraire* through the line until some 15 minutes after the *Victory*. He did not follow directly behind his flagship but turned to larboard a little later when opposite the French *Neptune*. She was greeted with a powerful broadside. As she luffed up into the wind she was unable to avoid accidentally colliding with the starboard side of the *Redoutable*, already entangled with the *Victory*, and immediately added the weight of her fire into the already battered hull of Lucas' ship. Within about 20 minutes of the *Téméraire* running aboard her the *Redoutable* struck to the *Victory*, but as noted above Nelson's flagship soon moved away and left her prize to Harvey.

When the *Fougueux* collided with the *Téméraire* at around 1.45 p.m. she had already been badly mauled by the *Royal Sovereign*, *Mars* and *Belleisle*. She had lost her topsail and lower yards and had drifted northwards through the smoke after cutting loose from the *Belleisle*. As the unmanageable French 74 closed the *Téméraire* fired her full starboard broadside into her. Harvey mustered boarding parties of seamen and marines and, aided by the firing of carronades, secured a foothold on the enemy deck. The report of second-in-command Commander Francois Bazin describes what happened on his ship.

> At almost the same time [as the collision] gallant Captain Baudoin was mortally wounded and fell unconscious. I took over the command, I continued firing from the gun-decks and only kept a few men with me to repel boarding ... . But the enemy by her superior fire riddled us with grape and in less than half an hour our decks were beaten in several places. ... I called for the 1st Lieutenant to assist me in this grievous situation; I was informed he was no longer alive; [of] the two next in seniority one was nearly dead and the other, M. Peltier, had a ball in the leg; I summoned the 4th Lieutenant, who informed me that his battery was nearly silenced. *Enseigne de vaissau* [sub-lieutenant] Drudesit sent me word that he had only 15 men left and all his guns dismounted; all the people I had on deck or in the tops were killed or wounded. Seeing moreover that the enemy had got on board ... having then very few people to fight the enemy who had succeeded in gaining possession of the deck, I gave orders to cease fire and I immediately went to the Captain's cabin to remove thence the leaden box containing confidential papers which I myself threw into the sea, and coming out on to the quarter-deck I saw that the enemy were in possession of it. I fell into their hands and they made me prisoner; I was at once conveyed on board their ship; the colours were then hauled down and gradually the slaughter ceased.

### Two Seamen from the *Téméraire* Are Offended

Shortly after the battle a special Thanksgiving Day was celebrated in the church at Plymouth, which was attended by two former *Téméraire* seamen. The clergymen in the course of his sermon mentioned the words 'glorious victory', at which one of the seamen observed to the other, 'Hear Jack, there's the *Victory*!' The clergyman pronounced the word 'victory' a second time, and the same seaman remarked, 'Mind Jack, there's the *Victory* again.' The clergyman, not long afterwards mentioned the word 'victory' a third time. The irritated sailor said to his companion, 'Damn my eyes, Jack, if we stop here any longer – that fellow has mentioned the *Victory* three times, and never mentioned the *Téméraire*, that was in the hottest part of the engagement; and took two ships.' Whereupon they immediately left the church.

Casualties were certainly catastrophic on the *Fougueux*, although many of the crew met their end by drowning when their ship was wrecked the following day. Out of a complement of 755 only 18 officers and about 100 men were eventually saved. The *Fougueux* had surrendered to Lieutenant Thomas Kennedy, who in accordance with his captain's orders hoisted the British colours and had the prize lashed to the *Téméraire*. The *Victory*'s prize, the *Redoutable* remained attached to her larboard side and was taken over by a prize crew led by Lieutenant Henry Coxen. *Téméraire*'s fighting was over. In addition to her 123 battle casualties 43 of the prize crew perished after the battle.

## Neptune

The *Neptune* (another powerful 98-gun ship) under Captain Thomas Freemantle, was third in Nelson's column. She sailed in with band playing and, with the exception of the musicians and the officers, everybody else on the upper decks lying down, a precaution of which Midshipman William Badcock approved:

> During the whole time we were going down into action and being raked by the enemy the whole crew, with the exception of the officers [and presumably the band], were made to lie flat on the deck to secure them from the raking shots, some of which came in at the bow and went out at the stern. Had it not been for this precaution many lives must have been sacrificed.

Freemantle saw the *Téméraire* ahead turn to break the line astern of the *Redoutable* but determined to follow Nelson's course into the gap ahead of her and astern of the *Bucentaure*. As the *Neptune* came through a second massive stern rake devastated the *Bucentaure*. Freemantle instructed Mr Keith to have the helm swung hard to starboard, bringing his ship abeam of Villeneuve's flagship. From less than 100 yards two more triple-shotted broadsides were fired from almost 50 guns. Then, just ahead through the smoke, Freemantle spotted the towering bulk of a four-decker – the *Santisima Trinidad* sailing away from him. It presented yet another opportunity for a stern rake, and Freemantle took it. He steered into a position on the Spanish flagship's starboard quarter and his larboard batteries had another perfect point-blank target. The *Neptune* maintained her position about 100 yards off the starboard beam of the Spaniard and continued to exchange broadsides while ship after ship of Nelson's column came through astern of her during the next hour, each one raking her in the process. The *Santisima Trinidad*, the pride of the Spanish Navy, found herself alone and surrounded by several enemies firing into her from all directions.

## Leviathan

The fourth ship in the weather column, the *Leviathan* came through the same gap as, and in the wake of, the *Neptune*. As she came level with the *Santisima Trinidad* she delivered yet another full broadside into her, by now, shattered stern. On clearing the banks of smoke Captain Henry Bayntun saw the 80-gun French

*Neptune* on his starboard bow and immediately came slightly to starboard to engage. The French ship had not long before been exchanging fire with the *Téméraire* and one or two broadsides from the *Leviathan* were sufficient to see her draw away to leeward. Bayntun turned north to seek fresh opponents.

## Conqueror

Captain Israel Pellew's ship was to be the one that gave the final *coup de grace* to the *Bucentaure*. Although the ships immediately following (*Britannia*, *Ajax* and *Agamemnon*) added several broadsides it was the *Conqueror*'s point-blank fire that finished her and it was a boarding party from the *Conqueror* that accepted Villeneuve's surrender.

Pellew, like the three ships before him, began his assault with a triple-shotted stern rake. He then luffed up to larboard and came up on the *Bucentaure*'s starboard quarter. At pistol-shot range he began to administer the pounding that finally proved too much for his gallant opponent. The first obvious signs that the end was near was the dramatic slackening of return fire. The Combined Fleet's flagship was becoming little more than a floating target, absorbing broadsides but unable to deliver anything effective in return. Next came the toppling of the mizzen- and mainmasts. Shots snatched huge chunks from them both and they began to wobble under the weight of the sails and spars. When they collapsed they did so over the starboard side, dragging with them shredded canvas and wreckage that obscured many gunports, and were soon followed by the foremast. Lieutenant Humphrey Stenhouse has left his account of the effectiveness of *Conqueror*'s guns.

> A cannonading commenced at so short a distance that every shot winged with death and destruction. Our men, who from constant practice had gained great quickness in the use of their guns, aimed with deliberate precision, as if they had only been firing at a mark, and tore their opponent to pieces. In ten minutes the *Bucentaure*'s main and mizzen masts went by the board, twenty minutes after her foremasts shared a similar fate; at half-past two she struck to the *Conqueror*.

Villeneuve had lost the ability to hoist signals. His flagship had become a helpless hulk, he could no longer control his fleet and was about to lose his command with nearly three hours of the battle still to run. He had realized how serious the situation was when he signalled to all ships to join the fight. Then, as he admitted in his report:

> It was impossible for me to distinguish the state of affairs in the centre and in the rear owing to the dense smoke which enveloped us. Two other three-deckers [*Neptune* and *Britannia*] had succeeded the *Victory* and several 74s [*Leviathan*, *Conqueror*, *Ajax*], which passed slowly in succession astern of the *Bucentaure*. I had just made the signal for the van to go about, when the main and mizzen masts fell. The ships which had passed astern of me ranged alongside to leeward, without suffering greatly from our fire, a great part of our guns being dismounted, and the rest masked by the fall of the masts.

With the *Bucentaure* unable to function as a flagship, Villeneuve sought to transfer his flag to another ship, but in vain. As he later wrote:

> ... but finally it [the foremast] fell. I had kept a boat lowered, foreseeing the possibility of being dismasted, with the intention of going aboard another vessel. As soon as the mainmast fell I gave orders for it to be made ready, but whether it had been sunk by shot or crushed by the falling of the masts, it could not be found. I had the *Santisima Trinidad*, which was ahead of us, hailed to know if she could send a boat and give us a tow. I had no reply; this ship was herself engaging vigorously with a three-decker [*Neptune*] that was firing into her quarter. In the end, surrounded by the enemy ships that had congregated on my quarters, astern, and abreast to leeward; being powerless to do them any injury, the upper works and the 24-pounder gun-deck being deserted and strewn with dead and wounded; the lower deck guns dismounted or masked by the fallen masts and rigging ... I was obliged to yield to my fate and put an end to the slaughter already vast, which was from henceforward useless.

The losses on board the *Bucentaure* had indeed been crippling and with the loss of all masts the colours had been nailed to a stump. The casualty figures were 197 killed and 85 wounded. The fact that dead outnumbered wounded by more than two to one testifies to the sheer volume of close-range fire that she received. Losses among the officers were, as Captain Magentie states, acute:

> I was wounded by a splinter [in the mouth], and M. Daudignon, my second-in-command, went aft by the Admiral's orders to take over the command of the ship, whilst my wound was being dressed. ... as this minute M. Prigny, the chief-of-staff, was wounded as well as M. Daudignon. M. Fournier, the 2nd lieutenant, took over the command. ... An instant later the foremast fell and M. Gaudran, the navigating officer, was wounded.

Mr Joseph Seymour, master of the *Conqueror*, recorded the historic event of the surrender of the enemy flagship with the customary brevity of all logs: 'At 2, shot away the *Bucentaure*'s main and mizzen masts ... Shot away the *Bucentaure*'s foremast. At 2.5, the *Bucentaure* struck. Sent a boat on board of her to take possession.' Pellew, not realizing his enemy was Villeneuve himself (perhaps because the admiral's pennant had fallen with the mainmast) and not wanting to denude his ship unnecessarily, sent only a small party in the cutter to take possession, consisting of Captain James Atcherley RM, a corporal, two marines and two seamen. He and his men clambered aboard and made their way to the quarterdeck, picking their way around and over the debris and bodies that littered the decks. Atcherley was immediately recognizable as a British officer by his red jacket and epaulettes. As he stepped up onto the quarterdeck he was confronted by three officers, all of whom bowed and offered him their sword hilts. The first was a thin man in admiral's uniform – Villeneuve; the second a short, fat naval captain with a bandaged face – Magentie; the third wore the uniform of an Army general – Contamine. Commander Prigny was too badly wounded to be present.

'To whom,' inquired Villeneuve in excellent English, 'have I the honour of surrendering?'

'To Captain Pellew of the *Conqueror*,' replied a startled Atcherley, who had certainly not anticipated taking so exalted a prisoner.

'It is a satisfaction to me to have been so fortunate to have struck my flag to Sir Edward Pellew.'

'It is his brother, sir,' answered Atcherley.

'His brother! What, are there two of them? *Hélas!*'

Magendie, who had already been a British prisoner twice, put the third time down to '*la fortune de la guerre*'. Perhaps the embarrassment of an Army general surrendering to a naval captain was what kept Contamine silent.

Somewhat overawed by the array of rank before him, Atcherley respectfully suggested that the swords of such senior officers would be best handed to Captain Pellew personally. In the meantime he excused himself as he wished to go below to secure the magazine. When he returned with the keys in his pocket he assembled the senior prisoners (Prigny was left lying below) and they climbed down into the cutter. It was only then that Atcherley realized the *Conqueror* had disappeared. Poor man. He was rowing around in a small boat amidst the smoke and floating wreckage of a major battle with the enemy commander-in-chief on board – and he had lost his ship! It had the makings of a splendid story for latter years but at the time must have been extremely disconcerting. He looked round desperately for the nearest British ship, and spotted the *Mars*. It was a startled Lieutenant William Hennah, commanding the ship after Captain Duff's death, who finally received the sword of Vice-Admiral Villeneuve – after the battle it was sent to Collingwood.

While his Royal Marine captain was away Pellew had moved north and then swung to starboard in order to engage the *Santisima Trinidad* carrying the flag of Rear-Admiral Cisneros. The Spanish four-decker now had up to 86 guns (the combined larboard broadsides of *Neptune* and *Conqueror*) smashing into her. Within minutes this storm of iron brought the mizzen-, main- and shortly afterwards the foremast down, dragging her huge red and gold ensign and admiral's pennant with them. An officer of the *Conqueror* wrote, 'Her immense topsails had every reef out. Her royals were sheeted home, but lowered; and the falling of this majestic mass of spars, sails and rigging, was one of the most magnificent sights I ever beheld. Immediately after this a Spaniard showed an English Union on the lee gangway, in token of surrender.'

Before this happened other ships had been arriving on the Spaniard's weather side. First the 64-gun *Africa*, somewhat battered from her journey down the line of the van squadron from whom she had received numerous broadsides. Then the 100-gun *Britannia* appeared to add her weight to the one-sided struggle. Again the log of the *Conqueror* reduces the horror of what was happening on this superb Spanish flagship as she wallowed helplessly from side to side to a few bland phrases. 'At 2.25 the four-decker's main and mizzen went by the board. At 2.32, shot her fore mast away. At 2.35, she struck to the *Neptune* and *Conqueror*. Left her in charge of the *Africa*.' As we shall see the last sentence was incorrect.

Perhaps the most realistic account of what it was like on the *Santisima Trinidad* that afternoon is contained in Don Peres Galdos's book *Trafalgar*, extracts of which were published in the *Cornhill Magazine* in October 1896 and are reproduced overleaf. Although Galdos used invented characters as narrators of incidents his words are based on authentic accounts drawn from official documents held in the Naval Archives in Madrid, private papers and letters in family collections and the published accounts of eyewitnesses, giving a realistic insight into what was happening on this huge four-decker at Trafalgar.

Every shot from a British broadside hit home. The Spaniard's masts had gone and as each heavy swell lifted the hulk she rocked first one way and then the other, her weed-coated sides exposed above the water. Below the waterline, holes were smashed through into the hold and orlop deck. Despite the carpenter's efforts water was soon sloshing around and crewmen had to be diverted to man the pumps. Rear-Admiral Cisneros had been wounded, Commodore Uriate was unconscious as a result of a blow from a flying splinter and the second-in-command, Lieutenant Oleata, was also hit. The *Santisima Trinidad* was dying. She was dismasted, unmanageable, hardly a gun could fire, while her pumps were fighting to prevent her sinking. There were 205 dead men awaiting disposal and 105 injured awaiting the surgeon. Surrender could not be postponed. Oleata dragged himself down to the cockpit to report the desperate situation to his admiral. Cisneros gave instructions that the third-in-command should make the decision, but only after consulting the surviving officers, and in a matter of minutes a man was waving a union jack from the gangway. He was seen by Freemantle on the *Neptune* as well as by Bayntun, and both ships ceased firing. However, there was still fighting to do in the north. Enemy ships could be glimpsed approaching so both the *Neptune* and *Conqueror* abandoned the Spaniard and sailed towards Dumanoir's oncoming van.

The *Africa*, on the weather side, had not spotted the surrender signal, although Captain Digby ceased firing when he realized the others had done so. Gradually the smoke around the Spaniard cleared. Digby assumed the silence indicated a surrender and ordered his first lieutenant, John Smith, across to take possession. He and a handful of men took a boat and climbed aboard but, despite the waving of the Union flag when Smith approached the quarterdeck, he was told the ship had not struck: the Spanish officers had seen some of Dumanoir's ships approaching and thus had had second thoughts about surrendering. Somewhat sheepishly Smith and his party departed back to the *Africa*, and Digby prepared to sail to meet the new threat. The *Santisima Trinidad* was left wallowing and waiting.

### *Africa*, *Britannia*, *Ajax* and *Agamemnon*

The *Africa* joined the battle from the north, while the others made up the last three ships in the first eight of Nelson's column of attack. They all arrived at the centre of the enemy line between 1.30 p.m. and 2.00 p.m. but although their effect on this phase of the action was helpful it was not crucial. The *Africa*'s larboard broadside had been busy exchanging fire with at least eight enemy ships as she sailed south down the line of the van, and thus was in action for much longer than the other three. As her log states: 'At 1, bore down to the assistance of the *Neptune*, engaging the *Santisima Trinidad*. At 1.30, commenced our fire on her.' By the end of the afternoon she had lost 18 killed and 44 wounded – moderate losses.

The *Britannia*, under Captain Charles Bullen, was the fifth in the line, a 100-gun three-decker with an admiral (Northesk) on board, but she did not contribute much to the victory, either in the central mêlée or overall. She joined what had by then become something of a 'turkey shoot' into the *Bucentaure* and undoubtedly fired at some others. According to her log she came through the enemy line at 3.00 p.m., which must surely be a mistake as it would indicate a very considerable hanging back; it has been suggested that had the battle not been such a resounding British triumph Northesk would have had some official explaining to do. She suffered a total of 10 dead and 42 injured and slight structural damage. It seems a fair proportion were the result of one shot. Lieutenant Lawrence Halloran RM tells us:

… between one and two o'clock, a shot struck the muzzle of the gun at which I was stationed (the aftermost gun on the larboard side of the lower deck), and killed or wounded everyone there stationed, myself and Midshipman Tomkyns only excepted. The shot was a very large one, and split into a number of pieces, each of which took its victim. We threw the mangled body of John Jolley, a marine, out of the stern port, his stomach being shot away; the other sufferers we left to be examined.

Unusually, a Royal Marine officer had been posted in charge of guns on the lower gun-deck. He was unlikely to have been trained in naval gunnery and his normal position would have been on the poop, quarterdeck or fore-castle. However, there were two RM captains (again exceptional) and three lieutenants so perhaps there were sufficient on the upper decks and Halloran's marines may have been forming part of the gun crews.

The *Ajax*, commanded by Lieutenant John Pilford, followed the *Britannia* into action. Like most other leading ships of Nelson's column she fired into the *Bucentaure* on passing and then, according to Mr Donaldson's log, 'brought the ship to the wind on the larboard tack to leeward of the enemy's line, engaging them on their star-board side'. This was, seemingly, the sum total of her efforts in the centre as the serious fighting in that area had slackened off considerably due to damage and casualties already inflicted. Her casualties for the day, two killed and nine wounded, indicate the *Ajax* did not endure much in the way of enemy fire.

The *Agamemnon* with her 64 guns was very much a lightweight in the central mêlée where so many heavyweights were involved. She was the eighth ship to reach the enemy line and Captain Sir Edward Berry briefly brought her into action against the *Bucentaure*. By this time, however, the French flagship was on the verge of striking. *Agamemnon* did not play a substantive part in the central battle around the opposing flagships and her casualty rate of only ten (two killed, eight wounded) was one of the three lightest of the battle.

## AB James West (*Britannia*) Is Wounded

There were not many casualties on the *Britannia* but among them were James West and several of his messmates. West, who was a member of a gun crew, wrote home of his experiences; his letter was quoted in the *Naval Chronicle* in 1806.

I am sorry to inform you that I am wounded in the left shoulder, and that William Hillman was killed at the same time. The shot that killed him and three others, wounded me and five more! – Another of my messmates, Thomas Crosby, was also killed; they both went to their guns like men and died close to me. Crosby was shot in three places. Pray inform their poor friends of their death, and remind them that they died at the same time as Nelson, and in the moment of glorious victory! – Remember me to all my relations and friends, and tell them I am wounded at last, but that I do not mind it much, for I had my satisfaction of my enemies, as I never fired my gun in pain; I was sure to hit them; I killed and wounded them in plenty. Should have written sooner but the pain in my shoulder would not let me.

of the central mêlée both Villeneuve's and Cisneros's flagships had to deal with three, even four, enemies at once. It was a classic example of the successful massing of naval firepower. Little wonder the enemy commander-in-chief and the largest warship in the world were out of the action before the battle was half over.

• A situation unique in naval history occurred when, for a time, four ships-of-the-line were locked together in a deadly sandwich. That the *Redoutable*, caught between two three-deckers, fought on for so long is a remarkable tribute to the gallantry and courage of her crew and the leadership of Captain Lucas.

• The mortal wounding of Nelson so early (around 1.15 p.m.) could have been equally wounding to the morale of the British Fleet had it become general knowledge. For obvious reasons no attempt was made to communicate this bad news, other than informing his second-in-command Collingwood by personal messenger. Nelson's fate emphasized how conspicuous and vulnerable were the officers on the upper decks at close range. The French tactics of smothering the enemy's upper works with musketry and grenades were effective, and contributed significantly to the losses on several British ships. Less successful were the French attempts to board British ships whose decks had been supposedly swept clean by muskets balls. There were always enough Royal Marines and seamen to beat them back.

• By 2.00 p.m., or shortly after, the score in ship losses in this small area of the battle was British two badly damaged (*Victory* and *Téméraire*, the latter unmanageable) and Combined Fleet four reduced to hulks and struck (Villeneuve's flagship *Bucentaure*, *Redoutable*, *Fougueux* and *Santisima Trinidad*).

• With regard to the commanders-in-chief Nelson was dying and Villeneuve was a prisoner – surely another situation unique in naval warfare.

By 2.00 p.m. the remaining six ships of Collingwood's column had arrived. The *Prince* was still a long way off. Before we look at Dumanoir's belated return in the north the battle at the southern end of the action needs explanation.

### Nelson's column, about 2.00 p.m.: comments

• Nelson had achieved his concentration on the centre. Within a matter of 30 minutes he had delivered a powerful punch with three three-deckers (*Victory*, *Téméraire* and *Neptune*) and two two-deckers (*Leviathan* and *Conqueror*) mounting 446 guns. This force was somewhat belatedly reinforced by the *Britannia*, *Ajax*, *Africa* and *Agamemnon* – another 302 guns. Initially this first concentration of five ships was directed primarily against the *Bucentaure*, *Redoutable* and then the *Santisima Trinidad* with 290 guns.

• This heavy blow was doubly effective because so many British ships were able to stern rake their enemy (*Bucentaure* and then *Santisima Trinidad*) at point-blank range. The victims of these double- or triple-shotted blasts never recovered and fought from them on in a seriously damaged condition. During this early part

## COLLINGWOOD'S SECOND GROUP OF SHIPS JOIN THE BATTLE

This second group of ships began to arrive shortly after 1.20 p.m. and were just in time to take the pressure off the *Revenge*, which had been under fire from *San Ildefonso*, *Achille* and *Principe de Asturias* for some 20 minutes. Four of these British ships (*Defence*, *Polyphemus*, *Thunderer* and *Swiftsure*) did not break the line but enveloped the rear – an event foreseen in Nelson's plan. Captain Durham's *Defiance* led into the action, but in try-ing to cut through the gap between the stern of the *Principe de Asturias* and the bows of the *Berwick* ran abroad the French ship as she closed the gap, costing the *Berwick* her bowsprit. Durham managed to get clear and followed after Gravina's flagship.

## Santisima Trinidad

Quotations are taken from Don Peres Galdos's *Trafalgar* (see p. 510)

### 'Preparation for Battle'

A number of sailors were posted on the ladders from the
hatchway to the hold and between decks, and in this way
were hauling up sacks of sand. Each man handed one to
the man next to him and so it was passed on. A great
quantity of sacks were thus brought up from hand to
hand, and were emptied out on the upper decks, the poop,
and the forecastle, the sand being spread out so as to cover
all the planking. The same thing was done between decks.

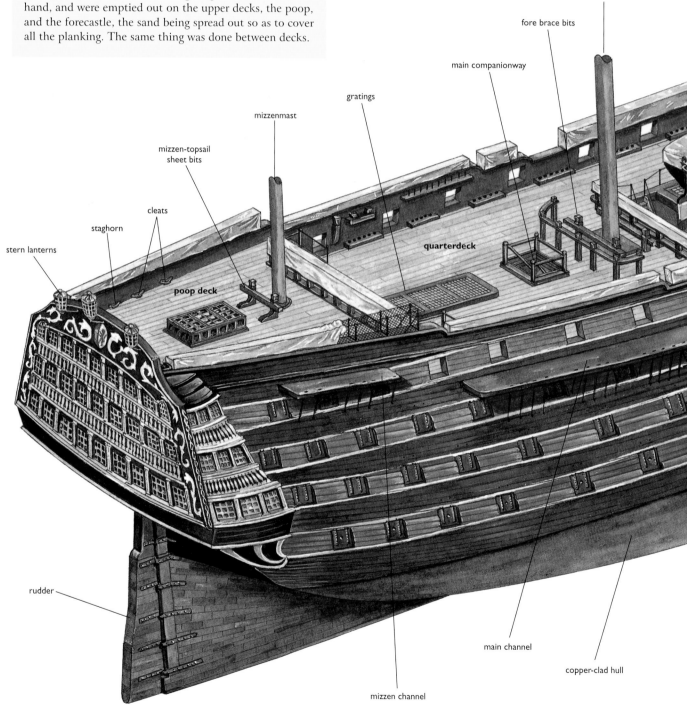

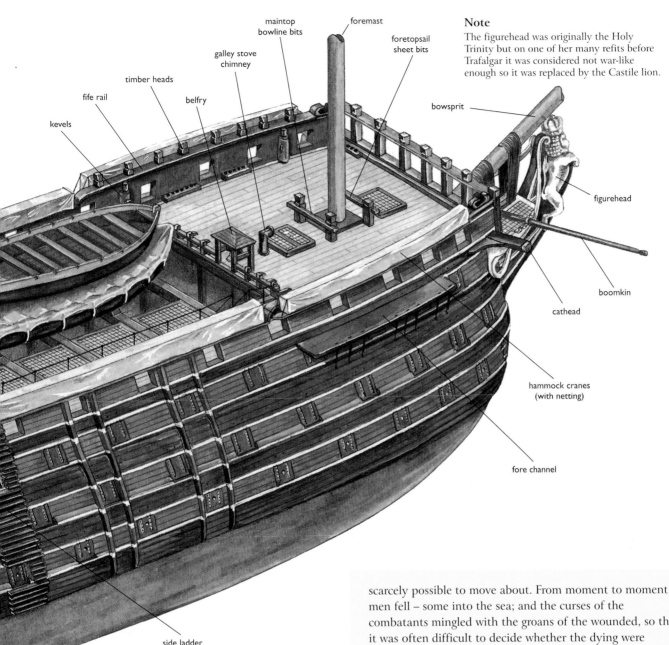

maintop
bowline bits

foremast

galley stove
chimney

foretopsail
sheet bits

timber heads

fife rail

belfry

kevels

**Note**
The figurehead was originally the Holy
Trinity but on one of her many refits before
Trafalgar it was considered not war-like
enough so it was replaced by the Castile lion.

bowsprit

figurehead

boomkin

cathead

hammock cranes
(with netting)

fore channel

side ladder

### 'At the Height of the Action'

The scene on board the *Trinidad* was a hellish one. No
attention was paid to the sails. The vessel, indeed, was
unmanageable. The energies of all were concentrated upon
the business of working the guns as quickly as possible …
The English shot had torn our sails to tatters. It was as if
huge invisible talons had been dragging at them. Fragments
of spars, splinters of wood, thick hempen cables cut as corn
is cut by the sickle, shreds of canvas, bits of iron, and
hundreds of other things that had been wrenched away by
the enemy's fire, were piled along the deck, where it was
scarcely possible to move about. From moment to moment
men fell – some into the sea; and the curses of the
combatants mingled with the groans of the wounded, so that
it was often difficult to decide whether the dying were
blaspheming God or the fighters were calling upon Him for
aid. I helped in the very dismal task of carrying the
wounded into the hold, where the surgeons worked. Some
died ere we could convey them thither; others had to
undergo frightful operations, ere their worn out bodies could
get an instant's rest. It was much more satisfying to be able
to assist the carpenter's crew in temporarily stopping some
of the holes torn by shot in the ship's hull. … Blood ran in
streams about the deck; and in spite of the sand, the rolling
of the ship carried it hither and thither until it made strange
patterns on the planks. The enemy's shot, fired, as they
were, from very short range, caused horrible mutilations. …
The ship creaked and groaned as she rolled – and through a
thousand holes and crevices in her strained hull the sea
spurted in, and began to flood the hold.

## Collingwood's Second Group of Ships Join Battle

### 1.30–2.00 p.m.

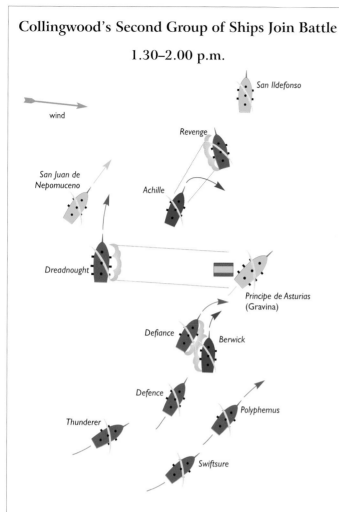

**Notes**
- The last group of Collingwood's ships do not break the line but rather envelop the rear as they join the mêlée.
- *Defiance* tries to bear away under the stern of *Principe de Asturias* but is prevented from doing so by *Berwick*, who runs aboard the British ship and loses her bowsprit in the process.
- *Dreadnought* approaches *San Juan Nepomuceno* and opens fire on *Principe de Asturias*.
- *Defence, Thunderer, Polyphemus* and *Swiftsure* have yet to be engaged.

The *Berwick* turned to leeward and was later (as described above) forced to strike to the British *Achille*. The *Revenge*, freed from her three to one battle, continued her struggle with the French *Achille* and then the *Aigle*. Shortly after this the *Defiance* broke off her chase of the *Principe de Asturias* and engaged the *Aigle* after she had drifted off from her action with the *Revenge*.

The *Defiance* came in close to the *Aigle* and an exchange of broadsides began. The British ship soon began to get the upper hand and firing from the *Aigle* became intermittent. Durham determined to take his enemy by boarding. However, this was difficult as lack of wind made coming alongside problematic and all his ship's boats were riddled with holes. The solution came in the form of Master's Mate James (Jack) Spratt, the officer in command of the assembled boarding party. This young man, described as a 'high-spirited Irishman' and 'one of the handsomest men in the service', volunteered to swim across. One of his shipmates later gave a graphic account of what happened next.

His offer being accepted, he instantly, with his sword in his teeth and his battle-axe in his belt, dashed into the sea, calling at the same time for the others to follow [a few did so] ... Spratt on reaching the French ship, contrived by means of the rudder chains, to enter the stern gun-room port, and thence to fight his way through all the decks until he reached the poop. Here he was charged by three grenadiers with fixed bayonets ... by the assistance of the signal halyards he got upon and arms-chest ... and disabled two of them. Seizing the third one he threw him from the poop down onto the quarter-deck, where he fell and broke his neck. He dragged Spratt with him, but the British officer escaped injury. ...

By this time other men from the *Defiance* had fought their way through to the upper decks.

Spratt joined in the desperate hand-to-hand conflict which raged on the quarter-deck, and had the happiness of saving the life of a French officer ... [then] an endeavour was made by a French grenadier to run him through with his bayonet. The thrust was parried, whereupon the Frenchman presented his musket at Spratt's breast, and fired. Although the midshipman [the Trafalgar Roll shows him as a master's mate] succeeded in striking the muzzle down with his cutlass, the charge passed through his right leg a little below the knee, shattering both bones. Spratt immediately backed in between two of the quarter-deck guns to prevent being cut down from behind, in which position he continued to defend himself against his old tormentor and two others, until, at length, relieved by some of his party.

Durham had by this time managed to warp the two ships together and lash them securely. Spratt was found bleeding heavily and leaning against the bulwark. On seeing Durham he called out: 'Captain, poor old Jack Spratt is done up at last!' He was carried back on board and down to the surgeon. The Tricolour was hauled down and a Union flag run up but the fight for the *Aigle* was not over. Although a vicious brawl with cutlass, axe, musket and pistol had cleared the upper works, sharpshooters remained on the tops, while attempts to clamber down the hatchways were greeted by a fusillade of musketry. Other Frenchmen below had stocks of grenades which were thrown through the gunports into the *Defiance*. Durham, realizing his boarding party was not strong enough to take the ship, recalled it and had the lines holding the two ships cut so they drifted apart. He then began a further process of softening up with close-range broadsides.

Command of the *Aigle* had fallen to Lieutenant Asmus Classen, whose report states:

As early as the first broadsides we had the affliction of carrying Captain Gourrege below to the cockpit; he had received 5 wounds of which two were mortal. He was succeeded by Commander Tempie ...

We still held out for some time, but the enemy's flaming sulphur-saturated wads having set the gun-room on fire close to the cable tier and to the stern galleries, the ship being stripped of her rigging, most of the guns dismounted, the captain and the commander killed, nearly all the naval officers wounded and two-thirds of the crew disabled, the ship moreover – by what misfortune I know not – being isolated from the rest of the fleet, we decided to haul down our colours in order to extinguish the flames.

The end for the *Aigle* came at around three o'clock. She had paid dearly for her prolonged resistance with some 270 killed and wounded (many more were to drown a few days later when she was wrecked in the storm).

Another major clash was between the 98-gun *Dreadnought* under Captain John Conn and the Spanish 74-gun *San Juan Nepomuceno* commanded by Commodore Churruca. The Spanish ship had just opened fire on the helpless *Bellerophon* when out of the smoke the towering bulk of the *Dreadnought* loomed alongside. It only took ten minutes of battering from her 46-gun broadsides to reduce her to a dismasted hulk. During those few minutes, however, Churruca fought his ship with the utmost gallantry, dying in agony and becoming a national hero remembered to this day. Before the action Churruca had told his nephew, who was on board as a volunteer: 'Write to your friends that you are going into a battle that will be desperate and bloody. Tell them also that they may be certain of this – that I, for my part, will meet my death there. Let them know that rather than surrender my ship I will sink her.'

According to a Spanish account:

Churruca, meanwhile, who was the brain of all, directed the battle with gloomy calmness. ... He saw to everything, settled everything, and the shot flew round him and over his head without his ever once changing colour even. ...

Seeing that no one could hit one of the enemy's ships which was battering us with impunity, he went down himself to judge of the line of fire and succeeded in dismasting her. He was returning to the quarter-deck when a cannon ball hit his right leg with such violence as almost to take it off, tearing it across the thigh in the most frightful manner. He fell to the ground, but the next moment he made an effort to raise himself, supporting himself on one arm. His face was as white as death, but he said, in a voice that was scarcely weaker than his ordinary tone: 'It is nothing – go on firing!'

He did all he could to conceal the terrible sufferings of his cruelly mangled frame. Nothing would induce him, it would seem, to quit the quarter-deck. At last he yielded to our entreaties and then he seemed to understand that he must give up the command. He called for Moyna, his second in command, but was told he was dead. Then he called for the officer in command on the main deck. That officer, though himself seriously wounded, at once came to the quarter-deck and took command.

## Jack Spratt Refuses to Have His Leg Amputated

Spratt had fought as a midshipman on the *Bellona* at Copenhagen in 1801 and then as a master's mate on the *Defiance* in Calder's action in July 1805 and at Trafalgar, where he was wounded in the leg by a close-range musket shot while leading a boarding party to capture the *Aigle*. After that ship struck Spratt was taken to the surgeon on the *Defiance*. Some days later a shipmate of Spratt described what happened.

A few days afterwards, Mr. Burnett, Surgeon on board the *Defiance*, came to Captain Durham and asked for a written order to cut off Mr. Spratt's leg, saying that it could not be cured, and that he refused to submit to the operation. The Captain replied that he could not give such an order, but that he would see Mr. Spratt, which he managed to do in spite of his own wounds. Upon the Captain remonstrating with him, Spratt held out the other leg (certainly a very good one) and exclaimed, 'Never! If I lose my leg, where shall I find a match for this?' He was a high-spirited young Irishman, and one of the handsomest men in the Navy. He was safely landed at Gibraltar, where he remained sixteen weeks in hospital.

Spratt kept his injured leg although he was lame for the rest of his life. He eventually became a commander before retiring to Devon where he was frequently seen riding around on a tiny Dartmoor pony; an acquaintance of his recalled, 'Captain Spratt had a useless leg, yet he was a splendid swimmer, and when nearly sixty years old, swam a fourteen mile race for a wager with a French gentleman and won it.' He died at Teignmouth in 1852 aged eighty-one, and his son became a vice-admiral.

It was just before he went below that Churruca, in the midst of his agonies, gave the order that the flag should be nailed to the mast. The ship, he said, must never surrender so long as he breathed. ...

He never lost consciousness till the very end, nor did he complain of his sufferings. His sole anxiety was that the crew should not know how dangerous his wound was; that no one should be daunted or fail in his duty. He specially desired that that the men be thanked for their heroic courage. Then he spoke a few words to Ruiz de Apodoca [his nephew], and after sending a farewell message to his poor young wife, whom he had married only a few days before he sailed, he fixed his thoughts on God, Whose name was ever on his lips. So with the calm resignation of a good man and the fortitude of a hero, Churruca passed away.

When the *San Juan Nepomuceno* struck she had lost her fore- and mizzenmasts, her rudder had been smashed and her decks were strewn with 103 dead men while another 131 lay wounded. Despite this she attempted to follow Gravina's 112-gun flagship when she made the signal to withdraw, but the *San Juan Nepomuceno* could neither sail nor steer – she had no option but to strike. The *Dreadnought*, however, was able to set off in pursuit of the *Principe de Asturias*.

Meanwhile the *Defence* had forced the *San Ildefonso* to surrender and the *Berwick* had struck to the British *Achille*. By 3.00 p.m. the *Principe de Asturias* was the only ship in the area that had not either disappeared through the smoke to leeward or struck. She had been heavily engaged by several ships when, at around 3.00, Captain Richard Grindall brought the latecomer 98-gun *Prince* into action against her. The *Prince* slammed two broadsides into the Spaniard. The log of the *Principe de Asturias* records:

... an English three-decker ... discharged all her guns, at grape-shot range, into our stern. The Major [General Gravina] was wounded in the left leg; he was obliged to go below but while it was being temporarily dressed, he gave orders that he should be conveyed back and placed sitting at his post on deck. Weakened by loss of blood, he fell fainting; but quickly coming to himself and not perceiving the national colours, he ordered them to be hoisted without delay and he resumed command. ... In this critical position we sighted the *Neptune* and *San Justo* that were coming to our aid, which was observed by the enemy who obliged them to sheer off.

The *Prince* was distracted by the nearby, but already badly damaged, French *Achille* and at around 4.00 p.m. turned her attention to the stricken ship. The *Achille* had lost her captain, Denieport, her mizzenmast, snapped off five feet above the poop deck, and the mainmast in her encounters with her British namesake, the *Revenge* and others. The *Prince*'s broadsides were to prove the death knell for the French *Achille* in the most spectacular and devastating manner – it was an event that marked the end of the Battle of Trafalgar in the south. Sub-Lieutenants Jean Lachase and Desire Clamart best describe it in their detailed report.

Very soon the three-decker *Prince* came up to engage us and to support her [the English *Achille*]. It was then 4 o'clock; an instant later we perceived that the foretop was on fire, and that the ship was making a great deal of water, having several shot holes above and below the water-line. Our situation was the more critical as our fire-engine having been rendered useless by a shot, there remained no means of arresting the progress of the fire. Several officers and midshipmen, accompanied by the few men that were left in the 18-pounder battery and part of those from the 36-pounder deck went forward with the carpenters to cut away the foremast; but the three-decker fired into us at such close quarters that with her second broadside she succeeded in bringing down our masts and swept us as bare as a hulk. We had the misfortune to see our two masts fall amidships, an event that was the more calamitous as our flaming foretop set fire to our boats. This cruel predicament did not deter us from redoubling our courage and from serving the 36-pounder battery with the greatest energy, whilst the men who were left in the upper works and in the 18-pounder battery were employed in extinguishing the fire. But this was in vain, its progress continually increasing and the flaming debris of the boats falling on the 36-pounder gun-deck [presumably via the main hatchway]. At 4.30 the 18-pounder battery hardly showed more than one port. The *Prince* sheered off from us, doubtless for fear of an explosion. All hands then came on deck and losing all hope of extinguishing the fire, we no longer attended to anything except saving the ship's company, by throwing overboard all the debris that might offer them the means of escaping from almost certain death and of awaiting the aid that the neighbouring ships might send them.

The English ship *Prince,* which had been the last to engage us, seeing the greater part of the crew in the water, lowered her boats to go to their rescue; a cutter [*Entreprenante*] and a schooner [*Pickle*] also came up for the same purpose.

At 5.30 a part of the men in the water were saved; at the same hour the explosion occurred. It was not very violent seeing

## The Rescue of 'Jeanette' from the French *Achille*

A plethora of stories exist about how this young woman survived the fire and explosion on the French *Achille* and was plucked from the sea while clinging to a spar. Probably the most authentic one is that of Captain Moorsom of the *Revenge* which was quoted in *The Journal of the Nelson Society* in October 2002. Apologies for the lack of punctuation.

... I must tell you an anecdote of a French woman the *Pickle* Schooner sent to me about Fifty people saved from the *Achille* which was burned & blew up amongst them was a young French woman about five and twenty & wife of one of the Main Topmen when the *Achille* was burning she got out of the gun room Port & and sat on the Rudder chains, till some melted lead ran down upon her, and forced her to strip & leap off; she swam to a spar where several men, but one of them bit & kicked her till she was obliged to quit & get to another, which supported her till she was taken up by the *Pickle* & sent on board the *Revenge* amongst the men she was lucky enough to find her Husband – We were not wanting in civility to the lady; I ordered her two Pussers shirts to make a Petticoat & most of the officers found something to clothe her; in a few hours Jeanette was perfectly happy & and hard at work making her Petticoats ...

we had taken the precaution of drowning the remainder of our powder. The ship disappeared with the tatters of her flag which had never been lowered ...

The losses of this disaster were estimated at around 480 men killed, wounded and drowned. Most of the survivors became prisoners of war.

There is no doubt many Frenchmen (and one woman, see box) were saved by the actions of the *Prince*, *Pickle* and *Entreprenante* in lowering their boats. The *Pickle*'s log states: 'one took fire and blew up. Out boats to save the men. ... Saved one hundred and twenty or thirty men.' The *Entreprenante*: 'Observed one of the enemy's ships on fire. Made all sail to her. Sent our boats to the assistance of the people which were overboard. At 5.30 the ship blew up. ... Preserved from different wrecks, &., upwards of 169 men.'

The *Prince* was the only ship at Trafalgar to have not a single casualty of any sort. The other three ships that arrived late, although well before the *Prince*, were the *Polyphemus* (Captain Robert Redmill), British *Swiftsure* (Captain William Rutherford) and the *Thunderer* (Lieutenant John Stockham). All suffered lightly as far as damage and casualties were concerned as none were engaged at close range for any length of time with an enemy that was not already crippled – or nearly so. The *Polyphemus* is thought to have fired at the *Berwick*, *Principe de Asturias*, French *Achille* and *Neptune* before eventually taking the Spanish *Argonauta* in tow. Her losses amounted to two killed and four wounded. The British *Swiftsure* also fired on the *Principe de Asturias*, *Berwick* and French *Achille*. She lost 17 killed and eight wounded. In his journal Mr Robert Cocks, the master of the *Thunderer,* managed to describe the entire battle in five short lines: 'P.M. Light breezes and hazy weather. At 15 minutes past noon the action commenced between the combined fleets of France and Spain, consisting of 33 sail of the line, and 27 of the English; and at 5, twenty sail of the line had struck to the English. At 8, took the *Santa Ana* on tow. Made sail.' He neglected to mention that his ship had at least been of some assistance to the *Revenge* and had briefly engaged the French *Neptune* and *Principe de Asturias* – all at a cost of seven dead and 26 wounded.

## DUMANOIR WEARS THE VAN

The final phase of the Battle of Trafalgar was fought in the late afternoon by the British against the ships of the Combined Fleet's van squadron under Rear-Admiral Dumanoir, who had finally turned round to come to Villeneuve's aid. Dumanoir's actions have generated heated arguments which continue up to the present day. The key question is: if all Dumanoir's ships (ten if all those ahead of the *Santisima Trinidad* are counted) had joined the battle at 1.00 p.m., rather than some of them after

## Trafalgar: The Combined Fleet Van Comes About, 2.30 to 2.45 p.m.

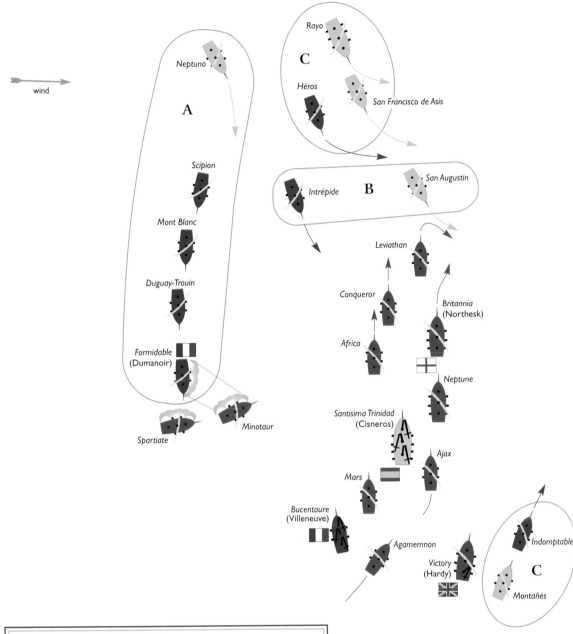

wind

**A**

Neptuno

Scipion

Mont Blanc

Duguay-Trouin

Formidable
(Dumanoir)

Spartiate

Minotaur

**C**

Rayo

Héros

San Francisco de Asis

**B**

Intrépide

San Augustin

Leviathan

Conqueror

Britannia
(Northesk)

Africa

Neptune

Santisima Trinidad
(Cisneros)

Ajax

Mars

Bucentaure
(Villeneuve)

Agamemnon

Victory
(Hardy)

Indomptable

**C**

Montañés

### Notes – Combined Fleet

**A** These 4 French ships and later 1 Spanish come south, keeping well to windward of the mêlée and making no real attempt to support Villeneuve. *Formidable* (Dumanoir) engages the British late arrivals *Minotaur* and *Spartiate*.

**B** Only *Intrépide* and *San Augustin* make a gallant attempt to involve themselves in the fight and relieve the pressure on *Bucentaure* and *Santisima Trinidad*.

**C** These two groups of ships have lost interest and are sailing to leeward out of the main action.

### Notes – British Fleet

• When Hardy sees the approach of Dumanoir's ships he signals for the fleet to come to the wind on the larboard tack to counter this new threat.

• Only 7 ships see the signal and are able to comply: *Leviathan*, *Conqueror*, *Britannia*, *Africa*, *Neptune*, *Ajax* and *Agamemnon*. They form a double line of battle and sail north.

• In fact, of the 10 ships that Dumanoir could have brought into the battle only 2 become seriously involved with the centre mêlée.

3.00 p.m., would the battle have ended differently? Many French and Spanish commentators are convinced the answer is yes. They maintain that had Dumanoir and his squadron joined battle as soon as they could, then Trafalgar would at least have been a draw – certainly not the disastrous defeat it was.

After the two British columns broke the line, all the ships to the north of the *Santisima Trinidad* continued to sail in that direction while all those to the south became, over the next 45 minutes, almost stationary and embroiled in a confused mêlée. A gap thus opened up between the ten ships in the north and the 23 in the centre and south. All accounts agree that the British broke the line in two places at 12.15 p.m. (Collingwood) and 12.30 p.m. (Nelson) and that Dumanoir's van began turning back at around 2.00 p.m., by which time, given an average speed of one to one and a half knots, the gap would have been about two miles wide, though by the time they turned many British ships had sailed north to meet them.

Villeneuve's instructions to his fleet could not have been clearer: 'Any captain commanding that is not under fire will not be at his post, [and] any whose next ahead or next astern is closer than he to the enemy will not be doing his duty and a signal recalling him will be a reflection on his honour.' During the engagement he made two signals that were, in effect, orders for Dumanoir to assist him. At 12.30 p.m. he made the general signal of a single flag representing Article 5 in the code, ordering all ships not closely engaging an enemy to do so immediately. Then, as Lieutenant Demay, commanding the brig *Furet* which repeated the signal, wrote in his report: 'At 1.45 p.m. the Admiral signalled to the Squadron that was in the van to wear together.' The *Santisima Trinidad* also repeated this signal, as did several ships in the van squadron. It was addressed specifically to Dumanoir and was Villeneuve's last act of command; a few minutes later his mizzen- and mainmasts fell.

Villeneuve could see very little of the battle from his flagship; as Commander Prigny wrote, 'the *Bucentaure* was constantly enveloped in smoke, which deprived us of the possibility of seeing what passed'. But Captain Delamare-Lamellerie of the frigate *Hortense* had been amazed to see Dumanoir's ships sailing away from the action, and informed the commander-in-chief immediately. His report states: 'At 1.30 seeing that the ten ships of the van were no longer having any enemy abeam [most had briefly engaged with the *Africa*], I signalled the same to the Admiral; he immediately [at 1.45 p.m.] ordered the van to wear in succession [in fact together]. At 1.50 the *Bucentaure*'s main and mizzen masts fell.'

At last, at around 2.00 p.m., Dumanoir began to come about. He afterwards claimed that he began to do so before Villeneuve's second, and direct, order. But why wait so long when it was obvious the centre was in action and he had no enemy? Why continue away from the battle when he knew the 'standing order' was, if in doubt, to engage the enemy? Dumanoir later claimed that the lack of wind prevented an earlier manoeuvre, and it was certainly true that the process of coming about took a long time. But this was surely an argument for coming about much earlier. Dumanoir must have known that entering the action two hours after it started was likely to be a futile gesture. In the event only two ships out of the ten (*San Augustin* and *Intrépide*) became seriously engaged in the centre.

---

### Dumanoir's First Court of Enquiry

Dumanoir escaped from Trafalgar with four ships but was then intercepted, defeated and captured by Captain Sir Richard Strachan's squadron on 4 November. When released in 1809 Dumanoir faced two courts of enquiry. The charges against him at the first (Trafalgar) court of inquiry were as follows:

1. Did the Rear-Admiral manoeuvre in conformity with the signals and with the dictates of duty and honour?
2. Did Rear-Admiral Dumanoir do all that he was able to do to relieve the centre of the Fleet and the flagship in particular?
3. Did the Rear-Admiral Dumanoir engage the enemy ship to ship and did he approach the action sufficiently to take part in the engagement at as close a range as he should have done?
4. Did Rear-Admiral Dumanoir quit the action when it was in his power to engage?

The Court received a long written statement from Dumanoir, the log of the *Formidable* and several captain's reports, notably those of Captain Delamare-Lameillerie of the frigate *Hortense* and Villeneuve's flag captain, Magendie. There appears to have been no examination of witnesses or the accused, and Dumanoir was absolved of blame for each charge.

For Dumanoir's second Court of Enquiry and subsequent court martial, see pp. 542–3.

---

Although the order was to 'wear together', several ships tacked, or tried to, and most, including the flagship, could not do either without using boats to pull the bows round – in itself a slow process. Several captains of the van mention this important sequence of events in their reports, all of which contradict Dumanoir's claim to have begun to turn before Villeneuve's signal.

**Captain Valdés (*Neptuno*):** 'At 1.45 I saw the signal which ordered the van to wear together and to assist in supporting the corps or division attacked, which I executed immediately without awaiting the moment when, a little later, I saw it hoisted by the *Formidable* ...'.

**Captain Berrenger (*Scipion*):** 'I attempted to tack; the wind being very light and the sea very high, the ship missed stays. It was impossible for me to wear, at least unless several ships, such as the *Intrépide* who was my next astern and the *San Augustin* which was to leeward, had gone about also, without the risk of running them aboard. The line being overcrowded, I had a boat to assist my manoeuvre. At the same instant General Dumanoir made the signal to the van to wear together and hoisted the executive [signal] at the same time. ...'

**Captain Infernet (*Intrépide*):** 'At 1.30 [it was 1.45] the *Formidable* signalled ... to go about and proceed into action; carried out this signal at once and went on the starboard tack. In manoeuvring to effect this evolution I ran aboard the *Mont Blanc*, who broke her flying jib-boom and she split my foresail ...'.

The three French and one Spanish ship that followed the *Formidable* kept well to windward of the main area of battle. Vice-Admiral Decrès in his report (undated) to Napoleon was particularly scathing of this, commenting: 'having executed this order [to wear], Rear-Admiral Dumanoir manoeuvred with four ships in such a manner as to pass to windward of the enemy instead of standing boldly into the thick of the fight'. As Dumanoir himself later explained his action, '[he] continued to crowd on sail in order to go to the rescue of the Admiral, and with the intention of cutting off two ships belonging to the enemy's northern column [*Minotaur* and *Spartiate*]'. If he had really been determined to 'rescue the admiral' he had no reason for working so far to windward (about 600 yards). Dumanoir continued, 'The Admiral was by then totally dismasted; I still had a hope that I might take him in tow and endeavour to get him out of fire. ... the two vessels that I had intended to cut off managed to pass ahead of me at pistol-shot and damaged me greatly; to crown all the misfortune, I found that the *Bucentaure* had been taken.'

After coming about, Dumanoir's ten ships had split into three groups. His flagship led four others south but well to windward (*Formidable, Duguay-Trouin, Scipion, Mont Blanc* and, at the rear, the *Neptuno*). Two ships headed straight for the centre of the approaching enemy (*Intrépide* and *San Augustin*) while the third group (*Héros*, *San Francisco de Asis* and *Rayo*) headed home.

Dumanoir's intention to cut off the *Minotaur* and *Spartiate* failed. The two British ships were able to fire several raking broadsides into the *Formidable* as she approached. As Dumanoir said, 'they damaged me greatly'. Both British ships came to the wind and engaged the three French ships astern of the *Formidable.* They then became embroiled in a close, if somewhat one-sided and lengthy, struggle with the Spanish *Neptuno* under Commodore Valdés. The log of Mr Francis Whitney, the *Spartiate*'s master, records:

> Lay onto her quarter … firing obliquely through her, she returning at times from her stern chase and quarter guns. At 4.10 Wore [now headed south], not being able to bring our guns to bear, to engage her on the other tack, the other four ships having left her [Dumanoir and his three French ships]. … 4.22 The Spanish ship engaged by the *Spartiate* and *Minotaur* had her mizzen mast shot away. 5.10 she struck, after having been very much disabled. She proved to be *El Neptuno*, 80 guns.

Mr Robert Duncan, master of the *Minotaur*, had this to say:

> At 2.10, observed four French and one Spanish ships bearing down towards the *Victory*. Hauled towards them, as did the *Spartiate,* and commenced firing on the Admiral's ship [*Formidable*]. Passed the four French ships and attacked the Spanish ship with a broad pennant flying [Commodore Valdés]. At 4, wore [just ahead of *Spartiate*] and got alongside of her, *Spartiate* in company. At 5.12 she struck; found her to be the *Neptuno* of 84 guns [in fact 80].

On the *Neptuno* Captain Valdés later recorded that at around 4.00 p.m.:

> the mizzen mast fell and in its fall I was wounded in the head and neck and lost consciousness and was carried below, where I had never thought to go, notwithstanding that I had already been wounded three times during the action. … finally a few minutes before sunset, having 30 dead [actually 42] and 47 wounded, totally dismasted and overwhelmed by the superior number of enemy who surrounded my ship – which was the only one in these waters – we decided to strike …

Dumanoir had not done well. Not all his ships followed him, and his late arrival meant he was unable to influence events in the centre. Of the five ships he led, only the *Neptuno* put up a serious fight and he failed to cut off the two British ships before they joined the action. He then gave up and sailed away to the southwest, leaving the *Neptuno* to face the combined broadsides of the *Minotaur* and *Spartiate* alone; the two British ships had been enough to see his five off. He later put the blame on those ships that did not follow him, saying:

> If I had had with me ten ships, however desperate our position, I should have been able to bear down on the scene of action and to fight the enemy to a finish … . But in consequence of this non-compliance I was left with four ships (the *Neptuno* was very far astern owing to the irresolution of her manoeuvres) … . To bear down on the enemy at this

moment would have been a desperate stroke which would have only served to increase the number of our losses, and to augment the advantages of the enemy to whom, on account of the depletion of my division, I could not have done much damage; it was therefore my duty in this painful situation to endeavour to effect the repairs of my division in the hope of more favourable chances on the morrow.

During the latter part of the afternoon the only serious fighting involved the *Neptuno*, *Intrépide* and *San Augustin* in the north. All three fought it out to the bitter end, all three were left isolated and unsupported in the midst of their enemies and all three only surrendered when further resistance was futile. The 74-gun *San Augustin* under the command of Commodore Felipe Cajigal had begun the battle just ahead and to the lee of the *Santisima Trinidad*. In this position she had become embroiled in the desperate mêlée around the Spanish flagship in the early afternoon. Cajigal's report refers to this stage of the fighting as:

> last[ing] more or less up to 3 o'clock [nearer 2.00 p.m.], at which hour the whole enemy line having defiled and attacked the *Trinidad* … in response to a signal from the *Trinidad* to bear up and support her in distress [I steered] straight for the three-decker which was engaging her to starboard [*Neptune*], and at our first discharge … we carried away part of her yards; but in the end the *Trinidad* struck …

The *San Augustin* had then moved north, and at the time that the van wore round in response to Villeneuve's final signal she was one of the ten ships that came about, although, like the *Intrépide* and *Héros*, she was not originally in Dumanoir's squadron. She came down on the lee side of the British ships heading north and clashed with the leading ship, the 74-gun *Leviathan* under Captain Henry Bayntun. As the two ships closed from opposite directions Bayntun had the helm put a-starboard and ran aboard the Spaniard. Mr John Trotter, the master, recorded the subsequent events with the customary brevity in his log. 'At about half-past 3 [it was earlier], laid the *San Augustin* aboard, carried her and towed her off.' After an exchange of muzzle-to-muzzle broadsides Bayntun had the ships lashed together and summoned his boarding parties led by Lieutenant John Baldwin. A brutal brawl with cutlass, axe and pistol took place as the British seamen swarmed along the yards and spars and clambered over the bulwarks. Twice they were beaten back, but on the third attempt the ship was taken. Commodore Cajigal recorded: 'it was inevitable to surrender to such superior numbers, and having been boarded twice I had not sufficient men left to repel a third boarding, the few who remained being on the gun-decks, continuing to fire into the other ships that were closing around me at pistol range …'.

One of the most gallant actions of the battle was fought by the French 74-gun *Intrépide* under Captain Louis Infernet, a rough, uneducated Provençal who had begun his career as a ship's boy. According to the young Maquis Gicquel des Touches, who was an officer on board, Infernet had been fuming at Dumanoir's sailing away from the battle and had several times tried unsuccessfully to wear on his own initiative. In his words: 'The leading division, however, although not a single British ship threatened it, remained inactive. Our captain, Infernet, with his eyes fixed on the *Formidable,* expected Admiral Dumanoir every moment to make the signal to go about and take part in the battle. But no signal went up.'

When the van did eventually come about Infernet was appalled to see the *Formidable* leading three ships to windward seemingly away from the action. He managed to wear his ship by using a boat and headed straight for the line of British ships that were coming north in pursuit of the *Rayo*, *Héros* and *San Francisco de Asis*. As she came steadily south the *Intrépide* exchanged broadsides with the *Conqueror*, *Britannia*, *Ajax*, *Agamemnon*, *Neptune* and then the 64-gun *Africa*, the first enemy to engage her at close range. Captain Digby wore round astern of the Frenchman, came onto the starboard tack and opened fire. It was the start of an hour-long duel. Infernet also had to take punishment from the *Leviathan*'s starboard batteries as he came close to the latter while she was engaging the *San Augustin*.

Next into the fray was Captain Edward Codrington's *Orion*. She had arrived into the mêlée around 2.00 p.m., by which time the fiercest of the fighting in the centre had abated somewhat, and Codrington at first had difficulty amidst the smoke and confusion in finding an opponent. The log of Mr Cass Halliday, *Orion*'s master, explains how the ship joined action with the *Intrépide*:

> Observed the *Leviathan* closely engaged with a Spanish ship [*San Augustin*], and the whole of the enemy's van wearing to attack her. Made sail to assist her. Observed a French 74 [*Intrépide*] bring to on the starboard tack [come about] and engage warmly betwixt the *Leviathan*, who was boarding a Spanish 74, and the *Africa*, who appeared to have almost ceased

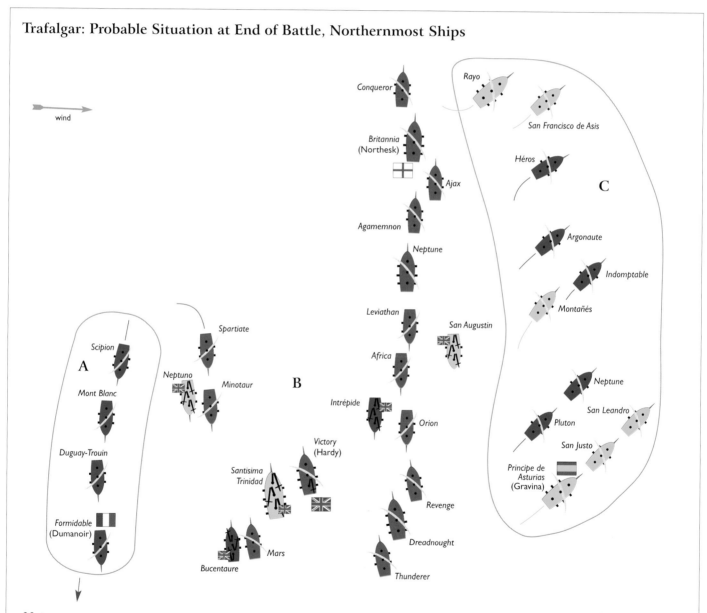

**Trafalgar: Probable Situation at End of Battle, Northernmost Ships**

### Notes

**A** These 4 ships under Dumanoir have briefly engaged *Minotaur* and *Spartiate* but are now sailing off to the south-west. They escape but are captured by Capt. Strachan's squadron on 4 November.

**B** After a valiant fight *Neptune*, *San Augustin* and *Intrépide* have now struck. *Intrépide* is the last ship of the Combined Fleet to surrender, after a prolonged fight against heavy odds.

**C** Adm. Gravina has signalled to those ships that can to rally to leeward and these 11 ships manage to escape from the scene of the battle and head towards Cadiz.

firing. Made all possible sail. ... At 4, opened our fire close on his starboard quarter, wore round his stern, and brought to on his lee bow ... At 4.45, he struck his colours. Sent the first lieutenant, Mr Croft, and a party of men to take possession of her. At 6, stood under her stern with a rope to take her in tow, but they slipped it. At 8, the *Ajax* took her in tow.

As with all logs this abbreviated account cannot do justice to the deadly and unequal struggle that took place from around 2.45 p.m. until after five o'clock. The best description of what occurred on the *Intrépide* is from the pen of Lieutenant Giquel des Touches. As a personal account it is in many ways unique and worth quoting in full.

When at length we drew near where the *Bucentaure* and the *Redoutable* lay, their masts had fallen, their fire was almost silenced ... [they were] fighting against ships that were practically undamaged, from the ports of which broadside after broadside flashed incessantly. ...

I passed the whole of the action on the forecastle, where I had charge of the head sails and of the musketry and the boarders. ... What took my attention was to prevent the masts and yards from coming down, by means of which we were able to manoeuvre the ship to some extent. While the fighting was very hot, the British *Orion* crossed our bows in order to pour in a raking fire. I got my men ready to board, and pointing out to a midshipman her position and what I wanted to do, I sent him to the captain with a request to have the ship laid on board the *Orion* ... With keen anxiety I waited; but there was no change in the *Intrépide's* course. Then I dashed off to the quarter-deck myself. On my way I found my midshipman lying flat on the deck, terrified at the sight of the *Téméraire* [in fact, *Britannia*], which ship had come abreast of us within pistol-shot and was thundering into us from her lofty batteries. I treated my emissary as he deserved – I gave him a hearty kick – and then hurried aft to explain my project personally to the captain. It was then too late. The *Orion* swept forward across our bows, letting fly a murderous broadside – and no second chance presented itself.

At the moment I reached the poop the brave Infernet was brandishing a small curved sabre which struck off one of the pieces of wooden ornamental work by the rail. The sword-blade went quite close to my face, and I said laughingly, 'Do you want to cut my head off captain?'

'No, certainly not you, my friend,' was the reply, 'but that's what I mean to do to the first man who speaks to me of surrender.'

Nearby was a gallant colonel of infantry, who had distinguished himself at Marengo. He was terribly perturbed at the broadside from the *Téméraire* [*Britannia*]. In vain he tried to dodge and shelter behind the stalwart form of the captain, who at length saw what he was doing. 'Ah, Colonel,' called out the captain, 'do you think I am sheathed in metal then?' In spite of the gravity of the moment we could not keep from laughing.

But by now, indeed, the decks had been almost swept clear; our guns were disabled, and the batteries heaped up with dead and dying. It was impossible to keep up a resistance, which meant the doom of what remained of our brave ship's company. Our flag was hauled down. It had been for some time the last flag to fly in our part of the battle, and I believe after us no other French or Spanish ship maintained resistance.

In this des Touches was correct. Captain Infernet left a blow-by-blow account of how his ship was finally battered into submission, although there is some doubt as to his timings.

At 4 o'clock I was dismantled to such a degree that all my rigging was cut to pieces and several guns on deck and in the batteries dismounted. At 4.45 I ordered the few hands remaining on deck to go below to the batteries in order to engage to starboard and larboard; at this minute the mizzen yard where my colours were flying was carried away by a shot; I immediately ordered a flag to be flown from the mizzen shrouds to starboard and to larboard and continued the fight. At 5 o'clock the wheel, the tiller sweep, the tiller ropes and the tiller were shattered to a thousand pieces; I at once had the spare tiller rigged and steered with it, always fighting desperately. At 5.15 the mizzen mast fell; four or five minutes later the main mast did the same; I still fought – and I am able to say so to the honour of those whom I commanded, undauntedly; I was then surrounded by seven [an exaggeration] enemy ships, which were all firing into me and I was making all possible resistance; I was firing with the stern-chasers, musketry from the upper works and from the fore-top. At 5.35 the fore-mast fell; I was left without masts or sails ... having about half my crew killed or wounded ... I was obliged to yield ... .

At 6 o'clock I saw a boat arrive from the *Orion* which took me off my ship ... the *Intrépide* was so crippled that the enemy were obliged to burn her two days after the battle ...

To the south, some half an hour earlier, Admiral Gravina had hoisted the signal on the *Principe de Asturias* for all ships able to do so to rally to leeward. Under tow by the frigate *Thémis*, the acting commander-in-chief began to struggle back towards Cadiz along with the *Rayo*, *San Francisco de Asis*, *Héros*, *Argonauta*, *Montañés* and *Indomptable*. Dumanoir and his four ships had disappeared to the south-west.

The Battle of Trafalgar was over.

## Post-Battle Lassitude

Lieutenant Paul Nicolas RM of the *Belleisle* later wrote of his fellow officers' reactions after the action.

About five o'clock the officers assembled in the captain's cabin to take some refreshment. The parching effects of the smoke made this a welcome summons, although some of us had been fortunate in relieving our thirst by plundering the captain's grapes which hung around his cabin; still four hours' exertion of body with the energies incessantly employed, occasioned a lassitude, both corporeally and mentally, from which the victorious termination now so near at hand, could not arouse us; moreover there sat a melancholy on the brows of some who mourned the messmates who had shared their perils and their vicissitudes for many years. Then the merits of the departed heroes were repeated with a sigh, but their errors sunk with them into the deep.

# THE RECKONING

Nelson had the battle he craved, and lived just long enough to know that he had achieved a splendid victory. His plan had worked, he had his pell-mell battle, his captains and crews had done their jobs magnificently and British seamanship and gunnery had, as he knew they would, proved greatly superior to both Spanish and French. However, as far as gallantry and courageous leadership was concerned there was nothing to choose between the two fleets. It is possible to argue that, with some notable exceptions, the Combined Fleet put up a much stiffer fight than had been expected. Despite their ill-trained crews, many inexperienced officers and ratings and serious shortages of seamen, a high proportion of Villeneuve's ships gave better accounts of themselves than is appreciated today. The battle was far from being a walkover and had Dumanoir's squadron turned back to join battle at 12.30 p.m. the outcome would have been less certain.

## The Combined Fleet: Ships
Villeneuve lost 18, or slightly over 54 per cent, of his line-of-battle fleet at Trafalgar, of which nine were French and nine Spanish. This was a big haul in battered prizes for the British. The fate of the Combined Fleet's 33 line-of-battle ships at the battle was:

| Struck/captured | Blew up | Escaped |
|---|---|---|
| Aigle | Achille | Argonaute |
| Algéciras | | Duguay-Trouin |
| Argonauta | | Formidable |
| Bahama | | Héros |
| Berwick | | Indomptable |
| Bucentaure | | Mont Blanc |
| Fougueux | | Montañés |
| Intrépide | | Neptune |
| Monarca | | Pluton |
| Neptuno | | Principe de Asturias |
| Redoutable | | Rayo |
| San Augustin | | San Francisco de Asis |
| San Ildefonso | | San Justo |
| San Juan Nepomuceno | | San Leandro |
| Santa Ana | | Scipion |
| Santisima Trinidad | | |
| Swiftsure | | |

## The French Fleet: Casualties
Official records of battle casualties, particularly those of the French, are seldom entirely reliable. This is normal with a losing side in any battle of this period, and in this instance accurate figures are even harder to obtain as many men were drowned when their ships were wrecked in the storm afterwards. The figures given do not take account of prisoners taken by the British, several hundred in total, most of whom ended up in prison hulks in England. Where only the total figure of losses is available, and this includes those drowned, then an attempt has been made to estimate battle casualties. The figures given below are therefore best estimates based on several sources.

| Ship | Killed | Wounded | Drowned | Total |
|---|---|---|---|---|
| Achille | 445 | – | 35 | 480 |
| Aigle* | 70 | 100 | 330 | 500[1] |
| Algéciras | 77 | 142 | – | 219 |
| Argonaute | 55 | 132 | – | 187 |
| Berwick* | 75 | 125 | 497 | 600[2] |
| Bucentaure | 197 | 85 | – | 282 |
| Duguay-Trouin | 12 | 24 | – | 36 |
| Formidable | 22 | 45 | – | 67 |
| Fougueux* | 60 | 75 | 502 | 637[3] |
| Héros | 12 | 24 | – | 36 |
| Indomptable* | 20 | 30 | 657 | 707[4] |
| Intrépide | 80 | 162 | – | 242 |
| Mont Blanc | 20 | 20 | – | 40 |
| Neptune | 15 | 39 | – | 54 |
| Pluton | 60 | 132 | – | 192 |
| Redoutable* | 120 | 130 | 275 | 525[5] |
| Scipion | 17 | 22 | – | 39 |
| Swiftsure | 68 | 123 | – | 191 |
| **Totals** | **1,425** | **1,410** | **2,296** | **5,133** |

*Killed and wounded have been roughly estimated as most losses were men drowned when the ship was wrecked after the battle.
1  Some two-thirds of the crew became casualties, most by drowning.
2  According to a muster roll of 12 November 1805, 58 crew escaped from the wreck.
3  18 officers/midshipmen and 100 seamen escaped from the wreck.
4  Records show that only 2 officers and 178 seamen were saved.
5  Out of a crew of 643. There were another 99 lightly wounded. All wounded were sent back to Cadiz and 35 men were taken to England as prisoners.

## 'Wind Farms Threaten Legacy of Trafalgar and Nelson'

The above was a headline in the *Daily Telegraph* of 6 June 2003. Extracts of the article are quoted below.

Spain is planning the world's biggest wind farm on the site of the Battle of Trafalgar. The scheme has enraged some British Nelson aficionados who fear it will desecrate a hallowed spot before the 200th anniversary in 2005 and impede important archeological work. For years there has been talk of harnessing the area's notorious wind power by planting turbines in its shallow waters.. Yesterday, the Spanish newspaper *El Mundo* published details of the Trafalgar Sea Project, which envisages the construction of 500 240ft-tall wind turbines off Cape Trafalgar.

The £1.5 billion project which is waiting final government approval could produce electricity for 750,000 families and would include fish farms in cages at the base of each turbine.

Not all Nelson enthusiasts disapprove. One is quoted as saying, 'Nelson would have approved. He harnessed the wind to his own advantage. It was wind that gave him the edge in the battle.' The article continues, 'Nelson certainly understood the power of the area's winds. Just before uttering his legendary last words imploring Hardy to kiss him, he ordered; "Anchor the ships. There's going to be a storm" [inaccurate quote]'.

*Comments*

• On the five frigates and two brigs present there were only two casualties – one officer killed on the *Argus* (brig) and one wounded on the *Furet* (brig).

• The approximate total French battle casualties were 1,425 killed and 1,410 wounded – total 2,835. The similarity between the numbers of dead and wounded is accounted for by the large number of killed when the *Achille* blew up. Moreover, surgeons were overwhelmed on the ships that fought throughout the battle so a substantial number of wounded bled to death or died of shock. Add in those drowned (approximately 2,296) and a grand total of French losses due to Trafalgar is 5,131. With battle losses the Combined Fleet suffered one killed to every 1.13 wounded – an extremely high ratio.

• The number of Frenchmen drowned (2,296) when six ships were wrecked was not far below the number of battle casualties (2,835). The French ships had a total complement of approximately 14,000 men, including officers and soldiers. Battle casualties were therefore some 20 per cent. If those drowned are included then French total losses represent nearly 37 per cent – high but not catastrophic.

• The French ships to suffer the least in the battle were the *Duguay-Trouin* and *Héros*, both with 36 casualties. Those that suffered the most were the *Achille*, which blew up with the loss of around 480 lives, the *Bucentaure*, with 282 (32 per cent), of which an exceptionally high percentage (70) were killed, and the *Redoutable*, which probably had more battle losses than the *Bucentaure* but for which exact figures are not available as she sank during the storm.

• The average number of battle casualties on each French ship was 157. This includes all the ships with very light losses (*San Justo*, *San Francisco de Asis*, *Rayo* and *San Leandro*). If only those ships with over 100 battle casualties are taken then the average for ships heavily engaged is 223. If the *Achille*'s 480 losses are included the average rises to 255 – almost exactly a third of a 74's complement.

## The Spanish Fleet: Casualties

Considerably fewer Spanish seamen drowned than French. This was because of the five ships that were wrecked or foundered (*Neptuno*, *Argonauta*, *Monarca*, *San Augustin* and *Santisima Trinidad*) three (*Argonauta*, *Monarca* and *San Augustin*) were sunk on Collingwood's orders and therefore their crews were taken on board other ships. The *Santisima Trinidad* foundered while under tow and although some wounded were drowned many of the crew were transferred before she went down.

| Ship | Killed | Wounded | Drowned | Total |
|---|---|---|---|---|
| *Argonauta* | 103 | 202 | – | 305 |
| *Bahama* | 75 | 67 | – | 142 |
| *Monarca* | 101 | 154 | – | 255 |
| *Montañés* | 20 | 29 | – | 49 |
| *Neptuno* | 42 | 47 | [some] | 89 |
| *Principe de Asturias* | 52 | 110 | – | 162 |
| *Rayo* | 4 | 14 | – | 18 |
| *San Augustin* | 184 | 201 | – | 385 |
| *San Francisco de Asis* | 5 | 12 | – | 17 |
| *San Ildefonso* | 34 | 126 | – | 160 |
| *San Juan Nepomuceno* | 103 | 131 | – | 234 |
| *San Justo* | – | 7 | – | 7 |
| *San Leandro* | 8 | 22 | – | 30 |
| *Santa Ana* | 97 | 141 | – | 238 |
| *Santisima Trinidad* | 205 | 108 | [some] | 313 |
| **Totals** | **1,033** | **1,371** | **[some]** | **2,404** |

*Comments*

• Spanish battle casualties totalled around 2,404 compared with 2,835 French. Thus the Combined Fleet's losses in terms of killed and wounded is estimated at 5,239. Undoubtedly some Spaniards were drowned but they are not specified in any returns, however, the number would be considerably less than the French, perhaps 400 or so. The Spanish crews numbered around 12,000 so their casualty rate was 20 per cent in the battle, 23 per cent if the notional figure of 400 drowned is added – a similar figure to the French casualty rate.

• The casualty rate varied enormously between ships. Three ships had over 300 casualties and another three well over 200. The *San Augustin* with 385 lost 54 per cent of her complement, and the *Santisima Trinidad* lost 30 per cent – high but not excessively so considering the intensity and closeness of the firing. In contrast the *San Justo*, with no one killed and only seven wounded, had the least casualties in the Combined Fleet. Perhaps most deserving of criticism was the three-decker, 100-gun *Rayo* under the Irish Commodore Macdonell, whose lack of engagement in the battle is reflected by her four killed and 14 wounded.

• The average battle losses for Spanish ships were 160, remarkably similar to the French 157 (discounting the *Achille*). If those with over 100 casualties are taken then the average rises to 244, slightly higher than the French 223.

• In summary Villeneuve's fleet lost approximately 8,000 at the battle and as a consequence of the storm in the days immediately afterwards. They are made up as follows:

| | Killed | Wounded | Drowned | Total |
|---|---|---|---|---|
| French | 1,425 | 1,410 | 2,296 | 5,131 |
| Spanish | 1,033 | 1,371 | 400 (E) | 2,804 |
| **Totals** | **2,458** | **2,781** | **2,696** | **7,935** |

## The British Fleet: Ships

While no British ships struck, a considerable number were in no fit condition to fight or sail at the end of the battle. No fewer than seven ships were so damaged that they had to be towed, and another four were severely damaged. This represents 41 per cent of the fleet – testimony to the fact that many of their French and Spanish adversaries fought hard. Nevertheless, 14 ships were only lightly damaged and remained, with running repairs, fully effective warships. The table below lists Nelson's ships under three categories of damage. Those with (T) after their name required a tow.

| Unmanageable/severe damage | Moderate damage | Light damage |
|---|---|---|
| *Africa* (T) | *Achille* | *Agamemnon* |
| *Belleisle* (T) | *Britannia* | *Ajax* |
| *Bellerophon* (T) | | *Conqueror* |
| *Colossus* | | *Defence* |
| *Defiance* | | *Dreadnought* |
| *Mars* | | *Leviathan* |
| *Revenge* | | *Minotaur* |
| *Royal Sovereign* (T) | | *Neptune* |
| *Téméraire* (T) | | *Orion* |
| *Tonnant* (T) | | *Polyphemus* |
| *Victory* (T) | | *Prince* |
| | | *Spartiate* |
| | | *Swiftsure* |
| | | *Thunderer* |

*Comments*
- In percentage terms 41 per cent were severely damaged, 7 per cent moderately and 52 per cent lightly. However, only three of the severely damaged ships (*Victory, Téméraire* and *Africa*) were in Nelson's column. This is largely attributable to the fact that none of Dumanoir's van squadron got into the action until around 2.30 p.m. and even then a mere three out of ten joined the central mêlée. Collingwood's column of 14, however, had to engage up to 16 enemy ships.
- Inevitably, the ships who reached the enemy line first had to fight hardest and longest and suffered accordingly. As Dumanoir sailed away from the battle in the centre Villeneuve had no support. Nelson, although initially outnumbered, was steadily reinforced until by one o'clock he outnumbered his enemies in the centre.

## The British Fleet: Casualties

Records of British losses are not difficult to obtain, as no ship was wrecked so virtually no men were lost by drowning.

| Ship | Killed | Wounded | Total |
|---|---|---|---|
| **Nelson's column** | | | |
| *Victory* | 57 | 102 | 159 |
| *Téméraire* | 47 | 76 | 123 |
| *Neptune* | 10 | 44 | 54 |
| *Leviathan* | 4 | 22 | 26 |
| *Conqueror* | 3 | 9 | 12 |
| *Britannia* | 10 | 42 | 52 |
| *Africa* | 18 | 44 | 62 |
| *Ajax* | 2 | 9 | 11 |
| *Agamemnon* | 2 | 8 | 10 |
| *Orion* | 1 | 23 | 24 |
| *Minotaur* | 3 | 22 | 25 |
| *Spartiate* | 3 | 20 | 23 |
| **Sub-total** | **161** | **377** | **538** |
| | | | |
| **Collingwood's column** | | | |
| *Royal Sovereign* | 47 | 94 | 141 |
| *Belleisle* | 33 | 93 | 126 |
| *Mars* | 29 | 69 | 98 |
| *Tonnant* | 26 | 50 | 76 |
| *Bellerophon* | 27 | 123 | 150 |
| *Colossus* | 40 | 160 | 200 |
| *Achille* | 13 | 59 | 72 |
| *Revenge* | 28 | 51 | 79 |
| *Defiance* | 17 | 53 | 70 |
| *Swiftsure* | 17 | 8 | 25 |
| *Dreadnought* | 7 | 26 | 33 |
| *Polyphemus* | 2 | 4 | 6 |
| *Thunderer* | 4 | 12 | 16 |
| *Defence* | 7 | 29 | 36 |
| *Prince* | 0 | 0 | 0 |
| **Sub-total** | **297** | **831** | **1,128** |
| **Totals** | **458** | **1,208** | **1,666** |

*Comments*
- There were no losses on any British frigate, schooner or cutter.
- Collingwood had only three more ships than Nelson but more than twice the losses. In terms of ship average Collingwood had 75 per ship and Nelson 45 – still a large difference. The casualty figures support the damage sustained. Collingwood's column had a tougher battle than Nelson's.

- The ratio of killed to wounded in the British Fleet was 1:2.6.
- Overall the British Fleet suffered some 10 per cent casualties from a complement of just over 17,000 – remarkably low. The average losses per ship were 62. *Colossus* with 200 had the highest, while the *Prince* was the only ship-of-the-line to have none at all.
- Six ships received over 100 casualties, two in Nelson's column (*Victory* and *Téméraire*) and four in Collingwood's (*Royal Sovereign, Belleisle, Bellerophon* and *Colossus*). Their 899 losses represent 54 per cent of the total for the fleet.

**Comparison of Battle Losses: British and Combined Fleets**
Overall the Combined Fleet sustained just over three times as many battle losses as the British.

| | British Fleet | Combined Fleet |
|---|---|---|
| Total killed | 458 | 2,458 |
| Total wounded | 1,208 | 2,781 |
| Total casualties | 1,666 | 5,239 |
| Ratio killed:wounded | 1:2.6 | 1:1.13 |
| Average losses per ship | 62 | 158 |
| Average losses for ships with over 100 | 150 | 255 |
| Losses as % of total fleet strength | 10 | 20 |
| Admirals killed/mortally wounded | 1 | 2 |
| Admirals wounded | 1 | 3 |
| Commodores/captains killed | 2 | 10 |
| Commodores/captains wounded | 4 | 10 |

### Senior Officer Casualties

| Admirals killed/ mortally wounded | Commodores/ captains killed | Commodores/ captains wounded |
|---|---|---|
| **British:** Nelson **French:** Magon **Spanish:** Gravina | **British:** Cooke, Duff | **British:** Durham, Moorsom, Morris, Tyler |
| **Admirals wounded** | **French:** Hubert, Baudouin, Poulain, Gourrège, Le | **French:** Magendie, Prigny, Lucas |
| **British:** Collingwood **Spanish:** Alava, Escano, Cisneros | Tourneur, Denieport, Camas **Spanish:** Galiano, Alcedo and Churruca | **Spanish:** Valdes, Cajigal, Uriate, Gardoqui, Argumosa, Pareja, Vargas |

### *Victory*'s Foretopsail

The largest single artefact remaining from the battle is *Victory*'s foretopsail, which measures 80 feet along the base, 54 feet at the head (top) and 54 feet deep, giving an area of 3,618 square feet. It is heavily pock-marked by some ninety shot holes and a much larger hole made by nineteenth-century souvenir hunters. In 1995 the Carpet Conservation Workshop at Salisbury took over preservation work and the collection of historical data from the sail, funded by the Society of Nautical Research. It was last seen by the public during the Festival of the Sea in 1997.

The intention is to display the sail as part of the 2005 celebrations, when it is hoped it will be fully opened, supported by a foretopsail yard with the foot spread on a fore yard. It will be rigged with standing and running rigging, associated blocks, deadeyes, foot-ropes and fittings. The public should be able to see it as it was during the action, although probably inside a large glass case with temperature and humidity control.

Information from www.hms-victory.com

# The Aftermath

*Silence is now upon the seas,*
*The stormy seas of yore;*
*The thunder of the cannonade*
*Awakes the wave no more!*

Anon

## AFTER THE BATTLE

### THE STORM

When the guns fell quiet on 21 October 1805, the British were left in possession of seventeen ships from the Combined Fleet and thousands of prisoners, representing enormous potential riches for the British crews. All the captured vessels required a prize crew on board and most needed a tow; arrangements for towing were made as follows:

| Prize | Towed by |
| --- | --- |
| Bucentaure | Conqueror |
| Fougueux | Phoebe |
| Intrépide | Ajax |
| Redoutable | Swiftsure (British) |
| Swiftsure (French) | Dreadnought |
| Berwick | Britannia |
| Santisima Trinidad | Prince |
| San Augustin | Leviathan |
| Neptuno | Minotaur |
| Santa Ana | Thunderer |
| Monarca | Achille |
| Bahama | Orion |
| San Ildefonso | Defence |
| Argonauta | Polyphemus |
| Aigle | uncertain |

The remaining two ships (*Algéciras* and *San Juan Nepomuceno*) were thought able to sail of their own accord with just a prize crew on board.

It was not only Combined Fleet ships that needed a tow immediately after the firing ceased. The *Royal Sovereign* had to be put under tow by the *Euryalus*, to which Collingwood transferred his flag, and later by the *Neptune*. The *Téméraire* was towed by *Sirius*, the *Belleisle* by the *Naiad*, the *Tonnant* by the *Spartiate* and *Colossus* by *Agamemnon*. This enormous, unwieldy fleet set sail for Gibraltar, the nearest British territory.

But the day after the battle the heavy swell began to develop into an increasingly violent storm. Soon former enemies were struggling side by side on the same ship to man pumps and make repairs as tons of water poured in through shot holes and huge waves crashed over the decks. Cables broke, ships were driven away from each other and on the 24th Collingwood decided that some captured ships that had broken away from their towing ship should be scuttled rather than allow the possibility of their escape. His letter written off Cadiz that day states:

> ... the bad weather continuing, determined me to destroy all the leewardmost [captured ships] that could be cleared of the men, considering that keeping possession of the Ships was a matter of little consequence compared with the chance of their falling again into the hands of the enemy: but even this was an arduous task in the high sea which was running.

In accordance with this order the *Intrépide* and *San Augustin* were set on fire to finish them off, while the *Argonauta* and the shattered hulk of the huge *Santisima Trinidad* were scuttled. The *Redoutable* went down without assistance while still under tow by the *Swiftsure*, and the *Monarca* too ran aground, totally dismasted. Of the enemy ships that broke free from their tow only the *Santa Ana* was to see the inside of Cadiz harbour. In order to prevent the violence of the wind driving them onto the lee shore, ships needed to anchor – as Nelson had insisted just before he died – but many had had their anchors and cables shot away during the battle, and the length and fury of the squalls made even anchors in good condition drag and lose their moorings. With brief periods of respite, the storms began on 22 October and continued until the 29th, destroying nine ships and drowning upwards of 2,700 men. Their savagery is not apparent from most ships' logs. One of the most comprehensive

## Experiences of the Prize Crew on the *Monarca*

The *Monarca* was wrecked during the storm off San Lucar, at which time there was a prize crew from the *Bellerophon* on board. A young midshipman later wrote of his experiences during that time.

You will imagine what have been our sufferings, in a crippled ship, with 500 prisoners on board and only 55 Englishmen, most of whom were in a constant state of intoxication. We rolled away all our masts except the foremast; were afterwards forced to cut away 2 anchors, heave overboard several guns, shot &c. to lighten her; and were, after all [that], in such imminent danger of sinking that, seeing no ship near to assist us, we at length determined to run the ship on shore on the Spanish coast, which we should have done had not the *Leviathan* fortunately fallen in with us and saved us, and all but about 150 Spaniards. The ship went ashore and was afterwards destroyed.

In a letter dated 2 December 1805 published in a Portsmouth newspaper, a midshipman (probably the same one) described his feelings on the *Monarca* before she was abandoned.

saved by the *Leviathan,* with all but 150 prisoners who were afraid of getting into the boats. I can assure you I felt not the least fear of death during the action, which I attribute to the general confidence of victory which I saw all round me; but in the prize, when I was in danger of and had time to reflect upon the approach of death, either from the rising up of the Spaniards ... or of what latterly appeared inevitable, from the violence of the storm. I was most certainly afraid, and at one time, when the ship made three feet of water in ten minutes, when our people were almost all lying drunk upon the deck, ... when the Spaniards [through exhaustion] would no longer work the only chain pump left serviceable ... I wrapped myself up in a Union Jack, and lay down upon the deck for a short time, quietly awaiting the approach of death ...

was that kept by Mr Ruckert, master of the *Euryalus*. Of the weather he wrote:

*Tuesday, October 22nd*
A.M. ... at noon, strong gales and cloudy with heavy rain ... P.M. ... Strong breezes and hazy; rain. ... At 4 strong gales and rain. ... At 8, ditto gales with heavy squalls and rain. ... At 12, do. weather ...
*Wednesday, October 23rd*
A.M. Do. weather with heavy squalls. The fore topmast staysail split and blown away by a heavy squall from the westward. ... Weather more moderate. ... At 8, heavy rain and squally. P.M. Variable and cloudy. ... At 5.30, ... strong breezes and rain, and a heavy swell from the westward. ... At 8, strong gales with rain and a heavy squall. ... From 10 to 11.45, heavy gales and rain. At 12, a little more moderate.
*Thursday, October 24th*
A.M. Ditto gales and rain. ... At noon, strong breezes and cloudy. P. M. At noon moderate and appeared for fine weather. ... Employed destroying the prizes between Cadiz and St. Lucia [San Lucar]. At 5.30, shortened sail and hove to. Sent Lieut. [John] Williams, the carpenter [Mr Thomas Parrott], and his crew, with 30 men on board the *Santisima Trinidad*, Spanish 4-decker, to destroy her. Sounded in 20 fathoms. At 9.15, boats returned. ... At 10.30 strong breezes and squally, with rain.
*Friday, October 25th*
A.M. At 4, strong breezes, and squalls with heavy rain from the southward and westward. At 8, ditto gales ... At 9.45 ... Heavy gales, and thick weather with rain ...
P.M. Heavy gales and thick with rain, and a heavy swell from the southward. At 12.15, the spritsail yard carried away by a heavy sea with all the rigging belonging to it ... At 8, more moderate... At 12, fresh gales and a great swell.
*Saturday, October 26th*
A.M. At 8, ditto gales. At 9.45 ... Heavy gales, and thick weather with rain. At noon, strong gales with heavy swell. ... P.M. Heavy gales, and thick with rain. At 4, ditto gales and rain. ... At 12, fresh gales and a great swell.

Superhuman efforts were made by British crews to save the lives of prize and enemy crews from sinking ships. Eyewitness accounts survive of the final moments of the greatest prize of all, the *Santisima Trinidad*, and they are quoted here in full. The two British witnesses are Midshipman William Badcock of the *Neptune* and Lieutenant John Edwards of the *Prince*.

Badcock:

I was sent on board the *Santisima Trinidad* a few days after the action to assist in getting out the wounded men previous to destroying her. She was a magnificent ship, and ought now to be in Portsmouth Harbour. Her top-sides it is true were perfectly riddled by our firing, and she had, if I recollect right, 550 killed and wounded [in fact, just over 300], but from the lower part of the sills of the lower-deck ports to the water's edge, a few shot of consequence had hurt her between wind and water, and those were all plugged up. She was built of cedar, and would have lasted for ages, a glorious trophy of the battle, but 'sink, burn and destroy' was the order of the day, and after a great deal of trouble [the *Euryalus*' log reckons it took some four hours], scuttling her in many places, hauling up her lower-deck ports – that when she rolled a heavy sea might fill her decks – she did at last unwillingly go to the bottom.

Edwards:

All the necessary signals were made to leave the prizes, and we, being effective, took the *Trinidad*, the largest ship in the world, in tow ... . Before four in the morn it blew so strong that we broke the hawsers twice, and from two such immense bodies as we were, found it difficult to secure her again; however, every exertion was made, and we got her again. By eight in the morning it blew a hurricane on the shore, and so close in that we could not weather the land either way ... After driving about four days [it was three] without any prospect of saving the ship or the gale abating, the signal was made to destroy the prizes. We had no time before to remove the prisoners, and it now became a most dangerous task; no boats could lie alongside, we got under her stern, and the men dropped in by ropes; but what a sight when we came to remove the wounded, which were between three and four hundred [actually about 108]. We had to tie the poor mangled wretches round their waists, or where we could, and lower them down into a tumbling boat, some without arms, others no legs, and lacerated all over in the most dreadful manner. About ten o'clock we had got all out but about thirty-three or four, which I believe it was impossible to remove without instant death. The water was now at the pilot deck, the weather deck, and boisterous, and taking in tons at every roll, when we quitted her, and supposed this superb ship could not remain afloat longer than ten minutes. Perhaps she sunk in less time, with the unfortunate victims, never to rise again.

The Spanish witness is the fictional character created by Perez Galdos in his book *Trafalgar*. His description of the terrifying conditions on the ship during her last few hours was composed from documents and letters of survivors.

Night fell, increasing the horror of our situation. ... A tremendous storm burst and the winds and waves tossed and buffeted our ship in their fury, while as she could not be worked, she was utterly at their mercy. The rolling was so terrible that it was very difficult even to work the pumps; and this combined with the exhausted condition of the men, made our condition grow worse every minute. An English vessel, which we learnt was the *Prince*, tried to take us in tow, but her efforts were in vain and she was forced to keep off for fear of a collision, which would have been fatal to both.

The same confusion prevailed below as on deck. On one side, covered with the Spanish flag, lay the bodies of the officers who had been killed; and in the midst of all this misery, surrounded by so much suffering, these poor corpses seemed really to be envied. ...

Never shall I forget the moment when the bodies were cast into the sea, by order of the English officer in charge of the ship. The dismal ceremony took place on the morning of the 22nd, when the storm seemed to be at its wildest ... The bodies of the officers were brought on deck, the priest said a short prayer ... . Each wrapped in a flag, with a cannonball tied to his feet, was dropped into the waves without any solemn or painful emotion. ... The sailors were thrown overboard with less ceremony. The regulation is that they shall be tied up in their hammocks, but there was no time to carry this out. Some indeed were wrapped round as the rules require, but most of them were thrown into the sea without any shroud or ball at their feet, for the simple reason there was not enough for all. ...

As the day advanced the *Prince* attempted once more to take the *Santisima Trinidad* in tow, but with no better success than before. Our situation was no worse, although the tempest raged with undiminished fury, for a good deal of the mischief had been patched up, and we thought that if the weather should mend, the hulk, at any rate, might be saved. The English made a great point of it, for they were very anxious to take the largest man-of-war ever seen afloat into Gibraltar as a trophy; so they willingly plied the pumps by

night and day and allowed us to rest awhile. All through the day on the 22nd the sea continued terrific, tossing the huge and helpless vessel as though it were a fishing boat; and the enormous mass of timber proved the soundness of her build by simply not falling to pieces under the furious lashing of the waters. At some moments she rolled so completely over on her beam ends that it seemed she must go to the bottom ... . Floating about were myriad fragments and masses of wreck – spars, timbers, broken boats, hatches, bulwarks and doors – besides two unfortunate sailors who were clinging to a plank, and who must have been swept off and drowned if the English had not hastened to rescue them.

It was decided that the ship would be scuttled, and the witness continued to describe the evacuation.

We set to work promptly with the launches of the *Trinidad* and *Prince*, and three other boats belonging to the English. The wounded were attended first, but though they were lifted with all possible care they could not be moved without much suffering, and some entreated with groans and shrieks to be left in peace, preferring immediate death to anything that could aggravate and prolong their torments. But there was no time for pity, and they were carried to the boats as ruthlessly as the cold corpses of their comrades had been flung into the sea.

I thought only of saving my life, and to stay on board a foundering vessel was not the best means to that end. Nor were my fears ill-founded; for not more than half the men had been taken off when a dull roar of terror echoed through the ship. 'She's going to the bottom! – to the boats, to the boats!' shouted some, and there was a rush to the ship's side, all looking out eagerly for the return of the boats. Every attempt at work or order was given up, the wounded were forgotten, and several who had been brought on deck dragged themselves to the side in a sort of delirium, to seek an opening and throw themselves into the sea. Up through the hatchways came a hideous shriek, which I think I can hear as I write. It came from the poor wretches on the lower deck, who already felt the waters rising to drown them and vainly cried for help to God or men – who can tell? Vainly indeed to men, for they had enough to do to save themselves. They jumped wildly into the boats ...

Despite the double defeat of the Combined Fleet – first by British guns, then by Atlantic gales – some captains still displayed commendable initiative in trying to retrieve something from the disaster. Foremost of these was Captain Cosmao-Kerjulien of the 74-gun *Pluton*. He had succeeded in reaching Cadiz on 22 October after anchoring during the night of 21/22 October off Rota. In his report to the Minister of Marine he explains events after the battle.

We stood north and in the course of the same night we anchored off Rota bay; the wind blowing a strong gale from the south-south-west prevented me from making any movement ...

In the night I heard signals of distress fired from the coast to the south; I was myself in danger of being cast away, two cables having parted and only one anchor holding, whose cable I knew to be much damaged; my boats having been shattered in the battle I found it impossible to render any assistance ... .

[the next day] The weather lifting, I sighted two dismasted ships offshore, one being towed by an English line-of-battle ship … . I immediately decided to hoist a senior officer's pendant and, in spite of the bad condition of my ship – which was leaking a great deal from the large number of shot-holes between wind and water, and my masts being barely secure – I made the signal to weigh and follow me. I got out followed by the French ships *Neptune* and *Héros* and by the Spanish ships *Rayo* and *San Francisco Asis* [the *Indomptable* also followed]. At our approach the English ship cast off the tow and made off. I directed the frigates to escort these ships, which were the three-decker *Santa Ana*, having Lieut.-General Alava on board, and the *Neptuno* [she was in fact wrecked]… . I did not think it my duty to run the risk of a skirmish, seeing the bad state of the ships which composed the division. We re-entered the bay, my ship in a sinking condition …

It was a brave sortie aimed at recovering some of the captured or disabled ships. Collingwood responded by collecting ten of his most serviceable ships to form a line a battle, and Cosmao wisely withdrew. However, perhaps understandably, he neglected to mention in his report that although he was able to bring in the *Santa Ana* the weather was too much for the *Indomptable*, *Neptuno* and *San Francisco de Asis* – all of which ended up wrecked or ashore around Rota. Additionally the *Rayo* got into severe difficulties, losing her masts and then being captured, only to be abandoned by the British and allowed to run ashore. Only four prizes eventually arrived at Gibraltar (the French *Swiftsure*, *Bahama*, *San Ildefonso* and *San Juan Nepomuceno*). Atrocious weather had deprived the victors of the spoils of war.

If most British crews behaved honourably and gallantly in doing their best to rescue enemy wounded and crews from stricken ships the same must be said of the Spaniards ashore in their endeavours to save prize crews of wrecked ships. Two examples will suffice. The first, by Captain Codrington of the *Orion*, concerns his master, Mr Cass Halliday, who was taken ashore from the wreck of the *Rayo*.

> The poor Spaniards behaved very credible indeed: they not only sent boats for them (English and all) as soon as the weather moderated, with bread and water for their immediate relief; but when the boat, in which the Master

of the ship was sent, had got into Cadiz harbour a carriage was backed into the water for him to step into from the boat, all sorts of cordials and confectionery were placed in the carriage for him, and clean linen, bed etc. prepared for him at a lodging on shore. … had he been wrecked on any part of the English coast he would never have received half the attention which he did from these poor Spaniards, whose friends we had just destroyed in such large numbers.

The second account is by a seaman of the *Spartiate* who was a member of a prize crew on a Spanish ship that was sunk – possibly the *Argonauta*, which had a lieutenant, four midshipmen and twenty seamen on board when she was scuttled. After he got ashore he was extremely well treated.

> [His former prisoners] came down to assist us, which they did, for they brought us some bread, and some figs, and some wine, to refresh us, which we wanted very much … the Spaniards behaved very kind to us. … [A Spanish man] lifted me up into one of the bullock-carts in which they had brought down the provisions for us, and covered me up with one of their great ponchos, and he tapped me on the shoulder, and said 'Bono English!' … I heard afterwards the French soldiers came down and marched the rest of my shipmates up to Cadiz, and put them into the Spanish prison. … I was taken up to Cadiz in the bullock-cart and my kind friend took me to his own house, and had me put to bed …

Collingwood paid great attention to alleviating the suffering of his wounded prisoners. Six days after the battle, with the storm abating somewhat, he wrote to the Spanish governor in Cadiz.

> *Euryalus*, off Cadiz, October 27, 1805
> My Lord Marquis
> A great number of Spanish subjects having been wounded in the late action between the British and the combined fleets of Spain and France, on the 21st instant, humanity, and my desire to alleviate the sufferings of these wounded men, dictate to me to offer to Your Excellency their enlargement, that they may be taken proper care of in the hospitals on shore provided Your Excellency will send

## The Final Hours of the *Intrépide*

Lieutenant des Touches had been among the last of the crew of the *Intrépide* to be removed from the stricken ship by a boat from the *Orion*, along with his captain, Infernet. The *Intrépide* had put up a magnificent fight against ever-mounting odds and had been the last ship of the Combined Fleet to surrender. Des Touches' description highlights the horror on board as they struggled to evacuate the wounded amid a breakdown of discipline.

> in the half-darkness, while the tempest was still gathering its forces, we had to pass through a leeward gunport more than eighty wounded who were incapable of movement. With infinite trouble we did it, by means of a bed-frame and capstan bars. We were then taken in tow by an English frigate [possibly *Phoebe*], which we followed, rolling from side to side and making water everywhere. At a certain point I noticed that the work of the pumps was slowing down, and I was told

> that the door of the storeroom had been forced and that everybody, French and English, had rushed there to get drunk. When I got to these men, reduced to the state of brutes, a keg of brandy had just been broken and the liquor was running along the deck and was lapping the base of a candle that had been put there. I only just had time to stamp out the flame, and in the darkness threatening voices were raised against me … With kicks and punches I made them get out of the storeroom, I barricaded the door, and reached an understanding with the English officer to avert the danger which seemed imminent.
>
> … I wished to stay on the *Intrépide* up to the last agonized minute of one of my friends, who had been judged too badly injured to be transferred. He was a sub-lieutenant called Poullain, with whom I was closely connected, and who had begged me not to leave him in the anguish of his last hour. …

# Trafalgar: The Storm, 22–27 October 1805

Map 27

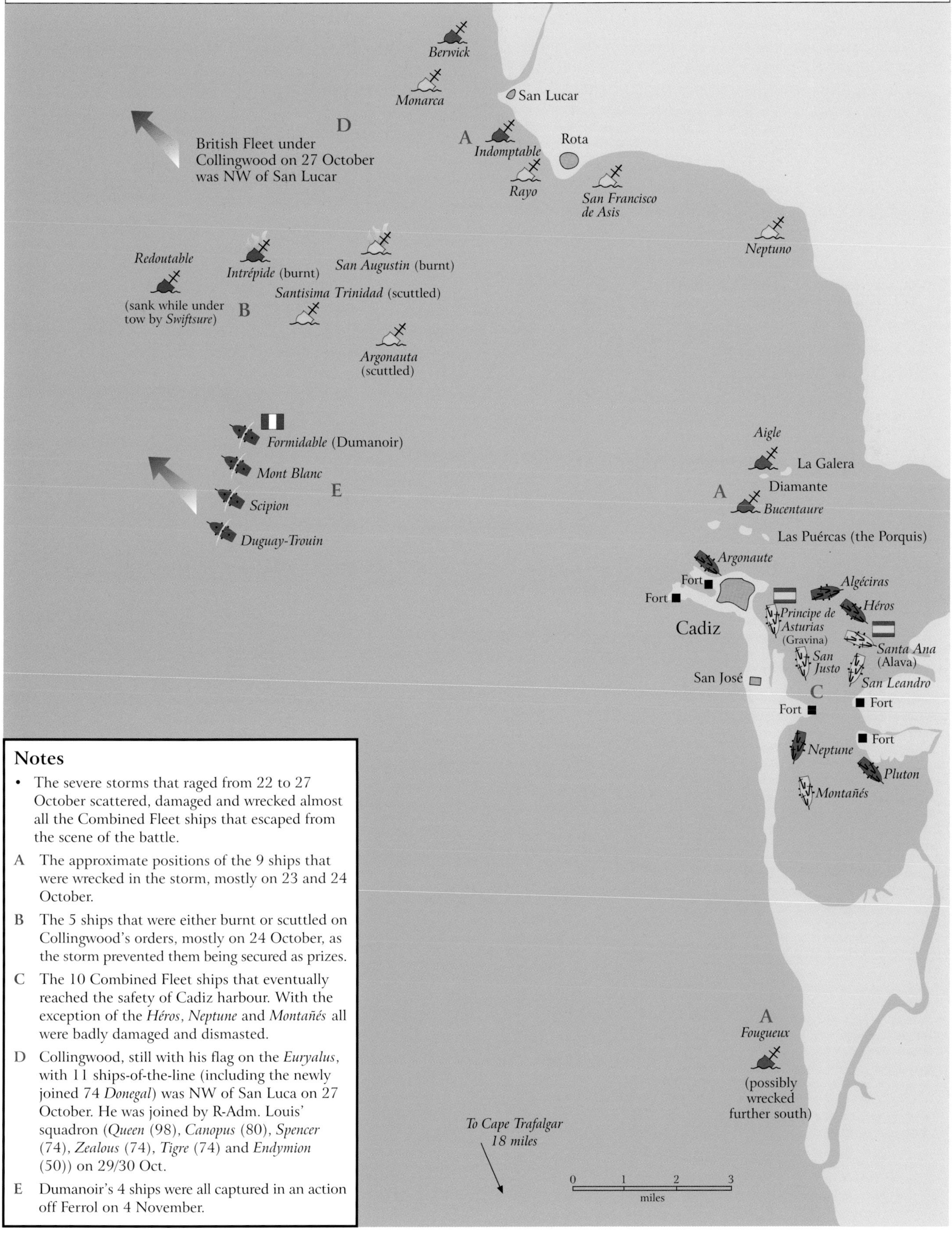

Berwick

Monarca

San Lucar

D

British Fleet under
Collingwood on 27 October
was NW of San Lucar

A

Indomptable

Rota

Rayo

San Francisco
de Asis

Neptuno

Redoutable

Intrépide (burnt)

San Augustin (burnt)

Santisima Trinidad (scuttled)

(sank while under
tow by Swiftsure)

B

Argonauta
(scuttled)

Formidable (Dumanoir)

Mont Blanc

Scipion

E

Duguay-Trouin

Aigle

La Galera

Diamante

A

Bucentaure

Las Puércas (the Porquis)

Argonaute

Fort

Fort

Algéciras

Héros

Principe de
Asturias
(Gravina)

Santa Ana
(Alava)

Cadiz

San
Justo

San Leandro

San José

C

Fort

Fort

Neptune

Fort

Pluton

Montañés

## Notes

- The severe storms that raged from 22 to 27 October scattered, damaged and wrecked almost all the Combined Fleet ships that escaped from the scene of the battle.

**A** The approximate positions of the 9 ships that were wrecked in the storm, mostly on 23 and 24 October.

**B** The 5 ships that were either burnt or scuttled on Collingwood's orders, mostly on 24 October, as the storm prevented them being secured as prizes.

**C** The 10 Combined Fleet ships that eventually reached the safety of Cadiz harbour. With the exception of the *Héros*, *Neptune* and *Montañés* all were badly damaged and dismasted.

**D** Collingwood, still with his flag on the *Euryalus*, with 11 ships-of-the-line (including the newly joined 74 *Donegal*) was NW of San Luca on 27 October. He was joined by R-Adm. Louis' squadron (*Queen* (98), *Canopus* (80), *Spencer* (74), *Zealous* (74), *Tigre* (74) and *Endymion* (50)) on 29/30 Oct.

**E** Dumanoir's 4 ships were all captured in an action off Ferrol on 4 November.

A

Fougueux

(possibly
wrecked
further south)

To Cape Trafalgar
18 miles

0   1   2   3
miles

boats to convey them, with a proper Officer to give receipts for the number, and acknowledge them in Your Excellency's answer to this letter, to be prisoners of war, to be exchanged before they serve again.

I beg to assure Your Excellency of my high consideration, and that                        I am, &. C.COLLINGWOOD
To his Excellency the Marquis de Solana,
Captain General of Andalusia, Governor,
&c., &c., Cadiz.

Significantly, no such consideration was suggested for the French wounded prisoners. The marquis readily accepted Collingwood's proposals and sent a senior officer to the *Euryalus* with authority to sign for the prisoners. The letter he signed is below.

I, Guillame Valverde, having been authorised and empowered by the Marquis de Solana, Governor-General of Andalusia and Cadiz, to receive from the English squadron the wounded prisoners, and such persons as may be necessary to their care [other unwounded prisoners], which release, and enlargement of the wounded &c. is agreed to, on the part of the Commander in Chief of the British squadron, on the positive condition, that none of the said prisoners shall be employed again, in any public service of the crown of Spain, either by sea or land, until they are regularly exchanged.
Signed on board His Britannic Majesty's Ship *Euryalus*, at Sea, 30 October, 1805.

GUILL. DE VALVERDE
Edecan de S. E.

## DUMANOIR'S DEFEAT

As will be recalled, Rear-Admiral Dumanoir le Pelley escaped almost unscathed from the battle with his flagship, the 80-gun Formidable, and three 74s – *Duguay-Trouin*, *Mont Blanc* and *Scipion*. His intention was to head for Toulon, Villeneuve's original destination on leaving Cadiz. However, on 22 October he reversed his decision, remembering that Rear-Admiral Louis' stronger squadron was probably in or near the Straits. With the storm gathering strength he altered course to the west, with the aim of clearing Cape St Vincent and steering north-west before finally swinging east across the Bay of Biscay to Rochefort. Like the other survivors of Trafalgar his already battle-damaged ships suffered several days of heavy pounding. On 2 November his exhausted crews entered

the Bay of Biscay. When about 40 miles north of Cape Ortegal (north-west Spain), with Rochefort still 350 miles away, he spotted a British frigate – the 36-gun *Phoenix* under Captain Thomas Baker. Dumanoir turned to attack. Baker, however, deliberately lured the French south towards Captain Sir Richard Strachan's squadron of five ships-of-the-line cruising off Ferrol. Strachan's flag was at the masthead of the 80-gun *Caesar* and with him were the 74s *Bellona*, *Hero*, *Namur* and *Courageux*. Although it was late at night on 2 November before Strachan was informed of the proximity of the French ships, and his own squadron was somewhat scattered, he immediately set course for the enemy with the *Caesar* while sending the *Phoenix* to round up the others.

By dawn on 4 November the wind was moderate from the south-east and the leading British line-of-battle ship was six miles astern of the nearest French ship, the *Scipion*. Strachan had with him his own ship, the *Caesar*, and the *Hero* and *Courageux*, with the *Namur* trailing some distance astern. He also had four frigates of which two (the 36-gun *Santa Margarita* and *Phoenix*) were well ahead, intent on harassing the *Scipion* at long range. The 32-gun *Aeolus* was with the battleships and the 38-gun *Revolutionaire* close to the *Namur*; the *Bellona* was not up with the squadron. Dumanoir was hoping to avoid action. His ships were battered by the storm, his crews depleted and exhausted, with the inevitable results of slow reactions and sluggish sailing. Even more importantly, he was heavily out-gunned. The *Formidable* had three guns dismounted at Trafalgar and, to lighten her load, had jettisoned twelve quarterdeck 12-pounders during the chase, leaving her 65 guns instead of 80. In total Dumanoir's squadron mounted 287 guns at most, whereas Strachan could count on 444 – ships-of-the-line 302, frigates 142.

Throughout the morning the British ships, aided by a shifting and slackening breeze, overhauled the French. By 10.00 a.m. the situation was approximately as shown opposite top left, with the frigates closing to yaw repeatedly to deliver broadsides into the *Scipion* and *Mont Blanc*. According to Captain Berrenger of the *Scipion*, the *Santa Margarita* and *Phoenix* had by then been in action for half an hour. 'At 9.30 the foremost frigates opened fire on us; we replied with our stern-chasers and with several of the starboard quarter-guns.' Snapping at the heels of their more powerful enemy from astern, these frigates gave a classic demonstration of how to damage and delay an enemy while avoiding the full weight of return broadsides. Ten years before in the Gulf of Genoa Nelson had harried the French 80-gun *Ça Ira* in the same manner with the same success (see p. 116).

---

## Vice-Admiral Decrès' Report to Napoleon

Decrès, in his undated report, puts the blame for defeat squarely on the actions of Dumanoir. It was this report that triggered the eventual Court of Enquiry on Dumanoir's behaviour at Trafalgar. Extracts are given below.

Everything that the Admiral [Villeneuve] had foreseen concerning the enemy took place, and if Rear-Admiral Dumanoir did not execute all the measures that he [Villeneuve] had prescribed for the defence, he is culpable. ...

It is clear that if this signal [for the van to come about] had to be made and if the division in the van was able to

anticipate it, the Commanding Officer of this van did not carry out the Instructions quoted above, which directed him to go to the assistance of the ships assailed and to close on the Admiral.

It is to this cause that the flag-captain of the *Bucentaure* [Magendie] attributes the disaster of the Fleet, and Captains Villemandrin, Lucas and Infernet have expressed the same opinion to me verbally. ...

To have stretched ahead [sailed on] when the Admiral had been engaged, dismasted and forced to surrender, is a crime in those who have acted so. ...

# Dumanoir's Defeat by Captain Strachan, 4 November 1805

## A – About 10.00 a.m.

### Notes

Dumanoir's squadron is in line abreast pursued by Strachan's four 74s and four frigates. The French ships have suffered substantial damage at Trafalgar and during the storm. Strachan's leading frigates are able to fire broadsides into *Scipion*, who can only reply with stern-chasers.

## B – About 11.30 a.m.

### Notes

Dumanoir has ordered line ahead on starboard tack with the British to windward. Shortly before noon action begins between the British and the rear ships of the French line. Strachan's leading frigates continue to harry *Scipion*.

## C – About 12.15 p.m.

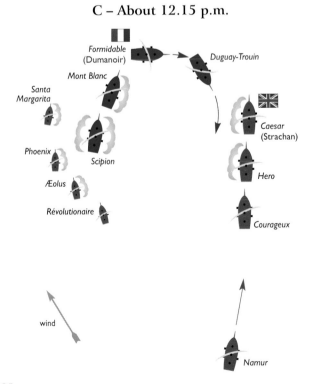

### Notes

Dumanoir orders his line to tack in succession. All four British frigates are now in the action and *Namur* is approaching.

## D – About 12.45–1.15 p.m.

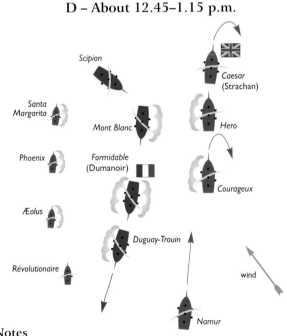

### Notes

The two opposing lines pass close to each other in opposite directions with the French hoping to cut off and concentrate on *Namur*. However, the British have doubled Dumanoir's line with the frigates to leeward. Strachan then orders his line to turn together. By this time the French, with the exception of the *Duguay-Trouin*, have suffered considerable damage and slowed.

## Dumanoir's Defeat by Captain Strachan

### E – About 1.30 p.m.

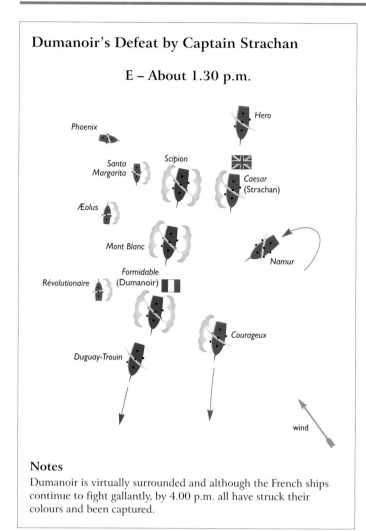

**Notes**

Dumanoir is virtually surrounded and although the French ships continue to fight gallantly, by 4.00 p.m. all have struck their colours and been captured.

arrived was one of the supposed misjudgements Dumanoir had to defend at his court martial. By around 11.30 a.m. Strachan, leading two of his three battleships, had come up and was starting to attack the centre and rear of Dumanoir's line. The *Duguay-Trouin* was left out of the action. Dumanoir again signalled to 'tack in succession preserving the order'. He wanted his line of battle on the larboard tack and foresaw the attack was threatening his rear and that his leading ship would be excluded, or take time to rejoin. Dumanoir was annoyed to see the *Duguay-Trouin* make no change of course. He repeated his signal but it was not until about 12.15 p.m. that his leading ship began to come round. By then some three-quarters of an hour had been lost, and the enemy frigates were engaging the *Scipion* and *Mont Blanc* from leeward while three of their line-of-battle ships had closed up.

Dumanoir wanted his line to come about before all four of Strachan's squadron had come up, and he wanted to cut off the *Namur*. He had abandoned all thought of escaping. His intention was to secure some advantage for the coming battle, to drive away the enemy frigates and concentrate all his ships before his enemy could do the same. The effect of the delay in coming about was that both squadrons passed within pistol shot of each other sailing on opposite tacks. Both lines fired into each other as they passed. Dumanoir held to his new course to isolate the *Namur*. For perhaps half an hour action virtually ceased as the squadrons drew apart. Strachan now needed to come round so gave the order to tack together. There was some delay and confusion. At this time, Strachan wrote in his dispatch, 'the *Namur* joined soon after we tacked, which we did as soon as we could get the Ships round, and I directed her by signal to engage the van'. By 1.30 p.m. the situation was approximately as shown left. The *Namur* had joined the line astern of the *Courageux* and the French line was doubled with British frigates to leeward and battleships to windward. The outcome could never be in doubt. By 3.30 p.m. all French ships had struck and a wounded Dumanoir was a prisoner.

The unequal slugging match was conducted at close range with Dumanoir's ships frequently subjected to broadsides from two directions simultaneously. The circumstances of their final surrender, as described by officers on board, make for interesting reading.

Much earlier that morning Dumanoir had considered ordering his ships to come about in succession to form a line of battle on the larboard tack. He hoisted the signal to do so about 8.00 a.m. but cancelled it before it could be obeyed. Instead, he ordered his squadron to adopt the 'larboard bow and quarter line' (echeloned back on the larboard side). This failure to come about and commence the action before all the ships of the British squadron had

## The Long Life of the *Duguay-Trouin*

After repairs the *Duguay-Trouin* was taken into Royal Naval service and renamed the *Implacable*. Within three years she was in action again, this time serving under the *Victory*, then flying the flag of Admiral Sir James Saumarez, and she captured the Russian ship *Sevolod*. Over thirty years later she was still an active member of the British Fleet, and in 1840 she played her part in the capture of Acre from the Turks. Her captain, Edward Harvey, was awarded a ceremonial sword and the St Jean d'Acre in gold by the Sultan of Turkey for his actions. Harvey was certainly something of an old sea dog. When awarded the Naval General Service Medal in 1848 he was entitled to just two clasps – for the battles of Camperdown and Syria, fought forty-three years apart!

In 1855 the *Implacable* became a training ship alongside the *Lion*, moored off Torpoint, Devonport, and remained so for almost a century. In December 1949 the Admiralty had a surfeit

of Second World War warships that required mothballing. Unfortunately the old *Implacable* was occupying one of the berths needed, and it was decided to sink her. She was towed out to sea some nine miles east of Selsey Bill (east of Portsmouth) and a naval party placed explosive charges in her hold. Both the White Ensign and Tricolour were hoisted. The explosion, when it came, appeared to have little effect. The gallant old lady remained upright, merely settling down in the water by one deck, the flags of the two nations under which she had served still fluttering proudly. Next, a powerful tug, appropriately called the *Alligator*, was summoned from Portsmouth to administer the coup de grace. Several rammings by the tug at speed were needed before the *Implacable* turned turtle and slipped silently below the surface. Those watching fell silent and one would like to think the officers saluted.

*Formidable*, Lieutenant Johannenc, who commanded the lower gundeck:

on opening fire from the lower deck the chain pumps were manned; that these pumps began by flooding the said deck mid-leg deep – at least six inches – and the said pump never ceased working on the opposite side to that engaged throughout the action, which greatly hampered serving the guns both in laying and running them out and in consequence their usual rate of fire was retarded. At four o'clock [almost certainly earlier], when I was summoned to replace the Commander on the forecastle I left the gun-deck with four pieces either dismounted or with their crews mostly killed or wounded, besides the one that had been condemned after the last engagement; that at this time the master-caulker had reported four feet of water in the hold. [After some time on the forecastle Johannenc was ordered by the captain to go below. He found] that many of the men were missing from the crews of the remaining guns who had been killed and were still lying where they fell; attendance on the wounded had been abandoned ... I ordered the master-caulker to report on the water in the hold; not withstanding that the chain-pump with great activity he informed me that there were six feet of water in the hold and that it was gaining continually.

Shortly after this reporting, and with 'two ships firing into us at pistol-range', the *Formidable*'s colours came down.

*Scipion*, Captain Berrenger's report:

Then the action began anew with these three ships and [the] frigates who almost totally dismasted me. My main topmast was shattered; it fell to starboard and a little while later the mizzen-mast fell on the taffrail which prevented me from using the stern-chasers to engage the three frigates ... .

After having been in action at musket range for three hours and forty-five minutes, the *Scipion*, having six feet of water in the hold according to the master-caulker's report; about 200 men disabled, several guns dismounted; ... the remaining masts tottering, all the sails without exception in the same condition; the *Formidable* being in the enemy's possession ... I gave orders to strike it [the colours] at 3.40 in the afternoon.

After the surrender of the *Formidable* and *Scipion* the remaining two ships attempted to escape. They were quickly overhauled and forced to submit.

### An Accident on the *Formidable*

The *Naval Chronicle* of July–December 1805 published the following article.

A MELANCHOLY accident lately happened on board le *Formidable*, of 84 guns [*sic*], Admiral Dumanoir, prize to Rear-Admiral Sir R. Strachan, lying in Hamoaze. As a fine young man, a royal marine, of the *Caesar*, was assisting to pack away the musketry and pistols in the arms chest, and to discharge those loaded, one musket by accident, under the arm of his comrade, went off; the bullet took the top off the thigh bone. He was conveyed to the Royal Naval Hospital. On the Surgeon's examining and probing the wound, he found the bone shattered so much as to form a mortification [become gangrenous], it being supposed the ball was lodged in the pulvis [*sic*]. The poor fellow, almost in the agonies of death, heroically declared he would not have minded being killed in the action – but to die from so foolish an accident was dreadful! He soon expired, and the Coroner's Inquest brought in a verdict of *Accidental Death*.

*Mont Blanc*, Captain Lavillegris' report:

the report from the gun-decks giving 200 men disabled, several guns dismounted, others on both decks with their entire crews out of action; our masts wounded in various places, not a shroud left to secure them; all our sails unserviceable, absolutely stripped of braces, sheets and bowlines; obliged to run free to keep the wind in our tattered sails; the ship threatening to founder, having seven feet of water in the hold, the powder magazine having several tiers of barrels already awash ... the master-caulker and carpenter having also reported that they could not manage to stop up the shot-holes below water; two enemy ships engaging us at point-blank ... the colours were hauled down at 3.50 in the afternoon.

*Duguay-Trouin*, *ensigne de vaisseau* Claude Rigodit's report:

Our loss in men was no less serious; gallant Captain Toufett had been killed at the beginning of the action and the second-in-command, M. Boisnard, severely wounded, MM. Lavenu, Cosse, Guillet and Tocqueville, who had successively commanded the ship, were disabled, and I saw myself within reach of the honour ... when M. Guillet, who had his cheek pierced by a bullet came up to deprive me of it. Half our 18-pounders and those on the upper works were dismounted or silenced by the death of those serving them; our 36-pounder battery alone had suffered but little and promised a prolonged resistance ... .

There was no hope left [after the *Formidable* and *Scipion* struck]; accordingly the *Duguay-Trouin* and the *Mont Blanc* attempted to set sail and quit the scene of action that they could no longer contest; but of our riddled sails nothing remained but the bolt-ropes and we were obliged to determine upon a final effort ...

So lengthy a resistance exasperated the English, who shouted to us to surrender, and very soon they pressed around us so closely that we feared lest we should be boarded from to windward and to leeward at the same moment; however M. Guillet was preparing to repel them when our main and mizzen masts – cut through ten feet above the deck – fell and masked our starboard battery.

The main chains then caught fire and required prompt attention; we had no sails left save the tatters of the foretopsail and the foresail; finally at about half past four we were forced to strike.

All four captured ships eventually took their place in the Royal Navy, while their crews faced an eternity in rotting prison hulks around southern England. The *Duguay-Trouin* continued to serve her new masters for another 144 years before she was finally scuttled (see box p. 532). Strachan reported his losses as:

| | |
|---|---|
| *Caesar* | 4 killed and 25 wounded |
| *Hero* | 10 killed and 51 wounded |
| *Courageux* | 1 killed and 13 wounded |
| *Namur* | 4 killed and 8 wounded |
| *Santa Margarita* | 1 killed and 1 wounded |
| *Revolutionaire* | 2 killed and 6 wounded |
| *Phoenix* | 2 killed and 4 wounded |
| *Aeolus* | 3 wounded |
| **Total** | **135 (24 killed and 111 wounded)** |

This was a very small price to pay for what had been a hard-fought action at extremely close range. The *Hero* seemed to have lived up to her name and borne the brunt of the enemy's fire. The action was an object lesson in the use of frigates, first to delay and harass larger ships from astern, then, in certain favourable circumstances, to join the main action and/or double an enemy line. That they did so on this occasion with so few losses is a remarkable tribute to their captains. This action was considered a part of the Battle of Trafalgar when awards were made.

## COLLINGWOOD'S VICTORY DISPATCH

The day following the battle Collingwood issued two General Orders to the fleet. The first, a very fulsome message, was to be read out on board every ship by its captains.

GENERAL ORDER

*Euryalus*, October 22, 1805

The ever-to-be-lamented death of Lord Visc. Nelson, Duke of Bronte, the Commander-in-Chief, who fell in the action of the 21st, in the arms of victory, covered with glory, whose memory will be ever dear to the British Navy, and the British Nation; whose zeal for the honour of his King, and for the interests of his Country, will be ever held up as a shining example for a British Seaman, – leaves me a duty to return my thanks to the Right Hon. Rear-Admiral [Northesk], the Captains, Officers, Seamen and detachments of Royal Marines serving on board His Majesty's squadron now under my command, for their conduct on that day; but where can I find language to express my sentiments of the valour and skill which were displayed by the Officers, the Seaman, and Marines in the battle with the enemy, where every individual appeared an Hero, on whom the glory of his Country depended; the attack was irresistible, and the issue of it adds to the page of Naval Annals a brilliant instance of what Britons can do, when their King and their Country need their service.

To the Right Honourable Rear-Admiral the Earl of Northesk, to the Captains, the Officers, and Seamen, and to the Officers, Non-commissioned Officers, and Privates of the Royal Marines, I beg to give my sincere and hearty thanks for their highly meritorious conduct, both in the action, and in their zeal and activity in bringing the captured Ships out from the perilous situation in which they were, after their surrender, among the shoals of Trafalgar, in boisterous weather.

And I desire that the respective Captains will be pleased to communicate to the Officers, Seamen, and Royal Marines, this public testimony of my high approbation of their conduct, and my thanks for it.

C. COLLINGWOOD

His second General Order, dated the same day, offered thanks to God for the victory and announced his intention to specify a day during which appropriate prayers and thanks might be made on all ships. However, the fleet had been dispersed by the gales so no date was actually named.

### The *Pickle* carries the dispatch

Not until 6 November, sixteen days after the battle, did the Admiralty in London receive the official news of the dramatic victory and Nelson's death. The officer chosen by Collingwood to carry his dispatch was Lieutenant John Richard Lapenotiere, commanding the schooner *Pickle*. Bringing the official news of a victory to their Lordships was a much-coveted mission, since by custom the officer concerned would receive immediate promotion and a financial reward – and in this case a name in British history books forever.

The morning entry of the *Pickle*'s log for 26 October read:

> A.M. – At 6, out middle jib boom and set the jib. Answered the signal 84 [to pass within hail]. Bore up and made sail towards the Commander-in-Chief. At 9, the Commander went on board of the Commander-in-Chief. At 10, discharged all prisoners into the *Revenge*. ...

It took some considerable time for the *Pickle* to work her way across the heavy seas and through the high wind and lashing rain to close with the *Euryalus* on her lee side. Those on the *Pickle* could just understand the bellowed instruction for the captain to come aboard. The schooner's jolly-boat was lowered and pulled across. As the tiny boat came amidships Lapenotiere, judging his moment with care, leapt into the frigate's entry port as he was lifted by the swell. In Collingwood's cabin he was handed his written instructions, which read:

> By Cuthbert Collingwood
> Vice Admiral of the Blue
> Commanding a squadron of His Majesty's Ships off Cadiz
>
> You are hereby required and directed to proceed in His Majesty's Schooner under your command to England, and on your arrival at Plymouth, you are immediately to forward the accompanying Dispatches to the Secretary of the Admiralty, by taking them yourself express to him, or if Quarantine Laws prevent it, by sending them the moment of your arrival to Vice Admiral Young, for the same purpose.
>
> Should you be prevented by Easterly Winds from fetching so high up as Plymouth, you are to make the first port you can in England, and act as is above directed, taking care to obtain receipts for the dispatches with which you are charged, and which are of the highest importance.
>
> As I trust you are fully aware of the great importance of these dispatches being forwarded as soon as possible, I rely on your using every exertion that a moment's time may not be lost in their delivery.
>
> Given on board the *Euryalus*
> Off Cadiz, 26 October 1805
> Cuthbert Collingwood
> To Lieutenant Lapenotiere
> Commanding His Majesty's Schooner The *Pickle*
> By command of the Vice Admiral
> If necessary, these dispatches are to be thrown overboard, and for which you are to be prepared.

Lapenotiere was then given a covering letter addressed to William Marsden, the Secretary to the Admiralty, which merely stated that the Secretary would receive the admiral's dispatches from Lapenotiere and that duplicates would follow. Next he was handed the sealed packet of dispatches and a number of personal letters, including several from Blackwood to his wife. His ship's log records, 'At noon the boat returned. In boat and made sail for England. The Commander-in-Chief south, 2 miles. Fresh breezes and cloudy with heavy swell from the westward.'

The thirty-five-year-old lieutenant must have been delighted when he realized why he had been called aboard. But why was he chosen, rather than the flag captain, Hardy, or Blackwood or another frigate captain? No doubt the most important factor was speed. The *Pickle* was probably the fastest ship in the fleet with her recently coppered bottom and no battle damage. Lapenotiere had also done this duty previously in the same ship carrying dispatches from Malta in 1803, and Blackwood could not be spared as Collingwood was still, on 26 October, using *Euryalus* as his flagship.

Plymouth was some 1,300 miles from Cadiz. The voyage involved crossing the notorious Bay of Biscay in bad weather and the risk of the tiny ship being intercepted by a more powerful enemy. Dumanoir was still at large, the French Admiral Allemande was at sea, while the hostile ports of Vigo, Corunna, Ferrol and Brest all lay along the route. On her second day (27 October) *Pickle*'s lookout sighted a strange sail and although Lapenotiere tried to outrun her the other vessel was faster and had set a course to intercept. She was soon identified as a ship-rigged sloop, and as the distance closed the *Pickle* hoisted her private identification signal. To her crew's relief the response was No. 451, the number of the 26-gun *Nautilus*. When the ships hove to alongside each other Captain Sykes of the *Nautilus* came aboard the *Pickle* to receive the news. On his return to his own ship Sykes headed for Lisbon to pass the news to a Mr Gambier, the British Consul. This done (via payment to the master of a Portuguese fishing boat), and unknown to Lapenotiere, Sykes set course for England, eager that the *Pickle* should not be the only ship bearing the vital tidings. It had developed into something of a race. Indeed, on 30 October the acting second master of the *Pickle*, Mr George Almy, noted in the log that the *Nautilus* was in sight when both ships were off the Burlings (rocks north-west of Lisbon).

The Bay of Biscay lived up to its foul reputation. Huge seas rolled in from across three thousand miles of Atlantic driven by screaming winds and accompanied by lashing rain. The *Pickle* was constantly rising up almost vertically to the crest of each mountainous wave before plunging sickeningly down to bury her bows in the depths of the trough. Permanently soaked, not a man on board could sleep or rest. The situation became critical on 31 October and 1 November when frantic pumping, plus the use of a human bucket chain for bailing, could not keep pace with the water flooding the forepeak. Lapenotiere began to think his ship might founder. In order to lighten her he ordered four carronades, weighing a ton in total, to be heaved over the side. This helped, but the *Pickle*'s survival

### Collingwood's Truce after the Battle

Collingwood opened negotiations with the Spanish authorities in Cadiz after the storm, by sending Captain Blackwood under a flag of truce to the governor. He was received in a most amicable way, dined and given accommodation overnight in the Governor's residence. Good relations were speedily developed and the Governor, the Marquis de Solana, sent a cask of wine to Collingwood. It was followed by more fruit – melons, grapes, figs and pomegranates. Collingwood returned the courtesy the best he could from his meagre resources, with a cheddar cheese and a cask of porter. Later, when the news of Gravina's death reached Gibraltar, Collingwood wrote a kind and sympathetic letter to Cadiz.

was probably due to the slight easing of the weather by mid-morning on 1 November. The next day, a Saturday, found the bruised and battered schooner with her bone-tired crew at the entrance to the Channel. There she faced the exact opposite of the storm – a calm. The wind dropped, the sails flapped and the *Pickle* wallowed on the gentle swell. Her captain, desperate to get ashore, ordered out the sweeps. Slowly, with three men to an oar, the ship began to crawl towards the Lizard. After several hours of rowing fortune smiled at last and a breeze sprang up – the sweeps were stowed.

On Sunday 3 November the *Pickle* exchanged identity signals with Captain Richard Keats' 74-gun *Superb*, which was on her way to join Nelson's fleet. Keats, it may be remembered, was one of the two men to whom Nelson had described his battle plan just a few weeks earlier. Now he was made wretched by Lapenotiere's news. Not only was his friend dead, but the *Superb* had missed playing a part in the glorious victory.

Dawn on 4 November, a grey Monday morning, revealed the Cornish port of Falmouth only a few miles away. Lapenotiere calculated he would make better progress ashore than sailing another 40 miles to Plymouth, which might take another eight to ten hours. Putting on his best uniform and buckling on his sword, the lieutenant gathered up the dispatches and letters, ordered the jolly-boat lowered and briefed Sub-Lieutenant John Kingdon to take the ship to Plymouth.

The *Pickle* was just ahead of the faster-sailing *Nautilus*, which had been delayed by a brief encounter with several enemy ships that necessitated beating to quarters and sailing a different course to avoid them. Sykes arrived at Plymouth some twelve hours after Lapenotiere had begun his ride to London. This mad dash through southern England is famous – the planned celebrations for the bicentenary in 2005 include a re-enactment following the precise route. Lapenotiere had a journey of about 265 miles, which he made in a hired post chaise drawn by four horses. It was the fastest means of transport available as unlike other coaches it kept going through the night, with only short stops for quick refreshments and to change horses. Because it was fast it was expensive – the bill for the whole journey was £46-19-1 (see box p. 536), including toll charges, tips and meals en route. Lapenotiere left Falmouth at noon on 4 November and arrived at the Admiralty at 1.00 a.m. on the 6th, thirty-seven hours later. An average speed of just over seven miles an hour was certainly faster that the *Pickle* could have managed going round by sea and up the Thames.

The final few miles into London were hampered by thick smog. Not many people were awake in the Admiralty at one o'clock in the morning when the coach clattered into the cobbled courtyard. A weary but excited Lapenotiere was admitted by the night porter and made his way up two flights of stairs to the Board Room, knocking at the door. The next few minutes are best described by Mr Marsden, the First Secretary to the Admiralty.

Admiral Collingwood's important despatches were delivered to me about one o'clock a.m. of the 6th of November, when I was in the act of withdrawing from the

Board Room to my private apartments. In accosting me the officer used these impressive words: 'Sir, we have gained a great victory, but we have lost Lord Nelson!'

Shocked into stillness for a moment, Marsden then realized it was his duty to inform the First Lord, Lord Barham. Leaving Lapenotiere alone, the Secretary, clutching a candle, set off to find his master's bedroom. Marsden takes up the story again:

The First Lord had retired to rest, as had his domestics, and it was not until after some research that I could discover the room in which he slept. Drawing aside his curtains with a candle in my hand, I woke the old peer from a sound slumber, and to the credit of his nerves be it mentioned that he showed no symptom of alarm or surprise, but calmly asked, 'What news Mr Marsden?' We then discussed, in few words, what was to be done, and I sat up the remainder of the night with such clerks as I could collect, in order to make the necessary communications, at an early hour, to the King, Prince of Wales, Duke of York, the Ministers, and other members of the Cabinet, and to the Lord Mayor, who communicated the intelligence to the shipping interest at Lloyd's Coffee House. A notice for the Royal salute was also necessary.

This vast amount of copying kept Marsden and his clerks scribbling well past daybreak.

At about 7.00 a.m. the news arrived at Windsor Castle. According to the King's private secretary, a Colonel Taylor, 'The King was so affected by it that some minutes elapsed before he could give utterance to his feelings. The Queen called the Princesses around her to read the despatches, while the whole royal group shed tears to the memory of Lord Nelson.' In replying to Mr Marsden Colonel Taylor wrote:

However His Majesty rejoices at the signal success of his gallant fleet, he has not heard without expressions of

## Lieutenant Lapenotiere's Journey from Falmouth to London

An article in the *Nelson Dispatch* of October 2002 by Derek Allen and Anthony Cross included Lapenotiere's 'Account of Expenses' for his famous ride. It was copied from the Public Record Office and reads as follows.

Account of Expenses of Lieut Lapendiere [*sic*] ..... for a ..... with Dispatch from Adm Lord Nelson [*sic*] to the Admiralty from Falmouth

| | | | |
|---|---|---|---|
| Falmouth to Truro | £1: | 2: | 6 |
| To the Blue Anchor | 2: | 17: | – |
| To Bodmin | 1: | 19: | – |
| To Launceston | 3: | 6: | 6 |
| To Oakhampton | 3: | 4: | – |
| To Crockenwell | 1: | 16: | 6 |
| To Exeter | 1: | 17: | 6 |
| To Honiton | 2: | 14: | – |
| To Axminster | 1: | 11: | 7 |
| To Bridport | 1: | 16: | 6 |
| To Dorchester | 2: | 14: | 6 |
| To Blandford | 2: | 10: | 6 |
| To Woodyates | 2: | 5: | – |
| To Salisbury | 1: | 17: | 6 |
| To Andover | 2: | 15: | – |
| To Overton | 1: | 13: | – |
| To Basingstoke | 1: | 14: | – |
| To Herford-bridge | 1: | 15: | 6 |
| To Bagshot | 1: | 12: | – |
| To Staines | 1: | 17: | 6 |
| To Hounslow | 1: | 14: | 6 |
| To the Admiralty | 2: | 5: | – |
| | 46: | 19: | 1 |

Signed J R Lapenotiere

He stopped briefly en route for a variety of reasons (to change horses, buy food and so on) twenty-two times or, on average, about every 12 miles.

very deep regret of the death of its valuable and distinguished Commander, although a life so replete with glory, and marked by a succession of such meritorious services and exertions, could not have ended more gloriously ... I have not upon any occasion seen His Majesty more affected. The King is of the opinion that the battle should be styled that of Trafalgar.

The Royal Family went to chapel immediately after hearing the news, 'to return thanks to Almighty God, for the success of His Majesty's arms; and, at about one o'clock, the Staffordshire Militia marched to the Little Park, where they fired three volleys in honour of the great event'. At a Privy Council meeting on the following day the King declared that Thursday 5 December was to be 'a day of General Thanksgiving throughout England, Scotland, and Ireland'.

The news triggered huge national celebrations, thanksgiving and mourning all at the same time. Salutes were fired, cathedral bells rang out and Collingwood's dispatch was published in a *Gazette Extraordinary*, 3,000 copies of which were sent to Yarmouth for despatch by fast cutter to the continent. As the news spread round the world in the coming weeks so did the dual celebratory and commemorative celebrations. Typical were the British ships off Kronborg Castle, who fired their guns to celebrate a magnificent victory and immediately afterwards lowered their flags to half-mast before firing three minute guns as a salute to Nelson. Less typical were the events ashore at Kingston in Jamaica. There a huge funeral pyre was build measuring 47 feet in height and 47 feet in width, representing Nelson's age. It was lit by 47 people simultaneously. The Governor then made a funeral oration with a backdrop of roaring flames and flying sparks, followed by the firing of 47 rockets and 47 minute guns.

Fanny, Nelson's wife, was informed officially in writing by Lord Barham. Emma never recovered from the news. As already recounted, the Government ignored Nelson's last plea that she be provided for and she died in poverty ten years later.

# REWARDS AND PUNISHMENTS

## REWARDS

### What Trafalgar meant to Britain

After Trafalgar the real riches in terms of captured ships were mostly lost during the week of wild weather that followed the battle. Out of thirty-three line-of-battle ships in the Combined Fleet the final British haul was eight: the French *Swiftsure* and the Spanish *Bahama*, *San Ildefonso* and *San Juan Nepomuceno* from the battle, and Dumanoir's four ships captured by Captain Strachan's squadron. Although it was exasperating to seize and then lose such magnificent trophies as the *Santisima Trinidad* and *Santa Ana*, Trafalgar had been a outstanding victory. The French Navy never fully recovered, although they maintained a squadron at Brest. Never again in the remaining ten years of the Napoleonic Wars would (or could) Napoleon seriously confront his enemies at sea. The only real risk came from the Treaty of Tilsit on 1 July 1807, which allied the Spanish, Russian and Dutch navies to that of the French; the Emperor also hoped to strong-arm neutral Denmark and Sweden into the alliance. Had he succeeded, a challenge to Britain might have been mounted. Britain ensured this did not happen with her second devastating attack on Copenhagen in September 1807, at which Britain captured eighteen ships-of-the-line. After Trafalgar Napoleon sought to 'conquer the sea by the power of the land' – a policy that entailed the closing of Continental ports to British shipping and a prohibition of trade. It failed.

Nelson's triumph gave Britain the huge strategic advantage of naval supremacy – something that was to last a hundred years. She could land her armies on hostile coasts as she did in Portugal in 1808, and she could evacuate armies in trouble as at Corunna in 1809. It was the virtually unchallenged Royal Navy that supplied and reinforced Britain's Peninsular Army throughout that six-year campaign, and enabled the Duke of Wellington to dramatically shorten his lines of communications by switching his main base from one port to another. Maritime sovereignty ensured the safety of Britain's trade and gave her unrivalled strategic flexibility in any conflict. There is a hackneyed old saying that 'Waterloo was won on the playing fields of Eton'. That final defeat of Napoleon on land owed as much, if not, more to the drama played out on the waters off Cape Trafalgar a decade earlier.

The scale of the victory was immediately recognized by the British Government and the entire nation. Honours and rewards were not long in coming. They can be conveniently divided into three categories: promotions, decorations and medals, and financial awards.

### Promotions

*To Vice-Admiral of the Red (a rank just reinstated in the Royal Navy)*
Vice-Admiral of the Blue Cuthbert Collingwood
Rear-Admiral of the White The Right Honourable William Earl of Northesk

*To Rear-Admiral of the Blue*
Captain Eliab Harvey (*Téméraire*)
Captain Richard Grindall (*Prince*)
Captain Sir Richard Strachan (*Caesar*)

*To post captain*
Lieutenant John Quilliam, first lieutenant, *Victory*
Lieutenant John Pilford, acting commander of the *Ajax*
Lieutenant John Stockham, acting commander of the *Thunderer*
Lieutenant William Hennah – assumed command of the *Mars* on death of Captain Duff
Lieutenant William Cumby – assumed command of the *Bellerophon* on death of Captain Cooke

*To commander*
All first lieutenants of ships-of-the-line and frigates at Trafalgar and Captain Strachan's action
Lieutenants John Pascoe, Edward Williams and John Yule of the *Victory*
Lieutenant Edward Barker of the *Royal Sovereign*

*To lieutenant*
Under the heading 'Promotions and Appointments' in the *Naval Chronicle* for January to June 1806, an extract reads:

> Four Midshipmen or Master's Mates of the *Victory*; three of the *Royal Sovereign*; two of the *Britannia*; one of each of the other line of battle ships and of the frigates, selected by their respective captains, according to merit, are made lieutenants, and will rank according to their seniority in passing.

Listed below are those who were promoted under this order. Of the nineteen listed only four were midshipmen. It seems captains mostly chose their most senior master's mates, with certain exceptions for especially meritorious conduct during the battle; some captains do not seem to have recommended anyone.

*Victory* – Master's Mates William Chasman, Thomas Robins, William Symons and Midshipman John Carslake
*Royal Sovereign* – Midshipman Robert Edwards
*Britannia* – Master's Mate Sylvester Austen
*Belleisle* – Master's Mate William Pierson
*Spartiate* – Master's Mate Flowers Beckett
*Mars* – Midshipman George Barclay
*Defiance* – Master's Mate James (Jack) Spratt, who showed great courage when wounded during the boarding of the *Aigle* (see p. 514)
*Minotaur* – Master's Mate James Eagle
*Achille* – Master's Mate John Man
*Defence* – Master's Mate Richard Marks
*Leviathan* – Master's Mate James Cumming
*Bellerophon* – Master's Mate Edward Hartley
*Swiftsure* – Master's Mate Henry Weekes
*Agamemnon* – Master's Mate John Sadler
*Euryalus* – Midshipman James Bayley (only the third senior midshipman)
*Naiad* – Master's Mate Hugh Montgomery

## Honours, awards and medals

*Rev. William Nelson*

Nelson's elder brother, a loud, fat and greedy individual, was the main family beneficiary of his death. On 9 November 1805 it was published that William was to be elevated to the peerage as with the titles of 'Viscount Merton and Earl Nelson, of Trafalgar, and of Merton, in the county of Surrey ...'. He also received a huge amount of money – see below under financial awards.

*Admiral Collingwood*

The same promulgation stated,

> His Majesty has also been pleased to grant the dignity of a Baron of the United Kingdom of Great Britain and Ireland, to Cuthbert Collingwood Esq., Vice-Admiral of the Blue Squadron of His Majesty's Fleet, and their heirs male of his body lawfully begotten, by the name, stile [*sic*] and title of Baron Collingwood, of Caldbourne and Hethpoole, in the county of Northumberland.

*The Earl of Northesk*

Northesk was made a Knight of the Bath (KB) at the same time as Sir Richard Strachan, but was far from satisfied. As Northesk was already an earl this was not an advancement in the peerage. An anonymous author wrote a biographical memoir in the early 1806 *Naval Chronicle* that was full of extravagant praise for Northesk's services and indignation that he was not showered with honours for his (in the present writer's view) decidedly mediocre performance at Trafalgar. An extract is worth quoting.

> What may be his [Northesk's] feelings, or private sentiments on the subject, the writer of these memoirs cannot pretend to develop. But ... he must, for *himself*, take the liberty to profess, as his decided opinion, 'that his Lordship's services remained far too long unnoticed, and ultimately have received a very frigid, and inadequate reward'. He by no means wishes to institute invidious comparisons; or, in the smallest degree, to detract from

the eminence of another most gallant and distinguished officer. Yet he conceives it must be obvious, that while a *private Captain* [Strachan], commanding a detached squadron, for having captured four previously-beaten ships, *with a superior force*, had received the same distinction as his Lordship, 'the Order of the Bath', accompanied by more *solid considerations*, a '*Flag Officer*', the second surviving Hero of the incomparable Battle of Trafalgar, has been most unequally remunerated, for the highly distinguished part he bore, in achieving, *with inferior numbers*, that most brilliant of British victories.

*The Lloyds Patriotic Fund awards for officers and ratings who fought at Trafalgar*

These awards were funded by commercial and public donations to reward gallantry by Royal Navy or Army personnel. The committee resolved as follows:

1. That a silver vase valued at £500, 'ornamented with emblematical devices, and appropriate inscriptions, illustrative of the transcendant and heroic achievements of the late Lord Viscount Nelson', be presented to his wife Lady Nelson.
2. That a similar £500 vase be presented to the present Earl Nelson (the Reverend William Nelson).
3. Another £500 vase was to be presented to Collingwood.
4. Vases to the value of £300, with appropriate inscriptions, were to be given to Rear-Admiral the Earl of Northesk and Rear-Admiral Sir Richard Strachan.
5. A vase valued at £300 to be presented to Mrs Cooke in memory of Captain Cooke, killed in action.
6. A ceremonial sword valued at £100, suitably inscribed on the blade, or a vase of the same value, to be presented to the captains of every ship present at the battle. Officers had a choice as to which award they received.

*Naval Gold Medals*

A very rare award instituted in 1795 and abolished in 1815, awarded to admirals and captains who were present at certain naval engage-

---

## The Last Survivors of Trafalgar

Definitive records are difficult to obtain, especially from French sources, but it is worth recording those available to the present writer.

1870 Spanish naval records indicate three veterans still alive. Manuel Alonso Munoz, aged ninety and formerly a soldier on the *Monarca*, Francisco Mendez y Sanchez, once a cabin boy on the *Santisima Trinidad*, and Pedro Antonio Zia Martinez, similarly employed on the *San Juan Nepomuceno*.

1875 Admiral Sir George Westphal, who had been wounded as a midshipman on the *Victory*, was the longest-surviving British officer when he died in this year, aged ninety.

1876 *Victory*'s longest surviving seaman, James Chapman, died in Dundee aged ninety-one. He had been a twenty-year-old landsman at the battle.

1878 In July of this year former Private David Newton Royal Marines died at Cholesbury, Buckinghamshire. He was in his ninetieth year and had fought on the *Revenge* during the battle.

1885 Admiral of the Fleet Sir George Sartorius, former midshipman on the *Tonnant*, died in this year aged ninety-five. He had three sons in the Army and lived to see two of them awarded

the Victoria Cross. Major Reginald Sartorius gained his in Ashanti, West Africa in 1874 and Captain Euston Sartorius in Afghanistan in 1879. For brothers to win the VC is almost, but not quite, unique. Both men later became major-generals.

1887 Lieutenant-Colonel James Fynmore RM died. He had been a Volunteer Class 1 on the *Africa* while his father, also James Fynmore, was the captain commanding the Royal Marine detachment.

1892 Gaspar Costela Vasquez died aged 105. He had fought on the *Santa Ana* as a seaman, and was given a full military funeral with a Marine Infantry band. He was thought to be the last survivor of the battle of any nationality but the authorities were not aware of the existence of Pedro Martinez.

1898 Pedro Antonio Zia Martinez died in Dallas, Texas at the astonishing age of 109.

Captain Churruca's sixteen-year-old cabin boy was probably the last survivor of Trafalgar. One wonders how much he remembered, ninety-three years after the battle, of the dreadful battering his ship received from the 98-gun *Dreadnought*.

ments during the Napoleonic Wars. The large medal measured 2 inches in diameter and the smaller one 1.3 inches. Only 22 large and 117 smaller medals were issued. For Trafalgar large ones were awarded to Nelson (posthumously), Collingwood and Northesk, with the smaller medals being going to all captains of ships-of-the-line – posthumously in the case of Captains Cooke and Duff.

## The Naval General Service Medal 1793–1840

This was sanctioned in 1848 and issued in 1849. Initially known as the Naval War Medal, it was to be awarded to veterans who had been present at specific battles between the years 1793 and 1840. It was silver suspended from a white ribbon with dark-blue edges. For each 'fleet' or 'ship' a separate clasp was issued, there being 231 in all, although seven were never issued due to lack of claimants. This was by far the largest number of clasps on any campaign medal. Some 21,000 medals and 24,000 clasps are known to have been awarded. Not until forty-three years after the battle did parliament finally sanction this award with the clasp 'Trafalgar'. After this huge lapse of time there were only some 1,700 applicants. Not all claims were approved. Of those that were, 119 went to former members of *Victory*'s crew. Of these four were officers (John Pasco and his assistant signals officer George Brown, Lewis Rotely RM and Lewis Reeves RM). Landsman John Roome, who helped hoist the famous signal, and John Saunders, Boy 3rd Class, were among the ratings. It is not generally well known that 55 'boat service' clasps were also issued, to men who went on 'cutting out' expeditions.

## Mr Boulton's Trafalgar Medal

Matthew Boulton was a wealthy manufacturer and owner of the Soho Mint in Birmingham. He had made at his personal expense a set of medals, gold for admirals, silver for officers (including midshipmen) and pewter for ratings, each to be suspended from a dark-blue ribbon. Over 16,000 were struck. The medal had the support of the government but as it was privately produced recipients were not allowed to wear it in uniform.

## Mr Davison's Trafalgar Medal

Alexander Davison was Nelson's prize agent and accountant. This was a pewter medal with a dark-blue ribbon, paid for by him and intended to be awarded to the ratings of the *Victory*. The number issued is uncertain.

## The Nelson Medal, 1845

This was awarded to commemorate the opening of Trafalgar Square and the building of Nelson's Column. The recipients, who also received a gratuity, were all those in-pensioners of the Naval Hospital at Greenwich who had fought under Nelson at St Vincent, Tenerife, the Nile, Copenhagen or Trafalgar. The medal bears the bust of Nelson with 'England expects every man will do his duty' around the circumference and a representation of Trafalgar Square and the Column on the reverse. A special award ceremony was held in the Painted Hall at Greenwich in April 1845. Between 340 and 350 veterans received their medals from the Governor, Admiral Sir Robert Stopford, who had served under Nelson during the chase to the West Indies as captain of the 74-gun *Spencer* in the summer of 1805, but who had missed Trafalgar.

## Financial rewards

Financial awards came from three sources: government grants, prize money and the Patriotic Fund.

### Government grant and prize money

The sum of £300,000 was authorised by Parliament to be divided amongst all ranks who fought at the battle, distributed in the same proportions as prize money. Captains received £2,389-7-6, about 15 times the reward of lieutenants and well over 500 times that of a seaman. Prize money was eventually distributed after the valuation, sale or taking into Royal Navy service of the eight captured ships. The final awards were as listed below – totals to the nearest pound.

> ## The Wounding of Thomas Main
>
> The following is an extract from a letter of Captain Bayntun (*Leviathan*) to the Lloyds Patriotic Fund Committee dated 1 December 1805. It was intended to support Main's possible entitlement to compensation.
>
> a shot took off the arm of Thomas Main, when at his gun on the forecastle; his messmates kindly offered to assist him in going to the Surgeon; but he bluntly said, 'I thank you, stay where you are; you will do more good there:' he then went down by himself to the cockpit. The Surgeon (who respected him) would willingly have attended him in preference to others whose wounds were less alarming; but Main would not admit of it, saying, 'Avast, not until it comes to my turn, if you please.' The Surgeon soon after amputated the shattered part of the arm, near the shoulder; during which, with great composure, smiling, and with a steady clear voice, he sang the whole of 'Rule Britannia.' ... I hope this recital may be of service to him.
>
> Plymouth December 1
> I am sorry to inform you, that the above-mentioned fine fellow died since writing the above, at Gibraltar Hospital, of a fever he caught, when the stump of his arm was nearly well.                                    H.B.

| Rank | Government grant | Prize money | Total |
|---|---|---|---|
| Captain | £2,389-7-6 | £973-0-0 | £2,362 |
| Lieutenants, master, RM captain | £161-0-0 | £65-11-0 | £226 |
| RM lieutenants, carpenter, boatswain gunner, master's mate, purser, surgeon, admiral's secretary | £108-12-0 | £44-4-6 | £153 |
| Midshipman, petty officers, cook, captains of foretop | £26-6-0 | £10-14-0 | £37 |
| Marines, seamen, landsmen, boys | £4-12-6 | £1-17-6 | £6 |

The government also awarded a huge pension of £5,000 per year to Nelson's elder brother, now the Reverend Earl Nelson. Because he had no estate worthy of his elevated status he was also given £90,000 with which to purchase Stanlynch Park, near Salisbury. Despite his being a multi-millionaire in today's money and a clergyman William Nelson gave not a penny to Emma or Horatia, though he was well aware of their poverty. Vice-Admiral Collingwood received an annual pension of £2,000, which since he had no male heirs passed to his daughters.

### Patriotic Fund grants

These were in the form of lump sums for wounded personnel. The amount varied according to the severity of the wound and whether the man was permanently disabled. The Committee announced the following awards at its meeting on 3 December 1805:

*RN lieutenants and RM captains*

£100 if severely wounded and £50 if slightly wounded. Lieutenant Pasco, with a bad grapeshot wound to the side, and Lieutenant Bligh, who was wounded in the head by a musket ball, both received the higher amount.

*RM lieutenants and warrant officers*

£50 if severely wounded and £30 if only slightly. Second Lieutenant Reeves RM was awarded £50 for his wound and Lieutenant Peake £30.

*Midshipmen and petty officers*

£40 and £25 for severe and slight wounds respectively, Midshipman Westphal being an example of the latter. These officers could receive an additional amount if they were disabled.

*Seamen and marines*

£40 if disabled, £20 if severely wounded and £10 if only slightly. Examples include AB David Buchan and Private James Burgess, both of whom had a leg amputated and received £40. The compound fracture of Private James Hines was worth £20, as was the gunshot wound of AB Thomas Green.

The Committee also resolved: 'That relief be afforded to the Widows, Orphans, Parents, and Relatives, depending for support on the Captains, Officers, Petty Officers, Seamen and Marines, who fell in these glorious engagements, as soon as their situation is made known to the Committee.'

## PUNISHMENTS

### Prisoners of war

Although many Spanish prisoners were captured, few were brought to England. Most were put ashore at Gibraltar under the terms and conditions agreed between Collingwood and the authorities in Cadiz after the battle. While off Cadiz he had made efforts to get rid of his French prisoners in the same way – on condition they would never serve again unless properly exchanged with British prisoners. However, the newly arrived Admiral Rosily claimed he had no power to make such an arrangement, so Collingwood had to send them to England. During November, the Spanish agent dealing with this matter signed an official receipt for 210 officers and 4,589 seamen and soldiers released from the British Fleet. These were in addition to the 1,087 wounded Spaniards of all ranks landed at Cadiz and 253 French officers and men who had been exchanged for the British taken prisoner when prizes were recaptured or had been wrecked ashore.

The first two French prisoners to step ashore in England were Vice-Admiral Villeneuve and his flag captain, Magendie, who disembarked from the *Euryalus* on 29 November at Gosport. Villeneuve appeared depressed, while Magendie, who had been a prisoner on parole in England twice before, seemed, according to the *Hampshire Telegraph*, 'a very spirited and excellent officer'. Villeneuve's dejection and 'spasms' on the journey inland seemed so serious that a doctor was called. Suitable accommodation for senior officers was found for them (and later for Captains Lucas and Infernet) at Reading. Villeneuve and Magendie were allowed to witness Nelson's funeral and the two other captains later made the most of London's social life. Villeneuve was only a prisoner on parole for just over five months before he was exchanged for four British captains.

Officers signed a parole, a promise not to escape, before disembarking. They were then sent off to their places of residence, mostly small country towns in southern England such as Bishop's Waltham, Andover, Winchester, Reading, Tiverton, Maidstone and Canterbury. They lived in lodgings, received a small pittance from the British Government and were free to come and go as they pleased, with certain restrictions: they could not walk more than a mile outside their place of internment and they had to keep to main roads. Minor breaches of these conditions were dealt with by local justices; a serious attempt to escape would mean being confined with ordinary prisoners.

Exchanges could be arranged with British prisoners held in France, although few were arranged as Napoleon refused to agree them (except for perhaps half a dozen officers). For Trafalgar prisoners this meant a wait of nine years until the end of the war in 1814. Any officer exchanges were arranged in accordance with an accepted scale for the various ranks, either rank for rank or against the release of a certain number of ratings. These rates were:

| | |
|---|---|
| Admiral (commander-in-chief) | 60 seamen |
| Vice-Admiral | 40 |
| Rear-Admiral | 30 |
| Captain | 15 |
| Commander | 8 |
| Senior lieutenant | 6 |
| Junior lieutenant | 4 |
| Midshipman | 3 |

---

### Dumanoir's 'Imprisonment'

A Lieutenant Gicquel des Touches, imprisoned after Trafalgar, described some aspects of his captivity in the company of Dumanoir and several other officers. He considered Tiverton, where they were paroled, a small, pleasant place but very boring. He was kindly treated and was even offered help if he wanted to break parole and escape. He mentioned one young lady who offered to escape with him if he would marry her on getting to France. Des Touches was not tempted and had to wait six years for an exchange, arranged through the good offices of Lord Northesk.

Dumanoir was lodged in a house in the town that was for years afterwards pointed out to visitors. The route Dumanoir and his fellow officers took for their daily exercise was afterwards known as 'Frenchman's Mile'. The only restrictions on their liberty was having to be within the turnpike gates by 8.00 p.m. in summer and 4.00 p.m. in winter., when a warning bell was rung from St George's Church. It was from Tiverton that Dumanoir took the unusual step for a prisoner of writing to *The Times* to protest against certain unflattering comments about his conduct at Trafalgar that appeared in English newspapers. He was determined to put across his version of events, knowing that once back in France he was certain to face a court martial.

The exact number of French prisoners from Trafalgar is uncertain, but large contingents were delivered at Chatham by the *Victory, Leviathan, Defence, Conqueror* and *Revenge*. There they were disgorged into four hulks, the largest, a three-decker named *Sandwich*, being able to take up to 1,200 men. The *Royal Sovereign, Belleisle, Achille* and *Bellerophon* landed their prisoners at Plymouth, where they were incarcerated in either Mill Bay Prison or one of the eight hulks then in the Hamoaze. Some of these Trafalgar prisoners ultimately ended up in Dartmoor Prison. Yet others were disembarked at Portsmouth from the *Téméraire, Colossus, Tonnant, Defiance, Mars* and *Spartiate*. They ended up in Porchester Castle (able to take 8,000), Forton Prison near Gosport (4,000) or seven hulks moored in Porchester Lake (700–800 each).

A Frenchman named Louis Garneray was captured from a privateer and spent several years in a hulk on Porchester Lake. He later became a writer and artist and he has left a gruesome description of the conditions under which prisoners suffered on these rotting hulks. Much of it is quoted in Edward Fraser's *The Enemy at Trafalgar*, from which comes the passage below.

> Entering on board between a double file of soldiers, the newcomers were abruptly hustled below, among the former arrivals, who seemed 'like the dead just out of their graves'; hollow-eyed, with pale and haggard faces, bowed backs, dishevelled, and with ragged unkempt beards, dressed in scanty yellow garments, emaciated and feeble-looking. He himself was at once taken charge of by two guards, stripped and made to take a chilly bath. Then he had to put on the same garb as the others; a coarse shirt, and orange-yellow vest and breeches, both too small for him, and stamped in immense letters 'T.O.' (Transport Office). ...

The seven to eight hundred prisoners on board were allowed on deck during daytime in the waist, says Garneray; space at their disposal being 44 ft. by 38 ft. 'The Park' was the name that the prisoners gave ... to their airing place. They might use a small space on the forecastle also, but the galley funnels opened there, and it was practically impossible to avoid the smoke. At night all were locked up in two divisions of between three and four hundred men each, on the lower and main decks [of a 74]; the space available for each division being 120 ft. long,

## Some French Prisoners Escape

While most officer prisoners were content to see out their parole in peace, tranquility and boredom, some were not. For an officer recapture meant losing all privileges and being treated like a common seaman with all the attendant filth, starvation rations and disease. Nevertheless, a number did escape. When they did so rewards were offered for their recapture and notices announced the fact to the public such as the one below. Of the five escapees, only the three naval officers, who were Trafalgar prisoners, have been named.

TRANSPORT OFFICE March 24 1806. WHEREAS the five French Prisoners of War, named and described at foot herof, have broken their parole, and absconded from the Towns of Thame in Oxfordshire, and Odiham in Hampshire. The Commissioners for conducting His Majesty's Transport Service, &c. do hereby give notice, that any person or persons, who shall apprehend the said prisoners or either of them, and deliver them or him at this Office, or otherwise cause them to be properly secured in any of the Public Gaols, shall receive for each prisoner, a REWARD of TEN GUINEAS. A further Reward of TEN GUINEAS will be paid to any person giving such information as may be the means of convicting any British Subject of aiding the said Prisoners of War, or either of them, in effecting their escape. FROM THAME VICTOR SERAIN, Ensigne de Vaisseau, 26 years of age, 5 feet 5 inches high, slight person, long visage, swarthy complexion; dark brown hair, grey eyes, scar on his right eye. ALEXANDER PERRAULT, Ensigne de Vaisseau, 20 years of age, 5 ft. 6 in. high, slight person, long visage, fair complexion, light brown hair, hazle [*sic*] eyes, ears pierced. ... ——— LE BOLLOCHE, Ensigne de Vaisseau, 23 years of age, 5 ft. 7½ in. high, slight person, oval visage, fair complexion, dark brown hair, hazle eyes, cut with a sword on right leg, marked with small-pox. ...

40 ft. wide, and 6 ft. high. They had to pack so close that the hammocks were hung in two tiers, with only a few inches between the upper and lower tiers. Some men slept on the deck as a third row. The heat and stench, according to Garneray, were indescribable; almost insupportable. The candles often went out for want of oxygen. The British officers, the naval lieutenant in charge, with the lieutenant in command of the fifty soldiers on board, and servants, with the main guard on duty for the day, were quartered aft. The remainder of the soldiers, with the twenty-five seamen and ship's boys forming the crew of the hulk, lived forward. Their quarters were stoutly barricaded off by bulkheads studded with huge iron nails; loopholes being cut in the bulkheads for musketry, and ports for a couple of guns, which were kept pointed to sweep the decks with case shot in case of trouble. Sentries were on duty on board by day at all points, and during the night prisoners were constantly visited by rounds and kept under continuous supervision. The hulk was carefully examined every evening against attempts to break out, and prisoners paraded on deck and counted one by one.

The food, undoubtedly, was the great grievance on board. ... The dietary, he tells us, was coarse, insufficient and repugnant. One and a quarter pound of dark bread and seven ounces of 'cow beef' was each man's ration; with a modicum of barley and onions for soup for each mess of four. Once a week the issue was a pound of red herring with a pound of potatoes; on another day salt cod instead of herring. Poor as the allowance was, the rogues of contractors who victualled the hulks gave short weight, or sent on board uneatable stuff. The herrings, indeed, describes Garneray, were often sold back to the contractor at a nominal price, to reappear again as another day's ration. ... The salt cod could be eaten, he says, but the bread was like lead, and was constantly short weight. A complaint meant going without anything until the evening, when the officer of the day heard complaints. Drinking water was brought alongside in casks by small boats and pumped on board by the prisoners themselves. Apart from stories, authentic in some cases, of the dogs of British officers paying a call on board, being decoyed below, killed and turned into cutlets, while their late masters were talking aft, it is a fact that the rats in the hold were as a regular thing fished for with hooks baited with bits of beef, and caught cooked and eagerly devoured. Gambling was a favourite means of passing the time; the usual stakes being the poor wretches' rations. One man at Porchester, it is on record, lost his rations for eight days running and died of starvation. …

Some Trafalgar prisoners from the Medway were moved north when fresh batches made it impossible to jam more into the hulks.

> They were sent round by sea to Yarmouth, to be thence marched inland to the central depots at Weedon in Northamptonshire, and Norman's Cross, near Yaxley, in Huntingdonshire, this last a huge establishment covering forty acres of ground, where six thousand prisoners in all were confined under a strong guard of yeomanry and two regiments of militia.

Thousands died in captivity. The dead from the hulks along the Thames were buried in the marshes beside St Mary's Creek opposite Gillingham and forgotten until excavations to extend the dockyard at Chatham unearthed their bones. They were collected and reinterred in the presence of the French naval attaché in an enclosure laid out with flower beds and paths, in the centre of which was a memorial stone. Unfortunately another move to a space in front of the Royal Naval Barracks at Chatham was necessary a few years later.

### Dumanoir's second court martial
Dumanoir's actions at Trafalgar and on 4 November 1805 were both the subject of Courts of Enquiry. The first has been discussed in Section Eight above (p. 518), along with the dismissal of the allegations described. The Court was established by imperial decree; its conclusions about Dumanoir's behaviour on 4 November are given below in full.

> THE COURT OF ENQUIRY DIRECTED TO INVESTIGATE THE CONDUCT OF REAR-ADMIRAL DUMANOIR ON THE DAYS OF BRUMARE 11TH, 12TH AND 13TH, YEAR XIV.
> [2, 3 and 4 November 1805]
> 1. Imperial Decree
> THE Court of Enquiry directed by Our sealed letter of September 7th last, to examine the conduct of Rear-Admiral Dumanoir in the Battle of Trafalgar will also investigate the events that took place on Brumaire 11th and 12th, Year xiv, when Our ships *Formidable*, *Scipion*, *Mont-Blanc* and *Duguay-Trouin* under the command of this flag-officer fell into the hands of the enemy.
> The above-mentioned Court of Enquiry will examine whether on these days Rear-Admiral Dumanoir did, both

---

### Memorial to French Prisoners Who Died in Captivity

A memorial to the French prisoners (Army and Navy) was erected outside the Royal Naval Barracks at Chatham, with an inscription as follows:

Here are gathered together
The remains of many brave soldiers and sailors
Who having once been the foes and afterwards
The captives of England
Now find rest in her soil
Remembering no more the animosities of war, or
The sorrows of imprisonment.
They were deprived of the consolation of closing
Their eyes
Among the countrymen they loved,
But they have been laid in an honoured grave
By a nation which knows how to respect valour
And to sympathise with misfortune.

---

> personally and by his manoeuvres, orders and signals, everything that was possible in this situation for the defence of the Squadron entrusted to his command, for that of the ship carrying his flag and for the honour of Our arms.
> The finding of this Court will be submitted to Us as has been ordained in regard to the subject of Our sealed letter of September 7th last.
> Given at Our Palace of the Tuileries, November 23rd, 1809.
>
> Signed: Napoleon.
>
> By the Emperor:
> The Secretary of State:
> Signed: H.B. Duc de Bassano.

After considering statements, reports, the journals of Dumanoir and his captains and the relevant ships' logs, the Court's findings were as quoted below:

> To sum up, the Court of Enquiry finds that Rear-Admiral Dumanoir was to blame:
>
> 1. In not having gone about as early as 7.30 in the morning, at the time when he himself proposed it to the Captain of the *Mont-Blanc*, who concurred in this manoeuvre and supported him with his counsel; in having annulled the execution shortly after having ordered it;
> 2. In allowing himself to be chased and fired upon for four hours by heavy frigates which were attacking his ships with overmuch advantage from astern, instead of having the same frigates engaged at close quarters by the best sailers in his Squadron;
> 3. In only going about when the enemy had already attacked his rear and under their fire.
> In conclusion, that the Rear-Admiral showed too much indecision in all his manoeuvres.
> Given at Paris, December 29th, 1809
> The Comte de Fleurieu
> The Comte Bougainville
> Vice-Admiral Thevenard
> Vice-Admiral Rosily

These findings landed on the desk of the Minister of Marine in early January 1810, having been seen by the Emperor. Napoleon wanted to make an example of Dumanoir but his minister was reluctant to proceed without further instructions: if Dumanoir was to face a court martial he wanted a direct order from the Emperor to that effect. Decrès was doubtful as to the strength of any charges framed on the evidence he had seen – strangely, as an entire squadron of four ships-of-the-line had been lost, and the Court of Enquiry had spelt out in some detail where it considered Dumanoir at fault. One suspects Decrès was anxious to shield his fellow admiral from the Emperor's anger. He responded as follows:

Your Majesty has done me the honour to refer this finding back to me with orders <u>to have the laws of the Empire executed.</u>

These laws contain nothing sufficiently definite in a case of this kind to enable me to act without having received Your Majesty's orders.

But in the case in question, the Court of Enquiry finds General Dumanoir guilty of <u>error</u> but does not in any way impute <u>misconduct</u> to him.

If Your Majesty thinks proper to adopt this opinion, it is none the less true that it will necessarily influence that which You hold concerning the ability and resolution of Rear-Admiral Dumanoir.

In this hypothesis of definitely adopting the opinion of the Court of Enquiry, I beg Your Majesty to inform me if You are of the opinion that Rear-Admiral Dumanoir should be immediately restored to employment or whether You think it well to ordain other arrangements concerning him.

1.    Should Rear-Admiral Dumanoir be restored to active service?

2.    Does Your Majesty think well to deprive him of employment by dismissal, placing him on half pay, or by suspending him from duty?

3.    Does Your Majesty desire that Rear-Admiral Dumanoir should be brought before a Court-Martial, in order to be tried upon the errors imputed to him in the finding of the Court of Enquiry?

I beg Your Majesty to give me Your orders on these questions …

Decrès then went on to explain why he thought the Emperor should be lenient, and ended by recommending that Dumanoir be placed on half pay. Napoleon, however, wanted Dumanoir and the surviving ships' captains (Berrenger and Le Tellier) to face a court martial, as was the usual fate of any captain who lost his ship. Captain Toufett of the *Duguay-Trouin* had died in the battle, his second-in-command was still a prisoner and Lavillegris of the *Mont Blanc* had died since the action.

Decrès' covering letter to the convening order for the court was a little more explicit as to the actual charge against Dumanoir. Article 1 merely states the Court was 'to try the conduct of Rear-Admiral Dumanoir on 2, 3 and 4 November 1805' – hopelessly vague. Article 2 refers only to the ships' captains and is more specific. They were to be tried 'for their conduct relative to the surrender of the ships under their command'. The minister wrote:

> [The Court is] to ascertain whether Rear-Admiral Dumanoir and each of the officers commanding under his orders <u>did personally and by their manoeuvres, orders and signals</u> everything that was possible in the circumstances for the defence of the Squadron, for that of their respective ships and for the honour of His Majesty's arms.

After hearing the evidence, questioning witnesses, reading the statements and relevant logs it was the task of the judge-advocate, M. Gourdon, to sum up to the Court. In effect he was both prosecutor and defender. He was required to advise on the law and highlight the strengths or weaknesses of the evidence presented. The final decision rested with the Court but the judge-advocate could, and did, make his own opinions known. Gourdon's speech was a long one. His key points were as follows.

•    With regard to Dumanoir's manoeuvres prior to the engagement on 2 and 3 November, when he was endeavouring to escape to Rochefort, the judge-advocate stated, 'I see nothing in these manoeuvres that should not meet with your approval.'

•    On the much more serious charge that Dumanoir should have gone about at 7.30 a.m. instead of changing his mind and waiting another four hours before doing so, Gourdon again found in the admiral's favour. He considered that 'in view of the state of his Division, which made it his imperative duty to avoid an engagement if he still retained a hope of doing so, General Dumanoir was not in fault in not going about at 8 o'clock in the morning'.

•    Gourdon agreed that tacking in succession 'entailed a great loss of time'. However, because of the delay from the hoisting of the signal and the *Duguay-Trouin* implementing it (about 45 minutes), Dumanoir, according to the judge-advocate, was not culpable.

•    In his summing up Gourdon stressed that the reason for the defeat lay 'simply in the superiority of the enemy force – both in number and the armament of their vessels – and in the superiority of their sailing qualities over that of our ships'.

•    Gourdon recommended that the Court acquit Dumanoir and hand him back his sword. Similarly both Le Tellier (Dumanoir's flag captain) and Berrenger (*Scipion*) were considered to have 'gallantly done the duty imposed on them' and should also have their swords returned.

The Court 'having deliberated in private, opinions being delivered individually, commencing with the junior officer, the President having delivered his opinion last upon the corresponding questions being put to him, approving the conclusions of His Majesty's Judge-Advocate, unanimously declare' the acquittal of all three officers. The person most upset by this verdict was Napoleon. Another dissenter was Cosmao, now a rear-admiral and a member of the Court, who as mentioned earlier was said to have broken his own sword when Dumanoir's was returned.

The Emperor, then celebrating his great victory on the Ulm, had taken the news of his navy's defeat at Trafalgar remarkably calmly. His only public reference to it was made five months after the battle in his Imperial Address from the throne to the Corps Legislatif on 2 March 1806, when he said, '*Les tempetes nous ont faites perdre quelques vaisseaux après un combat imprudemment engagé.*' ('We lost several ships in the gales after an action foolishly engaged in.') According to Edward Fraser, in his book *The Enemy at Trafalgar*, within four months of the battle Napoleon directed that all ships in the French Navy should have Nelson's Trafalgar signal painted up prominently on every man-of-war. In French it read, '*La France compte que chacun fera son devoir!*' The Emperor is said to have passed the order to Decrès with the words, 'It is the best of lessons.'

# *Epilogue*
## NELSON'S FUNERAL

### NELSON'S LAST JOURNEY

Nelson's death occurred at around 4.30 p.m. on 21 October 1805 but he was not finally lowered into his grave under the dome of St Paul's Cathedral until the early evening of 9 January 1806, eighty days after being struck down on his quarterdeck. The stages of his final journey were:

*21–28 October* From the scene of battle to Gibraltar, on *Victory.*

*29 October–2 November* In Gibraltar, with *Victory* partially refitting.

*3 November–4 December Victory* carries body from Gibraltar to St Helen's (Portsmouth) in the Solent.

*11 December Victory* sails for the Nore (Thames estuary). On the same day Beatty begins his autopsy on Nelson's body.

*12 December Victory* anchors west of Dover.

*16 December Victory* sails but bad weather prevents her from arriving off the Nore until 22 December.

*23 December* Nelson's body is transferred to the yacht *Chatham* and taken to Greenwich and thence to the Painted Hall for three days' lying in state.

*8 January 1806* A grand river procession takes the body from Greenwich to the Whitehall Stairs and thence to the Admiralty building.

*9 January* Funeral procession to St Paul's Cathedral, followed by the burial service.

### From Cape Trafalgar to St Helen's, 21 October–4 December

As he lay dying in the cockpit Nelson had whispered, 'Don't throw me overboard, Hardy.' His friend replied at once, 'Oh no! Certainly not.' For obvious practical reasons anybody who died on board ship at sea was buried at sea. In battle the bodies of the dead, including those of senior officers (such as Nelson's secretary Mr Scott and Captain Cooke of the *Bellerophon*), were immediately thrown overboard with no ceremony at all. A compromise seems to have been reached on the *Mars*, whose log of 22 October records, 'At 5.30 committed the body of Captain Duff to the deep', suggesting that a funeral was held the day after the battle. The corpses of those who died outside an action were invariably weighted down and, after a brief service, tipped over the side. Nelson was the sole exception to this rule, certainly as far as Trafalgar was concerned.

Collingwood wanted to get the body back to England as quickly as possible, so initially instructed that Nelson be transferred to the *Euryalus*, Captain Blackwood's frigate. When this

became known on the *Victory* the crew were horrified, and instantly demanded to be allowed to bring the body of their beloved admiral home on his own flagship. Colllingwood agreed.

The surgeon, Dr Beatty, then had to work out how to keep the body for several weeks without it decomposing. As there was no lead on board for a coffin he used a leaguer –the largest cask on board, and big enough to take Nelson, who was slightly built and of average height for the time (5 feet 6 inches). Before his body was put in the leaguer, most of his hair and his pigtail were cut off, to be sent ultimately to Emma – the pigtail is currently on display at the Royal Naval Museum, Portsmouth. Then all his clothes with the exception of his long shirt were removed; his uniform jacket had been taken off when he was still alive. Beatty then used a probe to try to determine the course and depth of the wound and to locate the ball. In this he was unsuccessful. Many years later in retirement Major Rotely RM gave a speech in which he described how he went below to the cockpit.

> On the morning after his death, I went below to view the body, and to procure a lock of his hair as a memento, but Captain Hardy had been before me and cut off the whole with the exception of a small lock at the back of the neck, which I secured. The hair, with the coat and waistcoat Nelson fell in were preserved and sent to Lady Hamilton; the breeches and stockings came into my possession, and I have preserved them as valuable relics for forty years. To preserve the body, a large cask was procured and lashed on its end on the middle deck. The body was brought up by two men from the cockpit. I received it and placed [it] head foremost in the cask. The head of the cask was then replaced and filled with brandy, and a marine sentinel placed over it by night or day …

To preserve the body, Beatty used brandy. When responding to later criticism that rum would have been better, he replied :

> Brandy was recommended in preference to rum, on which spirit there was plenty on board. The circumstance is here noticed, because a very general but erroneous opinion was found to prevail on *Victory*'s arrival in England, that rum preserves the body from decay much longer and more perfectly from decay than any other spirit, and ought therefore to have been used: but the fact is quite the reverse, for there are several kinds of spirit much better for

that purpose than rum; and as their appropriateness in this respect arises from their degree of strength, on which alone their antiseptic quality depends, brandy is superior. Spirit of wine [surgical spirit], however, is certainly by far the best when it can be procured.

There must have been a good stock of brandy on board as well as rum, as a very substantial amount would have been needed to fill a leaguer.

Rotely states the body was placed headfirst into the leaguer but gave no particular reason for this. Neither did he explain that the cask had an aperture cut in the side near the bottom, and another at the top. These were needed so that the brandy could be drawn off and the spirit renewed without difficulty and without disturbing the body. The leaguer was then left under the watchful eyes of the Royal Marine sentry – with Nelson seemingly standing on his head inside.

It took exactly a week for the *Victory* to reach Gibraltar. By evening on 23 October her log records, 'Strong gales and heavy squalls, a heavy sea from the westward.' At eleven o'clock the next morning the weather was the same, forcing the *Polyphemus* to take the struggling *Victory* in tow. At sometime the same day a worried marine came stumbling up from the middle deck to blurt out to the officer on watch that the lid on the leaguer was moving, seemingly being pushed up from inside! A dash down below revealed that the sentry had not been imagining things – the lid was indeed being pushed up. However, this was caused, not by Nelson straining to get out, but, as Beatty states, by the 'disengagement of air from the Body to such a degree' that it raised the head of the cask. The top was spiked to release the air and the reassured sentry resumed his vigil.

On 25 October the hawser from the *Polyphemus* parted and for twenty-four hours the *Victory* wallowed and struggled until the *Neptune* took over towing duty, though she was unable to maintain the tow for more than a day before her rope broke. Nevertheless, by 7.00 p.m. on the 28th *Victory* was able to drop anchor in Rosia Bay, Gibraltar. During the week the cask had been drained off and the brandy replenished once. While the ship was being refitted and repaired for the voyage home Walter Burke, the purser, was tasked, among many other items, with procuring spirit of wine and restocking the brandy. When she sailed on 3 November Nelson was submerged in a mixture of spirit of wine and brandy. When the level had been checked at Gibraltar, Beatty stated, 'the cask show[ed] a deficit produced by the Body's absorbing a considerable quantity of the brandy'. It was topped up with spirit of wine. However, due to 'adverse winds and tempestuous weather'

the voyage to Portsmouth took a full month, so two replenishments were necessary en route. On these occasions a mixture of two-thirds brandy and one-third spirit of wine was used.

*Victory* anchored in the Solent on 4 December. Captain Hardy wanted instructions on what to do with the body. Was it to be taken by land to the lying in state or should he take it to the Nore? The latter, came the reply, and during this time a leaden coffin was brought on board. Shortly afterwards the painter Arthur Devis clambered through the entry port. Devis had managed to talk his way out of debtor's prison in order to join the *Victory*, and he stayed on board for the voyage to the Nore and Nelson's autopsy. He made good use of his time, sketching Nelson's face before eventually painting his familiar 'Death of Nelson', which enabled him to clear his debts! The *Victory* finally sailed for the Thames estuary on 11 December.

### The autopsy

Like any autopsy this must have been a gruesome business, particularly for those like Arthur Devis who were not medical men, and for those who counted themselves Nelson's friends. Beatty began his task on the day *Victory* sailed. His statement records:

> On the 11th December, the day on which the *Victory* sailed from the Spithead to the Nore, Lord Nelson's body was taken from the cask in which it had been kept since the day after his death. On inspecting it externally, it exhibited a state of perfect preservation, without being in the smallest degree offensive.

Once the body was opened up the bowels, heart, lungs, liver and spleen were examined. The bowels were found to be 'much decayed and likely to spread putrefaction' and were removed.

---

## Nelson and *HMS Victory* Coins

In the *Nelson Dispatch* dated January 1985 was published a letter from Mr Alan Smith in which he recounted two issues of commemorative coins for Trafalgar:

> In 1980 the Gibraltar Government issued legal tender coinage in gold, silver and the standard cupronickel to commemorate the 175th anniversary of Trafalgar and the death of Nelson. The justification for such an issue is not as slight as it often is in many cases. The first news of Nelson's triumph and death came to Gibraltar, and it was from Gibraltar that *Victory* sailed to bring Nelson's body home. Some of the fleet's casualties [those who died of their wounds in the hospital] are buried in what was later named Trafalgar Cemetery, where an act of remembrance is still held annually. The coins issued comprise a £50 piece in gold (5,000 in 'proof' condition and 7,500 uncirculated); 15,000 'proof' crowns in sterling silver, plus the ordinary cupronickel crown which is still available at about £1.75. The obverse of these coins shows a standard Queen's head: the reverse a portrait of Nelson superimposed on *Victory*. The inscription is: 'Nelson 1758 – 1805'.

> The only other Nelson issue known to me is from the Isle of Man. In 1982 four crowns were issued with a 'Maritime Heritage' theme, depicting famous ships with associated famous Manxmen. The coin in question shows *Victory* with a small cartouche portrait of Captain John Quilliam ...

---

Beatty continued:

> Thoracic and abdominal viscera were not inflamed or diseased ... the heart was small and dense in its substance; its valves, pericardium, and the large vessels were sound and firm in their structure. The lungs were sound and free from adhesions. The liver was very small, in its colour natural, firm in its texture, and in every way free from the smallest appearance of disorganisation. The stomach, as well as the spleen and other abdominal contents, was alike free from the traces of disease. Indeed all the vital parts were so perfectly healthy, and so small, that they resembled more those of a youth, than a man who had attained his forty-seventh year ...

Beatty was also able to trace the course of the ball that had caused the mortal wound. It had passed through Nelson's spine and lodged in the muscles of his back, taking with it a considerable portion of gold lace, the lining of his epaulette and a piece of his coat. The lace was found still attached to the ball 'as if it had been inserted into the metal while in a state of fusion'. Examination of the ball established immediately that the sharpshooter responsible had been armed with a musket, not a rifle. Beatty described the course and lodgement site in some detail.

> The ball struck the fore part of His Lordship's epaulette; and entered the left shoulder immediately before the processus acromion scapulae, which it slightly fractured. It then descended obliquely into the thorax, fracturing the second and third ribs: and after penetrating the left lobe of the lungs, and dividing in its passage a large branch of the pulmonary artery, it entered the left side of the spine between the sixth and seventh dorsal vertebrae. It fractured the left transverse process of the sixth dorsal vertebra, wounded the medulla spinalis, and fracturing the right transverse process of the seventh vertebra. [It then] made its way from the right side of the spine, directing its course through the muscles of the back; and lodged therein, about two inches below the inferior angle of the right scapula ...

> The immediate cause of His Lordship's death was a wound of the left pulmonary artery, which poured out its blood into the cavity of the chest. The quantity of blood thus effused did not appear to be very great; but as the haemorrhage was from a vessel so near the heart, and the blood was consequently lost in a very short time, it produced death sooner than would have been effected by a larger quantity of blood lost from an artery in a more remote part of the body. The injury done to the spine must of itself proved mortal, but His Lordship might perhaps have survived this alone for two or three days; though his existence would have been miserable to himself, and highly distressing to the feelings of all around him.

Beatty then explained what happened to the body after the autopsy until delivery at the Nore.

> The remains [the body less the internal organs] were wrapped in cotton vestments, and rolled from head to foot with bandages of the same material, in the ancient mode of embalming. The Body was then put in a leaden coffin, filled with brandy holding in a solution of camphor and myrrh. (The spirit of wine on board was exhausted; and from the sound state of the Body, brandy was judged sufficient for its

preservation.) This coffin was enclosed in a wooden one, and placed in the after part of HIS LORDSHIP'S cabin; where it remained till the 21st of December, when an order was received from the Admiralty for the removal of the Body ...

The original plan had been for Nelson's body to be taken off the *Victory* at Portsmouth; this proposal was abandoned but the *Victory* could not sail until certain essential repairs were done. She sailed on the 11th, and anchored west of Dover until the 16th, when a unfavourable wind slowed progress. She finally arrived off the Nore on 22 December, when preparations were made on board for the handing over of the body. It was at this stage that use was made of the coffin that had been made from the mainmast of the *Orient* and presented to Nelson by his friend Captain Hallowell after the Battle of the Nile. There were many curious eyes gathered round, including visitors from ashore, when Nelson was, for the last time, exposed to human view. Beatty described what happened.

> the leaden coffin was opened, and the Body taken out; when it was found still in excellent condition, and completely plastic. The features were somewhat tumid [swollen], from absorption of the spirit; but on using friction with a napkin, they resumed a great degree their natural character. All the Officers of the ship, and several of HIS LORDSHIP'S friends, as well as some of Captain Hardy's, who had come on board the *Victory* that day from the shore, were present at the time of the Body's being removed from the leaden coffin; and witnessed its undecayed state after a lapse of two months since death, which excited the surprise of all who beheld it. This was the last time the mortal part of the lamented Hero was seen by human eyes; as the Body, after being dressed in a shirt, stockings, uniform small clothes and waistcoat, neckcloth, and night-cap, was then placed in the shell made from *L'Orient's* mast, and covered with the shrouding.

On 21 December a Mr Whitby, the Master Attendant at Woolwich, had brought the outer coffin to Sheerness. He was accompanied by Mr Tyson, who for several years had been secretary to Nelson. This coffin was an elaborate piece of craftsmanship (see box p. 293). According to the *Naval Chronicle* of the day:

> This coffin, which is considered as the most elegant and superb ever seen in Europe, is the production of Mr. France, undertaker of Pall Mall. The emblematical devices with which it is ornamented, were executed from designs, by Ackerman, of the Strand. The covering is of fine black velvet, with treble rows of double gilt nails, the whole finely enriched with gold matt, enclosed and chased.

---

## The Inscription on Nelson's Coffin

The inscription plate was 13 inches by 9 and made of gold. It read as follows:

DEPOSITUM.
The Most Noble Lord HORATIO NELSON,
Viscount and Baron NELSON of the NILE,
And of
Burnham Thorpe, in the County of Norfolk.
Baron NELSON of the Nile, and of
Hilborough, in the said County.
Knight Commander of the Most Honourable
Order of the Bath;
Vice-Admiral of the White Squadron of the Fleet;
And
Commander in Chief of His Majesty's Ships
and Vessels in the Mediterranean.
Also
Duke of BRONTE, in Sicily;
Knight Grand Cross of the Sicilian Order of
St Ferdinand,
And of Merit.
Member of the Ottoman Order of the Crescent;
And
Knight Grand Commander of the Order of
St Joachim.
Born September 29, 1758.
After a series of transcendent and Heroic
Services, this Gallant Admiral fell gloriously, in
the moment of a brilliant and decisive Victory
over the Combined Fleets of France and Spain,
off Cape Trafalgar, on the 21st October, 1805.

The reception plan ashore was for the Commissioner of the Royal Dockyard at Chatham, a Mr Grey, to take his yacht, the *Chatham,* from Sheerness to the Nore and then deliver the body to Lord Hood at Greenwich. There it would remain for the lying in state and until the funeral. The *Victory* had been sighted several miles off the Nore on the 22nd but a strong south-west wind prevented her coming any closer. Nevertheless, ships in harbour lowered their colours to half-mast. It was not until the next day that Nelson was transferred to the *Chatham*. The coffin was covered with an ensign and placed on deck. As it progressed slowly up the Thames all ships and vessels dipped their colours to half-mast as the yacht passed. Church bells tolled, while at Tilbury and Gravesend the forts fired minute guns in salute. In the evening the body was received by Admiral Lord Hood in his capacity as Governor of Greenwich. It was placed in a private apartment until completion of the arrangements for the lying in state in the Painted Hall.

## THE FUNERAL CEREMONIES
### Lying in state

It was not until 27 December that the date for the funeral was finally fixed for 9 January 1806. Before that would be a public lying in state for three days, from 5 to 7 January, and the afternoon of the 4th, a Saturday, was set aside for the private attendance of the Prince of Wales and certain other privileged persons admitted by the Governor. Mr Scott, Nelson's principal chaplain, remained in attendance throughout the night. At eleven o'clock on the Sunday the public began filing past. In total it was estimated that over 15,000 people were admitted – far fewer than those wanting to get in. Crowd control was rigidly enforced and at one stage Lord Hood asked the Home Secretary for more troops to control the situation. The last people into the chamber were a contingent of forty-six seamen and fourteen marines from the *Victory*, who arrived as it was getting dark on board the brig *Elizabeth and Mary*. The crowds watching gave them a rousing reception with much cheering and clapping. After stowing their hammocks – they were to be billeted overnight at the Hospital – they were escorted through the hall. Then the great doors were closed, leaving a long queue of disappointed members of the public outside.

Trafalgar was acknowledged by the whole of England as an outstanding triumph but all celebrations were muted as the public was so deeply shocked by the death of their hero. For some the price of victory was too high. During the week following the receipt of the news official celebrations were held at various ports and garrisons around the country. At all of them Army officers appeared in full mourning with their colours and band instruments draped in black crape ribbon. On 19 November all the ships in the Elsinore roads fired three broadsides in celebration but immediately afterwards their colours were lowered and three minute guns fired in salute. Even children at school regarded his

death as a personal loss. A Lady Wenlock, who died in 1869, recalled: 'I remember well the Battle of Trafalgar. I was seven years old then, but I knew the names of all the ships and captains.' On the day the news came, she had occasion to go to her sister's bedroom. '[My sister] was not up, and the newspaper was lying on the bed. "Oh, my dear", she said, "my father has sent me up the newspaper, and we have taken twenty ships of the line; but Nelson is dead!" Child as I was I burst into tears; one had been taught to think that nothing could go on without him.'

A Countess Brownlow remembered being in classroom at school when the news was announced – she dropped to the ground in horror although she had never seen Nelson. An old Christ's Hospital 'boy' who died aged 103 was also at school at the time. 'We let up fireworks for the victory and then drank a little glass of sherry for Lord Nelson in solemn silence.'

### Nelson Memorial Rings

After Nelson's death his executors distributed memorial rings to a number of his relatives and friends, made by the Strand jeweller John Salter who had long been Nelson's jeweller. They were made of enamelled gold with the gilt letters N.B. (Nelson and Bronte). The former was surmounted by a viscount's coronet, and the latter by a ducal coronet representing the Sicilian Dukedom of Bronte which had been conferred on Nelson by King Ferdinand IV of the Two Sicilies. Underneath in gold letters is the word 'Trafalgar', and round the circlet is engraved 'Palmam qui meruit ferat' – 'Let him who has deserved it bear the palm'. The inscription reads 'Lost to his Country 21 October 1805 aged 47'.

Some fifty-eight rings were produced, thirty-one going to immediate family members. Today at least one can be seen at each of the National Maritime Museum Greenwich, the Nelson Museum at Monmouth, the Royal Navy Museum at Portsmouth, Lloyds of London and the Victoria and Albert Museum London.

### The river procession

Early January was not a good time of the year for a public funeral of this magnitude. Rain, sleet, snow and icy winds, possibly all four, were likely; spectators spent ten hours of standing and shivering, with their only reward a glimpse of a barge or a carriage carrying a coffin. But no amount of wind or weather would stop the people of London coming to say their final farewell. On 8 January 1806 the rain held off (as it did the following day) but the wind was biting and bitter from the south-west, causing delays and some difficulties as oarsmen struggled to make headway. Londoners began to arrive early, while it was still dark. As the morning progressed tens of thousands lined the Thames to witness a procession of barges and boats that would never be seen again.

By ten o'clock on the morning of Wednesday 8 January Greenwich Hospital and the wharf had become the centre for the assembly of officials, boats and barges that would form the procession accompanying Nelson's body to the Whitehall Stairs in central London. Heralds, naval officers, the Mayor of London, the great Livery Companies, River Fencibles, Water Bailiffs, the Harbour Master, the Harbour Marine Corps – all had a part to play or were responsible for assembling the huge flotilla of barges and boats in the correct order. Life Guards, Greenwich Volunteers and Pikemen were responsible for local crowd control. It proved a difficult task. Pressure built up when people pushed forward to see the coffin carried from the Painted Hall down to the King's Stairs. The *Naval Chronicle* noted that 'many people were much hurt in their attempts to obtain a view'.

At 12.30 p.m. precisely the procession escorting the body began its slow march from the Hall to the river, between lines of the Deptford Volunteers who presented arms as the coffin was borne past. The River Fencibles fired minute guns throughout. The banks of the river were packed, and there were people on the decks and clinging to the yards, masts and rigging of every ship moored along the water's edge. The diagram shows the order of the principal barges

# The River Procession Taking Nelson's Body from Greenwich to the Whitehall Stairs

**1st Mourning Barge**
• The Standard at the head borne by Capt. Laforey (*Spartiate*) supported by 2 lieuts RN
• The Guidon at the door-place supported by Capt. Bayntun and 2 lieuts RN
• Rouge Croix and Blue Mantle (heralds) and Pursuivants (junior heralds)

**4th Mourning Barge**
• The Chief Mourner, Adm. of the Fleet Sir Peter Parker
• 6 assistant mourners (adms); 4 supporters of the Pall (v-adms), 6 supporters of the Canopy (r-adms)

• The Train-bearer of the Chief Mourner, Capt. Blackwood (*Euryalus*)
• The Windsor Herald
• The Banner of Emblems at the door-place supported by Capt. Hardy and 2 lieuts RN

**Admiralty Barge**
The Lords Commissioners for executing the office of the Lord High Admiral

To Whitehall Stairs

**2nd Mourning Barge**
• 4 Heralds of Arms bearing Nelson's Surcoat, Sword and Target, Helm and Crest and Gauntlet and Spurs
• The Banner of the deceased at the head borne by Capt. Rotherham (*Royal Sovereign*) and 2 lieuts RN
• The Great Banner at the door-place borne by Capt. Moorsom (*Revenge*) and 2 lieuts RN

**Nelson's Body**
A mourning barge, originally that of King Charles II. Draped in black with black plumes on the canopy, it had on board the Garter King of Arms carrying Nelson's coronet, 6 trumpets and 6 lieutenants carrying Nelson's bannerolls.

**His Majesty's Barge**
Dignitaries representing the King and members of the Royal Family

**City State Barge**
The Lord Mayor's barge, large, very ornate and covered in flags all at half-mast

**Goldsmiths' Company**

**Fishmongers' Company**

**Drapers' Company**

**Thames Navigation Committee Barge**
The committee was responsible for the control of river navigation markers and traffic.

**Corporation of London Committee Barge**
7 seamen of *Victory* carrying the Colours she wore at Trafalgar, all shot-holed and torn

**Skinners' Company**

**Merchant Taylors' Company**

**Ironmongers' Company**

**Stationers' Company**

**Apothecaries' Company**

From Greenwich

**Notes**
• This plan only shows the principal barges of the procession. It cannot show the scores of others including escorting gun-boats and Harbour Marine Corps boats that came up the river on either side of the main procession. The flags shown are representations of the hundreds worn at half-mast on all boats and barges.
• The Standard, Guidon, Banner of the deceased, Great Banner and Banner of Emblems were Nelson's personal standards and banners and were carried in the 1st, 2nd and 4th mourning barges, each by a Trafalgar captain supported by 2 RN lieutenants. Nelson's family bannerolls were carried by 6 RN lieutenants on the barge bearing the body.
• 7 of the 12 Great Livery Companies of London participated in the procession, along with the Apothecaries' Company.

but it cannot show the scores of smaller craft and gunboats that flanked and followed the procession as it moved off, the liveried oarsmen straining to keep on station in the face of the stiff wind.

The first four craft were the main mourning barges – all black. They carried not just Nelson's body but his personal Standard, Guidon and Banners, each borne by a Trafalgar captain and supported by two naval lieutenants. The first barge carried, at the head, Nelson's Standard borne by Captain Laforey of the *Spartiate,* his Guidon by Captain Bayntun of the *Leviathan* (it was supposed to be Captain Durham of the *Defiance* but he was ill). Also on this leading barge were two senior heralds (Rouge Croix and Blue Mantle) and several junior heralds (Pursuivants) from the College of Arms (see box). The second mourning barge carried four heralds bearing Nelson's Surcoat, Target and Sword, Helm and Crest, and Gauntlet and Spurs, and his Banner as a Knight of the Order of the Bath, borne by Captain Rotherham of the *Royal Sovereign,* together with the Great Banner with Augmentations 'at the doorplace' borne by Captain Moorsom of the *Revenge.* The third barge carried Nelson himself. It was covered in black velvet, with the top adorned with black plumes and in the centre four shields of the arms of the deceased. Three Bannerolls bearing the lineage of Nelson's family were fixed on either side of the barge, each carried by officers from the *Victory* who had fought at Trafalgar: Lieutenant Pasco, Lieutenant Yule, Lieutenant Williams, Lieutenant Brown, Mr Atkinson, master, and also Lieutenant Purches of the *Defiance.* The Norroy King of Arms, acting for the indisposed Clarenceux King of Arms (see box), bore a viscount's coronet on a black velvet cushion. The only flag on this barge was the Union flag at the head, at half-mast – as were all flags in the procession. The fourth and final official mourning barge carried the eighty-four-year-old chief mourner, Admiral of the Fleet Sir Peter Parker, who, as Commander-in-Chief in the West Indies, had first taken young Lieutenant Nelson on his flagship, the *Bristol,* in 1778. His barge was bursting with senior officers, including six admirals as assistant mourners, four vice-admirals as supporters of the pall and six rear-admirals as supporters of the canopy. In addition were the train-bearer of the chief mourner Captain Blackwood, the Windsor Herald and Captain Hardy bearing the Banner of Emblems.

Thereafter followed the barges of His Majesty with his representatives, the Lords Commissioners of the Lord High Admiral, the Lord Mayor, the Corporation of London, the Thames Navigation Committee and eight barges from the Great Livery Companies. There were twelve such companies but strangely only eight participated.

It took about three hours for the procession to arrive opposite the Whitehall Stairs. Its progress was intended to be slow and the stiff wind and choppy water assisted. As Nelson's barge came opposite the Tower at 2.45 p.m. the great guns were fired at minute intervals from the wharf, to be answered by the gunboats escorting the procession. As they neared their destination the wind seemed to strengthen and the by now exhausted rowers struggled to keep their place. There was more difficulty at the Whitehall Stairs at 3.30 p.m. as the barges manoeuvred to disembark people and the coffin. According to the *Naval Chronicle*:

> ... the whole of the boats drew up, and lay upon their oars, forming columns, in the order of a crescent, suffering the barge with the body to shoot ahead, and pass the stairs a short distance. This done the barge tacked and brought to, when the coffin was landed and received with military honours under the above described awning or canopy.

As the bearers were lifting the coffin ashore and onto the hearse the wind gusted and a heavy squall of rain lashed the party, the first since they had left Greenwich. From the Stairs it was but a short journey up Whitehall to the Admiralty where the body was to lie overnight, with the Reverend Scott maintaining his vigil. Only the body and the associated mourners in the leading barges landed at the Whitehall Stairs. The Lord Mayor and the various Livery Company barges proceeded to the Palace Yard Stairs where they rejoined their coaches to return to the City.

## The College of Arms

Nelson's funeral was arranged and organized by the College of Arms and its heralds. In early mediaeval times the chief function of heralds was the proclamation and organization of tournaments; they marshalled and introduced the contestants and kept a tally of the score. The knights jousting in tournaments or fighting in battle were recognized by the arms they bore on their shields and the crests they wore on their helmets. Heralds soon acquired an expert knowledge of these and became responsible for recording arms, and later for controlling their use.

Heralds under the Earl Marshal still organize certain ancient ceremonies. Familiar examples are the State Opening of Parliament, the procession and service of the Sovereign and the Knights Companion of the Order of the Garter at Windsor, the monarch's Coronation in Westminster Abbey and State Funerals. At these ceremonies heralds wear their distinctive mediaeval uniform – the tabard, a coat embroidered on its front, back and sleeves with the Royal Arms. The Earl Marshal, the Duke of Norfolk, whose office is hereditary, has powers of supervision over the heralds and College of Arms. The heralds with key roles in Nelson's funeral procession and service of burial were as follows:

• The three Kings of Arms – today under the Earl Marshal. The senior of the three was the Garter King of Arms. The office takes its name from the Order of the Garter instituted by Henry V in 1415. The next senior is the Clarenceux King of Arms whose English province has always been all England south of the River Trent. He was indisposed on 8 January 1806 and so did not participate in the river procession (though he had recovered to take part in the funeral the next day). His place was taken by the junior of the three, the Norroy (and today Ulster) King of Arms, whose province is England north of the Trent.
• Six 'heralds in ordinary' who derive their titles from the royal dukedoms of Chester, Lancaster, Richmond, Somerset, Windsor and York.
• The four 'pursuivants in ordinary' or junior heralds, whose titles derive from royal badges. They are: the Bluemantle Pursuivant, whose blue mantle derives from the blue mantle of the Order of the Garter, the Portcullis Pursuivant, the Rouge Croix Pursuivant, named for the red cross of St George, and the Rouge Dragon Pursuivant, a post instituted by Henry VII in 1485 in reference to the royal badge, the 'red dragon of Caldwallader'.

## Funeral Advertisements in *The Times*

Throughout the week prior to the funeral *The Times* carried numerous advertisements both from people with viewpoints for hire and from others wanting official tickets. Typical are the following:

FUNERAL OF LORD NELSON
Dundee Arms Tavern, Wapping High-street, in forms his Friends and the Public, he is preparing his LONG and COMMODIOUS ROOM with SEATS, for their accommodation, for the above Procession, it being the Best view on the River. Tickets 5s. to be had at the Bar, on any day preceding the Procession.

LORD NELSON'S FUNERAL – A Gentleman, who has engaged a large ROOM, on the First Floor, in the most eligible part of Ludgate-hill, will accommodate, upon fair terms, a respectable Family with PART of the Room, which is too large for the Advertiser and Friends. As profit is not the Advertiser's object, the most respectable references will be required. For particulars apply to Mr. Catter, Stationer, at the back of the Exchange.

LORD NELSON'S FUNERAL. – PALL MALL
a most desirable ROOM, commanding the best prospect in Pall-mall, will be LET, for viewing the Funeral, on Thursday next. Price for the whole Room 30 guineas, or 10 guineas each window [this appears dishonest as well as exorbitant as the procession did not go along Pall Mall]. A line addressed (post paid) to A.Z., No. 10, Bury-street, St James's, will meet immediate attention.

ST. PAUL'S CATHEDRAL – WANTED one or two TICKETS for the cupola or Body of the Cathedral, on the 9th instant. Any person having Tickets who, from illness, or any other cause, may be prevented from attending on the occasion, and may be willing, in consequence, to dispose of the same, may hear of a purchaser, by addressing a line to A.Z., No. 26 Bread-street-hill. Secresy [*sic*] may be relied on.

## The funeral procession

Nelson's state funeral was virtually indistinguishable in its grandeur from that accorded to royalty. The planning of this huge ceremonial event was a massive undertaking, organized via messengers carrying handwritten correspondence. It generated a blizzard of letters, documents and instructions. Countless clerks and copiers toiled long into the night for weeks on end to keep the plans on track. The occasion was under the overall charge of the College of Arms and its senior herald, the Garter King of Arms Sir Isaac Heard. From the Admiralty the procession made its way through Charing Cross, the Strand, Temple Bar (where the Lord Mayor's party joined the procession), Fleet Street and Ludgate Hill to the western entrance to St Paul's Cathedral, where the funeral service would be held and the body buried. It was a direct

## Nelson's Coat of Arms

The illustration is the final coat of arms Nelson used in his lifetime, produced after the Battle of Copenhagen. Nelson's use of a seaman as a supporter of his arms (on his shield) set a precedent. The other supporter, the lion tearing up the flags of France and Spain, was quite controversial as the original Spanish flag showed the arms of the Spanish royal family. In the final version neither flag is really recognizable and the Spanish coat of arms has gone. The palm tree and fronds held by both supporters refer to Nelson's victory at the Nile. Nelson also insisted that the rather gaudy 'chelengk', awarded by the Sultan of Turkey and which he often wore as a sort of capbadge in his hat, be included. The coat of arms was changed again after his death at Trafalgar.

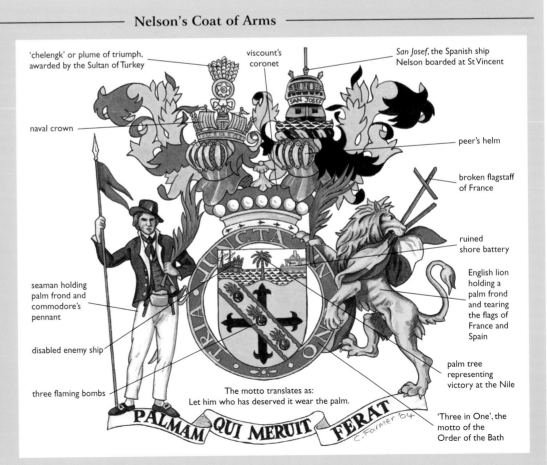

'chelengk' or plume of triumph, awarded by the Sultan of Turkey

viscount's coronet

*San Josef*, the Spanish ship Nelson boarded at St Vincent

naval crown

peer's helm

broken flagstaff of France

ruined shore battery

English lion holding a palm frond and tearing the flags of France and Spain

seaman holding palm frond and commodore's pennant

disabled enemy ship

three flaming bombs

palm tree representing victory at the Nile

'Three in One', the motto of the Order of the Bath

The motto translates as:
Let him who has deserved it wear the palm.

PALMAM QUI MERUIT FERAT

C. Farmer '04

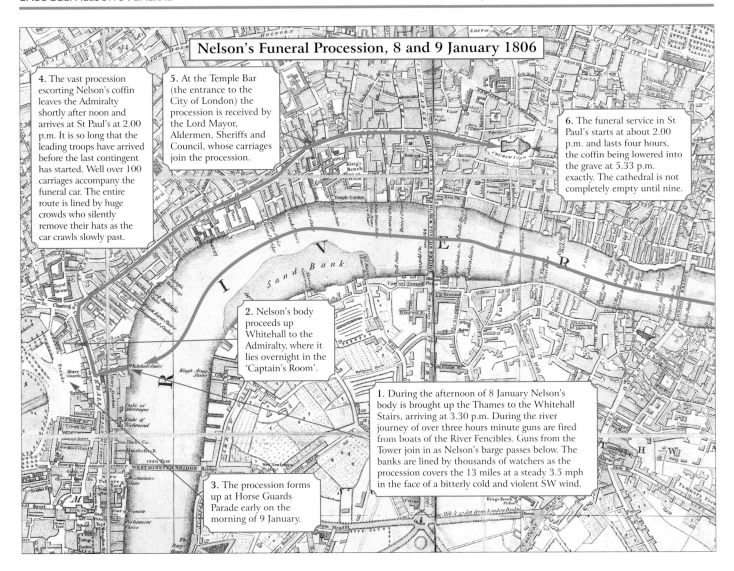

## Nelson's Funeral Procession, 8 and 9 January 1806

**4.** The vast procession escorting Nelson's coffin leaves the Admiralty shortly after noon and arrives at St Paul's at 2.00 p.m. It is so long that the leading troops have arrived before the last contingent has started. Well over 100 carriages accompany the funeral car. The entire route is lined by huge crowds who silently remove their hats as the car crawls slowly past.

**5.** At the Temple Bar (the entrance to the City of London) the procession is received by the Lord Mayor, Aldermen, Sheriffs and Council, whose carriages join the procession.

**6.** The funeral service in St Paul's starts at about 2.00 p.m. and lasts four hours, the coffin being lowered into the grave at 5.33 p.m. exactly. The cathedral is not completely empty until nine.

**2.** Nelson's body proceeds up Whitehall to the Admiralty, where it lies overnight in the 'Captain's Room'.

**1.** During the afternoon of 8 January Nelson's body is brought up the Thames to the Whitehall Stairs, arriving at 3.30 p.m. During the river journey of over three hours minute guns are fired from boats of the River Fencibles. Guns from the Tower join in as Nelson's barge passes below. The banks are lined by thousands of watchers as the procession covers the 13 miles at a steady 3.5 mph in the face of a bitterly cold and violent SW wind.

**3.** The procession forms up at Horse Guards Parade early on the morning of 9 January.

route not more than a mile and a quarter in length. Nelson's funeral car started its journey at about noon but did not arrive at the cathedral steps until 2.00 p.m. – by which time his private coach was just leaving the Admiralty!

The preparations began several hours before daylight on 9 January. There were three assembly areas. The first was Hyde Park, for all those in the procession (except those from the City of London and the military and naval contingents). It was here that, in the words of the official gazette:

> His Royal Highness the Prince of Wales, their Royal Highnesses the Dukes of the Blood Royal, with several of the great Officers, and the Nobility and Gentry in their carriages; the relations of the Deceased, with the Officers and others of his household, the Officers of Arms, and a number of Naval Officers, in mourning coaches assembled in Hyde Park; having been admitted at Cumberland and Grosvenor Gates upon producing tickets issued from the College of Arms.

The second was St James' Park. This was for the Army contingents with their bands and drums, all under the command of General Sir David Dundas, nicknamed 'Old Pivot' for his enthusiasm for the intricacies of Prussian drill. The infantry, cavalry and artillery were all represented and after much shouting and shuffling were formed up facing Horse Guards in the order they were to march off.

The third assembly area was Admiralty Yard. This was for all those closely associated with Nelson or playing a prominent ceremonial role in the funeral. These included the Chief Mourner (Admiral Parker) with his supporters and train-bearer (Captain Blackwood) and the naval officers bearing the Standard, Guidon and Banners (Captains Laforey, Rotherham, Durham, Moorsom, Hardy and Bayntun and Reverend Scott) with their supporters. Also parading here were the seamen and marines from *Victory*, the pensioners from Greenwich Hospital and Nelson's Watermen.

Perhaps because many ships were at sea the predominant colour in the procession was, unfortunately, military red rather than naval blue. The Army led the way, providing over 4,000 men for the procession itself and several thousand more from Militia and Volunteer units deployed on street-lining duties. Numerous admirals and a hundred naval captains participated, but only forty-eight Greenwich pensioners and forty-eight seamen and Royal Marines from the *Victory* – considered disappointingly inadequate by many of the watching public. The men from *Victory* carried her tattered, shot-torn colours, which they opened out from time to time to display their battle damage – something that invariably earned them a spontaneous burst of applause. Apart from the slow, solemn thump of bass drums and the regular boom of minute guns the procession was a silent affair, interrupted by faint rustling when hats were removed as Nelson's car carrying his coffin approached. Many of

## Nelson's Funeral Carriage

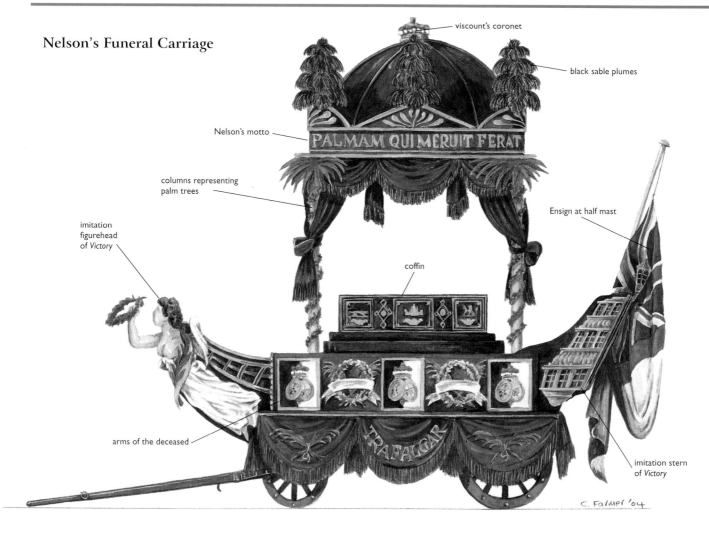

viscount's coronet

black sable plumes

Nelson's motto

PALMAM QUI MERUIT FERAT

columns representing
palm trees

Ensign at half mast

imitation
figurehead
of *Victory*

coffin

arms of the deceased

TRAFALGAR

imitation stern
of *Victory*

C. Farmer '04

those watching unashamedly wept. The car was an elaborate affair designed to resemble the *Victory* and hung with heraldic devices and trophies drawn by six black horses. It had been stripped of its pall to allow the spectators a more complete view of the coffin.

At Temple Bar there was a pause in proceedings. Here, on horseback and bearing the City Sword, was the Lord Mayor of London. His carriage and those of the Aldermen, Sheriffs, Council and Commercial Companies had to be guided into their proper positions. There was a longish halt for those at the rear, including Nelson's car, while all these coaches were slotted in and moved off.

At about 2.00 p.m. Nelson arrived at the door of his last resting place.

### The burial service

From the early hours of a bitterly cold morning St Paul's Cathedral had been the scene of a huge press of people. The doors, with the exception of the western entrance, had been thrown open as early as 7.00 a.m. but not before a number of would-be spectators had been injured in the crush. People admitted at seven o'clock had to wait six hours until the head of the procession arrived and another hour for the funeral car. The western entrance had been kept clear and on arrival the 92nd and 79th Foot (Highlanders) drew up fronting the cathedral. The Greenwich pensioners and the *Victory*'s contingent of seamen and marines ascended the steps and divided into a line on each side under the great western portico. The remainder of the procession entered as they arrived and were ushered to their reserved places.

These had been kept clear by 200 men of the West London Militia dispersed around the cathedral, some of whom were 'stationed at the several doors of the church, in order to prevent pressure or riot'. In preparation for the arrival of the coffin about 300 of the Highlanders filed in, marching in slow time, to deploy on either side of the route to be taken by the procession from the western gate, along the aisle, the dome and on to the gate of the choir. They carried their muskets and once in position turned inwards and rested on their arms reversed.

When the funeral car reached the western entrance the coffin was lifted from the car, covered with the pall, and borne by twelve seamen from the *Victory*. The pallbearers and supporters met it at the gate. First came the service of evensong. As the procession with the coffin moved slowly from the west door through the enclosed place in the centre of the dome, and over the grave on its way to the choir, the cathedral was filled with the wonderful words and music of William Croft's *Burial Sentences*: 'I am the resurrection and the life, saith the Lord: he that believeth in me, though he were dead, yet shall he live. And whosoever liveth and believeth in me shall never die …'. The choir consisted of 100 men and boys from St Paul's, Westminster Abbey and the Chapels Royal. The Reverend John Pridden, one of the Minor Canons of the cathedral, arranged the music. He was naturally anxious that the organ should strike up the opening bars exactly as the coffin was borne through the entrance. Pridden had arranged for an attendant to signal to the organist, Thomas Attwood (a former pupil of Mozart), by holding up a book.

Unfortunately, a member of the choir innocently held up a similar volume too early and Attwood played half a dozen bars before realizing his mistake. It was a trivial error and in no way detracted from a beautifully conducted service.

As evening approached it became necessary to illuminate the proceedings. Arrangements had been made to light the huge space under the dome with a large temporary wooden chandelier consisting of an octagonal frame, painted black, to which were attached 130 lamps. According to the *Naval Chronicle*, 'the grand central light, though inferior to the celebrated annual illuminated crucifix of St Peter's, had a most impressive and grand effect, and contributed greatly to the grandeur of [the] spectacle '.

At around five o'clock the procession returned from the choir to the grave under the dome. This was for the start of the burial service. Those gathered around were Nelson's male relatives (it was not customary for female family members to be present), the naval officers carrying his banners and close family friends such as Alexander Davison (Treasurer), William Hazelwood (Comptroller) and William Marsh (Steward). But perhaps most significant of all were the seamen from *Victory* holding the tattered battle colours that she wore at Trafalgar. Again the *Naval Chronicle* best describes the scene.

> On the return of the coffin from the choir, a grand funeral canopy of state was borne over it by six Admirals [actually rear-admirals]. It was composed of black velvet, supported by six small pillars covered with the same material, and crowned by six plumes of black ostrich feathers; the vallens [pelmets] were fringed with black, and decorated with devices of festoons and symbols of his Lordship's victories, his arms, crest and coronet, in gold.
>
> When the coffin was brought to the centre of the dome, it was placed on a platform sufficiently elevated to be visible from every part of the church – the state canopy was then withdrawn, and the pall taken off. The carpet and cushion on which the trophies were deposited, were laid by the Gentleman Usher who carried them, on a table placed near the grave, and behind the place which was occupied by the Chief Mourner. The coronet and cushion, borne by the Clarenceux King of Arms, was laid on the body [coffin]. ...

During the return of the corpse from the choir to the place of internment, a solemn dirge was performed on the organ; after which was sung the following

## ANTHEM

Man that is born of a woman, hath but a short time to live, and is full of misery. He cometh up, and is cut down like a flower: he fleeth as it were a shadow, and never continueth in one stay. ...

*Then the officiating Minister said*

Forasmuch as it hath pleased Almighty God, of his great mercy, to take unto himself the soul of our dear brother here departed, we therefore commit his body to the ground; earth to earth, ashes to ashes, dust to dust; in the sure and certain hope of resurrection to eternal life, through our Lord Jesus Christ ...'.

*After which was sung by the whole Choir*

I heard a voice from heaven saying unto me, 'Write, from henceforth blessed are the dead, which die in the Lord ...'.

*Concluding Anthem*

*Verse*. His body is buried in peace.
*Chorus*. But his name liveth evermore.

At the conclusion of the burial service the Garter King at Arms, Sir Isaac Heard, read the words: 'That it hath pleased Almighty God to take, out of this transitory life, unto his divine mercy, the Most Noble Lord Horatio Nelson ... [Nelson's titles were listed] Let us humbly trust, that he is now raised to bliss ineffable, and to a glorious immortality.' While Heard was speaking, the Trafalgar colours carried by *Victory*'s seamen were supposed to be furled up and placed in the grave. However, a large part of the ensign was seen to be ripped off and torn into smaller pieces that were quickly divided among the sailors as mementoes. Only what was left and the other flags were put on the coffin. At this point the Comptroller, Treasurer and Steward of Nelson's household broke their staves and handed the pieces to the Garter King at Arms, who threw them onto the coffin. Dean Henry Milman, who was a boy in the choir at the time, later wrote of this moment, 'As a youth I was present and I remember the solemn effect of the sinking of the coffin. I heard or fancied that I heard, the low wail of sailors who bore and encircled the remains of their admiral.'

The ceremony concluded just before six o'clock, although the cathedral was not clear until nine. Nelson had been put to rest in a manner befitting his glorious life.

### Trafalgar Square

The most important physical memorial to Nelson is probably the most famous square in the world, laid out between 1829 and 1841. Nelson's column in the centre is 170 feet high and the statue 17 feet. The column is surrounded by four bronze lions, on granite plinths sculpted by Sir Edwin Landseer and unveiled in 1868. Bronze reliefs at the base of the column depict scenes from Nelson's four famous battles – St Vincent, the Nile, Copenhagen and Trafalgar. As noted earlier in the text the wording on the base of the column of his famous signal is incorrect in that the 'that' is omitted.

The square was the centre for commemorative celebrations for the hundredth anniversary in 1905. On this occasion among the many wreaths laid at the foot of the column was one from New Zealand and another that bore the words 'To the memory of the gallant officers and men of France and Spain who died for their country at Trafalgar.' In August 1905 the French Fleet was visiting Portsmouth and a number of senior officers had been invited to a dinner at the Guildhall. En route their carriages passed through Trafalgar Square. As each carriage came abreast of Nelson's Column the officers turned towards it and saluted. One elderly officer went further. In addition to saluting he rose from his seat and, looking upwards, he raised his hat and bowed.

# Appendix 1 – TIMELINE OF NELSON'S LIFE

**1758** Horatio Nelson born at Burnham Thorpe, Norfolk.

**1767** 26 December His mother, Catherine Nelson, dies.

**1770** 27 November Entered as a midshipman on the 64-gun *Raisonnable*.

**1771** March Joins the *Raisonnable*.

15 May Transfers to 74-gun *Triumph* (Thames guard ship).

August Sails for West Indies on merchant ship.

**1772** Returns to England and rejoins *Triumph*.

**1773** June to September Sails with an expedition in bomb vessel *Carcass* in search of an Arctic route to the Pacific.

Joins 24-gun frigate *Seahorse* as midshipman and sails for East Indies.

**1775** Invalided from his ship with malaria.

American War of Independence begins.

**1776** August Returns to England.

24 September Appointed to 64-gun *Worcester*.

**1777** 9 April Passes promotion exam to lieutenant.

10 April Appointed to 32-gun frigate *Lowestoft*.

19 July Arrives Port Royal, Jamaica.

**1778** France allied with American rebels against Britain.

Commands small schooner *Little Lucy* as 'tender' to *Lowestoft*.

July Appointed first lieutenant in the 50-gun *Bristol*.

December Appointed commander of 16-gun armed brig *Badger*.

**1779** June Promoted post captain, appointed to 32-gun frigate *Hinchinbroke*.

Spain allied with France against Britain.

**1780** February to April Takes part in disastrous expedition to Nicaragua (capture of Fort San Juan).

Appointed to command 44-gun *Janus*.

Falls ill and sent home to England as passenger on 64-gun *Lion*, arriving Portsmouth 1 December.

**1781** August Appointed to command 28-gun frigate *Albemarle*.

Autumn Escorts Baltic convoy.

18 October General Cornwallis surrenders to Washington at Yorktown.

**1782** Joins North American Squadron. Visits Québec and New York.

Returns to West Indies.

**1783** March Fails to take Turks Island. American War of Independence ends.

June Returns home.

Visits St Omer, France.

**1784** Appointed to command 28-gun frigate *Boreas*. Sails for West Indies.

28 July Arrives Antigua.

**1785** May Meets Frances (Fanny) Nisbet.

**1786** Appointed ADC to Prince William Henry.

**1787** 11 March Marries Frances Nisbet at Nevis.

July Sails for England.

**1788** Placed on half pay. Lives at Burnham Thorpe with his wife.

**1789** French Revolution begins.

**1793** Start of French Revolutionary Wars.

Appointed to command 64-gun *Agamemnon*.

June Sails for Mediterranean.

September Visits Naples and meets Sir William and Lady (Emma) Hamilton.

22 October In action with French frigates.

**1794** January to August Corsican campaign. Right eye injured at Calvi.

**1795** 14 March *Agamemnon* in action against *Ça Ira* in the battle in the Gulf of Genoa.

**1796** March Appointed commodore. Hoists his pennant on the 64-gun *Diadem* in September then transfers in October to the 74-gun *Captain*.

**1797** January Temporarily hoists his flag on the 38-gun frigate *La Minerve*.

14 February Plays key role in the victory at the Battle of St Vincent on the *Captain*. Promoted rear-admiral and appointed Knight of the Bath.

Hoists flag on 74-gun *Theseus*. Returns home.

April to May Naval mutinies at Nore and Spithead.

July 3 to 5 Boat actions off Cadiz.

24 July Attack on Santa Cruz, Tenerife, fails. Loses right arm.

Returns home to Bath to recover as passenger on 38-gun frigate *Seahorse*.

**1798** March Hoists flag on 74-gun *Vanguard* and joins Lord St Vincent's fleet off Cadiz.

April Commands detached squadron in Mediterranean.

July In pursuit of French Toulon Fleet taking Napoleon to Egypt.

1 August Destroys French Fleet at Battle of the Nile (Aboukir Bay), where he is wounded in the head.

22 September Arrives at Naples.

6 November Created Baron Nelson of the Nile.

December 23 to 26 Rescues Neapolitan royal family and the Hamiltons from advancing French Army and takes them to Palermo.

**1799** 23 January French take Naples.

Begins relationship with Lady (Emma) Hamilton.

8 June Transfers his flag to 80-gun *Foudroyant*.

24 June Returns to Naples and cancels truce with rebels.

29 June Authorizes the execution of Neapolitan Admiral Caracciolo.

August to December Commands in the Mediterranean in absence of Lord Keith. Created Duke of Bronte and given Sicilian estate.

23 August Napoleon escapes from Egypt and reaches France 9 October.

**1800** 18 February Captures the *Le Généreux*.

April Visits Maltese waters with the Hamiltons.

June Recalled home.

13 July Strikes his flag in Mediterranean. Sails for Leghorn on 74-gun *Alexander*.

July to November Visits European cities on leisurely journey home with the Hamiltons.

6 November Lands at Yarmouth to hero's welcome and Freedom of Borough.

November Meets Lady Nelson in London but spends Christmas with Hamiltons.

**1801** January Promoted vice-admiral. Deserts his wife.

13 January Hoists flag on 114-gun *San Josef*.

End of January or early February Emma Hamilton gives birth to Nelson's illegitimate daughter Horatia.

12 February Transfers his flag to 98-gun *St George*.

6 March Joins Admiral Parker at Yarmouth and six days later sails for the Baltic.

2 April Battle of Copenhagen; Nelson commands the attack with his flag on the 74-gun *Elephant*.

6 May Assumes command in Baltic.

June Returns home on the 16-gun *Kite*, having been created Viscount Nelson of the Nile and Burnham Thorpe.

27 July Appointed to command anti-invasion forces in Channel.

Hoists flag on 36-gun frigate *Unite* but transfers to 32-gun *Medusa*.

15 August Failure of attack on Boulogne.

September Buys Merton Place.

1 October Britain and France sign armistice. Joins Hamiltons at Merton.

**1802** 25 March French Revolutionary Wars end with Treaty of Amiens.

26 April His father, Reverend Edmund Nelson, dies.

July to August Tours South Wales and the Midlands with the Hamiltons.

**1803** 6 April Sir William Hamilton dies.

16 May The Napoleonic Wars begin. Nelson appointed Commander-in-Chief Mediterranean.

18 May Hoists flag on 102-gun *Victory* but sails to Mediterranean on 32-gun frigate *Amphion* and joins fleet off Toulon on 6 July.

August French prepare to invade England.

**1804** Blockades Toulon with flag in *Victory*.

**1805** January to February Chases but fails to catch Villeneuve's fleet in Mediterranean.

April to July Chases Villeneuve to West Indies and back but fails to catch him.

22 July Rear-Admiral Calder engages Villeneuve in indecisive action off Cape Finisterre.

18 August Arrives Portsmouth and returns to Merton.

14 September Rejoins *Victory* at Portsmouth.

28 September Takes command of British Fleet off Cadiz.

21 October Killed at Battle of Trafalgar.

6 November News of Trafalgar and Nelson's death reaches England.

4 December *Victory* brings his body to Portsmouth.

5 December National day of thanksgiving for the victory at Trafalgar.

**1806** 8 January Funeral procession of barges on River Thames from Greenwich to Whitehall Stairs.

9 January Funeral procession from Admiralty to St Paul's Cathedral for burial service.

# BIBLIOGRAPHY

*Publication was in London unless otherwise stated.*

## BOOKS

Beatty, William, *The Authentic Narrative of the Death of Lord Nelson*, 1807
Beauchant, Lieutenant T.S. Royal Marine Artillery, *The Naval Gunner*, 1829
Bennett, Geoffrey, *The Battle of Trafalgar*, B.T. Batsford Ltd, 1977
Bennett, Geoffrey, *Nelson the Commander*, B.T. Batsford Ltd, 1972
Biesty, Stephen, *Cross-Sections Man-of-War*, Darling Kindersley, 1993
Boudriot, Jean, *The Seventy-Four Gun Ship* Vols 1–4, J. Boudriot, Paris, 1986–8
Bradford, Ernle, *Nelson: The Essential Hero*, Macmillan Ltd, 1977
Broardly A.M., *The Three Dorset Captains*, John Murray, 1906
Brooks, Richard, *The Royal Marines 1664 to the Present*, Constable and Robinson, 2002
Callo, Admiral Joseph F., *Legacy of Leadership: Lessons from Admiral Lord Nelson*, Hellgate Press, Oregon, USA, 1999
Cassin-Scott, Jack and Fabb, John, *Uniforms of Trafalgar*, B.T. Batsford Ltd, 1977
Chandler, David G., *Dictionary of the Napoleonic Wars*, Arms and Armour Press, 1979
Chartrand, René, *Napoleon's Sea Soldiers*, Osprey Publishing Ltd, 1995
Clarke, John D., *The Men of HMS* Victory *at Trafalgar*, Vintage Naval Library, 1999
Claver, Scott, *Under the Lash*, Torchstream Books, 1954
Corbett, Julian S., *The Campaign of Trafalgar*, Longmans and Green & Co., 1910
– (ed.), *Signals and Instructions 1776–1794*, Navy Records Society, 1908
Davies, David, *Fighting Ships – The Ships of the Line*, Constable, 1996
Desbriere, Edouard, *The Naval Campaign of 1805* Vols I & II, University Press, 1933
Eardley-Wilmot, S., *Our Flags*, Simpkin, Marshall, Hamilton, Kent & Co. Ltd, 1901
Falconer, William, *A Universal Dictionary of the Marine*, 1769
Feldbaek, Ole, *The Battle of Copenhagen 1801*, Leo Cooper, Barnsley, 2002
Field, Colonel C. Royal Marine Light Infantry, *Britain's Sea Soldiers* Vol. I, 1924
–, *Old Times Afloat*, Andrew Melrose Ltd, 1932
Fitchett W. H., *Deeds that Won the Empire*, John Murray, 1928
Fraser, Edward, *The Enemy at Trafalgar*, Hodder and Stoughton, 1906
–, *The Sailors Whom Nelson Led*, Methuen & Co. Ltd, 1913
Galdos, Benito Perez, *Trafalgar*, Madrid, 1907
Galiano, Pelayo Alcala, *El Combate de Trafalgar*, Madrid, 1930
Gardiner, Robert (ed.), *Fleet Battle and Blockade: The French Revolutionary War 1793–1797*, Chatham Publishing, 1996
– (ed.), *The Line of Battle: The Sailing Warship 1650–1840*, Conway Maritime Press Ltd, 1992
– (ed.), *The Campaign of Trafalgar 1803–1805*, Caxton Editions, 2002
Goldsmith-Carter, George, *Sailing Ships and Sailing Craft*, Paul Hamlyn, 1969
Goodwin, Peter, *Countdown to Victory*, Manuscript Press, Portsmouth, 2000
–, *Nelson's Ships*, Conway Maritime Press Ltd, 2002
Harbron, John D., *Trafalgar and the Spanish Navy*, Conway Maritime Press Ltd, 1988
Harland, John, *Seamanship in the Age of Sail*, Conway Maritime Press Ltd, 1984
Haythornthwaite, Philip, *Nelson's Navy*, Osprey Publishing Ltd, 1993
Henderson, James, *The Frigates*, Adland Coles Ltd, 1970
Hewitt, J. (ed.), *Eye-Witness to Nelson's Battles*, Osprey Publishing Ltd, 1972
Hill, J.R. (ed.), *The Oxford Illustrated History of the Royal Navy*, Oxford University Press, 1995
Hogg, Ian and Batchelor, John, *Naval Gun*, Blandford Press, Poole, Dorset, 1978
Howarth, David, *Trafalgar: The Nelson Touch*, World Books, 1970
Huskison, T., *Eye-Witness to Trafalgar*, Ellison's Editions, 1985
Jackson, S.T., *Logs of the Great Sea Fights* Vol. II, Navy Records Society, 1900
James, William, *The Naval History of Great Britain* Vol. IV, Richard Bentley, 1886
Jeans, Peter D. *Ship to Shore*, ABC-Clio Ltd, Oxford, 1998
Jenkins, E.H., *The History of the French Navy*, Macdonald & Jane's, 1973
Jolly, Rick, *Jackspeak: The Pusser's Rum Guide to Royal Navy Slanguage*, Palamanando Publishing, Totpoint, Cornwall, 1989
Kennedy, Ludovic, *Nelson and His Captains*, Collins, 1975
Kent, Captain Barry RN, *Signal!*, Hyden House Ltd, Clanfield, Hants, 1993
Lavery, Brian, *Nelson's Navy*, Conway Maritime Press Ltd, 1989
–, *The Arming and Fitting of English Ships of War 1600–1815*, Conway Maritime Press Ltd, 1987
–, *Anatomy of the Ship – The 74-gun Ship* BELLONA, Conway Maritime Press Ltd, 1985
Legg, Stuart (ed.), *Trafalgar*, Rupert Hart-Davis, 1966
Lewis, Michael, *England's Sea-Officers*, Allen & Unwin, 1948
Leyland, John (ed.), *Dispatches and Letters Relating to the Blockade of Brest, 1803–1805*, two vols, Navy Records Society, 1899–1902
Lyon, David, *Sea Battles in Close Up: The Age of Nelson*, Naval Institute Press, 1996
McKay, John, *The 100-Gun Ship* VICTORY, Conway Maritime Press Ltd, 1987
Mackenzie R.H., *The Trafalgar Roll*, George Allen & Co. Ltd, 1913

Mahan, A.T., *The Life of Nelson* Vols I & II, Sampson Low, Marston & Co., 1897
Mead, H.P., *Trafalgar Signals*, Percival Marshall & Co. Ltd, 1936
*Naval Chronicle The*, Vols 14 & 15, 1805–6
Newbolt, Henry, *The Year of Trafalgar*, John Murray, 1965
O'Brian, Patrick, *Men of War*, Collins, 1974
Oman, Carola, *Nelson*, Hodder & Stoughton, 1967
Padfield, Peter, *Guns at Sea*, Hugh Evelyn Ltd, 1973
–, *Nelson's War*, Hart-Davis, MacGibbon Ltd, 1976
Parsons, Lieutenant G.S., *Nelsonian Reminiscences*, Chatham Publishing, 1998
Pivka, Otto von, *Navies of the Napoleonic Era*, Hippocrene, New York, 1980
Pope, Dudley, *England Expects*, Chatham Publishing, 1959
–, *The Great Gamble*, Weidenfeld & Nicolson, 1972
–, *Life in Nelson's Navy*, Chatham Publishing, 1997
–, *The Black Ship*, Weidenfeld & Nicolson, 1963
Popham, Sir Home, *The Signal Book for the Ships of War 1799* (Admiralty Signal Book)
Pugh, Gordon P.D., *Nelson and His Surgeons*, E & S Livingstone Ltd, 1968
Raigersfeld, Rear-Admiral J., *The Life of a Sea Officer*, 1929
*Regulations and Instructions Relating to His Majesty's Service at Sea* – His Majesty in Council, 1806
Rodger, N.A.M., *The Wooden World*, Fontana Press, 1988
Schom, Alan, *Trafalgar*, Michael Joseph, 1990
Steel P., *Observations for the use of the commissioned, the junior and other officers of The Royal Navy on all the material points of professional duty*, 1804
Steele, Sir Robert, *The Marine Officer or Sketches of Service* Vol. I, Henry Colburn, 1840
Terraine, John, *Trafalgar*, Sidgwick & Jackson, 1976
Tucker, J.S., *Memoirs of Earl St Vincent*, 1844
Tunstall, Brian, *Naval Warfare in the Age of Sail*, Chatham Maritime Press Ltd, 1990
Vincent, Edgar, *Nelson – Love and Fame*, Yale University Press, New Haven, 2003
Warner, Oliver, *The Battle of the Nile*, B.T. Batsford Ltd, 1960
White, Colin, *The Nelson Encyclopaedia*, Chatham Publishing, 2002
–, *1797 – Nelson's Year of Destiny*, Sutton Publishing Ltd, Stroud, 1998
–, (ed.), *The Nelson Companion*, Sutton Publishing Ltd, Stroud, 1995
Wilson, Timothy, *Flags at Sea*, HMSO, National Maritime Museum, Greenwich, 1986
Wood, Walter, *The Battleship*, Kegan, Paul, Trench, Trubner & Co. Ltd, 1912

## PAPERS AND PERIODICALS

Anderson, R.C., 'The Lee Line at Trafalgar', *Mariner's Mirror* Vol. 57, 1971
Baudry, A., 'The Naval Battle: Studies of the Tactical Factors', Hugh Rees, 1914
Bridge, Admiral Sir Cyprian, 'Naval Strategy and Tactics at the Time of Trafalgar', paper read to the Institution of Naval Architects, 1905
Denton, Reverend Sydney, 'Admiral the Lord Collingwood', *United Service Magazine* Vol. XXXII, 1906
Douglas, General Sir Howard, 'A Treatise on Naval Gunnery', John Murray, 1860
Field, Vice-Admiral A.M., 'The Nelson Touch at Trafalgar', *Royal United Services Institute Journal* Vol. LV, 1911
Freemantle, Admiral the Hon. Sir E.R., 'Nelson's Tactics at Trafalgar', *United Service Magazine* Vol. XXXII, 1905/1906
Goodwin, Peter, 'Where Nelson Died: An Historical Riddle Resolved by Archaeology', *Mariner's Mirror* Vol. 85, 1999
'HMS *Victory*', Royal Naval Museum Trading Co. Ltd, 1994
Howarth, David, 'The Man Who Lost Trafalgar', *Trafalgar Chronicle*, 1979
Howarth, Stephen (ed.), 'Battle of Cape St Vincent', selected papers from the Bicentennial International Naval Conference, Portsmouth, 1997
Hutchinson, William, 'A Treatise on Naval Architecture', 1794
*Journal of the Royal Naval Medical Service* Vol. 86 No. 2, 2000
Laughton, Professor J.K., 'The Navy in 1805', *United Service Magazine* Vol. XXXII, 1905
'Letters and Documents Relating to the Service of Nelson's Ships 1780–1805: A Critical Report', Institute of Historical Research, 1997
'Methods of Blockade', *Royal United Services Institute Journal* Vol. LXI, 1908
Mountaine, William, 'The Practical Sea-Gunner's Companion', 1781
'Nelson Dispatch, The', *Journal of the Nelson Society* Vols 6,7 & 8, 1999–2003
Nicolls, Bruce, 'The Talking Flags at Trafalgar', paper presented to the 10th International Congress of Vexillology, New College Oxford, 1983
Taylor, Rear-Admiral A.H., paper on Trafalgar presented to Society of Nautical Research in 1936, *Mariner's Mirror* Vol. 36, 1950
Thursfield, James R., 'The Tactics at Trafalgar', *Brassey's Naval Annual*, 1911
'Trafalgar General Order Book of HMS *Mars*', *Mariner's Mirror* Vol. 22, 1936
Watts, Sir Percy, 'The Ships of the Royal Navy as They Existed at the Time of Trafalgar', paper presented to Institution of Naval Architects, 1905
Zulueta, Julian de, 'Trafalgar: The Spanish View', *Mariner's Mirror* Vol. 66, 1980

# INDEX

940.    Adkin, Mark
2745   The TRafalgar Companion
ADK

2/2/06                      $75.00

WITHDRAWN

**LONGWOOD PUBLIC LIBRARY**
**Middle Country Road**
**Middle Island, NY 11953**
**(631) 924-6400**

**LIBRARY HOURS**

| | |
|---|---|
| Monday-Friday | 9:30 a.m. - 9:00 p.m. |
| Saturday | 9:30 a.m. - 5:00 p.m. |
| Sunday (Sept-June) | 1:00 p.m. - 5:00 p.m. |